STATISTICAL PRINCIPLES IN
EXPERIMENTAL DESIGN

STATISTICAL PRINCIPLES IN EXPERIMENTAL DESIGN

Third Edition

B. J. Winer

Late Professor of Psychology
Purdue University

Donald R. Brown

Professor of Psychology
Purdue University

Kenneth M. Michels

Professor of Psychology
Florida Atlantic University

McGraw-Hill, Inc.

New York   St. Louis   San Francisco   Auckland   Bogotá
Caracas   Hamburg   Lisbon   London   Madrid   Mexico   Milan   Montreal
New Delhi   Paris   San Juan   São Paulo   Singapore   Sydney   Tokyo   Toronto

This book was set in Times Roman.
The editors were Maria E. Chiappetta, Jane Vaicunas,
and John M. Morriss;
the production supervisor was Annette Mayeski.
The cover was designed by Pencils Portfolio.
Project supervision was done by Universities Press.
R. R. Donnelley & Sons Company was printer and binder.

STATISTICAL PRINCIPLES IN EXPERIMENTAL DESIGN

234567890 DOC DOC 90987654321

ISBN 0-07-070982-3

Library of Congress Cataloging-in-Publication Data

Winer, B. J.
    Statistical principles in experimental design / B. J. Winer, Donald
R. Brown, Kenneth M. Michels. — 3rd ed.
      p.   cm.
    Includes bibliographical references and index.
    ISBN 0-07-070982-3
    1. Experimental design.   I. Brown, Donald R.   II. Michels,
Kenneth M.   III. Title.
QA279.W54   1991
519.5—dc20   90-27253

ABOUT THE AUTHORS

B. J. Winer was known for being a superb teacher and the author of two editions of *Statistical Principles in Experimental Design*. Upon completing his doctorate in 1951 at Ohio State University, he received a postdoctoral foundation fellowship in the Institute of Statistics at the University of North Carolina. He joined the faculty at Purdue University in 1954, and for thirty years, until his death in 1984, he taught graduate-level statistics and experimental design at Purdue. In 1983 he received the Distinguished Teaching of Quantitative Methods in Psychology Award from the American Psychological Foundation. He was president of the Psychometric Society and managing editor of the journal *Psychometrika*.

Donald R. Brown is Vice President and Dean of Academic Services at Purdue University. He completed his doctorate at Purdue in 1961, spent a year teaching and doing research at Ohio State University, then returned to Purdue, inspired by Ben Winer to become a faculty member there. He has taught statistics at the graduate and undergraduate levels, as well as experimental design, and perception. He serves on several university committees, and holds membership in an impressive list of local and national academic organizations. He has published his research extensively in the area of visual pattern perception, and has co-authored several papers with Kenneth Michels.

Kenneth M. Michels is a Professor of Psychology Emeritus at Florida Atlantic University. Author of more than 35 professional publications, he has served as major professor for numerous masters and doctoral students, including Donald Brown. He was an associate of Ben Winer for ten years at Purdue University, after which he moved to Florida Atlantic to chair the psychology department. He has since been dean of two different colleges, Director of the Institute for Epidemiological Studies of Health Care Delivery, and University Provost and Vice President for Academic and Student Affairs. He completed his doctorate at the University of Wisconsin at Madison (1953). His research and consulting activities include the areas of sensory and perceptual processes and systems design and evaluation.

CONTENTS

PREFACE

In 1984 Professor B. J. Winer died while working on the third edition of *Statistical Principles in Experimental Design*. Two of his colleagues for nearly twenty-five years, Drs. Donald R. Brown and Kenneth M. Michels, took on the task of organizing, editing, rewriting, and adding to the unfinished manuscript. For a number of years, Professors Winer and Brown taught, in alternate semesters, the graduate courses for which a major portion of the book was intended. In completing this edition, we have tried to preserve Professor Winer's intended purpose of the book as a teaching text, as well as a resource book for research workers primarily in the behavioral and biological sciences. The usefulness of previous editions has been broadly acknowledged. We hope that this edition will likewise be accepted.

As in previous editions, the logic basic to understanding principles underlying the statistical aspects of experimental design is emphasized rather than the details of mathematical and statistical proofs. As before, there is sufficient redundancy in the writing so that the more theoretical sections may be omitted without loss of the readability in the more applied sections.

The applied sections of the book have been written at a readability level for students having a mathematical background equivalent to having had freshman college algebra and a basic course in statistical inference.

Major changes have been made throughout this edition to increase readability and to incorporate new information.

Chapter 1 is new and is intended to introduce the topic of design within a broad context as well as to provide the student with a perspective for the rest of the book.

Although the student is presumed to have a background in statistical inference, Chapter 2 is included to provide a review or summary of material covered in such a prerequisite course.

Chapters 3 and 4 have been extensively rewritten. Chapter 3, which covers completely-randomized, single-factor experiments, has been expanded extensively to cover methods for controlling Type 1 error when multiple tests of significance are involved. In Chapter 4, the assumptions underlying repeated-measures designs are examined in much greater detail than they were in the previous edition.

Chapters 5 through 9, while similar in content to those in the second edition, have been modified to be consistent with the new material in Chapters 3 and 4.

In general, the discussion of principles, interpretation of illustrative examples, and computational procedures are included in successive sections within the same chapter. However, to facilitate the use of the book as a reference source, this procedure is not followed in Chapters 5 and 6. Rather, basic principles associated with a large class of designs for factorial experiments are discussed in Chapter 5, with associated illustrative examples presented in Chapter 6.

Chapter 10, which covers analysis of covariance, has been rewritten from a new perspective.

Considerable information involving the general linear model and least-squares estimation were included in the main body of the book in the previous editon (Chapter 2). Some of this material is presented in a new form in Appendices B and C. In Appendix B an introducton to matrix algebra is presented and in Appendix C selected aspects of the general linear model relevant to regression and analysis of variance are provided.

Appendix D contains relatively complete tables for sampling distributions of statistics used in the analysis of experimental designs. Tables of the Dunn-Bonferroni t statistic, Dunn-Sidák t statistic, the studentized maximum modulus, Mauchley's sphericity criterion W, Imhof F, and the generalized studentized range statistic are included in this edition.

The authors are indebted to E. S. Pearson and the trustees of *Biometrika* for permission to reproduce parts of Tables D.1, D.3, D.7, and D.9 from *Biometrika Tables for Statisticians,* vol. I, 2nd ed. We wish to thank H. L. Harter, D. S. Clem, and E. H. Guthrie for permission to reproduce Table D.4, which was taken from WADC Technical Report 58–484, vol. 2, 1959. We appreciate the cooperation of the editor of the *Journal of the American Statistical Association* and of C. W. Dunnett for Table D.6, D. B. Owen for Table D.13., M. L. Tiku for Table D.14, B. J. R. Bailey for Table D.15, and P. A. Games for Table D.16, C. Eisenhart, M. W. Hasty, and W. A. Wallis for Table D.8, which appears in *Techniques of Statistical Analysis,* 1947. We wish to thank L. S. Feldt and M. W. Mahmoud as well as the editor of *Psychometrika* for permission to reprint Table D.11, R. E. Bechover and C. W. Dunnett and the editor of *Technometrics* for Table D.17, the editor of the *Annals of Mathematical Statistics* and J. P. Imhof for Table D.18, B. N. Nagarsenker and K. C. S. Pillai and the editor of the *Journal of Multivariate Analysis* for Table D.19, and for Table D.20, J. L. Bryant and A. S. Paulson and the editor of *Biometrika.*

There are a number of individuals to whom we owe a debt of gratitude, singly and jointly. Margaret Binford and Marcia Weller provided outstanding proofreading skill and other editorial assistance in the preparation of the manuscript. Mark Senn is due our appreciation and recognition for his help in selecting the software and advising on the use of the computer to accommodate the needs of the manuscript.

Very special thanks are due to Winnie Walter for supervising the preparation and near-perfect rendering of this third editon manuscript.

For their encouragement, support, and guidance through the years, we wish to express our appreciation to E. J. Asher, Charles L. Darby, Norville M. Downie, and Allan J. Nash.

McGraw-Hill and the authors would like to thank the following reviewers for their many helpful comments and suggestions: Jennifer Gille; Arthur Kirsch, George Washington University; Donald Meyer, University of Pittsburgh; Allan J. Nash, Florida Atlantic University; Joseph S. Rossi, University of Rhode Island; and Marty Schmidt.

Donald R. Brown
Kenneth M. Michels

CHAPTER 1

INTRODUCTION TO DESIGN

1.1 INTRODUCTION

Science is concerned with understanding variability in nature, statistics is concerned with making decisions about nature in the presence of variability, and experimental design is concerned with reducing and controlling variability in ways which make statistical theory applicable to decisions made about nature.

It is the variability of experimental material, be it chunks of concrete, flasks of liquids, stalks of corn, or human beings, which provides a communality among all sciences (Federer, 1963) and poses the mysteries for which resolution is sought and lawfulness is discovered in the presence of previously unexplained differences. What discriminates among the sciences and among problems within a scientific discipline is not the presence or absence of variability of experimental material. It is the number and nature of the factors which contribute to the variability and, most important, it is the magnitude of variability which remains when all factors already known to influence differences are held constant. Regardless of the magnitude of the variation to be explained and regardless of the number of variables which can be systematically related to the variation, it is the purpose of science to discover patterns in the variability which simplify and permit accurate prediction. In this enterprise statistics may be useful in one of two ways.

First, there are content areas wherein logical theories are formulated in terms of statistical models. This is true, for example, of statistical learning theory and stochastic models of language usage (Luce et al., 1963). Where this is true, statistical models act as do all other theories. They have a role in the deductive process of reasoning. Statistical models provide the logical basis for the deduction of hypotheses which can be verified through experimentation.

There is a second role for statistical models in scientific inquiry. It is their use as the basis for the inductive process, the process of generalizing from a particular set of instances to a general phenomenon of which the instances are representative, which makes statistical theory of interest to discussions of experimental design. There are two sub-functions involved, *description* and *inference*. Statistics are useful to describe observations in summary fashion in numerical or graphical form. If the observations are of events, objects, or elements representative of larger classes, then they are samples and may be viewed as representing the populations from which they were selected. Statistics describe samples and are estimates of parameters which describe entire populations which may be impossible to measure directly because of size or accessibility. Beyond merely describing samples, the statistics also provide estimates of parameters. It is inferential statistical theory which then provides the foundation for using statistics to infer something about the magnitude of parameters. Thus, they provide the basis for inductive reasoning in that generalizations from samples to populations are a special case of generalizing from the particular and known to the general and unknown. Because such generalizations are imperfect, statistical theory also provides the foundation for specifying the relative frequency and magnitude of errors when conclusions about parameters are reached based upon statistics. Statistical inference, then, is the process of reaching conclusions about populations from samples in the face of uncertainty, uncertainty which is brought about by variability.

1.2 THE CONTROL OF INDEPENDENT, DEPENDENT, AND SUPPLEMENTARY VARIABLES

Life and behavioral scientists have at their disposal an array of research techniques which can be ordered on a continuum relative to the degree of control it is assumed the experimenter can exercise over the environment.

One extreme is most clearly characterized by survey research, wherein the major concern is with understanding population information which exists in its own right. That is, populations, the existence of which in no way depends upon actions taken by the researcher, are sampled and conclusions about the populations are reached based entirely upon content theories, sample data, and the statistical theories which tie sampling procedures to the data. The researcher does not control the environment, but observes it in its intact form.

At the other extreme, the structure of populations is created by the controlled conditions, the experimental design, established by the experimenter. It is this tradition which forms the basis for the material presented herein, which tradition has its foundations primarily in the work of R. A. Fisher and is exemplified in his classic book, *The Design of Experiments* (Fisher, 1951). That this work was carried out within the context of agricultural research accounts for the fact that much of the nomenclature of classical experimental design utilizes agricultural terminology. The logic, however, is totally general and has found widespread application in all research domains wherein control of experimental conditions is possible.

The essence of experimentation is the ability to control or manipulate variables in a systematic manner. In simplest terms, an experiment is performed when one variable, an independent variable, is systematically varied in order to assess its effects on another variable, the dependent variable. Less simply, experiments may involve more than a single independent or dependent variable. That is, experiments may be univariate or multivariate in either the independent or dependent variables.

An experimental design simply describes how an experiment is to be executed. It may be compared to an architect's plans for a structure, and in designing the structure, decisions must be made regarding the independent variable(s), the dependent variable(s), supplementary variables, and the experimental materials of interest. In many contexts outside of the life sciences, the term "experimental materials" is used to describe the basic unit of observation or object of study in an experiment. Herein, because the emphasis is upon the life and behavioral sciences, the word "subject" or "element" will be used to describe the basic unit of observation. Typically, the subject is a living organism and brings to the experimental setting a very wide array of characteristics which may affect performance on any particular dependent variable of interest.

Independent Variables

Independent variables must, by definition, be manipulable at levels of interest to the experimenter. The levels may vary in kind (qualitative variables) or in magnitude (quantitative variables). Of particular interest are the range of the independent variables included in the experiment, how the levels of the independent variables included in the experiment are selected from among all possible levels, and how different independent variables are combined in order to define treatment conditions.

The range of levels of the independent variables should assure that the hypothetical impact upon relevant dependent variables can be expressed clearly. The experimenter's interest may be more sophisticated than merely specifying that an independent variable has an impact upon the dependent variable. It may involve specifying the nature of the function which relates variation of the two variables as, for example, in the case of trend analysis. In that case, special attention needs to be given to both the range and spacing of levels of the independent variable(s).

How the particular levels of the independent variable(s) which are included in the experimental design are selected is important in that it determines the domain to which the results of the experiment may be generalized. When the levels of independent variable(s) can be considered a random sample from a population of all possible levels of the variable, it is possible to generalize the outcome to the entire population of levels of the independent variable(s). When sampling of the particular levels of the independent variable(s) is constrained, generalization of the results cannot be made beyond the levels actually studied in the experiment.

One of the major determinants of the structure of experimental designs is how the experimenter elects to combine different independent variables into treatment conditions. A treatment condition is the set of conditions under which a subject is observed. It may be defined in terms of combining any number of independent variables, each one of which is being held constant in order to define the treatment condition. In the case of an experimental design involving a single independent variable, treatment conditions and levels of the independent variable are synonymous. When different independent variables are combined, that is not the case. For example, if an experimenter were only studying the effects of drug dosages upon learning rates, a single factor experiment (Chapter 3) would be defined and each drug dosage would be a treatment condition under which some measure of learning rate would be taken on appropriate subjects. If, however, an experimenter were studying the effects of both drug dosages and types of drugs upon learning rate, a treatment condition would be defined by the combination of a particular kind of drug and a particular dosage of the drug.

Experimental designs in which treatment conditions are defined by combinations of levels of independent variables are critically important to behavioral scientists. Such designs may make it possible to assess interactions. Interactions are unique effects upon the dependent variable(s) which only occur when two or more variables are operating in concert. They are effects which cannot be assessed when independent variables are studied one at a time. Since much behavior may reasonably be contingent upon a variety of variables acting in concert, it is often critical that designs include the possibility of assessing interactions. Particular emphasis is placed upon such designs, factorial designs, in Chapters 4, 5, and 6.

Dependent Variables

An experiment involving a single dependent variable is typically referred to as univariate even though there may be multiple independent variables. The procedures discussed herein are primarily univariate in nature. Whether they are univariate or multivariate in nature, the selection of dependent variables is primarily a matter of sensitivity, concern with measurement issues, and concern with the amount and distributional properties of variability in the dependent variable.

It is obvious that the chosen dependent variable should be maximally sensitive to the treatment conditions.

Measurement, the assignment of labels or numbers to attributes of objects or events, is a topic which is as complex as is the topic of experimental design. Herein, it is simply assumed that the values of the dependent variable have meaning through the application of appropriate measurement procedures. However, it is important to point out that measurement theory has strong implications for statistical theory and can have very important significance for the interpretation of the results derived from any statistical analyses of experimental data.

A controversy that dates back at least to the 1940s has held the attention of a number of scholars (e.g., Stevens, 1946, 1951, 1959; Suppes, 1951; Suppes and Zinnes, 1963; Townsend and Ashby, 1984; Mitchell, 1986). "On one side is the view that the scale on which a set of measurements lies determines the type of statistical treatments that are suitable for application to the measurements. The opposing view is that there is no relation between the measurement scale and statistical procedures; essentially anything goes, relative to the measurement stipulations" (Townsend and Ashby, 1984, p. 394).

All other things being equal, it is desirable for the dependent variable to have small inherent variability from subject to subject. In general, this will increase the precision with which parameters can be estimated and contribute to increased statistical power for any given sample size. Moreover, it is desirable for the observations taken over samples of subjects to be normally distributed since many parametric inferential statistical procedures are based upon the assumption that the dependent variable(s) assume a univariate or multivariate normal distribution. If that is not true, one must assume that the statistical procedures are robust with regard to violations of that assumption, or that the variable(s) can be transformed to a normal distribution.

Supplementary Variables

In any given experiment, there are variables other than the independent variables which may affect the dependent variable but are not of primary interest to the experimenter. Such variables have also been referred to as "nuisance variables" (Kirk, 1982). The control of these variables in some fashion is necessary to increase the precision with which independent variable effects can be estimated or to remove bias effects from those estimates. In general, there are two ways in which supplementary or nuisance variables can be managed: directly (experimentally) or indirectly (statistically).

In the case of direct control, the experimenter can include the supplementary variable in the experimental design as a basis for forming blocks of subjects who are homogeneous with regard to the supplementary variable. Thus, if a dependent variable is thought to be related to the intelligence of subjects, one might simply create several blocks of subjects wherein within each block all subjects have the same IQ level but different blocks of subjects are characterized by different IQ levels. The basic experimental design by which this is accomplished is **the** randomized block design. A second, and very simple, direct control is exercised by holding the supplementary variable totally constant for all subjects. Direct control can also be accomplished through randomization, the purpose of randomization being to ensure that no systematic bias in the dependent variable is due to the supplementary variables. This will be true when treatments are assigned at random to a large number of subjects (or, more generally, replications).

When indirect, or statistical, control is chosen, supplementary variables are usually referred to as concomitant variables or covariates and the method of analysis is analysis of covariance (Chapter 10). A covariate is a variable which systematically varies with the dependent variable. The design goal is to assess the effects of independent variables upon the dependent variable independently of the covariate. Analysis of covariance accomplishes this through what amounts to a combination of regression and analysis of variance procedures.

1.3 EXPERIMENTAL DESIGN BASICS

It is possible to construct almost an unlimited number of different experimental designs. For that reason, no encompassing classification scheme will be presented here. Rather, the general principles by which designs are constructed and analyzed and those aspects of experimental design and analysis which are most useful to life and behavioral scientists will be emphasized.

Since Fisher's pioneering work was published in *The Design of Experiments,* a number of authors have presented classification schemes. What is perhaps the equivalent of a master collection of architects' plans is to be found in the work *Experimental Design* by W. G. Cochran and G. M. Cox (1957). Beyond that, several authors (e.g., Federer, 1963; Kirk, 1982) have emphasized that complex designs can be constructed from and classified in accordance with a few basic building block designs, the completely randomized design, the randomized complete block design, and the Latin square design. Kirk (1982) has presented the most complete classification scheme based upon the building block notion.

Nature is characterized by variation. The ideal of experimentation is to construct an environment in which all of the variation in the dependent variable is systematically related to the experimenter's manipulation of one or more independent variables. Were that ideal to be realized, there would be no need for statistics as an inductive tool for there would be no error component associated with the observations and the experimenter's task would be the mathematical one of describing the function relating the dependent and independent variables.

For the most part that ideal is never realized because the objects of study are so inherently variable or because the dependent variable is influenced by so many variables that it is impossible to hold all of them constant except the few of primary interest. Rather, observations can be conceived as having two major components, one associated with the effects of the independent variables (treatment effects) and another of unknown content which is called random error. Under these circumstances, the ideal is to design experiments in such a way that two goals are realized. First, the experiment should yield results in which systematic variation in the dependent variable can only be attributed to treatment effects. This ideal of removing all bias from estimates of treatment effects is extremely difficult to achieve. Cook and Campbell (1972) have best described those problems. However, when all bias *has* been removed, increasing the accuracy of estimating treatment effects is the same as increasing the precision with which treatment effects can be estimated, the latter being accomplished when the closeness with which measurers approach an estimate of treatment effects is increased. The second goal, then, is to reduce the non-systematic, random error components of the observations to their smallest possible value in order to increase the precision with which the treatment effects can be estimated. It is reasonable to think of treatment effects being viewed in a background of random noise. They are made understandable only when they become large relative to their noisy background.

The experimenter has an array of tools with which to attempt to achieve those two goals, some of which lie outside of the design of the experiment and others of which are integral to the design process. The best available discussion of the steps which researchers may take to reduce bias in research data and which lie outside of direct questions of experimental design is the presentation by Cook and Campbell (1979). That presentation will not be repeated here but is highly recommended.

Those tools which do fall directly under the purview of experimental design are randomization, replications, and error control.

Randomization as Control

It was Fisher who first elucidated the notion of randomization as a method of experimental control. Since that time, several authors have presented thorough explanations of the role of randomization in the design of experiments. The reader is referred to either Kempthorne (1952) or Cox (1958) for detailed accounts.

It is important to note at the outset that randomization may be called for at various points in an experiment. For example, if a series of treatments is to be presented to the same subjects, it may be desirable to randomize the sequence in which each subject receives the treatments if undesirable learning or fatigue effects occur over the treatments. The fundamental occasion for randomization, however, is the assignment of treatment conditions to subjects or, as preferred herein, assignment of subjects to treatment conditions.

As indicated earlier, variability of the dependent variable from subject to subject or from occasion to occasion may be large. Subject attributes may also interact with treatment conditions. Clearly, an experimenter cannot hope to control all subject attributes which may influence the outcome of the experiment. A decision can be made, however, about which of such attributes would best be controlled experimentally as independent variables, which can be controlled or measured as supplementary variables, and which can be "neutralized" by being allowed to vary at random. The principle in this latter case is that all variables not controlled experimentally or statistically should be allowed to vary completely at random. This is accomplished when the subjects are assigned at random to treatment conditions. The outcome is that over large numbers of subjects the unique characteristics of subjects which are not controlled are distributed evenly over the treatment conditions, the primary purpose of this being to remove bias from the estimates of treatment effects. Randomization also provides for unbiased estimates of error variance and for independence of errors.

Returning to our earlier statement that one can fruitfully conceptualize observations as having two components, one defined by treatment effects and one defined by random errors, we can identify treatment effects with those variables which the experimenter elects to manipulate as independent variables (plus possible interactions among those variables) and we can identify error effects with all of the unspecified and unmeasured variables which were randomized when subjects were assigned to treatment conditions. What error is, and how large it is, varies from study to study and from experimental design to experimental design, a point which will be emphasized as each design is discussed.

Replications as Control

To replicate an experiment or treatment condition is to repeat it under identical conditions. Normally, this means observing the treatment conditions with new subjects, each subject being treated as a replication. Replicating an experiment is required for two major purposes: it provides an estimate of variability due to error, and it allows one to increase the precision with which treatment effects are estimated.

In general, all uncontrolled sources of variation—variation not due to independent variables or supplementary variables controlled by the experimenter—are considered to be due to random assignment of subjects to the constant treatment conditions and are, by definition, error. Observations taken on two or more subjects under the same treatment conditions differ only because of error, such differences, then, providing estimates of variability due to error.

All other things being equal, the precision with which treatment effects can be estimated is directly proportional to the number of independent replications of the experiment. The question of the number of replications needed is dealt with in detail in Chapter 2.

Error Reduction

Error reduction is essential in order to detect small differences among treatment effects or to estimate treatment effects with precision. The topic of experimental design is essentially the topic of error reduction and control.

Error arises from all uncontrolled sources of variation, but can be attributed to three general sources: variability due to the very large number of ways in which living organisms differ, but which are not under experimental control; variability due to lack of constancy of experimental conditions; and variability due to the choice of a dependent variable. The latter two sources of error need not detain us long. Suffice it to say that dependent variables differ one from another with regard to their variability and, all other things being equal, preference should be to reduce error by selecting the least variable from among those which are valid measures of the construct of interest. Failure to standardize experimental conditions is a failure to hold treatment conditions constant and should, of course, be avoided. Sometimes that will be very difficult, but it will be assumed that it has been accomplished.

The third possibility for error reduction, reducing error due to heterogeneity of subjects, is accomplished through the use of supplementary variables to select subjects who are homogeneous with regard to that variable, by grouping subjects in homogeneous subgroups (blocking) based upon one or more supplementary variables, or by the use of analysis of covariance to remove the effects of supplementary variable(s) as covariates. The first two methods may be thought of as restrictions upon randomization.

The first method is simple, but severely restricts the generality of results. If, for example, the dependent variable is thought to be influenced by the motivation of subjects as well as by the treatments, one could simply select subjects at random for the experiment but with the restriction that all subjects have the same score on some measure of motivation. The outcome of the study of treatment effects, however, would be restricted to subjects with that particular level of motivation.

The second possibility for direct control of error, blocking, is of greatest interest as an experimental design tool. The basic notion is very simple: one or more supplementary variables are used to group subjects who are homogeneous with regard to those variables, creating differences between blocks with regard to the blocking variables but increasing the homogeneity of subjects within blocks. Since error is assessed between subjects within blocks and since subjects are homogeneous with regard to the variables used to form the blocks, there is no error due to the blocking variables and error is correspondingly reduced. Much of this book will be concerned with how blocking can be used to reduce error and, thereby, increase precision of the experiments.

Designs using blocks originated in agriculture, where blocks corresponded to areas of land and blocking was used to remove major differences in soil conditions from error, the requirement for accomplishing that being that soils within blocks are more homogeneous than are soil conditions between blocks. In those sciences wherein experimental materials are living organisms, blocking is most often used to remove differences between subjects from error with regard to one or more supplementary variables. For example, one might block to remove variation due to intelligence, motivation, or anxiety. However, blocking may not be with regard to any particular variable. It might involve a host of unspecified variables, as would be the case if blocks were formed with either litter mates or twins. This would also be true if blocks were used to control for such environmental variables as the time of day, season, or geographic location of the study.

A special case of blocking which is of particular interest to life, behavioral, and biological scientists is the case wherein blocks are individual subjects who are observed under all treatment conditions in either a random or specified sequence. The effect of such a design is that removing block effects from error is tantamount to removing all differences between people from error. Since it is a fundamental law that people are more like themselves than anyone else,[1] between-block (people) effects tend to be very large relative to the remaining within-block (people) error effects. The choice of a design in which each subject is randomly assigned to and observed under only a single treatment condition or a design in which subjects act as their own controls under all treatment conditions is a fundamental one; randomization procedures are different, error has a different meaning, and the assumptions underlying tests of hypotheses are quite different. Accordingly, throughout this text, these two classes of designs will be treated separately.

1.4   SUMMARY

Given a set of research hypotheses, one designs an experiment in such a way that valid conclusions can be reached regarding those hypotheses. The foundation purposes of design are to remove biases from treatment effects and to reduce error so that treatment effects can be estimated with precision and hypotheses can be tested with reasonable statistical power.

Beyond these basics, experiments must be designed in such a way that there is a high degree of correspondence between the conditions under which observations were taken, the design, and the conditions specified by a mathematical model useful for analysis. One postulates a model, imposes various conditions upon this model, and then derives consequences which are valid for the mathematical system. To the extent that the model and the conditions imposed upon the model approximate the actual experiment, the model can be used to draw inferences from the data.

The models and methods appropriate for experimental design are, for the most part, the models and methods of analysis of variance. As is the case with design, it was R. A. Fisher who provided the essentials for both analysis and inference. "Analysis of variance" is apt. It describes what the experimenter does in the design of an experiment, and it describes what is done in the analysis of the observations taken under the design.

---

[1] Consider the alternative that someone might be more like someone else than oneself.

In the design stage, the experimenter controls the answer to the question, "Why do these observations vary?" They vary because of the treatment effects which arose from manipulation of the independent variables and any interactions which may have resulted from independent variables. They also vary because of random error minus whatever reduction of error was accomplished through direct control of supplementary variables or was accomplished statistically through such techniques as analysis of covariance.

In the analysis stage appropriate mathematical procedures are invoked which partition the total variation of the observations into components associated with those various effects, i.e., analysis of the variance. From this partitioning of the variance, it is possible to evaluate the magnitude of treatment effects relative to the size of the error. If the mathematical models for inference have been appropriately mirrored in the empirical process of carrying out the research, the evaluation can be accurately carried out with the formal apparatus of statistical theory. It is that topic, the topic of design *and* analysis for the purpose of statistical inference, to which the rest of this volume is devoted.

CHAPTER 2

PRINCIPLES OF ESTIMATION AND INFERENCE: MEANS AND VARIANCES

2.1 BASIC TERMINOLOGY IN SAMPLING

It is important to establish clear definitions of many of the terms that will be used throughout this text. Since the basic domain of the subject matter is parametric inferential statistics (i.e., constructing estimates of, and testing hypotheses about, population parameters), the following designations are used to distinguish population characteristics from the samples drawn from them.

A statistical population is the collection of all elements about which one seeks information. Only a relatively small fraction, or *sample*, of the total number of elements in a statistical population can generally be observed. From data on the elements that are observed, conclusions or inferences are drawn about the characteristics of the entire population. In order to distinguish between quantities computed from observed data and quantities which characterize the population, the term *statistic* will be used to designate a quantity computed from sample data, and the term *parameter* will be used to designate a quantity characteristic of a population. Statistics are computed from sample data for two purposes: (1) to describe the data obtained in the sample, and (2) to estimate or test hypotheses about characteristics of the population.

If all the elements in a statistical population were measured on a characteristic of interest and if the measurements were then tabulated in the form of a frequency distribution, the result would be the population distribution for the characteristic measured. A description of the population distribution is made in terms of parameters. The number of parameters necessary depends on the form of the population distribution. If the form is that of the normal distribution, two parameters will completely specify the frequency distribution—the population mean, designated μ, and the population standard deviation, designated σ (or, population variance, σ^2). If the form is not normal, the mean and the standard deviation may not be sufficient to specify the distribution. Indeed these two parameters may provide relatively little information about the distribution; other parameters may be required. However, when emphasis is restricted to univariate statistical procedures, interest is almost exclusively restricted to means and variances because most parametric procedures involve the assumption that the population distribution of the variate is normal in form.

The sample mean, designated $\bar{X}$, generally provides an estimate of the population mean μ. In these same cases, the sample standard deviation, designated s, generally provides an estimate of the population standard deviation σ. The accuracy, and precision, of estimates of this kind depend upon the size of the sample from which such estimates are computed, the manner in which the sample was drawn from the population, the characteristics of the population from which the sample was drawn, and the principle used to estimate the parameter.

If a sample is drawn in such a way that (1) all elements in the population have an equal and constant chance of being drawn on all draws and (2) all possible samples have an equal (or a fixed and determinable) chance of being drawn, the resulting sample is a *random* sample from the specified population. By no means should a random sample be considered a haphazard, unplanned sample. Numerous other methods exist for drawing samples. Random samples have properties which are particularly important in statistical work. This importance stems from the fact that random sampling ensures constant and independent probabilities; the latter are relatively simple to handle mathematically.

2.2 BASIC TERMINOLOGY IN STATISTICAL ESTIMATION

Numerical values of parameters can be computed directly from observed data only when measurements on all elements in the population are available. Generally a parameter is estimated from statistics based upon one or more samples. Several criteria are used to evaluate how good a statistic is as an estimate of a parameter. One such criterion is lack of bias. A statistic is an *unbiased estimate* of a parameter if the expected value of the sampling distribution of the statistic is equal to the parameter of which it is an estimate. Thus the concept of unbiasedness is a property of the sampling distribution (see Sec. 2.6) and not strictly a property of a single statistic. When one says that a given statistic is an unbiased estimate of a parameter, what one implies is that in the long run the mean of such statistics computed from a large number of samples of equal size will be equal to the parameter. If the statistic

$\hat{\theta}$ is an estimator of the parameter θ, and if

$$E(\hat{\theta}) = \theta + c,$$

then the bias of the estimator is of magnitude c.

The mean $\bar{X}$ of a random sample from a normal population is an unbiased estimator of the population mean because the sampling distribution of $\bar{X}$ has an expected value equal to μ. Suppose that a random sample of size n is drawn from a specified normal population; suppose that the mean of this sample is 45. Then 45 is an unbiased estimate of the population mean. Suppose that a second random sample of size n is drawn from the same population; suppose that the mean of the second sample is 55. Then 55 is also an unbiased estimate of the population mean. Thus two random samples provide two unbiased estimates of the population mean; these estimates will not, in general, be equal to one another. There is no way of deciding which one, considered by itself, is the better estimate. The best single estimate of the population mean, given the two samples, is the average of the two sample means. This average is also an unbiased estimate of the population mean. It is a better estimate of μ in the sense that it has greater precision.

The *precision* of an estimator is generally measured by the standard error of its sampling distribution. The smaller the standard error, the greater the precision. Of two unbiased estimators whose sampling distributions have the same form, the better estimator is the one having the smaller standard error. The standard error of a sampling distribution is a good index of the precision only in those cases in which the form of the distribution approaches the normal distribution as the sample size increases. For statistics whose sampling distribution has this property, the *best* unbiased estimator is defined to be the one having the smallest standard error.

The *efficiency* of an unbiased estimator is measured relative to the square of the standard error of the best unbiased estimator. For example, if the squared standard error of one unbiased estimator is σ^2/n and the squared standard error of the best unbiased estimator is $\sigma^2/2n$, then the efficiency of the first estimator relative to the second is defined to be

$$E_f = \frac{\sigma^2/2n}{\sigma^2/n} = \frac{1}{2}.$$

The concept of *consistency* in an estimator is in a sense related to that of unbiasedness. An estimator is a *consistent* estimate of a parameter if the probability that it differs from the parameter by any amount approaches zero as the sample size increases. In other words, a statistic is a consistent estimator if the bias tends toward zero as the sample size increases. An unbiased estimator is a consistent estimator. On the other hand, a consistent estimator may be biased for small samples.

Properties of estimators which hold as the sample size increases are called *asymptotic* properties. How large the sample size must be before asymptotic properties can be reasonably expected to hold varies as a function of the characteristics of the population and the method of sampling being used. Consistent estimators are asymptotically unbiased estimators. Where the bias of a consistent estimator is low but its precision is high, the consistent statistic may be used in preference to an unbiased estimator having less precision.

A parameter is, in most cases, a number. It may be estimated by a number, called a *point estimate* of the parameter. Another way of estimating a parameter is to specify a range of numbers, or an interval, within which the parameter lies. This latter type of estimate is known as an *interval estimate* of the parameter. The difference between the largest and smallest numbers of the interval estimate defines the range, or width of the interval. The sampling distribution of a statistic obtained by means of purely mathematical considerations will provide information about the relative frequency (probability) of statistics in a given interval. Probabilities obtained directly from such sample distributions provide predictions about the relative frequency with which statistics of given magnitudes will occur, assuming that conditions specified in the mathematical derivation are true in the empirical population. Thus knowledge of sampling distributions permits one to argue from a specified population to consequences in a series of samples drawn from this population.

In statistical estimation, the objective is to obtain estimates of the parameters in the population, given the observations in the sample. The parameters are unknown. Given the magnitude of certain statistics computed from the observed data, from which of several possible alternative populations was this sample drawn? Concepts of likelihood, confidence, inverse probability, and fiducial probability are used by some statisticians to evaluate the answer to this last question. This question can be rephrased in terms of two of these concepts.

1 Given a sample, what is the *likelihood* that it was drawn from a population having a specified set of parameters?

2 Given a sample, with what *confidence* can it be said that the population from which it was drawn has a specified parameter within a given range?

The likelihood of obtaining a given sample is the probability of obtaining the sample as a function of different values of the parameters underlying the population. Admittedly there is only a single set of parameters underlying a specified population. These values are, however, unknown. The relative frequency with which certain samples will occur depends upon the true values of these parameters. Under one set of assumptions about the parameters' values a given sample may have very high probability of occurring, whereas under a second set of assumptions the probability of the occurrence of a given sample may be very low.

R. A. Fisher introduced a widely used principle in statistical estimation: one selects as an estimator of a parameter that value which will maximize the likelihood of the sample that is actually observed to occur. Estimators having this property are known as *maximum-likelihood estimators*. In many areas of statistics, the principle of maximum likelihood provides estimators having maximum precision (i.e., minimum standard error).

The *least-squares principle* is another widely used principle of estimation. Gauss (among others) introduced this principle into statistics. If an observation X has the structure

$$X = f(\theta_1, \ldots, \theta_\rho) + \varepsilon,$$

where

$f(\theta_1, \ldots, \theta_\rho)$ is some known function of the parameters $\theta_1, \ldots, \theta_\rho$,
ε is a random variable, say "error,"

then the least-squares estimators, $\hat{\theta}_1, \ldots, \hat{\theta}_\rho$, make

$$\sum_i [X_i - f_i(\hat{\theta}_1, \ldots, \hat{\theta}_\rho)]^2 = \text{minimum}$$

for the sample data. If $f(\theta_1, \ldots, \theta_\rho)$ is a linear function of the θ_i, then, in the class of all estimators which are linear functions of the sample observations, the least-squares estimators are minimum-variance, unbiased estimators.

Yet another widely used principle of estimation yields what are called *Bayes estimators*. For large sample sizes, Bayes estimators tend to differ very little from maximum-likelihood estimators. Under the Bayes principle, the parameter being estimated (say θ) is considered to be a random variable with a known distribution function, called the prior distribution for θ. Associated with different estimators of θ (say $\hat{\theta}_i$) there is a loss function. In many applications this loss function is taken to be proportional to $(\hat{\theta}_i - \theta)^2$. The expected value of this loss function is called the *risk*. A Bayes estimator of θ is some function of the sample observations that minimizes the expected value of the risk.

An interval estimate is frequently referred to as a *confidence interval* for a parameter. The two extreme points in this interval, the upper and lower confidence bounds, define a range of values within which there is a specified likelihood (or level or confidence) that the parameter will fall. Given information from a single sample, the parameter either does or does not lie within this range. The procedure by which the upper and lower confidence bounds are determined will, in the long run (if the study is repeated many times), ensure that the proportion of correct statements is equal to the level of confidence for the interval. The numerical values of the upper and lower confidence bounds change from sample to sample, since these bounds depend in part upon statistics computed from the samples.

An interval estimate of a parameter provides information about the precision of the estimate; a point estimate does not include such information. The principles underlying interval estimation for a parameter are closely related to the principles underlying tests of statistical hypotheses.

2.3 BASIC TERMINOLOGY IN TESTING STATISTICAL HYPOTHESES

A *statistical hypothesis* is a statement about a statistical population which, on the basis of information obtained from observed data, one seeks either to support or refute. A *statistical test* is a set of rules whereby a decision about the hypothesis is reached. Associated with the decision rules is some indication of the accuracy of the decisions reached by following the rules. The measure of the accuracy is a probability statement about making the correct decision when various conditions are true in the population in which the hypothesis applies.

The design of an experiment has a great deal to do with the accuracy of the decision based upon information supplied by an experiment. The decision rules depend in part upon what the experimenter considers critical bounds on arriving at the wrong decision. However, a statistical hypothesis does not become false when it exceeds such critical bounds, nor does the hypothesis become true when it does not exceed such bounds. Decision rules are guides in summarizing the results of a statistical test—following such guides enables the experimenter to attach probability statements to his decisions. In evaluating the outcome of a single experiment or in using the information in a single experiment as a basis for a course of action, whether an outcome exceeds an arbitrary critical value may or may not be relevant to the issue at hand. Probability statements that are associated with decision rules in a statistical test are predictions as to what may be expected to be the case if the conditions of the experiment were repeated a large number of times.

The logic of tests on statistical hypotheses is as follows. One assumes that the hypothesis that one desires to test is true. Then one examines the consequences of this assumption in terms of a sampling distribution which depends upon the truth of this hypothesis. If, as determined from the sampling distribution, observed data have a relatively high probability of occurring, the decision is made that the data do not contradict the hypothesis. On the other hand, if the probability of an observed set of data is relatively low when the hypothesis is true, the decision is that the data tend to contradict the hypothesis. Frequently the hypothesis that is tested is stated in such a way that, when the data tend to contradict it, the experimenter is actually demonstrating what it is that he is trying to establish. In such cases the experimenter is interested in being able to reject or nullify the hypothesis being tested.

The *level of significance* of a statistical test defines the probability level that is to be considered too low to warrant support of the hypothesis being tested. If the probability of the occurrence of observed data (when the hypothesis being tested is true) is smaller than the level of significance, then the data are said to contradict the hypothesis being tested, and a decision is made to reject this hypothesis. Rejection of the hypothesis being tested is equivalent to supporting one of the possible alternative hypotheses which are not contradicted.

The hypothesis being tested will be designated by the symbol H_0. The set of hypotheses that remain tenable when H_0 is rejected will be called the alternative hypothesis and will be designated by the symbol H_1. The decision rules in a statistical test are with respect to the rejection or nonrejection of H_0. The rejection of H_0 may be regarded as a decision to accept H_1; the nonrejection of H_0 may be regarded as a decision against the acceptance of H_1. If the decision rules reject H_0 when in fact H_0 is true, the rules lead to an erroneous decision. The probability of making this kind of error is at most equal to the level of significance of the test. Thus the level of significance sets an upper bound on the probability of making a decision to reject H_0 when in fact H_0 is true. This kind of erroneous decision is known as a *type 1 error*; the probability of making a type 1 error is controlled by the level of significance.

If the decision rules do not reject H_0, when in fact one of the alternative hypotheses is true, the rules also lead to an erroneous decision. This kind of error is known as a *type 2 error*. The potential magnitude of a type 2 error depends in part upon the level of significance and in part upon which one of the possible alternative hypotheses actually is true. Associated with each of the possible alternative hypotheses is a type 2 error of a different magnitude. The magnitude of a type 1 error is designated by the symbol α, and the magnitude of the type 2 error for a specified alternative hypothesis is designated by the symbol β. The definitions of type 1 and type 2 errors may be summarized as follows:

	State of affairs in the population	
Decision	H_0 **true**	H_0 **false**
Reject H_0	Type 1 error (α)	No error
Do not reject H_0	No error	Type 2 error (β)

In this summary, rejection of H_0 is regarded as being equivalent to accepting H_1 and nonrejection of H_0 equivalent to not accepting H_1. The possibility of a type 1 error exists only when the decision is to reject H_0; the possibility of a type 2 error exists only when the decision is not to reject H_0.

The experimenter has the level of significance (type 1 error) directly under his control. Type 2 error is controlled indirectly, primarily through the design of the experiment. If possible, the hypothesis to be tested is stated in such a way that the more costly error is type 1 error. It is desirable to have both types of error small. However, the two types of error are not independent—the smaller numerically the type 1 error, the larger numerically the potential type 2 error.

To see the relationship between the two types of error, consider Fig. 2.1. In part *a* of this figure the left-hand curve represents the sampling distribution of a relevant statistic when H_0 is true, and the right-hand curve represents the

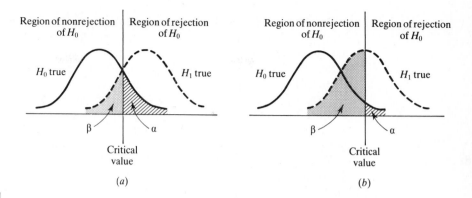

FIGURE 2-1

sampling distribution of the same statistic when a particular H_1 is true. The region of rejection of H_0 is defined with reference to the sampling distribution which assumes that H_0 is true. The decision rules specify that H_0 is to be rejected if an observed statistic has any value in the region of rejection. The probability of a statistic's falling in this region is equal to α when H_0 is true. The type 2 error associated with the particular H_1 represented in part *a* is numerically equal to the area under the right-hand curve which falls in the region of nonrejection of H_0.

In part *b* the numerical value of α is smaller than that in part *a*. This means that the decision rule has smaller type 1 error. The area under the right-hand curve in part *b* that falls in the region of nonrejection of H_0 is larger than the corresponding area in part *a*. Decreasing the numerical value of the type 1 error (level of significance) will increase the potential magnitude of the type 2 error.

The *power* of a test with respect to a specified alternative hypothesis is numerically equal to 1 minus the probability of a type 2 error. Represented geometrically, the power of a test is the area of the sampling distribution when H_1 is true that falls in the region of rejection of H_0. In part *a* of the figure, this is the area under the right-hand curve that is to the right of the critical value. The power of a test decreases as the numerical value of α decreases.

The power of a test may be defined symbolically as

$$\text{Power} = P(\text{decision rejects } H_0 \mid H_1 \text{ true}).$$

In words, power is the probability that the decision rule rejects H_0 when a specified H_1 is true. Each of the possible hypotheses in H_1 has its own power. The closer an alternative hypothesis is to H_0, that is, the greater the overlap of the corresponding sampling distributions, the lower will be the power of the test with respect to that alternative. A well-designed experiment will have relatively high power with respect to all alternatives which are different in a practical sense from H_0. For example, if H_0 states that there is zero difference between two means, then one of the possible alternative hypotheses is that the difference is 0.001 unit. For all practical purposes this alternative may not be different from H_0; hence power with respect to this alternative need not be of concern to the experimenter. However, an alternative hypothesis which states that the difference is 5 units may have practical consequences if true. Power with respect to this alternative would be a matter of concern to the experimenter.

In research in the area of the behavioral sciences, it is often difficult to evaluate the relative costs of type 1 and type 2 errors in terms of meaningful units. Both kinds of errors may be equally important, particularly in exploratory work. Too much emphasis has been placed upon the level of significance of a test and far too little emphasis upon the power of the test. In many cases where H_0 is not rejected, were the power of such tests studied carefully, the decisions might more appropriately have been that the experiment did not really provide an adequately sensitive (powerful) test of the hypothesis.

No absolute standards can be set up for determining the appropriate level of significance and power that a test should have. The level of significance used in making statistical tests should be gauged in part by the power of practically important alternative hypotheses at varying levels of significance. If experiments were conducted in the best of all possible worlds, the design of the experiment would provide adequate power for any predetermined level of significance that the experimenter were to set. However, experiments are conducted under the conditions that exist within the world in which one lives. What is needed to attain the demands of the well-designed experiment may not be realized. The experimenter must be satisfied with the best design feasible within the restrictions imposed by the working conditions. The frequent use of the 0.05 and 0.01 levels of significance is a matter of a convention having little scientific or logical basis. When the power of tests is likely to be low under these levels of significance, and when type 1 and type 2 errors are of approximately equal importance, the 0.30 and 0.20 levels of significance may be more appropriate than the 0.05 and 0.01 levels.

The evidence provided by a single experiment with respect to the truth or falsity of a statistical hypothesis is seldom complete enough to arrive at a decision which is free of all possible error. The potential risks in decisions based upon experimental evidence may in most cases be evaluated. What the magnitude of the risks should be before one takes a specified action in each case will depend upon existing conditions. The data from the statistical test will provide likelihoods associated with various actions.

2.4   VARIABLES WITH NORMAL DISTRIBUTIONS

Researchers rarely work directly with empirical distributions of variables because the number of elements (subjects) in a statistical population is usually quite large—there are frequently an infinite number of such elements assumed to exist either in reality or in principle. If the number of elements in a statistical population is infinite, the population distribution exists only in a mathematical sense; in practice, one cannot measure an infinite number of elements. One can, however, define the operations whereby this kind of measurement could be made and the operations whereby a population distribution could be constructed from those measurements. In general, the population distribution for a variable exists as a limiting process—the distribution is either represented by a mathematical model or is constructed from some form of operational definition.

Certain mathematical models for population distributions have been found to be particularly useful in inferential statistics because they provide convenient ways to test hypotheses of general interest. These include the binomial and multinomial distributions for categorical variables and the normal, t, chi-square, and F distributions for continuous variables. A more mathematically complete treatment of these distributions is provided in Appendix A. Their salience to inferences regarding means and variances is presented here.

Normal distributions, be they univariate, bivariate, or multivariate normal, have been particularly useful in parametric inferential statistics for several reasons. One reason is that they provide a reasonable model for a wide variety of biological, sociological, and behavioral phenomena because their original derivation was based upon the assumption that the variable under study is impacted by a very large number of independent events or processes. Another reason is that normal distributions are mathematically tractable and a large number of transformations of normal distributions are, themselves, normally distributed and are of interest in their own right. For example, any linear transformation of a normally distributed variable is normally distributed. One example is the sample mean, $\bar{X}$. Moreover, the *central-limit theorem* states that the sampling distribution of the means of random samples will be approximately normally distributed regardless of the form of the population distribution where the samples are large and the population variance is finite. Finally, the derivation of other important distributions, for example, t, chi-square, and F, are based upon the assumption that the random variable from which they are computed is normally distributed.

The Univariate Normal Distribution

The univariate normal distribution, which is generated by the normal probability model, may be regarded as a generalization of the binomial model where the number of independent contributors to a joint outcome is quite large. Alternatively, the normal probability model may be regarded as one which gives the probability that an outcome falls into one of an infinite number of mutually exclusive and quantitatively different categories.

The normal probability model defines a continuous distribution. This implies that a measurement X can be any value in a specified range—not necessarily an integer. The height (ordinate) Y of this distribution (probability density) at any value X is defined by the equation:

$$Y = f(X) = \frac{1}{\sigma\sqrt{2\pi}} \exp\left[\frac{-(X-\mu)^2}{2\sigma^2}\right].$$

Given a value of X, the corresponding value for Y can be obtained only if a value for μ and σ^2, the mean and variance of the distribution, can be specified. Therefore, the normal model represents a family of distributions—given different values for μ and σ^2 one obtains different members of the normal family.

Three members of this family are shown in Fig. 2-2. For each of these distributions $\mu = 0$, but the variances are different. In general, any member of the family may be specified by the symbol $N(\mu, \sigma^2)$ or $N(\mu, \sigma)$ where σ is the population standard deviation and σ^2 is the population variance.

All members of the normal family may be cast in standard form z. If z is a linear transformation of any normal distribution defined as

$$z = \frac{X-\mu}{\sigma},$$

FIGURE 2-2   Examples of the family of normal curves with means of zero and variances of 0.5, 1, and 2.

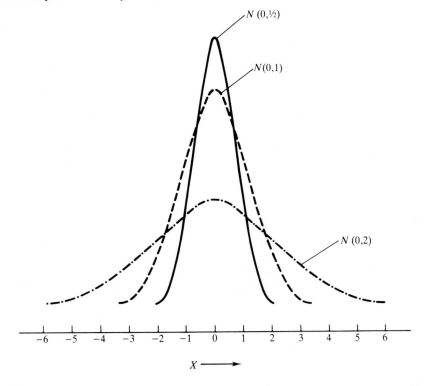

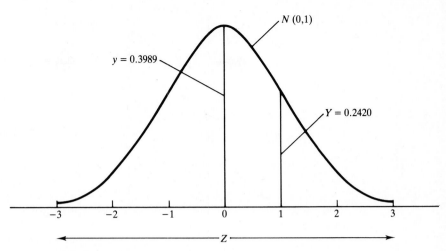

FIGURE 2-3   The unit normal distribution.

then the function becomes

$$Y = f(z) = \frac{1}{\sqrt{2\pi}} \exp\left[\frac{-z^2}{2}\right].$$

The mean and standard deviation of the z distribution are 0 and 1, respectively, and it is referred to as the unit, or standard, distribution. The height of the standard normal distribution at the point $z = 0$ is given by

$$Y = f(0) = \frac{1}{\sqrt{2\pi}} \exp[0] = 0.3989.$$

The height of this distribution at the point $z = 1$ is

$$Y = f(1) = \frac{1}{\sqrt{2\pi}} \exp\left[\frac{-1}{2}\right] = 0.2420.$$

The general form of the unit normal distribution is given in Fig. 2-3. The curve actually extends from $-\infty$ to $+\infty$, but beyond $z = \pm 3$ the height approaches zero very rapidly.

The total area under the curve in Fig. 2-3 is unity. The area under this curve over any range of values of z defines the probability that a measurement (standardized to the z scale) will have a value in this range. Equivalently, the area under the curve over the interval -1 to 1 defines the probability of z in this interval. As an example

Prob $(z \le 0) =$ area under the curve over the range from $-\infty$ to 0.

This area is represented by the shaded portion of the curve in Fig. 2-4.

Mathematically, the process of finding the area under a continuous curve

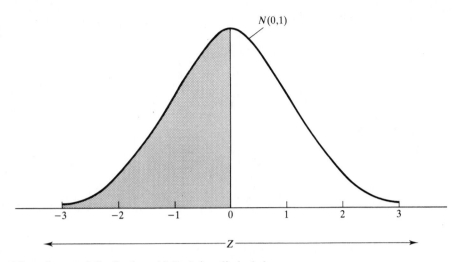

FIGURE 2-4   The unit normal distribution with Prob $(z \le 0)$ shaded.

over an interval corresponds to the process of integrating between the endpoints of the interval. The integral (area) between the limits $-\infty$ to 0 for the standard normal distribution is given by

$$\int_{-\infty}^{0} f(z)\, dz = 0.50.$$

Roughly, dz may be regarded as a small interval along the z scale and $f(z)$ as the average height of the curve in this small interval. Hence, $f(z)\, dz$ represents a column of area over a very small interval on the z scale and the integral from $-\infty$ to 0 represents the sum of all of the areas over these small intervals between $-\infty$ and 0. In dealing with discrete distributions, summation of columns of areas corresponds to integration.

In general, the integral

$$\int_{-\infty}^{m} f(z)\, dz$$

defines the cumulative probability of observing an outcome which has a measurement on the z scale which is less than or equal to m, i.e., Prob $(z \le m)$. The numerical values of this cumulative probability for some values of m are given in Appendix D.1.

The Bivariate Normal Distribution

The distributions that have been discussed up to this point are those corresponding to a single variable. Suppose that two dimensions of an outcome

TABLE 2.1. **Bivariate frequency distribution**

X_1	X_2 0	1	2	3	4	5	6	Total
5					1	1	2	4
4				1	3	3	1	8
3		1	4	9	3	1		18
2	1	6	8	4	2			21
1	2	3	1	2				8
0	1							1
Total	4	10	13	16	9	5	3	60

are considered simultaneously. For example, suppose X_1 represents the height of an element and X_2 represents the weight of an element; or X_1 may represent the blood pressure and X_2 may represent the heart rate of a subject under a given experimental condition; or X_1 may represent the score on one test and X_2 may represent the score on a second test on the same individual. Hence a measurement on a single element is represented by a pair of values designated (X_1, X_2). The joint distribution of X_1 and X_2 may, for example, take the form shown in Table 2.1.

This table represents a *bivariate* frequency distribution. Each cell entry gives the number of elements having a specified pair of values for X_1 and X_2. For example, consider the entry appearing in the row corresponding to $X_1 = 2$ and the column corresponding to $X_2 = 3$. This entry is 4; it indicates that there are four elements (of the total of 60 elements measured) for which $X_1 = 2$ and $x_2 = 3$. The relative frequency in the cell $(2, 3)$ is $4/60 = 0.067$.

The entries in the column headed "Total" represent the frequency distribution of the variable X_1 when variable X_2 is disregarded. Similarly the entries in the row headed "Total" give the frequency distribution for X_2 when X_1 is disregarded. These distributions are called the *marginal* distributions for X_1 and X_2, respectively.

Any column in Table 2.1 represents the distribution of X_1 for the value of X_2 corresponding to that column. This distribution is called the *conditional* distribution of X_1 for a specified value of X_2. Similarly any row of this table represents the conditional distribution for X_2 for the X_1 value.

In the bivariate normal probability model, the marginal distribution of X_1 is $N(\mu_1, \sigma_1^2)$, and the marginal distribution of X_2 is $N(\mu_2, \sigma_2^2)$. Not only are each of the marginal distributions normal in form but each of the conditional distributions are also normal in form. Further each of the conditional distributions for X_1 has variance $(1 - \rho^2)\sigma_1^2$, where ρ is the product-moment correlation between X_1 and X_2. It is also the case that each of the conditional distributions for X_2 has variance $(1 - \rho^2)\sigma_2^2$. Thus within each set of conditional distributions, the distributions are normal in form and have homogeneous (equal) variances. Homogeneity of variances of the conditional distributions is sometimes called *homoscedasticity*.

An additional important property of the conditional distributions of X_1 in a bivariate normal distribution is that the means of these distributions all lie on the line defined by the equation

$$X_1 = \rho \frac{\sigma_1}{\sigma_2}(X_2 - \mu_2) + \mu_1. \tag{2.1}$$

This line is called the regression of X_1 on X_2. The conditional distributions of X_2 have a similar property—the means of these distributions lie on the following line

$$X_2 = \rho \frac{\sigma_2}{\sigma_1}(X_1 - \mu_1) + \mu_2. \tag{2.2}$$

These two lines coincide when $\rho = \pm 1$; these lines are at right angles when $\rho = 0$.

If one defines,

$$z_1 = \frac{X_1 - \mu_1}{\sigma_1} \quad \text{and} \quad z_2 = \frac{X_2 - \mu_2}{\sigma_2},$$

then in terms of these standardized units of measurement (2.1) has the form

$$z_1 = \rho z_2 \tag{2.1'}$$

and (2.2) has the form

$$z_2 = \rho z_1. \tag{2.2'}$$

For example, if $\rho = 0.80$ in a bivariate normal distribution, then the mean of the conditional distribution of z_1 corresponding to $z_2 = 3$ is

$$z_1 = 0.80(3) = 2.4.$$

This implies that on the average, individuals having a z_2 measurement equal to 3 will have a z_1 measurement equal to 2.4.

The definition of the bivariate normal probability model, in terms of the standardized scale, has the following form.

$$Y = f(z_1, z_2) = \frac{1}{2\pi\sqrt{1-\rho^2}} \exp\left[\frac{-(z_1^2 + z_2^2 - 2\rho z_1 z_2)}{2(1-\rho^2)}\right] \tag{2.3}$$

In (2.3) Y represents the height (ordinate) of the bivariate normal distribution at a point (z_1, z_2). Expression (2.3) represents a family of standardized bivariate distributions—each member is defined by specifying a value of ρ. The general form of the distribution generated by (2.3) is shown in Fig. 2-5. This distribution is represented by a curved surface rather than a single curve since each cell in a two-way table defines an ordinate. In general, the parameters of a bivariate normal distribution are μ_1, μ_2, σ_1^2, σ_2^2, and ρ. Since in the

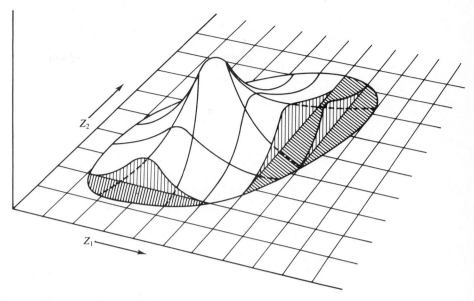

FIGURE 2-5   The bivariate normal distribution.

standardized case μ_1 and μ_2 are both 0 and σ_1^2 and σ_2^2 are both 1, this leaves only the specification of the parameter ρ to establish the distribution.

The total volume (relative frequency or probability) under this surface is unity. To obtain the cumulative volume (cumulative probability) over the area defined by $-\infty < z_1 < m_1$ and $-\infty < z_2 < m_2$, i.e., the area below and to the left of the point $z_1 = m_1$ and $z_2 = m_2$, requires the double integration

$$\int_{-\infty}^{m_2} \int_{-\infty}^{m_1} f(z_1 z_2) \, dz_1 \, dz_2.$$

Volume in the case of a bivariate distribution has the role that area has in the case of the distribution of a single variable. A cumulative bivariate probability has the form

$$\text{Prob} \, (-\infty < z_1 < m_1; \, -\infty < z_2 < m_2).$$

This probability defines the expected proportion of elements in a specified population for which the joint property $z_1 < m_1$ and $z_2 < m_2$ holds.

Before one can use the bivariate probability model to obtain such a proportion, some value for ρ must be specified. There is no single distribution in the bivariate case which corresponds to the standard normal distribution in the single-variable case. Each of the possible values of ρ between -1 and $+1$ specifies a different standard bivariate normal distribution. Hence there is a potentially infinite number of such distributions. A relatively complete set of tables of the standard bivariate normal distributions (say in 0.01 intervals for ρ) would fill a large volume; such a volume does exist.

When $\rho = 0$, then (2.3) becomes

$$Y = f(z_1, z_2) = \frac{1}{2\pi} \exp (z_1^2 + z_2^2)$$

$$= \left(\frac{1}{2\pi} \exp z_1^2 \right)\left(\frac{1}{2\pi} \exp z_2^2 \right)$$

$$= f(z_1)f(z_2).$$

In words, when $\rho = 0$, the height of the bivariate normal distribution at a point (z_1, z_2) is the product of the corresponding heights under the marginal distributions. The cumulative probability in this case is given by

$$\int_{-\infty}^{m_1} \int_{-\infty}^{m_2} f(z_1, z_2) \, dz_1 \, dz_2 = \int_{\infty}^{m_1} f(z_1) \, dz_1 \int_{-\infty}^{m_2} f(z_2) \, dz_2.$$

In words, when the product-moment correlation in a bivariate normal distribution is zero, the cumulative probability density up to the point $z_1 = m_1$, $z_2 = m_2$ is the product of the respective cumulative probabilities obtained from the marginal distributions of z_1 and z_2.

If the joint probability of two events is the product of their individual probabilities, then these two events are *statistically independent*. For the bivariate normal probability model, the condition that $\rho = 0$ is equivalent to the condition of statistical independence.

The Multivariate Normal Distribution

The normal probability model can be extended to any number of variables. If there are k variables, or dimensions of an observation that are to be considered simultaneously, the corresponding normal model is known as a k-variate normal distribution. The general expression for an element of volume (probability) has a relatively complex form unless matrix notation is used. There are k means, k variances, and $(k - 1)/2$ correlation coefficients required as parameters before any probability associated with this model can be computed. Multivariate normal distributions are presented in Appendix A.

2.5   OTHER DISTRIBUTIONS—CHI-SQUARE, t, AND F

Other than the normal distribution, there are three distributions which are fundamental to the evaluation of means and variances computed from random samples taken from a normally distributed variable. These are the chi-square, t, and F distributions.

The Chi-Square Distribution

An important class of empirical sampling distributions may be approximated by the chi-square distribution, which distribution is a special case of a gamma distribution with a single parameter k, the degrees of freedom (see Appendix A). Since the chi-square distribution is determined by a single parameter, its degrees of freedom k, all other parameters can be expressed in terms of k; the mean, or expected value, is equal to k and the variance is equal to $2k$. The probability density function is not symmetrical. The mode is $k - 2$ and the 50 percentile point is approximately $k - 0.7$.

Percentile points on the chi-square distribution may be approximated by means of a unit normal distribution, provided k is relatively large. The relation between corresponding percentile points is

$$\chi^2_{1-\alpha}(k) = \tfrac{1}{2}(\sqrt{2k - 1} + z_{1-\alpha})^2.$$

For example, the 90th percentile point on the chi-square distribution having 30 degrees of freedom, $\chi^2_{0.90}(30)$ is obtained from the 90th percentile point on the unit normal distribution ($z_{0.90} = 1.28$) as

$$\chi^2_{0.90}(30) = \tfrac{1}{2}(\sqrt{2(30) - 1} + 1.28)^2 = 40.2.$$

The larger the number of degrees of freedom, the closer the approximation.

A useful way to generate a chi-square distribution is in terms of z, a variable with a unit normal distribution. If single values of a random variable X are selected from a normally distributed population and transformed to

$$z_i = \frac{X_i - \mu}{\sigma},$$

the quantity z_i squared,

$$z_i^2 = \frac{(X_i - \mu)^2}{\sigma^2}$$

is a random variable with a chi-square distribution with a single degree of freedom, $\chi^2(1)$. It is shown graphically in Fig. 2-6. Since $\chi^2(1)$ is a squared unit normal variable, it ranges between 0 and $+\infty$ and highly skewed with an expected value of 1 and a variance of 2.

An important property of independent chi-square variables is their reproductive property; their sum is a chi-square variable with its form being determined by the sum of the independent degrees of freedom. Thus

$$\chi^2(2) = z_1^2 + z_2^2 = \frac{(X_1 - \mu)^2}{\sigma^2} + \frac{(X_2 - \mu)^2}{\sigma^2},$$

$$\chi^2(3) = z_1^2 + z_2^2 + z_3^2 = \frac{(X_1 - \mu)^2}{\sigma^2} + \frac{(X_2 - \mu)^2}{\sigma^2} + \frac{(X_3 - \mu)^2}{\sigma^2},$$

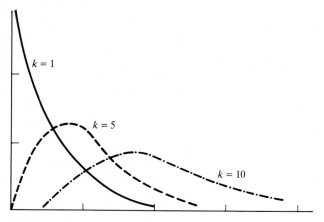

FIGURE 2-6   Chi-square distribution with 1, 5, and 10 degrees of freedom.

and, in general

$$\chi^2(k) = \sum_{i=1}^{k} z_i^2 = \frac{(X_1 - \mu)^2}{\sigma^2} + \frac{(X_2 - \mu)^2}{\sigma^2} + \cdots + \frac{(X_k - \mu)^2}{\sigma^2}.$$

Chi-square distributions with $k = 5$ and $k = 10$ are shown in Fig. 2-6.

The population mean μ is rarely known, but it is also possible to express the above relation as a chi-square distribution with the sample mean $\bar{X}$ substituted for μ. It can be shown that if random samples are selected from a population where $X = N(\mu, \sigma^2)$, then

$$\frac{\sum\limits_{i=1}^{n} (X_i - \bar{X})^2}{\sigma^2}$$

has a chi-square distribution with $k = n - 1$ degrees of freedom. Moreover, since the sample variance may be defined as an unbiased estimate of σ^2 as

$$s^2 = \frac{\sum (X_i - \bar{X})^2}{n - 1}$$

it follows that

$$\frac{(n - 1)s^2}{\sigma^2}$$

has a chi-square distribution with $n - 1$ degrees of freedom. This latter ratio for a random variable is particularly useful for testing hypotheses about and constructing confidence intervals for population variances.

Table D.9 contains selected percentiles of various chi-square distributions.

Student's t Distribution

Student's t derives its name from the fact that William Gosset, credited with its derivation, published under the pseudonym, Student.

The probability density function for Student's t distribution is discussed in detail in Appendix A. That function defines a family of distributions for a continuous variable, each specified by a single parameter, the degrees of freedom k. All central t distributions are symmetric about $E(t)$, which is

$$E(t) = 0.$$

The second moment of t is

$$E(t^2) = \sigma_t^2 = \frac{k}{k-2}.$$

It is convenient to define t in terms of a unit normal variable and a chi-square variable. In particular, if x is a unit normal variable, y is a chi-square variable with k degrees of freedom, and if x and y are independent, then

$$t = \frac{x}{\sqrt{y/k}}.$$

In words, t is a unit normal variable divided by the square root of a chi-square variable divided by its degrees of freedom.

The probability density functions for t are shown graphically in Fig. 2-7 for $k = 1$ and $k = 10$. Both curves extend from $-\infty$ to $+\infty$. The total area under each of the curves is unity. The form of the distribution resembles that of the normal; however, the t distribution is somewhat flatter than the normal when k is small and approaches the unit normal as k approaches infinity.

FIGURE 2-7   Student's t with 1 and 10 degrees of freedom.

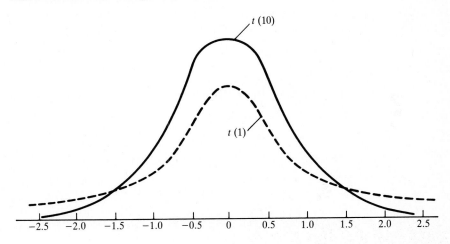

Student's t has been defined quite generally as the ratio of any unit normal variable to the square root of a chi-square variable divided by its degrees of freedom. There are many special cases of this general relation which make t particularly useful for testing hypotheses about means and for establishing confidence intervals for means. For example, the statistic

$$t = \frac{\bar{X} - \mu}{s/\sqrt{n}}$$

can be shown to be a special case of the general definition of t with $n - 1$ degrees of freedom when X and s are the means and standard deviations of random samples from a population in which $X = N(\mu, \sigma^2)$.

The F Distribution

The F distribution is a special case of the beta distribution (see Appendix A) and could be called Snedecor's F distribution. Snedecor transformed a distribution obtained by Fisher and assigned the letter F to the resulting distribution in honor of Fisher.

F may be defined mathematically as a transformed beta variable with the form

$$\int_0^{F'} CF^{(k_1/2)-1}\left(1 + \frac{k_1}{k_2} F\right)^{-(k_1+k_2)/2} dF,$$

where

$$C = \frac{(k_1 + k_2)^{k_1/2}}{\beta(k_1/2, k_2/2)}.$$

The denominator of C is known as a beta function. Tables of the F distribution are obtained by integrating this function. F defines a family of distributions determined by the parameters, k_1 and k_2, where k_1 and k_2 are the degrees of freedom of the numerator and denominator, respectively. Two F distributions are shown in Fig. 2-8, $F(10, \infty)$ and $F(10, 4)$. The first moment (expected value) of the F distribution is

$$E(F) = \frac{k_2}{k_2 - 2}, \qquad\qquad k_2 > 2.$$

The mode of the F distribution, for $k_1 > 2$, is at the point

$$\frac{k_1 - 2}{k_1} \frac{k_2}{k_2 + 2}.$$

The second central moment (variance) of the F distribution is

$$E[F - E(F)]^2 = \frac{2k_2^2(k_1 + k_2 - 2)}{k_1(k_2 - 2)^2(k_2 - 4)}, \qquad\qquad k_2 > 4.$$

Because of the skewness of the F distribution, left-hand areas are not tabled

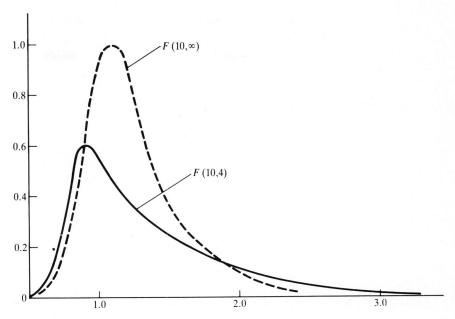

FIGURE 2-8   The F distribution with $(10, \infty)$ and $(10, 4)$ degrees of freedom.

but may be computed from the right-hand areas because F has a quasi-symmetry of the form

$$F_\alpha(k_2, k_1) = \frac{1}{F_{1-\alpha}(k_1, k_2)}.$$

That is, the left side of the distribution is the reciprocal of the right side with the degrees of freedom reversed. Thus, if one desires $F_{0.05}(10, 20)$, it may be obtained as

$$\frac{1}{F_{0.95}(20, 10)}.$$

It is very useful to know that F may be defined as the ratio of two independent chi-square variables, each divided by its respective degrees of freedom,

$$F = \frac{\chi_1^2/k_1}{\chi_2^2/k_2}.$$

We know that

$$\frac{(n-1)s^2}{\sigma^2}$$

is a chi-square variable with the degrees of freedom of s^2 being $n - 1$. If two independent random samples are taken from populations in which $X_1 = N(\mu_1, \sigma_1^2)$ and $X_2 = N(\mu_2, \sigma_2^2)$, then two chi-square variables could be defined

$$\chi_1^2(n_1 - 1) = \frac{(n_1 - 1)s_1^2}{\sigma^2},$$

$$\chi_2^2(n_2 - 1) = \frac{(n_2 - 1)s_2^2}{\sigma^2},$$

and

$$F = \frac{\chi_1^2/n_1 - 1}{\chi_2^2/n_2 - 1}$$

$$= \frac{\dfrac{(n_1 - 1)s_1^2}{\sigma^2} \Big/ n_1 - 1}{\dfrac{(n_2 - 1)s_2^2}{\sigma^2} \Big/ n_2 - 1}$$

$$= \frac{s_1^2}{s_2^2}.$$

In words, the ratio of two sample variances is an F distribution if both are unbiased estimates of the same population variance σ^2. This is an F distribution with the degrees of freedom of the variance in the numerator and denominator being k_1 and k_2, respectively. It is this latter expression of F as the ratio of two sample variances which explains its utility in the context of the analysis of variance.

Relations Among Distributions

It should be obvious that there are systematic relations which exist among the normal, chi-square, t, and F distributions. Basic among these is

$$z_{1-\alpha}^2 = \chi_{1-2\alpha}^2(1) = F_{1-2\alpha}(1, \infty) = t_{1-\alpha}^2(\infty).$$

This derives from the fact that

$$t_{1-\alpha}^2(k) = F_{1-2\alpha}(1, k)$$

$$t^2 = \frac{\text{unit normal}^2}{\chi^2/k}$$

$$= \frac{\chi^2/1}{\chi^2/k}$$

$$= F(1, k) \quad \text{and,}$$

$$t(\infty) = z.$$

Another relation of interest is:

$$\frac{1}{k}\chi^2_{1-\alpha}(k) = F_{1-\alpha}(k, \infty).$$

Equivalently,

$$\chi^2_\alpha(k) = kF_\alpha(k, \infty) = \frac{1}{F_{1-\alpha(\infty, k)}}$$

since

$$F_\alpha(k_1, k_2) = \frac{1}{F_{1-\alpha(k_2, k_1)}}.$$

2.6 INFERENCES CONCERNING MEANS

Means are measures of central tendency. Inferential tools for dealing with population means are special cases of more general procedures for making inferences about the central tendency of distributions. There are appropriate inferential tools for dealing with any number of means.

Single Means: The Sampling Distribution of $\bar{X}$

Hypothesis testing with regard to a single population mean takes the form,

H_0: μ = Something specified by the null hypothesis = μ_{H_0}
H_1: $\mu \neq \mu_{H_0}$

where "something specified by the null hypothesis" refers to any numerical value of interest to the researcher. Interval estimates of μ take the form of a confidence interval where l and L are,

$$C(l \leq \mu \leq L) = 1 - \alpha,$$

respectively, lower and upper bounds for μ, and the overall statement is a statement of confidence that those bounds actually bracket μ.

In the case of either hypothesis testing or interval estimation, the basis for inference is the sampling distribution of the statistic $\bar{X}$, the best unbiased estimate of μ.

Suppose that one were to draw a large number of samples (say 100,000), each having n elements, from a specified population. Suppose further that the procedures by which all of the samples are drawn are comparable. For each of the samples drawn, suppose that the sample mean $\bar{X}$ and the sample variance s^2 are computed. The frequency distribution of the $\bar{X}$'s defines operationally what is meant by the *sampling distribution* of the sample mean. A distribution constructed in this way provides an *empirically determined* sampling distribution for the mean. Sampling distributions of statistics are generally tabulated in terms of cumulative frequencies, relative frequencies, or probabilities. The characteristics of sampling distributions are also described by parameters. Frequently the parameters of sampling distributions are related to the parameters of the population from which the samples are drawn. As indicated earlier, the mean of the sampling distribution is called the *expected value* of the statistic; the standard deviation of the sampling distribution is called the *standard error* of the statistic. The form of the sampling distribution as well as the magnitude of its parameters depends upon (1) the distribution of the measurements in the basic population from which the sample was drawn, (2) the sampling plan followed in drawing the samples, and (3) the number of elements in the sample.

Suppose that the basic population from which sample elements are drawn can be considered to be approximately normal in form, with mean equal to some value μ, and with standard deviation equal to some value σ. If one were to draw a large number of random samples of size n from a population in which the measurements have the approximate form $N(\mu, \sigma)$, the sampling distribution of the statistic $\bar{X}$ would be approximately normal in form, with expected value approximately equal to μ, and with standard error approximately equal to $\sigma/\sqrt{n}$. Thus the sampling distribution of the mean of random samples of size n from the population $N(\mu, \sigma)$ would be $N(\mu, \sigma/\sqrt{n})$. When X is not normally distributed, by the central limits theorem the sampling distribution of the means would be approximately $N(\mu, \sigma/\sqrt{n})$.

The sampling distribution of the statistic, $\bar{X}$, assuming random sampling from the exact population $N(\mu, \sigma)$, can be derived mathematically from the properties of random samples; from purely mathematical considerations it can be shown that this sampling distribution is exactly $N(\mu, \sigma/\sqrt{n})$.[1] Herein lies the importance of random samples: they have properties which permit the estimation of sampling distributions from purely mathematical considerations without the necessity for obtaining empirical sampling distributions.

In general, the normal distribution has the property that any linear combination of independent normally distributed variables is normally distributed. Suppose that $X_1, X_2, \ldots, X_i, \ldots, X_n$ are jointly independent with densities

$$N(X_i \mid \mu = \mu_i, \sigma^2 = \sigma_i^2).$$

Suppose further that

$$C = w_1 X_1 + w_2 X_2 + \cdots + w_i X_i + \cdots + w_n X_n.$$

C is a linear combination of the X_i and the weights w are totally arbitrary. Then the density of C is

$$N(C \mid \mu_c = \sum w_i \mu_i, \sigma_c^2 = \sum w_i^2 \sigma_i^2).$$

---

[1] Strictly speaking, $\sigma_{\bar{x}} = \sigma/\sqrt{n}$ only when samples are taken with replacement. When samples are taken without replacement, $\sigma_{\bar{x}}^2 = (N - n)/(N - 1)\sigma^2/n$. This difference is practically consequential when populations are finite and small.

In words, the linear combination is normally distributed with its mean being a linear combination of the means of the original variables. The variance is a weighted sum of the variances of the original variables where the weights are the squares of the original weights w_i.

From this it follows that sums and differences of normally distributed variables are normally distributed, i.e.

$$X_1 + X_2 = N(\mu_1 + \mu_2, \sigma_1^2 + \sigma_2^2), \quad \text{since} \quad w_1 = w_2 = 1,$$

and

$$X_1 - X_2 = N(\mu_1 - \mu_2, \sigma_1^2 + \sigma_2^2), \quad \text{since} \quad w_1 = +1, \quad w_2 = -1.$$

It also follows that the sampling distribution of sample means $\bar{X}$ is normally distributed with expected value equal to μ and variance equal to σ^2/n. That is

$$\bar{X} = N(\mu, \sigma^2/n).$$

This follows from the fact that $\bar{X}$ is a linear combination of the X's wherein the weights are all equal to $1/n$. Thus, if the X's are a random sample of size n where $X = N(\mu, \sigma^2)$,

$$\bar{X} = \sum X/n$$

$$= \frac{1}{n}X_1 + \frac{1}{n}X_2 + \cdots \frac{1}{n}X_i + \cdots \frac{1}{n}X_n$$

and

$$E(\bar{X}) = \frac{1}{n}\mu + \frac{1}{n}\mu + \cdots + \frac{1}{n}\mu + \cdots + \frac{1}{n}\mu$$

$$= \frac{n}{n}\mu$$

$$= \mu$$

and

$$\sigma_{\bar{X}}^2 = \left(\frac{1}{n}\right)^2\sigma^2 + \left(\frac{1}{n}\right)^2\sigma^2 + \cdots + \left(\frac{1}{n}\right)^2\sigma^2 + \cdots + \left(\frac{1}{n}\right)^2\sigma^2$$

$$= \left(\frac{n}{n^2}\right)\sigma^2$$

$$= \frac{\sigma^2}{n}.$$

This is interesting. It means $\bar{X}$ is an unbiased estimate of μ since $E(\bar{X}) = \mu$. It also means that when $\bar{X}$ is used to estimate μ, precision of estimation is a direct function of the sample size n for any given population variance σ^2, since $\sigma_{\bar{X}}^2 = \sigma_X^2/n$.

If the population distribution is only approximately normal in form, the mathematical sampling distributions just discussed provide approximations to their operational counterparts; the larger the sample size, the better the approximation. One of the basic theorems in sampling theory, the *central-limit theorem,* states that the sampling distribution of the means of random samples will be approximately normal in form regardless of the form of the distribution in the population, provided that the sample size is sufficiently large and provided that the population variance is finite. The more the population distribution differs from the normal distribution, the larger the sample size must be for the theorem to hold.

Single Means: Testing Hypotheses—σ Assumed Known

To illustrate the basic procedures for making a statistical test, a highly simplified example will be used. Suppose that experience has shown that the form of the distribution of measurements on a characteristic of interest in a specified population is approximately normal. Further suppose, given data on a random sample of size 25 from this population, that information about the population mean μ is desired. In particular the experimenter is interested in finding out whether or not the data support the hypothesis that μ is greater than 50.

The first step in the test is to formulate H_0 and H_1. Suppose that an erroneous decision to reject the hypothesis that the population mean is 50 is more costly than an erroneous decision to reject the hypothesis that the mean is greater than 50. In this case H_0 is chosen to be $\mu = 50$; this choice for H_0 makes the more costly type of error the type 1 error, which is under the direct control of the experimenter. The alternative hypothesis in this case is $\mu > 50$. The decision rules for this test are to be formulated in such a way that rejection of H_0 is to provide evidence in favor of the tenability of H_1.

The choice for H_0 could also be $\mu \leq 50$. However, if the data tend to reject the hypothesis that $\mu = 50$ and support the hypothesis that $\mu > 50$, then the data will also tend to reject the hypothesis that $\mu < 50$. Thus, in formulating a decision rule which rejects H_0 only when the data support the hypothesis that $\mu > 50$, only the hypothesis that $\mu = 50$ need be considered. However, nonrejection of H_0 would imply $\mu \leq 50$.

When it is true that $\mu = 50$, the sampling distribution of the mean of random samples from a normal population is normal in form, with expected value equal to 50 and standard error equal to the population standard deviation divided by the square root of the sample size. In practice the value of the population standard deviation will not be known, but to keep this example simple, suppose that the population standard deviation σ is equal to 10. Then the standard error of the sampling distribution of the mean for samples of size 25 is $\sigma/\sqrt{n} = 10/\sqrt{25} = 2$. Decision rules must now be formulated to indicate when observed data are consistent with H_0 and when observed data are not consistent with H_0. The decision rules must indicate a range of potentially observable values of $\bar{X}$ for which the decision will be to reject H_0. This range of values of $\bar{X}$ will be called the region of rejection for H_0. The probability of observing an $\bar{X}$ in this region is to be at most equal to the level of significance of the test, i.e., the magnitude of the type 1 error. This sets an upper bound on the probability of reaching the wrong decision when H_0 is true. In addition to satisfying this condition with respect to type 1 error, the region of rejection for H_0 must have relatively high probability for the observed $\bar{X}$ when H_1 is true. Hence the decision rules must specify a range of values of potentially observable $\bar{X}$ in which (1) the probability of an observed $\bar{X}$'s falling in this region is at most equal to the level of significance when H_0 is true and (2) the probability of an $\bar{X}$'s falling in this region is relatively high when H_1 is true. The latter condition is necessary to assure the power of the test.

Probabilities associated with the sampling distribution of $\bar{X}$ when H_0 is true are required in order to construct the decision rules. In addition, some knowledge about the relative location of the sampling distribution of $\bar{X}$ when each of the possible alternative hypothesis is true is required. Consider Fig. 2-9. When H_0 is true, the sampling distribution of $\bar{X}$ is given by (1). When H_1 is true, (that is, μ is greater than 50), the sampling distribution of $\bar{X}$ will have an expected value somewhere to the right of 50. In particular, one possibility for this expected value is that $\mu = 54$. This possibility is represented by (2). Areas under these curves represent probabilities. The probability of observing an $\bar{X}$ in a range of values covered by the extreme right-hand tail of (1) is relatively low when H_0 is true but relatively higher when the alternative hypothesis is true.

Suppose that the experimenter wants to formulate a set of decision rules which, in the long run, will make the probability of an erroneous decision when H_0 is true less than 0.01. This is another way of saying that the level of significance of the test is to be 0.01. Suppose that the mean of the potentially observable sample is designated by the symbol $\bar{X}_{obs}$. Then the decision rules will take the following form:

Reject H_0 when $\bar{X}_{obs}$ is greater than L.

Do not reject H_0 otherwise.

L is the critical value for $\bar{X}_{obs}$; L must have the property that

$$P(\bar{X}_{obs} > L \mid H_0 \text{ true}) = 0.01.$$

FIGURE 2-9

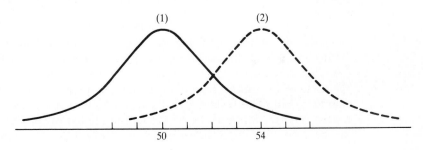

(1)   (2)

50   54

In words, the probability of drawing a sample whose mean is greater than L is to be 0.01 when H_0 is true.

Under the assumptions that have been made, when H_0 is true the form and parameters of the sampling distribution for sample means are known to be $N(50, 2)$, that is, normal in form with expected value equal to 50 and standard error equal to 2. The tabulated values of the normal distribution are directly appropriate only for the standard normal, $N(0, 1)$. From the table of the standard normal, the probability of observing a value 2.33 standard-error units or more above the mean of a population is 0.01. For the distribution $N(50, 2)$, 2.33 standard-error units above the mean would be $50 + 2.33(2) = 54.66$. Therefore,

$$P(\bar{X} > 54.66 \mid H_0 \text{ true}) = 0.01.$$

Thus the region of rejection for H_0 is $\bar{X} > 54.66$. When H_0 is true, the probability that a random sample of size 25 from $N(50, 10)$ will have a mean larger than 54.66 is less than 0.01. When one of the alternative hypotheses is true, i.e., when μ is greater than 50, the probability of a sample mean falling in this region will be higher than 0.01; the larger the difference between the true value of μ and 50, the higher the probability of an observed mean falling in the region of rejection.

The steps in formulation of the decision rule have been as follows:

1 Basic population of measurements assumed to be normal in form, with $\sigma = 10$.

2 Random sample of size $n = 25$ elements to be drawn from this population.

3 $\bar{X}_{\text{obs}}$ to be computed from sample data.

The hypothesis being tested, the alternative hypothesis, the level of significance of the test, and the decision rule are as follows:

$$H_0: \mu = 50.$$
$$H_1: \mu > 50.$$
$$\alpha = 0.01$$

Decision rules:

$$\text{Reject } H_0 \text{ when } \bar{X}_{\text{obs}} > 54.66.$$
$$\text{Do not reject } H_0 \text{ otherwise.}$$

The region of rejection for H_0 may be represented geometrically as the right-hand tail of the sampling distribution for $\bar{X}$ which assumes H_0 to be true (see Fig. 2-10).

There are many regions in which the probability is 0.01 for observing a sample mean. The level of significance of a test does not determine where the region of rejection is to be located. The choice of the extreme right-hand tail of the sampling distribution which assumes H_0 to be true was necessary in

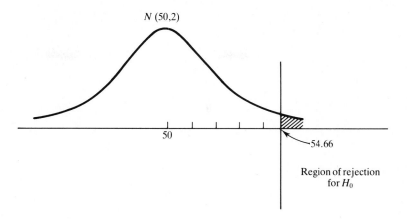

$N\,(50,2)$

50

54.66

Region of rejection
for H_0

FIGURE 2-10

order to minimize type 2 error (or, equivalently, to maximize the power). In general, the alternative hypothesis determines the *location* of the region of rejection, whereas the level of significance determines the size of the region of rejection. In this case the alternative hypothesis does not include the possibility that μ is less than 50. No matter how much smaller than 54.66 the observed sample mean is, H_0 is not rejected. Thus, if H_0 is not rejected, the evidence would indicate that μ is equal to or less than 50. On the other hand, if H_0 is rejected, the evidence would indicate that μ is greater than 50. Locating the region of rejection for H_0 in the right-hand tail provides maximum power with respect to the alternative hypothesis that μ is greater than 50.

The power of these decision rules with respect to various alternative hypotheses is readily computed. For example, the power with respect to the alternative hypothesis $\mu = 58$ is represented geometrically by the shaded area under curve (2) in Fig. 2-11. This area represents the probability of an observed mean's being greater than 54.66 when the true sampling distribution is $N(58, 2)$. With reference to the latter sampling distribution, the point 54.66, which determines the region of rejection, is $(54.66 - 58.00)/2$ or 1.67 standard-error units below the mean. The area from the mean to 1.67 standard-error units below the mean is 0.45. Hence the total shaded area is $0.45 + 0.50 = 0.95$. Thus the power of this test with respect to the alternative hypothesis $\mu = 58$ is 0.95. Conversely, the probability of a type 2 error when $\mu = 58$ is 0.05.

Instead of working directly with the sampling distribution of the statistic $\bar{X}$ and formulating the decision rules in terms of the statistic $\bar{X}$, it is more convenient to work with the statistic

$$z = \frac{\bar{X} - \mu_0}{\sigma/\sqrt{n}},$$

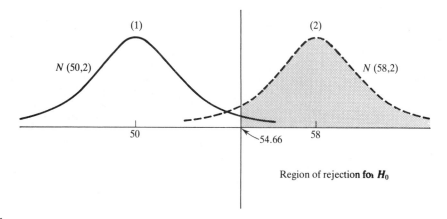

FIGURE 2-11

where μ_0 is the value specified by H_0. The sampling distribution of this z statistic is $N(0, 1)$. Given the mean of an observed sample, $\bar{X}_{\text{obs}}$, the corresponding value of the z statistic, when H_0 is $\mu = 50$ and $\sigma/\sqrt{n} = 2$, is

$$z_{\text{obs}} = \frac{\bar{X}_{\text{obs}} - 50}{2}.$$

If the alternative hypothesis is $H_1: \mu > 50$, then the decision rules for a test having level of significance 0.01 are as follows:

Reject H_0 when $z_{\text{obs}} > 2.33$.

Do not reject H_0 otherwise.

The value 2.33 satisfies the condition that

$$P(z_{\text{obs}} > 2.33 \mid H_0 \text{ true}) = 0.01.$$

This numerical value actually is the 99 percentile point on $N(0, 1)$ and will be designated by the symbol $z_{0.99}$. Thus $z_{0.99} = 2.33$. Since the level of significance for this test is $\alpha = 0.01$, the critical value for the decision rule can be designated $z_{1-\alpha}$, which in this case is $z_{0.99}$.

For the general case in which the region of rejection for H_0 is the right-hand tail of $N(0, 1)$ and the level of significance is equal to some value α, the decision rules that take the following form:

Reject H_0 when $z_{\text{obs}} > z_{1-\alpha}$.

Do not reject H_0 otherwise.

Suppose that the mean for the sample observed actually is 60. Then the

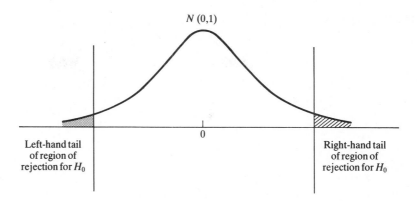

$N(0,1)$

0

Left-hand tail
of region of
rejection for H_0

Right-hand tail
of region of
rejection for H_0

FIGURE 2-12

numerical value of the z statistic (when H_0 is that $\mu = 50$ and $\sigma/\sqrt{n} = 2$) is

$$z_{obs} = \frac{60 - 50}{2} = 5.00.$$

Since z_{obs} is larger than 2.33, H_0 is rejected. Hence the observed data do not support the hypothesis that the population mean is 50. The data indicate that the mean in the population is greater than 50.

If the alternative hypothesis has the form $H_1: \mu \neq 50$, then the region of rejection for H_0 usually has the form

$$z_{obs} < z_{\alpha/2} \quad \text{and} \quad z_{obs} > z_{1-(\alpha/2)}.$$

For this kind of alternative hypothesis, the region of rejection for H_0 includes both the left-hand and right-hand extreme tails of the sampling distribution associated with H_0. The two parts of the region of rejection for H_0 are sketched in Fig. 2-12. For example, if $\alpha = 0.01$, the two-tailed region of rejection for H_0 would be z_{obs} smaller than $z_{0.005}$ and z_{obs} greater than $z_{0.995}$. Locating the region of rejection for H_0 in this manner provides power with respect to the possibility that μ is less than 50, as well as to the possibility that μ is greater than 50. An alternative hypothesis of this form is called a two-tailed alternative hypothesis, and tests which admit to the possibility of a two-tailed alternative hypothesis are called two-tailed tests. The size of either tail of the region of rejection is equal to one-half the level of significance; the total size of the region of rejection is equal to the level of significance.

Dividing α into two equal parts in this way provides equal power with respect to alternative hypotheses equidistant (on the left and right) from H_0. If there is reason to want different power for such equidistant alternative hypotheses, α should not be divided into equal parts. For example, if it is desired to have greater power with respect to alternative hypotheses to the

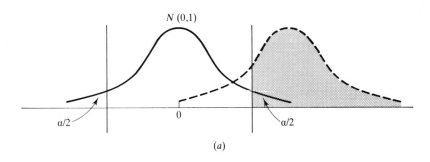

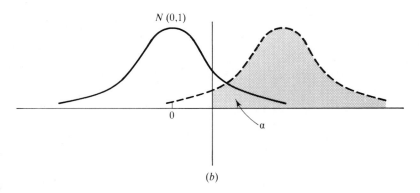

FIGURE 2-13

right of H_0, the size of the right-hand critical region may be $2\alpha/3$, whereas the size of the left-hand critical region may be $\alpha/3$.

In cases in which the experimenter is interested in rejecting H_0 only when the alternative hypothesis is one having a specified direction with respect to H_0, a one-tailed rather than a two-tailed alternative hypothesis is the more appropriate. Limiting the region of rejection to one tail of the sampling distribution for H_0 provides greater power with respect to an alternative hypothesis in the direction of that tail. This fact is illustrated geometrically in Fig. 2-13. The power under a two-tailed test with respect to a specified alternative hypothesis to the right of zero is shown by the shaded area in part *a*. The corresponding power with respect to a one-tailed test is shown in part *b*. Although the magnitude of the type 1 error is the same in both cases, the increased power in the one-tailed case is at the expense of zero power with respect to alternative hypotheses which are to the left of zero. In the latter case, all hypotheses corresponding to sampling distributions to the left of zero may be considered part of H_0.

Single Means: Testing Hypotheses—σ Unknown

If $\bar{X}$ is distributed as $N(\mu, \sigma_{\bar{X}}^2/n)$, the sampling distribution of

$$t = \frac{\bar{X} - \mu}{\sqrt{s^2/n}}, \quad \text{where} \quad s^2 = \frac{\sum (X_i - \bar{X})^2}{n - 1},$$

is Student's t with $n - 1$ degrees of freedom. The degrees of freedom for this distribution are those associated with s^2.[2]

It is noted that the normality assumption in the background of the t distribution is with respect to the sampling distribution of $\bar{X}$. Even though the distribution of X may not be normal, the distribution of $\bar{X}$ will tend to be normal in form asymptotically in n, that is, as n gets large. How large n has to be before this asymptotic property holds depends upon how far the distribution of X deviates from the normal distribution. If the latter distribution is normal in form, normality of the distribution of $\bar{X}$ holds for all n.

Since

$$t = \frac{\bar{X} - \mu}{\sqrt{s^2/n}}$$

contains the parameter μ, one may regard t as a parameter to be estimated. From data in a single sample, one obtains a set of numerical values for $\bar{X}$, s^2, and n. To estimate t one must specify a value for μ. The latter is given in terms of the hypothesis being tested. In testing hypotheses, Student's t distribution provides the statistical basis for setting up a region of rejection for H_0. The noncentral t distribution permits one to evaluate the power of the test with respect to alternative values for H_1.

For the one-tailed alternative hypothesis $\mu > \mu_0$, the region of rejection

---

[2] If $\mu' \neq \mu$, and if $\bar{X}$ is distributed as $N(\mu', \sigma_{\bar{X}}^2/n)$, then the statistic

$$t' = \frac{\bar{X} - \mu}{\sqrt{s^2/n}} = \frac{\bar{X} - \mu'}{\sqrt{s^2/n}} + \frac{\mu' - \mu}{\sqrt{\sigma^2/n}} \sqrt{\frac{\sigma^2}{s^2}}$$

$$= t + \delta \sqrt{\frac{\sigma^2}{s^2}},$$

where

$$\delta = (\mu' - \mu) \frac{\sqrt{n}}{\sigma},$$

is distributed as the *noncentral t* distribution with parameters $n - 1$ and δ, where δ is called the noncentrality parameter. Symbolically,

$$t' \text{ is distributed as } t(n - 1; \delta).$$

Note that when $\mu' = \mu$ then $\delta = 0$ and $t' = t$. Thus Student's t distribution is that special case of the noncentral t distribution for which the noncentrality parameter is zero.

of H_0 is given by

$$t_{obs} > t_{1-\alpha}(n-1),$$

where α is the level of significance and $t_{1-\alpha}(n-1)$ is the $1-\alpha$ percentile point on Student's t distribution having $n-1$ degrees of freedom. An alternative notation system for this percentile point is

$$t_{1-\alpha;n-1}.$$

To illustrate these procedures, suppose that the data observed in a random sample from the population of interest are

$$n = 25, \qquad \bar{X} = 60, \qquad s = 15.$$

Suppose that the statement of the hypothesis to be tested and the alternative hypothesis are

$$H_0: \mu = 50$$
$$H_1: \mu > 50$$

and that the level of significance of the test is 0.01. From the table of the distribution of the t statistic having 24 degrees of freedom one finds that

$$P(t_{obs} > 2.49 \mid H_0 \text{ true}) = 0.01.$$

That is, the table of the t distribution indicates that $t_{0.99}(24) = 2.49$. Hence the decision rules for this test are as follows:

Reject H_0 when t_{obs} is larger than 2.49.

Do not reject H_0 otherwise.

From the sample data, t_{obs} is found to be

$$t_{obs} = \frac{60-50}{15/\sqrt{25}} = 3.33.$$

Since t_{obs} is greater than the critical value 2.49, t_{obs} falls in the region of rejection for H_0. Hence the decision rules indicate that H_0 should be rejected.

The interpretation of this test is as follows: On the basis of the data in a random sample of size 25 from a population of interest, the hypothesis that $\mu = 50$ cannot be considered tenable when the test is made at the 0.01 level of significance. If this hypothesis were true, the probability of obtaining the data in the sample would be less than 0.01. The data obtained support the hypothesis that the mean of the population is greater than 50.

Single Means: Interval Estimates of μ

The sampling distribution of $\bar{X}$ can be transformed into either a z (σ known) or t (σ unknown) distribution in order to construct an interval estimate of μ. An interval estimate provides a lower and upper limit for a parameter along with a specification of a level of confidence for the statement. It answers the question, how confident are you that the parameter lies within the limits?

From the distributions of $\bar{X}$, z, and t (Fig. 2-14), it is obvious that all of the following probability statements are true

$$P(\bar{X}_{\alpha/2} \leq \bar{X}_{\text{obs}} \leq \bar{X}_{1-\alpha/2}) = 1 - \alpha$$
$$P(z_{\alpha/2} \leq z_{\text{obs}} \leq z_{1-\alpha/2}) = 1 - \alpha$$
$$P(t_{\alpha/2} \leq t_{\text{obs}} \leq t_{1-\alpha/2}) = 1 - \alpha.$$

That is, if a random sample of n observations is taken from a population in which $X = N(\mu, \sigma^2)$, then $1 - \alpha$ percent of $\bar{X}$'s computed from such samples would fall between $\bar{X}_{\alpha/2}$ and $\bar{X}_{1-\alpha/2}$. Transformed to z or t, the same statement can be made about those statistics. These are straightforward probability statements about the relative frequency of random variables. What is desired, however, is a statement about limits for a parameter which is a fixed value for any given population. Such a statement is a confidence statement. Confidence is sometimes referred to as inverse or fiducial probability. It can be constructed from the relations of Fig. 2-14 rather easily.

For example, the probability statement

$$P(t_{\alpha/2} \leq t_{\text{obs}} \leq t_{1-\alpha/2}) = 1 - \alpha$$

is still true if

$$P\left(t_{\alpha/2} \leq \frac{\bar{X} - \mu}{s/\sqrt{n}} \leq t_{1-\alpha/2}\right) = 1 - \alpha$$

and can be restated as

$$C\left(\bar{X} + t_{\alpha/2}\frac{s}{\sqrt{n}} \leq \mu \leq \bar{X} + t_{1-\alpha/2}\frac{s}{\sqrt{n}}\right) = 1 - \alpha$$

at which point it is a confidence statement, not a probability statement, because μ is a fixed value which does not vary. What do vary are the lower

$$l = \bar{X} + t_{\alpha/2}\frac{s}{\sqrt{n}}$$

and upper

$$L = \bar{X} + t_{1-\alpha/2}\frac{s}{\sqrt{n}}$$

limits. The confidence statement, then, is a statement about the relative frequency with which limits, which vary from sample to sample, will enclose the fixed parameter. The statement

$$C(20 \leq \mu \leq 50) = 0.95$$

means that if this experiment is repeated many times 95 percent of all limits computed would enclose the fixed value μ, while 5 percent would not include the parameter. The confidence level is often expressed as a confidence

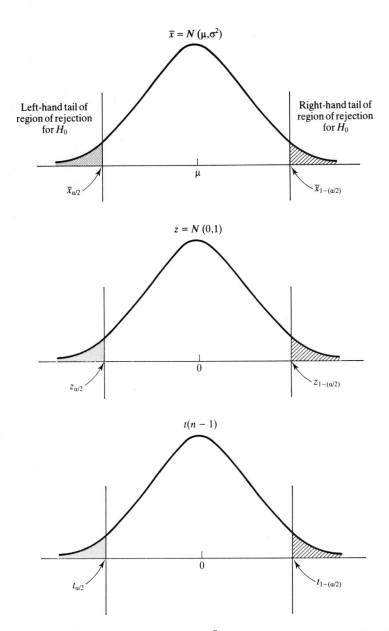

FIGURE 2-14   The probability that a random sample of $\bar{X}$, z, or t will fall between the $\alpha/2$ level and the $1 - \alpha/2$ level of the distribution.

coefficient

$$C = 100(1 - \alpha)\text{percent}.$$

Confidence intervals may involve only an upper or lower limit or they may involve both limits.

Another interpretation of a confidence statement is that it specifies the range of null hypotheses which would *not* be rejected from the same set of data used to construct the interval. It would not be logical to state that μ lies between 20 and 50, i.e.

$$C(20 \le \mu \le 50) = 0.95$$

and then reject the hypothesis H_0: $\mu = 30$ with $\alpha = 0.05$ from the same sample data.

Returning to our hypothesis testing example, having rejected the hypothesis that $\mu = 50$, suppose that the experimenter wanted to find the smallest value of μ_0 which would lead to nonrejection of H_0. The region of nonrejection for H_0 is defined by the inequality

$$\frac{\bar{X} - \mu_0}{s/\sqrt{n}} \le t_{1-\alpha}(n - 1).$$

Solving this inequality for μ_0 gives

$$\mu_0 \ge \bar{X} - \frac{s}{\sqrt{n}} t_{1-\alpha}(n - 1).$$

Thus any value of μ_0 equal to or greater than $\bar{X} - (s/\sqrt{n})t_{1-\alpha}(n - 1)$ will yield a t statistic that will fall in the region of nonrejection for H_0. For the numerical example just considered, any H_0 that specifies μ_0 to be equal to or greater than

$$60 - (3.00)(2.49) = 52.53$$

would, on the basis of the single sample observed, lead to a decision not to reject H_0. Thus, on the evidence supplied by the single sample observed, any value for μ_0 equal to or greater than 52.53 would make t_{obs} smaller than the critical value of 2.49. Therefore the experimenter may conclude that the population mean is likely to be greater than 52.53. If the experimenter were to test hypotheses specifying that μ_0 is any value equal to or less than 52.53, the decision in every case (for the data in the given sample) would be to reject H_0. This conclusion may be expressed in the form of a one-tailed confidence interval on the population mean. This confidence interval takes the general form

$$C\left[\mu \ge \bar{X} - \frac{s}{\sqrt{n}} t_{1-\alpha}(n - 1) \right] = 1 - \alpha.$$

The numerical values in terms of the observed sample data and $\alpha = 0.01$ are

$$C[\mu \ge 52.53] = 0.99.$$

The value 52.53 may be considered as the lower bound for μ. If one were to draw additional samples, the mathematical form of the lower bound would remain the same but its numerical value would change, since the numerical values of $\bar{X}$ and s would change. Once a sample has been drawn and numerical values for the confidence interval determined, the statement made in the confidence interval is either true or false. However, the procedure by which the confidence interval is constructed will, in the long run, lead to statements which are correct with probability equal to $1 - \alpha$.

The example that has just been considered involved a one-tailed alternative hypothesis. Suppose that the experimenter is willing to reject H_0 when μ is either smaller or larger than 50. In this case the alternative hypothesis takes the form $\mu \neq 50$. To provide power with respect to both tails of the alternative hypothesis, the decision rules for this case are as follows:

$$\text{Reject } H_0 \text{ when } t_{\text{obs}} \begin{cases} < t_{\alpha/2}(n-1). \\ > t_{1-(\alpha/2)}(n-1). \end{cases}$$

Otherwise do not reject H_0.

The region of rejection for H_0 for the case of a two-tailed alternative hypothesis is sketched in Fig. 2-15. The size of the region of rejection in each tail is equal to $\alpha/2$. The left-hand tail of the region of rejection makes provision for power with respect to alternative hypotheses $\mu < 50$; the right-hand tail of the region of rejection makes provision for power with respect to alternative hypotheses $\mu > 50$.

For $n - 1 = 24$ and $\alpha = 0.01$,

$$t_{\alpha/2} = t_{0.005} = -2.80,$$

and

$$t_{1-(\alpha/2)} = t_{0.995} = 2.80.$$

FIGURE 2-15

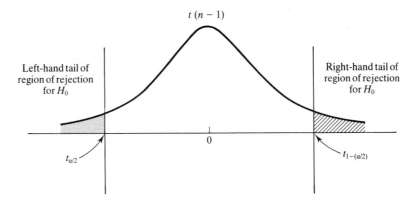

(Since Student's t distribution is symmetrical, $t_{\alpha/2} = -t_{1-(\alpha/2)}$.) For this case the decision rules are

$$\text{Reject } H_0 \text{ when } t_{\text{obs}} \begin{cases} < -2.80. \\ > 2.80. \end{cases}$$

Otherwise do not reject H_0.

For $\bar{X}_{\text{obs}} = 60$ and $s_{\text{obs}} = 15$, $t_{\text{obs}} = 3.33$. Hence the decision rules lead to rejecting H_0. Having rejected the hypothesis that $\mu = 50$, the experimenter may be interested in determining the range of values of μ which, on the basis of the observed sample data, would not be rejected by these decision rules. This range of values is defined by a two-tailed confidence interval on μ, which is given by

$$C[\bar{X} - c \le \mu \le \bar{X} + c] = 1 - \alpha,$$

where

$$c = \frac{s}{\sqrt{n}} t_{1-(\alpha/2)}(n - 1).$$

The numerical value of this confidence interval for the observed sample and $\alpha = 0.01$ is

$$C[51.60 \le \mu \le 68.40] = 0.99.$$

To illustrate the fact that any value of μ in this range which is selected for H_0 leads to a decision not to reject H_0, consider the hypothesis that $\mu = 68$. For this H_0

$$t_{\text{obs}} = \frac{60 - 68}{3} = -2.33.$$

Since t_{obs} is greater than -2.80 the hypothesis that $\mu = 68$ is not rejected.

This relationship between confidence intervals and tests of hypotheses applies to many classes of tests. Given a set of statistics computed from a sample, and given a confidence interval of size $1 - \alpha$ on a parameter, then the range of values within this interval will provide a range for the parameter in H_0 which will lead to a decision not to reject H_0 at level of significance α. If H_0 specifies values of the parameter outside this range, the decision will be to reject H_0. Two-tailed confidence intervals are associated with two-tailed tests and one-tailed confidence intervals with one-tailed tests. Thus confidence intervals provide information about the potential outcomes of a series of individual tests.

2.7   INFERENCES CONCERNING PAIRS OF MEANS

One problem common to many fields of research may be cast in the following form: which one of two procedures will produce the better results when used in a specified population? To provide information relevant for an answer, the experimenter may draw two samples from the specified population. His experiment might consist of following procedure A in one of the samples and procedure B in the other sample. (These procedures will be referred to as treatments A and B.) The question, which one of the two is the better, requires some criterion on which to base the answer. Several criteria may be relevant; treatment A may be better with respect to some of these criteria, treatment B better with respect to others. Techniques exist for the evaluation of several criteria simultaneously, but in this section methods for evaluating a single criterion at a time will be considered.

Suppose that the experimenter measures each of the elements in the two samples on a single criterion. The results may be that some of the scores under treatment A are higher than those under B, and vice versa. If the distribution of the scores within each of the samples is approximately normal in form, then a comparison of the means of the criterion scores provides one kind of information about which of the two treatments gives the better results.

In some experimental situations, the variability on the criterion within the samples assigned to different treatments is primarily a function of (1) differences in the elements observed that existed before the start of the experiment—such differences are not directly related to the experimental treatment—and (2) uncontrolled sources of variability introduced during the course of the experiment which are in no way related to the treatment itself. In such cases one might reasonably expect that the criterion variance within each of the samples assigned to the experimental treatments is due to common sources of variance. In more technical language, one might reasonably expect homogeneity of variance, i.e., that the sources of variance within each of the samples are essentially the same and that the variances in the corresponding populations are equal.

It is convenient to formalize the arguments just given in more mathematical terms. The formal mathematical argument will serve to make explicit what it is that one assumes to arrive at the conclusions that have just been reached. Let the criterion measure on element i in the sample given experimental treatment j be designated by the symbol X_{ij}. In this case there are two experimental treatments; so j stands for either treatment A or treatment B. Suppose that this measurement may be expressed as the sum of a quantity τ_j, which represents the effect of experimental treatment j, and a quantity ε_{ij}, which is not directly related to experimental treatment j. That is, suppose that

$$X_{ij} = \tau_j + \varepsilon_{ij}. \tag{2.4}$$

The effect ε_{ij} includes all the unique characteristics associated with the element i as well as all uncontrolled effects associated with the experimental conditions under which the measurement is made. The effect τ_j is assumed to be constant for all elements in the experimental group assigned to treatment j, whereas the effect ε_{ij} varies from element to element within the group and is in no direct way related to the experimental treatment. The effect ε_{ij} is frequently called the experimental error.

The term X_{ij} on the left-hand side of (2.4) represents a quantity that is observed. The terms on the right-hand side cannot be observed; they designate the variables that account for what is observed. The terms τ_j and ε_{ij} represent structural variables underlying the observed data; (2.4) is referred to as a structural model. The first basic assumption that has been made about the variables in the structural model is that they are uncorrelated. (Being uncorrelated is a less stringent assumption than statistical independence. The latter assumption is, however, required in making tests. For purposes of estimation, only the assumption of zero correlation is required.)

Let σ_a^2 and σ_b^2 designate the expected values of the criterion variance within the respective experimental groups. (That is, σ_a^2 represents the mean of the sampling distribution of the statistic s_a^2, the variance on the criterion for a sample of elements given treatment A.) Suppose the experiment is designed in such a way that in the long run there will be no difference in the unique characteristics of the group of elements assigned to treatments A and B. Suppose also that the experiment is conducted in such a manner that the uncontrolled sources of variability are comparable in the two expermental groups. These latter assumptions imply homogeneity of experimental error; i.e., they imply that $\sigma_a^2 = \sigma_b^2$. These latter assumptions also imply that the expected value of the mean of the experimental error within treatment groups A and B will be equal. That is, if $\bar\varepsilon_a$ and $\bar\varepsilon_b$ represent the respective means of the experimental error within the treatment groups, the expected values of these quantities will be equal if the assumptions are true. The quantities $\bar\varepsilon_a$ and $\bar\varepsilon_b$ are the means of structural variables and cannot be computed directly from a single sample.

Experience has shown that the model (2.4) and the assumptions made about the variables in the model are appropriate for a large class of experimental situations. The tests to be considered in this section are suitable for this class. In terms of this structural model, the mean of the criterion scores for a sample of elements given treatment A may be represented as

$$\bar{X}_a = \tau_a + \bar\varepsilon_a. \tag{2.5}$$

Since the effect τ_a is assumed to be constant for all elements in the sample, its mean effect will be simply τ_a. The corresponding mean for a sample of elements given treatment B may be represented by

$$\bar{X}_b = \tau_b + \bar\varepsilon_b. \tag{2.6}$$

The difference between the two sample means has the form

$$\bar{X}_a - \bar{X}_b = (\tau_a - \tau_b) + (\bar\varepsilon_a - \bar\varepsilon_b). \tag{2.7}$$

In words, (2.7) says that the observed difference between the criterion mean for the sample given treatment A and the criterion mean for the sample given treatment B is in part a function of the difference in effectiveness of the two treatments and in part a function of the difference between the average experimental error associated with each of the means. One purpose of a statistical test in this context is to find out whether the observed difference is of a magnitude that may be considered a function of experimental error alone or whether the observed difference indicates some effect larger than that due to experimental error.

The details in the analysis of an experiment designed to study the effects of treatments A and B on a specified criterion will now be considered. From the population of interest a random sample of n elements is drawn. The elements are subdivided at random into two subsamples—one of size n_a, the other of size n_b.

Note: In most cases n_a will be equal to n_b. The most sensitive design makes

$$n_a \sigma_b = n_b \sigma_a \quad \text{or} \quad \frac{n_a}{n_b} = \frac{\sigma_a}{\sigma_b} \quad (n_a + n_b = n).$$

This choice for n_a and n_b makes

$$\frac{\sigma_a^2}{n_a} - \frac{\sigma_b^2}{n_b} = \text{minimum}.$$

TABLE 2.2. **Outline of steps in an experiment**

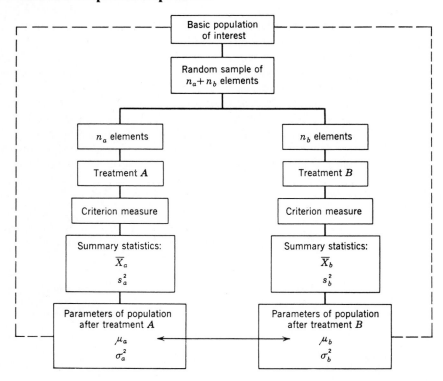

The sample of size n_a is assigned to experimental treatment A; the sample of size n_b is assigned to experimental treatment B. After the administration of the treatments, each of the elements in the experiment is measured on a common criterion. Suppose that experience in related research indicated that the distribution of such criterion measures tends to be approximately normal in the population of interest and suppose that inspection of the observed data does not contradict what past experimentation indicates about the form of the distribution of the criterion measures within each of the experimental conditions.

To summarize the information from the experiment, the sample mean and variance for each of the experimental groups are computed. The sample statistics $\bar{X}_a$ and s_a^2 provide, respectively, estimates of the parameters μ_a and σ_a^2. Similarly for treatment group B, $\bar{X}_b$ and s_b^2 provide, respectively, estimates of the parameters μ_b and σ_b^2. A schematic outline of this experiment is given in Table 2.2. If the form of the distribution of the measurements were not approximately bell-shaped, other statistics might be more appropriate to summarize the information in the samples.

The Sampling Distribution of $\bar{X}_a - \bar{X}_b$

If one were to repeat this experiment a large number of times, each time starting with a different random sample, and if one were to compute the statistic $\bar{X}_a - \bar{X}_b$ for each experiment, the sampling distribution of this statistic would be the sampling distribution of differences between pairs of independent means. If the observations in both treatment population A and treatment population B are normally distributed, then

$$\bar{X}_a - \bar{X}_b = N\left(\mu_a - \mu_b, \frac{\sigma_a^2}{n_a} + \frac{\sigma_b^2}{n_b}\right).$$

In words, $\bar{X}_a - \bar{X}_b$ is normally distributed with an expected value equal to the difference between the two population means of interest and variance equal to the sum of the variances for $\bar{X}_a$ and $\bar{X}_b$. If σ_a^2 equals σ_b^2 and if the common variance is designated σ_ε^2, then the variance

$$\sigma_{\bar{X}_a - \bar{X}_b}^2 = \sigma_\varepsilon^2\left(\frac{1}{n_a} + \frac{1}{n_b}\right).$$

These results are true because any linear combination of normally distributed variables is normally distributed with $\mathrm{E}(C) = \sum w_j \mu_j$ and $\sigma_c^2 = \sum w_j^2 \sigma_j^2$. If both treatment variables are normally distributed,

$$\bar{X}_a = N(\mu_a, \sigma_a^2)$$

and

$$\bar{X}_b = N(\mu_b, \sigma_b^2).$$

Even if the population distributions are not normal, both $\bar{X}_a$ and $\bar{X}_b$ may be normally distributed by virtue of the central limit theorem. If $\bar{X}_a$ and $\bar{X}_b$ are normally distributed, then $\bar{X}_a - \bar{X}_b$ is normally distributed because the difference is a linear combination with $w_1 = 1$ and $w_2 = -1$. Thus

$$E(\bar{X}_1 - \bar{X}_2) = w_1\mu_a + w_2\mu_b$$

$$= \mu_a - \mu_b$$

$$\sigma^2_{\bar{X}_1 - \bar{X}_2} = w_1^2\sigma^2_{\bar{X}_a} + w_2^2\sigma^2_{\bar{X}_b}$$

$$= \frac{\sigma^2_{\bar{X}_a}}{n_a} + \frac{\sigma^2_{\bar{X}_b}}{n_b}.$$

One could transform $\bar{X}_a - \bar{X}_b$ into a unit normal distribution

$$z = \frac{(\bar{X}_a - \bar{X}_b) - (\mu_a - \mu_b)}{\sqrt{\dfrac{\sigma_a^2}{n_a} + \dfrac{\sigma_b^2}{n_b}}}$$

and utilize z to test hypotheses regarding $\mu_a - \mu_b$ or establish confidence intervals for the difference between the population means. However, one does not normally know either σ_a^2 or σ_b^2; they are estimated by s_a^2 and s_b^2 and this makes it possible to utilize a t distribution for such purposes. Three cases will be considered, independent observations under treatments A and B, with and without homogeneity of error variances, and the case of non-independent observations which arises when the same elements are observed under both treatments.

Hypothesis Testing with Homogeneity of Variance

When one has homogeneity of variance, σ_ε^2 denotes the common variance for σ_a^2 and σ_b^2 and can be estimated by pooling the information available from sample A and sample B. Given s_a^2 and s_b^2, the best estimate of σ_ε^2 is a weighted average of the sample variance, the weights being the respective degrees of freedom $n_a - 1$ and $n_b - 1$. The pooled variance is s_p^2,

$$s_p^2 = \frac{(n_a - 1)s_a^2 + (n_b - 1)s_b^2}{(n_a - 1) + (n_b - 1)}.$$

This weighted average of the sample variances is known as the pooled within-class estimate of the common population variance. The degrees of freedom for s_p^2 are the sum of the respective degrees of freedom for the parts; i.e.,

$$(n_a - 1) + (n_b - 1) = n_a + n_b - 2.$$

The statistic used to test hypotheses about $\mu_a - \mu_b$ is

$$t = \frac{(\bar{X}_a - \bar{X}_b) - (\mu_a - \mu_b)}{\sqrt{s_p^2[(1/n_a) + (1/n_b)]}}.$$

The sampling distribution of this statistic, under the assumptions that have been made, is the t distribution having $n_a + n_b - 2$ degrees of freedom. Operationally, if this experiment were to be repeated a large number of times, each time with a different random sample from a specified population, and if one actually knew the value of $\mu_a - \mu_b$, then the distribution of the resulting t statistics could be approximated by the t distribution having $n_a + n_b - 2$ degrees of freedom. The latter degrees of freedom are those associated with s_p^2. In general one does not know the value of $\mu_a - \mu_b$. Its value is specified by H_0.

The denominator of the t statistic is often symbolized by $s_{\bar{X}_a - \bar{X}_b}$, that is,

$$s_{\bar{X}_a - \bar{X}_b} = \sqrt{s_p^2 \left(\frac{1}{n_a} + \frac{1}{n_b} \right)}.$$

Under this notation system,

$$t = \frac{(\bar{X}_a - \bar{X}_b) - (\mu_a - \mu_b)}{s_{\bar{X}_a - \bar{X}_b}}.$$

The t distribution is used to test hypotheses about $\mu_a - \mu_b$. In terms of the right-hand side of the structural model, the expected value of the numerator of the t statistic is $E(\bar{\varepsilon}_a - \bar{\varepsilon}_b) = 0$, and the expected value of the denominator is $\sigma_{\bar{\varepsilon}_a - \bar{\varepsilon}_b}$. Hence, when the hypothecated value of $\mu_a - \mu_b$ is actually the true value of the difference between these parameters, the t statistic provides a standardized measure of the difference in the average experimental error for the two experimental conditions.

Suppose that the experimenter is interested in testing the following hypothesis:

$$H_0: \mu_a - \mu_b = \delta.$$
$$H_1: \mu_a - \mu_b \neq \delta.$$

Level of significance $= \alpha$.

The numerical value of δ is the smallest practically important difference of interest to the experimenter. (This value is often taken to be zero.) Since the alternative hypothesis is two-tailed, a two-tailed region of rejection for H_0 is required. The region of rejection for H_0 is defined by the two tails of the sampling distribution which assumes H_0 to be true. The decision rules are as follows:

$$\text{Reject } H_0 \text{ when } t_{\text{obs}} \begin{cases} < t_{\alpha/2}(n_a + n_b - 2). \\ > t_{1-(\alpha/2)}(n_a + n_b - 2). \end{cases}$$

Do not reject H_0 otherwise.

The t statistic will be numerically large when (1) H_0 is not true or (2) H_0 is true but the difference between the mean experimental errors is unusually large relative to what is expected on the basis of the assumptions underlying the experimental design. The probability of rejecting H_0 when the latter contin-

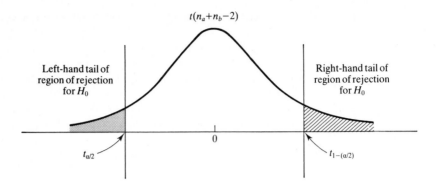

FIGURE 2-16

gency occurs is at most equal to the level of significance of the test. The region of rejection for H_0 is sketched in Fig. 2-16.

To illustrate the use of the t statistic and its sampling distribution in making a test about the difference $\mu_a - \mu_b$, suppose that the following data are obtained from an experiment designed and conducted under conditions such that the assumptions underlying the sampling distribution of the t statistic are satisfied.

Treatment	Sample size	Sample variance	Criterion mean
A	$n_a = 8$	$s_a^2 = 18$	$\bar{X}_a = 20$
B	$n_b = 10$	$s_b^2 = 12$	$\bar{X}_b = 25$

The experimenter is interested in making a two-tailed test on the hypothesis that $\mu_a - \mu_b = 0$. Since rejecting this hypothesis when it is true is considered by the experimenter to be a more costly error than not rejecting this hypothesis when it is false, H_0 has the form $\mu - \mu_b = 0$. The level of significance for this test is chosen to be 0.05. The pooled estimate of the common population variance will have 16 degrees of freedom. Hence the decision rules for this test will have the following form:

$$\text{Reject } H_0 \text{ when } t_{\text{obs}} \begin{cases} < -2.12 \\ > 2.12. \end{cases}$$

$$\text{Do not reject } H_0 \text{ otherwise.}$$

The value 2.12 is the 97.5 percentile point on the t distribution having 16 degrees of freedom, that is $t_{0.975}(16) = 2.12$. Since the t distribution is symmetrical, $t_{0.025}(16) = -2.12$.

For these data the estimate of the population variance is

$$s_p^2 = \frac{7(18) + 9(12)}{16} = 14.62.$$

The value of t_{obs} is given by

$$t_{obs} = \frac{(20 - 25) - 0}{\sqrt{14.62(\frac{1}{8} + \frac{1}{10})}} = \frac{-5}{\sqrt{14.62(\frac{18}{80})}} = \frac{-5}{1.82} = -2.75.$$

Since t_{obs} is less than the critical value -2.12, H_0 is rejected. Thus the hypothesis that treatments A and B are equally effective with respect to the criterion measure is not supported by the experimental data. Inspection indicates that treatment B has the higher mean. Hence the data support the alternative hypothesis that $\mu_a - \mu_b < 0$, that is, $\mu_a < \mu_b$.

The hypothesis that the difference between the population means is zero having been rejected, the tenable values for this difference are given by a confidence interval for $\mu_a - \mu_b$. This interval has the general form

$$C[(\bar{X}_a - \bar{X}_b) - c \leq \mu_a - \mu_b \leq (\bar{X}_a - \bar{X}_b) + c] = 1 - \alpha,$$

where

$$c = t_{1-(\alpha/2)} s_{\bar{X}_a - \bar{X}_b}.$$

For the numerical data being considered,

$$c = 2.12(1.82) = 3.86.$$

Hence a 0.95 confidence interval on the difference between the two treatment means is

$$C[-8.86 \leq \mu_a - \mu_b \leq -1.14] = 0.95.$$

For these sample data, any H_0 which specifies that $\mu_a - \mu_b$ is within this interval will lead to non-rejection of H_0 when $\alpha = 0.05$.

POWER OF THE t TEST. Consider the one-tailed hypothesis

$$H_0: \mu_a - \mu_b = 0,$$
$$H_1: \mu_a - \mu_b > 0,$$
$$\alpha = 0.01.$$

Suppose one has the following sample data:

$$n_a = 10, \qquad s_a^2 = 15.33,$$
$$n_b = 15, \qquad s_b^2 = 21.00.$$

Hence,

$$s_{pooled}^2 = \frac{(n_a - 1)s_a^2 + (n_b - 1)s_b^2}{n_a + n_b - 2} = 18.78,$$
$$\hat{\sigma} = s_{pooled} = \sqrt{s_{pooled}^2} = 4.33.$$

To obtain the power of this test with respect to the alternative hypothesis

$$(\mu_a - \mu_b)' = 6,$$

the noncentrality parameter is

$$\delta = \frac{6 - 0}{\sigma\sqrt{(1/n_a) + (1/n_b)}}.$$

One cannot evaluate this expression unless σ is known. If, however, one replaces σ by $\hat{\sigma}$, one obtains an approximate value for δ corresponding to $(\mu_a - \mu_b)' = 6$. Thus,

$$\delta \doteq \frac{6}{4.33\sqrt{\frac{1}{10} + \frac{1}{15}}} = 3.40.$$

The power of the test with respect to this value of δ may be obtained from Table D.13 for $\alpha = 0.01$. In this case $f = n_a + n_b - 2 = 23$. Reading over on line 23, the value 3.40 lies between 3.84 and 3.37. Corresponding to 3.37, $\beta = 0.20$; corresponding to 3.84, $\beta = 0.10$. Using linear interpolation,

$$\beta = 0.10 + \frac{3.84 - 3.40}{3.84 - 3.37}(0.20 - 0.10) = 0.194.$$

Hence, the power of this test when $\delta = 3.40$ is

$$\text{Power } (\delta = 3.40) = 1 - 0.194 = 0.806.$$

In Fig. 2-17, the power of the test when $\delta = 3.40$ is illustrated graphically. Note that $t_{0.99}(23) = 2.50$.

A relatively good approximation to percentile points on the noncentral t distribution may be obtained by the procedure illustrated in Fig. 2-18. If z is distributed as $N(0, 1)$, then

$$\Pr\left[t(f, \delta) \geq t_{1-\alpha}(f)\right] \doteq \Pr\left(z \geq z_\beta\right),$$

FIGURE 2-17   Schematic representation of power of t test when $\delta = 3.40$.

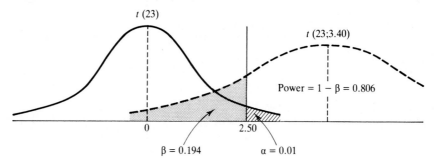

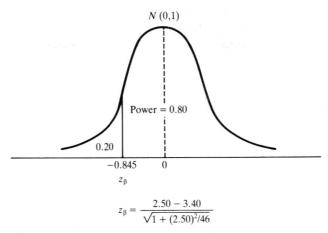

$$z_\beta = \frac{2.50 - 3.40}{\sqrt{1 + (2.50)^2/46}}$$

FIGURE 2-18   Normal approximation to noncentral t distribution.

where

$$z_\beta = \frac{t_{1-\alpha}(f) - \delta}{\sqrt{1 + [t_{1-\alpha}^2(f)/2f]}}.$$

In this case,

$$t_{1-\alpha}(f) = t_{0.99}(23) = 2.50.$$

Wilcox (1987) presents an interesting summary of work concerned with controlling statistical power and with determining sample sizes needed for that purpose.

Tests on Variances

The test on population means was based upon a structural model which assumed that $\sigma_a^2 = \sigma_b^2$. In the absence of extensive information from past experimentation in an area on which to base a judgment, the data obtained in the experiment are sometimes used to make preliminary tests on the model. Preliminary tests on structural models do not establish the appropriateness of the models; rather their appropriateness depends upon the design of the experiment and the nature of the sources of variation. The purpose of preliminary tests is to provide a partial check on whether or not the observed data tend to be consistent with the model.

Concern with homogeneity of variance as part of the model is a special case of the broader topic of evaluating inferences concerning variances. Behavioral scientists often state hypotheses in terms of means and their interest in variances is usually limited to assessing whether assumptions regarding variances which underlie tests on means have been met. Variances, however, can be of interest in their own right as indicators of important constructs. Just as is the case with means, there are procedures for evaluating hypotheses concerning single variances, pairs of variances, and multiple variances.

SINGLE VARIANCES: THE SAMPLING DISTRIBUTION OF s^2. If one were to draw a large number of samples each having n elements from a population in which $X = N(\mu, \sigma^2)$ and compute the statistic

$$s^2 = \frac{\Sigma (X_i - \bar{X})^2}{n - 1}$$

from each of the samples, s^2 would be an unbiased estimate of σ^2 which has a sampling distribution related to a chi-square distribution

$$\chi^2 = \frac{(n - 1)s^2}{\sigma^2}$$

with $n - 1$ degrees of freedom.

From this it follows that the χ^2 distribution may be used to test hypotheses regarding a specified value for σ^2 and to establish confidence intervals for σ^2. Under a random sampling plan from a normal distribution, the hypothesis

$$H_0: \ \sigma^2 = \sigma_0^2$$
$$H_1: \ \sigma^2 \neq \alpha_0^2$$

(or its one-tailed versions) can be tested at a level of significance α by the decision rule,

$$\text{Reject } H_0 \text{ if } \chi_{obs}^2 \geq \chi_{1-\alpha/2}^2(n - 1)$$
$$\leq \chi_{\alpha/2}^2(n - 1),$$

where

$$\chi_{obs}^2 = \frac{(n - 1)s^2}{\sigma_0^2}.$$

Chi-square may also be used to establish a confidence interval for σ^2. Starting with the probability statement

$$P\left[\chi_{\alpha/2}^2(n - 1) < \frac{(n - 1)s^2}{\sigma^2} < \chi_{1-\alpha/2}^2(n - 1)\right] = 1 - \alpha$$

by rearranging terms one arrives at a confidence statement about σ^2,

$$C\left[\frac{(n - 1)s^2}{\chi_{1-\alpha/2}^2} < \sigma^2 < \frac{(n - 1)s^2}{\chi_{\alpha/2}^2}\right] = 1 - \alpha.$$

This is a probability statement about the random variable s^2 since σ^2 is an unknown constant. For example, for a random sample of $n = 11$, suppose the observed variance, s^2, is found to be 20. A confidence interval on σ^2 with confidence coefficient $1 - \alpha = 0.90$ is

$$C\left[\frac{(11-1)20}{\chi^2_{0.95}(10)} < \sigma^2 < \frac{(11-1)(20)}{\chi^2_{0.05}(10)}\right] = 0.90,$$

$$C[10.93 < \sigma^2 < 50.76] = 0.90.$$

Unlike the confidence interval for μ, note that this interval is not symmetrical about the point estimator, s^2. This is because the χ^2 distribution is not symmetrical. This interval may be interpreted as a statement that 90 percent of such intervals actually bracket σ^2. It may also be interpreted that any null hypothesis which states that the variance is a value between 10.93 and 50.76 will not be rejected with these data at the $\alpha = 0.10$ level of significance.

HOMOGENEITY OF TWO VARIANCES. Regardless of the motivation for the test, as a preliminary test on the model or as a test of interest in its own right, the hypothesis that $\sigma^2_a = \sigma^2_b$ can be tested using an F distribution. In section 2.5 it was shown that an F distribution may be defined as the ratio of two sample variances both of which are unbiased estimates of the same population variance. Suppose that the following data are potentially available for random samples given treatment A and treatment B:

Treatment	Sample size	Sample variance
A	n_a	s^2_a
B	n_b	s^2_b

Assuming that the distribution of the measurements in the treatment populations is approximately normal, under the hypothesis that $\sigma^2_a = \sigma^2_b$ the statistic

$$F = \frac{s^2_a}{s^2_b}$$

has a sampling distribution which is approximated by $F(n_a - 1, n_b - 1)$, that is, an F distribution with $n_a - 1$ degrees of freedom for the numerator and $n_b - 1$ degrees of freedom for the denominator. Operationally, if the experiment yielding the potential set of data given above were to be repeated a large number of times, and if for each experiment an F statistic were computed, then the resulting distribution of the F statistics would be approximately $F(n_a - 1, n_b - 1)$. The region of rejection for the hypothesis $\sigma^2_a = \sigma^2_b$ against the alternative hypothesis $\sigma^2_a \neq \sigma^2_b$ is sketched in Fig. 2-19. The F distribution is not symmetrical, but there is a relationship by means of which percentile points in the left tail may be obtained from points in the right tail. This relationship is

$$F_{a/2}(n_a - 1, n_b - 1) = \frac{1}{F_{1-(\alpha/2)}(n_b - 1, n_a - 1)}.$$

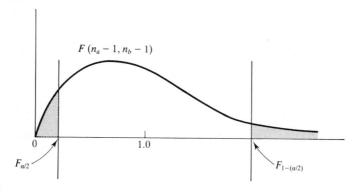

FIGURE 2-19

Most tables of the F distribution provide values only for the right-hand tail. Values for the left-hand tail are readily computed by means of this relation. There is, however, a procedure by which use of the left-hand tail may be avoided. It is actually immaterial which treatment is called A and which B. Suppose that F_{obs} is defined to be the ratio of the larger sample variance to the smaller sample variance. Hence F_{obs} will always fall toward the right-hand tail of the F distribution for which the degrees of freedom for the numerator are equal to the degrees of freedom for the larger sample variance and the degrees of freedom for the denominator are equal to the degrees of freedom for the smaller sample variance.

To illustrate this test, suppose that the following data were obtained in an experiment:

Treatment	Sample size	Sample variance
A	$n_a = 10$	$s_a^2 = 15.58$
B	$n_b = 8$	$s_b^2 = 28.20$

To test the hypothesis $\sigma_a^2 = \sigma_b^2$ against the alternative hypothesis $\sigma_a^2 \neq \sigma_b^2$,

$$F = \frac{s_{\text{larger}}^2}{s_{\text{smaller}}^2}$$

$$= \frac{28.20}{15.58} = 1.81.$$

Using this approach, the decision rule is to reject H_0 provided

$$F_{obs} \geq F_{1-\alpha/2}.$$

If the level of significance for this test is chosen to be $\alpha = 0.10$, then the critical value for the region of rejection is $F_{0.95}(7, 9) = 3.29$. Since F_{obs} does not exceed this value, the hypothesis that $\sigma_a^2 = \sigma_b^2$ is not contradicted by the observed data.

If one draws a large number of random samples of size n_a from an approximately normal population, then the sampling distribution of the statistic

$$\chi_a^2 = \frac{(n_a - 1)s_a^2}{\sigma_a^2}$$

is approximated by the chi-square distribution having $n_a - 1$ degrees of freedom. If one were to draw similar samples from the population which is approximately $N(\mu_b, \sigma_b^2)$, then the sampling distribution of the statistic

$$\chi_b^2 = \frac{(n_b - 1)s_b^2}{\sigma_b^2}$$

is approximated by the chi-square distribution having $n_b - 1$ degrees of freedom. Assuming that the two populations have no elements in common, the two chi-square statistics will be independent. In an actual experiment there will be one sample from the A population and one sample from the B population.

The statistic

$$F = \frac{\chi_a^2/(n_a - 1)}{\chi_b^2/(n_b - 1)} = \frac{s_a^2/s_b^2}{\sigma_a^2/\sigma_b^2}$$

has a sampling distribution given by $F(n_a - 1, n_b - 1)$. This statistic may be used to test any hypothesis about the relationship between σ_a^2 and σ_b^2. Under the hypothesis that $\sigma_a^2 = \sigma_b^2$, the ratio $\sigma_a^2/\sigma_b^2 = 1.00$, and the ratio assumes the form $F = s_a^2/s_b^2$. The ratio of two statistics whose sampling distributions are independent central chi-squares will have a sampling distribution given by an F distribution.

The region of rejection for this test under the hypothesis that $\sigma_a^2/\sigma_b^2 = 1$ is defined by

$$\Pr\left[\frac{s_a^2}{s_b^2} > F_{1-\alpha}(n_a - 1, n_b - 1)\right].$$

The power of this test under the alternative hypothesis

$$\frac{\sigma_a^2}{\sigma_b^2} = \theta,$$

where $\theta > 1$, is

$$\Pr\left[\theta\frac{s_a^2}{s_b^2} > F_{1-\alpha}(n_a - 1, n_b - 1)\right].$$

Thus the power function for this test is given by a noncentrality parameter, θ, times a central F distribution. This is the power function that comes into play in the variance-component model of the analysis of variance.

When concern with testing the hypothesis $\sigma_a^2 = \sigma_b^2$ is in the context of a preliminary test on the model, some cautions are in order. It is true that moderate departures from the hypothesis $\sigma_a^2 = \sigma_b^2$ do not seriously affect the accuracy of the decisions reached by means of the t test on differences between pairs of means given earlier. The t test is said to be *robust* with respect to moderate departures from the hypothesis of homogeneity of variance. This general conclusion derives from an extensive investigation of the effect of unequal variances upon the t test and the corresponding F test by Box (1954). The term moderate in this context is relative to the magnitude and difference in sample sizes. To illustrate the effect of unequal population variances upon the accuracy of the decision rule based upon the t test which assumes equal population variances, consider the case in which $\sigma_a^2 = 2\sigma_b^2$. If $n_a = 5$ and $n_b = 5$, then the 95th percentile point on the F distribution which assumes the population variances equal is approximately equal to the 94th percentile point on the sampling distribution which actually takes into account the difference in the population variances. Thus for an 0.05-level test with these sample sizes, this violation of the assumption that $\sigma_a^2 = \sigma_b^2$ results in an error in the level of significance of approximately 1 percent (in the direction of rejecting H_0 more often than should be the case).

The work of Box (1954) also indicates that the t test is robust with respect to the assumption of normality of the distributions within the treatment populations. That is, the type 1 error of the decision rule is not seriously affected when the population distributions deviate from normality. Even when population distributions are markedly skewed, the sampling distribution of the t statistic, which assumes normality provides a good approximation to the exact sampling distribution which takes into account the skewness. The caution is that the emphasis is upon moderate departures from the model. More recent work, summarized by Wilcox (1987), indicates that relatively large impact upon the nominal level of significance may occur when the right combinations of sample size, deviations from normality, and lack of homogeneity of variance occur. More will be said of this in Chapter 3.

HOMOGENEITY OF MORE THAN TWO VARIANCES. When there are k treatments, $k > 2$, one may be interested in testing the hypothesis that all variances are homogeneous

$$H_0 = \sigma_1^2 = \sigma_2^2 = \cdots = \sigma_j^2 = \cdots = \sigma_k^2.$$

This hypothesis may be of interest in its own right or as a preliminary test on the model for analysis of variance tests on a set of treatment effects defined in terms of means. There are many procedures for testing this null hypothesis as will be found in Chapter 3.

Testing Hypotheses About the Difference Between Two Means—Assuming Population Variances Not Equal

Earlier tests about $\mu_a - \mu_b$ were made under the assumption that $\sigma_a^2 = \sigma_b^2$. In this section, tests about $\mu_a - \mu_b$ make no assumption about the equality of the population variances.

The sampling distribution of the statistic

$$z = \frac{(\bar{X}_a - \bar{X}_b) - (\mu_a - \mu_b)}{\sqrt{(\sigma_a^2/n_a) + (\sigma_b^2/n_b)}} \qquad (2.8)$$

is $N(0, 1)$. Two sets of parameters are involved in this statistic. Hypotheses about $\mu_a - \mu_b$ cannot be tested unless values for σ_a^2 and σ_b^2 are known. If n_a and n_b are both large (say larger than 30), then s_a^2 and s_b^2 may be substituted for the corresponding parameters and the resulting statistic has a sampling distribution approximated by $N(0, 1)$. For small samples, however, the statistic

$$t^* = \frac{(\bar{X}_a - \bar{X}_b) - (\mu_a - \mu_b)}{\sqrt{(s_a^2/n_a) + (s_b^2/n_b)}} \qquad (2.9)$$

has a sampling distribution which is neither the normal distribution nor Student's t distribution.

Several workers have attempted to obtain the exact sampling distribution of the t^* statistic. The end products have differed slightly because of differing assumptions that were made in the course of the derivations. Behrens made one attempt to obtain the sampling distribution of the t^* statistic; Fisher enlarged upon the work of Behrens, and the resulting distribution is called the Behrens–Fisher distribution. Tables of the Behrens–Fisher distribution are given in Fisher and Yates (1953, p. 52). A method of approximating critical values of the Behrens–Fisher distribution by Student's t distribution is given by Cochran and Cox (1957, p. 101).

Not all mathematical statisticians agree with the logic underlying the derivation of the Behrens–Fisher distribution. Using a somewhat different approach to a related problem, Satterthwaite (1946) derived an approximation for the t^* distribution which involves Student's t distribution having degrees of freedom approximated by the quantity

$$f = \frac{U^2}{[V^2/(n_a - 1)] + [W^2/(n_b - 1)]}, \qquad (2.10)$$

where

$$V = \frac{s_a^2}{n_a}, \qquad W = \frac{s_b^2}{n_b} \quad \text{and} \quad U = V + W.$$

The critical values for the t^* statistic are obtained from tables of Student's t distribution having degrees of freedom equal to the nearest integer to f. A slightly different (and perhaps closer) approximation for f (Welch, 1947) is given by

$$f = \frac{U^2}{[V^2/(n_a + 1)] + [W^2/(n_b + 1)]} - 2. \qquad (2.11)$$

Welch derived an exact sampling distribution for the t^* statistic. Tables for this distribution have been prepared by Aspin (1949).

A numerical example of the use of the t^* statistic appears in Table 2.3. The approximate degrees of freedom are obtained from (2.10). The value of f

TABLE 2.3. **Numerical example**

	Treatments	
	A	**B**
Sample size	$n_a = 16$	$n_b = 8$
Sample mean	$\bar{X}_a = 30.00$	$\bar{X}_b = 21.00$
Sample variance	$s_a^2 = 32.00$	$s_b^2 = 80.00$

$H_0: \mu_a - \mu_b = 0$

$H_1: \mu_a - \mu_b \neq 0$ $\qquad t_{\text{obs}}^* = \dfrac{(30.00 - 21.00) - 0}{\sqrt{(32.00/16) + (80.00/8)}} = \dfrac{9}{\sqrt{12}} = 2.60$

$$f = \frac{(2 + 10)^2}{\frac{4}{15} + \frac{100}{7}} = 9.90$$

in (2.10) will be less than $f_a + f_b$, but greater than the smaller of f_a and f_b. If H_0 is rejected using the degrees of freedom equal to the smaller of f_a and f_b, the value of f need not be computed, since the decision reached by its use will be to reject H_0.

To test the hypothesis that $\mu_a - \mu_b = 0$ against a two-tailed alternative hypothesis, the decision rules for a test with level of significance equal to 0.05 are as follows:

$$\text{Reject } H_0 \text{ if } t_{\text{obs}}^* \begin{cases} <t_{0.025}(f). \\ >t_{0.975}(f). \end{cases}$$

Otherwise do not reject H_0.

The nearest integer to the numerical value of f computed in Table 2.3 is 10. From tables of Student's t distribution, $t_{0.975}(10) = 2.23$. The value of $t_{\text{obs}}^* = 2.60$ is greater than 2.23; hence the hypothesis that $\mu_a - \mu_b = 0$ is rejected. In this case it is not actually necessary to compute the value of f. The degrees of freedom for the variance associated with the smaller sample is 7; hence the numerical value of f will be larger than 7. Using $t_{0.975}(7) = 2.36$ as a critical value leads to the decision to reject H_0. This critical value is larger than that based upon f. Hence H_0 will also be rejected when the proper number of degrees of freedom is used in determining the critical value.

The critical value obtained from tables of the Behrens–Fisher distribution is 2.20. The use of the Cochran and Cox approximation to the Behrens–Fisher test will also be illustrated for the data in Table 2.3. The critical value for t_{obs}^* is given by

$$t_{\text{critical}} = \frac{w_a t_a + w_b t_b}{w_a + w_b}, \tag{2.12}$$

where $w_a = s_a^2/n_a$, $w_b = s_b^2/n_b$, $t_a = t_{1-(a/2)}(n_a - 1)$, and $t_b = t_{1-(a/2)}(n_b - 1)$. For the data in Table 2.3 when $\alpha = 0.05$, $w_a = 2.00$, $w_b = 10.00$, $t_a = 2.13$, $t_b = 2.36$, and

$$t_{\text{critical}} = \frac{2.00(2.13) + 10.00(2.36)}{12.00} = 2.32.$$

In general t_{critical} computed in this manner will differ only slightly from the critical value obtained by means of the Satterthwaite approximation.

Formula (2.11) is actually a modified version of (2.10). Using (2.11) to compute f for the numerical data in Table 2.3 gives

$$f = \frac{(12.00)^2}{[(2.00)^2/17] + [(10.00)^2/9]} - 2 = \frac{144}{11.35} - 2 = 10.69.$$

Use of formula (2.10) gave 9.90.

Testing Hypotheses About the Difference Between Two Means—Correlated Observations

In earlier sections the data from two independent samples were used as the basic data for tests. Elements in one of the samples were independent of (in no way related to) elements in the other sample. Hence the data in the two samples were uncorrelated. If the elements in a single sample of size n are observed under both treatments A and B, then the resulting data are generally correlated. In this case two measurements are made on each element; hence the term repeated measurements to describe this type of design. If the order in which the treatments are administered has no effect upon the final outcome, and this will generally be true when order is independently randomized for each subject, then the difference between the two measures on the same element on a common criterion provides a measure of the relative effectiveness of the treatments. This measure is free of variation due to unique but systematic effects associated with the elements themselves. In this respect, each element serves as its own control.

The following structural model, which describes the sources of variation that underlie an observation, is applicable in a variety of experimental situations:

$$X_{ia} = \tau_a + \pi_i + \varepsilon_{ia}, \tag{2.13}$$

where X_{ia} = criterion measure for element i under treatment A;
τ_a = assumed magnitude of effect of treatment A;
π_i = unique systematic effect associated with element i;
ε_{ia} = uncontrolled sources of variance affecting observation X_{ia} (the experimental error).

Each of the structural variables on the right-hand side of (2.13) is assumed to be independent of the others. The corresponding structural model for an observation on element i under treatment B has the form

$$X_{ib} = \tau_b + \pi_i + \varepsilon_{ib}. \qquad (2.14)$$

The structural model for independent observations

$$X_{ij} = \tau_j + \varepsilon_{ij},$$

combined the term π_i with the experimental error, since π_i could not be distinguished from experimental error. In experimental designs having repeated measures, this source of variance may be eliminated from experimental error. The difference between two measures on the same criterion made on a randomly selected element i is

$$d_i = X_{ia} - X_{ib} = (\tau_a - \tau_b) + (\varepsilon_{ia} - \varepsilon_{ib}). \qquad (2.15)$$

This difference does not involve the variable π_i. The term $\tau_a - \tau_b$ is assumed to be constant for all elements, whereas the term $\varepsilon_{ia} - \varepsilon_{ib}$ varies from element to element. Hence all variance of the d_i's is a function of $\varepsilon_{ia} - \varepsilon_{ib}$, which is assumed to be a measure of experimental error. The mean of the differences has the structural form

$$\bar{d} = \bar{X}_a - \bar{X}_b = (\tau_a - \tau_b) + (\bar{\varepsilon}_a - \bar{\varepsilon}_b). \qquad (2.16)$$

Thus $\bar{d}$ consists of the sum of two components. One of the components is a measure of the difference between the treatment effects; the other is a measure of the difference between the average experimental error associated with each of the treatments.

If the experimental error for the observations made under treatment A differs in no systematic way from the experimental error for the observations made under treatment B, then it is reasonable to assume that

$$E(\bar{\varepsilon}_a - \bar{\varepsilon}_b) = 0. \qquad (2.17)$$

Therefore,

$$E(\bar{d}) = \tau_a - \tau_b = \mu_a - \mu_b. \qquad (2.18)$$

In words, $\bar{d}$ provides an unbiased estimate of $\mu_a - \mu_b$. If the distribution of the d's is approximately normal with variance equal to σ_ε^2 the expected value of the variance of the term $\varepsilon_{ia} - \varepsilon_{ib}$ in the structural model, then the sampling distribution of the statistic

$$t = \frac{\bar{d} - (\mu_a - \mu_b)}{\sqrt{s_d^2/n}} \qquad (2.19)$$

may be approximated by Student's t distribution having $n-1$ degrees of freedom when $\mu_a - \mu_b = 0$, where n is the number of differences and s_d^2 is used as an estimate of σ_ε^2.

The application of this sampling distribution to testing hypotheses about $\mu_a - \mu_b$ will be illustrated by means of the data in Table 2.4. These data represent the measures on a common criterion before and after the ad-

TABLE 2.4   Numerical example

Person number	Before treatment	After treatment	Difference
1	3	6	3
2	8	14	6
3	4	8	4
4	6	4	−2
5	9	16	7
6	2	7	5
7	12	19	7

$$\sum d = 30 \quad \bar{d} = 4.29$$
$$\sum d^2 = 188$$

$$L_d = n \sum d^2 - (\sum d)^2$$
$$= 7(188) - (30)^2 = 416$$
$$s_d^2 = \frac{L_d}{n(n-1)} = \frac{416}{7(6)} = 9.90 \qquad \sqrt{s_d^2/n} = \sqrt{9.90/7} = 1.19$$

$$H_0: \mu_a - \mu_b = 0$$
$$H_1: \mu_a - \mu_b \neq 0 \qquad t_{obs} = \frac{4.29 - 0}{1.19} = 3.61$$
$$\alpha = 0.05$$

ministration of a treatment. In this type of experiment the question of which treatment is to be administered first is not relevant. For a two-tailed test at the 0.05 level of significance of the hypothesis $\mu_a - \mu_b = 0$, the decision rules are as follows:

$$\text{Reject } H_0 \text{ if } t_{obs} \begin{cases} < t_{0.025}(6) = -2.45. \\ > t_{0.975}(6) = 2.45. \end{cases}$$

Do not reject H_0 otherwise.

The value of $t_{obs} = 3.61$ falls in the region of rejection for H_0. Inspection of the data indicates that the difference in the population means is probably greater than zero.

A confidence interval for the difference between the population means takes the following general form,

$$C(\bar{d} - c \leq \mu_a - \mu_b \leq \bar{d} + c) = 1 - \alpha,$$

where

$$c = t_{1-(\alpha/2)}(n-1) \sqrt{\frac{s_d^2}{n}}.$$

The symbol $t_{1-(\alpha/2)}(n-1)$ is to be interpreted as the $[1 - (\alpha/2)]$-percentile point on the t distribution with $n-1$ degrees of freedom, not as $n-1$ times this value. For the data in Table 2.4,

$$c = 2.45(1.19) = 2.92.$$

The confidence interval is

$$C(1.37 \le \mu_a - \mu_b \le 7.21) = 0.95.$$

Hypotheses which specify that the difference in the population means lies in this range will lead to a decision not to reject H_0 when the data in Table 2.4 are used to make the test.

If a single element is to be given two different treatments for the purpose of evaluating the difference in the effectiveness, there is the question of which treatment is to be given first. It may make some difference in the results if the treatments are administered in the order A followed by B or B followed by A. That is, the carry-over effect, if any, from the sequence A followed by B, or vice versa, may be different. This kind of effect is known as a treatment by order interaction. To check upon the possibility of this interaction in a repeated-measure design, half the elements in the study may be given one sequence, the other half the reverse sequence. This design will permit the evaluation of order effects as well as treatment by order interactions. Tests associated with the evaluation of interaction effects are discussed in Chapter 5. However, if no interaction of this type exists, the t statistic in (2.19) may be used to test the difference in treatment effects when the order of administration of the treatments is counter-balanced. In the absence of any information about this interaction, the method of attack in Chapter 5 is to be preferred to the use of the t statistic in (2.19).

The variance s_d^2 in the denominator of (2.19) may be expressed in terms of the variances of the individual measures, s_a^2 and s_b^2. This relationship is

$$
\begin{aligned}
s_d^2 &= s_a^2 + s_b^2 - 2r_{ab}s_a s_b \\
&= \text{var}_a + \text{var}_b - 2\,\text{cov}_{ab},
\end{aligned}
\tag{2.20}
$$

where r_{ab} is the product-moment correlation between the measures, and where cov_{ab} is the covariance between the measures. The following relationship holds:

$$\text{cov}_{ab} = r_{ab}s_a s_b.$$

The notations var_a and var_b are sometimes used interchangeably with s_a^2 and s_b^2.

The computation of s_d^2 by means of this formula is illustrated by the numerical data in Table 2.5. A summary of the computational steps for the statistics needed is given in Table 2.5. Substituting the numerical values in Table 2.5 for the corresponding statistics in (2.20) gives

$$s_d^2 = 32.62 + 12.90 - 2(0.868)(5.71)(3.59) = 9.91.$$

Within rounding error, this is the value obtained by working directly with the difference measures.

TABLE 2.5 Numerical example (continued)

Before treatment (B)	After treatment (A)	Product of treatments
$\sum X_b = 44$	$\sum X_a = 74$	
$\sum X_b^2 = 354$	$\sum X_a^2 = 978$	$\sum X_a X_b = 572$
$L_b = n \sum X_b^2 - \left(\sum X_b\right)^2$	$L_a = n \sum X_a^2 - \left(\sum X_a\right)^2$	$L_{ab} = n \sum X_a X_b - \left(\sum X_a\right)\left(\sum X_b\right)$
$\quad = 7(354) - (44)^2$	$\quad = 7(978) - (74)^2$	$\quad = 7(572) - (74)(44)$
$\quad = 542$	$\quad = 1370$	$\quad = 748$
$s_b^2 = \dfrac{L_b}{n(n-1)}$	$s_a^2 = \dfrac{L_a}{n(n-1)}$	$r_{ab} = \dfrac{L_{ab}}{\sqrt{L_a L_b}}$
$\quad = 12.90$	$\quad = 32.62$	$\quad = \dfrac{748}{\sqrt{(1370)(542)}}$
$s_b = 3.59$	$s_a = 5.71$	$\quad = 0.868$

One of the primary advantages of repeated measures is the potential reduction in variance due to experimental error. For this design

$$s_d^2 = s_{\bar{X}_a - \bar{X}_b}^2 = \frac{s_d^2}{n} = \frac{s_a^2}{n} + \frac{s_b^2}{n} - \frac{2r_{ab}s_a s_b}{n}. \tag{2.21}$$

The corresponding estimate for the case of uncorrelated observations is

$$s_{\bar{X}_a - \bar{X}_b}^2 = \frac{s_a^2}{n} + \frac{s_b^2}{n}. \tag{2.22}$$

If the correlation is positive, and it will be positive if the model in (2.4) holds, then the estimate of the experimental error obtained from a design in which (2.21) is appropriate will be smaller than that obtained from a design involving uncorrelated observations by a factor of $2r_{ab}s_a s_b$. However, the degrees of freedom for the estimate in (2.21) are $n - 1$, whereas the degrees of freedom for the estimate in (2.22) are $2n - 2$. Before a repeated-measure design may be considered more efficient than a design which does not have repeated measures, the decrease in the experimental error must be sufficient to offset the reduction in degrees of freedom.

In areas of research in which the variance associated with the term π_i in the model in (2.13) is likely to be large, the control on this source of variation provided by a repeated-measure design will greatly increase the sensitivity of the experiment. The smaller the proportion of the total variance in an experiment due to effects which are not related to the treatments per se, the more sensitive the experiment.

CHAPTER 3

DESIGN AND ANALYSIS OF SINGLE-FACTOR EXPERIMENTS: COMPLETELY RANDOMIZED DESIGN

3.1 INTRODUCTION

The designs considered in this chapter are appropriate for single-factor experiments where comparisons are made of the relative effectiveness of two or more treatments on a common criterion. The term single-factor in this context is used in contrast to the term multifactor. In this latter type of experiment the primary objective is to compare the effect of combinations of treatments acting simultaneously on each of the elements.

In this chapter, only designs involving independent observations will be discussed; corresponding designs having correlated observations are considered in the next chapter. The designs in this chapter form a special case of what are called *completely randomized* designs. These form the building blocks for many other designs; they also provide a standard against which the efficiency of other types of designs is measured.

3.2 DEFINITIONS AND NUMERICAL EXAMPLE

A numerical example will illustrate the definitions of terms used in the analysis of a single-factor experiment. The actual analysis of this example will be given in detail. The rationale justifying this analysis will be discussed in the next section.

An experimenter is interested in evaluating the effectiveness of three methods of teaching a given course. A group of 24 subjects is available to the experimenter. This group is considered by the experimenter to be the equivalent of a random sample from the population of interest. Three

TABLE 3.1

	Method 1	Method 2	Method 3	
(i)	3	4	6	
	5	4	7	$n = 8$
	2	3	8	
	4	8	6	$k = 3$
	8	7	7	
	4	4	9	
	3	2	10	
	9	5	9	

(ii)	$T_1 = 38$	$T_2 = 37$	$T_3 = 62$	$G = \sum T_j = 137$
	$\sum X_1^2 = 224$	$\sum X_2^2 = 199$	$\sum X_3^2 = 496$	$\sum \left(\sum X_j^2 \right) = 919$

(iii)	$SS_1 = \sum X_1^2 - \dfrac{T_1^2}{n}$	$SS_2 = \sum X_2^2 - \dfrac{T_2^2}{n}$	$SS_3 = \sum X_3^2 - \dfrac{T_3^2}{n}$	$SS_w = \sum SS_j$
	$= 224 - \dfrac{38^2}{8}$	$= 199 - \dfrac{37^2}{8}$	$= 496 - \dfrac{62^2}{8}$	
	$= 43.50$	$= 27.88$	$= 15.50$	$SS_w = 86.88$

(iv)	$\bar{T}_1 = T_1/n$	$\bar{T}_2 = T_2/n$	$\bar{T}_3 = T_3/n$	$\bar{G} = G/nk$
	$= 38/8 = 4.75$	$= 37/8 = 4.62$	$= 62/8 = 7.75$	$= 137/24 = 5.71$

subgroups of eight subjects each are formed at random; the subgroups are then taught by one of the three methods. Upon completion of the course, each of the subgroups is given a common test covering the material in the course. The resulting test scores are given in part i of Table 3.1. The symbol n designates the number of subjects in a subgroup and k the number of methods.

In part ii of this table, the symbol T_j designates the sum of the test scores for the subjects who were taught by method j. For example, T_1 designates the sum of the test scores for the subjects taught by method 1. The symbol G designates the grand total of all observations in the experiment. G is most readily obtained by summing the T_j's; that is, $G = 38 + 37 + 62 = 137$. The symbol $\sum X_j^2$ designates the sum of the squares of the observations on the subjects taught by method j. For example, $\sum X_1^2 = 3^2 + 5^2 + \cdots + 9^2 = 224$.

In part iv, $\bar{T}_j$ designates the mean of the test scores for subjects taught by method j. For example, $\bar{T}_1 = 4.75$ is the mean test score for the subjects under method 1. The symbol $\bar{G}$ designates the grand mean of all test scores. When there is an equal number of subjects in each of the subgroups, $\bar{G} = (\sum \bar{T}_j)/k$, where k is the number of subgroups.

The symbol SS_j in part iii designates the sum of squares, or *variation*, of the test scores within the group under method j. By definition, the variation of the observations within method j is

$$SS_j = \sum_i (X_{ij} - \bar{T}_j)^2, \tag{3.1}$$

i.e., the sum of the squared deviations of the test scores under method j about the mean of subgroup j. This definition is algebraically equivalent to

$$SS_j = \sum X_j^2 - \frac{T_j^2}{n}, \tag{3.2}$$

which is a more convenient computational formula. Use of this formula is illustrated in part iii. The symbol SS_w designates the pooled within-method variation (or sum of squares). By definition, SS_w is the sum of the variation within each of the methods,

$$SS_w = \sum SS_j. \tag{3.3}$$

A computationally more convenient formula for SS_w is

$$SS_w = \sum \left(\sum X_j^2 \right) - \frac{\sum T_j^2}{n}. \tag{3.4}$$

For the data in the table, (3.4) is

$$SS_w = 919 - \frac{(38)^2 + (37)^2 + (62)^2}{8}$$

$$= 919 - \frac{6657}{8} = 919 - 832.12 = 86.88.$$

This value for SS_w is the same as that obtained in the table using (3.3).

The variation (or sum of squares) due to the methods of training is by definition

$$SS_{\text{methods}} = n \sum (\bar{T}_j - \bar{G})^2. \tag{3.5}$$

This statistic measures the extent to which the means for the subgroups differ from the grand mean. It is also a measure of the extent to which the subgroup means differ from one another. In terms of this latter interpretation, (3.5) may be shown to be algebraically equivalent to

$$SS_{\text{methods}} = \frac{n \sum (\bar{T}_j - \bar{T}_{j'})^2}{k}, \tag{3.6}$$

where the symbol $\bar{T}_j - \bar{T}_{j'}$ designates the difference between a pair of means. For the data in the table, (3.6) is

$$SS_{\text{methods}} = \frac{8[(4.75 - 4.62)^2 + (4.75 - 7.75)^2 + (4.62 - 7.75)^2]}{3}$$

$$= 50.08.$$

Using (3.5),

$$SS_{\text{methods}} = 8[(4.75 - 5.71)^2 + (4.62 - 5.71)^2 + (7.75 - 5.71)^2]$$

$$= 50.08.$$

Neither (3.5) nor (3.6) is a convenient computational formula for $SS_{methods}$; the latter is given by

$$SS_{methods} = \frac{\sum T_j^2}{n} - \frac{G^2}{nk}. \tag{3.7}$$

For the data in the table, (3.7) is numerically

$$SS_{methods} = \frac{(38)^2 + (37)^2 + (62)^2}{8} - \frac{(137)^2}{24}$$

$$= 832.12 - 782.04 = 50.08.$$

The variation due to experimental error is, by definition, the pooled within-method variation,

$$SS_{error} = SS_w = \sum SS_j. \tag{3.8}$$

This statistic measures the sum of the variation within each of the subgroups. Its computational formula is given by (3.4).

The total variation, or total sum of squares, is

$$SS_{total} = \sum \sum (X_{ij} - \bar{G})^2, \tag{3.9}$$

the sum of the squared deviation of each observation in the experiment about the grand mean. Its computational formula is

$$SS_{total} = \sum \left(\sum X_j^2 \right) - \frac{G^2}{nk}. \tag{3.10}$$

For the data in the table,

$$SS_{total} = 919 - \frac{(137)^2}{24}$$

$$= 136.96.$$

From these definitions of SS_{total}, $SS_{methods}$, and SS_{error}, it may be shown algebraically that

$$SS_{total} = SS_{methods} + SS_{error}, \tag{3.11}$$

$$\sum \sum (X_{ij} - \bar{G})^2 = n \sum (\bar{T}_j - \bar{G})^2 + \sum \sum (X_{ij} - \bar{T}_j)^2.$$

The relation (3.11) describes a *partition,* or division, of the total variation into two additive parts. One part is a function of differences between the mean scores made by the subgroups having different methods of training; the other part is the sum of the variation of scores within subgroups. Numerically,

$$136.96 = 50.08 + 86.88.$$

The partition represented by (3.11) is basic to the analysis of variance (ANOV). Its derivation is not difficult. Let

$$a_{ij} = X_{ij} - \bar{T}_j \quad \text{and} \quad b_j = \bar{T}_j - \bar{G}.$$

Then
$$a_{ij} + b_j = X_{ij} - \bar{G},$$

and
$$\sum_i \sum_j (X_{ij} - \bar{G})^2 = \sum_i \sum_j (a_{ij} + b_j)^2 = \sum_i \sum_j a_{ij}^2 + \sum_i \sum_j b_j^2 + 2 \sum_i \sum_j a_{ij}b_j.$$

The term at the extreme right is
$$\sum_i \sum_j a_{ij}b_j = \sum_j b_j \left(\sum_i a_{ij} \right) = 0,$$

since $\sum_i a_{ij} = 0$ for each j. (That is, $\sum_i$ is the sum of deviations about the mean of observations in class j.) Since b_j^2 is a constant for all i's in the same class,
$$\sum_i \sum_j b_j^2 = n \sum_j b_j^2.$$

Hence
$$\sum_i \sum_j (X_{ij} - \bar{G})^2 = \sum_i \sum_j a_{ij}^2 + n \sum_j b_j^2$$
$$= \sum_i \sum_j (X_{ij} - \bar{T}_j)^2 + n \sum_j (\bar{T}_j - \bar{G})^2.$$

A variance, in the terminology of analysis of variance, is more frequently called a *mean square* (abbreviated MS). By definition

$$\text{Mean square} = \frac{\text{variation}}{\text{degrees of freedom}} = \frac{\text{SS}}{\text{df}}. \tag{3.12}$$

In words, a mean square is the average variation per degree of freedom; this is also the basic definition for a variance. The term mean square is a more general term for the average of squared measures. Hence a variance is actually a special case of a mean square.

The term *degrees of freedom* originates from the geometric representation of problems associated with the determination of sampling distributions for statistics. In this context the term refers to the dimension of the geometric space appropriate in the solution of the problem. The following definition permits the computation of the degrees of freedom for any source of variation:

$$\text{Degrees of freedom} = \begin{pmatrix} \text{no. of independent} \\ \text{observations on} \\ \text{source of variation} \end{pmatrix} - \begin{pmatrix} \text{no. of independent} \\ \text{parameters estimated} \\ \text{in computing variation} \end{pmatrix}.$$
$$\tag{3.13}$$

In this context, a statistic may be used either as an estimate of a parameter or as a basic observation in estimating a source of variation. The source of variation being estimated will indicate what role a particular statistic will have in a specified context. More accurately,

$$\text{df} = (\text{no. of independent observations}) - (\text{no. of linear restraints}). \tag{3.13a}$$

Substituting an $\bar{X}_j$ for a μ_j in the computation of a mean square is equivalent to imposing a linear restraint upon the estimation procedure. The substitution restricts the sum of a set of observations to a specified number. For example, if the mean of four scores is required to be 10, and if the first three observations are

$$3, -5, \text{ and } 20,$$

then the fourth score must be 22; that is, the total must be 40. Under this restraint on the mean, only three of the four scores are free to vary. Hence the term *degrees of freedom*.

In the computation of $SS_{methods}$, the $\bar{T}_j$'s are considered to be the basic observations; $SS_{methods}$ is a measure of the variation of the $\bar{T}_j$'s. Thus, there are k independent observations in $SS_{methods}$. In the computation of this source of variation, $\bar{G}$ is used as a parameter estimating the mean of the $\bar{T}_j$'s. Hence one estimate of a parameter is used in the computation of $SS_{methods}$. Therefore, by (3.13), the degrees of freedom for this source of variation are $k - 1$.

An alternative, computational definition of the degrees of freedom for a source of variation is

$$\text{Degrees of freedom} = \begin{pmatrix} \text{no. of squared} \\ \text{deviations} \end{pmatrix} - \begin{pmatrix} \text{no. of independent points} \\ \text{about which deviations} \\ \text{are taken} \end{pmatrix}.$$

$$(3.13b)$$

For example, $SS_{methods} = n \sum (\bar{T}_j - \bar{G})^2$ involves k squared deviations all taken about the single point $\bar{G}$. Hence the degrees of freedom are $k - 1$. As another example, $SS_{error} = \sum SS_j$ involves n squared deviations for each of the k subgroups, or a total of kn squared deviations. Within each subgroup the deviations are taken about the $\bar{T}_j$ of that subgroup. Since there are k subgroups, there are k different points about which the deviations are taken. Hence the degrees of freedom are $nk - k$ for SS_{error}.

SS_{error} is the pooled variation within each of the subgroups. The variation within the subgroup j is a measure of the extent to which each of the n observations deviates from the mean of the subgroup, $\bar{T}_j$. For this source of variation, $\bar{T}_j$ is used as an estimate of the mean for population j. Hence the number of degrees of freedom for the variation within subgroup j is $n - 1$. The degrees of freedom for the pooled within-subgroup variation is the sum of the degrees of freedom for each of the subgroups. If the variation within each of k subgroups has $n - 1$ degrees of freedom, then the total degrees of freedom for k subgroups are $k(n - 1)$, that is, the sum $(n - 1) + (n - 1) + \cdots + (n - 1)$ for k terms.

SS_{total} is the variation of the nk independent observations about the grand mean $\bar{G}$. Here $\bar{G}$ is an estimate of the overall population mean. Hence SS_{total} is based upon $nk - 1$ degrees of freedom.

Corresponding to the partition of the total variation in (3.11), there is a

TABLE 3.2   **Summary of analysis of variance**

Source of variation	Sum of squares	Degrees of freedom	Mean square
Between methods	$\mathrm{SS_{methods}} = 50.08$	$k - 1 = 2$	$\mathrm{MS_{methods}} = 25.04$
Experimental error	$\mathrm{SS_{error}} = 86.88$	$kn - k = 21$	$\mathrm{MS_{error}} = 4.14$
Total	$\mathrm{SS_{total}} = 136.96$	$kn - 1 = 23$	

partition of the total degrees of freedom,

$$\mathrm{df_{total}} = \mathrm{df_{methods}} + \mathrm{df_{error}},$$
$$kn - 1 = (k - 1) + (kn - k). \tag{3.14}$$

A summary of the statistics used in the analysis of a single-factor experiment is given in Table 3.2. The numerical entries are those computed from the data in Table 3.1.

Assuming that there is no difference in the effectiveness of the methods of training, as measured by the mean scores on the test, and making additional assumptions which will become explicit in the next section, the statistic

$$F = \frac{\mathrm{MS_{methods}}}{\mathrm{MS_{error}}} \tag{3.15}$$

has the sampling distribution of an F distribution having $k - 1$ degrees of freedom for the numerator and $kn - k$ degrees of freedom for the denominator. Thus the F statistic may be used to test the hypothesis that the population means for the methods are equal. To test the hypothesis that the population means for the test scores are equal, that is, $\mu_1 = \mu_2 = \mu_3$, against a two-tailed alternative hypothesis, the decision rules are as follows:

Reject H_0 when $F_{obs} > F_{1-\alpha}(k - 1, kn - k)$.

Otherwise do not reject H_0.

For the data in Table 3.2, $F_{obs} = 25.04/4.14 = 6.05$. Critical values for $\alpha = 0.05$ and $\alpha = 0.01$ are, respectively, $F_{0.95}(2, 21) = 3.47$ and $F_{0.99}(2, 21) = 5.78$. In this case F_{obs} exceeds the critical value for $\alpha = 0.01$. Hence the data do not support the hypothesis that the population means are equal. Inspection of the means in Table 3.1 indicate that method 3 has the largest mean.

The experiment represented by the data in Table 3.1 is a special case of a single-factor experiment. For this case, the experimental variable is the method of training. In the general case the term *treatment* will be used interchangeably with the terms *experimental variable, experimental condition,* or whatever it is that distinguishes the manner in which the subgroups are handled (treated) in the experiment. The elements assigned to a treatment constitute what will be called a treatment class. A general notation for the observed data in a single-factor experiment having n observations in each

TABLE 3.3 **General notation**

Treatment 1	$\cdots$	Treatment j	$\cdots$	Treatment k	

(i)

X_{11}		X_{1j}		X_{1k}	
X_{21}		X_{2j}		X_{2k}	
$\vdots$		$\vdots$		$\vdots$	
X_{i1}		X_{ij}		X_{ik}	
$\vdots$		$\vdots$		$\vdots$	
X_{n1}		X_{nj}		X_{nk}	

(ii)

Treatment 1	$\cdots$	Treatment j	$\cdots$	Treatment k	
T_1		T_j		T_k	G
$\sum X_1^2$		$\sum X_j^2$		$\sum X_k^2$	$\sum (\sum X_j^2)$
$\bar{T}_1$		$\bar{T}_j$		$\bar{T}_k$	$\bar{G}$

(iii)

$$SS_{treat} = \frac{\sum T_j^2}{n} - \frac{G^2}{kn} \qquad\qquad df_{treat} = k - 1$$

$$SS_{error} = \sum \left(\sum X_j^2 \right) - \frac{\sum T_j^2}{n} \qquad\qquad df_{error} = kn - k$$

$$SS_{total} = \sum \left(\sum X_j^2 \right) - \frac{G^2}{kn} \qquad\qquad df_{total} = kn - 1$$

(iv)

Computational symbols	Sum of squares in terms of computational symbols
$(1) = G^2/kn$	$SS_{treat} = (3) - (1)$
$(2) = \sum \left(\sum X_j^2 \right)$	$SS_{error} = (2) - (3)$
$(3) = \left(\sum T_j^2 \right) \big/ n$	$SS_{total} = (2) - (1)$

treatment class is given in part i of Table 3.3. For example, an observation on the element i in treatment class j is designated X_{ij}. Notation for the totals required in the computation of the sums of squares appears in part ii. For example, T_j designates the sum of all observations in treatment class j, and $\sum X_j^2$ designates the sum of the squares of the observations in treatment class j.

In part iii the computational formulas for the sums of squares used in the analysis of variance and the associated degrees of freedom are given. A convenient method for summarizing the computational formulas is given in part iv in terms of what may be called computational symbols. For example, the symbol (2) designates the numerical value of $\sum(\sum X_j^2)$.

The degrees of freedom for a sum of squares may be computed directly from the computational formula by means of the following rule: Count the number of quantities which are squared in a term, and then replace this term by this number in the computational formula. For example, in the term $(\sum T_j^2)/n$ there are k quantities that are squared ($T_1, T_2, \ldots, T_k$). In the term

TABLE 3.4 **General form of summary data**

Source	SS	df	MS	F
Treatments	SS_{treat}	$k - 1$	MS_{treat}	$F = \dfrac{MS_{treat}}{MS_{error}}$
Experimental error	SS_{error}	$kn - k$	MS_{error}	
Total	SS_{total}	$kn - 1$		

G^2/kn there is just one term which is squared, namely, G. Hence the degrees of freedom of the sum of squares defined by $[(\sum T_j^2)/n - G^2/kn]$ are $k - 1$. As another example, in the term $\sum (\sum X_j^2)$ there are kn terms that are squared; namely, each of the kn individual observations. Hence the sum of squares defined by $[\sum (\sum X_j^2) - G^2/kn]$ has $kn - 1$ degrees of freedom.

The general form used in summarizing the analysis of variance for a single-factor experiment is given in Table 3.4. The F statistic is used in testing the hypothesis that $\mu_1 = \mu_2 = \cdots = \mu_k$ against the equivalent of a two-tailed alternative hypothesis. If this hypothesis is rejected, additional tests are required for more detailed information about which means are different from the others. Specialized tests for comparing individual means with each other are discussed in later sections.

The formal method for testing statistical hypotheses requires that the level of significance of a test be set in advance of obtaining the data. Convention in the analysis of variance is somewhat opposed to this procedure. The value of F_{obs} is generally compared with tabled critical values, and the outcome is described in terms of the statement: F_{obs} exceeds a specified percentile point (usually the 95 or the 99 percentile points). The choice of the level of significance is thus in part determined by the observed data. This procedure is not objectionable for purposes of estimating the probability of the observed outcome in terms of an assumed underlying sampling distribution.

3.3 STRUCTURAL MODEL: MODEL I (FIXED CONSTANTS)

A *treatment population* is defined hypothetically when all elements in a specified basic population are given a treatment. Suppose, for example, that all elements in a population are given treatment 1, after which the elements are measured on a criterion X_{ij} related to the effectiveness of the treatment. The distribution of the resulting measurements is the distribution for treatment population 1 and, if approximately normal in form, can be described by the parameters, μ_1 and σ_1^2. If, instead, treatment 2 is administered to all of the elements, the resulting distribution of criterion scores is the distribution for treatment population 2 and is assumed to be $N(\mu_2, \sigma_2^2)$.

In general, corresponding to each treatment about which the experimenter seeks to make inferences, there is assumed to be a population of approximately normally distributed criterion measures. The number of such populations is equal to the number of treatments. Assume that the number of treatments is K. In the experiment, data are obtained on k of the possible K treatments. If $k = K$, then observed data are available on all treatments in the domain of treatments to which inferences are to be made. If k is less than K, observed data are available on only some of the treatments about which inferences are to be drawn. The importance of this distinction is that it determines the nature of the generalizations which can be made by the researcher. In this section the case in which $k = K$ will be considered. This case is called Model I or the *fixed constants* model and limits the experimenter to making statements only about the levels of the treatment actually included in the experiment. Model II, the *variance components* model in which $k < K$, will be considered in the next section.

The parameters defining the treatment populations are summarized in Table 3.5. When $k = K$, the grand mean μ is

$$\mu = \frac{\sum \mu_j}{k}. \tag{3.16}$$

The effect of treatment j, designated τ_j, is the difference between the mean for treatment j and the grand mean of the population means,

$$\tau_j = \mu_j - \mu. \tag{3.17}$$

Thus τ_j is a parameter which measures the degree to which the mean for treatment j differs from the mean of all other relevant population means. Since the sum of the deviations about the mean of a set is zero, $\sum \tau_j = 0$; hence the mean of the τ_j's, designated $\bar{\tau}$, is equal to zero.

TABLE 3.5   **Parameters of population corresponding to treatments in the experiment**

Treatment	Population mean	Population variance	Treatment effect
1	μ_1	σ_1^2	$\tau_1 = \mu_1 - \mu$
2	μ_2	σ_2^2	$\tau_2 = \mu_2 - \mu$
$\vdots$	$\vdots$	$\vdots$	$\vdots$
j	μ_j	σ_j^2	$\tau_j = \mu_j - \mu$
$\vdots$	$\vdots$	$\vdots$	$\vdots$
j'	$\mu_{j'}$	$\sigma_{j'}^2$	$\tau_{j'} = \mu_{j'} - \mu$
$\vdots$	$\vdots$	$\vdots$	$\vdots$
$k = K$	μ_k	σ_k^2	$\tau_k = \mu_k - \mu$
	Grand mean $= \mu$		$\bar{\tau} = 0$

Let X_{ij} be the criterion measure on a randomly selected element i in the treatment population j. The following structural model is assumed for this measurement,

$$X_{ij} = \mu + \tau_j + \varepsilon_{ij}, \qquad (3.18)$$

where
$\mu = $ grand mean of treatment populations,

$\tau_j = $ effect of treatment j, $= \mu_j - \mu$

$\varepsilon_{ij} = $ experimental error, $= X_{ij} - \mu_j$.

The term μ is constant for all measurements in all treatment populations. The effect τ_j is constant for all measurements within population j; however, a different value, say $\tau_{j'}$, is associated with population j', where j' represents some treatment other than j. The experimental error ε_{ij} represents all the uncontrolled sources of variance affecting individual measurements; this effect is unique for each of the elements i in the basic population. This effect is further assumed to be independent of τ_j.

Since both μ and τ_j are constant for all measurements *within* population j, the only source of variance for these measurements is that due to experimental error. Thus

$$\sigma_j^2 = \sigma_{\varepsilon_j}^2, \qquad (3.19)$$

where $\sigma_{\varepsilon_j}^2$ designates the variance due to experimental error for the measurements within treatment population j. If $X_{ij'}$ represents a measurement in population j', then (3.18) takes the form

$$X_{ij'} = \mu + \tau_{j'} + \varepsilon_{ij'}. \qquad (3.20)$$

The variance within population j' is due solely to the experimental error; hence

$$\sigma_{j'}^2 = \sigma_{\varepsilon_j}^2. \qquad (3.21)$$

If the elements (subjects, animals) that are observed under each of the treatment conditions are assigned at random to these conditions, one has some degree of assurance that the error effects will be independent of the treatment effects—hence the importance of randomization in design problems. The elements, in this context, are called the experimental units. Random assignment of the experimental units to the experimental conditions tends to make the unique effects of the units *per se* independent of the treatment effects.

It is important to keep in mind what defines experimental error in each design. In this single factor design, the only thing the experimenter is controlling is each treatment level. Thus, error is the combined effects of all random variables in the universe which are impinging upon the subjects and influencing the magnitude of the dependent variable except for the one variable being controlled by the experimenter.

Under these conditions, it is reasonable to assume that the distribution of the ε_{ij}'s within population j will be approximately normal in form, with expected value $\mu_{\varepsilon_j} = 0$ and variance $\sigma_{\varepsilon_j}^2$. If the sources of experimental error are comparable in each of the treatment populations, it is also reasonable to assume that

$$\sigma_{\varepsilon_j}^2 = \sigma_{\varepsilon_j'}^2. \tag{3.22}$$

This last relationship may be written in more general form as

$$\sigma_{\varepsilon_1}^2 = \sigma_{\varepsilon_2}^2 = \cdots = \sigma_{\varepsilon_k}^2 = \sigma_\varepsilon^2, \tag{3.23}$$

where σ_ε^2 is the variance due to experimental error within any of the treatment populations. This is the assumption of homogeneity of error variance. The use of the F distribution to evaluate the ANOV hypothesis depends upon these assumptions being met.

To summarize the assumptions underlying the structural model (3.18), a measurement X_{ij} is expressed as the sum of three components: (1) a component μ which is constant for all treatments and all elements; (2) a component τ_j which is constant for all elements within a treatment population but may differ for different treatment populations; and (3) a component ε_{ij}, independent of τ_j, and distributed as $N(0, \sigma_\varepsilon^2)$ within each treatment population. The component μ in Model I is actually an unknown constant which is estimated by $\bar{G}$; the component τ_j is a systematic or fixed component which depends upon the difference between the means of the treatment populations and is estimated by $\bar{T}_j - \bar{G}$; the component ε_{ij} is a random component (or a random variable) depending upon uncontrolled sources of variances assumed to be drawn randomly from a population in which the distribution is $N(0, \sigma_\varepsilon^2)$. Errors are estimated by $X_{ij} - \bar{T}_j$.

A parameter indicating the extent to which the treatment effects differ is

$$\sigma_\tau^2 = \frac{\sum \tau_j^2}{k-1} = \frac{\sum (\mu_j - \mu)^2}{k-1}. \tag{3.24}$$

An equivalent definition in terms of differences between treatment effects is

$$\sigma_\tau^2 = \frac{\sum (\tau_j - \tau_{j'})^2}{k(k-1)} = \frac{\sum (\mu_j - \mu_{j'})^2}{k(k-1)}, \tag{3.25}$$

where the summation is over all the different possible pairs of means; there are $k(k-1)/2$ such distinct pairs. When the treatment effects are equal, i.e., when $\tau_1 = \tau_2 = \cdots = \tau_k$, σ_τ^2 will be zero. The larger the differences between the τ's, the larger will be σ_τ^2. Thus the hypothesis specifying that $\sigma_\tau^2 = 0$ is equivalent to the hypothesis that specifies $\tau_1 = \tau_2 = \cdots = \tau_k$ or $\mu_1 = \mu_2 = \cdots = \mu_k$.

Statistics useful in estimating the parameters in Table 3.5 are summarized in Table 3.6. Since Model I assumes that the population variances are all equal to $\sigma_{\varepsilon_i}^2$, the best estimate of this parameter is the pooled within-class sample variance

$$s_{\text{pooled}}^2 = \frac{\sum s_j^2}{k} = \text{MS}_{\text{error}}. \tag{3.26}$$

TABLE 3.6 **Estimates of parameters of treatment populations**

Sample size	Treatment	Sample mean	Sample variance	Treatment effect
n	1	$\bar{T}_1$	s_1^2	$t_1 = \bar{T}_1 - \bar{G}$
n	2	$\bar{T}_2$	s_2^2	$t_2 = \bar{T}_2 - \bar{G}$
$\vdots$	$\vdots$	$\vdots$	$\vdots$	$\vdots$
n	j	$\bar{T}_j$	s_j^2	$t_j = \bar{T}_j - \bar{G}$
$\vdots$	$\vdots$	$\vdots$	$\vdots$	$\vdots$
n	j'	$\bar{T}_{j'}$	$s_{j'}^2$	$t_{j'} = \bar{T}_{j'} - \bar{G}$
$\vdots$	$\vdots$	$\vdots$	$\vdots$	$\vdots$
n	k	$\bar{T}_k$	s_k^2	$t_k = \bar{T}_k - \bar{G}$
		Grand mean $= \bar{G}$		$\bar{t} = 0$

For this design the pooled within-class variance is designated $\mathrm{MS}_{\mathrm{error}}$. The latter is an unbiased estimate of σ_ε^2; that is,

$$E(\mathrm{MS}_{\mathrm{error}}) = \sigma_\varepsilon^2.$$

In terms of the structural model in (3.18), the treatment means for the samples of n observations may be expressed as

$$\bar{T}_1 = \mu + \tau_1 + \bar{\varepsilon}_1,$$
$$\bar{T}_2 = \mu + \tau_2 + \bar{\varepsilon}_2,$$
$$\ldots \tag{3.27}$$
$$\bar{T}_k = \mu + \tau_k + \bar{\varepsilon}_k,$$

where $\bar{\varepsilon}_j$ is the mean experimental error for a sample of n observations within treatment class j. For random samples, it is reasonable to assume that $E(\bar{\varepsilon}_j) = $ constant. Without any loss in generality, this constant may be assumed to be zero. Therefore,

$$E(\bar{T}_1) = \mu + \tau_1 = \mu + (\mu_1 - \mu) = \mu_1$$
$$E(\bar{T}_2) = \mu + \tau_2 = \mu + (\mu_2 - \mu) = \mu_2$$
$$\ldots \tag{3.28}$$
$$E(\bar{T}_k) = \mu + \tau_k = \mu + (\mu_k - \mu) = \mu_k.$$

The first relation in (3.28) may be interpreted as follows: If an infinite number of random samples of size n are given treatment 1 and the statistic $\bar{T}_1$ is computed for each of the samples, the distribution of the resulting statistic would have an expected value (or mean) equal to $\mu + \tau_1$. Equivalently, $E(\bar{T}_1) = \mu_1$.

The statistic t_j in Table 3.6 may be represented as

$$t_j = \bar{T}_j - \bar{G} = (\mu + \tau_j + \bar{\varepsilon}_j) - (\mu + \bar{\varepsilon})$$
$$= \tau_j + \bar{\varepsilon}_j - \bar{\varepsilon}. \tag{3.29}$$

where $\bar{\varepsilon}$ is the mean of the $\bar{\varepsilon}_j$'s. The expected value of t_j is equal to τ_j, since the expected value of the quantity $\bar{\varepsilon}_j - \bar{\varepsilon}$ equals 0.

A measure of the degree to which the sample means for the various treatments differ is provided by the statistic

$$\text{MS}_{\text{treat}} = \frac{n \sum (\bar{T}_j - \bar{G})^2}{k - 1} = \frac{n \sum t_j^2}{k - 1}. \tag{3.30}$$

Inspection of the right-hand side of the relation (3.29) indicates that differences among the $\bar{T}$'s depend upon differences among the τ_j's and differences among the $\bar{\varepsilon}_j$'s. Since the τ_j's and the $\bar{\varepsilon}_j$'s are assumed to be independent, the variance of the $\bar{T}$'s is the sum of the variance of the τ's and the variance of the $\bar{\varepsilon}$'s. Therefore n times the variance of the $\bar{T}$'s has the expected value

$$E(\text{MS}_{\text{treat}}) = \frac{n \sum \tau_j^2}{k - 1} + \frac{n \sum \bar{\varepsilon}_j^2}{k - 1}$$

$$= n\sigma_\tau^2 + n\sigma_{\bar{\varepsilon}}^2. \tag{3.31}$$

Since the variance of the mean of n observations is $1/n$ times the variance of the individual observations, using the relationship that $\sigma_\varepsilon^2 = n\sigma_{\bar{\varepsilon}}^2$ permits (3.31) to be written as

$$E(\text{MS}_{\text{treat}}) = n\sigma_\tau^2 + \sigma_\varepsilon^2. \tag{3.32}$$

Thus, when $\tau_1 = \tau_2 = \cdots = \tau_k$, the term σ_τ^2 is equal to zero and the expected value of MS_{treat} is σ_ε^2. This implies that MS_{treat} is an unbiased estimate of the variance due to experimental error when there are no differences among the treatment effects.

Note: For the case in which the sample size under treatment j is n_j, where n_j is not the same for all treatments, it can be shown that

$$E(\text{MS}_{\text{treat}}) = \frac{N^2 - \sum n_j^2}{N(k - 1)} \sigma_\tau^2 + \sigma_\varepsilon^2,$$

where $N = \sum n_j$. (See Graybill, 1961, pp. 353–354.) When $n_j = n$ for all treatments,

$$N = kn \qquad \text{and} \qquad \sum n_j^2 = kn^2.$$

Hence for the case of equal sample sizes,

$$\frac{N^2 - \sum n_j^2}{N(k - 1)} = \frac{k^2 n^2 - kn^2}{kn(k - 1)} = \frac{kn^2(k - 1)}{kn(k - 1)} = n.$$

A more general approach to the result obtained in (3.32) is to start from the relation

$$\bar{T}_j - \bar{T}_{j'} = (\tau_j - \tau_{j'}) + (\bar{\varepsilon}_j - \bar{\varepsilon}_{j'}). \tag{3.33}$$

This relation is obtained from (3.27). In this form, a difference between two treatment means estimates a difference between two treatment effects and a

TABLE 3.7 **Expected values of mean squares (n observations per treatment)**

Source	df	MS	E(MS)
Treatments	$k - 1$	MS_{treat}	$\sigma_\varepsilon^2 + n\sigma_\tau^2$
Experimental error	$kn - k$	MS_{error}	σ_ε^2

difference between two average error effects. Further, $\bar{T}_j - \bar{T}_{j'}$ provides an unbiased estimate of $\tau_j - \tau_{j'}$. MS_{treat} is readily expressed in terms of all possible pairs of differences among the $\bar{T}$'s. Similarly σ_τ^2 and σ_ε^2 may be expressed in terms of the differences on the right-hand side of (3.33). In the derivation of the expected values for the mean square due to treatments, the more direct approach is by means of relations analogous to (3.33).

The expected values of the mean squares which are used in the analysis of variance are summarized in Table 3.7. The ratio of the expected values has the form

$$\frac{E(MS_{treat})}{E(MS_{error})} = \frac{\sigma_\varepsilon^2 + n\sigma_\tau^2}{\sigma_\varepsilon^2}.$$

When $\sigma_\tau^2 = 0$, the expected value of the numerator is σ_ε^2. Thus, on condition that $\sigma_\tau^2 = 0$, numerator and denominator are unbiased, independent estimates of σ_ε^2. The independence of the estimators follows from the fact that the sampling distribution of the within-class variance is independent of the class means. MS_{error} is obtained from the within-class data, whereas MS_{treat} is obtained from the class means.

On condition that $\sigma_\tau^2 = 0$, under relatively weak assumptions, the sampling distribution of the statistic

$$F = \frac{MS_{treat}}{MS_{error}} \tag{3.34}$$

can be shown to be that of the F distribution having $k - 1$ degrees of freedom for the numerator and $kn - k$ degrees of freedom for the denominator. It should be noted that

$$E(F) \neq \frac{E(MS_{treat})}{E(MS_{error})}, \tag{3.35}$$

since, in general, the expected value of any ratio is not equal to the ratio of expected values, even though the latter may be equal. Actually,

$$E(F) = \frac{df_{denominator}}{df_{denominator} - 2} \quad \text{on condition that} \quad \sigma_\tau^2 = 0. \tag{3.36}$$

Thus, on condition that $\sigma_\tau^2 = 0$,

$$\frac{E(\mathrm{MS_{treat}})}{E(\mathrm{MS_{error}})} = 1 \quad \text{but} \quad E(F) > 1.$$

This F statistic may be used to test the hypothesis that $\sigma_\tau^2 = 0$, which is equivalent to the hypothesis that $\tau_1 = \tau_2 = \cdots = \tau_k$. The assumptions under which this test is valid are those underlying Model I. The effects of possible violations of these assumptions are discussed in Sec. 3.6.

When $\sigma_\tau^2 \neq 0$, the expected value of the F statistic will be greater than 1.00 by an amount which depends in part upon the magnitude of σ_τ^2. Thus, if the F ratio is larger than 1.00 by an amount having low probability when $\sigma_\tau^2 = 0$, the inference is that $\sigma_\tau^2 \neq 0$.

The notation ave (MS), read average value of a mean square, is used by some authors in place of the notation $E(\mathrm{MS})$. Also the notation σ_τ^2 is sometimes reserved for use in connection with Model II, and no special symbol is used to designate the quantity $n(\sum \tau_j^2)/(k - 1)$. Thus for Model I

$$E(\mathrm{MS_{treat}}) = \sigma_\varepsilon^2 + \frac{n \sum \tau_j^2}{k - 1}.$$

As long as the assumptions underlying the model are made explicit, no ambiguity will result from the use of the symbol σ_τ^2 in Model I.

3.4 METHODS OF DERIVING ESTIMATES AND THEIR EXPECTED VALUES: MODEL I

Under Model I, the structural equation for an observation has the form

$$X_{ij} = \mu + \tau_j + \varepsilon_{ij},$$

where μ is a constant for all observations, τ_j is a constant (or fixed variable) for observations under treatment j, and ε_{ij} is a random variable independent of τ_j having the distribution $N(0, \sigma_\varepsilon^2)$ for all treatments. Thus, there are k fixed variables and one random variable in the model. This model is similar to that underlying a k-variate (fixed) multiple regression equation; hence the methods for the solution of estimation problems in multiple regression are applicable. Indeed, both analysis of variance and multiple regression analysis can be shown to be special cases of the general linear model, which model simply states that one or more dependent variables can be expressed as a linear combination of one or more independent variables. In both analyses, one can view the problem as one of predicting the dependent variable from information contained in the independent variables. In the case of multiple regression analysis, the independent variables may contain quantitative information (e.g.,

$X_1 =$ height, $X_2 =$ IQ scores, $X_3 =$ blood volume) and the independent variables may be correlated with each other as well as with the dependent variable (Y). In the case of analysis of variance, the independent variable information used to predict the dependent variable is simply which treatment a particular subject receives. That is all that is known about each subject. Thus, the predictors are qualitative and they are uncorrelated in the case of an orthogonal experimental design. This simplifies computational procedures for analysis of variance as compared to regression analysis, but the underlying principles are the same for all special cases of the general linear model. The relevant matrix algebra and the general linear model approach are presented in detail in Appendixes B and C, respectively.

The method of least-squares yields unbiased minimum variance estimators when applied to estimation problems posed by Model I. The generalization of Model I forms a major part of classic analysis of variance; estimation problems in this area may be handled by means of least-squares analysis or by means of maximum likelihood methods. The two approaches lead to identical results for Model I.

To illustrate the principles, only a restricted version of Model I will be considered here—that special case in which the constraint $\sum \tau_j = 0$ is imposed upon the model. Without this constraint it is not possible to obtain unbiased estimators of the individual treatment effects τ_j. The more general approach to Model I, which does not impose this constraint on the τ_j, will be considered in Appendix C.

To illustrate the least-squares approach to the model, let $m, t_1, t_2, \ldots, t_k$, and e_{ij} designate the respective least-squares estimators of $\mu, \tau_1, \tau_2, \ldots, \tau_k$, and ε_{ij}. The method of least squares minimizes the quantity

$$\sum \sum e_{ij}^2 = \sum_i \sum_j (X_{ij} - m - t_j)^2 = \text{minimum.} \qquad (3.37)$$

By taking partial derivatives with respect to the estimators $m, t_1, t_2, \ldots, t_k$ (this is the procedure used to obtain the normal equations in the multiple regression problem for fixed variables) and setting these derivatives equal to zero, one obtains the normal equations

$$knm + n \sum t_j - G = 0,$$
$$nm + nt_1 - T_1 = 0,$$
$$nm + nt_2 - T_2 = 0, \qquad (3.38)$$
$$\cdots$$
$$nm + nt_k - T_k = 0.$$

There are $k + 1$ equations and $k + 1$ unknowns; however, the $k + 1$ equations are not independent, since the first equation may be obtained by summing the last k equations. A unique solution to these equations requires a restriction on the variables. Since $\sum \tau_j = 0$, a reasonable restriction is that $\sum t_j = 0$. The solutions to (3.38) now take the form

$$m = \frac{G}{kn} = \bar{G},$$

$$t_1 = \frac{T_1 - n\bar{G}}{n} = \bar{T}_1 - \bar{G},$$

$$t_2 = \frac{T_2 - n\bar{G}}{n} = \bar{T}_2 - \bar{G}, \qquad (3.39)$$

$$\cdots$$

$$t_k = \frac{T_k - n\bar{G}}{n} = \bar{T}_k - \bar{G}.$$

To show that these estimators are unbiased, one has

$$E(m) = E(\bar{G}) = E\left(m + \frac{\sum t_j}{k} + \frac{\sum \varepsilon_{ij}}{kn}\right)$$

$$= \mu + 0 + 0 = \mu,$$

$$E(t_j) = E(\bar{T}_j - \bar{G}) = E(\bar{T}_j) - E(\bar{G})$$

$$= E(\mu + \tau_j + \bar{\varepsilon}_j) - \mu = \tau_j.$$

Although the expected value of t_j is the parameter τ_j, in terms of the parameters of the model, t_j has the form

$$t_j = \bar{T}_j - \bar{G} = \left(\mu + \tau_j + \frac{\sum\limits_i \varepsilon_{ij}}{n}\right) - \left(\mu + \frac{n\sum \tau_j}{kn} + \frac{\sum\sum \varepsilon_{ij}}{kn}\right) = \tau_j + \bar{\varepsilon}_j - \bar{\varepsilon}, \quad (3.40)$$

where $\bar{\varepsilon}_j = (\sum\limits_i \varepsilon_{ij})/n$ and $\bar{\varepsilon} = (\sum\sum \varepsilon_{ij})/kn$. Thus,

$$\text{MS}_{\text{treat}} = \frac{n\sum t_j^2}{k-1} = \frac{n\sum (\tau_j + \bar{\varepsilon}_j - \bar{\varepsilon})^2}{k-1}. \qquad (3.41)$$

Since the τ's and the ε's are independent, the expected value of MS_{treat} will be n times the sum of the mean squares of the parameters on the right-hand side of (3.41), that is, $n(\sigma_\tau^2 + \sigma_{\bar{\varepsilon}}^2) = n\sigma_\tau^2 + \sigma_\varepsilon^2$. This is a general property of least-squares estimators: the expected value of the mean square of an estimator is the sum of the respective mean squares of the parameters estimated. The term

$$e_{ij} = X_{ij} - m - t_j = X_{ij} - \bar{G} - (\bar{T}_j - \bar{G})$$

$$= X_{ij} - \bar{T}_j = (\mu + \tau_j + \varepsilon_{ij}) - (\mu + \tau_j + \bar{\varepsilon}_j) \qquad (3.42)$$

$$= \varepsilon_{ij} - \bar{\varepsilon}_j.$$

Thus

$$E\left(\sum\sum e_{ij}^2\right) = E\left\{\frac{\sum\sum (X_{ij} - \bar{T}_j)^2}{kn - k}\right\} = \sigma_\varepsilon^2. \qquad (3.43)$$

3.5 STRUCTURAL MODEL—MODEL II (VARIANCE-COMPONENT MODEL)

One of the basic assumptions underlying Model I is that all treatments about which inferences are to be made are included in the experiment. Thus, if the experiment were to be replicated, the same set of treatments would be included in each of the replications. Model I is usually the most appropriate for a single-factor experiment. If, however, the k treatments that are included in a given experiment constitute a random sample from a collection of K treatments, where k is small relative to K, then upon replication a different random sample of k treatments will be included in the experiment. It is quite rare for experiments to be designed and executed with the treatments selected randomly from a population of treatments in the social, behavioral, and biological sciences. Accordingly, Model I is usually the appropriate model. One result is that the outcome of those studies cannot be generalized to a population of treatment levels. In principle, experiments can be carried out under the conditions specified by Model II and results may be generalized to the population of treatment levels when that occurs. Model II covers this case. The structural equation for Model II has the same form as that of Model I, namely,

$$X_{ij} = \mu + \tau_j + \varepsilon_{ij}.$$

However, the assumptions underlying this model are different. The term μ is still assumed to be constant for all observations; the term ε_{ij} is still assumed to have the distribution $N(0, \sigma_\varepsilon^2)$ for all treatments; but the term τ_j is now considered to be a random variable. The distribution of τ_j is assumed to be $N(0, \sigma_\tau^2)$. In the variance-component model, the primary objective is to estimate σ_τ^2 rather than the individual τ_j.

From the point of view of the computation of estimates of the various effects, the two models do not lead to different procedures. For samples of size n, the expected values of the mean squares of the estimators are as follows:

Source	df	MS	E(MS)
Treatments	$k - 1$	MS_{treat}	$\sigma_\varepsilon^2 + n\sigma_\tau^2$
Experimental error	$kn - k$	MS_{error}	σ_ε^2

Here the expected value of the mean square for treatments is the sum of the variances of two independent variables, that is, $\sigma_\varepsilon^2 + n\sigma_\tau^2$. This value was the one that was obtained under Model I. The test on the hypothesis $\sigma_\tau^2 = 0$ is identical with that made under Model I. In more complex designs, the F ratios for analogous tests do not have identical forms.

In spite of these similarities, the distribution theory underlying Model II is quite different from the corresponding theory underlying Model I. Model II, which has more than one random variable, does not permit the direct application of least-squares methods. Instead, maximum likelihood methods are used to obtain estimators and the expected values of the mean squares of those estimators. General methods for obtaining the expected values for mean squares under Model II are discussed by Crump (1951).

SOME SPECIAL FEATURES OF THE VARIANCE-COMPONENT MODEL. In the variance-component model,

$$X_{ij} = \mu + \tau_j + \varepsilon_{ij}, \qquad j = 1, \ldots, k; \qquad i = 1, \ldots, n,$$

μ is considered to be a fixed constant. τ_j and ε_{ij} are independently distributed random variables, with respective distributions $N(0, \sigma_\tau^2)$ and $N(0, \sigma_\varepsilon^2)$. Thus, as part of the model,

$$E(X_{ij}) = E(\mu) + E(\tau_j) + E(\varepsilon_{ij})$$
$$= \mu,$$

and
$$\mathrm{var}\,(X_{ij}) = \mathrm{var}\,(\mu) + \mathrm{var}\,(\tau_j) + \mathrm{var}\,(\varepsilon_{ij})$$
$$= \quad 0 \quad + \quad \sigma_\tau^2 \quad + \quad \sigma_\varepsilon^2.$$

The covariance structure of this model may be represented as follows: If $i = i'$,

$$\mathrm{cov}\,(X_{ij}, X_{i'j}) = \mathrm{var}\,(X_{ij}) = \sigma_\varepsilon^2 + \sigma_\tau^2.$$

If $i \neq i'$,

$$\mathrm{cov}\,(X_{ij}, X_{i'j}) = \sigma_\tau^2.$$

The *intraclass* correlation is, by definition,

$$\rho = \frac{\mathrm{cov}\,(X_{ij}, X_{i'j})}{\mathrm{var}\,(X_{ij})} = \frac{\sigma_\tau^2}{\sigma_\varepsilon^2 + \sigma_\tau^2}.$$

In the numerator of the expression for the intraclass correlation, $i \neq i'$.

If the n observations under treatment j are considered to be the components of a vector variable

$$\mathbf{x}_j = \begin{bmatrix} X_{1j} \\ \vdots \\ X_{nj} \end{bmatrix},$$

then the variance-component model assumes that the random variable $\mathbf{x}_j$ is multivariate normal with parameters

$$E(\mathbf{x}_j) = \begin{bmatrix} \mu \\ \mu \\ \vdots \\ \mu \end{bmatrix}, \qquad \sum_{n,n} = \begin{bmatrix} \sigma_\varepsilon^2 + \sigma_\tau^2 & \sigma_\tau^2 & \cdots & \sigma_\tau^2 \\ \sigma_\tau^2 & \sigma_\varepsilon^2 + \sigma_\tau^2 & \cdots & \sigma_\tau^2 \\ \vdots & \vdots & \vdots & \\ \sigma_\tau^2 & \sigma_\tau^2 & \cdots & \sigma_\varepsilon^2 + \sigma_\tau^2 \end{bmatrix}.$$

The corresponding matrix of intercorrelations is

$$\underset{n,n}{P} = \begin{bmatrix} 1 & \rho & \cdots & \rho \\ \rho & 1 & \cdots & \rho \\ \vdots & \vdots & & \vdots \\ \rho & \rho & \cdots & 1 \end{bmatrix},$$

where ρ is the intraclass correlation. In words, these results simply say that the variance among observations is due to error and treatment effects, and the covariances among observations are due solely to treatment effects.

The matrix Σ may be written in the form

$$\Sigma = \sigma_\varepsilon^2 I + \sigma_\tau^2 J,$$

where I = diagonal matrix with unity in the main diagonal,

J = square matrix whose elements are all unity.

The inverse of the matrix Σ may be shown to be

$$\Sigma^{-1} = \alpha_1 I + \alpha_2 J,$$

where

$$\alpha_1 = \frac{1}{\sigma_\varepsilon^2}, \qquad \alpha_2 = \frac{-\sigma_\tau^2}{\sigma_\varepsilon^2(\sigma_\varepsilon^2 + n\sigma_\tau^2)}.$$

This inverse has a role in obtaining the standard error of estimators. Under this type of covariance structure, the method of maximum likelihood may be used to obtain estimates of the parameters in the model.

An alternative path toward obtaining estimates of the parameters σ_ε^2 and σ_τ^2 is to set mean squares equal to their corresponding expected values and then solve the resulting equations. Thus, let

$$MS_{treat} = \hat{\sigma}_\varepsilon^2 + n\hat{\sigma}_\tau^2,$$
$$MS_{error} = \hat{\sigma}_\varepsilon^2.$$

Substituting the last result in the first expression gives

$$\hat{\sigma}_\tau^2 = \frac{1}{n}(MS_{treat} - MS_{error}).$$

In matrix notation,

$$\begin{bmatrix} 1 & n \\ 1 & 0 \end{bmatrix} \begin{bmatrix} \hat{\sigma}_\varepsilon^2 \\ \hat{\sigma}_\tau^2 \end{bmatrix} = \begin{bmatrix} MS_{treat} \\ MS_{error} \end{bmatrix}.$$

Hence

$$\begin{bmatrix} \hat{\sigma}_\varepsilon^2 \\ \hat{\sigma}_\tau^2 \end{bmatrix} = \begin{bmatrix} 0 & 1 \\ \dfrac{1}{n} & -\dfrac{1}{n} \end{bmatrix} \begin{bmatrix} MS_{treat} \\ MS_{error} \end{bmatrix},$$

or

$$\begin{bmatrix} \hat{\sigma}_\varepsilon^2 \\ \hat{\sigma}_\tau^2 \end{bmatrix} = \begin{bmatrix} MS_{error} \\ \dfrac{1}{n}(MS_{treat} - MS_{error}) \end{bmatrix}.$$

It can be shown (Graybill, 1961, pp. 338–347) that these estimators are the unbiased, maximum-likelihood estimators of the corresponding parameters. (The constant μ in the model is estimated by $\bar{G}$, the mean of all observations.) From the assumptions underlying the model

$$\frac{(k-1)\text{MS}_{\text{treat}}}{\sigma_\varepsilon^2 + n\sigma_\tau^2} \text{ is distributed as } \chi^2(k-1),$$

$$\frac{[k(n-1)]\text{MS}_{\text{error}}}{\sigma_\varepsilon^2} \text{ is distributed as } \chi^2[k(n-1)].$$

(3.44)

Further, these distributions are independent. Hence from (3.44) one has

$$F = \frac{\text{MS}_{\text{treat}}}{\text{MS}_{\text{error}}} \text{ is distributed as } \frac{\sigma_\varepsilon^2 + n\sigma_\tau^2}{\sigma_\varepsilon^2} \frac{\chi^2(k-1)/(k-1)}{\chi^2[k(n-1)]/k(n-1)}$$

$$= \frac{\sigma_\varepsilon^2 + n\sigma_\tau^2}{\sigma_\varepsilon^2} F[(k-1), k(n-1)].$$

(3.45)

One may rewrite (3.45) in the form

$$F = (1+n\theta)F[k-1, k(n-1)], \quad \text{where } \theta = \frac{\sigma_\tau^2}{\sigma_\varepsilon^2};$$

(3.46)

that is, the F statistic $\text{MS}_{\text{treat}}/\text{MS}_{\text{error}}$ is distributed as a multiple of the central F distribution. Under the hypothesis that σ_τ^2 is zero, this multiple is unity. Under the hypothesis that $\sigma_\tau^2 > 0$, this multiple is not unity.

Thus, whether or not θ is zero, the F statistic has a central F distribution. Hence the power of the test $\sigma_\tau^2 = 0$ with respect to nonzero θ is given by

$$\Pr\left\{F > \frac{F_{1-\alpha}[k-1, k(n-1)]}{1+n\theta}\right\}. \qquad \text{(See Fig. 3-1)}$$

Since
$$F = (1+n\theta)F[k-1, k(n-1)],$$

one may test any hypothesis of the form $\theta = \theta_0$ by means of the following decision rule:

Reject the hypothesis that $\theta = \theta_0$ if

$$F_{\text{obs}} > (1+n\theta_0)F_{1-\alpha}[k-1, k(n-1)].$$

From (3.46) one has

$$\Pr\left\{F_\alpha[k-1, k(n-1)] \le \frac{F}{1+n\theta} \le F_{1-\alpha}[k-1, k(n-1)]\right\} = 1-\alpha. \quad (3.47)$$

One may rewrite (3.46) in the form

$$\Pr\left\{\frac{F}{F_{1-\alpha}[k-1, k(n-1)]} \le 1+n\theta \le \frac{F}{F_\alpha[k-1, k(n-1)]}\right\} = 1-\alpha. \quad (3.48)$$

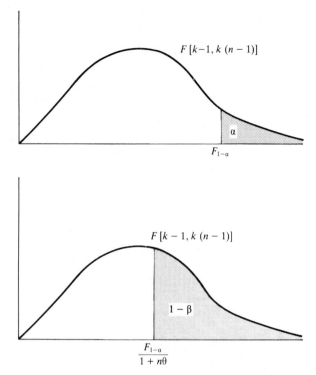

FIGURE 3-1 Power of F test under variance component model.

From (3.48) one obtains the following confidence interval on θ:

$$C(A \le \theta \le B) = 1 - \alpha, \qquad (3.49a)$$

where
$$A = \frac{1}{n}\left(\frac{MS_{\text{treat}}/MS_{\text{error}}}{F_{1-\alpha}[k-1,\, k(n-1)]} - 1\right),$$

$$B = \frac{1}{n}\left(\frac{MS_{\text{treat}}/MS_{\text{error}}}{F_{\alpha}[k-1,\, k(n-1)]} - 1\right).$$

In terms of the parameter θ, the intraclass correlations is given by

$$\rho = \frac{\theta}{1+\theta} = \frac{\sigma_\tau^2/\sigma_\varepsilon^2}{1+(\sigma_\tau^2/\sigma_\varepsilon^2)} = \frac{\sigma_\tau^2}{\sigma_\varepsilon^2 + \sigma_\tau^2}.$$

From (3.48) one obtains the following confidence interval on ρ:

$$C\left(\frac{A}{1+A} \le \rho \le \frac{B}{1+B}\right) = 1 - \alpha, \qquad (3.49b)$$

where A and B are defined in (3.48). A point estimate of the intraclass correlations is given by

$$\hat{\rho} = \frac{\hat{\sigma}_\tau^2}{\hat{\sigma}_\varepsilon^2 + \hat{\sigma}_\tau^2} = \frac{(MS_{treat} - MS_{error})/n}{MS_{error} + (MS_{treat} - MS_{error})/n}$$

$$= \frac{MS_{treat} - MS_{error}}{MS_{treat} + (n-1)MS_{error}}.$$

This estimate will be biased.

In problems involving variance components, it is of interest to obtain unbiased estimates of the ratio of variance components. Toward this end consider the problem of finding an unbiased estimate of the ratio $\theta = \sigma_\tau^2/\sigma_\varepsilon^2$. One will find that

$$E\left(\frac{\hat{\sigma}_\tau^2}{\hat{\sigma}_\varepsilon^2}\right) \neq \frac{\sigma_\tau^2}{\sigma_\varepsilon^2},$$

where $\hat{\sigma}_\tau^2$ and $\hat{\sigma}_\varepsilon^2$ are the estimators obtained earlier in this section.

From the relationship

$$\frac{MS_{treat}}{MS_{error}} = (1 + n\theta)F[k-1, k(n-1)],$$

one has

$$E\left(\frac{MS_{treat}}{MS_{error}}\right) = (1 + n\theta)\frac{k(n-1)}{k(n-1)-2}, \qquad (3.50)$$

since

$$E\{F[k-1, k(n-1)]\} = \frac{k(n-1)}{k(n-1)-2}.$$

Solving (3.50) for θ gives

$$E\left\{\frac{1}{n}\left[\frac{MS_{treat}}{MS_{error}}\frac{k(n-1)-2}{k(n-1)} - 1\right]\right\} = \theta. \qquad (3.51)$$

Hence an unbiased estimate of θ is

$$\hat{\theta} = \frac{1}{n}\left[\frac{MS_{treat}}{MS_{error}}\frac{k(n-1)-2}{k(n-1)} - 1\right]$$

$$= \frac{[k(n-1)-2]MS_{treat} - k(n-1)MS_{error}}{kn(n-1)MS_{error}}$$

$$= \frac{MS_{treat} - mMS_{error}}{nmMS_{error}} \quad \text{where} \quad m = \frac{k(n-1)}{k(n-1)-2}.$$

By way of contrast,

$$\frac{\hat{\sigma}_\tau^2}{\hat{\sigma}_\varepsilon^2} = \frac{MS_{treat} - MS_{error}}{mMS_{error}}.$$

To indicate the order of the magnitude of the bias in the estimator $\hat{\sigma}_\tau^2/\hat{\sigma}_\varepsilon^2$, consider the following numerical example:

$$k = 4 \qquad \text{MS}_{\text{treat}} = 250,$$
$$n = 10 \qquad \text{MS}_{\text{error}} = 50.$$

For this example,

$$\hat{\sigma}_\tau^2 = \tfrac{1}{10}(250 - 50) = 20, \qquad \hat{\sigma}_\varepsilon^2 = 50.$$

Hence

$$\frac{\hat{\sigma}_\tau^2}{\hat{\sigma}_\varepsilon^2} = 0.400.$$

Whereas

$$\hat{\theta} = \frac{250 - \frac{36}{34}(50)}{\frac{360}{34}(50)} = 0.372.$$

An estimate of ρ in terms of the unbiased estimate of θ is given by

$$\hat{\rho} = \frac{\hat{\theta}}{1 + \hat{\theta}}.$$

For the numerical example in the preceding paragraph,

$$\hat{\rho} = \frac{0.372}{1 + 0.372} = 0.271.$$

An estimate of ρ in terms of the estimators of σ_ε^2 and σ_τ^2 is

$$\hat{\rho}' = \frac{\hat{\sigma}_\tau^2}{\hat{\sigma}_\varepsilon^2 + \hat{\sigma}_\tau^2} = \frac{20}{50 + 20} = 0.286.$$

To obtain the variance of an estimate of a variance component, one notes that

$$E[\chi^2(k - 1)] = k - 1, \qquad \text{var}\,[\chi^2(k - 1)] = 2(k - 1);$$
$$E\{\chi^2[k(n - 1)]\} = k(n - 1), \qquad \text{var}\,\{\chi^2[k(n - 1)]\} = 2k(n - 1).$$

Since

$$k(n - 1)\frac{\hat{\sigma}_\varepsilon^2}{\sigma_\varepsilon^2} = \chi^2[k(n - 1)],$$

it follows that

$$\hat{\sigma}_\varepsilon^2 = \frac{\sigma_\varepsilon^2}{k(n - 1)}\chi^2[k(n - 1)].$$

Hence

$$\text{var}\,(\hat{\sigma}_\varepsilon^2) = \text{var}\,(\text{MS}_{\text{error}}) = \frac{\sigma_\varepsilon^4}{k^2(n - 1)^2}\,2k(n - 1) = \frac{2\sigma_\varepsilon^4}{k(n - 1)}.$$

Since

$$\frac{(k - 1)\text{MS}_{\text{treat}}}{\sigma_\varepsilon^2 + n\sigma_\tau^2} = \chi^2(k - 1),$$

it follows that

$$\text{MS}_{\text{treat}} = \frac{\sigma_\varepsilon^2 + n\sigma_\tau^2}{k - 1}\chi^2(k - 1).$$

Hence
$$\text{var (MS}_{\text{treat}}) = \frac{(\sigma_\varepsilon^2 + n\sigma_\tau^2)^2}{(k-1)^2} 2(k-1)$$

$$= \frac{2(\sigma_\varepsilon^2 + n\sigma_\tau^2)^2}{(k-1)}.$$

Since MS_{error} and MS_{treat} are distributed independently,

$$\text{var }(\hat{\sigma}_\tau^2) = \text{var } \frac{1}{n} (\text{MS}_{\text{treat}} - \text{MS}_{\text{error}})$$

$$= \frac{1}{n^2} [\text{var }(\text{MS}_{\text{treat}}) + \text{var }(\text{MS}_{\text{error}})].$$

Estimates of these variances are obtained by replacing parameters by their estimators. Thus,

$$\text{est var }(\text{MS}_{\text{error}}) = \frac{2\hat{\sigma}_\varepsilon^4}{k(n-1)} = \frac{2\text{MS}_{\text{error}}^2}{k(n-1)}.$$

It may happen that estimates of variance components will turn out to be negative. One may avoid using a negative number as an estimate of a variance component by setting the estimate at zero whenever the estimator is less than or equal to zero. However, if one adopts this procedure, the estimators given above will no longer be unbiased. Further, the distribution theory used to obtain the variance of the estimators will no longer be valid.

ALTERNATIVE APPROACH TO VARIANCE-COMPONENT MODEL. The E(MS) for the variance-component model may be obtained by constructing the analysis-of-variance table corresponding to the fixed model. That is, the sources of variation and mean squares are computed as though one were working with Model I. The E(MS) are then obtained by assuming that

1 The τ_j are uncorrelated random variables with

$$E(\tau_j) = 0 \quad \text{and} \quad \text{var }(\tau_j) = \sigma_\tau^2,$$

2 The ε_{ij} are uncorrelated with the τ_j and uncorrelated with each other with

$$E_i(\varepsilon_{ij}) = 0 \quad \text{and} \quad \text{var}_i(\varepsilon_{ij}) = \sigma_\varepsilon^2 \quad \text{for all } j.$$

The estimates of σ_τ^2 and σ_ε^2 that are obtained under this procedure are identical with those obtained under the variance-component model. Without any distribution assumptions, however, no F tests may be constructed. (Randomization tests on the experimental data can, of course, be made without prior distribution assumptions.) Even without distribution assumptions on the random variables, it may be shown that the estimators are unbiased and have minimum variance in the class of estimators that are quadratic functions of the basic observations.

From some points of view, the fixed model may be considered a limiting case of the variance-component model. It is that limiting case in which one is dealing with a finite population of size $k = K$. Methods of obtaining the E(MS) that are used in later chapters consider the fixed model as a limiting case of this type.

3.6 ANALYSIS OF VARIANCE ASSUMPTIONS

In earlier sections the assumptions which underlie the analysis of variance structural model, $X_{ij} = \mu + \tau_j + \varepsilon_{ij}$, have been discussed. Summarized, it is assumed that the observations can be represented as the sum of three components: (1) a component μ which is constant for all observations; (2) a treatment effect τ_j which is constant for all elements within a treatment population; (3) a component e_{ij} which is independent of τ_j and of other errors and is distributed as $N(0, \sigma_\varepsilon^2)$ within each treatment population. For Model I it is further assumed that all treatments of interest are included in the experiment; for Model II k treatments are assumed to have been sampled at random from a population of K possible treatments. Under Model I assumptions, τ_j is assumed to be fixed; under Model II the distribution of τ_j is assumed to be $N(0, \sigma_\tau^2)$. When random samples are taken from normally distributed populations and good experimental control is maintained throughout a study, the assumptions of both the structural model and the F ratio (assumed to be the ratio of two independent, unbiased estimates of the same population variance (σ_ε^2) when the null hypothesis is true) will tend to be met.

It is well to keep in mind, however, how restrictive those assumptions really are. First, they assume a simple additive model. No provision is made for effects to be combined in an interactive or multiplicative fashion. Beyond that, it is assumed that the treatments have no effect upon the shapes of the treatment populations (all are assumed to be normal) and that the treatments have no effect upon population variances (all are assumed to be equal to σ_ε^2).

In general, there are two sets of circumstances under which the reasonableness of this simple model needs to be considered.

In the first instance, there are circumstances under which it is *not* logical on theoretical grounds to consider the model assumptions to be reasonable. For example, there are contexts wherein the assumptions of normality and homogeneity of variance are not likely to be met because one expects treatments to affect both means and variances. In experiments wherein treatments engender different skill levels, one might expect the behavior of skilled subjects to be at a higher average level *and* to be less variable; means and variances are correlated under such circumstances. One might also expect the shape of the distributions to be affected; floor and ceiling effects would generate skewed distributions at the extremes of performance. When such outcomes are likely on logical grounds, the analysis of variance assumptions are inappropriate. Transformations of the observations may be in order or alternatives to the analysis of variance may need to be considered.

A second general set of circumstances arises when it is perfectly logical to expect the analysis of variance assumptions to be met, but for a variety of reasons the assumptions are violated to one degree or another. Indeed, it is highly unlikely that the assumptions will ever be met exactly in the real world of experimentation. When violations of assumptions do occur, there may be effects upon both statistical power and type I error rates. It is well, then, to consider the effects of such violations upon the F distribution and, therefore, upon error rates associated with decisions. When violating assumptions has relatively little effect upon the distribution of the test statistic, and, thus, upon type I and type II errors, the statistic is said to be *robust* with regard to violations of those assumptions.

Violating the assumption of random sampling of elements from a population and random assignment of the elements to the treatments may totally invalidate any study, since randomness provides the assurance that errors are independently distributed within and between treatment conditions and is also the mechanism by which bias is removed from treatment conditions.

The assumption of normality of the observations in the various treatment populations follows from the structured model; if the e_{ij}'s are normally distributed, the X_{ij}'s will be normally distributed. Conversely, if random samples are taken from normally distributed populations, the e_{ij}'s will be normally distributed when treatment effects are an additive constant. When observations are normally distributed, the variance estimates in the numerator and denominator of F are independent since the sampling distribution of the within-treatment variance is independent of the treatment means used to compute MS_{treat}. A reasonable statement is that the analysis of variance F statistic is robust with regard to moderate departures from normality when sample sizes are reasonably large and are equal (e.g., Lindquist, 1953; Lunney, 1970).

The study of the effects of violating the assumptions underlying parametric statistics in general, and the analysis of variance in particular, has created a large literature. Generally, the focus has been upon the level of significance and statistical power when various assumptions are violated and are violated to differing degrees. A thorough and thoughtful analysis of that literature has been presented by Glass et al. (1972). They have reviewed the literature for both analysis of variance and analysis of covariance (see Chap. 10). Table 3.8 presents their summary of the major implications of the studies which they reviewed. It is strongly recommended that the reader study this excellent article.

Tests for Homogeneity of Variance

One of the basic assumptions underlying both Models I and II is that the variance due to experimental error within each of the treatment populations is homogeneous; that is, $\sigma_{\varepsilon_1}^2 = \sigma_{\varepsilon_2}^2 = \cdots = \sigma_{\varepsilon_k}^2$. The experimental design literature is prone to emphasize that the analysis of variance F test is robust with regard

TABLE 3.8 Summary of consequences of violation of assumptions of the fixed-effects ANOVA†

Type of violation	Equal n's		Unequal n's	
	Effect on α	Effect on power	Effect on α	Effect on power
Non-independence of errors	Non-independence of errors seriously affects both the level of significance and power of the F-test regardless whether n's are equal or unequal.			
Non-normality: skewness	Skewed populations have very little effect on either the level of significance or the power of the fixed-effects model F-test; distortions of nominal significance levels of power values are rarely greater than a few hundredths. (However, skewed populations can seriously affect the level of significance and power of *directional*—or "one-tailed"—tests.)			
Kurtosis	Actual α is less than nominal α when populations are leptokurtic (i.e., $\beta_2 > 3$). Actual α exceeds nominal α for platykurtic populations. (Effects are slight.)	Actual power is less than nominal power when populations are platykurtic. Actual power exceeds nominal power when populations are leptokurtic. Effects can be substantial for small n.	Actual α is less than nominal α when populations are leptokurtic (i.e., $\beta_2 > 3$). Actual α exceeds nominal α for platykurtic populations. (Effects are slight.)	Actual power is less than nominal power when populations are platykurtic. Actual power exceeds nominal power when populations are leptokurtic. Effects can be substantial for small n's.
Heterogeneous variances	Very slight effect on α, which is seldom distorted by more than a few hundredths. Actual α seems always to be slightly increased over the nominal α.	(No theoretical power value exists when variances are heterogeneous.)	α may be seriously affected. Actual α exceeds nominal α when smaller samples are drawn from more variable populations; actual α is less than nominal α when smaller samples are drawn from less variable populations.	(No theoretical power value exists when variants are heterogeneous.)
Combined non-normality and heterogeneous variances	Non-normality and heterogeneous variances appear to combine additively ("non-interactively") to affect either level of significance or power. (For example, the depressing effect on α of leptokurtosis could be expected to be counteracted by the elevating effect on α of having drawn smaller samples from the more variable, leptokurtic populations.)			

† This table is produced from: G. V. Glass, P. D. Peckham, and J. R. Sanders. Consequences of failure to meet assumptions underlying the fixed effects analysis of variance and covariance. *Review of Educational Research*, 1972, 42, 3, 237–288 with permission of the editor.

102

to this assumption. This statement is usually based upon the work of Box (1954a, 1954b), wherein it was demonstrated that with equal sample sizes moderate departures from the assumption of homogeneity of variance do not seriously affect the sampling distribution of the F statistic. That is, when the variances in the population are not equal, the F statistic using a pooled variance has approximately the same distribution as the F statistic which takes the differences in the population variances into account. The following examples taken from Box (1954a, p. 299) illustrate the effect of lack of homogeneity of variance. In these examples $n = 5$ and $k = 3$.

| | **Populations** | | | **Probability of F** |
	1	**2**	**3**	**exceeding $F_{0.95}$**
(a) Variances	1	1	1	0.050
(b) Variances	1	2	3	0.058
(c) Variances	1	1	3	0.059

In (a) all variances are equal; hence an F statistic which pools variances has probability of 0.05 of exceeding $F_{0.95}$ when $\tau_1 = \tau_2 = \tau_3$. In (b) the variances have the ratio 1:2:3; that is, the variance for the second population is twice the variance of the first population, and the variance of the third population is three times the variance of the first population. For this case, the exact sampling distribution (assuming $\tau_1 = \tau_2 = \tau_3$) for the F statistic shows probability equal to 0.058 of exceeding $F_{0.95}$ obtained from the F statistic which assumes $\sigma_{\varepsilon_1}^2 = \sigma_{\varepsilon_2}^2 = \sigma_{\varepsilon_3}^2$. Using the ordinary F test when the population variances are in the ratio 1:2:3 gives a test having a small positive bias, since relatively more significant results will be obtained than the exact sampling distribution warrants. In (c) the ratio of the variances is 1:1:3; the F test in this case would also have a small positive bias, since the probability of exceeding $F_{0.95}$ is 0.059 rather than 0.050. When the number of observations in each treatment class varies considerably, Box indicates that the bias becomes somewhat larger and the direction of the bias is not always positive. Also, the greater the skewness in the distribution of the population variances, the more bias in the resulting tests.

A recent review by Wilcox (1987) points out that the situation regarding violations of the homogeneity of variance is much more complex than is implied by the usual interpretations of the work of Box. Indeed, Wilcox recommends that one should never use the conventional F test. That suggestion is dealt with at the end of this section and is based upon data which show that large differences among observed variances may occur in life and behavioral sciences research and that differences of those magnitudes can have important impact on the nominal levels of significance when the usual F ratio is computed. For example, Wilcox cites the results of Monte Carlo studies by Bishop (1976) wherein differences among variances larger than those reported by Box had considerable impact upon the nominal levels of significance. When $k = 4$ and $n = 12$ for all treatments, and with variances equal to 1, 1, 1, and 9 for σ_1^2 through σ_4^2, respectively, the actual levels of significance are 0.144, 0.101, and 0.046, corresponding to nominal levels of significance of 0.10, 0.05, and 0.01. Beyond that, it is known that large and equal sample sizes reduce, but do not eliminate, the impact of unequal variances upon the F ratio and that the problem is exacerbated when distributions are not normal in form.

In cases where the experimenter has no knowledge about the effect of the treatments upon the variance, tests for homogeneity of variances may be appropriate as preliminary tests on the model underlying the analysis.

A relatively simple test of the hypothesis that

$$\sigma_1^2 = \sigma_2^2 = \cdots = \sigma_k^2$$

is one proposed by Hartley (1940, 1950). When n is constant for all the k treatments in an experiment, this hypothesis may be tested by means of the statistic

$$F_{\max} = \frac{\text{largest of } k \text{ treatment variances}}{\text{smallest of } k \text{ treatment variances}}$$

$$= \frac{s_{\text{largest}}^2}{s_{\text{smallest}}^2}.$$

Under the hypothesis that $\sigma_1^2 = \sigma_2^2 = \cdots = \sigma_k^2$, the sampling distribution of the $F_{\max}$ statistic (assuming independent random samples from normal populations) has been tabulated by Hartley. This distribution is given in Table D.7. The parameters for this distribution are k, the number of treatments, and $n - 1$, the degrees of freedom for each of the treatment class variances. If the observed $F_{\max}$ is greater than the tabled value associated with an α-level test, then the hypothesis of homogeneity of variance is rejected. This test will be illustrated by use of the data in Table 3.9.

TABLE 3.9   **Numerical example ($n = 10$)**

	Treatment 1	Treatment 2	Treatment 3	Treatment 4
T_j	140	95	83	220
$\sum X_j^2$	2320	1802	869	6640
T_j^2/n	1960.00	902.50	688.90	4840.00
SS_j	360.00	899.50	180.10	1800.00
s_j^2	40.00	99.94	20.01	200.00

$$\sum SS_j = 3239.60$$
$$\sum s_j^2 = 359.95$$

In this table $k = 4$, and $n = 10$. SS_j is the variation within treatment class j and is given by

$$SS_j = \sum X_j^2 - \frac{T_j^2}{n}.$$

The variance within treatment class j is given by

$$s_j^2 = \frac{SS_j}{n-1}.$$

The largest of the within-class variances is 200.00; the smallest is 20.01. Thus, the numerical value of the F_{max} statistic for these data is

$$F_{max} = \frac{200.00}{20.01} = 10.0.$$

From the tables of the F_{max} distribution $F_{max_{0.99}}(4, 9) = 9.9$. Since the observed value of the F_{max} statistic is greater than the critical value for a 0.01-level test, the hypothesis of homogeneity of variance is rejected. This test, referred to as Hartley's test, is in practice sufficiently sensitive for use as a preliminary test in situations where such a test is in order. When the number of observations in each of the treatment classes is not constant but the n_j's are relatively close to being equal, the largest of the sample sizes may be used instead of n in obtaining the degrees of freedom required for use in the Hartley tables. This procedure leads to a slight positive bias in the test, i.e., rejecting H_0 more frequently than should be the case.

Another relatively simple test for homogeneity of variance, developed by Cochran (1941), uses the statistic

$$C = \frac{s_{largest}^2}{\sum s_j^2}.$$

The parameters of the sampling distribution of this statistic are k, the number of treatments, and $n - 1$, the degrees of freedom for each of the variances. Tables of the 95th and 99th percentile points of the distribution of the C statistic are given in Table D.8. For the data in Table 3.9,

$$C = \frac{200.00}{359.95} = 0.56.$$

For a 0.01-level test the critical value is $C_{0.99}(4, 9) = 0.57$. The observed value of C is quite close to the critical value but does not exceed it. However, the experimenter should on the basis of this result seriously question the tenability of the hypothesis of homogeneity of variance.

In most situations encountered in practice, the Cochran and Hartley tests will lead to the same decisions. Since the Cochran test uses more of the information in the sample data, it is generally somewhat more sensitive than is the Hartley test. In cases where n_j, the number of observations in each treatment class, is not constant but is relatively close, the largest of the n_j's may be used in place of n in determining the degrees of freedom needed to enter the tables.

Bartlett's (1937) test for homogeneity of variance is perhaps the most widely used. The routine use of Bartlett's test as a preliminary test on the model underlying the analysis of variance is not, however, recommended. From the computational point of view, it is more complex than is either the Hartley or the Cochran test. In Bartlett's test the n_j's in each of the treatment classes need not be equal; however, no n_j should be smaller than 3, and most n_j's should be larger than 5. The statistic used in Bartlett's test is

$$\chi^2 = \frac{2.303}{c}\left(f \log MS_{error} - \sum f_j \log s_j^2\right),$$

where
$$f_j = n_j - 1 = \text{degrees of freedom for } s_j^2, j = 1, \ldots, k,$$
$$f = \sum f_j = \text{degrees of freedom for } MS_{error},$$
$$c = 1 + \frac{1}{3(k-1)}\left(\sum \frac{1}{f_j} - \frac{1}{f}\right),$$
$$MS_{error} = \frac{\sum SS_j}{\sum f_j}.$$

When $\sigma_1^2 = \sigma_2^2 = \cdots = \sigma_k^2$, the sampling distribution of the χ^2 statistic is approximated by the χ^2 distribution having $k - 1$ degrees of freedom.

The data in Table 3.9 will be used to illustrate the computation of the χ^2 statistic. Computations will be indicated for the case in which the n_j's are not assumed to be equal. For this case MS_{error} is most readily obtained from

$$MS_{error} = \frac{\sum SS_j}{\sum f_j} = \frac{3239.60}{36} = 89.99,$$

since $\sum f_j = 9 + 9 + 9 + 9 = 36$. Other items required for the computation of the χ^2 statistic are

$$f \log MS_{error} = 36 \log \ 89.99 = 36(1.954) = \underline{70.344}$$

$$
\begin{aligned}
f_1 \log s_1^2 \quad &= \ 9 \log \ 40.00 = \ 9(1.602) = 14.418 \\
f_2 \log s_2^2 \quad &= \ 9 \log \ 99.94 = \ 9(1.999) = 17.991 \\
f_3 \log s_3^2 \quad &= \ 9 \log \ 20.01 = \ 9(1.301) = 11.709 \\
f_4 \log s_4^2 \quad &= \ 9 \log 200.00 = \ 9(2.301) = \underline{20.709}
\end{aligned}
$$

$$\sum f_j \log s_j^2 \qquad\qquad\qquad\qquad\qquad\qquad 64.827$$

$$c = 1 + \frac{1}{3(3)}\left(\frac{1}{9} + \frac{1}{9} + \frac{1}{9} + \frac{1}{9} - \frac{1}{36}\right)$$
$$= 1 + \tfrac{1}{9}\left(\tfrac{15}{36}\right)$$
$$= 1.046.$$

From these terms, the χ^2 statistic in Bartlett's test is

$$\chi^2 = \frac{2.303}{1.046}(70.344 - 64.827) = 12.14.$$

The larger the variation between the s_j^2's, the larger will be the value of the χ^2 statistic. For a 0.01-level test of the hypothesis that $\sigma_1^2 = \sigma_2^2 = \cdots = \sigma_k^2$ the critical value is $\chi_{0.99}^2(3) = 11.3$. Since the observed value of the χ^2 statistic is larger than the critical value, the experimental data do not support the hypothesis being tested.

For the data in Table 3.9, the Hartley, Cochran, and Bartlett tests give comparable results. The Hartley test uses the equivalent of the range of the sample variances as a measure of heterogeneity, whereas the Bartlett test uses the equivalent of the ratio of the arithmetic mean to the geometric mean of the variances. The sampling distribution of the latter measure has a smaller standard error and hence provides a more powerful test of the hypothesis being tested. For purposes of detecting large departures from the hypothesis of homogeneity of variance, either the Hartley or the Cochran test is adequate in most cases in practice.

There is evidence that the Hartley, Cochran, and Bartlett tests are all sensitive to violations of the assumption of normality of population treatment distributions. That being the case, it is probably reasonable to consider them rough screening devices for evaluating the homogeneity assumptions when the shape of the distributions is in question.

Another test for homogeneity of variance which is relatively insensitive to departure from normality is one suggested by Box (1953) and Scheffé (1959). In essence this procedure represents an analysis of variance on the logarithm of a set of variances (Scheffé, 1959, pp. 83–87). The hypothesis being tested under the procedure to be described is $\sigma_1^2 = \sigma_2^2 = \cdots = \sigma_k^2 = \sigma^2$. The computations to be described are essentially those of Table 3.9, with the exception of a system of weights.

Let the sample sizes under the treatments be denoted

$$n_1, n_2, \ldots, n_j, \ldots, n_k.$$

Suppose the n_j elements under treatment j are subdivided into subsamples of size

$$n_{1j}, n_{2j}, \ldots, n_{ij}, \ldots, n_{p_jj}.$$

(See part i of Table 3.10.) The number of subsamples p_j is arbitrary. As a rule of thumb, each of the subsamples should be of approximately equal size; each subsample should be larger than three. Also as a rule of thumb, $\sum (p_j - 1)$ should be 10 or more to assure reasonable power for the test.

For each of the subsamples compute

$$s_{ij}^2 = \frac{\sum (X_{ijk} - \bar{X}_{ij})^2}{n_{ij} - 1} = \frac{\sum_k X_{ijk}^2 - \left[\sum_k (X_{ijk})\right]^2 / n_{ij}}{n_{ij} - 1},$$

TABLE 3.10 **Scheffé test for homogeneity of variance**

		Treatment 1		Treatment 2	$\cdots$	Treatment k		
(i)		n_{11}	y_{11}	n_{12} $\quad$ y_{12}	$\cdots$	n_{1k}	y_{1k}	
		n_{21}	y_{21}	n_{22} $\quad$ y_{22}	$\cdots$	n_{2k}	y_{2k}	
		$\vdots$	$\vdots$	$\vdots$ $\quad$ $\vdots$		$\vdots$	$\vdots$	
		$n_{p_1 1}$	$y_{p_1 1}$	$n_{p_2 2}$ $\quad$ $y_{p_2 2}$	$\cdots$	$n_{p_k k}$	$y_{p_k k}$	
	Total	n_1		n_2	$\cdots$	n_k		
(ii)		$f_{i1} = n_{i1} - 1$		$f_{i2} = n_{i2} - 1$	$\cdots$	$f_{ik} = n_{ik} - 1$		
		$f_1 = \sum f_{i1}$		$f_2 = \sum f_{i2}$	$\cdots$	$f_k = \sum f_{ik}$		$f = \sum f_j$
		$T_1 = \sum f_{i1} y_{i1}$		$T_2 = \sum f_{i2} y_{i2}$	$\cdots$	$T_k = \sum f_{ik} y_{ik}$		$G = \sum T_j$
		$\bar{T}_1 = T_1/f_1$		$\bar{T}_2 = T_2/f_2$	$\cdots$	$\bar{T}_k = \sum T_k/f_k$		$\bar{G} = G/f$
(iii)		$(1) = G^2/f$		$(2) = \sum \sum f_{ij} y_{ij}^2$		$(3) = \sum (T_j^2/f_j)$		

that is, the variance for the subsample of size n_{ij}. Let

$$y_{ij} = \ln s_{ij}^2.$$

The data for the analysis of variance are shown in part i of Table 3.10. In essence one now carries out an analysis of variance with the y_{ij} as the basic observations. Each y_{ij} is considered to have $f_{ij} = n_{ij} - 1$ degrees of freedom. Hence one carries out a weighted analysis of variance, the weights being the f_{ij}. The y_{ij} are assumed to be approximately normally distributed.

Additional notation is defined in part ii. One has

$$f_j = \sum_i f_{ij}, \qquad T_j = \sum_i f_{ij} y_{ij}.$$

Convenient computational symbols are defined in part iii. The analysis of variance is

$$\text{SS}_{\text{treat}} = \sum f_j (\bar{T}_j - \bar{G})^2 = (3) - (1),$$

$$\text{SS}_{\text{error}} = \sum \sum f_{ij} (y_{ij} - \bar{T}_j)^2 = (2) - (3).$$

To test the hypothesis $\sigma_1^2 = \sigma_2^2 = \cdots = \sigma_k^2$, one uses the test statistic

$$F = \frac{\text{SS}_{\text{treat}}/(k-1)}{\text{SS}_{\text{error}}/\sum (p_j - 1)}.$$

When the hypothesis being tested is true, this F statistic is approximately an F distribution with degrees of freedom $k - 1$ and $\sum (p_j - 1)$.

As an example of the application of this test, suppose that $k = 5$ and that there are $n = 12$ observations under each treatment. One may subdivide (at random) each set of 12 observations into $p_j = 3$ subsamples, each of size $n_{ij} = 4$. Under each treatment condition there will be three variances. The degrees of freedom for the resulting F ratio will be $k - 1 = 4$ and $\sum (p_j - 1) = 10$. The sample size under each treatment need not be equal. If the sample sizes are not equal, generally the sizes of the subgroups within the treatments cannot be equal. But each subgroup should be three or larger. However each of the subgroups should be approximately equal—or as equal as the sample sizes will allow. In order to ensure adequate power for the overall F test, the denominator of the latter should be larger than 10.

Based upon the work of Conover and his colleagues (Conover et al., 1981), Wilcox (1987) recommends another test as being robust with regard to the normality assumption, which test was proposed by Brown and Forsythe (1974) and has more power than the Scheffé test. The Brown–Forsythe test has the virtue of simplicity. One transforms the original observations X_{ij} to a new variable

$$Z_{ij} = |X_{ij} - M_j|,$$

where M_j is the sample median for treatment j, and carries out an analysis of variance of the variable Z_{ij}. The analysis of variance F tests the hypothesis that the k variances are homogeneous.

Finally, one may take advantage of an approximation to the F distribution suggested by Box (1954, p. 300). Even if the variances are not homogeneous, the sampling distribution of the statistic

$$F = \frac{\mathrm{MS_{treat}}}{\mathrm{MS_{error}}}$$

may be approximated by an F distribution having parameters

$$F[(k-1)\varepsilon', \, k(n-1)\varepsilon],$$

where
$$\varepsilon' = \left[1 + \frac{k-2}{k-1}c^2\right]^{-1}, \qquad \varepsilon = (1+c^2)^{-1},$$

$$c^2 = \frac{1}{k}\frac{\sum (\sigma_j^2 - \bar{\sigma}^2)^2}{(\bar{\sigma}^2)^2}, \qquad \bar{\sigma}^2 = \frac{1}{k}\sum \sigma_j^2.$$

The value of c^2 may be shown to lie in the interval

$$0 \le c^2 \le k - 1.$$

If c^2 assumes its maximum value, then

$$\varepsilon' = \frac{1}{k-1} \quad \text{and} \quad \varepsilon = \frac{1}{k}.$$

Hence, when $c^2 = k - 1$, then

$$F = \frac{\mathrm{MS_{treat}}}{\mathrm{MS_{error}}} \text{ is distributed approximately as } F[1, n-1].$$

The decision rule

$$\text{Reject } H_0 \text{ when } \quad F_{\mathrm{obs}} > F_{1-\alpha}[1, n-1]$$

will be extremely conservative in the sense that the critical value will probably be larger than it should be to represent level of significance α. This conservatism follows from the fact that the degrees of freedom for the distribution used to approximate the exact distribution are set equal to their lower bounds.

What, then, should the experimenter do with regard to the assumption of homogeneity of variance? There is no substitute for a knowledge of how the dependent variable should behave under the various treatments based upon theory or previous work with the same variables. Based upon such knowledge, when there is doubt about homogeneity of variance the experimenter should strive for large and equal sample sizes as one way of assuring that the nominal level of significance is approximated. When that is not possible, the Box approximation may be used, but will result in an unwarranted loss of statistical power in many instances. Alternatives to the analysis of variance F have been proposed, but additional work is required before they should be recommended as routine alternatives to the usual F distribution as a test of the analysis of variance hypothesis.

TRANSFORMATIONS

It may be beneficial to systematically alter, i.e., transform, all observations prior to carrying out the analysis of variance in order to meet analysis of variance assumptions. It is well to keep in mind that many of the characteristics of data are a function of the particular scale of measurement chosen for the dependent variable. When one cannot meet the assumptions of homogeneity of variance, normality of treatment population distributions, or additivity of effects, it may be reasonable to select a new dependent variable or to consider transforming the selected dependent variable in such a way that the assumptions are met. A discussion of transformations is presented in Chapter 5, Sec. 5.21.

UNEQUAL SAMPLE SIZES

The plan of an experiment may call for an equal number of observations under each treatment, but the completed experiment may not meet this objective for a variety of reasons that do not compromise the experiment. For comparable precision in the evaluation of each treatment effect equal sample sizes are desirable, assuming that the variances for the treatment classes are equal. Circumstances not related to the experimental treatments often prevent the experimenter from having an equal number of observations under each treatment. For example, in animal research, deaths may occur from causes in no way related to the experimental treatments. In areas of research in which people are the subjects, it may be that only intact groups can be handled; such intact groups may vary in size.

In the earlier sections of this chapter, it is generally assumed that random

TABLE 3.11 **Notation**

	Treatment 1	Treatment 2	$\cdots$	Treatment j	$\cdots$	Treatment k	
Number of observations	n_1	n_2	$\cdots$	n_j	$\cdots$	n_k	$N = \sum n_j$
Sum of observations	T_1	T_2	$\cdots$	T_j	$\cdots$	T_k	$G = \sum T_j$
Mean of observations	$\bar{T}_1$	$\bar{T}_2$	$\cdots$	$\bar{T}_j$	$\cdots$	$\bar{T}_k$	$\bar{G} = G/N$
Sum of squares of observations	$\sum X_1^2$	$\sum X_2^2$	$\cdots$	$\sum X_j^2$	$\cdots$	$\sum X_k^2$	$\sum \left(\sum X_j^2 \right)$
T_j^2/n_j	T_1^2/n_1	T_2^2/n_2	$\cdots$	T_j^2/n_j	$\cdots$	T_k^2/n_k	
Within-class variation	SS_1	SS_2	$\cdots$	SS_j	$\cdots$	SS_k	
Within-class variance	$s_1^2 = \dfrac{SS_1}{n_1 - 1}$	$s_2^2 = \dfrac{SS_2}{n_2 - 1}$	$\cdots$	$s_j^2 = \dfrac{SS_j}{n_j - 1}$	$\cdots$	$s_k^2 = \dfrac{SS_k}{n_k - 1}$	

samples of size n were assigned to each of the treatments. In this section it will be assumed that a random sample of size n_1 is assigned to treatment 1, a random sample of size n_2 is assigned to treatment 2, etc. The size of the random sample is not assumed to be constant for all treatments. The form of the definitions of the sums of squares is different from those appropriate for the case in which the sample size is constant. The notation that will be used is outlined in Table 3.11. The number of treatments in the experiment is k. The treatments are designated by the symbols $1, 2, \ldots, j, \ldots, k$, where the symbol j represents any treatment within the set. The size of the sample observed under treatment j is designated by the symbol n_j. The total number of elements in the experiment is

$$n_1 + n_2 + \cdots + n_k = N.$$

To obtain estimates of the variation due to error and treatment effects, one starts with the model

$$X_{ij} = \mu + \tau_j + \varepsilon_{ij}.$$

The usual assumptions underlying the general linear model apply here.

Least-squares estimates of the parameters μ and τ_j are obtained by making

$$\sum \hat{\varepsilon}_{ij}^2 = \sum (X_{ij} - \hat{\mu} - \hat{\tau}_j)^2 = \text{minimum}.$$

Without constraints on the model, the least-squares estimators are not unique. When the estimators of parameters are not unique, they are said to be *nonestimable*. When sample sizes are equal, the constraint $\sum \hat{\tau}_j = 0$ is placed on the model, but this constraint does not lead to a simple solution to the normal equations in the case of unequal sample sizes. A convenient constraint with unequal sample sizes is $\sum n_j \hat{\tau}_j = 0$.

The normal equations are obtained from

$$\sum \hat{\varepsilon}_{ij}^2 = \sum (X_{ij} - \hat{\mu} - \hat{\tau}_j)^2 = \text{minimum}$$

by taking the partial derivatives with respect to each of the parameters and then setting the partial derivatives equal to zero. Since the solution to the normal equations represents both necessary and sufficient conditions for this minimization, all solutions to the normal equations will lead to the same minimum. Solutions with two different constraints will be illustrative.

The general form of the normal equations is

$$N\hat{\mu} + \sum n_j \hat{\tau}_j = G,$$
$$n_j \hat{\mu} + n_j \hat{\tau}_j = T_j \qquad j = 1, \ldots, k.$$

For the case $k = 2$, the normal equations have the form

$$N\hat{\mu} + n_1 \hat{\tau}_1 + n_2 \hat{\tau}_2 = G$$
$$n_1 \hat{\mu} + n_1 \hat{\tau}_1 \qquad\quad = T_1$$
$$n_2 \hat{\mu} \qquad\quad + n_2 \hat{\tau}_2 = T_2.$$

Under a first constraint that $\hat{\mu} = 0$, a solution to the normal equations is

$$n_1 \hat{\tau}_1 = T \quad \text{or} \quad \hat{\tau}_1 = \bar{T}_1,$$
$$n_2 \hat{\tau}_2 = T_2 \quad \text{or} \quad \hat{\tau}_2 = \bar{T}_2.$$

In words, the treatment effects are estimated by their respective observed treatment means under the constraint that $\hat{\mu} = 0$.

Under a second constraint that $\sum n_j \hat{\tau}_j = 0$, a second solution to the normal equations is

$$N\hat{\mu} = G \quad \text{or} \quad \hat{\mu} = G/N = \bar{G}$$
$$n_1 \bar{G} + n_1 \hat{\tau}_1 = T_1 \quad \text{or} \quad \hat{\tau}_1 = \bar{T}_1 - \bar{G}$$
$$n_2 \bar{G} + n_2 \hat{\tau}_2 = T_2 \quad \text{or} \quad \hat{\tau}_2 = \bar{T}_2 - \bar{G}.$$

In this case, the solution is identical to that obtained with equal sample sizes under the constraint that $\sum \tau_j = 0$. It is worth noting that under both solutions, *differences* between estimates of treatment effects are the same,

$$\hat{\tau}_1 - \hat{\tau}_2 = \bar{T}_1 - \bar{T}_2.$$

In terms of the structural model

$$\bar{T}_1 = \mu + \tau_1 + \bar{\varepsilon}_1,$$
$$\bar{T}_2 = \mu + \tau_2 + \bar{\varepsilon}_2,$$
$$\overline{\bar{T}_1 - \bar{T}_2 = (\tau_1 - \tau_2) + (\bar{\varepsilon}_1 - \bar{\varepsilon}_2)}$$
$$E(\bar{T}_1 - \bar{T}_2) = \tau_1 - \tau_2.$$

In general, differences between estimates of treatment effects are the same for *all* solutions to the normal equations. Functions of the estimators which are invariant for all solutions to the normal equations define estimable parametric functions. Thus, in spite of the fact that the individual parameters are nonestimable, sources of variation due to the parameters will be invariant for all solutions to the normal equations. From the solution with the restriction $\hat{\mu} = 0$, the variation due to μ, τ_1, and τ_2 is given by

$$
\begin{aligned}
R(\mu, \tau_1, \tau_2) &= \hat{\mu}G + \hat{\tau}_1 T_1 + \hat{\tau}_2 T_2 \\
&= 0G + \bar{T}_1 T_1 + \bar{T}_2 T_2 \\
&= \sum (T_j^2/n_j).
\end{aligned}
$$

From the solution with the restriction that $\sum n_j \tau_j = 0$, this same source of variation is given by

$$
\begin{aligned}
R(\mu, \tau_1, \tau_2) &= \hat{\mu}G + \hat{\tau}_1 T_1 + \hat{\tau}_2 T_2 \\
&= \bar{G}G + (\bar{T}_1 - \bar{G})T_1 + (\bar{T}_2 - \bar{G})T_2 \\
&= (G^2/N) + (T_1^2/n_1) + (T_2^2/n_2) - \bar{G}(T_1 - T_2) \\
&= \sum (T_j^2/n_j) + (G^2/N) - (G^2/N) \\
&= \sum (T_j^2/n_j).
\end{aligned}
$$

To return to the analysis of variance, then, the variation due to error is

$$
\text{SS}_{\text{error}} = \sum X^2 - R(\mu, \tau_1, \tau_2) = \sum X^2 - \sum (T_j^2/n),
$$

and the variation due to treatments adjusted for μ is

$$
\begin{aligned}
\text{SS}_{\text{treat}} &= R(\tau_1, \tau_2/\mu) = R(\mu, \tau_1, \tau_2) - R(\mu) \\
&= \sum (T_j^2/n_j) - (G^2/N) = \sum n_j (\bar{T}_j - \bar{G})^2,
\end{aligned}
$$

where $R(\mu)$ is the variation due to μ and is

$$
R(\mu) = \hat{\mu}G = \bar{G}G = G^2/N.
$$

The same outcomes would result under maximum likelihood procedures assuming the τ_j were random variates having a joint multivariate normal distribution as is the case for Model II. Thus, the basic partition of the overall variation has the form

$$
\sum \sum (X_{ij} - \bar{G})^2 = \sum n_j (\bar{T}_j - \bar{G})^2 + \sum \sum (X_{ij} - \bar{T}_j)^2,
$$
$$
\text{SS}_{\text{total}} = \text{SS}_{\text{treat}} \qquad + \text{SS}_{\text{error}}.
$$

In the computation of SS_{treat}, each $(\bar{T}_j - \bar{G})^2$ is weighted by n_j. Hence, SS_{treat} is a weighted sum of the squared deviations about $\bar{G}$. Further, $\bar{G}$ is itself a weighted average of the treatment means. That is,

$$
\bar{G} = \frac{n_1 \bar{T}_1 + n_2 \bar{T}_2 + \cdots + n_k \bar{T}_k}{N}.
$$

TABLE 3.12 **Computational formulas**

$$(1) = \frac{G^2}{N} \qquad (2) = \sum \left(\sum X_j^2 \right) \qquad (3) = \sum \left(\frac{T_j^2}{n_j} \right)$$

$SS_{treat} = (3) - (1)$	$df_{treat} = k - 1$
$SS_{error} = (2) - (3)$	$df_{error} = N - k$
$SS_{total} = (2) - (1)$	$df_{total} = N - 1$

An analysis of variance procedure for unequal sample sizes which does not weight the $\bar{T}_j$ in obtaining $\bar{G}$ and which does not weight the $(\bar{T}_j \bar{G})^2$ by n_j is defined at the end of this section. This latter definition is to be preferred in cases where differences in the n_j have no meaning in terms of the population about which inferences are being drawn. This would be the case wherein unequal sample sizes occur essentially at random.

Computational formulas are summarized in Table 3.12. Symbols (1) and (2) have the same general form as they do for the case of equal n's. However, symbol (3) is different; that is,

$$(3) = \frac{T_1^2}{n_1} + \frac{T_2^2}{n_2} + \cdots + \frac{T_k^2}{n_k}.$$

Thus each T_j^2 must be divided by its n_j before the summation is made. The degrees of freedom for each of the sums of squares are also shown in Table 3.12. For SS_{error} the number of degrees of freedom is the pooled degrees of freedom for the variation within each of the treatments, i.e.,

$$df_{error} = (n_1 - 1) + (n_2 - 1) + \cdots + (n_k - 1)$$
$$= N - k.$$

The computational formulas given in Table 3.12 become those for the case of equal sample sizes when n_j is constant for all treatments. Hence the computational formulas for equal n's are simplified special cases of those given in Table 3.12.

A numerical example is given in Table 3.13. Data in part i represent the basic observations. Detailed summary data are given in part ii. The symbols used in part ii are defined in Table 3.11. For example,

$$SS_1 = \sum X_1^2 - \frac{T_1^2}{n_1} = 64 - 54.00 = 10.00.$$

Use of the computational formulas is illustrated in part iii. There are alternative methods for computing these sums of squares. SS_{error} may be obtained from

$$SS_{error} = \sum SS_j = 73.21.$$

TABLE 3.13 **Numerical example**

	Treatment 1	Treatment 2	Treatment 3	Treatment 4
	3	7	3	10
	2	8	2	12
(i)	4	4	1	8
	3	10	2	5
	1	6	4	12
	5		2	10
			3	9
			1	

(ii)

$n_1 = 6$	$n_2 = 5$	$n_3 = 8$	$n_4 = 7$	$N = 26$
$T_1 = 18$	$T_2 = 35$	$T_3 = 18$	$T_4 = 66$	$G = 137$
$\sum X_1^2 = 64$	$\sum X_2^2 = 265$	$\sum X_3^2 = 48$	$\sum X_4^2 = 658$	$\sum \left(\sum X_j^2 \right) = 1035$
$\dfrac{T_1^2}{n_1} = 54.00$	$\dfrac{T_2^2}{n_2} = 245.00$	$\dfrac{T_3^2}{n_3} = 40.50$	$\dfrac{T_4^2}{n_4} = 622.29$	$\sum \left(\dfrac{T_j^2}{n_j} \right) = 961.79$
$SS_1 = 10.00$	$SS_2 = 20.00$	$SS_3 = 7.50$	$SS_4 = 35.71$	$\sum SS_j = 73.21$
$s_1^2 = 2.00$	$s_2^2 = 5.00$	$s_3^2 = 1.07$	$s_4^2 = 5.95$	
$\bar{T}_1 = 3.00$	$\bar{T}_2 = 7.00$	$\bar{T}_3 = 2.25$	$\bar{T}_4 = 9.43$	$\bar{G} = \frac{137}{26} = 5.27$

(iii)

$(1) = G^2/N = (137)^2/26 = 721.88$ $(2) = \sum\sum X^2 = 1035$ $(3) = \sum (T_j^2/n_j) = 961.79$

$$SS_{\text{treat}} = (3) - (1) = 239.91$$
$$SS_{\text{error}} = (2) - (3) = \underline{73.21}$$
$$SS_{\text{total}} = (2) - (1) = 313.12$$

From the definition,

$$SS_{\text{treat}} = \sum n_j (\bar{T}_j - \bar{G})^2$$
$$= 6(3.00 - 5.27)^2 + 5(7.00 - 5.27)^2 + 8(2.25 - 5.27)^2$$
$$+ 7(9.43 - 5.27)^2$$
$$= 239.95.$$

For purposes of showing just what it is that forms the sum of squares for error and treatments, these alternative computational methods are more revealing, but they also involve more computational effort.

The analysis of variance is summarized in Table 3.14. A test of the

TABLE 3.14 **Analysis of variance**

Source of variation	SS	df	MS	F
Treatments	239.91	3	79.97	24.02**
Experimental error	73.71	22	3.33	
Total	313.12	25		

$** \ F_{0.99}(3, 22) = 4.82$

hypothesis that all the treatment effects are equal is given by the F ratio,

$$F = \frac{\text{MS}_{\text{treat}}}{\text{MS}_{\text{error}}} = \frac{79.97}{3.33} = 24.02.$$

The critical value for a 0.01-level test is $F_{0.99}(3, 22) = 4.82$. The data contradict the hypothesis of no differences in treatment effects.

As a rough check for homogeneity of variance,

$$F_{\text{max}} = \frac{s^2_{\text{largest}}}{s^2_{\text{smallest}}} = \frac{5.95}{1.07} = 5.56.$$

The largest of the n_j's is 8. For a 0.05-level test, an approximate critical value is $F_{\text{max}_{0.95}}(k = 4, \text{df} = 8 - 1 = 7) = 8.44$. The data do not contradict the hypothesis of homogeneity of variance.

A detailed explanation of methods for comparing means is presented in Sec. 3.10. The example presented here in terms of unequal sample sizes may be combined with that information for a complete treatment.

A comparison has the same form as that for the case of equal n's (see Sec. 3.10); that is, in terms of an observed comparison:

$$C = c_1 \bar{T}_1 + c_2 \bar{T}_2 + \cdots + c_k \bar{T}_k, \quad \text{where} \quad \sum c_j = 0.$$

A component of variation corresponding to a comparison is in this case

$$\text{SS}_C = \frac{C^2}{(c_1^2/n_1) + (c_2^2/n_2) + \cdots + (c_k^2/n_k)}.$$

Two comparisons,

$$C_1 = c_{11} \bar{T}_1 + c_{12} \bar{T}_2 + \cdots + c_{1k} \bar{T}_k,$$
$$C_2 = c_{21} \bar{T}_1 + c_{22} \bar{T}_2 + \cdots + c_{2k} \bar{T}_k,$$

are orthogonal if

$$\frac{c_{11} c_{21}}{n_1} + \frac{c_{12} c_{22}}{n_2} + \cdots + \frac{c_{1k} c_{2k}}{n_k} = 0.$$

These definitions reduce to those given for equal n's when all the n_j's are equal.

Computational procedures for comparisons will be illustrated through use of the data in Table 3.13. The component of variation corresponding to the difference between treatments 2 and 4 is

$$\text{SS}_C = \frac{(\bar{T}_2 - \bar{T}_4)^2}{[(1)^2/n_2] + [(-1)^2/n_4]} = \frac{(7.00 - 9.43)^2}{\frac{1}{5} + \frac{1}{7}} = 17.20.$$

To test the hypothesis that $\tau_2 = \tau_4$, the statistic used is

$$F = \frac{\text{SS}_C}{\text{MS}_{\text{error}}} = \frac{17.20}{3.33} = 5.17.$$

The numerator of this statistic has 1 degree of freedom, the denominator has 22 degrees of freedom (the degrees of freedom for MS_{error}). For a 0.01-level test the critical value is $F_{0.99}(1, 22) = 7.94$. Since the observed F statistic does not exceed the critical value, the data do not contradict the hypothesis that $\tau_2 = \tau_4$.

As another example, suppose a meaningful comparison planned in advance of the experiment is that between treatment 4 and all others combined; i.e., does treatment 4 differ from the average of all other treatment effects? This comparison is given by

$$SS_C = \frac{(3\bar{T}_4 - \bar{T}_1 - \bar{T}_2 - \bar{T}_3)^2}{(c_4^2/n_4) + (c_1^2/n_1) + (c_2^2/n_2) + (c_3^2/n_3)}$$

$$= \frac{[3(9.43) - (3.00) - (7.00) - (2.25)]^2}{\frac{9}{7} + \frac{1}{6} + \frac{1}{5} + \frac{1}{8}} = 144.54.$$

To test the hypothesis that $\tau_4 = (\tau_1 + \tau_2 + \tau_3)/3$, the statistic used is

$$F = \frac{SS_C}{MS_{error}} = \frac{144.54}{3.33} = 43.40.$$

The critical value for a 0.01-level test is $F_{0.99}(1, 22) = 7.94$. Hence the data clearly contradict the hypothesis that the effect of treatment 4 is equal to the average effect of the other three treatments.

When the n_j's do not differ markedly, the Newman–Keuls, the Duncan, or the Tukey method (see Sec. 3.11) may be adapted for use in making tests on differences between all pairs of means. The Newman–Keuls method will be used to illustrate the principles involved. With unequal sample sizes it is convenient to work with the treatment means. (For the case of equal sample sizes it is more convenient to work with the treatment totals.) The example in Table 3.13 will be used to illustrate the numerical operations. Part i of Table 3.15 gives the treatment means arranged in order of increasing magnitude. The differences between all possible pairs of means are shown. For example, the entry 7.18 in the first row is the difference $9.43 - 2.25$. The entry 4.75 is the difference $7.00 - 2.25$. In general an entry in this table is the difference between the mean at the top of the column and the mean at the left of the row.

The statistic to be used in making tests on these differences is

$$q_r = \frac{\bar{T}_j - \bar{T}_{j'}}{\sqrt{MS_{error}/n}},$$

where r is the number of steps apart the two means are on an ordered scale. The n in the expression $\sqrt{MS_{error}/n}$ refers to the number of observations in each of the means and is assumed to be constant. If the n_j's do not differ markedly from each other, the harmonic mean of the n_j's may be used instead of n in this expression. The harmonic mean $\bar{n}$ is defined as

$$\bar{n} = \frac{k}{(1/n_1) + (1/n_2) + \cdots + (1/n_k)}.$$

TABLE 3.15 **Tests on differences between all pairs of means**

	Treatments		3	1	2	4
		Means	2.25	3.00	7.00	9.43
(i)	3	2.25	—	0.75	4.75	7.18
	1	3.00		—	4.00	6.43
	2	7.00			—	2.43
	4	9.43				—

		$r = 2$	$r = 3$	$r = 4$
(ii) (iii)	$q_{0.99}(r, 22)$	3.99	4.59	4.96
	$\sqrt{\text{MS}_{\text{error}}/\tilde{n}}\, q_{0.99}(r, 22)$	2.90	3.34	3.61

		3	1	2	4
(iv)	3			**	**
	1			**	**
	2				
	4				

For the numerical example,

$$\tilde{n} = \frac{4}{\frac{1}{6} + \frac{1}{5} + \frac{1}{8} + \frac{1}{7}} = 6.30.$$

Note: An alternative procedure is to replace n by the harmonic mean of the sample sizes corresponding to the two extreme means. That is, n is replaced by $\dot{n}$, where

$$\dot{n} = \frac{2}{(1/n_{(1)}) + (1/n_{(k)})},$$

where $n_{(1)}$ = sample size corresponding to smallest treatment mean,

$n(k)$ = sample size corresponding to largest treatment mean.

This alternative procedure tends to be conservative in the sense of erring on the side of reducing the nominal value of the level of significance. That is, a test having nominal value $\alpha = 0.05$ relative to equal n tends to have actual $\alpha = 0.04$ (approximately) for unequal n, provided the sample sizes are relatively close to each other.

Since the degrees of freedom for MS_{error} are 22, the critical values for the q_r statistic are found in the tables of the studentized range statistic (Appendix D.4) in the row corresponding to 22 degrees of freedom. The critical values for a 0.01-level test are given in part ii of Table 3.15. Thus 3.99 is the critical value for the q_r statistic when $r = 2$, that is, when the means are two steps apart; 4.59 is the critical value for q_r when $r = 3$. In making several tests it is convenient to work with the critical value of the difference between a pair of means rather than the critical value of q_r. Since

$$\sqrt{\frac{MS_{error}}{\bar{n}}}\, q_r = \bar{T}_j - \bar{T}_{j'},$$

the critical value for the difference between two means is

$$q_{1-\alpha}(r, \text{df})\sqrt{\frac{MS_{error}}{\bar{n}}}.$$

The numerical value of $\sqrt{MS_{error}/\bar{n}}$ is in this case $\sqrt{3.33/6.30} = 0.727$. Hence the critical values for 0.01-level tests on the differences between pairs of means are given by multiplying the entries in part ii of Table 3.15 by 0.727. These values are given in part iii. For example, the entry $2.90 = (0.727)(3.99)$.

The sequence in which the tests must be made is given in Sec. 3.11. This sequence must be followed here. The sequence indicated in the following steps is equivalent to that in Sec. 3.11.

1 The first test made is on the difference 7.18 in the upper right of part i. Since this entry is the difference between two means that are four steps apart, the critical value is 3.61. Hence the hypothesis that $\tau_3 = \tau_4$ is contradicted by the experimental data.

2 The next test is on the entry 4.75, the difference between two means which are three steps apart. The critical value for this test is 3.34. Hence the data contradict the hypothesis that $\tau_2 = \tau_3$.

3 The entry 0.75, which is the difference between two means that are two steps apart, is tested next. The critical value is 2.90. Hence the data do not contradict the hypothesis that $\tau_1 = \tau_3$.

4 The entry 6.43 is tested against the critical value 3.34, since this entry is the difference between two means which are three steps apart. Hence the data contradict the hypothesis that $\tau_1 = \tau_4$.

5 The entry 4.00 is tested against the critical value 2.90. The data contradict the hypothesis that $\tau_1 = \tau_2$.

6 The entry 2.43 is tested against the critical value 2.90. The data do not contradict the hypothesis that $\tau_2 = \tau_4$.

A summary of the tests is given in part iv. The cells with asterisks indicate that the corresponding differences are statistically significant at the 0.01 level. Schematically this summary may be represented as follows:

$$\underline{3 \quad 1} \qquad \underline{2 \quad 4}.$$

Treatments underlined by a common line do not differ; treatments not underlined by a common line do differ. Hence treatments 2 and 4 differ from treatments 3 and 1, but there is no difference between treatments 2 and 4 and no difference between 3 and 1.

In adapting the Duncan method or either of the Tukey methods to the case of unequal sample sizes, the harmonic mean $\bar{n}$ is used in place of n. For example, in the Tukey test the critical value for 0.01-level tests on all differences would be $\sqrt{\text{MS}_{\text{error}}/\bar{n}}\, q_{0.99}(k, \text{df})$, where k is the number of treatments and df is the degrees of freedom for MS_{error}. For the numerical example, this critical value is 3.61. In this case the Tukey test would give outcomes identical with those obtained by means of the Newman–Keuls test.

Unweighted-Means Analysis

The definition of SS_{treat} given earlier in this section requires that each $(\bar{T}_j - \bar{G})^2$ be weighted by n_j. If the error variances for each of the treatments are equal, this weighting procedure gives each squared deviation a weight which is proportional to the reciprocal of its squared standard error, which is n_j. If, however, the n_j's are in no way related to the hypothesis being tested and it is desirable to give each treatment mean a numerically equal weight in determining SS_{treat}, then the latter source of variation may be defined as

$$\text{SS}_{\text{treat}} = \bar{n} \sum (\bar{T}_j - \bar{G})^2,$$

where
$$\bar{G} = \frac{\sum \bar{T}_j}{k}.$$

This definition of $\bar{G}$ differs from that used earlier in this section. If the latter definition of SS_{treat} is used, $\text{SS}_{\text{treat}} + \text{SS}_{\text{error}}$ will not be numerically equal to SS_{total}. This solution weights all treatment effect estimates on an equal amount, the weight being the harmonic mean of the sample sizes $\bar{n}$.

3.9   POWER, TREATMENT EFFECT SIZE, AND THE DETERMINATION OF SAMPLE SIZE

Statistical power was introduced in Chapter 2 as the probability of correctly rejecting the null hypothesis. If β is the probability of a Type II error—the probability of incorrectly retaining the null hypothesis as tenable—statistical power is $1 - \beta$. Given the logical structure of hypothesis testing, power is essentially the ability of an experiment to detect treatment effects—the ability to demonstrate that a phenomenon exists. More generally, it is the ability of an experiment to demonstrate the magnitude of treatment effects. It is an answer to the question, "With this experiment, what is the probability that I can detect a treatment effect of a specified magnitude?" Since experiments are performed in order to specify that treatment effects exist or, preferably, to establish the magnitude of treatment effects, assessment of power is fundamental to the evaluation of the adequacy of an experimental design. As Cohen (1988) has noted, however, the topic is often neglected. He presents data to support the conclusion that for many areas of research in the social sciences the experimental designs lack reasonable levels of statistical power.

As a practical matter, evaluation of statistical power requires the experimenter to establish a level of significance, sample size(s), magnitude (and, where appropriate, direction) of the treatment effects which (s)he wishes to detect, and the within-class variance associated with the observations. Variance is, among other things, a function of the nature and reliability of the dependent variable and of the nature of the experimental design. The level of significance is typically set by convention. Hence, the question of power is often framed in terms of the sample size required to detect a deviation from the null hypothesis which is of interest on theoretical or practical grounds.

It is intuitively appealing that emphasis should be placed upon sample size; all other things being equal, sample size determines the precision with which parameters can be estimated. Since treatment effects are defined in terms of parameters and estimated from statistics, sample size determines the accuracy with which the estimation proceeds. Cohen (1988, Chapter 1) presents an excellent discussion of the relations among α, n, effect size, and statistical power. It is also fundamental to specify how the magnitude of treatment effects will be defined and estimated.

Measuring Treatment Effects and Strengths of Association

An experimental design with a numerically high level of statistical power can lead to rejection of the analysis of variance null hypothesis even though treatment effects are trivial from a practical or theoretical point of view. For example, Wilcox (1987) points out that recent studies which demonstrate that cholesterol-lowering drugs significantly reduce heart attack rates ($\alpha = 0.001$) also reflect differences in the number of heart attacks which are very small. The differences may or may not justify drug usage as a practical matter.

Whether treatment effects are large or small is a relative matter which should be assessed in terms of some external criterion of practical or theoretical utility. The measures of the size of treatment effects presented here assess the magnitude of treatment effects relative to the error in the data. Generally speaking, one can approach the question of the magnitude of treatment effects as a question concerning the strength of association between the dependent and independent variables which can in turn be expressed in terms of some kind of correlation coefficient.

With experimental designs wherein treatment conditions are fixed (Model I) interest centers upon estimating particular treatment effects, since the treatments in the study are of particular interest. When treatment levels are random (Model II), the focus is upon estimating components of variance (see Sec. 3.5). Hence, for the two models estimates of treatment effects are different, as are methods for computing statistical power. For a variety of reasons, procedures for fixed treatment levels are better known.

MODEL I: FIXED TREATMENTS. How one should assess the size of treatment effects is not always obvious, and the study of different measures constitutes an active area of research due in part from an increased interest in evaluating statistical power and from an interest in meta-analysis (e.g., Hedges and Olkin, 1985). Cohen (1988) and others (e.g., Kraemer and Thiemann, 1985; Maxwell and Delaney, 1990; Wilcox, 1987) present interesting discussions of the topic. The approach followed here is closely related to Cohen's very useful and general approach to measuring effect size and determining statistical power. The reader is urged to study his presentation in detail and to follow new developments in this important area of research.

When $k = 2$, the simplest measure of effect size is the difference between the two means, $\mu_1 - \mu_2$, an unbiased estimate of which is $\bar{T}_1 - \bar{T}_2$. Taking this approach one step further, Cohen (1988) utilizes a standardized difference between means,

$$d = \frac{\mu_1 - \mu_2}{\sigma}$$

or

$$d = \frac{|\mu_1 - \mu_2|}{\sigma}$$

as an index of treatment effect size for one-tailed and two-tailed differences, respectively.[1] The denominator, σ, refers to the population within-treatment standard deviation which is assumed to be homogeneous for the two treatment populations. Thus, by d the mean difference is standardized to the common standard deviation and is, in that sense, unitless.

Hedges (1981) has derived the sampling distribution of the estimator of d,

$$\hat{d} = \frac{\bar{T}_1 - \bar{T}_2}{s^2_{pooled}},$$

$$s^2_{pooled} = \frac{(n_1 - 1)s_1^2 + (n_2 - 1)s_2^2}{n_1 + n_2 - 2}.$$

Computed thusly, $\hat{d}$ is a biased estimator. As explained by Wilcox (1987) most of the bias is removed if $\hat{d}$ is computed as

$$\hat{d} = A(\bar{T}_1 - \bar{T}_2)/s^2_{pooled},$$

where

$$A = 1 - 3[4(n_1 + n_2 - 2) - 1]^{-1}.$$

Cohen (1988, p. 21) has interpreted d in terms of the percent of overlap between the two treatment population distributions, under the assumption that the distributions are normal in form and the populations have equal size. He has also shown that d may be interpreted as the point biserial correlation coefficient between treatment group membership and the dependent variable (1988, p. 24). The square of this correlation coefficient may be interpreted as

---

[1] The quantity d (sometimes denoted δ) is sometimes referred to as Glass's effect size because Glass (1976) and then Cohen (1977) suggested its use.

the proportion of the variance of the dependent variable which can be predicted through knowing group membership. Related to d, the point biserial correlation is

$$r = \frac{d}{\sqrt{d^2 + (1/pq)}},$$

and

$$r^2 = \frac{d^2}{d^2 + (1/pq)},$$

where p is the proportion of the total number of elements in treatment population 1 and q is the proportion in treatment population 2. When $n_1 = n_2$,

$$r^2 = \frac{d^2}{d^2 + 4}.$$

The interpretation of d in terms of r provides continuity between the index d and its generalization to f, a useful measure of effect size when $k > 2$ and to other more complicated experimental designs.

The index d may be easily generalized to the analysis of variance context wherein $k > 3$. Let

$$\sigma_\mu^2 = \frac{\Sigma (\mu_j - \mu)^2}{k} = \frac{\Sigma \tau_j^2}{k}$$

be the population treatment variance (Cohen, 1988, refers to σ_μ as σ_m). Then, the standard deviation of the treatment means, or treatment effects, is

$$\sigma_\mu = \sqrt{\frac{\Sigma (\mu_j - \mu)^2}{k}} = \sqrt{\frac{\Sigma \tau_j^2}{k}}.$$

Given σ_μ,

$$f = \frac{\sigma_\mu}{\sigma_\varepsilon}$$

is the generalization of d to $k > 2$, the standard deviation of the means standardized by the common within-treatment population variance. The common variance is due to random error when the analysis of variance model holds. The effect size, f, is unitless and has a lower bound of zero when there are no population treatment effects. It is worth noting that

$$f^2 = \frac{\sigma_\mu^2}{\sigma_\varepsilon^2}$$

expresses the variance of the means relative to error variance.

Just as d may be interpreted in terms of correlation coefficients and proportions of variance, f may be interpreted in the same terms and may be shown to be closely related to other measures of degree of association between treatment group means and the dependent variable.

The most general measure of association between treatment group membership and the dependent variable is the correlation ratio eta (η), the square of which (η^2) may be interpreted as the proportion of population variance attributable to treatment group membership. If σ^2_{total} is the variance of the dependent variable computed about a common mean, μ, σ^2_ε is the variance of the observations taken about their respective treatment population means, and σ^2_μ is the variance of the treatment means, then

$$\eta^2 = \frac{\sigma^2_\mu}{\sigma^2_{total}} = \frac{\sigma^2_\mu}{\sigma^2_\mu + \sigma^2_\varepsilon}.$$

Hence, η^2 is the porportion of population variance which may be accounted for by treatment population means.

As d is related to the point biserial correlation coefficient for two-group membership, f is related to η^2 for k-group membership:

$$\eta^2 = \frac{f^2}{1 + f^2},$$

and

$$f^2 = \frac{\eta^2}{1 - \eta^2}.$$

For purposes of generalizing, it is important to note that η^2 is the "function-free" correlation which expresses the total (linear and curvilinear) regression of the dependent variable upon the treatments. It is the sum of the variation components which are predictable by a polynomial of any degree (see Sec. 3.13). It is function-free in the sense that the regression function is the line of means and no particular function is implied. Stated another way, it is the squared multiple correlation which obtains when multiple regression techniques are used to predict the dependent variable from treatment group membership (see Appendix C). In analysis of variance terms, the descriptive statistic is

$$R^2 = \frac{SS_{treat}}{SS_{total}},$$

the observed proportion of total variation in the dependent variable predictable by treatment membership. Computed thusly, R^2 is an overestimate of η^2 in the population. An index which is equivalent to the "shrunken multiple" (Wherry, 1931) is epsilon squared (ε^2), where

$$\varepsilon^2 = \frac{SS_{treat} - (k - 1)MS_{error}}{SS_{total}}.$$

Two other measures of association, which are related to η^2, are important. When treatments are fixed, the predictable proportion of variance is expressed by omega squared (ω^2) (Hays, 1981); when treatments are random, the intraclass correlation coefficient expresses the same concept.

For fixed treatments, omega squared is

$$\omega^2 = \frac{\theta}{\sigma^2_\varepsilon + \theta},$$

where, for equal sample sizes,

$$\theta = \sum \tau_j^2/k,$$

and

$$\omega^2 = \frac{\sum \tau_j^2/k}{\sigma_\varepsilon^2 + \sum \tau_j^2/k}.$$

One notes that

$$\theta = \frac{k-1}{k}\sigma_\tau^2 = \frac{k-1}{k}\left(\frac{\sum \tau_j^2}{k-1}\right) = \frac{\sum \tau_j^2}{k}.$$

One heuristic approach to estimating ω^2 is to estimate θ and σ_ε^2 separately and then define

$$\hat{\omega}^2 = \frac{\hat{\theta}}{\hat{\sigma}_\varepsilon^2 + \hat{\theta}}.$$

This approach leads to a biased estimator of the ratio,[2] but the resulting estimator is satisfactory for most practical purposes. One has

$$\mathrm{MS}_{\mathrm{error}} = \hat{\sigma}_\varepsilon^2.$$

For the fixed model

$$E(\mathrm{MS}_{\mathrm{treat}}) = \sigma_\varepsilon^2 + n\sigma_\tau^2 = \sigma_\varepsilon^2 + n\left[\sum \tau_j^2/(k-1)\right]$$

$$= \sigma_\varepsilon^2 + \frac{nk}{k-1}\left(\sum \tau_j^2/k\right)$$

$$= \sigma_\varepsilon^2 + \frac{nk}{k-1}\theta.$$

Hence, it follows that

$$E(\mathrm{MS}_{\mathrm{treat}} - \mathrm{MS}_{\mathrm{error}}) = \frac{nk}{k-1}\theta.$$

Thus, one may take

$$\hat{\theta} = \frac{k-1}{nk}(\mathrm{MS}_{\mathrm{treat}} - \mathrm{MS}_{\mathrm{error}}),$$

and the heuristic estimator of ω^2 is given by

$$\hat{\omega}^2 = \frac{\dfrac{k-1}{kn}(\mathrm{MS}_{\mathrm{treat}} - \mathrm{MS}_{\mathrm{error}})}{\mathrm{MS}_{\mathrm{error}} + \dfrac{k-1}{kn}(\mathrm{MS}_{\mathrm{treat}} - \mathrm{MS}_{\mathrm{error}})} = \frac{\mathrm{SS}_{\mathrm{treat}} - (k-1)\mathrm{MS}_{\mathrm{error}}}{\mathrm{SS}_{\mathrm{total}} + \mathrm{MS}_{\mathrm{error}}}.$$

---

[2] Abu Libdeh (1984) has derived the distribution for $\hat{\omega}^2$ and has studied the degree of bias of estimation.

If one divides the numerator and denominator by MS_{error} and then lets $F = MS_{treat}/MS_{error}$, this expression takes the following form:

$$\hat{\omega}^2 = \frac{(k-1)(F-1)}{kn + (k-1)(F-1)}.$$

For the random model, the intraclass correlation is

$$\rho_I = \frac{\sigma_\tau^2}{\sigma_\varepsilon^2 + \sigma_\tau^2}, \quad \text{where} \quad \sigma_\tau^2 = \frac{\sum \tau_j^2}{k-1}.$$

A heuristic biased estimator of $\rho_{intraclass}$ takes the general form

$$\hat{\rho}_{intraclass} = \frac{\hat{\sigma}_{treat}}{\hat{\sigma}_\varepsilon^2 + \hat{\sigma}_{treat}^2}.$$

$$= \frac{MS_{treat} - MS_{error}}{MS_{treat} + (n-1)MS_{error}}.$$

The intraclass correlation is essentially a measure of the extent to which the observations within a treatment are similar (or dependent) relative to observations in different treatments.

EFFECT SIZE: SUMMARY REMARKS. The presentation here has relied heavily upon Cohen's work because the approach can be generalized to experimental designs of any degree of complexity and to other applications of the general linear model such as multiple linear regression and analysis of covariance. Other important work is occurring. Wilcox (1987) has summarized research designed to develop nonparametric measures of treatment effects and Kraemer and Thiemann (1987) present a detailed account of a simple approach to determining sample sizes needed to achieve a specified level of power which is applicable to a variety of research environments. Rosenthal and Rubin (1982) have suggested an alternative to measures which reflect proportions of variance called a binomial effect size display. Another alternative is the use of various graphical displays (e.g. Cleveland, 1985).

Estimating Power: Fixed Treatments

The most extensive treatment of statistical power for social and behavioral science is Cohen's work (1988). He presents tables wherein power is estimated given values of the level of significance (α), his effect size measure (f), the sample size (n), and the degrees of freedom of the numerator of F ratios. He also presents tables wherein sample sizes are provided for experimenters who establish α, f, df, and the desired level of power. The basis for these tables (when sample sizes are equal) is

$$f = \frac{\sigma_\mu}{\sigma_\varepsilon} = \frac{\sqrt{\sum (\mu_j - \mu)^2/k}}{\sigma_\varepsilon} = \frac{\sqrt{\sum \tau_j^2/k}}{\sigma_\varepsilon}.$$

This is important because it makes clear that an experimenter must have enough knowledge of the research area to estimate σ_μ and σ_ε. Given some pilot data, σ_μ may be estimated by obtaining an estimate of $\sum \tau_j^2$. An unbiased estimate for this design is

$$\sum \hat{\tau}_j^2 = \frac{k-1}{n} (\text{MS}_{\text{treat}} - \text{MS}_{\text{error}})$$

based upon the expected value of the mean squares for Model I. An unbiased estimate of σ_ε is

$$\hat{\sigma}_\varepsilon = \text{MS}_{\text{error}}.$$

Ideally, one studies an area of research extensively enough that good estimates of f are available and power may, therefore, be established for a new experiment during the design stages. When that is not possible, Cohen suggests the convention that $f = 0.10$, 0.25, and 0.40 may be viewed as small, medium, and large effect measures, respectively. These f values correspond to η^2 values of 0.01, 0.06, and 0.14. For example, if one wishes to detect small differences—σ_μ is 0.10 of σ_ε, or one can predict 1 percent of the variance in the dependent variable—then power should be assessed for $f = 0.10$. The suggestion is a reasonable one. However, it would be unfortunate if these f values were to become rigid standards or were to substitute for thorough knowledge of what to expect for effect sizes based upon prior research.

Power computations used herein are based upon the charts presented in Appendix D, Table 14, or the power charts of Table 11. Instead of Cohen's index of effect size,

$$f = \frac{\sqrt{\sum \tau_j^2/k}}{\sigma_\varepsilon},$$

these tables are based upon the noncentrality parameter of the noncentral F distribution, λ. In particular, they are based upon ϕ, where

$$\phi = \sqrt{\frac{n \sum \tau_j^2}{k \sigma_\varepsilon^2}} = \sqrt{\frac{\lambda}{k}},$$

where the noncentrality parameter is

$$\lambda = n \sum \tau_j^2 / \sigma_\varepsilon^2.$$

The quantity ϕ is closely related to f:

$$f = \phi/\sqrt{n},$$

and

$$\phi = f\sqrt{n}.$$

In words, f is standardized relative to σ_ε and ϕ is standardized to the standard error of the mean $\sigma_\varepsilon/\sqrt{n}$.

In terms of a single-factor experiment (fixed model) having k treatments and n experimental units per treatment, the expected values of the mean squares for the overall F ratio have the form

$$\frac{E(MS_{\text{treat}})}{E(MS_{\text{error}})} = \frac{\sigma_\varepsilon^2 + n(\sum \tau_j^2)/(k-1)}{\sigma_\varepsilon^2} = 1 + \frac{n(\sum \tau_j^2)/(k-1)}{\sigma_\varepsilon^2} = 1 + \frac{\lambda}{k-1},$$

where

$$\lambda = \frac{n \sum \tau_j^2}{\sigma_\varepsilon^2}.$$

The parameters τ_j are assumed to be scaled so that $\sum \tau_j = 0$. Under the hypothesis that $\tau_1 = \tau_2 = \cdots = \tau_k = 0$, it follows that $\lambda = 0$, and the sampling distribution of the overall F ratio has the *central F* distribution $F[(k-1), k(n-1)]$. When $\lambda \neq 0$, the sampling distribution of the F ratio is a *noncentral F* distribution $F[(k-1), k(n-1); \lambda]$. That is, the distribution depends upon the parameter λ. If f_2 is the degrees of freedom for the denominator of an F statistic, then

$$E(\text{central } F) = \frac{f_2}{f_2 - 2}.$$

For the noncentral F,

$$E(\text{noncentral } F) = \frac{f_2}{f_2 - 2} \left[1 + \frac{(f_1 + 1)\phi^2}{f_1} \right],$$

where

$$\phi = \sqrt{\frac{n \sum \tau_j^2}{k \sigma_\varepsilon^2}} = \sqrt{\frac{\lambda}{k}}.$$

One notes that when $\lambda = 0$.

$$E(\text{central } F) = E(\text{noncentral } F).$$

When $\lambda > 0$
$$E(\text{central } F) < E(\text{noncentral } F).$$

The larger λ is, the larger the variance of the noncentral F.

To compute the power of the overall F test with respect to alternative hypotheses specified by the noncentrality parameter λ, tables of the noncentral F distribution corresponding to specified values of λ are needed. Such tables are available for a limited number of values for λ. (See Tiku, 1967.) Most tables of the noncentral F distribution are tabulated in terms of the quantity

$$\phi = \sqrt{\frac{n \sum \tau_j^2}{k \sigma_\varepsilon^2}} = \sqrt{\frac{\lambda}{k}}.$$

The corresponding noncentral F distribution is symbolized $F[(k-1), k(n-1); \phi]$. The noncentral F distribution is given in Appendix D, Table 14. Charts prepared by Pearson and Hartley are also available to evaluate the power of the overall F test. The Pearson–Hartley charts are also oriented in terms of the parameter ϕ.

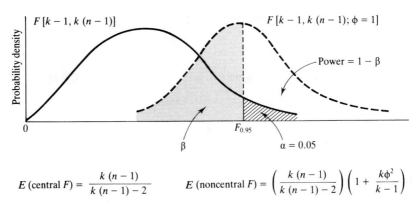

$$E \text{ (central } F) = \frac{k(n-1)}{k(n-1)-2} \qquad E \text{ (noncentral } F) = \left(\frac{k(n-1)}{k(n-1)-2}\right)\left(1 + \frac{k\phi^2}{k-1}\right)$$

FIGURE 3-2   Power of F test under fixed model.

The power of an overall F test (having $\alpha = 0.05$) with respect to an alternative hypothesis specified by $\phi = 1.00$ is indicated graphically in Fig. 3-2. The magnitude of the type 2 error is represented by the area β. The power of the test is numerically equal to $1 - \beta$.

Since ϕ depends in part upon n, the power of the overall F test also depends upon n. By making n suitably large, the power of the overall F test can be made suitably large for any nonzero specified value of $\sum \tau_j^2 / \sigma_\varepsilon^2$. That is, for a fixed value of $\sum \tau_j^2 / \sigma_\varepsilon^2$, the larger n, the larger ϕ becomes. The larger ϕ is, for a fixed level of significance, the smaller β; hence the larger is the power.

Once $\sum \tau_j^2 / \sigma_\varepsilon^2$ and k have been specified, the power of the overall F test becomes a function solely of n. The problems of estimating σ_ε^2 and specifying $\sum \tau_j^2$ can both be partially resolved by carrying out a pilot study with relatively few subjects. Such a study can provide data from which estimates of the magnitude of both error variance and treatment effects can be computed. For purposes of what follows, $\sum \tau_j^2$ should be taken as the smallest value that is considered of practical importance. The sample size n will then be determined so as to make the power of the overall F test adequately high (say, power equal to 0.80 or 0.90) with respect to this specified value for $\sum \tau_j^2$. Equivalently, the sample size will be determined so as to make the experiment sensitive enough to detect differences in the parameters τ_j that are considered large enough to be of practical importance—if indeed such differences exist. (Procedures that make it possible to determine n without specifying either $\sum \tau_j^2$ or σ_ε^2 have been published by Bratcher, Moran, and Zimmer (1970) and reproduced by Kirk (1982).)

To illustrate geometrically the power of the overall F test, suppose that

$$k = 4, \qquad n = 5, \qquad \lambda = 10.24, \qquad \phi = \sqrt{\frac{\lambda}{k}} = \sqrt{\frac{10.24}{4}} = 1.60.$$

In the corresponding analysis of variance,

$$f_1 = k - 1 = 3,$$
$$f_2 = k(n - 1) = 4(4) = 16.$$

The F ratio in the overall test of the hypothesis that all $\tau_j = 0$, the central F (when H_0 is true), is distributed as

$$F(f_1, f_2) = F(3, 16).$$

The critical value for this test is ($\alpha = 0.05$)

$$F_{0.95}[3, 16] = 3.24.$$

The decision rule for this test is indicated in Fig. 3-3. The decision rule is

$$\text{Reject } H_0 \text{ if } F_{\text{obs}} > 3.24.$$

The noncentral F distribution

$$F[3, 16; \phi = 1.60]$$

is sketched at the right of Fig. 3-3. The area under the noncentral F to the left of the point 3.24 represents the magnitude of the type 2 error. This area may be found in tables of the noncentral F given in Appendix D. In this case

$$\beta = \Pr(\text{type 2 error}/\phi = 1.60) = 0.34.$$

FIGURE 3-3   Power of F test under fixed model—numerical example.

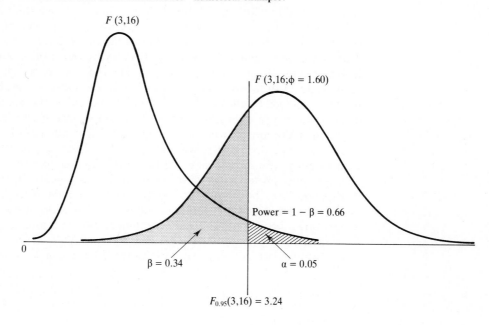

The power of the test is represented by the area under the noncentral F distribution to the right of 3.24. In this case,

$$\text{Power (with respect to } \phi = 1.60) = 1 - \beta = 0.66.$$

For this numerical example,

$$E[\text{central } F] = \frac{f_2}{f_2 - 2} = \frac{16}{14} = 1.14,$$

$$E[\text{noncentral } F] = \frac{f_2}{f_2 - 2}\left[1 + \frac{(f_1 + 1)\phi^2}{f_1}\right] = 5.05.$$

With reference to Fig. 3-3, the points corresponding to these expectations will be just a little to the right of the high points of the respective distributions.

As a numerical example, consider the case in which $k = 2$ and the overall F test is to be made at level of significance $\alpha = 0.05$. From tables of the noncentral F distribution, the power of the overall test may be evaluated for various combinations of ϕ and n. A summary of the latter is presented in Table 3.16.

If the minimum value of τ_j to be considered of practical importance is 3, then $\sum \tau_j^2 = 9 + 9 = 18$. If σ_ε^2 is estimated to be equal to 20, then

$$\frac{\sum \tau_j^2}{\sigma_\varepsilon^2} = \frac{18}{20} = 0.90.$$

Hence

$$\phi = \sqrt{\frac{n \sum \tau_j^2}{k\sigma_\varepsilon^2}} = \sqrt{0.45n}.$$

TABLE 3.16 **Power of the overall F test in the analysis of variance when $k = 2$ and $\alpha = 0.5$†**

ϕ	$n = 5$ $F(1, 8; \phi)$	$n = 10$ $F(1, 18; \phi)$	$n = 15$ $F(1, 28; \phi)$	$n = 20$ $F(1, 38; \phi)$	$n = 25$ $F(1, 48; \phi)$
0.00	0.05	0.05	0.05	0.05	0.05
0.50	0.10	0.10	0.10	0.11	0.11
1.00	0.24	0.27	0.28	0.28	0.29
1.20	0.32	0.36	0.37	0.38	0.38
1.40	0.41	0.47	0.48	0.49	0.49
1.60	0.51	0.57	0.59	0.60	0.60
1.80	0.61	0.67	0.69	0.70	0.70
2.00	0.70	0.76	0.78	0.79	0.79
2.20	0.78	0.84	0.85	0.86	0.86
2.60	0.89	0.94	0.94	0.95	0.95
3.00	0.96	0.98	0.98	0.99	0.999

† The value of n, in part, determines the degrees of freedom for MS_{error}, which is $k(n - 1)$. These values are obtained from the Tiku (1967) tables. Part of these tables appears in Appendix D, Table 14.

For this special case, the value of ϕ associated with various values of n and the corresponding power are as follows:

n:	5	10	15	20	25
ϕ:	1.50	2.12	2.60	3.25	3.35
Power:	0.46	0.81	0.94	0.99	0.999

If power 0.80 is considered to be appropriate for $\sum \tau_j^2 = 18$, then letting $n = 10$ will provide a test having this power. If power 0.90 is desired for this alternative hypothesis, then n should be between 10 and 15. It will be found that when $n = 13$,

$$F(1, 24; 2.42) = 0.90.$$

To avoid the necessity of having to prepare summary tables such as Table 3.16 from tables of the noncentral F distribution, charts like those in Table D.11 in Appendix D have been prepared. Let

$$\phi' = \sqrt{\frac{\sum \tau_j^2}{k\sigma_\varepsilon^2}}.$$

For the special case $k = 2$, $\sum \tau_j^2 = 18$, and $\sigma_\varepsilon^2 = 20$,

$$\phi' = 0.67.$$

From Table D.11 ($k = 2$), for $\alpha = 0.05$ and $\phi' = 0.67$, to find n required for power 0.90, one reads up from the point $\phi' = 0.67$ until one intersects the curve corresponding to $P = 0.9$. The point of intersection corresponds to approximately $n = 13$ on the scale for n at the left. If the overall tests are to be made with level of significance $\alpha = 0.01$, one reads up on the same chart at $\phi' = 0.67$ on the scale for $\alpha = 0.01$. For power 0.90 in this case, n must be approximately 18.

As a second numerical example, suppose $k = 3$. Assume $\sigma_\varepsilon^2 = 50$ and that the minimal value for $\sum \tau_j^2 = 75$. Hence the value of ϕ corresponding to $\sum \tau_j^2 = 75$ is

$$\phi = \sqrt{\frac{n \sum \tau_j^2}{k\sigma_\varepsilon^2}} = \sqrt{\frac{n(75)}{3(50)}} = \sqrt{0.50n}.$$

In Table 3.17 are tabulated the powers corresponding to various combinations of n and ϕ obtained from tables of the noncentral F distributions.

Given below are the values of ϕ for different values of n corresponding to the alternative hypothesis $\sum \tau_j^2 = 75$ for $k = 3$ and $\sigma_\varepsilon^2 = 50$. Associated with these values of ϕ and n is the power for specified level of significance.

n:	5	10	15	20
ϕ:	1.58	2.24	2.74	3.16
Power ($\alpha = 0.01$):	0.29	0.73	0.92	0.99
Power ($\alpha = 0.05$):	0.58	0.91	0.98	0.99

TABLE 3.17 **Power of the overall F test in the analysis of variance when $k = 3$**

ϕ	$n=5$ $F(2,12;\phi)$ $\alpha=0.01$	$\alpha=0.05$	$n=10$ $F(2,27;\phi)$ $\alpha=0.01$	$\alpha=0.05$	$n=15$ $F(2,42;\phi)$ $\alpha=0.01$	$\alpha=0.05$	$n=20$ $F(2,57;\phi)$ $\alpha=0.01$	$\alpha=0.05$
0.00	0.01		0.01		0.01		0.01	
		0.05		0.05		0.05		0.05
0.50	0.02		0.03		0.03		0.03	
		0.10		0.11		0.11		0.11
1.00	0.09		0.11		0.12		0.13	
		0.26		0.29		0.30		0.31
1.20	0.14		0.18		0.19		0.20	
		0.36		0.40		0.42		0.43
1.40	0.20		0.27		0.29		0.31	
		0.47		0.53		0.54		0.55
1.60	0.29		0.38		0.41		0.43	
		0.58		0.65		0.66		0.68
1.80	0.39		0.50		0.53		0.55	
		0.69		0.75		0.77		0.78
2.00	0.49		0.62		0.65		0.68	
		0.78		0.84		0.86		0.87
2.20	0.60		0.73		0.76		0.78	
		0.86		0.91		0.92		0.92
2.60	0.78		0.89		0.91		0.93	
		0.95		0.98		0.98		0.98
3.00	0.91		0.97		0.98		0.98	
		0.99		0.99		0.99		0.99

The power for a specified α is obtained from the appropriate column of Table 3.17.

Thus, if $n = 10$ is chosen, the power corresponding to the alternative hypothesis $\sum \tau_j^2 = 75$ is 0.73 when $\alpha = 0.01$ and 0.91 when $\alpha = 0.05$. If $n = 15$, the corresponding power is 0.91 when $\alpha = 0.01$ and 0.98 when $\alpha = 0.05$.

If one were to use the charts in Appendix D, Table 11,

$$\phi' = \sqrt{\frac{\sum \tau_j^2}{k\sigma_\varepsilon^2}} = \sqrt{\frac{75}{3(50)}} = \sqrt{0.50} = 0.7.$$

On the chart for $k = 3$, on the scale for which $\alpha = 0.01$, corresponding to power 0.90, n is 15. For power 0.70, the approximate n is 10. The values of n determined from these charts will, except for interpolation errors, be the same as those obtained directly from the noncentral F distributions—indeed the charts were prepared from the latter.

APPROXIMATING PERCENTILE POINTS ON THE NONCENTRAL F. Very close approximations to percentile points on the noncentral F distribution may be obtained from tables of the central F distribution, provided relatively

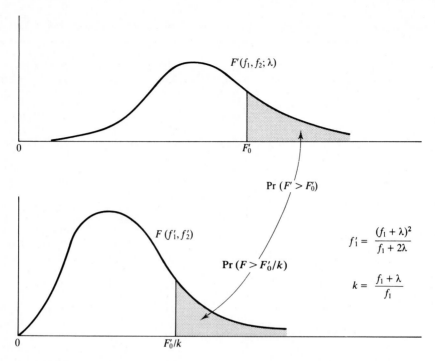

FIGURE 3-4 Approximating noncentral F.

complete tables of the latter are available. The approximation to be outlined here is one suggested by Patnaik (1949).

At the top of Fig. 3-4 is a sketch of a noncentral F distribution with parameters f_1, f_2 and λ, denoted $F'(f_1, f_2; \lambda)$. The area to the right of the point F_0' is the probability

$$\Pr(F' \geq F_0'),$$

that is, the probability of obtaining an F' statistic larger than F_0'. This probability is approximated by

$$\Pr\left(F \geq \frac{F_0'}{k}\right)$$

from the F distribution specified in the lower half of Fig. 3-4. In general, f_1' will not be an integer. Hence, interpolation in tables of the central F distribution will be necessary.

To illustrate this approximation procedure, suppose one desires

$$\Pr(F' \geq 6.55)$$

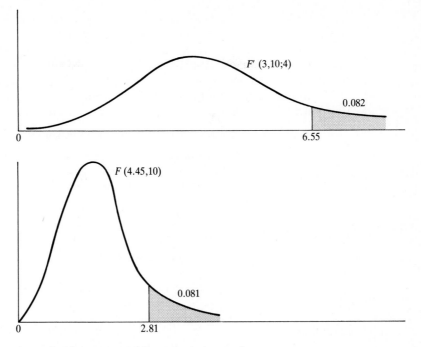

FIGURE 3-5   Approximating noncentral F—numerical example.

for the distribution $F'(3, 10; 4)$. For this case,

$$f_1' = \frac{(3+4)^2}{3+8} = 4.45; \qquad k = \frac{3+4}{3} = 2.33; \qquad \frac{F'}{k} = 2.81.$$

Hence, $\Pr(F' > 6.55) \doteq \Pr(F > 2.81),$

where F has the central F distribution $F(4.45, 10)$. (See Fig. 3-5.) By interpolation in tables of the central F,

$$\Pr(F \geq 2.81) \doteq 0.81.$$

From tables of the noncentral F, the exact probability is 0.082.

To illustrate the degree of accuracy of the approximation procedure, from Patnaik (1949) one has the following:

| f_1 | f_2 | λ | F_0' | \multicolumn{2}{c}{$\Pr(F' \geq F_0')$} |
				Approx.	Exact
3	10	4	3.708	0.248	0.254
3	10	4	6.552	0.081	0.082
8	10	9	5.057	0.091	0.092
8	30	9	3.173	0.185	0.187

A more accurate approximation of the noncentral F from the central F distribution may be obtained from a method given by Tiku (1967). The approximation method used by Patnaik has the first two moments of the central F in common with the noncentral F; the Tiku approximation method has the first three moments of the central F in common with the noncentral F.

Another simple and reasonably accurate approximation is based upon the unit normal distribution. To illustrate the use of this approximation suppose

$$f_1 = \text{degrees of freedom for numerator of } F \text{ ratio,}$$

$$f_2 = \text{degrees of freedom for denominator of } F \text{ ratio,}$$

$$\lambda = \text{noncentrality parameter} = \frac{n \sum \tau_j^2}{\sigma_\varepsilon^2},$$

$$\phi = \sqrt{\lambda/(f_1 + 1)}.$$

If F_0 is a point on $F(f_1, f_2; \lambda)$, then

$$\Pr(F > F_0) \doteq \Pr(z > z_0),$$

where

$$z_0 = \frac{\sqrt{(2f_2 - 1)B} - \sqrt{2(f_1 + \lambda) - A}}{\sqrt{B + A}},$$

and where

$$A = \frac{f_1 + 2\lambda}{f_1 + \lambda}, \qquad B = f_1 F_0 / f_2.$$

To illustrate how close the approximation is, consider the example in Fig. 3-3. For this figure,

$$f_1 = 3, \qquad f_2 = 16, \qquad \lambda = 10.24, \qquad \phi = 1.60, \qquad F_0 = 3.24.$$

Hence

$$A = \frac{3 + 2(10.24)}{3 + 10.24} = 1.7766, \qquad B = \frac{3(3.24)}{16} = 0.6075.$$

$$z_0 = \frac{\sqrt{(31)(0.6075)} - \sqrt{26.4800} - 1.7766}{\sqrt{0.6075 + 1.7766}} = -0.4118.$$

From tables of the unit normal distribution,

$$\Pr(z > z_0) = \Pr(z > -0.41) = 0.66.$$

Hence

$$\Pr(F > 3.24) \doteq 0.66.$$

To two decimal places, this is the value obtained from tables of the noncentral F distribution.

Some indication of how well the approximation works in general is given in Table 3.18. Inspection of this table indicates that the approximation is indeed a very good one. When $\lambda = 0$, the procedure gives one an approximation to the central F distribution.

ALTERNATE APPROACH TO NONCENTRAL F. The approach taken earlier in this section to justify the use of the noncentral distribution in terms of the

TABLE 3.18   **Normal approximation to noncentral F distribution**

f_1	f_2	ϕ	λ	$\alpha = 0.05$ Exact	$\alpha = 0.05$ Approx.	$\alpha = 0.01$ Exact	$\alpha = 0.01$ Approx.
2	12	1.20	4.32	0.36	0.36	0.14	0.14
3	16	1.60	10.24	0.66	0.66	0.36	0.36
3	20	1.40	7.84	0.55	0.56	0.28	0.29
4	12	2.00	20.00	0.85	0.85	0.58	0.57
6	20	0	0	0.05	0.05	0.01	0.01
1	10	2.00	8.00	0.72	0.76	0.42	0.40

expected value of the mean squares can be somewhat misleading. (It will be found that the power function for the variance-component model involves the central F distribution rather than the noncentral F (see Sec. 3.5); yet approached from the expected values of the mean squares, the two models appear quite similar.)

Under the model which assumes no treatment effects,

$$X_{ij} = \mu + \varepsilon_{ij},$$

the estimate of the variation due to error is

$$\text{SS}' = \text{SS}_{\text{total}} = \sum (X_{ij} - \bar{G})^2.$$

Under the model, assuming that the τ_j are fixed constants,

$$X_{ij} = \mu + \tau_j + \varepsilon_{ij},$$

the estimate of the variation due to error is

$$\text{SS}'' = \text{SS}_{\text{error}} = \sum (X_{ij} - \bar{T}_j)^2.$$

A measure of deviation from the hypothesis that all $\tau_j = 0$ is

$$\text{SS}' - \text{SS}'' = \text{SS}_{\text{total}} - \text{SS}_{\text{error}} = \text{SS}_{\text{treat}} = n \sum (\bar{T}_j - \bar{G})^2.$$

It may be shown (Scheffé, 1959, p. 38) that

$$\text{SS}_{\text{total}} - \text{SS}_{\text{error}} = \sum_{j=1}^{k-1} z_j^2,$$

where the z_j are independently distributed as $N(\xi_j, \sigma^2/n)$ where ξ_j is the $E(z_j)$. Hence

$$\frac{n \sum z_j^2}{\sigma_\varepsilon^2} \text{ is distributed as } \chi^2\left(k - 1; \frac{n \sum \xi_j^2}{\sigma_\varepsilon^2}\right).$$

That is,

$$\frac{(k - 1)\text{MS}_{\text{treat}}}{\sigma_\varepsilon^2}$$

is distributed as a noncentral chi square with noncentrality parameter

$$\frac{n \sum \xi_j^2}{\sigma_\varepsilon^2} = \frac{n \sum \tau_j^2}{\sigma_\varepsilon^2}.$$

That is,

$$\frac{(k-1)\mathrm{MS_{treat}}}{\sigma_\varepsilon^2} = \frac{\sum_{j=1}^{k-1} z_j^2}{\sigma_\varepsilon^2}$$

is distributed as a noncentral chi square with parameters $k-1$ and

$$\lambda = \frac{n \sum \xi_j^2}{\sigma_\varepsilon^2}.$$

The z_j represent linear transformations on $\tau_j + \varepsilon_{ij}$. Under a model which assumes that $\underset{i}{E}(\varepsilon_{ij}) = 0$ for all j, $\mathrm{MS_{error}}$ is distributed as a central F. Thus the F statistic in the analysis of variance is symbolically

$$F = \frac{\text{noncentral chi-square}}{\text{central chi-square}},$$

where the two chi-squares are independent. This ratio defines a noncentral F distribution with a noncentrality parameter equal to the noncentrality parameter of the noncentral chi-square distribution in the numerator.

Estimating Power: Random Treatments

When treatment effects are random, emphasis is upon estimating variance components. Reasonably, the researcher has no interest in the effects of any particular treatment. Some features of the variance-component model were presented in Sec. 3.5. In that section and in the preceding section, it was mentioned that the equivalent to ω^2 for fixed designs is the intraclass correlation coefficient, an estimator of which is:

$$\hat{\rho}_I = \frac{\mathrm{MS_{treat}} - \mathrm{MS_{error}}}{\mathrm{MS_{treat}} + (n-1)\mathrm{MS_{error}}}.$$

Tables for computing power and for sample sizes have been less available for the variance-components model, but power is relatively simple to compute. Unlike the case for fixed treatment effects, when treatments are random, F is distributed as a multiple of the F distribution whether or not the ANOV null hypothesis is true. That is, only the central F distribution is involved in power calculations. In particular, one may write the distribution of

$$F = \frac{\mathrm{MS_{treat}}}{\mathrm{MS_{error}}},$$

$$F = (1 + n\theta)F[(k-1), k(n-1)],$$

where
$$\theta = \frac{\sigma_\tau^2}{\sigma_\varepsilon^2}$$

is the measure of effect size for Model II. Hence, F is distributed as a multiple $(1 + n\theta)$ of the central F distribution.[3] When $\sigma_\tau^2 = 0$, this multiple is unity; when $\sigma_\tau^2 > 0$, the multiple is not unity. The power of the test that $\sigma_\tau^2 = 0$ with respect to some nonzero θ is given by

$$\Pr\left\{F > \frac{F_{1-\alpha}[(k-1), k(n-1)]}{1 + n\theta}\right\}.$$

(See footnote 4.)

The experimenter must estimate θ in order to estimate power. An unbiased estimate is provided from experimental data by

$$\hat{\theta} = \frac{MS_{treat} - mMS_{error}}{nmMS_{error}} \quad \text{where} \quad m = \frac{k(n-1)}{k(n-1)-2}.$$

Unlike the fixed effects model, it is not always appreciated by researchers that there are two random processes involved—treatment levels and subjects. That is, τ_j and ε_{ij} have distributions $N(0, \sigma_\tau^2)$ and $N(0, \sigma_\varepsilon^2)$, respectively. Hence, power is a function of both k and n. Barcikowski (1973) has provided some very useful tables which provide power estimates for the random model for specified values of θ_0, θ, nk, k and α. A small part is reproduced here as Table 3.19.

As an example, if an experimenter wants to test the simple hypothesis that there are no treatment effects ($\theta_0 = 0$), and previous research has led to the expectation that if θ is as large as 1.0 s(he) wants to reject the null hypothesis at $\alpha = 0.05$ with a high probability, Table 3.19 makes it possible to select values for nk and k which makes this possible. For example, when $\theta = 1.0$, with a total of 100 subjects assigned at random to 20 treatment conditions ($nk = 100$, $k = 20$, $n = 5$) power is numerically equal to 0.998; with a total of 40 subjects with 5 assigned to each of 8 treatment conditions, the power is estimated to be 0.904. These power values may seem large for the values of k and n, but one should note that $\theta = 1.0$ is a large treatment effect which should be easy to detect. When θ is relatively small (e.g., 0.2), a total of 300 subjects assigned to 20 treatment levels is required for $1 - \beta$ to exceed

---

[3] In general, the multiple of central F is the ratio of the expected values of the mean squares of the numerator and denominator of F (Scheffé, 1959).

[4] This value is specific to the null hypothesis, $H_0: \sigma_\tau^2 = 0$. Hence $\theta_0 = 0$; where θ_0 is a specific value, an experimenter may specify in a more general null hypothesis, $H_0: \sigma_\tau^2 \le \theta_0\sigma_\varepsilon^2$. In this general case, power is:

$$\Pr\left\{F > F_{1-\alpha}[k-1, k(n-1)]\frac{1 + n\theta_0}{1 + n\theta}\right\}.$$

TABLE 3.19   **Power values and optimum number of levels for fixed total numbers of observations in the one-way random-effects analysis of variance**

	$\alpha = 0.05$							
	$\theta_0 = 0.00$							
θ nk	0.2	0.4	0.6	0.8	1.0	2.0	3.0	4.0
10	2, 0.142	2, 0.220	2, 0.282	2, 0.333	2, 0.374	3, 0.518	3, 0.622	5, 0.693
20	2, 0.241	4, 0.386	4, 0.507	4, 0.596	4, 0.662	5, 0.847	5, 0.914	5, 0.945
30	3, 0.342	5, 0.530	5, 0.666	6, 0.756	6, 0.818	10, 0.949	10, 0.984	10, 0.994
40	4, 0.424	5, 0.645	8, 0.768	8, 0.854	8, 0.904	10, 0.984	13, 0.996	13, 0.999
50	5, 0.495	5, 0.724	10, 0.843	10, 0.914	10, 0.950	16, 0.994	16, 0.999	12, 1.000
60	5, 0.564	6, 0.792	10, 0.900	12, 0.950	12, 0.974	20, 0.999	12, 1.000	10, 1.000
70	5, 0.621	7, 0.843	10, 0.934	14, 0.971	14, 0.987	23, 1.000	10, 1.000	8, 1.000
80	5, 0.668	10, 0.883	10, 0.955	16, 0.983	16, 0.993	13, 1.000	9, 1.000	8, 1.000
90	6, 0.715	10, 0.913	15, 0.965	18, 0.990	18, 0.997	11, 1.000	8, 1.000	7, 1.000
100	7, 0.746	10, 0.933	14, 0.980	20, 0.995	20, 0.998	10, 1.000	8, 1.000	7, 1.000
300	20, 0.989	23, 1.000	8, 1.000	7, 1.000	6, 1.000	5, 1.000	5, 1.000	5, 1.000
500	10, 1.000	7, 1.000	7, 1.000	6, 1.000	6, 1.000	5, 1.000	5, 1.000	5, 1.000
	$\theta_0 = 0.10$							
θ nk	0.3	0.5	0.7	0.9	1.0	2.0	3.0	4.0
10	2, 0.112	2, 0.169	2, 0.220	2, 0.263	2, 0.282	3, 0.436	3, 0.547	5, 0.628
20	4, 0.163	5, 0.283	4, 0.386	5, 0.473	5, 0.512	5, 0.753	5, 0.854	10, 0.907
30	5, 0.211	5, 0.377	6, 0.513	6, 0.618	6, 0.661	10, 0.884	10, 0.962	10, 0.984
40	5, 0.255	8, 0.445	8, 0.616	8, 0.727	10, 0.771	10, 0.952	13, 0.988	13, 0.996
50	7, 0.290	10, 0.526	10, 0.698	10, 0.806	10, 0.843	16, 0.978	16, 0.996	16, 0.999
60	10, 0.325	10, 0.592	12, 0.764	15, 0.863	15, 0.897	20, 0.993	20, 0.999	14, 1.000
70	10, 0.364	10, 0.644	14, 0.816	14, 0.904	14, 0.930	23, 0.997	17, 1.000	13, 1.000
80	10, 0.397	16, 0.692	16, 0.857	20, 0.934	20, 0.955	26, 0.999	15, 1.000	11, 1.000
90	10, 0.426	15, 0.738	18, 0.890	18, 0.954	18, 0.969	30, 1.000	14, 1.000	10, 1.000
100	11, 0.453	20, 0.771	20, 0.915	25, 0.969	25, 0.981	20, 1.000	12, 1.000	10, 1.000
300	37, 0.821	50, 0.991	48, 1.000	26, 1.000	21, 1.000	15, 1.000	8, 1.000	7, 1.000
500	71, 0.949	29, 1.000	17, 1.000	13, 1.000	12, 1.000	9, 1.000	8, 1.000	7, 1.000

This table is abridged from Table 2 in R. S. Barcikowski, (1973), Optimum sample size and number of levels in a one-way random-effects analysis of variance. *The Journal of Experimental Education*, **41, 4,** 10–16 with permission of the author.

0.90! The reader is referred to Barcikowski's original article for the remainder of his tables.

3.10   COMPARISONS AMONG TREATMENT MEANS

Often one is interested in testing a variety of hypotheses about differences among means. This interest may arise because of the outcome of the analysis of variance. Rejecting the analysis of variance hypothesis merely asserts that there is a difference somewhere among the k means which is large enough to have a very small probability of occurring under the null hypothesis. It says nothing about the source of the difference. Tests may also arise because of particular hypotheses the experimenter has which (s)he wants to evaluate. Those hypotheses can be evaluated with or without the overall analysis of variance.

When one of a series of tests of significance is carried out, a number of issues arise. There are various ways of dealing with those issues and a variety of techniques available. Moreover, the questions involved are the subject of debate and considerable current reseach.

At the foundation of all of the issues is the question of controlling the level of significance. Since statistical power varies inversely with the level of significance, the experimenter would like to control the level of significance while maximizing statistical power for the particular set of comparisons of interest. All of the techniques for accomplishing this discussed herein make the assumption that sampling was random from populations in which $X_{ij} = N(\mu_j, \sigma_j^2)$ and that there is homogeneity of treatment population variances. If those assumptions are not met, the control over the level of significance may be lost.

Definitions and Relationships

A linear function of the treatment effects τ_j is an expression of the form

$$\theta = c_1\tau_1, +c_2\tau_2 + \cdots + c_k\tau_k,$$

where the c_j are arbitrary constants. If one adds the constraint that

$$\sum c_j = 0$$

then the linear function is called a *comparison* or *contrast* among the τ_j and is denoted

$$\psi = c_1\tau_1 + c_2\tau_2 + \cdots + c_k\tau_k \quad \left(\sum c_j = 0 \right).$$

For example, if $k = 2$, a comparison takes the form

$$\psi = (1)\tau_1 + (-1)\tau_2$$
$$= \tau_1 - \tau_2.$$

In this case, the comparison is a simple difference between the two τ's. If $k = 3$, some possible comparisons are:

$$\psi_a = \tau_1 - \tau_2 \qquad (c_1 = 1, c_2 = -1, c_3 = 0),$$
$$\psi_b = \tau_1 - \tau_3 \qquad (c_1 = 1, c_2 = 0, c_3 = -1),$$
$$\psi_c = \tau_2 - \tau_3 \qquad (c_1 = 0, c_2 = 1, c_3 = -1),$$
$$\psi_d = 2\tau_1 - \tau_2 - \tau_3 \qquad (c_1 = 2, c_2 = -1, c_3 = -1),$$
$$\psi_e = -\tau_1 + 2\tau_2 - \tau_3 \quad (c_1 = -1, c_2 = 2, c_3 = -1),$$
$$\psi_f = -\tau_1 - \tau_2 + 2\tau_3 \quad (c_1 = -1, c_2 = -1, c_3 = 2).$$

The comparisons ψ_a through ψ_c are called simple comparisons or pairwise comparisons.

In general, a comparison has the form

$$\psi = \sum c_j \tau_j \quad \left(\sum c_j = 0 \right),$$

where the c_j are known constants. The least-squares estimate of a linear function of a set of τ_j is the corresponding linear function of the least-squares estimators of the τ_j. Hence, the least-squares estimator of ψ is

$$\hat{\psi} = C = \sum c_j (\bar{T}_j - \bar{G})$$

$$= \sum c_j \bar{T}_j - \bar{G} \left(\sum c_j \right)$$

$$= \sum c_j \bar{T}_j \quad \text{since} \quad \sum c_j = 0$$

$$= c_1 \bar{T}_1 + c_2 \bar{T}_2 + \cdots + c_k \bar{T}_k.$$

Hereafter, both ψ and C will be referred to as comparisons with the context making it clear that C is an estimate of ψ.

When the number of observations in each treatment is equal to n, it is more convenient to work with totals rather than means. A comparison among the treatment totals with equal sample sizes is defined by

$$\sum c_j T_j \quad \left(\sum c_j = 0 \right).$$

Consider the two comparisons

$$\psi_1 = c_{11} \tau_1 + c_{12} \tau_2 + \cdots + c_{1k} \tau_k,$$

$$\psi_2 = c_{21} \tau_1 + c_{22} \tau_2 + \cdots + c_{2k} \tau_k.$$

If
$$c_{2j} = m c_{1j},$$

where m is any arbitrary constant, then ψ_1 and ψ_2 are *equivalent comparisons*. The corresponding estimators are equivalent if $C_2 = m C_1$.

A comparison may always be cast in the form of the difference between two weighted averages. Hence, a comparison is sometimes called a "generalized" difference. For example, consider the following difference between two weighted averages of the τ's

$$\frac{2\tau_1 + \tau_2 + \tau_3}{4} - \frac{2\tau_4 + 2\tau_5 + 3\tau_6}{7}.$$

This difference may be rewritten in the form

$$\tfrac{1}{28} [14\tau_1 + 7\tau_2 + 7\tau_3 - 8\tau_4 - 8\tau_5 - 12\tau_6],$$

making it clear that the difference is a comparison with coefficients given by

$$c_1 = \frac{14}{28}, \qquad c_2 = \frac{7}{28}, \qquad c_3 = \frac{7}{28}, \qquad c_4 = \frac{-8}{28}, \qquad c_5 = \frac{-8}{28}, \qquad c_6 = \frac{-12}{28}.$$

By definition of equivalent comparisons, this is equivalent to

$$14\tau_1 + 7\tau_2 + 7\tau_3 - 8\tau_4 - 8\tau_5 - 12\tau_6.$$

Let

$$\psi_1 = c_{11}\tau_1 + c_{12}\tau_2 + \cdots + c_{1k}\tau_k \quad \left(\sum c_{1j} = 0 \right),$$

$$\psi_2 = c_{21}\tau_1 + c_{22}\tau_2 + \cdots + c_{2k}\tau_k \quad \left(\sum c_{2j} = 0 \right).$$

Comparisons which convey independent information concerning differences among means are *orthogonal*. When sample sizes are equal, ψ_1 and ψ_2 are orthogonal if

$$\sum c_{1j}c_{2j} = 0.$$

In words, with equal n, two comparisons are orthogonal if the sum of products of their corresponding coefficients is zero. For example, if

$$\psi_1 = 3\tau_1 + 1\tau_2 - 1\tau_3 - 3\tau_4$$
$$\psi_2 = 1\tau_1 - 3\tau_2 + 3\tau_3 - 1\tau_4$$
$$\sum c_{1j}c_{2j} = (3)(1) + (1)(-3) + (-1)(3) + (-3)(-1) = 0,$$

and ψ_1 and ψ_2 are orthogonal. If two comparisons are orthogonal, their corresponding least-squares estimates are orthogonal. When sample sizes are not equal, two comparisons are orthogonal if

$$\frac{c_{11}c_{21}}{n_1} + \frac{c_{12}c_{22}}{n_2} + \cdots + \frac{c_{1k}c_{2k}}{n_k} = 0.$$

The members of a set of comparisons are *mutually orthogonal* if each member of the set is orthogonal to every other member of the set. If there are k treatments, there cannot be more than $k-1$ mutually orthogonal comparisons in a set and the $k-1$ comparisons are a *complete orthogonal set*. For example, if $k = 3$, the following coefficients define a complete orthogonal set of comparisons:

$$[2, \quad -1, \quad -1]$$
$$[0, \quad 1, \quad -1].$$

Another complete orthogonal set for $k = 3$ is

$$[-1, \quad 0, \quad 1]$$
$$[1, \quad -2, \quad 1].$$

Note that the coefficients within each set are orthogonal but between sets they are not orthogonal. There exist many complete orthogonal sets but the number of comparisons within a complete set cannot exceed $k - 1$. All other comparisons can be expressed as a linear combination of those in *any* complete orthogonal set.

Comparisons which are not orthogonal are correlated, with the correlation between two comparisons $_i$ and $_{i'}$ being

$$\rho_{ii'} = \frac{\sum c_{ij}c_{i'j}}{\sqrt{\left(\dfrac{\sum c_{ij}^2}{n_j}\right)\left(\dfrac{\sum c_{i'j}^2}{n_j}\right)}}.$$

One may view SS_{treat} of the analysis of variance as the total orthogonal variation due to comparing all treatment means. That being the case, one may define the variation due to a comparison as a component of SS_{treat} and the variation due to $k - 1$ mutually orthogonal comparisons will totally "account for" the variation between treatments. In general the variation due to a comparison among means $C_{\bar{T}}$ is

$$SS_{C_{\bar{T}}} = \frac{C_{\bar{T}}^2}{\sum c_j^2/n}$$

when sample sizes are equal, and when sample sizes are unequal,

$$SS_{C_{\bar{T}}} = \frac{C_{\bar{T}}^2}{(c_1^2/n_1) + (c_2^2/n_2) + \cdots + (c_k^2/n_k)}.$$

If, however, a comparison C_T is among totals, since

$$C_T = nC_{\bar{T}},$$

$$SS_{C_T} = \frac{C_T^2}{n \sum c_j^2}$$

$$= SS_{C_{\bar{T}}}.$$

For example, suppose $n = 5$ and the experimental data are:

	Treatments			
	1	**2**	**3**	**4**
Totals (T_j)	10	15	20	25
Means ($\bar{T}_j$)	2	3	4	5

Define

$$\psi = 3\tau_1 - 1\tau_2 - 1\tau_3 - 1\tau_4.$$

Then

$$C_{\bar{T}} = 3\bar{T}_1 - 1\bar{T}_2 - 1\bar{T}_3 - 1\bar{T}_4$$

$$= (3)(2) - (1)(3) - (1)(4) - (1)(5) = -6,$$

and
$$C_T = 3T_1 - 1T_2 - 1T_3 - 1T_4$$
$$= (3)(10) - (1)(5) - (1)(20) - (1)(25) = -30.$$

Using $C_{\bar{T}}$ to compute SS_C, one has

$$SS_C = \frac{C_{\bar{T}}^2}{\dfrac{\sum c_j^2}{n}} = \frac{(-6)^2}{\dfrac{12}{5}} = 15.$$

Using C_T to compute SS_C,

$$SS_C = \frac{C_T^2}{n \sum c_j^2} = \frac{(-30)^2}{(5)(12)} = 15.$$

It is usually more convenient to work with totals.

A component of the sums of squares for treatments is SS_C and since a comparison may always be represented as a difference between two weighted means, this source of variation has one degree of freedom. Since SS_{treat} has $k - 1$ degrees of freedom, if the variation is computed for all comparisons of a complete orthogonal set, the variation will always sum to SS_{treat}.

To illustrate this point, suppose that the following data were obtained:

	Treatments		
	1	**2**	**3**
Totals (T_j)	6	16	14
n_j	6	6	6

For these data,

$$SS_{\text{treat}} = \frac{\sum T_j^2}{n} - \frac{G^2}{nk} = 81.33 - 72.00 = 9.33$$

with $k - 1$ degrees of freedom. The variation due to a complete set of orthogonal comparisons is:

	T_1	T_2	T_3			
	6	16	14	$C_T = \sum c_{ij} T_j$	$SS_C = \dfrac{C^2}{n \sum c_{ij}^2}$	**df**
c_{1j}	2	−1	−1	$C_1 = -18$	9.00	1
c_{2j}	0	1	−1	$C_2 = 2$	0.33	1

$$\sum SS_{C_i} = 9.33 = SS_{\text{treat}}$$

Using different complete sets of orthogonal comparisons, one may partition SS_{treat} in a variety of ways. In general the partition of the variation should be the one of most interest to the experimenter. It need not be in terms of orthogonal sets, but in many instances keeping the comparisons orthogonal simplifies the interpretation of both the outcome of the tests on comparisons and the level of significance of tests.

Inferences with Respect to Individual (*a priori*) Comparisons

One of the issues with regard to inferences on comparisons among means selected from a larger set is the question of whether comparisons are of interest on an *a priori* or *a posteriori* basis. In general this distinction is based upon whether or not the tests are related to the structure of the obtained data. An *a priori* hypothesis is one which an experiment was designed to test. It is sometimes called a *planned* comparison. Tests that derive from the structure of the outcome—for example, because an overall *F* test was significant and the experimenter wants to "track down" possible sources of the outcome—are *a posteriori* tests. These latter tests are also referred to as *unplanned*, *post hoc*, or *post mortem* tests.

A procedure which is appropriate for a series of planned comparisons is simply to carry out a series of *t* tests, where *t* is appropriately defined for the experimental design used. An equivalent procedure is to use an *F* statistic since comparisons involve a single degree of freedom and $t^2_{1-\alpha/2}(f) = F_{1-\alpha}(1, f)$.

A *t* statistic can be constructed by defining an appropriate denominator. The standard error of a mean is

$$\sigma_{\bar{x}} = \frac{\sigma_x}{\sqrt{n}},$$

and it is estimated by

$$s_{\bar{x}} = \frac{s_x}{\sqrt{n}}.$$

In an analysis of variance wherein homogeneity of variance is assumed, it is appropriate to use MS_{error} as a pooled estimate of σ^2_ε. Thus

$$s^2_{\bar{T}} = \frac{s^2_X}{n} = \frac{MS_{error}}{n}$$

is an estimate of the square of the standard error for all single means $\bar{T}_j$.

The standard error of the difference between independent treatment means is

$$\sigma_{\bar{x}-\bar{x}_2} = \sqrt{\frac{\sigma^2_1}{n_1} + \frac{\sigma^2_2}{n_2}}$$

and it is estimated by

$$s_{\bar{x}_1-\bar{x}_2} = \sqrt{\frac{s_1^2}{n_1} + \frac{s_2^2}{n_2}},$$

which becomes

$$s_{\bar{x}_1-\bar{x}_2} = \sqrt{\frac{s_p^2}{n} + \frac{s_p^2}{n}}$$

$$= \sqrt{\frac{2s_p^2}{n}}$$

with the use of a pooled variance under the assumption of homogeneity of variance and the use of equal sample sizes. In the analysis of variance context, this expression becomes

$$s_{\bar{T}_1-\bar{T}_2} = \sqrt{\frac{2\text{MS}_{\text{error}}}{n}}.$$

This is a special case. In general the estimate of the standard error of any linear function of k independent means in the analysis of variance is

$$s_{C_{\bar{T}}} = \sqrt{\frac{\sum c_j^2 \text{MS}_{\text{error}}}{n}},$$

and has $k(n-1)$ degrees of freedom.

It follows, then, that the t statistic used to test the hypothesis that two independent means are equal can be specialized for any comparison in the analysis of variance to test the hypothesis $H_0: |\psi| = 0$. Alternative expressions of this null hypothesis are

$$H_0: \sum c_j\mu_j = 0 \quad \text{and} \quad H_0: \sum c_j\tau_j = 0.$$

Under the null hypothesis, and if the assumptions of the analysis of variance have been met, the statistic

$$t = \frac{|\hat{\psi}|}{s_{\hat{\psi}}}$$

$$= \frac{|C|}{\sqrt{\text{MS}_{\text{error}}(\sum c_j^2/n_j)}}$$

$$= \frac{|\sum c_j\bar{T}_j|}{\sqrt{\text{MS}_{\text{error}}(\sum c_j^2/n_j)}}$$

is distributed as Student's t with $k(n-1)$ degrees of freedom.

Since

$$t_{1-\alpha/2}^2[k(n-1)] = F_{1-\alpha}[1, k(n-1)],$$

the statistic

$$t^2 = \frac{C_T^2}{MS_{error}(\sum c_j^2/n_j)}$$

$$= \frac{C_T^2/\sum c_j^2/n_j}{MS_{error}}$$

$$= \frac{SS_C}{MS_{error}}$$

$$= F[1, k(n-1)]$$

may also be used to test hypotheses regarding comparisons. The decision rule is to reject the null hypothesis if

$$F_{obs} > F_{1-\alpha}[1, k(n-1)] = t_{1-\alpha/2}^2[k(n-1)].$$

These test procedures are illustrated in Table 3.20.

TABLE 3.20 **Numerical example of tests on individual comparisons**

	$n=8$,	$k=4$,		$SS_{treat} = 131.08$,		$MS_{error} = 4.14$		
	T_1	T_2	T_3	T_4				
(i)	38	31	62	70	$C_T = \sum c_j T_j$ $\quad n\sum c_j^2$	$MS_{comp} = \dfrac{C_T^2}{n\sum c_j^2}$	$F = \dfrac{MS_{comp}}{MS_{error}}$	
(1)	−1	−1	1	1	63 $\quad$ 32	124.03	$F_1 = 29.96**$	
(2)	1	−1	0	0	7 $\quad$ 16	3.06	$F_2 = 0.74$	
(ii) (3)	0	0.	1	−1	−8 $\quad$ 16	4.00 / 131.09 = SS_{treat}	$F_3 = 0.97$	

(iii)

$$s_{C_T}^{(1)} = \sqrt{nMS_{error}\left(\sum c_{1j}^2\right)} = \sqrt{8(4.14)(4)} = 11.51 \quad [F_{0.99}(1, 28) = 7.64]$$

$$s_{C_T}^{(2)} = \sqrt{nMS_{error}\left(\sum c_{2j}^2\right)} = \sqrt{8(4.14)(2)} = 8.14$$

$$s_{C_T}^{(3)} = \sqrt{nMS_{error}\left(\sum c_{3j}^2\right)} = \sqrt{8(4.14)(2)} = 8.14$$

$$t^{(1)} = \frac{|C_T^{(1)}|}{s_{C_T}^{(1)}} = \frac{63}{11.51} = 5.473 \quad (t^{(1)})^2 = 29.96 \quad t_{0.995}(28) = 2.76$$

$$t^{(2)} = \frac{|C_T^{(2)}|}{s_{C_T}^{(2)}} = \frac{7}{8.14} = 0.86 \quad (t^{(2)})^2 = 0.74 \quad t_{0.995}^2(28) = 7.64$$

$$t^{(3)} = \frac{|C_T^{(3)}|}{s_{C_T}^{(3)}} = \frac{8}{8.14} = 0.98 \quad (t^{(3)})^2 = 0.97$$

The first hypothesis is

$$H_0: \psi_1 = 0$$
$$= \tau_3 + \tau_4 - \tau_1 - \tau_2 = 0$$
$$= (\tau_3 + \tau_4) - (\tau_1 + \tau_2) = 0$$
$$= (\mu_3 + \mu_4) - (\mu_1 + \mu_2) = 0$$
$$H_1: \psi \neq 0.$$

If $\alpha = 0.01$, $F_{0.99}(1, 28) = 7.64$, and $F_{\text{obs}} = 29.96$ leads to rejection of the null hypothesis.

Comparison (2) is used to test the hypothesis

$$H_0: \psi_2 = 0$$
$$= \tau_1 - \tau_2 = 0$$
$$= \mu_1 - \mu_2 = 0$$
$$H_1: \psi_2 \neq 0.$$

With $F_{\text{obs}} = 0.74$, this null hypothesis is not rejected.

Comparison (3) is used to test the hypothesis that $\mu_3 = \mu_4$. The F statistic in this case is 0.97 and the conclusion is that the data do not contradict the null hypothesis.

In part iii of the table, the tests made in part ii are carried out in terms of the t statistic. The estimates of the standard errors of comparisons (1) through (3) are computed in the upper half of part iii. The t statistics corresponding to comparisons (1) through (3) are computed in the lower half of part iii. One notes that the square of $t^{(1)}$ is F_1. In each case the critical value for the t statistic is $t_{0.995}(28) = 2.76$. One notes that $t_{0.995}^2(28) = F_{0.99}[1, 28]$.

The F-test in part ii is equivalent to a two-tailed t-test. If one desired to make a one-tailed t-test of the following form:

$$H_0: \psi_1 = \tau_3 + \tau_4 - \tau_1 - \tau_2 = 0$$
$$H_1: \psi_1 > 0$$

one would compute

$$t^{(1)} = \frac{C_T^{(1)}}{s^{(1)}} = 5.473.$$

For this one-tailed t-test and with 0.01 as the level of significance, the decision rule is

$$\text{Reject } H_0 \text{ if } \quad t_{\text{obs}} > t_{0.99}(28) > 2.47.$$

The equivalent F-test would be

$$\text{Reject } H_0 \text{ if } \quad F_{\text{obs}} > F_{0.98}[1, 28] = 6.10.$$

OVERALL ANOV F AS A COMPARISON. It is possible to construct a comparison C_{max} such that $\text{SS}_C = \text{SS}_{\text{treat}}$ of the analysis of variance. An F

statistic can then be used to test the analysis of variance hypothesis based upon this single comparison. Consider the following comparison:

$$C = c_1 \bar{T}_1 + c_2 \bar{T}_2 + \cdots + c_k \bar{T}_k, \qquad \sum c_j = 0.$$

Assuming equal sample sizes under each of the treatments, the variation due to this comparison is

$$SS_C = \frac{C^2}{(\sum c_j^2)/n}.$$

The answer to the following question is of considerable interest: What choice of $c_1, c_2, \ldots, c_k$ will make SS_C a maximum? The maximum value of SS_C (when it is equal to SS_{treat}) will be attained (Scheffé, 1959, p. 118) if one sets

$$c_j = \frac{n(\bar{T}_j - \bar{G})}{\sqrt{SS_{\text{treat}}}}.$$

For this choice of c_j, one notes that

$$\frac{\sum c_j^2}{n} = \frac{\sum n(\bar{T}_j - \bar{G})^2}{SS_{\text{treat}}} = 1.$$

A comparison for which the denominator of SS_C is equal to unity is called a *normalized* comparison.

If one lets $C_{\text{max}} = $ normalized comparison for which SS_C is maximum, then

$$C_{\text{max}} = \frac{\sum n(\bar{T}_j - \bar{G})}{\sqrt{SS_{\text{treat}}}} \bar{T}_j = \frac{1}{\sqrt{SS_{\text{treat}}}} \sum n(\bar{T}_j - \bar{G})\bar{T}_j$$
$$= \sqrt{SS_{\text{treat}}},$$

since $n \sum (\bar{T}_j - \bar{G})\bar{T}_j = SS_{\text{treat}}$. Hence

$$SS_{C_{\text{max}}} = C_{\text{max}}^2 = SS_{\text{treat}}.$$

For example, suppose

$$n = 5, \qquad \bar{T}_1 = 5, \qquad \bar{T}_2 = 10, \qquad \bar{T}_3 = 30, \qquad \bar{G} = 15.$$

For these data,

$$SS_{\text{treat}} = n \sum (\bar{T}_j - \bar{G})^2 = 5(100 + 25 + 225) = 1750.$$

To find C_{max}, let

$$c_1 = \frac{5(-10)}{\sqrt{1750}}, \qquad c_2 = \frac{5(-5)}{\sqrt{1750}}, \qquad c_3 = \frac{5(15)}{\sqrt{1750}}.$$

Hence $\qquad C_{\text{max}} = c_1(5) + c_2(10) + c_3(30) = \dfrac{1750}{\sqrt{1750}} = \sqrt{1750}.$

Thus
$$SS_{C_{\max}} = C^2_{\max} = 1750 = SS_{\text{treat}}.$$

If one were to test the hypothesis that the comparison, of which $C_{\max}$ is an estimate, is zero, for the case of equal sample size, the region of rejection for this test (as obtained from the Scheffé simultaneous-confidence-interval approach in Sec. 3.11) is

$$F = \frac{SS_{C_{\max}}}{MS_{\text{error}}} > (k-1)F_{1-\alpha}(k-1, kn-k),$$

or equivalently,

$$F = \frac{SS_{C_{\max}}/(k-1)}{MS_{\text{error}}} = \frac{MS_{\text{treat}}}{MS_{\text{error}}} > F_{1-\alpha}(k-1, kn-k).$$

In the latter form, one notes that the test of the hypothesis that the comparison estimated by $C_{\max}$ is zero is identical to the test of no variation due to treatments. If the hypothesis being tested in terms of the comparison is not rejected, the implication is the corresponding population comparison is not significantly different from zero. If the comparison having maximum sum of squares is not significantly different from zero, then no other comparison will be significantly different from zero when tested by means of the Scheffé approach. If the hypothesis being tested is rejected, the implication is that the corresponding comparison (and possibly others) is significantly different from zero.

For the collection of all tests on comparisons, considered as a single test, the Scheffé approach has level of significance α. That is, the probability of a type 1 error on the entire collection is α.

For the case of unequal sample sizes,

$$SS_C = \frac{C^2}{(c_1^2/n_1) + (c_2^2/n_2) + \cdots + (c_k^2/n_k)}.$$

To maximize SS_C in this case one sets

$$c_j = \frac{n_j(\bar{T}_j - \bar{G})}{\sqrt{\sum n_j(\bar{T}_j - \bar{G})^2}}.$$

The maximum value of SS_C will be found to be

$$SS_{C_{\max}} = \sum n_j(\bar{T}_j - \bar{G})^2 = SS_{\text{treat}}.$$

CONFIDENCE INTERVALS FOR COMPARISONS. Like single means and differences between pairs of means, comparisons are normally distributed variables under the assumption that the original X variable was normally distributed or under the central limit theorem. That being the case, either z (if σ_ε^2 were actually known) or t may be used to set up a confidence interval for a comparison

$$C(C_{\bar{T}} + t_{\alpha/2}s_{C_{\bar{T}}} \le \psi \le C_{\bar{T}} + t_{1-\alpha/2}s_{C_{\bar{T}}}) = 1 - \alpha,$$

where
$$s_{C_{\bar{T}}} = \sqrt{\frac{\sum c_j^2 MS_{error}}{n}}$$

is an estimate of the standard error of the comparison. For example, if the information in Table 3.20 is used to construct a confidence interval for the difference between totals for treatments 1 and 2, Comparison 2, the result is

$$C[(T_1 - T_2) + t_{0.005}(28)s_{c_T} \le \psi_2 \le (T_1 - T_2) + t_{0.995}(28)s_{c_T}] = 0.99$$
$$C[7 + (-2.76)(8.14) \le \psi_2 \le 7 + (2.76)(8.14)] = 0.99$$
$$C[-15.47 \le \psi_2 \le 29.47] = 0.99.$$

THE LEVEL OF SIGNIFICANCE FOR INFERENCES ON COMPARISONS. When comparisons are *a priori* comparisons, the level of significance with regard to each individual test is α, the nominal level of significance, if the assumptions have been met. However, there is another type 1 error rate which is relevant when more than a single test of significance is computed. It is the level of significance for the entire set of m tests; it is an answer to the question, "What is the probability that one or more type 1 errors have been made out of the entire set of m tests?"

The level of significance is α for each hypothesis tested on an *a priori* comparison. Therefore, the probability of not making a type 1 error is $1 - \alpha$. For independent events, the probabilities of joint outcomes are the products of the respective probabilities for individual events. Thus the probability of *not* making a type 1 error on a series of tests is

$$(1 - \alpha)(1 - \alpha) = (1 - \alpha)^2 \quad (m = 2),$$
$$(1 - \alpha)(1 - \alpha)(1 - \alpha) = (1 - \alpha)^3 \quad (m = 3),$$
$$\vdots$$
$$(1 - \alpha)(1 - \alpha) \cdots (1 - \alpha) = (1 - \alpha)^m \quad (m).$$

Consequently, the probability of making one or more type 1 errors is

$$1 - (1 - \alpha)^m$$

for a series of independent tests. When α is numerically small, $1 - (1 - \alpha)^m$ is very closely approximated by $m\alpha$. For example when $\alpha = 0.05$ and $m = 2$, $1 - (1 - \alpha)^m = 0.0925$ and $m\alpha = 0.10$. This relation applies to a series of tests on *a priori* comparisons. Thus, if an experimenter makes 5 independent tests each at the 0.05 level of significance, the probability of a type 1 error in one or more of the five decisions is $1 - (0.95)^5 = 0.23$. If ten tests are made, $1 - (0.95)^{10} = 0.40$. Clearly, when a large number of tests is made, type 1 errors are likely to occur. Using the approach of multiple t's or F's for a series of tests on orthogonal comparisons maximizes power. However, if one wants to avoid making type 1 errors on the collection of tests, the total number of tests must be minimized, or one must set the level of significance so low on each test that statistical power is very low.

Strictly speaking, even if tests are made on only mutually orthogonal comparisons, the tests are not independent because a common estimate of σ_ϵ^2 is used. When sample sizes are large, in this case when $k(n-1)$ is large, tests may be considered to be essentially independent. When comparisons are not orthogonal, the probability of making one or more type 1 errors also increases for the set of m tests, but is less than or equal to $1 - (1 - \alpha)^m$.

3.11 METHODS OF ERROR CONTROL FOR SETS OF MULTIPLE COMPARISONS

There are numerous procedures for controlling type 1 error rates for inferences involving some particular set of comparisons. For example, the set may be all planned, pair-wise comparisons, comparisons between a control group and a set of experimental conditions, or all possible comparisons which can be constructed. Generally, which procedure is most appropriate will depend upon whether the hypotheses are *a priori* or *post mortem* and the values of m, the number of tests, and/or k, the number of means in the set. In making the choice among alternative procedures, it is well for the researcher to consider the relative loss of statistical power associated with controlling the level of significance. When all other things are equal, the procedure which controls the level of significance *and* yields the highest degree of precision, i.e., the shortest confidence intervals, for the set of comparisons of interest is to be preferred.

As discussed in the previous section, when a series of tests is made regarding *a priori* comparisons, one may control the level of significance for individual tests, but in so doing the probability of making one or more type 1 errors for the entire set of m tests increases with m to $1 - (1 - \alpha)^m$ for independent tests and less than $1 - (1 - \alpha)^m$ otherwise. This relation serves to define one of the issues surrounding tests of significance on multiple comparisons, the issue being the choice of a unit for type 1 errors. The unit can be set for individual tests and will be referred to in this section as α_{ind}. The unit for type 1 errors can also be set for an entire experiment or for a series of replications of an experiment.

To examine the issue more closely, one can focus upon joint decisions or joint confidence intervals. Suppose that $m = 3$ independent tests are to be made with $\alpha_{\text{ind}} = 0.05$. Suppose further that the joint probability is computed as the probability on the condition that all three null hypotheses are true and a joint decision will be declared correct only if all of its parts are correct. The possible joint or simultaneous decisions and the probability of each of the possible joint decisions are as follows (A = accept H_0, R = reject H_0):

Joint decision	Probability of joint decision	Joint decision correct?
R_1 R_2 R_3	α^3	No
R_1 R_2 A_3	$\alpha^2(1-\alpha)$	No
R_1 A_2 R_3	$\alpha^2(1-\alpha)$	No
A_1 R_2 R_3	$\alpha^2(1-\alpha)$	No
R_1 A_2 A_3	$\alpha(1-\alpha)^2$	No
A_1 R_2 A_3	$\alpha(1-\alpha)^2$	No
A_1 A_2 R_3	$\alpha(1-\alpha)^2$	No
A_1 A_2 A_3	$(1-\alpha)^3$	Yes
	1.00	

The probabilities follow from the fact that the joint probability of independent outcomes is the product of the probabilities of their individual parts. Since the joint outcomes on the left are both mutually exclusive as well as mutually exhaustive, the sum of the probabilities will be unity.

When all null hypotheses are true, only the decision to accept all three null hypotheses is correct. Thus, for the case of $m = 3$ individual decisions

$$\text{Pr (joint decision is correct} - \text{all } H_0\text{'s are true)} = (1 - \alpha)^3.$$

This probability is called the *joint confidence*. The joint level of significance is defined as

$$\alpha_{\text{joint}} = 1 - \text{joint confidence}$$
$$= 1 - (1 - \alpha)^3.$$

Thus, the probability of making any one of the joint decisions other than $A_1 A_2 A_3$ (all of which contain errors) is equal to $1 - (1 - \alpha)^3$. Generalized to any number of independent tests m the result is:

$$\text{Joint confidence} = (1 - \alpha_{\text{ind}})^m$$

$$\alpha_{\text{joint}} = \text{Pr (Joint Type I Error)} = 1 - (1 - \alpha_{\text{ind}})^m.$$

For example, for the three joint decisions made above at $\alpha_{\text{ind}} = 0.05$

$$\alpha_{\text{joint}} = 1 - (1 - 0.05)^3 = 0.14.$$

As another example if $m = 4$ independent tests are each made with $\alpha_{\text{ind}} = 0.05$ then

$$\alpha_{\text{joint}} = 1 - (1 - 0.05)^4 = 0.19.$$

One notes that α_{joint} is determined by two things, α_{ind} and m. Thus, one can reduce α_{joint} by numerically decreasing α_{ind} or by reducing the number of tests. When α_{ind} becomes smaller, power is decreased on each individual test. Thus, a heavy burden is placed upon careful planning to reduce the number of tests of significance.

Of considerable practical importance is the question, given m, what should α_{ind} be in order to make α_{joint} some specified value? To answer this question, one solves

$$\alpha_{\text{joint}} = 1 - (1 - \alpha_{\text{ind}})^m$$

for α_{ind} and obtains

$$\alpha_{\text{ind}} = 1 - (1 - \alpha_{\text{joint}})^{1/m}$$
$$= 1 - \sqrt[m]{1 - \alpha_{\text{joint}}}.$$

For example, if $m = 4$ independent tests are to be made, what should α_{ind} be if it is desired to have $\alpha_{\text{joint}} = 0.05$? One has

$$\alpha_{\text{ind}} = 1 - \sqrt[4]{1 - 0.05} = 0.01274.$$

Thus, each of the four tests would be made at the 0.01274 level of significance. As another example, if $m = 8$ independent tests are to be made and the desire is to control α_{joint} at 0.05, then one should make

$$\alpha_{\text{ind}} = 1 - (1 - \alpha)^{1/m}$$
$$= 1 - \sqrt[8]{1 - 0.05}$$
$$= 0.0064$$

for each test. The Šidák procedure, to be discussed later, utilizes this approach to control the level of significance.

In some contexts, α_{joint} will be referred to as the experimentwise error rate,

$$\alpha_{\text{expw}} = \alpha_{\text{joint}} \leq 1 - (1 - \alpha_{\text{ind}})^m$$

$$= \frac{\text{Number of experiments having}}{\text{one or more type 1 errors}} \Big/ \text{Number of experiments} .$$

The logic of this is simply that when one considers an entire experiment, m tests may be made, which tests may or may not be independent, and α_{expw} is the experimentwise error rate or the probability of one or more type 1 errors for the entire experiment.

In other contexts, α_{joint} may be referred to as the familywise error rate. This would be appropriate when some subset of an entire experiment is being analyzed in terms of m tests and the experimenter wishes to control α_{joint} for that family, i.e., subset, of tests. In that case, α_{joint} or α_{fam} refers to the probability of type 1 error for the family of interest. In an analysis of variance of an experiment involving two treatments and their interaction, for example, the analysis of variance provides tests on the three sources of variation. The overall test made at α_{ind} for each effect, treatments A and B, and their interaction, provides a familywise error rate equal to α_{fam}. If further comparisons are constructed in order to isolate more detailed effects within each family, the error rate can be set within that family.

$$\alpha_{\text{fam}} = 1 - (1 - \alpha_{\text{ind}})^m$$

$$= \frac{\text{Number of families having}}{\text{one or more type 1 errors}} \Big/ \text{Number of families} .$$

For this control, set

$$\alpha_{\text{ind}} = 1 - \sqrt[m]{1 - \alpha_{\text{fam}}}.$$

In the analysis of variance, tests of significance are not normally independent. However, when the tests involve a set of orthogonal comparisons, the tests within that set will tend to be more independent. If tests are not independent,

$$\alpha_{\text{joint}} \leq 1 - (1 - \alpha_{\text{ind}})^m$$

and using

$$\alpha_{\text{ind}} = 1 - \sqrt[m]{1 - \alpha_{\text{joint}}}$$

will provide values for α_{ind} which are too small.

Various other approaches have been used to define the equivalent of a level of significance on a collection of tests. One such approach, suggested by Fisher (1951) and known as the least significant difference (lsd) method, has been studied extensively by Dunn (e.g., 1961). The Dunn approach is based upon the Bonferroni inequality which, in its simplest form, is this: If A_1 and A_2 are two outcomes, then

$$\text{Pr}(A_1 \text{ or } A_2) = \text{Pr}(A_1) + \text{Pr}(A_2) - \text{Pr}(A_1 \cap A_2)$$
$$\leq \text{Pr}(A_1) + \text{Pr}(A_2),$$

where $\text{Pr}(A_1 \cap A_2)$ represents the probability that the outcome is simultaneously in both A_1 and A_2. If $\text{Pr}(A_1 \cap A_2) = 0$, then the events are said to be independent. Thus, for independent events,

$$\text{Pr}(A_1 \text{ or } A_2) = \text{Pr}(A_1) + \text{Pr}(A_2),$$

otherwise

$$\text{Pr}(A_1 \text{ or } A_2) = \text{Pr}(A_1) + \text{Pr}(A_2) - \text{Pr}(A_1 \cap A_2),$$

and the greater $\text{Pr}(A_1 \cap A_2)$, the less accurate is $\text{Pr}(A_1) + \text{Pr}(A_2)$ as an estimate of $\text{Pr}(A_1 \text{ or } A_2)$.

To illustrate the general approach taken by Fisher, suppose, for example, that m independent tests are made on simple differences in each experiment at the level of significance α_{ind}. Further suppose the experiment is replicated r times with independent random samples and that all differences specified by the null hypotheses are zero. Schematically, one has for the entire experiment

	Test			
Replication	**1**	**2**	$\cdots$	**m**
1				
2				
$\vdots$				
r				
Expected no. type 1 errors	$r\alpha_{\text{ind}}$	$r\alpha_{\text{ind}}$	$\cdots$	$r\alpha_{\text{ind}}$

Total no. type 1 errors $= mr\alpha_{\text{ind}}$

The per experiment type 1 error is

$$\alpha_{exp} = \frac{mr\alpha_{ind}}{r} = \frac{\text{number of type 1 errors with respect to tests on simple differences}}{\text{number of experiments}}.$$

$$= m\alpha_{ind}.$$

For this example, if $\alpha_{ind} = 0.05$ and $m = 10$, then

$$\alpha_{exp} = (10)(0.05) = 0.50,$$

and is not a probability. Rather, it is the average number of type 1 errors expected to be made per experiment.

Since

$$\alpha_{ind} = \frac{\alpha_{exp}}{m},$$

if m independent tests are to be made and the desire is to keep α_{exp} at the 0.05 level, then one can set

$$\alpha_{ind} = \frac{0.05}{10} = 0.005.$$

As another example suppose that an experiment consists of making $m = 16$ tests, each with $\alpha_{ind} = 0.05$. Suppose further that the experiment is replicated 100 times. If all H_0's were true, then one would expect

Experiment	Test ($\alpha_{ind} = 0.05$)					
	1	2	3	$\cdots$	16	
1						
2						
$\vdots$						
100						
E(no. of type 1 errors)	5	5	5	$\cdots$	5	E(total no. of type 1 errors) $= 16 \times 5 = 80$

That is, the expected number of type 1 errors per test would be $100 \times 0.05 = 5$. If the tests were independent, then the expected total number of type 1 errors would be $16 \times 5 = 80$. Let

$$\alpha_{exp} = \frac{\text{Total number of type 1 errors}}{\text{Total number of experiments}}.$$

For this example,

$$\alpha_{exp} = \frac{80}{100} = 0.80.$$

Suppose that one chose $\alpha_{\text{ind}} = 0.05/16$. Then the last line in the preceding summary would take the following form.

E(no. of type 1 errors)	5/16	5/16	5/16	$\cdots$	5/16	E(total no. of type 1 errors) $= 16 \times 5/16 = 5$

For this choice of α_{ind}, one has

$$\alpha_{\text{exp}} = \frac{5}{100} = 0.05$$

If the tests are not independent, then from the Bonferroni inequality one has

$$\alpha_{\text{exp}} \leq 0.05.$$

In general if m tests are made in an experiment and $\alpha_{\text{ind}} = \alpha_{\text{exp}}/m$, then

$$\alpha_{\text{exp}} = m\alpha_{\text{ind}} \text{ if the tests are independent,}$$

$$\alpha_{\text{exp}} < m\alpha_{\text{ind}} \text{ if the tests are not independent.}$$

How much less α_{exp} will be than $m\alpha_{\text{ind}}$ depends upon the degree of overlap between classes. The Dunn–Bonferroni procedure described below uses this approach to controlling the level of significance for a set of tests. That is, $\alpha_{\text{ind}} = \alpha_{\text{exp}}/m$.

As was the case for α_{expw}, a per-family error rate can be defined corresponding to α_{exp} wherein the desire is to control the level of significance for some meaningful subset of an entire experiment using

$$\alpha_{\text{ind}} = \frac{\alpha_{\text{fam}}}{m}.$$

Since some techniques to be discussed below use α_{joint} or α_{expw} to control the level of significance and others use α_{exp}, it is of interest to compare the magnitude of α_{ind} corresponding to fixed values of α_{joint} and α_{exp}. This is done in Table 3.21 and one notes that the two procedures for controlling the buildup of type 1 errors yield values for α_{ind} which are almost identical for small levels of significance for α_{joint} and α_{exp}.

Control of type 1 error can also be based upon sampling distributions which take into account the order of magnitude of the observed outcomes. Such control would be based upon the sampling distribution of order statistics. These are discussed in more detail in conjunction with the Newman–Keuls procedure, a method for testing all pairwise differences among a set of means described later in this section.

Multiple *a priori* Comparisons: Dunn–Bonferroni Procedure

Dunn (1961) has developed a procedure which is appropriate for testing a series of *a priori* hypotheses while controlling α_{expw}. As mentioned above, it is

TABLE 3.21 α_{ind} **necessary to control** α_{joint} **and** α_{exp}

m	$\alpha_{joint} = 0.05$ $\alpha_{ind} = 1 - (1 - \alpha_{joint})^{1/m}$	$\alpha_{exp} = 0.05$ $\alpha_{ind} = \alpha_{exp}/m$
2	0.0253	0.0254
4	0.0127	0.0125
8	0.0064	0.0062
12	0.0043	0.0042
20	0.00256	0.00250
	$\alpha_{joint} = 0.01$	$\alpha_{exp} = 0.01$
2	0.00501	0.00500
4	0.00251	0.00250
8	0.00126	0.00125
12	0.00837	0.000833
20	0.000500	0.000500

based upon the demonstration that the type 1 error rate does not exceed the sum of α_{ind} for a set of m tests of significance ($\alpha_{exp} \leq m\alpha_{ind}$). Thus, the familywise or experimentwise error rate can be controlled by the simple expedient of dividing the desired α_{expw} into m parts; $\alpha_{ind} = \alpha_{expw/m}$.

This result is very general. Let

$$\theta_s = c_{s1}\tau_1 + c_{s2}\tau_2 + \cdots + c_{sk}\tau_k$$

where

$$s = 1, 2, \ldots, m.$$

Thus, θ_s represents a set of m linear functions of the treatment effects. Those linear functions need not be comparisons. The estimator of θ_s is

$$\hat{\theta}_s = c_{s1}\bar{T}_1 + c_{s2}\bar{T}_2 + \cdots + c_{sj}\bar{T}_j + \cdots + c_{sk}\bar{T}_k.$$

Using the Bonferroni inequality on the probability of a series of joint outcomes, Dunn was able to show that a joint confidence interval on the set of m linear functions is given by

$$C[\hat{\theta}_s - A^s_{Bon} \leq \theta \leq \hat{\theta}_s + A^s_{Bon}] \geq (1 - \alpha).$$

Rather than working with a series of tests of significance, the experimenter may construct such a set of confidence intervals. For this purpose it is convenient to introduce the concept of what Tukey has called an allowance, designated by the symbol A. In this particular context an allowance is defined by

$$A^s_{Bon} = t_{1-(\alpha/2m)}(f)\sqrt{MS_{error}(\sum c^2_{sj/n_j})}$$

and

$$f = \text{the degrees of freedom for MS}_{error}$$
$$= k(n - 1).$$

This joint confidence interval may be converted into a series of m joint tests with a joint level of significance denoted α_{Bon}. Assuming the θ's are comparisons, the decision rule for these tests is

$$\text{Reject } H_0: |\theta| = 0 \quad \text{if} \quad |\hat{\theta}| > A_{\text{Bon}}.$$

When θ is a comparison, this procedure is identical to using the Student's t statistic developed in Sec. 3.10 to test hypotheses regarding *a priori* comparisons, but using

$$\alpha = \frac{\alpha}{m}$$

as α_{ind}. That is,

$$t = \frac{\sum c_j \bar{T}_j}{\sqrt{\text{MS}_{\text{error}}\left(\dfrac{\sum c_j^2}{n_j}\right)}},$$

and the decision rule is to reject H_0 if

$$t \geq t_{1-(\alpha/2m)}(f)$$

for a two-tailed test. As was noted earlier

$$\alpha/m \doteq (1 - (1 - \alpha)^{1/m}).$$

Accordingly α_{ind} for the Bonferroni procedure is very close to α_{ind} for the level of significance associated with m independent tests. For example, if $\alpha = 0.01$, one has

m	$0.01/m$	$1 - (1 - 0.01)^{1/m}$
2	0.005	0.005
4	0.0025	0.0025
8	0.001250	0.001256
16	0.000625	0.000628
32	0.000313	0.000314

Thus, use of the Dunn–Bonferroni procedure requires percentile points on the Student's t distribution of the form

$$t_{1-(\alpha/2m)}(f) = t_{1-\alpha}^{\text{Bon}}(m, f).$$

For example, if

$$\alpha = 0.05, \quad m = 9, \quad f = 15,$$

one would need

$$t_{0.95}^{\text{Bon}}(9, 15) = t_{1-(0.05/18)}(15) = t_{0.9972}(15).$$

This percentile point does not appear in the usual tables of Student's t distribution. Special tables known as tables of the Bonferroni t (Bailey, 1977) are provided in Appendix D.15. Moreover, one may approximate the

TABLE 3.22 **Values of $z_{1-(\alpha/2m)}$ for use in approximating Bonferroni t**

m	$\alpha = 0.05$	$\alpha = 0.01$	m	$\alpha = 0.05$	$\alpha = 0.01$
1	1.9600	2.5758	21	3.0381	3.4938
2	2.2414	2.8070	28	3.1237	3.5699
3	2.3940	2.9352	36	3.1970	3.6352
4	2.4977	3.0233	45	3.2608	3.6923
5	2.5758	3.0902	55	3.3172	3.7430
6	2.6383	3.1440	66	3.3678	3.7886
7	2.6901	3.1888	78	3.4136	3.8299
8	2.7344	3.2272	91	3.4554	3.8676
9	2.7729	3.2608	105	3.4938	3.9024
10	2.8070	3.2905	120	3.5293	3.9346
11	2.8376	3.3172	136	3.5623	3.9646
12	2.8653	3.3415	153	3.5931	3.9926
13	2.8905	3.3636	171	3.6219	4.0189
14	2.9137	3.3840	190	3.6491	4.0436
15	2.9352	3.4029			
16	2.9552	3.4205			
17	2.9738	3.4370			
18	2.9913	3.4524			
19	3.0078	3.4670			
20	3.0233	3.4808			

This table is abridged from Tables 1 and 2 from B. J. R. Bailey, Tables of the Bonferroni t Statistic, *Journal of the American Statistical Association*, 1977, **72**, 469–478.

percentile points needed for the Bonferroni t from special tables of the unit normal distribution. A portion of those tables is given in Table 3.22.

The values in Table 3.23 are based upon values of $z_{1-(\alpha/2m)}$ given in Table 3.22.

To illustrate the use of these tables, suppose that

$$\alpha = 0.05, \qquad m = 10, \qquad f = 20.$$

Then

$$t_{1-(0.05/2m)}(20) \doteq z_{1-(0.05/2m)} + \frac{z^3_{1-(0.05/2m)} + z_{1-(0.05/2m)}}{4(f-2)}.$$

Entering Table 3.22 with $m = 10$ and $\alpha = 0.05$, one has

$$t_{0.9975}(20) \doteq 2.8070 + \frac{[(2.8070)^3 + 2.8070]}{72} = 3.15.$$

The exact value of $t_{0.9975}$ as obtained from tables of the Bonferroni t is 3.17. Table 3.23 provides an indication of how well the approximation holds.

TABLE 3.23 **Normal approximation to Bonferroni** t: $t_{1-(\alpha/2m)}(f) = z_{1-\alpha/2m} + [z^3_{1-(\alpha/2m)} + z_{1-(\alpha/2m)}]/4(f-2)$

		$\alpha_{\text{Bon}} = 0.05$		$\alpha_{\text{Bon}} = 0.01$	
m	f	Exact t	Approx. t	Exact t	Approx. t
1	10	2.23	2.26	3.17	3.19
	15	2.13	2.14	2.95	2.95
	20	2.09	2.09	2.85	2.85
	∞	1.9600	1.9600	2.5758	2.5758
2	10	2.63	2.66	3.58	3.59
	15	2.49	2.50	3.29	3.29
	20	2.42	2.43	3.15	3.15
	60	2.30	2.30	2.91	2.91
	∞	2.2414	2.2414	2.8070	2.8070
3	15	2.69	2.70	3.48	3.48
	20	2.61	2.62	3.33	3.33
	60	2.46	2.46	3.06	3.06
	∞	2.3940	2.3940	2.9352	2.9352
4	15	2.84	2.85	3.62	3.61
	20	2.74	2.75	3.46	3.45
	60	2.58	2.57	3.16	3.16
	∞	2.4977	2.4977	3.0233	3.0233
10	20	3.17	3.15	3.85	3.83
	60	2.91	2.91	3.46	3.46
	100	2.87	2.87	3.39	3.39
	∞	2.8070	2.8070	3.2905	3.2905
15	30	3.19	3.19	3.80	3.79
	60	3.06	3.06	3.59	3.58
	100	3.01	3.01	3.51	3.51
	∞	2.9352	2.9352	3.4029	3.4029
105	30	3.92	3.91	4.50	4.47
	60	3.70	3.69	4.18	4.17
	100	3.61	3.61	4.06	4.07
	∞	3.4938	3.4938	3.9024	3.9024

As a numerical example of the Dunn–Bonferroni procedure, consider the values in Table 3.24. In this experiment there are four treatment conditions, one of which is a control, ($k = 4$); three observations ($n = 3$) are made under each of the treatment conditions. One of the treatments represents a standard manufacturing process; the other three represent different methods of manufacturing the same product. The criterion measure in each case is an index of quality of the manufactured product. The overall $F = 7.05$ exceeds the critical value for a 0.05 level test.

TABLE 3.24 Numerical example

	Methods				
	Standard	**I**	**II**	**III**	
	55	55	55	50	
	47	64	49	44	$n = 3$; $k = 4$
	48	64	52	41	
T_j	150	183	156	135	$G = 624$
$\sum (X_j^2)$	7538	11217	8130	6117	$\sum \left(\sum X^2 \right) = 33{,}002$
$\bar{T}_j$	50	61	52	45	

$$(1) = G^2/kn = (624)^2/12 = 32{,}448.00$$

$$(2) = \sum \left(\sum X^2 \right) = 33{,}002$$

$$(3) = \left(\sum T_j^2 \right) \Big/ n = (150^2 + 183^2 + 156^2 + 135^2)/3 = 32{,}850.00$$

$$SS_{\text{methods}} = (3) - (1) = 402.00$$
$$SS_{\text{error}} = (2) - (3) = \underline{152.00}$$
$$SS_{\text{total}} = (2) - (1) = 554.00$$

Source of variation	SS	df	MS	F
Methods	402.00	3	134.00	7.05
Experimental error	152.00	8	19.00	
Total	554.00	11		

$$F_{0.95}(3, 8) = 4.07$$

Suppose the experimenter is interested in comparing treatments as follows:

$$\psi_1 = 2\tau_1 - \tau_2 - \tau_3$$
$$\psi_2 = \tau_{\text{standard}} - (\tau_2 + \tau_3)/2$$
$$\psi_3 = \tau_{\text{standard}} - \tau_3.$$

For this set of $m = 3$ tests, a set of confidence intervals can be constructed in which all three statements are simultaneously true $100(1 - \alpha)$ percent of the time; one or more of the statements will be false at most 100α percent of the time under replications of the experiment. To accomplish this, the intervals are

$$C(\hat{\psi}_s - A^s_{\text{Bon}} \le \psi \le \hat{\psi}_s + A^s_{\text{Bon}}) \ge 100(1 - \alpha),$$

where

$$\hat{\psi}_s = C_s = \sum c_j \bar{T}_j \qquad \sum c_j = 0,$$

and

$$A^s_{\text{Bon}} = t_{t-(\alpha/2m)}(f) \sqrt{\text{MS}_{\text{error}}\left(\sum c_j^2/n_j\right)}.$$

More succinctly the interval is defined by

$$C_s \pm A^s_{\text{Bon}}.$$

For the comparisons of interest,

$$
\begin{aligned}
C_1 &= (2)\bar{T}_1 + (-1)(\bar{T}_2) + (-1)(\bar{T}_3) \\
&= (2)(61) + (-1)(52) + (-1)(45) = 25 \\
C_2 &= (1)(\bar{T}_{\text{standard}}) + (-\tfrac{1}{2})(\bar{T}_2) + (-\tfrac{1}{2})(\bar{T}_3) \\
&= (1)(50) + (-\tfrac{1}{2})(52) + (-\tfrac{1}{2})(45) = 1.5 \\
C_3 &= (1)(\bar{T}_{\text{standard}}) + (-1)(\bar{T}_3) \\
&= (1)(50) + (-1)(45) = 5.
\end{aligned}
$$

For a joint level of significance equal to $\alpha_{\text{Bon}} = 0.05$,

$$A^s_{\text{Bon}} = t_{1-(0.05/(2)(3))}(8) \sqrt{19.0\left(\sum c_j^2/n_j\right)}$$

$$= t_{0.9917}(8) \sqrt{19.0\left(\sum c_j^2/n_j\right)}.$$

From the tables of $t^{\text{Bon}}_{1-\alpha}(m, f)$, the value for $t^{\text{Bon}}_{0.95}(3, 8)$ is required. Approximated from the values in Table 3.22,

$$t^{\text{Bon}}_{0.95}(3, 8) = z_{0.95} + \frac{(z^3_{0.95} + z_{0.95})}{(4)(6)}$$

$$= 2.3940 + \frac{(2.3940^3 + 2.3940)}{24}$$

$$= 3.06.$$

Thus, the interval for the first comparison is:

$$C(C_1 - A^s_{\text{Bon}} \le \psi_1 \le C_1 + A^s_{\text{Bon}}) = 0.95,$$

where

$$A^s_{\text{Bon}} = (3.06) \sqrt{19.00\left(\frac{2^2 + 1^2 + 1^2}{3}\right)}$$

$$= (3.06)(6.16) = 18.85,$$

and the interval is

$$6.15 \le \psi_1 \le 43.85.$$

For the second and third comparisons, the intervals are, respectively,

$$-6.29 \le \psi_2 \le 10.93$$
$$-5.91 \le \psi_3 \le 15.91.$$

An interpretation of these results is that the experimenter can be confident at the 95 percent level that all three of these statements are true.

It is not necessary, but one can test hypotheses regarding those three comparisons using t_{Bon}^s. The hypothesis

$$H_0: |\psi| = 0$$

can be rejected if the comparison C is greater than A_{Bon}. Equally, if

$$t = \frac{\sum c_j \bar{T}_j}{\sqrt{MS_{error}(\sum c_j^2/n_j)}}$$

exceeds $t_{1-\alpha}^{Bon}$, one can reject the hypothesis that a comparison is zero. We already know that the null hypothesis would be rejected in the case of the first comparison, but would not be rejected for the second and third comparisons, because the limits do not include zero in the first instance but do for the other two comparisons. For illustrative purposes, however

$$t_{obs_1} = \frac{25}{\sqrt{(19)(\frac{6}{3})}} = 4.06,$$

$$t_{obs_2} = \frac{1.5}{\sqrt{(19)\left(\frac{1.5}{3}\right)}} = 0.49, \quad \text{and}$$

$$t_{obs_3} = \frac{5}{\sqrt{(19)(\frac{2}{3})}} = 1.40$$

for comparisons 1, 2, and 3 respectively. Since

$$t_{0.95}^{Bon}(3, 8) = 3.06,$$

the decisions are to reject H_0 only in the case of the first comparison. The level of significance for this set of all three tests is $\alpha_{Bon} = 0.05$.

A procedure which is slightly more powerful (yields shorter confidence intervals) than the Dunn–Bonferroni procedure was developed by Šidák (1967) as a modification of the Dunn–Bonferroni procedure. As we have seen, the Dunn–Bonferroni procedure is based upon the additive inequality

$$\alpha_{expw} \le m\alpha_{ind}$$

for m tests each made at the same α_{ind}. More generally, if the m tests were each made at a level of significance α_{ind}, then

$$\alpha_{expw} \le \sum_{i=1}^{m} \alpha_{ind}.$$

The Dunn procedure then simply establishes an individual level of significance as

$$\alpha_{\text{ind}} = \frac{\alpha_{\text{expw}}}{m} = \frac{\alpha_{\text{Bon}}}{m}$$

to achieve a desired level of significance for the set of tests. Thus, if the desire is to have $\alpha_{\text{expw}} = 0.01$ for a set of $m = 8$ tests, then α_{ind} for each test is

$$\alpha_{\text{ind}} = \frac{0.01}{8} = 0.001250.$$

Šidák shows that the multiplicative inequality for a set of non-orthogonal comparisons

$$\alpha_{\text{expw}} \leq 1 - (1 - \alpha_{\text{ind}})^m$$

can be used by making the level of significance for each test equal to

$$\alpha_{\text{ind}} = 1 - (1 - \alpha_{\text{expw}})^{1/m}.$$

Thus, if the experimenter uses this approach for $\alpha_{\text{expw}} = 0.01$ and $m = 8$, the level of significance for each test is

$$\alpha_{\text{ind}} = 1 - (1 - 0.01)^{\frac{1}{8}} = 0.001256.$$

Obviously, α_{Bon} and $\alpha_{\text{Šidák}}$ are almost identical when the level of significance is small. For example, suppose that $m = 4$, $f = 20$, and the level of significance for the entire set of four tests is to be 0.05. For a two-tailed test using the Dunn–Bonferroni procedure, one would use $t_{0.99375}(20)$; for the Šidák procedure, the t would be $t_{0.99363}(20)$. Clearly, the difference between these values is very small, but the Šidák critical values will always be smaller.

In order to use the Šidák values, the procedures used for the Dunn–Bonferroni can be used to test hypotheses and to establish confidence limits. However, critical values of t based upon the multiplicative inequality are used. Such tables have been provided by Games (1977). They are reproduced here in Appendix D.16. Since $\alpha_{\text{Šidák}} > \alpha_{\text{Bon}}$, the use of those tables provides a slightly more powerful test on each comparison for any given value of α_{expw}.

Multiple Orthogonal *a priori* Comparisons: Bechhofer–Dunnett Procedure

The Dunn–Bonferroni procedure applies to any set of planned comparisons whether or not the set is mutually orthogonal. When multiple comparisons are orthogonal, it is not true that the statistics used to evaluate those comparisons are independent (Tong, 1980; Wilcox, 1987). Were that true, then a set of m comparisons each tested at the $1 - (1 - \alpha)^{1/m}$ level would yield an exact α_{expw}. Bechhofer and Dunnett (1982) have provided tables of the distribution of the studentized maximum modulus statistic which do control α_{joint} for a set of m orthogonal contrasts, the critical values of which give shorter confidence intervals than do the Bonferroni or Šidák values.

Suppose that $z_1, z_2, \ldots, z_m$ represents a random sample of size m of independent observations from a population in which z is distributed as $N(0, \sigma^2)$. Suppose that s^2 is an estimate of σ^2 based upon f degrees of freedom. The distribution of the statistic

$$h = \frac{\max |z_j|}{s}$$

will be that of the studentized maximum modulus with parameters m and f. Tables of this distribution, prepared by Bechhofer and Dunnett, are presented in Appendix D.17. These values assure that α_{expw} equals a level established for the set of tests when the comparisons are orthogonal.

These tables may be used to construct a joint confidence interval on a set of m orthogonal comparisons. Bechhofer and Dunnett have shown that if

$$\psi_s = \sum c_{sj} \tau_j \qquad j = 1, 2, \ldots, k; \qquad s = 1, 2, \ldots, m;$$

and

$$\hat{\psi}_s = \sum c_{sj} \bar{T}_j$$

represent a set of m orthogonal comparisons and estimates of those comparisons, respectively, then a joint confidence interval on the set is

$$C[\hat{\psi}_s - A_{\text{Bech}}^s \leq \psi_s \leq \hat{\psi}_s + A_{\text{Bech}}^s] = 100(1 - \alpha),$$

where

$$A_{\text{Bech}}^s = h_{1-\alpha}(m, f) \sqrt{\text{MS}_{\text{error}}\left(\sum c_j^2/n\right)}.$$

In this relation, $h_{1-\alpha}(m, f)$ is the $1 - \alpha$ percentile point on the distribution of the studentized maximum modulus with parameters m and f.

Since the term on the right hand side of A_{Bech}^s is the same as the term which appears in A_{Bon}^s, the difference in the width of the Bonferroni and the Bechhofer–Dunnett confidence intervals is a function of the difference between

$$t_{1-\alpha}^{\text{Bon}}(m, f) \quad \text{and} \quad h_{1-\alpha}(m, f).$$

Heuristically, one might expect that a set of m orthogonal comparisons would have shorter confidence bounds than would a set of nonorthogonal comparisons. As already mentioned, such is the case, but the improvement in the bounds is small. A comparison of some corresponding percentile points on these distributions appears in Table 3.25. Unless sample sizes are very small, one notes that the corresponding values of t^{Bon} and h differ only slightly. With the exception of the case where $f_{\text{error}} = \infty$, percentile points on the studentized maximum modulus distribution are always smaller. Although there may be other reasons for keeping the set of comparisons orthogonal, insofar as improvement in the bounds of the joint confidence interval is of concern, there seems to be very little to gain.

TABLE 3.25 **Bonferroni t and studentized maximum modulus (in parentheses)**

f_{error}	α	$m = 2$	$m = 5$	$m = 10$	$m = 15$	$m = 20$
5	0.05	3.16 (3.09)	4.03 (3.79)	4.77 (4.31)	5.25 (4.61)	4.60 (4.82)
	0.01	4.77 (4.70)	5.89 (5.63)	6.87 (6.33)	7.50 (6.74)	7.98 (7.03)
10	0.05	2.63 (2.61)	3.17 (3.10)	3.58 (3.47)	3.83 (4.68)	4.00 (3.82)
	0.01	3.58 (3.57)	4.14 (4.10)	4.78 (4.50)	4.85 (4.74)	5.05 (4.91)
16	0.05	2.47 (2.46)	2.92 (2.88)	3.25 (3.20)	3.44 (3.38)	3.58 (3.50)
	0.01	3.25 (3.25)	3.69 (3.67)	4.02 (3.99)	4.20 (4.14)	4.35 (4.30)
20	0.05	2.42 (2.41)	2.85 (2.82)	3.15 (3.11)	3.33 (3.28)	3.46 (3.38)
	0.01	3.15 (3.15)	3.55 (3.54)	3.85 (3.83)	4.02 (4.00)	4.11 (4.10)
30	0.05	2.36 (2.35)	2.75 (2.73)	3.03 (3.00)	3.19 (3.16)	3.30 (3.27)
	0.01	3.03 (3.03)	3.39 (3.38)	3.65 (3.64)	3.80 (3.78)	3.90 (3.89)
∞	0.05	2.24 (2.24)	2.58 (2.57)	2.81 (2.80)	2.94 (2.93)	3.02 (3.02)
	0.01	2.81 (2.81)	3.09 (3.09)	3.29 (3.29)	3.40 (3.40)	3.48 (3.48)

$$t^{Bon} = t_{1-(\alpha/2m)}(f_{error}) \qquad\qquad h_{1-\alpha}(m, f_{error})$$

As a numerical example, suppose that

$$n = 6, \qquad k = 6, \qquad f_{error} = k(n-1) = 30, \qquad MS_{error} = 4.00,$$
$$\alpha = 0.05, \quad \text{and} \quad m = 5.$$

Suppose that one of the $m = 5$ orthogonal comparisons in the set is

$$H_0: \psi = 3\tau_1 - 2\tau_2 - \tau_3 = 0$$
$$H_1: \text{not } H_0.$$

Suppose further that

$$|\hat{\psi}| = |3\bar{T}_1 - 2\bar{T}_2 - \bar{T}_3| = 9.00.$$

Under the Bechhofer–Dunnett approach

$$A_{Bech} = h_{0.95}(5, 30) \sqrt{MS_{error}\left(\sum c_j^2 / n\right)}$$
$$= 2.73\sqrt{4.00(14/6)} = 8.34.$$

Since
$$|\hat{\psi}| > 8.34,$$

H_0 is rejected under the Bechhofer–Dunnett procedure with a joint $\alpha = 0.05$ on a specified set of $m = 5$ comparisons of which the comparison presented here is only one.

Under the Dunn–Bonferroni approach to this same problem, the critical value should be slightly larger than 8.34. Under the Dunn–Bonferroni approach

$$A_{\text{Bon}} = [t_{1-(0.05/10)}(5, 30)]\sqrt{\text{MS}_{\text{error}}\left(\sum c_j^2/n\right)}$$

$$= 2.75(3.055) = 8.40.$$

Since
$$|\hat{\psi}| > 8.40$$

the decision is to also reject H_0 under the Dunn–Bonferroni procedure.

Comparing All Treatments with a Single Control: Dunnett Procedure

It is often sensible and of interest to compare each of a set of $k - 1$ treatment condition means $\bar{T}_j$ to the mean for a control condition $\bar{T}_0$. A procedure which controls α_{joint} for that collection of $k - 1$ tests of the form

$$H_0: |\tau_j - \tau_0| = 0 \qquad j = 1, 2, \ldots, k - 1$$

has been developed by Dunnett (1955). He has shown that the following simultaneous confidence interval holds

$$C[|\bar{T}_j - \bar{T}_0| - A_{1-\alpha}^{\text{Dunnett}} \le |\tau_j - \tau_0|] = 100(1 - \alpha),$$

where
$$A_{1-\alpha}^{\text{Dunnett}} = t_{1-(\alpha/2)}^{\text{Dunnett}}[k, k(n - 1)]\sqrt{2\text{MS}_{\text{error}}/n}.$$

Tabled values for t^{Dunnett} are presented in Appendix D.6. The parameters of Dunnett's distribution for the t statistic are:

$k = $ numbers of treatments (including the control),

$k(n - 1) = $ degrees of freedom for MS_{error}.

Since each of the tests uses the same information on the control condition and a common estimate of error, the tests are not independent.

This joint confidence interval may be converted into a series of m joint tests with a controlled joint level of significance. The test statistic for the Dunnett procedure is the t statistic developed in Sec. 3.10 for *a priori* comparisons (also used for the Dunn–Bonferroni and Dunn–Šidák procedure)

$$t = \frac{\sum c_j \bar{T}_j}{\sqrt{\text{MS}_{\text{error}}(\sum c_j^2/n_j)}}.$$

For comparisons of the form $\bar{T}_j - \bar{T}_0$, the coefficients are $(+1)$ and (-1) for $\bar{T}_j$ and $\bar{T}_0$ respectively. Thus, when specialized for the Dunnett procedure, this statistic becomes

$$t = \frac{|\bar{T}_j - \bar{T}_0|}{\sqrt{2\text{MS}_{\text{error}}/n}}$$

when sample sizes are equal. The decision rule is to reject the hypothesis $|\tau_j - \tau_0| = 0$ if $t > t_{1-(\alpha/2)}^{\text{Dunnett}}[k, k(n - 1)]$ for a two-tailed test.

The numerical example in Table 3.24 will be used to illustrate the application of Dunnett's t statistic. In this experiment there are four treatment conditions, one of which is a control, $(k = 4)$; three observations $(n = 3)$ are made under each of the treatment conditions. The t statistic for the difference between method j and the standard method is

$$t = \frac{\bar{T}_j - \bar{T}_0}{\sqrt{2MS_{error}/n}}.$$

The critical value for the collection of $k - 1$ statistics of this form that may be computed is obtained from the Dunnett tables. For the data in Table 3.24 the critical value for a two-tailed 0.05-level test is ± 2.88 [that is, $t_{0.975}(4, 8) = 2.88$]. This value is found under the column headed 4 and the row corresponding to degrees of freedom equal to 8 (Table D.6). For example, in comparing method I with the standard,

$$t = \frac{61 - 50}{\sqrt{2(19)/3}} = \frac{11}{3.56} = 3.09.$$

Since the observed t statistic exceeds the critical value, the hypothesis that the two methods of manufacturing yield products having an equal average quality index is rejected. The level of significance for this single test is not 0.05; it is approximately 0.02. The critical value of 2.88 is associated with the collection of the three tests that would be made. The other two tests are:

$$t = \frac{52 - 50}{3.56} = 0.56,$$

$$t = \frac{45 - 50}{3.56} = 1.41,$$

and neither hypothesis can be rejected since neither value exceeds 2.88. These three tests may be summarized in the statement that method I differs significantly from the standard but methods II and III do not. This summary decision has significance level equal to 0.05. In the long run the summary decision reached by the procedures followed will have the equivalent of a type 1 error equal to, at most, 0.05.

Rather than working with a series of tests of significance, the experimenter may construct a series of confidence intervals. In this context an allowance is defined by

$$A^{Dunnett} = t_{1-(\alpha/2)}^{Dunnett} \sqrt{\frac{2MS_{error}}{n}},$$

where $t_{1-(\alpha/2)}$ is a value obtained from the Dunnett tables. The general form for the lower and upper confidence limits is

$$(\bar{T}_j - \bar{T}_0) \pm A^{Dunnett}.$$

For the data in Table 3.24, with $\alpha = 0.05$, $A = 2.88(3.56) = 10.25$, and 95 percent confidence limits for the collection of confidence statements on the difference $\mu_j - \mu_0$ are as follows:

> For method I: $(61 - 50) \pm 10.25 = 0.75$ and 21.15,
> For method II: $(52 - 50) \pm 10.25 = -8.25$ and 12.25,
> For method III: $(45 - 50) \pm 10.25 = -15.25$ and 5.25.

The joint (simultaneous) confidence coefficient for the intervals defined by these limits is 0.95. The confidence interval for method I takes the form

$$0.75 \le \mu_1 - \mu_0 \le 21.25.$$

In words, the difference between the mean quality indices for method I and the standard method is between 0.25- and 21.25-quality index units. This statement and the additional confidence statements for methods II and III have a joint confidence coefficient of 0.95.

It is of interest to compare the distribution of Dunnett's t statistic with that of Student's t statistic. For the case in which $k = 2$, the two distributions are identical. For k greater than 2, corresponding critical values in the Dunnett tables are larger. For example, with the degrees of freedom for error equal to 10 and $k = 7$, two-tailed tests with joint significance level 0.05 are equivalent to individual two-tailed tests are the 0.01 level.

It might be expected that the Dunn–Bonferroni and Dunn–Šidák procedures would yield results quite close to those of the Dunnett procedure when applied to the same problem. Such does turn out to be the case. For example, the Dunn–Bonferroni procedure will be applied to the data in Table 3.24. Suppose that the following $m = 3$ tests are made using the Dunn–Bonferroni procedure with $\alpha_{\text{Bon}} = 0.01$:

$$H_0: |\tau_0 - \tau_j| = 0, \qquad j = 1, 2, 3.$$

Using tables of the Bonferroni t, one has

$$t_{0.99}^{\text{Bon}}(3, 8) = 4.12.$$

The critical value for a Bonferroni test is

$$
\begin{aligned}
A_{0.99}^{\text{Bon}} &= t_{0.99}^{\text{Bon}}(3, 8)\sqrt{2\text{MS}_{\text{error}}/n} \\
&= 4.12\sqrt{12.67} = 14.67.
\end{aligned}
$$

The decision rule under the Dunn–Bonferroni procedure is:

> Reject the hypothesis that $|\tau_0 - \tau_j| = 0$ if $|\hat{T}_0 - T_j| > 14.67$.

The critical value under the Dunnett procedure is 13.42. In general the Dunn–Bonferroni and Dunn–Šidák critical values will be slightly larger than the Dunnett critical value. Since the Dunnett procedure was specifically designed for testing each treatment with a single control, one would expect that the confidence bounds on the simultaneous confidence interval would be smaller than the corresponding confidence bounds under the Dunn–Bonferroni and Dunn–Šidák procedures which control α for any set of m tests.

It would not be unusual for a control condition to have a variance different from the variances of the treatment conditions, but for there to be homogeneity of variances among treatment conditions. Under those circumstances, the t statistic for the Dunnett procedure can take the following form:

$$t' = \frac{\bar{T}_j - \bar{T}_0}{\sqrt{\dfrac{MS_{error_{treat}}}{n} + \dfrac{MS_{error_{control}}}{n}}}.$$

The approximate degrees of freedom for the denominator of this t statistic are

$$df' = \frac{\dfrac{MS_{error_{treat}}}{n}(df_{error_{treat}}) + \dfrac{MS_{error_{control}}}{n}(df_{error_{control}})}{\dfrac{MS_{error_{treat}}}{n} + \dfrac{MS_{error_{control}}}{n}}.$$

There is a slight bias in this method of computing df' in the direction of making df' slightly too large. Dunnett (1964) gives a method for removing this bias.

All Pairwise Comparisons

It is often of interest to determine whether any of the $k(k-1)/2$ pairwise differences from among k means are significant. Under some limited circumstances, one could consider these as tests on *a priori* or planned comparisons, but most often these tests are made because the F test of the overall null hypothesis leads to the conclusion that there are some treatment effects present and the desire is to seek out the source of those differences among the simple differences between pairs of means. One would like to control the level of significance with regard to this set of tests. There are numerous procedures for accomplishing this goal.

TUKEY (HSD) PROCEDURE. Tukey (1953) developed a procedure for testing all comparisons which has been very widely used as a procedure for testing all pairwise comparisons. The procedure is called the honestly significant difference (hsd) test, to contrast it with a procedure suggested earlier by Fisher (1951) referred to as the least significant difference (lsd) test. The lsd test consists of simply using an appropriate t statistic (Sec. 3.10) to evaluate all pairwise differences following a significant F obtained in the overall analysis of variance.

The Tukey hsd procedure uses the studentized range statistic, q, as the test statistic. This statistic owes its name to the fact that it uses the range of differences among means and was originally derived by Gossett, who also derived the t distribution. The studentized range statistic may be used for a variety of purposes including testing the overall ANOV hypothesis. The studentized range statistic is

$$q = \frac{\bar{T}_{\text{largest}} - \bar{T}_{\text{smallest}}}{s_{\bar{T}}},$$

where $s_{\bar{T}} = \sqrt{\text{MS}_{\text{error}}/n}$ is the sample estimate of the standard error of a mean based upon n observations in the analysis of variance. The numerator of the q statistic is the range of the k means; the range is "studentized" by dividing by the estimate of the standard error of a $\bar{T}_j$.

In the present context, q is defined by

$$q = \frac{\bar{T}_{\text{largest}} - \bar{T}_{\text{smallest}}}{\sqrt{\text{MS}_{\text{error}}/n}},$$

where n is the number of observations in each $\bar{T}$. A numerically equivalent form of the q statistic is given by

$$q = \frac{T_{\text{largest}} - T_{\text{smallest}}}{\sqrt{n\text{MS}_{\text{error}}}}.$$

It may readily be shown that q is equal to

$$q = \sqrt{2F_{\text{range}}},$$

where F_{range} is an F statistic based upon a comparison of the largest and smallest means. Since $t^2 = F$, when F has a single degree of freedom in the numerator, $t = (1/\sqrt{2})q$, and since $t_{(\infty)} = z$, from the tables of the studentized range statistic (Table D.4), one notes that

$$\frac{1}{\sqrt{2}} q_{0.95}(2, \infty) = \frac{2.77}{\sqrt{2}} = 1.96 = z_{0.975} = t_{0.975}(\infty).$$

This implies that both tails of the unit normal distribution fold over into one tail of the studentized range distribution. If one works with ordered differences, all values of the q statistic will be greater than zero. Hence the critical value for ordered differences will always be in the right-hand tail. The potentially negative differences are converted to positive differences if one works with absolute values.

Under the hypothesis that $\tau_1 = \tau_2 \cdots = \tau_k$ and under all of the assumptions underlying either Model I or Model II, the sampling distribution of the q statistic is approximated by the studentized range distribution having parameters $k = $ number of treatments and $f = $ degrees of freedom for MS_{error}. The symbol $q_{0.99}(k, f)$ designates the 99th percentile point on the q distribution. In contrast to the overall F ratio, which uses all the k treatment means to obtain the numerator, the q statistic uses only the two most extreme means in the set of k. Thus, the q statistic uses less of the information from the experiment than does the F statistic and the use of the F statistic generally leads to a more powerful test with respect to a broader class of alternative hypotheses than does the use of the q statistic. However, there are some alternative hypotheses

TABLE 3.26   **Numerical example**

Treatments...	a	b	c	d	e	
T_j..........	10	14	18	14	14	$k = 5; n = 4$
$\bar{T}_j$..........	2.50	3.50	4.50	3.50	3.50	

Source	SS	df	MS	F
Treatments	8.00	4	2.00	4.00
Experimental error	7.50	15	0.50	
Total	15.50	19		

$$F_{0.99}(4, 15) = 4.89$$

for which the q statistic leads to a more powerful test. Whether or not the two tests lead to the same decision with respect to the hypothesis being tested depends upon the distributions in the populations from which the means were obtained. If the distributions are each $N(\mu, \sigma^2)$, the use of either the F or the q statistic will lead to the same decision. In other cases the decision reached may differ.

The numerical example summarized in Table 3.26 provides an illustration of a case in which the two tests lead to different decisions. Each T_j in this table represents the sum over 4 observations ($n = 4$) under each of 5 treatments ($k = 5$). Since the observed overall F ratio (4.00) does not exceed the critical value (4.89) for a 0.01-level test, the data do not contradict the hypothesis that the treatment effects are all equal. The q statistic is

$$q = \frac{4.50 - 2.50}{\sqrt{0.50/4}} = 5.67.$$

The critical value for a 0.01-level test is $q_{0.99}(5, 15) = 5.56$. Since the observed q statistic exceeds the critical value, the data contradict the hypothesis that the treatment effects are all equal. In this case the F statistic and the q statistic lead to conflicting decisions. This is so because the means for treatments b, d, and e fall at a single point.

In contrast to the example in Table 3.24, consider the example in Table 3.27. In this table the means tend to be more evenly distributed between the highest and lowest values. SS_{treat} for this case is larger than it is for the case in which the means concentrate at a single point within the range. The experimental error in this example is numerically equal to that in Table 3.26. The overall F value exceeds the critical value for a 0.01-level test. Since the ranges are the same in the two examples and since the error is also the same, there is no numerical change in the value of the q statistic. If, in practice, the overall F leads to nonrejection of the hypothesis being tested but the q test leads to rejection of the hypothesis being tested, the experimenter should

TABLE 3.27 **Numerical example**

Treatments . . .	a	b	c	d	e	
T_j	10	12	18	16	14	$k = 5; n = 4$
$\bar{T}_j$	2.50	3.00	4.50	4.00	3.50	

Source	SS	df	MS	F
Treatments	10.00	4	2.50	5.00
Experimental error	7.50	15	0.50	
Total	17.50	19		

$$**F_{0.99}(4, 15) = 4.89$$

examine his data quite carefully before attempting any interpretation. In most cases, the F test is more powerful than the corresponding q test.

Under the assumptions of the analysis of variance, the statistic

$$q = \frac{\bar{T}_{\max} - \bar{T}_{\min} - (\tau_{\max} - \tau_{\min})}{\sqrt{MS_{error}/n}}$$

has the studentized range distribution with parameters k and $k(n-1)$, where $k(n-1)$ are the degrees of freedom for MS_{error}.

If one defines

$$A_{Tukey} = q_{1-\alpha}[k, k(n-1)]\sqrt{MS_{error}/n}$$

then from the distribution of q when all $\tau_j = 0$,

$$\Pr[\bar{T}_{\max} - \bar{T}_{\min} \leq A_{Tukey}] = 1 - \alpha.$$

This probability statement implies that

$$\Pr[|\bar{T}_j - \bar{T}_{j'}| \leq A_{Tukey}] \geq 1 - \alpha \quad \text{for all } j \neq j'$$

since

$$|\bar{T}_j - \bar{T}_{j'}| \leq \bar{T}_{\max} - \bar{T}_{\min}.$$

This latter probability holds jointly for all $j \neq j'$, and may therefore be used as the basis for testing the $k(k-1)/2$ unique simple comparisons of the form $H_0: |\tau_j - \tau_{j'}| = 0$.

For values of $\bar{T}_j - \bar{T}_{j'}$ which are smaller than the range, probability statements of this form are conservative in the sense that A_{Tukey} is too large. Hence using the confidence interval as a basis for constructing tests on differences of the form $\tau_j - \tau_{j'} = 0$, where $\tau_j - \tau_{j'}$ is smaller than the range of the differences, will lead to conservative tests in the sense that the critical value will be too large. Such tests are called negatively biased tests since they will yield too few statistically significant results. Procedures which will be discussed in later sections are designed to remove some of this bias.

To illustrate these points in more concrete terms, consider an analysis of variance in which $k = 3$ with n observations under each of the treatments. For this case MS_{error} will have $3(n - 1)$ degrees of freedom. Suppose that the treatment means are ordered $\bar{T}_1 \le \bar{T}_2 \le \bar{T}_3$. If the assumptions underlying the analysis of variance model are met, then the statistic

$$q = \frac{\bar{T}_3 - \bar{T}_1}{\sqrt{MS_{error}/n}}$$

will have the studentized range distribution with parameters $r = k$ and degrees of freedom $k(n - 1)$, where r = number of ordered steps between the smallest and largest means. The difference between the largest and smallest of the sample means defines the range of the means.

From this distribution fact, one may construct the following confidence interval on the difference between $\mu_3 - \mu_1$ or equivalently $\tau_3 - \tau_1$:

$$C[(\bar{T}_3 - \bar{T}_1) - A_{Tukey} \le \mu_3 - \mu_1 \le (\bar{T}_3 - \bar{T}_1) + A_{Tukey}] = 1 - \alpha.$$

This represents a confidence statement on the range of a sample of size $k = 3$ means, each mean being based upon sample size n. $q_{1-\alpha}[3, 3(n - 1)]$ is the $100(1 - \alpha)$ percentile point on the corresponding studentized range distribution. This confidence statement on the range implies the following two confidence statements with respect to the two sub-ranges:

$$C[(\bar{T}_2 - \bar{T}_1) - A_{Tukey} \le \mu_2 - \mu_1 \le (\bar{T}_2 - \bar{T}_1) + A_{Tukey}] > 1 - \alpha,$$
$$C[(\bar{T}_3 - \bar{T}_2) - A_{Tukey} \le \mu_3 - \mu_2 \le (\bar{T}_3 - \bar{T}_2) + A_{Tukey}] > 1 - \alpha.$$

The principle on which these last two confidence statements is based is this: If the upper and lower confidence limits are broad enough to include the maximum difference in the set of three means with confidence $1 - \alpha$, then these same limits are sufficiently broad to include differences which are smaller than the maximum with confidence greater than $1 - \alpha$. Hence one has the following joint or simultaneous confidence statement covering all of the possible differences:

$$C[(\bar{T}_j - \bar{T}_{j'}) - A_{Tukey} \le \mu_j - \mu_{j'} \le (\bar{T}_j - \bar{T}_{j'}) + A_{Tukey}] \ge 1 - \alpha,$$
$$\text{for all } j, j', \quad j > j'.$$

In terms of the parameters in the analysis of variance model, the simultaneous confidence intervals take the form

$$C[(\bar{T}_j - \bar{T}_{j'}) - A_{Tukey} \le \tau_j - \tau_{j'} \le (\bar{T}_j - \bar{T}_{j'}) + A_{Tukey}] \ge 1 - \alpha,$$
$$\text{for all } j, j', \quad \bar{T}_j > \bar{T}_{j'}.$$

There is a maximum of $k(k - 1)/2$ such pairwise differences. For the maximum of such differences, the confidence coefficient is $1 - \alpha$; for all other differences, the confidence coefficient will be greater than $1 - \alpha$.

In terms of the usual hypothesis testing situation, a confidence interval represents the range of all values of a parameter (or some function thereof) which will lead to the decision to not reject H_0. One can therefore translate a set of confidence intervals into a set of tests whose decisions are formulated in terms of the upper and lower confidence limits. In the present case, the level of significance associated with the corresponding tests will be denoted α_{Tukey}, since the set of confidence intervals based upon the studentized range is due to Tukey.

One may formulate a decision rule for testing the $k(k-1)/2$ hypotheses of the form

$$H_0: |\tau_j - \tau_{j'}| = 0 \qquad H_1: |\tau_j - \tau_{j'}| > 0 \qquad \alpha_{Tukey} = 0.01$$

as follows:

$$\text{Reject } H_0 \text{ if } \quad |\bar{T}_j - \bar{T}_{j'}| > A_{Tukey}$$

where

$$A_{Tukey} = \sqrt{MS_{error}/n}\, q_{0.99}[k, k(n-1)].$$

An equivalent decision rule in terms of the differences between treatment totals is:

$$\text{Reject } H_0 \text{ if } \quad |T_j - T_{j'}| > q_{1-\alpha}[k, k(n-1)]\sqrt{nMS_{error}}.$$

If tests of this form are made on the collection of all the $k(k-1)/2$ unique pairwise differences among k means, then Pr (one or more type 1 errors in the collection) $\leq \alpha_{Tukey}$. The method by which the simultaneous confidence intervals were constructed implies the last probability statement. Thus α_{Tukey} is a measure of the joint type 1 error rate associated with the collection of all tests on simple differences.

It is of interest to illustrate the difference in decision rules for an "ordinary" t test, where α_{ind} is the comparisonwise error rate for each test considered singly, and the Tukey procedure where α_{Tukey} is the experimentwise error rate with regard to the Tukey collection of all unique pairwise differences.

Consider an example wherein $k = 10$, $n = 5$, and $MS_{error} = 20$. If one computes

$$t = \frac{|\bar{T}_j - \bar{T}_{j'}|}{\sqrt{2MS_{error}/n}} = \frac{|\bar{T}_j - \bar{T}_{j'}|}{\sqrt{8}},$$

for $\alpha_{ind} = 0.01$, the decision rule is:

$$\text{Reject } H_0 \text{ if } \quad |\bar{T}_j - \bar{T}_{j'}| > t_{0.995}(40)\sqrt{8}$$
$$= 2.70\sqrt{8} = 7.64.$$

Now consider the Tukey procedure with $\alpha_{Tukey} = 0.01$. Here the level of significance is a joint probability with respect to type 1 errors in the collection of all tests on simple differences. One computes the statistic

$$q = \frac{|\bar{T}_j - \bar{T}_{j'}|}{\sqrt{MS_{error}/n}} = \frac{|\bar{T}_j - \bar{T}_{j'}|}{\sqrt{20/5}} = \frac{|\bar{T}_j - \bar{T}_{j'}|}{2}.$$

With $\alpha_{\text{Tukey}} = 0.01$, the decision rule is

$$\text{Reject } H_0 \text{ if } \quad |\bar{T}_j - \bar{T}_{j'}| > q_{0.99}(10, 40)\sqrt{\text{MS}_{\text{error}}/n}$$
$$= (5.60)(2) = 11.20.$$

For this example, then, the critical value for a test considered singly ($\alpha_{\text{ind}} = 0.01$) is 7.64; with $\alpha_{\text{Tukey}} = 0.01$, the critical value is 11.20.

Which one of the two approaches should be taken in any given data analysis problem depends upon the purpose of the analysis. No one approach is to be preferred in all cases. Further, there may be an advantage to using both approaches in handling the same set of data—provided the domain of the inferences is stated in unambiguous terms. Joint probability statements and joint confidence intervals are not meant to be used simply because procedures for doing such have a degree of statistical elegance which is lacking in individual tests or confidence statements.

An example of the Tukey approach to testing the $k(k-1)/2$ simple differences in a single-factor design is given in Table 3.28.

TABLE 3.28 **Tukey procedure for testing all simple differences** ($k = 7$, $n = 5$)

	Treatment	a	b	c	d	e	f
	Total ($n = 5$)	12	18	10	13	24	25

(i)

Source	SS	df	MS	F
Treatments	43.09	6	7.52	9.40**
Error	22.40	28	0.80	
Total	67.49	34		

(ii)

Order:	(1)	(2)	(3)	(4)	(5)	(6)	(7)
Treatment:	c	a	d	b	g	e	f
Total:	10	12	13	18	22	24	25
10	—	2	3	8	12**	14**	15**
12		—	1	6	10	12**	13**
13			—	5	9	11**	12**
18				—	4	6	7
22					—	2	3
24						—	1
25							—

(iii)

$$q_{0.99}(7, 28) = 5.44 \text{ (from table of studentized range)}$$
$$A_{\text{Tukey}} = \sqrt{\text{MS}_{\text{treat}}/n}\, q_{0.99}(7, 28)$$
$$= \sqrt{0.80/5}\,(5.44) = 2.176$$
$$\text{critical value} = nA_{\text{Tukey}} = \sqrt{n\text{MS}_{\text{error}}}\, q_{0.99}(7, 28)$$
$$= 10.88$$

Rather than using the decision rule:

$$\text{Reject } H_0 \text{ if } \quad |\bar{T}_j - \bar{T}_{j'}| > A_{\text{Tukey}} = \sqrt{\text{MS}_{\text{error}}/n} \, q_{0.99}[k, k(n-1)],$$

in applications it is more convenient to use the equivalent decision rule formulated in terms of totals:

$$\text{Reject } H_0 \text{ if } \quad n\,|\bar{T}_j - \bar{T}_{j'}| > A_{\text{Tukey}} = \sqrt{n\text{MS}_{\text{error}}} \, q_{0.99}[k, k(n-1)],$$

or $$\text{Reject } H_0 \text{ if } \quad |T_j - T_{j'}| > \sqrt{n\text{MS}_{\text{error}}} \, q_{0.99}[k, k(n-1)].$$

It is this latter decision rule which is used in Table 3.28.

There are $k = 7$ treatments in this example, which are labeled $a, b, \ldots, f$. The total of the $n = 5$ observations under each treatment is given at the top of the table, but the individual observations are not given. A summary of the analysis of variance is given in part i. The overall $F(9.40)$ is statistically significant beyond the 0.01 level, $F_{0.99}(6, 28) = 3.53$. To probe the $k(k-1)/2$ simple differences, it is convenient to construct a matrix of ordered differences as is done in part ii of Table 3.28. The symbol (1) here denotes the smallest total, which corresponds to treatment c; the symbol (7) denotes the largest total, which corresponds to treatment f.

In the table in the lower part of part ii the entries in the first row are the differences between each treatment total and the smallest total. For example in column (5), row (1) is entry

$$T_{(5)} - T_{(1)} = T_g - T_c = 22 - 10 = 12,$$

and in column 7, row 1 is the entry

$$T_{(7)} - T_{(1)} = T_f - T_c = 25 - 10 = 15.$$

This entry is the range of the treatment totals. Note that all differences in this table are positive. The lower half of this table (if it were filled in) would be the negative mirror image of the upper half.

The Tukey critical value for tests with level of significance $\alpha_{\text{Tukey}} = 0.01$ is constructed in part iii. From tables of the studentized range one will find

$$q_{0.99}[k, k(n-1)] = q_{0.99}[7, 28] = 5.44.$$

Hence $$A_{\text{Tukey}} = \sqrt{\text{MS}_{\text{error}}/n} \, q_{0.99}[7, 28] = \sqrt{0.80/5} \, (5.44)$$
$$= 2.176,$$

and $$nA_{\text{Tukey}} = 5(2.176) = 10.88.$$

The decision rule for testing each of the 21 entries in part ii is thus:
Reject the hypothesis that $|\tau_j - \tau_{j'}| = 0$ if

$$|T_j - T_{j'}| > 10.88.$$

Those seven entries in the table with double asterisks satisfy this inequality.

Thus, the following statistical hypotheses are rejected:

$$|\tau_g - \tau_c| = 0, \qquad |\tau_e - \tau_c| = 0, \qquad |\tau_f - \tau_c| = 0,$$
$$|\tau_e - \tau_a| = 0, \qquad |\tau_f - \tau_a| = 0,$$
$$|\tau_e - \tau_d| = 0, \qquad |\tau_f - \tau_d| = 0.$$

The range of the $\bar{T}_j - \bar{T}_{j'}$ is $\bar{T}_{max} - \bar{T}_{min} = 5.00 - 2.00 = 3.00$. Under the Tukey procedure unless the difference is significant at a specified α_{Tukey}, no other difference can be statistically significant at that specified α_{Tukey}. Often, but not always, if the overall F is statistically significant, at least one simple difference will also be statistically significant. Since the overall F test in the analysis of variance is based upon MS_{treat} and the Tukey procedure is based upon the range, a statistically significant overall F does not necessarily imply that the range will be statistically different from zero. For the special case $k = 2$, however, the overall F test and the Tukey procedure are identical.

As an example, suppose that $k = 2$ and $n = 5$. To test the hypothesis that $|\tau_1 - \tau_2| = 0$, the decision rule is: Reject the hypothesis being tested at level of significance 0.01 if

$$F = \frac{(T_1 - T_2)^2}{2nMS_{error}} > F_{0.99}(1, 8) = 11.3.$$

Under the Tukey procedure, the decision rule is:
Reject the hypothesis being tested at level of significance $\alpha = 0.01$ if

$$q = \frac{|T_1 - T_2|}{\sqrt{nMS_{error}}} > q_{0.99}(2, 8) = 4.74.$$

When $k = 2$, one notes that

$$F = \frac{q^2}{2}.$$

One also notes that

$$F_{0.99}(1, 8) = 11.3; \qquad \frac{q_{0.99}^2(2, 8)}{2} = \frac{(4.74)^2}{2} = 11.2.$$

These percentile points differ only because of rounding error. Hence the overall F test and the Tukey procedure are identical when $k = 2$.

The procedure followed in Table 3.28 is known as the Tukey hsd method or the Tukey (a) procedure. Recognizing the negative bias in this test procedure, Tukey proposed a modification, known as the Tukey (b) procedure, for reducing this bias. That method will not be presented here. Rather, the Student–Newman–Keuls procedure, also designed to reduce this bias, will be presented later in this section.

The Tukey approach to making tests on multiple comparisons while controlling the joint level of significance may be extended to the set of all possible comparisons, simple and otherwise. If one defines a comparison as

$$\psi = \sum c_j \tau_j \qquad \left(\sum c_j = 0\right),$$

then a joint confidence interval on all possible comparisons that may be constructed among the k treatments is given by

$$C[\hat{\psi} - A''_{\text{Tukey}} \leq \psi \leq \hat{\psi} + A''_{\text{Tukey}}] = 100(1 - \alpha)$$

where

$$\hat{\psi} = \sum c_j \bar{T}_j$$

and

$$A''_{\text{Tukey}} = \tfrac{1}{2} \sum |c_j| \sqrt{MS_{\text{error}}/n} \, q_{1-\alpha}[k, k(n - 1)].$$

For the case of a simple comparison,

$$\tfrac{1}{2} \sum |c_j| = \tfrac{1}{2}(|1| + |-1|) = \tfrac{1}{2}(2) = 1.$$

Hence for the case of a simple comparison,

$$A''_{\text{Tukey}} = A_{\text{Tukey}}.$$

In a later section, the Scheffé procedure for testing hypotheses regarding all comparisons will be presented. Where the Tukey procedure is used to test all possible comparisons, Tukey-type confidence intervals on comparisons have wider confidence bounds than do Scheffé type confidence bounds when the comparisons involve coefficients (c_j) which differ rather widely from each other. For example, the Tukey-type confidence interval will have slightly shorter confidence bounds for a comparison of the form

$$\psi = 2\tau_1 - \tau_2 - \tau_3;$$

whereas the Scheffé-type confidence interval will have considerably shorter bounds for a comparison of the form

$$\psi = 4\tau_1 + 4\tau_2 - 2\tau_3 - 2\tau_4 - 2\tau_5 - 2\tau_6.$$

The Tukey-type confidence interval requires that n be constant for all treatments. If the sample sizes do not differ markedly from each other with $n_{\text{smallest}} > 10$ and

$$\frac{n_{\text{largest}}}{n_{\text{smallest}}} < 1.25,$$

a reasonably good approximation to the Tukey procedures may be obtained by setting n equal to the harmonic mean of the sample sizes. The harmonic mean of the sample sizes, denoted $\bar{n}$, is defined by

$$\bar{n} = \frac{k}{\sum (1/n)}.$$

Another approximation for unequal sample sizes sets n equal to

$$\frac{2}{\dfrac{1}{n_{\text{smallest}}} + \dfrac{1}{n_{\text{largest}}}}.$$

In using these approximations one cannot work with the treatment totals but must work with the treatment means.

Beyond these simple adjustments for unequal sample sizes, Spjøtvoll and Stoline (1973) have suggested another way of handling unequal sample sizes in conjunction with the Tukey approach to testing all pairwise comparisons. Under this approach the simultaneous confidence intervals take the following form:

$$C[\bar{T}_j - \bar{T}_{j'} - A_{jj'} \leq \tau_j - \tau_{j'} \leq \bar{T}_j - \bar{T}_{j'} + A_{jj'}] = 1 - \alpha,$$

where

$$A_{jj'} = \sqrt{\frac{\text{MS}_{\text{error}}}{\min{(n_j, n_{j'})}}} \, q_{1-\alpha}(k, f_{\text{error}}),$$

$$f_{\text{error}} = \frac{\text{degrees of freedom for MS}_{\text{error}} \text{ in the}}{\text{analysis of variance}}.$$

Each of the $A_{jj'}$ will depend upon n_j and $n_{j'}$, hence the width of the confidence intervals will differ. However, the decision rule (with simultaneous level of significance equal to α) is as follows:

Reject the hypothesis that $\tau_j - \tau_{j'} = 0$ if the
confidence interval does not contain 0.

If the variation among the n_j is relatively extreme

$$\left(\text{say } \frac{\max{(n_j)}}{\min{(n_j)}} > 3\right),$$

the indications are that this latter method for handling unequal sample sizes is to be preferred to modified Tukey procedures which use a constant A for the allowance factor.

STUDENT–NEWMAN–KEULS PROCEDURE. The Student–Newman–Keuls procedure represents an attempt to remove the negative bias in the Tukey approach (although, as mentioned by Kirk (1982), historically the procedure was suggested prior to Tukey's work, the Newman–Keuls procedure having been developed from work by Student in 1927, Newman in 1939, and Keuls in 1952).

The Student–Newman–Keuls procedure takes into account the order of a set of k means. In general, for any set of statistics there are marked differences in sampling distributions for statistics constructed in a way which takes into account the order of magnitude of the observed outcomes. Before introducing the Newman–Keuls procedure, it is of interest to examine such distributions.

Consider a population having the following five elements:

Element	X
1	10
2	15
3	20
4	25
5	30

The collection of all possible samples of size $n = 3$, the sequence within the sample being disregarded, that can be constructed by sampling without replacement after each draw is enumerated in part i of Table 3.29.

In each sample in Table 3.29, the observations are arranged in order of magnitude. Thus

$$X_{(1)} < X_{(2)} < X_{(3)}.$$

Different order statistics are computed for each of the samples. The statistic d_3 is defined to be the difference between the largest and the smallest of the sample values. The statistic d_2 is the difference between the next largest and the smallest. Under a sampling plan which gives each of the samples in part i an equal chance of being drawn, the sampling distributions for d_2 and d_3 are the cumulative relative-frequency distributions in part ii. From the latter, one obtains the following probability statements:

$$P(d_2 > 10) = 0.10,$$
$$P(d_3 > 10) = 0.70.$$

In words, the probability of large values for d_3 is greater than the corresponding probability for d_2. In general the larger the range over which an ordered

TABLE 3.29   **Sampling distributions for ordered differences**

	Sample	d_2	d_3	Sample	d_2	d_3
	10, 15, 20	5	10	10, 25, 30	15	20
	10, 15, 25	5	15	15, 20, 25	5	10
(i)	10, 15, 30	5	20	15, 20, 30	5	15
	10, 20, 25	10	15	15, 25, 30	10	15
	10, 20, 30	10	20	20, 25, 30	5	10

	d_2		Cumulative rel. frequency	d_3		Cumulative rel. frequency
	20		1.00	20	III	1.00
	15	I	1.00	15	IIII	0.70
(ii)	10	III	0.90	10	III	0.30
	5	IIIII I	0.60	5		0.00

$$E(d_2) = 7.50 \qquad E(d_3) = 15.00$$
$$\text{Var}(d_2) = 11.25 \qquad \text{Var}(d_3) = 15.00$$

difference is taken, the larger the probability for a large value of that d. One notes that

$$\text{var}\,(d_3) = 15 \quad \text{is larger than} \quad \text{var}\,(d_2) = 11.25.$$

In general the larger the range over which d_j is taken, the larger the variance of the sampling distribution of that order statistic, given a specified population distribution.

The statistical principle which emerges from this example is this: When one attempts to draw inferences from statistics determined by taking into account the order of magnitude of the observations within an experiment, the approximate sampling distribution depends in part upon the number of ordered steps between the observations from which the statistic was computed. This sampling distribution also depends upon the form of the distribution in the basic population.

As a further illustration of the nature of the sampling distribution of what are called order statistics, consider random samples of size n from a normal population in which $\mu = 0$ and $\sigma = 1$. Suppose that one arranges the observations within these samples in rank order from low to high as illustrated below:

$$X^{(1)}_{\text{smallest}} \quad X_{(2)} \quad \cdots \quad X_{(k)} \quad \cdots \quad X_{(n-1)} \quad X^{(n)}_{\text{largest}}.$$

Consider the distribution of $X_{(k)}$ for these random samples. This distribution defines the sampling distribution of the (k)th order statistic. The shapes of these distributions will depend in part upon k. The expected values and standard errors of the (k)th order statistic for various values of n are given in Table 3.30.

From this table one may conclude that the expected value of an order statistic depends upon both k and n. Further, the difference between the expected value of the (k)th and the $(k+1)$th order statistic depends upon k—the larger k, the larger the magnitude of the differences between expected values. Still further, one notes that the standard error of the sampling distribution depends upon k as well as n—in general, the larger k, the larger $\sigma_{(k)}$. As one might expect, the larger n, the smaller $\sigma_{(k)}$.

The direct use of the sampling distribution of the (k)th order statistic in tests of statistical hypotheses about sets of means in the analysis-of-variance setting is of somewhat limited utility since the standard error depends upon k and the sampling distribution of the (k)th order statistic is not independent of the $(k+i)$th-order statistic, where $i \leqq 1$. (However, the covariance between such order statistics can be obtained.) A more useful approach to the problem of tests on a set of means obtained in the analysis of variance which takes into account order is through use of the studentized range statistic and a procedure known as the Newman–Keuls test. This test procedure focuses upon a series of ranges rather than a collection of differences between the expected values of order statistics.

The basic strategy underlying the Newman–Keuls approach is that the set

TABLE 3.30   **Expected value and standard error of order statistics from** $N(0, 1)$

n	(k)	$E(X_{(k)})$	$\sigma_{X_{(k)}}$	n	(k)	$E(X_{(k)})$	$\sigma_{X_{(k)}}$
3	(3)	0.85	0.75	8	(8)	1.42	0.61
	(2)	0.00	0.67		(7)	0.85	0.49
					(6)	0.47	0.45
4	(4)	1.03	0.70		(5)	0.15	0.43
	(3)	0.30	0.60				
5	(5)	1.16	0.67	9	(9)	1.49	0.60
	(4)	0.50	0.56		(8)	0.93	0.48
	(3)	0.00	0.54		(7)	0.57	0.43
					(6)	0.27	0.41
6	(6)	1.27	0.63		(5)	0.00	0.41
	(5)	0.64	0.51				
	(4)	0.20	0.50	10	(10)	1.54	0.59
					(9)	1.00	0.46
7	(7)	1.35	0.63		(8)	0.66	0.42
	(6)	0.76	0.51		(7)	0.38	0.40
	(5)	0.35	0.47		(6)	0.12	0.39
	(4)	0.00	0.46				

Note: $E(X_{(n-k+1)}) = -E(X_{(k)})$
For $n = 10$, $E(5) = -0.012$, $E(4) = -0.38$, etc.

of ranked treatment means (or totals) is divided into subsets which are consistent with the hypothesis of no differences. Within any specified subset no tests are made unless the range of the set containing the specified subset is statistically different from zero. The procedure controls the level of significance at α for each range, or ordered set, of means; for each range, the probability of a type 1 error for the test that all means are equal in each set is α.

For this purpose, the q_r statistic will be used, where r is the number of steps apart two means (or totals) are on an ordered scale. Consider the following treatment totals arranged in increasing order of magnitude:

Order	1	2	3	4	5	6	7
T_j	$T_{(1)}$	$T_{(2)}$	$T_{(3)}$	$T_{(4)}$	$T_{(5)}$	$T_{(6)}$	$T_{(7)}$

In this notation $T_{(1)}$ designates the smallest treatment total and $T_{(7)}$ the largest treatment total. $T_{(7)}$ is defined as being seven steps from $T_{(1)}$, $T_{(6)}$ is six steps from $T_{(1)}$, etc.; $T_{(7)}$ is six steps from $T_{(2)}$, $T_{(6)}$ is five steps from $T_{(2)}$, etc. In general, the number of steps between the ordered totals $T_{(j)}$ and $T_{(i)}$ is $j - i + 1$. Thus,

$$q_7 = \frac{T_{(7)} - T_{(1)}}{\sqrt{n\mathrm{MS}_{\mathrm{error}}}}.$$

There is only one q_7 statistic. There are, however, two q_6 statistics,

$$q_6 = \frac{T_{(7)} - T_{(2)}}{\sqrt{n\,\mathrm{MS}_{\mathrm{error}}}} \quad \text{and} \quad q_6 = \frac{T_{(6)} - T_{(1)}}{\sqrt{n\,\mathrm{MS}_{\mathrm{error}}}}.$$

q_7 corresponds to the ordinary studentized range statistic when $k = 7$, but q_r, where r is less than k, is a modified or truncated studentized range statistic. Critical values for q_r are obtained from tables of the studentized range statistic by setting r equal to the range. For example, the critical value for q_6 in a 0.01-level test is $q_{0.99}(6, f)$; the corresponding critical value for q_4 is $q_{0.99}(4, f)$, where f is the degrees of freedom for $\mathrm{MS}_{\mathrm{error}}$. Tables of the q statistic are given in Appendix D.4.

In terms of treatment means,

$$q_7 = \frac{\bar{T}_{(7)} - \bar{T}_{(1)}}{\sqrt{\mathrm{MS}_{\mathrm{error}}/n}}.$$

Also, $$q_6 = \frac{\bar{T}_{(7)} - \bar{T}_{(2)}}{\sqrt{\mathrm{MS}_{\mathrm{error}}/n}}, \qquad q_6 = \frac{\bar{T}_{(6)} - \bar{T}_{(1)}}{\sqrt{\mathrm{MS}_{\mathrm{error}}/n}}.$$

Rather than working directly with the critical value for the q_r statistic, it is more convenient in making a large number of tests to obtain a critical value for the difference between two totals. For example,

$$T_{(7)} - T_{(2)} = q_6\sqrt{n\,\mathrm{MS}_{\mathrm{error}}}.$$

Since the critical value for q_6 is $q_{1-\alpha}(6, f)$, the critical value for $T_{(7)} - T_{(2)}$ will be $q_{1-\alpha}(6, f)\sqrt{n\,\mathrm{MS}_{\mathrm{error}}}$. In general, the critical value for the difference between two treatment totals which are r steps apart on an ordered scale will be $q_{1-\alpha}(r, f)\sqrt{n\,\mathrm{MS}_{\mathrm{error}}}$.

The use of the q_r statistic in testing the difference between all pairs of means following a significant overall F will be illustrated by the numerical example in Table 3.31. The summary of the analysis of variance appears in part i. Since the observed F ratio (9.40) exceeds the critical value for a 0.01-level test, the hypothesis that the effects of the seven treatments are all equal is rejected.

The seven treatments are designated by the symbols a through g. The totals of the five observations under each of the treatments are arranged in increasing order of magnitude in part ii of this table. For example, treatment c has the smallest total; treatment f has the largest total. A table of differences between the treatment totals also appears in part ii. For example, the entry in column a, row c, is $T_a - T_c = 12 - 10 = 2$; the entry in column g, row a, is $T_g - T_a = 22 - 12 = 10$. In general, the entry in column j, row i, is $T_j - T_i$.

The critical values for the q_r statistic (when $\alpha = 0.01$) are given in part iii of Table 3.31. Since the mean square for experimental error has 28 degrees of freedom, $f = 28$. The entry 3.91 is obtained from tables of the studentized range statistic in which $k = 2$ and $f = 28$. The entry 4.48 is obtained from the same row of the tables, but from the column in which $k = 3$. Similarly the entry

TABLE 3.31   **Tests on all ordered pairs of means**

(i)

Sources of variation	SS	df	MS	F
Treatments	45.09	6	7.52	9.40
Experimental error	22.40	28	0.80	
Total	67.49	34		

Order	1	2	3	4	5	6	7
Treat in order of T_j	c	a	d	b	g	e	f

(ii)

T_j	10	12	13	18	22	24	25					r	$q_{0.99}(r, 28)\sqrt{n\mathrm{MS}_{\mathrm{error}}}$
	c	a	d	b	g	e	f						
c	—	2	3	8	12	14	15	—	—	—	7	— — — —	10.90
a		—		6	10	12	13	—	—	—	6	— — — —	10.56
d			—	5	9	11	12	—	—	—	5	— — — —	10.18
b				—	4	6	7	—	—	—	4	— — — —	9.68
g					—	2	3	—	—	—	3	— — — —	8.96
e						—	1	—	—	—	2	— — — —	7.82

(iii)

Truncated range r	2	3	4	5	6	7
$q_{0.99}(r, 28)$	3.91	4.48	4.84	5.09	5.28	5.45
$q_{0.99}(r, 28)\sqrt{n\mathrm{MS}_{\mathrm{error}}}$	7.82	8.96	9.69	10.18	10.56	10.90

(iv)

	c	a	d	b	g	e	f
c				**	**	**	
a				**	**	**	
d				**	**	**	

4.84 is obtained from the column in which $k = 4$. These entries are critical values for q_r; to obtain the critical value for the difference between treatment totals which are r steps apart, the critical values are multiplied by

$$\sqrt{n\mathrm{MS}_{\mathrm{error}}} = \sqrt{5(0.80)} = \sqrt{4.00} = 2.00.$$

Thus the entry $7.82 = q_{0.99}(2, 28)\sqrt{n\mathrm{MS}_{\mathrm{error}}} = (3.91)(2.00)$. Similarly the entry $10.90 = q_{0.99}(7, 28)\sqrt{n\mathrm{MS}_{\mathrm{error}}} = (5.45)(2.00)$. Hence the critical value for the difference between two treatment totals that are $r = 2$ steps apart is 7.82, whereas the critical value for the difference which is $r = 7$ steps apart is 10.90. Differences between totals an intermediate number of steps apart have critical values between these two limits.

The farther apart two means (or totals) are on an ordered scale, the larger the difference between them must be before their range exceeds its critical value. Thus, if one examines the data obtained from an experiment and decides to test the difference between the largest and the smallest mean in a set of k means, the critical value for a test of this kind is larger than the critical value for two means which are adjacent to each other on an ordered scale. The larger critical value is required because the sampling distribution of the difference between the largest and smallest means in a set of k will have a greater relative frequency of more extreme values than will the sampling distribution of two adjacent means in a set of k.

In part ii of the table of ordered differences, entries on a diagonal running from upper left to lower right have the same r value. For example, for the diagonal having the entries 2, 1, 5, 4, 2, 1, one has $r = 2$; for the diagonal having the entries 3, 6, 9, 6, 3, one has $r = 3$. The critical value for these entries appears at the extreme right. In order to avoid a type of contradiction that is explained later in this section, there is a prescribed sequence in which tests on differences between the ordered totals should be made.

1 The first test is made on the difference in the upper right-hand corner. This is the difference for which r has its maximum value, which in this case is $r = 7$. The critical value for a 0.01-level test is 10.90. Since the observed difference exceeds this critical value, the hypothesis that $\tau_{(7)} - \tau_{(1)} = \tau_f - \tau_c = 0$ is rejected. Two asterisks are placed in the cell (c, f) in part iv to indicate that this hypothesis is rejected at the 0.01 level of significance. If this hypothesis had not been rejected, no further tests would be made. If there is no significant difference between the two most extreme treatment totals, the implication is that there is no significant difference between two totals which are less extreme.

2 Tests are now made on all differences for which $r = 6$. The critical value for these tests is 10.56. The entries on the diagonal for which $r = 6$ are 14 and 13. Both entries exceed the appropriate critical value. Hence two asterisks are placed in the cells (c, e) and (a, f) in part iv.

3 Tests are next made on all differences for which $r = 5$. In this case the critical value is 10.18. The diagonal corresponding to this value of r has the entries 12, 12, 12. Since all entries on this diagonal exceed this critical value, double asterisks are entered in the corresponding cells in part iv.

4a Tests are now made on all differences for which $r = 4$. The appropriate critical value is 9.68. The entries for which $r = 4$ are 8, 10, 11, 7.

4b The entry 8 does not exceed the critical value. No further tests are made in the triangular region defined by the rows and columns of which the entry 8 forms the upper right-hand corner.

4c The entry 7 does not exceed the critical value. No further tests are made in the triangular region defined by the rows and columns of which 7 forms the upper right-hand corner.

4d The entries 10 and 11 do exceed the critical value. Hence double asterisks are placed in the corresponding cells in part iv.

5 Tests are now made on entries on the diagonal corresponding to $r = 3$ which are not in the triangular regions defined by 4b and 4c. There is just one entry to be checked, namely, 9. The critical value is 8.96, hence the corresponding ordered difference is statistically significant. No additional tests are made.

The information with respect to the significant differences summarized in part iv may be presented schematically as follows:

$$c\ a\ d\ b\ g\ e\ f.$$

Treatments underlined by a common line do not differ from each other; treatments not underlined by a common line do differ. Thus, treatment f differs from treatments c, a, and d but does not differ from b, g, e.

This sequence for making the tests prevents one from arriving at contradictory decisions of the following type: Suppose there are four means in an ordered set and that the difference $T_{(4)} - T_{(1)}$ is close to being significant but does not quite "make it." Further suppose that the difference $T_{(3)} - T_{(1)}$ is just larger than the appropriate critical value. In this case one might be tempted to conclude that there is no significant difference between the largest and the smallest means in the set but that there is a significant difference between the next to the largest and the smallest. Geometrically this conclusion would be equivalent to inferring that the distance between the largest and smallest of four means is zero but that the distance from the smallest to the next to the largest is greater than zero. Yet the latter distance has to be smaller than the former. Clearly this kind of inference leads to a contradiction.

In general, if the sequence indicated above is followed in making tests on all possible pairs of ordered means, the patterns of significant differences indicated below will *not* occur:

(1)	(2)	(3)	(4)	(5)	(1)	(2)	(3)	(4)	(5)
	*	—	*	*		*	*	—	*
		—	*	*			—	*	—
			*	—			*	—	*
			—	—				*	—

That is, between any two asterisks in the same row or column there can be no gaps (non-significant differences). Further, if the extreme position at the right of a row is a gap, then there can be no asterisks in that row or any row below that row.

When the n's do not differ markedly, as was the case with the Tukey procedure, the Newman–Keuls and Duncan methods (see next section) may be adapted for use in making tests on differences between all pairs of means. A simple approximation can be obtained by substituting the harmonic mean

$$\tilde{n} = \frac{k}{(1/n_1) + (1/n_2) + \cdots + (1/n_k)}$$

of the sample sizes for n in the equation

$$q_r = \frac{\bar{T}_j - \bar{T}_{j'}}{\sqrt{\text{MS}_{\text{error}}/n}}.$$

Alternatively, one may replace n by the harmonic mean of the sample sizes corresponding to the two extreme means. That is, n is replaced by $\dot{n}$, where

$$\dot{n} = \frac{2}{(1/n_{(1)}) + (1/n_{(k)})},$$

and $n_{(1)}$ and $n_{(k)}$ are the sample sizes corresponding to the smallest and largest treatment means, respectively. This latter procedure tends to reduce the nominal level of significance leading to a conservative bias.

DUNCAN PROCEDURE. The Newman–Keuls procedure keeps the level of significance at most α for sets of ranges and subsets of ranges within an overall inclusive range. However, the level of significance with respect to the collection of all tests considered as a single test is less than α. Thus, the power of the collection of all tests is less than that associated with an ordinary α-level test. Duncan (1955) has developed a procedure, the Duncan New Multiple Range Test (which no longer need be called new), which uses a *protection level* of α for the collection of all tests. [Scheffé (1959, p. 78) takes issue with the principles underlying the development of the sampling distributions which Duncan uses].

Duncan's procedure is based upon the argument that as the number of means increases, there should be more significant comparisons. Accordingly, as k, the number of treatment conditions increases, the power of the tests should increase systematically. This protection level corresponds to the experimentwise error rate of $1 - (1 - \alpha)^r$ for r independent tests, but is adjusted to the level for orthogonal comparisons among k means. That is, α is equal to $1 - (1 - \alpha)^{r-1}$ for means which are r steps apart corresponding to $\alpha_{\text{expw}} = 1 - (1 - \alpha)^{k-1}$ for $k - 1$ orthogonal comparisons. Thus, in terms of individual tests, a protection level with $\alpha = 0.01$ provides a level of significance equal to 0.01 for means which differ by two ordered steps; for means differing by three steps, the level of significance is equal to $1 - (0.99)^2 = 0.02$; for means differing by four steps, $\alpha = 1 - (0.99)^3 = 0.03$. In general, $\alpha = 1 - (1 - \alpha)^{r-1}$ for means which are r steps apart; with a protection level equal to α, the level of significance is numerically higher than α when the pairs are more than two steps apart.

The statistic used in the Duncan procedure is the same as that used in the Newman–Keuls test, namely, q_r, where r is the number of steps apart of two means or totals in an ordered sequence. The steps followed in using the Duncan procedure are identical to those followed in the Newman–Keuls procedure. However, the critical values for the q_r statistic are obtained from tables prepared by Duncan for use with protection levels.

For the case of $k = 7$ and degrees of freedom for experimental error equal to 28, critical values for the 0.01-level Newman–Keuls tests and the 0.01-level protection level are as follows:

k	2	3	4	5	6	7
Newman–Keuls	3.91	4.48	4.84	5.09	5.28	5.45
Duncan	3.91	4.08	4.18	4.28	4.34	4.39

When $k = 2$, the two procedures have identical critical values. For values of k larger than 2, the Duncan procedure has the smaller critical value. The larger the value of r, the larger the difference between the critical values for the two procedures. Thus, on the average, a larger difference between two means (or two totals) is required for statistical significance under the Newman–Keuls procedure.

When the Duncan procedure values are utilized to evaluate the differences in Table 3.31, the outcome is the same as for the Newman–Keuls procedure, but, in general, one would expect to declare more differences significant with the Duncan procedure.

Making Any Comparison: Scheffé Procedure

A very popular procedure for making *any* of the possible comparisons among means, not just simple comparisons between pairs of means, has been developed by Scheffé. It is widely used because it controls the level of significance for unfettered data snooping, because it is robust with regard to violations of the ANOV assumptions, and because it does not require equal sample sizes. Earlier, it was pointed out that the Tukey (hsd) procedure can be used to test hypotheses regarding any of the infinite number of comparisons among k means. However, under a variety of circumstances of interest, the Scheffé procedure is more powerful (provides shorter confidence intervals).

Of the approaches considered for controlling type 1 error in multiple comparisons, the Scheffé method is the only one which rests upon the same statistical foundation as does the overall F test in the analysis of variance (Scheffé, 1959). It is also the most conservative in the sense of requiring wider confidence bounds when applied to the problem of setting a simultaneous confidence interval on any subset of all possible differences among means. The approach has much in common with the Tukey approach; both are concerned with constructing a simultaneous confidence interval.

The Scheffé method uses a confidence interval on the maximum normalized comparison. In Sec. 3.10, the maximum comparison among k means was defined and it was pointed out that the analysis of variance test is equivalent to testing the hypothesis that the comparison corresponding to $\hat{\psi}_{max}$ is significant under the Scheffé procedure.

The Scheffé approach to multiple comparisons is actually based upon using the maximum *normalized* comparison to establish a confidence interval.

A normalized comparison is one in which $\sum (c_j^2/n_j) = 1.0$. If a comparison is

$$C = \sum c_j \bar{T}_j = c_1 \bar{T}_1 + c_2 \bar{T}_2 + \cdots + c_k \bar{T}_k, \qquad \sum (c_j/n_j) = 0,$$

then the corresponding normalized comparison is

$$C^* = \sum c_j^* \bar{T}_j = c_1^* \bar{T}_1 + c_2^* \bar{T}_2 + \cdots + c_k^* \bar{T}_k$$

where
$$c_j^* = \frac{c_j}{\sqrt{\sum (c_j^2/n_j)}} \qquad \begin{array}{l} \sum (c_j^*/n_j) = 0 \\ \sum (c_j^{*2}/n_j) = 1. \end{array}$$

One notes that

$$\mathrm{MS}_c = \frac{C^2}{\sum c_j^{*2}/n_j} = C^{*2},$$

since $\sum (c_j^{*2}/n_j) = 1$. Thus, if C^* is maximum for any set of data, MS_c will be maximum.

The maximum normalized comparison is defined when

$$c_j^* = \frac{n_j(\bar{T}_j - \bar{G})}{\sqrt{\mathrm{SS}_{\mathrm{treat}}}}.$$

Hence,
$$\sum (c_j^{*2}/n_j) = \frac{\sum n_j^2(\bar{T}_j - \bar{G})^2/n_j}{\mathrm{SS}_{\mathrm{treat}}} = \frac{\mathrm{SS}_{\mathrm{treat}}}{\mathrm{SS}_{\mathrm{treat}}} = 1.$$

For the normalized comparison

$$C_{\max}^* = \sum c_j^* \bar{T}_j = \frac{\sum n_j(\bar{T}_j - \bar{G})\bar{T}_j}{\sqrt{\mathrm{SS}_{\mathrm{treat}}}} = \sqrt{\mathrm{SS}_{\mathrm{treat}}},$$

and
$$C_{\max}^{*2} = \mathrm{SS}_{\mathrm{treat}}.$$

Suppose that $C_{\max}^*$ is the maximum normalized comparison for a set of k means; $\psi_{\max}^*$ is the corresponding comparison among population means. Scheffé has shown that the following confidence statement holds:

$$C[C_{\max}^* - A_{\mathrm{Scheffé}}^* \leq \psi_{\max}^* \leq C_{\max}^* + A_{\mathrm{Scheffé}}] = 1 - \alpha,$$

where
$$A_{\mathrm{Scheffé}}^* = \sqrt{(k-1)F_{1-\alpha}[(k-1), (N-k)]\mathrm{MS}_{\mathrm{error}}},$$

and $k = $ number of treatments in the analysis of variance,

$n_j = $ sample size under treatment j,

$N = \sum n_j$,

$\mathrm{MS}_{\mathrm{error}} = $ mean square due to error in the analysis of variance.

If this confidence statement holds for the maximum comparison, it will hold simultaneously for all comparisons. Thus, one has the following joint confidence statement:

$$C[C^* - A_{\mathrm{Scheffé}}^* \leq \psi^* \leq C^* + A_{\mathrm{Scheffé}}^*] \geq 1 - \alpha$$

for any normalized comparison. In terms of non-normalized comparisons, the joint confidence interval takes the form

$$C[C - A_{\text{Scheffé}} \leq \psi \leq C + A_{\text{Scheffé}}] \geq 1 - \alpha,$$

where $A_{\text{Scheffé}} = \sqrt{(k - 1)F_{1-\alpha}[(k - 1), (N - k)]} \sqrt{MS_{\text{error}}/(\sum c_j^2/n_j)},$

and the estimate of the standard error of the comparison is

$$\sqrt{MS_{\text{error}}/\sum (c_j^2/n_j)}.$$

Since this latter value depends upon both c_j and n_j, the allowance factor depends upon both.

   This confidence interval on a collection of comparisons is true only if all of the statements it contains are true simultaneously $100(1 - \alpha)$ percent of the time. One or more of the statements will be false at most 100α percent of the time under replications of the experiment. The confidence interval is exact for the maximum value of ψ. For all other ψ, the confidence interval is conservative in the sense that the confidence coefficient is actually greater than $1 - \alpha$. Since one is always evaluating a subset of all possible comparisons, the procedure is very conservative.

   If the overall test in the analysis of variance is significant, then one or more comparisons will be significant under the Scheffé procedure.

   It was noted in Sec. 3.10 that the overall test in the analysis of variance is equivalent to testing the hypothesis that ψ_{max} is significant under the Scheffé procedure. To test the hypothesis

$$H_0: |\psi^*_{\text{max}}| = 0,$$

reject H_0 if $\quad |\hat{\psi}^*_{\text{max}}| > \sqrt{(k - 1)F_{1-\alpha}(k - 1, f)} \sqrt{MS_{\text{error}}}.$

If one squares both sides of this last decision rule, one obtains:

Reject H_0 if $\quad \hat{\psi}^{*2}_{\text{max}} > (k - 1)F_{1-\alpha}(k - 1, f)MS_{\text{error}}.$

Equivalently,

Reject H_0 if $\quad SS_{\text{treat}} > (k - 1)F_{1-\alpha}(k - 1, f)MS_{\text{error}},$

which may be cast in the form

$$\text{Reject } H_0 \text{ if } \quad F = \frac{SS_{\text{treat}}/(k - 1)}{MS_{\text{error}}} > F_{1-\alpha}(k - 1, f).$$

This decision rule is identical to the overall F test in the analysis of variance.

   For other tests of significance, the Scheffé confidence interval may be converted into a collection of tests on all possible comparisons with $\alpha_{\text{Scheffé}}$ at some specified value as follows:

$$\text{Reject } \quad H_0: |\psi| = 0 \quad \text{if} \quad |\hat{\psi}| > A_{\text{Scheffé}}.$$

This procedure is exactly equivalently to computing the F statistic used for individual comparisons in Sec. 3.10 and rejecting the null hypothesis if

$$F_{\text{obs}} > (k-1)F_{1-\alpha}[k-1, k(n-1)],$$

where

$$F_{\text{obs}} = \frac{SS_{\hat{\psi}}}{MS_{\text{error}}},$$

and

$$F_{1-\alpha}[k-1, k(n-1)]$$

is the critical value of F used to test the overall analysis of variance hypothesis.

As a numerical example, suppose a researcher were interested in testing the hypothesis

$$H_0: 3\tau_f + 3\tau_e - 2\tau_b - 2\tau_c - 2\tau_d = 0$$

$$H_1: \text{Not } H_0$$

$$\alpha_{\text{Scheffé}} = 0.01.$$

Using the information from Table 3.31 and working with totals instead of means, one has

$$\hat{\psi}_{\text{Totals}} = C_T = \sum c_j T_j = 3T_f + 3T_e - 2T_b - 2T_c - 2T_d$$

$$= 3(25) + 3(24) - 2(18) - 2(16) - 2(13) = 65.$$

Since $F_{0.99}(6, 28) = 3.53$,

$$A_{\text{Scheffé(Totals)}} = \sqrt{n \sum c_j^2 MS_{\text{error}}} \sqrt{(k-1)F_{1-\alpha}[k-1, k(n-1)]}$$

$$= \sqrt{(5)(30)(0.80)} \sqrt{(6)(3.53)} = 50.41.$$

Thus, $|\hat{\psi}_{\text{Totals}}| = 65$ is greater than $A_{\text{Scheffé(Totals)}} = 50.41$ and the decision is to reject H_0 with the probability of type 1 error being at most equal to 0.01.

An alternative procedure would be to compute

$$F = \frac{SS_c}{MS_{\text{error}}}$$

$$= \frac{C_T^2/n \sum c_j^2}{MS_{\text{error}}}$$

$$= \frac{(\sum c_j T_j)^2}{MS_{\text{error}}(n)(\sum c_j^2)}$$

and reject H_0 if $F > (k-1)F[k-1, k(n-1)]$.

Thus

$$F_{\text{obs}} = \frac{65^2}{(0.80)(5)(30)} = 35.21$$

and since $F_{\text{obs}} = 35.21 > (k-1)F_{0.99}[k-1, k(n-1)] = 21.18$, the decision is to reject H_0.

Another advantage of the Scheffé method over the Tukey method is that the power function of the tests made under the Scheffé method is well known—this power function is a slight modification of the power function of the usual F test. The power function of tests based upon the Tukey method has not been studied extensively.

3.12 COMPARING COMPARISON METHODS

The different procedures which have been presented for evaluating comparisons are each optimal for some particular situation and should be used accordingly. It may be instructive, however, to compare them in common situations.

In Table 3.32, the critical values of various test techniques are presented scaled to the common unit of t statistics when they are used with equal sample sizes for multiple tests on simple differences with two-tailed tests.

TABLE 3.32   **Comparison of critical values for test procedures on simple differences**

	Test statistic	Critical value
(1)	*A priori* $t = |\bar{T}_j - \bar{T}_{j'}|/\sqrt{2MS_{error}/n}$	$t_{1-(\alpha/2)}(f_{error})$
(2)	Dunnet $t = |\bar{T}_0 - \bar{T}_j|/\sqrt{2MS_{error}/n}$	$t_{1-(\alpha/2)}^{Dunnett}(k, f_{error})$
(3)	Bechhofer–Dunnett $t = |\bar{T}_j - \bar{T}_{j'}|/\sqrt{2MS_{error}/n}$	$t_{1-\alpha}^{Bech}(m, f_{error}),\quad m = k - 1$
(4)	Dunn–Bonferroni $t = |\bar{T}_j - \bar{T}_{j'}|/\sqrt{2MS_{error}/n}$	$t_{1-\alpha}^{Bon}(m, f_{error}),\quad m = k - 1$
(5)	Tukey (hsd) $t = \dfrac{1}{\sqrt{2}}q = \dfrac{1}{\sqrt{2}}|\bar{T}_j - \bar{T}_{j'}|/\sqrt{MS_{error}/n}$	$t = \dfrac{1}{\sqrt{2}}q_{1-\alpha}(k, f_{error})$
(6)	Newman–Keuls $t = \dfrac{1}{\sqrt{2}}q = \dfrac{1}{\sqrt{2}}|\bar{T}_j - \bar{T}_{j'}|/\sqrt{MS_{error}/n}$	$t = \dfrac{1}{\sqrt{2}}q_{1-\alpha}(r, f_{error})\quad m = k(k-1)/2$
(7)	Scheffé $t = \sqrt{F} = \bar{T}_j - \bar{T}_{j'}/\sqrt{2MS_{error}/n}$	$t = \sqrt{(k-1)F_{1-\alpha}(k-1, f_{error})}$

k	n	$f=k(n-1)$	α	(1)	(2)	(3)	(4)	(5)	(6)	(7)
3	5	12	0.05	2.18	2.50	2.54	2.56	2.67	2.78	2.79
			0.01	3.05	3.39	3.42	3.43	3.56	3.65	3.72
4	5	16	0.05	2.12	2.59	2.65	2.67	2.86	3.01	3.12
			0.01	2.92	3.39	3.43	3.44	3.67	3.77	3.98
6	5	24	0.05	2.06	2.70	2.77	2.80	3.09	3.26	3.62
			0.01	2.80	3.40	3.46	3.47	3.80	3.91	4.41
7	5	28	0.05	2.05	2.74	2.82	2.84	3.18	3.34	3.83
			0.01	2.76	3.43	3.47	3.48	3.87	3.95	4.60
5	11	50	0.05	2.01	2.53	2.58	2.59	2.83	2.94	3.59
			0.01	2.67	3.16	3.18	3.18	3.44	3.50	3.87
10	11	100	0.05	1.98	2.70	2.82	2.83	3.31	3.36	4.24
			0.01	2.63	3.29	3.38	3.56	3.80	3.83	4.87
15	5	60	0.05	2.00	2.93	3.02	3.03	3.54	3.70	5.11
			0.01	2.58	3.33	3.56	3.59	3.85	3.90	5.40
15		∞	0.05	1.96	2.81	2.91	2.91	3.39	3.49	4.87
			0.01	2.58	3.33	3.38	3.38	3.85	3.90	5.40
20		∞	0.05	1.96	2.90	3.00	3.01	3.54	3.65	5.51
			0.01	2.58	3.41	3.47	3.47	3.99	4.04	6.01

It is apparent from Table 3.32 that the methods appear in increasing order of conservativeness when applied to a set of simple differences between means. Least conservative, and providing no control over the level of significance for a set of tests, is a series of t (or F) tests [Column (1)]. Dunnett's t, because it controls α for only the small subset of $k - 1$ tests on differences between a control condition mean and a set of $k - 1$ treatment condition means, is the next most liberal with regard to α. It was previously mentioned that the Bechhofer–Dunnett procedure is more powerful than the Dunn–Bonferroni procedure since control of α is for only orthogonal comparisons in the first case and for all comparisons in the latter case. The Tukey (hsd) and Scheffé procedures are the most conservative.

Even though the Scheffé procedure is the most conservative when applied to these simple differences, it does not give the widest confidence interval for all comparisons. In general, when k is large relative to m, the Dunn–Bonferroni or Bechhofer–Dunnett confidence intervals will be narrower than the Scheffé confidence bounds. When k is small and m is large relative to k, the Scheffé confidence bounds will be shorter. When Scheffé bounds are compared to the Tukey (hsd) confidence intervals, Tukey confidence intervals have wider bounds when comparisons involve c_j which differ markedly from each other; Scheffé bounds are wider for comparisons wherein the c_j are similar.

Another interesting comparison among methods is provided in Table 3.33. Using the numerical example for testing all $k(k - 1)/2$ simple differences between pairs of means presented in Tables 3.28 and 3.31, Table 3.33 presents the critical values for differences between pairs of ordered totals. Table 3.33 compares only those procedures which are in some sense optimal for this particular set of comparisons [Duncan, Newman–Keuls, Tukey (hsd)] to individual t or F tests for *a priori* comparisons and to the Scheffé procedure. For purposes of constructing this table, all values were corrected to q using the relation

$$q_r = \sqrt{2F}.$$

The critical value for a test on individual components of variation for totals

TABLE 3.33 **Comparison of methods of comparison**

Method	k:	2	3	4	5	6	7
Scheffé		13.02	13.02	13.02	13.02	13.02	13.02
Tukey (hsd)		10.90	10.90	10.90	10.90	10.90	10.90
Newman–Keuls		7.82	8.96	9.69	10.18	10.56	10.90
Duncan		7.82	8.16	8.36	8.56	8.68	8.78
Individual comparisons		7.82	7.82	7.82	7.82	7.82	7.82

which are two steps apart $(r = 2)$ would be used for all tests for individual comparisons. Thus, $q_{2_{(1-\alpha)}} = \sqrt{2F_{0.99}(1, 28)} = \sqrt{2.64} = 3.91$ is the critical value for all comparisons, and 7.82 is the critical value for differences between all treatment totals. For the Scheffé procedure,

$$q_{r_{(1-\alpha)}} = \sqrt{2(k-1)F_{0.99}[(k-1), k(n-1)]}$$
$$= \sqrt{2(6)(3.53)} = 6.51$$

and the critical value for differences is 13.02 for all pairs. When applied to these data, the individual F statistics yield ten "significant" differences, the Duncan and Newman–Keuls procedures each detect nine differences, and the Tukey (hsd) and Scheffé procedures lead to the conclusion that there are seven and two differences, respectively. What is happening, of course, is that the real levels of significance vary markedly with the values presented in Table 3.33.

To illustrate the difference in the size of type 1 error associated with individual tests which disregard the order of differences, the q_r statistic may be transformed into an F statistic by the relation

$$F = \frac{q_r^2}{2}.$$

For example, for the case where $k = 7$ and $k(n-1) = 28$, critical values for the 0.01-level Newman–Keuls and 0.01-level Duncan protection level are 5.45 and 4.39, respectively, for means which are $r = 7$ steps apart. These q_r values are equivalent to F's of 14.85 and 8.63. Relative to the critical value for an individual comparison made by means of an F statistic, the type 1 error associated with the difference between two totals which are seven steps apart is:

	Critical F value	"Actual" α
Individual comparison	7.64	0.01
Newman–Keuls	14.85	0.0005
Duncan	8.63	0.007

In other words, if a 0.01-level test were made on the difference between two means that are seven steps apart on an ordered scale, assuming that MS_{error} has 28 degrees of freedom, and if the order of the means in the sample were disregarded, the critical value would be $F = 7.64$. If, however, the order were taken into account, the equivalent critical value would be 14.85. With a protection level equal to 0.01, the equivalent critical value would be 8.63. Clearly, the "level of significance" varies markedly depending upon the choice of the testing procedure.

3.13 TREATMENT MAGNITUDE—DEPENDENT VARIABLE RELATIONSHIPS: TREND ANALYSIS AND STRENGTH OF ASSOCIATION

The overall analysis of variance provides limited information about the outcome of an experiment. The test of significance merely tells one whether or not there are population treatment effects. Knowing that there are, indeed, treatment effects, other questions arise; two of these concern the nature and magnitude of the association between the treatment condition and the dependent variable.

Trend Analysis

At the heart of scientific analysis is the goal of establishing the nature of the functions which relate the magnitudes of independent and dependent variables. In the context of experimental design, this goal may be pursued when treatments are quantitative; when treatments are qualitative in nature, the form of the relationship is meaningless.

One way to express the nature of the relationship between treatments and the dependent variable is to use polynomials. At the simplest level, the relationship may be linear. If so, a first degree equation of the form

$$\text{Response} = b_0 + b_1 \text{ (treatment magnitude)}$$

could be used to fit the observed data and to estimate the linear equation needed to fit the population data. If the relationship is quadratic, a second-degree equation of the form

$$\text{Response} = b_0 + b_1 \text{ (treatment magnitude)} + b_2 \text{ (treatment magnitude)}^2$$

would be required. In general, one wants to know the equation of the lowest degree which is required to fit the relationship from the general polynomial

$$X = b_0 + b_1 t + b_2 t^2 + b_3 t^3 + \cdots + b_{k-1} t^{k-1}$$

where

X = dependent variable magnitudes

t = treatment conditions magnitudes

b_0 = a constant

$b_1 t$ = linear component

$b_2 t^2$ = quadratic component

$b_3 t^3$ = cubic component

$$\vdots$$

$b_{k-1} t^{k-1} = k - 1$th component.

Consider the data presented in Fig. 3-6, which are typical of what one might expect from an experiment. The observed treatment means vary and the observations vary within treatments. If F leads to rejection of the overall

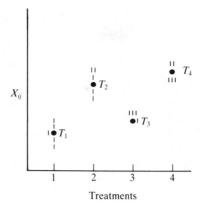

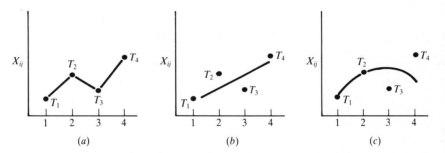

FIGURE 3-6   Fitting line of means ($n = 5$, $k = 4$) with a cubic (a), linear (b), or quadratic (c) function.

hypothesis that the four treatment population means are equal, the conclusion is that the treatments *do* influence the dependent variable means. This conclusion is equivalent to the conclusion that there is *some* trend to the relationship between treatment magnitudes and the dependent variable means. The questions to be answered have to do with the nature of that trend.

In general, one can always fit k data points perfectly with a polynomial of degree $k - 1$. For example, with only $k = 2$ points, one can fit the two points without error by connecting them with a straight line. Consider the means in Fig. 3-6. They can be fit perfectly with a cubic equation (Fig. 3-6a). However, some of the variations among the means may be due to random error and a reasonable fit may be possible with a linear (Fig. 3-6b) or quadratic (Fig. 3-6c) equation. The goal with real data is to fit the data points with the polynomial of the smallest possible degree. One way to determine the simplest equation is through the use of trend analysis using orthogonal polynomials.

Orthogonal polynomials are polynomials, the various terms of which are independent, making it possible to reconceptualize the general polynomial

$$X = b_0 + b_1 t + b_2 t^2 + b_3 t_3^2 + \cdots + b_{k-1} t^{k-1},$$

as
$$X = b_0' + b_1' c_{1j} + b_2' c_{2j} + b_3' c_{3j} + \cdots + b_{k-1}' c_{k-1,j}.$$

In this latter equation, b_0' is a scaling constant. The b_1' through b_{k-1}' are coefficients in the polynomial corresponding to trends of different degrees (i.e., $b_1' = $ linear, $b_2' = $ quadratic, etc.). The c_{ij}'s are orthogonal polynomial coefficients which are transformations of the treatment condition magnitudes t_j which are derived so that each product $b_i c_{ij}$ is an orthogonal component of the overall trend of the observations. Since it is really the trend of the treatment *means* which is of interest here, the *population* trend equation is

$$\mu_j = \beta_0' + \beta_1' c_{1j} + \beta_2' c_{2j} + \beta_3' c_{3j} + \cdots + \beta_{k-1}' c_{k-1,j}$$

and the estimate of that equation based upon fitting the observed treatment means is

$$\bar{T}_j = b_0' + b_1' c_{1j} + b_2' c_{2j} + b_3' c_{3j} + \cdots + b_{k-1}' c_{k-1,j}.$$

It is the c_{ij}'s which are of interest. In general,

$$c_{1j} = a_1 + t_j$$
$$c_{2j} = a_2 + b_2 t_j + t_j^2$$
$$c_{3j} = a_3 + b_3 t_j + c_3 t_j^2 + t_j^3$$
$$\vdots$$
$$c_{k-1,j} = a_{k-1} + b_{k-1} t_j + c_{k-1} t_j^2 + d_{k-1} t_j^3 + \cdots + t_j^{k-1}.$$

The c_{ij}'s must be chosen to meet the constraints of orthogonality of trend components. Tables of orthogonal polynomial coefficients have been published for the case where treatment condition magnitudes are equally spaced (e.g., drug dosages of 1, 2 or 3 cc) and sample sizes are equal. The most complete set of coefficients is in the work of Anderson and Houseman (1942). The Fisher and Yates tables (1953) have an adequate set. Table 10, Appendix D provides values for $k = 3 - 10$ and trends up to quintic. When treatment conditions are not equally spaced and/or sample sizes are not equal, coefficients may be derived (Gaito, 1965; Grandage, 1958; Kirk, 1982; Robson, 1959).

In Sec. 3.10 a comparison among treatments was defined

$$\psi_i = c_{i1} \tau_1 + c_{i2} \tau_2 + \cdots + c_{ij} \tau_j + \cdots + c_{ik} \tau_k$$

and was estimated as

$$\hat{\psi}_i = C_i = c_{i1} \bar{T}_1 + c_{i2} \bar{T}_2 + \cdots + c_{ij} \bar{T}_j + \cdots + c_{ik} \bar{T}_k$$

when the coefficients are chosen with the restriction that $\sum c_{ij} = 0$. When two comparisons are defined, they are orthogonal when $\sum c_{ij} c_{i'j} = 0$. Further, it was shown that the total variation among the k means could be partitioned into $k - 1$ orthogonal components, each component being associated with a particular comparison. An F statistic was used to test the hypothesis H_0: $\psi = 0$ for each comparison. Exactly the same logic can be used to evaluate the various components of the overall polynomial equation by using orthogonal polynomial coefficients to construct the comparisons.

Consider the orthogonal polynomial coefficients for the case of $k = 4$ treatments (from Table D 10):

	Treatments			
Trend	**1**	**2**	**3**	**4**
Linear	−3	−1	1	3
Quadratic	1	−1	−1	1
Cubic	−1	3	−3	1

Note that each set of coefficients forms a trend corresponding to an equation of its respective degree. Note also that for each trend, $\sum c_{ij} = 0$ and that the comparisons are all mutually orthogonal (i.e., $\sum c_{ij}c_{i'j} = 0$). Since these coefficients define mutually orthogonal comparisons, $k - 1$ orthogonal components of SS_{treat} are defined by

$$SS_{trend_i} = \frac{C_i^2}{\sum c_{ij}^2/n},$$

and
$$SS_{treat} = SS_{linear} + SS_{quad} + SS_{cubic} + \cdots + SS_{k-1}.$$

SS_{linear} is the variation between treatments (variation of the line of means) which can be accounted for by a linear trend; $SS_{quadratic}$ is the increase in predictability due to adding a quadratic term to a linear function; SS_{cubic} provides the increment in predictability due to adding a cubic term to the polynomial; etc.; through SS_{k-1}.

To illustrate, suppose that an experimenter is interested in approximating the form of the relationship between the degree of complexity of a visual display (i.e., an instrument panel containing a series of dials) and the reaction time of subjects in responding to the displacement of one or more of the dials. After deciding upon a definition of the complexity scale, the experimenter constructs six displays representing six equal steps along this scale. The treatments in this experiment correspond to the degree of complexity of the displays. Random samples of 10 subjects are assigned to each of the displays; each sample is observed under only one of the displays. The criterion used in the analysis is the mean reaction time (or some transformation thereof) for each subject to a series of trials which are as comparable as the displays permit.

Summary data for this experiment are presented in Table 3.34. Steps in the computation of the sums of squares are given in part ii.

The analysis of variance appears in Table 3.35. Since there are six displays,

TABLE 3.34 **Numerical examples**

	Complexity of display	1	2	3	4	5	6	$k = 6; n = 10$ Total
(i)	T_j	100	110	120	180	190	210	$910 = G$
	$\sum X_j^2$	1180	1210	1600	3500	3810	4610	$15{,}910 = \sum \left(\sum X^2 \right)$
	$\bar{T}_j$	10.0	11.0	12.0	18.0	19.0	21.0	

(ii)

$$(1) = G^2/kn = (910)^2/60 \qquad\qquad = 13{,}801.67$$

$$(2) = \sum \left(\sum X^2 \right) \qquad\qquad = 15{,}910$$

$$(3) = \left(\sum T_j^2 \right) \Big/ n = (100^2 + 110^2 + \cdots + 210^2)/10 = 14{,}910.00$$

$$\text{SS}_{\text{displays}} = (3) - (1) = 1108.33$$
$$\text{SS}_{\text{error}} \;\; = (2) - (3) = 1000.00$$

$$\text{SS}_{\text{total}} \;\; = (2) - (1) = 2108.33$$

the degrees of freedom for the displays are $6 - 1 = 5$. Ten subjects were used under each display. Hence the sum of squares within a single display has degrees of freedom equal to 9; the pooled within-display variation has $6 \times 9 = 54$ degrees of freedom. The pooled within-display variation defines the experimental error. To test the hypothesis that the mean reaction times (or the means of the transformed measures) for the displays are equal,

$$F = \frac{\text{MS}_{\text{displays}}}{\text{MS}_{\text{error}}} = \frac{221.67}{18.52} = 11.97.$$

The critical value for this test, using the 0.01 level of significance, is

$$F_{0.99}(5, 54) = 3.38.$$

Clearly the data indicate that reaction times for the displays differ. Inspection of the T_j's in Table 3.34 shows that the greater the degree of complexity, the

TABLE 3.35 **Summary of analysis of variance**

Source of variation	SS	df	MS	F
Displays	1108.33	5	221.67	11.97**
Experimental error	1000.00	54	18.52	
Total	2108.33	59		

$^{**}\ F_{0.99}(5, 54) = 3.38$

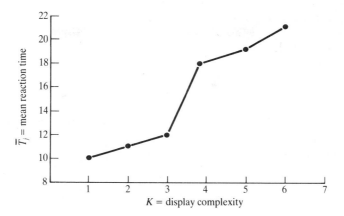

FIGURE 3-7

slower the reaction time. The means corresponding to the $\bar{T_j}$'s are plotted in Fig. 3-7. Since there are six treatment conditions, the data points can be perfectly fit by a fifth-order equation regardless of the arrangement of the means. That is, if the variation were to be computed for all trends, for these data

$$SS_{displays} = SS_{lin} + SS_{quad} + SS_{cubic} + SS_{quartic} + SS_{quintic}.$$

The goal, however, is to determine the lowest level of trend which is required to fit the data. In that regard, this figure shows a strong linear relationship between display complexity and reaction time. There is also the suggestion that an S-shaped curve might be the best-fitting curve; an S-shaped curve corresponds to an equation having degrees 3 (cubic).

In the upper left part of Table 3.36 are the coefficients for linear, quadratic and cubic comparisons for $k = 6$ obtained from Appendix D, Table 10. Notice that the sum of the linear coefficients is zero, that each coefficient differs by 2 units from its neighbor, and that only once in the sequence from -5 to $+5$ does the sign change. For the coefficients defining the quadratic comparison, the signs change twice in the sequence from $+5$ to $+5$; in the cubic comparison there are three changes of sign in the sequence from -5 to $+5$. The number of times the signs change corresponds to the degree of the polynomial.

The numerical value of a comparison for a trend of any degree i is

$$C_{trend} = \sum c_{ij}\bar{T_j} \qquad \left(\sum c_{ij} = 0\right),$$

where the c_{ij} are the orthogonal polynomial coefficients. Thus, the numerical

TABLE 3.36 **Tests for trend**

	Complexity	1	2	3	4	5	6	$\sum c^2$	C	$n\sum c^2$	$SS_{trend} = \dfrac{C^2}{n\sum c_{ij}^2}$
	T_j	100	110	120	180	190	210				
	Linear	−5	−3	−1	1	3	5	70	850	700	1032.14
(i)	Quadratic	5	−1	−4	−4	−1	5	84	50	840	2.98
	Cubic	−5	7	4	−4	−7	5	180	−250	1800	34.72
											1069.84

(ii)

Test for linear trend: $F = \dfrac{1032.14}{18.52} = 55.73**$

Test for quadratic trend: $F = \dfrac{2.98}{18.52} = 0.16$

Test for cubic trend: $F = \dfrac{34.72}{18.52} = 1.87$

$$** F_{0.99}(1, 54) = 7.14$$

values for the first three comparisons are:

$$C_{lin} = (-5)(100) + (-3)(110) + (-1)(120)$$
$$+ (1)(180) + (3)(190) + (5)(210) = 850,$$
$$C_{quad} = (5)(100) + (-1)(110) + (-4)(120)$$
$$+ (-4)(180) + (-1)(190) + (5)(210) = 50, \quad \text{and}$$
$$C_{cubic} = (-5)(100) + (7)(110) + (4)(120)$$
$$+ (-4)(180) + (-7)(190) + (5)(210) = -250.$$

The component of variation (of means) corresponding to a trend of any degree is

$$SS_{trend} = \frac{C_{trend}^2}{\sum c_{ij}^2 / n}.$$

The component of variation corresponding to the linear comparison (of totals) is

$$SS_{lin} = \frac{C_{lin}^2}{n \sum c_{1j}^2}$$

$$= \frac{850^2}{10[(-5)^2 + (-3)^2 + (-1)^2 + 1^2 + 3^2 + 5^2]}$$

$$= \frac{850^2}{10(70)} = 1032.14.$$

The other two components of variation of interest, SS_{quad} and SS_{cubic}, are 2.98 and 34.72. Thus, the three trends collectively "account for" 1069.84 units of the total variation between displays ($SS_{displays} = 1108.33$). This is 96.5 percent of the treatment variation. Ninety-three percent ($1032.14/1108.33$) of the variation in the mean reaction time for the displays may be predicted from a linear equation.

The test of significance for any trend is

$$F = \frac{SS_{trend}}{MS_{error}},$$

and provides a test of the null hypothesis, H_0: $\psi_{trend} = 0$. For the linear trend,

$$F = \frac{\text{linear component}}{MS_{error}} = \frac{1032.14}{18.52} = 55.73.$$

The critical value for a 0.01-level test is $F_{0.99}(1, f)$, where f is the degrees of freedom for MS_{error}. In this case $f = 54$, and the critical value is 7.14. Clearly the linear trend is statistically significant. However,

$$1108.33 - 1032.14 = 76.19$$

units of reaction-time variation are not predicted by the linear regression equation. There is still the possibility that a higher-order trend might be statistically significant.

In general, one may evaluate for any trend whether a higher-order trend is needed to fit the data by computing the variation $SS_{deviation\ from\ trend}$ and evaluating that source of variation for significance with an F ratio. For example, an overall measure of deviation from linearity is given by

$$SS_{nonlin} = SS_{displays} - SS_{lin} = 1108.33 - 1032.14 = 76.19.$$

The degrees of freedom for this source of variation are $k - 2$. An overall test for nonlinearity is given by

$$F = \frac{SS_{nonlin}/(k - 2)}{MS_{error}} = \frac{76.19/4}{18.52} = \frac{19.05}{18.52} = 1.03.$$

For a 0.01-level test, the critical value is $F_{0.99}(4.54) = 3.68$. Since the F ratio does not exceed this critical value, the data do not indicate significant deviations from linearity. However, when the degrees of freedom for MS_{nonlin} are large, the overall test may mask a significant higher-order component. In spite of the fact that the overall test indicates no significant deviations from linearity, if there is *a priori* evidence that a higher-order component might be meaningful, tests may continue beyond the linear component. Caution is required in the interpretation of significant higher-order trend components when the overall test for nonlinearity indicates no significant nonlinear trend. In the absence of a strong theory which predicts an equation of higher order than a linear trend, these particular data should not be examined for higher-order trends. It is well to keep in mind that the tests of significance being used here are appropriate only for *a priori* hypotheses and that the level of significance for the total set of m tests is increasing at the rate $1 - (1 - \alpha)^m$. Be that as it may, it is interesting to continue the analysis for illustrative purposes.

The quadratic comparison is orthogonal to the linear comparison, since the sum of the products of corresponding coefficients is zero, i.e.,

$$(-5)(5) + (-3)(-1) + (-1)(-4) + (1)(-4) + (3)(-1) + (5)(5) = 0.$$

Therefore the quadratic component of variation is part of the 76.19 units of variation which are not predicted by the linear component. This is the increase in predictability that would accrue for the sample data by using a second-degree instead of a first-degree equation. A test on whether or not this increase in predictability is significantly greater than zero uses the statistic

$$F = \frac{\text{quadratic component}}{\text{MS}_{\text{error}}} = \frac{2.98}{18.52} = 0.16.$$

The critical value for a 0.01-level test is $F_{0.99}(1, f)$; in this case the critical value is 7.14. The F statistic for quadratic trend is 0.16. Hence, the increase in predictability due to the quadratic component is not significantly different from zero.

It is readily verified that the cubic comparison is orthogonal to both the linear and quadratic components. Thus, the cubic component is part of the $1108.33 - 1032.14 - 2.98 = 73.21$ units of variation not predicted by the linear or quadratic trends. A test of the hypothesis, H_0: $\psi_{\text{cubic}} = 0$ is

$$F = \frac{34.72}{18.52} = 1.87,$$

leading to the expected conclusion that no improvement in goodness of fit occurs when a cubic component is added to the prediction equation.

Of the total of 1108.33 units of variation due to differences in complexity of the displays, 1069.84 units are predictable from the linear, quadratic, and cubic components. The remaining variation is due to higher-order components, none of which would be significantly different from zero. In summary, the linear trend appears to be the only trend that is significantly greater than zero. Hence a first-degree equation (linear equation) is the form of the best-fitting curve.

Having determined the degree of equation needed to fit the relation between the line of means of the dependent variable and the magnitudes of the independent variable, a next goal may be to actually fit an equation of the appropriate degree to the data. Subsequent to that, one may want to evaluate how well that equation actually fits the data.

In this case the linear equation will have the form

$$X = bK + a,$$

where X = predicted reaction time,

K = degree of complexity of display,

b, a = regression coefficients.

The regression coefficient b is given by the relation

$$b = \sqrt{\frac{\text{linear component}}{\text{SS}_K}} = \sqrt{\frac{\text{SS}_{\text{lin}}}{\text{SS}_K}}.$$

Equivalently,
$$b = \frac{\lambda_1 C_{\text{lin}}}{D_{\text{lin}}},$$

where λ_1 is a constant which depends upon k; tables of coefficients for the orthogonal polynomials will give values of λ_1. The numerical value of the regression coefficient a is given by the relation

$$a = \bar{X} - b\bar{K}.$$

Computation of the coefficients for the regression equation is summarized in Table 3.37.

Note that since the degree of complexity of the displays is assumed to be equally spaced along a complexity dimension, the degree of complexity may conveniently be indicated by the integers $1, 2, \ldots, 6$. The sum of squares for the complexity variable is given by

$$\text{SS}_K = \frac{n(k^3 - k)}{12},$$

where k is the number of displays and n is the number of observations under each display. The entry 12 is constant for all values of n and k.

In general, in working with higher-order regression equations, to predict V from U it is convenient to work with the equation in the second of the following forms:

$$V = a_0 + a_1 U + a_2 U^2 + a_3 U^3$$
$$= A_0' \xi_0' + A_1' \xi_1' + A_2' \xi_2' + A_3' \xi_3'.$$

TABLE 3.37 **Computation of regression equation**

X = reaction time $\qquad$ K = display complexity

$\bar{X} = G/kn = 15.17$ $\qquad$ $\bar{K} = (k+1)/2 = 3.50$

$$\text{SS}_K = \frac{n(k^3 - k)}{12} = \frac{(10)(216 - 6)}{12} = 175$$

$$b = \sqrt{\frac{\text{SS}_{\text{lin}}}{\text{SS}_K}} = \sqrt{\frac{1032.14}{175}} = 2.43$$

$$a = \bar{X} - b\bar{K} = 15.17 - (2.43)(3.50) = 6.67$$

Regression equation: $X = bK + a = 2.43K + 6.67$

In this latter form,

$$A_0' = \bar{V}, \qquad \xi_0' = 1,$$

$$A_1' = \frac{C_{\text{lin}}}{\sum c_{1j}^2}, \qquad \xi_1' = \lambda_1(U - \bar{U}),$$

$$A_2' = \frac{C_{\text{quad}}}{\sum c_{2j}^2}, \qquad \xi_2' = \lambda_2\left[(U - \bar{U})^2 - \frac{k^2 - 1}{12}\right],$$

$$A_3' = \frac{C_{\text{cubic}}}{\sum c_{3j}^2}, \qquad \xi_3' = \lambda_3\left[(U - \bar{U})^3 - (U - \bar{U})\frac{3k^2 - 7}{20}\right].$$

The numerical values of the λ_j's depend upon the value of k, the number of treatments. Numerical values for λ_j will be found in tables of the coefficients.

The square of the correlation between the independent variable and the line of means of the dependent variable is the proportion of the total variation which is accounted for by a trend of any given degree. Thus, the linear correlation between degree of complexity and reaction time is given by

$$r = \sqrt{\frac{SS_{\text{lin}}}{SS_{\text{total}}}} = \sqrt{\frac{1032.11}{2108.33}} = 0.70.$$

The actual fit of the linear regression equation to the points in Fig. 3-7 is shown in Fig. 3-8.

The correlation associated with the cubic relationship is

$$r = \sqrt{\frac{SS_{\text{lin}} + SS_{\text{quad}} + SS_{\text{cubic}}}{SS_{\text{total}}}}$$

$$= \sqrt{\frac{1032.14 + 2.98 + 34.72}{2108.33}} = 0.71.$$

FIGURE 3-8

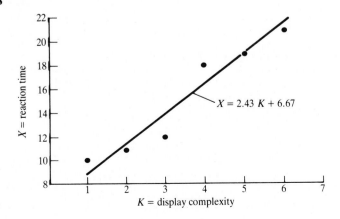

$X = 2.43\ K + 6.67$

X = reaction time

K = display complexity

The tests that have been made indicate that the cubic correlation does not differ significantly from the linear correlation.

Returning to the material concerning estimation of the magnitude of treatment effects in Sec. 3.9, recall that the correlation ratio η^2 expresses the proportion of the variation which can be accounted for by a polynomial of any degree. For these data a (biased) estimate of η^2 is

$$\hat{\eta}^2 = \frac{SS_{\text{treat}}}{SS_{\text{total}}} = \frac{1108.33}{2108.33} = 0.526;$$

the line of means accounts for 52.6 percent of the total variation in the dependent variable. In units comparable to the linear correlation used earlier

$$\hat{\eta} = \sqrt{\frac{1108.33}{2108.33}} = \sqrt{0.526} = 0.725.$$

A closely-related measure of association is defined by

$$\omega^2 = \frac{\theta}{\sigma_\varepsilon^2 + \theta},$$

where, for equal sample sizes,

$$\theta = \sum \tau_j^2 / k,$$

and

$$\omega^2 = \frac{\sum \tau_j^2 / k}{\sigma_\varepsilon^2 + \sum \tau_j^2 / k}.$$

The heuristic (biased) estimator of ω^2 is given by

$$\hat{\omega}^2 = \frac{\dfrac{k-1}{kn}(MS_{\text{treat}} - MS_{\text{error}})}{MS_{\text{error}} + \dfrac{k-1}{kn}(MS_{\text{treat}} - MS_{\text{error}})}$$

$$= \frac{(k-1)(F-1)}{kn + (k-1)(F-1)}.$$

As a numerical example, consider the data in Table 3.35. For these data,

$$\hat{\omega}^2 = \frac{(5)(10.97)}{60 + (5)(10.97)} = 0.47.$$

This index may be interpreted as the extent to which knowing the treatment in which a subject appears allows one to predict the response of that individual. Stated otherwise, it is the proportion of variance which can be accounted for on the basis of treatment group memberships.

For the random model, ω^2 corresponds to another measure of association, the intraclass correlation, which is defined by

$$\rho_I = \frac{\sigma_\tau^2}{\sigma_\varepsilon^2 + \sigma_\tau^2}, \quad \text{where} \quad \sigma_\tau^2 = \frac{\sum \tau_j^2}{k-1}.$$

Again considering the numerical example in Table 3.35, a heuristic estimator of $\rho_{\text{intraclass}}$ takes the form

$$\hat{\rho}_{\text{intraclass}} = \frac{\hat{\sigma}_{\text{displays}}^2}{\hat{\sigma}_\varepsilon^2 + \hat{\sigma}_{\text{displays}}^2}$$

$$= \frac{20.31}{18.52 + 20.31} = 0.5230.$$

This result is based upon the fact that for this example,

$$E(MS_{\text{displays}}) = \sigma_\varepsilon^2 + 10\sigma_{\text{displays}}^2,$$
$$E(MS_{\text{error}}) = \sigma_\varepsilon^2.$$

Thus, $\hat{\sigma}_\varepsilon^2 = 18.52,$

$$\hat{\sigma}_\varepsilon^2 + 10\hat{\sigma}_{\text{displays}}^2 = 221.67 \quad \text{or} \quad \hat{\sigma}_{\text{displays}}^2 = \frac{221.67 - 18.52}{10}$$

$$= 20.31.$$

In units comparable to the product–moment correlation

$$\sqrt{\hat{\rho}_{\text{intraclass}}} = \sqrt{0.5230} = 0.723.$$

Recall that for these same data and in comparable units, the estimate of the correlation ratio,

$$\hat{\eta} = \sqrt{\frac{SS_{\text{displays}}}{SS_{\text{total}}}} = 0.725.$$

This is the correlation associated with a polynomial of degree $k - 1 = 5$. The indices $\hat{\omega}^2$ or $\hat{\rho}_I$ can differ appreciably from $\hat{\eta}^2$ since the latter does not involve degrees of freedom.

Overall, then, for this problem, we have the result that overall association measured by $\hat{\eta}^2$ states that a polynomial equation of degree $k - 1 = 5$ results in a correlation of 0.725. A linear function yields a correlation of 0.70 and a third degree equation yields a correlation of 0.71. In terms of hypotheses tested, one concludes that there are no significant differences among these correlations since the line of means ($\hat{\eta} = 0.725$) is linear ($\hat{\rho}_{\text{lin}} = 0.70$) and nothing is added by including a cubic trend ($\hat{\rho}_{\text{cubic}} = 0.71$).

3.14 RANDOMIZED COMPLETE-BLOCK DESIGNS

In a completely randomized design, represented schematically for $n = 3$ observations in Table 3.38, the random error component of observations

TABLE 3.38   Structural model detail

Treatment 1	Treatment 2	Treatment 3
$X_{11} = \mu + \tau_1 + \varepsilon_{11}$	$X_{12} = \mu + \tau_2 + \varepsilon_{12}$	$X_{13} = \mu + \tau_3 + \varepsilon_{13}$
$X_{21} = \mu + \tau_1 + \varepsilon_{21}$	$X_{22} = \mu + \tau_2 + \varepsilon_{22}$	$X_{23} = \mu + \tau_3 + \varepsilon_{23}$
$X_{31} = \mu + \tau_1 + \varepsilon_{31}$	$X_{32} = \mu + \tau_2 + \varepsilon_{32}$	$X_{33} = \mu + \tau_3 + \varepsilon_{33}$

within each treatment arises because of all of the variables in the universe which effect the dependent variable with the exception of the one controlled variable, the treatment condition.

It should be emphasized that such within-treatment differences include all of the variation due to differences between people; X_{1j} is an observation on person 1, X_{2j} is an observation on person 2.

Suppose the experimenter wants to reduce the errors which account for differences among observations within each treatment. It is emphasized in Chapter 1 that one of the ways in which this can be accomplished is through blocking. The simplest design by which this could be accomplished is the *randomized complete-block* design. For three treatments arranged in two complete blocks, a simple illustration is:

Block 1	Block 2
Treatment 3	Treatment 2
Treatment 1	Treatment 3
Treatment 2	Treatment 1

Each block is divided into k subblocks of equal size. Within each block the k treatments are assigned at random to the subblocks. The purpose of arranging treatments in blocks is to eliminate variation due to differences between blocks from error. The terminology originated in an agricultural setting wherein a "block" corresponded to an area of land and blocking was used to remove differences in soil conditions from error, the requirement for accomplishing this being that soils within blocks are more homogeneous than are soil conditions between blocks. In those sciences wherein experimental materials are living organisms, blocking is most often used to remove differences between subjects from error with regard to one or more supplementary variables. For example, one might block to remove variation due to intelligence, motivation, or anxiety. However, blocking may not be with regard to any particular variable. It might involve a host of unspecified variables as would be the case if blocks were formed with either litter mates or twins. This would also be true if blocks were used to control for such environmental variables as the time of day, season, or geographic location of the study.

Each block is divided into k subblocks of equal size. The treatments are then assigned at random to the subblocks. Thus, each block contains all k treatments. In this sense each block is "complete." In so-called *incomplete-block designs*, each block is divided into $m < k$ subblocks so that each block contains only a specified fraction of all treatments. In general, a block corresponds to a repetition of an experiment under essentially comparable conditions. The number of blocks, say n, will be equal to the number of repetitions called for by the design.

Although the blocks are often considered to represent a random factor (in the sense that the blocks actually included in the experiment are a random sample from a population of blocks), in what follows in this section the blocks will be considered to represent a fixed factor. As long as a primary interest lies in the elimination of block effects from experimental error and as long as statistical tests are restricted to treatment effects, handling blocks as a fixed factor will not alter the principal features of the analysis.

Suppose the observed data from a design in which treatments are arranged in n complete blocks are symbolized as follows:

	Treatment 1	Treatment 2	$\cdots$	Treatment k	Total
Block 1	X_{11}	X_{12}	$\cdots$	X_{1k}	B_1
Block 2	X_{21}	X_{22}	$\cdots$	B_{2k}	B_2
$\vdots$	$\vdots$	$\vdots$		$\vdots$	$\vdots$
Block n	X_{n1}	X_{n2}	$\cdots$	X_{nk}	B_n
Total	T_1	T_2	$\cdots$	T_k	G

$$\bar{B}_i = B_i/k, \qquad \bar{T}_j = T_j/n, \qquad \bar{G} = G/kn$$

Suppose the following model is appropriate for an observation on treatment j in block i:

$$X_{ij} = \mu + \beta_i + \tau_j + \varepsilon_{ij}, \quad i = 1, \ldots, n; \quad j = 1, \ldots, k. \tag{3.52}$$

If m, b_1, and t_j are least-squares estimators of the corresponding parameters, the least squares estimators of the parameters in (3.52) are obtained by solving the following set of normal equations:

$$
\begin{aligned}
\mu: & \quad knm + k \sum b_i + n \sum t_j = G, \\
\beta_i: & \quad km + kb_i + \sum t_j = B_i, \\
\tau_j: & \quad nm + \sum b_i + nt_j = T_j.
\end{aligned}
\tag{3.53}
$$

For the special case $n = 2$, $k = 3$, the normal equations may be written schematically as follows:

	m	b_1	b_2	t_1	t_2	t_3	
m:	6	3	3	2	2	2	G
b_1:	3	3	0	1	1	1	B_1
b_2:	3	0	3	1	1	1	B_2
t_1:	2	1	1	2	0	0	T_1
t_2:	2	1	1	0	2	0	T_2
t_3:	2	1	1	0	0	2	T_3

$$(3.54)$$

The first line in the above schematic representation corresponds to the equation

$$6m + 3b_1 + 3b_2 + 2t_1 + 2t_2 + 2t_3 = G.$$

The set of equations (3.54) represents six equations in six unknowns, namely m, b_1, b_2, t_1, t_2, and t_3. These unknowns correspond to the parameters in the model given by (3.52). One will find, however, that these equations are not linearly independent. The

(i) Sum of equations b_1 and b_2 = sum of equations t_1, t_2, and t_3,
(ii) Equation m = sum of equations b_1, b_2, t_1, t_2, and t_3.

Thus there are two linear relationships among the $k + n + 1$ normal equations in which there are $k + n + 1$ unknowns. Hence, two linearly independent constraints on the unknowns will be needed before the system (3.53) will have a unique solution. There are many possible choices for the constraints. Different choices will yield different solutions. However, there will be certain functions of the estimators which will be invariant for all admissible choices of the constraints.

A relatively simple solution to the system of equations is obtained if one imposes the constrains

$$\sum b_i = 0 \quad \text{and} \quad \sum t_j = 0. \tag{3.55}$$

If the constraints

$$\sum \beta_i = 0 \quad \text{and} \quad \sum \tau_j = 0$$

are imposed upon the model in (3.52), as they sometimes are, then the constraints in (3.55) automatically follow. The solution to the normal equations (3.53) corresponding to the constraints in (3.55) is

$$\hat{\mu} = m = \frac{G}{kn} = \bar{G},$$

$$\hat{\beta}_i = b_i = \frac{B_i - km}{k} = \bar{B}_i - \bar{G}, \qquad (3.56)$$

$$\hat{\tau}_j = t_j = \frac{T_j - nm}{n} = \bar{T}_j - \bar{G}.$$

The reduction in sums of squares due to $\mu, \beta_1, \ldots, \beta_n, \tau_1, \ldots, \tau_k$ is given by

$$R(\mu, \beta, \tau) = mG + \sum b_i B_i + \sum t_j T_j. \qquad (3.57)$$

Although the estimators in (3.56) do depend upon the choice of the constraints, the estimate of the variation due to the corresponding parameters does not depend upon the constraints chosen.

If one uses the models indicated below, least-squares procedures will provide the variations indicated.

Disregarding treatments:

$$X_{ij} = \mu + \beta_i + \varepsilon_{ij}, \qquad R(\mu, \beta) = mG + \sum b_i B_i.$$

Disregarding blocks:

$$X_{ij} = \mu + \tau_j + \varepsilon_{ij}, \qquad R(\mu, \tau) = mG + \sum t_j T_j.$$

Disregarding treatments and blocks:

$$X_{ij} = \mu + \varepsilon_{ij}, \qquad R(\mu) = mG.$$

If the constraints $\sum b_i = 0$ and $\sum t_j = 0$ are used in solving the normal equations associated with these models, then

$$m = \bar{G}, \qquad b_i = \bar{B}_i - \bar{G}, \qquad t_j = \bar{T}_j - \bar{G}.$$

Hence, one has the following relationships for complete-block designs:

$$R(\beta \mid \mu) = \text{SS}_{\text{blocks}} = R(\mu, \beta, \tau) - R(\mu, \tau)$$

$$= \sum b_i B_i$$

$$= k \sum (\bar{B}_i - \bar{G})^2 = \frac{\sum B_i^2}{k} - \frac{G^2}{kn}.$$

$$R(\tau \mid \mu) = \text{SS}_{\text{treat}} = R(\mu, \beta, \tau) - R(\mu, \beta)$$

$$= \sum t_j T_j$$

$$= n \sum (\bar{T}_j - \bar{G})^2 = \frac{\sum T_j^2}{n} - \frac{G^2}{kn}.$$

$$SS_{error} = \sum X_{ij}^2 - R(\mu, \beta, \tau) = \sum X_{ij}^2 - mG - \sum b_i B_i - t_j T_j$$
$$= \sum (X_{ij} - \bar{G})^2 - SS_{blocks} - SS_{treat}$$
$$= SS_{total} - SS_{blocks} - SS_{treat}$$
$$= \sum (X_{ij} - \bar{B}_i - \bar{T}_j + \bar{G})^2.$$

It should be noted from $SS_{error} = \sum (X_{ij} - \bar{B}_i - \bar{T}_j - \bar{G})^2$ that error for this design takes the form of a two-factor interaction between blocks and treatments. More will be said of this point in Chapter 4. It should also be noted that

$$R(\tau, \beta \mid \mu) = R(\mu, \beta, \tau) - R(\mu) = \sum b_i B_i + \sum t_j T_j$$
$$= R(\beta \mid \mu) + R(\tau \mid \mu).$$

In general, when

$$R(u, v) = R(u) + R(v),$$

the design is said to be *orthogonal* with respect to u and v. In a complete-block design, the block effects and the treatment effects are orthogonal. (In what are called incomplete-block designs, the block effects are not orthogonal to the treatment effects.)

The analysis of variance associated with a randomized, complete-block design is summarized in Table 3.39. The degrees of freedom for SS_{error} are obtained as follows: There are kn observations in all. There are $(k + n + 1) - 2$ linearly independent normal equations. Hence, the number of linearly independent estimators obtained from the normal equations is $(k + n + 1) - 2$. The degrees of freedom for SS_{error} are given by

$$kn - [(k + n + 1) - 2] = kn - k - n + 1$$
$$= (k - 1)(n - 1).$$

TABLE 3.39 **Analysis of variance for complete-block design**

Sources of variation	SS	df	MS	E(MS)
Blocks	SS_{blocks}	$n - 1$	MS_{blocks}	$\sigma_\varepsilon^2 + k\sigma_\beta^2$
Treatments	SS_{treat}	$k - 1$	MS_{treat}	$\sigma_\varepsilon^2 + n\sigma_\tau^2$
Error	SS_{error}	$(k - 1)(n - 1)$	MS_{error}	σ_ε^2
Total	SS_{total}	$kn - 1$		

$$(1) = G^2/kn \qquad (3) = \left(\sum T_j^2\right) \Big/ n$$

$$(2) = \sum X^2 \qquad (4) = \left(\sum B_i^2\right) \Big/ k$$

$$SS_{blocks} = (4) - (1) \qquad SS_{error} = (2) - (3) - (4) + (1)$$
$$SS_{treat} = (3) - (1) \qquad SS_{total} = (2) - (1)$$

An alternative rationale for obtaining these degrees of freedom is as follows:

$$df_{error} = df_{total} - df_{blocks} - df_{treat}$$
$$= (kn - 1) - (n - 1) - (k - 1) = (k - 1)(n - 1).$$

Such designs potentially offer an increase in statistical power, but the assumptions are much more stringent than those of the completely randomized design.

It should be noted that the error variation of the complete-block design is smaller than the error variation of the completely randomized design. This is because the variation due to the variable which was used for blocking has been eliminated. Thus, if SS_{error} is the error variation after blocking,

$$SS_{error} = SS_{error} - SS_{blocks},$$

it is a residual variation left when within treatment variation has block effects eliminated. Provided there is no real interaction between blocks and treatments, this remainder may be reasonably considered to be due to error. If the variation due to the blocking variable is large relative to other sources of error, the complete block design provides a more powerful test for treatment effects than does the completely randomized design.

In Chapter 4, the logic for single-factor experiments having repeated measures on the same experimental subjects is presented. Those designs are equivalent to the randomized complete-block design with the experimental subjects (usually people or other living organisms) each considered to be a block.

3.15   EXERCISES

1. Assume that there are very small *populations* wherein $n = 5$ for $k = 3$ treatment populations.
   (a) For these populations, generate numerical values for observations on each element which satisfy all of the Model I structural model requirements for
   $$X_{ij} = \mu + \tau_j + \varepsilon_{ij}.$$
   (b) What is the numerical value of τ_2?
   (c) What is the numerical value of ε_{32}?
   (d) What is the numerical value of $\sum \tau_j$?
   (e) What is the numerical value of $\sum_{i=1}^{5} \varepsilon_{i2}$?

2. The management of a large regional airport is concerned about possible lapses of attention by air traffic controllers under conditions of heavy traffic. Because of your expertise in the areas of attention and visual pattern perception research, you have been retained as a consultant. A simulation of the traffic control environment has been established in your laboratory and you have developed three training conditions designed to enhance selective attention when air traffic is heavy. There is a fourth condition—a control condition—in which no training is administered. You have selected a random sample of 44 trainees as subjects, randomly assigned them in equal numbers to the four conditions and recorded their accuracy scores in detecting

potential collisions during a series of displays. Those scores are:

Conditions

1	2	3	Control
10.0	11.4	11.9	10.0
10.6	10.7	12.6	9.7
9.4	12.2	12.2	10.5
9.8	11.8	13.2	10.3
11.0	11.7	12.9	9.9
10.4	11.3	12.8	9.6
10.0	11.5	11.8	10.1
9.2	11.0	12.1	9.5
10.2	10.9	12.4	10.2
10.8	12.0	13.0	9.8
9.6	11.1	12.5	10.4

(a) Complete the analysis of variance and test H_0: $\mu_1 = \mu_2 = \mu_3 = \mu_c$, assuming that treatment conditions are fixed. Use $\alpha = 0.05$.

(b) What is the power of this test (a, above) assuming that $f = 0.10, 0.25$, and 0.40, respectively?

(c) Test the assumption of homogeneity of variance using the F_{max} statistic, and using the Brown–Forsythe test. Use $\alpha = 0.5$.

(d) Construct comparisons among the observed means using the following coefficients:

Comparison	t_1	t_2	t_3	$t_{control}$
1	$\frac{1}{3}$	$\frac{1}{3}$	$\frac{1}{3}$	-1
2	1	-1	0	0
3	$\frac{1}{2}$	$\frac{1}{2}$	-1	0

(1) Are these comparisons orthogonal?

(2) Compute SS_{C_1}, SS_{C_2}, SS_{C_3}, and show numerically that

$$SS_{C_1} + SS_{C_2} + SS_{C_3} = \frac{n \sum (\bar{T}_j - \bar{G})^2}{k-1} = SS_{treat} \quad \text{(from 2a).}$$

(3) You are interested in evaluating the hypothesis that the control mean is different from the mean of the other three conditions. Test the hypothesis,

$$H_0: \psi = \frac{\mu_1 + \mu_2 + \mu_3}{3} - \mu_c = 0,$$

using an F statistic ($\alpha_{ind} = 0.5$).

(4) Test the hypotheses associated with C_1 and C_2 ($\alpha_{ind} = 0.5$) using an F statistic.

(5) What is the numerical value of α_{joint} for this set of three tests of significance? What is the numerical value of α_{exp}?

(6) For the Bonferroni procedure, what is the numerical value of α_{ind} if $\alpha_{expw} = 0.05$ for those three tests?

(7) What is the numerical value of α_{ind} if $\alpha_{expw} = 0.05$ for these three tests using the Šidák procedure?

(8) Using the Newman–Keuls procedure, compare all unique pairs of means with appropriate tests of significance. ($\alpha = 0.05$.)

(9) Using Dunnett's t, test all hypotheses of the form $H_0: \mu_j - \mu_C = 0$, ($\alpha = 0.05$), where μ_C is the mean for the control group.

3. Assume that observations were lost *at random* (from the data set presented in Problem 2) for Subjects 1 and 2 in Treatment 1, Subject 6 in Treatment 2, and Subject 4 in the control condition. Carry out an unweighted-means analysis of variance with these new data and unequal sample sizes.

4. For a fixed model, compute the power for ($\alpha = 0.05$):
   (*a*) $k = 4$, $n = 6$, $\sigma_\tau^2 = 25$, $\sigma_\epsilon^2 = 25$.
   (*b*) $k = 4$, $n = 3$, $\sigma_\tau^2 = 25$, $\sigma_\epsilon^2 = 25$.
   (*c*) $k = 4$, $n = 15$, $\sigma_\tau^2 = 25$, $\sigma_\epsilon^2 = 25$.
   (*d*) $k = 4$, $n = 6$, $\sigma_\tau^2 = 100$, $\sigma_\epsilon^2 = 25$.

5. An experimenter is interested in maximizing power in an experiment wherein the levels of the treatments were selected at random from a population of possible levels. (S)he is interested in detecting any deviation from $\theta_0 = \sigma_\tau^2/\sigma_\epsilon^2 = 0$ in the null hypothesis. What are appropriate values for n and k if power is to exceed 0.90 and $\alpha = 0.05$. For the alternative hypothesis, $\theta = 1.0$?

6. Three methods for facilitating learning mathematical structures were investigated. From a total of $nk = 30$ subjects selected at random from a large school, 10 were assigned at random to each of the three treatment conditions. After training, performance was assessed on a set of 100 problems and the number of correct solutions was scored. The data were:

Treatments		
1	**2**	**3**
48	46	78
30	40	60
50	40	70
20	30	80
40	80	60
80	70	70
40	40	90
30	20	100
90	50	90
47	47	77

(*a*) Carry out an analysis of variance. Assuming the treatments are fixed, test the hypothesis, $H_0: \mu_1 = \mu_2 = \mu_3$. ($\alpha = 0.05$.)

(*b*) What is the power of this test assuming $f = 0.10$?

(*c*) Compute $\hat{\eta}^2$ and $\hat{\omega}^2$.

(*d*) Using the Newman–Keuls procedure, compare all unique pairs of means with $\alpha = 0.05$.

(e) Construct two orthogonal comparisons, and
    (1) Compute SS_{C_1} and SS_{C_2}.
    (2) Test the hypotheses ($\alpha_{ind} = 0.5$)

$$H_0: \psi_1 = \sum c_{1j}\mu_j = 0$$
$$H_0: \psi_2 = \sum c_{2j}\mu_j = 0.$$

(f) What is α_{expw} equal to for the two tests in (e) above?
(g) What is α_{exp} equal to for the two tests in (e) above?

CHAPTER 4

SINGLE-FACTOR EXPERIMENTS HAVING REPEATED MEASURES ON THE SAME ELEMENTS

4.1 INTRODUCTION

In Chapter 1, and again in the discussion of randomized complete-block designs, the advantages of blocking as a method for reducing experimental error were discussed. The designs to be discussed in this chapter are special cases of the randomized complete-block design wherein each subject is considered to be a block and is observed under all treatment conditions. In general when blocks are constructed, error is reduced when subjects are more homogeneous with regard to the dependent variable within blocks than they are between blocks. Since people are more like themselves than they are like anyone else, maximum within-block homogeneity tends to be realized when each subject acts as his or her own control, i.e., forms a block. Homogeneity within blocks could be achieved, albeit usually to a lesser degree, by using litter mates, twins or siblings within each block for each treatment or by matching subjects used in each block with regard to one or more relevant ancillary measures.

In general, repeated measures designs can be used in two different settings, as a matter of choice when a completely randomized design could have been used, or in situations wherein the nature of the experiment dictates that each subject must be observed under all treatment conditions. In the first case, the designs are sometimes referred to as *subject-by-treatments designs*; in the latter case, they may be called *subjects-by-trials* designs. In cases where the sequence of the treatments is not dictated by the nature of the experimental material, the order of the treatments is usually randomized independently for each subject. When relatively large numbers of subjects are used, this has the effect of eliminating order effects from estimates of treatment effects. More elaborate schemes for controlling order or sequence effects can be used and will be discussed in Chapter 7. In subject-by-trials studies, prime examples of which would be learning or adaptation experiments, the sequence of treatments (e.g., trials) is fixed for all subjects and it is precisely the sequence effects which are of interest.

Repeated measures designs are very important in experimental work in the behavioral sciences because the elements forming the statistical population are frequently people. Because of large differences in experience and background, the responses of people to the same experimental treatment may show relatively large variability. In many cases, much of this variability is due to differences existing between people prior to the experiment. If this latter source of variability can be separated from treatment effects and experimental error, the sensitivity of the experiment may be increased. If the source of variability cannot be estimated, as is the case with completely randomized designs, it remains part of the uncontrolled sources of variability and is thus automatically part of the experimental error.

One of the primary purposes of experiments in which the same subject is observed under each of the treatments is to provide a control on differences between subjects. In this type of experiment, treatment effects for subject i are measured relative to the average response made by subject i on all treatments. In this sense each subject serves as his own control—responses of individual subjects to the treatments are measured in terms of deviations about a point which measures the average performance of that individual subject. Hence variability due to differences in the average responsiveness of the subjects is eliminated from the experimental error (if an additive model is appropriate).

Experiments in which the same elements are used under all the k treatments require k observations on each element, hence, the term *repeated measurements* to describe this kind of design. To the extent that unique characteristics of the individual elements remain constant under the different treatments, pairs of observations on the same elements will tend to be positively correlated. More generally, the observations will be *dependent* rather than independent. If the population distributions involved are multivariate normal, the terms *dependent* and *correlated* are synonymous; analogously, the terms independent and uncorrelated are synonymous in this context. Since the models that will be used are assumed to have underlying multivariate normal distributions, correlated measurements imply statistically dependent measurements. The designs in this chapter may be said to involve correlated, or dependent, observations. This is in contrast to completely randomized designs wherein all observations are independent and this distinction has strong implications for both the efficiency of the two designs and for the assumptions which underlie the tests of significance.

4.2 NOTATION AND COMPUTATIONAL PROCEDURES

Notation for this type of design will be illustrated in terms of people as the elements of the statistical population. However, the notation is not restricted to this case. In Table 4.1 the symbol X_{11} represents the measurement on person 1 under treatment 1, X_{12} the measurement on person 1 under treatment 2, X_{1j} the measurement of person 1 under treatment j. In general the first subscript to an X indicates the person observed and the second subscript the treatment under which the observation is made.

The symbol P_1 represents the sum of the k observations on person 1, P_2 the sum of the k observations on person 2, P_i the sum of the k observations on person i. In summation notation,

$$P_i = \sum_j X_{ij};$$

that is, P_i is the sum of the k entries in row i. Summation over the subscript j is equivalent to summing over all columns within a single row. The mean of the observations on person i is

$$\bar{P}_i = \frac{P_i}{k}.$$

The symbol T_1 represents the sum of the n observations under treatment 1, T_2 the sum of the n observations under treatment 2, T_j the sum of the n observations under treatment j. In summation notation,

$$T_j = \sum_i X_{ij}.$$

Summation over the subscript i is equivalent to summing all entries in a single column. The mean of the n observations under treatment j, designated $\bar{T}_j$, is

$$\bar{T}_j = \frac{T_j}{n}.$$

TABLE 4.1   Notation

Person	Treatment 1	2	$\cdots$	j	$\cdots$	k	Total	Mean
1	X_{11}	X_{12}		X_{1j}		X_{1k}	P_1	$\bar{P}_1$
2	X_{21}	X_{22}		X_{2j}		X_{2k}	P_2	$\bar{P}_2$
$\vdots$	$\vdots$	$\vdots$		$\vdots$		$\vdots$	$\vdots$	$\vdots$
i	X_{i1}	X_{i2}		X_{ij}		X_{ik}	P_i	$\bar{P}_i$
$\vdots$	$\vdots$	$\vdots$		$\vdots$		$\vdots$	$\vdots$	$\vdots$
n	X_{n1}	X_{n2}		X_{nj}		X_{nk}	P_n	$\bar{P}_n$
Total	T_1	T_2	$\cdots$	T_j	$\cdots$	T_k	G	
Mean	$\bar{T}_1$	$\bar{T}_2$	$\cdots$	$\bar{T}_j$	$\cdots$	$\bar{T}_k$		$\bar{G}$

The sum of the kn observations in the experiment, designated G, is

$$G = \sum P_i = \sum T_j = \sum \sum X_{ij}.$$

The symbol $\sum \sum X_{ij}$ represents the sum over all observations in the experiment. The grand mean of all observations, designated $\bar{G}$, is

$$\bar{G} = \frac{G}{kn} = \frac{\sum \bar{P}_i}{n} = \frac{\sum \bar{T}_j}{k}.$$

The total variation in this design is

$$\text{SS}_{\text{total}} = \sum_i \sum_j (X_{ij} - \bar{G})^2.$$

This source of variation measures how different each X is from every other X. The degrees of freedom for SS_{total} are $kn - 1$. It is customary in this type of design to partition the total variation into two non-overlapping (orthogonal) parts.

One part is called the between-people variation and is defined by

$$\text{SS}_{\text{b. people}} = k \sum (\bar{P}_i - \bar{G})^2.$$

In words, the between-people variation is a function of the squared deviations of the means for the people about the grand mean. Alternatively, this source of variation may be viewed as due to the differences between all possible pairs of $\bar{P}_i$; the larger such differences, the larger this source of variation. Since there are n means, this source of variation has $n - 1$ degrees of freedom.

The second part is called the within-people variation and is defined by

$$\text{SS}_{\text{w. people}} = \sum_i \sum_j (X_{ij} - \bar{P}_i)^2.$$

This is a pooling of the variations from within each of the rows. That is, $\text{SS}_{\text{w. people}}$ is the sum of the following variations:

$$\text{SS}_{\text{w. people 1}} = \sum_j (X_{1j} - \bar{P}_1)^2$$

$$\text{SS}_{\text{w. people 2}} = \sum_j (X_{2j} - \bar{P}_2)^2$$

$$\vdots$$

$$\text{SS}_{\text{w. people } n} = \sum_j (X_{nj} - \bar{P}_n)^2$$

$$\sum_i \text{SS}_{\text{w. person } i} = \sum_i \sum_j (X_{ij} - \bar{P}_i)^2 = \text{SS}_{\text{w. people}}.$$

The degrees of freedom for the variation within a single person are $k - 1$. The degrees of freedom for the pooled within people variation are, therefore, $n(k - 1)$.

It is readily shown that the between- and within-people sources of variation are statistically independent and that

$$SS_{total} = SS_{b.\ people} + SS_{w.\ people}.$$

The degrees of freedom corresponding to these sources of variation are also additive,

$$kn - 1 = (n - 1) + n(k - 1).$$

To show this partition of SS_{total} algebraically, let

$$b_{ij} = X_{ij} - \bar{P}_i,$$
$$a_i = \bar{P}_i - \bar{G}.$$

Then,

$$\sum_j b_{ij} = 0 \quad \text{for all } i, \qquad \sum_i a_i = 0, \qquad \sum_j a_i = ka_i.$$

Hence,

$$\sum_i \sum_j a_i b_{ij} = \sum_i a_i \left(\sum_j b_{ij} \right) = \sum_j (0) = 0.$$

From the definitions of b_{ij} and a_i, it follows that

$$X_{ij} - \bar{G} = b_{ij} + a_i.$$

Hence,

$$SS_{total} = \sum_i \sum_j (X_{ij} - \bar{G})^2 = \sum_i \sum_j (b_{ij} + a_i)^2$$

$$= \sum_i \sum_j b_{ij}^2 + \sum_i \sum_j a_i^2 + 2 \sum_i \sum_j a_i b_{ij}$$

$$= \sum_i \sum_j b_{ij}^2 + k \sum_i a_i^2 + 2(0)$$

$$= SS_{w.\ people} + SS_{b.\ people}.$$

The difference between two observations on the same person (which generates within-people variation) depends in part upon the difference in treatment effects and in part upon uncontrolled or residual sources of variation. Specifically, such differences may be expressed as (see Sec. 4.5 for model)

$$X_{ij} - X_{ij'} = (\mu + \tau_j + \pi_i + \varepsilon_{ij}) - (\mu + \tau_{j'} + \pi_i + \varepsilon_{ij'})$$
$$= (\tau_j - \tau_{j'}) + (\varepsilon_{ij} + \varepsilon_{ij'}).$$

Since the τ's and the ε's are assumed to be independent, $SS_{w.\ people}$ may be partitioned into two orthogonal parts, one source due to the $(\tau_j - \tau_{j'})$, the other due to the $(\varepsilon_{ij} - \varepsilon_{ij'} = \text{residuals})$.

Thus

$$SS_{\text{w. people}} = \sum_i \sum_j (X_{ij} - \bar{P}_i)^2$$

$$= \sum_i \sum_j (X_{ij} - \bar{P}_i - \bar{T}_j + \bar{T}_j - \bar{G} + \bar{G})^2$$

$$= \sum_i \sum_j (X_{ij} - \bar{P}_i - \bar{T}_j + \bar{G} + \bar{T}_j - \bar{G})^2$$

$$= \sum_i \sum_j (X_{ij} - \bar{P}_i - \bar{T}_j + \bar{G})^2 + \sum_i \sum_j (\bar{T}_j - \bar{G})^2$$

$$+ 2 \sum_i \sum_j (X_{ij} - \bar{P}_i - \bar{T}_j + \bar{G})(\bar{T}_j - \bar{G}).$$

Since the last term on the right is zero,

$$SS_{\text{w.people}} = \sum_i \sum_j (X_{ij} - \bar{P}_i - \bar{T}_j + \bar{G})^2 + n \sum_j (\bar{T}_j - \bar{G})^2$$

$$= SS_{\text{res}} + SS_{\text{treat}}.$$

One notes that the degrees of freedom are also additive:

$$df_{\text{w. people}} = df_{\text{res}} + df_{\text{treat}}$$

$$n(k-1) = (k-1)(n-1) + k - 1.$$

Note that

$$n(k-1) - (k-1)(n-1) = nk - n - nk + k + n - 1$$

$$= k - 1.$$

Thus, that part of $SS_{\text{w. people}}$ which depends upon differences between treatment effects is defined as

$$SS_{\text{treat}} = n \sum (\bar{T}_j - \bar{G})^2, \text{ with } k - 1 \text{ degrees of freedom.}$$

Alternatively, this source of variation may be expressed as

$$SS_{\text{treat}} = \frac{n \sum (\bar{T}_j - \bar{T}_{j'})^2}{k}.$$

The expression $\bar{T}_j - \bar{T}_{j'}$ represents the difference between a pair of treatment means; the summation is with respect to all possible pairs of treatment means, order within the pair being disregarded. For example, if $k = 3$,

$$SS_{\text{treat}} = \frac{n[(\bar{T}_1 - \bar{T}_2)^2 + (\bar{T}_1 - \bar{T}_3)^2 + (\bar{T}_2 - \bar{T}_3)^2]}{3}.$$

To demonstrate that

$$\frac{n \sum (\bar{T}_j - \bar{T}_{j'})^2}{k} = n \sum (\bar{T}_j - \bar{G})^2 \qquad (j < j'),$$

consider the special case $k = 2$. For this special case

$$n \sum (\bar{T}_j - \bar{G})^2 = n[(\bar{T}_1 - \bar{G})^2 + (\bar{T}_2 - \bar{G})^2]$$

$$= n \left[\left(\bar{T}_1 - \frac{\bar{T}_1 + \bar{T}_2}{2} \right)^2 + \left(\bar{T}_2 - \frac{\bar{T}_1 + \bar{T}_2}{2} \right)^2 \right]$$

$$= n \left[\left(\frac{2\bar{T}_1 - \bar{T}_1 - \bar{T}_2}{2} \right)^2 + \left(\frac{2\bar{T}_2 - \bar{T}_1 - \bar{T}_2}{2} \right)^2 \right]$$

$$= \frac{n}{4} [(\bar{T}_1 - \bar{T}_2)^2 + (\bar{T}_2 - \bar{T}_1)^2]$$

$$= \frac{n}{4} [2(\bar{T}_1 - \bar{T}_2)^2]$$

$$= \frac{n(\bar{T}_1 - \bar{T}_2)^2}{2}.$$

Demonstration of the general case involves the same sort of thing in a slightly more complicated form. The special case $k = 2$ illustrates the variation due to a comparison.

The residual variation is

$$\mathrm{SS}_{\mathrm{res}} = \sum \sum [(X_{ij} - \bar{G}) - (\bar{P}_i - \bar{G}) - (\bar{T}_j - \bar{G})]^2.$$

In this form it is clear the residual is that which is left from total variation when people and treatment effects are removed. Alternatively, the term that is squared in $\mathrm{SS}_{\mathrm{res}}$ may be written

$$X_{ij} - \bar{P}_i - \bar{T}_j + \bar{G}.$$

This term has expectation

$$E(X_{ij} - \bar{P}_i - \bar{T}_j + \bar{G}) = (\mu + \tau_j + \pi_i + \varepsilon_{ij}) - (\mu + \pi_i + \bar{\tau} + \bar{\varepsilon}_i)$$
$$- (\mu + \tau_j + \bar{\pi} + \bar{\varepsilon}_j) + (\mu + \bar{\pi} + \bar{\tau} + \bar{\varepsilon})$$
$$= \varepsilon_{ij} - \bar{\varepsilon}_i - \bar{\varepsilon}_j + \bar{\varepsilon}.$$

Hence under this model, $\mathrm{SS}_{\mathrm{res}}$ is a function of experimental error.

The degrees of freedom for $\mathrm{SS}_{\mathrm{res}}$ may also be expressed by subtraction from $\mathrm{df}_{\mathrm{total}}$,

$$\mathrm{df}_{\mathrm{res}} = \mathrm{df}_{\mathrm{total}} - \mathrm{df}_{\mathrm{b.\,people}} - \mathrm{df}_{\mathrm{treat}}$$
$$= (kn - 1) - (n - 1) - (k - 1)$$
$$= kn - n - k + 1 = n(k - 1) - (k - 1)$$
$$= (k - 1)(n - 1).$$

The analysis of the sources of variation and the corresponding degrees of freedom are shown schematically in Fig. 4-1.

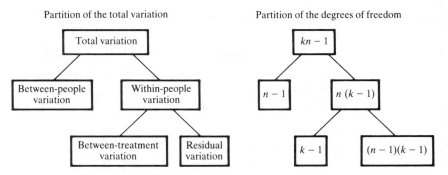

FIGURE 4-1 Schematic representation of the analysis.

The definitions of the sources of variation do not provide the most convenient formulas for their computation. Formulas for this purpose are summarized in Table 4.2. The symbols (1), (2), and (3) are identical to those used in the case of single-factor experiments which do not have repeated measures. Symbol (4) occurs only in experiments having repeated measures. In each case the divisor in a term is the number of observations that are summed to obtain an element in the numerator. For example, G is the sum of kn observations; T_j is the sum of n observations; P_i is the sum of k observations. A summary of the analysis of variance appropriate for this design is given in part ii of this table. Mean squares are obtained from corresponding sums of squares by dividing the latter by their respective degrees of freedom.

The F ratio

$$F = \frac{\text{MS}_{\text{treat}}}{\text{MS}_{\text{res}}}$$

provides a test of the hypothesis that $\tau_1 = \tau_2 = \cdots = \tau_k$, where the τ's

TABLE 4.2 **Summary of computational procedures**

(i) $\quad (1) = G^2/kn \qquad (2) = \sum\sum X^2 \qquad (3) = \left(\sum T_j^2\right)\Big/n \qquad (4) = \left(\sum P_i^2\right)\Big/k$

Source of variation	SS		df
Between people	$\text{SS}_{\text{b. people}}$	$= (4) - (1)$	$n - 1$
Within people	$\text{SS}_{\text{w. people}}$	$= (2) - (4)$	$n(k - 1)$
Treatments	SS_{treat}	$= (3) - (1)$	$k - 1$
Residual	SS_{res}	$= (2) - (3) - (4) + (1)$	$(n - 1)(k - 1)$
Total	SS_{total}	$= (2) - (1)$	$kn - 1$

(ii) appears to the left of the Treatments/Residual rows.

represent treatment effects and are defined in the same manner as for the case of designs not having repeated measures. The rationale underlying the use of this statistic for this test is discussed in Sec. 4.4 and 4.5.

Under one set of assumptions (made explicit in Sec. 4.4) about the underlying sources of variation, the F ratio has a sampling distribution which is approximated by the F distribution having $k - 1$ and $(n - 1)(k - 1)$ degrees of freedom. This is the usual test. When the assumptions underlying the model are violated, the sampling distribution of this F statistic may, in some cases, be approximated by an F distribution having adjusted degrees of freedom. It will be found that the assumptions underlying the repeated-measure design are considerably more restrictive than the assumptions underlying a design which does not have repeated measures.

4.3 NUMERICAL EXAMPLE

The computational procedures described in the last section will be illustrated by means of the numerical example in Table 4.3. The statistical basis for the

TABLE 4.3 **Numerical example**

	Person	Drug 1	Drug 2	Drug 3	Drug 4	Total
	1	30	28	16	34	$108 = P_1$
	2	14	18	10	22	$64 = P_2$
(i)	3	24	20	18	30	$92 = P_3$
	4	38	34	20	44	$136 = P_4$
	5	26	28	14	30	$98 = P_5$
		132	128	78	160	$498 = G$
		T_1	T_2	T_3	T_4	

$$(1) \quad = \frac{G^2}{kn} = \frac{(498)^2}{4(5)} = \frac{248{,}004}{20} \qquad = 12{,}400.20$$

(ii)

$$(2) \quad = \sum \sum X^2 \qquad\qquad = 13{,}892$$

$$(3) \quad \frac{\sum T_j^2}{n} = \frac{132^2 + 128^2 + 78^2 + 160^2}{5} = \frac{65{,}492}{5} \qquad = 13{,}098.40$$

$$(4) \quad = \frac{\sum P_i^2}{k} = \frac{108^2 + 64^2 + 92^2 + 136^2 + 98^2}{4} = \frac{52{,}324}{4} \qquad = 13{,}081.00$$

(iii)

$SS_{\text{b. people}}$ $= (4) - (1) = 13{,}081.00 - 12{,}400.20$ $= 680.80$

$SS_{\text{w. people}}$ $= (2) - (4) = 13{,}892 - 13{,}081.00$ $= 811.00$

SS_{drugs} $= (3) - (1) = 13{,}098.40 - 12{,}400.20$ $= 698.20$

SS_{res} $= (2) - (3) - (4) + (1)$

$= 13{,}892 - 13{,}098.40 - 13{,}081.00 + 12{,}400.20$ $= 112.80$

SS_{total} $= (2) - (1) = 13{,}892 - 12{,}400.20$ $= 1491.80$

analysis is discussed in the next section. The purpose of this experiment was to study the effects of four drugs upon reaction time to a series of standardized tasks. All subjects had been given extensive training on these tasks prior to the experiment. The five subjects used in the experiment are a random sample from a population of interest to the experimenter.

Each subject was observed under each of the drugs; the order in which a subject was administered a given drug was randomized. (In designs considered in later chapters, the order in which treatments are given to the same subject is either controlled or counterbalanced.) A sufficient time was allowed between the administration of the drugs to avoid the effect of one drug upon the effects of subsequent drugs, i.e., an interaction effect. The numerical entries in Table 4.3 represent the score (mean reaction time) on the series of standardized tasks. Thus person 1 had scores of 30, 28, 16, and 34 under the respective drug conditions. The total of these scores is 108; thus the numerical value of P_1 is 108. The other values for the P's are obtained by summing the entries in the respective rows in part i. The numerical values for the T's are obtained by summing the columns. For example, T_1 is the sum of the five entries under drug 1. The grand total, G, is obtained either by summing the P's or by summing the T's. A check on the arithmetic work is provided by computing G by both methods.

Quantities required in the computation of the sums of squares are given in part ii. The first three of these are identical to those computed for designs which do not involve repeated measures. Symbol (4) is obtained from the P's. Each P is the sum over $k = 4$ drugs; hence the divisor associated with the symbol (4) is 4. The computation of the sums of squares required in the analysis of variance is illustrated in part iii. An alternative method for computing SS_{res} is

$$SS_{res} = SS_{w. \, people} - SS_{drugs}$$
$$= 811.00 - 698.20 = 112.80.$$

The latter method is actually simpler than the method used in part iii; however, the method in part iii provides a partial check on the numerical work, since the sum of SS_{drugs} and SS_{res} should equal total $SS_{w. \, people}$.

The analysis of variance is summarized in Table 4.4. The F ratio

$$F = \frac{MS_{treat}}{MS_{res}} = \frac{232.73}{9.40} = 24.76$$

is used in testing hypotheses about reaction time as a function of the effects of the drugs. For a 0.01-level test on the hypothesis that $\tau_1 = \tau_2 = \tau_3 = \tau_4$, the critical value for the F ratio is $F_{0.99}(3, 12) = 5.95$. The experimental data contradict this hypothesis.

Inspection of the totals for the drugs in Table 4.3 indicates that drug 3 is associated with the fastest reaction.

TABLE 4.4 **Analysis of variance**

Source of variation	SS	df	MS	F
Between people	680.80	4	170.20	
Within people	811.00	15		
Drugs	690.20	3	232.73	24.76**
Residual	112.80	12	9.40	
Total	1491.80	19		

$$** F_{0.99}(3, 12) = 5.95$$

Differences Among Means

All of the procedures for making *a priori* or *post mortem* tests presented in Sections 3.10, 3.11, and 3.13 of Chapter 3 may be generalized to the single factor design with repeated measures by simply substituting MS_{res} for MS_{error} and using the appropriate degrees of freedom, $(n-1)(k-1)$, instead of $k(n-1)$.

For example, suppose that it had been anticipated before conducting the experiment that drug 3 would have a different effect from all others.

The null hypothesis of interest is

$$H_0: \tau_3 = (\tau_1 + \tau_2 + \tau_4)/3.$$

The comparison (of totals) that would be used in testing this hypothesis is

$$C = 3T_3 - T_1 - T_2 - T_4 = 3(78) - 132 - 128 - 160 = -186.$$

The component of variation corresponding to this comparison is

$$SS_C = \frac{C^2}{n \sum c^2} = \frac{(-186)^2}{5[3^2 + (-1)^2 + (-1)^2 + (-1)^2]} = 576.60.$$

Thus, of the total of 698.20 units of variation due to all differences among drug means, 576.60 units are due to comparing only drug 3 and the average of the others. The F statistic

$$F = \frac{SS_C}{MS_{res}} = \frac{579.60}{9.40} = 61.34$$

is used to test the hypothesis that $\tau_3 = (\tau_1 + \tau_2 + \tau_4)/3$. The critical value for a 0.01-level test of this hypothesis $F_{0.99}(1, 12) = 9.33$. The observed data contradict this hypothesis. If this comparison were suggested by inspection of the data, the procedure given by Scheffé would be used to obtain the critical value. The latter critical value for a 0.01-level test is $(k-1)F_{0.99}(k-1, df_{res}) = 3F_{0.99}(3, 12) = 3(5.95) = 17.85$. Even with this critical value, the data indicate that drug 3 is different in its effect on reaction time from the effects of the other three drugs.

To test another hypothesis of some possible interest, that $\tau_1 = \tau_2 = \tau_4$, the sum of squares for those three drugs is given by

$$
\begin{aligned}
\text{SS}_{\text{drugs 1, 2, 4}} &= \frac{T_1^2 + T_2^2 + T_4^2}{n} - \frac{(T_1 + T_2 + T_4)^2}{3n} \\
&= \frac{132^2 + 128^2 + 160^2}{5} - \frac{(132 + 128 + 160)^2}{15} \\
&= 121.60.
\end{aligned}
$$

The mean square corresponding to this sum of squares is

$$
\text{MS}_{\text{drugs 1, 2, 4}} = \frac{121.60}{2} = 60.80.
$$

The statistic used in the test is

$$
F = \frac{\text{MS}_{\text{drugs 1, 2, 4}}}{\text{MS}_{\text{res}}} = \frac{60.80}{9.40} = 6.47.
$$

For a 0.01-level *a priori* test, the critical value is $F_{0.99}(2, 12) = 6.93$. Although the observed F statistic does not quite exceed the critical value, the observed F is large enough to make one question the hypothesis that drugs 1, 2, and 4 are equally effective with respect to their influence on reaction time. Inspection of the drug totals in Table 4.3 indicates that drug 4 has a somewhat longer reaction time, but the evidence is not quite strong enough to establish this conclusion at the 0.01 level of significance.

The data in this case can be adequately summarized in terms of a few selected comparisons. Analogous conclusions can be reached by somewhat more systematic probing procedures. Any of the methods discussed in Chapter 3 may be used to test differences between all possible pairs of means. In such procedures MS_{res} takes over the role played by MS_{error}. Application of the Student–Newman–Keuls procedure is illustrated in Table 4.5.

With repeated measures, barring missing data, the number of observations under each treatment will be equal. In this case treatment totals may be used rather than treatment means. The drug totals in increasing order of magnitude are given in part i. The entry in a cell of part i is the difference between a total at the head of a column and a total to the left of a row, with negative entries being deleted. Critical values for the statistic

$$
q_r = \frac{T_j - T_{j'}}{\sqrt{n\text{MS}_{\text{res}}}},
$$

where r is the number of steps two totals are apart on an ordered scale, are given in part ii. These values are obtained from the first three columns of tables for the 99th percentile point for the q statistic; the degrees of freedom for this q statistic are the degrees of freedom of MS_{res}. Critical values for

$$
T_j - T_{j'} = q_r\sqrt{n\text{MS}_{\text{res}}}
$$

TABLE 4.5 **Tests on differences between pairs of means**

	Drugs		3	2	1	4
		Totals	78	128	132	160
(i)	3	78	—	50	54	82
	2	128		—	4	32
	1	132			—	28
	4	160				—
(ii)		$q_{0.99}(r, 12)$		4.32	5.04	5.50
(iii)		$\sqrt{n\mathrm{MS}_{\mathrm{res}}}\, q_{0.99}(r, 12)$		29.64	34.57	37.73
			3	2	1	4
(iv)	3			**	**	**
	2			—	—	—
	1				—	—
	4					—

are given part iii. In this case

$$\sqrt{n\mathrm{MS}_{\mathrm{res}}} = \sqrt{5(9.40)} = \sqrt{47.00} = 6.86.$$

Thus the entries in part iii are 6.86 times the corresponding entries in part ii.

The order in which tests are made is given in Sec. 3.8. The critical value for the difference $T_4 - T_3 = 82$ is 37.73. Hence the data contradict the hypothesis that $\tau_4 = \tau_3$. The difference $T_1 - T_3 = 54$ has the critical value 34.57, and the difference $T_2 - T_3 = 50$ has the critical value 29.64. The difference $T_4 - T_2 = 32$ has the critical value 34.57; this difference does not quite exceed the critical value. No further tests are made. The tests which yield statistically significant results are summarized in part iv. Drug 3 appears to be different from the other drugs in its effect on reaction time. Although the differences between drug 4 and drugs 2 and 1 are relatively large, the differences do not exceed critical values of a 0.01-level test. This result is consistent with the outcome of the test of the hypothesis that $\tau_1 = \tau_2 = \tau_4$. This hypothesis was not rejected at the 0.01-level of significance, but the observed F statistic was close to the critical value.

Under the Scheffé procedure the critical value of all differences is

$$\sqrt{(k-1)F_{0.99}[k-1, (k-1)(n-1)]}\,\sqrt{2n\mathrm{MS}_{\mathrm{res}}}$$
$$= \sqrt{3F_{0.99}(3, 12)}\,\sqrt{2(5)(9.40)}$$
$$= \sqrt{3(5.95)}\,\sqrt{94.0} = 40.96$$

TABLE 4.6 **Analysis of learning data**

Source of variation	SS	df	MS	F
Between subjects	90.00	9	10.00	
Within subjects	155.24	60		
Blocks	103.94	6	17.32	18.23
Residual	51.30	54	0.95	
Total	254.24			

Trend Analysis

All of the points discussed with regard to trend analysis for the completely randomized design (Sec. 3.13) are applicable to this design with the exception that MS_{res} is used for all tests of significance instead of MS_{error}.

A sample of 10 subjects is used in the experiment to be described. Each subject is given 28 trials in which to learn a discrimination problem. The trials are grouped into blocks of 4 trials each. The block is considered the observational unit. Hence the data are analyzed as if there were 7 observations on each subject, an observation being the outcome of a series of 4 trials. The degrees of freedom for the between-subject variation are 9; the degrees of freedom for the within-subject variation are 60, 6 degrees of freedom for each of the 10 subjects.

A summary of the overall analysis appears in Table 4.6. For $\alpha = 0.01$ the critical value for a test of the hypothesis that there is no difference in the block means is $F_{0.99}(6, 54) = 3.28$. The data indicate that there are significant differences between the block means. A graph of the block totals is given in Fig. 4-2. Inspection of this figure indicates that a straight line would provide a good fit to the points, but there is also some evidence to indicate that an S-shaped (cubic) curve would provide a better fit. The nature of the subject

FIGURE 4-2

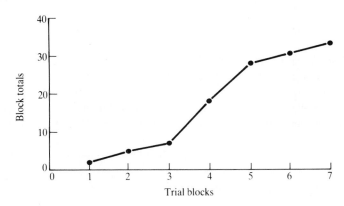

TABLE 4.7   **Tests for trends**

	Blocks:	1	2	3	4	5	6	7	$\sum c^2$	C	MS
	Block totals:	2	5	7	18	28	31	33			
Linear		−3	−2	−1	0	1	2	3	28	166	98.41**
Quadratic		5	0	−3	−4	−3	0	5	84	−2	0.00
Cubic		−1	1	1	0	−1	−1	1	6	−16	4.27*
											102.68

matter also suggests that a cubic curve would be more appropriate for these data. Hence a point to be investigated is whether or not a cubic curve provides a better fit than a straight line (within the range of blocks included in this study).

Toward this end, the mean squares corresponding to the linear, quadratic and cubic trends are computed in Table 4.7. The block totals for these experimental data are given near the top of Table 4.7. Each of these totals is the sum over 10 observations. Since there are seven blocks, the coefficients corresponding to the linear, quadratic, and cubic trends are obtained from the set of coefficients for which $k = 7$ in Appendix D, Table 10. The entries under the column headed $\sum c^2$ represent the sums of the squares of the coefficients in the corresponding rows. The entries under the column headed C represent the numerical value of the comparisons. For example, the linear comparison is

$$(-3)(2) + (-2)(5) + (-1)(7) + (0)(18) + (1)(28) + (2)(31) + (3)(33) = 166.$$

The mean square corresponding to the linear comparison is

$$MS_{lin} = \frac{C_{lin}^2}{n \sum c^2} = \frac{(166)^2}{10(28)} = 98.41.$$

A test on the significance of the linear trend is given by the F ratio

$$F = \frac{MS_{lin}}{MS_{res}} = \frac{98.41}{0.95} = 103.59.$$

The sampling distribution of this statistic (assuming no linear trend) may be approximated by an F distribution having degrees of freedom $(1, 54)$. The linear trend is significant beyond the 0.01 level.

For these data the numerical value of the quadratic comparison is zero to two decimal places. The mean square corresponding to the cubic comparison is

$$MS_{cubic} = \frac{C_{cubic}^2}{n \sum c^2} = \frac{(-16)^2}{10(6)} = 4.27.$$

A test on whether or not the cubic trend adds significant predictability beyond that already given by the linear and quadratic trends employs the statistic

$$F = \frac{MS_{cubic}}{MS_{res}} = \frac{4.27}{0.95} = 4.49.$$

The sampling distribution of this statistic (assuming no cubic trend) may be approximated by an F distribution having $(1, 54)$ degrees of freedom. The critical value when $\alpha = 0.05$ is 4.03. Hence the data indicate that within the range of blocks included in the experiment the cubic comparison adds significant predictability to that given by the linear trend ($\alpha = 0.05$).

The total variation between blocks (as given in Table 4.6) is 103.94. Of this total, 102.68 is accounted for by the linear and cubic trends. The remaining between-block variation appears negligible relative to experimental error. The between-block variation due to higher-order trend components is

$$SS_{higher\ order} = SS_{blocks} - SS_{lin} - SS_{quad} - SS_{cubic}$$
$$= 1.23.$$

The corresponding mean square is

$$MS_{higher\ order} = \frac{1.23}{3} = 0.41.$$

The F ratio in the test for trend components higher than the third is

$$F = \frac{MS_{higher\ order}}{MS_{res}} = \frac{0.41}{0.95} < 1.$$

Since this ratio is less than unity, the data indicate that no component higher than the third is relevant.

An alternative, more widely used testing procedure for trends is possible (Table 4.8). In this procedure the error term in the test for linear trend is obtained from

$$SS_{dev\ lin} = SS_{res} + (SS_{blocks} - SS_{lin})$$
$$= 51.30 + (103.94 - 98.41) = 56.83.$$

TABLE 4.8   **Summary of alternative tests for trend**

Source of variation	SS	df	MS	F
Linear trend	98.41	1	98.41	102.51**
Dev from lin	56.83	59	0.96	
Quadratic trend	0.00	1		
Dev from quad	56.83	58		
Cubic trend	4.27	1	4.27	4.64*
Dev from cubic	52.56	57	0.92	

The degrees of freedom for $SS_{dev\ lin}$ in this type of design are $n(k-1)-1$. For the case under consideration, the degrees of freedom are $60-1=59$. The mean square for deviations from linearity is

$$MS_{dev\ lin} = \frac{SS_{dev\ lin}}{59} = 0.96.$$

Under this testing procedure the statistic used in the test for linear trend is

$$F = \frac{MS_{lin}}{MS_{dev\ lin}} = \frac{98.41}{0.96} = 102.61.$$

The sampling distribution for this statistic may be approximated by an F distribution having degrees of freedom $(1, 59)$. This test procedure has a slight negative bias; i.e., if $F_{0.95}(1, 59)$ is used as a critical value for a test having $\alpha = 0.05$, this critical value will tend to be slightly larger than the exact critical value if the trend is actually different from linear.

Under the alternative test procedure, the test for cubic trend uses a denominator obtained from

$$SS_{dev\ cubic} = SS_{res} + (SS_{blocks} - SS_{lin} - SS_{quad} - SS_{cubic})$$
$$= 51.30 + (103.94 - 98.41 - 0.00 - 4.27) = 52.56.$$

The degrees of freedom for this source of variation are $n(k-1)-3$, which in this case is $60-3=57$. The mean square corresponding to this source of variation is

$$MS_{dev\ cubic} = \frac{SS_{dev\ cubic}}{57} = \frac{52.56}{57} = 0.92.$$

The test for cubic trend uses the statistic

$$F = \frac{MS_{cubic}}{MS_{dev\ cubic}} = \frac{4.27}{0.92} = 4.64.$$

The sampling distribution of this statistic may be approximated by an F distribution having $(1, 57)$ degrees of freedom. The critical value for this test ($\alpha = 0.05$) is 4.01. Hence the data contradict the hypothesis that the cubic trend adds no predictability to the linear and quadratic trends.

From some points of view, this alternative test procedure is to be preferred to that which has a constant denominator. Under this procedure, the denominator of F ratios tends to err on the side of being too large. When the degrees of freedom for MS_{res} are large (say over 30), the first approach presented differs only slightly from the alternative approach.

In those cases where the experimental data provide a direct estimate of σ_ε^2, tests on trend may be viewed as a special case of testing *a priori* hypotheses. Tests on trend of the kind discussed here focus on individual comparisons that make up the overall main effect.

Covariance Matrix

The important role of the variance–covariance (or, more briefly, the covariance matrix) in the assumptions under which the F statistic is distributed as an F distribution will be discussed later.

The computational formula for MS_{res} is algebraically equivalent to the expression

$$MS_{res} = \overline{var} - \overline{cov},$$

where $\overline{var}$ is the mean of the variances within each of the drug conditions and $\overline{cov}$ is the mean of the covariances between the pairs of observations under any two drug conditions. To show this equivalence for the numerical data in Table 4.3, the variance–covariance matrix for these data is given in Table 4.9.

The variance of the observations made under each of the drugs appears along the main diagonal of this table. For example, the variance of the observations made under drug 1 is

$$var\ X_1 = \frac{\sum X_1^2 - (T_1^2/n)}{n-1} = \frac{3792 - (132^2/5)}{4} = 76.80.$$

The covariances appear above the main diagonal. For example, the covariance between the observations under drug 1 and those made under drug 2 is

$$cov_{X_1 X_2} = \frac{\sum (X_{i1} X_{i2}) - (T_1 T_2/n)}{n-1}$$

$$= \frac{(30)(28) + \cdots + (26)(28) - [(132)(128)/5]}{4} = 53.20.$$

The mean of the variances is 49.60; the mean of the covariances is 40.20. Thus,

$$\overline{var} - \overline{cov} = 49.60 - 40.20 = 9.40.$$

The numerical value of MS_{res} obtained by the computational formula is also 9.40. It is considerably more work to obtain MS_{res} from the variance–covariance matrix than it is to obtain MS_{res} by means of the computational formula. However, in order to check certain of the assumptions underlying the F test, computation of the variance–covariance matrix is sometimes required and is often enlightening in its own right.

TABLE 4.9 **Variance–covariance matrix**

	Drug 1	Drug 2	Drug 3	Drug 4
Drug 1	76.80	53.20	29.20	69.00
Drug 2		42.80	15.80	47.00
Drug 3			14.80	27.00
Drug 4				64.00

$MS_{b.\ people}$ is also related to $\overline{var}$ and $\overline{cov}$. This relationship is

$$MS_{b.\ people} = \overline{var} + (k-1)\overline{cov}.$$

From Table 4.4,

$$MS_{b.\ people} = \frac{SS_{people}}{n-1} = \frac{680.80}{4} = 170.20.$$

In terms of the average variance and the average covariance,

$$MS_{b.\ people} = 49.60 + 3(40.20) = 170.20.$$

From the covariance matrix one may compute the correlation matrix from the following relationship:

$$r_{jm} = \frac{cov_{jm}}{\sqrt{var_j\ var_m}}.$$

For example,

$$r_{23} = \frac{15.80}{\sqrt{(42.80)(14.80)}} = 0.628.$$

The correlation matrix is given in Table 4.10. The average of the off-diagonal entries is

$$\bar{r} = 0.86.$$

Had a common estimate of the population variance been used, namely $\overline{var}$, the average of the correlation would be

$$\bar{r}' = \frac{\overline{cov}}{\overline{var}} = \frac{40.20}{49.60} = 0.8105.$$

In terms of the latter average correlation,

$$MS_{res} = \overline{var}(1 - \bar{r}') = 49.60(1 - 0.8105) = 9.40.$$

The relationship,

$$MS_{res} = \overline{var} - \overline{cov}$$

provides a convenient way to compare the outcome of this experiment to the outcome which would have occurred if the experiment had been carried out as

TABLE 4.10   **Intercorrelation matrix**

	Drug 1	Drug 2	Drug 3	Drug 4
Drug 1	1.000	0.928	0.866	0.984
Drug 2		1.000	0.628	0.898
Drug 3			1.000	0.877
Drug 4				1.000

a single-factor design without repeated measures. Under those circumstances, there is no correlation between observations under the different treatments, i.e., $\overline{\text{cov}} = 0$. Therefore

$$MS_{res} = \overline{var},$$

and

$$\overline{var} = MS_{error}$$

of the completely randomized design. Thus,

$$MS_{res} = MS_{error} = 49.60.$$

The effect of using each subject as his own control was, therefore, to generate $\bar{r} = 0.81$, which in turn reduced the error estimate from 49.60 to 9.40. In general, the larger the average intercorrelation (or covariance), the smaller will be MS_{res} compared to MS_{error} (or $\bar{s}^2$) of the completely randomized design.

In general, since one can expect MS_{res} to be quite small relative to MS_{error} of the completely randomized design, it would seem that efficiency considerations would always dictate the use of repeated-measures designs over completely-randomized designs. That is not true for several reasons. First, one must be concerned with possible order effects in some studies. Independently randomizing sequences of the treatments for each subject will solve that problem in some, but not all, cases. More importantly, MS_{error} has $k(n-1)$ degrees of freedom; MS_{res} has $k(n-1) - (n-1) = (n-1)(k-1)$ degrees of freedom. That is, removing $SS_{b.\,subjects}$ from SS_{error} leads to the loss of $n-1$ degrees of freedom. In the case of the numerical example in Table 4.4, for example, MS_{error} would have had 16 degrees of freedom; MS_{res} has 12 degrees of freedom. In summary, the average covariance must be large enough so that $MS_{res} = MS_{error} - \overline{cov}$ is reduced enough to compensate for the loss of degrees of freedom in order for the repeated-measures design to show a gain in efficiency. Finally, and very critically, the assumptions underlying the completely randomized designs are relatively simple. One assumes random samples from normally distributed populations with homogeneous error variances. The assumptions underlying the F distribution for the randomized-block design or, more specifically, repeated-measures designs, are much more restrictive. We now turn to those.

4.4 ANALYSIS OF VARIANCE ASSUMPTIONS FOR REPEATED MEASURES DESIGNS

The validity of the F test used in the last section rests upon a set of assumptions concerning the nature of the underlying sources of variation and covariation or, equivalently, variances and covariances. Those, in turn, follow in part from assumptions made about the model assumed to underlie the observations.

Matrices to Summarize Assumptions About Variances and Covariances

The variance–covariance matrix for a design with k treatment conditions (e.g., Table 4.9) is:

$$\hat{\Sigma}_x = S_x = \begin{bmatrix} s_{11} & s_{12} & \cdots & s_{1k} \\ s_{21} & s_{22} & \cdots & s_{2k} \\ \vdots & & & \vdots \\ s_{k1} & s_{k2} & \cdots & s_{kk} \end{bmatrix}.$$

The entries on the main diagonal are the within-treatment variances and may be written

$$s_1^2, s_2^2, \ldots, s_k^2,$$

or

$$\text{var}_1, \text{var}_2, \ldots, \text{var}_k.$$

In the context of the analysis of variance, these entries may also be written $MS_{\text{w. treat 1}}, MS_{\text{w. treat 2}}, \ldots, MS_{\text{w. treat k}}$. The entries off the main diagonal of S_x are the covariances and are sometimes written in the general form $\text{cov}_{jj'}$.

S_x is an estimate of the population covariance matrix Σ_z which is defined as

$$\underset{k,k}{\Sigma_x} = \begin{bmatrix} \sigma_{11} & \sigma_{12} & \cdots & \sigma_{1k} \\ \sigma_{21} & \sigma_{22} & \cdots & \sigma_{2k} \\ \vdots & & & \vdots \\ \sigma_{k1} & \sigma_{k2} & \cdots & \sigma_{kk} \end{bmatrix}.$$

The entries on the main diagonal are the population variances, which are sometimes written

$$\sigma_1^2, \sigma_2^2, \ldots, \sigma_k^2.$$

A covariance matrix will always be symmetric. That is,

$$\Sigma_x = \Sigma_x'.$$

Also

$$S_x = S_x'.$$

Certain patterned covariance matrices are of interest in order to make explicit the assumptions underlying repeated-measures designs.[1] In particular, the analysis of variance makes certain assumptions about the variances and covariances in a repeated-measures design and about the relationships among those values. The most general matrix which best represents the case when all

---

[1] Matrix concepts used in this section are explained in Appendix B.

of those assumptions are met is called a type H matrix. In general a type H matrix will have the property that

$$\sigma_{jj} + \sigma_{j'j'} - 2\sigma_{jj'} = 2\lambda \qquad \text{for all} \qquad j \neq j'.$$

This relationship defines what is called *circularity*. Thus, type H matrices define a general class of matrices which includes circular matrices. That is, circularity requires that the sum of any two treatment variances minus twice their covariance equals a constant (2λ) and that this is true for all pairs of treatments on which there are repeated measures. The scalar λ depends upon the relationship between treatments and the scale of measurement, as do the variances and covariances.

To illustrate, suppose that a set of k, X variates has a covariance matrix Σ_x which has a pattern generated by

$$\Sigma_x_{k,k} = A + A' + \lambda I_k,$$

where

$$A_{k,k} = \begin{bmatrix} a_1 & a_1 & \cdots & a_1 \\ a_2 & a_2 & \cdots & a_2 \\ \vdots & & & \vdots \\ a_k & a_k & \cdots & a_k \end{bmatrix},$$

and where

$$a_1, a_2, \ldots, a_k, \text{ and } \lambda \text{ are any known arbitrary constants.}$$

A matrix Σ_x having the pattern defined thusly will be called a type H matrix.

As an example, suppose that $k = 3$, $\lambda = 5$ and

$$A = \begin{bmatrix} 2 & 2 & 2 \\ 3 & 3 & 3 \\ 4 & 4 & 4 \end{bmatrix},$$

then the covariance matrix is

$$\Sigma_x = \begin{bmatrix} 2 & 2 & 2 \\ 3 & 3 & 3 \\ 4 & 4 & 4 \end{bmatrix} + \begin{bmatrix} 2 & 3 & 4 \\ 2 & 3 & 4 \\ 2 & 3 & 4 \end{bmatrix} + \begin{bmatrix} 5 & 0 & 0 \\ 0 & 5 & 0 \\ 0 & 0 & 5 \end{bmatrix}$$

$$= \begin{bmatrix} 9 & 5 & 6 \\ 5 & 11 & 7 \\ 6 & 7 & 13 \end{bmatrix} = \begin{bmatrix} \sigma_{11} & \sigma_{12} & \sigma_{13} \\ \sigma_{21} & \sigma_{22} & \sigma_{23} \\ \sigma_{31} & \sigma_{32} & \sigma_{33} \end{bmatrix}.$$

For this numerical example of a type H matrix, please note that the circularity property holds since

$$\sigma_{11} + \sigma_{22} - 2\sigma_{12} = 9 + 11 - (2)(5) = 10,$$
$$\sigma_{11} + \sigma_{33} - 2\sigma_{13} = 9 + 13 - (2)(6) = 10,$$
$$\sigma_{22} + \sigma_{33} - 2\sigma_{23} = 11 + 13 - (2)(7) = 10.$$

The circularity relationship also implies that

$$\sigma^2_{X_j - X_{j'}} = 2\lambda \quad \text{for all} \quad j \ne j'.$$

In words, circularity implies that the variance of the difference between any two X variates is a constant. Finally, for any type H matrix, the average variance σ_{jj} and the average covariance $\sigma_{jj'}$ differ by a constant,

$$\bar{\sigma}_{jj} - \bar{\sigma}_{jj'} = \lambda.$$

For the numerical example under consideration,

$$\bar{\sigma}_{jj} = \frac{9 + 11 + 13}{3} = 11,$$

$$\bar{\sigma}_{jj'} = \frac{5 + 6 + 7}{3} = 6.$$

Hence

$$\bar{\sigma}_{jj} - \bar{\sigma}_{jj'} = 5 = \lambda.$$

Since $\bar{\sigma}_{jj} - \bar{\sigma}_{jj'}$ is the difference between an average variance and an average covariance, it expresses a residual error variance and since this difference is a constant ($\lambda = 5$), the requirement of homogeneity of residual error variances for all pairs of treatments is met. Recall computing $\text{MS}_{\text{residual}}$ as a pooled residual error variance. That is, $\text{MS}_{\text{residual}} = \bar{s}^2 - \overline{\text{Cov}}$.

A type H matrix which has the property of circularity, but in addition has the property that both the variances (σ_{jj}) and covariances ($\sigma_{jj'}$) are constant, defines a matrix which has *compound symmetry,* which property is a special case of circularity. For example, suppose that the matrix A takes the form

$$A = \begin{bmatrix} 2 & 2 & 2 \\ 2 & 2 & 2 \\ 2 & 2 & 2 \end{bmatrix}.$$

That is, the matrix A contains just one arbitrary constant. Suppose further that $\lambda = 5$. Then the matrix Σ_x generated by the relation

$$\Sigma_x = A + A' + \lambda I_k$$

$$\begin{bmatrix} 9 & 4 & 4 \\ 4 & 9 & 4 \\ 4 & 4 & 9 \end{bmatrix} = \begin{bmatrix} 2 & 2 & 2 \\ 2 & 2 & 2 \\ 2 & 2 & 2 \end{bmatrix} + \begin{bmatrix} 2 & 2 & 2 \\ 2 & 2 & 2 \\ 2 & 2 & 2 \end{bmatrix} + 5 \begin{bmatrix} 1 & 0 & 0 \\ 0 & 1 & 0 \\ 0 & 0 & 1 \end{bmatrix}.$$

This matrix, in addition to being circular, has the additional property of compound symmetry. That is, σ_{jj} and $\sigma_{jj'}$ are both constant; they need not be equal to each other. A matrix which has compound symmetry will have circularity, but a circular matrix need not have compound symmetry; the condition of compound symmetry is more restrictive than circularity. For example, the matrix

$$\Sigma_x = \begin{bmatrix} 6 & 4 & 4 \\ 4 & 6 & 4 \\ 4 & 4 & 6 \end{bmatrix}$$

has compound symmetry and is, of course, circular since $\sigma_{jj} + \sigma_{j'j'} - 2\sigma_{jj'}$ is constant. That is,

$$\sigma_{11} + \sigma_{22} - 2\sigma_{12} = 6 + 6 - 2(4) = 4,$$
$$\sigma_{11} + \sigma_{33} - 2\sigma_{13} = 6 + 6 - 2(4) = 4,$$
$$\sigma_{22} + \sigma_{33} - 2\sigma_{23} = 6 + 6 - 2(4) = 4.$$

In contrast, the matrix

$$\Sigma_x = \begin{bmatrix} 8 & 3 & 5 \\ 3 & 10 & 6 \\ 5 & 6 & 14 \end{bmatrix}$$

does not have compound symmetry, but is circular since

$$\sigma_{jj} + \sigma_{j'j'} - 2\sigma_{jj'} = \text{constant} = 2\lambda.$$

For this latter matrix

$$\sigma_{11} + \sigma_{22} - 2\sigma_{12} = 8 + 10 - 2(3) = 12,$$
$$\sigma_{11} + \sigma_{33} - 2\sigma_{13} = 8 + 14 - 2(5) = 12,$$
$$\sigma_{22} + \sigma_{33} - 2\sigma_{23} = 10 + 14 - 2(6) = 12.$$

Another way to represent the condition for circularity is that

$$\sigma_{jj'} = \frac{\sigma_{jj} + \sigma_{j'j'}}{2} - \lambda.$$

For this example

$$\sigma_{12} = \frac{\sigma_{11} + \sigma_{22}}{2} - \lambda = \frac{8 + 10}{2} - 6 = 3,$$

$$\sigma_{13} = \frac{\sigma_{11} + \sigma_{33}}{2} - \lambda = \frac{8 + 14}{2} - 6 = 5,$$

$$\sigma_{23} = \frac{\sigma_{22} + \sigma_{33}}{2} - \lambda = \frac{10 + 14}{2} - 6 = 6.$$

In order to fully develop and to evaluate the assumptions of repeated measures designs, it is helpful to define the matrix property of *sphericity* from the property of circularity. This can be accomplished in terms of a normalized orthogonal transformation of the covariance matrix Σ_x, which transformation converts Σ_x to an orthonormal matrix Σ_y.

A matrix is said to be orthonormal if its rows are both orthogonal and in normal form. One could construct an orthonormal matrix by using as rows the coefficients for orthogonal comparisons and then normalizing those coefficients. For example, with $k = 3$, the coefficients for two orthogonal comparisons would be

$$c_{11} = -1 \qquad c_{12} = 0 \qquad c_{13} = 1$$
$$c_{21} = 1 \qquad c_{22} = -2 \qquad c_{23} = 1.$$

Since $\sum c_{1j} = \sum c_{2j} = 0$ and $\sum c_{1j} c_{2j} = 0$, these two sets of coefficients can be used to define comparisons and the comparisons are orthogonal. They would be *orthonormal* if they were also normalized, i.e., of unit length. A vector is normalized by dividing each entry by the norm, or length, of the vector. If, for example, $\mathbf{c}'_1$ is the row vector

$$\mathbf{c}'_1 = [-1, 0, 1],$$

the norm is

$$\|\mathbf{c}'\| = \mathbf{c}'\mathbf{c} = \left(\sum c_j^2 \right)^{\frac{1}{2}} = [(-1)^2 + (0)^2 + (1)^2]^{\frac{1}{2}} = \sqrt{2},$$

and the normalized vector is

$$\mathbf{c}^{*'} = \frac{1}{\|\mathbf{c}'\|} \mathbf{c}' = \frac{1}{\sqrt{2}}[-1, 0, 1]$$
$$= \left[\frac{-1}{\sqrt{2}}, 0, \frac{1}{\sqrt{2}} \right].$$

Note that the normalized vector has unit length. That is

$$\|\mathbf{c}^{*'}\| = \left[\left(-\frac{1}{\sqrt{2}} \right)^2 + (0)^2 + \left(\frac{1}{\sqrt{2}} \right)^2 \right]^{\frac{1}{2}} = 1.$$

The second vector,

$$\mathbf{c}'_2 = (1, -2, 1),$$

has length

$$\|\mathbf{c}'_2\| = \left(\sum c_j^2 \right)^{\frac{1}{2}} = [(1^2) + (-2)^2 + (1)^2]^{\frac{1}{2}} = \sqrt{6},$$

and in normalized form is

$$\mathbf{c}_2^{*'} = \left[\frac{1}{\sqrt{6}}, \ -\frac{2}{\sqrt{6}}, \ \frac{1}{\sqrt{6}} \right].$$

Thus, we may define an orthonormal coefficient matrix as

$$M^* = \begin{bmatrix} \dfrac{-1}{\sqrt{2}} & 0 & \dfrac{1}{\sqrt{2}} \\ \dfrac{1}{\sqrt{6}} & -\dfrac{2}{\sqrt{6}} & \dfrac{1}{\sqrt{6}} \end{bmatrix}.$$

Each row in M^* provides the coefficients for a normalized comparison which in general is an expression of the form

$$c_1^* X_1 + c_2^* X_2 + c_3^* X_3,$$

where

$$\sum c_j^* = 0 \quad \text{and} \quad \sum c_j^{*2} = 1.0.$$

In M^*, then, the rows are orthogonal and of unit lengths; the matrix M^* is orthonormal. For an orthonormal matrix,

$$M^* M^{*'} = I$$

since $\mathbf{c}_j' \mathbf{c}_j = 0$ (i.e., rows are orthogonal) and $\mathbf{c}_j' \mathbf{c}_j = 1$ (i.e., rows are normalized). An orthonormal matrix need not be square; in applications to problems associated with repeated-measures designs, M^* will not typically be square.

If M^* is orthonormal and Σ_x is circular, then

$$M^* \Sigma_x M^{*'} = \lambda I$$

where

$$\lambda = (\sigma_{jj} + \sigma_{j'j'} - 2\sigma_{jj'})/2$$

and I is an identity matrix. A matrix having the form λI is said to be *spherical*. There is nothing complicated about a spherical matrix; it is simply a matrix with λ on the main diagonal and zero elsewhere. In obtaining $\Sigma_y = \lambda I$, one has the covariance matrix of a set of variables which are orthogonal (all covariances are zero) with constant variance. If Σ_x is circular,

$$\Sigma_y = M^* \Sigma_x M^{*'} = \lambda I$$

will have those simple properties.

In terms of the numerical example

$$\underset{M^*}{\begin{bmatrix} -1/\sqrt{2} & 0 & 1/\sqrt{2} \\ 1/\sqrt{6} & -2/\sqrt{6} & 1/\sqrt{6} \end{bmatrix}} \underset{\Sigma_x}{\begin{bmatrix} 8 & 3 & 5 \\ 3 & 10 & 6 \\ 5 & 6 & 14 \end{bmatrix}} \underset{M^{*'}}{\begin{bmatrix} 1/\sqrt{2} & 1/\sqrt{6} \\ 0 & -2/\sqrt{6} \\ 1/\sqrt{2} & 1/\sqrt{6} \end{bmatrix}}$$

$$= \underset{M^* \Sigma_x}{\begin{bmatrix} -3/\sqrt{2} & 3/\sqrt{2} & 9/\sqrt{2} \\ 7/\sqrt{6} & -11/\sqrt{6} & 7/\sqrt{6} \end{bmatrix}} \underset{M^{*'}}{\begin{bmatrix} 1/\sqrt{2} & 1/\sqrt{6} \\ 0 & -2/\sqrt{6} \\ 1/\sqrt{2} & 1/\sqrt{6} \end{bmatrix}}$$

$$= \underset{\lambda I}{6 \begin{bmatrix} 1 & 0 \\ 0 & 1 \end{bmatrix}} = \begin{bmatrix} 6 & 0 \\ 0 & 6 \end{bmatrix}.$$

Matrix Properties and Analysis of Variance Assumptions

Huynh and Mandeville (1979) have presented a succinct discussion of the assumptions regarding variance–covariance matrices with repeated-measures designs. Summarized, the validity of the F statistic is assured when the covariance matrix of the observations is *circular* in form. Equivalently, the covariance matrix of a variable which is a normalized orthogonal transformation of the observations is *spherical* in form when the assumptions are met.

The matrix

$$M^* \Sigma_x M^{*'} = \lambda I$$

is important because when Σ_x is circular, $M^* \Sigma_x M^{*'}$ is spherical. The analysis of variance assumption of circularity of Σ_x is tested by evaluating whether $M \Sigma_x M^{*'}$ is spherical by a procedure to be presented later. To make what is being presented here specific to the analysis of variance, the matrix

$$M^* \Sigma_x M^{*'} = \lambda I$$

will be considered as the covariance matrix Σ_y of $k - 1$, Y variables which are normalized orthogonal transformations of the original k, X variables. That is, one may transform the analysis of variance X variables into new variables which are orthogonal. Σ_y is the variance covariance matrix of those $k - 1$, orthogonal Y variables. When Σ_x is circular, Σ_y is spherical. That is, Σ_y has a single variance on the main diagonal and zero for all covariances. It is *not* necessary to transform X to Y or Σ_x to Σ_y in order to evaluate the analysis of variance assumptions. The presentation here is for illustrative purposes only to help clarify the analysis of variance assumptions.

The analysis of variance hypothesis H_0: $\mu_1 = \mu_2 = \cdots = \mu_j = \cdots = \mu_k = \mu$ can always be recast in terms of a set of $k - 1$ mutually orthogonal comparisons. For example, if $k = 3$, then two orthogonal comparisons can be used to evaluate the hypotheses

$$H_0^1: \mu_1 - \mu_2 = 0$$
$$H_0^2: \mu_1 + \mu_2 - 2\mu_3 = 0.$$

The coefficients for these comparisons are

$$
\begin{array}{ccc}
c_{11} = 1 & c_{21} = -1 & c_{31} = 0 \\
c_{12} = 1 & c_{22} = 1 & c_{32} = -2,
\end{array}
$$

and M^* as one possible coefficient matrix whose rows are a set of $k - 1$ mutually orthogonal normalized comparisons is, then,

$$
M^* = \begin{bmatrix} \dfrac{1}{\sqrt{2}} & -\dfrac{1}{\sqrt{2}} & 0 \\[2ex] \dfrac{1}{\sqrt{6}} & \dfrac{1}{\sqrt{6}} & -\dfrac{2}{\sqrt{6}} \end{bmatrix},
$$

since the norm of the first row vector (comparison 1) is $\sqrt{2}$ and for the second comparison it is $\sqrt{6}$.

As a second example, if $k = 4$, the coefficients for three normalized, mutually orthogonal comparisons are provided by

$$
M^* = \begin{bmatrix}
\dfrac{1}{\sqrt{2}} & -\dfrac{1}{\sqrt{2}} & 0 & 0 \\[2mm]
0 & 0 & \dfrac{1}{\sqrt{2}} & -\dfrac{1}{\sqrt{2}} \\[2mm]
\dfrac{1}{2} & \dfrac{1}{2} & -\dfrac{1}{2} & -\dfrac{1}{2}
\end{bmatrix}.
$$

This particular M^* corresponds to evaluating the analysis of variance hypothesis in terms of the $k - 1 = 3$ null hypotheses,

$$H_0^1: \mu_1 - \mu_2 = 0$$

$$H_0^2: \mu_3 - \mu_4 = 0$$

$$H_0^3: (\mu_1 + \mu_2)/2 - (\mu_3 + \mu_4)/2 = 0.$$

In the general case there are k, X variates; under a normalized orthogonal transformation, the X variates may be transformed into a set of $k - 1$, Y variates,

$$\underset{n,k-1}{Y} = \underset{n,k}{X}\ \underset{k,k-1}{M^{*'}},$$

where $\underset{k,k-1}{M^*} = $ a matrix whose rows are a set of normalized orthogonal

comparisons, i.e., M^* is orthonormal $(M^{*'}M = I_{k-1})_j$

$\underset{x,k}{X} = $ a matrix of basic observations j

$\underset{n,k-1}{Y} = $ a matrix of transformed scores.

If S_x is the observed covariance matrix for the X variates, then S_y, the covariance matrix for the Y variates, is given by

$$\underset{k-1,k-1}{S_y} = M^* S_x M^{*'}.$$

Since the set of $k - 1$ normalized orthogonal comparisons are not unique, the Y matrix will not be unique. However, many of the important properties of the Y variates will be invariant for all possible choices of M^*. In particular, any property of S_y which depends upon the characteristic roots will be invariant for all choices of M^*. These include the trace and determinants of S_y.

S_x estimates Σ_x and S_y estimates Σ_y. It is important to remember that if Σ_x is a type H matrix, Σ_y will be spherical. To demonstrate this,

$$\Sigma_y = M^* \Sigma_x M^{*'},$$

and since Σ_x is a type H matrix, one may rewrite

$$\Sigma_y = M^*(A + A' + \lambda I_k)M^{*'},$$
$$= M^*AM^{*'} + M^*A'M^{*'} + \lambda M^*M^{*'}.$$

From the definition of the matrix A, it follows that

$$M^*A' = [0] \quad \text{and} \quad AM^{*'} = [0]$$

since the sum of the entries in any row of M^* is zero. Hence,

$$\Sigma_y = \lambda M^*M^{*'}$$
$$= \lambda I_{k-1}.$$

Thus, the X variables with a covariance matrix which is a type H matrix have been transformed into a set of Y variables, the covariance matrix of which is λI. That is, all of the Y variables have a common variance λ and all of the covariances of Y are zero. A matrix with these properties is spherical. Although a set of X variates having a multivariate normal distribution may always be transformed to a set of independently distributed variates, the resulting variates need not have the same variance. It is only for the special case in which Σ_x is circular that Σ_y will be spherical.

A numerical example is presented in Table 4.11 where there are $k = 3$ treatments.

TABLE 4.11 **Numerical example—normalized orthogonal transformation**

Observed Data:

Person	Treat. 1 X_1	Treat. 2 X_2	Treat. 3 X_3	Total	$SS_{\text{within person}}$
1	40	30	25	95	116.67
2	70	50	40	160	466.67
3	60	45	50	155	116.67
4	30	25	20	75	50.00
5	80	75	60	215	216.67

(i)

$\sum (\ )$:	$280 = T_1$	$225 = T_2$	$195 = T_3$	$700 = G$	966.68
$\sum (\ )^2$:	17400	11675	8725	110500	

$$\sum X_1X_2 = 14150 \quad \sum X_1X_3 = 12200$$
$$\sum X_2X_3 = 10000$$

TABLE 4.11 *(Continued)*

(ii)

$(1) = G^2/15 \qquad = 32,666.67$

$(2) = \sum X^2 \qquad = 37,800.00$

$(3) = \left(\sum T_j^2\right)\big/5 \ = 33,410.00$

$(4) = \left(\sum P_i^2\right)\big/3 \ = 36,833.33$

$$S_X = \begin{bmatrix} 430.00 & 387.50 & 320.00 \\ 387.50 & 387.50 & 306.25 \\ 320.00 & 306.25 & 280.00 \end{bmatrix}$$

(iii)

Source of variation		SS	df
Between people	$(4) - (1) =$	4165.66	4
Within people	$(2) - (4) =$	966.67	10
Treatments	$(3) - (1) =$	743.33	2
Residual	$(2) - (3) - (4) + (1) =$	223.34	8

Transformed data:

$$Y_1 = 1 = \left(\frac{1}{\sqrt{2}}\right)X_1 + \left(\frac{-1}{\sqrt{2}}\right)X_2 + (0)X_3$$

$$Y_2 = \left(\frac{1}{\sqrt{6}}\right)X_1 + \left(\frac{1}{\sqrt{6}}\right)X_2 + \left(\frac{-2}{\sqrt{6}}\right)X_3$$

(iv)

Person	Y_1	Y_2	Total	$\sum Y_i^2 = SS_i$
1	7.071	8.165	15.236	116.67
2	14.142	16.330	30.472	466.67
3	10.607	2.041	12.648	116.67
4	3.536	6.124	9.660	50.01
5	3.536	14.289	17.825	216.68

$\sum(\ ):\quad$ 38.892 $\quad$ 46.949 $\quad$ 85.841 $\qquad$ 966.70

$\qquad\qquad\ T_{Y_1} \qquad\quad T_{Y_2}$

$\sum(\ )^2:\quad$ 387.510 $\quad$ 579.181 $\qquad\qquad$ 966.69

$$\sum Y_1 Y_2 = 382.505$$

(v)

Source of variation	SS	df
Due to $\bar{Y}_1 = T_{Y_1}^2/5 = 302.52$		1
Due to $\bar{Y}_2 = T_{Y_2}^2/5 = 440.84$		1
Treatments	743.36	2
$\quad SS_{Y_1} = \ 84.99$		
$\quad SS_{Y_2} = 138.34$		
Residual	223.33	8
Within people	966.69	10

(vi)

$$S_y = \begin{bmatrix} 21.248 & 4.330 \\ 4.330 & 34.585 \end{bmatrix}$$

$tr S_y = 55.839 \qquad \hat{\varepsilon} = 0.925$

$|S_y| = 716.113$

Parts i–iii of Table 4.11 present the basic data for the treatment condition variable X. Parts iv–vii present analogous data for the Y variables resulting from the normalized orthogonal transformation of the treatment data.

One choice for the Y variates is

$$Y_{i1} = \left(\frac{1}{\sqrt{2}}\right)X_{i1} + \left(-\frac{1}{\sqrt{2}}\right)X_{i2} + (0)X_{i3}$$

$$Y_{i2} = \left(\frac{1}{\sqrt{6}}\right)X_{i1} + \left(\frac{1}{\sqrt{6}}\right)X_{i2} + (-2/\sqrt{6})X_{i3}.$$

In matrix form

$$\underset{2\times 3}{M^*} = \begin{bmatrix} \dfrac{1}{\sqrt{2}} & -\dfrac{1}{\sqrt{2}} & 0 \\[2mm] \dfrac{1}{\sqrt{6}} & \dfrac{1}{\sqrt{6}} & -\dfrac{2}{\sqrt{6}} \end{bmatrix},$$

and

$$\underset{n,2}{Y} = \underset{n,3}{X} \; \underset{3,2}{M^{*'}}$$

For the Y variables $SS_{\text{within person } i}$ is given by

$$Y_{i1}^2 + Y_{i2}^2 = \sum Y_i^2.$$

$$Y_{11}^2 + Y_{12}^2 = 116.67 = SS_{\text{w. person 1}}$$

$$Y_{21}^2 + Y_{22}^2 = 466.67 = SS_{\text{w. person 2}}$$

$$\vdots$$

$$Y_{51}^2 + Y_{52}^2 = 216.68 = SS_{\text{w. person 5}}$$

$$\sum\sum Y_{ij}^2 = 966.70 = SS_{\text{w. people of } X \text{ variables}}.$$

The treatment variation is equal to the treatment variation of the X variables

$$SS_{\text{treat}} = \frac{T_{y_1}^2 + T_{y_2}^2}{n} = \frac{(38.892)^2 + (46.949)^2}{5} = 743.36.$$

Actually, $T_{y_1}^2/n$ and $T_{y_2}^2/n$ are the variation due to Y_1 and Y_2, respectively, and are additive because Y_1 and Y_2 are orthogonal.

The residual variation of the analysis of the X variables is the variation within the Y variables,

$$SS_{y1} = \sum Y_1^2 - T_{y_1}^2/n = 84.99$$

$$SS_{y2} = \sum Y_2^2 - T_{y_2}^2/n = 138.34$$

$$SS_{y_1} + SS_{y_2} = 223.33 = SS_{\text{res}}.$$

This SS_{res} has the same meaning as does SS_{error} of the non-repeated measures design because the Y variates, unlike the X variates, are independent.

From the point of view of the assumptions, S_y is of interest. S_y estimates Σ_y and the assumption underlying the distribution theory of the F ratio on the treatment effects is that

$$E(S_y) = \Sigma_y = \lambda I_{k-1}.$$

That is, Σ_y is spherical and S_y provides an estimate of that spherical matrix.

The matrix S_y is presented in part vi of Table 4.11. S_y can be obtained directly from the Y variables. However, the Y variables are not normally computed except for illustrative purposes and S_y is, therefore, normally obtained as

$$M^* S_x M^{*'}.$$

If S_y were exactly spherical, the variances would be equal and the covariance would be zero. Equivalently, $r_{y_1 y_2}$ would be zero. In fact, for S_y, $r_{y_1 y_2} = 0.160$. However, S_y only estimates Σ_y and can differ from a spherical matrix by chance even if Σ_y is, in fact, spherical and Σ_x is, therefore, circular.

DEPARTURE FROM ASSUMPTIONS. A measure of the extent to which Σ_x departs from circularity (and, therefore, Σ_y departs from sphericity) has been proposed by Box (1954):

$$\varepsilon = \frac{k^2 (\bar{\sigma}_{jj} - \bar{\sigma}_{..})^2}{(k-1) \sum \sum (\sigma_{jj'} - \sigma_{j.} - \sigma_{.j} + \sigma_{..})}.$$

The measure may also be expressed in terms of λ_i the characteristic roots of the matrix Σ_y, as

$$\varepsilon = \frac{(\sum \lambda_i)^2}{(k-1) \sum \lambda_i^2}.$$

For example,

$$\Sigma_x = \begin{bmatrix} 1.00 & 0.50 & 1.50 \\ 0.50 & 3.00 & 2.50 \\ 1.50 & 2.50 & 5.00 \end{bmatrix}$$

is a matrix which is circular since

$$\sigma_{jj} + \sigma_{j'j'} - 2\sigma_{jj'} = 3$$

for all $j \neq j'$.

For this example,

$$\Sigma_y = M^* \Sigma_x M^{*'} = \lambda I_2 = 1.50 I_2$$

$$= \begin{bmatrix} 1.50 & 0 \\ 0 & 1.50 \end{bmatrix}$$

is a spherical matrix. The characteristic roots of Σ_y are $\lambda_1 = \lambda_2 = 1.50$.

Thus, one may compute ε from either Σ_x or Σ_y. From Σ_x,

$$\Sigma_x = \begin{bmatrix} 1.00 & 0.50 & 1.50 \\ 0.50 & 3.00 & 2.50 \\ 1.50 & 2.50 & 5.00 \end{bmatrix} \begin{array}{l} \bar{\sigma}_{1.} = 1.0 \\ \bar{\sigma}_{2.} = 2.0 \\ \bar{\sigma}_{3.} = 3.0 \end{array}$$

$$\bar{\sigma}_{.1} = 1.0 \qquad \bar{\sigma}_{.2} = 2.0 \qquad \bar{\sigma}_{.3} = 3.0 \qquad \bar{\sigma}_{..} = 2.0$$

$$\bar{\sigma}_{jj} = 3.0$$

where $\bar{\sigma}_{.j}$ = mean for column j
  $\bar{\sigma}_{j.}$ = mean for row j
  $\bar{\sigma}_{..}$ = mean of all entries
  $\bar{\sigma}_{jj}$ = mean of main-diagonal entries.

The matrix of terms of the form $\sigma_{jj'} - \bar{\sigma}_{j.} - \bar{\sigma}_{.j} + \bar{\sigma}_{..}$ is

$$\begin{bmatrix} 1.00 & -0.50 & -0.50 \\ -0.50 & 1.00 & -0.50 \\ -0.50 & -0.50 & 1.00 \end{bmatrix}.$$

Note that the form of the last matrix corresponds to compound symmetry. In general if Σ_x is circular, the matrix whose elements are $\sigma_{jj'} - \bar{\sigma}_{j.} - \bar{\sigma}_{.j'} + \bar{\sigma}_{..}$ will have compound symmetry. From this information, then,

$$\varepsilon = \frac{9(3.0 - 2.0)^2}{2(4.50)} = 1.0.$$

Thus, Σ_x is circular; when Σ_x is circular, $\varepsilon = 1.0$.
  Equivalently, from the characteristic roots of Σ_y, one has

$$\varepsilon = \frac{\sum \lambda_i^2}{(k-1) \sum \lambda_i^2}$$

$$= \frac{(1.50 + 1.50)^2}{(2)[1.50^2 + 1.50^2]} = \frac{9}{9} = 1.0.$$

When Σ_x has maximum departure from circularity, Σ_y will have maximum departure from sphericity and will take the form (for $k = 4$)

$$\Sigma_y = \begin{bmatrix} c & c & c \\ c & c & c \\ c & c & c \end{bmatrix}$$

where c is some constant. The characteristic roots of this equation are

$$\lambda_1 = 3c, \qquad \lambda_2 = 0, \qquad \lambda_3 = 0.$$

In this case

$$\varepsilon = \frac{9c^2}{(k-1)(9c^2)} = \frac{1}{k-1}.$$

Thus, the range of the measure of departure from circularity is

$$\frac{1}{k-1} = \varepsilon \le 1.0.$$

In general Σ_x is unknown but may be estimated by S_x, the sample covariance matrix. In terms of the latter, one may estimate ε (Collier et al. 1967) as

$$\hat{\varepsilon} = \frac{k^2(\bar{s}_{jj} - s_{..})^2}{[(k-1)(\Sigma \Sigma s_{jj'}^2 - 2k \Sigma s_{j.}^2 + k^2\bar{s}_{..}^2)]},$$

where $\Sigma \Sigma s_{jj'}^2 = $ sum of the squares of *all* entries of S_x

$\bar{s}_{..} = (\Sigma \Sigma s_{jj'})/k^2 = $ grand mean of all entries

$\bar{s}_{j.} = \Sigma s_{jj'}^2/k = $ row means

$\bar{s}_{jj} = \Sigma s_{jj}/k = $ main diagonal mean.

This estimate of ε tends to be biased for larger values of ε. Others (Huynh and Feldt, 1976; Huynh, 1978) recommend a less biased estimate of ε,

$$\bar{\varepsilon} = \frac{n(k-1)\hat{\varepsilon} - 2}{(k-1)[n-1-(k-1)\hat{\varepsilon}]}.$$

This latter measure, $\bar{\varepsilon}$, may exceed 1. When this occurs, set $\bar{\varepsilon} = 1.0$. It will be found that $\bar{\varepsilon} \ge \hat{\varepsilon}$; $\bar{\varepsilon}$ will always be equal to $\hat{\varepsilon}$ when $\hat{\varepsilon} = 1/(k-1)$.

Box (1954) has shown that the overall F statistic in the repeated measures designs is distributed as

$$F[(k-1)\varepsilon, (n-1)(k-1)\varepsilon].$$

In terms of $\hat{\varepsilon}$, F is approximately distributed as

$$F[(k-1)\hat{\varepsilon}, (n-1)(k-1)\hat{\varepsilon}].$$

That is, by adjusting the degrees of freedom to take into account the degree to which the circularity assumption has been violated, an F distribution can be approximated with any arbitrary covariance matrix.

If one assumes that $\varepsilon = 1$, then the degrees of freedom for F are $k-1$, $(n-1)(k-1)$. That is, the assumption of circularity is met and no adjustment is required. If the assumption has not been met, this gives the F test a positive bias and the real level of significance will exceed the nominal level established by the experimenter. If one sets ε at its minimum value, the assumption is that Σ_x deviates maximally from circularity and $\varepsilon = 1/(k-1)$. At this extreme, one uses $F(1, n-1)$ since

$$(k-1)\varepsilon = (k-1)\frac{1}{(k-1)} = 1$$

$$(n-1)(k-1)\varepsilon = (n-1)(k-1)\left(\frac{1}{k-1}\right) = n-1.$$

In most instances, this adjustment is too extreme and the F will have a negative bias. However, it is reasonable to use this procedure, and if H_0 is rejected no further steps are required since this test would have minimum statistical power and any other value for ε would lead to rejection of the null hypothesis. The use of $F(1, n-1)$ has been labeled the Geisser–Greenhouse conservative test (Geisser–Greenhouse, 1958; Kirk, 1982).

If one uses the unadjusted F and does *not* reject the null hypothesis, no further steps are necessary since that F has maximum power and the use of other values for ε would lead to non-rejection of H_0.

Uncertainty arises when the unadjusted F leads to rejection of the null hypothesis, and the maximum correction leads to non-rejection. It is under those circumstances that ε should be estimated and the adjusted degrees of freedom should be used. For example if $\alpha = 0.05$, $k = 3$, and $n = 5$, and $\hat{\varepsilon} = 0.80$, the critical value for the test is

$$F_{0.95}[(2)(0.80), (4)(2)(0.80)] = F_{0.95}(1.6, 6.40)$$

$$= 5.21.$$

If one were to use $\bar{\varepsilon}$ to estimate ε, then

$$\bar{\varepsilon} = \frac{(5)(2)(0.80)}{2[4 - 2(0.80)]} = 1.36,$$

which would be set equal to 1.00 and the unadjusted degrees of freedom would be used. The maximum correction yields $\varepsilon = 1/k - 1 = 0.50$. Thus, to summarize, with $k = 3$ and $n = 5$:

ε	Critical Value	
$\bar{\varepsilon} = 1.0$	$F_{0.95}(2, 9)$	$= 4.46$
$\hat{\varepsilon} = 0.80$	$F_{0.95}(1.6, 6.4)$	$= 5.21$
$\dfrac{1}{(k-1)} = 0.50$	$F_{0.95}(1, 4)$	$= 7.71.$

For small degrees of freedom, it is difficult to double interpolate in tables of the ordinary F distribution to use adjusted degrees of freedom. However, this interpolation may be avoided by using the Imhof tables, which are in Appendix D. For the example at hand, with $\hat{\varepsilon} = 0.80$, $k = 3$, and $n = 5$, the corrected F of interest is

$$F[(k-1)\hat{\varepsilon}, (k-1)(n-1)\hat{\varepsilon}] = F(1.6, 6.40).$$

This F is presented in the Imhof tables in terms of the parameters

$$h = (k-1)\hat{\varepsilon} = 1.6, \text{ and}$$

$$m = n - 1 = 4.$$

From the Imhof tables, then,

$$F_{0.95}(h = 1.60, m = 4) = 5.21.$$

TABLE 4.12 **Monte Carlo study of effect of Box correction for degrees of freedom on level of significance**

ε	n	k	α:	$\hat{\varepsilon}$ 0.10	0.05	0.01	α:	$\tilde{\varepsilon}$ 0.10	0.05	0.01
0.363	10	5		0.096	0.052	0.012		0.105	0.060	0.018
	15	5		0.096	0.051	0.012		0.101	0.054	0.015
	20	5		0.098	0.054	0.012		0.101	0.033	0.015
0.752	10	5		0.080	0.034	0.007		0.102	0.055	0.013
	15	5		0.082	0.038	0.008		0.096	0.051	0.013
	20	5		0.094	0.044	0.011		0.102	0.051	0.014
0.831	10	5		0.078	0.036	0.006		0.101	0.053	0.013
	15	5		0.085	0.040	0.009		0.101	0.053	0.014
	20	5		0.091	0.046	0.080		0.103	0.053	0.012
1.00	10	5		0.071	0.029	0.003		0.095	0.046	0.009
	15	5		0.081	0.034	0.005		0.095	0.047	0.009
	20	5		0.093	0.046	0.006		0.105	0.050	0.010

From Huynh and Feldt (1979).

A Monte Carlo study (Huynh and Feldt, 1979) illustrating how well the Box correction for degrees of freedom works with respect to the level of significance, is shown in Table 4.12. One notes that when $\varepsilon = 1$, the adjustment procedure using $\hat{\varepsilon}$ errs on the side of making the actual level of significance too small relative to the nominal level of significance. Since $\tilde{\varepsilon}$ is set equal to 1.00 when it exceeds 1.00, this bias disappears when one uses $\tilde{\varepsilon}$ in the adjustment procedure. When $\varepsilon = 0.752$, using $\hat{\varepsilon}$ in the adjustment procedure tends to make the actual level of significance too small relative to the nominal level of significance. There is little or no bias when $\tilde{\varepsilon}$ is used.

TEST OF ASSUMPTIONS. Mauchley (1940) has published a procedure for testing the hypothesis that

$$\Sigma_{M^*\Sigma_x M^{*'}} = \Sigma_y = \lambda I.$$

The test statistic used in the Mauchley test is

$$W = \frac{|M^* S_x M^{*'}|}{[tr(M^* S_x M^{*'})/k - 1]^{k-1}}$$

$$= \frac{|S_y|}{[tr S_y/k - 1]^{k-1}},$$

where

$$|M^* S_x M^{*'}| = |S_y|$$

is the determinant of S_y, and

$$trM^*S_xM^{*'} = tr\,|S_y|$$

is the trace of S_y. The range of W is

$$0 \le W \le 1,$$

the lower limit occurring when there is maximum departure from sphericity and the upper limit $W = 1$ corresponding to S_y being spherical. The smaller the numerical value of W, the greater is the departure of S_y from sphericity. Tables of the exact sampling distribution of the statistic W (under the hypothesis that Σ_y is spherical) have been prepared by Nargarsenker and Pillai (1973) and are presented in Appendix D.

A good approximation of the exact distribution of W may be obtained by the maximum-likelihood statistic

$$L = -(n - 1)d(\ln W),$$

where

$$d = \frac{(2p^2 + p + 2)}{6p(n - 1)}, \qquad p = k - 1.$$

The statistic L is approximately distributed as chi square with degrees of freedom equal to

$$[p(p + 1)/2] - 1.$$

As an example of the application of the Mauchley test, suppose that $k = 3$, $n = 11$, and

$$S_x = \begin{bmatrix} 12 & 6 & 14 \\ 6 & 32 & 28 \\ 14 & 28 & 45 \end{bmatrix}.$$

(This example is taken from Huynh, H. and L. S. Feldt, 1970, p. 1588.)

First, it is interesting to examine the extent to which this matrix departs from circularity. Since a matrix in which

$$\sigma_{jj} + \sigma_{j'j'} - 2\sigma_{jj'} = 2\lambda$$

is circular, one can examine the extent to which

$$s_{jj} + s_{j'j'} - 2s_{jj'}$$

is constant. One has for this example

$$s_{11} + s_{22} - 2s_{12} = 12 + 32 - 12 = 32$$
$$s_{11} + s_{33} - 2s_{13} = 12 + 45 - 28 = 29$$
$$s_{22} + s_{33} - 2s_{23} = 32 + 45 - 56 = 21.$$

These values are similar and with small sample sizes deviations from equality for $s_{x_j - x_{j'}}$ of this size may be expected even if Σ_x is circular.

A more formal measure is provided by the measure of departure from sphericity

$$\hat{\varepsilon} = \frac{k^2(\bar{s}_{jj} - s_{..})^2}{k - 1(\sum\sum s_{jj'}^2 - 2k\sum s_{j.}^2 + k^2\bar{s}_{..}^2)},$$

where

$$\bar{s}_{jj} = (12 + 32 + 45)/3 = 29.67$$
$$\bar{s}_{..} = (12 + 6 + 14 + \cdots + 45)/9 = 20.55$$
$$\bar{s}_{1.} = (12 + 6 + 14)/3 = 10.67$$
$$\bar{s}_{2.} = (6 + 32 + 28)/3 = 22.00$$
$$\bar{s}_{3.} = (14 + 28 + 45)/3 = 29.67$$
$$\sum\sum s_{jj'}^2 = (12^2 + 6^2 + 14^2 + \cdots + 45^2) = 5225,$$

and

$$\hat{\varepsilon} = \frac{(9)(29.67 - 20.55)^2}{(2)[5225 - (2)(3)(10.67^2 + 22.00^2 + 29.67^2) + (9)(20.55^2)]}$$

$$= \frac{747.13}{790.17} = 0.945.$$

The Mauchley test may be used to test the hypothesis that Σ_x is circular by testing for sphericity in Σ_y. For example, under a normalized orthogonal transformation of S_x, one obtains

$$S_y = \begin{bmatrix} 16 & 2.31 \\ 2.31 & 11.33 \end{bmatrix}.$$

To test the hypothesis that Σ_y is spherical, one computes

$$W = \frac{|S_y|}{[(tr S_y)/(k - 1)]^{k-1}}$$

$$= \frac{[(16)(11.33) - (2.31)(2.31)]}{[(16.80 + 11.33)/2]^2}$$

$$= 0.942.$$

From tables of the exact distribution of W one finds

$$W_{0.95}(k - 1, n) = W_{0.95}(2, 11) = 0.514.$$

For a test having $\alpha = 0.05$, the decision rule is:

Reject the hypothesis of sphericity if

$$W < 0.514.$$

In this case the decision is to not reject the hypothesis that Σ_y is spherical. That is, the observed covariance matrix S_y could have been obtained with relatively high probability (with sample size $n = 11$) from a population in which Σ_y is spherical. From tables of the sampling distribution of W, one notes that

$$W_{0.75}(2, 11) = 0.735;$$

even with level of significance $\alpha = 0.25$, the hypothesis of sphericity would not be rejected for this case.

To use the chi-square approximation to the sampling distribution of W, for these data one transforms W to L as follows:

$$d = 1 - \frac{2p^2 + p + 2}{6(p - 1)} = 0.90, \quad p = k - 1 = 2,$$

$$f = \frac{p(p + 1)}{2} - 1 = 2, \quad \ln W = \ln 0.942 = -0.05975.$$

Hence

$$L = -(n - 1)(d)(\ln W) = -(10)(0.90)(-0.05975) = 0.5379.$$

In this case for a test having $\alpha = 0.05$, the decision rule is:

Reject the hypothesis of sphericity if

$$L > \chi^2_{0.95}(2) = 5.99.$$

As expected, the data do not contradict the hypothesis that Σ_y is spherical.

To indicate how close the maximum-likelihood approximation is to the exact test, if one replaces W in the formula for L by $W_{0.95}(2, 11)$, for this example one obtains

$$L = -(10)(0.90)(\ln 0.514)$$
$$= -(10)(0.90)(-0.66553) = 5.99.$$

In this case the exact and the maximum-likelihood approximation yield critical values which are identical to two decimal places.

If the test described here were made at $\alpha = 0.01$, from tables of W one finds

$$W_{0.99}(2, 11) = 0.3594.$$

The corresponding percentile point in terms of the maximum-likelihood approximation is

$$L = -(10)(0.90)(\ln 0.3594) = -(10)(0.90)(-1.0222)$$
$$= 9.21.$$

From tables of chi square, one finds

$$\chi^2_{0.99}(2) = 9.21.$$

Again the chi-square approximation to the exact critical value is correct to two decimal places. Additional comparisons with the exact tables are shown in Table 4.13.

TABLE 4.13 **Comparison of chi-square approximation with exact values of sampling distribution of Mauchley's W statistic**

p	n	d	f	$-\ln W_{0.05}(p, n)$	Exact value $L_{0.05} = (n-1)(d)(-\ln W_{0.05})$	Approx. $\chi^2_{0.95}(f)$
3	11	0.872	5	1.2774	11.14	11.07
4	21	0.921	9	0.9231	16.41	16.92
6	21	0.889	20	1.7825	31.69	31.41

p	n	d	f	$-\ln W_{0.01}(p, n)$	$L_{0.01} = (n-1)(d)(-\ln W_{0.01})$	$\chi^2_{0.95}(f)$
3	11	0.872	5	1.7433	15.20	15.09
4	21	0.921	9	1.1823	21.78	21.67
6	21	0.889	20	2.328	37.92	37.57

Routine use of the Mauchley test is not recommended. The use of $\hat{\varepsilon}$ and adjusted degrees of freedom is preferred when there is reason to suspect that the assumptions have not been met.

SUMMARY OF ASSUMPTIONS. The necessary and sufficient condition that the F statistic in the overall test in a repeated-measure design has an F distribution is that an orthonormal transformation on Σ_x define a set of Y variates which have a covariance matrix that is spherical in form. That is

$$\Sigma_y = \lambda I_{k-1} \quad \text{where} \quad \Sigma_y = M^* \Sigma_x M^{*'},$$

M^* being an orthonormal matrix of order $(k-1) \times k$. In particular if Σ_x has compound symmetry, the orthonormal transformation will lead to a spherical matrix. More generally if Σ_x is circular in form, an orthonormal transformation on X will yield a spherical matrix Σ_y.

Given a matrix of order $n \times k$ of observed data (repeated measures) from the population $N_k(\mu_x, \Sigma_x)$, where Σ_x is unknown, an estimate of Σ_x based upon the sample data is

$$\hat{\Sigma}_x = S_x.$$

S_x is the sample covariance matrix. An orthonormal transformation on the X variates yields a set of $k - 1$, Y variates given by

$$Y = M^* X'.$$

The covariance matrix for the Y variates will be given by

$$S_y = M^* S_x M^{*'}.$$

Even though Σ_x may be circular in form, S_x may differ from circularity by sampling error. Hence S_y may differ from sphericity by sampling error. One may test the hypothesis that Σ_y is spherical in form through use of the Mauchley test.

As an alternative or supplement to the use of the Mauchley test, a measure of deviation from circularity, $\hat{\varepsilon}$, may be used to correct the degrees of freedom of the F distribution as a way of compensating for violation of the assumptions.

Pooling Covariance Matrices

For the design at hand, there is only one covariance matrix S_x. For more complex repeated-measures designs discussed in later chapters, there will be numerous covariance matrices which are pooled together in the process of carrying out the analyses. In some important applications sampling distribution assumptions demand equivalence of covariance matrices which are to be pooled. To demonstrate the relevant equivalence, consider the three covariance matrices in Table 4.14. In Table 4.14, $\Sigma_x^{(3)}$ is related to $\Sigma_x^{(1)}$ and $\Sigma_x^{(2)}$ as follows:

$$\Sigma_x^{(3)} = \tfrac{1}{2}(\Sigma_x^{(1)} + \Sigma_x^{(2)}).$$

That is, $\Sigma_x^{(3)}$ is obtained by pooling the other two matrices. Both $\Sigma_x^{(1)}$ and $\Sigma_x^{(1)}$ are circular matrices with the property that

$$\bar{\sigma}_{ii} - \bar{\sigma}_{ij} = 2.$$

This property is also shared by the pooled covariance matrix $\Sigma_x^{(3)}$. In general if two circular covariance matrices having identical values for $\bar{\sigma}_{jj} - \bar{\sigma}_{jj'}$ are pooled, the pooled covariance matrix will also be circular. For this example, all three matrices have one of their characteristic roots equal to 2. This follows from that fact that all three matrices are circular and have

$$\bar{\sigma}_{ii} - \bar{\sigma}_{ij} = 2.$$

TABLE 4.14 **Properties of three covariance matrices**

$$\Sigma_X^{(1)} = \begin{bmatrix} 3 & 2 & 3 \\ 2 & 5 & 4 \\ 3 & 4 & 7 \end{bmatrix} \qquad \Sigma_X^{(2)} = \begin{bmatrix} 4 & 3 & 4 \\ 3 & 6 & 5 \\ 4 & 5 & 8 \end{bmatrix} \qquad \Sigma_X^{(3)} = \begin{bmatrix} 3.5 & 2.5 & 3.5 \\ 2.5 & 5.5 & 4.5 \\ 3.5 & 4.5 & 7.5 \end{bmatrix}$$

$\bar{\sigma}_{ii} = 5$	$\bar{\sigma}_{ii} = 6$	$\bar{\sigma}_{ii} = 5.5$
$\bar{\sigma}_{ij} = 3$	$\bar{\sigma}_{ij} = 4$	$\bar{\sigma}_{ij} = 3.5$
$\bar{\sigma}_{ii} - \bar{\sigma}_{ij} = 2$	$\bar{\sigma}_{ii} - \bar{\sigma}_{ij} = 2$	$\bar{\sigma}_{ii} - \bar{\sigma}_{ij} = 2$
$\lambda_1 = 11.623$	$\lambda_1 = 14.480$	$\lambda_1 = 13.129$
$\lambda_2 = 2.000$	$\lambda_2 = 2.000$	$\lambda_2 = 2.000$
$\lambda_3 = 1.377$	$\lambda_3 = 1.519$	$\lambda_3 = 1.371$
$\Sigma_Y^{(1)} = 2I_2$	$\Sigma_Y^{(2)} = 2I_2$	$\Sigma_Y^{(3)} = 2I_2$

$$\Sigma_Y^{(1)} = \Sigma_Y^{(2)} = \Sigma_Y^{(3)} = 2I_2$$

Although $\Sigma_x^{(1)}$, $\Sigma_x^{(2)}$, and $\Sigma_x^{(3)}$ are not equal, they are equivalent in the sense that

$$M^*\Sigma_x^{(1)}M^{*'} = M^*\Sigma_x^{(2)}M^{*'} = M^*\Sigma_x^{(3)}M^{*'} = 2I_2.$$

4.5 STATISTICAL MODELS AND THE ASSUMPTIONS

Different models for the observations lead to different outcomes for the covariance matrix. A simple additive model leads to an underlying covariance matrix which has compound symmetry. A somewhat more complicated model is required to lead to circularity, and other covariance matrix patterns may occur.

Model Leading to Compound Symmetry

A *strictly* additive model contains no interaction terms. Consider the model

$$X_{ij} = \mu + \pi_i + \tau_j + \varepsilon_{ij}.$$

In this model

X_{ij} = an observation on person i under treatment j.

μ = grand mean of all potential observations and is constant for all observations.

π_i = a constant associated with person i in the experiment. Whether or not person i is included in the experiment depends upon random selection from the population of interest. Thus, $\pi: N(0, \sigma_\pi^2)$;

τ_j = a treatment effect which is constant for each treatment and is defined as $\tau_j = \mu_j - \mu$, where μ_j is the mean of all potential observations under treatment j. $\sum \tau_j = \sum (\mu_j - \mu) = 0$.

ε_{ij} = experimental error associated with each observation X_{ij}. ε_{ij} is defined by all sources of variation in X_{ij} except those accounted for by the treatment effects τ_j and element effects π_i. For each treatment j, $\varepsilon_{ij}: N(0, \sigma_\varepsilon^2)$. That is, errors are assumed to be normally distributed within each treatment and $\sigma_{\varepsilon_1}^2 = \sigma_{\varepsilon_2}^2 = \cdots = \sigma_{\varepsilon_k}^2 = \sigma_\varepsilon^2 \cdot \varepsilon_{ij}$ is uncorrelated with all other terms in the model.

Thus, the observations are a strictly additive function of the model elements; no provision is made for interactions among the components of the model. For the special case wherein $k = 3$, this model is made explicit for a sample of n people in Table 4.15.

Since μ and τ_1 are constant for all observations under treatment 1, the variance of the X's within treatment population 1 is a function of the variance due to π_i and ε_{i1}. Assuming π_i and ε_{i1} are uncorrelated,

$$\sigma_{x_1}^2 = \sigma_\varepsilon^2 + \sigma_\pi^2.$$

In words, under the assumptions that have been made the variance of the potential observations under treatment 1 is the sum of the variance due to

TABLE 4.15 **Additive model for repeated-measure design** $(k = 3)$

Person	Treatment 1	Treatment 2	Treatment 3
1	$X_{11} = \mu + \pi_1 + \tau_1 + \varepsilon_{11}$	$X_{12} = \mu + \pi_1 + \tau_2 + \varepsilon_{12}$	$X_{13} = \mu + \pi_1 + \tau_3 + \varepsilon_{13}$
2	$X_{21} = \mu + \pi_2 + \tau_1 + \varepsilon_{21}$	$X_{22} = \mu + \pi_2 + \tau_2 + \varepsilon_{22}$	$X_{23} = \mu + \pi_2 + \tau_3 + \varepsilon_{23}$
$\vdots$			
i	$X_{i1} = \mu + \pi_i + \tau_1 + \varepsilon_{i1}$	$X_{i2} = \mu + \pi_i + \tau_2 + \varepsilon_{i2}$	$X_{i3} = \mu + \pi_i + \tau_3 + \varepsilon_{i3}$
$\vdots$			
n	$X_{n1} = \mu + \pi_n + \tau_1 + \varepsilon_{n1}$	$X_{n2} = \mu + \pi_n + \tau_2 + \varepsilon_{n2}$	$X_{n3} = \mu + \pi_n + \tau_3 + \varepsilon_{n3}$
Totals	$T_1 = n\mu + \sum \pi_i + n\tau_1 + \sum \varepsilon_{i1}$	$T_2 = n\mu + \sum \pi_i + n\tau_2 + \sum \varepsilon_{i2}$	$T_3 = n\mu + \sum \pi_i + n\tau_3 + \sum \varepsilon_{i3}$
Means	$\bar{T}_1 = \mu + \bar{\pi} + \tau_1 + \bar{\varepsilon}_1$	$\bar{T}_2 = \mu + \bar{\pi} + \tau_2 + \bar{\varepsilon}_2$	$\bar{T}_3 = \mu + \bar{\pi} + \tau_3 + \bar{\varepsilon}_3$

experimental error and the variance due to differences between the π's. Similarly the variance due to the potential observations under treatment 2 is

$$\sigma_{x_2}^2 = \sigma_\varepsilon^2 + \sigma_\pi^2,$$

and under treatment 3 is

$$\sigma_{x_3}^2 = \sigma_\varepsilon^2 + \sigma_\pi^2.$$

In general, within any column the terms which vary are ε_{ij} and π_i. Hence the expected value of the variance within any column is

$$E(\text{column variance}) = \sigma_{x_j}^2 = \sigma_\varepsilon^2 + \sigma_\pi^2.$$

Since the term π_i is common to two measurements on the same person, the covariance between X_1 and X_2 will not in general be equal to zero. Indeed, the only terms that covary across columns are the π_i. Hence all covariance between X_j and $X_{j'}$ is due to π_i, and the expected value of the covariance between columns is, therefore,

$$E(\text{covariance between columns}) = \sigma_{x_j x_{j'}} = \sigma_\pi^2.$$

In words, the covariance is due solely to the variance of person effects. Since the ε_{ij} are uncorrelated with the π_i, the expectation of the covariance terms does not include σ_ε^2.

From this, it follows that under a strictly additive model the covariance structure has the population form

$$\Sigma_x = \begin{bmatrix} \sigma_\varepsilon^2 + \sigma_\pi^2 & \sigma_\pi^2 & \sigma_\pi^2 & \cdots & \sigma_\pi^2 \\ & \sigma_\varepsilon^2 + \sigma_\pi^2 & \sigma_\pi^2 & \cdots & \sigma_\pi^2 \\ & & \sigma_\varepsilon^2 + \sigma_\pi^2 & \cdots & \sigma_\pi^2 \\ & & & \vdots & \\ & & & & \sigma_\varepsilon^2 + \sigma_\pi^2 \end{bmatrix}.$$

That is, all the variances are equal and are equal to $\sigma_\varepsilon^2 + \sigma_\pi^2$, and all the covariances are equal and are equal to σ_π^2. This matrix obviously has compound symmetry.[2]

It is of interest to express the same relations in terms of the matrix of intercorrelations. Given the assumptions, the correlation between any two treatments can be defined as

$$\rho = \frac{\sigma_{x_j x_{j'}}}{\sigma_x^2}$$

$$= \frac{\sigma_\pi^2}{\sigma_\varepsilon^2 + \sigma_\pi^2},$$

and

$$\rho \sigma_x^2 = \sigma_{x_j x_{j'}} = \sigma_\pi^2.$$

Hence, the matrix of intercorrelations takes the form

$$R = \frac{1}{\sigma_\varepsilon^2 + \sigma_\pi^2} \Sigma_x = \begin{bmatrix} 1 & \rho & \rho & \cdots & \rho \\ & 1 & \rho & \cdots & \rho \\ & & 1 & \cdots & \rho \\ & & & \vdots & \\ & & & & 1 \end{bmatrix}.$$

That is, compound symmetry (homogeneity of variances and covariances) for Σ_x implies homogeneity of correlations between observations under all pairs of treatment conditions.

The matrix Σ_x for the potential observations under treatments $1, \ldots, k$ is estimated by the matrix

$$\hat{\Sigma}_x = S_x^* = \begin{bmatrix} \overline{\text{var}} & \overline{\text{cov}} & \overline{\text{cov}} & \cdots & \overline{\text{cov}} \\ & \overline{\text{var}} & \overline{\text{cov}} & \cdots & \overline{\text{cov}} \\ & & \overline{\text{var}} & \cdots & \overline{\text{cov}} \\ & & & \vdots & \\ & & & & \overline{\text{var}} \end{bmatrix},$$

where $\overline{\text{var}}$ and $\overline{\text{cov}}$ are respectively the mean of the variances and the mean of the covariances in S_x. The matrix also has compound symmetry. In this estimate of Σ_x

$$E(\overline{\text{var}}) = \sigma_x^2 = \sigma_\varepsilon^2 = \sigma_\pi^2,$$

---

[2] When Σ_x has compound symmetry its inverse, which is involved in some key relationships, takes the relatively simple form

$$\Sigma_x^{-1} = \frac{1}{\text{var} - \text{cov}} \left[I - \frac{\text{cov}}{\text{var} + (k-1)\,\text{cov}} J \right]$$

where $\text{var} = \sigma_\varepsilon^2 + \sigma_\pi^2$, $\text{cov} = \sigma_\pi^2$,

J = square matrix all of the elements of which are unity.

and

$$E(\overline{\text{cov}}) = \sigma_{x_j x_{j'}} = \sigma_\pi^2 \quad \text{for all} \quad j \neq j',$$

and

$$E\left(\frac{\overline{\text{cov}}}{\overline{\text{var}}}\right) = \frac{\sigma_\pi^2}{\sigma_\varepsilon^2 + \sigma_\pi^2} = \rho.$$

It is of interest to express the expectation of all of the observed variances (mean squares) in the analysis of variance in terms of the parameters of the covariance matrix Σ_x.

Consider first the expectation for MS_{res}. Under the assumptions of this model, MS_{res} estimates error variance. This result may be arrived at by examining the model as summarized in Table 4.15. From the model, one has

$$(X_{ij} - \bar{P}_i - \bar{T}_j + \bar{G}) = \varepsilon_{ij} - \bar{\varepsilon}_{i.} - \bar{\varepsilon}_{.j} + \bar{\varepsilon}_{..}.$$

Since

$$\text{MS}_{\text{res}} = \frac{1}{(n-1)(k-1)} \sum \sum (X_{ij} - \bar{P}_i - \bar{T}_j + \bar{G})^2,$$

it follows that

$$E(\text{MS}_{\text{res}}) = \sigma_\varepsilon^2.$$

This result may also be approached from the point of view of the variance–covariance matrix. It may be shown that the computational formula for MS_{res} is equivalent to

$$\text{MS}_{\text{res}} = \overline{\text{var}} - \overline{\text{cov}}.$$

From this, it follows that

$$\begin{aligned}
E(\text{MS}_{\text{res}}) &= E(\overline{\text{var}} - \overline{\text{cov}}) \\
&= \sigma_x^2 - \sigma_\pi^2 \\
&= (\sigma_\pi^2 + \sigma_\varepsilon^2) - \sigma_\pi^2 \\
&= \sigma_\varepsilon^2.
\end{aligned}$$

Finally, the same result may be expressed in terms of the correlation matrix. Since

$$\rho \sigma_x^2 = \sigma_\pi^2,$$
$$\begin{aligned}
E(\text{MS}_{\text{res}}) &= \sigma_x^2 - \sigma_\pi^2 \\
&= \sigma_x^2(1 - \rho) \\
&= \sigma_\varepsilon^2 + \sigma_\pi^2 - \rho \sigma_x^2 \\
&= \sigma_\varepsilon^2.
\end{aligned}$$

$\text{MS}_{\text{b. people}}$ may also be developed directly in terms of the model. In terms of the additive model,

$$\bar{P}_i = \frac{1}{k} \sum_j X_{ij} = \mu + \pi_i + \bar{\varepsilon}_i.$$

Hence,

$$kE[\mathrm{var}(\bar{P}_i)] = E(\mathrm{MS}_{\mathrm{b.\ people}})$$
$$= k(\sigma_{\bar{\varepsilon}}^2 + \sigma_{\pi}^2)$$
$$= \sigma_{\varepsilon}^2 + k\sigma_{\pi}^2.$$

Since it may also be shown that the computational formula for $\mathrm{MS}_{\mathrm{b.\ people}}$ is equivalent to

$$\mathrm{MS}_{\mathrm{b.\ people}} = \overline{\mathrm{var}} + (k-1)\,\overline{\mathrm{cov}},$$

it follows that

$$E(\mathrm{MS}_{\mathrm{b.\ people}}) = E[\overline{\mathrm{var}} + (k-1)\,\overline{\mathrm{cov}}]$$
$$= \sigma_x^2 + (k-1)\sigma_{\pi}^2$$
$$= \sigma_{\varepsilon}^2 + \sigma_{\pi}^2 + k\sigma_{\pi}^2 - \sigma_{\pi}^2$$
$$= \sigma_{\varepsilon}^2 + k\sigma_{\pi}^2.$$

In terms of the correlation matrix, this result may be expressed as

$$E(\mathrm{MS}_{\mathrm{b.\ people}}) = \sigma_x^2[1 + (k-1)\rho].$$

Finally, $\mathrm{MS}_{\mathrm{treat}}$ is defined in terms of differences among treatment means. From the structural model, one has

$$\bar{T}_j - \bar{T}_{j'} = (\tau_j - \tau_{j'}) + (\bar{\varepsilon}_{.j} - \bar{\varepsilon}_{.j'}).$$

Since the same people are observed under all treatments, differences between treatment means are free of any effects associated with the $\bar{\pi}$'s. The variance of differences among treatment means when the experiment is replicated with random samples of people has the form (assuming the treatment and error effects are uncorrelated)

$$\sigma_{\bar{T}}^2 = \sigma_{\tau}^2 + \sigma_{\bar{\varepsilon}}^2.$$

Since $\mathrm{MS}_{\mathrm{treat}}$ is defined in terms of $n \sum (\bar{T}_j - \bar{T}_{j'})^2$, one has

$$E(\mathrm{MS}_{\mathrm{treat}}) = n\sigma_{\bar{T}}^2 = n\sigma_{\tau}^2 + n\sigma_{\bar{\varepsilon}}^2$$
$$= n\sigma_{\tau}^2 + \sigma_{\varepsilon}^2.$$

In terms of the parameters of the covariance matrix, this result may be expressed as

$$E(\mathrm{MS}_{\mathrm{treat}}) = \sigma_x^2(1 - \rho) + n\sigma_{\tau}^2.$$

To summarize, under the additive model being considered one has the following $E(\mathrm{MS})$:

$$\mathrm{MS}_{\mathrm{b.\ people}}:\ \sigma_{\varepsilon}^2 + k\sigma_{\pi}^2 = \sigma_x^2[1 + (k-1)\rho],$$
$$\mathrm{MS}_{\mathrm{treat}}:\ \sigma_{\varepsilon}^2 + n\sigma_{\tau}^2 = \sigma_x^2(1 - \rho) + n\sigma_{\tau}^2,$$
$$\mathrm{MS}_{\mathrm{res}}:\ \sigma_{\varepsilon}^2 = \sigma_x^2(1 - \rho).$$

The $E(\mathrm{MS})$ at the extreme right are in terms of the parameters of the variance–covariance matrix for the X_j. The correspondence between the parameters of this covariance matrix and the parameters in the model was established by a set of assumptions on the parameters in the model. It will be found that the $E(\text{MS})$ at the extreme right hold for a class of models of which this is a special case.

One notes that

$$\frac{E(\text{MS}_{\text{treat}})}{E(\text{MS}_{\text{res}})} = \frac{\sigma_\varepsilon^2 + n\sigma_\tau^2}{\sigma_\varepsilon^2} = 1 \quad \text{when} \quad \sigma_\tau^2 = 0.$$

Further, the ratio

$$F = \frac{\text{MS}_{\text{treat}}}{\text{MS}_{\text{res}}}$$

is distributed as a central F distribution when $\sigma_\tau^2 = 0$. Hence, to test the hypothesis that $\sigma_\tau^2 = 0$, the F ratio indicated is appropriate. Since τ_j corresponds to a fixed factor, it is understood that

$$\sigma_\tau^2 = \frac{\sum \tau_j^2}{k - 1}.$$

When $\sigma_\tau^2 > 0$, the F ratio indicated has a noncentral F distribution with noncentrality parameter

$$\lambda = \frac{n \sum \tau_j^2}{\sigma_\varepsilon^2}.$$

The development presented here has been based upon the assumption that the treatments were a fixed variable and people were a random variable. This is a so-called mixed model (Model III). There are other possibilities. A fixed-effects model (Model I) would result if both subjects and treatments were considered to be fixed $(\sum_j \tau_j = 0, \; \sum_i \pi_i = 0)$. Under those circumstances the inferences one can make are restricted to both the treatments and subjects actually included in the study. Such a study would be of very little interest since one would like to at least generalize to a population of subjects. Where the subjects are actually blocks defined by some control variable other than each subject acting as his own control, Model I may be more useful.

A random-effects model (Model II) is one in which both elements and treatments are random variables. Thus, $\tau_j\colon N(0, \sigma_\tau^2)$ and $\pi_i\colon N(0, \sigma_\pi^2)$. When both subjects and treatments are taken as random samples from some population, the results may be generalized to populations of both subjects and treatments.

Table 4.16 presents the expected values of the mean squares for these various conditions. It is worth noting that regardless of which variables are fixed or random, for the strictly additive model under consideration, MS_{res} is the denominator for all tests on treatment effects. The nature of the inferences does, however, change.

TABLE 4.16 $E(MS)$ **for Models I, II, and III**

Mean Square	Model I	Model II	Model III†
$MS_{b.\ people}$	$\sigma_\varepsilon^2 + k \sum_i \pi_i^2/n - 1$	$\sigma_\varepsilon^2 + k\sigma_\pi^2$	$\sigma_\varepsilon^2 + k\sigma_\pi^2$
MS_{treat}	$\sigma_\varepsilon^2 + n \sum \tau_j^2/k - 1$	$\sigma_\varepsilon^2 + n\sigma_\tau^2$	$\sigma_\varepsilon^2 + n \sum \tau_j^2/k - 1$
MS_{res}	σ_ε^2	σ_ε^2	σ_ε^2

† Treatments fixed, people random.

Model with Interaction and the Assumption of Circularity

The necessary and sufficient condition for meeting the analysis of variance distribution assumptions is circularity of the covariance matrix. As demonstrated above, however, the strictly additive model for the observations leads logically to the more restrictive outcome that the covariance matrix have compund symmetry. This latter outcome is sufficient to meet the distribution assumptions, but is unnecessarily restrictive. It is possible that the less restrictive circularity outcome could result from a model which includes an interaction term. Such a model has a *person by treatment* interaction.

Consider the model

$$X_{ij} = \mu + \pi_i + \tau_j + \pi\tau_{ij} + \varepsilon_{ij}, \qquad \begin{array}{l} i = 1, \ldots, n. \\ j = 1, \ldots, k. \end{array}$$

where $X_{ij} =$ a score for person i under treatment level j
$\mu =$ the population grand mean
$\tau_j = \mu_j - \mu =$ a treatment effect for treatment j. Assume τ_j corresponds to a fixed factor with $\sum \tau_j = 0$, $\sigma_\tau^2 = \sum \tau_j^2/k - 1$
$\pi_i =$ the effect for person i and is a random variable. Thus, $\pi_i\colon N(0, \sigma_\pi^2)$. The π_i are assumed to be independent of ε_{ij} and $\pi\tau_{ij}$.
$\pi\tau_{ij} =$ a person by treatment interaction. $\pi\tau_{ij}$ is a random variable. The variables $\pi\tau_{ij}$ have the constraint $\sum_j \pi\tau_{ij} = 0$. The distribution of the $\pi\tau_{ij}$ is

$$\pi\tau_{ij}\colon N\left(0, \frac{k-1}{k}\sigma_{\pi\tau}^2\right).$$

The $\pi\tau_{ij}$ are assumed to be independent of the π_i and ε_{ij}.

The $\pi\tau_{ij}$ are not, however, independent. The covariance between $\pi\tau_{ij}$ and $\pi\tau_{ij'}$ is

$$\text{cov}\,(\pi\tau_{ij}, \pi\tau_{ij'}) = -\frac{1}{k}\sigma_{\pi\tau}^2, \qquad j \neq j'.$$

However,

$$\text{cov}\,(\pi\tau_{ij}, \pi\tau_{i'j}) = 0, \qquad i \neq i'.$$

Note that under this covariance structure on the $\pi\tau_{ij}$ it follows that

$$\text{var}\,(\pi\tau_{i1} + \cdots + \pi\tau_{ik}) = k\left(\frac{k-1}{k}\right)\sigma^2_{\pi\tau} + (k-1)\left(-\frac{1}{k}\,\sigma^2_{\pi\tau}\right)$$

$$= 0.$$

Under the constraint

$$\sum_j \pi\tau_{ij} = 0$$

this sum will always be zero. Hence the constraint implies the covariance structure, and the covariance structure implies that this sum will be constant.

ε_{ij} = a random error variable with distribution $\varepsilon: N(0,\, \sigma^2_\varepsilon)$
    which is independent of all other terms in the model.

As stated, this is a mixed model with treatments considered to be a fixed factor and elements a random factor.

It is the interaction terms which makes this model a nonadditive model. The inclusion of interaction in the model expresses the possibility that the trend of the observations may not be the same for each person over the k treatments.

Under this approach,

$$\bar{P}_i = \frac{1}{k}\sum_j X_{ij} = \mu + \pi_i + \bar{\varepsilon}_{i.}.$$

Hence

$$kE[\text{var}(\bar{P}_i)] = k(\sigma^2_{\bar{\varepsilon}} + \sigma^2_\pi) = \sigma^2_\varepsilon + k\sigma^2_\pi,$$

$$= E(\text{MS}_{\text{b. people}}).$$

Also from the model,

$$\bar{T}_j - \bar{T}_{j'} = (\tau_j - \tau_{j'}) + (\overline{\pi\tau}_{.j} - \overline{\pi\tau}_{.j'}) + (\bar{\varepsilon}_{.j} - \bar{\varepsilon}_{.j'}).$$

Note that

$$\overline{\pi\tau}_{.j} - \overline{\pi\tau}_{.j'} = \frac{1}{n}[(\pi\tau_{1j} - \pi\tau_{1j'}) + \cdots + (\pi\tau_{nj} - \pi\tau_{nj'})].$$

$$E[\text{var}(\overline{\pi\tau}_{.j} - \overline{\pi\tau}_{.j'})] = \frac{n}{n^2}\left[2\left(\frac{k-1}{k}\right)\sigma^2_{\pi\tau} - 2\left(-\frac{1}{k}\,\sigma^2_{\pi\tau}\right)\right]$$

$$= \frac{2}{n}\,\sigma^2_{\pi\tau}.$$

Since MS_{treat} is a function of $n(\bar{T}_j - \bar{T}_{j.})^2$, one has

$$E(\text{MS}_{\text{treat}}) = \sigma^2_\varepsilon + \sigma^2_{\pi\tau} + n\sigma^2_\tau.$$

The person by treatment interaction may be defined as that part of an observation which is not an additive function of the person and treatment main effects. In this model

$$\widehat{\pi\tau}_{ij} = X_{ij} - \bar{P}_i - \bar{T}_j + \bar{G},$$

TABLE 4.17 $E(MS)$ **for mixed model**

Sources of variation	df	$E(MS)$
Between people	$n - 1$	$\sigma_\varepsilon^2 + k\sigma_\pi^2$
Treatments	$k - 1$	$\sigma_\varepsilon^2 + \sigma_{\pi\tau}^2 + n\sigma_\tau^2$
Person × treatment (res.)	$(n-1)(k-1)$	$\sigma_\varepsilon^2 + \sigma_{\pi\tau}^2$

and

$$MS_{people \times treat} = \frac{\sum_i \sum_j (\widehat{\pi\tau}_{ij})^2}{(n-1)(k-1)}.$$

But this was the definition of MS_{res} in the analysis of variance. Hence, for this model,

$$MS_{res} = MS_{person \times treat}.$$

Under this model

$$\widehat{\pi\tau}_{ij} = \pi\tau_{ij} - \overline{\pi\tau}_j + \varepsilon_{ij} - \bar{\varepsilon}_{i.} - \bar{\varepsilon}_{.j} + \bar{\varepsilon}_{..}.$$

Thus

$$E(\widehat{\pi\tau}_{ij}) = \pi\tau_{ij},$$

$$E(MS_{person \times treat}) = \sigma_\varepsilon^2 + \sigma_{\pi\tau}^2.$$

The expected values of the mean squares are summarized in Table 4.17 for the mixed model with treatments fixed and people randomly selected. It is possible to consider all alternatives (Model I, II, or III) with the non-additive structural model, but there is an appropriate F ratio for testing treatment effects only when people (more generally, blocks) are considered to be a random variable. That is shown in Table 4.18. It is apparent from these expected values that when interactions are actually present ($\sigma_{\pi\tau}^2 > 0$) and when people are a fixed variable, MS_{res} in an F ratio constructed to test for treatment effects is

TABLE 4.18 $E(MS)$ **when interactions are present**

Mean square	Model I (fixed)	Model II (random)	Model III treatments fixed people random	Model III treatments random people fixed
$MS_{b.\,people}$	$\sigma_\varepsilon^2 + k\sum_i \pi_i^2/n-1$	$\sigma_\varepsilon^2 + \sigma_{\pi\tau}^2 + k\sigma_\pi^2$	$\sigma_\varepsilon^2 + k\sigma_\pi^2$	$\sigma_\varepsilon^2 + \sigma_{\pi\tau}^2 + k\sum_i \pi_i^2/n-1$
MS_{treat}	$\sigma_\varepsilon^2 + n\sum_j \tau_j^2/k-1$	$\sigma_\varepsilon^2 + \sigma_{\pi\tau}^2 + n\sigma_\tau^2$	$\sigma_\varepsilon^2 + \sigma_{\pi\tau}^2 + n\sum_j \tau_j^2/k-1$	$\sigma_\varepsilon^2 + n\sigma_\tau^2$
MS_{res}	$\sigma_\varepsilon^2 + \sum_i \sum_j (\pi\tau)_{ij}^2/(n-1)(k-1)$	$\sigma_\varepsilon^2 + \sigma_{\pi\tau}^2$	$\sigma_\varepsilon^2 + \sigma_{\pi\tau}^2$	$\sigma_\varepsilon^2 + \sigma_{\pi\tau}^2$

inappropriately large, resulting in a negatively biased test of significance. Since it is most sensible to consider subjects a random variable, that does not pose a serious problem for the design presented here. However, when blocks are formed by some other control variable it may be a consideration, since it may not be reasonable to consider the blocking variable to be random. Tukey (1949) has published a test for nonadditivity which has some usefulness in deciding whether MS_{res} estimates σ_ε^2 or includes some estimate of a non-zero interaction variance which might negatively bias such a test.

The $k \times k$ variance–covariance matrix Σ which was made explicit with the additive model is actually in the background of the present model. If the matrix Σ has the symmetry properties indicated under the additive approach, then the F ratio for testing the hypothesis $\sigma_\tau^2 = 0$ suggested by Table 4.16, namely

$$F = \frac{MS_{treat}}{MS_{person \times treat}},$$

will have the distribution $F[k - 1, (n - 1)(k - 1)]$ when $\sigma_\tau^2 = 0$. If the matrix Σ does not have the symmetry properties indicated, then the test based upon the F distribution is an approximate one.

There are circumstances, albeit somewhat unrealistic, wherein this model with interactions may lead to a covariance matrix with circularity. Such a model may be formulated as follows. Consider a difference between two observations on person i:

$$X_{ij} - X_{ij'} = (\tau_j - \tau_{j'}) - (\varepsilon_{ij} - \varepsilon_{ij'}).$$

Since this difference is taken on the same person, the ε's are assumed to be correlated. Further the variance of this difference is assumed to be equal to

$$\sigma_{x_{ij} - x_{ij'}}^2 = \sigma_j^2 + \sigma_{j'}^2 - 2\sigma_{jj'}$$
$$= \sigma_{jj} + \sigma_{j'j'} - 2\sigma_{jj'}$$
$$= \text{constant for all } j \neq j'.$$

In this case the variances do not necessarily have to be equal nor are the covariances assumed to be equal. One only assumes that the variance of the difference scores is constant. (This is consistent with the assumption made when one works with Fisher's t test for correlated data.) Differences in the magnitudes of the variances may be offset by compensating differences in the covariances. Under an orthonormal transformation this kind of model is transformed into a model which meets the assumption of homogeneity of variance and uncorrelated error. In terms of the transformed data, the usual assumptions of an analysis of variance without repeated measures are met when this model actually holds.

If one focuses on differences in responsiveness of an individual and assumes that the variance of such differences remains constant over a set of treatments, then the assumption of circularity of the underlying covariance matrix becomes, in addition to being a necessary and sufficient condition for certain distribution assumptions, a realistic model for a repeated-measure design. It may be that the inclusion of a person by treatment interaction term in the model can contribute to making the circularity model plausible. Such a covariance term will contribute to making the within-treatment variances unequal. However, it is difficult to see how these interactions will give the covariances the required pattern relative to the variances. Because of this, the strictly additive model that leads to compound symmetry appears to be more realistic.

Simplex Pattern of Covariance Matrix

In addition to compound symmetry and circularity, there are other patterns for the covariance matrix which may be reasonable under certain experimental circumstances. One of those is a simplex pattern.

If repeated measures are made on the same variate over a series of time intervals, it is sometimes found that the observations close to each other in time are more highly correlated than observations which are farther apart in time. The correlation will change with time or trials in a repeated measures design if the people effects π_i are a function of the treatments (or time) and a simplex pattern may be generated. For example if there are $k = 4$ time periods (the time periods correspond to treatments) the covariance matrix might have the following pattern:

$$\Sigma_x = \sigma_\varepsilon^2 \begin{bmatrix} 1 & \rho & \rho^2 & \rho^3 \\ \rho & 1 & \rho & \rho^2 \\ \rho^2 & \rho & 1 & \rho \\ \rho^3 & \rho^2 & \rho & 1 \end{bmatrix}.$$

That is, all of the variances are equal to σ_ε^2 and ρ is the correlation between adjacent time periods. For example, if

$$\sigma_\varepsilon^2 = 10 \quad \text{and} \quad \rho = 0.80,$$

then Σ_x would be

$$\Sigma_x = \begin{bmatrix} 10.00 & 8.00 & 6.40 & 5.12 \\ 8.00 & 10.00 & 8.00 & 6.40 \\ 6.40 & 8.00 & 10.00 & 8.00 \\ 5.12 & 6.40 & 8.00 & 10.00 \end{bmatrix}.$$

This pattern is called a *simplex* pattern. One notes that the entries on the diagonals running from upper left to lower right are equal. One also notes that

$$\rho = \frac{\sigma_{j,j+1}}{\sigma_\varepsilon}, \qquad \rho^2 = \frac{\sigma_{j,j+2}}{\sigma_\varepsilon^2}.$$

The simplex pattern does not have circularity unless $\rho = 0$.

TABLE 4.19 **Values of ε when Σ_x has simplex pattern**

			k			
ρ	3	4	5	7	10	25
0.10	0.996	0.992	0.990	0.987	0.985	0.982
0.20	0.985	0.971	0.961	0.949	0.940	0.929
0.30	0.968	0.940	0.919	0.892	0.872	0.848
0.40	0.948	0.901	0.866	0.822	0.782	0.745
0.50	0.925	0.859	0.809	0.743	0.692	0.629
0.60	0.900	0.814	0.749	0.663	0.594	0.507
0.70	0.875	0.769	0.689	0.584	0.499	0.387
0.80	0.849	0.724	0.631	0.510	0.411	0.275
0.90	0.824	0.661	0.551	0.410	0.298	0.138

Lower bound

$\varepsilon^* =$	0.800	0.641	0.526	0.381	0.266	0.103
$\dfrac{1}{(k-1)} =$	0.500	0.333	0.350	0.167	0.111	0.042

From Wallenstein and Fleiss (1979).

Assuming that Σ_x does have a simplex pattern with a specified value for ρ, the measure of departure from circularity ε is given in Table 4.19.

These values of ε may be computed from the matrix of correlations in the same manner in which they are computed from a covariance matrix corresponding to a simplex pattern. For example, if $k = 3$ and $\rho = 0.80$ then

$$R = \begin{bmatrix} 1 & 0.80 & 0.64 \\ 0.80 & 1 & 0.80 \\ 0.64 & 0.80 & 1 \end{bmatrix} = [\rho_{ij}].$$

From this matrix one has

$$\sum \rho_{ij} = 7.4800, \qquad \sum \rho_{ij}^2 = 6.3792,$$

$$\bar{\rho}_{..} = 0.8311, \qquad \bar{\rho}_{1.} = 0.8133,$$

$$\bar{\rho}_{jj} = 1.0000, \qquad \bar{\rho}_{2.} = 0.8667,$$

$$\bar{\rho}_{3.} = 0.8133.$$

Hence

$$\varepsilon = \frac{9[1.0000 - 0.8311]^2}{2[6.3792 - 6(2.074133) + 9(0.690745)]}$$

$$= \frac{0.2567}{0.3022} = 0.8494.$$

This is the value one will find in Table 4.19.

The Box adjusted degrees of freedom technique may be used to obtain the critical value for the overall test. As indicated at the bottom of Table 4.19 the lower bound for ε, say ε^*, for the case of the simplex pattern is higher than the corresponding lower bound for ε when Σ_x is arbitrary. If one uses ε^* to obtain the critical value, one has an ultraconservative test in the sense that the critical value will be too large. That critical value is given by

$$F_{1-\alpha}[(k-1)\varepsilon^*, \quad (k-1)\varepsilon^*(n-1)].$$

This lower bound for the case of a simplex pattern is

$$\varepsilon^* = \frac{5(k+1)}{2k^2+7}.$$

For example, if $k = 4$,

$$\varepsilon^* = \frac{5(5)}{39} = 0.641.$$

In general for the simplex pattern, the Box adjusted degrees of freedom approach will have the critical value

$$F_{1-\alpha}[(k-1)\varepsilon, \quad (k-1)\varepsilon(n-1)],$$

where ε is determined from k and the estimated value for ρ. One way of estimating ρ is to compute the intercorrelation matrix and then use the first two supradiagonal elements for estimation purposes. Suppose, for example, that $k = 4$ and that the sample correlation matrix is

$$R_x = \begin{bmatrix} 1 & 0.80 & 0.58 & 0.30 \\ & 1 & 0.76 & 0.60 \\ & & 1 & 0.83 \\ & & & 1 \end{bmatrix}.$$

Then

$$\hat{\rho} = \frac{0.80 + 0.76 + 0.83 + 0.58 + 0.60}{5} = 0.785.$$

Then the estimate of the population correlation matrix under the hypothesis that Σ_x has a simplex pattern is

$$R_x = \begin{bmatrix} 1 & 0.785 & 0.616 & 0.484 \\ & 1 & 0.785 & 0.616 \\ & & 1 & 0.785 \\ & & & 1 \end{bmatrix}.$$

If Σ_x has a simplex pattern and ρ is large (say greater than 0.70), Monte Carlo studies have found that the Box adjusted degrees of freedom procedure tends to err on the side of making the critical value too small. When ρ tends to be less than 0.50, the Box approximation tends to work quite well.

4.6 MEASURES OF ASSOCIATION AND POWER

The preceding discussion of the expected values of mean squares forms a basis for computing power and measures of association. Table 4.16 summarizes the expected values of the mean squares for the strictly additive model,

$$X_{ij} = \mu + \pi_i + \tau_j + \varepsilon_{ij}.$$

Tables 4.17 and 4.18 summarize for the model with interaction between people and treatments,

$$X_{ij} = \mu + \pi_i + \tau_j + \pi\tau_{ij} + \varepsilon_{ij}.$$

Vaughan and Corballis (1969), Dodd and Schultz (1973) and Koele (1982) have all presented very useful discussions of measures of association and power using those values. Scheffé (1959) provided the foundation for those discussions.

Measures of Association

In Sec. 3.9, the general goal of constructing measures of association which estimate the proportion of total variance accounted for by treatments was discussed. Two measures, $\hat{\omega}^2$ for the case wherein treatments are fixed, and $\hat{\rho}_I^2$, when treatments are random, were introduced. In general terms, those discussions also apply to the repeated measures design.

In principle one might consider Model I, wherein both subjects and treatments are fixed. However, it is not a particularly useful case since one would wish to at least generalize to a population of elements. Accordingly, four alternate cases will be considered here. Subjects will be considered random and treatments either fixed or random. Those two conditions will be combined with both the additive model and the model with interaction between people and treatments.

ADDITIVE MODEL. For the additive model, the expected values of mean squares are provided in Table 4.16 for both randomly-selected and fixed treatment levels.

When treatments are random,

$$\hat{\sigma}_\tau^2 = (MS_{treat} - MS_{res})/n$$
$$\hat{\sigma}_\pi^2 = (MS_{b.\ people} - MS_{res})/k$$
$$\hat{\sigma}_\varepsilon^2 = MS_{res}.$$

The estimated proportion of total variance associated with treatments is

$$\hat{\rho}_I^2 = \frac{\hat{\sigma}_\tau^2}{\hat{\sigma}_\varepsilon^2 + \hat{\sigma}_\tau^2 + \hat{\sigma}_\pi^2}.$$

Using the numerical example summarized in Table 4.4 to illustrate,

$$\hat{\sigma}_\tau^2 = (MS_{treat} - MS_{res})/n = \frac{(232.70 - 9.40)}{5} = 44.67$$

$$\hat{\sigma}_\pi^2 = (MS_{b.\,people} - MS_{res})/k = \frac{(170.20 - 9.40)}{4} = 40.20$$

$$\hat{\sigma}_\varepsilon^2 = MS_{res} = 9.40.$$

Hence,

$$\hat{\rho}_I^2 = \frac{44.67}{44.67 + 40.20 + 9.40} = \frac{44.67}{94.27} = 0.47.$$

Instead of computing $\hat{\rho}_I^2$ by summing separate estimates for σ_τ^2, σ_π^2, and σ_ε^2, one may compute directly (Dodd and Schultz, 1973):

$$\hat{\rho}_I^2 = \frac{k(MS_{treat} - MS_{res})}{SS_{total} + MS_{treat} + MS_{b.\,people} - MS_{res}}$$

$$= \frac{4(232.73 - 9.40)}{1491.80 + 232.73 + 170.20 - 9.40}$$

$$= \frac{893.32}{1885.33} = 0.47.$$

When treatments are fixed,

$$\hat{\sigma}_\tau^2 = \frac{(k-1)}{nk}(MS_{treat} - MS_{res}) = \tfrac{3}{20}(232.73 - 9.40) = 33.50$$

$$\sigma_\pi^2 = (MS_{b.\,people} - MS_{res})/k = 40.20$$

$$\sigma_\varepsilon^2 = MS_{res} = 9.40.$$

Thus,

$$\hat{\omega}^2 = \frac{33.50}{33.50 + 40.20 + 9.40} = \frac{33.50}{83.10} = 0.40.$$

Computed directly,

$$\hat{\omega}^2 = \frac{k - 1(MS_{treat} - MS_{res})}{SS_{total} + MS_{b.\,people}}$$

$$= \frac{SS_{treat} - (k-1)MS_{res}}{SS_{total} + MS_{b.\,people}}$$

$$= \frac{698.20 - (3)(9.40)}{1491.80 + 170.20} = \frac{670.00}{1662.00} = 0.40.$$

Hence, 40 percent of the variance is due to treatments.

NONADDITIVE MODEL. For the model,

$$X_{ij} = \mu + \pi_i + \tau_j + \pi\tau_{ij} + \varepsilon_{ij},$$

the expected values of mean squares are provided in Table 4.18.

When treatments are random, the results are the same as for the additive model (note that it is not possible to obtain separate estimates of σ_ε^2 and $\sigma_{\pi\tau}^2$, their sum being estimated by MS_{res}):

$$\hat{\sigma}_\tau^2 = (MS_{treat} - MS_{res})/n = 44.67,$$

$$\hat{\sigma}_\pi^2 = (MS_{b.\,people} - MS_{res})/k = 40.20,$$

and

$$\hat{\sigma}_\varepsilon^2 + \hat{\sigma}_{\pi\tau}^2 = MS_{res} = 9.40.$$

Hence,

$$\hat{\rho}_I^2 = \frac{44.67}{44.67 + 40.20 + 9.40} = \frac{44.67}{94.27} = 0.47.$$

When treatments are fixed for the nonadditive model,

$$\hat{\sigma}_\tau^2 = \frac{(k-1)}{nk}(MS_{treat} - MS_{res})$$

$$\hat{\sigma}_\pi^2 + \frac{\hat{\sigma}_\varepsilon^2}{k} = \frac{MS_{b.\,people}}{k}$$

$$\sigma_{\pi\tau}^2 + \sigma_\varepsilon^2 = MS_{res}.$$

For the numerical example,

$$\hat{\sigma}_\tau^2 = \frac{3}{20}(232.73 - 9.40) = 33.50$$

$$\hat{\sigma}_\pi^2 + \frac{\hat{\sigma}_\varepsilon^2}{k} = \frac{170.20}{4} = 42.55$$

$$\hat{\sigma}_{\pi\tau}^2 + \hat{\sigma}_\varepsilon^2 = 9.40.$$

If one attempts to estimate the proportion of variance due to the treatments by summing all three values, the estimate of total variance will be too large by $\hat{\sigma}_\varepsilon^2/k$. That is,

$$\hat{\sigma}_{total}^2 = \hat{\sigma}_{treat}^2 + (\hat{\sigma}_\pi^2 + \hat{\sigma}_\varepsilon^2/k) + (\hat{\sigma}_{\pi\tau}^2 + \hat{\sigma}_\varepsilon^2).$$

Hence,

$$\hat{\omega}^2 = \frac{33.50}{33.50 + 42.55 + 9.40} = 0.39$$

is negatively biased by $\hat{\sigma}_\varepsilon^2/k$. The same is true if the $\hat{\omega}^2$ is computed directly as

$$\hat{\omega}^2 = \frac{SS_{treat} - (k-1)(MS_{res})}{SS_{total} + MS_{b.\,people} + nMS_{res}}$$

$$= \frac{698.20 - (3)(9.40)}{1491.80 + 170.20 + (5)(9.40)} = 0.39.$$

Estimating Power

As was pointed out in Chapter 3, when treatments are fixed the observed F statistic follows a noncentral F distribution with noncentrality parameter

$$\lambda = \frac{n \sum \tau_j^2 / k}{\sigma_\varepsilon^2}.$$

Power is given by

$$\text{Probability } \{F > F_{1-\alpha}[k-1, (n-1)(k-1); \lambda]\}.$$

Hence, when treatments are fixed, one must specify values for λ which, in turn, requires the experimenter to estimate treatment effects for either the additive or nonadditive model. For both the additive and nonadditive models,

$$\hat{\sigma}_\tau^2 = \frac{(k-1)}{nk} (\text{MS}_{\text{treat}} - \text{MS}_{\text{res}})$$

may be used as a basis for estimating treatment effects. One may proceed as in Sec. 3.9 to obtain power and sample-size estimates from appropriate tables and/or charts. One must remember that the F distribution has $(n-1)(k-1)$ instead of $k(n-1)$ degrees of freedom in the denominator when power or sample sizes are estimated.

When treatments are random, the observed F statistic follows a multiple of the central F distribution where the multiple of the F distribution is given by the ratio of the expected values of the mean squares of the numerator and denominator of the F statistic. Hence, the power of the test is given by

$$\text{Probability } \left\{ \frac{E(\text{MS}_{\text{treat}})}{E(\text{MS}_{\text{res}})} F > F_{1-\alpha}[k-1, (n-1)(k-1)] \right\}.$$

To compute power, then, requires the experimenter to have estimates of all of the variance components of both MS_{treat} and MS_{res}. Otherwise, there are no special problems associated with estimating power or sample sizes.

Designs in which each subject acts as its own control potentially offer increases in statistical power over completely randomized designs. This is most clearly seen by comparing error estimates for the two designs. For the completely randomized design, everything in the universe which affects the dependent variable except for the treatment effects is called error. Thus

$$E(\text{MS}_{\text{within treatment}}) = \sigma_x^2 = \sigma_\varepsilon^2.$$

That is, *all* variance from within the constant treatment condition is due to error.

With subjects held constant, error no longer includes people effects; they are removed from the error estimate. Formally, all variance due to people effects is shown to be covariance between treatments and

$$E(\text{MS}_{\text{res}}) = \sigma_\varepsilon^2 = \sigma_x^2(1 - \rho)$$
$$= \sigma_x^2 - \rho\sigma_x^2.$$

Thus, the size of the error associated with repeated measures is a function of the size of the average correlation (covariance, variance due to people effects) arising between treatments.

As has been emphasized, the reduction of error and, therefore, increased efficiency is accomplished at the expense of simplicity of assumptions. The repeated measures analysis is based upon a set of assumptions concerning the structure of the variance–covariance matrices which are difficult to meet in many experimental situations. When those assumptions are in question, the recommended procedure is to adjust the degrees of freedom of the F ratio. In so doing, however, the increased statistical power gained by controlling subjects may be lost due to the reduction of degrees of freedom. Another possibility is to use a multivariate analysis of variance when the assumptions of the univariate, repeated-measures design cannot be met. It is difficult, however, to formulate a set of rules whereby one type of analysis will always or clearly be preferred to the other. Vonesh and Schork (1986) have presented a discussion of methods of estimating sample sizes in the multivariate analysis of repeated measures.

4.7 HOTELLING'S T^2 MULTIVARIATE ANALYSIS OF DATA THAT DO NOT MEET THE CIRCULARITY ASSUMPTION

In Sec. 4.4 it was indicated that tests in the analysis of variance are exact only if the population covariance matrix Σ has a specified pattern. Exact procedures for testing the hypothesis that $\sigma_\tau^2 = 0$, where Σ is arbitrary, will be described in this section. Here the basic assumption is that the variables have a joint multivariate normal distribution with arbitrary covariance matrix Σ. If the pattern assumption on Σ is appropriate, the test to be described will be less powerful than the corresponding test in the analysis of variance.

When the *sample* covariance matrix is replaced by a matrix which has compound symmetry, the T^2 statistic to be computed in this section will actually be equal to $(k-1)F_a$, where F_a is the F ratio obtained in the analysis of variance. For small deviations from compound symmetry, T^2 will be quite close to $(k-1)F_a$.

In what follows it is assumed that k, the number of treatments, is four. Generalization to k equal to any number is direct. Throughout, it will be assumed that $n > k$. Let

$$\underset{4,4}{S} = \text{covariance matrix for observations,}$$

$$\bar{\mathbf{t}}' = [\bar{T}_1 \quad \bar{T}_2 \quad \bar{T}_3 \quad \bar{T}_4] = \text{vector of treatment means,}$$

$$\underset{3,4}{C} = \begin{bmatrix} 1 & 0 & 0 & -1 \\ 0 & 1 & 0 & -1 \\ 0 & 0 & 1 & -1 \end{bmatrix},$$

$$\underset{3,3}{S_y} = CSC',$$

$$\underset{3,1}{\bar{\mathbf{y}}} = C\bar{\mathbf{t}}.$$

There are many possible choices for the matrix C. All that is required is that matrix C have rank $k - 1$, and that for each row the sum must be zero. For example, an alternative choice for C might be

$$C^{(1)} = \begin{bmatrix} 1 & -1 & 0 & 0 \\ 0 & 1 & -1 & 0 \\ 0 & 0 & 1 & -1 \end{bmatrix}.$$

It will be found that the T^2 statistic will be invariant for all choices of C.

One notes that

$$\bar{\mathbf{y}} = C\bar{\mathbf{t}} = \begin{bmatrix} \bar{T}_1 - \bar{T}_4 \\ \bar{T}_2 - \bar{T}_4 \\ \bar{T}_3 - \bar{T}_4 \end{bmatrix}.$$

Under the hypothesis that $\tau_1 = \tau_2 = \tau_3 = \tau_4$,

$$E(\bar{\mathbf{y}}) = \begin{bmatrix} 0 \\ 0 \\ 0 \end{bmatrix}.$$

One also notes that

$$\bar{\mathbf{y}}^{(1)} = C^{(1)}\bar{\mathbf{t}} = \begin{bmatrix} \bar{T}_1 - \bar{T}_2 \\ \bar{T}_2 - \bar{T}_3 \\ \bar{T}_3 - \bar{T}_4 \end{bmatrix},$$

and under the hypothesis specified above,

$$E(\bar{\mathbf{y}}^{(1)}) = \begin{bmatrix} 0 \\ 0 \\ 0 \end{bmatrix}.$$

The covariance matrix associated with $\bar{\mathbf{y}}$ is $(1/n)CSC' = (1/n)S_y$.

Under the hypothesis indicated, the statistic

$$T^2 = n\bar{\mathbf{y}}'S_y^{-1}\bar{\mathbf{y}}$$

is distributed as Hotelling's (central) T^2. Equivalently, under the hypothesis that $\sigma_\tau^2 = 0$,

$$\frac{n - k + 1}{(n - 1)(k - 1)} T^2 \quad \text{is distributed as} \quad F(k - 1, n - k + 1).$$

One should note that in the analysis of variance the F distribution involved is $F[k - 1, (n - 1)(k - 1)]$.

What has been done here is to transform the hypothesis

$$\tau_1 = \tau_2 = \cdots = \tau_k$$

into the equivalent hypothesis

$$\boldsymbol{\mu} = \begin{bmatrix} \tau_1 - \tau_k \\ \tau_2 - \tau_k \\ \vdots \\ \tau_{k-1} - \tau_k \end{bmatrix} = \begin{bmatrix} 0 \\ 0 \\ \vdots \\ 0 \end{bmatrix}.$$

Given a $k - 1$ multivariate normal population, the T^2 distribution represents the sampling distribution for the vector of sample means $\bar{\mathbf{y}}$ when $\boldsymbol{\mu} = \mathbf{0}$ on the population. The covariance matrix Σ in this population is estimated by S_y. Percentile points on the T^2 distribution can be obtained from the F distribution.

The computation of Hotelling's T^2 for the numerical data in Table 4.3 is illustrated in Table 4.20. In part i, the components of the vector $\bar{\mathbf{t}}'$ are those obtained from Table 4.3. S_y is obtained from the covariance matrix in Table 4.9. The T^2 statistic is computed in part ii. Converted to an F statistic, $F = 28.39$. The sampling distribution of this F statistic has $k - 1$ and $n - k + 1$ degrees of freedom, or three and two degrees of freedom. With only two degrees of freedom for the denominator, the resulting test will have very low power. Whenever k is large relative to n, the power of a test involving the T^2 statistic will be low. The resulting T^2 statistic exceeds the critical value for a test

TABLE 4.20   Computation of Hotelling's T^2 ($n = 5$, $k = 4$)

$\bar{\mathbf{t}}' = [26.40 \quad 25.60 \quad 15.60 \quad 32.00]$

$\bar{\mathbf{t}}'C' = [-5.60 \quad -6.40 \quad -16.40]$

$S_y = CSC'$

$$= \begin{bmatrix} 1 & 0 & 0 & -1 \\ 0 & 1 & 0 & -1 \\ 0 & 0 & 1 & -1 \end{bmatrix} \begin{bmatrix} 76.80 & 53.20 & 29.20 & 69.00 \\ 53.20 & 42.80 & 15.80 & 47.00 \\ 29.20 & 15.80 & 14.80 & 27.00 \\ 69.00 & 57.00 & 27.00 & 64.00 \end{bmatrix} \begin{bmatrix} 1 & 0 & 0 \\ 0 & 1 & 0 \\ 0 & 0 & 1 \\ -1 & -1 & -1 \end{bmatrix}$$

(i)

$$= \begin{bmatrix} 2.80 & 1.20 & -2.80 \\ 1.20 & 13.00 & 5.80 \\ -2.80 & 5.80 & 24.80 \end{bmatrix}$$

$$S_y^{-1} = \begin{bmatrix} 0.45690 & -0.07280 & 0.06861 \\ -0.07280 & 0.09749 & -0.03102 \\ 0.06861 & -0.03102 & 0.05532 \end{bmatrix}$$

$$T^2 = n\bar{\mathbf{y}}'S_y - 1\bar{\mathbf{y}}' = 170.36$$

(ii)

$$F = \frac{n - k + 1}{(n - 1)(k - 1)}\, T^2 = 28.39 \qquad \begin{array}{l} F_{0.95}(3, 2) = 19.2 \\ F_{0.99}(3, 2) = 99.2 \end{array}$$

TABLE 4.21 **Computation of Hotelling's T^2—assuming Σ has compound symmetry**

(i)

$$\bar{\mathbf{y}} = [-5.60 \quad -6.40 \quad -16.40]$$

$$S^* = \begin{bmatrix} 49.60 & 40.20 & 40.20 & 40.20 \\ 40.20 & 49.60 & 40.20 & 40.20 \\ 40.20 & 40.20 & 49.60 & 40.20 \\ 40.20 & 40.20 & 40.20 & 49.60 \end{bmatrix}$$

$$S_y^* = (CSC')^{-1} = \begin{bmatrix} 0.07980 & -0.02662 & -0.02662 \\ -0.02662 & 0.07980 & -0.02662 \\ -0.02662 & -0.02662 & 0.07980 \end{bmatrix}$$

(ii)

$$T^2 = n\mathbf{y}S_v^{*-1}\mathbf{y} = 74.29$$

$$F_a = \frac{1}{k-1} T^2 = \tfrac{1}{3}(74.29) = 24.76$$

having level of significance 0.05. (The analysis-of-variance test exceeded the 0.01 level, but the latter test had a larger number of degrees of freedom in the denominator—resulting from a pooling under the assumption of compound symmetry.) The model under which the test using Hotelling's T^2 statistic is applicable is a more general one in the sense that it involves fewer assumptions about symmetry in the underlying parameters.

It will be instructive to compute Hotelling's T^2 statistic for the case in which the sample covariance matrix is replaced by a matrix which has compound symmetry. Toward this end, suppose the S matrix in Table 4.20 is replaced by the S^* matrix in Table 4.21. The latter has $\overline{\text{var}}$ on the main diagonal and $\overline{\text{cov}}$ off the main diagonal. This matrix would be an estimate of Σ under the hypothesis of compound symmetry. The resulting T^2 statistic is shown in part ii. One notes that $T^2 = 74.29$. From Table 4.4 one has $F_a = 24.76$. Hence

$$T^2 = (k-1)F_\alpha = 3(24.76) = 74.28.$$

Under the hypothesis of compound symmetry,

$$\frac{1}{k-1} T^2 \qquad \text{is distributed as} \qquad F[k-1, (n-1)(k-1)].$$

A more detailed discussion of the use of the T^2 statistic will be found in T. W. Anderson (1958, pp. 107–112) and Morrison (1967, pp. 133–141).

4.8 TOPICS CLOSELY RELATED TO REPEATED-MEASURES ANOV

There are a number of problems which can be addressed in a manner closely related to the repeated-measures analysis of variance. Those include use of the variance-component model to estimate reliability of measurements, analysis of variance of ranked data, and analysis of dichotomous data. Those topics are all covered in Appendix E.

4.9 EXERCISES

1. An experimenter was interested in evaluating the response to motivation upon errors in a learning task. Four levels of motivation were defined in terms of task complexity and time constraints. A random sample of $n = 8$ subjects was selected and each subject was tested under all four motivation conditions in an independent random order. Total errors were scored over a period of 20 minutes of performance under each treatment condition. Those scores are:

	Motivation conditions			
Person	1	2	3	4
1	24	20	18	30
2	26	28	14	30
3	26	25	16	32
4	30	28	16	34
5	14	18	10	22
6	27	24	17	31
7	26	25	15	33
8	25	26	13	30

(a) Carry out the analysis of variance and test the hypothesis $H_0: \mu_1 = \mu_2 = \mu_3 = \mu_4$ ($\alpha = 0.05$).

(b) Assume that the first motivation level was a control condition designed to minimize motivation and the other three conditions were designed to represent increased motivational levels.

  (1) Test the *a priori* hypothesis, $H_0: \mu_1 = (\mu_2 + \mu_3 + \mu_4)/3$ ($\alpha = 0.05$).

  (2) Compare each of the treatments, t_2, t_3 and t_4 to the control condition using an appropriate procedure to control ($\alpha_{joint} = 0.05$).

(c) Carry out a trend analysis, evaluating the linear, quadratic and cubic trends ($\alpha_{ind} = 0.05$).

(d) Compute S, the observed variance–covariance matrix. Show numerically that $MS_{res} = \overline{var} - \overline{cov}$ from that matrix.

(e) Compute $\hat{\varepsilon}$ and adjust the degrees of freedom using $\hat{\varepsilon}$.

(f) Compute $s_{jj} - s_{j'j'} - 2s_{jj'}$ to inspect the extent to which the values are constant for all possible values $j \geq j'$.

(g) On balance, using the information from (e) and (f), is it reasonable for the experimenter to conclude that the assumptions were met?

(h) Assume that the motivation conditions were fixed. What proportion of the total variance (estimated) is accounted for by the treatment conditions, assuming:

  a. $X_{ij} = \mu + \pi_i + \tau_j + \varepsilon_{ij}$,

  b. $X_{ij} = \mu + \pi_i + \tau_j + \pi\tau_{ij} + \varepsilon_{ij}$.

2. The analysis summarized in Table 4.6 is of data from a discrimination learning study wherein $n = 10$ and $k = 7$. Given the nature of the study, blocks of trials should be considered to be fixed.

   (a) Were the assumptions of the repeated-measures design met for these data?

   (b) The experimenter has shown that a function with a cubic component would provide a good fit to the data using a trend analysis. What is the magnitude of association between learning and the seven trial blocks when trends of all possible degree are assessed?

   (c) What would have been the outcome of this study if it had been carried out as a completely randomized design with $n = 10$ independent observations under each treatment?

3. A social psychologist was interested in the accumulative impact of a particular mode of interaction between teachers and students upon academic achievement. Under one mode of interaction, for 6 randomly selected students who were observed over four one-week sessions, the achievement scores were:

	Weeks			
Students	**1**	**2**	**3**	**4**
1	10	10	15	13
2	13	10	15	14
3	14	13	16	12
4	14	12	17	18
5	15	14	16	16
6	17	15	18	19

   (a) Complete an analysis of variance of these data and test the hypothesis, $H_0: \mu_1 = \mu_2 = \mu_3 = \mu_4$. ($\alpha = 0.05$.)

   (b) Compute $\hat{\omega}^2$.

   (c) Calculate the power of the test in (a) above.

   (d) Use the Newman–Keuls procedure to compare all unique pairs of treatment means ($\alpha = 0.05$).

   (e) Carry out a trend analysis to determine the degree of the function needed to best fit these data. ($\alpha = 0.05$.)

   (f) Compute (assuming an additive model):

   (1) $\hat{\sigma}_\tau^2$

   (2) $\hat{\sigma}_\pi^2$

   (3) $\hat{\sigma}_{\pi\tau}^2 + \hat{\sigma}_e^2$.

   (g) Evaluate the efficiency of this design relative to a completely randomized design with the same data.

   (h) Evaluate the hypothesis in (a) above assuming the assumptions regarding the pattern of the variance–covariance matrices have *not* been met.

CHAPTER 5

DESIGN AND ANALYSIS OF FACTORIAL EXPERIMENTS: COMPLETELY RANDOMIZED DESIGNS

5.1 GENERAL PURPOSE

Basic principles underlying factorial designs are discussed in this chapter. Examples and detailed computational procedures associated with these designs are given in Chapter 6.

Factorial experiments permit the experimenter to evaluate the combined effect of two or more experimental variables that are used simultaneously. Information obtained from factorial experiments is more complete than that obtained from a series of single-factor experiments, in the sense that factorial experiments permit the evaluation of *interaction* effects. An interaction effect is an effect attributable to the combination of variables above and beyond that which can be predicted from the variables considered singly.

For example, many of the properties of the chemical substance H_2O (water) cannot be predicted from the properties of oxygen and the properties of hydrogen studied in isolation. Most of the properties of water are attributable to the effect of the interaction between oxygen and hydrogen. The compound formed by this interaction has properties which are not given by simply adding the properties of oxygen to the properties of hydrogen.

At the end of a factorial experiment, the experimenter has information which permits decisions to be made which have a broad range of applicability. In addition to the information about how the experimental variables operate in isolation, the experimenter can predict what will happen when two or more variables are used in combination. Apart from the information about interactions, the estimates of the effects of the individual variables are, in a sense, more practically useful ones; these estimates are obtained by averaging over a relatively broad range of other relevant experimental variables. By contrast, in a single-factor experiment some relevant experimental variables may be held constant, while others may be randomized. In the case of a factorial experiment, the population to which inferences can be made is more inclusive than the corresponding population for a single-factor experiment.

In working with factorial experiments in the behavioral science area, a sharp distinction must be drawn between experiments involving repeated measures on the same elements and those which do not involve repeated measures. The material in this chapter will be concerned primarily with experiments which do not involve repeated measures. These are completely randomized factorial designs. However, many of the basic principles to be developed in this chapter will be applicable, with only slight modification, to the case in which there are repeated measures.

R. A. Fisher (1951, p. 51) defined *factors* as the elementary ingredients of observable effects. These ingredients are assumed to be the underlying causes for what is being observed. The term *factorial* implies that all possible combinations of the factors under study are included in the design. Ideally, the factors to be included in a design are chosen on the basis of prior knowledge or theory about what potentially "causes" an observable outcome. Herein, the term factor will be used in a broad sense. For some purposes a distinction will be made between treatment and classification factors. The latter group the experimental units into classes which are homogeneous with respect to what is being classified. In contrast, treatment factors define the experimental conditions applied to an experimental unit. The administration of the treatment factors is under the direct control of the experimenter, whereas classification factors are not. The effects of the treatment factors are of primary interest to the experimenter, whereas classification factors are included in an experiment to reduce experimental error and clarify interpretation of the effects of the treatment factors. That is, classification factors are used for blocking of experimental units. An experimental unit is the element to which a treatment is administered. The experimental unit may be a single person, a group of people, an individual rat, a litter of rats. The manner in which the treatments are administered determines what the experimental unit is. The allocation of the treatment factor to the units is under the direct control of the experimenter, whereas the class to which an experimental unit belongs is not under direct control. For example, the sex of an animal at the start of an experiment may be either male or female; sex may be a classification factor. The drug under which an animal is observed may be assigned to an animal by an experimenter; hence, drug is a treatment factor.

The design of factorial experiments is concerned with answering the following questions:

1 What factors should be included?
2 How many levels of each factor should be included?
3 How should the levels of the factors be spaced?

4 How should the experimental units be selected?

5 How many experimental units should be selected for each treatment combination?

6 What steps should be taken to control experimental error?

7 What criterion measures should be used to evaluate the effects of the treatment factors?

8 Can the effects of primary interest be estimated adequately from the experimental data that will be obtained?

The answers to these questions will be considered in some detail in this chapter and the chapters that follow. An excellent and readable overview of the planning of factorial experiments will be found in Cox (1958, Chapter 7).

The estimation and hypothesis-testing problems in experimental design work may be approached in two ways. Under one approach, a hypothetical population of elements is postulated. If the treatments were administered to all elements of the population, the resulting population could be described in terms of distributions having specified forms with specified sets of parameters. The experiment consists in drawing a sample from this hypothetical population. The problem is to make inferences about the population from the experiment. In this context, a given experiment may be considered as a sample from a potential population of replications of the experiment.

On the other hand, one may approach the same problems in terms of a (linear) model for a basic observation. Associated with this model are one or more random variables and a set of distribution assumptions on the random variables. In the latter case one is concerned with estimating and testing hypotheses about the parameters in the model. In most cases the two approaches lead to similar results. However, in the approach postulating a hypothetical population of elements, certain constraints appear as a natural part of the system. Both approaches are used in the discussion that follow in this chapter.

5.2 TERMINOLOGY AND NOTATION

The term *factor* will be used interchangeably with the terms *treatment* and *experimental variable*. More specifically, a factor is a series of related treatments or related classifications. The related treatments making up a factor constitute the *levels* of that factor. For example, a factor *color* may consist of three levels: red, green, and yellow. A factor *size* may consist of two levels: small and large. A factor *dosage* may consist of four levels: 1, 3, 5, and 7 cc. The number of levels within a factor is determined largely by the thoroughness with which an experimenter desires to investigate the factor. Alternatively, the levels of a factor are determined by the kind of inferences the experimenter desires to make upon conclusion of the experiment. The levels of a factor may be quantitative variations in an essentially quantitative variable, or they may be qualitatively different categories within an essentially qualitative variable. Basically, a factor is a qualitative variable; in special cases it becomes a quantitative variable.

The *dimensions* of a factorial experiment are indicated by the number of factors and the number of levels of each factor. For example, a factorial experiment in which there are two factors, one having three levels and the other having four levels, is called a 3×4 (read "three by four") factorial experiment. In a $2 \times 3 \times 5$ factorial experiment there are three factors, having respective levels of two, three, and five. The treatment combinations in a 2×3 factorial experiment may be represented schematically as follows:

Levels of factor B

	b_1	b_2	b_3
a_1	ab_{11}	ab_{12}	ab_{13}
a_2	ab_{21}	ab_{22}	ab_{23}

Levels of factor A

In this schema, a_1 and a_2 designate the levels of factor A; b_1, b_2, and b_3 designate the levels of factor B. In general, the levels of factors in the experiment are designated

Factor	Typical level	Numbers of levels
A	a_i	$i = 1, \ldots, p$
B	b_j	$j = 1, \ldots, q$
C	c_k	$k = 1, \ldots, r$
D	d_l	$l = 1, \ldots, s$

for 1-, 2-, 3-, and 4-factor experiments, respectively. For larger designs, the progression is continued with a factor $E, F,$ etc.

In a factorial experiment, *treatment conditions* are defined by combinations of the levels of factors. In the 2×3 factorial experiment illustrated above, there are six possible combinations of the two levels of factor A and the three levels of factor B. These treatment conditions are labeled ab_{ij}, with the first subscript designating the level of factor A which is combined with the level of factor B indicated by the second subscript. Thus, ab_{12} refers to level 1 of factor A combined with level 2 of factor B. In general, there are p levels of factor A and q levels of factor B. Thus, one may form pq treatment conditions in a $p \times q$ factorial design.

One may generalize to larger designs:

Number of factors	Number of treatment conditions	Typical treatment conditions
Three	pqr	abc_{ijk}
Four	$pqrs$	$abcd_{ijkl}$
Five	$pqrst$	$abcde_{ijklm}$
$\vdots$		

It is obvious that factorial experiments can become quite large as the number of levels of each factor increases or as the number of factors increases. For example, in a three-factor $p \times q \times r$ factorial experiment, there are pqr treatment conditions. With only five levels of each factor, there are $5 \times 5 \times 5 = 125$ treatment conditions.

In a completely randomized factorial design, the elements observed under each of the treatment combinations will generally be a random sample from some specified population. This specified population will, in most cases of interest, contain a potentially infinite number of elements. If n elements are to be observed under each treatment combination in a $p \times q$ factorial experiment, a random sample of npq elements from the population is required (assuming no repeated measurements on the same elements). The npq elements are then subdivided at random into pq subsamples of size n each. These subsamples are then assigned at random to the treatment combinations.

The potential (or population) levels of factor A will be designated by the symbols $a_1, a_2, \ldots, a_I, \ldots, a_P$. The number of such potential levels, P, may be quite large. The experimenter may group the P potential levels into p levels ($p < P$) by either combining adjoining levels or deliberately selecting what are considered to be representative levels. For example, if factor A represents the dimension of age, the experimenter may choose to group the levels into 1-year intervals; alternatively, the experimenter may choose to group the levels into 2-year intervals. On the other hand, if factor A represents a dosage dimension, the experimenter may deliberately select a series of representative dosages; i.e., in terms of previous research the levels selected may be representative of low, middle, and high dosages.

When p, the number of levels of factor A included in the experiment, is equal to P, then factor A is called a *fixed* factor. When the selection of the p levels from the potential P levels is determined by some systematic, non-random procedure, then factor A is also considered a fixed factor. In this latter case, the selection procedure reduces the potential P levels to p *effective* levels. Under this type of selection procedure, the effective, potential number of levels of factor A in the population may be designated $P_{\text{effective}}$, and $P_{\text{effective}} = p$.

In contrast to this systematic selection procedure, if the p levels of factor A included in the experiment represent a random sample from the potential P levels, then factor A is considered a *random* factor. For example, in an experiment designed to test the effectiveness of various drugs upon categories of patients, the factor A may be the hospitals in which the patients are located. Potentially, the number of different hospitals may be quite large. If a random sample of p of the P potential hospitals are included in the experiment, then factor A is a random factor. (If, further, the sampling within each of the hospitals selected is proportional to the number of patients within the hospital, then conclusions drawn from this kind of experiment will be relevant to the domain of all patients and not just to the domain of all hospitals.) In most practical situations in which random factors are encountered, p is quite small relative to P, and the ratio p/P is quite close to zero.

Similar definitions apply to factor B. Let the potential level of factor B be designated $b_1, b_2, \ldots, b_J, \ldots, b_Q$. Of these Q potential levels, let the number of levels actually in an experiment be q. If $q = Q$, or if the effective number of levels of factor B is reduced from Q to q by some systematic, nonrandom procedure, then factor B is considered fixed. (The reduction from Q potential levels to q effective levels is a function of the experimental design.) The actual levels of factor B included in an experiment will be designated by the notation $b_1, b_2, \ldots, b_j, \ldots, b_q$. If the q levels in an experiment are a random sample from the Q potential levels, then factor B is considered a random factor. In most practical cases in which factor B is a random factor, Q will be quite large relative to q, and the ratio q/Q will be close to zero.

The ratio of the number of levels of a factor in an experiment to the potential number of levels in the population is called the *sampling fraction* for a factor. In terms of this sampling fraction, the definitions of fixed and random factors may be summarized as follows:

Sampling fraction		Factor
$p/P = 1$	or $p/P_{\text{effective}} = 1$	A is a fixed factor
	$p/P = 0$	A is a random factor
$q/Q = 1$	or $q/Q_{\text{effective}} = 1$	B is a fixed factor
	$q/Q = 0$	B is a random factor

Cases in which the sampling fraction assumes a value between 0 and 1 do occur in practice. However, cases in which the sampling fraction is either 1 or very close to 0 are encountered more frequently.

The symbol a_I will be used to refer to a representative level of factor A when the frame of reference is the potential P levels of factor A. The symbol a_i will be used to refer to any level of factor A when the frame of reference is the p levels actually included in the experiment. A similar distinction will be made between the symbols b_J and b_j. The first symbol has as its frame of reference the potential Q levels of factor B, whereas the second symbol has as its frame of reference the q levels of factor B in the actual experiment. In those cases in which factor A is a random factor, the symbol a_1, when the frame of reference is the potential population levels, refers to a specified population level. However, when the frame of reference is the experiment, the symbol a_1 refers to a specified level in the experiment. Thus the symbol a_1 may refer to different levels of the same factor, depending upon the frame of reference. The context in which the notation is used will clarify the ambiguity of the symbol considered in isolation.

To illustrate additional notation, assume that all the potential elements are included in all the potential cells of a factorial experiment. (Generally only a random sample of the potential elements is included in a cell of a factorial experiment.) Assume further that, after the treatment combinations have been administered, each of the elements is measured (observed) on the characteristic being studied (the *criterion* or dependent variable). The mean of the observations made under each treatment combination will be denoted by the following notation:

	b_1	b_2	$\cdots$	b_J	$\cdots$	b_Q	
a_1	μ_{11}	μ_{12}	$\cdots$	μ_{1J}	$\cdots$	μ_{1Q}	$\mu_{1.}$
a_2	μ_{21}	μ_{22}	$\cdots$	μ_{2J}	$\cdots$	μ_{2Q}	$\mu_{2.}$
$\vdots$	$\vdots$	$\vdots$		$\vdots$		$\vdots$	$\vdots$
a_I	μ_{I1}	μ_{I2}	$\cdots$	μ_{IJ}	$\cdots$	μ_{IQ}	$\mu_{I.}$
$\vdots$	$\vdots$	$\vdots$		$\vdots$		$\vdots$	$\vdots$
a_P	μ_{P1}	μ_{P2}	$\cdots$	μ_{PJ}	$\cdots$	μ_{PQ}	$\mu_{P.}$
	$\mu_{.1}$	$\mu_{.2}$	$\cdots$	$\mu_{.J}$	$\cdots$	$\mu_{.Q}$	$\mu_{..}$

In this notation, μ_{IJ} denotes the mean on the criterion for the potential population of elements under treatment combination ab_{IJ}. Equivalently, μ_{IJ} represents the population mean for the dependent variable in cell ab_{IJ}. It will be assumed that the potential number of elements in each of the cells is the same for all cells.

The average of the cell means appearing in row I is

$$\mu_{I.} = \frac{\sum_{J} \mu_{IJ}}{Q}.$$

In words, $\mu_{I.}$ is the mean of the dependent variable averaged over all potential treatment combinations in which factor A is at level a_I. Similarly, the mean of the dependent variable averaged over all potential treatment combinations in which factor B is at level b_J is

$$\mu_{.J} = \frac{\sum_{I} \mu_{IJ}}{P}.$$

The grand mean on the dependent variable is

$$\mu_{..} = \frac{\sum_{I} \sum_{J} \mu_{IJ}}{PQ} = \frac{\sum_{I} \mu_{I.}}{P} = \frac{\sum_{J} \mu_{.J}}{Q}.$$

The grand mean may also be defined as the mean of the dependent variable for all potential observations under all potential treatment combinations. These are the *parameters* of a $p \times q$ factorial experiment in terms of which the elements of an appropriate structural model may be defined.

These parameters are estimated by corresponding statistics obtained from an experiment, assuming that an experiment has been carried out with n randomly assigned subjects under each treatment condition. Notation for the statistics obtained from actual experimental data is as follows. (It is assumed that each cell mean is based upon an independent random sample of size n.)

	b_1	b_2	$\cdots$	b_j	$\cdots$	b_q	
a_1	$\overline{AB}_{11}$	$\overline{AB}_{12}$	$\cdots$	$\overline{AB}_{1j}$	$\cdots$	$\overline{AB}_{1q}$	$\bar{A}_1$
a_2	$\overline{AB}_{21}$	$\overline{AB}_{22}$	$\cdots$	$\overline{AB}_{2j}$	$\cdots$	$\overline{AB}_{2q}$	$\bar{A}_2$
$\vdots$	$\vdots$	$\vdots$		$\vdots$		$\vdots$	$\vdots$
a_i	$\overline{AB}_{i1}$	$\overline{AB}_{i2}$	$\cdots$	$\overline{AB}_{ij}$	$\cdots$	$\overline{AB}_{iq}$	$\bar{A}_i$
$\vdots$	$\vdots$	$\vdots$		$\vdots$		$\vdots$	$\vdots$
a_p	$\overline{AB}_{p1}$	$\overline{AB}_{p2}$	$\cdots$	$\overline{AB}_{pj}$	$\cdots$	$\overline{AB}_{pq}$	$\bar{A}_p$
	$\bar{B}_1$	$\bar{B}_2$	$\cdots$	$\bar{B}_j$	$\cdots$	$\bar{B}_q$	$\bar{G}$

The symbol $\overline{AB}_{ij}$ represents the mean of the measurements on the dependent variable for the n elements under treatment combination ab_{ij}. The average of all observations at level a_i is

$$\bar{A}_i = \frac{\sum_j \overline{AB}_{ij}}{q}.$$

Similarly, the average of all observations at level b_j is

$$\bar{B}_j = \frac{\sum_i \overline{AB}_{ij}}{p}.$$

The grand mean $\bar{G}$ is the mean of all means. Thus

$$\bar{G} = \frac{\sum_i \sum_j \overline{AB}_{ij}}{pq} = \frac{\sum_i \bar{A}_i}{p} = \frac{\sum_j \bar{B}_j}{q}.$$

When factors A and B are fixed, each observed mean is an unbiased estimate of its corresponding parameter. That is,

$$\mathrm{E}(\overline{AB}_{ij}) = \mu_{ij}, \qquad \mathrm{E}(\bar{A}_i) = \mu_{i.}, \quad \text{and} \quad \mathrm{E}(\bar{B}_j) = \mu_{.j}.$$

5.3   STRUCTURAL MODEL

It is assumed that there is a very large number of observations N in each of the PQ treatment populations and that n of those have been assigned at random to each of the pq treatment conditions in the experiment. The structural model provides a theoretical rationale for the magnitude of those individual observations which is logical in terms of the way the experiment was carried out.

Some of the assumptions that will be made for purposes of estimation and analysis in a two-factor experiment are summarized by the following structural model:

$$X_{IJK} = \mu_{..} + \alpha_I + \beta_J + \alpha\beta_{IJ} + \varepsilon_{IJK}. \tag{5.1}$$

In this model, X_{IJK} is an observation made in the experiment on element K under treatment combination ab_{IJ}. In the population there are $K = 1, \ldots, N$ elements; in the sample, there are $k = 1, \ldots, n$ elements. On the right-hand side of (5.1) are the factorial effects and the experimental error. This model assumes that the factorial effects as well as the experimental error are additive, i.e., that an observation is a linear function of the factorial effects and the experimental error. Expression (5.1) is a special case of the general linear hypothesis. Each of the terms on the right-hand side is assumed to be statistically independent of the others.

The left-hand side of (5.1) represents an observation on the dependent variable made in the experiment. The terms on the right-hand side are parameters underlying the independent variables. The terms on the right-hand side cannot be observed directly; however, data from an experiment will give unbiased estimators of these parameters, provided a set of constraints is added to the model. If these constraints are not included, only certain linear functions of the parameters can be estimated. Tests of hypotheses are possible only with respect to estimable functions of the parameters. In the analysis of variance, the constraints necessary to obtain unbiased estimators of the individual parameters are usually considered part of the model.

In this model, $\mu_{..}$ is the grand mean of all observations and is constant for all observations; it is estimated by $\bar{G}$, the grand mean of all observations. It is worth noting that if the structural model is restated as

$$X_{IJK} - \mu_{..} = \alpha_I + \beta_J + \alpha\beta_{IJ} + \varepsilon_{IJK}, \tag{5.2}$$

it is clear that the observations vary in this experiment (i.e., they differ from their grand mean $\mu_{..}$ and, therefore, from each other) because of α_I, β_J, $\alpha\beta_{IJ}$, and ε_{IJK}. What, then, are these components of the model which underlie variation among the observations?

Experimental Error

Experimental error ε_{IJK} is associated with each observation and is part of the model representing the influence of all uncontrolled sources of variation upon an observation under a specified treatment combination. In a factorial experiment, everything in the universe except for the controlled levels of the factors included in the experiment potentially contributes to experimental error. Experimental error is defined as

$$\varepsilon_{IJK} = X_{IJK} - \mu_{IJ}.$$

That is, the model states that the only reason all of the observations in a particular treatment condition vary (i.e., are not equal to their own treatment mean μ_{IJ}) is because of error.

It follows from this definition of error that since observations differ within a treatment condition, they differ only because of random error. It is reasonable to assume that the observations within each treatment population are normally distributed; a large number of variables impinging upon the observations logically generate random errors which are normally distributed. The variance of the observations in the cell ab_{ij} is given by

$$s_{ij}^2 = \frac{\sum_k (X_{ijk} - \overline{AB}_{ij})^2}{n-1}.$$

Assuming that the experimental error in the population is σ_ε^2 for all cells, s_{ij}^2 provides an estimate of σ_ε^2. A better estimate of σ_ε^2 is obtained by averaging the within-cell variances for each of the pq cells in the experiment. This average within-cell variance, denoted by the symobl s_{pooled}^2, may be represented as

$$s_{\text{pooled}}^2 = \frac{\sum \sum s_{ij}^2}{pq}.$$

Under the assumptions made, s_{pooled}^2 will be an unbiased estimate of σ_ε^2. Further, the sampling distribution of $pq(n-1)s_{\text{pooled}}^2/\sigma_\varepsilon^2$ will be a chi-square distribution having $pq(n-1)$ degrees of freedom. [Since the variance within each of the pq cells in the experiment is based upon n independent observations, each of the within-cell variances has $n-1$ degrees of freedom. The pooled variance, s_{pooled}^2, has degrees of freedom equal to the combined degrees of freedom for each of the within-cell variances, that is, $pq(n-1)$.] Because the observations within each of the cells are independent, the degrees of freedom are additive for each of the variances that has been averaged.

The statistic s_{pooled}^2 is called the within-cell mean square, abbreviated $MS_{\text{w.cell}}$. Alternatively, this source of variance is designated as MS_{error} in designs which do not have repeated measures. It is worth noting that with this definition of error, the other elements of the structural model (α_I, β_J and $\alpha\beta_{IJ}$) account for differences among the treatment means. That is, since

$$X_{IJK} = \mu_{..} + \alpha_I + \beta_J + \alpha\beta_{IJ} + \varepsilon_{IJK},$$

$$X_{IJK} - \varepsilon_{IJK} = \mu_{..} + \alpha_I + \beta_J + \alpha\beta_{IJ},$$

$$X_{IJK} - (X_{IJK} - \mu_{IJ}) = \mu_{..} + \alpha_I + \beta_J + \alpha\beta_{IJ},$$

$$\mu_{IJ} = \mu_{..} + \alpha_I + \beta_J + \alpha\beta_{IJ},$$

and $$\mu_{IJ} - \mu_{..} = \alpha_I + \beta_J + \alpha\beta_{IJ}.$$

In words, all differences among treatment means (equivalently, $\mu_{IJ} - \mu_{..}$) are due to the parameters α_I, β_J, and $\alpha\beta_{IJ}$, the main effects and interactions.

Main Effects

Main effects are average, additive effects which are associated with each particular level of each factor; α_I is a mean effect associated with level I of factor A and β_J is a main effect associated with level J of factor β. Main effects are analogous to treatment effects of single factor designs discussed in Chapters 3 and 4.

Main effects are defined in terms of parameters. Direct estimates of these parameters will, in most cases, be obtainable from corresponding statistics. The main effect of level a_I of factor A is by definition

$$\alpha_I = \mu_{I.} - \mu_{...}.$$

In words, the main effect for level a_I is the difference between the mean of all potential observations on the dependent variable at level a_I and the grand mean of all potential observations. The main effect for level a_I may be either positive or negative. The main effect for level $a_{I'}$, where I' designates a level of factor A different from I, is

$$\alpha_{I'} = \mu_{I'.} - \mu_{...}.$$

For most practical purposes, only the difference between two main effects will be needed. The *differential* main effect is defined to be

$$\alpha_I - \alpha_{I'} = \mu_{I.} - \mu_{I'.}.$$

In terms of what are called *estimable parametric functions* in the general linear model, differential main effects are estimable, whereas the individual main effects are not estimable.

Analogous definitions hold for the main effects of the levels of factor B. Thus, the main effect for level b_J is

$$\beta_J = \mu_{.J} - \mu_{...}.$$

The differential main effect for levels b_J and $b_{J'}$ is

$$\beta_J - \beta_{J'} = \mu_{.J} - \mu_{.J'}.$$

A differential main effect measures the extent to which criterion means for two levels within the same factor differ. Thus, if all the means for the various levels of a factor are equal, all the differential main effects for the levels of that factor will be zero. It should be pointed out that equality of the population means does not imply equality of the sample main effects because observed data contain error. Hence estimates of differential main effects may not be zero even though the population values are zero. However, when the population differential main effects are zero, their sample estimates will differ from zero by amounts which are functions of experimental error.

Assuming hypothetical populations defined earlier, unbiased estimators of the main effects are given by

$$\hat{\alpha}_I = \bar{A}_I - \bar{G},$$
$$\hat{\beta}_J = \bar{B}_J - \bar{G}.$$

Estimators of differential main effects are

$$\hat{\alpha}_I - \hat{\alpha}_{I'} = \bar{A}_I - \bar{A}_{I'}; \qquad \hat{\beta}_J - \hat{\beta}_{J'} = \bar{B}_J - \bar{B}_{J'}.$$

These estimators, in addition to being unbiased, also have minimum standard error.

A measure of how different the main effects due to a factor are is given by the variance due to the main effects. (Even though α_I and β_J are not random variables, it is convenient to think of differences in variance terms.)

The variance of the main effects due to factor A is, by definition,

$$\sigma_\alpha^2 = \frac{\sum_I (\mu_{I.} - \mu_{..})^2}{P-1} = \frac{\sum_I \alpha_I^2}{P-1}.$$

An equivalent definition in terms of the differential main effects is

$$\sigma_\alpha^2 = \frac{\sum (\alpha_I - \alpha_{I'})^2}{P(P-1)}, \qquad\qquad I < I'.$$

The symbol $I < I'$ indicates that the summation is over different pairs of α's; that is, $\alpha_1 - \alpha_2$ is not considered to be different from $\alpha_2 - \alpha_1$. The variance of the main effects of factor A measures the extent to which the criterion means for the various levels of factor A differ. Equivalently, the variance of the main effects may be regarded as an overall measure of the differential main effects for that factor. Thus, σ_α^2 will be small when all the differential main effects are small; σ_α^2 will be large when one or more of the differential main effects are large. When all the $\mu_{I.}$ are equal, σ_α^2 will be zero.

Analogous definitions hold for the variance of the main effects of factor B.

$$\sigma_\beta^2 = \frac{\sum_J (\mu_{.J} - \mu_{..})^2}{Q-1} = \frac{\sum_J \beta_J^2}{Q-1}.$$

In terms of the differential main effects,

$$\sigma_\beta^2 = \frac{\sum_J (\beta_J - \beta_{J'})^2}{Q(Q-1)}, \qquad\qquad J < J'.$$

To illustrate the definitions of main effects and their variances, suppose the population means on the dependent (criterion) variable are those given in the following table. Here $P = 2$ and $Q = 3$.

	b_1	b_2	b_3	Mean
a_1	10	5	15	10
a_2	20	5	5	10
Mean	15	5	10	10

For the data in this table, $\mu_{1.} = 10$, $\mu_{2.} = 10$, and $\mu_{..} = 10$. Hence $\alpha_1 = 0$, and $\alpha_2 = 0$. It is also noted that $\mu_{.1} = 15$, $\mu_{.2} = 5$, $\mu_{.3} = 10$. Hence

$$\beta_1 = 15 - 10 = 5,$$

$$\beta_2 = 5 - 10 = -5,$$

$$\beta_3 = 10 - 10 = 0.$$

The differential main effects for factor B are

$$\beta_1 - \beta_2 = 10, \qquad \beta_1 - \beta_3 = 5, \qquad \beta_2 - \beta_3 = -5.$$

[In the general case there will be $Q(Q-1)/2$ distinct differential main effects for factor B.]

The variance due to the main effects of factor B is

$$\sigma_\beta^2 = \frac{\sum_J \beta_J^2}{Q - 1} = \frac{5^2 + (-5)^2 + 0^2}{3 - 1} = 25.$$

In terms of the differential main effects of factor B, the variance is

$$\sigma_\beta^2 = \frac{\sum (\beta_J - \beta_{J'})^2}{Q(Q - 1)}$$

$$= \frac{10^2 + 5^2 + (-5)^2}{3(3 - 1)} = 25.$$

In summary, main effects as well as differential main effects are defined in terms of a special population and not in terms of individual treatments within the population. Thus a main effect is *not* a parameter associated with a specified level of a specified factor; rather, a main effect depends upon all the other factors that may be present, as well as the number of levels assumed for the specified factor. It should also be noted that main effects are estimated from means which are obtained by averaging over the totality of other factors present in the population to which inferences are to be made.

Interaction Effects

The major advantage of factorial designs is that they make it possible to assess interactions among the factors in the design. Interactions are unique effects which occur when a particular level of one factor is combined with a particular level of one or more other factors. Thus, the interaction between level a_I and level b_J, designated by the symbol $\alpha\beta_{IJ}$, is a measure of the extent to which the criterion mean for treatment combination ab_{IJ} *cannot* be predicted from the sum of the corresponding main effects. From many points of view, interaction is a measure of the nonadditivity of the main effects. To some extent the existence or nonexistence of interaction depends upon the scale of measurement. For example, in terms of a logarithmic scale of measurement, interaction may not be present, whereas in terms of some other scale of measurement an interaction effect may be present. The choice of a scale of measurement for the dependent variable is generally at the discretion of the experimenter. If alternative choices are available, then that scale which leads to the simplest additive model will generally provide the most complete and adequate summary of the experimental data.

In terms of the population means and main effects, since

$$\mu_{IJ} - \mu_{..} = \alpha_I + \beta_J + \alpha\beta_{IJ},$$
$$\alpha\beta_{IJ} = (\mu_{IJ} - \mu_{..}) - (\alpha_I + \beta_J).$$

That is, interactions are defined as the differences among treatment means which are left when main effects are removed from those differences. An interaction effect is associated with each of the PQ treatment combinations. If

$$(\mu_{IJ} - \mu_{..}) = \alpha_I + \beta_J,$$

then all interactions are zero. Thus, one may view an interaction as a measure of departure from additivity of the main effects.

An equivalent definition of interaction is given by

$$\alpha\beta_{IJ} = \mu_{IJ} - \mu_{I.} - \mu_{.J} + \mu_{..},$$

since $\alpha_I = \mu_{I.} - \mu_{..}$ and $\beta_J = \mu_{.J} - \mu_{..}$. Thus, if

$$\mu_{IJ} = \mu_{I.} + \mu_{.J} - \mu_{..},$$

then all $\alpha\beta_{IJ}$ will be zero and the cell means are an additive function of the marginal means.

From the way in which $\mu_{I.}$ and $\mu_{.J}$ were defined, it follows that

$$\sum_I \alpha\beta_{IJ} = \sum_I \mu_{IJ} - \sum_I \mu_{I.} - \sum_I \mu_{.J} + \sum_I \mu_{..}$$
$$= P\mu_{.J} - P\mu_{..} - P\mu_{.J} + P\mu_{..}$$
$$= 0.$$

It also follows that

$$\sum_J \alpha\beta_{IJ} = 0.$$

In words, the sum of the interaction effects within any row or any column of the population cells is zero.

Differential interaction effects are defined by the following examples.

(i) $\qquad\qquad \alpha\beta_{12} - \alpha\beta_{34} = \mu_{12} - \mu_{34} - (\alpha_1 - \alpha_3) - (\beta_2 - \beta_4),$

(ii) $\qquad\qquad \alpha\beta_{12} - \alpha\beta_{13} = \mu_{12} - \mu_{13} - (\beta_2 - \beta_3),$

(iii) $\qquad\qquad \alpha\beta_{12} - \alpha\beta_{32} = \mu_{12} - \mu_{32} - (\alpha_1 - \alpha_3),$

(iv) $\quad (\alpha\beta_{12} - \alpha\beta_{13}) - (\alpha\beta_{22} - \alpha\beta_{23}) = \mu_{12} - \mu_{13} - \mu_{22} + \mu_{23}.$

Of these examples only (iv) does not involve main effects. In (iv) one has a difference between two differences, which is called a second-order difference. The first difference in (iv) is at level a_1, the second difference is at level a_2 but at the same levels of b as the first difference. The general form of the second-order difference represented by (iv) is

$$(\alpha\beta_{IJ} - \alpha\beta_{IM}) - (\alpha\beta_{KJ} - \alpha\beta_{KM}).$$

This type of second-order difference will not involve any main effects. If

$$\mu_{IJ} - \mu_{IM} = \mu_{KJ} - \mu_{KM} \quad \text{for all } I, J, K, M$$

then all $\alpha\beta_{IJ}$ will be zero. Geometrically this implies that the profiles of the row means will be parallel; the relation also implies that the profiles of the column means will be parallel. Functions of the cell means having the general form

$$(\mu_{IJ} - \mu_{IM}) - (\mu_{KJ} - \mu_{KM})$$

are said to "belong" to the interaction effect since they do not involve main effects.

For the numerical example the interaction effects are

$$\alpha\beta_{11} = 10 - 10 - 15 + 10 = -5, \qquad \alpha\beta_{12} = 5 - 10 - 5 + 10 = 0,$$

$$\alpha\beta_{13} = 15 - 10 - 10 + 10 = 5, \qquad \alpha\beta_{21} = 20 - 10 - 15 + 10 = 5,$$

$$\alpha\beta_{22} = 5 - 10 - 5 + 10 = 0, \qquad \alpha\beta_{23} = 5 - 10 - 10 + 10 = -5.$$

The variance due to the interaction effects is by definition

$$\sigma_{\alpha\beta}^2 = \frac{\sum \sum (\alpha\beta_{IJ})^2}{(P-1)(Q-1)}.$$

Unbiased, minimum variance estimators of the interaction effects may be obtained from corresponding estimators of the cell and marginal means. Thus

$$\widehat{\alpha\beta}_{IJ} = \hat{\mu}_{IJ} - \hat{\mu}_{I.} - \hat{\mu}_{.J} + \hat{\mu}_{..}$$
$$= \overline{AB}_{IJ} - \bar{A}_I - \bar{B}_J + \bar{G}.$$

The estimators will have the same constraints as the parameters, namely

$$\sum_I \widehat{\alpha\beta}_{IJ} = 0, \qquad \sum_J \widehat{\alpha\beta}_{IJ} = 0.$$

5.4   ESTIMATING ELEMENTS OF THE MODEL

Some of the assumptions that will be made for purposes of estimation and analysis in a two-factor experiment are summarized by the structural model:

$$X_{ijk} = \mu_{..} + \alpha_i + \beta_j + \alpha\beta_{ij} + \varepsilon_{ijk}. \tag{5.3}$$

From this model and the definitions of main effects and interactions, one has the result that variability of *observations* is a function of main effects, interactions, and random error,

$$X_{ijk} - \mu_{..} = \alpha_i + \beta_j + \alpha\beta_{ij} + \varepsilon_{ijk},$$

whereas differences among treatment condition *means* is a function of main effects and interactions,

$$\mu_{ij} - \mu_{..} = \alpha_i + \beta_j + \alpha\beta_{ij}.$$

It is this variability among observations and means that is addressed by the analysis of variance.

Estimating Error

One of the primary purposes of well-designed experiments is to provide a clear-cut definition for the experimental error associated with effects about which inferences are desired.

All uncontrolled sources of variance influencing the estimation of parameters contribute to what is known as experimental error. The greater the number of relevant sources of variance which are controlled, the smaller the variance due to the experimental error. The standard error of estimators depends upon both the variance due to experimental error and sample size. In factorial designs of the type being considered in this chapter, the variance of the observations within a specified treatment combination is assumed to be due to experimental error (provided there are no repeated measures). This variance is in large part a function of *individual differences* among the experimental units and in smaller part due to uncontrolled conditions surrounding the individual observations. Careful experimentation will keep the latter sources of variation to a minimum and make them comparable for all observations. Any unique interaction effects between the units and the treatments will also add to the variance due to experimental error.

Formally, the experimental error associated with observation X_{IJK} is

$$\varepsilon_{IJK} = X_{IJK} - \mu_{IJ} \quad \text{or} \quad \varepsilon_{IJK} = X_{IJK} - \mathrm{E}(X_{IJK}).$$

Since μ_{IJ} cannot be observed, neither can ε_{IJK}. An estimate based upon the sample of size n observations in cell ab_{IJ} is given by

$$\hat{\varepsilon}_{ijk} = X_{ijk} - \overline{AB}_{ij}.$$

The experimental error is considered to be the sum over a large number of independent, uncontrolled variables that can potentially affect an observation. Hence it is reasonable to assume that ε_{IJK} is distributed as $N(0, \sigma_\varepsilon^2)$ for all I, J. The variance due to experimental error within cell ab_{IJ} is defined to be

$$\sigma_\varepsilon^2 = \frac{\sum\limits_K (X_{IJK} - \mu_{IJ})^2}{N - 1} = \frac{\sum\limits_K \varepsilon_{IJK}^2}{N - 1} \quad \text{for all } I, J.$$

That is,

$$\sigma^2_{\varepsilon_{11}} = \sigma^2_{\varepsilon_{12}} = \cdots = \sigma^2_{\varepsilon_{IJ}} = \cdots = \sigma^2_{\varepsilon_{PQ}} = \sigma^2_{\varepsilon}.$$

This relationship defines homogeneity of variance due to experimental error. If there are treatment by unit interactions or the uncontrolled sources of variance are not comparable from cell to cell, then the variance due to experimental error will not be homogeneous. Further, if the treatment effects are correlated with the experimental error, the within-cell variances will not be homogeneous.

In the definition of σ^2_{ε}, a divisor of $N - 1$ is used. In the usual definition of a population variance, the divisor is N rather than $N - 1$. If N is infinite, the difference between N and $N - 1$ is zero. If N is finite, this definition of a population variance runs counter to the usual definition. However, σ^2_{ε} as defined above is consistent with that adopted by Cornfield and Tukey (1956, p. 916).

An estimate of σ^2_{ε} based upon the n observations in cell ab_{ij} is provided by the observed variance of the observations in cell ab_{ij},

$$s^2_{ij} = \frac{\sum_k (X_{ijk} - \overline{AB}_{ij})^2}{n - 1} = \frac{\sum_k \hat{\varepsilon}^2_{ijk}}{n - 1}.$$

Since there is the constraint,

$$\sum_k (X_{ijk} - \overline{AB}_{ij}) = 0,$$

s^2_{ij} has $n - 1$ degrees of freedom. Under the assumption of homogeneity of variance, a better estimate of σ^2_{ε} is

$$\hat{\sigma}^2_{\varepsilon} = s^2_{\text{pooled}} = \frac{\sum \sum s^2_{ij}}{pq}.$$

This estimate will be unbiased; it will have $pq(n - 1)$ degrees of freedom. The statistic s^2_{pooled} is called the within-cell mean square and is denoted by the symbol $MS_{\text{within cell}}$. Alternatively, in designs which do not have repeated measures, the pooled within-class variance is denoted MS_{error}. The latter is also given by

$$MS_{\text{error}} = \frac{\sum \sum \sum \hat{\varepsilon}^2_{ijk}}{pq(n - 1)}.$$

Under the normality assumption on the distribution of the ε and the independence of the observations within each cell,

$$\frac{pq(n - 1)MS_{\text{error}}}{\sigma^2_{\varepsilon}} \quad \text{is distributed as } \chi^2[pq(n - 1)].$$

Estimation of Mean Squares Due to Main Effects and Interaction Effects

In the structural model there are $p + q + pq$ parameters. All of the parameters are defined in terms of the cell means in the hypothetical population and all are linear functions of the μ_{IJ}. Since the μ_{IJ} will be estimable, all of the other parameters will be estimable. In terms of the structural model, the observed treatment mean $\overline{AB}_{ij}$ provides an unbiased estimate of the corresponding population treatment mean μ_{IJ}. Thus,

$$\hat{\mu}_{ij} = \overline{AB}_{ij} = \frac{\sum\limits_{k} X_{ijk}}{n} = \mu_{..} + \alpha_i + \beta_j + \alpha\beta_{ij} + \bar{\varepsilon}_{ij},$$

where

$$\bar{\varepsilon}_{ij} = \frac{\sum\limits_{k} \varepsilon_{ijk}}{n}$$

If the observations in cell ab_{ij} were to be replicated with independent samples of size n, $\bar{\varepsilon}_{ij}$ would be a random variable distributed as $N(0, \sigma_\varepsilon^2/n)$. However, all of the other terms on the right-hand side would remain constant. Hence

$$E(\overline{AB}_{ij}) = E(\mu_{..}) + E(\alpha_i) + E(\beta_j) + E(\alpha\beta_{ij}) + E(\bar{\varepsilon}_{ij})$$

$$= \mu_{..} + \alpha_i + \beta_j + \alpha\beta_{ij} + 0.$$

In this context, the expected value of terms on the right-hand side is the average value of a large number of replications for cell ab_{ij} with independent samples. Although the mean experimental error $\bar{\varepsilon}_{ij}$ has expected value equal to zero, it varies from one replication to the next. Hence the variance of $\bar{\varepsilon}_{ij}$ is not zero; $\sigma_{\bar{\varepsilon}}^2 = \sigma_\varepsilon^2/n =$ squared standard error of μ_{ij}.

From the structural model and the definitions of the various parameters, it is simple to provide a statement of the parameters of the structural model which are estimated by those statistics. Since interest is centered upon variability—upon differences among statistics—Table 5.1 provides the structural variables estimated by differences among observed means.

TABLE 5.1 **Structural parameters estimated by various statistics**

Statistic	Structural parameters estimated
$\bar{A}_i - \bar{A}_{i'}$	$(\alpha_i + \alpha_{i'}) + (\overline{\alpha\beta}_i - \overline{\alpha\beta}_{i'}) + (\bar{\varepsilon}_i - \bar{\varepsilon}_{i'})$
$\bar{B}_j - \bar{B}_{j'}$	$(\beta_j - \beta_{j'}) + (\overline{\alpha\beta}_j - \overline{\alpha\beta}_{j'}) + (\bar{\varepsilon}_j - \bar{\varepsilon}_{j'})$
$\overline{AB}_{ij} - \overline{AB}_{i'j'}$	$(\alpha_i - \alpha_{i'}) + (\beta_j - \beta_{j'}) + (\alpha\beta_{ij} - \alpha\beta_{i'j'}) + (\bar{\varepsilon}_{ij} - \bar{\varepsilon}_{i'j'})$
$(\overline{AB}_{ij} - \bar{A}_i - \bar{B}_j) -$ $(\overline{AB}_{i'j'} - \bar{A}_{i'} - \bar{B}_{j'})$	$(\alpha\beta_{ij} - \alpha\beta_{i'j'}) + (\bar{\varepsilon}_{ij} - \bar{\varepsilon}_{i'j'})$

As noted earlier, differences between observed treatment condition means $\overline{AB}_{ij}$ reflect differences in main effects due to both factors A and B, differences in interactions, and differences in average errors.

Differences between means at different levels of factor A and B estimate differences between main effects, average interactions, and average errors. It is worth commenting about the differences in average interactions, $\overline{\alpha\beta}_i - \overline{\alpha\beta}_{i'}$ in the case of $\bar{A}_i - \bar{A}_{i'}$ and $\overline{\alpha\beta}_j - \overline{\alpha\beta}_{j'}$ in the case of $\bar{B}_j - \bar{B}_{j'}$. The notation $\overline{\alpha\beta}_i$ denotes the average for level a_i of the $\alpha\beta_{ij}$ effects over the levels of factor B included in the experiment. If $q = Q$ (that is, if factor B is fixed), then $\overline{\alpha\beta}_i$ is zero. If $q \neq Q$, $\overline{\alpha\beta}_i$ need not be zero for any single experiment. To illustrate this point, suppose that there are six levels of factor B in the population of such levels, and suppose that the interaction effects associated with level a_i are those given below:

	b_1	b_2	b_3	b_4	b_5	b_6
a_i	$\alpha\beta_{i1} = 3$	$\alpha\beta_{i2} = 2$	$\alpha\beta_{i3} = -3$	$\alpha\beta_{i4} = -2$	$\alpha\beta_{i5} = 5$	$\alpha\beta_{i6} = -5$

In this case, $Q = 6$. Note that $\sum_j \alpha\beta_{ij} = 0$. Suppose that only a random sample of $q = 3$ levels of factor B is included in any single experiment. Suppose that the levels b_2, b_4, and b_5 are included in an experiment which is actually conducted. For this experiment

$$\overline{\alpha\beta}_i = \frac{\sum_j \alpha\beta_{ij}}{q} = \frac{\alpha\beta_{i2} + \alpha\beta_{i4} + \alpha\beta_{i5}}{3} = \frac{5}{3}.$$

For a large number of random replications of this experiment, where an independent random sample of levels of B is drawn for each replication, the expected value of $\overline{\alpha\beta}_i$ will be zero. The variation of the distribution of $\overline{\alpha\beta}_i$ generated by this kind of sampling procedure depends upon n, q, Q, and the variance $\sigma^2_{\alpha\beta}$.

The notation $\overline{\alpha\beta}_j$ denotes the average of the $\alpha\beta_{ij}$ effects over the levels of factor A present in an experiment at level b_j of factor B. If factor A is a fixed factor, $\overline{\alpha\beta}_j = 0$. However, if factor A is not a fixed factor, $\overline{\alpha\beta}_j$ is not necessarily equal to zero for any single experiment. Over a large number of random replications of the experiment, the expected value of $\overline{\alpha\beta}_j$ will be equal to zero. If factor A is a fixed factor, $\sigma^2_{\overline{\alpha\beta}_j}$ will be zero for all replications. If factor A is a random factor, $\sigma^2_{\overline{\alpha\beta}_j}$ will be a function of n, p, P, and $\sigma^2_{\alpha\beta}$.

The mean square due to the main effects of factor A in the experiment is defined to be

$$\text{MS}_a = \frac{nq \sum (\bar{A}_i - \bar{G})^2}{p - 1}.$$

Defined thusly, MS_a is simply the variance of the means for levels of factor A premultiplied by the number of observations upon which each A mean is based,

$$\text{MS}_a = nqs_{\bar{A}}^2.$$

An equivalent definition in terms of differences between pairs of means is

$$\text{MS}_a = \frac{nq \sum (\bar{A}_i - \bar{A}_{i'})^2}{p(p-1)}.$$

The summation in this last expression is with respect to all distinct pairs of means, no pair being included twice. The multiplier nq is the number of observations in each $\bar{A}_i$. The expected value of $\bar{A}_i - \bar{A}_{i'}$ (for independent, random replications of the experiment) is

$$\text{E}(\bar{A}_i - \bar{A}_{i'}) = \text{E}(\alpha_i - \alpha_{i'}) + \text{E}(\overline{\alpha\beta_i} - \overline{\alpha\beta_{i'}}) + \text{E}(\bar{\varepsilon}_i - \bar{\varepsilon}_{i'})$$
$$= \alpha_i - \alpha_{i'} \qquad + 0 \qquad\qquad + 0.$$

The expected value of MS_a may be shown to be

$$\text{E}(\text{MS}_a) = \left(\frac{N-n}{N}\right)\sigma_\varepsilon^2 + \left(\frac{Q-q}{Q}\right)n\sigma_{\alpha\beta}^2 + nq\sigma_\alpha^2.$$

Detailed steps in the derivation of this latter expected value are given by Cornfield and Tukey (1956).

The mean square due to factor B is defined as the variance of the B means premultiplied by np, the number of observations upon which each B mean is based. Hence,

$$\text{MS}_b = nps_{\bar{B}}^2$$
$$= \frac{np \sum (\bar{B}_j - \bar{G})^2}{q-1}$$
$$= \frac{np \sum (\bar{B}_j - \bar{B}_{j'})^2}{q(q-1)}.$$

The expected value of this mean square in terms of the parameters in the structural model is given in Table 5.2.

The mean square due to interaction effects in the experiment is defined as

$$\text{MS}_{ab} = \frac{n \sum \sum (\overline{AB}_{ij} - \bar{A}_i - \bar{B}_j + \bar{G})^2}{(p-1)(q-1)}.$$

TABLE 5.2   Expected values of mean squares

Mean square as obtained from experimental data	Expected value of mean square in terms of parameters of (1)
MS_a	$(1-n/N)\sigma_\varepsilon^2 + n(1-q/Q)\sigma_{\alpha\beta}^2 + nq\sigma_\alpha^2$
MS_b	$(1-n/N)\sigma_\varepsilon^2 + n(1-p/P)\sigma_{\alpha\beta}^2 + np\sigma_\beta^2$
MS_{ab}	$(1-n/N)\sigma_\varepsilon^2 + n\sigma_{\alpha\beta}^2$
MS_{error}	$(1-n/N)\sigma_\varepsilon^2$

An equivalent definition can be given in terms of differential interaction effects. The multiplier n is the number of observations in each $\overline{AB}_{ij}$.

The expected value of a mean square represents the average of the MS computed from a large number of independent, random replications of the experiment expressed in terms of functions of the variances of parameters in the general linear model. These, in turn, represent the sources of variance underlying observations and the conditions under which levels of the factors are included in the experiment. With regard to this latter point, certain of the coefficients in Table 5.2 are either zero or unity, depending upon whether a factor is fixed or random. It will generally be assumed that the number of elements observed in an experiment is small relative to the number of potential elements in the population of elements, i.e., that the ratio n/N for all practical purposes is equal to zero. Hence, the coefficient $1 - n/N$ is assumed to be equal to unity.

If factor A is fixed, the ratio p/P will be equal to unity and the coefficient $1 - p/P$ will be equal to zero. If, on the other hand, factor A is random, the ratio p/P will be equal to zero and the coefficient $1 - p/P$ will be equal to unity. In an analogous manner, the coefficient $1 - q/Q$ is equal to zero when factor B is a fixed factor and equal to unity when factor B is a random factor.

Special cases of the expected values of the mean squares are summarized in Table 5.3. Each of these cases is obtained from the general values given in Table 5.2 by evaluating the coefficients which depend upon the ratios n/N, p/P, and q/Q. Several different approaches may be used to obtain the special cases given in Table 5.3. Specialization of the generalized approach represented by Table 5.2 provides the simplest method of evaluating more complex experimental designs.

Case 1, in which both factors are fixed, has been designated by Eisenhart (1947) as Model I. Case 2, in which one factor is fixed and the second is random, is called the mixed model. Case 3, in which both factors are random, is called Model II, or the *variance-component* model. Model I has been more extensively studied than the other two models. In its most general form, the statistical principles underlying Model I are identical to those underlying the general regression model having any number of fixed variates and one random variate. As such, the best estimates of various parameters can readily be

TABLE 5.3 **Special cases of expected values of mean squares**

Mean squares	Case 1 Factor A fixed Factor B fixed	Case 2 Factor A fixed Factor B random	Case 3 Factor A random Factor B random
MS_a	$\sigma_\varepsilon^2 + nq\sigma_\alpha^2$	$\sigma_\varepsilon^2 + n\sigma_{\alpha\beta}^2 + nq\sigma_\alpha^2$	$\sigma_\varepsilon^2 + n\sigma_{\alpha\beta}^2 + nq\sigma_\alpha^2$
MS_b	$\sigma_\varepsilon^2 + np\sigma_\beta^2$	$\sigma_\varepsilon^2 \qquad\quad + np\sigma_\beta^2$	$\sigma_\varepsilon^2 + n\sigma_{\alpha\beta}^2 + np\sigma_\beta^2$
MS_{ab}	$\sigma_\varepsilon^2 + n\sigma_{\alpha\beta}^2$	$\sigma_\varepsilon^2 + n\sigma_{\alpha\beta}^2$	$\sigma_\varepsilon^2 + n\sigma_{\alpha\beta}^2$
$\mathrm{MS}_{\mathrm{error}}$	σ_ε^2	σ_ε^2	σ_ε^2

obtained by the method of least-squares. For the case of the generalized Model I, application of the method of least-squares is straightforward and leads to no difficulties. For the generalized mixed model, application of the principles of maximum likelihood is more direct.

Since the statistical tests made on the experimental data depend upon what these expected values are assumed to be, it is particularly important to specify the conditions under which these expected values are derived. To obtain the general expected values given in Table 5.4, the following assumptions are made:

1 There is a population of size P and variance σ_a^2 of main effects of factor A, of which the effects $(\alpha_1, \alpha_2, \ldots, \alpha_p)$ occurring in the experiment constitute a random sample (sampling without replacement) of size p. The sample may include all the levels of factor A in the population; that is, p may be equal to P.

2 There is a population of size Q and variance σ_β^2 of main effects of factor B, of which the effects $(\beta_1, \beta_2, \ldots, \beta_q)$ occurring in the experiment constitute a random sample of size q. The sample may include all the levels of factor B in the population; that is, q may be equal to Q.

3 There is a population of interaction effects of size PQ and variance $\sigma_{\alpha\beta}^2$; the $\alpha\beta_{ij}$'s which occur in the experiment correspond to the combinations of the levels of factor A and factor B that occur in the experiment. That is, one does not have a random sample of pq interaction effects; rather, the interaction effects in the experiment are tied to the levels of factor A and factor B that occur in the experiment. It is assumed that the average (in the population) of the interaction effects over all levels of one factor is independent of the main effects of the other factor; that is, $\overline{\alpha\beta}_i$ is independent of α_i, and $\overline{\alpha\beta}_j$ is independent of β_j.

4 The sampling of the levels of factor A is independent of the sampling of the levels of factor B.

5 The experimental error is independent of all main effects and all interactions. Further, within each cell in the population, ε, the experimental error, is assumed to be normally distributed, with mean equal to zero and variance equal to σ_ε^2 for all cells in the population.

6 The n observations within each cell of the experiment constitute a random sample of size n from a population of size N (assumed infinite in most cases). The n observations within each cell constitute independent random samples from a random sample of npq independent elements drawn from the basic population.

For purposes of deriving the expected values of mean squares, some of these assumptions may be relaxed. The assumption of normality of the distribution of the experimental error is not required for the derivation of the expected values. However, all these assumptions are needed for the validity of the tests involving the use of F ratios, which are based upon the expected values of the mean squares. In particular, the assumption that the distribution of the experimental error is normal is required in order that the sampling distributions of mean squares be chi-square distributions.

Under the conditions that have been stated, the mean squares computed in the analysis of variance have the following sampling distributions:

Statistic	Sampling distribution
$(p-1)\text{MS}_a/\text{E}(\text{MS}_a)$	Chi square with $p-1$ df
$(q-1)\text{MS}_b/\text{E}(\text{MS}_b)$	Chi square with $q-1$ df
$(p-1)(q-1)\text{MS}_{ab}/\text{E}(\text{MS}_{ab})$	Chi square with $(p-1)(q-1)$ df

Principles Underlying Derivation of Expected Values for Mean Squares

To provide some insight into the principles underlying the derivation of the expected values for mean squares, a nonrigorous derivation will be outlined. From finite sampling theory, one has the following theorem:

$$\sigma_{\bar{X}}^2 = \frac{N-n}{N-1}\frac{\sigma_X^2}{n}. \tag{5.4}$$

Under random sampling without replacement after each draw, (5.4) relates the square of the standard error of a mean, $\sigma_{\bar{X}}^2$, to the population size N, the sample size n, and the variance σ_X^2 of the variable X in the population.

In (5.4), the population variance is defined to be

$$\sigma_X^2 = \frac{\Sigma (X-\mu)^2}{N}.$$

If one uses as the definition of the population variance

$$\sigma_X^2 = \frac{\Sigma (X-\mu)^2}{N-1},$$

then (5.4) has the form

$$\sigma_{\bar{X}}^2 = \frac{N-n}{N-1}\frac{\Sigma (X-\mu)^2}{nN}\frac{N-1}{N-1}$$

$$= \frac{N-n}{N}\frac{\Sigma (X-\mu)^2}{n(N-1)}$$

$$= \left(1-\frac{n}{N}\right)\frac{\sigma_X^2}{n} \quad \text{where} \quad \sigma_X^2 = \frac{\Sigma (X-\mu)^2}{N-1}. \tag{5.5}$$

To simplify the notation, the present development will define a population variance using $N-1$ as the divisor. This definition is consistent with that used by Cornfield and Tukey (1956).

In terms of the right-hand side of the structural model given at the beginning of this section, the mean of all observations made at level a_i in an experiment is

$$\bar{A}_i = \mu_{..} + \alpha_i + \bar{\beta} + \overline{\alpha\beta_i} + \bar{\varepsilon}_i. \tag{5.6}$$

In this notation $\bar{\beta}$ represents the average effect of all levels of factor B included in the experiment; $\bar{\beta}$ is constant for all levels of factor A. The notation $\overline{\alpha\beta_i}$ represents the average interaction effect associated with level a_i; $\overline{\alpha\beta_i}$ may differ for the various levels of factor A. The notation $\bar{\varepsilon}_i$ denotes the average experimental error associated with each $\bar{A}_i$.

The variance of $\bar{A}_i$ is defined to be

$$s_{\bar{A}}^2 = \frac{\Sigma \, (\bar{A}_i - \bar{G})^2}{p - 1}.$$

Under the assumption that the terms on the right-hand side of (5.6) are statistically independent, the expected value of the variance of the left-hand side of (5.6) will be equal to the sum of the variances of the terms on the right-hand side. Terms which are constants have zero variance. Thus

$$E(s_{\bar{A}}^2) = \sigma_\alpha^2 + \sigma_{\alpha\beta}^2 + \sigma_{\bar{\varepsilon}}^2. \tag{5.7}$$

The mean square due to the main effect of factor A may be written as

$$\mathrm{MS}_a = nqs_{\bar{A}}^2.$$

Hence (5.7) becomes

$$E(\mathrm{MS}_a) = E(nqs_{\bar{A}}^2) = nqE(s_{\bar{A}}^2) = nq\sigma_\alpha^2 + nq\sigma_{\alpha\bar{\beta}}^2 + nq\sigma_{\bar{\varepsilon}}^2. \tag{5.8}$$

The analog of the theorem stated in (5.4) may now be applied to each of the variances in (5.8) which have a mean as a subscript. Thus, $\bar{\varepsilon}$ is the mean of the experimental error associated with the nq observations from which $\bar{A}_i$ is computed. Therefore,

$$nq\sigma_{\bar{\varepsilon}}^2 = \frac{nq(1 - n/N)\sigma_\varepsilon^2}{nq} = \left(1 - \frac{n}{N}\right)\sigma_\varepsilon^2.$$

(The experimental error in the basic linear model is associated with each element in the basic population from which the elements are drawn. Hence the sampling fraction associated with the experimental error is n/N.)

The mean interaction effect in (5.7) represents the average over the q values of $\alpha\beta_{ij}$ present at level a_i. Hence $\overline{\alpha\beta_i}$ may be considered to be the mean of a sample of size q levels from a population of size Q levels of factor B. The analog of the theorem in (5.4) now takes the form

$$nq\sigma_{\alpha\bar{\beta}}^2 = \frac{nq(1 - q/Q)\sigma_{\alpha\beta}^2}{q} = n\left(1 - \frac{q}{Q}\right)\sigma_{\alpha\beta}^2.$$

Since the main effects and interaction effects are assumed to be independent, restricting the sample of q values of $\alpha\beta_{ij}$ to level a_i does not invalidate the theorem summarized in (5.4).

The expression for the expected value of the mean square of the main effect of factor A may now be written as

$$E(MS_\alpha) = \left(1 - \frac{n}{N}\right)\sigma_\varepsilon^2 + n\left(1 - \frac{q}{Q}\right)\sigma_{\alpha\beta}^2 + nq\sigma_\alpha^2. \tag{5.9}$$

Each of the variances in (5.9) is associated with the parameters in the general linear model, whereas in (5.8) some of the variances were in terms of parameters which are not explicitly in the general linear model. The purpose of defining MS_a as nqs_A^2 now becomes clear. By adding the multiplier nq, one may conveniently express each of the variances in (5.8) in terms of parameters which are explicitly in the linear model.

Derivation of the expected values of the mean squares for the main effects of B and for the AB interaction follows the same general line of reasoning. The algebraic procedures whereby the various means are obtained from the experimental data are carried through in terms of the right-hand side of the basic structural model for an observation. Then, using the assumptions underlying the model, one obtains the expected values of the mean squares by the principles that have just been outlined.

The principles underlying the derivation of expected values of the mean squares will be illustrated for the case of a 2×2 factorial experiment having n observations in each cell. In terms of a general linear model, the cell means and the marginal means for the levels of factor B may be represented as follows:

$$
\begin{array}{ll}
\qquad\qquad b_1 & \qquad\qquad b_2 \\
\overline{AB}_{11} = \mu_{..} + \alpha_1 + \beta_1 + \alpha\beta_{11} + \bar{\varepsilon}_{11} & \overline{AB}_{12} = \mu_{..} + \alpha_1 + \beta_2 + \alpha\beta_{12} + \bar{\varepsilon}_{12} \\
\overline{AB}_{21} = \mu_{..} + \alpha_2 + \beta_1 + \alpha\beta_{21} + \bar{\varepsilon}_{21} & \overline{AB}_{22} = \mu_{..} + \alpha_2 + \beta_2 + \alpha\beta_{22} + \bar{\varepsilon}_{22} \\
\hline
\bar{B}_1 \;= \mu_{..} + \bar{\alpha} + \beta_1 + \overline{\alpha\beta}_{.1} + \bar{\varepsilon}_{.1} & \bar{B}_2 \;= \mu_{..} + \bar{\alpha} + \beta_2 + \overline{\alpha\beta}_{.2} + \bar{\varepsilon}_{.2}
\end{array}
$$

The difference between the two marginal means for factor B estimates the following parameters:

$$\bar{B}_1 - \bar{B}_2 = (\beta_1 - \beta_2) + (\overline{\alpha\beta}_{.1} - \overline{\alpha\beta}_{.2}) + (\bar{\varepsilon}_{.1} - \bar{\varepsilon}_{.2}).$$

Multiplying each side of the above expression by np gives

$$np(\bar{B}_1 - \bar{B}_2) = np(\beta_1 - \beta_2) + np(\overline{\alpha\beta}_{.1} - \overline{\alpha\beta}_{.2}) + np(\bar{\varepsilon}_{.1} - \bar{\varepsilon}_{.2}).$$

Since the terms on the right-hand side of the above expression are assumed to be statistically independent, the variance of the term on the left-hand side will estimate the sum of the variances of the terms on the right-hand side. Hence,

$$E(MS_b) = np\sigma_\beta^2 + np\sigma_{\overline{\alpha\beta}}^2 + np\sigma_{\bar{\varepsilon}}^2.$$

Using the analog of the relation given in (5.4),

$$np\sigma_{\overline{\alpha\beta}}^2 = n\left(1 - \frac{p}{P}\right)\sigma_{\alpha\beta}^2, \quad \text{and} \quad np\sigma_{\bar{\varepsilon}} = \left(1 - \frac{n}{N}\right)\sigma_\varepsilon^2.$$

Thus,
$$E(MS_b) = np\sigma_\beta^2 + n\left(1 - \frac{p}{P}\right)\sigma_{\alpha\beta}^2 + \left(1 - \frac{n}{N}\right)\sigma_\varepsilon^2.$$

In most experimental designs the potential number of experimental units, N, is considered to be infinite. Hence $1 - n/N = 1$.

Least-Squares Estimates of Parameters in Model

In a $p \times q$ factorial experiment having n observations per cell, assume factors A and B to be fixed. The least-squares principle leads quite directly to estimators of the parameters in a linear model, provided a set of constraints is imposed upon the model. Let the linear model have the form

$$X_{ijk} = \mu + \alpha_i + \beta_j + \alpha\beta_{ij} + \varepsilon_{ijk}, \tag{5.10}$$

with the constraints

$$\sum_i \alpha_i = 0, \qquad \sum_j \beta_j = 0, \qquad \sum_i \alpha\beta_{ij} = 0, \qquad \sum_j \alpha\beta_{ij} = 0.$$

It is also assumed that

$$E_k(\varepsilon_{ijk}) = 0 \qquad \text{for all } i, j,$$

$$E_k(\varepsilon_{ijk}^2) = \sigma_\varepsilon^2 \qquad \text{for all } i, j.$$

That is, σ_ε^2 does not depend upon i or j.

If the least-squares estimators are denoted $\hat{\mu}$, $\hat{\alpha}_i$, $\hat{\beta}_j$, and $\widehat{\alpha\beta}_{ij}$, the least-squares criterion makes

$$\sum \hat{\varepsilon}_{ijk}^2 = \sum (X_{ijk} - \hat{\mu} - \hat{\alpha}_i - \hat{\beta}_j - \widehat{\alpha\beta}_{ij})^2 = \text{minimum} \tag{5.11}$$

for the experimental data. Taking the partial derivative of (5.11) with respect to each of the estimators and then setting each of the partial derivatives equal to zero yields the following set of normal equations:

$$\mu: \quad npq\hat{\mu} + nq\sum_i \hat{\alpha}_i + np\sum_j \hat{\beta}_j + n\sum_i\sum_j \widehat{\alpha\beta}_{ij} = G,$$

$$\alpha_i: \quad nq\hat{\mu} + nq\hat{\alpha}_i + n\sum_j \hat{\beta}_j + n\sum_j \widehat{\alpha\beta}_{ij} = A_i, \qquad i = 1, \ldots, p,$$

$$\beta_j: \quad np\hat{\mu} + n\sum_i \hat{\alpha}_i + np\hat{\beta}_j + n\sum_i \widehat{\alpha\beta}_{ij} = B_j, \qquad j = 1, \ldots, q, \tag{5.12}$$

$$\alpha\beta_{ij}: \quad n\hat{\mu} + n\hat{\alpha}_i + n\hat{\beta}_j + n\widehat{\alpha\beta}_{ij} = AB_{ij}.$$

The set of linear equations represented by (5.12) contains

$$1 + p + q + pq$$

individual equations in the same number of unknowns. However, the equations are not linearly independent. To illustrate one linear dependency in the set, one notes that the sum of the p equations represented by α_i is the equation represented by μ. Another linear dependency in the set is noted by the fact that the sum over j of the pq, $\alpha\beta_{ij}$ equations yields the equation corresponding to α_i. Because of these and other linear dependencies in the set (5.12), there is no unique solution to the system without imposing a set of constraints on the unknowns.

If one imposes upon the estimators the same set of constraints that are imposed upon the parameters in (5.10), namely,

$$\sum_i \hat{\alpha}_i = 0, \qquad \sum_j \hat{\beta}_j = 0, \qquad \sum_i \widehat{\alpha\beta}_{ij} = 0, \qquad \sum_j \widehat{\alpha\beta}_{ij} = 0,$$

then the solution to the set of equations in (5.12) has the following relatively simple solution:

$$\hat{\mu} = \bar{G}, \qquad \hat{\alpha}_i = \bar{A}_i - \bar{G} \qquad\qquad i = 1, \ldots, p,$$

$$\hat{\beta}_j = \bar{B}_j - \bar{G} \qquad\qquad j = 1, \ldots, q,$$

$$\widehat{\alpha\beta}_{ij} = \overline{AB}_{ij} - \bar{A}_i - \bar{B}_j + G.$$

From the Gauss–Markov theorem, it follows that these estimators are unbiased and are the *best* unbiased estimators, which are linear in the X_{ijk}, in the sense of having minimum standard errors.

The estimators obtained here are identical to those that are obtained if one sets up a hypothetical population of elements and levels of factors A and B. In this hypothetical population, the key constructs were the cell variances and the cell and marginal means. Estimates of the parameters in the linear model were expressed in terms of corresponding estimates of the cell and the marginal means obtained from the experimental data.

From the properties of the general linear model, the variation due to the mean is

$$R(\mu) = \hat{\mu}G = \frac{G^2}{npq}.$$

The sum of squares due to the main effects of factor A, adjusted for the mean, is

$$\mathrm{SS}_a = R(\alpha \mid \mu) = \sum \hat{\alpha}_i A_i = \sum (\bar{A}_i - \bar{G})A_i$$

$$= \frac{\sum A_i^2}{nq} - \frac{G^2}{npq}.$$

Similarly, the sum of squares due to the main effects of factor B, adjusted for the mean, is

$$SS_b = R(\beta \mid \mu) = \sum \hat{\beta}_j B_j$$

$$= \frac{\sum B_j^2}{np} - \frac{G^2}{npq}.$$

The sum of squares due to the interaction effects, adjusted for the mean, is

$$SS_{ab} = R(\alpha\beta \mid \mu) = \sum \widehat{\alpha\beta}_{ij} AB_{ij}$$

$$= \frac{\sum AB_{ij}^2}{n} - \frac{\sum A_i^2}{nq} - \frac{\sum B_j^2}{np} + \frac{G^2}{npq}.$$

If the cell frequencies are not equal, the solution to the normal equations and the estimation of the variation due to various effects are somewhat more complex. The case of unequal cell frequencies is considered in detail in Sec. 5.20.

5.5 PRINCIPLES FOR CONSTRUCTING F RATIOS

For either Model I (all factors assumed fixed) or Model II (all factors assumed random) the sampling distributions of the mean squares for main effects and interactions are independent chi-square distributions. For Model III (some factors fixed, some factors random) all required sampling distributions are independent chi-square distributions only if highly restrictive assumptions on covariances are made. The principles for testing hypotheses to be presented in this section hold rigorously for Models I and II. In practice, tests under Model III follow the principles presented here; however, interpretations under Model III require special care. Scheffé (1959, pp. 264, 288), in particular, has questioned principles for constructing F tests of the type to be presented here for special cases of Model III. Under the mixed model, it is the test on the main effects of the fixed factor that is only approximate unless a set of homogeneity assumptions on covariances are satisfied. The latter are discussed in Chapter 4. Indications are, however, that the operating characteristics of the approximate tests are quite close to the exact tests under relatively weak assumptions on the relevant covariances.

The hypothesis that $\alpha_1 = \alpha_2 = \cdots = \alpha_P$ (that is, the hypothesis of no differences between the main effects of factor A) is equivalent to the hypothesis that $\sigma_\alpha^2 = 0$. This hypothesis is in turn equivalent to the following hypotheses:

1 All possible comparisons (or contrasts) among the main effects of factor A are equal to zero.

2 $\mu_{1.} = \mu_{2.} = \cdots = \mu_{P.} = \mu_{..}$.

To test this hypothesis against the alternative hypothesis that $\sigma_\alpha^2 > 0$ requires the construction of an F ratio. In terms of the expected value of mean squares, the F ratio for this test has the general form

$$\frac{E(\text{numerator})}{E(\text{denominator})} = \frac{u + c\sigma_\alpha^2}{u},$$

where u is some linear function of the variances of other parameters in the model and c is some coefficient. In words, $E(\text{MS}_{\text{numerator}})$ must be equal to $E(\text{MS}_{\text{denominator}})$ when $\sigma_\alpha^2 = 0$.

For the tests under consideration, the mean square in the numerator of the F ratio must be MS_a. The mean square that is in the denominator depends upon the expected value of MS_a under the proper model. For Model I, the appropriate denominator for this F ratio is MS_{error}; for Model II, the appropriate denominator (in a two-factor factorial experiment) is MS_{ab}. Thus, in order to form an F ratio in the analysis of variance, knowledge of the expected value of mean squares under the appropriate model is needed. This, in essence, implies that the F ratio depends upon the design of the experiment.

If the numerator and denominator of an F ratio satisfy the structural requirements in terms of the expected values of the mean squares, and if the sampling distributions of these mean squares are independent chi squares when the hypothesis being tested is true, then the resulting F ratio will have a sampling distribution given by an F distribution. The degrees of freedom for the resulting F distribution are, respectively, the degrees of freedom for the numerator mean square and the degrees of freedom for the denominator mean square. General principles for setting up F ratios are illustrated in Table 5.4.

The expected values in this table are those appropriate for Model II. In terms of these expected values, the F ratio used to test the hypothesis that $\sigma_\alpha^2 = 0$ has the form

$$\frac{E(\text{numerator})}{E(\text{denominator})} = \frac{\sigma_\varepsilon^2 + n\sigma_{\alpha\beta}^2 + nq\sigma_\alpha^2}{\sigma_\varepsilon^2 + n\sigma_{\alpha\beta}^2}.$$

When the hypothesis being tested is true (that is, when $\sigma_\alpha^2 = 0$), the expected value of the numerator is equal to the expected value of the denominator. Thus $E(\text{MS}_a) = E(\text{MS}_{ab})$ when $\sigma_\alpha^2 = 0$. When σ_α^2 is greater than zero, the expected value of the numerator is greater than the expected value of

TABLE 5.4   **Tests of hypotheses under Model II**

Source of variation	E(MS)	Hypothesis being tested	F ratio
Main effect of factor A	$\sigma_\varepsilon^2 + n\sigma_{\alpha\beta}^2 + nq\sigma_\alpha^2$	$H_0: \sigma_\alpha^2 = 0$	$F = \text{MS}_a/\text{MS}_{ab}$
Main effect of factor B	$\sigma_\varepsilon^2 + n\sigma_{\alpha\beta}^2 + np\sigma_\beta^2$	$H_0: \sigma_\beta^2 = 0$	$F = \text{MS}_b/\text{MS}_{ab}$
$A \times B$ interaction	$\sigma_\varepsilon^2 + n\sigma_{\alpha\beta}^2$	$H_0: \sigma_{\alpha\beta}^2 = 0$	$F = \text{MS}_{ab}/\text{MS}_{\text{error}}$
Error	σ_ε^2		

the denominator by an amount which depends upon the term $nq\sigma_\alpha^2$. From the structure of the F ratio, the numerator can be less than the denominator only because of sampling error associated with the estimation of MS_a and MS_{ab}; for any single experiment each of these statistics may be independently either less than or greater than its expected value. Alternatively, the F ratio may be less than unity when some of the assumptions about the model do not hold.

The F ratio appropriate for testing the hypothesis $\sigma_{\alpha\beta}^2 = 0$ has the structure

$$\frac{E(\text{numerator})}{E(\text{denominator})} = \frac{\sigma_\varepsilon^2 + n\sigma_{\alpha\beta}^2}{\sigma_\varepsilon^2}.$$

When the hypothesis being tested is true, numerator and denominator have the same expected value. When $\sigma_{\alpha\beta}^2 > 0$, the expected value of this ratio will be greater than unity by an amount which depends in part upon the term $n\sigma_{\alpha\beta}^2$. The ratio obtained from the experimental data has the form

$$F = \frac{MS_{ab}}{MS_{\text{error}}}.$$

When the hypothesis being tested is true, the sampling distribution of this F ratio is the F distribution having $(p-1)(q-1)$ degrees of freedom for the numerator and $pq(n-1)$ degrees of freedom for the denominator.

5.6 HIGHER-ORDER FACTORIAL EXPERIMENTS

When a factorial experiment includes three or more factors, different orders of interaction are possible. For example, in a $2 \times 3 \times 5$ factorial experiment having 10 independent observations in each cell, the analysis of variance generally has the form given in Table 5.5.

TABLE 5.5 **Analysis of variance for $2 \times 3 \times 5$ factorial experiment having 10 observations per cell**

Source of variation	Sum of squares	df	df (general)
A main effects	SS_a	1	$p-1$
B main effects	SS_b	2	$q-1$
C main effects	SS_c	4	$r-1$
AB interaction	SS_{ab}	2	$(p-1)(q-1)$
AC interaction	SS_{ac}	4	$(p-1)(r-1)$
BC interaction	SS_{bc}	8	$(q-1)(r-1)$
ABC interaction	SS_{abc}	8	$(p-1)(q-1)(r-1)$
Experimental error (within cell)	SS_{error}	270	$pqr(n-1)$
Total	SS_{total}	299	$npqr-1$

In a three-factor experiment, there are three interactions which involve two factors: $A \times B$, $A \times C$, $B \times C$. There is one three-factor interaction. The $A \times B \times C$ interaction represents the unique effects attributable to the combination of the three factors, i.e., the effects that cannot be predicted from a knowledge of the main effects and two-factor interactions. The notation that was introduced for the case of a two-factor experiment can be extended as follows:

	Levels in population	Levels in experiment
Factor A	$a_1, a_2, \ldots, a_I, \ldots, a_P$	$a_1, a_2, \ldots, a_i, \ldots, a_p$
Factor B	$b_1, b_2, \ldots, b_J, \ldots, b_Q$	$b_1, b_2, \ldots, b_j, \ldots, b_q$
Factor C	$c_1, c_2, \ldots, c_K, \ldots, c_R$	$c_1, c_2, \ldots, c_k, \ldots, c_r$

The definitions of fixed and random factor given in Sec. 5.2 also apply to factor C. If $r = R$, then factor C is a fixed factor. If the r levels of factor C in the experiment are a random sample from the R levels in the population, and if R is quite large relative to r, then factor C is a random factor. If the R levels are reduced to $R_{\text{effective}}$ levels by some systematic, nonrandom procedure, then factor C is considered fixed when $r = R_{\text{effective}}$.

The notation for cell means used for the case of a two-factor experiment may also be extended. An observation on element m under treatment combination abc_{ijk} is designated by X_{ijkm}. Notation for cell means is summarized in Table 5.6. In this notation system, μ_{ijk} designates the mean of the N potential observations that could be made under treatment combination abc_{ijk}. The notation $\mu_{ij.}$ designates the mean of the NR potential observations that could be made under the treatment combinations $abc_{ij1}, abc_{ij2}, \ldots, abc_{ijR}$ (N potential observations under each of the R treatment combinations). In terms of symbols,

$$\mu_{ij.} = \frac{\sum\limits_{K} \mu_{ijK}}{R}.$$

(The subscript K is used here to indicate that the average is over all potential levels of factor C and not just those in any single experiment.)

TABLE 5.6 **Notation for means in a three-factor experiment**

	Population mean	Experiment mean
Elements in cell abc_{ijk}	μ_{ijk}	$\overline{ABC}_{ijk}$
Elements under ab_{ij}	$\mu_{ij.}$	$\overline{AB}_{ij}$
Elements under ac_{ik}	$\mu_{i.k}$	$\overline{AC}_{ik}$
Elements under bc_{jk}	$\mu_{.jk}$	$\overline{BC}_{jk}$
Elements under a_i	$\mu_{i..}$	$\overline{A}_i$
Elements under b_j	$\mu_{.j.}$	$\overline{B}_j$
Elements under c_k	$\mu_{..k}$	$\overline{C}_k$

The notation $\mu_{i..}$ designates the mean of the NQR potential observations that could be made under the treatment combinations in which factor A is at level a_i. Thus,

$$\mu_{i..} = \frac{\sum\limits_{J} \sum\limits_{K} \mu_{iJK}}{QR}.$$

(The subscripts J and K indicate that the average is over all levels of factors B and C, not just those included in the experiment.) Similarly, $\mu_{..k}$ denotes the mean of the potential NPQ observations that could be made under level c_k, that is,

$$\mu_{..k} = \frac{\sum\limits_{I} \sum\limits_{J} \mu_{IJk}}{PQ}.$$

The notation k refers to a level of factor C actually included in an experiment. If all the factors in an experiment are fixed factors, there is no need to make the distinction between I, J, and K and i, j, and k.

The numerical data given in Table 5.7 will be used to illustrate the

TABLE 5.7   Population means for $2 \times 3 \times 2$ factorial experiment

(i)

		b_1		b_2		b_3	
		c_1	c_2	c_1	c_2	c_1	c_2
	a_1	20	0	30	10	70	50
	a_2	60	40	40	20	50	30
	Mean	40	20	35	15	60	40

(ii)

	c_1	c_2	Mean
a_1	40	20	30
a_2	50	30	40
Mean	45	25	35

(iii)

	b_1	b_2	b_3	Mean
a_1	10	20	60	30
a_2	50	30	40	40
Mean	30	25	50	35

(ia)

		b_1		b_2		b_3		
		c_1	c_2	c_1	c_2	c_1	c_2	Mean
	a_1	μ_{111}	μ_{112}	μ_{121}	μ_{122}	μ_{131}	μ_{132}	$\mu_{1..}$
	a_2	μ_{211}	μ_{212}	μ_{221}	μ_{222}	μ_{231}	μ_{232}	$\mu_{2..}$
	Mean	$\mu_{.11}$	$\mu_{.12}$	$\mu_{.21}$	$\mu_{.22}$	$\mu_{.31}$	$\mu_{.32}$	

(iia)

	c_1	c_2	Mean
a_1	$\mu_{1.1}$	$\mu_{1.2}$	$\mu_{1..}$
a_2	$\mu_{2.1}$	$\mu_{2.2}$	$\mu_{2..}$
Mean	$\mu_{..1}$	$\mu_{..2}$	$\mu_{...}$

(iiia)

	b_1	b_2	b_3	Mean
a_1	$\mu_{11.}$	$\mu_{12.}$	$\mu_{13.}$	$\mu_{1..}$
a_2	$\mu_{21.}$	$\mu_{22.}$	$\mu_{23.}$	$\mu_{2..}$
Mean	$\mu_{.1.}$	$\mu_{.2.}$	$\mu_{.3.}$	$\mu_{...}$

definitions of main effects and interactions in a three-factor experiment. The data in this table include all levels of each of the factors, and the entries in the cells are the means of all the potential observations that could be in each of the cells. Thus the numerical entries represent the parameters for a specified population.

In part i the cell entries may be designated by the symbol μ_{IJK}. For example, $\mu_{211} = 60$. In symbols,

$$\mu_{211} = \frac{\sum\limits_{M} X_{211M}}{N} = 60.$$

The entries along the lower margin of part i represent the means of the respective columns. Thus the entry 40 at the extreme left represents the mean of all potential observations in which factor B is at level b_1 and factor C is at level c_1; in symbols, this mean is $\mu_{.11}$. Thus,

$$\mu_{.11} = \frac{\sum\limits_{I} \mu_{I11}}{P} = \frac{20 + 60}{2} = 40.$$

Part i*a* summarizes the symbols for the entries in part i.

In part ii each of the numerical entries in the cells represents a mean which has the general symbol $\mu_{I.K}$. For example, the entry in cell ac_{21} is

$$\mu_{2.1} = \frac{\sum\limits_{J} \mu_{2J1}}{Q} = \frac{60 + 40 + 50}{3} = 50.$$

Each of the marginal entries to the right of the cells in part ii has the general symbol $\mu_{I..}$. For example, the entry 30 is the mean of the entries in row a_1; in symbols, $\mu_{1..} = 30$. Thus,

$$\mu_{1..} = \frac{\sum\limits_{K} \mu_{1.K}}{R} = \frac{40 + 20}{2} = 30.$$

The entries along the bottom margin of part ii represent the means of all potential observations at specified levels of factor C. Thus,

$$\mu_{..2} = \frac{\sum\limits_{I} \mu_{I.2}}{P} = \frac{20 + 30}{2} = 25.$$

Part ii*a* summarizes the symbols for corresponding entries in part ii.

In part iii each of the cell entries has the general designation $\mu_{IJ.}$. The marginal entries at the right may be designated $\mu_{I..}$; the marginal entries at the bottom may be designated $\mu_{.J.}$. Thus the entry 50 at the bottom of part iii is

$$\mu_{.3.} = \frac{\sum\limits_{I} \mu_{I3.}}{P} = \frac{60 + 40}{2} = 50.$$

The main effects and interaction effects for a three-factor experiment will be defined in terms of the data in Table 5.7.

Main Effects

All main effects in all experimental designs of any degree of complexity are defined in precisely the same way. A main effect is always the difference between the mean of all observations at a particular level of a factor and the grand mean. Thus, in the two-factor $p \times q$ design, $\alpha_I = \mu_I. - \mu_{..}$ and $\beta_J = \mu_{.J} - \mu_{..}$.

In a three-factor design the main effect of level a_I is

$$\alpha_I = \mu_{I..} - \mu_{...}.$$

Thus, for the data in Table 5.7,

$$\alpha_1 = \mu_{1..} - \mu_{...} = 30 - 35 = -5$$

$$\alpha_2 = \mu_{2..} - \mu_{...} = 40 - 35 = +5.$$

In words, the main effect of level a_I is a measure of the extent to which the mean of all potential observations at level a_I, averaged over all potential levels of factors B and C, differs from the grand mean of all potential observations.

The main effect of level b_J of factor B is

$$\beta_J = \mu_{.J.} - \mu_{...},$$

and
$$\beta_1 = \mu_{.1.} - \mu_{...} = 30 - 35 = -5$$
$$\beta_2 = \mu_{.2.} - \mu_{...} = 25 - 35 = -10$$
$$\beta_3 = \mu_{.3.} - \mu_{...} = 50 - 35 = +15.$$

For factor C the main effects are in general

$$\gamma_K = \mu_{..K} - \mu_{...},$$

and

$$\gamma_1 = \mu_{..1} - \mu_{...} = 45 - 35 = +10$$
$$\gamma_2 = \mu_{..2} - \mu_{...} = 25 - 35 = -10.$$

Note in all cases the sum of main effects is zero:

$$\sum_I \alpha_I = (-5) + (5) = 0$$

$$\sum_J \beta_J = (-5) + (-10) + (15) = 0$$

$$\sum_K \gamma_K = (10) + (-10) = 0.$$

In each case the summation is over all the potential levels of the factors. If, for example, $k \neq K$, then

$$\sum_k \gamma_k \neq 0.$$

The variance due to the main effects of factor A is

$$\sigma_\alpha^2 = \frac{\sum\limits_I \alpha_I^2}{P-1}.$$

Similarly, the variances due to the main effects of factors B and C are, respectively,

$$\sigma_\beta^2 = \frac{\sum\limits_J \beta_J^2}{Q-1},$$

$$\sigma_\gamma^2 = \frac{\sum\limits_K \gamma_K^2}{R-1}.$$

When the main effects within any factor are all equal, the variance corresponding to these main effects will be zero. Hence the equality of main effects implies that the variance corresponding to these main effects is zero.

Two-Factor Interactions

In general, there are as many two-factor interactions as there are the number of combinations of the factors taken two at a time. Thus, in a three-factor experiment, the number of combinations of three factors taken two at a time, $_3C_2$, is three. Those interactions are the $A \times B$, $A \times C$, and $B \times C$ interactions. In a four-factor design,

$$_4C_2 = \frac{4 \cdot 3}{1 \cdot 2} = 6,$$

and those interactions are $A \times B$, $A \times C$, $A \times D$, $B \times C$, $B \times D$, and $C \times D$. This relation can be generalized to a design of any size. In general, if there are k factors in a design, the number of two-factor interactions is $_kC_2$.

All two-factor interactions have the same form and all measure the extent to which the two-factor means cannot be accounted for as the sum of the relevant main effects. Thus, in the two-factor experiment

$$\alpha\beta_{IJ} = (\mu_{IJ} - \mu_{..}) - (\alpha_I + \beta_J),$$
$$= \mu_{IJ} - \mu_{I.} - \mu_{.J} + \mu_{..}.$$

In the three-factor experiment, the three two-factor interactions have exactly this same form when considered in terms of their respective two-factor table of means. The ab_{ij} summary table (part iii and iiia in Table 5.7) is a case in point. From that table, the interaction of level a_i with level b_j is by definition

$$\alpha\beta_{IJ} = (\mu_{IJ.} - \mu_{...}) - (\alpha_I + \beta_J)$$
$$= \mu_{IJ.} - \mu_{I..} - \mu_{.J.} + \mu_{...}.$$

Thus, for example,

$$\alpha\beta_{13} = 60 - 30 - 50 + 35 = 15.$$

The interaction of levels of factor A with levels of factor C is defined in precisely the same way, but with regard to the ac_{IK} summary table. The interaction of a_I with c_K is

$$\alpha\gamma_{IK} = (\mu_{I.K} - \mu_{...}) - (\alpha_I + \gamma_K),$$

the extent to which the two-factor mean ($\mu_{I.K}$) differences are not due to the sum of the A and C main effects. This interaction may be written as

$$\alpha\gamma_{IK} = \mu_{I.K} - \mu_{I..} - \mu_{..K} + \mu_{...}.$$

Thus, for example,

$$\alpha\gamma_{22} = (\mu_{2.2} - \mu_{...}) - (\alpha_2 + \gamma_2)$$
$$= \mu_{2.2} - \mu_{2..} - \mu_{..2} + \mu_{...}$$
$$= 30 - 40 - 25 + 35 = 0.$$

The two-factor interaction of levels of factor B with levels of factor C is defined in terms of the bc_{JK} summary table shown (indirectly) in part (i) and part (ia) of Table 5.7.

$$\beta\gamma_{JK} = (\mu_{.JK} - \mu_{...}) - (\beta_J + \gamma_K)$$
$$= \mu_{.JK} - \mu_{.J.} - \mu_{..K} + \mu_{...}.$$

For example,

$$\beta\gamma_{31} = \mu_{.31} - \mu_{.3.} - \mu_{..1} + \mu_{...}$$
$$= 60 - 50 - 45 + 35 = 0.$$

Because of the nature of the definitions,

$$\sum_I \alpha\beta_{IJ} = \sum_J \alpha\beta_{IJ} = \sum_I \alpha\gamma_{IK} = \sum_K \alpha\gamma_{IK} = \sum_J \beta\gamma_{JK} = \sum_K \beta\gamma_{JK} = 0.$$

The variances due to two-factor interactions are defined as follows:

$$\sigma^2_{\alpha\beta} = \frac{\sum_I \sum_J (\alpha\beta_{IJ})^2}{(P-1)(Q-1)},$$

$$\sigma^2_{\alpha\gamma} = \frac{\sum_I \sum_K (\alpha\gamma_{IK})^2}{(P-1)(R-1)},$$

$$\sigma^2_{\beta\gamma} = \frac{\sum_J \sum_K (\beta\gamma_{JK})^2}{(Q-1)(R-1)}.$$

Three-Factor Interactions

In designs with more than two factors, interactions of factors taken three at a time—three-factor interactions—occur. In a three-factor experiment, there is only one such interaction, the interaction of a_I, b_J, and c_K. The interaction of a_I, b_J, and c_K is defined to be

$$\alpha\beta\gamma_{IJK} = \mu_{IJK} - \mu_{...} - (\alpha\beta_{IJ} + \alpha\gamma_{IK} + \beta\gamma_{JK} + \alpha_I + \beta_J + \gamma_K)$$

$$= \mu_{IJK} - \mu_{IJ.} - \mu_{I.K} - \mu_{.JK} + \mu_{I..} + \mu_{.J.} + \mu_{..K} - \mu_{...}.$$

In words, the interaction of three factors measures the difference between the mean of all potential observations under a specified combination, μ_{IJK}, and the sum of two-factor interactions, main effects, and the grand mean. The three-factor interaction is in essence a measure of the non-additivity of two-factor interactions and main effects. For example, for the data in Table 5.7, the interaction of a_1, b_3, and c_2 is

$$\alpha\beta\gamma_{132} = \mu_{132} - \mu_{13.} - \mu_{1.2} - \mu_{.32} + \mu_{1..} + \mu_{.3.} + \mu_{..2} - \mu_{...}$$

$$= 50 - 60 - 20 - 40 + 30 + 50 + 25 - 35$$

$$= 0.$$

Equivalently,

$$\alpha\beta\gamma_{132} = \mu_{132} - \mu_{...} - (\alpha\beta_{13} + \alpha\gamma_{12} + \beta\gamma_{32} + \alpha_1 + \beta_3 + \gamma_2)$$

$$= 50 - 35 - [15 + 0 + 0 + (-5) + 15 + (-10)]$$

$$= 0.$$

In larger experimental designs, there are more three-factor interactions. For example, in a four-factor experiment, there are four three-factor interactions, $A \times B \times C$, $A \times B \times D$, $A \times C \times D$, and $B \times C \times D$. There is also one four-factor interaction, $A \times B \times C \times D$. In general, the number of three-factor interactions is given by the number of combinations of the total number of factors taken three at a time, $_kC_3$. Thus, with a four-factor experiment,

$$_4C_3 = \frac{4 \cdot 3 \cdot 2}{1 \cdot 2 \cdot 3} = 4.$$

For the three-factor interaction, by definition

$$\sum_I \alpha\beta\gamma_{IJK} = \sum_J \alpha\beta\gamma_{IJK} = \sum_K \alpha\beta\gamma_{IJK} = 0.$$

The variance due to the three-factor interaction is

$$\sigma^2_{\alpha\beta\gamma} = \frac{\sum_I \sum_J \sum_K (\alpha\beta\gamma_{IJK})^2}{(P-1)(Q-1)(R-1)}.$$

Experimental Error

Experimental error has the same general definition as that given for two-factor experiments; it is the deviation of an observation from its own treatment population mean,

$$\varepsilon_{ijkM} = X_{ijkM} - \mu_{ijk}.$$

The variance due to the experimental error also has the same general definition as that given for two-factor experiments; it is the variance of the measurements on the N potential elements within each potential cell of the experiment. Thus for cell abc_{ijk},

$$\sigma^2_{\varepsilon_{ijk}} = \frac{\sum_M (X_{ijkM} - \mu_{ijk})^2}{N - 1},$$

where the subscript M represents a potential element in the cell specified. Assuming that the variance due to experimental error is equal for all potential cells in the experiment, the overall variance due to experimental error is

$$\sigma^2_\varepsilon = \frac{\sum_I \sum_J \sum_K \sigma^2_{\varepsilon_{IJK}}}{PQR}$$

Extension to Four-Factor Designs

The extension of the notation and definitions to four-factor experiments is direct. There are

$_4C_1 = 4$	main effects,
$_4C_2 = 6$	two-factor interactions,
$_4C_3 = 4$	three-factor interactions, and
$_4C_4 = 1$	four-factor interaction.

All main effects, two-factor interactions, and three-factor interactions have the same form as those defined for simpler designs.

For example, the main effect of level d_m of factor D is

$$\delta_m = \mu_{...m} - \mu_{....}.$$

This effect is estimated by

$$\text{est}(\delta_m) = \bar{D}_m - \bar{G}.$$

The notation est (δ_m) denotes an estimate of the parameter δ_m obtained from the data in the experiment. The interaction effect associated with levels a_i and d_m is

$$\alpha\delta_{ij} = \mu_{i..m} - \mu_{....} - (\alpha_i + \delta_m).$$

This interaction effect is estimated by

$$\text{est}\,(\alpha\delta_{im}) = \overline{AD}_{im} - \bar{A}_i - \bar{D}_m + \bar{G}.$$

The interaction of levels a_i, b_j, and d_m is defined to be

$$\alpha\beta\delta_{ijm} = \mu_{ij.m} - \mu_{....} - (\alpha\beta_{ij} + \alpha\delta_{im} + \beta\delta_{jm}) - (\alpha_i + \beta_j + \delta_m).$$

This interaction effect is estimated by

$$\text{est}\,(\alpha\beta\delta_{IJM}) = \overline{ABD}_{IJM} - \overline{AB}_{IJ} - \overline{AD}_{IM} - \overline{BD}_{JM} + \bar{A}_I + \bar{B}_J + \bar{D}_M - \bar{G}.$$

The last estimate has the general form

$$(\text{3-factor mean}) - \sum (\text{2-factor means}) + \sum (\text{1-factor means}) - \bar{G}.$$

The estimate of a four-factor interaction has the general form (4-factor means) $- \sum$ (3-factor means) $+ \sum$ (2-factor means) $- \sum$ (1-factor means) $+ \bar{G}$. For example, the interaction of levels a_1, b_2, c_3, d_4 is estimated by

$$\begin{aligned}
\text{est}\,(\alpha\beta\gamma\delta_{1234}) = {} & \overline{ABCD}_{1234} - (\overline{ABC}_{123} + \overline{ABD}_{124} + \overline{ACD}_{134} + \overline{BCD}_{234}) \\
& + (\overline{AB}_{12} + \overline{AC}_{13} + \overline{AD}_{14} + \overline{BC}_{23} + \overline{BD}_{24} + \overline{CD}_{34}) \\
& - (\bar{A}_1 + \bar{B}_2 + \bar{C}_3 + \bar{D}_4) + \bar{G}.
\end{aligned}$$

The term $\sum$ (3-factor means) in the general expression for the estimate of a four-factor interaction effect includes all possible means of the form UVW_{rst}, where r, s, and t are the subscripts for corresponding terms in the interaction effect being estimated. In a four-factor experiment, the number of terms in $\sum$ (3-factor means) is equal to the number of combinations of four things taken three at a time. This number is

$$_4C_3 = \frac{4 \cdot 3 \cdot 2}{1 \cdot 2 \cdot 3} = 4.$$

For a four-factor experiment the number of terms in the summation $\sum$ (2-factor means) is

$$_4C_2 = \frac{4 \cdot 3}{1 \cdot 2} = 6.$$

In a k-factor experiment, the estimate of the k-factor interaction effect has the general form

$$(k\text{-factor mean}) - \sum [(k-1)\text{-factor means}] + \sum [(k-2)\text{-factor means}]$$

$$- \sum [(k-3)\text{-factor means}] + \sum [(k-4)\text{-factor means}]$$

$$- \cdots.$$

The last term is $\pm[(k-k)\text{-factor means}] = \pm\bar{G}$. If k is an even number, the last term is $+\bar{G}$; if k is an odd number, the last term is $-\bar{G}$. The number of terms in the summation $\sum [(k-1)\text{-factor means}]$ is $_kC_{k-1}$; the number of terms in the summation $\sum [(k-2)\text{-factor means}]$ is $_kC_{k-2}$. For example, if $k = 5$,

$$_kC_{k-2} = {_5C_3} = \frac{5 \cdot 4 \cdot 3}{1 \cdot 2 \cdot 3} = 10; \qquad _kC_{k-1} = {_5C_4} = \frac{5 \cdot 4 \cdot 3 \cdot 2}{1 \cdot 2 \cdot 3 \cdot 4} = 5.$$

5.7 ESTIMATION AND TESTS OF SIGNIFICANCE FOR THREE-FACTOR EXPERIMENTS

For purposes of demonstrating the principles underlying the analysis to be made, it is convenient to formulate a structural model for an observation. For a three-factor experiment, the structural model has the form

$$X_{ijkm} = f(abc_{ijk}) + \varepsilon_{ijkm}. \tag{5.13}$$

The observation on element m under treatment combination abc_{ijk} is designated by the symbol X_{ijkm}. The symbol $f(abc_{ijk})$ denotes the hypothetically true effect of the treatment combination abc_{ijk}. The symbol ε_{ijkm} is the experimental error associated with the measurement on element m. In this context the experimental error is considered to be the difference between the observed measurement and the predicted measurement given by $f(abc_{ijk})$.

For purposes of the analysis that follows, it will be assumed that the predicted measurement is a linear function of the main effects and interaction effects. Specifically,

$$f(abc_{ijk}) = \mu_{...} + \alpha_i + \beta_j + \gamma_k + \alpha\beta_{ij} + \alpha\gamma_{ik} + \beta\gamma_{jk} + \alpha\beta\gamma_{ijk}. \tag{5.14}$$

If (5.13) and (5.14) are combined, the resulting structural model is a generalization of the model given in Sec. 5.3 for a two-factor experiment. The assumptions that will be made about this model in the course of the analysis are direct generalizations of those summarized in Sec. 5.3.

It will be assumed that p levels of factor A are selected at random from a population of P levels. It will further be assumed that an independent random sample of q levels of factor B is selected from a population of Q levels and that a third independent random sample of size r is selected from a population of R levels of factor C. The treatments in the experiment are the pqr combinations that result when each of the selected levels of one factor is combined with each of the selected levels from the other factors. For example, if level a_1 is used in combination with b_2 and c_3, the resulting treatment is designated abc_{123}. In a $p \times q \times r$ factorial experiment, there are pqr treatment combinations.

It will also be assumed that a random sample of $npqr$ elements is drawn from a specified population. Random subsamples of size n each are assigned to each of the pqr treatment combinations to be studied in the experiment. After administration of the treatments, each of the elements is measured on a criterion of effectiveness (the dependent variable). The scale of measurement for the criterion is assumed to be given in terms of an experimentally meaningful unit.

From the data obtained in the experiment, mean squares are computed to estimate variances due to the structural variables on the right-hand side of the model. For a three-factor experiment, the definitions of the mean squares for main effects, interactions, and experimental error are summarized in Table 5.8. With the exception of multipliers and the ranges of summation, these definitions perform on the experimental data the same operations that would be carried out on the population to obtain the variance due to main effects, interactions, and experimental error.

For example, in the population the variance due to the main effects of factor A is

$$\sigma_\alpha^2 = \frac{\sum\limits_I (\mu_{I..} - \mu_{...})^2}{P - 1}.$$

The mean square due to the main effects of factor A as computed from the data in the experiment is

$$\mathrm{MS}_a = \frac{nqr \sum\limits_i (\bar{A}_i - \bar{G})^2}{p - 1}.$$

As another example, in the population the variance due to the BC interaction is

$$\sigma_{\beta\gamma}^2 = \frac{\sum\limits_J \sum\limits_K (\mu_{.JK} - \mu_{.J.} - \mu_{..K} + \mu_{...})^2}{(Q - 1)(R - 1)}.$$

TABLE 5.8   Definition of mean squares

A main effect	$\mathrm{MS}_a = nqr \sum (\bar{A}_i - \bar{G})^2/(p - 1)$
B main effect	$\mathrm{MS}_b = npr \sum (\bar{B}_j - \bar{G})^2/(q - 1)$
C main effect	$\mathrm{MS}_c = npq \sum (\bar{C}_k - \bar{G})^2/(r - 1)$
AB interaction	$\mathrm{MS}_{ab} = nr \sum\limits_i \sum\limits_j (\overline{AB}_{ij} - \bar{A}_i - \bar{B}_j + \bar{G})/(p - 1)(q - 1)$
AC interaction	$\mathrm{MS}_{ac} = nq \sum\limits_i \sum\limits_k (\overline{AC}_{ik} - \bar{A}_i - \bar{C}_k + \bar{G})^2/(p - 1)(r - 1)$
BC interaction	$\mathrm{MS}_{bc} = np \sum\limits_j \sum\limits_k (\overline{BC}_{jk} - \bar{B}_j - \bar{C}_k + \bar{G})^2/(q - 1)(r - 1)$
ABC interaction	$\mathrm{MS}_{abc} = n \sum \sum \sum (\overline{ABC}_{ijk} - \overline{AB}_{ij} - \overline{AC}_{ik} - \overline{BC}_{jk}$ $+ \bar{A}_i + \bar{B}_j + \bar{C}_k - \bar{G})^2/(p - 1)(q - 1)(r - 1)$
Experimental error	$\mathrm{MS}_{\mathrm{error}} = \sum\limits_i \sum\limits_j \sum\limits_k \sum\limits_m (X_{ijkm} - \overline{ABC}_{ijk})^2/pqr(n - 1)$

The mean square due to the BC interaction as obtained from the data in the experiment is

$$MS_{bc} = \frac{np \sum_j \sum_k (\overline{BC}_{jk} - \bar{B}_j - \bar{C}_k + \bar{G})^2}{(q-1)(r-1)}.$$

In each case, with the exceptions noted, the mean square duplicates for the data obtained from the experiment the definitions for the variance due to main effects and interactions in the population.

The expected values for the mean squares defined in Table 5.8 are summarized in Table 5.9. Part i of this table gives general values; part ii specializes these general values for specific cases. The last column is one of several possible special cases of the mixed model; for example, two factors may be random and one factor fixed, or one factor may be random, and two factors fixed. In all these cases it is assumed that the sample of elements observed under any treatment combination is a random sample of size n from a potentially infinite population of elements. Tests of significance in a three-factor experiment follow the same general rules as those for a two-factor experiment. Appropriate F ratios are determined from the structure of the expected values of the mean squares which correspond to the design of the experiment.

For the case of Model I, all F ratios have a simple structure; all use

TABLE 5.9 **Expected value for mean squares in a three-factor experiment having n observations per cell**

(i)

MS_a	$(1-n/N)\sigma_\varepsilon^2 + n(1-q/Q)(1-r/R)\sigma_{\alpha\beta\gamma}^2 + nq(1-r/R)\sigma_{\alpha\gamma}^2 + nr(1-q/Q)\sigma_{\alpha\beta}^2 + nqr\sigma_\alpha^2$
MS_b	$(1-n/N)\sigma_\varepsilon^2 + n(1-p/P)(1-r/R)\sigma_{\alpha\beta\gamma}^2 + np(1-r/R)\sigma_{\beta\gamma}^2 + nr(1-p/P)\sigma_{\alpha\beta}^2 + npr\sigma_\beta^2$
MS_c	$(1-n/N)\sigma_\varepsilon^2 + n(1-p/P)(1-q/Q)\sigma_{\alpha\beta\gamma}^2 + np(1-q/Q)\sigma_{\beta\gamma}^2 + nq(1-p/P)\sigma_{\alpha\gamma}^2 + npq\sigma_\gamma^2$
MS_{ab}	$(1-n/N)\sigma_\varepsilon^2 + n(1-r/R)\qquad\quad \sigma_{\alpha\beta\gamma}^2 + nr\sigma_{\alpha\beta}^2$
MS_{ac}	$(1-n/N)\sigma_\varepsilon^2 + n(1-q/Q)\qquad\quad \sigma_{\alpha\beta\gamma}^2 + nq\sigma_{\alpha\gamma}^2$
MS_{bc}	$(1-n/N)\sigma_\varepsilon^2 + n(1-p/P)\qquad\quad \sigma_{\alpha\beta\gamma}^2 + np\sigma_{\beta\gamma}^2$
MS_{abc}	$(1-n/N)\sigma_\varepsilon^2 + n\sigma_{\alpha\beta\gamma}^2$
MS_{error}	$(1-n/N)\sigma_\varepsilon^2$

Special Cases ($n/N = 0$ in all cases)

(ii)

Mean square	Model I All factors fixed	Model II All factors random	Model III Factor A random, all others fixed
MS_a	$\sigma_\varepsilon^2 + nqr\sigma_\alpha^2$	$\sigma_\varepsilon^2 + n\sigma_{\alpha\beta\gamma}^2 + nq\sigma_{\alpha\gamma}^2 + nr\sigma_{\alpha\beta}^2 + nqr\sigma_\alpha^2$	$\sigma_\varepsilon^2 + nqr\sigma_\alpha^2$
MS_b	$\sigma_\varepsilon^2 + npr\sigma_\beta^2$	$\sigma_\varepsilon^2 + n\sigma_{\alpha\beta\gamma}^2 + np\sigma_{\beta\gamma}^2 + nr\sigma_{\alpha\beta}^2 + npr\sigma_\beta^2$	$\sigma_\varepsilon^2 + nr\sigma_{\alpha\beta}^2 + npr\sigma_\beta^2$
MS_c	$\sigma_\varepsilon^2 + npq\sigma_\gamma^2$	$\sigma_\varepsilon^2 + n\sigma_{\alpha\beta\gamma}^2 + nq\sigma_{\alpha\gamma}^2 + np\sigma_{\alpha\gamma}^2 + npq\sigma_\gamma^2$	$\sigma_\varepsilon^2 + nq\sigma_{\alpha\gamma}^2 + npq\sigma_\gamma^2$
MS_{ab}	$\sigma_\varepsilon^2 + nr\sigma_{\alpha\beta}^2$	$\sigma_\varepsilon^2 + n\sigma_{\alpha\beta\gamma}^2 + nr\sigma_{\alpha\beta}^2$	$\sigma_\varepsilon^2 + nr\sigma_{\alpha\beta}^2$
MS_{ac}	$\sigma_\sigma^2 + nq\sigma_{\alpha\gamma}^2$	$\sigma_\varepsilon^2 + n\sigma_{\alpha\beta\gamma}^2 + nq\sigma_{\alpha\gamma}^2$	$\sigma_\varepsilon^2 + nq\sigma_{\alpha\gamma}^2$
MS_{bc}	$\sigma_\varepsilon^2 + np\sigma_{\beta\gamma}^2$	$\sigma_\varepsilon^2 + n\sigma_{\alpha\beta\gamma}^2 + np\sigma_{\beta\gamma}^2$	$\sigma_\varepsilon^2 + n\sigma_{\alpha\beta\gamma}^2 + np\sigma_{\beta\gamma}^2$
MS_{abc}	$\sigma_\varepsilon^2 + n\sigma_{\alpha\beta\gamma}^2$	$\sigma_\varepsilon^2 + n\sigma_{\alpha\beta\gamma}^2$	$\sigma_\varepsilon^2 + n\sigma_{\alpha\beta\gamma}^2$
MS_{error}	σ_ε^2	σ_ε^2	σ_ε^2

MS_{error} for a denominator. This is a general result. For all completely randomized factorial designs of any degree of complexity, with Model I, MS_{error} is the denominator of all F ratios.

With Model II, it should be apparent that the situation is more complicated. As stated, MS_{error} provides a denominator for testing H_0: $\sigma^2_{\alpha\beta\gamma} = 0$, MS_{abc} may be used as a denominator to test two-factor interactions for significance, but there are no appropriate F ratios to test main effects for significance. With this model, tests on main effects may require constructing quasi F ratios. Those are discussed in Sec. 5.17.

In a mixed model such as the case of Model III in Table 5.9, F ratios for main effects have the following structure:

$$H_0: \sigma^2_\alpha = 0, \qquad F = \frac{MS_a}{MS_{error}};$$

$$H_0: \sigma^2_\beta = 0, \qquad F = \frac{MS_b}{MS_{ab}};$$

$$H_0: \sigma^2_\gamma = 0, \qquad F = \frac{MS_c}{MS_{ac}}.$$

The general rule is that in a mixed model, main effects of random factors (e.g., A) are tested with MS_{error} as a denominator and main-effects of fixed factors are tested with a MS in the denominator which involves interaction with a random factor. Thus, to test $\sigma^2_\beta = 0$, MS_{ab}, which involves an interaction with the random factor A, serves as the denominator; similarly, $\sigma^2_\gamma = 0$ uses MS_{ac} as the denominator. A generalization of the same rule applies to tests on two-factor interactions. The appropriate F ratio to test the hypothesis $\sigma^2_{\beta\gamma} = 0$ is

$$F = \frac{MS_{bc}}{MS_{abc}}.$$

This is an F ratio involving both fixed variables in the numerator; the denominator utilizes an interaction with the random factor. The appropriate F ratio for a test on the hypothesis that $\sigma^2_{\alpha\beta} = 0$ has the form

$$F = \frac{MS_{ab}}{MS_{error}},$$

since the $A \times B$ interaction involves the random factor A. The F ratios constructed for tests on fixed effects under Model III are only approximately distributed as the corresponding F distributions. The distribution theory in this case is exact only under a set of homogeneity conditions on a set of covariances—or equivalently on a set of intraclass correlations.

5.8 SIMPLE EFFECTS AND THEIR TESTS

When interactions are present, the interpretation of main effects is ambiguous without a full understanding of the nature of the interaction. Because an interaction means that there are unique effects associated with combining particular levels of factors, the effects of a particular level of a factor cannot be assumed to be true for all levels of the factors with which it interacts. In the presence of significant interactions, it is appropriate to examine the outcome of an experiment in terms of individual levels of factors. This is an analysis of simple effects. Simple effects are associated with both main effects and interaction effects. The former are called simple main effects, the latter are simple interactions.

Simple main effects are main effects of one factor which are limited to a particular level of other factors. As an example, consider the 2×3 factorial design summary of means

$$
\begin{array}{c|ccc|c}
 & b_1 & b_2 & b_3 & \\
\hline
a_1 & \mu_{11} & \mu_{12} & \mu_{13} & \mu_{1.} \\
a_2 & \mu_{21} & \mu_{22} & \mu_{23} & \mu_{2.} \\
\hline
 & \mu_{.1} & \mu_{.2} & \mu_{.3} & \mu_{..}
\end{array}
$$

Simple main effects for levels of factor A at all levels of factor B defined in terms of these means are shown in Table 5.10 along with the A main effects. It should be clear from Table 5.10 that simple main effects for levels of factor A are main effects limited to a particular level of factor B.

The variances of simple main effects are shown in the lower portion of Table 5.10. The point of the whole analysis is that when there is no interaction, there are no unique effects for the levels of factor A at any of the levels of factor B. Thus, an hypothesis tested with regard to σ_α^2 will yield the same result when applied to $\sigma_{\alpha(b_1)}^2$, $\sigma_{\alpha(b_2)}^2$, or $\sigma_{\alpha(b_3)}^2$. When there are significant interactions that is not the case, and tests on hypotheses of this general form, $\sigma_{\alpha(b_j)} = 0$, will yield different outcomes at different levels of factor B.

The simple main effects of levels of factor B may be defined at each level of factor A. Those definitions are shown in Table 5.11.

One of the more fruitful ways to view an analysis of simple effects is in terms of a series of analyses of a larger design carried out at individual levels of one (or more) of the other factors in the design. Thus, in Table 5.10, one may

TABLE 5.10   *A* **simple main effects**

	A simple main effects, $(\alpha_{i(b_j)} = \mu_{ij} - \mu_{.j})$			*A* main effects
	b_1	b_2	b_3	
a_1	$\alpha_{1(b_1)} = \mu_{11} - \mu_{.1}$	$\alpha_{1(b_2)} = \mu_{12} - \mu_{.2}$	$\alpha_{1(b_3)} = \mu_{13} - \mu_{.3}$	$\alpha_1 = \mu_{1.} - \mu_{..}$
a_2	$\alpha_{2(b_1)} = \mu_{21} - \mu_{.1}$	$\alpha_{2(b_2)} = \mu_{22} - \mu_{.2}$	$\alpha_{2(b_3)} = \mu_{23} - \mu_{.3}$	$\alpha_2 = \mu_{2.} - \mu_{..}$
		Variances		
	$\sigma_{\alpha(b_1)}^2 = \dfrac{\sum_i \alpha_{i(b_1)}^2}{p-1}$	$\sigma_{\alpha(b_2)}^2 = \dfrac{\sum_i \alpha_{i(b_2)}^2}{p-1}$	$\sigma_{\alpha(b_3)}^2 = \dfrac{\sum_i \alpha_{i(b_3)}^2}{p-1}$	$\sigma_\alpha^2 = \dfrac{\sum \alpha_i^2}{p-1}$

TABLE 5.11 *B* **Simple main effects**

	Simple main effects, $\beta_{j(a_i)} = \mu_{ij} - \mu_{i\cdot}$			Variances
	b_1	b_2	b_3	
a_1	$\beta_{1(a_1)} = \mu_{11} - \mu_{1\cdot}$	$\beta_{2(a_1)} = \mu_{12} - \mu_{1\cdot}$	$\beta_{3(a_1)} = \mu_{13} - \mu_{1\cdot}$	$\sigma^2_{\beta(a_1)} = \dfrac{\sum_j \beta^2_{j(a_1)}}{Q - 1}$
a_2	$\beta_{1(a_2)} = \mu_{21} - \mu_{2\cdot}$	$\beta_{2(a_2)} = \mu_{22} - \mu_{2\cdot}$	$\beta_{3(a_2)} = \mu_{23} - \mu_{2\cdot}$	$\sigma^2_{\beta(a_2)} = \dfrac{\sum_j \beta^2_{j(a_2)}}{Q - 1}$

	Main effects			
	$\beta_1 = \mu_{\cdot 1} - \mu_{\cdot\cdot}$	$\beta_2 = \mu_{\cdot 2} - \mu_{\cdot\cdot}$	$\beta_3 = \mu_{\cdot 3} - \mu_{\cdot\cdot}$	$\sigma^2_{\beta} = \dfrac{\sum_j \beta^2_j}{Q - 1}$

view the analysis as three analyses of a single-factor experiment (Factor *A*) each carried out with the other factor (factor *B*) held constant. In Table 5.11, one has the analysis of two single-factor experiments comparing levels of factor *B*, each one of which involves holding a level of factor *A* constant. Stated in terms of analyses of variance summary tables, the results are presented in Table 5.12 for this example.

Note that in the case of both simple-effects analyses there is no variation due to interactions. That is because single-factor experiments provide no information about interactions. What actually occurs in the simple effects analyses is that the variation of both main effects and the interactions of the two-factor analysis are included in the sum of the variation due to simple main effects. Thus

$$\sum_j \text{SS}_{a \text{ for } b_j} = \text{SS}_a + \text{SS}_{ab}, \quad \text{and}$$

$$\sum_i \text{SS}_{b \text{ for } a_i} = \text{SS}_b + \text{SS}_{ab}.$$

TABLE 5.12 **Analyses of variance summary tables**

Two-factor analysis		A simple effects		B simple effects	
Source of variation	df	Source of variation	df	Source of variation	df
A	$p - 1 = 1$	$A(b_1)$	$p - 1 = 1$	$B(a_1)$	$q - 1 = 2$
B	$q - 1 = 2$	$A(b_2)$	$p - 1 = 1$	$B(a_2)$	$q - 1 = 2$
AB	$(p - 1)(q - 1) = 2$	$A(b_3)$	$p - 1 = 1$	Error	$pq(n - 1)$
Error	$pq(n - 1)$	Error	$pq(n - 1)$		
Total	$npq - 1$	Total	$npq - 1$	Total	$npq - 1$

Note that the same is true for the degrees of freedom. Hence, tests on simple main effects are actually tests concerning both main effects and interactions of the complete factorial design.

For larger experimental designs, the same logic applied. A $p \times q \times r$ factorial experiment can be viewed as a series of two-factor experiments, each carried out at particular levels of the third factor. Thus, one could analyze the data as r, $p \times q$ experiments, as p, $q \times r$ experiments, or as q, $p \times r$ experiments. Consider, for example, a $2 \times 2 \times 2$ factorial experiment as a series of $r = 2$, 2×2 factorial experiments combining levels of factor A with levels of factor B. The analysis as a three-factor experiment and as two, two-factor experiments is summarized in Table 5.13. The analyses of the three-factor experiment as a series of two-factor experiments would be appropriate if the ABC interaction were significant, implying that the effects observed for A and B depend upon the particular level of factor C with which they are combined.

The main effects for the two analyses of A and B effects at c_1 and c_2 are simple main effects; the interactions are simple interactions. The relation between the simple effects analyses and the analysis of the total three-factor design is

$$\sum_k SS_{a \text{ for } c_k} = SS_a + SS_{ac}$$

$$\sum_k SS_{b \text{ for } c_k} = SS_b + SS_{bc}$$

$$\sum_k SS_{ab \text{ for } c_k} = SS_{ab} + SS_{abc}$$

In words, the sum of the variation due to the simple main effects of A at the various levels of factor C is equal to the variation due to the overall main effect

TABLE 5.13   **Analysis of variance summaries**

Three-factor summary		A&B simple effects for c_1		A&B simple effects for c_2	
Source of variation	df	Source of variation	df	Source of variation	df
A	$p - 1 = 1$	$A(c_1)$	$p - 1 = 1$	$A(c_2)$	$p - 1 = 1$
B	$q - 1 = 1$	$B(c_1)$	$q - 1 = 1$	$B(c_2)$	$q - 1 = 1$
C	$r - 1 = 1$	$AB(c_1)$	$(p - 1)(q - 1) = 1$	$AB(c_2)$	$(p - 1)(q - 1) = 1$
AB	$(p - 1)(q - 1) = 1$				
AC	$(p - 1)(r - 1) = 1$	$Error(c_1)$	$pq(n - 1)$	$Error(c_2)$	$pq(n - 1)$
BC	$(q - 1)(r - 1) = 1$				
ABC	$(p - 1)(q - 1)(r - 1) = 1$				
Error	$pqr(n - 1)$				
Total	$npqr - 1$	$Total(c_1)$	$npq - 1$	$Total(c_2)$	$npq - 1$

TABLE 5.14 **Definition of effects**

Effect	Definition
Overall main effect of a_i	$\alpha_i = \mu_{i..} - \mu_{...}$
Simple main effect of a_i for c_k	$\alpha_{i(c_k)} = \mu_{i.k} - \mu_{..k}$
Overall main effect of b_j	$\beta_j = \mu_{.j.} - \mu_{...}$
Simple main effect of b_j for c_k	$\beta_{j(c_k)} = \mu_{.jk} - \mu_{..k}$
Overall interaction effect of ab_{ij}	$\alpha\beta_{ij} = \mu_{ij.} - \mu_{...} - \alpha_i \quad - \beta_j$
Simple interaction effect of ab_{ij} for c_k	$\alpha\beta_{ij(c_k)} = \mu_{ijk} - \mu_{..k} - \alpha_{i(c_k)} - \beta_{j(c_k)}$

of factor A and the overall AC interaction. When the variation due to the AC interaction is zero, the sum of the variation for these simple effects is equal to the overall main effects. The same is true for simple main effects of B and the simple AB interactions.

The definitions of the simple effects, in terms of population means, are given in Table 5.14. It will be noted that simple effects have the same general form as overall factorial effects; simple effects, however, are restricted to a single level of one or more of the factors. The degree to which overall effects approximate simple effects depends upon magnitudes of interactions. In the absence of interaction, overall effects will be equal to corresponding simple effects.

The definition of simple effects will be illustrated by the numerical data given in Table 5.15. The data in this table represent population means. An entry in a cell of part i has the general symbol μ_{ijk}; an entry in a cell of part ii has the general symbol $\mu_{ij.}$; an entry in a cell of part iii has the general symbol $\mu_{i.k}$. It is assumed that $p = q = r = 2$. The simple main effects for factor A at

TABLE 5.15 **Population means for $2 \times 2 \times 2$ factorial design**

(i)

		c_1			c_2		
		b_1	b_2	Mean	b_1	b_2	Mean
	a_1	60	20	40	80	40	60
	a_2	0	0	0	20	20	20
	Mean	30	10	20	50	30	40

(ii)

	b_1	b_2	Mean
a_1	70	30	50
a_2	10	10	10
Mean	40	20	30

(iii)

	c_1	c_2	Mean
a_1	40	60	50
a_2	0	20	10
Mean	20	40	30

(iv)

	c_1	c_2	Mean
b_1	30	50	40
b_2	10	30	20
Mean	20	40	30

levels c_1 and c_2 are most readily obtained from part iii. It will be found that

$$\alpha_1 = 50 - 30 = 20, \qquad \alpha_2 = 10 - 30 = -20;$$
$$\alpha_{1(c_1)} = 40 - 20 = 20, \qquad \alpha_{2(c_1)} = \ \ 0 - 20 = -20;$$
$$\alpha_{1(c_2)} = 60 - 40 = 20, \qquad \alpha_{2(c_2)} = 20 - 40 = -20.$$

In each case the simple main effect is equal to the corresponding overall main effect. This finding indicates that the two-factor interaction effects $\alpha\gamma_{ik}$ are all zero and hence that $\sigma^2_{\alpha\gamma} = 0$. The $\alpha\gamma_{ik}$'s are most readily obtained from part iii.

$$\alpha\gamma_{11} = 40 - 50 - 20 + 30 = 0,$$
$$\alpha\gamma_{12} = 60 - 50 - 40 + 30 = 0,$$
$$\alpha\gamma_{21} = \ \ 0 - 10 - 20 + 30 = 0,$$
$$\alpha\gamma_{22} = 20 - 10 - 40 + 30 = 0.$$

Conversely, when two-factor interaction effects are found to be zero, corresponding simple main effects will be equal to overall main effects.

The simple main effects for factor A at levels b_1 and b_2 are most readily obtained from part ii. These overall and simple main effects are

$$\alpha_1 = 50 - 30 = 20, \qquad \alpha_2 = 10 - 30 = -20;$$
$$\alpha_{1(b_1)} = 70 - 40 = 30, \qquad \alpha_{2(b_1)} = 10 - 40 = -30;$$
$$\alpha_{1(b_2)} = 30 - 20 = 10, \qquad \alpha_{2(b_2)} = 10 - 20 = -10.$$

In this case, simple main effects are not equal to corresponding overall main effects. This finding indicates that the two-factor interactions $\alpha\beta_{ij}$ are not all zero and hence that $\sigma^2_{\alpha\beta} \neq 0$. The $\alpha\beta_{ij}$'s are obtained from part ii.

$$\alpha\beta_{11} = 70 - 50 - 40 + 30 = 10,$$
$$\alpha\beta_{12} = 30 - 50 - 20 + 30 = -10,$$
$$\alpha\beta_{21} = 10 - 10 - 40 + 30 = -10,$$
$$\alpha\beta_{22} = 10 - 10 - 20 + 30 = 10.$$

The fact that the $\alpha\beta_{ij}$'s are not all equal to zero implies that the simple main effects are not equal to the corresponding overall main effects.

The overall two-factor interaction effects are related to corresponding simple effects. Specifically,

$$\alpha\beta_{ij} = \alpha_{i(b_j)} - \alpha_i. \tag{5.15}$$

For example,

$$\alpha\beta_{12} = \alpha_{1(b_2)} - \alpha_1 = 10 - 20 = -10,$$
$$\alpha\beta_{21} = \alpha_{2(b_1)} - \alpha_2 = -30 - (-20) = -10.$$

Similarly,

$$\alpha\beta_{ij} = \beta_{j(a_i)} - \beta_j. \tag{5.16}$$

These last relationships indicate that two-factor interaction effects will be zero when simple main effects are equal to overall main effects and, conversely, that when two-factor interaction effects are zero, corresponding simple main effects will be equal to overall main effects.

The simple two-factor interaction effects $\alpha\beta_{ij(c_k)}$ are most readily obtained from part i. For example,

$$\alpha\beta_{11(c_1)} = 60 \quad -40 \quad -30 \quad +20 = 10$$
$$= \mu_{111} - \mu_{1.1} - \mu_{.11} + \mu_{..1},$$
$$\alpha\beta_{11(c_2)} = 80 \quad -60 \quad -50 \quad +40 = 10$$
$$= \mu_{112} - \mu_{1.2} - \mu_{.12} + \mu_{..2}.$$

Thus it is noted that

$$\alpha\beta_{11(c_k)} = \alpha\beta_{11} = 10, \qquad\qquad k = 1, 2.$$

In general, the overall three-factor interaction effect is related to simple two-factor interaction effects by means of the relation

$$\alpha\beta\gamma_{ijk} = \alpha\beta_{ij(c_k)} - \alpha\beta_{ij}. \qquad\qquad (5.17)$$

Thus, when the simple interaction effect is equal to the overall interaction effect, the corresponding three-factor interaction effect will be zero.

For the data in part i in Table 5.15,

$$\alpha\beta_{11(c_1)} = \alpha\beta_{11}.$$

Hence, from relation (5.17) it follows that $\alpha\beta\gamma_{111} = 0$. In general, for the data in part i, it will be found that

$$\alpha\beta_{ij(c_k)} = \alpha\beta_{ij}, \qquad \text{for all } k\text{'s.}$$

From relation (5.17) it follows that all $\alpha\beta\gamma_{ijk}$'s are equal to zero. Hence, $\sigma^2_{\alpha\beta\gamma} = 0$. Analogous to (5.17) are the relations

$$\alpha\beta\gamma_{ijk} = \alpha\gamma_{ik(b_j)} - \alpha\gamma_{ik}, \qquad\qquad (5.18)$$
$$\alpha\beta\gamma_{ijk} = \beta\gamma_{jk(a_i)} - \beta\gamma_{ik}. \qquad\qquad (5.19)$$

That the relation (5.17) implies (5.18) and (5.19) is illustrated geometrically in the next section.

It should be apparent that the analyses of the form summarized in Table 5.13 can be further reduced to a series of analyses of the form summarized in Table 5.12. That is, a series of two-factor analyses can be further analyzed as a series of single-factor experiments. Such effects would be called simple-simple effects. This could be appropriate if any of the simple interactions of Table 5.13 were found to be significant.

Estimation of Simple Effects

As is true for main effects and interactions, simple main effects and simple interactions are estimated from observed means corresponding to the population means used in their definitions. Thus, for example, the simple effects defined in Table 5.10 are estimated as

$$\hat{\alpha}_{1(b_1)} = \overline{AB}_{11} - \bar{B}_1 \qquad \hat{\alpha}_{1(b_2)} = \overline{AB}_{12} = \bar{B}_2 \qquad \hat{\alpha}_{1(b_3)} = \overline{AB}_{13} - \bar{B}_3$$
$$\hat{\alpha}_{2(b_1)} = \overline{AB}_{21} - \bar{B}_1 \qquad \hat{\alpha}_{2(b_2)} = \overline{AB}_{22} - \bar{B}_2 \qquad \hat{\alpha}_{2(b_3)} = \overline{AB}_{23} - \bar{B}_3.$$

As further examples,

$$\hat{\alpha}_{i(c_k)} = \overline{AC}_{ik} - \bar{C}_k,$$
$$\hat{\beta}_{j(c_k)} = \overline{BC}_{jk} - \bar{C}_k,$$
$$\widehat{\alpha\beta}_{ij(c_k)} = \overline{ABC}_{ijk} - \overline{AC}_{ik} - \overline{BC}_{jk} + \bar{C}_k.$$

Variation due to simple effects is given by the general formula

$$\sum [\text{est (simple effect)}]^2.$$

Computational formulas for such variation are given in Chapter 6.

Tests of Significance for Simple Effects

It is well to keep in mind that the variation due to simple main effects actually includes both treatment effects and interaction effects. Thus, for example, from Tables 5.10 and 5.12 the simple main effects comparing the A effects at b_1 has the hypothesis

$$\mu_{11} = \mu_{21}.$$

If these means differ, it can be because of differences in the simple main effects $\alpha_{1(b_1)}$ vs $\alpha_{2(b_1)}$ or because the interactions $\alpha\beta_{11}$ and $\alpha\beta_{21}$ differ. Tests on simple effects depend upon expected values of mean squares for such effects. In general, appropriate expected values of mean squares for simple effects may be obtained from the expected values appropriate for experiments of lower dimension than the original experiment, i.e., by considering the simple effects as overall effects of experiments of lower dimension. F ratios are constructed from expected values thus obtained.

One must be cognizant of the fact that simple effects tests may involve making relatively large numbers of tests of significance, that the tests are not independent, and that there are questions regarding the appropriate unit for the error rate. Chapter 6 will discuss those matters in more detail.

5.9 GEOMETRIC INTERPRETATION OF HIGHER-ORDER INTERACTIONS

Various orders of interactions may be represented geometrically. In terms of such representation, interesting aspects of the meaning of interactions will become clearer. In particular, it will be noted how simple interactions are related to overall interactions. It will also be noted how simple interactions are

TABLE 5.16 **Population means**

		c_1					c_2			
	b_1	b_2	b_3	**Mean**		b_1	b_2	b_3	**Mean**
a_1	20	30	70	40	a_1	0	10	50	20
a_2	60	40	50	50	a_2	40	20	30	30
Mean	40	35	60	45	Mean	20	15	40	25

(i)

	(ii)					**(iii)**			
	b_1	b_2	b_3	**Mean**		b_1	b_2	b_3	**Mean**
a_1	10	20	60	30	c_1	40	35	60	45
a_2	50	30	40	40	c_2	20	15	40	25
Mean	30	25	50	35	Mean	30	25	50	35

related to higher-order interactions. The numerical data in Table 5.16 will be used for this purpose. It will be assumed that these data represent population means.

Data necessary to plot the profiles for the BC interactions for the two levels of factor A are given in part i. The left-hand side of Fig. 5-1 represents the profiles of means which are in the a_1 row of part i. The dotted line

FIGURE 5-1 $SS_{bc} = 0$, $SS_{abc} = 0$.

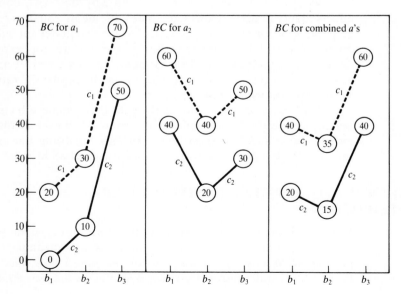

represents the means of the form μ_{1j1}; the solid line represents means of the form μ_{1j2}. Thus the two profiles on the left represent the BC means for level a_1. These two profiles have the same shape (i.e., are parallel). This finding implies that all simple interaction effects $\beta\gamma_{jk(a_1)}$ are zero.

In general, the simple two-factor interaction at level a_i has the definition

$$\beta\gamma_{jk(a_i)} = \mu_{ijk} - \mu_{ij.} - \mu_{i.k} + \mu_{i..}. \tag{5.20}$$

For the data in Table 5.16

$$\beta\gamma_{11(a_1)} = 20 - 10 - 40 + 30 = 0,$$

$$\beta\gamma_{21(a_1)} = 30 - 20 - 40 + 30 = 0,$$

$$\beta\gamma_{31(a_1)} = 70 - 60 - 40 + 30 = 0.$$

The observation that the profiles on the left are parallel has the algebraic counterpart

$$\mu_{1j1} - \mu_{1j2} = \text{constant} \qquad \text{for all } j\text{'s.}$$

Hence the variation arising from such differences will be zero. This source of variation is that due to the BC interaction for a_1.

It is noted that the profiles of the BC means for level a_2 are parallel. This finding implies that all $\beta\gamma_{jk(a_2)}$'s are zero. Hence

$$\text{SS}_{bc \text{ for } a_1} + \text{SS}_{bc \text{ for } a_2} = 0 + 0 = 0.$$

In words, the sum of variations due to the simple interaction effects for the levels of factor A is zero. Since

$$\sum_i \text{SS}_{bc \text{ for } a_i} = \text{SS}_{bc} + \text{SS}_{abc},$$

when $\sum_i \text{SS}_{bc \text{ for } a_i} = 0$, both SS_{bc} and SS_{abc} must be equal to zero.

The profiles of the overall BC means, obtained from part iii of Table 5.16, are given at the right in Fig. 5-1. The two profiles here are also parallel. This finding implies that

$$\beta\gamma_{jk} = 0, \qquad \text{for all } j\text{'s and } k\text{'s.}$$

Hence SS_{bc} must be zero. This latter result was implied by the fact that all the simple interaction effects of the $\beta\gamma_{jk(a_i)}$'s are zero. The fact that the BC profiles for a_1 and a_2 are parallel actually implies that the BC profiles for the combined levels of factor A are also parallel. To summarize, when the simple interactions of two factors at various levels of a third factor are all zero, the corresponding two-factor and three-factor interactions will also be zero.

It is, however, possible for two-factor interactions to be nonzero and yet have zero three-factor interaction. The profiles in Fig. 5-2 illustrate this case. These profiles represent the AB means for the two levels of factor C (Table 5.16). The profiles of AB for c_1 are not parallel; the profiles AB for c_2 are not

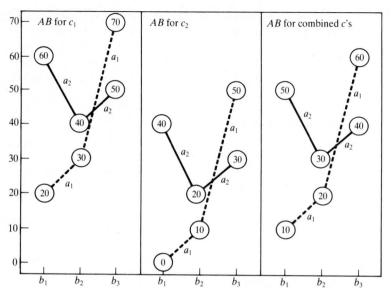

FIGURE 5-2 $SS_{ab} \neq 0$, $SS_{abc} = 0$.

parallel. Hence

$$\sum_{k} SS_{ab \text{ for } c_k} \neq 0.$$

Although the profiles within each level of factor C are not parallel, the a_1 profile for c_1 is parallel to the a_1 profile for the combined levels of factor C. Similarly, the a_1 profile for c_2 is parallel to the a_1 profile for the combined levels of factor C. The a_2 profiles for each level of factor C are also parallel to the a_2 profile for the combined data. This finding implies that SS_{abc} will be zero. The fact that the AB profiles for the combined data are not parallel indicates that SS_{ab} will not be zero.

To summarize the implications of the profiles with respect to the three-factor interaction, the latter will be zero when (1) the profiles of the two-factor means are parallel within each level of the third factor or when (2) the pattern of profiles for the two-factor means is geometrically similar to the pattern for the combined levels. In order that patterns be geometrically similar, corresponding profiles must be parallel.

A set of profiles in which the three-factor interaction is nonzero but the two-factor interaction is zero is given in Fig. 5-3. (These profiles are *not* based upon the data in Table 5.16). The profiles within level c_1 are not parallel to each other, nor is the profile at a_1 parallel to the a_1 profile for the combined levels of factor C. Hence the three-factor interaction is nonzero. However, the AB profiles for the combined levels of factor C are parallel. Thus $SS_{ab} = 0$.

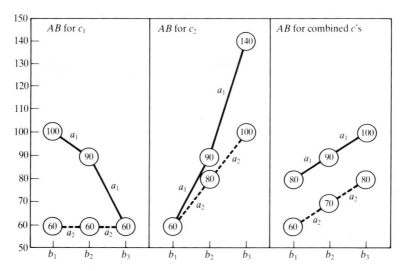

FIGURE 5-3 $SS_{ab} = 0$, $SS_{abc} \neq 0$.

The geometric relationships between the simple two-factor interactions, the three-factor interaction, and the overall two-factor interaction are seen more clearly by drawing three-dimensional profiles. The following data will be used for illustrative purposes:

	c_1		c_2	
	b_1	b_2	b_1	b_2
a_1	60	20	80	40
a_2	0	0	20	20

(These data are the same as those in part i of Table 5.15.) These data represent the population means for a $2 \times 2 \times 2$ factorial experiment. A geometric representation of the patterns formed by these means is given in Fig. 5-4. The left-hand panel represents the four means in which factor C is at level c_1. This panel is denoted AB for c_1. The right-hand panel represents the four means in which factor C is at level c_2. The line $(60, 20)$ in the left panel is parallel to the line $(80, 40)$ in the right panel. The line $(0, 0)$ in the left panel is parallel to the line $(20, 20)$ in the right panel. The vertical lines in these panels are automatically parallel by the method of construction. Since corresponding sides of the left and right panels are parallel, the two panels are geometrically similar.

Geometric similarity of the left and right panels forces similarity of the front and back panels as well as similarity of the top and bottom panels. In analysis-of-variance terms, similarity of panels implies that the profiles of the

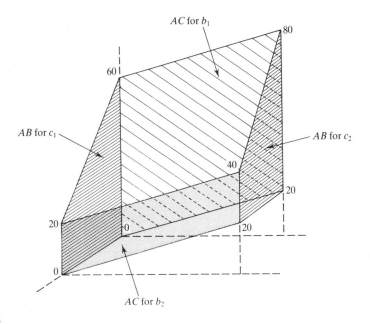

FIGURE 5-4

simple two-factor interactions have the same patterns for all levels of a third factor. Thus the fact that the panel AB for c_1 is similar to the panel AB for c_2 implies that the simple AB interactions have the same pattern for c_1 as they do for c_2. This in turn implies that $SS_{abc} = 0$.

The fact that $SS_{abc} = 0$ is implied by the similarity of any two opposite panels—in turn, similarity of one pair of opposite panels implies the similarity of all other pairs. This geometric fact illustrates why one cannot distinguish between the interactions $(AB) \times C$, $(AC) \times B$, and $(BC) \times A$. Similarity of the left and right panels actually implies that $(AB) \times C$ is zero. But similarity of the left and right panels forces similarity of the front and back panels. The latter similarity implies that $(AC) \times B$ is zero. Thus, when $(AB) \times C$ is zero, $(AC) \times B$ must also be zero; one implies the other. More emphatically, one is not distinguishable from the other.

When the three-factor interaction is zero, inspection of individual panels will provide information about the two-factor interactions. In Fig. 5-4 the line $(60, 20)$ is not parallel to the line $(0, 0)$. This implies that the variance due to the AB interaction is not zero. In the front panel, the line $(20, 40)$ is parallel to the line $(0, 20)$. This implies that the variance due to the AC interaction is zero. In the top panel, the line $(60, 80)$ is parallel to the line $(20, 40)$. This implies that $SS_{bc} = 0$. When the three-factor interaction is not zero, inspection of the individual panels does not provide information with respect to the two-factor interactions. The individual panels in pairs must be averaged in order to obtain information relevant to the overall two-factor interaction.

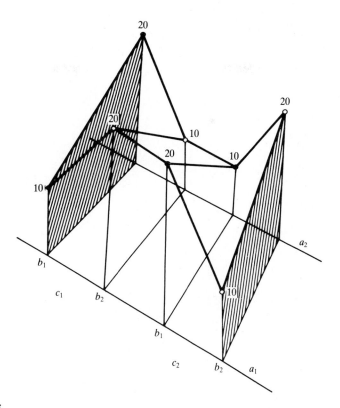

FIGURE 5-5

An example of a set of cell means which defines a population in which all main effects and all two-factor interactions are zero but the three-factor interaction is not zero is given below. A three-dimensional plot of these means appears in Fig. 5-5. Another view of the configuration in Fig. 5-5 is shown in Fig. 5-6. In the latter figure, the information on the levels of factor B appears as profiles. Figures 5-7 and 5-8 present somewhat different views of Fig. 5-5. In Fig. 5-8, the left-hand panel represents the relationship between the responses to combinations of factors A and B for level c_1; the right-hand panel represents the corresponding relationships for level c_2.

	c_1		c_2	
	b_1	b_2	b_1	b_2
a_1	10	20	20	10
a_2	20	10	10	20

Another way of representing Fig. 5-8 appears in Fig. 5-9. Here the left-

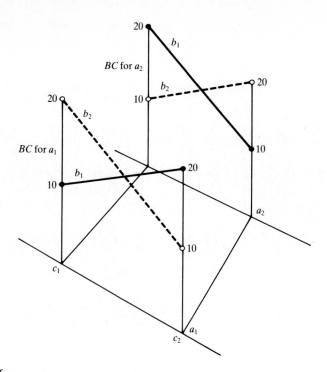

FIGURE 5-6

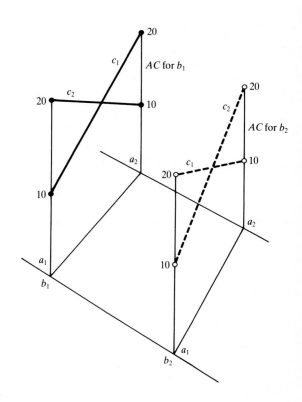

FIGURE 5-7

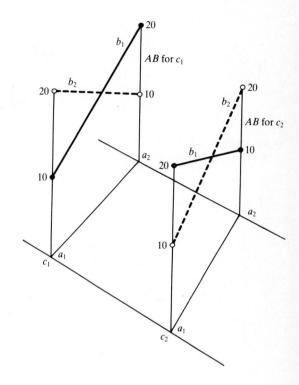

FIGURE 5-8

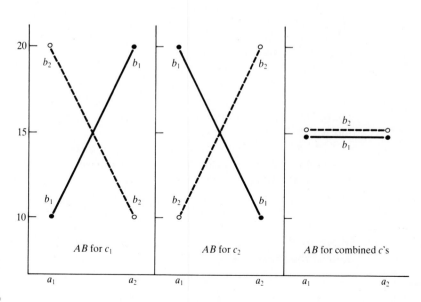

FIGURE 5-9

and right-hand panels of Fig. 5-8 appear side by side in two dimensions. The combined profiles appear at the extreme right. The fact that the combined profiles are parallel (actually identical in this case) indicates that the variation due to the AB interaction is zero. The fact that the combined profiles are identical and horizontal indicates that variation due to the main effects of factors A and B are both zero.

5.10   INDIVIDUAL COMPARISONS

Procedures discussed in Chapter 3 for making individual and multiple comparisons among means can be extended rather directly to factorial experiments. A significant overall F test on a main effect, for example, indicates that one or more of a multitude of possible comparisons is significant. (In particular, a significant overall main effect implies that the maximum normalized comparison among the relevant marginal means is statistically significant.)

The specific comparisons which are built into the design or suggested by the theoretical basis for the experiment can and should be made individually, regardless of the outcome of the corresponding overall F test. Seldom, if ever, should *a posteriori* comparisons be made when the overall F is non-significant. (In this context an *a posteriori* comparison is one suggested by deliberate inspection of the data.) Should such comparisons be made, statistically significant outcomes should be interpreted with extreme caution, but the experimenter should not hesitate to describe fully all aspects of his experimental results.

An experimenter may have an interest in testing differences among any of the means in the design. These may include differences between $\bar{A}$'s, $\bar{B}$'s, or $\overline{AB}_{ij}$'s. Following the procedures discussed in Chapter 3, in general an F statistic may be constructed as

$$F = \frac{\text{MS}_{\text{comparison}}}{\text{MS}_{\text{denominator}}},$$

where $\text{MS}_{\text{denominator}}$ depends upon the means being compared in the numerator and which factors are fixed or random.

In constructing $\text{MS}_{\text{comparisons}}$ for $p \times q$ factorial experiments having n observations in each cell, the mean square for a comparison among the main effects of factor A has the general form

$$\frac{(c_1 A_1 + c_2 A_2 + \cdots + c_p A_p)^2}{nq \sum c_i^2},$$

where $\sum c_i = 0$. The case in which $c_1 = 1$, $c_2 = -1$, and all other c's are zero defines the mean square

$$\frac{(A_1 - A_2)^2}{2nq}.$$

The case in which $c_1 = 1$, $c_2 = 1$, and $c_3 = -2$ defines the mean square

$$\frac{(A_1 + A_2 - 2A_3)^2}{6nq}.$$

The general mean square corresponding to a comparison among the main effects of factor B has the form

$$\frac{(c_1B_1 + c_2B_2 + \cdots + c_qB_q)^2}{np \sum c_j^2},$$

where $\sum c_j = 0$.

The general mean square for a comparison among the AB_{ij}'s has the form

$$\frac{(c_{11}AB_{11} + c_{12}AB_{12} + \cdots + c_{pq}AB_{pq})}{n \sum \sum c_{ij}^2}.$$

For example, the mean square for a comparison among the simple effects of factor A for level b_j has the form

$$\frac{(c_1AB_{1j} + c_2AB_{2j} + \cdots + c_pAB_{pj})^2}{n \sum c_i^2}.$$

A comparison involving marginal totals (or means) may always be expressed in terms of cell totals (or means). For example, the comparison

$$\frac{(AB_{11} + AB_{12} + \cdots + AB_{1q} - AB_{21} - AB_{22} - \cdots - AB_{2q})^2}{n(2q)}$$

reduces to

$$\frac{(A_1 - A_2)^2}{2nq}.$$

The appropriate $MS_{\text{denominator}}$ used to construct an F varies with the conditions of the experiment. For the case in which A and B are both fixed factors, $MS_{\text{w. cell}}$ is the appropriate MS to test differences among *any* of the means. The statistic is

$$F = \frac{MS_{\text{comparison}}}{MS_{\text{w. cell}}}.$$

Under the assumption that the hypothesis being tested is true, this statistic has a sampling distribution which is given by an F distribution. The critical value for this test is $F_{1-\alpha}[1, pq(n-1)]$.

This statistic is an appropriate one for planned comparisons, keeping in mind the discussion in Chapter 3 regarding the level of significance with regard to the collection of tests. In cases where the comparisons are *a posteriori* type, the appropriate critical value, as suggested by Scheffé (1953), for tests on main effects due to factor A is

$$(p - 1)F_{1-\alpha}[(p - 1), pq(n - 1)].$$

An analogous critical value for comparisons among the main effects of factor B is

$$(q - 1)F_{1-\alpha}[(q - 1), pq(n - 1)].$$

The critical value for comparisons of the *a posteriori* type among cell means is

$$(pq - 1)F_{1-\alpha}[(pq - 1), pq(n - 1)].$$

To illustrate the magnitude of the difference between the two types of critical values, consider the case in which $p = 10$ and $pq(n - 1) = 40$. For $\alpha = 0.01$,

$$F_{0.99}(1, 40) = 7.31$$

is the critical value for an *a priori* type of comparison. For an *a posteriori* type,

$$9F_{0.99}(9, 40) = 9(2.8876) = 25.99.$$

The difference between the two critical values is quite marked—but then the difference in the underlying logic is also quite marked. Whenever a relatively large number of tests of significance are to be made, or whenever comparisons suggested by the data are made, the usual sampling distributions (that is, t or F) associated with tests of significance no longer apply. The critical value for the *a posteriori* comparison is much larger because the sampling distribution appropriate for this type of comparison must take into account sources of variation which are not relevant to the *a priori* comparison.

When either factor A or B is not fixed, the appropriate $\text{MS}_{\text{denominator}}$ for tests on A and B means varies. To test the hypothesis that $\alpha_i = \alpha_{i'}$ against the two-tailed alternative hypothesis $\alpha_i \neq \alpha_{i'}$, one may use the test statistic

$$F = \frac{(\bar{A}_i - \bar{A}_{i'})^2}{\text{MS}_{\bar{A}_i - \bar{A}_{i'}}}.$$

The best estimate of $\text{MS}_{\bar{A}_i - \bar{A}_{i'}}$ depends upon whether factor B is fixed or random. For the case in which factor B is fixed,

$$\text{MS}_{\bar{A}_i - \bar{A}_{i'}} = \frac{2\text{MS}_{\text{w. cell}}}{nq}.$$

For the case in which factor B is random and $\sigma^2_{\alpha\beta} \neq 0$,

$$\text{MS}_{\bar{A}_i - \bar{A}_{i'}} = \frac{2\text{MS}_{ab}}{nq}.$$

For the first case, the degrees of freedom for $\text{MS}_{\bar{A}_i - \bar{A}_{i'}}$ are $pq(n - 1)$; for the second case, the degrees of freedom are $(p - 1)(q - 1)$. In either case

$$t = \sqrt{F} = \frac{\bar{A}_i - \bar{A}_{i'}}{\sqrt{\text{MS}_{\bar{A}_i - \bar{A}_{i'}}}}.$$

Either one-tailed or two-tailed tests may be made by using the t statistic. An equivalent but computationally simpler form of the F statistic for the case in which factor B is fixed, in terms of totals rather than means, is

$$F = \frac{(A_i - A_{i'})^2}{2nq\,MS_{\text{w. cell}}}.$$

For the case in which factor B is random,

$$F = \frac{(A_i - A_{i'})^2}{2nq\,MS_{ab}}.$$

Similarly for tests involving B means,

$$F = \frac{(\bar{B}_j - \bar{B}_{j'})^2}{MS_{\bar{B}_j - \bar{B}_{j'}}},$$

where

$$MS_{\bar{B}_j - \bar{B}_{j'}} = \frac{2MS_{\text{w. cell}}}{np}$$

when factor A is fixed, and

$$MS_{\bar{B}_j - \bar{B}_{j'}} = \frac{2MS_{ab}}{np}$$

when factor A is random. Regardless of whether factors A or B are fixed or random, a test on the difference between cell means has the form

$$F = \frac{(AB_{ij} - AB_{km})^2}{2n\,MS_{\text{w. cell}}}.$$

In making the tests indicated in this section, the denominators use data from all cells in the experiment, not just those from which the means have been computed. If the experimental error is homogeneous, use of information from all cells to estimate experimental error is justified.

Individual Comparisons Involving Interactions

It was seen earlier that in the presence of significant interactions it may be useful to carry out tests on simple main effects or, in the case of designs with three or more factors, simple main effects and/or simple interactions. A different view of interactions may be obtained by defining a comparison or contrast of interest and then evaluating whether that contrast varies over the levels of the other factors, i.e., interacts with the other factor. A *treatment-contrast* interaction is one which arises because a comparison among levels of one factor varies at different levels of the other factor.

In general, a comparison among the A means

$$\sum c_i \mu_{i.} \qquad \sum c_i = 0$$

is estimated by

$$\sum c_i \bar{A}_i = c_1 \bar{A}_1 + c_2 \bar{A}_2 + \cdots + c_p \bar{A}_p \qquad \sum c_i = 0.$$

This same comparison can be estimated separately at each level of factor B as

$$C_{\bar{A}(b_1)} = \sum c_i \overline{AB}_{i1}$$

$$C_{\bar{A}(b_2)} = \sum c_i \overline{AB}_{i2}$$

$$\vdots$$

$$C_{\bar{A}(b_q)} = \sum c_i \overline{AB}_{iq}.$$

If the comparison of interest varies for the different levels of factor B, that variation can be evaluated for significance. When significant variations exist, the conclusion is that one way to account for the significant overall interaction is in terms of the interaction of this particular contrast with the levels of the other factor.

For this purpose the variation among the comparisons of the A means at the different levels of factor B is given by

$$SS_{C_{\bar{A}(b_j)}} = n\left[\sum_j C^2_{\bar{A}(b_j)} - \left(\sum_j C^2_{\bar{A}(b_j)}\right)^2 \Big/ q\right] \Big/ \sum_i c_i^2.$$

The statistic

$$F = \frac{SS_{C_{\bar{A}(b_j)}}/q - 1}{MS_{\text{w. cell}}} = F[(q-1)pq(n-1)]$$

can be used to evaluate whether there is interaction with this particular comparison.

In a two-factor design, analogous relations may be defined for comparisons among the levels of factor B and their possible treatment–contrast interactions with levels of factor A.

A comparison among B means

$$\sum c_j \mu_{.j} \qquad \sum c_j = 0$$

is estimated by

$$\sum c_j \bar{B}_j,$$

and is estimated at each level of factor A as

$$C_{\bar{B}(a_1)} = \sum c_j \overline{AB}_{1j}$$

$$C_{\bar{B}(a_2)} = \sum c_j \overline{AB}_{2j}$$

$$\vdots$$

$$C_{\bar{B}(a_p)} = \sum c_j \overline{AB}_{pj}.$$

The variation due to differences in this comparison at the different levels of factor B is

$$SS_{C_{\bar{B}(a_i)}} = \left[\sum_i C_{\bar{B}(a_i)}^2 - \left(\sum_i C_{\bar{B}(a_i)}^2 \right)^2 \Big/ p \right] \sum_j c_j^2.$$

The statistic

$$F = \frac{SS_{C_{\bar{B}(a_i)}}/p - 1}{MS_{\text{w. cell}}} = F[(p-1)pq(n-1)]$$

tests the null hypothesis that this particular comparison is equal at all levels of factor B against the alternative that the contrast interacts with levels of factor A.

It is an interesting aspect of treatment-contrast interactions that they may be used to partition the overall interaction variation into orthogonal components. In the case of simple effects analysis, the variation due to simple main effects represents a partition of variation due to both main effects and interactions. That is, in a two-factor design

$$\sum_j SS_{a \text{ for } b_j} = SS_A + SS_{AB},$$

and

$$\sum_i SS_{b \text{ for } a_i} = SS_B + SS_{AB}.$$

In the case of variation due to treatment-contrast interactions, the variation from $p-1$ mutually orthogonal contrasts on the A main effect sums to SS_{AB} when computed over the levels of factor B for each contrast. The same is true for the variation from $q-1$, mutually orthogonal contrasts among B main effects summed over the levels of Factor A. A numerical example will be presented in Chapter 6 to clarify this point. The literature includes a number of discussions of the components of interactions (Boik, 1979; Gabriel et al., 1973; Kirk, 1982; Marascuilo and Levin, 1970) which may be useful to the interested reader.

Controlling Significance Levels

Obviously, when simple main effects analyses or comparisons are used to evaluate the outcome of the overall analyses of variance, the results can be complicated from the point of view of controlling type 1 error. This can be particularly true when factorial designs involve a number of factors and the number of tests of significance can be quite large, tests may not be independent, and tests may be either *a priori* or *post mortem* in nature.

In general, all of the techniques for controlling type 1 errors discussed in Sec. 3.11 may be applied to comparing means within a factorial design. Specific numerical examples will be presented in Chapter 6.

5.11 PARTITION OF MAIN EFFECTS AND INTERACTION INTO TREND COMPONENTS

In Chapters 3 and 4, procedures were presented for dividing treatment effects into trend components. In factorial designs, it is possible and sometimes desirable to divide main effects as well as interactions into components associated with functional forms assumed to account for trends in the criterion responses. As an example, consider a 3×4 factorial experiment in which the levels of both factors may be regarded as steps along an underlying continuum. The magnitudes of the criterion scores within each of the cells may be considered to define a response surface. It is frequently of interest to explore regions on this response surface, particularly when one is seeking an optimum combination of treatments. In order to better understand the nature of the problem, it may be helpful to refer back to figures such as Figs. 5-4 and 5-5. They present response surfaces which make it possible to visualize the interactions and other effects. The surface in Fig. 5-4 is linear by linear; the surface shown in Fig. 5-5 is quite complex, but is linear with regard to levels of factor A, as it must be with only two levels, and quadratic with regard to levels of factor B.

Main effects and interactions in a 3×4 factorial experiment may be subdivided as indicated below:

Source	df			
A	2			
Linear	1			
Quadratic	1			
B	3			
Linear	1			
Quadratic	1			
Cubic	1			
AB				6
Linear × linear	1	Quadratic × linear	1	
Linear × quadratic	1	Quadratic × quadratic	1	
Linear × cubic	1	Quadratic × cubic	1	

The components of the variation due to the main effects of factor A can be expressed in the form

$$\text{SS}_{A \text{ component}} = \frac{(\sum c_i A_i)^2}{nq \sum c_i^2},$$

where the c_i are the coefficients of trend comparisons corresponding to the main effects of factor A. The computational work is simplified if the levels of factor A are equally spaced along the underlying continuum; in this case the coefficients are defined by appropriate entries in Table D.10, the so-called coefficients of orthogonal polynomials. In the case of unequal spacing, these coefficients may be modified by using methods described by Robson (1959).

In a similar manner, the components of the variation due to the main effects of factor B may be expressed in the form

$$\text{SS}_{B \text{ component}} = \frac{(\sum c_j B_j)^2}{np \sum c_j^2}.$$

The trend components of the variation due to the interaction have the general form

$$\text{SS}_{AB \text{ component}} = \frac{(\sum c_i A B_{ij})^2}{n \sum c_{ij}^2},$$

where $c_{ij} = c_i c_j$ and c_i and c_j are the respective trend components of the main effects. (See Table 5.17.)

The response surface defined by such trend components is that described by a polynomial in which the independent variates are mutually uncorrelated.

TABLE 5.17 **Some trend comparisons in a 3 × 4 factorial experiment**

	A_lin						B_quad				
	b_1	b_2	b_3	b_4	Total		b_1	b_2	b_3	b_4	Total
a_1	−1	−1	−1	−1	−4	a_1	1	−1	−1	1	0
a_2	0	0	0	0	0	a_2	1	−1	−1	1	0
a_3	1	1	1	1	4	a_3	1	−1	−1	1	0
Total	0	0	0	0	0	Total	3	−3	−3	3	0

	$A_\text{lin} \times B_\text{quad}$				
	b_1	b_2	b_3	b_4	Total
a_1	−1	1	1	−1	0
a_2	0	0	0	0	0
a_3	1	−1	−1	1	0
Total	0	0	0	0	0

For the case of a 3×4 factorial experiment, an exact fit to the surface on which the cell means lie can always be obtained by a polynomial having the following form:

$$\overline{AB} = b_0 + b_{1,0}P_{1,0} + b_{2,0}P_{2,0} + b_{0,1}P_{0,1} + b_{0,2}P_{0,2} + b_{0,3}P_{0,3}$$
$$+ b_{1,1}P_{1,1} + b_{1,2}P_{1,2} + b_{1,3}P_{1,3}$$
$$+ b_{2,1}P_{2,1} + b_{2,2}P_{2,2} + b_{2,3}P_{2,3},$$

where each $P_{i.}$ is uncorrelated with each of the others. The $P_{i,j}$ actually correspond to polynomials of degree i in a variate Z_1 and of degree j in a variate Z_2. However, for prediction purposes the $P_{i,j}$ may be regarded as a set of independent variates. Because the $P_{i,j}$ are uncorrelated, the sources of variation associated with each of the $b_{i,j}$ are orthogonal.

The variation due to the regression coefficient

$b_{1,0}$ corresponds to that due to A_{lin},

$b_{2,0}$ corresponds to that due to A_{quad},

$b_{0,1}$ corresponds to that due to B_{lin},

$b_{0,2}$ corresponds to that due to B_{quad},

$b_{1,1}$ corresponds to that due to $A_{\text{lin}} \times B_{\text{lin}}$,

$b_{2,3}$ corresponds to that due to $A_{\text{quad}} \times B_{\text{cubic}}$.

In terms of the $P_{i,j}$ variates, the components of the regression analysis and the components of the analysis of variance are identical. However, this identity is not readily established if the regression analysis is carried out in terms of a correlated set of regression variates.

The components of the interaction obtained in this way describe features of a response surface that might be described in a more parsimonious form by means of functions other than polynomials. More extensive methods for exploring response surfaces are available. A survey of some of these methods is given in Cochran and Cox (1957, Chapter 8A).

If only one of the factors—say, factor B—is continuous, then the following analysis is possible:

Source		df
A		2
B		3
Linear	1	
Quadratic	1	
Cubic	1	
AB		6
Difference in lin trend	2	
Difference in quad trend	2	
Difference in cubic trend	2	

This method of partitioning the interaction is particularly appropriate when attempting to interpret differences in shapes of profiles. Computational details for this kind of partition are given in Secs. 6.9 and 7.6. In Sec. 7.6, computational steps are given in terms of a design calling for repeated measures.

5.12   THE CASE $n = 1$ AND A TEST FOR NONADDITIVITY

If there is only one observation in each cell of a $p \times q$ factorial experiment, there can be no within-cell variation and hence no direct estimate of experimental error. Among other models, the following two may be postulated to underlie the observed data:

$$X_{ij} = \mu + \alpha_i + \beta_j + \varepsilon_{ij}, \tag{5.21}$$

or
$$X_{ij} = \mu + \alpha_i + \beta_j + \alpha\beta_{ij} + \varepsilon_{ij}. \tag{5.22}$$

In (5.21) no interaction effect is postulated; hence, all sources of variation other than main effects are considered to be part of the experimental error. In (5.22) an interaction term is postulated. From some points of view the interaction term may be considered a measure of nonadditivity of the main effects. In this context, (5.21) will be considered the additive model, whereas (5.22) will be considered the nonadditive model.

It is sometimes difficult to know whether an experiment should include interactions. The social and behavioral sciences literature is probably confusing because many researchers have failed to appreciate this complexity, and although a number of writers have addressed problems associated with interpreting interactions, the problems remain. One problem is that the choice of a scale of measurement for the basic criterion measurements will to some extent determine whether interactions will occur in the data; when dependent variables and the theoretical constructs they purport to measure are only monotonically related, a permissible transformation of the dependent variable may eliminate or add interactions (Busemeyer, 1980). The best guide to which model is most appropriate is a strong theory regarding the nature of the variables under study. That and subject matter knowledge and experience gained from past experimentation about the functional form of the underlying sources of variation are the best guides for deciding between models (5.21) and (5.22). To supplement these sources of information, the experimenter may want to use information provided by preliminary tests before specifying the model. So far in this chapter such tests have been considered only for the case in which direct estimates of experimental error were available from the experimental data.

Tukey (1949) developed a test applicable to the case in which there is a single observation per cell. This test is discussed in detail by Scheffé (1959, pp. 130–134) and by Rao (1965, pp. 207–209).

Tukey's test is called a test for *nonadditivity*. Its purpose is to help in the decision between models (5.21) and (5.22). This test has also been used to choose between alternative scales of measurement, the decision being made in favor of the scale for which model (5.21) is the more appropriate.

In Tukey's approach to the problem, he starts with the model

$$X_{ij} = \mu + \alpha_i + \beta_j + \lambda\alpha_i\beta_j + \varepsilon_{ij},$$

where $\alpha_i\beta_j$ is the product of the main effects and λ is a regression coefficient. Here the product term is that part of the interaction which can be expressed as the product of main effects. A test on the hypothesis that $\lambda = 0$ is equivalent to a test on the hypothesis that product terms of this form do not contribute to the prediction of the X_{ij}.

Assuming that the α_i and the β_j are known, a least-squares estimate of λ is obtained by making

$$\sum \hat{\varepsilon}_{ij}^2 = \sum (X_{ij} - \mu - \alpha_i - \beta_j - \hat{\lambda}\alpha_i\beta_j)^2 = \text{minimum}.$$

Solving the normal equation yields the following estimate for λ,

$$\hat{\lambda} = \frac{\sum \alpha_i\beta_j(X_{ij} - \mu - \alpha_i - \beta_j)}{\sum \alpha_i^2\beta_j^2},$$

all summations being over i and j. If one then replaces μ, α_i, and β_j with their respective least-squares estimates,

$$\hat{\mu} = \bar{G}, \qquad \hat{\alpha}_i = \bar{A}_i - \bar{G}, \qquad \hat{\beta}_j = \bar{B}_j - \bar{G},$$

one obtains, after simplication,

$$\hat{\lambda} = \frac{\sum \hat{\alpha}_i\hat{\beta}_j X_{ij}}{\sum \hat{\alpha}_i^2\hat{\beta}_j^2}.$$

If one lets

$$k_{ij} = \hat{\alpha}_i\hat{\beta}_j,$$

from the definitions of $\hat{\alpha}_i$ and $\hat{\beta}_j$, one finds that

$$\sum k_{ij} = 0 \quad \text{and} \quad \sum k_{ij}^2 = \sum \hat{\alpha}_i^2\hat{\beta}_j^2,$$

where all summations are over both i and j. In terms of the k_{ij}, the expression for $\hat{\lambda}$ takes the form

$$\hat{\lambda} = \frac{\sum k_{ij}X_{ij}}{\sum k_{ij}^2}.$$

Let
$$D = \lambda \sum k_{ij}^2 = \sum k_{ij}X_{ij}.$$

Since $\sum k_{ij} = 0$, D represents a comparison or contrast among the X_{ij}. The component of variation çorresponding to this comparison has the form

$$SS_D = \frac{D^2}{\sum k_{ij}^2} = \hat{\lambda}^2(\sum k_{ij}^2) = \frac{(\sum k_{ij}X_{ij})^2}{\sum k_{ij}^2}.$$

This source of variation Tukey calls the nonadditivity component. Upon replacing the k_{ij} by their basic definitions one has

$$SS_{\text{nonadd}} = \hat{\lambda}^2(\sum k_{ij}^2) = \frac{(\sum \alpha_i\beta_j X_{ij})^2}{(\sum \hat{\alpha}_i^2)(\sum \hat{\beta}_j^2)} = \frac{pq(\sum \hat{\alpha}_i\hat{\beta}_j X_{ij})^2}{SS_a SS_b},$$

since $SS_a = q \sum \hat{\alpha}_i^2$ and $SS_b = p \sum \hat{\beta}_j^2$.

In the application of Tukey's test for nonadditivity to the case of a $p \times q$ factorial experiment having one observation per cell, the analysis of variance takes the following form:

Source of variation	SS	df	MS
A	SS_a	$p - 1$	MS_a
B	SS_b	$q - 1$	MS_b
Residual	SS_{res}	$(p - 1)(q - 1)$	
Nonadditivity	SS_{nonadd}	1	MS_{nonadd}
Balance	SS_{bal}	$(p - 1)(q - 1) - 1$	MS_{bal}

In this table

$$SS_{\text{bal}} = SS_{\text{res}} - SS_{\text{nonadd}},$$

and

$$SS_{\text{res}} = SS_{\text{total}} - SS_a - SS_b.$$

The test for nonadditivity is given by

$$F = \frac{MS_{\text{nonadd}}}{MS_{\text{bal}}}.$$

When this F ratio exceeds the critical value defined by the level of significance of the test, the hypothesis that model (5.21) is appropriate is rejected. Tukey's test for nonadditivity is sensitive to only one source of nonaddivity—that associated with a component of the interaction represented by $\alpha_i\beta_j$. (This component is somewhat related to the linear $\times$ linear component of interaction in the analysis of trend.) In working with this component there is an implicit assumption that the larger the main effects of the individual levels in a treatment combination, the larger the potential interaction effect for the treatment combination, if this does exist. This assumption appears reasonable in some cases. In other cases it might be that the equivalent of the linear $\times$ quadratic or the quadratic $\times$ quadratic component could more appropriately be used as a measure of nonadditivity. A numerical example is given in Sec. 6.8.

The principles underlying Tukey's test for a two-factor experiment can be extended to higher-order factorial experiments. For the three-factor case, the comparison for nonadditivity is given by

$$D = \sum c_{ijk} X_{ijk}$$

where
$$c_{ijk} = (\bar{A}_i - \bar{G})(\bar{B}_j - \bar{G})(\bar{C}_k - \bar{G}).$$

The corresponding component of variation is

$$SS_D = SS_{nonadd} = \frac{D^2}{\sum c_{ijk}^2} = \frac{pqrD^2}{SS_a SS_b SS_c}.$$

In this case the residual variation is partitioned as follows:

Source of variation	df
$SS_{residual}$	$(p-1)(q-1)(r-1)$
SS_{nonadd}	1
$SS_{balance}$	$(p-1)(q-1)(r-1)-1$

5.13 THE CHOICE OF A SCALE OF MEASUREMENT AND TRANSFORMATIONS

In the analysis of variance of a factorial experiment, the total variation of the criterion variable is subdivided into nonoverlapping parts which are attributable to main effects, interactions, and experimental error. The relative magnitude of each of the corresponding variances depends upon the scale of measurement as well as the spacing of the levels of the factors using the experiment. When alternative choices of a scale of measurement appear equally justifiable on the basis of past experience and theory, analysis in terms of each of the alternative scales is warranted providing each scale satisfies the assumptions underlying the respective analyses.

It may happen that within-cell variances will be homogeneous in terms of one scale of measurement but heterogeneous in terms of a second scale. The within-cell distributions may be highly skewed in terms of one scale but approximately normal in terms of a second scale. In terms of one scale of measurement, an additive (i.e., no interaction terms) model may be appropriate, whereas in terms of a second scale the additive model will not be appropriate.

In determining the choice of a scale of measurement for the observed data, two cases will be contrasted. In one case, *a priori* theory and experience determine the appropriate model as well as the appropriate scale. In the second case, where there is neither adequate theory nor experience to serve as guides, the appropriate model and the proper scale of measurement are determined only after the experimental data have been partially analyzed. In the latter case the design of the experiment should provide the experimenter with sufficient data to permit the evaluation of alternative formulations of the model.

A readable summary of methods for determining appropriate transformations will be found in Olds et al. (1956). A series of alternative methods is also given by Tukey (1949). A transformation in this context is a change in the scale of measurement for the criterion. For example, rather than time in seconds, the scale of measurement may be logarithm time in seconds; rather than number of errors, the square root of the number of errors may be used as the criterion score. There are different reasons for making such transformations. Some transformations have as their primary purpose the attainment of homogeneity of error variance.

Another reason for using transformations is to obtain normality to within-cell distributions. Often non-normality and heterogeneity of variance occur simultaneously. The same transformation will sometimes normalize the distributions as well as make the variances more homogeneous. The work of Box (1953) has shown that the sampling distribution of the F ratio is relatively insensitive to moderate departures from normality. Hence, transformations whose primary purpose is to attain normal within-cell distributions are now considered somewhat less important than was the case previously.

A third reason for transformations is to obtain additivity of effects. In this context *additivity of effects* implies a model which does not contain interaction terms. In some of the designs which are discussed in later chapters, a strictly additive model is required. In designs of this type certain interaction effects are completely confounded with experimental error. For those designs which do permit independent estimation of interaction effects and error effects, the strictly additive model is not essential. There are, however, advantages to the strictly additive model, if it is appropriate, over the nonadditive model—particularly when fixed and random factors are in the same experiment. The interaction of the random factors with the fixed factors, if these exist, will tend to increase the variance of the sampling distribution of the main effects. Tukey (1949) has pointed out rather vividly the influence of the scale of measurement upon existence or nonexistence of interaction effects.

The use of transformations in order to obtain additivity has received more attention in recent works than it has in the past. Tukey's test for nonadditivity has been used, in part, as a guide for deciding between alternative possible transformations. It is not possible to find transformations which will eliminate nonadditivity in all cases. In some cases there is an intrinsic interaction between the factors which cannot be considered a function of the choice of the scale of measurement. These cases are not always easily distinguished from cases in which the interaction is essentially an artifact of the scale of measurement. Busemeyer (1980) and others (e.g., Krantz and Tversky, 1971; Townsend and Ashby, 1984) have discussed in depth some of the problems measurement scales can generate for statistics.

A *monotonic* transformation is one which leaves ordinal relationships (i.e., greater than, equal to, or less than) unchanged. If the means for the levels of factor A have the same rank for all levels of factor B, then a monotonic transformation can potentially remove the $A \times B$ interaction. When such rank order is not present, a monotonic transformation cannot remove the $A \times B$ interaction. Only monotonic transformations will be discussed in this section. Nonmonotonic transformations in this connection would be of extremely limited utility.

There are some overall guides in selecting a scale of measurement which will satisfy the assumptions of homogeneity of error variance. These guides will be considered in terms of the relationship between the cell means and the cell variances. The latter relationship will be presented in terms of a $p \times q$ factorial experiment; the principles to be discussed hold for all designs.

Case (i): $\sigma_{ij}^2 = c^2 \mu_{ij}$. In case (i) the cell variances tend to be functions of the cell means: the larger the mean, the larger the variance. This kind of relationship exists when the within-cell distribution is Poisson in form. For this case, a square-root transformation will tend to make the variances more homogeneous. This transformation has the form

$$X'_{ijk} = \sqrt{X_{ijk}},$$

where X is the original scale and X' is the transformed scale. If X is a frequency—number of errors, number of positive responses—and if X is numerically small in some cases (say less than 10) then a more appropriate transformation is

$$X'_{ijk} = \sqrt{X_{ijk}} + \sqrt{X_{ijk} + 1}.$$

The following transformation is also used for frequency data in which some of the entries are numerically small:

$$X'_{ijk} = \sqrt{X_{ijk} + \tfrac{1}{2}}.$$

Either of the last two transformations is suitable for the stated purpose.

Case (ii): $\sigma_{ij}^2 = \mu_{ij}(1 - \mu_{ij})$. Case (ii) occurs in practice when the basic observations have a binomial distribution. For example, if the basic observations are proportions, variances and means will be related in the manner indicated. The following transformation is effective in stabilizing the variances,

$$X'_{ijk} = 2 \arcsin \sqrt{X_{ijk}},$$

where X_{ijk} is a proportion. In many cases only a single proportion appears in a cell. Tables are available for this transformation (See Appendix D, Table 5). Numerically, X'_{ijk} is an angle measured in radians. For proportions between 0.001 and 0.999, X'_{ijk} assumes values between 0.0633 and 3.0783. The notation $\sin^{-1}$ (read inverse sine) is equivalent to the notation arcsin. For values of X close to zero or close to unity, the following transformation is recommended:

$$X'_{ijk} = 2 \arcsin \sqrt{X_{ijk} \pm [1/(2n)]},$$

where n is the number of observations on which X is based. The plus sign is used for X_{ijk} close to zero; the minus sign is used for X_{ijk} close to unity.

Case (iii): $\sigma_{ij}^2 = k^2 \mu_{ij}^2$. In case (iii) the logarithmic transformation will stabilize the variances,

$$X'_{ijk} = \log X_{ijk}.$$

To avoid values of X close to zero, an alternative transformation

$$X'_{ijk} = \log (X_{ijk} + 1)$$

is often used when some of the measurements are equal to or close to zero. The logarithmic transformation is particularly effective in normalizing distributions which have positive skewness. Such distributions occur in psychological research when the criterion is in terms of a time scale, i.e., number of seconds required to complete a task.

The rationale underlying the choice of a transformation is the following: Let m be a cell mean in terms of an original scale of measurement. Let the cell variance be

$$\sigma_m^2 = f(m).$$

That is, the cell variances are some function of the cell means. Let $\phi(m)$ define a transformation. In terms of the transformed scale, the cell variances will be approximately

$$\sigma_\phi^2 = \left(\frac{d\phi}{dm}\right)^2 f(m) \quad \text{or} \quad d\phi = \frac{\sigma_\phi}{\sqrt{f(m)}} dm.$$

In order that the cell variances be some constant—say k^2—in terms of the transformed scale, one must have

$$\phi(m) = \int \frac{k\,dm}{\sqrt{f(m)}}.$$

For example, suppose

$$\sigma_m^2 = f(m) = c^2 m.$$

Then

$$\frac{df}{dm} = c^2 \quad \text{and} \quad dm = \frac{df}{c^2}.$$

Hence

$$\phi(m) = \int \frac{k}{\sqrt{c^2 m}} \frac{df}{c^2} = \frac{2k}{c^3} \int \frac{1}{2\sqrt{m}} df$$

$$= \frac{2k}{c^3} \sqrt{m}.$$

If all that is wanted is a transformation that will make σ_m^2 some constant, then one may use

$$\phi(m) = \sqrt{m}.$$

In terms of the basic observations, this information takes the form

$$\phi(X_{ijk}) = X'_{ijk} = \sqrt{X_{ijk}}.$$

Use of the Range in Deciding Between Alternative Transformations

In deciding which one of several possible transformations to use in a specific problem, one may investigate several before deciding which one puts the data in a form that most nearly satisfies the basic assumptions underlying the analysis of variance. The use of the range statistic (or the truncated range statistic) provides a relatively simple method for inspecting the potential usefulness of several transformations with a minimum of computational effort. An example given by Rider et al. (1956, pp. 47–55) will be used to illustrate the method.

In this example, eight operators individually measured the resistance of each of four propeller blades with each of two instruments. Order was randomized. The range of the 16 measurements on each blade in terms of the original scale as well as in terms of transformed scales is given below. (Only the end points of the ranges in terms of the original scale need to be transformed in order to obtain the following data.)

	Scale of measurement			
Blade	Original	Square root	Logarithm	Reciprocal
1	3.10	0.61	0.21	0.077
2	0.10	0.08	0.12	0.833
3	0.15	0.12	0.17	1.111
4	11.00	1.01	0.16	0.015

The logarithmic transformation is seen to make the ranges more uniform. In many practical cases the range tends to be proportional to the variance. A transformation which tends to make the ranges uniform will also tend to make the variances more uniform. As a further step in checking on the adequacy of the logarithmic transformation, the authors applied Tukey's test for nonadditivity to each of the four interaction terms. On the original scale of measurement, two of the four F ratios for nonadditivity were significant at the 5 percent level. None of the F ratios for nonadditivity was significant at the 5 percent level in terms of the logarithmic scale.

5.14 NESTED FACTORS (HIERARCHAL DESIGNS)

Sometimes it is neither possible nor desirable to construct complete factorial designs in which all levels of all factors are combined to define the treatment conditions. One class of such designs is defined by hierarchal designs wherein levels of one factor are *nested* within levels of one or more other factors.

Consider an experiment conducted to evaluate the relative effectiveness of two drugs with respect to some specified criterion. Suppose that the design calls for the administration of drug 1 to n patients from each of hospitals 1, 2, and 3; drug 2 is to be administered to n patients from each of hospitals 4, 5, and 6. This design can be represented schematically as follows:

Drug 1			Drug 2		
Hosp. 1	Hosp. 2	Hosp. 3	Hosp. 4	Hosp. 5	Hosp. 6
n	n	n	n	n	n

The difference between the mean effect of drug 1 and the mean effect of drug 2 will be due in part to differences between the unique effects associated with hospitals 1, 2, and 3 and the unique effects associated with hospitals 4, 5, and 6.

The unique effects associated with hospitals 1, 2, and 3 are confined to drug 1 whereas the unique effects associated with hospitals 4, 5, and 6 are confined to drug 2. Effects which are restricted to a single level of a factor are said to be *nested* within that factor. In the experimental design being considered, the hospital effects are nested under the drug factor. Since a given hospital appears only under one of the two drugs, there is no way of evaluating the interaction effect between the hospital and the drug. Before such an interaction effect can be evaluated, each hospital must appear under both levels of the drug factor.

Thus, in a two-factor experiment having one factor nested under the other, the interaction effect cannot be evaluated. For the general case of a two-factor experiment in which factor B is nested under factor A, the structural model is

$$\overline{AB}_{ij} = \mu_{..} + \alpha_i + \beta_{j(i)} + \bar{\varepsilon}_{ij}.$$

The notation $\beta_{j(i)}$ indicates that the effect of level b_j is nested under level a_i. Note that no interaction term of the form $\alpha\beta_{ij(i)}$ appears in the model. Inferences made from this type of design assume implicitly that the variation associated with this latter interaction is either zero or negligible relative to the variation associated with the main effects.

The analysis of variance for the design outlined at the beginning of this section takes the following form:

	Factor	df	df for general case
A	Drug	1	$p - 1$
$B(\text{w. } a_1)$	Hospitals within drug 1	2	$q - 1$
$B(\text{w. } a_2)$	Hospitals within drug 2	2	$q - 1$
	Within hospital	$6(n - 1)$	$pq(n - 1)$

The expected values of the mean squares in this analysis are as follows:

Source of variation	df	E(MS)
A	$p - 1$	$\sigma_\varepsilon^2 + nD_q\sigma_\beta^2 + nq\sigma_\alpha^2$
B (pooled)	$p(q - 1)$	$\sigma_\varepsilon^2 + n\sigma_\beta^2$
Experimental error (within cell)	$pq(n - 1)$	σ_ε^2

The symbol D_q is used to designate the expression $1 - q/Q$. Numerically $D_q = 0$ when $q = Q$ (that is, when factor B is fixed), and $D_q = 1$ when $q/Q = 0$ (that is, when factor B is random). To test the hypothesis that $\sigma_\alpha^2 = 0$,

$$F = \frac{MS_a}{MS_b}, \qquad \text{when factor B is random;}$$

$$F = \frac{MS_a}{MS_{\text{error}}}, \qquad \text{when factor B is fixed.}$$

By way of contrast, in a two-factor factorial experiment each level of one of the factors is associated with each level of the second factor. If the design outlined at the beginning of this section were changed to a two-factor factorial experiment, the new design could be represented schematically as follows:

	Hosp. 1	Hosp. 2	Hosp. 3	Hosp. 4	Hosp. 5	Hosp. 6
Drug 1	$n/2$	$n/2$	$n/2$	$n/2$	$n/2$	$n/2$
Drug 2	$n/2$	$n/2$	$n/2$	$n/2$	$n/2$	$n/2$

This factorial experiment requires n subjects from each of the hospitals, but $n/2$ of the subjects from each hospital are given drug 1, and $n/2$ of the subjects are given drug 2. In many cases the two-factor factorial experiment is to be preferred to the two-factor design in which the hospital factor is nested under the drug factor—particularly in those cases in which an interaction effect might be suspected. However, there are some instances in which the experimenter may be forced to use a design in which one factor is nested within another.

As another illustration of nested effects, consider the following experimental design:

	Drug 1			Drug 2		
	Hosp. 1	Hosp. 2	Hosp. 3	Hosp. 4	Hosp. 5	Hosp. 6
Category 1	n	n	n	n	n	n
Category 2	n	n	n	n	n	n

This design calls for a sample of n patients in category 1 and n patients in category 2 (random samples) from each of the hospitals. Patients from hospitals 1, 2, and 3 receive drug 1; patients from hospitals 4, 5, and 6 receive drug 2. In this design the hospital factor is nested under the drug factor. Since some patients from each category receive drug 1 and some patients from each category receive drug 2, the category factor is not nested under the drug factor. Further, since patients from each of the categories are obtained from each hospital, the category factor is not nested under the hospital factor.

In this case the hospital factor is nested under the drug factor but the hospital factor is crossed with the category factor. The drug factor is also crossed with the category factor. One may indicate the nesting and crossing schematically as follows:

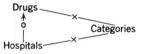

The design that has just been sketched may be considered as a three-factor experiment, the factors being drugs (A), hospitals (B), and categories (C). In this case, factor B is nested under factor A, but all other relationships are those of a bona fide factorial experiment, namely, crossing. The model for this type of experiment has the following form:

$$\overline{ABC}_{ijk} = \mu + \alpha_i + \beta_{j(i)} + \gamma_k + \alpha\gamma_{ik} + \beta\gamma_{j(i)k} + \bar{\varepsilon}_{ijk}.$$

No interaction in which the superscript i appears twice occurs in this model. That is, the interactions $\alpha\beta_{ij(i)}$ and $\alpha\beta\gamma_{ij(i)k}$ do not appear. Hence the utility of this type of design is limited to situations in which such interactions are either zero or negligible relative to other sources of variation of interest.

The analysis of variance for this design takes the form given in Table 5.18. In making tests by means of the F ratio, the appropriate ratios are determined from the expected values of the mean squares. The latter are in part a function of whether the factors in the experiment are fixed or random.

TABLE 5.18   **Analysis of three-factor experiment in which factor B is nested under factor A**

Source of variation		df	df for general case
A	Drugs	1	$p - 1$
$B(\text{w. } a_1)$	Hospital w. drug 1	2	$q - 1$
$\vdots$		$\vdots$ $\Big\}4$	$\vdots$ $\Big\}p(q-1)$
$B(\text{w. } a_p)$	Hospital w. drug 2	2	$q - 1$
C	Categories	1	$r - 1$
AC	Drug $\times$ category	1	$(p-1)(r-1)$
$(B \text{ w. } A) \times C$	Hospital $\times$ category	4	$p(q-1)(r-1)$
Error	Within cell	$12(n-1)$	$pqr(n-1)$
	Total	$11 + 12(n-1)$	$npqr - 1$

TABLE 5.19   **Expected values of mean squares, factor B nested under factor A**

Source of variation	df	Expected value of mean square
A	$p-1$	$\sigma_\varepsilon^2 + nD_qD_r\sigma_{\beta\gamma}^2 + nqD_r\sigma_{\alpha\gamma}^2 + nrD_q\sigma_\beta^2 + nqr\sigma_\alpha^2$
B w. A	$p(q-1)$	$\sigma_\varepsilon^2 + nD_r\sigma_{\beta\gamma}^2 + nr\sigma_\beta^2$
C	$r-1$	$\sigma_\varepsilon^2 + nD_q\sigma_{\beta\gamma}^2 + nqD_p\sigma_{\alpha\gamma}^2 + npq\sigma_\gamma^2$
AC	$(p-1)(r-1)$	$\sigma_\varepsilon^2 + nD_q\sigma_{\beta\gamma}^2 + nq\sigma_{\alpha\gamma}^2$
$(B$ w. $A)C$	$p(q-1)(r-1)$	$\sigma_\varepsilon^2 + n\sigma_{\beta\gamma}^2$
Within cell	$pqr(n-1)$	σ_ε^2

General expressions for the expected values of mean squares appropriate for this type of design are given in Table 5.19. In this table the symbol D_p is used to designate $1-p/P$, D_q is used to designate $1-q/Q$, and D_r is used to designate $1-r/R$. Each of these D's is either 0 or 1 depending, respectively, on whether the corresponding factor is fixed or random.

In this table, the source of variation B w. A (the main effects due to factor B, which is nested within factor A) is actually the sum of the following main effects:

$$
\begin{array}{cc}
 & \text{df} \\
B \text{ w. } a_1 & q-1 \\
\cdots & \cdots \\
B \text{ w. } a_p & q-1 \\
\hline
\text{Sum} = B \text{ w. } A & p(q-1)
\end{array}
$$

Similarly, the interaction $(B$ w. $A) \times C$ represents a pooling of the following interactions:

$$
\begin{array}{cc}
 & \text{df} \\
(B \text{ w. } a_1)C & (q-1)(r-1) \\
\cdots & \cdots \\
(B \text{ w. } a_p)C & (q-1)(r-1) \\
\hline
\text{Sum} = (B \text{ w. } A)C & p(q-1)(r-1)
\end{array}
$$

If this pooled interaction is used in the denominator of an F ratio, the variations which are pooled must be homogeneous if the resulting F ratio is to have an F distribution when the hypothesis being tested is true.

As another illustration of nested effects, consider an experiment in which the subjects have been classified as follows:

Company 1				Company 2			
Dept. 1		Dept. 2		Dept. 3		Dept. 4	
Job 1	Job 2	Job 3	Job 4	Job 5	Job 6	Job 7	Job 8
n	n	n	n	n	n	n	n

Suppose that n people from each job are included in an experiment in which attitude toward a retirement plan is being studied. This design may be considered as a three-factor experiment in which the department factor (B) is nested under the company factor (A). The job factor (C) is nested under both factors B and A. This type of design is referred to as a *hierarchal* design. In a three-factor hierarchal experiment, factor B is nested under factor A, and factor C is nested under both factors B and A. (The design in Table 5.18 is only partially hierarchal, since factor C was not nested under either factor A or factor B.)

The model for a three-factor hierarchal experiment has the form

$$\overline{ABC}_{ijk} = \mu_{...} + \alpha_i + \beta_{j(i)} + \gamma_{k(ij)} + \bar{\varepsilon}_{ijk}.$$

The notation $\gamma_{k(ij)}$ indicates that factor C is nested under both factors A and B. It should be noted that no interaction terms appear explicitly in this model. The expected values of the mean squares for this design are summarized in Table 5.20. The numerical values of the D's in these expected values depend upon the respective sampling fractions for the levels of the factors.

The expected values of the mean squares for a completely hierarchal design are readily obtained, once the expected value of the mean square for the factor within which all other factors are nested is determined. The expected value for each succeeding factor is obtained from the one above by dropping the last term and making D in the next to the last term unity.

The following design represents a partially hierarchal design:

	City 1		City 2	
	School 1	School 2	School 3	School 4
Method 1	n	n	n	n
Method 2	n	n	n	n

Suppose that the purpose of this experiment is to evaluate the relative effectiveness of two different methods of teaching a specified course. Since both methods of training are given within each of the schools and within each

TABLE 5.20 **Expected values of mean squares for three-factor hierarchal experiment**

Source of variation	df	Expected value of mean square
A	$p - 1$	$\sigma_\varepsilon^2 + nD_r\sigma_\gamma^2 + nrD_q\sigma_\beta^2 + nqr\sigma_\alpha^2$
B w. A	$p(q - 1)$	$\sigma_\varepsilon^2 + nD_r\sigma_\gamma^2 + nr\sigma_\beta^2$
C w. (A and B)	$pq(r - 1)$	$\sigma_\varepsilon^2 + n\sigma_\gamma^2$
Experimental error	$pqr(n - 1)$	σ_ε^2
Total	$npqr - 1$	

TABLE 5.21 **Expected values of mean squares for three-factor partially hierarchal experiment**

Source of variation	df	Expected value of mean square
A Methods	$p - 1$	$\sigma_\varepsilon^2 + nD_r\sigma_{\alpha\gamma}^2 + nrD_q\sigma_{\alpha\beta}^2 + nqr\sigma_\alpha^2$
B Cities	$q - 1$	$\sigma_\varepsilon^2 + nD_rD_p\sigma_{\alpha\gamma}^2 + nrD_p\sigma_{\alpha\beta}^2 + npD_r\sigma_\gamma^2 + npr\sigma_\beta^2$
C w. B Schools within cities	$q(r - 1)$	$\sigma_\varepsilon^2 + nD_p\sigma_{\alpha\gamma}^2 + np\sigma_\gamma^2$
AB	$(p - 1)(q - 1)$	$\sigma_\varepsilon^2 + nD_r\sigma_{\alpha\gamma}^2 + nr\sigma_{\alpha\beta}^2$
$A \times (C$ w. $B)$	$q(p - 1)(r - 1)$	$\sigma_\varepsilon^2 + n\sigma_{\alpha\gamma}^2$
Within cell	$pqr(n - 1)$	σ_ε^2

of the cities, there is no nesting with respect to the methods factor. The school factor is, however, nested within the city factor. The expected values of the mean squares for this design have the form given in Table 5.21. This design enables the experimenter to eliminate systematic sources of variation associated with differences between cities and differences between schools within cities from the experimental error—at the cost, however, of reduced degrees of freedom for experimental error.

As still another example of a useful design involving a nested factor, consider an experiment with the following schematic representation:

Period	Method 1			Method 2		
	Person 1	Person 2	Person 3	Person 4	Person 5	Person 6
1						
2						
3						
4						

In this design persons 1, 2, and 3 are observed under method of training 1; criterion measures are obtained at four different periods during the training process. Persons 4, 5, and 6 are observed at comparable periods under training method 2. This design may be considered as a three-factor experiment in which the person factor is nested under the methods factor. If methods is considered to be factor A, persons factor B, and periods factor C, the model for this design is

$$ABC_{ijk} = \mu_{...} + \alpha_i + \beta_{j(i)} + \gamma_k + \alpha\gamma_{ik} + \beta\gamma_{j(i)k} + \varepsilon_{ijk}.$$

For this design there is only one observation in each cell of the experiment. Hence there is no within-cell variation. The analysis of variance is identical in form with that given in Table 5.18 if the within-cell variation is deleted. The expected values of the mean squares are also identical to those given in Table 5.18, with n set equal to unity. Specializing this design to the case in which factors A (methods) and C (periods) are fixed and factor B

TABLE 5.22 **Three-factor partially hierarchal design** (Factors A and C fixed, B random)

	Source of variation	df	Expected value of mean square
A	Methods	$p - 1$	$\sigma_\varepsilon^2 + r\sigma_\beta^2 + qr\sigma_\alpha^2$
B w. A	People within methods	$p(q - 1)$	$\sigma_\varepsilon^2 + r\sigma_\beta^2$
C	Periods	$r - 1$	$\sigma_\varepsilon^2 + \sigma_{\beta\gamma}^2 + pq\sigma_\gamma^2$
AC	Method × period	$(p - 1)(r - 1)$	$\sigma_\varepsilon^2 + \sigma_{\beta\gamma}^2 + q\sigma_{\alpha\gamma}^2$
$(B$ w. $A)C$		$p(q - 1)(r - 1)$	$\sigma_\varepsilon^2 + \sigma_{\beta\gamma}^2$

(persons) is random, one obtains the expected values given in Table 5.22. In this table, the source of variation due to B w. A represents the pooled variation of people within methods. A homogeneity assumption is required for this pooling. The interaction term $(B$ w. $A)C$ also represents a pooling of different sources of variation. The homogeneity assumption required for pooling in this case is equivalent to the assumption that the correlation between periods be constant within each of the methods. The F tests for the analysis in Table 5.22 have the following form:

$$H_0: \quad \sigma_\alpha^2 = 0, \quad F = \frac{\mathrm{MS_{methods}}}{\mathrm{MS_{people\ w.\ methods}}};$$

$$H_0: \quad \sigma_\gamma^2 = 0, \quad F = \frac{\mathrm{MS_{periods}}}{\mathrm{MS_{(B\ w.\ A)C}}};$$

$$H_0: \quad \sigma_{\alpha\gamma}^2 = 0, \quad F = \frac{\mathrm{MS_{method\times period}}}{\mathrm{MS_{(B\ w.\ A)C}}}.$$

Rather than considering this last experiment as three-factor partially hierarchal, there are other ways of classifying this type of experiment. In particular, it can be considered as a two-factor experiment in which there are repeated measurements on one of the factors. This latter type of classification will receive more extensive treatment in Chapter 7.

5.15 SPLIT-PLOT DESIGNS

The *split-plot* design has much in common with the partially hierarchal design. The term split-plot comes from agricultural experimentation in which a single level of one treatment is applied to a relatively large plot of ground (the whole plot) but all levels of a second treatment are applied to subplots within the whole plot. For example, consider the following design, in which the levels of factor A are applied to the whole plots and the levels of factor B are applied to the subplots:

a_1	a_2	a_1	a_2
Plot 1	Plot 2	Plot 3	Plot 4
b_2	b_1	b_2	b_3
b_3	b_3	b_1	b_2
b_1	b_2	b_3	b_1

In this design, differences between the levels of factor A cannot be estimated independently of differences between groups of plots. That is,

$$6 \text{ est } (\alpha_1 - \alpha_2) = (\text{plot } 1 + \text{plot } 3) - (\text{plot } 2 + \text{plot } 4)$$
$$= \quad A_1 \quad - \quad A_2.$$

For this reason the variation due to the levels of factor A is part of the between-plot effects. However, comparisons among the levels of factor B are part of the within-plot variation. From the information within each of the plots, estimates of the main effects due to the factor B may be obtained. These estimates are free of variation due to whole plots. In the analysis of this type of design, sources which are part of the whole-plot variation are usually grouped separately from those which are part of the within-plot variation.

The model for this experiment is

$$X_{ijk} = \mu_{...} + \alpha_i + \pi_{k(i)} + \beta_j + \alpha\beta_{ij} + \pi'_{k(ij)} + \varepsilon_{ijk}.$$

The notation $\pi_{k(i)}$ designates the effect of plot k within level a_i. (This notation indicates that the plot effects are nested within the levels of factor A.) The notation $\pi'_{k(ij)}$ designates residual subplot effects. For the special, but frequently occurring, case in which A and B are fixed factors and the plots are a random sample from a specified population of plots, the analysis of variance assumes the form given in Table 5.23. In this design, each of the p levels of factor A is assigned at random to n plots. Within each plot, the levels of factor B are assigned at random to the subplots. The expected values of the mean squares in this table are actually identical in form with those given in Table 5.22 if plots are assigned the role of factor B in this latter design.

There is a distinction between the designs usually placed in the hierarchal category and designs in the split-plot category. In the hierarchal designs, generally (but not always) all except one of the factors are modes of classifying the experimental units rather than treatments which are administered to the units by the experimenter. Such modes of classification are set up primarily to eliminate, in part, differences among the experimental units from the experimental error. Interaction between the treatment and the classifications is generally considered to be negligible. The usual hierarchal experiment may be regarded as a single-factor experiment with controls on the grouping of the experimental units.

TABLE 5.23 **Expected values of mean squares for split-plot design** (A and B fixed, plots random)

Source of variation	df	Expected value of mean square
Between plots	$np - 1$	
$\quad A$	$p - 1$	$\sigma_\varepsilon^2 + q\sigma_\pi^2 + nq\sigma_\alpha^2$
$\quad$ Plots w. a_1 $\rbrace$		
$\quad$ ...	$p(n - 1)$	$\sigma_\varepsilon^2 + q\sigma_\pi^2$
$\quad$ Plots w. a_p		
Within plots	$np(q - 1)$	
$\quad B$	$q - 1$	$\sigma_\varepsilon^2 + \sigma_{\pi'}^2 + np\sigma_\beta^2$
$\quad AB$	$(p - 1)(q - 1)$	$\sigma_\varepsilon^2 + \sigma_{\pi'}^2 + n\sigma_{\alpha\beta}^2$
$\quad B \times$ plots w. a_1 $\rbrace$		
$\quad$ ...	$p(q - 1)(n - 1)$	$\sigma_\varepsilon^2 + \sigma_{\pi'}^2$
$\quad B \times$ plots w. a_p		

In contrast, the split-plot design has two treatment factors. Whole plots are the experimental units for one of the factors, whereas the subplots are the experimental units for the second factor. If this distinction is made, the final design considered in the last section should be placed in the split-plot rather than the partially hierarchal category.

By inspection of the design outlined at the beginning of this section it is not obvious that the AB interaction is free of variation due to whole-plot effects. To demonstrate that such is the case, consider only the whole-plot effects in each of the following means:

Mean	Whole-plot effects
$\bar{A}_1$	$\pi_1 + \pi_3$
$\bar{B}_1$	$\pi_1 + \pi_2 + \pi_3 + \pi_4$
$\overline{AB}_{11}$	$\pi_1 + \pi_3$
$\bar{G}$	$\pi_1 + \pi_2 + \pi_3 + \pi_4$

An estimate of the interaction effect associated with treatment combination ab_{11} is

$$\text{est } \alpha\beta_{11} = \overline{AB}_{11} - \bar{A}_1 - \bar{B}_1 + \bar{G}.$$

The whole-plot effects associated with est $\alpha\beta_{11}$ are

$$(\pi_1 + \pi_3) - (\pi_1 + \pi_3) - (\pi_1 + \pi_2 + \pi_3 + \pi_4) + (\pi_1 + \pi_2 + \pi_3 + \pi_4) = 0.$$

Thus the whole-plot effects for this interaction sum to zero. In general, the whole-plot effects for est $\alpha\beta_{ij}$ will sum to zero for all i's and j's. Hence the variation due to whole-plot effects does not influence variation due to the AB interaction.

It should be noted, however, that the variation due to the AB interaction is not free of variation, if any, associated with the $B \times$ plot interaction. This latter source of variation may be analyzed as follows:

$B \times$ plot	$(q-1)(np-1)$

AB	$(p-1)(q-1)$
$B \times$ plots w. a_1	
$\cdots$	$p(q-1)(n-1)$
$B \times$ plots w. a_p	

This analysis of the $B \times$ plot interaction shows the AB interaction as part of this source of variation. This actually follows directly from the fact that the effects of factor A are confounded with groups of plots.

Several variations of the split-plot design are possible. One such variation is a double-split or split-split-plot design. In this type of design each level of factor A is assigned at random to n whole plots. (A total of np whole plots is required for this design.) Each of the whole plots is divided into q subplots. The q levels of factor B are then assigned at random to the subplots within each whole plot, and each subplot is divided into r sub-subplots. The r levels of factor C are then assigned at random to each of the sub-subplots. Part of a split-split-plot design is illustrated schematically below:

Thus the experimental unit for factor A is the whole plot; the experimental unit for factor B is the subplot; and the experimental unit for factor C is the sub-subplot. Since the sub-subplots are nested within the subplots and the latter are nested within the whole plots, factor C is nested under the subplots and factor B is nested under the whole plots. Factor A is partially confounded with groups of whole plots.

The model for this type of design may be written

$$X_{ijkm} = \mu_{...} + \alpha_i + \pi_{m(i)} + \beta_j + \alpha\beta_{ij} + \pi'_{m(ij)} + \gamma_k$$
$$+ \alpha\gamma_{ik} + \beta\gamma_{jk} + \alpha\beta\gamma_{ijk} + \pi''_{m(ijk)} + \varepsilon_{ijkm}.$$

The notation $\pi''_{m(ij)}$ designates the residual sub-subplot effect. (This latter may also be regarded as the pooled $\gamma\pi_{km(i)}$ and $\beta\gamma\pi_{jkm(i)}$ interaction effects.) The analysis of this type of experiment takes the form given in Table 5.24. The

TABLE 5.24 **Expected values of mean squares for split-split-plot design** (A, B, C fixed, plots random)

Source of variation	df	Expected value of mean square
Between whole plots	$np - 1$	
A	$p - 1$	$\sigma_\varepsilon^2 + qr\sigma_\pi^2 + nqr\sigma_\alpha^2$
Whole-plot residual	$p(n - 1)$	$\sigma_\varepsilon^2 + qr\sigma_\pi^2$
Within subplots	$np(q - 1)$	
B	$q - 1$	$\sigma_\varepsilon^2 + r\sigma_{\pi'}^2 + npr\sigma_\beta^2$
AB	$(p - 1)(q - 1)$	$\sigma_\varepsilon^2 + r\sigma_{\pi'}^2 + nr\sigma_{\alpha\beta}^2$
Subplot residual	$p(n - 1)(q - 1)$	$\sigma_\varepsilon^2 + r\sigma_{\pi'}^2$
Within sub-subplots	$npq(r - 1)$	
C	$r - 1$	$\sigma_\varepsilon^2 + \sigma_{\pi''}^2 + npq\sigma_\gamma^2$
AC	$(p - 1)(r - 1)$	$\sigma_\varepsilon^2 + \sigma_{\pi''}^2 + nq\sigma_{\alpha\gamma}^2$
BC	$(q - 1)(r - 1)$	$\sigma_\varepsilon^2 + \sigma_{\pi''}^2 + np\sigma_{\beta\gamma}^2$
ABC	$(p - 1)(q - 1)(r - 1)$	$\sigma_\varepsilon^2 + \sigma_{\pi''}^2 + n\sigma_{\alpha\beta\gamma}^2$
Sub-subplot residual	$pq(n - 1)(r - 1)$	$\sigma_\varepsilon^2 + \sigma_{\pi''}^2$

expected values of the mean squares given in this table are for the special case in which factors A, B, and C are fixed and plots are random. The numbers of levels of factors A, B, and C are, respectively, p, q, and r; each level of factor A is assigned to n whole plots.

The expected values of the mean squares indicate the structure of appropriate F ratios. It will be noted that the sub-subplot residual mean square is the appropriate denominator for the main effect and all interactions involving factor C. More extensive consideration of split-plot designs is given in connection with designs having repeated measures on the same people. These designs form the subject matter of Chapter 7.

The design summarized in Table 5.24 involves pqr cells. Within each cell there are n independent observations. Hence the within-cell variation has $pqr(n - 1)$ degrees of freedom. It is of interest to note that the sum of the degrees of freedom for the residuals is the degrees of freedom for the within-cell variation.

Source	df
Whole-plot residual	$p(n - 1)$
Subplot residual	$p(n - 1)(q - 1)$
Sub-subplot residual	$pq(n - 1)(r - 1)$
Total	$pqr(n - 1)$

5.16 RULES FOR DERIVING THE EXPECTED VALUES OF MEAN SQUARES

Given an experiment in which the underlying variables can be assumed to satisfy the conditions of the general linear model, the expected values of the mean squares computed from the experimental data can be obtained by means of a relatively simple set of rules. Although these rules lead to an end product which has been proved to be statistically correct when the assumptions underlying the general linear model are met, the rules themselves provide little insight into the mathematical rationale underlying the end product. The assumptions that underlie the general linear model under consideration have been stated in Sec. 5.6. The rules which will be outlined in this section are those developed by Cornfield and Tukey (1956). A similar set of rules will also be found in Bennett and Franklin (1954).

As the rules will be given, no distinction will be made between random and fixed factors. However, certain of the terms become either 0 or 1 depending upon whether an experimental variable corresponds to a fixed or random factor. For purposes of simplifying the expressions that will result, the following notation will be used:

$$D_p = 1 - \frac{p}{P}, \qquad i = 1, \ldots, p.$$

$$D_q = 1 - \frac{q}{Q}, \qquad j = 1, \ldots, q.$$

$$D_r = 1 - \frac{r}{R}, \qquad k = 1, \ldots, r.$$

If $p = P$, that is, if factor A is fixed, then D_p is zero. On the other hand, if factor A is random, D_p is unity. Similarly, the other D's are either 0 or 1 depending upon whether the corresponding factor is fixed or random. In the application of these rules to designs of special interest, the appropriate evaluation of the D's should be used rather than the D's themselves. The general statement of the rules is followed by a series of examples.

Rule 1.   Write the appropriate model for the design, making explicit in the notation those effects which are nested.

Rule 2.   Construct a two-way table in which the terms in the model (except the grand mean) are the row headings and the subscripts appearing in the model are the column headings. The number of columns in this table will be equal to the number of different subscripts in the model. The number of rows will be equal to the number of terms in the model which have subscripts. The row headings should include all subscripts associated with terms in the model.

Rule 3.   To obtain the entries in column i, enter D_p in those rows having headings containing an i which is not nested, enter unity in those rows having headings containing an i which is nested, enter p in those rows having headings which do not contain an i.

Rule 4.   To obtain entries in column j, enter D_q in those rows having headings containing a j which is not nested, enter unity in those rows having headings containing a j which is nested, enter q in those rows having headings which do not contain a j.

Rule 5.   Entries in all other columns follow the general pattern outlined in rules 3 and 4. For example, the possible entries in column k would be D_r, unity, and r.

Rule 6.   The expected value of the mean square for the main effect of factor A is a weighted sum of the variances due to all effects which contain the subscript i. If a row heading contains a subscript i, then the weight for the variance due to this row effect is the product of all entries in this row, the entry in column i being omitted. (For nested effects, see rule 10.)

Rule 7.   The expected value of the mean square for the main effect of factor B is a weighted sum of the variances due to all effects which contain the subscript j. If a row heading contains a j, the weight for the variance due to this effect is the product of all entries in this row, the entry in column j being omitted. (See rule 10.)

Rule 8.   The expected value of the mean square for the AB interaction is a weighted sum of the variances due to all effects which contain both the subscripts i and j. If a row heading contains both the subscripts i and j, then the weight for the variance corresponding to this effect is the product of all entries in this row, the entries in both columns i and j being omitted.

Rule 9.   In general, the expected value of a mean square for an effect which has the general representation XYZ_{uvw} is a weighted sum of the variances due to all effects in the model which contain all the subscripts u, v, and w (and possibly other subscripts). If a row heading does contain all three of the three subscripts u, v, and w, then the weight for the variance due to the corresponding row effects is the product of all entries in this row, the entries in columns u, v, and w being omitted.

Rule 10.   If an effect is nested, the expected value of its mean square is a weighted sum of variances corresponding to all effects containing the same subscripts as the nested effect. For example, if the main effect of factor B appears as $\beta_{j(i)}$ in the model, then the relevant effects are those which contain both the subscripts i and j. Similarly, if the term $\beta\gamma_{j(i)k}$ appears in the model, in considering the set of relevant variances, row headings must contain all three of the subscripts i, j, and k.

The application of these rules will be illustrated by means of a $p \times q \times r$ partially hierarchal factorial design having n observations per cell. In this design, it will be assumed that factor B is nested under factor A. This type of design may be represented schematically as follows:

	a_1			a_2		
	$b_{1(1)}$	$b_{2(1)}$	$b_{3(1)}$	$b_{1(2)}$	$b_{2(2)}$	$b_{3(2)}$
c_1						
c_2			n observations in each cell			
c_3						
c_4						

The notation $b_{j(i)}$ indicates that factor B is nested under factor A. The structural model for this design may be written as

$$X_{ijkm} = \mu_{...} + \alpha_i + \beta_{j(i)} + \gamma_k + \alpha\gamma_{ik} + \beta\gamma_{j(i)k} + \varepsilon_{m(ijk)}.$$

In accordance with rule 1, the notation in the structural model makes explicit those effects which are nested. Thus, the notation $\beta_{j(i)}$ indicates that the levels of factor B are nested under the levels of factor A. The notation $\varepsilon_{m(ijk)}$ indicates that the unique effects associated with an observation on element m in cell abc_{ijk} are nested under all effects; i.e., the experimental error is nested under all factors.

The two-way table called for by rule 2 is given in Table 5.25. The row headings are the terms in the model, the term $\mu_{...}$ being omitted. The column headings are the different subscripts that appear in the model.

The entries that appear in column i of this table were obtained in accordance with rule 3. Since rows α_i and $\alpha\gamma_{ik}$ contain a subscript i which is not in parentheses, the entry in column i for each of these rows is D_p. Since rows $\beta_{j(i)}$, $\beta\gamma_{j(i)k}$, and $\varepsilon_{m(ijk)}$ each contain the subscript i in parentheses, the entry in column i for each of these rows is unity. All other entries in column i are p, since none of the remaining row headings contain the subscript i.

The entries that appear in column j were obtained in accordance with rule 4. The entries that appear in column m follow from rule 5—with one exception. From rule 5 the entry in row $\varepsilon_{m(ijk)}$ would be D_n. Since the experimental error will always be considered a random variable, $D_n = 1 - (n/N)$ will always be considered equal to unity. Thus the n observations that

TABLE 5.25 **Expected value of mean squares for partially hierarchal factorial design**

Effect	i	j	k	m	E(MS)
α_i	D_p	q	r	n	$\sigma_\varepsilon^2 + nD_qD_r\sigma_{\beta\gamma}^2 + nqD_r\sigma_{\alpha\gamma}^2 + nrD_q\sigma_\beta^2 + nqr\sigma_\alpha^2$
$\beta_{j(i)}$	1	D_q	r	n	$\sigma_\varepsilon^2 + nD_r\sigma_{\beta\gamma}^2 + nr\sigma_\beta^2$
γ_k	p	q	D_r	n	$\sigma_\varepsilon^2 + nD_q\sigma_{\beta\gamma}^2 + nqD_p\sigma_{\alpha\gamma}^2 + npq\sigma_\gamma^2$
$\alpha\gamma_{ik}$	D_p	q	D_r	n	$\sigma_\varepsilon^2 + nD_q\sigma_{\beta\gamma}^2 + nq\sigma_{\alpha\gamma}^2$
$\beta\gamma_{j(i)k}$	1	D_q	D_r	n	$\sigma_\varepsilon^2 + n\sigma_{\beta\gamma}^2$
$\varepsilon_{m(ijk)}$	1	1	1	1	σ_ε^2

appear within a cell in this design are considered to be a random sample from a potentially infinite number of observations that could be made within a cell.

In accordance with rule 6, the expected value of the mean square for the main effect of factor A is a weighted sum of the variances due to all row effects which contain the subscript i. Thus $E(MS_a)$ is a weighted sum of the following variances:

$$\sigma_\varepsilon^2, \ \sigma_{\beta\gamma}^2, \ \sigma_{\alpha\gamma}^2, \ \sigma_\beta^2, \ \sigma_\alpha^2.$$

The weight for σ_α^2, which is given by the product of all terms in row α_i, the term in column i being omitted, is nqr. The weight for σ_β^2, which is the product of all terms in row $\beta_{j(i)}$, the term in column i being omitted, turns out to be nrD_q. The weight for $\sigma_{\alpha\gamma}^2$ is the product of all terms in row $\alpha\gamma_{ik}$, the term in column i being omitted; this weight is nqD_r. The properly weighted sum for $E(MS_a)$ appears to the right of row α_i. Thus,

$$E(MS)_a = \sigma_\varepsilon^2 + nD_qD_r\sigma_{\beta\gamma}^2 + nqD_r\sigma_{\alpha\gamma}^2 + nrD_q\sigma_\beta^2 + nqr\sigma_\alpha^2.$$

In words, the expected value of the mean square for the main effect of factor A is a weighted sum of a set of variances; the variances included in this set and the weights for each are determined by application of rule 6.

Since, in this design, factor B is nested under factor A, the main effect of factor B is denoted by the symbol $\beta_{j(i)}$. In this case the expected value of the mean square for the main effect of factor B is a weighted sum of the variances of terms containing both the subscripts i and j. These variances are

$$\sigma_\varepsilon^2, \ \sigma_{\beta\gamma}^2, \quad \text{and} \quad \sigma_\beta^2.$$

The weight for σ_β^2 is the product of all terms in row $\beta_{j(i)}$, the terms in columns i and j being omitted; this weight is nr. The weight for $\sigma_{\beta\gamma}^2$ is the product of all terms in row $\beta\gamma_{j(i)k}$, the terms in columns i and j being omitted. This weight is nD_r. The expected value for the mean square of the main effect of factor B (which is nested under factor A) is given at the right of the row $\beta_{j(i)}$.

The other terms under the heading $E(MS)$ in Table 5.25 were obtained by application of rules 9 and 10. For example, the variances that enter into the expected value of MS_{ac} are

$$\sigma_\varepsilon^2, \ \sigma_{\beta\gamma}^2, \quad \text{and} \quad \sigma_{\alpha\gamma}^2.$$

These are the variances corresponding to those effects which contain the subscripts i and k.

The expected values for the mean squares in Table 5.25 may be specialized to cover specific designs by evaluating the D's. For example, if factors A and C are fixed and factor B is random, $D_p = 0$, $D_r = 0$, and $D_q = 1$. For this case,

$$E(MS_a) = \sigma_\varepsilon^2 + nr\sigma_\beta^2 + nqr\sigma_\alpha^2.$$

This expected value was obtained from the corresponding expected value, in

TABLE 5.26 **Expected value of mean squares for partially hierarchal factorial design** (Factors A and C fixed, factor B random)

Effect	i	j	k	m	E(MS)
α_i	0	q	r	n	$\sigma_\varepsilon^2 + nr\sigma_\beta^2 + nqr\sigma_\alpha^2$
$\beta_{j(i)}$	1	1	r	n	$\sigma_\varepsilon^2 + nr\sigma_\beta^2$
γ_k	p	q	0	n	$\sigma_\varepsilon^2 + n\sigma_{\beta\gamma}^2 + npq\sigma_\gamma^2$
$\alpha\gamma_{ik}$	0	q	0	n	$\sigma_\varepsilon^2 + n\sigma_{\beta\gamma}^2 + nq\sigma_{\alpha\gamma}^2$
$\beta\gamma_{j(i)k}$	1	1	0	n	$\sigma_\varepsilon^2 + n\sigma_{\beta\gamma}^2$
$\varepsilon_{m(ijk)}$	1	1	1	1	σ_ε^2

Table 5.25 by evaluating the D_p, D_q, and D_r. By a similar procedure

$$\text{E(MS}_b) = \sigma_\varepsilon^2 + nr\sigma_\beta^2.$$

The expected values of mean squares for specialized designs may be obtained by evaluating the D's prior to the application of the rules. For the special case under consideration, the expected values of the mean squares are derived in Table 5.26. The expected values of the mean squares shown on the right are identical to those obtained by specializing the E(MS) given at the right of Table 5.25. For special cases of interest to the experimenter, the simplest method of deriving the expected values of the mean squares is that illustrated in Table 5.26.

5.17 QUASI F RATIOS

In some cases the appropriate F ratio cannot be constructed by direct application of the rules based upon expected values of mean squares. For example, consider the case of a $p \times q \times r$ factorial experiment having n observations per cell. If all factors are random, the expected values of the mean squares are those given in Table 5.27.

TABLE 5.27 **Expected values of mean squares**

Source of variation	E(MS)
A	$\sigma_\varepsilon^2 + n\sigma_{\alpha\beta\gamma}^2 + nq\sigma_{\alpha\gamma}^2 + nr\sigma_{\alpha\beta}^2 + nqr\sigma_\alpha^2$
B	$\sigma_\varepsilon^2 + n\sigma_{\alpha\beta\gamma}^2 + np\sigma_{\beta\gamma}^2 + nr\sigma_{\alpha\beta}^2 + npr\sigma_\beta^2$
C	$\sigma_\varepsilon^2 + n\sigma_{\alpha\beta\gamma}^2 + np\sigma_{\beta\gamma}^2 + nq\sigma_{\alpha\gamma}^2 + npq\sigma_\gamma^2$
AB	$\sigma_\varepsilon^2 + n\sigma_{\alpha\beta\gamma}^2 + nr\sigma_{\alpha\beta}^2$
AC	$\sigma_\varepsilon^2 + n\sigma_{\alpha\beta\gamma}^2 + nq\sigma_{\alpha\gamma}^2$
BC	$\sigma_\varepsilon^2 + n\sigma_{\alpha\beta\gamma}^2 + np\sigma_{\beta\gamma}^2$
ABC	$\sigma_\varepsilon^2 + n\sigma_{\alpha\beta\gamma}^2$
Experimental error	σ_ε^2

In practice preliminary tests on the model are made on the higher-order interactions before proceeding with the tests on main effects. In many cases which arise in practice, tests on main effects may be relatively meaningless when interactions are significantly different from zero. If none of the interaction terms may be dropped from the model, then no single mean square can serve as a denominator in a test on main effects due to factor A. The proper denominator for a test in this case should have the expected value

$$\sigma_\varepsilon^2 + n\sigma_{\alpha\beta\gamma}^2 + nq\sigma_{\alpha\gamma}^2 + nr\sigma_{\alpha\beta}^2.$$

None of the individual mean squares in Table 5.27 has this expected value. However, by adding and subtracting certain of the mean squares one may obtain a composite mean square which has the required expected value. One such composite, assuming each of the mean squares is independent of the other, may be constructed as follows:

$$
\begin{array}{rl}
E(MS_{ac}) = & \sigma_\varepsilon^2 + n\sigma_{\alpha\beta\gamma}^2 + nq\sigma_{\alpha\gamma}^2 \\
E(MS_{ab}) = & \sigma_\varepsilon^2 + n\sigma_{\alpha\beta\gamma}^2 \qquad\qquad\quad + nr\sigma_{\alpha\beta}^2 \\
-E(MS_{abc}) = & -\sigma_\varepsilon^2 - n\sigma_{\alpha\beta\gamma}^2 \\
\hline
E(MS_{ac} + MS_{ab} - MS_{abc}) = & \sigma_\varepsilon^2 + n\sigma_{\alpha\beta\gamma}^2 + nq\sigma_{\alpha\gamma}^2 + nr\sigma_{\alpha\beta}^2
\end{array}
$$

A quasi F ratio, which has the proper structural requirements in terms of expected values of mean squares, for a test on the main effect of factor A is

$$F' = \frac{MS_a}{MS_{ac} + MS_{ab} - MS_{abc}}.$$

The symbol F' is used for this ratio rather than the symbol F. Since the denominator is a composite of different sources of variation, the sampling distribution of the F' ratio is not the usual F distribution, although the latter distribution may be used as an approximation. The denominator of this F' ratio calls for subtracting a mean square. This could lead to the possibility of obtaining a negative denominator. According to the population model, it is not possible to have a negative denominator in terms of parameters. However, in terms of the estimates of these parameters it is possible to have a negative denominator.

The following quasi F ratio avoids the possibility of a negative denominator and still satisfies the structural requirements for a test on the main effect of factor A:

$$F'' = \frac{MS_a + MS_{abc}}{MS_{ac} + MS_{ab}}.$$

In terms of expected values of the mean squares, the ratio of the expectations has the form

$$\frac{2\sigma_\varepsilon^2 + 2n\sigma_{\alpha\beta\gamma}^2 + nq\sigma_{\alpha\gamma}^2 + nr\sigma_{\alpha\beta}^2 + nqr\sigma_\alpha^2}{2\sigma_\varepsilon^2 + 2n\sigma_{\alpha\beta\gamma}^2 + nq\sigma_{\alpha\gamma}^2 + nr\sigma_{\alpha\beta}^2}.$$

Under the hypothesis that $\sigma_\alpha^2 = 0$, E(numerator) = E(denominator). Similarly, the following F'' ratio has the structural requirements in terms of the expected values of mean squares for a test of the hypothesis that $\sigma_\beta^2 = 0$:

$$F'' = \frac{MS_b + MS_{abc}}{MS_{ab} + MS_{bc}}.$$

Although these F'' ratios satisfy the structural requirements in terms of expected values, the sampling distributions of these F'' ratios can only be roughly approximated by the usual F distributions, provided that special degrees of freedom are used for numerator and denominator. Suppose that the F'' ratio has the following general form,

$$F'' = \frac{u + v}{w + x},$$

where u, v, w, and x are appropriate mean squares. Let respective degrees of freedom for these mean squares be f_u, f_v, f_w, and f_x. Then the degrees of freedom for the numerator are approximated by the nearest integral value to

$$\frac{(u + v)^2}{(u^2/f_u) + (v^2/f_v)}.$$

The degrees of freedom for the denominator are approximated by

$$\frac{(w + x)^2}{(w^2/f_w) + (x^2/f_x)}.$$

This approximation to the F distribution and the associated degrees of freedom are those suggested by Satterthwaite (1946).

The F' ratio has the following general form:

$$F' = \frac{u}{w + x - v}.$$

If the F distribution is used to approximate the sampling distribution of the F' statistic, the degrees of freedom for the denominator are

$$\frac{(w + x - v)^2}{(w^2/f_w) + (x^2/f_x) + (v^2/f_v)}.$$

The numerator of this expression may be expressed as

$$\left(\sum a_i MS_i \right)^2 \quad \text{where} \quad a_1 = 1, \ a_2 = 1, \quad \text{and} \quad a_3 = -1.$$

The denominator has the form

$$\sum_i \frac{(a_i MS_i)^2}{f_i}.$$

When one or more of the a_i are negative, the Satterthwaite procedure may lead to relatively poor estimates of the appropriate degrees of freedom. A study of the consequences of negative a_i appears in Gaylor and Hopper (1969).

5.18 PRELIMINARY TESTS ON THE MODEL AND POOLING PROCEDURES

In deriving the expected values for the mean squares, extensive use is made of a model which is assumed to be appropriate for an experiment. The model indicates the relevant sources of variability. A question might be raised about why certain terms appear in the model and why other possible terms are omitted. If in fact there is no interaction effect of a given kind in the population of interest, why should such an interaction term be included in the model? Including such an interaction term in the model can potentially affect the expected values of several mean squares. The latter in turn determine the structure of F ratios.

Decisions about what terms should appear in the model and what terms should be omitted are generally based upon experience in an experimental area and knowledge about what are reasonable expectations with respect to underlying sources of variation—in short, subject-matter information. All sources of variation not specifically included in the model are in reality classified as part of the experimental error. In most cases the latter variation is the residual variation after all controlled sources have been estimated. Previous experimentation in an area may indicate that no interaction between two factors is to be expected; hence in designing a new experiment in this area such an interaction term may be omitted from the model. However, any variation due to this interaction, if it exists, is automatically included as part of the experimental error or automatically confounds other estimates, depending upon the experimental design.

Lacking knowledge about interaction effects from past experimentation, one might ask whether or not data obtained in a given factorial experiment could be used as a basis for revising an initial model. The specification of the parameters in the initial model could be considered incomplete or left open to more complete specification. Tests designed to revise or complete the specification of parameters to be included in the model are called *preliminary* tests on the model. Such tests are particularly appropriate when one is dealing with experiments in which interactions between fixed and random factors or interactions between random factors are potentially in the model. Such terms may turn out to be denominators for F ratios. If such terms have a relatively small number of degrees of freedom, corresponding F ratios will have very low power. Since the mean squares for interactions between two or more fixed factors can never form the denominator in an F ratio, preliminary tests on such interactions are not generally required.

The procedure of making preliminary tests on higher-order interactions before proceeding with tests of lower-order interactions and main effects may be regarded as a multistage decision rule. Depending upon the outcome of a sequence of tests, the parameters in the model become more completely specified; in turn the expected values for the mean squares are revised sequentially.

If a preliminary test does not reject the hypothesis that the variance due to an interaction effect is zero, one proceeds as if this variance were actually zero and drops the corresponding term from the model. The expected values of the mean squares are then revised in accordance with the new model, and additional preliminary tests, if necessary, are made. Care must be taken in such tests to avoid type 2 error, i.e., accepting the hypothesis of zero interaction when it should be rejected. Type 2 error can be kept numerically small by making preliminary tests at a numerically high type 1 error, that is, $\alpha = 0.20$ or 0.30.

The sequence in which preliminary tests on the model are made will be illustrated for the case of a $p \times q \times r$ factorial experiment in which factor A is considered fixed and factors B and C are considered random. The initial model for this experiment is the following:

$$X_{ijkm} = \mu + \alpha_i + \beta_j + \gamma_k + \alpha\beta_{ij} + \alpha\gamma_{ik} + \beta\gamma_{jk}$$
$$+ \alpha\beta\gamma_{ijk} + \varepsilon_{m(ijk)}. \tag{5.23}$$

The question of whether or not all the interactions between random factors and between fixed and random factors should be included in the model is left unanswered for the time being. Assuming the complete model, the expected values of the mean squares are those given in Table 5.28. Suppose that the experimental work is completed and the analysis-of-variance table prepared. Tests of hypotheses depend upon the model and associated expected values. The model as given in (5.23) is tentative and subject to change. Associated with this model are the expected values given in Table 5.28. Inspection of this model indicates that the appropriate denominator for tests on the hypotheses $\sigma^2_{\alpha\beta\gamma} = 0$ and $\sigma^2_{\beta\gamma} = 0$ is $MS_{\text{w. cell}}$. Suppose both of these tests are made at the 25 percent level of significance. Suppose that these tests do not reject the respective hypotheses and that *a priori* information indicates no good basis for

TABLE 5.28   **Expected values of mean squares for model in (1)** (A fixed, B and C random)

Source of variation	df	E(MS)
A	$p-1$	$\sigma^2_\varepsilon + n\sigma^2_{\alpha\beta\gamma} + nq\sigma^2_{\alpha\gamma} + nr\sigma^2_{\alpha\beta} + nqr\sigma^2_\alpha$
B	$q-1$	$\sigma^2_\varepsilon + np\sigma^2_{\beta\gamma} + npr\sigma^2_\beta$
C	$r-1$	$\sigma^2_\varepsilon + np\sigma^2_{\beta\gamma} + npq\sigma^2_\gamma$
AB	$(p-1)(q-1)$	$\sigma^2_\varepsilon + n\sigma^2_{\alpha\beta\gamma} + nr\sigma^2_{\alpha\beta}$
AC	$(p-1)(r-1)$	$\sigma^2_\varepsilon + n\sigma^2_{\alpha\beta\gamma} + nq\sigma^2_{\alpha\gamma}$
BC	$(q-1)(r-1)$	$\sigma^2_\varepsilon + np\sigma^2_{\beta\gamma}$
ABC	$(p-1)(q-1)(r-1)$	$\sigma^2_\varepsilon + n\sigma^2_{\alpha\beta\gamma}$
Within cell	$pqr(n-1)$	σ^2_ε

TABLE 5.29   **Expected values of mean squares for model in (5.24)**

Source of variation	df	E(MS)
A	$p - 1$	$\sigma_\varepsilon^2 + nq\sigma_{\alpha\gamma}^2 + nr\sigma_{\alpha\beta}^2 + nqr\sigma_\alpha^2$
B	$q - 1$	$\sigma_\varepsilon^2 + npr\sigma_\beta^2$
C	$r - 1$	$\sigma_\varepsilon^2 + npq\sigma_\gamma^2$
AB	$(p - 1)(q - 1)$	$\sigma_\varepsilon^2 + nr\sigma_{\alpha\beta}^2$
AC	$(p - 1)(r - 1)$	$\sigma_\varepsilon^2 + nq\sigma_{\alpha\gamma}^2$
BC $\left.\begin{array}{c} \\ \\ \\ \\ \end{array}\right\}$ residual ABC Within cell	$npqr - pq - pr + p$	σ_ε^2

expecting that such interactions exist. On these grounds $\alpha\beta\gamma_{ijk}$ and $\beta\gamma_{jk}$ are now dropped from the model.

The revised model now has the form

$$X_{ijkm} = \mu + \alpha_i + \beta_j + \gamma_k + \alpha\beta_{ij} + \alpha\gamma_{ik} + \varepsilon_{ijkm}. \tag{5.24}$$

The term ε now includes the interaction terms which were dropped from the model in (5.23). The revised expected values of the mean squares are obtained by dropping $\sigma_{\alpha\beta\gamma}^2$ and $\sigma_{\beta\gamma}^2$ from the terms in Table 5.28. When this is done, MS_{bc}, MS_{abc}, and $MS_{w.\ cell}$ are all estimates of σ_ε^2. These three mean squares may be pooled to provide a single estimate of σ_ε^2 as shown in Table 5.29. The pooled estimate is

$$MS_{res} = \frac{SS_{bc} + SS_{abc} + SS_{w.\ cell}}{(q - 1)(r - 1) + (p - 1)(q - 1)(r - 1) + pqr(n - 1)}.$$

The degrees of freedom for the denominator are the sum of the degrees of freedom for the sources of variation which are pooled. This sum is equal to $npqr - pq - pr + p$.

Inspection of Table 5.29 indicates that the hypotheses $\sigma_{\alpha\gamma}^2 = 0$ and $\sigma_{\alpha\beta}^2 = 0$ may both be tested with MS_{res} as a denominator. Suppose that these tests are made at the 25 percent level of significance. Suppose that the outcome of these tests does not reject the hypothesis that $\sigma_{\alpha\gamma}^2 = 0$ but that the hypothesis that $\sigma_{\alpha\beta}^2 = 0$ is rejected. The revised model now has the form

$$X_{ijkm} = \mu + \alpha_i + \beta_j + \gamma_k + \alpha\beta_{ij} + \varepsilon_{ijkm}. \tag{5.25}$$

The experimental error in (5.25) includes variation due to $\alpha\gamma$ as well as the interaction terms included in model (5.24). The expected values associated with (5.25) are given in Table 5.30. These expected values may be taken as those appropriate for final tests.

If there is *a priori* evidence to indicate interaction between factors, preliminary tests on such interactions should in general be avoided and tests

TABLE 5.30 **Expected values of mean squares for model in (5.25)**

Source of variation	df	E(MS)
A	$p - 1$	$\sigma_\varepsilon^2 + nr\sigma_{\alpha\beta}^2 + nqr\sigma_\alpha^2$
B	$q - 1$	$\sigma_\varepsilon^2 + npr\sigma_\beta^2$
C	$r - 1$	$\sigma_\varepsilon^2 + npq\sigma_\gamma^2$
AB	$(p - 1)(q - 1)$	$\sigma_\varepsilon^2 + nr\sigma_{\alpha\beta}^2$
Residual (pooled AC, BC, ABC, and within cell)	$npqr - pq - r + 1$	σ_ε^2

should be made in accordance with the original formulation. When preliminary tests are made, only interactions in which random factors appear are considered in such tests. (Only interactions with random factors can potentially form the denominator of an F ratio.) If an adequate number of degrees of freedom (say 20 or more) is available for the denominator of F ratios constructed in terms of the original model, preliminary tests should also be avoided. However, if the denominator of an F ratio constructed in accordance with the original model has relatively few degrees of freedom (say less than 10), in the absence of *a priori* knowledge preliminary tests are in order.

A numerical example will be used to illustrate the pooling procedures associated with Tables 5.28, 5.29, and 5.30. Part i of Table 5.31 represents the analysis of variance for a $4 \times 2 \times 3$ factorial experiment having two observations per cell. Assume factor A fixed and factors B and C random. If the model in (5.23) is assumed, the expected values of the mean squares given in Table 5.28 are appropriate. Preliminary tests on $\sigma_{\alpha\beta\gamma}^2$ and $\sigma_{\beta\gamma}^2$ are made in part i. These tests indicate that the hypotheses that $\sigma_{\alpha\beta\gamma}^2 = 0$ and $\sigma_{\beta\gamma}^2 = 0$ cannot be rejected at the 25 percent level of significance. Hence the corresponding terms are dropped from the model in (5.23).

The residual term in part ii is obtained as follows:

Source	SS	df	MS
BC	18.00	2	
ABC	72.00	6	
Within cell	240.00	24	
Residual (ii)	330.00	32	10.31

The variation due to residual ii corresponds to variation due to experimental error in the model given in (5.24). The expected values for the mean squares in part ii are those given in Table 5.29. Second-stage tests are made in accordance with the latter expected values. As a result of the tests in part ii, the variation associated with the AC interaction is pooled with the experimental error, but the variation due to the AB interaction is not pooled.

TABLE 5.31 **Numerical example of pooling procedures** ($n = 2$, $p = 4$, $q = 2$, $r = 3$)

First-stage preliminary tests: H_0: $\sigma^2_{\alpha\beta\gamma} = 0$; H_0: $\sigma^2_{\beta\gamma} = 0$

	Source	SS	df	MS	F	
	A	120.00	3	40.00		
	B	60.00	1	60.00		
	C	40.00	2	20.00		
	AB	96.00	3	32.00		
(i)	AC	72.00	6	12.00		
	BC	18.00	2	9.00	0.90	$F_{0.75}(2, 24) = 1.47$
	ABC	72.00	6	12.00	1.20	$F_{0.75}(6, 24) = 1.41$
	Within cell	240.00	24	10.00		

Second-stage preliminary tests: H_0: $\sigma^2_{\alpha\beta} = 0$; H_0: $\sigma^2_{\alpha\gamma} = 0$

	Source	SS	df	MS	F	
	A	120.00	3	40.00		
	B	60.00	1	60.00		
	C	40.00	2	20.00		
(ii)	AB	96.00	3	32.00	3.10	$F_{0.75}(3, 32) = 1.44$
	AC	72.00	6	12.00	1.16	$F_{0.75}(6, 32) = 1.39$
	Residual (ii)	330.00	32	10.31		

Analysis for final tests:

	Source	SS	df	MS	F	
	A	120.00	3	40.00	1.25	$F_{0.95}(3, 3) = 9.28$
	B	60.00	1	60.00	5.67	$F_{0.95}(1, 38) = 4.10$
(iii)	C	40.00	2	20.00	1.89	$F_{0.95}(2, 38) = 3.25$
	AB	96.00	3	32.00	3.02	$F_{0.95}(3, 38) = 2.85$
	Residual (iii)	402.00	38	10.58		

The residual term in part iii is obtained as follows:

Source	SS	df	MS
AC	72.00	6	
Residual (ii)	330.00	32	
Residual (iii)	402.00	38	10.58

Statistical tests in part iii are based upon the expected values in Table 5.30. The denominator for the F ratio in the test on the main effect of factor A is MS_{ab}; all other F ratios have MS_{res} as a denominator. As distinguished from parts i and ii, the tests in part iii are final tests rather than preliminary tests; hence the difference in the level of significance.

The sampling distributions of the statistics used in tests made following preliminary tests are actually different from the sampling distributions associated with tests which are not preceded by preliminary tests. What is really required in the second stage of a sequential decision procedure is the sampling distribution of the statistic in question under the condition that specified decisions have been made in the first stage. Using sampling distributions which do not have such conditions attached generally introduces a slight bias into the testing procedure. Specified percentile points on the unconditional sampling distribution are probably slightly lower than corresponding points on the conditional sampling distribution. That is, a statistic which falls at the 95th percentile point when referred to the unconditional distribution may fall at only the 92d percentile point when referred to the conditional distribution. Hence use of the unconditional distributions for sequential tests probably gives tests which have a slight positive bias; i.e., the type 1 error is slightly larger than the specified level of significance.

By way of summary, it should be noted that there is no widespread agreement among statisticians on the wisdom of the pooling procedures which have been discussed in this section. Those statisticians who adhere to the "never pool" rule demand a completely specified model prior to the analysis of the experimental data. This position has much to recommend it. The inferences obtained from adopting this point of view will be based upon exact sampling distributions, provided that the model that has been specified is appropriate for the experiment.

Using data from the experiment to revise the model introduces contingencies which are difficult to evaluate statistically. However, working from a revised model which more adequately fits the data may potentially provide more powerful tests than those obtained from the "never pool" rule. Admittedly the change in power cannot be evaluated with precision. The conservative attitude toward pooling adopted in this section attempts to take middle ground: One departs from the initial model only if the experimental data strongly suggest that the initial model is not appropriate. The position taken by the authors in this section is quite close to that adopted by Green and Tukey (1960). It is also in line with the point of view developed by Bozivich et al. (1956).

5.19 REPLICATED EXPERIMENTS

A replication of an experiment is an independent repetition under as nearly identical conditions as the nature of the experimental material will permit. *Independent* in this context implies that the experimental units in the repetitions are independent samples from the population being studied. That is, if the elements are people, in a replication of an experiment an independent sample of people is used in the replication. Inferences made from replicated experiments are with respect to the outcomes of a series of replications of the experiment. In a sense that will be indicated, inferences from replicated experiments have a broader scope than do inferences from nonreplicated experiments.

An experiment in which there are n observations per cell is to be distinguished from an experiment having n replications with one observation per cell. The total number of observations per treatment is the same, but the manner in which the two types of experiments are conducted differs. Consequently the relevant sources of variation will differ; hence a change in the model for the experiment is needed. Associated with the latter change is a different set of expected values for the mean squares.

In conducting an experiment having n observations per cell, all observations in a single cell are generally made within the same approximate time interval or under experimental conditions that can be considered to differ only as a function of experimental error. In a $p \times q$ factorial experiment having n observations per cell (no repeated measures) the total variation may be subdivided as follows.

Source	df
Between cells	$pq - 1$
Within cells	$pq(n - 1)$

In this partition it is assumed that differences between observations within the same cell are attributable solely to experimental error. On the other hand, differences among cells are attributed to treatment effects and experimental error. Should there be systematic sources affecting between-cell variation, other than treatment effects and experimental error, such variation is completely or partially confounded with the treatment effects.

The purpose of a replicated experiment, in contrast to an experiment having n observations per cell, is to permit the experimenter to maintain more uniform conditions within each cell of the experiment, as well as to eliminate possible irrelevant sources of variation between cells. For example, the replications may be repetitions of the experiment at different times or at different places. In this case, sources of variation which are functions of time or place are eliminated from both between- and within-cell variation.

Instead of having n replications with one observation per cell, one may have two replications in which there are $n/2$ observations per cell, one may have three replications with $n/3$ observations per cell, etc. The number of observations per cell for any single replication should be the maximum that will permit uniform conditions within all cells of the experiment and, at the same time, reduce between-cell sources of variation which are not directly related to the treatment effects.

As an example of a replicated experiment, suppose that it is desired to have 15 observations within each cell of a 2×3 factorial experiment. Suppose that the experimental conditions are such that only 30 observations can be made within a given time period; suppose further that there are, potentially, differences in variation associated with the time periods. To eliminate sources of variation directly related to the time dimension, the experiment may be set up in three replications as follows (cell entries indicate the number of observations):

	Replication 1				Replication 2				Replication 3		
	b_1	b_2	b_3		b_1	b_2	b_3		b_1	b_2	b_3
a_1	5	5	5	a_1	5	5	5	a_1	5	5	5
a_2	5	5	5	a_2	5	5	5	a_2	5	5	5

If the replications are disregarded, there are 15 observations under each treatment combination. Within each replication, conditions may be relatively uniform with respect to uncontrolled sources of variation; between replication, conditions may not be uniform. In essence, a replicated experiment adds another dimension or factor to the experiment—a replication factor. The latter is a random factor.

In Table 5.32 the analysis of a $p \times q$ factorial experiment having n observations per cell is contrasted with a $p \times q$ factorial experiment in which there are r replications of a $p \times q$ factorial experiment having n/r observations per cell. In both designs there are n observations under treatment combination and a total of $npq - 1$ degrees of freedom. The degrees of freedom in braces in part i are often pooled in a replicated experiment. Part ii gives an alternative partition of the variation. In the nonreplicated experiment the between-cell

TABLE 5.32 **Comparison of analysis for replicated and nonreplicated factorial experiments**

	$p \times q$ factorial experiment with n observations per cell	df	r replications of $p \times q$ factorial experiment with n/r observations per cell	df
	A	$p - 1$	A	$p - 1$
	B	$q - 1$	B	$q - 1$
	AB	$(p - 1)(q - 1)$	AB	$(p - 1)(q - 1)$
			Reps	$r - 1$
(i)			$A \times$ rep	$(p - 1)(r - 1)$
			$B \times$ rep	$(q - 1)(r - 1)$
			$AB \times$ rep	$(p - 1)(q - 1)(r - 1)$
	Within cell	$pq(n - 1)$	Within cell	$pqr[(n/r) - 1]$
	Total	$npq - 1$	Total	$npq - 1$
	Between cells	$pq - 1$	Between cells	$pqr - 1$
			Treatments	$pq - 1$
(ii)			Reps	$r - 1$
			Treat $\times$ rep	$(pq - 1)(r - 1)$
	Within cell	$pq(n - 1)$	Within cell	$pqr[(n/r) - 1]$

variation defines the estimates of variation due to treatment effects. On the other hand, in the replicated experiment part of the between-cell variation is due to replication effects as well as interactions with replications. The within-cell variations in both designs is considered to be due to experimental error. Since observations in the replicated experiment are made under somewhat more controlled conditions, the within-cell variation in a replicated experiment is potentially smaller than the corresponding variation in a nonreplicated experiment.

The partition of the total variation given in part ii may be illustrated numerically. Consider a 3×4 factorial experiment in which there are to be 10 observations under each treatment combination. The design calling for 10 observations per cell is contrasted with the design calling for five replications with 2 observations per cell in the following partition:

10 observations per cell		5 reps, 2 observations per cell	
Between cells	11	Between cells	59
		Treatments	11
		Reps	4
		Treat $\times$ rep	44
Within cell	108	Within cell	60

In a replicated design of this kind interactions with replications are often considered to be part of the experimental error. However, preliminary tests on the model may be used to check upon whether or not such pooling is justified.

There are both advantages and disadvantages to replicated experiments when contrasted with those in which there are n observations per cell. The advantages of being able to eliminate sources of variation associated with replications depend upon the magnitude of the latter relative to treatment effects and effects due to experimental error. One possible disadvantage of a replicated design might arise in situations requiring precise settings of experimental equipment. Considerable time and effort may be lost in resetting equipment for each of the replications, rather than making all observations under a single set of experimental conditions before moving to the next experimental condition. However, the inferences which can be drawn from the replicated experiment are stronger when possible variations in the resettings are considered as a relevant source of variation in the conduct of the experiment.

5.20 UNEQUAL CELL FREQUENCIES

Unweighted Means Analysis

Although an experimental design in its initial planning phases may call for an equal number of observations per cell, the completed experiment may not have an equal number of observations in all cells. There may be many reasons for such a state of affairs. The experimenter may be forced to work with intact groups having unequal size; the required number of individuals in a given category may not be available to the experimenter at a specified time; subjects may not show up to complete their part in an experiment; laboratory animals may die in the course of an experiment. If the original plan for an experiment calls for an equal number of observations in each cell and if the loss of observations in cells is essentially random (in no way directly related to the experimental variables), then the experimental data may appropriately be analyzed by the method of unweighted means. In essence the latter method considers each cell in the experiment as if it contained the same number of observations as all other cells (at least with regard to the computation of main effects and interaction effects).

Under the conditions that have been specified, the number of observations within each cell will be of the same order of magnitude. The procedures for an unweighted-means analysis will be described in terms of a 2×3 factorial experiment. These procedures may be generalized to higher-order factorial experiments. The number of observations in each cell may be indicated as follows:

	b_1	b_2	b_3
a_1	n_{11}	n_{12}	n_{13}
a_2	n_{21}	n_{22}	n_{23}

The harmonic mean of the number of observations per cell is

$$\bar{n} = \frac{pq}{(1/n_{11}) + (1/n_{12}) + \cdots + (1/n_{pq})}.$$

In the computation of main effects and interactions, each cell is considered to have $\bar{n}$ observations. (The harmonic mean rather than the arithmetic mean is used here because the standard error of a mean is proportional to $1/n_{ij}$ rather than n_{ij}.)

The mean for each of the cells may be represented as follows:

	b_1	b_2	b_3
a_1	$\overline{AB}_{11}$	$\overline{AB}_{12}$	$\overline{AB}_{13}$
a_2	$\overline{AB}_{21}$	$\overline{AB}_{22}$	$\overline{AB}_{23}$

The estimate of the mean μ_1 is

$$\bar{A}_1 = \frac{\sum\limits_{j} \overline{AB}_{1j}}{q}.$$

That is, $\bar{A}_1$ is the mean of the means in row a_1, not the mean of all observations at level a_1. These two means will differ when each cell does not have the same number of observations. The estimate of $\mu_{.1}$ is

$$\bar{B}_1 = \frac{\sum_i \overline{AB}_{i1}}{p}.$$

Again, there will be a difference between the mean of the means within a column and the mean of all observations in a column. The grand mean in the population is estimated by

$$\bar{G} = \frac{\sum \bar{A}_i}{p} = \frac{\sum \bar{B}_j}{q} = \frac{\sum \sum \overline{AB}_{ij}}{pq}.$$

Variation due to main effects and interactions is estimated by the following sums of squares:

$$SS_a = \bar{n}q \sum (\bar{A}_i - \bar{G})^2,$$

$$SS_b = \bar{n}p \sum (\bar{B}_j - \bar{G})^2,$$

$$SS_{ab} = \bar{n} \sum (\overline{AB}_{ij} - \bar{A}_i - \bar{B}_j + \bar{G})^2.$$

These sums of squares have the same form as corresponding sums of squares for the case of equal cell frequencies. However, $\bar{A}_i$, $\bar{B}_j$, and $\bar{G}$ are computed in a different manner. If all cell frequencies are equal, both computational procedures will lead to identical results.

The variation within cell ij is

$$SS_{ij} = \sum_m X_{ijm}^2 - \frac{\left(\sum_m X_{ijm}\right)^2}{n_{ij}}.$$

The pooled within-cell variation is

$$SS_{\text{w. cell}} = \sum \sum SS_{ij}.$$

The degrees of freedom for this latter source of variation are

$$df_{\text{w. cell}} = \left(\sum \sum n_{ij}\right) - pq.$$

Other methods are available for handling the analysis for unequal cell frequencies. If, however, the differences in cell frequencies are primarily functions of sources of variation irrelevant to the experimental variables, there are no grounds for permitting such frequencies to influence the estimation of population means. On the other hand, should the cell frequencies be directly related to the size of corresponding population strata, then such frequencies should be used in estimating the mean of the population composed of such strata.

Unequal Cell Frequencies—Least-Squares Estimation

As long as the cell frequencies in a factorial experiment are equal (or proportional in a sense that is defined later in this section) the variations due to overall main effects and interactions are additive. That is, the joint variation due to the main effects is the sum of the variations due to the separate main effects:

$$SS_{a+b} = SS_a + SS_b.$$

Additivity in this sense corresponds to orthogonality of the separate variations. Further, for the case of equal or proportional cell frequencies,

$$SS_{a+b+ab} = SS_a + SS_b + SS_{ab}.$$

That is, the interaction is orthogonal to the main effects.

Orthogonality of the various sources of variation simplifies the interpretation of the outcome of an experiment; because of orthogonality one may interpret one source of variation independently of the others. This simplicity of interpretation disappears (in part) in a nonorthogonal design. Disproportionate cell frequencies will give rise to nonorthogonality.

Throughout this section it is assumed that the factors are fixed. Computational details for what is presented in this section will be found in Sec. 6.14.

An interesting discussion of some possible interpretations associated with the various methods discussed in this section will be found in Overall and Spiegel (1969).

NOTATION. In this section the following notation system will be used for the cell and marginal frequencies:

$$
\begin{array}{c|ccc|c}
 & b_1 & \cdots & b_q & \\
\hline
a_1 & n_{11} & \cdots & n_{1q} & n_{1.} \\
\vdots & \vdots & \vdots & \vdots & \vdots \\
a_p & n_{p1} & \cdots & n_{pq} & n_{p.} \\
\hline
 & n_{.1} & \cdots & n_{.q} & n_{..}
\end{array}
$$

The cell and marginal totals will be denoted as follows:

$$
\begin{array}{c|ccc|c}
 & b_1 & \cdots & b_q & \\
\hline
a_1 & AB_{11} & \cdots & AB_{1q} & A_1 \\
\vdots & \vdots & & \vdots & \vdots \\
a_p & AB_{p1} & \cdots & AB_{pq} & A_p \\
\hline
 & B_1 & \cdots & B_q & G
\end{array}
$$

Cell and marginal means will be defined as follows unless indicated otherwise:

$$\overline{AB}_{ij} = \frac{AB_{ij}}{n_{ij}}, \qquad \bar{A}_i = \frac{A_i}{n_{i.}}, \qquad \bar{B}_j = \frac{B_j}{n_{.j}}, \qquad \bar{G} = \frac{G}{n_{..}}.$$

The observations within cell ab_{ij} will be denoted

$$Y_{ij1} \quad Y_{ij2} \cdots Y_{ijn_{ij}}.$$

PRINCIPLES FROM GENERAL LINEAR MODEL. Consider the following linear function of the variables $X_0, X_1, \ldots, X_p$:

$$\hat{Y} = b_0 X_0 + b_1 X_1 + \cdots + b_p X_p = \mathbf{b}'\mathbf{x}. \tag{5.26}$$

The least-squares definitions of the components of $\mathbf{b}' = [b_0 \ b_1 \cdots b_p]$ are obtained by solving the system of normal equations

$$(X'X)\mathbf{b} = X'\mathbf{y}. \tag{5.27}$$

The solution to (5.27) has the form

$$\mathbf{b} = (X'X)^{-1}X'\mathbf{y} \tag{5.28}$$

if $X'X$ is nonsingular. If $X'X$ is singular, then a generalized inverse replaces $(X'X)^{-1}$; a generalized inverse is not unique. That part of $\sum Y^2$ which can be predicted from the linear system (5.26) is given by

$$\sum \hat{Y}^2 = \mathbf{b}'X'\mathbf{y}, \tag{5.29}$$

where $\mathbf{b}$ is any solution to the system (5.27). It is noted that (5.27) represents both a necessary and sufficient condition for minimizing $\sum (Y - \hat{Y})^2$. Hence, any solution for (5.27) will minimize $\sum (Y - \hat{Y})^2$. It is found that

$$\sum Y^2 = \sum \hat{Y}^2 + \sum (Y - \hat{Y})^2.$$

Hence, any solution which minimizes $\sum (Y - \hat{Y})^2$ will maximize $\sum \hat{Y}^2$. For a given set of sample data both $\sum (Y - \hat{Y})^2$ and $\sum \hat{Y}^2$ will be unique.

In applying the linear function represented by (5.26) to experimental designs, $X_0, X_1, \ldots, X_p$ are *indicator* (or counter) variables which may be defined as follows:

$$X_0 = 1 \quad \text{for all observations,}$$
$$X_j = \begin{cases} 1 & \text{if effect } j \text{ is present,} \\ 0 & \text{if effect } j \text{ is not present,} \end{cases} \qquad j = 1, \ldots, p.$$

ESTIMATION OF PARAMETERS UNDER DIFFERENT (FIXED) MODELS. Consider the model

$$Y_{ijk} = \mu + \varepsilon_{ijk}. \tag{5.30}$$

In terms of the general linear model, (5.30) is equivalent to

$$Y = \mu X_0 + \varepsilon_{ijk}, \tag{5.30a}$$

where μ has the role of β_0. In terms of matrix notation,

$$\mathop{\mathbf{y}}_{n_{..},1} = \begin{bmatrix} Y_{111} \\ \vdots \\ Y_{pqn_{pq}} \end{bmatrix}, \qquad \mathop{\mathbf{x}_0}_{n_{..},1} = \begin{bmatrix} 1 \\ \vdots \\ 1 \end{bmatrix}.$$

The normal equations for this model have the form

$$(\mathbf{x}_0'\mathbf{x}_0)\hat{\mu} = \mathbf{x}_0'\mathbf{y} \quad \text{or} \quad n_{..}\,\hat{\mu} = G. \tag{5.30b}$$

Hence the least-squares estimate of μ is

$$\hat{\mu} = \frac{G}{n_{..}} = \bar{G}. \tag{5.30c}$$

That part of $\sum Y^2$ which can be predicted from the model in (5.30) is

$$R(\mu) = \hat{\mu}(\mathbf{x}_0'\mathbf{y}) = \bar{G}G = \frac{G^2}{n_{..}}. \tag{5.30d}$$

Consider the model

$$Y_{ijk} = \mu + \alpha_i + \varepsilon_{ijk}. \tag{5.31}$$

This model is equivalent to

$$Y = \mu X_0 + \alpha_1 X_1 + \cdots + \alpha_p X_p + \varepsilon_{ijk}, \tag{5.31a}$$

where $X_0, X_1, \ldots, X_p$ are indicator variables. For this case the normal equations have the form

$$
\begin{array}{ccc}
(X'X) & \boldsymbol{\beta} & = X'\mathbf{y}, \\
\begin{bmatrix} n_{..} & n_{1.} & n_{2.} & \cdots & n_{p.} \\ n_{1.} & n_{1.} & 0 & \cdots & 0 \\ n_{2.} & 0 & n_{2.} & \cdots & 0 \\ \vdots & \vdots & \vdots & & \vdots \\ n_{p.} & 0 & 0 & \cdots & n_{p.} \end{bmatrix} & \begin{bmatrix} \mu \\ \alpha_1 \\ \alpha_2 \\ \vdots \\ \alpha_p \end{bmatrix} & = \begin{bmatrix} G \\ A_1 \\ A_2 \\ \vdots \\ A_p \end{bmatrix}.
\end{array} \tag{5.31b}
$$

In this case $X'X$ is singular. If one imposes the constraint

$$n_{1.}\hat{\alpha}_1 + \cdots + n_{p.}\hat{\alpha}_p = 0$$

upon the system in (5.31b), one obtains the following solution:

$$\hat{\mu} = \bar{G}, \qquad \hat{\alpha}_i = \bar{A}_i - \bar{G}.$$

That part of $\sum Y^2$ which is predictable from the model in (5.31) is thus

$$\sum \hat{Y}^2 = R(\mu, \alpha) = \hat{\mu}G + \hat{\alpha}_1 A + \cdots + \hat{\alpha}_p A_p$$

$$= \bar{G}G + (\bar{A}_1 - \bar{G})A_1 + \cdots + (\bar{A}_i - \bar{G})A_p$$

$$= \frac{G^2}{n_{..}} + \frac{A_1^2}{n_{1.}} + \cdots + \frac{A_p^2}{n_{p.}} - \bar{G}(A_1 + \cdots + A_p)$$

$$= \frac{A_1^2}{n_{1.}} + \cdots + \frac{A_p^2}{n_{p.}}. \tag{5.31c}$$

Had the constraint $\hat{\mu} = 0$ been imposed upon the system (5.31b) the following solution would have been obtained:

$$\hat{\mu} = 0, \qquad \hat{\alpha}_i = \bar{A}_i.$$

For this solution,

$$R(\mu, \boldsymbol{\alpha}) = 0G + \bar{A}_i A_i + \cdots + \bar{A}_p A_p$$

$$= \frac{A_1^2}{n_{1.}} + \cdots + \frac{A_p^2}{n_{p.}}.$$

This result is identical with that in (5.31c) since $R(\mu, \boldsymbol{\alpha})$ is a constant for all solutions to the system (5.31b).

Consider now the linear model

$$Y_{ijk} = \mu + \beta_j + \varepsilon_{ijk} \tag{5.32}$$

or the equivalent form

$$Y = \mu X_0 + \beta_1 X_1 + \cdots + \beta_q X_q + \varepsilon. \tag{5.32a}$$

Here the indicator variable X_j indicates the presence or absence of the treatment effect corresponding to the parameter β_j (the main effect of treatment b_j). In this case the normal equations are

$$
\begin{array}{ccc}
(X'X) & \boldsymbol{\beta} & = \quad X'\mathbf{y},
\end{array}
$$

$$
\begin{bmatrix}
n_{..} & n_{.1} & n_{.2} & \cdots & n_{.q} \\
n_{.1} & n_{.1} & 0 & \cdots & 0 \\
n_{.2} & 0 & n_{.2} & \cdots & 0 \\
\vdots & \vdots & \vdots & & \vdots \\
n_{.q} & 0 & 0 & \cdots & n_{.q}
\end{bmatrix}
\begin{bmatrix}
\mu \\
\beta_1 \\
\beta_2 \\
\vdots \\
\beta_q
\end{bmatrix}
=
\begin{bmatrix}
G \\
B_1 \\
B_2 \\
\vdots \\
B_q
\end{bmatrix}. \tag{5.32b}
$$

Under the constraint

$$n_{.1}\hat{\beta}_1 + \cdots + n_{.q}\hat{\beta}_q = 0,$$

a solution to the system (5.32b) is given by

$$\hat{\mu} = \bar{G}, \qquad \hat{\beta}_j = \bar{B}_j - \bar{G}.$$

That part of $\sum \hat{Y}^2$ which is predictable from the model (5.32) is

$$\sum \hat{Y}^2 = R(\mu, \boldsymbol{\beta}) = \hat{\mu} G + \hat{\beta}_1 B_1 + \cdots + \hat{\beta}_q B_q$$

$$= \frac{B_1^2}{n_{.1}} + \cdots + \frac{B_q^2}{n_{.q}}. \tag{5.32c}$$

Consider now the model

$$Y_{ijk} = \mu + \tau_{ij} + \varepsilon_{ijk}, \tag{5.33}$$

where τ_{ij} is an effect associated with cell ab_{ij}. In terms of main effects and interactions,

$$\tau_{ij} = \alpha_i + \beta_j + \alpha\beta_{ij}.$$

In terms of indicator variables, (5.33) has the form

$$Y = \mu X_0 + \tau_{11} X_{11} + \tau_{12} X_{12} + \cdots + \tau_{pq} X_{pq} + \varepsilon. \tag{5.33a}$$

For the linear function in (5.33a) the normal equations have the form

$$(X'X) \qquad\qquad \boldsymbol{\beta} \quad = \quad X'y,$$

$$\begin{bmatrix} n_{..} & n_{11} & n_{12} & \cdots & n_{pq} \\ n_{11} & n_{11} & 0 & \cdots & 0 \\ n_{12} & 0 & n_{12} & \cdots & 0 \\ \vdots & \vdots & \vdots & & \vdots \\ n_{pq} & 0 & 0 & \cdots & n_{pq} \end{bmatrix} \begin{bmatrix} \mu \\ \tau_{11} \\ \tau_{12} \\ \vdots \\ \tau_{pq} \end{bmatrix} = \begin{bmatrix} G \\ AB_{11} \\ AB_{12} \\ \vdots \\ AB_{pq} \end{bmatrix}. \tag{5.33b}$$

Under the constraint

$$n_{11} \hat{\tau}_{11} + \cdots + n_{pq} \hat{\tau}_{pq} = 0,$$

a solution to the system (5.33b) is given by

$$\hat{\mu} = \bar{G}, \qquad \hat{\tau}_{ij} = \overline{AB}_{ij} - \bar{G}.$$

The part of $\sum Y^2$ which is predictable from the model in (5.33) is

$$R(\mu, \boldsymbol{\tau}) = R(\mu, \boldsymbol{\alpha}, \boldsymbol{\beta}, \boldsymbol{\alpha\beta}) = \hat{\mu} G + \hat{\tau}_{11} AB_{11} + \cdots + \hat{\tau}_{pq} AB_{pq}$$

$$= \frac{AB_{11}^2}{n_{11}} + \cdots + \frac{AB_{pq}^2}{n_{pq}}. \tag{5.33c}$$

In terms of predictable *variation* rather than the uncorrected sum of squares one has

$$R(\boldsymbol{\alpha} \mid \mu) = R(\mu, \boldsymbol{\alpha}) - R(\mu) = \sum \left(\frac{A_i^2}{n_{i.}} \right) - \frac{G^2}{n_{..}} = SS_a(\text{unadjusted}), \tag{5.31d}$$

$$R(\boldsymbol{\beta} \mid \mu) = R(\mu, \boldsymbol{\beta}) - R(\mu) = \sum \left(\frac{B_j^2}{n_{.j}} \right) - \frac{G^2}{n_{..}} = SS_b(\text{unadjusted}), \tag{5.32d}$$

$$R(\boldsymbol{\tau} \mid \mu) = R(\mu, \boldsymbol{\tau}) - R(\mu) = \sum \left(\frac{AB_{ij}^2}{n_{ij}} \right) - \frac{G^2}{n_{..}} = SS_{b.\,\text{cell}}. \tag{5.33d}$$

Consider now a fifth model given by

$$Y_{ijk} = \mu + \alpha_i + \beta_j + \varepsilon_{ijk}, \tag{5.34}$$

or, in terms of indicator variables,

$$Y = \mu X_0 + \alpha_1 X_1 + \cdots + \alpha_p X_p + \beta_1 X_{p+1} + \cdots + \beta_q X_{p+q} + \varepsilon. \tag{5.34a}$$

This model is somewhat more complex than those considered up to this point. Hence a more elaborate notation system will be needed in order to obtain the type of solution desired. The notation system that will be used is summarized in Table 5.33. In this table one notes that

$$\underset{p,q}{C} = \text{matrix of cell frequencies.}$$

$$\underset{p,1}{\mathbf{u}_p} = \text{vector of unities.}$$

$$\underset{q,1}{\mathbf{u}_q} = \text{vector of unities.}$$

$$C\mathbf{u}_q = \text{vector of row totals of } C = [n_{i.}].$$
$$C'\mathbf{u}_p = \text{vector of column totals of } C = [n_{.j}].$$
$$D_a = \text{diagonal matrix with elements } n_{i.}.$$
$$D_b = \text{diagonal matrix with elements } n_{.j}.$$

TABLE 5.33   **Notation and relationships**

(i)	$\underset{p,q}{C} = \begin{bmatrix} n_{11} & \cdots & n_{1q} \\ \vdots & & \vdots \\ n_{p1} & \cdots & n_{pq} \end{bmatrix}$ $\quad$ $\underset{p,1}{\mathbf{u}_p} = \begin{bmatrix} 1 \\ \vdots \\ 1 \end{bmatrix}$ $\underset{q,1}{\mathbf{u}_q} = \begin{bmatrix} 1 \\ \vdots \\ 1 \end{bmatrix}$ $\quad$ $\underset{p,p}{D_a} = \begin{bmatrix} n_{1.} & & 0 \\ & \ddots & \\ 0 & & n_{p.} \end{bmatrix}$ $\quad$ $\underset{q,q}{D_b} = \begin{bmatrix} n_{.1} & & 0 \\ & \ddots & \\ 0 & & n_{.q} \end{bmatrix}$
(ii)	$C\mathbf{u}_q = \begin{bmatrix} n_{1.} \\ \vdots \\ n_{p.} \end{bmatrix}$ $\qquad$ $C'\mathbf{u}_p = \begin{bmatrix} n_{.1} \\ \vdots \\ n_{.q} \end{bmatrix}$
(iii)	$CD_b^{-1} = \begin{bmatrix} \dfrac{n_{11}}{n_{.1}} & \cdots & \dfrac{n_{1q}}{n_{.q}} \\ \vdots & & \vdots \\ \dfrac{n_{p1}}{n_{.1}} & \cdots & \dfrac{n_{pq}}{n_{.q}} \end{bmatrix}$ $\qquad$ $(CD_b^{-1})(C'\mathbf{u}_p) = \begin{bmatrix} n_{1.} \\ \vdots \\ n_{p.} \end{bmatrix} = C\mathbf{u}_q$
(iv)	$C'D_a^{-1} = \begin{bmatrix} \dfrac{n_{11}}{n_{1.}} & \cdots & \dfrac{n_{p1}}{n_{p.}} \\ \vdots & & \vdots \\ \dfrac{n_{1q}}{n_{1.}} & \cdots & \dfrac{n_{pq}}{n_{p.}} \end{bmatrix}$ $\qquad$ $(C'D_a^{-1})(C\mathbf{u}_q) = \begin{bmatrix} n_{.1} \\ \vdots \\ n_{.q} \end{bmatrix} = C'\mathbf{u}_p$

One notes that

$$(CD_b^{-1})(C'\mathbf{u}_p) = \left[\frac{n_{ij}}{n_{.j}}\right][n_{.j}] = [n_{i.}] = C\mathbf{u}_q.$$

Similarly,

$$(CD_a^{-1})(C\mathbf{u}_q) = \left[\frac{n_{ij}}{n_{i.}}\right][n_{i.}] = [n_{.j}] = C'\mathbf{u}_p.$$

In terms of the notation system that has just been defined, the normal equations corresponding to the system in (5.34a) take the form

$$
\begin{array}{cc}
(X'X) & \gamma = X'\mathbf{y}, \\
\begin{array}{c}(i)\\(ii)\\(iii)\end{array}
\begin{bmatrix} n_{..} & \mathbf{u}_q'C' & \mathbf{u}_p'C \\ C\mathbf{u}_q & D_a & C \\ C'\mathbf{u}_p & C' & D_b \end{bmatrix}
\begin{bmatrix} \mu \\ \alpha \\ \beta \end{bmatrix}
=
\begin{bmatrix} G \\ \mathbf{a} \\ \mathbf{b} \end{bmatrix},
\end{array}
\qquad (5.34b)
$$

where $\mathbf{a}' = [A_1 \cdots A_p]$ and $\mathbf{b}' = [B_1 \cdots B_q]$. If one multiplies row (iii) in (5.34b) by CD_b^{-1} and then subtracts the product from row (ii) one will obtain the following system:

$$(D_a - CD_b^{-1}C')\alpha = \mathbf{a} - CD_b^{-1}\mathbf{b},$$

or, equivalently,

$$M_a\alpha = \mathbf{v}_a, \qquad (5.34c)$$

where
$$M_a = D_a - CD_b^{-1}C',$$
$$\mathbf{v}_a = \mathbf{a} - CD_b^{-1}\mathbf{b}.$$

The system in (5.34c) is called the *reduced* set of normal equations for α. The matrix M_a will be symmetric; it will also be singular since each row will sum to zero.

The reduced set of normal equations corresponding to β is obtained by multiplying row (ii) in (5.34b) by $C'D_a^{-1}$ and then subtracting the product from row (iii). The result is

$$M_b\beta = \mathbf{v}_b, \qquad (5.34d)$$

where
$$M_b = D_b - C'D_a^{-1}C,$$
$$\mathbf{v}_b = \mathbf{b} - C'D_a^{-1}\mathbf{a}.$$

The matrix M_b will be symmetric; it will also be singular since the row sums will all be zero.

A convenient generalized inverse of M_a is obtained by first forming the matrix M_a^*, given by

$$M_a^* = \begin{bmatrix} M_a & \mathbf{u}_p \\ \mathbf{u}_p' & 0 \end{bmatrix}.$$

Forming the matrix M_a^* is equivalent to imposing the constraint

$$\hat{\alpha}_1 + \cdots + \hat{\alpha}_p = 0$$

on the system. The matrix M_a^* will be nonsingular. Suppose its regular inverse is represented schematically as follows:

$$(M_a^*)^{-1} = \begin{bmatrix} E_a & \mathbf{e}_a \\ \mathbf{e}_a' & 0 \end{bmatrix}.$$

The matrix E_a will be a generalized inverse of M_a. To show this, from the properties of the regular inverse of M_a^* one has

$$\begin{bmatrix} M_a E_a + \mathbf{u}_p \mathbf{e}_a' = I & M_a \mathbf{e}_a + \mathbf{u}_p 0 = \mathbf{0} \\ \mathbf{u}_p' E_a + 0\mathbf{e}_a' = \mathbf{0}' & \mathbf{u}_p' \mathbf{e}_a = I \end{bmatrix}.$$

Hence

$$M_a E_a = I - \mathbf{u}_p \mathbf{e}_a'.$$

Postmultiplying both sides of the last expression by M_a gives

$$M_a E_a M_a = M_a - \mathbf{u}_p \mathbf{e}_a' M_a = M_a$$

since $\mathbf{e}_a' M_a = \mathbf{0}'$.

A solution to the system in (5.34c) is given by

$$\hat{\boldsymbol{\alpha}} = E_a \mathbf{v}_a. \tag{5.34e}$$

The corresponding predictable sum of squares is

$$R(\boldsymbol{\alpha} \mid \mu, \boldsymbol{\beta}) = \hat{\boldsymbol{\alpha}}' \mathbf{v}_a = \mathbf{v}_a' E_a \mathbf{v}_a. \tag{5.34f}$$

In the course of obtaining the reduced set of normal equations the estimators were "adjusted" for the effects of μ and $\boldsymbol{\beta}$; hence (5.34f) represents $R(\boldsymbol{\alpha} \mid \mu, \boldsymbol{\beta})$ rather than $R(\boldsymbol{\alpha})$.

A solution to the system (5.34d) is given by

$$\hat{\boldsymbol{\beta}} = E_b \mathbf{v}_b, \tag{5.34g}$$

where

$$M_b^* = \begin{bmatrix} M_b & \mathbf{u}_q \\ \mathbf{u}_q' & 0 \end{bmatrix}, \qquad (M_b^*)^{-1} = \begin{bmatrix} E_b & \mathbf{e}_b \\ \mathbf{e}_b' & 0 \end{bmatrix}.$$

The corresponding predictable variation associated with the reduced system in (5.34d) is

$$R(\boldsymbol{\beta} \mid \mu, \boldsymbol{\alpha}) = \hat{\boldsymbol{\beta}}' \mathbf{v}_b = \mathbf{v}_b' E_b \mathbf{v}_b. \tag{5.34h}$$

One may now combine the results from models (1) through (5) to obtain the following relationships:

$$R(\mu, \boldsymbol{\alpha}, \boldsymbol{\beta}) = R(\mu, \boldsymbol{\alpha}) + R(\boldsymbol{\beta} \mid \mu, \boldsymbol{\alpha})$$
$$= R(\mu, \boldsymbol{\beta}) + R(\boldsymbol{\alpha} \mid \mu, \boldsymbol{\beta}). \tag{5.35}$$

$$R(\boldsymbol{\alpha}, \boldsymbol{\beta} \mid \mu) = R(\boldsymbol{\alpha} \mid \mu) + R(\boldsymbol{\beta} \mid \mu, \boldsymbol{\alpha})$$
$$= R(\boldsymbol{\beta} \mid \mu) + R(\boldsymbol{\alpha} \mid \mu, \boldsymbol{\beta}). \tag{5.36}$$

Relationship (5.36) expresses the joint predictability due to α and β in terms of the predictability due to the parts. In terms of variation, (5.36) has the form

$$SS_{a+b} = SS_a(\text{unadjusted}) + SS_b(\text{adjusted for } A)$$

$$= SS_b(\text{unadjusted}) + SS_a(\text{adjusted for } B). \qquad (5.36a)$$

If one combines the results in (5.36) and (5.36a) with those associated with the model in (5.33) one obtains

$$R(\alpha\beta \mid \mu, \alpha, \beta) = R(\mu, \alpha, \beta, \alpha\beta) - R(\mu, \alpha, \beta)$$

$$= R(\alpha, \beta, \alpha\beta \mid \mu) - R(\alpha, \beta \mid \mu). \qquad (5.37)$$

In terms of variation, (5.37) has the form

$$SS_{ab}(\text{adjusted for } A \text{ and } B) = SS_{\text{b. cell}} - SS_{a+b}. \qquad (5.37a)$$

The procedures that have been discussed in this subsection have been called the *method of fitting constants*. The approach used here shows that this method is a direct application of the least-squares criterion to the general linear model, the variables being indicator variables for the levels of the factors (or the presence or absence of an effect associated with a cell). Which one of the several models is appropriate depends upon the purpose of the analysis. Under the hypothesis of no interaction, the model given in (5.34) is appropriate for estimation of variation due to main effects. A test for interaction requires an estimate of the variation due to interaction adjusted for main effects. The latter is obtained from (5.37). If interaction is present, procedures for testing main effects are discussed in a later subsection.

A readable summary of some of the problems encountered in the analysis of variance of disproportionate data when interaction is present is contained in Gosslee and Lucas (1965). An approach to the problem of handling unequal cell frequencies in a mixed model is considered in Mielke and McHugh (1965).

Some numerical details of the principles discussed in this section appear in Sec. 6.14. A summary of the results for the various models is provided in Table 5.34.

TABLE 5.34 **Summary of analyses for various models**

Model	Predictable sum of squares	Estimator
(1) $Y_{ijk} = \mu + \varepsilon_{ijk}$	$R(\mu) = \hat{\mu}G$	$\hat{\mu} = \bar{G}$
(2) $Y_{ijk} = \mu + \alpha_i + \varepsilon_{ijk}$	$R(\mu, \alpha) = \sum \hat{\alpha}_i A_i$	$\hat{\alpha}_i = \bar{A}_i + \hat{\mu}G$
(3) $Y_{ijk} = \mu + \beta_j + \varepsilon_{ijk}$	$R(\mu, \beta) = \sum \hat{\beta}_j B_j$	$\hat{\beta}_j = \bar{B}_j + \hat{\mu}G$
(4) $Y_{ijk} = \mu + \tau_{ij} + \varepsilon_{ijk}$	$R(\mu, \tau) = R(\mu, \alpha, \beta, \alpha\beta)$	$\hat{\tau}_{ij} = \overline{AB}_{ij} + \hat{\mu}G$
	$= \sum \hat{\tau}_{ij} AB_{ij}$	
(5) $Y_{ijk} = \mu + \alpha_i + \beta_j + \varepsilon_{ijk}$	$R(\mu, \alpha, \beta) = \gamma'(X'\mathbf{y})$	
	$R(\alpha \mid \mu, \beta) = \hat{\alpha}'\mathbf{v}_a$	$\hat{\alpha} = E_a\mathbf{v}_a$
	$R(\beta \mid \mu, \alpha) = \hat{\beta}'\mathbf{v}_b$	$\hat{\beta} = E_b\mathbf{v}_b$

TESTS ON INTERACTION AND MAIN EFFECTS. The procedure for testing interaction is outlined in Table 5.35. To obtain an estimate of error one uses the model

$$Y_{ijk} = \mu + \tau_{ij} + \varepsilon_{ijk},$$

where
$$\tau_{ij} = \alpha_i + \beta_j + \alpha\beta_{ij}.$$

Variation due to error is given by

$$SS_{error} = \sum Y^2 - R(\mu, \tau)$$

$$= \sum Y^2 - \sum \frac{AB_{ij}^2}{n_{ij}} = SS_{\text{w. cell}}.$$

Variation due to interaction adjusted for main effects, $R(\alpha\beta \mid \mu, \alpha, \beta)$, is obtained from relationship (5.37).

A test on the hypothesis of no interaction is given by

$$F = \frac{MS_{ab}}{MS_{error}}.$$

If, either on *a priori* grounds or on the basis of the test indicated above, it is reasonable to assume that no interaction exists, variation due to main effects may be estimated from a model which does not include an interaction term. Since the variation due to main effects are not orthogonal in this case, the adjusted variation due to main effects are obtained as indicated earlier. The latter are summarized in Table 5.35.

One form of test on main effects is

$$F = \frac{MS_a}{MS_{error}}, \qquad F = \frac{MS_b}{MS_{error}},$$

where MS_{error} is that in Table 5.35. An alternative form of the test on main effects uses the error estimated from the model which does not include an

TABLE 5.35   **Test on interaction**

Source of variation	SS	df	MS	F
Mean	$R(\mu)$	1		
A (adj. for B)	$R(\alpha \mid \mu, \beta)$			
	$= R(\mu, \alpha, \beta) - R(\mu, \beta)$	$p - 1$		
B (adj. for A)	$R(\beta \mid \mu, \alpha)$			
	$= R(\mu, \alpha, \beta) - R(\mu, \alpha)$	$q - 1$		
AB (adj. for A and B)	$R(\alpha\beta \mid \mu, \alpha, \beta)$			
	$= R(\mu, \tau) - R(\mu, \alpha, \beta)$	$(p-1)(q-1)$	MS_{ab}	MS_{ab}/MS_{error}
Error	$\sum Y^2 - R(\mu, \tau)$	$n_{..} - pq$	MS_{error}	

interaction term. This estimate of error is obtained from

$$\sum Y^2 - R(\mu, \alpha, \beta).$$

This error may be estimated by pooling the variation due to error and the variation due to interaction in Table 5.35.

If interaction is present, it generally makes more sense to test simple main effects rather than main effects, since interaction implies that the effect of one factor is dependent upon the level of the other factors. However, if tests on main effects are wanted even though interaction is present, the variation due to main effects as given in Table 5.35 cannot be used. Since these sources of variation were estimated from a model which did *not* include an interaction term, they will be biased as estimates of variation due to main effects in a model which does include an interaction term.

One possible approach to testing variation due to main effects when interaction is present is to obtain

$$R(\alpha \mid \mu, \beta, \alpha\beta) = R(\mu, \alpha, \beta, \alpha\beta) - R(\mu, \beta, \alpha\beta),$$

where $R(\mu, \beta, \alpha\beta)$ is obtained by using the model

$$X_{ijk} = \mu + \beta_j + \alpha\beta_{ij} + \varepsilon_{ijk}.$$

In this context, $R(\alpha \mid \mu, \beta, \alpha\beta)$ represents that part of the variation due to the main effects of factor A which are orthogonal to the main effects of factor B as well as the AB interaction. Similarly, one may obtain

$$R(\beta \mid \mu, \alpha, \alpha\beta) = R(\mu, \alpha, \beta, \alpha\beta) - R(\mu, \alpha, \alpha\beta).$$

An alternative method for making a test on main effects is described below. Under this approach the variation due to the main effects is not orthogonal in the sense that

$$SS_{a+b} \neq SS_a + SS_b.$$

The test procedure on interaction outlined earlier in this section may be cast in the form of the general test principle given in Sec. 5.12. Let Ω be the set of conditions associated with the linear model

$$X_{ijk} = \mu + \alpha_i + \beta_j + \alpha\beta_{ij} + \varepsilon_{ijk}. \tag{5.38}$$

Under least-squares estimation procedures, the variation due to error (under Ω) is

$$Q_\Omega = \sum (X_{ijk} - \overline{AB}_{ij})^2$$

$$= SS_{\text{total}} - R(\alpha, \beta, \alpha\beta \mid \mu)$$

$$= SS_{\text{w. cell}}.$$

Let ω be the set of conditions associated with the model

$$X_{ijk} = \mu + \alpha_i + \beta_j + \varepsilon_{ijk}. \tag{5.39}$$

Under the hypothesis that all $\alpha\beta_{ij} = 0$, (5.38) reduces to (5.39). Hence

$$\omega = \Omega + (H: \text{all } \alpha\beta_{ij} = 0).$$

Under least-squares estimation procedures, variation due to error in this case is

$$Q_\omega = \text{SS}_{\text{total}} - R(\alpha, \beta \mid \mu).$$

Thus,
$$F = \frac{(Q_\omega - Q_\Omega)/(f_{\omega-\Omega})}{Q_\Omega/f_\Omega}$$

$$= \frac{[R(\alpha, \beta, \alpha\beta \mid \mu) - R(\alpha, \beta \mid \mu)]/(p-1)(q-1)}{\text{SS}_{\text{w. cell}}/(n_{..} - pq)}.$$

METHOD OF WEIGHTED SQUARES OF MEANS. The estimation procedures to be described in this subsection lead to unbiased estimates of the variation due to main effects even though interaction may be present.

Under the method of weighted squares of means, the estimators of the main effects are

$$\hat{\alpha}_i = \bar{A}_i - \bar{G} \quad \text{and} \quad \hat{\beta}_j = \bar{B}_j - \bar{G}$$

where
$$\bar{A}_i = \frac{\sum_j \overline{AB}_{ij}}{q}, \qquad \bar{B}_j = \frac{\sum_i \overline{AB}_{ij}}{p}, \qquad \bar{G} = \frac{\sum_i \sum_j \overline{AB}_{ij}}{pq}.$$

That is, $\bar{A}_i$ is an unweighted mean of the cell means at level a_i. Let

$$h_i = \frac{q}{\sum_j (1/n_{ij})} = \text{harmonic mean of cell frequencies at level } a_i,$$

$$h_j = \frac{p}{\sum_i (1/n_{ij})} = \text{harmonic mean of cell frequencies at level } b_j.$$

Also let
$$w_i = \frac{h_i}{q} \quad \text{and} \quad w_j = \frac{h_j}{p}.$$

The variation due to the main effects of factor A is defined as

$$\text{SS}_a = q \left[\sum h_i \hat{\alpha}_i^2 - \frac{(\sum h_i \hat{\alpha}_i)^2}{\sum h_i} \right]$$

$$= q^2 \left[\sum w_i \bar{A}_i^2 - \frac{(\sum w_i \bar{A}_i)^2}{\sum w_i} \right]. \tag{5.40}$$

It will be noted that, when $n_{ij} = n$ for all cell frequencies, $h_i = n$. Hence in (5.40) $\sum h_i \hat{\alpha}_i = n \sum \hat{\alpha}_i = 0$, and (5.40) becomes

$$nq \sum \hat{\alpha}_i^2,$$

which is the least-squares estimator of SS_a when the cell frequencies are equal.

Under the method of weighted squares of means,

$$SS_b = p \left[\sum h_j \hat{\beta}_j^2 - \frac{(\sum h_j \hat{\beta}_j)^2}{\sum h_j} \right]$$

$$= p^2 \left[\sum w_j \bar{B}_j^2 - \frac{(\sum w_j \bar{B}_j)^2}{\sum w_j} \right]. \tag{5.41}$$

For the case of equal cell frequencies, (5.41) reduces to

$$SS_b = np \sum \hat{\beta}_j^2.$$

By way of contrast, in the method of *unweighted* means (or more accurately *equally* weighted means)

$$h_i \text{ is replaced by } \bar{n} \quad \text{and} \quad h_j \text{ is replaced by } \bar{n},$$

where $\bar{n}$ is the harmonic mean of all cell frequencies and not just those frequencies in a single row or a single column. Under both methods,

$$SS_{error} = SS_{w.\ cell}.$$

For the special case in which factor A has only two levels, the method of weighted squares of means reduces to constructing that comparison among the cell means corresponding to the main effect of factor A. For the case of a 2×3 factorial, the variation due to this comparison is given by

$$SS_a = \frac{(\overline{AB}_{11} + \overline{AB}_{12} + \overline{AB}_{13} - \overline{AB}_{21} - \overline{AB}_{22} - \overline{AB}_{23})^2}{\sum (1/n_{ij})}$$

In general, if

$$\bar{A}_i = \frac{1}{q} \sum_j \frac{AB_{ij}}{n_{ij}},$$

then a comparison among the $\bar{A}_i$ has the form

$$C = \sum_i c_i \bar{A}_i = \sum_i \sum_j u_{ij} \overline{AB}_{ij},$$

where

$$\sum_i c_i = 0, \qquad u_{ij} = \frac{c_i}{q}.$$

The variation due to this comparison is

$$SS_C = \frac{C^2}{\sum (u_{ij}^2/n_{ij})}.$$

If one defines

$$u_{ij}^* = \frac{u_{ij}}{k}, \quad \text{where} \quad k = \sqrt{\sum_{ij} \frac{u_{ij}^2}{n_{ij}}},$$

and if one defines

$$C^* = \sum \sum u_{ij}^* \overline{AB}_{ij},$$

then

$$SS_{C^*} = \frac{(C^*)^2}{\sum (u_{ij}^{*2}/n_{ij})} = (C^*)^2$$

since

$$\frac{\sum u_{ij}^{*2}}{n_{ij}} = 1.$$

C^* is called a normalized comparison.

It may be shown that the weighted sum of squares of means corresponds to the variation due to the maximum normalized comparison (Scheffé, 1959, p. 118).

STANDARD ERRORS OF ESTIMATORS. When considering the model

$$Y_{ijk} = \mu + \alpha_i + \beta_j + \varepsilon_{ijk}$$

it was shown that

$$\hat{\boldsymbol{\alpha}} = E_a \mathbf{v}_a, \qquad \sum \hat{\alpha}_i = 0.$$

Here E_a is the generalized inverse of M_a obtained from the regular inverse of M_a^*. From the general property of least-squares estimation in a model assuming var $(\boldsymbol{\varepsilon}) = \sigma_\varepsilon^2 I$, the covariance matrix associated with the vector of estimators is given by

$$\text{cov}(\hat{\boldsymbol{\alpha}}) = \sigma_\varepsilon^2 E_a. \tag{5.42}$$

Thus,

$$\sigma_{\hat{\alpha}_i}^2 = \sigma_\varepsilon^2 e_{ii}, \quad \text{where } e_{ii} \text{ is a diagonal element of } E_a. \tag{5.43}$$

Also

$$\sigma_{\hat{\alpha}_i - \hat{\alpha}_k}^2 = \sigma_\varepsilon^2 (e_{ii} + e_{kk} - 2e_{ik}), \tag{5.44}$$

where e_{ik} is the element in row i, column k of E_a. If σ_ε^2 is replaced by $\hat{\sigma}_\varepsilon^2$, then one has an estimate of $\sigma_{\hat{\alpha}_i - \hat{\alpha}_k}^2$. One estimate of σ_ε^2 is given by

$$\hat{\sigma}_\varepsilon^2 = \frac{\sum Y^2 - R(\mu, \boldsymbol{\alpha}, \boldsymbol{\beta})}{n_{..} - p - q + 1}.$$

Alternatively, one may use

$$\hat{\sigma}_\varepsilon^2 = \frac{SS_{\text{w. cell}}}{n_{..} - pq}.$$

The latter estimator will have fewer degrees of freedom than the former since it does not include the variation due to interaction, which in a model that does not include an interaction term is considered part of error.

By analogy,

$$\text{cov}(\hat{\boldsymbol{\beta}}) = \sigma_\varepsilon^2 E_b, \tag{5.45}$$

$$\sigma_{\hat{\beta}_j - \hat{\beta}_k}^2 = \sigma_\varepsilon^2 (e_{jj} + e_{kk} - 2e_{jk}), \tag{5.46}$$

where e_{jk} is the element in row j, column k of E_b.

SPECIAL CASE OF PROPORTIONAL CELL FREQUENCIES. That special case in which the cell frequencies are proportional (in a sense that will be defined later) has a particularly elegant solution. It will be found that

$$SS_{a+b} = SS_a + SS_b;$$

that is, the variations due to the main effects of factors A and B are additive. This kind of additivity holds for equal cell frequencies. In this context, equal cell frequencies are a special case of proportional cell frequencies.

Consider the following numerical example:

	b_1	b_2	b_3	Total
a_1	5	15	10	$30 = n_{1.}$
a_2	10	30	20	$60 = n_{2.}$
Total	15	45	30	$90 = n_{..}$
	$n_{.1}$	$n_{.2}$	$n_{.3}$	

Let

$$r_1 = \frac{n_{1.}}{n_{1.}} = 1, \qquad r_2 = \frac{n_{2.}}{n_{1.}} = 2.$$

Also let

$$s_1 = \frac{n_{.1}}{n_{.1}} = 1, \qquad s_2 = \frac{n_{.2}}{n_{.1}} = 3, \qquad s_3 = \frac{n_{.3}}{n_{.1}} = 2.$$

If one lets

$$k = \frac{n_{1.}n_{.1}}{n_{..}} = \frac{(30)(15)}{90} = 5,$$

one notes that the cell frequencies given above may be expressed as follows:

$$n_{11} = kr_1 s_1 \qquad n_{12} = kr_1 s_2 \qquad n_{13} = kr_1 s_3$$
$$n_{21} = kr_2 s_1 \qquad n_{22} = kr_2 s_2 \qquad n_{23} = kr_2 s_3$$

In general, if cell frequencies are such that

$$n_{ij} = kr_i s_j = \frac{n_{i.}n_{.j}}{n_{..}},$$

the cell frequencies are said to be *proportional*. If the cell frequencies are proportional, then

$$n_{i.} = \sum_j kr_i s_j = kr_i \sum_j s_j = kSr_i \quad \text{where} \quad S = \sum_j s_j,$$

$$n_{.j} = \sum_i kr_i s_j = ks_j \sum_i r_i = kRs_j \quad \text{where} \quad R = \sum_i r_i, \qquad (5.47)$$

$$n_{..} = \sum_i n_{i.} = kS \sum_i r_i = kRS.$$

In terms of the numerical example given above,

$$R = \sum r_i = 3, \qquad S = \sum s_j = 6, \qquad kRS = 5(3)(6) = 90 = n_{..}.$$

Under the model

$$X_{ijk} = \mu + \alpha_i + \beta_j + \varepsilon_{ijk},$$

the normal equations take the following form:

$$\mu: \quad kRS\hat{\mu} + ks \sum_i r_i \hat{\alpha}_i + kR \sum_j s_j \hat{\beta}_j = G,$$

$$\alpha_i: \quad kSr_i \hat{\mu} + kSr_i \hat{\alpha}_i + kr_i \sum_j s_j \hat{\beta}_j = A_i, \qquad i = 1, \ldots, p, \qquad (5.48)$$

$$\beta_j: \quad kRs_j \hat{\mu} + ks_j \sum_i s_i \hat{\alpha}_i + kRs_j \hat{\beta}_j = B_j, \qquad j = 1, \ldots, q.$$

Here $\quad A_i = \sum_j AB_{ij}, \qquad B_j = \sum_i AB_{ij}, \quad \text{and} \quad G = \sum_i \sum_j AB_{ij}.$

If one imposes the constraints

$$\sum_i r_i \hat{\alpha}_i = 0, \qquad \sum_j s_j \hat{\beta}_j = 0,$$

one obtains the following solutions:

$$\hat{\mu} = \frac{G}{kRS} = \bar{G},$$

$$\hat{\alpha}_i = \frac{A_i - kSr_i \hat{\mu}}{kSr_i} = \bar{A}_i - \bar{G}, \quad \text{where} \quad \bar{A}_i = \frac{A_i}{kSr_i}, \qquad (5.49)$$

$$\hat{\beta}_j = \frac{B_j - kRs_j \hat{\mu}}{kRs_j} = \bar{B}_j - \bar{G}, \quad \text{where} \quad \bar{B}_j = \frac{B_j}{kRs_j}.$$

Hence

$$R(\mu, \boldsymbol{\alpha}, \boldsymbol{\beta}) = \hat{\mu}G + \sum \hat{\alpha}_i A_i + \sum \hat{\beta}_j B_j$$

$$= \frac{G^2}{n_{..}} + \sum A_i (\bar{A}_i - \bar{G})^2 + \sum B_j (\bar{B}_j - \bar{G})^2$$

$$= \frac{G^2}{n_{..}} + \sum \frac{A_i^2}{n_{i.}} + \sum \frac{B_j^2}{n_{.j}} - \frac{2G^2}{n_{..}}$$

$$= \sum \frac{A_i^2}{n_{i.}} + \sum \frac{B_j^2}{n_{.j}} - \frac{G^2}{n_{..}}. \qquad (5.50)$$

From earlier discussion, one has the following:

$$R(\mu) = \frac{G^2}{n_{..}},$$

$$R(\boldsymbol{\alpha} \mid \mu) = \sum \frac{A_i^2}{n_{i.}} - \frac{G^2}{n_{..}} = \sum n_{i.}(\bar{A}_i - \bar{G})^2,$$

$$R(\boldsymbol{\beta} \mid \mu) = \sum \frac{B_j^2}{n_{.j}} - \frac{G^2}{n_{..}} = \sum n_{.j}(\bar{B}_j - \bar{G})^2.$$

Combining (5.49) and (5.50) one has for the case of proportional cell frequencies

$$R(\boldsymbol{\alpha}, \boldsymbol{\beta} \mid \mu) = R(\mu, \boldsymbol{\alpha}, \boldsymbol{\beta}) - R(\mu)$$

$$= \sum \frac{A_i^2}{n_{i.}} + \sum \frac{B_j^2}{n_{.j}} - \frac{G^2}{n_{..}} - \frac{G^2}{n_{..}}$$

$$= R(\boldsymbol{\alpha} \mid \mu) + R(\boldsymbol{\beta} \mid \mu)$$

$$= SS_a + SS_b. \tag{5.51}$$

The analysis of variance for the case of proportional cell frequencies is summarized in Table 5.36.

It is readily verified that the variation due to interaction which is defined by

$$SS_{ab} = SS_{b.\ cell} - SS_a - SS_b$$

may be expressed in the algebraically equivalent form

$$SS_{ab} = \sum n_{ij}(\overline{AB}_{ij} - \bar{A}_i - \bar{B}_j + \bar{G})^2.$$

Estimability in a general sense is covered in Appendix C.

TABLE 5.36 **Analysis of variance (least squares) for proportional cell frequencies**

$(1) = G^2/n_{..}$ $\quad$ $(2) = \sum X_{ijk}^2$ $\quad$ $(3) = \sum (A_i^2/n_{i.})$ $(4) = \sum (B_j^2/n_{.j})$ $\quad$ $(5) = \sum [(AB_{ij})^2/n_{ij}]$		
Source of variation	**SS**	**df**
A	$(3) - (1)$	$p - 1$
B	$(4) - (1)$	$q - 1$
AB	$(5) - (3) - (4) + (1)$	$(p-1)(q-1)$
Within cell	$(2) - (5)$	$n_{..} - pq$

5.21 ESTIMATION OF THE MAGNITUDE OF EXPERIMENTAL EFFECTS AND STATISTICAL POWER

For completely randomized factorial designs with equal sample sizes, procedures for estimating treatment effects and computing statistical power are generalizations of the procedures presented for the single-factor design in Sec. 3.9.

Fixed Factors

If one uses omega squared as a measure of strength of association

$$\hat{\omega}^2_{\text{effect}} = \frac{\text{variance estimate for effect of interest}}{\text{total variance estimate}}.$$

The basis for constructing such estimates is the expected values of the mean squares. As pointed out by Dodd and Schultz (1973), to compute $\hat{\omega}^2_{\text{effect}}$ for *any* size completely randomized design, one may use the computational formula

$$\hat{\omega}^2_{\text{effect}} = \frac{\text{SS}_{\text{effect}} - (\text{df}_{\text{effect}})(\text{MS}_{\text{error}})}{\text{SS}_{\text{total}} + \text{MS}_{\text{error}}}.$$

The discussion which follows will be cast in terms of a two-factor design, but may be generalized to fixed-factor designs of any size. The results of an analysis of a 3×6 factorial experiment having $n = 5$ independent observations per cell are summarized in Table 5.37.

It is convenient to define the parameter θ^2_α, θ^2_β, and $\theta^2_{\alpha\beta}$ in order to translate between the fixed effects and the variance of effects. For levels of factor A,

$$\theta^2_\alpha = \frac{\sum \alpha_i^2}{p}$$

provides an index of the overall effects of the levels of factor A. Since

$$\sigma^2_\alpha = \frac{\sum \alpha_i^2}{p - 1},$$

TABLE 5.37 **Numerical example**

Source of variation	SS	df	MS	E(MS)	F
A	96.00	2	48.00	$\sigma^2_\varepsilon + nq\sigma^2_\alpha$	$F_\alpha = 12.00$
B	200.00	5	40.00	$\sigma^2_\varepsilon + np\sigma^2_\beta$	$F_\beta = 10.00$
AB	60.00	10	6.00	$\sigma^2_\varepsilon + n\sigma^2_{\alpha\beta}$	$F_{\alpha\beta} = 1.50$
Error	288.00	72	4.00	σ^2_ε	
Total	644.00	89			

one has
$$\theta_\alpha^2 = \frac{p-1}{p} \sigma_\alpha^2.$$

In terms of the parameter θ_α^2,
$$E(MS_a) = \sigma_\varepsilon^2 + nq\sigma_\alpha^2 = \sigma_\varepsilon^2 + \frac{npq}{p-1} \theta_\alpha^2.$$

Similarly, if one defines
$$\theta_\beta^2 = \frac{\sum \beta_j^2}{q}, \quad \text{then} \quad \theta_\beta^2 = \frac{q-1}{q} \sigma_\beta^2.$$

Thus
$$E(MS_b) = \sigma_\varepsilon^2 + np\sigma_\beta^2 = \sigma_\varepsilon^2 + \frac{npq}{q-1} \theta_\beta^2.$$

Similarly,
$$E(MS_{ab}) = \sigma_\varepsilon^2 + n\sigma_{\alpha\beta}^2 = \sigma_\varepsilon^2 + \frac{npq}{(p-1)(q-1)} \theta_{\alpha\beta}^2,$$

where
$$\theta_{\alpha\beta}^2 = \frac{(p-1)(q-1)}{pq} \sigma_{\alpha\beta}^2 = \frac{\sum (\alpha\beta_{ij})^2}{pq}.$$

One has
$$\hat{\sigma}_\varepsilon^2 = MS_{error}.$$

Using this estimate of σ_ε^2 in $E(MS_a)$, one has
$$\theta_\alpha^2 = \frac{(p-1)(MS_a - MS_{error})}{npq} = \frac{(p-1)(F_a - 1)MS_{error}}{npq},$$

where $F_a = MS_a/MS_{error}$. Similarly, one has
$$\theta_\beta^2 = \frac{(q-1)(MS_b - MS_{error})}{npq} = \frac{(q-1)(F_b - 1)MS_{error}}{npq}$$

and
$$\theta_{\alpha\beta}^2 = \frac{(p-1)(q-1)(MS_{ab} - MS_{error})}{npq} = \frac{(p-1)(q-1)(F_{ab} - 1)MS_{error}}{npq}.$$

One index (of several possible) of the relative magnitude of the effect of treatment A is
$$\omega_\alpha^2 = \frac{\theta_\alpha^2}{\theta_\alpha^2 + \theta_\beta^2 + \theta_{\alpha\beta}^2 + \sigma_\varepsilon^2}.$$

The numerator represents a measure of the main effects due to factor A; the denominator represents the sum of all effects underlying an observation. A heuristic principle for estimating this ratio is to replace each parameter by its estimator. The resulting estimator of ω_α^2, although biased, will be consistent. In this case
$$\hat{\omega}_\alpha^2 = \frac{(p-1)(F_a - 1)}{(p-1)(F_a - 1) + (q-1)(F_b - 1) + (p-1)(q-1)(F_{ab} - 1) + npq}.$$

For the numerical data in Table 5.37,

$$\hat{\omega}_\alpha^2 = \frac{2(12-1)}{2(12-1) + 5(10-1) + 2(5)(1.50-1) + 5(3)(6)}$$

$$= \frac{22}{162}$$

$$= 0.1358.$$

Hence, in terms of $\hat{\omega}^2$, 13.58 percent of the total variance is estimated to be due to the main effects of factor A. Using the alternative and simpler general computational formula, one obtains the same result:

$$\hat{\omega}_\alpha^2 = \frac{SS_a - (p-1)(MS_{error})}{SS_{total} + MS_{error}}$$

$$= \frac{96.00 - (2)(4.00)}{644.00 + 4.00} = 0.1358.$$

If one defines

$$\omega_\beta^2 = \frac{\theta_\beta^2}{\theta_\alpha^2 + \theta_\beta^2 + \theta_{\alpha\beta}^2 + \sigma_\varepsilon^2}$$

$$\hat{\omega}_\beta^2 = \frac{(q-1)(F_b - 1)}{(p-1)(F_a - 1) + (p-1)(F_b - 1) + (p-1)(q-1)(F_{ab} - 1) + npq}.$$

For the numerical data in Table 5.37, one has

$$\hat{\omega}_\beta^2 = \frac{(5)(9)}{162} = 0.2778.$$

Equivalently, in terms of the general computational formula,

$$\hat{\omega}_\beta^2 = \frac{SS_b - (q-1)MS_{error}}{SS_{total} + MS_{error}}$$

$$= \frac{200.00(5)(4)}{644.00 + 4} \frac{180}{648} = 0.2778.$$

One may account for 27.78 percent of the variance with the B main effects. For the interaction effects,

$$\hat{\omega}_{\alpha\beta}^2 = \frac{(p-1)(q-1)(F_{ab} - 1)}{(p-1)(F_a - 1) + (q-1)(F_b - 1) + (p-1)(q-1)(F_{ab} - 1) + npq}$$

$$= \frac{(10)(0.50)}{(2)(11) + (5)(9) + (10)(0.50) + 90}$$

$$= \frac{5}{162} = 0.0309.$$

Again, one may use the general computational formula to obtain the same result:

$$\hat{\omega}_{\alpha\beta}^2 = \frac{\text{SS}_{ab} - (p-1)(q-1)\text{MS}_{\text{error}}}{\text{SS}_{\text{total}} + \text{MS}_{\text{error}}}$$

$$= \frac{60 - (10)(4)}{644 + 4} = \frac{20}{648} = 0.0309.$$

Finally, one may define

$$\omega_{\text{all effects}}^2 = \frac{\theta_\alpha^2 + \theta_\beta^2 + \theta_{\alpha\beta}^2}{\theta_\alpha^2 + \theta_\beta^2 + \theta_{\alpha\beta}^2 + \sigma_\varepsilon^2}.$$

For the numerical example,

$$\hat{\omega}_{\text{all effects}}^2 = \frac{162 - 90}{162} = 0.4444.$$

Thus 44.44 percent of the variance is due to treatment effects, and 55.56 percent of the variance is due to error variance.

To help generalize, the estimates of variances (adjusted from fixed effects) for the three-factor design are provided in Table 5.38.

For power computations, under Model I, the sampling distribution of the F statistic when the hypothesis being tested is not true is the noncentral F with the appropriate noncentrality parameter.

Tables of the noncentral F are usually oriented in terms of the quantity ϕ which, in very general terms, is

$$\phi_{\text{effect}} = \sqrt{\lambda \text{ effect/number of effect levels}}.$$

For example, in testing the hypothesis that $\sigma_\alpha^2 = 0$ (for a two-factor completely randomized design),

$$\lambda_\alpha = \frac{nq \sum \alpha_i^2}{\sigma_\varepsilon^2},$$

and

$$\phi = \sqrt{\lambda_\alpha/p}$$

$$= \sqrt{\frac{nq \sum \alpha_i^2}{\sigma_\varepsilon^2} \Big/ p}$$

$$= \sqrt{\frac{nq \sum \alpha_i^2}{p\sigma_\varepsilon^2}}.$$

This last form emphasizes that, in general, one may compute ϕ as

$$\phi_{\text{effect}} = \frac{\text{no. of observations } [\sum (\text{deviation})^2]}{(\text{df}_{\text{effect}} + 1)\sigma_{\text{error}}^2},$$

TABLE 5.38   **Estimates of variance components in three-way designs†**

Model‡	Variance component
ABC	$\hat{\sigma}_\alpha^2 = (p-1)(\mathrm{MS}_a - \mathrm{MS}_{\mathrm{error}})/npqr$
	$\hat{\sigma}_\beta^2 = (q-1)(\mathrm{MS}_b - \mathrm{MS}_{\mathrm{error}})/npqr$
	$\hat{\sigma}_\gamma^2 = (r-1)(\mathrm{MS}_c - \mathrm{MS}_{\mathrm{error}})/npqr$
	$\hat{\sigma}_{\alpha\beta}^2 = (p-1)(q-1)(\mathrm{MS}_{ab} - \mathrm{MS}_{\mathrm{error}})/npqr$
	$\hat{\sigma}_{\alpha\gamma}^2 = (p-1)(r-1)(\mathrm{MS}_{ac} - \mathrm{MS}_{\mathrm{error}})/npqr$
	$\hat{\sigma}_{\beta\gamma}^2 = (q-1)(r-1)(\mathrm{MS}_{bc} - \mathrm{MS}_{\mathrm{error}})/npqr$
	$\hat{\sigma}_{\alpha\beta\gamma}^2 = (p-1)(q-1)(r-1)(\mathrm{MS}_{abc} - \mathrm{MS}_{\mathrm{error}})/npqr$
	$\hat{\sigma}_\varepsilon^2 = \mathrm{MS}_{\mathrm{error}}$
aBC	$\hat{\sigma}_\alpha^2 = (\mathrm{MS}_a - \mathrm{MS}_{\mathrm{error}})/nqr$
	$\hat{\sigma}_\beta^2 = (q-1)(\mathrm{MS}_b - \mathrm{MS}_{ab})/npqr$
	$\hat{\sigma}_\gamma^2 = (r-1)(\mathrm{MS}_c - \mathrm{MS}_{ac})/npqr$
	$\hat{\sigma}_{\alpha\beta}^2 = (\mathrm{MS}_{ab} - \mathrm{MS}_{\mathrm{error}})/nr$
	$\hat{\sigma}_{\alpha\gamma}^2 = (\mathrm{MS}_{ac} - \mathrm{MS}_{\mathrm{error}})/nq$
	$\hat{\sigma}_{\beta\gamma}^2 = (q-1)(r-1)(\mathrm{MS}_{bc} - \mathrm{MS}_{abc})/npqr$
	$\hat{\sigma}_{\alpha\beta\gamma}^2 = (\mathrm{MS}_{abc} - \mathrm{MS}_{\mathrm{error}})/n$
	$\hat{\sigma}_\varepsilon^2 = \mathrm{MS}_{\mathrm{error}}$
abC	$\hat{\sigma}_\alpha^2 = (\mathrm{MS}_a - \mathrm{MS}_{ab})/nqr$
	$\hat{\sigma}_\beta^2 = (\mathrm{MS}_b - \mathrm{MS}_{ab})/npr$
	$\hat{\sigma}_\gamma^2 = (r-1)(\mathrm{MS}_c - \mathrm{MS}_{ac} - \mathrm{MS}_{bc} + \mathrm{MS}_{abc})/npqr$
	$\hat{\sigma}_{\alpha\beta}^2 = (\mathrm{MS}_{ab} - \mathrm{MS}_{\mathrm{error}})/nr$
	$\hat{\sigma}_{\alpha\gamma}^2 = (\mathrm{MS}_{ac} - \mathrm{MS}_{abc})/nq$
	$\hat{\sigma}_{\beta\gamma}^2 = (\mathrm{MS}_{bc} - \mathrm{MS}_{abc})/np$
	$\hat{\sigma}_{\alpha\beta\gamma}^2 = (\mathrm{MS}_{abc} - \mathrm{MS}_{\mathrm{error}})/n$
	$\hat{\sigma}_\varepsilon^2 = \mathrm{MS}_{\mathrm{error}}$
abc	$\hat{\sigma}_\alpha^2 = (\mathrm{MS}_a - \mathrm{MS}_{ab} - \mathrm{MS}_{ac} + \mathrm{MS}_{abc})/nqr$
	$\hat{\sigma}_\beta^2 = (\mathrm{MS}_b - \mathrm{MS}_{ab} - \mathrm{MS}_{bc} + \mathrm{MS}_{abc})/npr$
	$\hat{\sigma}_\gamma^2 = (\mathrm{MS}_c - \mathrm{MS}_{ac} - \mathrm{MS}_{bc} + \mathrm{MS}_{abc})/npq$
	$\hat{\sigma}_{\alpha\beta}^2 = (\mathrm{MS}_{ab} - \mathrm{MS}_{abc})/nr$
	$\hat{\sigma}_{\alpha\gamma}^2 = (\mathrm{MS}_{ac} - \mathrm{MS}_{abc})/nq$
	$\hat{\sigma}_{\beta\gamma}^2 = (\mathrm{MS}_{bc} - \mathrm{MS}_{abc})/np$
	$\hat{\sigma}_{\alpha\beta\gamma}^2 = (\mathrm{MS}_{abc} - \mathrm{MS}_{\mathrm{error}})/n$
	$\hat{\sigma}_\varepsilon^2 = \mathrm{MS}_{\mathrm{error}}$

† This table is modified from Vaughan, G. M. & Corballis, M. C. Beyond tests of significance: estimating strength of effects in selected ANOV designs. *Psychological Bulletin*, 1969, **72**, 3, 204–213, with permission of the editor.

‡ Capital letters denote fixed factors; small letters denote random factors.

where "no. of observations" refers to the number of observations on which each effect estimate is based and "deviations" refers to the definition of the effect of interest. For example, each *A* main effect estimate is based upon nq observations and the deviation of interest is α. The quantity ϕ is related to Cohen's *f* as

$$\phi = f\sqrt{\text{"number of observations"}}.$$

Using these general relations for a two-factor completely randomized design, one may estimate ϕ as,

$$\hat{\phi}_\alpha = \sqrt{\frac{nq \sum \hat{\alpha}_i^2}{[(p-1)+1]\hat{\sigma}_\varepsilon^2}} = \sqrt{\frac{nq \sum \hat{\alpha}_i^2}{p\hat{\sigma}_\varepsilon^2}}$$

$$\hat{\phi}_\beta = \sqrt{\frac{np \sum \hat{\beta}_j^2}{[(q-1)+1]\hat{\sigma}_\varepsilon^2}} = \sqrt{\frac{np \sum \hat{\beta}_j^2}{q\hat{\sigma}_\varepsilon^2}}$$

$$\hat{\phi}_{\alpha\beta} = \sqrt{\frac{n \sum \sum \hat{\alpha\beta}_{ij}^2}{[(p-1)(q-1)+1]\hat{\sigma}_\varepsilon^2}}.$$

It is worth noting that the power associated with each effect varies in proportion to the total number of observations on which an effect estimate is based. Hence, the interaction effect tests will always have less power than will main effect tests since interaction effect estimates are based upon n observations and main effects are based upon nq and np values for factors A and B, respectively.

For purposes of estimating power or sample sizes, appropriate tables may be entered with $\hat{\phi}$. Numerical examples will be presented in Chapter 6.

Random Factors

For the special case of a single-factor experiment, the problem of estimating variance components was discussed in Sec. 3.5. The discussion in this section is limited largely to balanced designs wherein sample sizes are equal for all treatment conditions.

The estimation problems that are encountered in unbalanced designs having one or more random factors have been summarized by Searle (1968). In the statistical literature there are three methods for estimating components of variance for the case of disproportional cell frequencies. All three methods were studied in some detail by Henderson (1953). Most of the difficulties that are encountered occur in the mixed model. When the cell frequencies are equal, all three methods of estimation are equivalent.

Consider a two-factor experiment in which factors A and B are both random. The expected values of the mean squares for main effects and interactions (when cell frequencies are equal) have the following form:

$$E(MS_a) = \sigma_\varepsilon^2 + n\sigma_{\alpha\beta}^2 + nq\sigma_\alpha^2,$$

$$E(MS_b) = \sigma_\varepsilon^2 + n\sigma_{\alpha\beta}^2 + np\sigma_\beta^2,$$

$$E(MS_{ab}) = \sigma_\varepsilon^2 + n\sigma_{\alpha\beta}^2,$$

$$E(MS_{\text{w. cell}}) = \sigma_\varepsilon^2. \tag{5.52}$$

(5.52) may be written in matrix form as

$$
E\begin{bmatrix} MS_a \\ MS_b \\ MS_{ab} \\ MS_{\text{w. cell}} \end{bmatrix} = \begin{bmatrix} 1 & n & 0 & nq \\ 1 & n & np & 0 \\ 1 & n & 0 & 0 \\ 1 & 0 & 0 & 0 \end{bmatrix} \begin{bmatrix} \sigma^2_\varepsilon \\ \sigma^2_{\alpha\beta} \\ \sigma^2_\beta \\ \sigma^2_\alpha \end{bmatrix} \tag{5.53}
$$

$$
E(\mathbf{s}^2) \quad = \quad M \quad \quad \boldsymbol{\sigma}^2
$$

Estimators of the components of $\boldsymbol{\sigma}^2$ may be obtained by equating mean squares to their expectations. If this is done, (5.53) becomes

$$
\begin{bmatrix} MS_a \\ MS_b \\ MS_{ab} \\ MS_{\text{w. cell}} \end{bmatrix} = \begin{bmatrix} 1 & n & 0 & nq \\ 1 & n & np & 0 \\ 1 & n & 0 & 0 \\ 1 & 0 & 0 & 0 \end{bmatrix} \begin{bmatrix} \sigma^2_\varepsilon \\ \sigma^2_{\alpha\beta} \\ \sigma^2_\beta \\ \sigma^2_\alpha \end{bmatrix} \tag{5.54}
$$

$$
\mathbf{s}^2 \quad = \quad M \quad \quad \boldsymbol{\sigma}^2.
$$

For the case of balanced designs, solution of the system (5.54) will lead to unbiased estimators.

The general solution to the system is given by

$$
\hat{\boldsymbol{\sigma}}^2 = M^{-1}\mathbf{s}^2, \tag{5.55}
$$

provided M is nonsingular.[1] For the special case represented by (5.54), the solution is readily obtained by inspection. From the last equation in (5.54) one has

$$
\hat{\sigma}^2_\varepsilon = MS_{\text{w. cell}}.
$$

Substituting this result in the equation corresponding to MS_{ab} gives

$$
\hat{\sigma}^2_{\alpha\beta} = \frac{MS_{ab} - MS_{\text{w. cell}}}{n}.
$$

If one subtracts the equation corresponding to MS_{ab} from the equation corresponding to MS_b, one obtains

$$
\frac{MS_b - MS_{ab}}{np} = \frac{\hat{\sigma}^2_\varepsilon + n\hat{\sigma}^2_{\alpha\beta} + np\hat{\sigma}^2_\beta - \hat{\sigma}^2_\varepsilon - n\hat{\sigma}^2_{\alpha\beta}}{np} = \hat{\sigma}^2_\beta.
$$

---

[1] This procedure for estimating variance components may lead to negative estimators for variance components. Estimates of the variances and covariances of the estimators are readily obtained by methods developed by Tukey (1956). If the assumption is made that the random effects are independently and normally distributed, the variance and covariance of the estimators are obtained by a direct extension of the methods used in Sec. 3.5. Similar procedures are given in Scheffé (1959, pp. 228–229).

Similarly,

$$\frac{MS_a - MS_{ab}}{nq} = \hat{\sigma}_\alpha^2.$$

Hence, when sample sizes are equal and all factors are random, estimating variance components is simple. One may generalize the results from the two-factor design to larger designs. Table 5.39 provides that generalization to the three-factor design.

TABLE 5.39 **Computational components for estimates of magnitude of effect for random and mixed designs†**

Design‡	Source	Numerator	Denominator
Random			
a	A	$p(MS_a - MS_{error})$	$SS_{total} + MS_a$
ab	A	$p(MS_a - MS_{ab})$	
	B	$q(MS_b - MS_{ab})$	$SS_{total} + MS_a + MS_b - MS_{ab}$
	AB	$pq(MS_{ab} - MS_{error})$	
abc	A	$p(MS_a - MS_{ab} - MS_{ac} + MS_{abc})$	
	B	$q(MS_b - MS_{ab} - MS_{bc} + MS_{abc})$	
	C	$r(MS_c - MS_{ac} - MS_{bc} + MS_{abc})$	$SS_{total} + MS_a + MS_b + MS_c$
	AB	$pq(MS_{ab} - MS_{abc})$	$- MS_{ab} - MS_{ac} - MS_{bc}$
	AC	$pr(MS_{ac} - MS_{abc})$	$+ MS_{abc}$
	BC	$qr(MS_{bc} - MS_{abc})$	
	ABC	$pqr(MS_{abc} - MS_{error})$	
Mixed			
aB	A	$p(MS_a - MS_{error})$	
	B	$SS_b - (df_b \times MS_{ab})$	$SS_{total} + MS_a + pMS_{ab} - pMS_{error}$
	AB	$pq(MS_{ab} - MS_{error})$	
aBC	A	$P(MS_a - MS_{error})$	
	B	$SS_b - (df_b \times MS_{ab})$	
	C	$SS_c - (df_c \times MS_{ac})$	$SS_{total} + MS_a + pMS_{ab} + pMS_{ac}$
	AB	$pq(MS_{ab} - MS_{error})$	$+ p(q + r - 1)MS_{abc}$
	AC	$pr(MS_{ac} - MS_{error})$	$- p(q + r + 1)MS_{error}$
	BC	$SS_{bc} - (df_{bc} \times MS_{abc})$	
	ABC	$pqr(MS_{abc} - MS_{error})$	
abC	A	$p(MS_a - MS_{ab})$	
	B	$q(MS_b - MS_{ab})$	
	C	$SS_c - [df_c \times (MS_{ab} + MS_{bc} - MS_{abc})]$	$SS_{total} + MS_a + MS_b - MS_{ab}$
	AB	$pq(MS_{ab} - MS_{error})$	$+ pMS_{ac} + pMS_{bc}$
	AC	$pr(MS_{ac} - MS_{abc})$	$+ (pq - p - q)MS_{abc}$
	BC	$qr(MS_{bc} - MS_{abc})$	$- pqMS_{error}$
	ABC	$pqr(MS_{abc} - MS_{error})$	

† This table is modified from Dodd, D. H. and Schultz, R. F. Jr. Computational procedures for estimating magnitude of effect for some analysis of variance designs, *Psychological Bulletin*, 1975, **79**, 6, 391–395, with permission of the editor.

‡ Capital letters denote fixed factors; lowercase letters denote random factors.

If one wishes to construct estimates of the degree of association between treatment effects and the dependent variable, for the random model the intraclass correlation ρ_I is appropriate. To do so, in general one may estimate each of the variance components separately and then construct the estimate

$$\rho_I^2 = \frac{\hat{\sigma}^2_{\text{effect}}}{\hat{\sigma}^2_{\text{total}}}.$$

For example, for the two-factor design for the A effects, one has

$$\rho_I^2 = \frac{\hat{\sigma}^2_\alpha}{\hat{\sigma}^2_\alpha + \hat{\sigma}^2_\beta + \hat{\sigma}^2_{\alpha\beta} + \hat{\sigma}^2_\varepsilon}.$$

Using the data from Table 5.37, one obtains

$$\hat{\sigma}^2_\alpha = \frac{\text{MS}_a - \text{MS}_{ab}}{nq} = \frac{48 - 6}{(5)(6)} = 1.40$$

$$\hat{\sigma}^2_\beta = \frac{\text{MS}_b - \text{MS}_{ab}}{np} = \frac{40 - 6}{(5)(3)} = 2.27$$

$$\hat{\sigma}^2_{\alpha\beta} = \frac{\text{MS}_{ab} - \text{MS}_{\text{error}}}{n} = \frac{6 - 4}{5} = 0.40$$

$$\hat{\sigma}^2_{\text{error}} = \text{MS}_{\text{error}} = 4.$$

Hence,

$$\rho_I^2 = \frac{1.40}{1.40 + 2.27 + 0.40 + 4} = 0.1736.$$

One may also compute estimates of the interclass correlation directly. Table 5.39 from Dodd and Schultz (1973) provides the appropriate computations for random and mixed models for the single-factor experiment and for two- and three-factor designs. For example, under Model II, for a two-factor design for the effects of factor A,

$$\rho_I = \frac{p(\text{MS}_a - \text{MS}_{ab})}{\text{SS}_{\text{total}} + \text{MS}_a + \text{MS}_b - \text{MS}_{ab}}.$$

When applied to the numerical values of Table 5.37, one obtains

$$\rho_I = \frac{3(48 - 6)}{644 + 48 + 40 - 6} = 0.1736,$$

which is the same as the value obtained by summing the individual estimates.

When sample sizes are not equal, estimation of variance components becomes more complex. To illustrate the nature of the problem of estimating variance components for the case of disproportionate cell frequencies, consider an experiment for which the following additive model is appropriate:

$$X_{ijk} = \mu + \alpha_i + \beta_j + \varepsilon_{ijk},$$

where factors A and B are random. Suppose that there are n_{ij} observations in the cell corresponding to treatment ab_{ij}.

Let the total variation be partitioned as follows:

$$\sum (X_{ijk} - \bar{G})^2 = \left[\left(\frac{A_i^2}{n_{i.}} \right) - \frac{G^2}{n_{..}} \right] + \left[\sum \left(\frac{B_j^2}{n_{.j}} \right) - \frac{G^2}{n_{..}} \right] + SS_{rem},$$

$$SS_{total} = SS_a + SS_b + SS_{rem},$$

where
$$SS_{rem} = SS_{total} - SS_a - SS_b.$$

(It is possible that SS_{rem} will be negative.) The expected values of the mean squares corresponding to this partition may be shown to those given in Table 5.40. If one equates the expected values of the mean squares to their expectations, replacing parameters by their estimators, one obtains the following system of equations:

$$\begin{bmatrix} MS_a \\ MS_b \\ MS_{rem} \end{bmatrix} = \begin{bmatrix} 1 & C_{ab} & C_{aa} \\ 1 & C_{ba} & C_{bb} \\ 1 & C_{ea} & C_{eb} \end{bmatrix} \begin{bmatrix} \hat{\sigma}_\varepsilon^2 \\ \hat{\sigma}_\beta^2 \\ \hat{\sigma}_\alpha^2 \end{bmatrix}.$$

Solution of the system (5.56) provides a set of estimators for the variance components σ_ε^2, σ_β^2, and σ_α^2. For the unbalanced case, optimum properties of the estimators have not been studied in detail. The estimators will be consistent.

For purposes of computing power, recall that under Model II the

TABLE 5.40 Expected value of mean squares

Source of variation	df	E(MS)
A	$p-1$	$\sigma_\varepsilon^2 + c_{ab}\sigma_\beta^2 + c_{aa}\sigma_\alpha^2$
B	$q-1$	$\sigma_\varepsilon^2 + c_{bb}\sigma_\beta^2 + c_{ba}\sigma_\alpha^2$
Remainder	$n_{..} - p - q + 1$	$\sigma_\varepsilon^2 + c_{eb}\sigma_\beta^2 + c_{ea}\sigma_\alpha^2$

$$c_{aa} = \frac{1}{p-1} \left(n_{..} - \sum_i \frac{n_{i.}^2}{n_{..}} \right) \qquad c_{ab} = \frac{1}{p-1} \left(\sum_{i,j} \frac{n_{ij}^2}{n_{i.}} - \sum_j \frac{n_{.j}^2}{n_{..}} \right)$$

$$c_{bb} = \frac{1}{q-1} \left(n_{..} - \sum_j \frac{n_{.j}^2}{n_{..}} \right) \qquad c_{ba} = \frac{1}{q-1} \left(\sum_{i,j} \frac{n_{ij}^2}{n_{.j}} - \sum_i \frac{n_{i.}^2}{n_{..}} \right)$$

$$c_{eb} = \frac{1}{n_{..} - p - q + 1} \left(\sum_j \frac{n_{.j}^2}{n_{..}} - \sum_{i,j} \frac{n_{ij}^2}{n_{i.}} \right)$$

$$c_{ea} = \frac{1}{n_{..} - p - q + 1} \left(\sum_i \frac{n_{i.}^2}{n_{..}} - \sum_{i,j} \frac{n_{ij}^2}{n_{.j}} \right)$$

sampling distribution of the F statistic when the hypothesis being tested is not true is a multiple of the F distribution. The multiple is the ratio of the expected values of the mean squares of the numerator and denominator of the observed F statistic. For example, the statistic

$$\frac{MS_a}{MS_{ab}} \quad \text{is distributed as} \quad cF[p-1, (p-1)(q-1)],$$

where
$$c = \frac{\sigma_\varepsilon^2 + n\sigma_{\alpha\beta}^2 + nq\sigma_\alpha^2}{\sigma_\varepsilon^2 + n\sigma_{\alpha\beta}^2} = 1 + \frac{nq\sigma_\alpha^2}{\sigma_\varepsilon^2 + n\sigma_{\alpha\beta}^2}.$$

Under the hypothesis that $\sigma_\alpha^2 = 0$, then $c = 1$; under the hypothesis that $\sigma_\alpha^2 > 0$, then $c > 1$.

In general, there are no problems associated with generalizing to more complex Model II designs other than being able to estimate the expected values of relevant mean squares. It is well to keep in mind, however, that the power associated with Model II studies may be significantly smaller than for studies in which all factors are fixed. Further, when factors are random power depends upon sample size *and* the number of levels of the factors which are sampled.

Mixed Models

In general, when larger designs contain both fixed and random factors, it may be difficult to estimate power for certain effects (Koele, 1982). Recall from earlier discussions that in mixed-model designs, main effects of random factors are tested with MS_{error}, but main effects of fixed factors are tested with a MS in the denominator which involves interaction with a random variable. For example, if factor A is fixed and B is random, to test the hypothesis $\sigma_\alpha^2 = 0$,

$$F = \frac{MS_a}{MS_{ab}}.$$

This ratio does not follow an F distribution and treating this F statistic as if it has the central F distribution when the hypothesis being tested is true requires a set of highly restrictive assumptions about the covariance structure of the parameters in the model. Evaluation of power in this case involves the use of the noncentral F distribution. Monte Carlo studies as well as randomization tests indicate that treating the F ratio suggested by the E(MS) as if it does have an F distribution results in a good approximation to these tests, even though the homogeneity assumptions on the covariance structure may be violated. Koele (1982) points out that problems also arise when tests are made on interactions of fixed and random factors. He does not recommend computing power on those tests because of those problems.

5.22 EXERCISES

1. Consider the following numbers to represent *population* data wherein (unrealistically) $P = 2$, $Q = 2$, $N = 3$:

		b_1	b_2
	a_1	$X_{111} = 110$	$X_{121} = 95$
		$X_{112} = 109$	$X_{122} = 90$
		$X_{113} = 108$	$X_{123} = 85$
	a_2	$X_{211} = 88$	$X_{221} = 114$
		$X_{212} = 85$	$X_{222} = 118$
		$X_{213} = 82$	$X_{223} = 116$

Using these numbers, compute numerical values for:

(a) $X_{111} = \mu + \alpha_1 + \beta_1 + \alpha\beta_{11} + \varepsilon_{111}$.

(b)

	b_1	b_2
a_1	$\alpha\beta_{11}$	$\alpha\beta_{12}$
a_2	$\alpha\beta_{21}$	$\alpha\beta_{22}$

(c)

	b_1	b_2	
a_1	μ_{11}	μ_{12}	$\mu_{1.}$
a_2	μ_{21}	μ_{22}	$\mu_{2.}$
	$\mu_{.1}$	$\mu_{.2}$	$\mu_{..}$

(d) α_1, α_2, β_1, β_2, $\alpha_1(b_1)$, $\beta_1(a_1)$

(e) σ_α^2, σ_β^2, $\sigma_{\alpha\beta}^2$, σ_ε^2.

(f) $\sigma_{\alpha(b_1)}^2$

2. For each of the designs listed below, set up a table with the expected values of the mean squares for all factorial effects. Use numbers for p, q, r, n in those E(MS).

(a) Model I, 2×3 factorial, $n = 20$
   Model II, 2×3 factorial, $n = 20$
   Model III, 2×3 factorial, $n = 20$ (A random, B fixed).

(b) Model I, $2 \times 3 \times 4$ factorial, $n = 10$
   Model II, $2 \times 3 \times 4$ factorial, $n = 10$
   Model III, $2 \times 3 \times 4$ factorial, $n = 10$ (A and B random, C fixed).

3. How many are there?

(a) Two-factor interactions in a 4-factor factorial design?

(b) Three-factor interactions in a 5-factor factorial design?

(c) Two-factor interactions in a 5-factor factorial design wherein factors D and E are nested in levels of factor A.

4. Construct appropriate F ratios for each of the following situations by selecting an appropriate MS$_{\text{numerator}}$ and MS$_{\text{denominator}}$:

	Effect tested	Number of factors	Model	Other information
(a)	$H_0: \sigma_\alpha^2 = 0$	$p \times q$	I	
(b)	$H_0: \sigma_\beta^2 = 0$	$p \times q$	III (A fixed, B random)	
(c)	$H_0: \sigma_{\alpha\beta}^2 = 0$	$p \times q \times r$	III (A and B fixed, C random)	
(d)	$H_0: \sigma_{\alpha(b_1)}^2 = 0$	$p \times q \times r$	II	
(e)	$H_0: \sigma_\alpha^2 = 0$	$p \times q$	II	B nested in A
(f)	$H_0: \sigma_{\alpha\beta\gamma}^2 = 0$	$p \times q \times r$	I	

5. Draw graphs which geometrically represent each of the following outcomes of an experiment.

	Design	Effect	Effect size
(a)	2×3	A	>0
		B	0
		AB	>0
		B at a_1	>0
		B at a_2	>0
(b)	$2 \times 2 \times 2$	A	0
		B	0
		C	>0
		AB	0
		AC	0
		BC	0
		ABC	>0

6. Set up an F ratio to test each of the following comparison hypotheses with its specified design. Consider all tests to be *a priori* tests.

	Hypothesis	Design	Model
(a)	$H_0: \dfrac{\mu_{1.} + \mu_{2.}}{2} - \mu_{3.} = 0$	3×3 factorial	I
(b)	$H_0: \mu_{11} - \mu_{12} = 0$	2×3 factorial	II
(c)	$H_0: \mu_{11} - \mu_{22} = 0$	2×2 factorial	II

7. Match the coefficients to appropriate trends:

Trends	Coefficients				
Linear	2	-1	-2	-1	2
Quadratic	-1	2	0	-2	1
Cubic	1	-4	6	-4	1
Quartic	-2	-1	0	1	2

8. An experimenter was interested in evaluating clinical treatment procedures for different classes of patients who were located in different regions of the country. S(he) wanted to evaluate all three variables, but was quite sure there were no interactions involving geography and types of patients. There were two different classes of patients in each of three locations, and two different treatment types for each class of patients in each location.

(a) What does the design look like?

(b) What is the structural model?

(c) What are the expected values of all mean squares assuming all factors are fixed?

9. In an experiment involving the quality of judgments made in a decision task, the amount of information available for the decisions (factor A) was combined factorially with an academic achievement index of the subjects (factor B). Ten subjects were randomly selected and randomly assigned to each of the $2 \times 3 = 6$ treatment conditions. The summary data were:

Source of variation	SS	df	MS
A	100	1	100
B	204	2	102
AB	64	2	32
Within treatment	270	54	5
Total	640	59	

Consider both factors A and B fixed and
(a) Compute:

$$\hat{\omega}_\alpha^2 \quad \hat{\phi}_\alpha$$
$$\hat{\omega}_\beta^2 \quad \hat{\phi}_\beta$$
$$\hat{\omega}_{\alpha\beta}^2 \quad \hat{\phi}_{\alpha\beta}$$

(b) Compute power for the tests of significance on the hypotheses $\sigma_\alpha^2 = 0$, $\sigma_\beta^2 = 0$, and $\sigma_{\alpha\beta}^2 = 0$ ($\alpha = 0.05$).
(c) Compute power for all three tests assuming Model II ($\alpha = 0.05$).

CHAPTER 6

FACTORIAL EXPERIMENTS— COMPUTATIONAL PROCEDURES AND NUMERICAL EXAMPLES

6.1 GENERAL PURPOSE

In this chapter the principles discussed in Chapter 5 will be illustrated by numerical examples; detailed computational procedures will be given for a variety of factorial experiments. It should be noted that the formulas convenient for computational work are not necessarily those which are most directly interpretable. For purposes of interpretation the basic definitions given in Chapter 5 are the important sources for reference; however, in all cases the computational formulas are algebraically equivalent to the basic definitions. The algebraic proofs underlying this equivalence are not difficult. Factorial experiments in which there are repeated measures are discussed in Chapter 7.

6.2 $p \times q$ FACTORIAL EXPERIMENT HAVING n OBSERVATIONS PER CELL

The treatment combinations in this type of experiment are represented in the cells of the following table:

	b_1	b_2	$\cdots$	b_j	$\cdots$	b_q
a_1	ab_{11}	ab_{12}	$\cdots$	ab_{1j}	$\cdots$	ab_{1q}
a_2	ab_{21}	ab_{22}	$\cdots$	ab_{2j}	$\cdots$	ab_{2q}
$\vdots$	$\vdots$	$\vdots$		$\vdots$		$\vdots$
a_i	ab_{i1}	ab_{i2}	$\cdots$	ab_{ij}	$\cdots$	ab_{iq}
$\vdots$	$\vdots$	$\vdots$		$\vdots$		$\vdots$
a_p	ab_{p1}	ab_{p2}	$\cdots$	ab_{pj}	$\cdots$	ab_{pq}

The cell in row a_i and column b_j corresponds to that part of the experiment in which treatment a_i is used in combination with b_j to yield the treatment combination ab_{ij}. The first subscript in this notation system refers to the level of factor A, the second subscript to the level of factor B.

Within each cell of the experiment there are n observations. The observations made under treatment combination ab_{ij} may be symbolized as follows:

$$b_j$$

$$a_i \quad \boxed{X_{ij1} \quad X_{ij2} \quad \cdots \quad X_{ijk} \quad \cdots \quad X_{ijn}}$$

The symbol X_{ij1} denotes a measurement on the first element in this cell. The symbol X_{ij2} denotes a measurement on the second element in this cell. The measurement on element k is denoted by the symbol X_{ijk}. The subscript k assumes the values $1, 2, \ldots, n$ within each of the cells. The sum of the n observations within cell ab_{ij} will be denoted by the symbol AB_{ij}; thus,

$$AB_{ij} = \sum_k X_{ijk}.$$

The following table summarizes the notation that will be used for sums of basic measurements:

	b_1	b_2	$\cdots$	b_j	$\cdots$	b_q	Row sum $= \sum_j$
a_1	AB_{11}	AB_{12}	$\cdots$	AB_{1j}	$\cdots$	AB_{1q}	$A_1 = \sum AB_{1j}$
a_2	AB_{21}	AB_{22}	$\cdots$	AB_{2j}	$\cdots$	AB_{2q}	A_2
$\vdots$	$\vdots$	$\vdots$		$\vdots$		$\vdots$	$\vdots$
a_i	AB_{i1}	AB_{i2}	$\cdots$	AB_{ij}	$\cdots$	AB_{iq}	A_i
$\vdots$	$\vdots$	$\vdots$		$\vdots$		$\vdots$	$\vdots$
a_p	AB_{p1}	AB_{p2}	$\cdots$	AB_{pj}	$\cdots$	AB_{pq}	A_p
Column sum	B_1	B_2	$\cdots$	B_j	$\cdots$	B_q	G

The sum of the nq measurements in row i, that is, the sum of all measurements made at level a_i, is denoted by the symbol A_i. Thus,

$$A_i = \sum_j AB_{ij} = \sum_j \sum_k X_{ijk}.$$

The double summation symbol $\sum_j \sum_k$ indicates that one sums within each cell as well as across all cells in row i. (Summing over the subscripts j and k is equivalent to summing over all observations within a given row.) The sum of the np measurements in column j, that is, the sum of all measurements made under level b_j, is denoted by the symbol B_j. Thus,

$$B_j = \sum_i AB_{ij} = \sum_i \sum_k X_{ijk}.$$

The grand total of all measurements is denoted by the symbol G. Thus,

$$G = \sum_i A_i = \sum_j B_j = \sum_i \sum_j AB_{ij} = \sum_i \sum_j \sum_k X_{ijk}.$$

The mean of all measurements under treatment combination ab_{ij} is

$$\overline{AB}_{ij} = \frac{AB_{ij}}{n}.$$

The mean of all measurements at level a_i is

$$\bar{A}_i = \frac{A_i}{nq}.$$

The mean of all measurements at level b_j is

$$\bar{B}_j = \frac{B_j}{np}.$$

The grand mean of all observations in the experiment is

$$\bar{G} = \frac{G}{npq}.$$

To summarize the notation, a capital letter with a subscript ijk represents an individual observation; a pair of capital letters with the subscript ij represents the sum over the n observations represented by the subscript k. A capital letter with the subscript i represents the sum of nq observations within a row of the experimental plan; a capital letter with the subscript j represents the sum of the np observations within a column of the experimental plan. A widely used equivalent notation system is summarized below:

Notation	Equivalent notation
X_{ijk}	X_{ijk}
AB_{ij}	$X_{ij.}$
A_i	$X_{i..}$
B_j	$X_{.j.}$
G	$X_{...}$

In the equivalent notation system, the periods indicate the subscript over which the summation has been made.

An alternative notation system for the levels of the factors and the combinations of the levels is the following:

$$
\begin{array}{llllll}
A: & a_1 & a_2 & \cdots & a_i & \cdots & a_I \\
B: & b_1 & b_1 & \cdots & b_j & \cdots & b_J \\
AB: & ab_{11} & ab_{12} & \cdots & ab_{ij} & \cdots & ab_{IJ}
\end{array}
$$

Thus $i = 1, \ldots, I$ and $j = 1, \ldots, J$.

In this notation system, the number of levels of factor A in the experiment is I, and no distinction is made between the number of levels of factor A in the experiment and the number of levels of A in the population of levels.

In some notation systems, an individual observation is denoted by Y_{ijk}, and the observations within cell ab_{ij} takes the form

$$b_j$$

$$a_i \quad \boxed{Y_{ijl} \quad Y_{ij2} \quad \cdots \quad Y_{ijk} \quad \cdots \quad Y_{ijn_{ij}}}$$

where n_{ij} is the number of observations in cell ab_{ij}. For the case of equal cell frequencies

$$n_{ij} = n \quad \text{for all } i, j.$$

Definition of computational symbols

In order to simplify the writing of the computational formulas for the sums of squares needed in the analysis of variance, it is convenient to introduce a set of computational symbols. The symbols appropriate for a $p \times q$ factorial experiment having n observations per cell are defined in Table 6.1. The computational procedures for this case are more elaborate than they need be, but the procedures to be developed here can be readily extended to more complex experimental plans in which they are not more elaborate than they need be.

In using the summation notation, where the index of summation is not indicated it will be understood that the summation is over all possible

TABLE 6.1 **Definition of computational symbols**

(i)

$$(1) = G^2/npq \qquad (3) = \left(\sum A_i^2\right)\Big/nq$$

$$(2) = \sum X_{ijk}^2 \qquad (4) = \left(\sum B_j^2\right)\Big/np$$

$$(5) = \left[\sum (AB_{ij})^2\right]\Big/n$$

(ii)

Source of variation	Computational formula for SS
A	$SS_a = (3) - (1)$
B	$SS_b = (4) - (1)$
AB	$SS_{ab} = (5) - (3) - (4) + (1)$
Experimental error (within cell)	$SS_{error} = (2) - (5)$
Total	$SS_{total} = (2) - (1)$

subscripts. For example, the notation $\sum_i \sum_j \sum_k X_{ijk}^2$ will be abbreviated $\sum X_{ijk}^2$; similarly the notation $\sum_i \sum_j (AB_{ij})^2$ will be abbreviated $\sum (AB_{ij})^2$. Where the summation is restricted to a single level of one of the subscripts, the index of the summation will be indicated. Thus

$$\sum_i (AB_{ij})^2 = (AB_{1j})^2 + (AB_{2j})^2 + \cdots + (AB_{ij})^2 + \cdots + (AB_{pj})^2,$$

$$\sum_j (AB_{ij})^2 = (AB_{i1})^2 + (AB_{i2})^2 + \cdots + (AB_{ij})^2 + \cdots + (AB_{iq})^2.$$

In the definitions of the computational formulas given in part i of Table 6.1, the divisor in each case is the number of observations summed to obtain one of the terms that is squared. For example, n observations are summed to obtain an AB_{ij}. Hence the denominator n of the term $[\sum (AB_{ij})^2]/n$. There are nq observations summed to obtain an A_i. Hence the denominator nq in the term $(\sum A_i^2)/nq$.

An estimate of the variation due to the main effects of factor A is given by

$$SS_a = nq \sum (\bar{A}_i - \bar{G})^2.$$

This is not a convenient computational formula for this source of variation. An algebraically equivalent form is

$$SS_a = \frac{\sum A_i^2}{nq} - \frac{G^2}{npq} = (3) - (1).$$

The other sources of variation in the analysis of variance are as follows:

$$SS_b = np \sum (\bar{B}_j - \bar{G})^2 \qquad = (4) - (1),$$

$$SS_{ab} = n \left(\sum \overline{AB}_{ij} - \bar{A}_i - \bar{B}_j + \bar{G} \right)^2 = (5) - (3) - (4) + (1),$$

$$SS_{w. \text{ cell}} = \sum (X_{ijk} - \overline{AB}_{ij})^2 \qquad = (2) - (5),$$

$$SS_{\text{total}} = \sum (X_{ijk} - \bar{G})^2 \qquad = (2) - (1).$$

These computational formulas are summarized in part ii of Table 6.1.

Should the interaction term in the analysis of variance prove to be statistically significant, it is generally desirable to analyze the simple main effects rather than the overall main effects. Computational symbols for variation due to simple main effects are summarized in Table 6.2. By definition

TABLE 6.2 **Definition of computational symbols for simple effects**

(i)

$(3a_1) = A_1^2/nq$	$(4b_1) = B_1^2/np$
$(3a_2) = A_2^2/nq$	$(4b_2) = B_2^2/np$
$\cdots$	$\cdots$
$(3a_p) = A_p^2/nq$	$(4b_q) = B_q^2/np$
$(3) = (\sum A_i^2)/n)$	$(4) = (\sum B_j^2)/np$

$(5a_1) = \left[\sum_j (AB_{1j})^2\right]\Big/n$	$(5b_1) = \left[\sum_i (AB_{i1})^2\right]\Big/n$
$(5a_2) = \left[\sum_j (AB_{2j})^2\right]\Big/n$	$(5b_2) = \left[\sum_i (AB_{i2})^2\right]\Big/n$
$\cdots$	$\cdots$
$(5a_p) = \left[\sum_j (AB_{pj})^2\right]\Big/n$	$(5b_q) = \left[\sum_i (AB_{iq})^2\right]\Big/n$
$(5) = [\sum (AB_{ij})^2]/n$	$(5) = [\sum (AB_{ij})^2]/n$

(ii)

Source of variation	Computational formula for SS
Simple effects for A:	
For level b_1	$(5b_1) - (4b_1)$
For level b_2	$(5b_2) - (4b_2)$
$\cdots$	$\cdots$
For level b_q	$(5b_q) - (4b_q)$
Simple effects for B:	
For level a_1	$(5a_1) - (3a_1)$
For level a_2	$(5a_2) - (3a_2)$
$\cdots$	$\cdots$
For level a_p	$(5a_p) - (3a_p)$

the variation due to the simple main effect of factor A for level b_1 is

$$SS_{a \text{ for } b_1} = n \sum (\overline{AB}_{i1} - \bar{B}_1)^2$$

$$= \frac{\sum (AB_{i1})^2}{n} - \frac{B_1^2}{np} = (5b_1) - (4b_1).$$

By definition, the variation due to the simple main effect of factor B for level a_1 is

$$SS_{b \text{ for } a_1} = n \sum (\overline{AB}_{1j} - \bar{A}_1)^2$$

$$= \frac{\sum (AB_{1j}^2)^2}{n} - \frac{A_1^2}{nq} = (5a_1) - (3a_1).$$

Numerical Example

A numerical example of a 2×3 factorial experiment having three observations per cell will be used to illustrate the computational procedures. Suppose that an experimenter is interested in evaluating the relative effectiveness of three drugs (factor B) in bringing about behavioral changes in two categories, schizophrenics and depressives, of patients (factor A). What is considered to be a random sample of nine patients belonging to category a_1 (schizophrenics) is divided at random into three subgroups, with three patients in each subgroup. Each subgroup is then assigned to one of the drug conditions. An analogous procedure is followed for a random sample of nine patients belonging to category a_2 (depressives). Criterion ratings are made on each patient before and after the administration of the drugs. The numerical entries in part i of Table 6.3 represent the difference between the two ratings on each of the patients. (An analysis of covariance might be more appropriate for this plan; covariance analysis is discussed in Chapter 10.)

As a first step in the analysis, the AB summary table in part ii is

TABLE 6.3   Numerical example

Observed data:

(i)

	Drug b_1			Drug b_2			Drug b_3		
Category a_1	8	4	0	10	8	6	8	6	4
Category a_2	14	10	6	4	2	0	15	12	9

AB summary table:

(ii)

	b_1	b_2	b_3	Total
a_1	12	24	18	$54 = A_1$
a_2	30	6	36	$72 = A_2$
Total	42	30	54	$126 = G$
	B_1	B_2	B_3	

(iii)

$$(1) = (126)^2/18 = 882.00$$
$$(2) = (8^2 + 4^2 + 0^2 + \cdots + 15^2 + 12^2 + 9^2) = 1198$$
$$(3) = (54^2 + 72^2)/9 = 900.00$$
$$(4) = (42^2 + 30^2 + 54^2)/6 = 930.00$$
$$(5) = (12^2 + 24^2 + 18^2 + 30^2 + 6^2 + 36^2)/3 = 1092.00$$

(iv)

$$SS_a = (3) - (1) = 900.00 - 882.00 = 18.00$$
$$SS_b = (4) - (1) = 930.00 - 882.00 = 48.00$$
$$SS_{ab} = (5) - (3) - (4) + (1)$$
$$= 1092.00 - 900.00 - 930.00 + 882.00 = 144.00$$
$$SS_{w.\,cell} = (2) - (5) = 1198 - 1092.00 = 106.00$$

$$SS_{total} = (2) - (1) = 1198 - 882.00 = 316.00$$

TABLE 6.4 **Summary of analysis of variance**

Source of variation	SS	df	MS	F
A (category of patient)	18.00	1	18.00	2.04
B (drug)	48.00	2	24.00	2.72
AB	144.00	2	72.00	8.15
Within cell	106.00	12	8.83	
Total	316.00	17		

obtained. The entry in row a_1, column b_1 is

$$AB_{11} = 8 + 4 + 0 = 12.$$

The entry in row a_2, column b_3 is

$$AB_{23} = 15 + 12 + 9 = 36.$$

Data for all computational symbols except (2) are in part ii; computational symbol (2) is obtained from data in part i. The analysis of variance is summarized in Table 6.4.

The structure of the F ratios used in making tests depends upon the expected values of mean squares appropriate for the experimental data. If the categories and drugs are fixed factors, i.e., if inferences are to be made only with respect to the two categories of patients represented in the experiment and only with respect to the three drugs included in the experiment, then the appropriate expected values of the mean squares are given in Table 6.5. The structure of F ratios is determined in accordance with the principles given in Sec. 6.5.

If tests are made at the 0.05 level of significance, the critical value for the test of the hypothesis that the action of the drugs is independent of the category of patient (i.e., zero interaction) is $F_{0.95}(2, 12) = 3.89$. In this case $F_{obs} = 8.15$ exceeds the critical value. Hence, the experimental data do not support the hypothesis of zero interaction. The data indicate that the effect of a drug differs for the two types of patients—the effect of a drug depends upon the category of patient to which it is administered. Hence, analysis of simple main effects are required to further elucidate the nature of the overall outcome

TABLE 6.5 **Expected values for mean squares**

Source	MS	E(MS)	F
Main effect of A	MS_a	$\sigma_\varepsilon^2 + 9\sigma_\alpha^2$	$MS_a/MS_{\text{w. cell}}$
Main effect of B	MS_b	$\sigma_\varepsilon^2 + 6\sigma_\beta^2$	$MS_b/MS_{\text{w. cell}}$
AB interaction	MS_{ab}	$\sigma_\varepsilon^2 + 3\sigma_{\alpha\beta}^2$	$MS_{ab}/MS_{\text{w. cell}}$
Within cell	$MS_{\text{w. cell}}$	σ_ε^2	

of the experiment. First, however, it is well to examine the strength of association between the various treatment effects and the dependent variable and to determine the statistical power of the test of significance.

The degree of association between treatment effects and the dependent variable may be assessed using omega squared (see Sec. 5.21).

$$\hat{\omega}_\alpha^2 = \frac{SS_a - (p-1)(MS_{error})}{SS_{total} + MS_{error}}$$

$$= \frac{18 - (1)(8.83)}{316 + 8.83} = \frac{9.17}{324.83} = 0.0282,$$

$$\hat{\omega}_\beta^2 = \frac{SS_b - (q-1)(MS_{error})}{SS_{total} + MS_{error}}$$

$$= \frac{48 + (2)(8.83)}{316 + 8.83} = \frac{65.66}{324.83} = 0.2021,$$

$$\hat{\omega}_{\alpha\beta}^2 = \frac{SS_{ab} - (p-1)(q-1)(MS_{error})}{SS_{total} + MS_{error}}$$

$$= \frac{144 + (2)(8.83)}{316 + 8.83} = \frac{161.66}{324.83} = 0.4977,$$

and
$$\hat{\omega}_{all\ effects}^2 = 0.0282 + 0.2021 + 0.4977 = 0.7280.$$

The overall conclusion is that one may account for 72.8 percent of the total variance through treatment effects and 27.2 percent from error variance. Of this total, 2.82, 20.21, and 49.77 percent are due to A, B, and AB effects, respectively. When interpreting these numbers, it is well to keep in mind that they are products of the particular spacing of the means and the selection of the particular levels of factors A and B included in the study.

To compute power for the test of significance of the main effects of factor A, from Sec. 5.21, one has

$$\hat{\phi}_\alpha = \sqrt{\frac{nq \sum \hat{\alpha}_i^2/p}{\hat{\sigma}_\varepsilon^2}}.$$

The expected values of the mean squares for $MS_{within\ cell}$ and MS_a are:

$$E(MS_{within\ cell}) = \sigma_\varepsilon^2$$

$$E(MS_a) = \sigma_\varepsilon^2 + nq \sum \alpha_i^2/p - 1.$$

Hence, an unbiased estimate of $\sum \alpha_i^2$ is provided by

$$\sum \hat{\alpha}_i^2 = \frac{p-1}{nq}(MS_a - MS_{within\ cell})$$

$$= \frac{1}{(3)(3)}(18.00 - 8,83)$$

$$= 1.0189.$$

The estimated noncentrality parameter is:

$$\hat{\lambda} = \frac{nq \sum \hat{\alpha}_i^2}{\hat{\sigma}_\varepsilon^2} = \frac{(9)(1.0189)}{8.83} = 1.04.$$

Hence, the power of the test is computed in terms of the noncentral F distribution as:

$$\text{Probability } \{F > F_{1-\alpha}[p - 1, pq(n - 1); \lambda]\}.$$

Table E.14 displays power in terms of

$$\hat{\phi}_\alpha = \sqrt{\frac{\lambda_\alpha}{\rho}} = \sqrt{\frac{nq \sum \hat{\alpha}_i^2/\rho}{\hat{\sigma}_\varepsilon^2}},$$

$$\hat{\phi}_\alpha = \sqrt{\frac{1.04}{2}} = 0.72,$$

given values of α and the degrees of freedom of the F statistic. With $\alpha = 0.05$, $df_{numerator} = 1$, $df_{denominator} = 12$, and $\hat{\phi} = 0.72$, one notes that the power lies between 0.10 and 0.26. By linear interpolation, power is estimated to be 0.17. This value is very small but is to be expected with small treatment effects and sample sizes. Even if the sample size were set at ∞, the power would still be very small. Alternatively, with this sample size, ϕ would have to be tripled to reach a power level of approximately 0.80.

For the test of significance of the β main effects,

$$\sum \hat{\beta}_j^2 = \frac{q - 1}{np} (MS_b - MS_{within cell})$$

$$= \frac{2}{(3)(2)} (24.00 - 8.83)$$

$$= 5.06,$$

and

$$\hat{\phi}_\beta = \sqrt{\frac{\hat{\lambda}_\beta}{q}} = \sqrt{\frac{np \sum \hat{\beta}_j^2/q}{\hat{\sigma}_\varepsilon^2}}$$

$$= \sqrt{\frac{(3)(2)(5.06)/3}{8.83}}$$

$$= 1.07.$$

Referring to Table E.14 with $\alpha = 0.05$, $df_{numerator} = 2$, and $df_{numerator} = 12$, the power is estimated to be between 0.26 and 0.36. Were the experimenter to increase the sample size with ϕ equal to 1.07, there would be very little increase in power.

The power of the test on the interactions may be estimated using the relation

$$\hat{\phi}_{\alpha\beta} = \sqrt{\frac{n \sum \sum \hat{\alpha}\beta_{ij}^2/[(p - 1)(q - 1) + 1]}{\hat{\sigma}_\varepsilon^2}}.$$

Since

$$\sum \sum \hat{\alpha}\beta_{ij}^2 = \frac{(p-1)(q-1)}{n}(MS_{ab} - MS_{\text{within cell}})$$

$$= \tfrac{2}{3}(72.00 - 8.83)$$

$$= 42.11,$$

then,

$$\hat{\phi}_{\alpha\beta} = \sqrt{\frac{(3)(42.11)/3}{8.83}} = 2.18.$$

Entering Table E.14 with this value of ϕ, $\alpha = 0.05$, $df_{\text{numerator}} = 2$, and $df_{\text{denominator}} = 12$, power is approximately 0.86.

From these total results, one concludes that the experimenter had little chance of detecting significant main effects in this study because the main effects are very small. For any given effect size, tests on interactions are expected to have less power (because n is smaller than nq or np). In this instance, because interaction effects are large, the power level is reasonable for that test.

A significant interaction indicates that a given drug has different effects for one category of patient compared to a second category. The nature of the interaction effects is indicated by inspecting the cell means. These means are given below:

	Drug 1	Drug 2	Drug 3
Category 1	4	8	6
Category 2	10	2	12

A geometric representation of these means is given in Fig. 6-1. This figure represents the profiles corresponding to the simple effects of the drugs (factor B) for each of the categories (factor A). A test for the presence of interaction is equivalent to a test on the difference in the shapes of the profiles of these simple effects. An equivalent geometric representation of the table of means is given in Fig. 6-2. This figure represents the profiles corresponding to the simple effects of the categories for each of the drugs. The profile for drug 2 appears to have a slope which is different from the slopes of the profiles for the other drugs. As an aid in the interpretation of interactions, geometric representation of the profiles corresponding to the means is generally of considerable value.

Tests on differences between means within the same profile are given by tests on simple effects. Computational procedures for obtaining the variation due to simple effects are summarized in Table 6.6. Data from which the symbols in part ii are obtained are given in part i; the latter is the AB summary of Table 6.3.

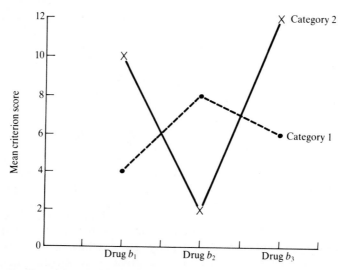

FIGURE 6-1   Profiles of simple effects for drugs.

The analysis of variance for the simple effects of the drugs for each of the categories is summarized in Table 6.7. The structure of the F ratios for simple effects is dependent upon appropriate expected values for the mean squares. Assuming that factors A and B are fixed factors, expected values for the mean squares of simple effects are given in Table 6.8. It should be noted, in terms of the general linear model, that a simple main effect is actually a sum of an

FIGURE 6-2   Profiles of simple effects for categories.

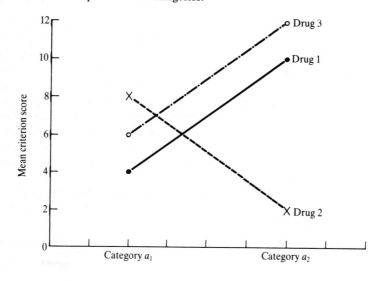

TABLE 6.6   Computation of simple effects

AB summary table:

(i)

	b_1	b_2	b_3	Total
a_1	12	24	18	54
a_2	30	6	36	72
Total	42	30	54	126

$(3a_1) = (54^2)/9 = 324.00$ $(4b_1) = (42^2)/6 = 294.00$
$(3a_2) = (72^2)/9 = 576.00$ $(4b_2) = (30^2)/6 = 150.00$
                                 $(4b_3) = (54^2)/6 = 486.00$

(ii)

$(3) = \qquad 900.00$ $(4) = \qquad 930.00$
$(5a_1) = (12^2 + 24^2 + 18^2)/3 = 348.00$ $(5b_1) = (12^2 + 30^2)/3 = 348.00$
$(5a_2) = (30^2 + 6^2 + 36^2)/3 = 744.00$ $(5b_2) = (24^2 + 6^2)/3 = 204.00$
                                                         $(5b_3) = (18^2 + 36^2)/3 = 540.00$

$(5) = \qquad 1092.00$ $(5) = \qquad 1092.00$

Simple effects of A:
    For level b_1 $SS_{a \text{ for } b_1} = (5b_1) - (4b_1) = 54.00$
    For level b_2 $SS_{a \text{ for } b_2} = (5b_2) - (4b_2) = 54.00$
    For level b_3 $SS_{a \text{ for } b_3} = (5b_3) - (4b_3) = 54.00$

                                162.00

(iii)   Simple effects of B:
    For level a_1 $SS_{b \text{ for } a_1} = (5a_1) - (3a_1) = 24.00$
    For level a_2 $SS_{b \text{ for } a_2} = (5a_2) - (3a_2) = 168.00$

                                192.00

Check: $SS_a + SS_{ab} = \sum SS_{a \text{ for } b_j}$ Check: $SS_b + SS_{ab} = \sum SS_{b \text{ for } a_i}$

$18.00 + 144.00 = 162.00$ $48.00 + 144.00 = 192.00$

TABLE 6.7   Analysis of variance for simple effects

Source of variation	SS	df	MS	F
B for a_1 (drugs for category a_1)	24.00	2	12.00	1.36
B for a_2 (drugs for category a_2)	168.00	2	84.00	9.51
Within cell	106.00	12	8.83	

TABLE 6.8 **Expected values for mean squares of simple effects**

Source of variation	E(MS)
Simple effects of factor A:	
For level b_1	$\sigma_\varepsilon^2 + 3\sigma_{\alpha \text{ for } b_1}^2$
For level b_2	$\sigma_\varepsilon^2 + 3\sigma_{\alpha \text{ for } b_2}^2$
For level b_3	$\sigma_\varepsilon^2 + 3\sigma_{\alpha \text{ for } b_3}^2$
Simple effects for factor B:	
For level a_1	$\sigma_\varepsilon^2 + 3\sigma_{\beta \text{ for } a_1}^2$
For level a_2	$\sigma_\varepsilon^2 + 3\sigma_{\beta \text{ for } a_2}^2$

overall main effect and an interaction. For example,

$$\overline{AB}_{ij} - \overline{B}_j \qquad \text{estimates} \qquad \alpha_i + \alpha\beta_{ij} = \alpha_i \text{ for } b_j.$$

A test on the simple effect of factor A for level b_j is equivalent to a test that $\sigma_{\alpha \text{ for } b_j}^2 = 0$. The appropriate F ratio for this test would have an estimate of σ_ε^2 as denominator; the latter estimate is given by $MS_{\text{w. cell}}$.

By using the 0.05 level of significance for the data in Table 6.7, the critical value for an F ratio is $F_{0.95}(2, 12) = 3.89$. The experimental data indicate that there are differences between the drugs for category a_2 ($F_{\text{obs}} = 9.51$). Inspection of the profile of the drugs for category a_2 in Fig. 6-2 indicates that the effect of drug b_2 is different from the effects of the other drugs.

Returning to the analysis in Table 6.4, neither of the main effects is statistically significant. However, in the presence of interaction, inferences made with respect to main effects must be interpreted with caution. The data indicate that the main effects due to drugs do not differ. However, this does not mean that the drugs are equally effective for each of the categories considered separately. Because of the significant interaction effect, conclusions with respect to main effects due to drugs cannot be applied separately to each of the categories.

The drugs are differentially effective only when one considers comparisons within each of the categories separately. It must be noted and emphasized that statistical inference is a tool to help the experimenter in drawing scientifically meaningful conclusions from his experiment. Too frequently the tool is allowed to become the master rather than the servant. The primary objective of the experiment should determine which tests are to be made and which tests are to be avoided for lack of meaning. Statistical elegance does not necessarily imply scientifically meaningful inferences.

INDIVIDUAL COMPARISONS. To make comparisons among means, the procedures given in Secs. 3.10, 3.11 and 5.10 may be used.

As one simple example, to test the hypothesis that drugs 1 and 2 are equally effective for category 2, one may use the following statistic (data from the last numerical example will be used for illustrative purposes):

$$F = \frac{n(\overline{AB}_{21} - \overline{AB}_{22})^2}{2MS_{\text{w. cell}}} = \frac{(AB_{21} - AB_{22})^2}{2nMS_{\text{w. cell}}} = \frac{(30 - 6)^2}{6(8.83)} = 10.87.$$

For a 0.05-level test, the critical value is $F_{0.95}(1, 12) = 4.75$. Hence the hypothesis that $\mu_{21} = \mu_{22}$ is not supported by the experimental data. Using this test with a level of significance set at 0.05 assumes that an *a priori* test was appropriate. If this same test were carried out as "data snooping" on a purely *post mortem* basis, it would be appropriate to use the Scheffé procedure. That is, the decision rule would be to reject the null hypothesis if

$$F_{\text{obs}} > (q - 1)F_{0.95}[q - 1, pq(n - 1)]$$

$$> (2)F_{0.95}(2, 12) = (2)(3.89) = 7.78.$$

Thus, if this test is made as a *post hoc* comparison, one still concludes that the difference is significant at the 0.05 level of significance.

It is often reasonable to want to test differences between all possible pairs of means in a *logical grouping* of means. A logical grouping of means could be any set of means of interest because of theory or because of the outcome of previous analyses. The logical grouping may involve main effects, simple main effects, or interactions, and any of the techniques for controlling error rates may be applied. For example, suppose that it is desired to test differences between all possible means for levels of factor B for category a_2. The Newman–Keuls procedure could be applied to that problem and is illustrated here for the numerical example. The procedure for such multiple comparisons is outlined in Table 6.9.

In part i the means to be compared are first arranged in rank order, from low to high. Then differences between all possible pairs which give a positive value are obtained. An estimate of the standard error of a single mean is computed in part ii. This estimate is based upon data in all cells in the experiment, not just those from which the means are obtained. (If there is any real question about homogeneity of variance, only cells from which the means

TABLE 6.9   **Comparisons between means for category a_2**

	$\overline{AB}_{22}$	$\overline{AB}_{21}$	$\overline{AB}_{23}$		Critical
Ordered means:	2	10	12	r	value
(i)	2 —	8*	10* ----- 3 -----		6.45
	10	—	2 ----- 2 -----		5.27

(ii) $s_{\overline{AB}} = \sqrt{MS_{\text{w. cell}}/n} = \sqrt{8.83/3} = 1.71$

	r:	2	3
(iii)	$q_{0.95}(r, 12)$:	3.08	3.77
	Critical value $= s_{\overline{AB}}q_{0.95}(r, 12)$:	5.27	6.45

are obtained may be used in estimating the standard error of a mean.) If the within-cell variance from all cells in the experiment is used, degrees of freedom for $s_{\overline{AB}}$ are $pq(n-1)$, which in this case is equal to 12.

To obtain critical values for a 0.05-level test, one first obtains values of the $q_{0.95}(r, 12)$ statistic, where 12 is the degrees of freedom for $s_{\overline{AB}}$ and r is the number of steps two means are apart in an ordered sequence. These values are obtained from tables of the q statistic in Table D.4. The actual critical values are $s_{\overline{AB}}q_{0.95}(r, 12)$. For example, the difference

$$\overline{AB}_{23} - \overline{AB}_{22} = 10.$$

These are three steps apart in the ordered sequence ($r = 3$); hence the critical value is 6.45. The difference

$$\overline{AB}_{23} - \overline{AB}_{21} = 2,$$

for which $r = 2$, has the critical value 5.27. Tests of this kind must be made in a sequence which is specified in Sec. 3.11.

From the outcome of the tests in part iii one concludes that, for category a_2, drugs 1 and 3 differ from drug 2, but there is no statistically significant difference (on the criterion used) between drugs 1 and 3. The differences evaluated in this numerical example involve simple main effects, thus main effects of drugs plus the interaction between drugs and patient categories are analyzed.

As another example, one may want to analyze the significant AB interaction. In the analysis of variance summary table, Table 6.4, one sees that there are 144 units of variation associated with the 2 interaction degrees of freedom. It is possible to partition this variation into orthogonal components by evaluating treatment-contrast interactions as discussed in Sec. 5.10.

It may be logical to want to compare the two types of patients separately for each drug. In terms of main effects, the comparison of interest is

$$C_{\bar{A}} = \sum c_i \bar{A}_i = (1)\bar{A}_1 + (-1)\bar{A}_2 = \bar{A}_1 - \bar{A}_2.$$

The question of interest is whether this particular comparison (and since there are only two levels of factor A, the only comparison) between levels of factor A interacts with levels of factor B. To evaluate this notion, one computes the comparison for each level of factor B:

$$C_{\bar{A}(b_1)} = \sum c_i \overline{AB}_{i1} = \overline{AB}_{11} - \overline{AB}_{21} = 4 - 10 = -6$$

$$C_{\bar{A}(b_2)} = \sum c_i \overline{AB}_{i2} = \overline{AB}_{12} - \overline{AB}_{22} = 8 - 2 = 6$$

$$C_{\bar{A}(b_3)} = \sum c_i \overline{AB}_{i3} = \overline{AB}_{13} - \overline{AB}_{23} = 6 - 12 = -6.$$

Are these comparisons different? That is, do they interact? The variation among the comparisons is

$$SS_{C_{\bar{A}(bj)}} = n\left[\sum_j C^2_{\bar{A}(b_j)} - \left(\sum_j C^2_{\bar{A}(b_j)}\right)^2 \Big/ q\right]\Big/ \sum_i c_i^2$$

$$= 3\left[(-6^2) + (6^2) + (-6)^2 - \frac{(-6)^2}{3}\right]\Big/[1^2 + (-1)^2]$$

$$= 144.$$

Note that the variation due to the comparisons between the $\bar{A}$'s, 144, is equal to SS_{AB} and has $q - 1 = (p - 1)(q - 1) = 2$ degrees of freedom. If there were more levels of factor A, then there would be more mutually orthogonal comparisons (in general, $p - 1$), the variation of each set of which would sum to SS_{AB}. In order to evaluate the hypothesis that there are no treatment-contrast interactions, the statistic

$$F = \frac{SS_{A_{\bar{A}(b_j)}}/q - 1}{MS_{w. \text{ cell}}} = F[(q - 1), pq(n - 1)]$$

may be used. Numerically,

$$F = \frac{144/2}{8.83} = 4.08$$

may be compared to $\qquad F_{0.95}(2, 12) = 3.89.$

Thus, one concludes that there are interactions (as was already known) due to this single contrast; the test is identical to the test on the overall interaction because there are only two A means.

To make this example more complex, it may be instructive to look at it from the point of view of comparing B means. Since there are three levels of factor B, the experimenter can define two (in general, $q - 1$) orthogonal contrasts among the B means. The experimenter is interested in knowing whether drugs 1 and 2 differ. He is also interested in knowing whether the mean for drugs 1 and 2 is different from the mean for drug 3. Hence, stated in terms of B main effects, there are two orthogonal contrasts:

$$C_B^{(1)} = \sum c_{1j}\bar{B}_j = (1)\bar{B}_1 + (-1)\bar{B}_2 + (0)\bar{B}_3$$

$$C_B^{(2)} = \sum c_{2j}\bar{B}_j = (\tfrac{1}{2})\bar{B}_1 + (\tfrac{1}{2})\bar{B}_2 + (-1)\bar{B}_3.$$

Note that $\sum c_{1j}c_{2j} = 0$, meaning the two contrasts are orthogonal.

Looking at these contrasts separately for each level of factor B, one has for the first comparison:

$$C_{\bar{B}(a_1)}^{(1)} = \sum c_{1j}\overline{AB}_{1j} = (1)4 + (-1)8 + (0)6 = -4$$

$$C_{\bar{B}(a_2)}^{(1)} = \sum c_{1j}\overline{AB}_{2j} = (1)10 + (-1)2 + (0)6 = 8.$$

The variation due to treatment-contrast interaction is

$$SS_{C_{B(a_i)}^{(1)}} = n\left[\sum_i C_{\bar{B}(a_i)}^2 - \left(\sum C_{\bar{B}(a_i)}\right)^2 \Big/ p\right]\Big/ \sum_j c_{1j}^2$$

$$= 3\left[(-4)^2 + (8)^2 - \frac{(4)^2}{2}\right]\Big/[(1)^2 + (-1)^2] = 108.$$

For the second comparison

$$C_{\bar{B}(a_1)}^{(2)} = \sum c_{2j}\overline{AB}_{1j} = (\tfrac{1}{2})4 + (\tfrac{1}{2})8 + (-1)6 = 0$$

$$C_{\bar{B}(a_2)}^{(2)} = \sum c_{2j}\overline{AB}_{2j} = (\tfrac{1}{2})10 + (\tfrac{1}{2})2 + (-1)12 = -6,$$

and the variation is

$$SS_{C_{\bar{B}(a_i)}^{(2)}} = 3[(0)^2 + (-6)^2 - (-6)^2/2]/[(\tfrac{1}{2})^2 + (\tfrac{1}{2})^2 + (-1)^2]$$
$$= 36.$$

Note, then, that

$$SS_{C_{B(a_i)}^{(1)}} + SS_{C_{B(a_i)}^{(2)}} = 108 + 36 = 144 = SS_{AB}.$$

That is, the overall interaction variation SS_{AB} has been partitioned into two orthogonal components, each component measuring the interactions of a particular comparison. It appears that the difference between drugs 1 and 2 interacts much more with patient types than does the second comparison.

Tests of significance for the two sources of interaction are

$$F = \frac{SS_{C_{\bar{B}(a_i)}}/p - 1}{MS_{\text{w. cell}}}.$$

For the first comparison,

$$F = \frac{108/1}{8.83} = 12.23;$$

for the second comparison,

$$F = \frac{36/1}{8.83} = 4.08.$$

What critical value one wishes to use to evaluate these observed statistics depends upon how type 1 error is to be controlled. As *a priori* comparisons, it is appropriate to use

$$F_{1-\alpha}[(p-1), pq(n-1)]$$

for the comparison. Thus, $F_{0.95}(1, 12) = 4.75$, and both hypotheses are rejected. If these contrasts are considered to be pure data snooping, appropriate, but highly conservative, control would be gained from a Scheffé

F. An alternative view is one in which the experimenter considers the appropriate error rate for all tests (in this case, 2) considered as a set to be the one used for the family of which they are a part. Thus, since the *AB* interaction was the variation partitioned and since it was tested at $\alpha = 0.05$, one can hold the set of two tests at this level using the Dunn–Bonferroni procedure. The appropriate statistic in general would be

$$F_{1-(\alpha/q-1)}[(p-1), pq(n-1)]$$

for the set of tests on *B* treatment contrast interactions computed at each level of factor *A*. Specific to this example, the critical value for an 0.05 level test is

$$F_{1-(0.05/2)}(1, 12) = F_{0.975}(1, 12) = 7.18.$$

By this criterion, only the first hypothesis is rejected, the criterion being that the level of significance for the set of 2 tests is 0.05.

TEST FOR HOMOGENEITY OF VARIANCE. A rough but simple check may be made on the assumption of homogeneity of variance through the use of the $F_{\max}$ statistic. Apart from the use of this statistic, the variances of the individual cells should be inspected for any kind of systematic pattern between treatments and variances. In cases having a relatively large number of observations within each cell, within-cell distributions should also be inspected.

Use of the $F_{\max}$ test for homogeneity of variance will be illustrated for the data in part i of Table 6.3. For this purpose the within-cell variation for each of the cells is required. In the computational procedures given in Table 6.3, the pooled within-cell variation from all cells is computed. The variation within cell *ij* has the form

$$SS_{ij} = \sum_k (X_{ijk} - \overline{AB}_{ij})^2$$

$$= \sum X_{ijk}^2 - \frac{(AB_{ij})^2}{n}.$$

For example,

$$SS_{11} = (8^2 + 4^2 + 0^2) - \frac{(12)^2}{3}$$

$$= \quad 80 \qquad - 48 \quad = 32.$$

Similarly, the variation within cell ab_{21} is given by

$$SS_{21} = (14^2 + 10^2 + 6^2) - \frac{(30)^2}{3}$$

$$= \quad 332 \qquad - 300 \quad = 32.$$

The other within-cell sums of squares are

$$SS_{12} = 8, \qquad SS_{22} = 8, \qquad SS_{13} = 8, \qquad SS_{23} = 18.$$

As a check on the computational work,

$$\sum SS_{ij} = SS_{w.\ cell} = 106.$$

Since the number of observations in each cell is constant, the F_{max} statistic is given by

$$F_{max} = \frac{SS(\text{largest})}{SS(\text{smallest})} = \frac{32}{8} = 4.00.$$

The critical value for a 0.05-level test is $F_{0.95}(pq, n-1)$, which in this case is $F_{0.95}(6, 2) = 2.66$. Since the observed F_{max} statistic exceeds the critical value, the hypothesis of homogeneity of variance may not be considered tenable. In cases in which the assumptions of homogeneity of variance cannot be considered tenable, a transformation on the scale of measurement may provide data which are amenable to the assumptions underlying the analysis model.

Approximate F Tests When Cell Variances Are Heterogeneous

A procedure suggested by Box (1954, p. 300) may be adapted for use in testing simple effects for factor A, even though variances may be heterogeneous. The F ratio in this case has the form

$$F = \frac{MS_{a\ for\ b_j}}{MS_{error(b_j)}},$$

where $MS_{error\ (b_j)}$ is the pooled within-cell variance for all cells at level b_j. The approximate degrees of freedom for this F ratio are

$$1 \quad \text{for numerator,}$$
$$n - 1 \quad \text{for denominator.}$$

In testing simple effects for factor B at level a_i, the F ratio has the form

$$F = \frac{MS_{b\ for\ a_i}}{MS_{error\ (a_i)}},$$

where $MS_{error\ (a_i)}$ is the pooled within-cell variance for all cells at level a_i. The approximate degrees of freedom for this F ratio are $(1, n-1)$. In the usual test (assuming homogeneity of variance) the degrees of freedom for the F ratio are $[(q-1), pq(n-1)]$ if all cell variances are pooled and $[(q-1), q(n-1)]$ if only variances from cells at level a_i are pooled.

6.3 $p \times q$ FACTORIAL EXPERIMENT—UNEQUAL CELL FREQUENCIES

Computational procedures for an unweighted-means analysis will be described in this section. The conditions under which this kind of analysis is appropriate are given in Sec. 5.20. For illustrative purposes the computational procedures are cast in terms of a 2×4 factorial experiment; these procedures may, however, be generalized to any $p \times q$ factorial experiment. Computational procedures for the least-squares solution are given in Sec. 6.14.

Suppose that the levels of factor A represent two methods for calibrating dials and levels of factor B represent four levels of background illumination. The criterion measure is an accuracy score for a series of trials. The original experiment called for five observations per cell. However, because of conditions not related to the experimental variables, the completed experiment had three to five observations per cell. The observed criterion scores are given in part i of Table 6.10. Summary of within-cell information required in the analysis is given in part ii. The variation within cell ab_{11} is

$$SS_{11} = 110 - \frac{(20)^2}{4} = 10.00.$$

The harmonic mean of the cell frequencies is computed in part iii. The

TABLE 6.10 **Numerical example**

Observed data:

	b_1	b_2	b_3	b_4
a_1	3, 4, 6, 7	5, 6, 6, 7, 7	4, 6, 8, 8	8, 10, 10, 7, 11
a_2	2, 3, 4	3, 5, 6, 3	9, 12, 12, 8	9, 7, 12, 11

(i) above rows

Cell data:

		b_1	b_2	b_3	b_4
a_1	n_{ij}	4	5	4	5
	$\sum X$	20	31	26	46
	$\sum X^2$	110	195	180	434
	SS_{ij}	10.00	2.80	11.00	10.80
a_2	n_{ij}	3	4	4	4
	$\sum X$	9	17	41	39
	$\sum X^2$	29	79	433	395
	SS_{ij}	2.00	6.75	12.75	14.75

(ii)

(iii)

$$\tilde{n} = \frac{8}{0.25 + 0.20 + 0.25 + 0.20 + 0.33 + 0.25 + 0.25 + 0.25}$$

$$= 4.04$$

$$SS_{\text{w. cell}} = \sum \sum SS_{ij} = 10.00 + 2.80 + \cdots + 14.75 = 70.85$$

TABLE 6.11   **Numerical example (continued)**

Cell means:

	b_1	b_2	b_3	b_4	Total
a_1	5.00	6.20	6.50	9.20	26.90
a_2	3.00	4.25	10.25	9.75	27.25
Total	8.00	10.45	16.75	18.95	54.15

(i) (left of first two rows)

$$(1) = G^2/pq = (54.15)^2/8 \qquad\qquad = 366.53$$

$$(2) = \sum X^2 \text{ (see part ii, Table 6.10)}$$

(ii)

$$(3) = \left(\sum A_i^2\right)\Big/q = (26.90^2 + 27.25^2)/4 \qquad = 366.54$$

$$(4) = \left(\sum B_j^2\right)\Big/p = (8.00^2 + 10.45^2 + 16.75^2 + 18.95^2)/2 = 406.43$$

$$(5) = \sum (\overline{AB}_{ij})^2 = 5.00^2 + 6.20^2 + \cdots + 9.75^2 \qquad = 417.52$$

(iii)

$$\text{SS}_a = \tilde{n}[(3) - (1)] = 4.04[366.54 - 366.53] = \quad 0.04$$

$$\text{SS}_b = \tilde{n}[(4) - (1)] = 4.04[406.43 - 366.53] = 161.20$$

$$\text{SS}_{ab} = \tilde{n}[(5) - (3) - (4) + (1)] \qquad\qquad = 44.76$$

computational formula used is

$$\tilde{n} = \frac{pq}{\sum\sum (1/n_{ij})}.$$

The pooled within-cell variation is also computed in part iii.

The data in the cells of part i of Table 6.11 are means of the respective n_{ij} observations in the cells. All the computational symbols in part ii are based upon these means and row and column totals of these means. In defining the computational symbols in (ii), each of the cell means is considered as if it were a single observation. Computational formulas for the main effects and interaction are given in part iii. The analysis of variance is summarized in Table 6.12. The degrees of freedom for the within-cell variation are $\sum\sum n_{ij} - pq = 33 - 8 = 25$. If factors A and B are fixed, then $\text{MS}_{\text{w. cell}}$ is the proper denominator for all tests. By using the 0.05 level of significance, the critical value for the test on the interaction is $F_{0.95}(3, 25) = 2.99$. Since the observed F

TABLE 6.12   **Summary of analysis of variance**

Source of variation	SS	df	MS	F
A (method of calibration)	0.04	1	0.04	
B (background illumination)	161.20	3	53.73	18.99
AB	44.76	3	14.92	5.27
Within cell	70.85	25	2.83	

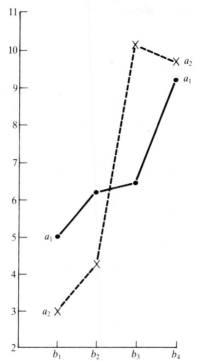

FIGURE 6-3   Profiles of simple effects for factor B.

ratio, $F = 5.27$, is larger than the critical value, the data tend to contradict the hypothesis of zero interaction. The test on the main effects for factor B has the critical value 2.99. The observed F ratio, $F = 18.99$, is larger than the critical value for a 0.05-level test. Hence the data contradict the hypothesis that the main effects of factor B are zero. Inspection of profiles (Fig. 6-3) of the simple effects of B for levels a_1 and a_2 indicates why the effects of factor A are masked by the interaction. For the first two levels of factor B the means for level a_1 are higher than the corresponding means for level a_2, and for the other two levels the means for level a_1 are lower than the the corresponding means for level a_2. Opposite algebraic signs of such differences tend to make their sum close to zero in the main effects for factor A.

   To illustrate the computation of the simple effects, the variation due to the simple effects of B for level a_2 is obtained as follows (data for the computations are obtained from part ii of Table 6.11):

$$(5a_2) = 3.00^2 + 4.25^2 + 10.25^2 + 9.75^2 = 227.19,$$
$$(3a_2) = (27.25)^2/4 \qquad\qquad = 185.64,$$
$$\text{SS}_{b \text{ for } a_2} = \bar{n}[(5a_2) - (3a_2)] = 167.86,$$
$$\text{MS}_{b \text{ for } a_2} = \frac{\text{SS}_{b \text{ for } a_2}}{q - 1} = 55.95.$$

A test of the hypothesis that the variance of the simple effects of factor B at level a_2 is zero is given by the F ratio

$$F = \frac{MS_{b \text{ for } a_2}}{MS_{\text{w. cell}}} = \frac{55.95}{2.83} = 19.77.$$

The degrees of freedom for this F ratio are $(3, 25)$.

In comparing two means, the actual number of observations upon which the mean is based may be used. For example,

$$t = \frac{\overline{AB}_{14} - \overline{AB}_{11}}{\sqrt{MS_{\text{w. cell}}[(1/n_{14}) + (1/n_{11})]}} = \frac{9.20 - 5.00}{\sqrt{2.83(\frac{1}{5} + \frac{1}{4})}} = \frac{4.20}{\sqrt{1.27}} = 3.73.$$

The degrees of freedom for this t statistic are those for $MS_{\text{w. cell}}$. In making all possible tests between ordered means within a logical grouping the procedures given in Sec. 6.2 may be followed, assuming $\bar{n}$ observations per cell.

6.4   EFFECT OF SCALE OF MEASUREMENT ON INTERACTION

In Chap. 5 it was indicated that interactions were in part a function of the choice of the scale of measurement. When this is the case, interaction effects may be "removed" by proper choice of a scale. A numerical example will be used to illustrate this point.

TABLE 6.13   **Analysis of variance in terms of original scale of measurement**

		Observed data			AB summary table			
		b_1	b_2	b_3	b_1	b_2	b_3	Total
(i)	a_1	1, 0	12, 14	20, 27	a_1 1	26	47	74
	a_2	9, 9	32, 30	40, 55	a_2 18	62	95	175
	a_3	30, 34	64, 70	100, 96	a_3 64	134	196	394
					Total 83	222	338	643

(ii) $(1) = 22{,}969.39$ $(3) = 31{,}889.50$ $(5) = 38{,}273.50$
$(2)\ 38{,}449$ $(4) = 28{,}402.83$

Source of variation	SS	df	MS	F
A	8,920.11	2	4460.06	
B	5,433.44	2	2716.72	
AB	950.56	4	237.64	12.19
Within cell	175.50	9	19.50	
Total	15,479.61	17		

(iii)

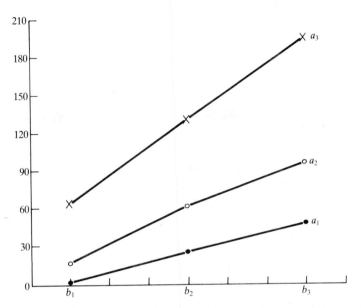

FIGURE 6-4   Profiles of factor B for levels of factor A. (Original scale of measurement.)

The data at the left in part i of Table 6.13 represent observed criterion scores obtained from a 3×3 factorial experiment having two observations per call. The symbols in part ii are defined in Table 6.1. The analysis of variance for these data is summarized in part iii. The critical value for a 0.01-level test on the interaction is $F_{0.99}(4, 9) = 6.42$. Since the observed F ratio exceeds the critical value, the experimental data tend to contradict the hypothesis that the interaction effects are zero. The profiles of factor B for each level of factor A are shown in Fig. 6-4. Within the range of the data, the profiles do not cross. Further, each profile is approximately linear in form. The major difference in these profiles is in the slopes of the respective best-fitting lines.

A square-root transformation on the original scale of measurement will make the slopes in this kind of configuration approximately equal. From the AB summary table, the ranges of the respective rows, in terms of a square-root transformation, are as follows.

Row a_1: $\sqrt{47} - \sqrt{1} \doteq 6$

Row a_2: $\sqrt{95} - \sqrt{18} \doteq 6$

Row a_3: $\sqrt{196} - \sqrt{64} \doteq 6$

The fact that these ranges are approximately equal provides partial evidence that the square-root transformation, when applied to the original observations, will yield profiles having approximately equal slopes.

TABLE 6.14 **Analysis of variance in terms of transformed scale of measurement**

Observed data (transformed scale):

	b_1	b_2	b_3		b_1	b_2	b_3	Total
a_1	1.0, 0.0	3.5, 3.7	4.5, 5.2	a_1	1.0	7.2	9.7	17.9
a_2	3.0, 3.0	5.7, 5.5	6.3, 7.4	a_2	6.0	11.2	13.7	30.9
a_3	5.5, 5.8	8.0, 8.4	10.0, 9.8	a_3	11.3	16.4	19.8	47.5
				Total	18.3	34.8	43.2	96.3

(i) label for left table and right table.

(ii)
$$(1) = 515.20 \qquad (3) = 588.58 \qquad (5) = 642.38$$
$$(2) = 643.91 \qquad (4) = 568.70$$

(iii)

Source of variation	SS	df	MS	F
A	73.38	2	36.69	
B	53.50	2	26.75	
AB	0.30	4	0.075	$F < 1$
Within cell	1.53	9	0.170	
Total	128.71	17		

In terms of the transformed scale of measurement, the observed data are given in part i of Table 6.14. The transformation has the following form:

$$X'_{ijk} = \sqrt{X_{ijk}}.$$

Each entry in the table at the left of part i is the square root of the corresponding entry in part i of Table 6.13. The analysis of variance for the

FIGURE 6-5 Profiles of factor B for levels of factor A. (Transformed scale of measurement.)

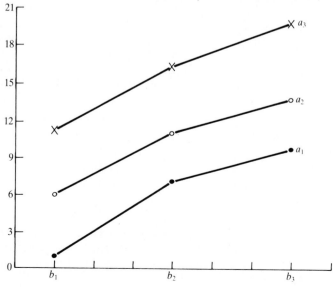

transformed data is summarized in part ii of Table 6.14. It will be noted that the F ratio in the test on the AB interaction is less than unity in this case. In contrast, the F ratio for the analysis in terms of the original scale was 12.19. The profiles in terms of the transformed scale of measurement are shown in Fig. 6-5. The magnitude of the mean squares for the main effects, relative to the within-cell mean square, is approximately constant for both scales of measurement.

Not all interaction effects can be regarded as functions of the scale of measurement. In cases where profiles cross, or in cases where the profiles have quite different shapes, transformations on the scale of measurement will not remove interaction effects. If, however, interaction effects can be removed by transformations, there are many advantages in working with a model which contains no interaction terms. This is particularly true in the mixed model, which has both fixed and random variables, since interactions between fixed and random factors form denominators for F ratios.

6.5 $p \times q \times r$ FACTORIAL EXPERIMENT HAVING n OBSERVATIONS PER CELL

The notation and computational procedures developed in Sec. 6.2 may be extended to three-factor experiments as well as higher-order factorial experiments. In this section the extension will be made to a $p \times q \times r$ factorial experiment. It will be assumed that there are n observations in each cell. Notation will be indicated for the special case of a $2 \times 3 \times 2$ factorial experiment. There are $pqr = 2(3)(2) = 12$ treatment combinations in this experiment. The notation for the treatment combinations is illustrated in the following table:

		c_1			c_2	
	b_1	b_2	b_3	b_1	b_2	b_3
a_1	abc_{111}	abc_{121}	abc_{131}	abc_{112}	abc_{122}	abc_{132}
a_2	abc_{211}	abc_{221}	abc_{231}	abc_{212}	abc_{222}	abc_{232}

A typical treatment combination in this experiment is designated by the notation abc_{ijk}, where i indicates the level of factor A, j the level of factor B, and k the level of factor C.

The n observations under treatment combination abc_{ijk} are represented as follows:

$$X_{ijk1} \quad X_{ijk2} \quad \cdots \quad X_{ijkm} \quad \cdots \quad X_{ijkn}$$

Thus the notation X_{ijkm} denotes an observation on element m under treatment combination abc_{ijk}. For the general case,

$$i = 1, 2, \ldots, p; \qquad j = 1, 2, \ldots, q; \qquad k = 1, 2, \ldots, r;$$

$$m = 1, 2, \ldots, n.$$

The sum of the n observations under treatment combination abc_{ijk} will be designated by the symbol ABC_{ijk}. Thus,

$$ABC_{ijk} = \sum_{m} X_{ijkm}.$$

A table of such sums will be called an ABC summary table. For the case of a $2 \times 3 \times 2$ factorial experiment, the ABC summary table has the following form:

	c_1			c_2			
	b_1	b_2	b_3	b_1	b_2	b_3	Total
a_1	ABC_{111}	ABC_{121}	ABC_{131}	ABC_{112}	ABC_{122}	ABC_{132}	A_1
a_2	ABC_{211}	ABC_{221}	ABC_{231}	ABC_{212}	ABC_{222}	ABC_{232}	A_2
Total	BC_{11}	BC_{21}	BC_{31}	BC_{12}	BC_{22}	BC_{32}	G

The column totals in this ABC summary table have the general form

$$BC_{jk} = \sum_{i} ABC_{ijk} = \sum_{i} \sum_{m} X_{ijkm}.$$

That is, a column total represents the sum of all observations under treatment combination bc_{jk}, the levels of factor A being disregarded. The BC summary table has the following form:

	b_1	b_2	b_3	Total
c_1	BC_{11}	BC_{21}	BC_{31}	C_1
c_2	BC_{12}	BC_{22}	BC_{32}	C_2
Total	B_1	B_2	B_3	G

Treatment combination ab_{ij} is defined to be the collection of treatment combinations $abc_{ij1}, abc_{ij2}, \ldots, abc_{ijr}$. The sum of all observations at level ab_{ij} is the sum of all observations in this collection. The sum of all observations at level ab_{ij} is thus

$$AB_{ij} = \sum_{k} ABC_{ijk} = \sum_{k} \sum_{m} X_{ijkm}.$$

For the case being considered,

$$AB_{11} = ABC_{111} + ABC_{112},$$
$$AB_{23} = ABC_{231} + ABC_{232}.$$

The AB summary table has the following form:

	b_1	b_2	b_3	Total
a_1	AB_{11}	AB_{12}	AB_{13}	A_1
a_2	AB_{21}	AB_{22}	AB_{23}	A_2
Total	B_1	B_2	B_3	G

The symbol AC_{ik} will be used to designate the sum of all observations at level ac_{ik}. Thus,

$$AC_{ik} = \sum_j ABC_{ijk} = \sum_j \sum_m X_{ijkm}.$$

For example, the treatment combinations at level ac_{12} for the case being considered are abc_{112}, abc_{122}, and abc_{132}. Thus,

$$AC_{12} = ABC_{112} + ABC_{122} + ABC_{132}.$$

The AC summary table has the following form:

	c_1	c_2	Total
a_1	AC_{11}	AC_{12}	A_1
a_2	AC_{21}	AC_{22}	A_2
Total	C_1	C_2	G_3

The sum of all observations at level a_i may be obtained as follows:

$$A_i = \sum_j AB_{ij} = \sum_k AC_{ik} = \sum_j \sum_k ABC_{ijk} = \sum_j \sum_k \sum_m X_{ijkm}.$$

The sum of all observations at level b_j is given by

$$B_j = \sum_i AB_{ij} = \sum_k BC_{jk} = \sum_i \sum_k ABC_{ijk} = \sum_i \sum_k \sum_m X_{ijkm}.$$

Similarly

$$C_k = \sum_i AC_{ik} = \sum_j BC_{jk} = \sum_i \sum_j ABC_{ijk} = \sum_i \sum_j \sum_m X_{ijkm}.$$

To summarize, two-way summary tables are most readily obtained from three-way summary tables by combining levels of one of the factors. Thus the BC summary table is obtained from the ABC summary table by adding totals in the latter table which are at the same levels of factors B and C but at different levels of factor A. The AB summary table is obtained from the ABC summary table by adding totals in the latter table which are at the same levels of factors A and B but at different levels of factor C. The AC summary table is obtained in an analogous manner.

Symbols in terms of which computational formulas may be conveniently written are summarized in part i of Table 6.15. With the exception of symbol

TABLE 6.15   **Definition of computational symbols**

(i)

$$(1) = G^2/npqr \qquad (6) = \left[\sum (AB_{ij})^2\right]\Big/nr$$

$$(2) = \sum X_{ijkm}^2 \qquad (7) = \left[\sum (AC_{ik})^2\right]\Big/nq$$

$$(3) = \left(\sum A_i^2\right)\Big/nqr \qquad (8) = \left[\sum (BC_{jk})^2\right]\Big/np$$

$$(4) = \left(\sum B_j^2\right)\Big/npr \qquad (9) = \left[\sum (ABC_{ijk})^2\right]\Big/n$$

$$(5) = \left(\sum C_k^2\right)\Big/npq$$

(ii)

$$SS_a = nqr \sum (\bar{A}_i - \bar{G})^2 = (3) - (1)$$

$$SS_b = npr \sum (\bar{B}_j - \bar{G})^2 = (4) - (1)$$

$$SS_c = npq \sum (\bar{C}_k - \bar{G})^2 = (5) - (1)$$

$$SS_{ab} = nr \sum (\overline{AB}_{ij} - \bar{A}_i - \bar{B}_j + \bar{G})^2$$

$$\quad = nr \sum (\overline{AB}_{ij} - \bar{G})^2 - SS_a - SS_b = (6) - (3) - (4) + (1)$$

$$SS_{ac} = nq \sum (\overline{AC}_{ik} - \bar{A}_i - \bar{C}_k + \bar{G})^2$$

$$\quad = nq \sum (\overline{AC}_{ik} - \bar{G})^2 - SS_a - SS_c = (7) - (3) - (5) + (1)$$

$$SS_{bc} = np \sum (\overline{BC}_{jk} - \bar{B}_j - \bar{C}_k + G)^2$$

$$\quad = np \sum (\overline{BC}_{jk} - \bar{G})^2 - SS_b - SS_c = (8) - (4) - (5) + (1)$$

$$SS_{abc} = n \sum (\overline{ABC}_{ijk} - \overline{AB}_{ij} - \overline{AC}_{ik} - \overline{BC}_{jk} + \bar{A}_i + \bar{B}_j + \bar{C}_k - \bar{G})^2$$

$$\quad = n \sum (\overline{ABC}_{ijk} - \bar{G})^2 - SS_{ab} - SS_{ac} - SS_{bc} - SS_a - SS_b - SS_c$$

$$\quad = (9) - (6) - (7) - (8) + (3) + (4) + (5) - (1)$$

$$SS_{w. cell} = \sum (X_{ijkm} - \overline{ABC}_{ijk})^2 = (2) - (9)$$

$$SS_{total} = \sum (X_{ijkm} - \bar{G})^2 = (2) - (1)$$

(2), all are obtained from either the two-way or the three-way summary tables. In each case the divisor for a computational symbol is the number of basic observations summed to obtain a term which is squared in the numerator. For example, in computational symbol (3), A_i is squared. There are nqr observations summed to obtain A_i.

There is a relatively simple method of determining the number of basic observations summed to obtain a total of the form A_i. In a $p \times q \times r$ factorial experiment a basic observation is represented by the symbol X_{ijkm}. In A_i the subscripts j, k, and m are missing. The numbers of levels corresponding to these missing subscripts are, respectively, q, r, and n. The number of observations summed to obtain A_i is the product of these missing subscripts, qrn. In the total B_j, the subscripts i, k, and m are missing. The corresponding numbers of levels are p, r, and n; hence the number of observations summed is *prn*. In the total BC_{jk} the subscripts i and m are missing. Hence pn observations are summed in this total. In the total AC_{ik} the subscripts j and m are missing. Hence the number of observations summed in this total is qn.

Where the index of summation does not appear under the summation symbol, it is understood that the summation is over all possible terms of the form specified. For example, the notation $\sum (AB_{ij})^2$ indicates that the sum is over all the pq cell totals in a two-way summary table of the form AB_{ij}. Similarly, the notation $\sum (BC_{jk})^2$ indicates that the sum is over all the qr cell totals having the form BC_{jk}. The basic definitions of the estimates of variation due to main effects and interactions are summarized in part ii of Table 6.15. Corresponding computational formulas are also given.

In a three-factor factorial experiment there are various orders of simple effects. Computational formulas for these sources of variation may be obtained by specializing the symbols given in part i of Table 6.15. The symbol $(6a_i)$ is defined to be the equivalent of symbol (6), in which the summation is restricted to level a_i. For example,

$$(6a_1) = \frac{(AB_{11})^2 + (AB_{12})^2 + \cdots + (AB_{1q})^2}{nr},$$

$$(6a_2) = \frac{(AB_{21})^2 + (AB_{22})^2 + \cdots + (AB_{2q})^2}{nr}.$$

Similarly the symbol $(7c_k)$ is defined to be computational symbol (7), in which the summation is limited to level c_k—that is, the summation is restricted to row c_k of the BC summary table.

The computational symbol $(9a_i)$ restricts the summation in (9) to row a_i of the ABC summary table. Computational symbol $(9ab_{ij})$ restricts the summation in (9) to just those totals in which the factor A is at level a_i and factor B is at level b_j. For example,

$$(9ab_{12}) = \frac{(ABC_{121})^2 + (ABC_{122})^2 + \cdots + (ABC_{12r})^2}{n},$$

$$(9ab_{23}) = \frac{(ABC_{231})^2 + (ABC_{232})^2 + \cdots + (ABC_{23r})^2}{n}.$$

In terms of computational symbols defined in this manner, computational formulas for various orders of simple effects are given in Table 6.16.

The following relationships hold for the computational symbols:

$$(6) = (6a_1) + (6a_2) + \cdots + (6a_p),$$

$$(7) = (7a_1) + (7a_2) + \cdots + (7a_p),$$

$$(9) = (9a_1) + (9a_2) + \cdots + (9a_p),$$

$$(9) = \sum_i \sum_j (9ab_{ij}).$$

Analogous relations hold for other computational symbols.

TABLE 6.16   **Computational formulas for simple effects**

Effects	Sum of squares
Simple interactions:	
AB for level c_k	$(9c_k) - (7c_k) - (8c_k) + (5c_k)$
AC for level b_j	$(9b_j) - (6b_j) - (8b_j) + (4b_j)$
BC for level a_i	$(9a_i) - (6a_i) - (7a_i) - (3a_i)$
Simple main effects:	
A for level b_j	$(6b_j) - (4b_j)$
A for level c_k	$(7c_k) - (5c_k)$
B for level a_i	$(6a_i) - (3a_i)$
B for level c_k	$(8c_k) - (5c_k)$
C for level a_i	$(7a_i) - (3a_i)$
C for level b_j	$(8b_j) - (4b_j)$
Simple, simple main effects:	
A for level bc_{jk}	$(9bc_{jk}) - (8bc_{jk})$
B for level ac_{ik}	$(9ac_{ik}) - (7ac_{ik})$
C for level ab_{ij}	$(9ab_{ij}) - (6ab_{ij})$

Computational checks:

$$\sum_k \text{SS}_{a \text{ for } c_k} = \text{SS}_a + \text{SS}_{ac}$$

$$\sum_k \text{SS}_{ab \text{ for } c_k} = \text{SS}_{ab} + \text{SS}_{abc}$$

$$\sum_j \sum_k \text{SS}_{a \text{ for } bc_{jk}} = \text{SS}_a + \text{SS}_{ab} + \text{SS}_{ac} + \text{SS}_{abc}$$

Numerical Example

The computational procedures will be illustrated by means of a $2 \times 3 \times 2$ factorial experiment. The purpose of this experiment is to evaluate the relative effectiveness of three methods of training (factor B). Two instructors (factor C) are used in this experiment; subjects in the experiment are classified on the basis of educational background (factor A). The plan for this experiment may be represented as follows:

Instructor:		c_1			c_2		
Training method:		b_1	b_2	b_3	b_1	b_2	b_3
Educational	a_1	G_{111}	G_{121}	G_{131}	G_{112}	G_{122}	G_{132}
level	a_2	G_{211}	G_{221}	G_{231}	G_{212}	G_{222}	G_{232}

In this plan G_{111} represents a group of subjects at educational level a_1 assigned to instructor c_1 to be trained under method b_1. The symbol G_{132} denotes the group of subjects at educational level a_1 assigned to instructor c_2 to be trained under method b_3. Thus each instructor teaches groups from both educational levels under each of the training methods. It will be assumed that there are 10 subjects in each of the groups, a total of 120 subjects in all.

In this experiment the methods of training (factor B) and the levels of education (factor A) will be considered fixed factors. Factor A is a classification variable included in the experiment to control potential variability in the experimental units, which is a function of level of education. (All relevant levels of the education factor must be covered if this factor is fixed.) Factor B is the treatment variable of primary interest; this factor is directly under the control of the experimenter. There is some question about whether or not factor C should be considered a fixed variable. If it is the purpose of the experiment to draw inferences about the methods of training which potentially hold for a population of instructors, of which the two instructors in the experiment can be considered a random sample, then the instructor factor is random. If inferences about the methods are to be limited to the two instructors in the experiment, then the instructor factor is fixed. Often in this type of experiment, inferences are desired about the methods over a population of specified instructors. Hence the instructor factor should be considered as a random factor, and suitable randomization procedures are required in the selection of the instructors.

The expected values for the mean squares for the case under consideration are given in Table 6.17. The model from which these expected values were obtained includes interaction terms with the instructor factor. According to these expected values, the test on the main effect of factor B has the form

$$F = \frac{MS_b}{MS_{bc}}.$$

This F ratio has degrees of freedom $[(q - 1), (q - 1)(r - 1)]$, which in this case is $(2, 2)$. When the denominator of an F ratio has only two degrees of freedom, the power of the resulting test is extremely low. This F does not provide a sufficiently powerful test of the main effects of factor B to be of much practical use.

TABLE 6.17   **Expected values of mean squares for numerical example** (A, B fixed; C random)

Effect	i	j	k	m	Expected value of mean square
a_i	0	3	2	10	$\sigma_\varepsilon^2 + 30\sigma_{\alpha\gamma}^2 + 60\sigma_\alpha^2$
β_j	2	0	2	10	$\sigma_\varepsilon^2 + 20\sigma_{\beta\gamma}^2 + 40\sigma_\beta^2$
γ_k	2	3	1	10	$\sigma_\varepsilon^2 + 60\sigma_\gamma^2$
$\alpha\beta_{ij}$	0	0	2	10	$\sigma_\varepsilon^2 + 10\sigma_{\alpha\beta\gamma}^2 + 20\sigma_{\alpha\beta}^2$
$\alpha\gamma_{ik}$	0	3	1	10	$\sigma_\varepsilon^2 + 30\sigma_{\alpha\gamma}^2$
$\beta\gamma_{jk}$	2	0	1	10	$\sigma_\varepsilon^2 + 20\sigma_{\beta\gamma}^2$
$\alpha\beta\gamma_{ijk}$	0	0	1	10	$\sigma_\varepsilon^2 + 10\sigma_{\alpha\beta\gamma}^2$
$\varepsilon_{m(ijk)}$	1	1	1	1	σ_ε^2

If, however, it can be assumed that interactions with the random factor (C) are negligible relative to the other uncontrolled sources of variation which are included in the experimental error, then interactions with factor C may be dropped from the original model. In terms of a model which does not include such interactions, relatively powerful tests on factor B are available. Inspection of Table 6.17 indicates that MS_{ac}, MS_{bc}, MS_{abc}, and $MS_{w. cell}$ are all estimates of variance due to experimental error if interactions with factor C are not included in the model. Preliminary tests on the model may be made to check on whether or not such interactions may be dropped.

Suppose that the ABC summary table for the data obtained in the experiment is that given in part i of Table 6.18. Each of the entries in this table is the sum of the 10 criterion scores for the corresponding group of subjects. For example, the entry in cell abc_{132} is the sum of the 10 criterion scores for the subjects in group G_{132}, that is, the subjects at education level a_1, trained

TABLE 6.18 **Data for numerical example**

(i)

ABC summary table

	c_1			c_2			
	b_1	b_2	b_3	b_1	b_2	b_3	Total
a_1	20	30	12	16	33	8	119
a_2	36	38	40	40	44	42	240
Total	56	68	52	56	77	50	359

AB summary table

	b_1	b_2	b_3	Total
a_1	36	63	20	119
a_2	76	82	82	240
Total	112	145	102	359

BC summary table

	b_1	b_2	b_3	Total
c_1	56	68	52	176
c_2	56	77	50	183
Total	112	145	102	359

AC summary table

	c_1	c_2	Total
a_1	62	57	119
a_2	114	126	240
Total	176	183	359

(ii)

$(1) = (359^2)/120$ $= 1074.01$
$(2) = (\text{not available from above data})$ $= 1360$
$(3) = (119^2 + 240^2)/60$ $= 1196.02$
$(4) = (112^2 + 145^2 + 102^2)/40$ $= 1099.32$
$(5) = (176^2 + 183^2)/60$ $= 1074.42$
$(6) = (36^2 + 63^2 + 20^2 + 76^2 + 82^2 + 82^2)/20 = 1244.45$
$(7) = (62^2 + 57^2 + 114^2 + 126^2)/30$ $= 1198.83$
$(8) = (56^2 + 68^2 + 52^2 + 56^2 + 77^2 + 50^2)/20 = 1101.45$
$(9) = (20^2 + 30^2 + \cdots + 44^2 + 42^2)/10$ $= 1249.30$

(iii)

$SS_a = (3) - (1) = 122.01$ $SS_{ab} = (6) - (3) - (4) + (1) = 23.12$
$SS_b = (4) - (1) = 25.31$ $SS_{ac} = (7) - (3) - (5) + (1) = 2.40$
$SS_c = (5) - (1) = 0.41$ $SS_{bc} = (8) - (4) - (5) + (1) = 1.72$
$SS_{abc} = (9) - (6) - (7) - (8) + (3) + (4) + (5) - (1) = 0.32$
$SS_{w. cell} = (2) - (9) = 110.70$
$SS_{total} = (2) - (1) = 285.99$

under method b_3 by instructor c_2. The two-way summary tables given in part i are obtained from the three-way summary table. For example, the entry ab_{11} in the AB summary table is given by

$$AB_{11} = ABC_{111} + ABC_{112}$$
$$= \quad 20 \quad + \quad 16 \quad = 36.$$

The computational symbols defined in part i of Table 6.15 are obtained in part ii in Table 6.18. Data for all these computations, with the exception of symbol (2), are contained in part i. Symbol (2) is obtained from the individual criterion scores; the latter are not given in this table. The computation of the sums of squares is completed in part iii.

The analysis of variance is summarized in Table 6.19. Preliminary tests on the model will be made on the interactions with factor C (instructors) before proceeding with other tests. According to the expected values of the mean squares given in Table 6.17, tests on interactions with factor C all have $MS_{\text{w. cell}}$ as a denominator. These tests have the following form:

$$F = \frac{MS_{abc}}{MS_{\text{w. cell}}} = \frac{0.16}{1.02} = 0.15,$$

$$F = \frac{MS_{ac}}{MS_{\text{w. cell}}} = \frac{2.40}{1.02} = 2.33,$$

$$F = \frac{MS_{bc}}{MS_{\text{w. cell}}} = \frac{0.86}{1.02} = 0.85.$$

Only the F ratio for the test on the AC interaction is greater than unity. By use of the 0.10 level of significance, the critical value for the latter test is $F_{0.90}(1,108) = 2.76$.

TABLE 6.19 **Summary of analysis of variance**

Source of variation	SS	df	MS
A (level of education)	122.01	$p - 1 = 1$	122.01
B (methods of training)	25.31	$q - 1 = 2$	12.66
C (instructors)	0.41	$r - 1 = 1$	0.41
AB	23.12	$(p - 1)(q - 1) = 2$	11.56
AC	2.40	$(p - 1)(r - 1) = 1$	2.40
BC	1.72	$(q - 1)(r - 1) = 2$	0.86
ABC	0.32	$(p - 1)(q - 1)(r - 1) = 2$	0.16
Within cell (experiment error)	110.70	$pqr(n - 1) = 108$	1.02
Total	285.99	119	

The outcome of these preliminary tests on the model does not contradict the hypothesis that interactions with factor C may be considered negligible. (The AC interaction is a borderline case). On *a priori* grounds, if the instructors are carefully trained, interaction effects with instructors may often be kept relatively small. On these bases, the decision is made to drop interactions with factor C from the model. The expected values corresponding to this revised model are obtained from Table 6.17 by dropping the terms $\sigma^2_{\alpha\gamma}$, $\sigma^2_{\beta\gamma}$, and $\sigma^2_{\alpha\beta\gamma}$ from the expected values in this table. Since the degrees of freedom for the within-cell variation (108) are large relative to the degrees of freedom for the interactions with factor C, which total 5, pooling these interactions with the within-cell variation will not appreciably affect the magnitude of $MS_{w.\,cell}$ or the degrees of freedom for the resulting pooled error term. Hence $MS_{w.\,cell}$ is used under the revised model for final tests on factors A and B. These tests have the following form:

$$F = \frac{MS_{ab}}{MS_{w.\,cell}} = 11.33, \qquad F_{0.99}(2,108) = 4.82;$$

$$F = \frac{MS_b}{MS_{w.\,cell}} = 12.41, \qquad F_{0.99}(2,\,108) = 4.82;$$

$$F = \frac{MS_a}{MS_{w.\,cell}} = 119.62, \qquad F_{0.99}(1,108) = 6.90.$$

Because of the significant AB interaction, care must be taken in interpreting the main effects due to factor B. The manner in which educational level is related to method of training is most readily shown by the profiles of the simple effects for the methods at each of the levels of education. These profiles are drawn in Fig. 6-6. Data for these profiles are obtained from the AB summary table. Inspection of these profiles indicates that differences between the methods of training for groups at level a_2 are not so marked as the corresponding differences for groups at level a_1.

Variation due to differences between training methods for groups at level a_1 is given by (data are obtained from row a_1 of the AB summary table)

$$SS_{b\,for\,a_1} = \frac{36^2 + 63^2 + 20^2}{20} - \frac{119^2}{60} = 47.23.$$

This source of variation has $q - 1 = 2$ degrees of freedom. Hence the mean square of the simple effect of factor B for level a_1 is

$$MS_{b\,for\,a_1} = \frac{47.23}{2} = 23.62.$$

To test the hypothesis of no difference between the methods of training for groups at educational level a_1,

$$F = \frac{MS_{b\,for\,a_1}}{MS_{w.\,cell}} = \frac{23.62}{1.02} = 23.15.$$

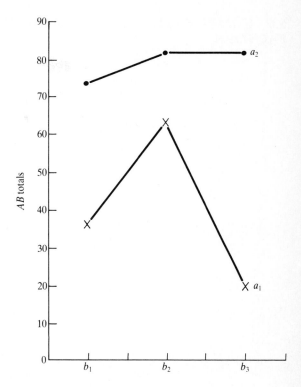

FIGURE 6-6   Profiles of simple main effects for training methods.

The degrees of freedom for this F ratio are (2, 108). The data clearly indicate a significant difference between the methods for level a_1. The test on the simple effects of methods for level a_2 indicates no significant difference between the methods; the F for this test will be found to be $F = 0.60/1.02$.

The levels of factor C (instructors) in this design may be considered to be replications. As indicated by the expected values for the mean squares, the proper denominator for tests on fixed effects is the corresponding interaction with replications, provided that such interactions cannot be pooled. When tests are made by using a pooled error term (this is essentially what has been done in the example that has just been considered), it is implicitly assumed that interactions with replications (instructors) do not exist.

There are potentially many reasons for the presence of interaction in this kind of experiment. Inspection of the $A \times B$ summary table indicates that groups at level a_2 are uniformly good under all the training methods. In part, this may be a function of a ceiling effect on the criterion. If the latter is the case, then the interaction is an artifact of the way in which performance is measured. Care is required in constructing the criterion to avoid this kind of artifact.

6.6   COMPUTATIONAL PROCEDURES FOR NESTED FACTORS

Factorial designs in which one or more factors are nested were discussed in Chapter 5. Computational procedures in which one factor is nested under a second will be illustrated from the case of a $p \times q \times r$ factorial experiment having n observations in each cell. Assume that factor B is nested under factor A. The analysis of variance for this case generally takes the following form:

Source of variation	df
A	$p - 1$
B within A	$p(q - 1)$
C	$r - 1$
AC	$(p - 1)(r - 1)$
$(B$ within $A) \times C$	$p(q - 1)(r - 1)$
Within cell	$pqr(n - 1)$

The variation due to B within A is defined to be

$$SS_{b(a)} = nr \sum_i \sum_j (\overline{AB}_{ij} - \bar{A}_i)^2.$$

This source of variation is actually a sum of simple main effects of factor B at each level of factor A. In terms of the computational symbols defined in Table 6.15,

$$SS_{b(a)} = (6) - (3).$$

For a design in which factor B is not nested under factor A,

$$
\begin{array}{ll}
 & \text{df} \\
SS_b = (4) - 1 & q - 1 \\
SS_{ab} = (6) - (3) - (4) + 1 & (p - 1)(q - 1) \\
\hline
\text{Sum} = \quad (6) - (3) & p(q - 1)
\end{array}
$$

Thus $SS_{b(a)}$ in a design in which factor B is nested under factor A is numerically equal to $SS_b + SS_{ab}$ in the corresponding factorial design in which factor B is not nested under factor A.

The variation due to the interaction $(B$ with $A) \times C$ is defined to be

$$SS_{b(a)c} = n \sum \sum \sum (\overline{ABC}_{ijk} - \overline{AB}_{ij} - \overline{AC}_{ik} + \bar{A}_i)^2.$$

This source of variation is actually a sum of simple interactions. In terms of the computational symbols defined in Table 6.15,

$$SS_{b(a)c} = (9) - (6) - (7) + (3).$$

For a $p \times q \times r$ factorial experiment in which there is no nested factor,

$$
\begin{array}{ll}
 & \text{df} \\
\mathrm{SS}_{bc} = (8) - (4) - (5) + (1) & (q-1)(r-1) \\
\mathrm{SS}_{abc} = (9) - (6) - (7) - (8) + (3) + (4) + (5) - (1) & (p-1)(q-1)(r-1) \\
\hline
\mathrm{Sum} = \quad (9) - (6) - (7) + (3) & p(q-1)(r-1)
\end{array}
$$

Thus $\mathrm{SS}_{b(a)c}$ is numerically equal to $\mathrm{SS}_{bc} + \mathrm{SS}_{abc}$. In general, if factor V is nested under factor U,

$$
\mathrm{SS}_{v(u)w} = \mathrm{SS}_{vw} + \mathrm{SS}_{uvw}.
$$

In a four-factor experiment in which factor C is nested under both factors A and B,

$$
\mathrm{SS}_{c(ab)} = \mathrm{SS}_c + \mathrm{SS}_{ac} + \mathrm{SS}_{bc} + \mathrm{SS}_{abc},
$$

$$
\mathrm{SS}_{c(ab)d} = \mathrm{SS}_{cd} + \mathrm{SS}_{acd} + \mathrm{SS}_{bcd} + \mathrm{SS}_{abcd}.
$$

Returning to a three-factor factorial experiment, consider the case of a $2 \times 2 \times 3$ factorial experiment having five observations per cell. Assume that factor B is nested under factor A and that factor B is a random factor. Assume also that factors A and C are fixed factors. Under these assumptions, the expected values of the mean squares for this design are given in Table 6.20. From these expected values it will be noted that the test on the main effects due to factor A has the form

$$
F = \frac{\mathrm{MS}_a}{\mathrm{MS}_{b(a)}}.
$$

If this denominator has relatively few degrees of freedom, the power of the test will be low. Preliminary tests on the model are often called for in this situation.

TABLE 6.20 **Expected values of mean squares (factor B nested under factor A; A and C fixed, B random)**

Effect	i	j	k	m	E(MS)
α_i	0	2	3	5	$\sigma_\varepsilon^2 + 15\sigma_{\beta(\alpha)}^2 + 30\sigma_\alpha^2$
$\beta_{j(i)}$	1	1	3	5	$\sigma_\varepsilon^2 + 15\sigma_{\beta(\alpha)}^2$
γ_k	2	2	0	5	$\sigma_\varepsilon^2 + 5\sigma_{\beta(\alpha)\gamma}^2 + 20\sigma_\gamma^2$
$\alpha\gamma_{ik}$	0	2	0	5	$\sigma_\varepsilon^2 + 5\sigma_{\beta(\alpha)\gamma}^2 + 10\sigma_{\alpha\gamma}^2$
$\beta\gamma_{j(i)k}$	1	1	0	5	$\sigma_\varepsilon^2 + 5\sigma_{\beta(\alpha)\gamma}^2$
$\varepsilon_{m(ijk)}$	1	1	1	1	σ_ε^2

Numerical Example

A $2 \times 2 \times 3$ factorial experiment having five observations per cell will be used to illustrate the computational procedures. To make this example concrete, suppose that the experiment has the following form:

Drugs:	a_1						a_2					
Hospitals:	$b_1(a_1)$			$b_2(a_1)$			$b_1(a_2)$			$b_2(a_2)$		
Category of patients:	c_1	c_2	c_3	c_1	c_2	c_3	c_1	c_2	c_3	c_1	c_2	c_3
n:	5	5	5	5	5	5	5	5	5	5	5	5

Schematically, one has the following crossing and nesting relationships among the factors:

Suppose that the purpose of this experiment is to test the relative effectiveness of two drugs on patients in different diagnostic categories. Patients from hospitals $b_{1(a_1)}$ and $b_{2(a_1)}$ are given drug a_1; patients from hospitals $b_{1(a_2)}$ and $b_{2(a_2)}$ are given drug a_2. Since only one of the drugs under study is administered within a hospital, the hospital factor is nested under the drug factor. The diagnostic categories are considered to be comparable across all hospitals; hence factor C is not nested. Only a random sample of the population of hospitals about which inferences are to be drawn is included in the experiment; hence factor B is random.

Suppose that the ABC and AC summary tables for the data obtained in this experiment are those in part i of Table 6.21. With the exception of symbol (2), which is computed from the individual observations, data for the computations are given in part i. (The definitions of these symbols appear in Table 6.15.) Symbols (4) and (8) are not required for this case. The analysis of variance is summarized in Table 6.22.

The expected values of the mean squares are given in Table 6.20. Before testing the main effects and interaction of the fixed factors, preliminary tests on the model are made with respect to factor B and its interaction with factor C. These preliminary tests will be made at the 0.10 level of significance. Inspection of the expected values of the mean squares indicates that the preliminary tests have the following form:

$$F = \frac{MS_{b(a)}}{MS_{w.\ cell}} = 2.05, \qquad F_{0.90}(2, 48) = 2.42;$$

$$F = \frac{MS_{b(a)c}}{MS_{w.\ cell}} = 1.00, \qquad F_{0.90}(4, 48) = 2.07.$$

TABLE 6.21   **Numerical example**

ABC summary table:

	a_1		a_2		
	$b_{1(a_1)}$	$b_{2(a_1)}$	$b_{1(a_2)}$	$b_{2(a_2)}$	Total
c_1	15	18	30	35	98
c_2	22	25	24	21	92
c_3	38	41	10	14	103
Total	75	84	64	70	293

(i) AC summary table:

	a_1	a_2	Total
c_1	33	65	98
c_2	47	45	92
c_3	79	24	103
Total	159	134	293

(ii)

$$(1) = (293)^2/60 = 1430.82$$
$$(2) \text{ (not obtained from above summary tables)} = 1690$$
$$(3) = (159^2 + 134^2)/30 = 1441.23$$
$$(5) = (98^2 + 92^2 + 103^2)/20 = 1433.85$$
$$(6) = (75^2 + 84^2 + 64^2 + 70^2)/15 = 1445.13$$
$$(7) = (33^2 + 47^2 + \cdots + 45^2 + 24^2)/10 = 1636.50$$
$$(9) = (15^2 + 22^2 + \cdots + 21^2 + 14^2)/5 = 1644.20$$

TABLE 6.22   **Summary of analysis of variance**

(i)

$$SS_a = (3) - (1) = 10.41$$
$$SS_{b(a)} = (6) - (3) = 3.90$$
$$SS_c = (5) - (1) = 3.03$$
$$SS_{ac} = (7) - (3) - (5) + (1) = 192.24$$
$$SS_{b(a)c} = (9) - (6) - (7) + (3) = 3.80$$
$$SS_{w.\ cell} = (2) - (9) = 45.80$$

(ii)

Source of variation	SS	df	MS
A (drugs)	10.41	1	10.41
B (hospitals within A)	3.90	2	1.95
C (categories)	3.03	2	1.52
AC	192.24	2	96.12
$B(A) \times C$	3.80	4	0.95
Within cell	45.80	48	0.95
Pooled error	53.50	54	0.99

Neither of the F ratios exceeds specified critical values. Hence variation due to $B(A)$ and $B(A) \times C$ is pooled with the within-cell variation. Thus,

$$SS_{\text{pooled error}} = SS_{b(a)} + SS_{b(a)c} + SS_{\text{w. cell}}.$$

The degrees of freedom for this term are the sum of the respective degrees of freedom for the parts.

The denominator for all final tests is $MS_{\text{pooled error}}$. For this case the final tests are

$$F = \frac{MS_{ac}}{MS_{\text{pooled error}}} = 102.26, \qquad F_{0.99}(2, 54) = 5.00;$$

$$F = \frac{MS_a}{MS_{\text{pooled error}}} = 11.07, \qquad F_{0.99}(1, 54) = 7.10;$$

$$F = \frac{MS_c}{MS_{\text{pooled error}}} = 1.62, \quad F_{0.99}(2, 54) = 5.00.$$

In spite of the significant AC interaction, the main effect for factor A is significant. An analysis of the simple effects is required for an adequate interpretation of the effects of the drugs. Inspection of the AC summary table indicates that drug a_2 has the higher criterion total for category c_1; there appears to be little difference between the criterion scores for category c_2; drug a_1 has the higher criterion total for category c_3. Formal tests on these last statements have the following form:

$$F = \frac{(AC_{11} - AC_{21})^2}{2nq MS_{\text{pooled error}}} = \frac{(33 - 65)^2}{2(5)(2)(0.99)} = 54.47,$$

$$F = \frac{(AC_{12} - AC_{22})^2}{2nq MS_{\text{pooled error}}} = \frac{(47 - 45)^2}{2(5)(2)(0.99)} = 0.21,$$

$$F = \frac{(AC_{13} - AC_{23})^2}{2nq MS_{\text{pooled error}}} = \frac{(79 - 24)^2}{(5)(2)(0.99)} = 160.90.$$

6.7 FACTORIAL EXPERIMENT WITH A SINGLE CONTROL GROUP

A design closely related to one reported by Levison and Zeigler (1959) will be used to illustrate the material that will be considered in this section. The purpose of this experiment is to test the effect of amount and time of irradiation upon subsequent learning ability. Different dosages (factor B) of irradiation are administered at different age levels (factor A). When all subjects reach a specified age, they are given a series of learning tasks. Separate analyses are made of the criterion scores for each task. (A multivariate analysis of variance might also have been made.) The plan for the experiment may be represented as follows:

		Dosage of irradiation		
		b_1	b_2	
	a_1	G_{11}	G_{12}	
Age at which	a_2	G_{21}	G_{22}	
irradiation is	a_3	G_{31}	G_{32}	$n = 10$
administered	a_4	G_{41}	G_{42}	

G_{ij} represents a group of subjects under treatment ab_{ij}. Suppose that each group contains $n = 10$ subjects. In addition to these eight groups there is a group G_0, having $n_0 = 20$ subjects, which receives no irradiation treatment. G_0 represents the control group. In this case the control condition may be considered to represent level b_0 of the dosage dimension; however, the control condition cannot be classified along the age dimension.

Thus there are nine groups in all, eight groups in the cells of a 4×2 factorial experiment plus a control group. For the general case there will be $pq + 1$ groups. The analysis of variance for this experimental plan may take the following form:

Source of variation		df
Between cell		$(pq + 1) - 1$
Control vs. all others	1	
A (age)	$p - 1$	
B (dosage)	$q - 1$	
AB	$(p - 1)(q - 1)$	
Within cell		$pq(n - 1) + (n_0 - 1)$

The factorial part of this plan follows the usual computation procedures for any factorial experiment of this type. The contrast between the control group and all experimental groups is given by

$$C = pq\bar{C}_0 - \sum \overline{AB}_{ij} = \frac{pqC_0}{n_0} - \frac{\sum AB_{ij}}{n},$$

where C_0 is the sum of the observations in the control group. The corresponding mean square is

$$\text{MS}_{\text{control vs. all others}} = \frac{C^2}{[(pq)^2/n_0] + (pq/n)}.$$

The within-cell variation is obtained by pooling the within-cell variation from the factorial part of the experiment with the within-cell variation from the control group. The between-cell variation is given by

$$\text{SS}_{\text{b. cell}} = \frac{C_0^2}{n_0} + \frac{\sum (AB_{ij})^2}{n} - \frac{(G + C_0)^2}{npq + n_0},$$

where G is the sum of the observations in the factorial part of the experiment and C_0 is the sum of the observations in the control group.

In this case the control group may be considered as a zero-level condition of the dosage factor. Hence, as an alternative to the variation due to the main effects of factor B in the factorial part of the experiment, the following may be computed:

$$SS_b = \frac{C_0^2}{n_0} + \frac{\sum B_j^2}{np} - \frac{(G + C_0)^2}{npq + n_0},$$

where G is the sum of all observations in the factorial part of the experiment. In this type of experiment it is also of interest to contrast the control group with each of the experimental groups or with selected sets. The procedure described in Sec. 3.11 may be adapted for this purpose. In this case the t statistic has the form

$$t = \frac{\bar{C}_0 - \overline{AB}_{ij}}{\sqrt{MS_{w.\,cell}[(1/n_0) + (1/n)]}}.$$

Critical values (Dunnett) are given in Table D.6. The degrees of freedom for this statistic are those of $MS_{w.\,cell}$; k corresponds to the total number of groups, which in this case is $pq + 1$. If comparisons are restricted to selected sets, then k is the number of groups in a set.

Numerical Example

Suppose data obtained from the eight experimental groups and the control in the experiment which has just been described are those given in Table 6.23. The computational symbols at the right of part i are defined in Table 6.15. (Data for the computation of symbol (2) are not given.) Summary data for the control group are given in part ii. The between-cell variation (including the control) is computed in part iii.

As a partial check for homogeneity of the within-cell variance for the factorial and the control parts of the experiment, one has for the factorial part

$$MS_{w.\,cell} = \frac{1092.40}{8(9)} = 15.17.$$

For the control group,

$$MS_{w.\,cell} = \frac{300.00}{19} = 15.79.$$

For these data, there is little question about the appropriateness of pooling the within-cell variations.

Under the definition of the variation due to main effects of factor B

TABLE 6.23 **Numerical example**

(i)

AB summary table ($n_0 = 20$; $n = 10$):

b_0		b_1	b_2	Total		
	a_1	380	310	690	A_1	(1) = 143,143.20
	a_2	405	340	745	A_2	(2) = 148,129
	a_3	485	470	955	A_3	(3) = 146,559.30
	a_4	504	490	994	A_4	(4) = 143,479.40
						(5) = 147,036.60
1000	Total	1774	1610	3384		
C_0		B_1	B_2	G		

Data for control group ($n_0 = 20$):

(ii) $$C_0 = \sum X = 1000, \quad \sum X^2 = 50.300, \quad SS_0 = 50,300 - \frac{(1000)^2}{20} = 300.00$$

(iii) $$SS_{b.\,cell} = \frac{(1000)^2}{20} + 147036.60 - \frac{(3384 + 1000)^2}{100} = 4842.04$$

(iv) $$SS_{control\,vs.\,all\,others} = \frac{[8(50) - 338.40]^2}{\frac{64}{20} + \frac{8}{10}} = 948.64$$

(v)

Source of variation	SS	df	MS	F
Between cell	4842.04	8		
Control vs. all others	948.64	1	948.64	62.00
A (age)	3416.10	3	1138.70	379.57
B (dosage)	336.20	1	336.20	21.97
AB	141.10	3	47.03	3.07
Within cell 1092.40 + 200.00 =	1392.40	91	15.30	

(dosage), which includes the control group as the zero level,

$$SS'_b = \frac{(1000)^2}{20} + \frac{(1174)^2}{40} + \frac{(1610)^2}{40} - \frac{(4384)^2}{100} = 1284.84.$$

Thus,

$$MS'_b = \frac{1284.84}{2} = 642.2 \quad \text{and} \quad F = \frac{MS'_b}{MS_{w.\,cell}} = 41.99.$$

The corresponding F ratio in the analysis-of-variance table is 21.97.

The test on the interaction indicates that this source of variation is significantly greater than zero, $F_{0.95}(3, 91) = 2.71$. The profiles for factor A at levels b_1 and b_2 as well as the control are plotted in Fig. 6-7. (Data for the control group are in units which are comparable with those in the experimental groups.) Inspection of these profiles indicates relatively large differences between the control group and the groups that were irradiated at ages a_1 and a_2. There is relatively little difference between the control group and groups

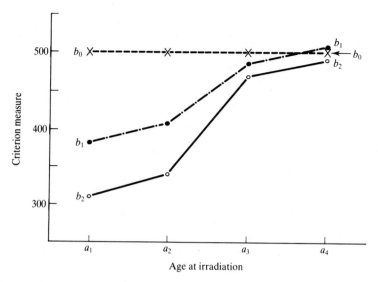

FIGURE 6-7 Profiles for different dosages.

irradiated at ages a_3 and a_4. Further, for groups given irradiation at ages a_1 and a_2, the groups given the larger dosage (b_2) showed the greater decrement in performance. A formal test on the latter statement uses the statistic

$$F = \frac{[AB_{11} + AB_{21} - AB_{12} - AB_{22}]^2}{4n\,\mathrm{MS_{w.\ cell}}}$$

$$= \frac{[380 + 405 - 310 - 340]^2}{40(15.30)} = 29.78.$$

The critical value for a 0.05-level (two-tailed) test on this comparison is $F_{0.95}(1, 91) = 3.95$.

To test the hypothesis that groups given irradiation at ages a_3 and a_4 do not differ from the control group, one may use the comparison

$$C = 2\bar{C}_0 - \bar{A}_3 - \bar{A}_4$$

$$= 2(50.00) - 47.75 - 49.70 = 2.55.$$

The mean square corresponding to this comparison is

$$\mathrm{MS}_C = \frac{C^2}{(4/n_0) + (2/nq)} = \frac{(2.55)^2}{(4/20) + (2/20)} = 21.67.$$

The F ratio is given by

$$F = \frac{\mathrm{MS}_C}{\mathrm{MS_{w.\ cell}}} = \frac{21.67}{15.30} = 1.42.$$

For a (two-tailed) test at the 0.05-level of significance, the critical value for this statistic is $F_{0.95}(1, 91) = 3.95$. Thus the data indicate that there is no statistically significant difference in performance decrement between the groups irradiated at ages a_3 and a_4 and the control group with respect to the criterion of performance measured.

Additional suggestions for analyzing data of the kind discussed in this section are given in Kempthorne (1952, pp. 364–369).

6.8 TEST FOR NONADDITIVITY

The assumptions underlying this test were discussed in Chapter 5. It should be remembered that only one of several possible sources of nonadditivity is checked in this test, namely, that source which is defined by the linear by linear cross product $\alpha_i\beta_j$. The numerical details of this test will be considered in this section.

In some cases which arise in practice, a factorial experiment may have only one observation in each cell. If the strictly additive model (no interaction effects) is appropriate, then what are computationally equivalent to interaction effects may be used as estimates of the experimental error. Computational procedures will be illustrated for the case of a 3×4 factorial experiment having one observation per cell. Suppose that the basic data for this illustration are those given at the left of part i in Table 6.24.

TABLE 6.24   Numerical example

		b_1	b_2	b_3	b_4	Sum	$\bar{A}_i$	$c_i = \bar{A}_i - \bar{G}$	$\sum_j c_j X_{ij} = d_i$
	a_1	8	12	16	20	56	14	3	104
	a_2	2	2	14	18	36	9	−2	168
	a_3	5	4	9	22	40	10	−1	166
(i)	Sum	15	18	39	60	132	$11 = \bar{G}$		$\sum_i c_i d_i = -190$
	$\bar{B}_j$	5	6	13	20			$\sum c_i^2 = 14$	
$c_j = \bar{B}_j - \bar{G}$		−6	−5	2	9	$\sum c_j^2 = 146$			

$(1) = 1452 \qquad\qquad (2) = 1998 \qquad\qquad (3) = 1508 \qquad\qquad (4) = 1890$

(ii)
$$S_{nonadd} = \frac{(\sum c_i d_i)^2}{(\sum c_i^2)(\sum c_j^2)} = \frac{(-190)^2}{(14)(146)} = 17.66$$

	Source of variation	SS	df	MS	F
	A	56.00	2		
	B	438.00	3		
(iii)	AB	52.00	6		
	Nonadd 17.66		1	17.66	2.57
	Balance 34.34		5	6.87	

In the column headed $\bar{A}_i$, the mean of the observations in the corresponding row is entered. In the column headed c_i, an entry has the form $\bar{A}_i - \bar{G}$. For example,

$$c_1 = 14 - 11 = \quad 3,$$
$$c_2 = \quad 9 - 11 = -2.$$

The entries in the row headed c_j have the form $\bar{B}_j - \bar{G}$.

An entry in the column headed d_i is a weighted sum of the entries in the corresponding row, the weights being respective entries in row c_j. For example,

$$d_1 = (-6)(8) + (-5)(12) + (2)(16) + (9)(20) = 104,$$
$$d_2 = (-6)(2) + (-5)(2) \quad + (2)(14) + (9)(18) = 168,$$
$$d_3 = (-6)(5) + (-5)(4) \quad + (2)(9) \quad + (9)(22) = 166.$$

The numerical value of the comparison for nonadditivity is

$$\sum_i c_i \left(\sum_j c_j X_{ij} \right) = \sum_i c_i d_i$$
$$= (3)(104) + (-2)(168) + (-1)(166) = -190.$$

The sum of squares corresponding to this comparison is computed in part ii. The numerical values for the computational symbols defined in Table 6.1 are also given in part ii.

As a partial check on the computation of SS_{nonadd}, the following relationships must hold:

$$pq \left(\sum c_i^2 \right) \left(\sum c_j^2 \right) = (SS_a)(SS_b),$$
$$8(14)(146) = (56)(438),$$
$$24,528 = 24,528$$

The balance, or residual variation, is given by

$$SS_{bal} = SS_{ab} - SS_{nonadd}.$$

Since SS_{nonadd} is a component having a single degree of freedom, SS_{bal} has $(p-1)(q-1) - 1$ degrees of freedom. The F ratio in the test for nonadditivity has the form

$$F = \frac{MS_{nonadd}}{MS_{bal}} = \frac{17.66}{6.87} = 2.57.$$

If the decision rule leads to accepting the hypothesis of additivity, then the strictly additive model is used in subsequent analyses. On the other hand, if this hypothesis is rejected, the more complete model is used in subsequent analyses. The latter model is generally the more conservative in the sense that higher F ratios are required for significance at a specified level. If the level of significance is set at a numerically high value (say, $\alpha = 0.25$ rather than $\alpha = 0.05$ or 0.01), the type 2 error becomes relatively low. In this case low type 2 error implies low probability of using the additive model when in fact it is inappropriate.

If this test is made at the 0.25-level of significance, the critical value is $F_{0.75}(1, 5) = 1.69$. Since the observed value of the F statistic exceeds this critical value, the hypothesis of a strictly additive model is rejected at the 0.25-level of significance. If, however, MS_{ab} is used as the denominator in testing main effects, the resulting test will be biased in the direction of giving too few "significant" results.

There is an alternative method for computing SS_{nonadd} which lends itself more readily to direct generalization to higher-order interaction effects. As a first step in the computation of the comparison desired, one sets up a table in which the entry in cell ij is $c_i c_j$. For the data in Table 6.24 the resulting table is as follows:

	b_1	b_2	b_3	b_4	Total
a_1	-18	-15	6	27	0
a_2	12	10	-4	-18	0
a_3	6	5	-2	-9	0
Total	0	0	0	0	

The entry in cell $ab_{11} = (3)(-6) = -18$; the entry $ab_{12} = (3)(-5) = -15$. As a check on the numerical work, each row total must be zero; each column total must also be zero. Since the row sums and the column sums are zero, the entries in this table define a comparison which belongs to the interaction rather than to either of the main effects.

The comparison in the test for nonadditivity is a weighted sum of the data in the upper left-hand portion of part i of Table 6.24, the weight being the corresponding cell entry in the table given above. Thus,

$$\sum \sum c_i c_j X_{ij} = (-18)(8) + (-15)(12) + \cdots + (-2)(9) + (-9)(22)$$

$$= -190.$$

As a check on the numerical work,

$$\sum \sum (c_i c_j)^2 = \left(\sum c_i^2\right)\left(\sum c_j^2\right).$$

The sum on the left is given by

$$(-18)^2 + (-15)^2 + \cdots + (-2)^2 + (-9)^2 = 2044.$$

The term on the right is given by

$$(14)(146) = 2044.$$

TABLE 6.25 **Numerical example**

		c_1			c_2			c_3			
		b_1	b_2	b_3	b_1	b_2	b_3	b_1	b_2	b_3	Total
(i)	a_1	3	6	9	6	9	12	9	12	15	81
	a_2	6	9	12	12	18	21	15	21	21	135
	a_3	9	9	3	18	21	12	18	18	12	120
	Total	18	24	24	36	48	45	42	51	48	336

(ii)

AB summary table

	b_1	b_2	b_3	Total
a_1	18	27	36	81
a_2	33	48	54	135
a_3	45	48	27	120
Total	96	123	117	336

AC summary table

	c_1	c_2	c_3	Total
a_1	18	27	36	81
a_2	27	51	57	135
a_3	21	51	48	120
Total	66	129	141	336

BC summary table

	c_1	c_2	c_3	Total
b_1	18	36	42	96
b_2	24	48	51	123
b_3	24	45	48	117
Total	66	129	141	336

(iii)

(1) = 4181.33	(4) = 4226.00	(7) = 4758.00
(2) = 4986.00	(5) = 4542.00	(8) = 4590.00
(3) = 4354.00	(6) = 4572.00	(9) = 4986.00

(iv)

$\bar{G} = 12.4$		$\bar{A}_i$	$\bar{B}_j$	$\bar{C}_k$	c_i	c_j	c_k	$\sum c_i^2 = 18.62$
	1	9	10.7	7.3	−3.4	−1.8	−5.1	$\sum c_j^2 = 5.04$
	2	15	13.7	14.3	2.5	1.2	1.9	
	3	13.3	13	15.7	0.9	0.6	3.2	$\sum c_k^2 = 39.86$

		c_1			c_2			c_3			
		b_1	b_2	b_3	b_1	b_2	b_3	b_1	b_2	b_3	Total
(v)	a_1	−31.2	20.8	10.4	11.6	−7.7	−3.9	19.6	−13.1	−6.5	0.0
	a_2	23.0	−15.3	−7.7	−8.6	5.7	2.9	−14.4	9.6	4.8	0.0
	a_3	8.2	−5.5	−2.7	−3.0	2.0	1.0	−5.2	3.5	1.7	0.0
	Total	0.0	0.0	0.0	0.0	0.0	0.0	0.0	0.0	0.0	

This latter computational scheme is readily extended to the case of a $p \times q \times r$ factorial experiment. The data in Table 6.25 will be used to indicate the numerical details. These data represent a $3 \times 3 \times 3$ factorial experiment in which there is one observation per cell. The usual summary tables for a three-factor factorial experiment are given in part ii. Data for the latter are given in part i. Numerical values of the computational symbols defined in Table 6.15 are given in part ii. Since there is only one observation per cell, symbols (2) and (9) are identical, i.e.,

$$\sum X_{ijk}^2 = \sum (ABC_{ijk})^2.$$

(The letter c is used for two different concepts, but the context should make clear what is meant. In one context c_1, c_2, and c_3 represent the levels of factor C. In a second context c_i, c_j, and c_k represent deviations from the grand mean.)

Means and the deviations of the means from the grand mean are computed in part iv. In this context $c_k = \bar{C}_k - \bar{G}$. Similarly, $c_i = \bar{A}_i - \bar{G}$. The entry in cell abc_{ijk} in part v has the general form $c_i c_j c_k$. Thus the entry in cell abc_{111} is $(-3.4)(-1.8)(-5.1) = -31.2$. The entry in cell abc_{123} is $(-3.4)(1.2)(3.2) = -13.1$. As a check on the computational work,

$$\sum_i c_i c_j c_k = \sum_j c_i c_j c_k = \sum_k c_i c_j c_k = 0.$$

That is, the sum of any column in part v must be zero; also the sum over b_j within any fixed level of ac_{ik} must be zero. For example, for level ac_{11}

$$-31.2 + 20.8 + 10.4 = 0.0.$$

For level ac_{12},

$$11.6 + (-7.7) + (-3.9) = 0.0.$$

The comparison associated with nonadditivity is a weighted sum of the entries in the cell of part i, the weights being the corresponding entries in part v. Thus the comparison used in the test for nonadditivity is

$$(-31.2)(3) + (20.8)(6) + (10.4)(9) + \cdots + (1.7)(12) = 60.60.$$

The sum of squares for this comparison has the form

$$SS_{nonadd} = \frac{(60.60)^2}{\sum (c_i c_j c_k)^2}.$$

The divisor is given by

$$\sum (c_i c_j c_k)^2 = (-31.2)^2 + (20.8)^2 + \cdots + (1.7)^2 = 3742.$$

Within rounding error, the following relation must hold:

$$\sum (c_i c_j c_k)^2 = \left(\sum c_i^2 \right) \left(\sum c_j^2 \right) \left(\sum c_k^2 \right).$$

TABLE 6.26 **Summary of analysis of variance**

Source of variation	SS	df	MS	F
A	172.67	2		
B	44.67	2		
C	360.67	2		
AB	173.33	4		
AC	43.33	4		
BC	3.33	4		
ABC	6.67	8		
Nonadd 0.98		1	0.98	1.21
Balance 5.69		7	0.81	

The right-hand side of this last expression is

$$(18.62)(5.04)(39.86) = 3740.7.$$

The analysis of variance is summarized in Table 6.26.
The test for nonadditivity is given by

$$F = \frac{0.98}{0.81} = 1.21.$$

The critical value of this statistic for a 0.25-level test is $F_{0.75}(1, 7) = 1.57$. Since the observed value of the F statistic does not exceed this critical value, there is no reason to reject the hypothesis of additivity. The evidence from this test supports the hypothesis that the components of the three-factor interaction are homogeneous. If the assumptions underlying the test are met, the component for nonadditivity would tend to be large relative to the other components, provided that the three-factor interaction estimated a source of variation different from experimental error. In this case, the three-factor interaction may be considered as an estimate of experimental error (granting the validity of the assumptions). Hence the three-factor interaction term may be dropped from the model. In the latter case, MS_{abc} provides an estimate of σ_ε^2.

6.9 COMPUTATION OF TREND COMPONENTS

Computational procedures for trends for the case of a single-factor experiment were discussed in Sec. 3.3. These procedures generalize to factorial experiments. Principles underlying this generalization were discussed in Sec. 5.11; the actual computation of trend components in a factorial experiment are considered in this section. Computational procedures will be illustrated for the case of a 3×4 factorial experiment having five observations in each cell.

It will be assumed that (1) both factors are fixed, (2) the levels of both factors represent steps along an underlying quantitative scale, and (3) the respective levels represent equally spaced steps along the respective scales. The latter assumption, which is not essential to the development, permits a simplification of the numerical work, since coefficients of orthogonal polynomials may be used to obtain desired sums of squares. For this case, the coefficients for the levels of factor A are as follows (see Table D.10):

Linear: c_i'	-1	0	1
Quadratic: c_i''	1	-2	1

The coefficients for the levels of factor B are as follows:

Linear: c_j'	-3	-1	1	3
Quadratic: c_j''	1	-1	-1	1
Cubic: c_j'''	-1	3	-3	1

The data given in part i of Table 6.27 will be used as a numerical example. [Assume that each entry in the AB summary table is the sum of five observations; data for the computation of symbol (2) are not given.] The analysis of variance is summarized in part iii. This particular analysis does not necessarily give the experimenter all the information he seeks. There are many other ways in which the overall variation may be analyzed.

In spite of the significant interaction, it may be of interest to study the trend components of the main effects. For illustrative purposes, the trend components of the B main effect will be obtained. The comparison associated with the linear component is a weighted sum of B_j totals, the weights being the linear coefficients. For data in part i of Table 6.27, the linear comparison is

$$C_{\text{lin}} = (-3)(19) + (-1)(21) + (1)(28) + (3)(37) = 61.$$

TABLE 6.27   **Numerical example**

(i)

AB summary table ($n = 5$):

	b_1	b_2	b_3	b_4	Total
a_1	3	5	9	14	31
a_2	7	11	15	20	53
a_3	9	5	4	3	21
Total	19	21	28	37	105

(ii)

(1) = 183.75   (3) = 210.55   (5) = 247.40
(2) = 280.00   (4) = 197.00

(iii)

Source of variation	SS	df	MS	F
A	26.80	2	13.40	19.71
B	13.25	3	4.42	6.50
AB	23.60	6	3.93	5.78
Within cell	32.40	48	0.68	

TABLE 6.28 **Trends of B main effects**

(i)

c'_j	-3	-1	1	3	$\sum (c'_j)^2 = 20$
c''_j	1	-1	-1	1	$\sum (c''_j)^2 = 4$
c'''_j	-1	3	-3	1	$\sum (c'''_j)^2 = 20$

(ii)

$$B_j: \quad 19 \quad 21 \quad 28 \quad 37$$

$$SS_{b(\text{lin})} = \frac{(\sum c'_j B_j)^2}{np \sum (c'_j)^2} = \frac{(61)^2}{5(3)(20)} = 12.40$$

$$SS_{b(\text{quad})} = \frac{(\sum c''_j B_j)^2}{np \sum (c''_j)^2} = \frac{(7)^2}{5(3)(4)} = 0.82$$

$$SS_{b(\text{cubic})} = \frac{(\sum c'''_j B_j)^2}{np \sum (c'''_j)^2} = \frac{(-3)^2}{5(3)(20)} = 0.03$$

$$SS_b \qquad\qquad\qquad\qquad\qquad 13.25$$

The linear component of the variation due to the main effects of factor B is

$$SS_{b(\text{lin})} = \frac{C_{\text{lin}}^2}{np \sum (c'_j)^2} = \frac{(61)^2}{5(3)(20)} = 12.40.$$

Computational formulas for the quadratic and cubic components of the B main effect are summarized in Table 6.28. It is noted that the linear component accounts for 12.40/13.25, or 94 percent, of the variation due to the main effect. This means that on the average over levels of factor A the criterion measure predominantly is a linear function of levels of factor B. A test on whether a trend component differs significantly from zero uses the statistic

$$F = \frac{MS_{\text{trend}}}{MS_{\text{w. cell}}}.$$

For example, a test on the quadratic trend is given by

$$F = \frac{MS_{b(\text{quad})}}{MS_{\text{w. cell}}} = \frac{0.82}{0.68} = 1.21.$$

The critical value for a 0.05-level test is $F_{0.95}(1, 48) = 4.04$. Hence the experimental data indicate that the hypothesis of no quadratic trend in the main effect of factor B is tenable.

A significant interaction implies that the response surface for different levels of factor B (or A) is not homogeneous, i.e, that profiles are not parallel. The linear × linear, linear × qudaratic, etc., components of interaction indicate the fit of variously shaped surfaces, i.e., different patterns of profiles. Computational procedures are summarized in Table 6.29. The weights for the linear × linear comparison are given in part i. An entry in cell ab_{ij} of this table

TABLE 6.29 **Trends within AB interaction**

Linear × Linear

	b_1	b_2	b_3	b_4
a_1	3	1	−1	−3
a_2	0	0	0	0
a_3	−3	−1	1	3

(i)

$$SS_{\text{lin}\times\text{lin}} = \frac{[\sum d_{ij}(AB_{ij})]^2}{n(\sum d_{ij}^2)}$$

$$= \frac{(-56)^2}{5(40)} = 15.68$$

Quadratic × Linear

	b_1	b_2	b_3	b_4
a_1	−3	−1	1	3
a_2	6	2	−2	−6
a_3	−3	−1	1	3

(ii)

$$SS_{\text{quad}\times\text{lin}} = \frac{[\sum d_{ij}(AB_{ij})]^2}{n(\sum d_{ij}^2)}$$

$$= \frac{(-68)^2}{5(120)} = 7.71$$

Linear × Quadratic

	b_1	b_2	b_3	b_4
a_1	−1	1	1	−1
a_2	0	0	0	0
a_3	1	−1	−1	1

(iii)

$$SS_{\text{lin}\times\text{quad}} = \frac{[\sum d_{ij}(AB_{ij})]^2}{n(\sum d_{ij}^2)}$$

$$= \frac{(0)^2}{5(8)} = 0$$

has the form

$$d_{ij} = c_i' c_j'.$$

For example,

$$d_{11} = (-1)(-3) = 3, \qquad d_{12} = (-1)(-1) = 1,$$
$$d_{21} = (0)(-3) \;\; = 0, \qquad d_{22} = (0)(-1) \;\; = 0.$$

The weights for the quadratic × linear comparison are given in part ii. An entry in this latter table is given by

$$d_{ij} = c_i'' c_j'.$$

(Although the symbol d_{ij} is used for the typical entry in different tables, the context will make it clear which table is meant. A more explicit, but more cumbersome, notation for the latter d_{ij} would be $d_{i''j'}$.) The entries in part ii are obtained as follows:

$$d_{11} = (1)(3) = 3, \qquad d_{12} = (1)(-1) = -1,$$
$$d_{21} = (-2)(3) = -6, \qquad d_{22} = (-2)(-1) = 2,$$
$$d_{31} = (1)(3) = 3, \qquad d_{32} = (1)(-1) = -1.$$

Computational formulas for some of the trend components of the AB interaction are summarized in Table 6.29. With suitable definition of d_{ij}, the other components have the same general form. In each case d_{ij} refers to an entry in a different table of weights. Of the total variation due to AB, the linear × linear component accounts for 15.68/23.60, or 66 percent. The sum of the linear × linear component and the quadratic × linear components accounts for

$$\frac{15.68 + 7.71}{23.60} = 0.99,$$

or 99 percent. Tests on trend components of the interaction have the following general form:

$$F = \frac{MS_{\text{trend}}}{MS_{\text{w. cell}}}.$$

It is sometimes of interest to study differences in trends for the simple effects of one factor at different levels of a second factor. For illustrative purposes, differences between trends for the simple effects of factor B at different levels of factor A will be obtained. (The degrees of freedom for such differences in trend are $p - 1 = 2$ for each trend.) Computational formulas for these sources of variation are given in Table 6-30.

TABLE 6.30   **Difference in trends for simple effects of factor B**

	b_1	b_2	b_3	b_4	Total	d_i'	d_i''	d_i'''
a_1	3	5	9	14	31	37	3	−1
a_2	7	11	15	20	53	43	1	1
a_3	9	5	4	3	21	−19	3	−3
(i) Total	19	21	28	37	105	61	7	−3
c_j'	−3	−1	1	3	$\sum (c_j')^2 = 20$			
c_j''	1	−1	−1	1	$\sum (c_j'')^2 = 4$			
c_j'''	−1	3	−3	1	$\sum (c_j''')^2 = 20$			

$$\mathrm{SS}_{\text{diff in lin trend}} = \frac{\sum (d_i')^2}{n \sum (c_j')^2} - \frac{(\sum d_i')^2}{np \sum (c_j')^2} = 35.79 - 12.40 = 23.39$$

(ii) $\quad \mathrm{SS}_{\text{diff in quad trend}} = \dfrac{\sum (d_i'')^2}{n \sum (c_j'')^2} - \dfrac{(\sum d_i'')^2}{np \sum (c_j'')^2} = 0.95 - 0.82 = 0.13$

$$\mathrm{SS}_{\text{diff in cubic trend}} = \frac{\sum (d_i''')^2}{n \sum (c_j''')^2} - \frac{(\sum d_i''')^2}{np \sum (c_j''')^2} = 0.11 - 0.03 = 0.08$$

$$\mathrm{SS}_{ab} = 23.60$$

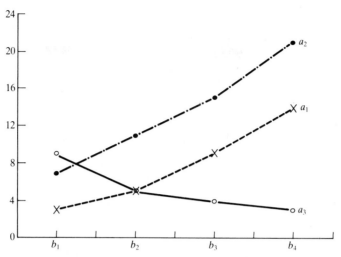

FIGURE 6-8   Profiles of factor B at levels of factor A.

In this table the symbol d_i' is defined as follows:

$$d_i' = \sum_j c_j'(AB_{ij}).$$

For example,

$$d_i' = (-3)(3) + (-1)(5) + (1)(9) + (3)(14) = 37.$$

The symbols d_i'' and d_i''' are defined as follows:

$$d_i'' = \sum_j c_j''(AB_{ij}),$$

$$d_i''' = \sum_j c_j'''(AB_{ij}).$$

The variation due to differences in linear trends in simple effects of factor B explains 23.39/23.60, or 99 percent, of the total variation of the AB interaction. This means that 99 percent of the AB interaction arises from differences between the linear trends in the profiles of factor B at the different levels of factor A. These profiles are shown in Fig. 6-8. If these profiles were plotted in a three-dimensional space, the response surface represented by the AB summary table would be obtained. This response surface is shown in Fig. 6–9. From this surface it is seen that profiles for factor A at fixed levels of factor B are predominantly quadratic in form. However, the profiles for factor B at fixed levels of factor A tend to be linear in form. Hence the shape of this surface is predominantly quadratic × linear.

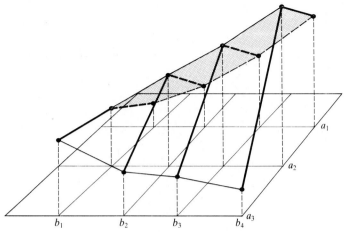

FIGURE 6-9 Response surface.

6.10 GENERAL COMPUTATIONAL FORMULAS FOR MAIN EFFECTS AND INTERACTIONS

The following notation will be used in this section:

A_i = sum of all observations at level a_i.

n_a = number of observations summed to obtain A_i; n_a is assumed constant for all levels of factor A.

AB_{ij} = sum of all observations at level ab_{ij}.

n_{ab} = number of observations summed to obtain AB_{ij}; n_{ab} is assumed constant for all ab_{ij}'s.

ABC_{ijk} = sum of all observations at level abc_{ijk}.

n_{abc} = number of observations summed to obtain ABC_{ijk}; n_{abc} is assumed constant for all abc_{ijk}'s.

In terms of this notation, a general formula for the main effect due to factor A is

$$SS_a = \frac{\sum A_i^2}{n_a} - \frac{G^2}{n_g},$$

where G is the grand total of all observations and n_g is the number of observations summed to obtain G. (In this context an observation is a measurement on the experimental unit.) A general formula for the main effect due to factor B has the form

$$SS_b = \frac{\sum B_j^2}{n_b} - \frac{G^2}{n_g}.$$

The general computational formula for the variation due to the AB interaction is

$$SS_{ab} = \frac{\sum (AB_{ij})^2}{n_{ab}} - \frac{G^2}{n_g} - (SS_a + SS_b).$$

The general computational formula for the variation due to the AC interaction has the form

$$SS_{ac} = \frac{\Sigma (AC_{ik})^2}{n_{ac}} - \frac{G^2}{n_g} - (SS_a + SS_c).$$

(Unless otherwise indicated, the range of summation is over all possible values of the terms being summed.)

The general computational formula for the variation due to the ABC interaction has the form

$$SS_{abc} = \frac{\Sigma (ABC_{ijk})^2}{n_{abc}} - \frac{G^2}{n_g} - (SS_a + SS_b + SS_c + SS_{ab} + SS_{ac} + SS_{bc}).$$

The computational formula for the variation due to the UVW interaction is

$$SS_{uvw} = \frac{\Sigma (UVW)^2}{n_{uvw}} - \frac{G^2}{n_g} - (SS_u + SS_v + SS_w + SS_{uv} + SS_{uw} + SS_{vw}).$$

Variation due to a four-factor interaction has the general formula

$$\begin{aligned}
SS_{uvwx} = \frac{\Sigma (UVWX)^2}{n_{uvwx}} - \frac{G^2}{n_g} &- (SS_u + SS_v + SS_w + SS_x) \\
&- (SS_{uv} + SS_{uw} + SS_{ux} + SS_{vw} + SS_{vx} + SS_{wx}) \\
&- (SS_{uvw} + SS_{uvx} + SS_{uwx} + SS_{vwx}).
\end{aligned}$$

In a factorial experiment having t factors there are

$$\binom{t}{2} \text{ two-factor interactions,}$$

$$\binom{t}{3} \text{ three-factor interactions,}$$

$$\cdots$$

$$\binom{t}{m} m\text{-factor interactions.}$$

For example, in a four-factor experiment, the number of possible two-factor interactions is

$$\binom{4}{2} = \frac{4(3)}{1(2)} = 6.$$

In a four-factor experiment the number of possible three-factor interactions

$$\binom{4}{3} = \frac{4(3)(2)}{1(2)(3)} = 4.$$

Alternatively, give a t-factor interaction, the formulas that have been given above indicate the number of different two-factor, three-factor, etc., interactions that may be formed from the t letters in the t-factor interaction.

The general formula for variation due to a five-factor interaction is

$$SS_{uvwxy} = \frac{\sum (UVWXY)^2}{n_{uvwxy}} - \frac{G^2}{n_g} - [(i) + (ii) + (iii) + (iv)],$$

where (i) $= \sum SS_{\text{main effect}}$—there are five terms in this sum;
  (ii) $= \sum SS_{\text{two-factor int}}$—there are $[5(4)]/[1(2)] = 10$ terms;
  (iii) $= \sum SS_{\text{three-factor int}}$—there are $[5(4)(3)]/[1(2)(3)] = 10$ terms;
  (iv) $= \sum SS_{\text{four-factor int}}$—there are $[5(4)(3)(2)]/[1(2)(3)(4)] = 5$ terms.

The general formulas given above assume that no factor is nested under any other. In case factor C is nested under factor B, the general formula for the main effect due to C within B is

$$SS_{c\,\text{w.}\,b} = \frac{\sum (BC)^2}{n_{bc}} - \frac{\sum B^2}{n_b}$$

$$= SS_c + SS_{bc},$$

where SS_c is the variation due to the main effect of factor C if the nesting is disregarded and SS_{bc} has an analogous definition. The general formula for the $A \times (C$ within $B)$ variation is

$$SS_{a(c\,\text{w.}\,b)} = \frac{\sum (ABC)^2}{n_{abc}} - \frac{\sum (AB)^2}{n_{ab}} - \frac{\sum (BC)^2}{n_{bc}} + \frac{\sum B^2}{n_b}$$

$$= SS_{ac} + SS_{abc},$$

where SS_{abc} is the three-factor variation computed with the nesting disregarded. In general,

$$SS_{uv(x\,\text{w.}\,w)} = SS_{uvx} + SS_{uvxw},$$

where the terms on the right are computed as if there were no nesting.

For the case in which factor C is nested under factor B and factor D is nested under factor C,

$$SS_{d\,\text{w.}\,b\,\text{and}\,c} = \frac{\sum (BCD)^2}{n_{bcd}} - \frac{\sum (BC)^2}{n_{bc}}$$

$$= SS_d + SS_{bd} + SS_{cd} + SS_{bcd}.$$

The terms in this last line are computed as if there were no nesting. Also,

$$SS_{a(d\,\text{w.}\,b\,\text{and}\,c)} = \frac{\sum (ABCD)^2}{n_{abcd}} - \frac{\sum (ABC)^2}{n_{abc}} - \frac{\sum (BCD)^2}{n_{bcd}} + \frac{\sum (BC)^2}{n_{bc}}$$

$$= SS_{ad} + SS_{abd} + SS_{acd} + SS_{abcd}.$$

The degrees of freedom for the variation on the left are the sum of the degrees of freedom of the variations on the right. The degrees of freedom may be checked as follows:

$$\begin{aligned}
df &= pqrs - pqr - qrs + qr \\
&= pqr(s-1) - qr(s-1) \\
&= qr(s-1)(p-1).
\end{aligned}$$

The terms in the first line of the above expression are obtained as follows:

$$pqrs = \text{number of } ABCD \text{ terms,}$$

$$pqr = \text{number of } ABC \text{ terms,}$$

$$qrs = \text{number of } BCD \text{ terms,}$$

$$qr = \text{number of } BC \text{ terms.}$$

6.11 MISSING DATA

For a factorial experiment in which the cell frequencies are not equal but all n_{ij}'s are approximately equal, the analysis by the method of unweighted means presents no particular problems, provided that all cells contain at least one observation. In the unweighted-means analysis, the mean of each cell is estimated by the observations actually made within that cell. In cases where the number of observations within a particular cell is small relative to the number of observations in other cells in the same row and column or adjacent rows and adjacent columns, then information provided by these other cells may be used in estimating the mean of a specified cell. In an unweighted-means analysis, such information is not utilized in the estimation process.

In an experiment having no observed data in given cells, estimates of such cell means may have to be obtained from other cells in the experiment. If the form of the response surface were known, estimates of the missing entries could be obtained by using a multiple regression equation. This solution is generally not practical. One method, having somewhat limited utility, is to estimate the missing mean in cell ij by the following formula,

$$\overline{AB}'_{ij} = \bar{A}'_i + \bar{B}'_j - \bar{G}',$$

where $\bar{A}'_i$ is the mean of the observations actually made under level a_i; similar definitions hold for $\bar{B}'_j$ and $\bar{G}'$. This method of estimating missing data assumes no interaction present. Because this method of estimation does not take into account trends in the row and column of the missing entry, its utility is limited. For the case of a three-factor experiment, the method that has just been described takes the form

$$\overline{ABC}'_{ijk} = \bar{A}'_i + \bar{B}'_j + \bar{C}'_k - 2\bar{G}'.$$

The presence of interaction effects is a stumbling block in all methods for estimating missing cell entries. A review of methods that have been proposed and an extensive bibliography on the topic of missing data are given in Federer

TABLE 6.31 **Numerical example**

	b_1	b_2	b_3	b_4	Total
a_1	28	20	11	10	69
a_2	u_{21}	16	15	8	$39 + u_{21}$
a_3	29	13	16	u_{34}	$58 + u_{34}$
a_4	27	10	18	11	66
a_5	28	11	15	10	64
Total	112 + u_{21}	70	75	39 + u_{34}	$296 + u_{21} + u_{34}$

(1955, pp. 124–127, 133–134). Caution and judgment are called for in the use of any method for estimating missing data. Each of the proposed methods has a set of assumptions that must be considered with care.

Consider the numerical data given in Table 6.31. These data represent the available observations in a 5×4 factorial experiment. Assume the levels of the factors represent steps along a quantitative scale. There is a single measurement in 18 of the 20 cells. Entries in cells ab_{21} and ab_{34} are missing. The unknown values of these cell entries are designated u_{21} and u_{34}. (The data in this table appear in Bennett and Franklin (1954, p. 383).) A method of estimating missing observations, which minimizes the interaction effect in the analysis resulting when such estimates are used in place of the missing data, is described by Bennett and Franklin (1954, pp. 382–383). Using this method, Bennett and Franklin arrive at the following estimates:

$$u_{21} = 28.6, \qquad u_{34} = 10.2.$$

If these two estimates of the missing entries are inserted in their proper places and the usual analysis of variance computed as if all data were observed, the variation due to AB will be a minimum. In essence, this principle for estimating the missing entries keeps the profiles of the simple effects as parallel as possible.

A simplified version of this latter principle utilizes information from only those cells adjacent to the cell in which data are missing. For example,

$$\frac{u_{21}}{16} = \frac{\left(\frac{28}{20}\right) + \left(\frac{29}{13}\right)}{2}.$$

Solving for u_{21} gives

$$u_{21} = 29.0.$$

This method of estimation assumes that the slope of the profiles for levels b_1 and b_2 at level a_2 is the mean of corresponding slopes at levels a_1 and a_3. The latter two slopes can be obtained from the observed data. Analogously,

$$\frac{u_{34}}{16} = \frac{(\frac{8}{15}) + (\frac{11}{18})}{2},$$

from which

$$u_{34} = 9.2.$$

To use the first method discussed in this section for estimating missing entries, one proceeds as follows:

$$\bar{A}_2' = \frac{39}{3} = 13.0, \qquad \bar{A}_3' = 19.3;$$

$$\bar{B}_1' = \frac{112}{4} = 28.0, \qquad \bar{B}_4' = 9.8;$$

$$\bar{G}' = \frac{296}{18} = 16.4.$$

In each case the denominator is the number of observations in the corresponding total. The estimates of the unknown entries are

$$u_{21} = 13.0 + 28.0 - 16.4 = 24.6,$$
$$u_{34} = 19.3 + 9.8 - 16.4 = 12.6.$$

If the analysis of variance were to be carried out with estimated values substituted for the missing values, the degrees of freedom for the resulting two-factor interaction would be

$$df_{ab} = (p-1)(q-1) - (\text{number of missing values}).$$

For the numerical example in Table 6.31,

$$df_{ab} = 4(3) - 2 = 10.$$

By way of summary, there are mathematically elegant methods for estimating missing cell entries. None of these methods is satisfactory unless the experimenter has information about the nature of the response surface being studied. There is, however, no real substitute for experimental data. In the example given in Table 6.31, the experimentally determined values of the missing entries were

$$u_{21} = 23, \qquad u_{34} = 24.$$

None of the methods considered yielded values relatively close to the observed value for u_{34}.

6.12 SPECIAL COMPUTATIONAL PROCEDURES WHEN ALL FACTORS HAVE TWO LEVELS

When each factor in a factorial experiment has two levels, the computational formulas for main effects and interactions may be simplified. For the case of a

2×2 factorial experiment having n observations per cell,

$$SS_a = \frac{(A_1 - A_2)^2}{4n},$$

$$SS_b = \frac{(B_1 - B_2)^2}{4n},$$

$$SS_{ab} = \frac{[(AB_{11} + AB_{22}) - (AB_{12} + AB_{21})]^2}{4n}.$$

In the expression for the interaction, note that the sum of the subscripts of each term in the first set of parentheses is an even number, whereas the sum of the subscripts for each term in the second set of parentheses is an odd number.

For the case of a $2 \times 2 \times 2$ factorial experiment having n observations per cell,

$$SS_a = \frac{(A_1 - A_2)^2}{8n},$$

$$SS_b = \frac{(B_1 - B_2)^2}{8n},$$

$$SS_c = \frac{(C_1 - C_2)^2}{8n},$$

$$SS_{ab} = \frac{[(AB_{11} + AB_{22}) - (AB_{12} + AB_{21})]^2}{8n},$$

$$SS_{ac} = \frac{[(AC_{11} + AC_{22}) - (AC_{12} + AC_{21})]^2}{8n},$$

$$SS_{bc} = \frac{[(BC_{11} + BC_{22}) - (BC_{12} + BC_{21})]^2}{8n},$$

$$SS_{abc} = \frac{[(ABC_{111} + ABC_{122} + ABC_{212} + ABC_{221}) - (ABC_{112} + ABC_{121} + ABC_{211} + ABC_{222})]^2}{8n}.$$

Again note that in expressions for interactions the sum of the subscripts for each term within a pair of parentheses is an odd number in one case and an even number in the other case.

The computations for a three-factor experiment may be made without obtaining two-factor summary tables by following the scheme given in Table 6.32.

The ABC summary table is given in part i. The symbol s_1' in part i' represents the sum of the entries in the first column of part i; s_2', s_3', and s_4' represent sums of entries in the respective columns of part i. These sums should be arranged as indicated in part i'. The symbol d_1' represents the difference between the two entries in the first column in part i, that is,

TABLE 6.32 **Computational scheme for $2 \times 2 \times 2$ factorial experiment**

		c_1		c_2	
		b_1	b_2	b_1	b_2
(i)	a_1	ABC_{111}	ABC_{121}	ABC_{112}	ABC_{122}
	a_2	ABC_{211}	ABC_{221}	ABC_{212}	ABC_{222}
		(1)	(2)	(3)	(4)
(i′)		s_1'	s_3'	d_1'	d_3'
		s_2'	s_4'	d_2'	d_4'
(i″)		s_1''	s_3''	d_1''	d_3''
		s_2''	s_4''	d_2''	d_4''
(i‴)		s_1'''	s_3'''	d_1'''	d_3'''
		s_2'''	s_4'''	d_2'''	d_4'''
(ii)		$SS_a = (s_2''')^2/8n$		$SS_c = (d_1''')^2/8n$	
		$SS_b = (s_3''')^2/8n$		$SS_{ac} = (d_2''')^2/8n$	
		$SS_{ab} = (s_4''')^2/8n$		$SS_{bc} = (d_3''')^2/8n$	
				$SS_{abc} = (d_4''')^2/8n$	

$d_1' = ABC_{111} - ABC_{211}$. The symbols d_2', d_3', and d_4' represent corresponding differences between entries in corresponding columns in part i. For example, $d_4' = ABC_{122} - ABC_{222}$.

The entries in part i″ are obtained from the entries in part i′ in the same general manner as corresponding entries were obtained from part i. That is,

$$s_1'' = s_1' + s_2', \qquad s_3'' = d_1' + d_2',$$
$$s_2'' = s_3' + s_4', \qquad s_4'' = d_3' + d_4'.$$

Also,

$$d_1'' = s_1' - s_2', \qquad d_3'' = d_1' - d_2',$$
$$d_2'' = s_3' - s_4', \qquad d_4'' = d_3' - d_4'.$$

The entries in part i‴ are obtained from the entries in part i″ by means of the same general pattern.

$$s_1''' = s_1'' + s_2'', \qquad s_3''' = d_1'' + d_2'',$$
$$s_2''' = s_3'' + s_4'', \qquad s_4''' = d_3'' + d_4''.$$

Also

$$d_1''' = s_1'' - s_2'', \qquad d_3''' = d_1'' - d_2'',$$
$$d_2''' = s_3'' - s_4'', \qquad d_4''' = d_3'' - d_4''.$$

Computational formulas for the sums of squares are given in part ii. These

TABLE 6.33 **Numerical example**

		c_1		c_2	
(i)		b_1	b_2	b_1	b_2	$(n = 5)$
a_1		10	15	20	10
a_2		20	30	30	10
		(1)	(2)	(3)	(4)
(i′)		30	50	−10	−10
		45	20	−15	0
(i″)		75	−25	−15	5
		70	−10	30	−10
(i‴)		145	15	5	−45
		−35	−5	−15	15

(ii)

$SS_a = (-35)^2/40 = 30.62$ $SS_c = (5)^2/40 = 0.62$

$SS_b = (15)^2/40 = 5.62$ $SS_{ac} = (-15)^2/40 = 5.62$

$SS_{ab} = (-5)^2/40 = 0.62$ $SS_{bc} = (-45)^2/40 = 50.62$

$SS_{abc} = (15)^2/40 = 5.62$

computational formulas are identical to those given earlier in this section. A numerical example of this computational scheme is given in Table 6.33. As a check on the computational work,

$$SS_{b.cells} = \frac{\sum (ABC)_2}{n} - \frac{G^2}{8n}$$

$$= \sum (\text{main effects}) + \sum (\text{two-factor int})$$

$$+ \sum (\text{three-factor int}).$$

For the data in Table 6.33,

$$SS_{b. cells} = 625.00 - 525.62 = 99.38.$$

Within rounding error, this is the numerical value of the sum of the variations computed in part ii.

The computational scheme that has just been illustrated may be generalized to any 2^k factorial experiment, where k is the number of factors. The generalization to a $2^4 = 2 \times 2 \times 2 \times 2$ factorial experiment is illustrated in Table 6.34. In part i the $ABCD$ summary table is represented schematically. In part i′ each $s′$ represents the sum of the entries in the corresponding columns of part i; each $d′$ represents the difference between the elements in the corresponding columns of part i. Entries in part i″ are obtained from the

TABLE 6.34 **Computational scheme for 2^4 factorial experiment**

| | | d_1 | | | | d_2 | | |
| | c_1 | | c_2 | | c_1 | | c_2 | |
	b_1	b_2	b_1	b_2	b_1	b_2	b_1	b_2
(i) a_1 a_2								
	(1)	(2)	(3)	(4)	(5)	(6)	(7)	(8)
(i′)	s_1' s_2'	s_3' s_4'	s_5' s_6'	s_7' s_8'	d_1' d_2'	d_3' d_4'	d_5' d_6'	d_7' d_8'
(i″)	s_1'' s_2''	s_3'' s_4''	s_5'' s_6''	s_7'' s_8''	d_1'' d_2''	d_3'' d_4''	d_5'' d_6''	d_7'' d_8''
(i‴)	s_1''' s_2'''	s_3''' s_4'''	s_5''' s_6'''	s_7''' s_8'''	d_1''' d_2'''	d_3''' d_4'''	d_5''' d_6'''	d_7''' d_8'''
(i^{iv})	s_1^{iv} s_2^{iv}	s_3^{iv} s_4^{iv}	s_5^{iv} s_6^{iv}	s_7^{iv} s_8^{iv}	d_1^{iv} d_2^{iv}	d_3^{iv} d_4^{iv}	d_5^{iv} d_6^{iv}	d_7^{iv} d_8^{iv}
(ii)	— A	B AB	C AC	BC ABC	D AD	BD ABD	CD ACD	BCD $ABCD$

entries in the columns of part i′ in an analogous manner. That is,

$$s_1'' = s_1' + s_2', \qquad d_1'' = s_1' - s_2';$$
$$s_2'' = s_3' + s_4', \qquad d_2'' = s_3' - s_4';$$
$$\cdots \qquad\qquad \cdots \quad ;$$
$$s_8'' = d_7' + d_8', \qquad d_8'' = d_7' - d_8'.$$

This procedure continues until part i^k is completed, in this case until part i^{iv} is completed. Computational formulas for the variation due to the sources indicated in part ii may be obtained from the corresponding entry in part i^{iv}. For example,

$$SS_c = \frac{(s_5^{iv})^2}{16n}, \qquad SS_{abd} = \frac{(d_4^{iv})^2}{16n}.$$

The general formula is

$$\frac{(s^k)^2}{2^k n} \quad \text{or} \quad \frac{(d^k)^2}{2^k n}.$$

This computational procedure is particularly useful when k is 4 or larger.

6.13 UNEQUAL CELL FREQUENCIES—LEAST-SQUARES SOLUTION

The data in Table 6.35 will be used to illustrate the computational procedures associated with the least-squares estimates of the sums of squares. The rationale underlying these procedures was discussed in Sec. 5.20. Definitions of the basic symbols are also given in the latter section.

These data have been taken from Anderson and Bancroft (1952, p. 243). The levels of factor A represent sex of animal; levels of factor B represent four successive generations of animals. In this type of experiment, the cell frequencies are, in a real sense, an integral part of the design. Hence a least-squares analysis is more appropriate than an unweighted-means analysis. In part iii, with the exception of symbol (2), data from which the numerical values of the symbols are computed are given in parts i and ii. The raw data for symbol (2) are not given.

When one of the factors has only two levels, the simplest approach (see Rao, 1952, pp. 95–100) is to obtain $SS_{ab(\text{adj})}$ directly from part i of Table 6.35 and from Table 6.36. In the latter table,

$$d_j = \overline{AB}_{1j} - \overline{AB}_{2j} \qquad \text{and} \qquad w_j = \frac{n_{1j}n_{2j}}{n_{1j} + n_{2j}}.$$

For example,
$$w_1 = \frac{(21)(27)}{48} = 11.8125.$$

TABLE 6.35 **Numerical example with unequal cell frequencies ($p = 2$)**

Cell frequencies:

		b_1	b_2	b_3	b_4	Total
(i)	a_1	$n_{11} = 21$	$n_{12} = 15$	$n_{13} = 12$	$n_{14} = 7$	$n_{1.} = 55$
	a_2	$n_{21} = 27$	$n_{22} = 25$	$n_{23} = 23$	$n_{24} = 19$	$n_{2.} = 95$
		$n_{.1} = 48$	$n_{.2} = 40$	$n_{.3} = 35$	$n_{.4} = 26$	$n_{..} = 149$

Cell totals:

		b_1	b_2	b_3	b_4	Total
(ii)	a_1	$AB_{11} = 3716$	$AB_{12} = 2422$	$AB_{13} = 1868$	$AB_{14} = 1197$	$A_1 = 9203$
	a_2	$AB_{21} = 2957$	$AB_{22} = 2852$	$AB_{23} = 2496$	$AB_{24} = 2029$	$A_2 = 10{,}334$
	Total	$B_1 = 6673$	$B_2 = 5274$	$B_3 = 4364$	$B_4 = 3226$	$G = 19{,}537$

(iii)

$$\begin{aligned}
(1) &= G^2/n_{..} &&= 2{,}561{,}707 \\
(2) &= \sum X^2 &&= 2{,}738{,}543 \\
(3) &= \sum (A_i^2/n_{i.}) = 1{,}539{,}913 + 1{,}136{,}080 &&= 2{,}675{,}993 \\
(4) &= \sum (B_j^2/n_{.j}) &&= 2{,}567{,}463 \\
(5) &= \sum\sum (AB_{ij}^2/n_{ij}) &&= 2{,}680{,}848
\end{aligned}$$

TABLE 6.36   **Direct computation of $SS_{ab(\text{adj})}$**

Cell means:

	b_1	b_2	b_3	b_4	
a_1	176.9524	161.4667	155.6667	171.0000	
a_2	109.5185	114.0900	108.5217	106.7895	
d_j	67.4339	47.3867	47.1450	64.2105	
w_j	11.8125	9.3750	7.8857	5.1154	$34.1886 = \sum w_j$
$w_j d_j$	796.5629	444.2344	371.7713	328.4624	$1941.0310 = \sum w_j d_j$
					$113{,}384.04 \quad = \sum w_j d_j^2$

The adjusted sum of squares due to interaction is given by

$$SS_{ab(\text{adj})} = \sum w_j d_j^2 - \frac{(\sum w_j d_j)^2}{\sum w_j}.$$

The first term on the right is most readily obtained from the terms $w_j d_j$, that is,

$$\sum w_j d_j^2 = d_1(w_1 d_1) + d_2(w_2 d_2) + \cdots + d_4(w_4 d_4)$$

$$= 113{,}384.$$

Thus

$$SS_{ab(\text{adj})} = 113{,}384 - \frac{(1941.0310)^2}{34.1886} = 3183.$$

From part iii of Table 6.35, the unadjusted sums of squares are

$$SS_{\text{cells}} = (5) - (1) = 119{,}141,$$

$$SS_a = (3) - (1) = 114{,}286,$$

$$SS_b = (4) - (1) = 5756.$$

The adjusted sum of squares due to factor A is

$$SS_{a(\text{adj})} = SS_{\text{cells}} - SS_{ab(\text{adj})} - SS_b = 110{,}202.$$

Similarly,

$$SS_{b(\text{adj})} = SS_{\text{cells}} - SS_{ab(\text{adj})} - SS_a = 1672.$$

As a partial check on the numerical work,

$$\sum w_j d_j^2 = R(\alpha \mid \mu, \beta) + R(\alpha\beta \mid \mu, \alpha, \beta) = SS_{a(\text{adj})} + SS_{ab(\text{adj})}$$

$$= 110{,}202 + 3183$$

$$= 113{,}385.$$

Also

$$\frac{(\sum w_j d_j)^2}{\sum w_j} = SS_{a(\text{adj})} = 110{,}202.$$

TABLE 6.37 **Summary of analysis of variance (least squares)**

Source of variation	SS	df	MS
$R(\alpha \mid \mu, \beta) = A(\text{adj})$	110,202	1	110,202
$R(\beta \mid \mu, \alpha) = B(\text{adj})$	1672	3	557
$R(\alpha\beta \mid \mu, \alpha, \beta) = AB(\text{adj})$	3183	3	1060
Error	57,695	141	409.2

From part iii of Table 6.35 one obtains

$$\text{SS}_{\text{error}} = (2) - (5) = 57,695.$$

A summary of the analysis of variance is given in Table 6.37. Tests follow the same pattern as that of the usual factorial experiment in which model I is appropriate.

The computation of

$$\text{SS}_{b(\text{adj})} = R(\beta \mid \mu, \alpha)$$

by means of the procedures discussed in Sec. 5.20 is illustrated in Table 6.38. In Sec. 5.20 it was indicated that the reduced normal equation for $\hat{\beta}$ was

$$\hat{\beta} M_b = \mathbf{v}_b,$$

and that
$$\hat{\beta} = E_b \mathbf{v}_b,$$

where E_b was a generalized inverse of M_b. Hence

$$R(\beta \mid \mu, \alpha) = \beta' \mathbf{v}_b.$$

One may, however, obtain $R(\beta \mid \mu, \alpha)$ without first obtaining an explicit solution for $\hat{\beta}$. The algorithm for doing this is outlined in Table 6.38.

In part i of this table are the cell and marginal frequencies corresponding to those given in Table 6.35. In part ii, the diagonal elements of D_a are the marginal frequencies for the levels of factor A; similarly, D_b contains the marginal frequencies for the levels of factor B. The elements of the matrix C are the cell frequencies. The elements of the vector $\mathbf{a}$ are the totals A_1 and A_2 as given in part ii of Table 6.35. The elements of the vector $\mathbf{b}$ are the treatment totals B_1, B_2, B_3, B_4 as given in Table 6.35.

The matrix M_b is computed in part iii. Note that the row totals are zero. The entries in the matrix M_b are the coefficients of $\hat{\beta}_1, \ldots, \hat{\beta}_4$ in the reduced normal equations for the levels of factor B. The reduced normal equations are those obtained from the complete set (which includes the levels of both factors A and B) when the effects of the levels of factor A are "swept out" of the complete set. What remains in the reduced set is that part of the effects of the levels of factor B which is orthogonal to the effects associated with the levels of factor A. The components of the vector $\mathbf{v}_b$ represent the right-hand side of the reduced normal equations.

TABLE 6.38 **Computation of** $SS_{b(\text{adj})}$

Cell frequencies:

(i)

	b_1	b_2	b_3	b_4	Total
a_1	21	15	12	7	55
a_2	27	25	23	19	94
Total	48	40	35	26	149

(ii)

$$D_a = \begin{bmatrix} 55 & 0 \\ 0 & 94 \end{bmatrix} \qquad D = \begin{bmatrix} 48 & 0 & 0 & 0 \\ 0 & 40 & 0 & 0 \\ 0 & 0 & 35 & 0 \\ 0 & 0 & 0 & 26 \end{bmatrix}$$

$$C = \begin{bmatrix} 21 & 15 & 12 & 7 \\ 27 & 25 & 23 & 19 \end{bmatrix} \qquad \mathbf{a} = \begin{bmatrix} 9203 \\ 10334 \end{bmatrix} \qquad \mathbf{b} = \begin{bmatrix} 6673 \\ 5274 \\ 4364 \\ 3226 \end{bmatrix}$$

(iii)

$$M_b = D_b - C'D_a^{-1}C = \begin{bmatrix} 32.2265 & -12.9081 & -11.1882 & -8.1302 \\ & 29.2602 & -9.3897 & -6.9623 \\ & \text{symmetric} & 26.7542 & -6.1762 \\ & & & 21.2687 \end{bmatrix}$$

$$\mathbf{v}_b = \mathbf{b} - C'D_a^{-1}\mathbf{a} = \begin{bmatrix} 190.85 \\ 15.69 \\ -172.46 \\ -34.08 \end{bmatrix}$$

(iv)

	b_1	b_2	b_3	b_4	v_b
b_1	32.2265	-12.9081	-11.1882	-8.1302	190.85
b_2		29.2602	-9.3897	-6.9623	15.69
b_3			26.7542	-6.1762	-172.46
b_4				21.2687	-34.08
b_1'	5.6769	-2.2739	-1.9708	-1.4322	33.6187
b_2'		4.9081	-2.8262	-2.0821	18.7721
b_3'			3.8578	-3.8579	-13.7774

$$R(\boldsymbol{\beta} \mid \mu, \boldsymbol{\alpha}) = (33,6187)^2 + (18.7721)^2 + (-13.7774)^2 = 1672.43$$

In part iv of Table 6.38 the Dwyer algorithm (as described in Appendix C) is applied to the first three rows of the matrix

$$[M_b \quad \mathbf{v}_b],$$

that is, the matrix M_b augmented by the column vector $\mathbf{v}_b$. Since the matrix M_b is singular (actually of rank $q - 1$), the Dwyer algorithm cannot proceed beyond the third row. The entries in column $\mathbf{v}_b$ in the lower half of part iv represent the following:

$$(33.6187)^2 = R(\beta_1 \mid \mu, \boldsymbol{\alpha}),$$
$$(18.7721)^2 = R(\beta_2 \mid \mu, \boldsymbol{\alpha}, \beta_1),$$
$$(-13.7774)^2 = R(\beta_3 \mid \mu, \boldsymbol{\alpha}, \beta_1, \beta_2).$$

Hence $R[\boldsymbol{\beta} \mid \mu, \boldsymbol{\alpha})$ may be computed as indicated in the last row of part iv. One has

$$SS_{b(\text{adj})} = R(\boldsymbol{\beta} \mid \mu, \boldsymbol{\alpha}) = 1672.$$

From the latter value, one obtains

$$SS_{a(\text{adj})} = SS_a - SS_b + SS_{b(\text{adj})}$$
$$= 114{,}286 - 5756 + 1672 = 110{,}202.$$

Also
$$SS_{ab(\text{adj})} = SS_{\text{cells}} - SS_a - SS_{b(\text{adj})}$$
$$= 119{,}141 - 114{,}286 - 1672 = 3183.$$

This last value is equal to that obtained from the direct computation in Table 6.36.

By way of contrast to the least-squares approach, the unweighted-means analysis for the data in Table 6.35 is summarized in Table 6.39. The cell entries in part i are the cell means. The rows and marginal totals for the cell means are also given in part i. Thus

$$A_1 = \sum \overline{AB}_{1j} = 665.0858,$$

$$B_1 = \sum \overline{AB}_{i1} = 286.4709.$$

TABLE 6.39 **Unweighted-means analysis**

Cell means and marginal totals of cell means:

	b_1	b_2	b_3	b_4	Total
(i) a_1	176.9524	161.4667	155.6667	171.0000	665.0858
a_2	109.5185	114.0900	108.5217	106.7895	438.9197
Total	286.4709	275.5567	264.1884	277.7895	1104.0055
	B_1	B_2	B_3	B_4	G

$$(1) = G^2/8 = 152{,}353.52 \qquad (4) = \sum B^2/2 = 152{,}479.79$$
(ii)
$$(3) = \sum A^2/4 = 158{,}747.41 \qquad (5) = \sum (\overline{AB})^2 = 159{,}049.19$$
$$\bar{n} = 15.575687$$

(iii)
$$SS_a = \bar{n}[(3) - (1)] \qquad\qquad = 99{,}589$$
$$SS_b = \bar{n}[(4) - (1)] \qquad\qquad = 1967$$
$$SS_{ab} = \bar{n}[(5) - (3) - (4) + (1)] = 2744$$

TABLE 6.40 **Summary of unweighted-means analysis of variance**

Source of variation	SS	df	MS
A	99,589	1	99,589
B	1,967	3	656
AB	2,744	3	915
Error		141	409.2

The computational symbols are defined and computed in part ii of the table. The harmonic mean of the cell frequencies is also given in part ii. Thus

$$\bar{n} = \frac{8}{\sum (1/n_{ij})}.$$

In part iii the variations due to main effects and interaction are computed. A summary of the analysis of variance appears in Table 6.40.

In this case the unweighted-means analysis and the least-squares analysis give roughly comparable results. The variance due to error is the same in both analyses.

TABLE 6.41 **Weighted-means analysis for main effects**

		a_1	a_2	
(i)	$h_i = \dfrac{q}{\sum (1/n_{ij})}$	11.7483	23.1011	
	$w_i = h_i/q$	2.9371	5.7753	$\sum w_i = 8.7124$
	$\bar{A}_i$	166.2714	109.7299	
	$w_i\bar{A}_i$	488.3557	633.7231	$\sum w_i\bar{A}_i = 1122.0788$

(ii)

$$SS_a = q^2\left[\sum w_i\bar{A}_i^2 - \frac{(\sum w_i\bar{A}_i)^2}{\sum w_i}\right]$$

$$= 16(150,737.9583 - 144,513.6625) = 99,588.73$$

		b_1	b_2	b_3	b_4	
(iii)	$h_j = \dfrac{p}{\sum\limits_i (1/n_{ij})}$	23.6250	18.7500	15.7714	10.2308	
	$w_j = h_j/p$	11.8125	9.3700	7.8857	5.1154	$\sum w_j = 34.1836$
	$\bar{B}_j$	143.2354	137.7783	132.0942	138.8947	
	$w_j\bar{B}_j$	1691.9682	1290.9827	1041.6552	710.5019	$\sum w_j\bar{B}_j = 4735.1084$

(iv)

$$SS_b = p^2\left[\sum w_j\bar{B}_j^2 - \frac{(\sum w_j\bar{B}_j)^2}{\sum w_j}\right]$$

$$= 4(656,500.4380 - 655,906.5684) = 2375.48$$

The weighted-means analysis for main effects (as described in Sec. 5.20) is illustrated in Table 6.41. In part i, the entries in row h_i are the harmonic means of the cell frequencies in row a_i. The entries in row $\bar{A}_i$ are the unweighted means of the cell means at level a_i. Thus, from Table 6.39, one has

$$\bar{A}_i = \frac{\sum\limits_j \overline{AB}_{1j}}{q} = \frac{665.0858}{4} = 166.2714.$$

Following the procedures outlined in Sec. 5.20, the variation due to the main effects of factor A is computed in part ii.

Since factor A has only two levels in this case, one may use the following comparison to obtain SS_a:

$$C_a = \sum\limits_j \overline{AB}_{1j} - \sum\limits_j \overline{AB}_{2j}.$$

Thus

$$SS_a = \frac{C_a^2}{\sum (1/n_{ij})}.$$

From the data in Table 6.39,

$$C_a = 665.0858 - 438.9197 = 226.1661,$$

$$SS_a = \frac{(226.1661)^2}{0.513621} = 99{,}589.$$

6.14 ANALYSIS OF VARIANCE IN TERMS OF POLYNOMIAL PROGRESSION

The sources of variation in both orthogonal and nonorthogonal experiments may be obtained using the techniques of polynomial regression, provided that appropriate terms are included in the polynomial. This is true if the factors in the design are qualitative, quantitative, or a mixture of qualitative and quantitative variables. Appendix C relates analysis of variance to regression.

6.15 EXERCISES

1. An experimenter was interested in evaluating the effects of reinforcement contingencies at $p = 2$ levels and magnitude of reward at $q = 3$ levels upon performance in a discrimination learning task. A total of 30 rats was selected randomly from a large colony and assigned at random in equal numbers to the $2 \times 3 = 6$ treatment conditions of a factorial design. The performance data were:

Reinforcement contingency	Reward magnitude		
	b_1	b_2	b_3
a_1	10, 6, 2, 6, 7	12, 10, 8, 10, 11	10, 8, 6, 8, 9
a_2	6, 4, 2, 4, 5	16, 12, 8, 12, 13	17, 14, 11, 14, 15

(*a*) Carry out the analysis of variance and test the hypotheses

$$H_0: \mu_1 = \mu_2$$

$$H_0: \mu_{.1} = \mu_{.2} = \mu_{.3}$$

$$H_0: \sigma^2_{\alpha\beta} = 0$$

($\alpha = 0.05$). Assume A and B are both fixed factors.

(*b*) Plot the $\overline{AB}_{ij}$ values to visually examine the outcome of the study.

(*c*) Carry out analyses of simple main effects comparing reward magnitudes for reinforcement contingencies a_1 and a_2, respectively. Test

$$H_0: \sigma^2_{\beta \text{ at } a_1} = 0$$

$$H_0: \sigma^2_{\beta \text{ at } a_2} = 0$$

with $\alpha = 0.05$.

(*d*) Show numerically that $SS_{b \text{ for } a_1} + SS_{b \text{ for } a_2} = SS_b + SS_{ab}$.

(*e*) What is the numerical value of α_{expw} for the total set of tests carried out in (*a*) and (*c*) above?

(*f*) Compute

$$\hat{\omega}^2_\alpha, \ \hat{\omega}^2_\beta, \text{ and } \hat{\omega}^2_{\alpha\beta}.$$

(*g*) Compute statistical power for the three tests of significance carried out in (*a*) above.

(*h*) Assuming that these data provide reliable measures of effect sizes and $\hat{\sigma}^2_\varepsilon$, what sample size would have been required for power $= 0.90$ on each of the three tests carried out in (*a*) above?

(*i*) The experimenter had reason to believe on the basis of prior research that the following comparisons should be nonzero.

$$\psi_1 = \mu_{11} - \mu_{12}$$

$$\psi_2 = \mu_{21} - \mu_{22}$$

$$\psi_3 = (\mu_{11} + \mu_{12})/2 - \mu_3$$

$$\psi_4 = \mu_{21} - \mu_{13}$$

(1) Which of these comparisons are orthogonal?

(2) Compute the variation associated with each comparison and use an F statistic to test the hypothesis that each comparison is zero ($\alpha_{\text{ind}} = 0.05$).

(3) What is the probability that at least one Type 1 error has been made in the set of tests in (2) above?

(*j*) Assume that three rats died during the experiment due to causes which are unrelated to the treatment conditions. No data are available, therefore, for observations X_{112}, X_{223}, and X_{234}. Use an unweighted-means analysis to re-analyze the data.

2. What are the expected values of the mean squares for each of the following completely-randomized designs?
   (a) 2×3 factorial, $n_{ij} = 10$, A and B random.
   (b) $3 \times 2 \times 4$ factorial, $n_{ijk} = 20$, A fixed, B and C random.
   (c) A and B completely crossed, C nested under B, A and B fixed, C random.
   $p = 2$, $q = 3$, $r =$ number of levels of factor C under each level of factor $B = 2$. The total number of levels of factor C is six. Sample size is $n = 10$.

3. For each graph of an experimental outcome indicate which effects are zero or greater than zero. (Assume that for any difference between means which can be seen, the effect associated with that difference is greater than zero.)

Mean criterion score

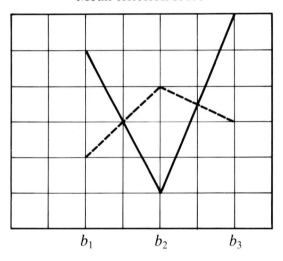

$b_1 \qquad b_2 \qquad b_3$

(Legend: _____ $= a_1$, _ _ _ _ _ _ _ $= a_2$).

Effects	> 0	$= 0$
A main effect	_____	_____
B main effect	_____	_____
AB interaction	_____	_____
A at b_1	_____	_____
A at b_2	_____	_____
A at b_3	_____	_____
B at a_1	_____	_____
B at a_2	_____	_____

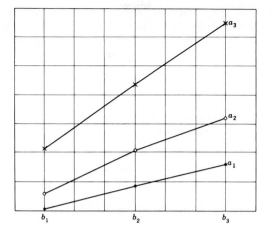

c_1

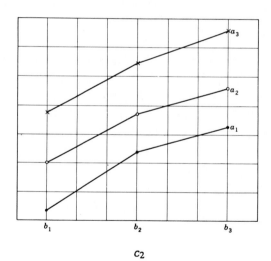

c_2

Effects	**> 0**	**= 0**
AB at c_1	————	————
AB at c_2	————	————
ABC	————	————
AC	————	————
AB	————	————
A at bc_{12}	————	————
B at ac_{12}	————	————

4. The experimenter who carried out the study in Problem 1 summarized above decided that the outcome might be unique to the particular strain of rats used. Accordingly, the study was repeated with a second strain of rats. The following data were collected:

Strain 2 (c_2)

Reinforcement contingency	Reward magnitude		
	b_1	b_2	b_3
a_1	14, 12, 5, 10, 11	16, 13, 12, 15, 15	13, 12, 10, 13, 13
a_2	10, 7, 8, 8, 9	21, 16, 11, 16, 17	20, 18, 14, 18, 19

(a) Plot the treatment-condition means. What are the effects of strain upon the outcome?

(b) Consider strain to be levels of a third factor with the data above in 1 obtained from strain 1(c_1) and the data presented here in problem 4 from strain 2(c_2). Analyze all of the data as a single, 3-factor experiment and test the significance of all experimental effects (with $\alpha = 0.05$). Assume factors A and C are fixed, but factor B is random.

(c) What is the statistical power associated with testing the significance of the B main effect?

(d) Carry out analyses of sample effects as follows ($\alpha = 0.05$):

$$\left.\begin{array}{c} A \\ B \\ AB \end{array}\right\} \text{at } c_1 \qquad \left.\begin{array}{c} A \\ B \\ AB \end{array}\right\} \text{at } c_2.$$

CHAPTER 7

MULTIFACTOR EXPERIMENTS HAVING REPEATED MEASURES ON THE SAME ELEMENTS

7.1 GENERAL PURPOSE

The designs discussed in this chapter are special cases of designs which had their origins in agricultural research. In general, these are designs in which blocks, or plots, of land are used to create relatively homogeneous within-block, soil-related conditions so that the effects of some treatments can be examined under relatively homogeneous within-block conditions. Between-block differences may either be removed from experimental error to increase precision, or may be confounded with differences between groups or between treatment effects of interest.

Examples of such applications have already been discussed. Chapter 1 presents a general discussion of blocking as a tool for reducing error; Chapter 3, Sec. 3.14 presents randomized complete-block designs, and Chapter 4 devotes its entirety to a presentation of the special case of a randomized complete-block design in which each subject is a block, the single-factor design with repeated measures for the subjects.

These notions concerning error reduction and blocking may be extended to factorial experiments of any size. In general, one may use blocking to partition the total variation into two overall components, within-block variation and between-block variation, and can assign treatments in such a way that main effects and interactions are part of either overall component of variation. In disciplines wherein the experimental materials are living organisms, differences between subjects or groups of subjects are often organismic or classification variables such as age, sex, or intelligence which define between-block differences. In those designs, individual subjects may be viewed as blocks, each acting as his or her own control. Because in the social and behavioral sciences it is very common to encounter factorial designs in which individual subjects have repeated measures on some or all of the factors, herein those designs will be presented as they are typically used in those disciplines—as multifactor, factorial experiments having repeated measures on the same subjects.

Repeated measures on the same elements may arise in different ways. In experiments designed to study rates of learning as a function of treatment effects, for example, repeated measures on the same subject are a necessary part of the design. Further, the order in which the observations are made is dictated by the experimental variables. On the other hand, in experiments designed to evaluate the joint effect of two or more treatments the experimenter may have the option of whether or not to observe the elements under more than one treatment combination. Further, the order in which the elements appear under the treatment combinations may also be under the control of the experimenter. The utility of designs calling for repeated measures is limited where carry-over effects are likely to confound results. In some cases such effects may be controlled by counterbalancing the order in which treatment combinations are given to the elements. (Designs of this kind are discussed in Sec. 9.7.)

Unless the nature of the experimental variables dictates the order in which treatments are administered to subjects, it will be assumed that the order of administration is randomized independently for each of the subjects. Further, it will be assumed that the n elements in a group are a random sample from a specified population of elements. If there are no carry-over effects, a repeated-measure design in the area of the behavioral sciences is to some degree analogous to a split plot design in the area of agricultural experimentation. Where additive carry-over effects are present, repeated-measure designs are analogous to crossover designs.

Aside from designs having the form of learning experiments, the primary purpose of repeated measures on the same elements is the control that this kind of design provides over individual differences between experimental units. In the area of the behavioral sciences, differences between such units often are quite large relative to differences in treatment effects which the experimenter is trying to evaluate.

Another (somewhat doubtful) advantage of a repeated-measure design is in terms of economy of subjects. Using different subjects under each of the treatment combinations in a factorial experiment has the *marked advantage* of providing statistically independent estimates of treatment effects from all cells in the experiment. Increasing the number of statistically independent observations is very likely to be the best way of increasing the precision of estimators. By having each subject serve as his own control, the experimenter attempts to work with a smaller sample size. However, the simple additive model underlying the usual analysis for the case of repeated measures may not be an adequate representation of the experimental phenomena. A more inclusive multivariate regression model is often required to represent fully the underlying experimental variables.

Several cautions are in order with regard to the use of these designs.

First, a strong word of warning is required in connection with order (or sequence) effects. Practice, fatigue, transfer of training, the effects of an immediately preceding success or failure are examples of what fall in the latter category. If such effects exist, randomizing or counterbalancing does not remove them; rather, such procedures completely entangle them with treatment effects. There is some chance that sequence effects will balance out—they generally will if a simple additive model is realistic. However, in experiments (other than those primarily concerned with learning or carry-over effects) where the sequence effects are likely to be marked and where primary interest lies in evaluating the effect of individual treatments in the absence of possible sequence effects, a repeated-measure design should be avoided.

In cases where sequence effects are likely to be small relative to the treatment effects, repeated-measure designs may be used. Counterbalancing or randomizing order of administration in this case tends to prevent sequence effects from being completely confounded with one or just a selected few of the treatments. Instead, such sequence effects may serve to mask treatment effects; however, the potential advantages can outweigh the potential disadvantages, particularly if the variance–covariance assumptions can be satisfied.

Second, designs which provide for partitioning total variation into between- and within-block variation (herein, between- and within-subject variation) can result in large differences in statistical power for effects which are part of these two overall sources of variation. Tests on effects which are part of between-subject variation typically have much less power than do tests on effects which are part of within-subject variation when assumptions are met.

Finally, the assumptions which justify the form of the sampling distributions of the final F ratio used in making tests differ for between- and within-subject effects. Those associated with the within-subject effects are highly restrictive.

Just as in the case of single-factor designs having repeated measures, the designs that are discussed in this chapter are sometimes handled more efficiently through the techniques of multivariate rather than univariate analysis of variance. However, under a set of restrictions on the pattern of the parameters in the variance–covariance matrices associated with these designs, the multivariate procedures become equivalent to those used in the univariate analysis of variance.

General Characteristics

It is desirable to have a general understanding of multifactor designs with repeated measures on the same elements, because there are many ways to construct such designs and the number increases as the number of factors of interest increases.

The design variety arises because of options with regard to which variables may have repeated measures. If any of the variables of interest are classification variables, by definition they give rise to between-subject effects and do not involve repeated measures on the same subjects. Such variables as sex, age, disease states, or intelligence may be used to define groups and may be included in the design as nuisance variables in order to reduce error, or may be of interest in their own right. In contrast, genuine treatment variables provide the option of being in the design as between-subject or within-subject variables. In this latter case, with only two treatment factors, there are three design options; the experiment may involve repeated measures on only factor A, only factor B, or both factors A and B. In general, if nCr is the number of combinations of n things taken r at a time, the number of design possibilities is

$$nC_1 + nC_2 + \cdots + nCn.$$

Thus, for a three-factor experiment (with no classification variables) there are three single variables on which repeated measures may be taken ($nC_1 = A$, B, or C), three pairs of variables on which there may be repeated measures ($nC_2 = AB$, AC, or BC), and one set of three variables on which there may be repeated measures ($3C_1 = ABC$). There are these seven possibilities with three variables. With four variables, there are 14 between- and within-subject design possibilities; with five variables, there are 31 possibilities. Clearly, one must seek to understand all such designs as a class of events.

One generalization has already been introduced. Variables on which there are repeated measures define within-subject sources of variation (main effects *and* all interactions); variables without repeated measures define between-subject effects (main effects and interactions involving only non-repeated measures variables). To clarify this and related points, consider the three ways in which a two-factor, 2×3 factorial experiment can be carried out if there are no inherent, between-subject variables.

(i)

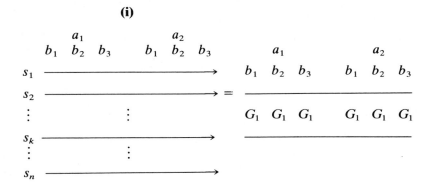

(ii)

(iii)

In these diagrams, arrows indicate repeated measures. Hence, in (i) there are repeated measures on both factors A and B, in (ii) there are repeated measures only on the levels of factor B, and in (iii) there are repeated measures only on levels of factor A. (The design (i) is sometimes labeled a randomized block factorial design, while (ii) and (iii) are examples of split-plot factorials (e.g., Kirk, 1982).) Considering *only* the factorial effects of factors A

and B (A and B main effects, AB interaction), the outcome is:

	(i)	(ii)	(iii)
Between-subject effects	—	A	B
Within-subject effects	A	B	A
	B	AB	AB
	AB		

A second generalization can be made clear by referring to these designs; subjects are nested within the group to which they are assigned. In (ii), G_1 represents a group of n subjects with each subject designated as $S_{k(1)}$; the second subscript shows that subject k is in group 1. The symbol G_2 represents a second group of n subjects with $S_{k(2)}$ indicating membership in G_2 for S_k. The subjects in both groups are observed under all levels of factor B in the experiment, but each group is observed under only a single level of factor A. In (iii), this relation is reversed; groups are assigned to levels of factor B and observed under all levels of factor A. In both cases, subjects are nested in their respective groups.

In these designs, subjects may be considered to define a third factor having n levels. As such, in (ii) the "subject" factor is crossed with factor B but nested under factor A. Schematically,

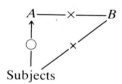

where $\times$ indicates a crossing relationship,
$\bigcirc$ indicates a nesting relationship.

In (iii), the relation with subjects is reversed:

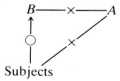

Nested variables are discussed in Chapter 5 in conjunction with hierarchal designs. That discussion may be generalized to subjects as a nested variable. Thus, subject main effects are generally defined separately within each group. For example, in (ii), one defines

$$SS_{\text{subjects within } a_1}$$
$$SS_{\text{subjects within } a_2}$$
$$\vdots$$
$$SS_{\text{subjects within } a_p},$$

and in (iii) one defines

$$SS_{\text{subjects within } b_1}$$
$$SS_{\text{subjects within } b_2}$$
$$\vdots$$
$$SS_{\text{subjects within } b_q}.$$

Nested variables do not interact with variables within which they are nested. They do interact with variables with which they are crossed, but do so separately for each "nesting." Thus, in (ii) subjects do not interact with A, but do interact with B separately for each level of A. One may define,

$$SS_{\text{subjects within } a_1} \times B$$
$$SS_{\text{subjects within } a_2} \times B$$
$$\vdots$$
$$SS_{\text{subjects within } a_p} \times B.$$

In (iii), subjects do not interact with B, but one may define an interaction with A at each level of B,

$$SS_{\text{subjects within } b_1} \times A$$
$$SS_{\text{subjects within } b_2} \times A$$
$$\vdots$$
$$SS_{\text{subjects within } b_q} \times A.$$

These principles may be generalized to more complex designs wherein subjects may be doubly or triply nested.

A third generalization becomes apparent from considering (ii) and (iii). In (ii), comparisons between treatment combinations at different levels of factor A involve differences between groups as well as differences associated with factor A; comparisons between different levels of factor B at the same level of A do not involve differences between groups. In (iii), differences between levels of B include group differences. In designs of this type, the main effects of factor A (ii) or B (iii) are said to be completely confounded with differences between groups. Both the variables on which there are repeated measures and the AB interaction are free of such confounding. This may or may not pose a problem. When groups are formed by randomly selecting subjects from some population and are randomly assigned to treatment levels, in principle there is no confounding since there should be no group effects other than the experimental variable effects of interest. In practice, randomization should be effective when group sizes are reasonably large. When intact groups are assigned to the levels of factors, there is no way to separate between-group treatment effects from whatever differences exist among the groups and impact the dependent variable. For example, in (ii) if a_1 were administered to pupils in one classroom and a_2 were administered to students in a different classroom, any interpretation of A effects would be hazardous without a thorough knowledge of all the ways the two groups differ other than the levels of factor A. In practice, when designs such as (ii) and (iii) are used, the between-class variable is typically a classification variable; subjects should be randomly selected to be representative of that group. For example, in (ii) if a_1 refers to male college sophomores and a_2 refers to female college sophomores, subjects should be randomly selected for G_1 and G_2 if the results are to be free of confounding by other variables. When no confounding with the group factor is present, there are fewer sources of uncontrolled error variance and more sensitive (powerful) tests.

A fourth generalization has to do with how the components of variation and their associated degrees of freedom may be conceptualized. A helpful way to do this is to compare the analysis of repeated measures designs with completely randomized designs of the same size. For example, suppose there were ten observations under each of the $p \times q = 2 \times 3 = 6$ treatment conditions used to construct (i), (ii), and (iii). A comparison of the analysis of variance summary table for the completely-randomized design to the analyses for the designs in (i), (ii) and (iii) is provided in Table 7.1.

In all analyses, there are 60 observations and, therefore, the total variation has 59 degrees of freedom and is defined in the same way, the variation of the individual observations around the grand mean. What is important about Table 7.1 is that it shows that the factorial effects, herein A and B main effects and the AB interaction are identical in all analyses. In each case, their variation is part of the total variation among the pq, treatment condition means $\overline{AB}_{ij}$. What is different among these analyses is how error variation is conceptualized. In the completely randomized design, it is the total variation among observations from within the treatment conditions. This is variation due to everything in the universe except for A, B, and AB. The important thing is that it includes all individual differences among subjects, which differences are typically quite large relative to all other sources of error. In contrast, in the analyses of (i), (ii), and (iii), this within-treatment variation of the completely randomized design is broken down into meaningful components involving the subjects, since subjects, like levels of factor A and B, are also controlled (held constant). These effects include the nested main effects and nested interactions. In short, subject main effects are separated from other sources of error which may involve interactions between the subjects and the experimental treatments. It is these components of variation which define "error terms" and appear as the mean squares used in F ratios to test the various treatment effects. The data presented in Table 7.1 may be

TABLE 7.1   Summaries comparing analysis of factorial designs

Completely randomized		Repeated measures (i)	
Source of variation	**df**	**Source of variation**	**df**
Between treatment means	$pq - 1 = 5$	Between treatment means	$pq - 1 = 5$
A	$(p - 1) = 1$	A	$(p - 1) = 1$
B	$(q - 1) = 2$	B	$(q - 1) = 2$
AB	$(p - 1)(q - 1) = 2$	AB	$(p - 1)(q - 1) = 2$
Within treatments		Within treatments	$pq(n - 1) = 54$
"error"	$pq(n - 1) = 54$	Between subjects	$n - 1 = 9$
		$A \times$ subjects	$(n - 1)(p - 1) = 9$
		$B \times$ subjects	$(n - 1)(q - 1) = 18$
		$AB \times$ subjects	$(n - 1)(p - 1)(q - 1) = 18$
Total	$npq - 1 = 59$	Total	$npq - 1 = 59$

Repeated measures (ii)		Repeated measures (iii)	
Source of variation	**df**	**Source of variation**	**df**
Between treatment means	$pq - 1 = 5$	Between treatment means	$pq - 1 = 5$
A	$(p - 1) = 1$	A	$(p - 1) = 1$
B	$(q - 1) = 2$	B	$(q - 1) = 2$
AB	$(p - 1)(q - 1) = 2$	AB	$(p - 1)(q - 1) = 2$
Within treatments	$pq(n - 1) = 54$	Within treatments	$pq(n - 1) = 54$
Between subjects (a_1)	$(n - 1) = 9$	Between subjects (b_1)	$(n - 1) = 9$
Between subjects (a_2)	$(n - 1) = 9$	Between subjects (b_2)	$(n - 1) = 9$
$B \times$ subjects (a_1)	$(n - 1)(q - 1) = 18$	Between subjects (b_3)	$(n - 1) = 9$
$B \times$ subjects (a_2)	$(n - 1)(q - 1) = 9$	$A \times$ subjects (b_1)	$(n - 1)(p - 1) = 9$
		$A \times$ subjects (b_2)	$(n - 1)(p - 1) = 9$
		$A \times$ subjects (b_3)	$(n - 1)(p - 1) = 9$
Total	$npq - 1 = 59$	Total	$npq - 1 = 59$

extended to all other factorial designs involving repeated measures on some or all of the factors.

In practice, the analyses of variance summary tables are not typically presented as in Table 7.1. Rather, it is traditional to separate the analysis in terms of the sources of variation which involve independent observations (between blocks, between subjects) and those which involve correlated observations (within blocks, within subjects, repeated measures), the dependence among which arises because of the repeated measures on the same elements. Thus, Table 7.2 would be the typical presentations of the analyses of (i), (ii), and (iii).

TABLE 7.2 **Analysis of variance summaries for repeated measures designs**

(i)		(ii)		(iii)	
Source of variation	df	Source of variation	df	Source of variation	df
Between subjects	$n - 1 = 9$	Between subjects	$np - 1 = 19$	Between subjects	$nq - 1 = 29$
Within subjects	$n(pq - 1) = 50$	A	$p - 1 = 1$	B	$q - 1 = 2$
A	$(p - 1) = 1$	Subjects (a_1)	$n - 1 = 9$	Subjects (b_1)	$(n - 1) = 9$
B	$(q - 1) = 2$	Subjects (a_2)	$n - 1 = 9$	Subjects (b_2)	$(n - 1) = 9$
AB	$(p - 1)(q - 1) = 2$	Within subjects	$np(q - 1) = 40$	Subjects (b_3)	$(n - 1) = 9$
$A \times$ subjects	$(p - 1)(n - 1) = 9$	B	$(q - 1) = 2$	With subjects	$nq(p - 1) = 30$
$B \times$ subjects	$(q - 1)(n - 1) = 18$	AB	$(p - 1)(q - 1) = 2$	A	$(p - 1) = 1$
$AB \times$ subjects	$(p - 1)(q - 1)(n - 1) = 18$	$B \times$ subjects (a_1)	$(q - 1)(n - 1) = 18$	AB	$(p - 1)(q - 1) = 2$
		$B \times$ subjects (a_2)	$(q - 1)(n - 1) = 18$	$A \times$ subjects (b_1)	$(p - 1)(n - 1) = 9$
				$A \times$ subjects (b_2)	$(p - 1)(n - 1) = 9$
				$A \times$ subjects (b_3)	$(p - 1)(n - 1) = 9$
Total	$npq - 1 = 59$	Total	$npq - 1 = 59$	Total	$npq - 1 = 59$

The pattern in Table 7.2 which can be generalized has already been discussed: between-subject effects do not involve repeated measures, within-subject effects do involve repeated measures.

Finally, there are very important generalizations which may be made regarding the assumptions which must be made in order to justify the structure of the F ratios. One generalization has already been mentioned: the assumptions regarding between-subject tests are much simpler and less restrictive than are those involving tests of significance on within-subject effects.

In Chapter 4, the assumptions involving the pattern of the variance–covariance matrix are examined in detail and are concerned with within-subject effects since the single factor involves repeated measures. In multifactor designs, the same assumption that variance–covariance matrices have a particular structure must be made, but the situation is more complex because there may be numerous sets of multiple variance–covariance matrices and for each set there are *two* restrictive assumptions which must be made. One assumption is that all matrices in a set are homogeneous; the other is that they have a particular form.

The generalization which may be made is that there is a set of variance–covariance matrices for each variable and for each combination of variables on which there are repeated measures, and in each set there are as many matrices as there are groups of subjects. This may be clarified with regard to designs (i), (ii), and (iii).

For (i), there is a single group of subjects with repeated measures on factors A and B, (and, therefore, AB combinations). Thus, there are three (sets of one) variance–covariance matrices. In population terms they are,

$$\Sigma_A = \begin{array}{c} a_1 \\ a_2 \end{array} \begin{array}{cc} a_1 & a_2 \\ \left[\begin{array}{cc} \sigma_{11} & \sigma_{12} \\ & \sigma_{22} \end{array} \right] \end{array} \quad \Sigma_B = \begin{array}{c} b_1 \\ b_2 \\ b_3 \end{array} \begin{array}{ccc} b_1 & b_2 & b_3 \\ \left[\begin{array}{ccc} \sigma_{11} & \sigma_{12} & \sigma_{13} \\ & \sigma_{22} & \sigma_{23} \\ & & \sigma_{33} \end{array} \right] \end{array}$$

$$\Sigma_{AB} = \begin{array}{c} ab_{11} \\ ab_{12} \\ ab_{13} \\ ab_{21} \\ ab_{22} \\ ab_{23} \end{array} \begin{array}{cccccc} ab_{11} & ab_{12} & ab_{13} & ab_{21} & ab_{22} & ab_{23} \\ \left[\begin{array}{cccccc} \sigma_{11} & \sigma_{12} & \sigma_{13} & \sigma_{14} & \sigma_{15} & \sigma_{16} \\ & \sigma_{22} & \sigma_{23} & \sigma_{24} & \sigma_{25} & \sigma_{26} \\ & & \sigma_{33} & \sigma_{34} & \sigma_{35} & \sigma_{36} \\ & & & \sigma_{44} & \sigma_{45} & \sigma_{46} \\ & & & & \sigma_{55} & \sigma_{56} \\ & & & & & \sigma_{66} \end{array} \right] \end{array}.$$

In each case, the entry on the main diagonal is a variance for the observations within that particular column and row heading; the off-diagonal entries are the covariances. Each of these matrices is assumed to have the property of circularity.

In (ii), there are repeated measures on only the B variable. Therefore, there is only one set of covariance matrices but there are $p = 2$ matrices in that set. Thus,

$$\Sigma_{B(a_1)} = \begin{array}{c} ab_{11} \\ ab_{12} \\ ab_{13} \end{array} \begin{array}{ccc} ab_{11} & ab_{12} & ab_{13} \\ \left[\begin{array}{ccc} \sigma_{11} & \sigma_{12} & \sigma_{13} \\ & \sigma_{22} & \sigma_{23} \\ & & \sigma_{33} \end{array} \right] \end{array},$$

and

$$\Sigma_{B(a_2)} = \begin{array}{c} ab_{21} \\ ab_{22} \\ ab_{23} \end{array} \begin{array}{ccc} ab_{21} & ab_{22} & ab_{23} \\ \left[\begin{array}{ccc} \sigma_{11} & \sigma_{12} & \sigma_{13} \\ & \sigma_{22} & \sigma_{23} \\ & & \sigma_{33} \end{array} \right] \end{array},$$

are the covariance matrices for groups 1 and 2, respectively, taken over the levels of factor B. The assumptions are that these matrices are both circular and homogeneous and may, therefore, be pooled into a single matrix

$$\Sigma_B = \begin{array}{c} b_1 \\ b_2 \\ b_3 \end{array} \begin{array}{ccc} b_1 & b_2 & b_3 \\ \left[\begin{array}{ccc} \sigma_{11} & \sigma_{12} & \sigma_{13} \\ & \sigma_{22} & \sigma_{23} \\ & & \sigma_{33} \end{array} \right] \end{array}.$$

For design (iii) there is one set of three matrices,

$$
\Sigma_{A(b_1)} =
\begin{array}{c}
\\ ab_{11} \\ ab_{22}
\end{array}
\begin{array}{cc}
ab_{11} & ab_{21} \\
\sigma_{11} & \sigma_{12} \\
 & \sigma_{22}
\end{array} \ ,
$$

$$
\Sigma_{A(b_2)} =
\begin{array}{c}
\\ ab_{12} \\ ab_{22}
\end{array}
\begin{array}{cc}
ab_{12} & ab_{22} \\
\sigma_{11} & \sigma_{12} \\
 & \sigma_{22}
\end{array} \ ,
$$

and

$$
\Sigma_{A(b_3)} =
\begin{array}{c}
\\ ab_{13} \\ ab_{23}
\end{array}
\begin{array}{cc}
ab_{13} & ab_{23} \\
\sigma_{11} & \sigma_{12} \\
 & \sigma_{22}
\end{array} \ ,
$$

each matrix being for a single level of factor B (group) and computed among levels of factor A. These three matrices are assumed to be circular. They are also assumed to be homogeneous and, therefore, can be pooled to form

$$
\Sigma_{A} =
\begin{array}{c}
\\ a_1 \\ a_2
\end{array}
\begin{array}{cc}
a_1 & a_2 \\
\sigma_{11} & \sigma_{12} \\
 & \sigma_{22}
\end{array} \ .
$$

This set of double assumptions can quickly generate a complex array even in experiments with reasonably modest goals. For example, it would not be unusual for an experimenter to want to classify subjects based upon two variables and, then, to examine the effects of two experimental variables using repeated measures. For example, one may want to control for sex (factor A) and age (factor B) to examine the effects of two experimental variables, factors C and D. Thus, the design, with $n = 4$ subjects in each group and only two levels of each factor, is:

The point here is that this relatively ordinary experiment generates three sets of matrices (C, D, CD, respectively) each set having four matrices (G_{11}, G_{12}, G_{21}, and G_{22}, respectively). Each set is assumed to be homogeneous and to be circular. It may even be advantageous to assume that the three sets are also homogeneous and circular. These are, indeed, restrictive assumptions.

The details of these generalizations will be represented as particular designs are presented throughout the remainder of this chapter.

7.2 TWO-FACTOR EXPERIMENT WITH REPEATED MEASURES ON ONE FACTOR

This kind of experiment is illustrated in the last section. The general case may be represented as follows:

	b_1	$\cdots$	b_j	$\cdots$	b_q
a_1	G_1	$\cdots$	G_1	$\cdots$	G_1
$\vdots$	$\vdots$		$\vdots$		$\vdots$
a_i	G_i	$\cdots$	G_i	$\cdots$	G_i
$\vdots$	$\vdots$		$\vdots$		$\vdots$
a_p	G_p	$\cdots$	G_p	$\cdots$	G_p

Each G represents a random sample of size n from a common population of subjects. Each subject in G_i is observed under q different treatment combinations, all involving factor A at level a_i. The actual observations on the subjects within group i may be represented as follows:

	Subject	b_1	$\cdots$	b_j	$\cdots$	b_q
	1	X_{i11}	$\cdots$	X_{ij1}	$\cdots$	X_{iq1}
	$\vdots$	$\vdots$		$\vdots$		$\vdots$
a_i	k	X_{i1k}	$\cdots$	X_{ijk}	$\cdots$	X_{iqk}
	$\vdots$	$\vdots$		$\vdots$		$\vdots$
	n	X_{i1n}	$\cdots$	X_{ijn}	$\cdots$	X_{iqn}

The symbol X_{ijk} denotes a measurement on subject k in G_i under treatment combination ab_{ij}. A more complete notation for subject k would be $k(i)$; the latter notation distinguishes this subject from subject k in some other group. Similarly, a more complete notation for X_{ijk} would be $X_{ijk(i)}$. The latter notation is rather cumbersome; in cases in which there is no ambiguity, the symbol X_{ijk} will be used to indicate an observation on subject k in G_i made under treatment combination ab_{ij}.

For special cases, the notation for a subject may be made more specific. For example, consider the case in which $p = 2$, $q = 3$, and $n = 2$. The experimental data may be represented as follows:

	Subject	b_1	b_2	b_3
a_1	1	X_{111}	X_{121}	X_{131}
	2	X_{112}	X_{122}	X_{132}
a_2	3	X_{213}	X_{223}	X_{233}
	4	X_{214}	X_{224}	X_{234}

In this notation scheme subject 3 is the first subject in G_2, and subject 4 is the second subject in G_2.

The linear model upon which the analysis will be based has the following form:

$$X_{ijk} = \mu + \alpha_i + \pi_{k(i)} + \beta_j + \alpha\beta_{ij} + \beta\pi_{jk(i)} + \varepsilon_{m(ijk)}.$$

The notation $\pi_{k(i)}$ indicates that the effect of subject k is nested under level a_i. Note that the linear model does not include any carry-over effects. From the Cornfield–Tukey algorithm as described in Sec. 5.16, the E(MS) associated with the model given above have the following form. (The dummy subscript m in the term $\varepsilon_{m(ijk)}$ is introduced in order to indicate that the experimental error is nested within the individual observation.)

Effect	i	j	k	m	Expected value of mean square
α_i	D_p	q	n	1	$\sigma_\varepsilon^2 + D_n D_q \sigma_{\beta\pi}^2 + n D_q \sigma_{\alpha\beta}^2 + q D_n \sigma_\pi^2 + nq\sigma_\alpha^2$
$\pi_{k(i)}$	1	q	D_n	1	$\sigma_\varepsilon^2 + D_q \sigma_{\beta\pi}^2 + q\sigma_\pi^2$
β_j	p	D_q	n	1	$\sigma_\varepsilon^2 + D_n \sigma_{\beta\pi}^2 + n D_p \sigma_{\alpha\beta}^2 + np\sigma_\beta^2$
$\alpha\beta_{ij}$	D_p	D_q	n	1	$\sigma_\varepsilon^2 + D_n \sigma_{\beta\pi}^2 + n\sigma_{\alpha\beta}^2$
$\beta\pi_{jk(i)}$	1	D_q	D_n	1	$\sigma_\varepsilon^2 + \sigma_{\beta\pi}^2$
$\varepsilon_{m(ijk)}$	1	1	1	1	σ_ε^2

Here

$$D_n = 1 - \frac{n}{N}, \qquad D_p = 1 - \frac{p}{P}, \qquad D_q = 1 - \frac{q}{Q}.$$

Each D is either 0 or 1 depending upon whether the corresponding factor is fixed or random, respectively. If factors A and B are fixed and the subject factor is random, then

$$D_n = 1, \qquad D_p = 0, \qquad D_q = 0.$$

If one makes this substitution for the D's in the E(MS) given above, the result is the E(MS) in Table 7.3.

TABLE 7.3   Summary of analysis of variance

Source of variation	df	E(MS)
Between subjects	$np - 1$	
$\quad A$	$p - 1$	$\sigma_\varepsilon^2 + q\sigma_\pi^2 + nq\sigma_\alpha^2$
$\quad$ Subjects within groups	$p(n - 1)$	$\sigma_\varepsilon^2 + q\sigma_\pi^2$
Within subjects	$np(q - 1)$	
$\quad B$	$q - 1$	$\sigma_\varepsilon^2 + \sigma_{\beta\pi}^2 + np\sigma_\beta^2$
$\quad AB$	$(p - 1)(q - 1)$	$\sigma_\varepsilon^2 + \sigma_{\beta\pi}^2 + n\sigma_{\alpha\beta}^2$
$\quad B \times$ subject within groups	$p(n - 1)(q - 1)$	$\sigma_\varepsilon^2 + \sigma_{\beta\pi}^2$

As noted earlier, the manner in which the total variation is partitioned in this table is quite similar to that used in a $p \times q$ factorial experiment in which there are no repeated measures. A comparison of the two partitions is shown in Table 7.4. It will be noted that partition of the between-cell variation is identical. However, in an experiment having repeated measures, the within-cell variation is divided into two orthogonal (nonoverlapping) parts. One part is a function of experimental error plus the main effects of subjects within groups, i.e., individual differences. The other part is a function of experimental error and $B \times$ subject-within-group interaction. If the latter interaction is negligible, then the second part of the within-cell variation is a function solely of experimental error.

The assumption that A and B are both fixed factors and that subjects are random is reasonable. It presumes that one can generalize the results of the study to the population of subjects from which these were selected. Under those assumptions, and using the E(MS) in Table 7.3 to test the hypothesis that $\sigma_\alpha^2 = 0$,

$$F = \frac{\text{MS}_a}{\text{MS}_{\text{subj w. groups}}}.$$

The mean square in the denominator of the above F ratio is sometimes

TABLE 7.4   Comparison of partitions

$p \times q$ factorial (no repeated measures)		$p \times q$ factorial (repeated measures on factor B)	
Total	$npq - 1$	Total	$npq - 1$
Between cells	$pq - 1$	Between cells	$pq - 1$
$\quad A \quad p - 1$		$\quad A \quad p - 1$	
$\quad B \quad q - 1$		$\quad B \quad q - 1$	
$\quad AB \quad (p - 1)(q - 1)$		$\quad AB \quad (p - 1)(q - 1)$	
Within cells	$pq(n - 1)$	Within cells	$pq(n - 1)$
		$\quad$ Subject within groups	$p(n - 1)$
		$\quad B \times$ subjects within groups	$p(n - 1)(q - 1)$

designated $MS_{error\ (between)}$. To test the hypothesis that $\sigma_\beta^2 = 0$,

$$F = \frac{MS_b}{MS_{B \times subj\ w.\ groups}}.$$

To test the hypothesis that $\sigma_{\alpha\beta}^2 = 0$, the appropriate F ratio is

$$F = \frac{MS_{ab}}{MS_{B \times subj\ w.\ groups}}.$$

The mean square in the denominator of the last two F ratios is sometimes called $MS_{error\ (within)}$, since it forms the denominator of F ratios used in testing effects which can be classified as part of the within-subject variation.

Assumptions

It has been stressed that the assumptions regarding between-subject and within-subject effects are different. Regarding the between-subject test on the A main effects, the mean square used as a denominator represents a pooling of different sources of variation; the variation due to subjects within groups is the sum of the following sources of variation:

Source	df
Subjects within groups	$p(n-1)$
Subjects within G_1	$n-1$
Subjects within G_2	$n-1$
. . .	. . .
Subjects within G_p	$n-1$

One of the assumptions required in order that the F ratio actually follow an F distribution is that these sources of variation be homogeneous. A partial check on this assumption may be made through use of the statistic

$$F_{max} = \frac{\text{maximum } (SS_{subj\ w.\ G_i})}{\text{minimum } (SS_{subj\ w.\ G_i})},$$

i.e., the ratio of the largest of these sources of variation to the smallest. The critical value for this statistic in a test having level of significance equal to α is

$$F_{max\ (1-\alpha)}(p, n-1).$$

These critical values are given in Table D.7.

With regard to the within-subject variation, the variation due to

$B \times$ subjects within groups represents a pooling of the following sources of variation:

Source	df
$B \times$ subjects within groups	$p(n-1)(q-1)$
$B \times$ subjects within G_1	$(n-1)(q-1)$
$B \times$ subjects within G_2	$(n-1)(q-1)$
$\cdots$	$\cdots$
$B \times$ subjects within G_p	$(n-1)(q-1)$

A test on the homogeneity of these sources is given by

$$F_{\max} = \frac{\text{maximum } (\text{SS}_{B \times \text{subj w. } G_i})}{\text{minimum } (\text{SS}_{B \times \text{subj w. } G_i})}.$$

The critical value for this test is

$$F_{\max(1-\alpha)}[p, (n-1)(q-1)].$$

If the scale of measurement for the original criterion data does not satisfy these homogeneity assumptions, a transformation may often be found which will satisfy these assumptions. Indications are, however, that the F tests given above are robust with respect to minor violations of these assumptions (see Box [1954]).

However, as discussed in general in Sec. 7.1, for the sampling distribution of the F ratio for within-subject effects to be the F distribution with the usual degrees of freedom requires additional assumptions about the pattern of elements in $q \times q$ covariance matrices.

EQUALITY AND SYMMETRY OF COVARIANCE MATRICES. Huynh and Feldt (1970) and Huynh and Mandeville (1979) are among those who have presented detailed discussions of the conditions under which the within-subject F tests are valid. Chapter 4 presented the assumptions concerning the required structure of the covariance matrix for a single-factor experiment. Essentially the requirement for that simple design is that the covariance matrix Σ_x of the original dependent variable be circular. Stated in terms of a normalized orthogonal transformation of the dependent variable X,

$$Y = XM^*,$$

the requirement is that the covariance matrix of Y be spherical. That is,

$$\Sigma_y = M^{*'}\Sigma_x M^* = \lambda I.$$

This simply states that if Σ_x is circular, Σ_y will have all zeros off the diagonal (i.e., have zero covariances) and a constant λ on the main diagonal (i.e., homogeneous variances equal to λ).

As indicated earlier in general terms, for the designs under consideration in this chapter, the assumptions are more complex. In general, there are two assumptions. One is that all covariance matrices in a set are homogeneous. The other is that when these homogeneous matrices are pooled, the pooled covariance matrix is circular.

For the particular design under consideration here, the first assumption is that the $q \times q$ covariance matrices are homogeneous over the levels of factor A,

$$\Sigma_{a_1} = \Sigma_{a_2} = \cdots = \Sigma_{a_p} = \Sigma.$$

Stated in terms of Y, a normalized orthogonal transformation of the dependent variable, the assumption is that

$$M_B^{*\prime} \Sigma_{a_1} M_B^* = M_B^{*\prime} \Sigma_{a_2} M_B^* = \cdots = M_B^{*\prime} \Sigma_{a_p} M_B^* = M_B^{*\prime} \Sigma M_B^*,$$

where M_B^* is the orthonormal transformation matrix for comparing levels of factor B and Σ_{a_i} is the $q \times q$ covariance matrix among levels of factor B.

This first assumption may be evaluated by a procedure suggested by Box (1950). To consider that in detail, the data at level a_i may be represented as follows:

	Subject	b_1	b_2	$\cdots$	b_q
	1	X_{i11}	X_{i21}	$\cdots$	X_{iq1}
a_i	2	X_{i12}	X_{i22}	$\cdots$	X_{iq2}
	$\vdots$	$\vdots$	$\vdots$		$\vdots$
	n	X_{i1n}	X_{i2n}	$\cdots$	X_{iqn}

From these data one may obtain the following $q \times q$ covariance matrix.

$$S_{a_i} = \hat{\Sigma}_{a_i} = \begin{bmatrix} \hat{\sigma}_{11} & \hat{\sigma}_{12} & \cdots & \hat{\sigma}_{1q} \\ \hat{\sigma}_{21} & \hat{\sigma}_{22} & \cdots & \hat{\sigma}_{2q} \\ \vdots & \vdots & & \vdots \\ \hat{\sigma}_{q1} & \hat{\sigma}_{q2} & \cdots & \hat{\sigma}_{qq} \end{bmatrix}$$

There is such an observed covariance matrix for each level of factor A $(i = 1, \ldots, p)$. It can be shown that for each matrix,

$$E(\hat{\Sigma}_{a_i}) = \Sigma_{a_i},$$

under random assignment of subjects to the levels of factor A. That is, $\hat{\Sigma}_{a_i}$ is unbiased as an estimate of Σ_{a_i}. Assume that there are n_1 subjects in the group (G_1) assigned to level a_1, n_2 subjects in the group (G_2) of subjects assigned to level a_2, etc. Let $N' = n_1' + n_2' + \cdots + n_p'$, where $n_i' = n_i - 1$.

The following additional notation will be used in this section.

$$S_1 = q \times q \text{ matrix of covariances for level } a_1 \qquad = \hat{\Sigma}_{a_1}.$$
$$S_2 = q \times q \text{ matrix of covariances for level } a_2 \qquad = \hat{\Sigma}_{a_2}.$$
$$\cdots \qquad\qquad\qquad\qquad\qquad\qquad\qquad\qquad \cdots$$
$$S_p = q \times q \text{ matrix of covariances for level } a_p \qquad = \hat{\Sigma}_{a_p}.$$

$S_{\text{pooled}} = q \times q$ matrix of pooled covariances; i.e., each entry is a weighted average of corresponding entries in S_1 through S_p, the weights being the corresponding degrees of freedom $= \hat{\Sigma}$.

The variables included in the covariance matrix at level a_i are assumed to have an underlying q-variate normal distribution.

To test the hypothesis that the covariance matrices $S_1, S_2, \ldots, S_p$ are random samples for populations in which the covariance matrices are $\Sigma_1 = \Sigma_2 = \cdots = \Sigma_p = \Sigma$ (that is, that the population covariance matrices are equal), one computes the following statistics:

$$M_1 = N' \ln |S_{\text{pooled}}| - \Sigma \, n_i' \ln |S_i|, \tag{7.1}$$

$$C_1 = \frac{2q^2 + 3q - 1}{6(q + 1)(p - 1)} \left[\Sigma \left(\frac{1}{n_i} \right) - \frac{1}{N} \right], \tag{7.2}$$

$$f_1 = \frac{q(q + 1)(p - 1)}{2} \tag{7.3}$$

Under the hypothesis that the univariate normal populations have equal covariance matrices, the statistic

$$\chi_1^2 = (1 - C_1) M_1 \tag{7.4}$$

has a sampling distribution which is approximated by a chi-square distribution having f_1 degrees of freedom. Rejection of this hypothesis rules against pooling covariance matrices. If the populations have a common covariance matrix Σ, then S_{pooled} is an unbiased estimate of Σ. This test procedure is a multivariate analog of Bartlett's test for homogeneity of variance. Its power is adequate only if each n_i' is large relative to q.

The second assumption is that for the common covariance matrix, Σ,

$$\sigma_{\bar{B}_j - \bar{B}_{j'}}^2 = \text{constant for all } j \text{ and } j', \text{ where } j \neq j'.$$

This is the assumption of circularity which is discussed in detail in Chapter 4. Stated in terms of Y, the assumption is that

$$M_B^{*\prime} \Sigma M_B^* = \Sigma_y = \lambda I,$$

i.e. that Σ_y is spherical. This assumption is somewhat related to the first one in that if circular covariance matrices are pooled, the pooled covariance matrix will be circular. Thus, if one has homogeneous, circular covariance matrices for each group of subjects, this second assumption is met (see Sec. 4.4). (However, circular matrices need not be equivalent, and equal covariance matrices need not be circular.)

A measure of the extent to which a covariance matrix departs from this requirement is given by ε, where

$$\varepsilon = \frac{q^2(\bar{\sigma}_{jj} - \bar{\sigma})^2}{(q-1)(\Sigma \Sigma \sigma_{jk}^2 - 2q \Sigma \bar{\sigma}_j^2 + q^2 \bar{\sigma}^2)}$$

$\bar{\sigma}$ = mean of all entries in Σ,

$\bar{\sigma}_{jj}$ = mean of all entries of main diagonal of Σ,

$\bar{\sigma}_j$ = mean of all entries in row j of Σ,

σ_{jk} = entry in row j, column k of Σ.

In this case, ε can range from 1 to $1/(q-1)$; ε will be equal to 1 if the covariance matrix meets the requirement

$$\sigma_{\bar{B}_j - \bar{B}_k}^2 = \text{constant for all } j \text{ and } k.$$

One notes that ε may be approximated from the sample estimate of Σ, in order to provide the basis for a critical value which does not assume that ε is at its lower bound. For example, if $\hat{\Sigma}(q = 3)$ is

$$\hat{\Sigma} = \begin{bmatrix} 4.00 & 3.00 & 2.00 \\ 3.00 & 5.00 & 2.00 \\ 2.00 & 2.00 & 6.00 \end{bmatrix},$$

then

$$\hat{\varepsilon} = \frac{9(5.00 - 3.22)^2}{2[111 - 6(3.00^2 + 3.33^2 + 3.33^2) + 9(3.22)^2]}$$

$$= 0.83.$$

The lower bound for ε in this case is $1/(q-1) = 0.50$.

As another example, if $\hat{\Sigma}(q = 3)$ is

$$\hat{\Sigma} = \begin{bmatrix} 2.00 & 1.00 & 1.50 \\ 1.00 & 3.00 & 2.00 \\ 1.50 & 2.00 & 4.00 \end{bmatrix},$$

then

$$\hat{\varepsilon} = \frac{9(3.00 - 2.00)^2}{2[43.50 - 6(1.50^2 + 2.00^2 + 2.50^2) + 9(4.00)]}$$

$$= 1.00.$$

The entries in the matrix $\hat{\Sigma}$ will be found to be related as follows:

$$\hat{\sigma}_{jj} + \hat{\sigma}_{kk} - 2\hat{\sigma}_{jk} = 3.00 \qquad \text{for all } j \text{ and } k, \qquad j \neq k.$$

Thus, $\hat{\Sigma}$ is exactly circular in this instance.

One may test the hypothesis that the pooled covariance matrix is circular ($M_B^{*'}\Sigma M_B^*$ is spherical)

$$H_0: M_B^* \Sigma M_B^* = \lambda I$$

by modifying the Mauchley test presented in Chapter 4. Equivalently, one may modify the χ^2 approximation to that test. Using the latter approach, one computes the following statistics:

$$M_2 = -(N - p) \ln \frac{|S_{\text{pooled}}|}{|S_0|},$$ (7.5)

$$C_2 = \frac{q(q + 1)^2(2q - 3)}{6(N - p)(q - 1)(q^2 + q - 4)},$$ (7.6)

$$f_2 = \frac{q^2 + q - 4}{2}.$$ (7.7)

Under the hypothesis that Σ has the specified form,[1] the statistic

$$\chi_2^2 = (1 - C_2)M_2$$ (7.8)

has a sampling distribution which can be approximated by a chi-square distribution having f_2 degrees of freedom.

The test of the two assumptions will be illustrated through the use of the numerical data given in Table 7.5. In this table, $p = 2$, $q = 3$, and $n_1 = n_2 = 5$. The covariance matrices obtained from the data in part i of this table are given at the left in Table 7.6. For example, the entry 1.75 in the covariance matrix at level a_1 is the covariance between the observations in columns b_1 and b_2 at level a_1. (The symbols in part iii of Table 7.5 are defined in Table 7.9.)

The matrix corresponding to S_{pooled} is given at the right of Table 7.6. The entry 3.10 is the mean of corresponding entries at levels a_1 and a_2, that is, $(2.50 + 3.70)/2 = 3.10$. Similarly, the entry 1.92 is the mean of corresponding entries at a_1 and a_2. The numerical values of the determinants corresponding to S_1, S_2, and S_{pooled} are

$$|S_1| = 1.08, \qquad |S_2| = 17.51, \qquad |S_{\text{pooled}}| = 11.28.$$

The statistic defined in (7.4) is obtained from

$$M_1 = 8 \ln (11.28) - 4 \ln (1.08) - 4 \ln (17.51)$$
$$= 8(2.421) - 4(0.077) - 4(2.863)$$
$$= 7.608$$

$$C_1 = \frac{18 + 9 - 1}{6(4)(1)} \left(\frac{1}{4} + \frac{1}{4} + \frac{1}{8}\right) = 0.406$$

$$f_1 = \frac{3(4)(1)}{2} = 6.$$

Hence

$$\chi_1^2 = (1 - 0.406)(7.608) = 4.52.$$

---

[1] This statistic actually tests the more restrictive assumption that Σ has compound symmetry.

TABLE 7.5   Numerical example

	Subject	b_1	b_2	b_3	Total
	1	4	7	2	13
	2	3	5	1	9
a_1	3	7	9	6	22
	4	6	6	2	14
	5	5	5	1	11
	Total	25	32	12	69
	6	8	2	5	15
	7	4	1	1	6
a_2	8	6	3	4	13
	9	9	5	2	16
	10	7	1	1	9
	Total	34	12	13	59

(i)

$128 = G$

(ii)

	b_1	b_2	b_3	Total
a_1	25	32	12	69
a_2	34	12	13	59
Total	59	44	25	128

(iii)

$$(2a_1) = 397 \qquad (2a_2) = 333$$
$$(3a_1) = 317.40 \qquad (3a_2) = 232.07$$
$$(5a_1) = 358.60 \qquad (5a_2) = 293.80$$
$$(6a_1) = 350.33 \qquad (6a_2) = 255.67$$

(iv)

$$\text{SS}_{B \times \text{subj w. } a_1} = (2a_1) - (5a_1) - (6a_1) + (3a_1) = 5.47$$
$$\text{SS}_{B \times \text{subj w. } a_2} = (2a_2) - (5a_2) - (6a_2) + (3a_2) = 15.60$$
$$\text{SS}_{B \times \text{subj (pooled)}} = 21.07$$

$$\text{MS}_{B \times \text{subj w. } a_1} = 5.47/8 = 0.684$$
$$\text{MS}_{B \times \text{subj w. } a_2} = 15.60/8 = 1.950$$
$$\text{MS}_{B \times \text{subj (pooled)}} = 21.07/16 = 1.315$$

TABLE 7.6   Covariance matrices associated with data in Table 7.5

	a_1				a_2				Pooled		
	b_1	b_2	b_3		b_1	b_2	b_3		b_1	b_2	b_3
b_1	2.50	1.75	2.50	b_1	3.70	2.10	1.15	b_1	3.10	1.92	1.82
b_2	1.75	2.80	3.30	b_2	2.10	2.80	0.70	b_2	1.92	2.80	2.00
b_3	2.50	3.30	4.30	b_2	1.15	0.70	3.30	b_3	1.82	2.00	3.80

$\overline{\text{var}} - \overline{\text{cov}} = 0.68 \qquad\qquad \overline{\text{var}} - \overline{\text{cov}} = 1.95 \qquad\qquad \overline{\text{var}} - \overline{\text{cov}} = 1.32$

If $\alpha = 0.05$, the critical value for the test of homogeneity of population covariance matrices is $\chi^2_{0.95}(6) = 12.6$. Since the observed chi-square statistic does not exceed this value, the hypothesis of homogeneity of covariances may be considered tenable.

To obtain the statistic defined in (7.8), one must compute the matrix

$$S_0 = \begin{bmatrix} \overline{\text{var}} & \overline{\text{cov}} & \cdots & \overline{\text{cov}} \\ \overline{\text{cov}} & \overline{\text{var}} & \cdots & \overline{\text{cov}} \\ \vdots & \vdots & & \vdots \\ \overline{\text{cov}} & \overline{\text{cov}} & \cdots & \overline{\text{var}} \end{bmatrix},$$

where $\overline{\text{var}}$ = mean of entries on main diagonal of S_{pooled},
$\overline{\text{cov}}$ = mean of entries off main diagonal of S_{pooled}.

For these data the matrix S_0 is given by

$$S_0 = \begin{bmatrix} 3.23 & 1.91 & 1.91 \\ 1.91 & 3.23 & 1.91 \\ 1.91 & 1.91 & 3.23 \end{bmatrix}.$$

Then, to obtain the statistic defined in (7.8),

$$M_2 = -(10 - 3) \ln \frac{11.28}{12.30} = -7(-0.0866) = 0.692,$$

$$C_2 = \frac{3(16)(3)}{6(7)(2)(8)} = 0.21,$$

$$f_2 = \frac{9 + 3 - 4}{2} = 4.$$

Hence

$$\chi^2_2 = (1 - 0.21)(0.692) = 0.55.$$

The critical value for a 0.05-level test on the hypothesis that all the diagonal values of Σ are σ^2 and all the off-diagonal entries are $\rho\sigma^2$ is $\chi^2_{0.95}(4) = 9.5$. These data do not contradict this hypothesis, the exact hypothesis being that

$$\Sigma = \begin{bmatrix} \sigma^2 & \rho\sigma^2 & \cdots & \rho\sigma^2 \\ \rho\sigma^2 & \sigma^2 & \cdots & \rho\sigma^2 \\ \vdots & \vdots & & \vdots \\ \rho\sigma^2 & \rho\sigma^2 & \cdots & \sigma^2 \end{bmatrix}.$$

That is, each entry on the main diagonal is equal to σ^2, and each entry off the main diagonal is equal to $\rho\sigma^2$. If, in fact, Σ has this form, then matrix S_0 provides an unbiased estimate of Σ.

It is of interest to note from S_0 that, within rounding error,

$$\text{MS}_{B \times \text{subj}} = \overline{\text{var}} - \overline{\text{cov}} = 3.23 - 1.91 = 1.32;$$

$$\text{MS}_{\text{subj w. } a_1} = \overline{\text{var}}_{a_1} + (q - 1)\overline{\text{cov}}_{a_1} = 3.20 + (2)(2.52) = 8.24;$$

$$\text{MS}_{\text{subj w. } a_2} = \overline{\text{var}}_{a_2} + (q - 1)\overline{\text{cov}}_{a_2} = 3.27 + (2)(1.32) = 5.91.$$

ASSUMPTIONS: SUMMARY REMARKS. As a practical matter, how should an experimenter proceed in view of these rather complicated and restrictive assumptions? Basically, there are three options.

First, one may utilize the F distributions considering that the assumptions have been met. This can be done based upon the tests of the assumptions or upon one's knowledge of the area of research. There is no substitute for extensive knowledge of how data "behave" in a particular research environment through having investigated a particular set of questions extensively. The tests of the assumptions are weak substitutes for such knowledge. If the usual F is used and the assumptions have been violated, a positive bias results and the analysis of variance hypotheses will be rejected more often than the true state of affairs warrants for the nominal level of significance.

Second, one can use the assumption that the covariance matrix departs maximally from circularity. That is, $\varepsilon = 1/(q-1)$, and the critical values for F become

$$F_{1-\alpha}[(q-1)\varepsilon, p(n-1)(q-1)\varepsilon] = F_{1-\alpha}[1, p(n-1)]$$

and

$$F_{1-\alpha}[(p-1)(q-1)\varepsilon, p(n-1)(q-1)\varepsilon] = F_{1-\alpha}[(p-1), p(n-1)],$$

for the tests that $\sigma_\beta^2 = 0$ and $\sigma_{\alpha\beta}^2 = 0$, respectively. Setting ε at its lower bound makes the test procedure conservative relative to the usual F test, resulting in rejecting too few null hypotheses for the true state of affairs in the population. Monte Carlo studies have indicated that the usual tests suggested by the analysis of variance tend to give results closer to the nominal significance levels than do results under this Greenhouse-Geisser conservative approach, provided the degree of heterogeneity of the covariances is relatively moderate (see Collier et al., 1967).

Since the usual F may be positively biased and setting ε at its minimal level may result in a negative bias, the third alternative is to estimate ε and use $\hat\varepsilon$ to adjust the degrees of freedom. Thus, one may consult the F tables for critical values of F as follows for testing σ_β^2 and $\sigma_{\alpha\beta}^2$, respectively:

$$F_{1-\alpha}[(q-1)\hat\varepsilon, \qquad p(n-1)(q-1)\hat\varepsilon],$$
$$F_{1-\alpha}[(p-1)(q-1)\hat\varepsilon, p(n-1)(q-1)\hat\varepsilon].$$

On balance, the best approach may be that suggested by Kirk (1982): use the usual F and if H_0 is not rejected, stop, because the other two procedures have less power. If H_0 is rejected, using the usual F, use the most conservative degrees of freedom to check for significance. If H_0 is still rejected, stop, if H_0 is not rejected, use $\hat\varepsilon$ to adjust the degrees of freedom and test H_0 with those degrees of freedom.

Numerical Example

To illustrate the computational procedures for this plan, consider a factorial experiment in which the levels of factor A are two methods for calibrating dials

TABLE 7.7   **Numerical example**

(i)

Observed data:

	Subject	b_1	b_2	b_3	b_4	Total
a_1	1	0	0	5	3	$8 = P_1$
	2	3	1	5	4	$13 = P_2$
	3	4	3	6	2	$15 = P_3$
a_2	4	4	2	7	8	$21 = P_4$
	5	5	4	6	6	$21 = P_5$
	6	7	5	8	9	$29 = P_6$
	Total	23	15	37	32	$107 = G$

(ii)

AB summary table:

	b_1	b_2	b_3	b_4	Total
a_1	7	4	16	9	36
a_2	16	11	21	23	71
Total	23	15	37	32	107

(iii)

Computational symbols:

$$(1) = G^2/npq \qquad = (107)^2/3(2)(4) \qquad\qquad = 477.04$$
$$(2) = \Sigma X^2 \qquad = 0^2 + 0^2 + 5^2 + \cdots + 8^2 + 9^2 \quad = 615$$
$$(3) = (\Sigma A_i^2)/nq \quad = (36^2 + 71^2)/3(4) \qquad\qquad = 528.08$$
$$(4) = (\Sigma B_j^2)/np \quad = (23^2 + 15^2 + 37^2 + 32^2)/3(2) \quad = 524.50$$
$$(5) = [\Sigma(AB_{ij})^2]/n = (7^2 + 4^2 + \cdots + 21^2 + 23^2)/3 \quad = 583.00$$
$$(6) = (\Sigma P_k^2)/q \qquad = (8^2 + 13^2 + \cdots + 21^2 + 29^2)/4 = 545.25$$

and the levels of B are four shapes for the dials. Suppose that the data obtained are those given in part i of Table 7.7. Entries are accuracy scores on a series of trials on each dial. Thus, for this experiment $p = 2$, $q = 4$, and $n = 3$.

The order in which subjects are observed under the dials is randomized independently.

From the data in part i, the AB summary table given in part ii is readily obtained. Computational symbols are defined and computed in part iii. The only symbol that does not occur in a $p \times q$ factorial experiment without repeated measures is (6). This symbol involves P_k, which is the sum of the q observations made on subject k. These sums are given at the right of part i. In each case the divisor in a computational symbol is the number of observations summed to obtain an entry which is squared in the numerator.

The analysis of variance is summarized in Table 7.8. In terms of means,

$$\text{SS}_{\text{subj w. groups}} = q \sum_k \sum_i (\bar{P}_{k(i)} - \bar{A}_i)^2,$$

$$\text{SS}_{B \times \text{subj w. groups}} = \sum_k \sum_j \sum_i (X_{ijk} - \bar{P}_{k(i)} - \overline{AB}_{ij} + \bar{A}_i)^2.$$

TABLE 7.8   **Analysis of variance for numerical example**

Source of variation	Computational formula	SS	df	MS	F
Between subjects	$(6) - (1) =$	68.21	5		
$\quad A$ (calibration)	$(3) - (1) - $	51.04	1	51.04	11.90
$\quad$ Subjects within groups	$(6) - (3) = $	17.17	4	4.29	
Within subjects	$(2) - (6) = $	69.75	18		
$\quad B$ (shape)	$(4) - (1) = $	47.46	3	15.82	12.76
$\quad AB$	$(5) - (3) - (4) + (1) = $	7.46	3	2.49	2.01
$\quad B \times$ subjects within groups	$(2) - (5) - (6) + (3) = $	14.83	12	1.24	

The computational formulas given in Table 7.7 are equivalent to these operations on the means.

The F ratios were obtained under the assumption that both factors A and B were fixed, but subjects are random. Those assumptions result in the E(MS) shown in Table 7.3. If the level of significance for tests is set at 0.05, one rejects the hypothesis that $\sigma_\alpha^2 = 0$, since $F_{0.95}(1, 4) = 7.71$; the hypothesis that $\sigma_\beta^2 = 0$ is also rejected, since $F_{0.95}(3, 12) = 3.49$. However, the experimental data do not contradict the hypothesis that $\sigma_{\alpha\beta}^2 = 0$.

It is interesting to compare the differential power of the between-subject and within-subject effects and to compare the power of those tests to the power which would have obtained with a completely randomized design. In a completely randomized design, $MS_{within\ cell}$ would have been the denominator for all F tests with $pq(n - 1) = 16$ degrees of freedom. Table 7.4 makes it clear that

$$SS_{w.\ cells} = SS_{subjects\ within\ groups} + SS_{B \times subjects\ within\ groups}$$
$$= 17.17 + 14.83 = 32.00.$$

Thus, $MS_{within\ cells} = 2.00$, in contrast to 4.29 and 1.24 for the between-subject and within-subject "error estimates" respectively. It is clear that removing subject effects from the within-cell error estimate reduced the power of the test on the A main effect, but increased the power of the test on σ_β^2 and $\sigma_{\alpha\beta}^2$, with the condition that the assumptions were actually met.

If the experimenter has reason (often there is) to question the pattern assumptions on the covariance matrix in the underlying population, the critical values for the within-subject tests are as follows:

Hypothesis	Conservative test	Ordinary test
$\sigma_\beta^2 = 0$	$F_{0.95}[1, 4] = 7.71$	$F_{0.95}[3, 12] = 3.49$
$\sigma_{\alpha\beta}^2 = 0$	$F_{0.95}[1, 4] = 7.71$	$F_{0.95}[3, 12] = 3.49$

Even under the more conservative test (i.e., negatively biased test) the main effects due to the shapes of the dials remain statistically significant.

If the experimenter has reason to question the homogeneity of the parts that are pooled to form the denominators of the F ratios, a check on homogeneity would logically precede the tests. Computational procedures for partitioning the relevant sums of squares are given in Table 7.9. A symbol of the form $(6a_1)$ has the same general definition as (6), but summations are restricted to level a_1. The computational procedures for parts which are pooled are given in part ii. As a check on the homogeneity of $SS_{subj\ w.\ groups}$,

$$F_{max} = \frac{10.67}{6.50} = 1.64.$$

TABLE 7.9   Partition of error terms

$(6a_1) = \left(\sum\limits_{a_1} P_k^2\right)\Big/q = (8^2 + 13^2 + 15^2)/4$	$= 114.50$
$(6a_2) = \left(\sum\limits_{a_2} P_k^2\right)\Big/q = (21^2 + 21^2 + 29^2)/4$	$= 430.75$
	$(6) = 545.25$

(i)

$(3a_1) = (A_1^2)/nq = 36^2/3(4)$	$= 108.00$
$(3a_2) = (A_2^2)/nq = 71^2/3(4)$	$= 420.08$
	$(3) = 528.08$

$(5a_1) = \left[\sum\limits_{a_1} (AB_{ij})^2\right]\Big/n = [7^2 + 4^2 + 16^2 + 9^2]/3$	$= 134.00$
$(5a_2) = \left[\sum\limits_{a_2} (AB_{ij})^2\right]\Big/n = (16^2 + 11^2 + 21^2 + 23^2)/3$	$= 449.00$
	$(5) = 583.00$

$(2a_1) = \sum\limits_{a_1} X^2 = 0^2 + 0^2 + \cdots + 6^2 + 2^2$	$= 150$
$(2a_2) = \sum\limits_{a_2} X^2 = 4^2 + 2^2 + \cdots + 8^2 + 9^2$	$= 465$
	$(2) = 615$

(ii)

$SS_{subj\ w.\ G_1} = (6a_1) - (3a_1)$	$= 6.50$
$SS_{subj\ w.\ G_2} = (6a_2) - (3a_2)$	$= 10.67$
	17.17
$SS_{B \times subj\ w.\ G_1} = (2a_1) - (5a_1) - (6a_1) + (3a_1)$	$= 9.50$
$SS_{B \times subj\ w.\ G_2} = (2a_2) - (5a_2) - (6a_2) + (3a_2)$	$= 5.33$
	14.83

The critical value for a 0.05-level test here is

$$F_{\max_{0.95}}(2, 2) = 39.00.$$

Since the computed $F_{\max}$ statistic does not exceed the critical value, the test does not contradict the hypothesis that the parts are homogeneous. Since each of the parts in this case has only two degrees of freedom, the power of a test of this kind is extremely low.

As a check on the homogeneity of the parts of $SS_{B \times \text{subj w. groups}}$,

$$F_{\max} = \frac{9.50}{5.33} = 1.78.$$

The critical value here is

$$F_{\max_{0.95}}(2.6) = 5.82.$$

Again, the computed value of the statistic does not exceed the critical value. Hence, the hypothesis of homogeneity is not contradicted by the experimental data.

COVARIANCE MATRICES ASSOCIATED WITH THIS NUMERICAL EXAMPLE. Consider the following data from part i of Table 7.7:

	Subject	b_1	b_2	b_3	b_4
	1	0	0	5	3
a_1	2	3	1	5	4
	3	4	3	6	2
		7	4	16	9

The variance of the observations made under b_1 is

$$\text{var}_{b_1} = \frac{(0^2 + 3^2 + 4^2) - (7^2/3)}{2} = 4.33.$$

Similarly, the variance of the observations made under b_2 is

$$\text{var}_{b_2} = \frac{(0^2 + 1^2 + 3^2) - (4^2/3)}{2} = 2.33.$$

The covariance of the observations made under b_1 and b_2 is

$$\text{cov}_{b_1 b_2} = \frac{(0)(0) + (3)(1) + (4)(3) - (7)(4)/3}{2} = 2.83.$$

Similarly, the covariance of the observations under b_1 and b_3 is

$$\text{cov}_{b_1 b_3} = \frac{(0)(5) + (3)(5) + (4)(6) - (7)(16)/3}{2} = 0.83.$$

The variance–covariance matrix for level a_1 of factor A is

		b_1	b_2	b_3	b_4
$\hat{\Sigma}_{a_1} = B_{a_1}$	b_1	4.33	2.83	0.83	−0.50
	b_2		2.33	0.83	−1.00
	b_3			0.33	−0.50
	b_4				1.00

A similar variance–covariance matrix for the data at level a_2 is given below:

		b_1	b_2	b_3	b_4
$\hat{\Sigma}_{a_2} = B_{a_2}$	b_1	2.33	2.17	1.00	1.17
	b_2		2.33	0.50	0.33
	b_3			1.00	1.50
	b_4				2.33

If the underlying population variance–covariance matrices for B_{a_1} and B_{a_2} are equal but not necessarily of the form indicated above, the best estimate of the common underlying population variance–covariance matrix is the pooled sample matrices. The pooled matrix is obtained by averaging corresponding entries in the individual matrices. For the data under consideration, the pooled variance–covariance matrix is given below:

		b_1	b_2	b_3	b_4
$\hat{\Sigma} = B_{\text{pooled}}$	b_1	3.33	2.50	0.92	0.33
	b_2		2.33	0.67	−0.33
	b_3			0.67	0.50
	b_4				1.67

The matrix of intercorrelations as computed from the pooled covariance matrix is given below:

$$
\begin{bmatrix}
1.00 & 0.90 & 0.62 & 0.14 \\
 & 1.00 & 0.54 & -0.17 \\
 & & 1.00 & 0.47 \\
\text{Symmetric} & & & 1.00
\end{bmatrix}.
$$

It is interesting to relate the values from the covariance matrix $\hat{\Sigma}$ to the differential power of between-subject and within-subject effects. Recall that

$$ MS_{B \times \text{subj w. groups}} = \overline{\text{var}} - \overline{\text{cov}}, $$

and

$$ MS_{\text{subj w. groups}} = \overline{\text{var}} + (q - 1)\,\overline{\text{cov}}, $$

where $\overline{\text{var}}$ and $\overline{\text{cov}}$ are the mean values from $\hat{\Sigma}$. For these data, $\overline{\text{var}} = 2.00$ and

$\overline{\text{cov}} = 0.76$, thus

$$\text{MS}_{B \times \text{subj w. groups}} = 2.00 - 0.76 = 1.24$$
$$\text{MS}_{\text{subj w. groups}} = 2.00 + 3(0.76) = 4.28.$$

It is clear, then, that the within-subject tests depend upon $\overline{\text{cov}}$ for their power advantage over the between-subject effects. This, in turn, depends upon the existence of subject main effects. Note that if there are no subject effects, $\overline{\text{cov}} = 0$, and both within- and between-subject effects will use $\overline{\text{var}}$ as the denominator of F ratios. That is because $\overline{\text{var}} = \text{MS}_{\text{w. cell}}$ of the non-repeated measures design; in the absence of subject effects, repeated measures and completely-randomized designs are identical in outcome.

There are two stages in testing for homogeneity with respect to the variance–covariance matrices. Those tests are illustrated earlier in this section. First, one is interested in finding out whether or not the B_{a_i}'s can be pooled. Second, if these matrices can be pooled, one is interested in finding out whether or not the population matrix has the required property of circularity (or, more restrictively, compound symmetry). In the case of these data, there is no reason for concern since the outcome of the tests of significance would not change regardless of the test procedure used.

Exploring Differences Among Means

Any of the procedures illustrated in earlier chapters may be used to examine hypotheses regarding differences among the pq treatment means. Thus, one may want to explore the nature of interactions by examining simple effects or treatment-contrast interactions (see Chapters 5 and 6), carry out trend analyses (see Sec. 7.6), or examine differences among sets of means using procedures which provide appropriate control over error rates (see primarily Chapter 3). In applying these procedures, the only major considerations remaining are the choice of the appropriate denominator for test statistics, and the question of adjusting for the possibility that the assumptions have not been met.

In general, the choice of a denominator for test statistics is determined by the partition of variation which is involved with the differences among means under consideration. The general rule is that the appropriate error term is the error term used in the overall analysis of variance to test the same source(s) of variation; when different denominators are used, they are pooled into a single MS. Using this rule one arrives at:

Mean difference	$\text{MS}_{\text{denominator}}$
$\bar{A}_i - \bar{A}_{i'}$	$\text{MS}_{\text{subj w. groups}}$
$\bar{B}_j - \bar{B}_{j'}$	$\text{MS}_{B \times \text{subj w. groups}}$
$\overline{AB}_{ij} - \overline{AB}_{i'j}$	$\text{MS}_{\text{pooled}} = \text{MS}_{\text{w. cell}} = \dfrac{\text{SS}_{\text{subj w. groups}} + \text{SS}_{B \times \text{subj w. groups}}}{p(n-1) + p(n-1)(q-1)}$
$\overline{AB}_{ij} - \overline{AB}_{ij'}$	$\text{MS}_{B \times \text{subj w. groups}}$
$\overline{AB}_{ij} - \overline{AB}_{i'j'}$	$\text{MS}_{\text{pooled}} = \text{MS}_{\text{w. cell}}.$

The first difference, $\bar{A}_i - \bar{A}_{i'}$, is simply part of SS_A and uses the between-subject MS denominator for F; the difference $\bar{B}_j - \bar{B}_{j'}$ is part of SS_B and uses $MS_{B \times \text{subj. w. groups}}$ as a MS denominator. A component of the simple main effects of A at a particular level of factor B is represented by $\overline{AB}_{ij} - \overline{AB}_{i'j}$. Since

$$\sum_j SS_{A \text{ at } b_j} = SS_A + SS_{AB},$$

this difference involves a partition of both between-subject (SS_A) and within-subject (SS_{AB}) variation. Thus, the appropriate error estimate pools between- and within-subject variation. (The result is $MS_{\text{w. cell}}$ of the non-repeated measures design). In contrast, $\overline{AB}_{ij} - \overline{AB}_{ij'}$ is a component of the simple main effects of B variation, $SS_{B \text{ at } a_i}$. This variation is related to the overall analysis as

$$\sum_i SS_{b \text{ at } a_i} = SS_B + SS_{AB}.$$

Since both SS_B and SS_{AB} are within-subject sources of variation, the appropriate denominator is $MS_{B \times \text{subj w. groups}}$. Finally, any difference $\overline{AB}_{ij} - \overline{AB}_{i'j'}$, involves both between- and within-subject effects; an appropriate denominator is, therefore, $MS_{\text{w. cell}}$. This information can be used to construct a t, F, or q statistic to be used for any of the test procedures, the degrees of freedom being those of the appropriate $MS_{\text{denominator}}$.

A second consideration is the assumptions. When the homogeneity assumptions cannot be met, it may be appropriate to use the information only from the treatment conditions being compared to construct the test statistic; when the circularity assumption does not obtain, the degrees of freedom may be adjusted.

The Newman–Keuls procedure is utilized in Table 7.10 to test differences among all $\bar{B}_j$'s.

In part i, the $\bar{B}_j$'s are arranged in rank order from low to high. Differences between all possible pairs of ordered means are computed. For example,

$$6.17 - 2.50 = 3.67, \qquad 5.33 - 2.50 = 2.83, \text{ etc.}$$

In part ii critical values for the ordered differences between pairs are computed. Since the main effect of factor B is a within-subject effect, the standard error of the mean for all observations at a given level of factor B is

$$s_{\bar{B}} = \sqrt{\frac{MS_{B \times \text{subj w. groups}}}{np}} = \sqrt{\frac{1.24}{6}} = \sqrt{2.07} = 0.46.$$

The degrees of freedom associated with this standard error are those of $MS_{B \times \text{subj w. groups}}$, which in this case are 12. To obtain the critical value for the difference between two ordered means which are r steps apart in an ordered

TABLE 7.10 **Tests on means using Newman–Keuls procedure**

Shapes	b_2	b_1	b_4	b_3
Ordered means	2.50	3.83	5.33	6.17

		b_2	b_1	b_4	b_3	r	$s_{\bar{B}}q_{0.95}(r, 12)$
(i)	b_2		1.33	2.83	3.67 -	4	----- 1.93
	b_1			1.50	2.34 -	3	----- 1.73
	b_4				0.84 -	2	----- 1.42

(ii)

$s_{\bar{B}} = 0.46$	$r =$	2	3	4
$q_{0.95}(r, 12)$:		3.08	3.77	4.20

(iii)

	b_2	b_1	b_4	b_3
b_2	—		*	*
b_1			*	*
b_4				—

sequence, one first finds the tabled values for

$$q_{1-\alpha}(r, \mathrm{df_{error}}),$$

where $\mathrm{df_{error}}$ represents the degrees of freedom associated with $s_{\bar{B}}$. These values are obtained from Table D.4. For level of significance 0.05, the relevant values of q are given in part ii. The critical value for an ordered difference between two means r steps apart is

$$s_{\bar{B}}q_{1-\alpha}(r, \mathrm{df_{error}}).$$

These critical values appear at the extreme right of part i. For example,

$$s_{\bar{B}}q_{0.95}(4, 12) = 0.46(4.20) = 1.93,$$
$$s_{\bar{B}}q_{0.95}(3, 12) = 0.46(3.77) = 1.73,$$
$$s_{\bar{B}}q_{0.95}(2, 12) = 0.46(3.08) = 1.42.$$

The pairs of means which can be considered different are indicated in part iii. The mean performance on shape b_3 is statistically different from the mean performance on shapes b_2 and b_1. The mean performance on shape b_4 is also statistically different from the mean performance on shapes b_2 and b_1. No other differences are statistically significant at the 0.05 level for the Newman–Keuls tests.

Tests on all possible ordered differences of the form $\bar{A}_i - \bar{A}_{i'}$ follow the same general pattern. For such tests,

$$s_{\bar{A}} = \sqrt{\frac{\mathrm{MS_{subj\ w.\ groups}}}{nq}}.$$

The degrees of freedom associated with $s_{\bar{A}}$ are $p(n-1)$.

If the AB interaction is significant, tests on simple main effects are called for, rather than direct tests on main effects. The computation of the variation due to the simple main effect of factors A and B is identical to that of a two-factor factorial experiment which does not have repeated measures. To test the simple main effect of factor B, the F ratio has the form

$$F = \frac{MS_{b \text{ at } a_i}}{MS_{B \times \text{subj w. groups}}} .$$

The denominator of this F ratio is the same as that used in testing the main effects of factor B. The F ratio for the test on the simple main effects of factor A has the form

$$F = \frac{MS_{a \text{ at } b_j}}{MS_{\text{w. cell}}} .$$

The denominator of this last F ratio requires special note—it is not the denominator used in testing the main effects of factor A. For each level of factor B considered individually, this plan reduces to a single-factor experiment in which there are no repeated measures. In this type of experiment $MS_{\text{w. cell}}$ is the appropriate denominator for the variation due to the treatment effects.

The within-cell variation is given by

$$SS_{\text{w. cell}} = SS_{\text{subj w. groups}} + SS_{B \times \text{subj w. groups}}.$$

Within the context of a repeated-measure design, $SS_{\text{w. cell}}$ represents a pooling of what will often be heterogeneous sources of variance. Hence, the F test on the simple main effects for factor A, which uses $MS_{\text{w. cell}}$ as a denominator, will tend to be biased. However, when the degrees of freedom for the within-cell variation are large (say greater than 30), the bias will be quite small. The magnitude of the bias depends in part upon the ratio of $MS_{\text{subj w. groups}}$ to $MS_{B \times \text{subj w. groups}}$.

Variation due to the simple main effects is most readily computed from the AB summary table given in part ii of Table 7.7. For example,

$$SS_{a \text{ at } b_1} = \frac{7^2 + 16^2}{3} - \frac{23^2}{6} = 13.50;$$

$$MS_{a \text{ at } b_1} = \frac{SS_{a \text{ at } b_1}}{p - 1} = 13.50.$$

The denominator for the appropriate F ratio is

$$MS_{\text{w. cell}} = \frac{SS_{\text{w. cell}}}{pq(n - 1)} = \frac{17.17 + 14.83}{16} = 2.00;$$

$$F = \frac{MS_{a \text{ at } b_1}}{MS_{\text{w. cell}}} = 6.75.$$

In this context $MS_{w.\ cell}$ represents an average of heterogeneous sources of variance. Hence, for purposes of making tests, $MS_{w.\ cell}$ cannot be considered as having $pq(n-1) = 16$ degrees of freedom. Further, the ratio does not have an F distribution. However, the distribution of the F ratio (under the null hypothesis) may be approximated by an F distribution having degrees of freedom equal to $p-1$ and f, where f is given by (Satterthwaite, 1946)

$$f = \frac{(u+v)^2}{(u^2/f_1) + (v^2/f_2)},$$

where

$$u = p(n-1)MS_{subj\ w.\ groups},$$
$$v = p(n-1)(q-1)MS_{B \times subj\ w.\ groups},$$
$$f_1 = p(n-1),$$
$$f_2 = p(n-1)(q-1).$$

For the data in this example,

$$u = 17.17, \qquad v = 14.83, \qquad f_1 = 4, \qquad \text{and} \qquad f_2 = 12.$$

Hence

$$f = \frac{(17.17 + 14.83)^2}{[(17.17)^2/4] + [(14.83)^2/12]} = 11.12.$$

To the nearest integer, $f = 11$. Thus, under the appropriate null hypothesis, the F ratio

$$F = \frac{MS_{a\ at\ b_j}}{MS_{w.\ cell}} \text{ is distributed approximately as } F[(p-1), f].$$

It will be found that

$$p(n-1) \leq f \leq p(n-1) + p(n-1)(q-1).$$

For this example,

$$4 \leq f \leq 16.$$

f will achieve its upper bound only when

$$MS_{subj\ w.\ groups} = MS_{B \times subj.\ w.\ groups}.$$

Note that

$$MS_{w.\ cell} = \frac{p(n-1)MS_{subj\ w.\ groups} + p(n-1)(q-1)MS_{B \times subj\ w.\ groups}}{p(n-1) + p(n-1)(q-1)}$$

Thus $MS_{w.\ cell}$ is a weighted average of two mean squares. Dividing numerator and denominator of this fraction by $p(n-1)$, one obtains

$$MS_{w.\ cell} = \frac{MS_{subj\ w.\ groups} + (q-1)MS_{B \times subj\ w.\ groups}}{q}.$$

If one sets

$$u = \text{MS}_{\text{sub w. groups}} \quad \text{and} \quad v = (q-1)\text{MS}_{B \times \text{subj w. groups}}$$

in the expression for f, the numerical value will be identical with that obtained in the preceding paragraph.

The variation due to the simple main effects for factor B at level a_1 is

$$\text{SS}_{b \text{ at } a_1} = \frac{7^2 + 4^2 + 16^2 + 9^2}{3} - \frac{36^2}{12} = 26.00;$$

$$\text{MS}_{b \text{ at } a_1} = \frac{\text{SS}_{b \text{ at } a_1}}{q-1} = \frac{26.00}{3} = 8.67.$$

A test on the simple main effects of factor B at level a_1 uses the statistic

$$F = \frac{\text{MS}_{b \text{ at } a_1}}{\text{MS}_{B \times \text{subj w. groups}}} = \frac{8.67}{1.24} = 6.99.$$

The critical value for a test having level of significance 0.05 is

$$F_{0.95}[(q-1), p(n-1)(q-1)] = F_{0.95}(3, 12) = 3.49.$$

Hence the experimental data tend to reject the hypothesis that there are no differences in the effects of factor B when all observations are made at level a_1.

7.1 THREE-FACTOR EXPERIMENT WITH REPEATED MEASURES (CASE I)

As discussed in Sec. 7.1, there are seven different design combinations possible for between- and within-subject variables when there are three factors, and no restrictions on the experimenter because of the nature of the independent variables. In this section and the next, two of those cases will be considered. The first case will be that of a $p \times q \times r$ factorial experiment in which there are repeated observations on the last two factors. In the second case, repeated measures will be restricted to the last factor. A schematic representation of the first case is given below:

	b_1			$\cdots$	b_q		
	c_1	$\cdots$	c_r	$\cdots$	c_1	$\cdots$	c_r
a_1	G_1	$\cdots$	G_1	$\cdots$	G_1	$\cdots$	G_1
a_2	G_2	$\cdots$	G_2	$\cdots$	G_2	$\cdots$	G_2
$\vdots$	$\vdots$		$\vdots$		$\vdots$		$\vdots$
a_p	G_p	$\cdots$	G_p	$\cdots$	G_p	$\cdots$	G_p

There are n subjects in each group. Each subject is observed under all qr combinations of factor B and C but only under a single level of factor A. Thus, there are p groups of n subjects each (np subjects in all); there are qr observations on each subject.

The observations on subjects in group i may be represented as follows:

a_i	Subject	b_1			$\cdots$	b_q			Total
		c_1	$\cdots$	c_r	$\cdots$	c_1	$\cdots$	c_r	
	$1(i)$	X_{i111}	$\cdots$	X_{i1r1}	$\cdots$	X_{iq11}	$\cdots$	X_{iqr1}	$P_{1(i)}$
	$\vdots$	$\vdots$		$\vdots$		$\vdots$		$\vdots$	$\vdots$
	$m(i)$	X_{i11m}	$\cdots$	X_{i1rm}	$\cdots$	X_{iq1m}	$\cdots$	X_{iqrm}	$P_{m(i)}$
	$\vdots$	$\vdots$		$\vdots$		$\vdots$		$\vdots$	$\vdots$
	$n(i)$	X_{i11n}	$\cdots$	X_{i1rn}	$\cdots$	X_{iq1n}	$\cdots$	X_{iqrn}	$P_{n(i)}$

The notation X_{ijkm} indicates an observation on subject $m(i)$ under treatment combination abc_{ijk}. The notation $P_{m(i)}$ denotes the sum of the qr observations on subject m in group i. Unless there is some ambiguity about which group is under discussion, the notation P_m will be used to denote this total.

In this design the subjects may be viewed as defining a fourth factor having n levels. The "subject" factor is crossed with factors B and C but is nested under factor A. Schematically,

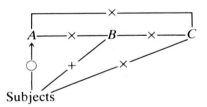

The structural model on which the analysis is based is

$$X_{ijkm} = \mu + \alpha_i + \pi_{m(i)} + \beta_j + \gamma_k + \alpha\beta_{ij} + \alpha\gamma_{ik} + \beta\gamma_{jk} + \alpha\beta\gamma_{ijk}$$

$$+ \beta\pi_{jm(i)} + \gamma\pi_{km(i)} + \beta\gamma\pi_{jkm(i)}.$$

The subject variable is nested in levels of factor A and cannot, therefore, interact with levels of A.

Assuming that A, B, and C are fixed factors, the analysis of variance generally takes the form shown in Table 7.11. The expected values of the mean squares indicate appropriate F ratios, provided that the sampling distributions of the statistics involved are actually what they are assumed to be. What is assumed will be made explicit later in this section. [The general E(MS) of which those in Table 7.11 are a special case are given in Table 7.18. If $D_n = 1$, $D_p = 0$, $D_q = 0$, $D_r = 0$ in the latter table, the results will be the E(MS) in Table 7.11.]

TABLE 7.11   **Summary of analysis of variance**

Source of variation	df	E(MS)†
Between subjects	$np - 1$	
A	$p - 1$	$\sigma_\varepsilon^2 + qr\sigma_\pi^2 + nqr\sigma_\alpha^2$
Subj w. groups	$p(n - 1)$	$\sigma_\varepsilon^2 + qr\sigma_\pi^2$
Within subjects	$np(qr - 1)$	
B	$q - 1$	$\sigma_\varepsilon^2 + r\sigma_{\beta\pi}^2 + npr\sigma_\beta^2$
AB	$(p - 1)(q - 1)$	$\sigma_\varepsilon^2 + r\sigma_{\beta\pi}^2 + nr\sigma_{\alpha\beta}^2$
B × subj w. groups	$p(n - 1)(q - 1)$	$\sigma_\varepsilon^2 + r\sigma_{\beta\pi}^2$
C	$r - 1$	$\sigma_\varepsilon^2 + q\sigma_{\gamma\pi}^2 + npq\sigma_\gamma^2$
AC	$(p - 1)(r - 1)$	$\sigma_\varepsilon^2 + q\sigma_{\gamma\pi}^2 + nq\sigma_{\alpha\gamma}^2$
C × subj w. groups	$p(n - 1)(r - 1)$	$\sigma_\varepsilon^2 + q\sigma_{\gamma\pi}^2$
BC	$(q - 1)(r - 1)$	$\sigma_\varepsilon^2 + \sigma_{\beta\gamma\pi}^2 + np\sigma_{\beta\gamma}^2$
ABC	$(p - 1)(q - 1)(r - 1)$	$\sigma_\varepsilon^2 + \sigma_{\beta\gamma\pi}^2 + n\sigma_{\alpha\beta\gamma}^2$
BC × subj w. groups	$p(n - 1)(q - 1)(r - 1)$	$\sigma_\varepsilon^2 + \sigma_{\beta\gamma\pi}^2$

† Assumes A, B, and C fixed factors.

An alternative partition of the total degrees of freedom is as follows:

Source of variation	Degrees of freedom	
	General case	Special case $p = 2, q = 3, r = 4, n = 5$
Between cells	$pqr - 1$	23
Within cells	$pqr(n - 1)$	96
Subj w. groups	$p(n - 1)$	8
B × subj w. groups	$p(n - 1)(q - 1)$	16
C × subj w. groups	$p(n - 1)(r - 1)$	24
BC × subj w. groups	$p(n - 1)(q - 1)(r - 1)$	48

A cell in this context contains the n observations under treatment combination abc_{ijk}. There are pqr cells. Treatment and interaction variation are obtained by partitioning the between-cell variation. The latter partition is identical for all $p \times q \times r$ factorial experiments whether or not there are repeated measures. The manner in which the within-cell variation is partitioned depends upon the pattern of the repeated measures. For the case being considered, each of the parts of the within-cell variation forms a denominator for some F ratio. Hence the following alternative notation system

$$\text{MS}_{\text{subj w. groups}} = \text{MS}_{\text{error}(a)},$$

$$\text{MS}_{B \times \text{subj w. groups}} = \text{MS}_{\text{error}(b)},$$

$$\text{MS}_{C \times \text{subj w. groups}} = \text{MS}_{\text{error}(c)},$$

$$\text{MS}_{BC \times \text{subj w. groups}} = \text{MS}_{\text{error}(bc)}.$$

The alternative notation system has the advantage of being more compact as well as more indicative of the role of the error term in the F tests for the special case being considered. However, the F tests will change as a function of what model is appropriate for the data being analyzed. Thus the alternative notation has the disadvantage of not indicating how each of the terms is computed.

The expected values for mean squares given in Table 7.11 are obtained from a model which includes interactions with the subject factor. If in fact such interactions do not exist (or are negligible relative to the magnitude of σ_ε^2), then

$$E(MS_{error(b)}) = \sigma_\varepsilon^2 \quad \text{if} \quad \sigma_{\beta\pi}^2 = 0,$$

$$E(MS_{error(c)}) = \sigma_\varepsilon^2 \quad \text{if} \quad \sigma_{\gamma\pi}^2 = 0,$$

$$E(MS_{error(bc)}) = \sigma_\varepsilon^2 \quad \text{if} \quad \sigma_{\beta\gamma\pi}^2 = 0.$$

In words, if all interactions with the subject factor are zero, each of the above mean squares is an estimate of the same variance, namely, that due to experimental error. Further, these estimates are independent and may be pooled to provide a single estimate of σ_ε^2. Thus,

$$MS_{error(within)} = \frac{SS_{error(b)} + SS_{error(c)} + SS_{error(bc)}}{p(n-1)(qr-1)}$$

provides an estimate of σ_ε^2 having $p(n-1)(qr-1)$ degrees of freedom.

If the experiment provides a relatively large number of degrees of freedom (say over 30) for estimating the variance due to each of the interactions with subjects, there is generally no need to consider pooling procedures. When there are relatively few degrees of freedom for such estimates, the decision about pooling should depend largely on previous experimental work. In the absence of such background information, preliminary tests on the model are useful. The purpose of such tests is to provide the experimenter with *a posteriori* information about whether certain interactions with random factors should be included in the model for the experiment. Such tests should be made at numerically high levels of significance (that is, $\alpha = 0.20$ or $\alpha = 0.30$). This procedure does not drop a term from the model unless the data clearly indicate that such terms can be dropped. Since terms are dropped when tests on the model do not reject the hypothesis being tested, high power is required. Bartlett's test for homogeneity of variance may be used to indicate whether interactions with subjects can be pooled. (Pooling is equivalent to dropping terms from the model.)

Any of the procedures for analyzing differences among means may be adopted for this design, provided that care is used in constructing estimates of standard errors. The general rules are the same as those introduced for a two-factor design in Sec. 7.2; differences which involve components of variation which were tested using different MS in the denominator of F ratios in the overall analysis of variance require that those be pooled in structuring t,

TABLE 7.12 **Denominator of F ratio for simple effects**

	Simple effect	Denominator of F ratio
A at b_j	$\overline{AB}_{1j} - \overline{AB}_{2j}$	$[MS_{error(a)} + (q-1)MS_{error(b)}]/q$
A at c_k	$\overline{AC}_{1k} - \overline{AC}_{2k}$	$[MS_{error(a)} + (r-1)MS_{error(c)}]/r$
B at a_i	$\overline{AB}_{i1} - \overline{AB}_{i2}$	$MS_{error(b)}$
C at a_i	$\overline{AC}_{i1} - \overline{AC}_{i2}$	$MS_{error(c)}$
B at c_k	$\overline{BC}_{1k} - \overline{BC}_{2k}$	$[MS_{error(b)} + (r-1)MS_{error(bc)}]/r$
C at b_j	$\overline{BC}_{j1} - \overline{BC}_{j2}$	$[MS_{error(c)} + (q-1)MS_{error(bc)}]/q$
A at bc_{jk}	$\overline{ABC}_{1jk} - \overline{ABC}_{2jk}$	$MS_{w.\ cell}$

F, or q statistics. Pooling in this context can always be accomplished by adding the variation and degrees of freedom. MS_{pooled} is the pooled variation divided by the pooled degrees of freedom. For example, tests on simple main effects have denominators of the form shown in Table 7.12. These denominators can be derived by considering the overall sources of variation included in these simple effects. Since

$$\sum_j SS_{a\ at\ b_j} = SS_a + SS_{ab},$$

the F ratio for tests on the simple main effects of A at level b_j involves a mixture of the appropriate denominators for tests on the main effect of A and the AB interaction. Thus, MS_{error} for A at b_j is given by

$$\frac{SS_{error(a)} + SS_{error(b)}}{p(n-1) + p(n-1)(q-1)} = \frac{MS_{error(a)} + (q-1)MS_{error(b)}}{q}.$$

Similarly, since

$$\sum_k SS_{b\ at\ c_k} = SS_b + SS_{bc},$$

the denominator of the F test on the variance due to the main effects of B at c_k is given by

$$\frac{SS_{error(b)} + SS_{error(bc)}}{p(n-1)(q-1) + p(n-1)(q-1)(r-1)} = \frac{MS_{error(b)} + (r-1)MS_{error(bc)}}{r}.$$

For tests on variance due to C at b_j,

$$\sum_j SS_{c\ at\ b_j} = SS_c + SS_{bc},$$

both MS_c and MS_{bc} have as their denominator $MS_{error(c)}$. Hence

$$MS_{error\ for\ c\ at\ b_j} = MS_{error(c)}.$$

A more rigorous rationale for the denominators of F ratios for simple effects is developed later in this chapter.

The same logic may be used to construct t, F, or q statistics to examine comparisons among meaningful subsets of means. For example, t statistics to test differences among means at different levels of factor A, but at the same level of factor B, take the form

$$t = \frac{\overline{AB}_{ij} - \overline{AB}_{i'j}}{\sqrt{2[\text{MS}_{\text{error}(a)} + (q-1)\text{MS}_{\text{error}(b)}]/nrq}} ;$$

to test differences between A means at the same level of factor C,

$$t = \frac{\overline{AC}_{ik} - \overline{AC}_{i'k}}{\sqrt{2[\text{MS}_{\text{error}(a)} + (r-1)\text{MS}_{\text{error}(c)}]/nrq}} .$$

It is easiest to generalize these statistics in terms of F. For any comparison among the $\bar{A}_i$'s, $\bar{B}_j$'s, $\bar{C}_k$'s, $\overline{AB}_{ij}$, $\overline{AC}_{ik}$, $\overline{BC}_{jk}$, or $\overline{ABC}_{ijk}$,

$$F = \frac{\text{SS}_c}{\text{MS}_{\text{appropriate}}} = F(1, \text{df}_{\text{appropriate}}),$$

where $\text{MS}_{\text{appropriate}}$ can be deduced from Table 7.12 and

$$\text{SS}_c = \frac{C^2}{\sum c_i^2 / N},$$

is the variation associated with the comparison C among means, $\sum c_i^2$ is the sum of the squares of the coefficients associated with the comparison, and "N" is the number of observations on which the means are based ($N = n$, np, nq, npq, etc). Since $t = \sqrt{F}$, $q = \sqrt{2F}$, this general F statistic may be converted to t or q to use any of the previously-discussed techniques to compare means.

Since pooling mean squares may involve pooling heterogeneous sources of between- and within-subject variation [e.g., $\text{MS}_{\text{error}(a)}$ and $\text{MS}_{\text{error}(b)}$], an approximation to the distribution of the test statistic may be in order. For the t statistics above, an approximate critical value of a t statistic of this kind is obtained as follows: Let t_a and t_b be the critical values for a test of level of significance equal to α for the degrees of freedom corresponding to $\text{MS}_{\text{error}(a)}$ and $\text{MS}_{\text{error}(b)}$ respectively. Then an approximate critical value for the t statistic is

$$t_{\text{critical}} = \frac{t_a \text{MS}_{\text{error}(a)} + t_b(q-1)\text{MS}_{\text{error}(b)}}{\text{MS}_{\text{error}(a)} + (q-1)\text{MS}_{\text{error}(b)}} .$$

This critical value is suggested by Cochran and Cox (1957, p. 299). In cases in which the degrees of freedom for the mean squares are both large (say over 30), the critical value may be obtained directly from tables of the normal distribution instead of t.

Alternatively, one may enter the usual t table with degrees of freedom

TABLE 7.12a **Approximate degrees of freedom for denominators indicated in Table 7.12**

A at b_j	$\dfrac{[MS_{error(a)} + (q-1)MS_{error(b)}]^2}{MS^2_{error(a)}/p(n-1) + [(q-1)MS_{error(b)}]^2/p(n-1)(q-1)}$
A at c_k	$\dfrac{[MS_{error(a)} + (r-1)MS_{error(c)}]^2}{MS^2_{error(a)}/p(n-1) + [(r-1)MS_{error(c)}]^2/p(n-1)(r-1)}$
B at c_k	$\dfrac{[MS_{error(b)} + (r-1)MS_{error(bc)}]^2}{MS^2_{error(b)}/p(n-1)(q-1) + [(r-1)MS_{error(bc)}]^2/p(n-1)(r-1)(q-1)}$
C at b_j	$\dfrac{[MS_{error(c)} + (q-1)MS_{error(bc)}]^2}{MS^2_{error(c)}/p(n-1)(r-1) + [(q-1)MS_{error(bc)}]^2/p(n-1)(r-1)(q-1)}$

	Lower limit for df	Upper limit for df
A at b_j	$p(n-1)$	$pq(n-1)$
A at c_k	$p(n-1)$	$pr(n-1)$
B at c_k	$p(n-1)(q-1)$	$pr(n-1)(q-1)$
C at b_j	$p(n-1)(r-1)$	$pq(n-1)(r-1)$

given by the Satterthwaite approximation, which in this case has the form

$$f = \frac{[MS_{error(a)} + (q-1)MS_{error(b)}]^2}{MS^2_{error(a)}/p(n-1) + [(q-1)MS_{error(b)}]^2/p(n-1)(q-1)}.$$

The Satterthwaite approximation is discussed in some detail in Sec. 5.17. A summary of the degrees of freedom, as obtained from the Satterthwaite approach, is given in Table 7.12a.

Computational Procedures

With the exception of the breakdown of the within-cell variation, computational procedures are identical with those of a $p \times q \times r$ factorial experiment having n observations per cell. These procedures will be illustrated by the data in Table 7.13.

TABLE 7.13 **Basic data for numerical example**

		Periods:	b_1			b_2			b_3			
	Subjects	**Dials:**	c_1	c_2	c_3	c_1	c_2	c_3	c_1	c_2	c_3	**Total**
	1		45	53	60	40	52	57	28	37	46	418
a_1	2		35	41	50	30	37	47	25	32	41	338
	3		60	65	75	58	54	70	40	47	50	519
	4		50	48	61	25	34	51	16	23	35	343
a_2	5		42	45	55	30	37	43	22	27	37	338
	6		56	60	77	40	39	57	31	29	46	435

TABLE 7.14 **Summary tables for numerical example**

ABC summary table

| | b_1 | | | b_2 | | | b_3 | | |
	c_1	c_2	c_3	c_1	c_2	c_3	c_1	c_2	c_3
a_1	140	159	185	128	143	174	93	116	137
a_2	148	153	193	95	110	151	69	79	118
Total	288	312	378	223	253	325	162	195	255

(i)

AB summary table

	b_1	b_2	b_3	Total
a_1	484	445	346	1275
a_2	494	356	266	1116
Total	978	801	612	2391

AC summary table

	c_1	c_2	c_3	Total
a_1	361	418	496	1275
a_2	312	342	462	1116
Total	673	760	958	2391

BC summary table

	c_1	c_2	c_3	Total
b_1	288	312	378	978
b_2	223	253	325	801
b_3	162	195	255	612
Total	673	760	958	2391

(ii)

$B \times$ subj w. G_1 summary table

Subject	b_1	b_2	b_3	Total
1	158	149	111	418
2	126	114	98	338
3	200	182	137	519
Total	484	445	346	1275

$B \times$ subj w. G_2 summary table

Subject	b_1	b_2	b_3	Total
4	159	110	74	343
5	142	110	86	338
6	193	136	106	435
Total	494	356	266	1116

$C \times$ subj w. G_1 in summary table

Subject	c_1	c_2	c_3	Total
1	113	142	163	418
2	90	110	138	338
3	158	166	195	519
Total	361	418	496	1275

$C \times$ subj w. G_2 summary table

Subject	c_1	c_2	c_3	Total
4	91	105	147	343
5	94	109	135	338
6	127	128	180	435
Total	312	342	462	1116

Suppose that the levels of factor A represent the noise background under which subjects monitor three dials. The dials define factor C. Subjects are required to make adjustments on the respective dials whenever needles swing outside a specified range. Accuracy scores are obtained for each during three consecutive 10-minute time periods (factor B).

The basic data for this experiment are given in Table 7.13. Subjects 1, 2,

TABLE 7.15 **Definitions and numerical values of computational symbols**

$$(1) = G^2/npqr \qquad = (2391)^2/3(2)(3)(3) \qquad = 105\,868.17$$

$$(2) = \sum X^2 \qquad = 45^2 + 53^2 + 60^2 + \cdots + 31^2 + 29^2 + 46^2 = 115\,793.00$$

$$(3) = \left(\sum A_i^2\right)\bigg/nqr \qquad = (1275^2 + 1116^2)/3(3)(3) \qquad = 106\,336.33$$

$$(4) = \left(\sum B_j^2\right)\bigg/npr \qquad = (978^2 + 801^2 + 612^2)/3(2)(3) \qquad = 109\,590.50$$

$$(5) = \left(\sum C_k^2\right)npq \qquad = (673^2 + 760^2 + 958^2)/3(2)(3) \qquad = 108\,238.50$$

$$(6) = \left[\sum (AB_{ij})^2\right]\bigg/nr \qquad = (484^2 + 445^2 + \cdots + 266^2)/3(3) \qquad = 110\,391.67$$

$$(7) = \left[\sum (AC_{ik})^2\right]\bigg/nq \qquad = (361^2 + 418^2 + \cdots + 462^2)/3(3) \qquad = 108\,757.00$$

$$(8) = \left[\sum (BC_{jk})^2\right]\bigg/np \qquad = (288^2 + 312^2 + \cdots + 255^2)/3(6) \qquad = 111\,971.50$$

$$(9) = \left[\sum (ABC_{ijk})^2\right]n \qquad = (140^2 + 159^2 + \cdots + 118^2)/3 \qquad = 112\,834.33$$

$$(10) = \left(\sum P_m^2\right)\bigg/qr \qquad = (418^2 + 338^2 + \cdots + 435^2)/3(3) \qquad = 108\,827.44$$

$$(11) = \left[\sum (BP_{jm})^2\right]\bigg/r \qquad = (158^2 + 149^2 + \cdots + 106^2)/3 \qquad = 113\,117.67$$

$$(12) = \left[\sum (CP_{km})^2\right]\bigg/q \qquad = (113^2 + 142^2 + \cdots + 180^2)/3 \qquad = 111\,353.67$$

$$(10a_1) = \left(\sum_{a_1} P_m^2\right)\bigg/qr \qquad = (418^2 + 338^2 + 519^2)/3(3) \qquad = 62\,036.56$$

$$(10a_2) = \left(\sum_{a_2} P_m^2\right)\bigg/qr \qquad = (343^2 + 338^2 + 435^2)/3(3) \qquad = 46\,790.89$$

$$108\,827.45$$

$$(11a_1) = \left[\sum_{a_1} (BP_{jm})^2\right]\bigg/r \qquad = (158^2 + 149^2 + \cdots + 137^2)/3 \qquad = 63\,285.00$$

$$(11a_2) = \left[\sum_{a_2} (BP_{jm})^2\right]\bigg/r \qquad = (159^2 + 110^2 + \cdots + 106^2)/3 \qquad = 49\,832.67$$

$$113\,117.67$$

and 3 comprise G_1; subjects 4, 5, and 6 comprise G_2. To illustrate the meaning of the data, during the first 10-minute interval (b_1) subject 1 had scores of 45, 53, and 60 on dials c_1, c_2, and c_3, respectively.

Summary tables prepared from these basic data are given in Table 7.14. In part i are summary tables that would be obtained for any $2 \times 3 \times 3$ factorial experiment having n observations per cell. Part ii is unique to a factorial experiment having repeated measures on factors B and C. In the $B \times$ subjects within G_1 summary table a cell entry will be denoted by the symbol BP_{jm}. For example, $BP_{11} = 158$, and $BP_{13} = 111$. Similarly, an entry in a cell of the $C \times$ subjects within group summary table will be denoted by the symbol CP_{km}.

Convenient computational symbols are defined and computed in Table 7.15. Symbols (1) through (9) are identical to those used in any $p \times q \times r$ factorial experiment in which there are n observations in each cell. Symbols (10) through (12) are unique to a factorial experiment in which there are repeated measures on factors B and C. By using these symbols, computational formulas take the form given in Table 7.16. In terms of means,

$$\text{SS}_{B \times \text{subj w. groups}} = r \sum_i \sum_j \sum_m (\overline{BP}_{km(i)} - \overline{AB}_{ij} - \bar{P}_{m(i)} + \bar{A}_i)^2.$$

The formula for this source of variation given in Table 7.16 leads to simpler computations. This source of variation is also designated $\text{SS}_{\text{error}(b)}$.

There is an overall computational check that can be be made on the sum

TABLE 7.16 **Summary of analysis of variance**

Source of variation	Computational formula	SS	df	MS	F
Between subjects	(10) − (1)	2959.27	5		
A	(3) − (1)	468.16	1	468.16	
Subj w. groups [error (a)]	(10) − (3)	2491.11	4	622.78	
Within subjects	(2) − (10)	6965.56	48		
B	(4) − (1)	3722.33	2	1861.16	63.39*
AB	(6) − (3) − (4) + (1)	333.00	2	166.50	5.67*
B × subj w. groups [error (b)]	(11) − (6) − (10) + (3)	234.89	8	29.36	
C	(5) − (1)	2370.33	2	1185.16	89.78*
AC	(7) − (3) − (5) + (1)	50.34	2	25.17	1.91
C × subj w. groups [error (c)]	(12) − (7) − (10) + (3)	105.56	8	13.20	
BC	(8) − (4) − (5) + (1)	10.67	4	2.67	
ABC	(9) − (6) − (7) − (8) + (3) + (4) + (5) − (1)	11.32	4	2.83	
BC × subj w. groups [error (bc)]	(2) − (9) − (11) − (12) + (6) + (7) + (10) − (3)	127.11	16	7.94	

of the error terms. The following relationship exists:

$$SS_{error\,(a)} = (10) - (3)$$
$$SS_{error\,(b)} = (11) - (6) - (10) + (3)$$
$$SS_{error\,(c)} = (12) - (7) - (10) + (3)$$
$$SS_{error\,(bc)} = (2) - (9) - (11) - (12) + (6) + (7)$$
$$+ (10) - (3)$$

$$\overline{SS_{w.\,cell} = (2) - (9)}$$

The computational symbols on the right may be treated as algebraic symbols; that is, $(3) + (3) = 2(3)$, $(3) - (3) = 0$. The algebraic sum of the symbols on the right is $(2) - (9)$. The latter is the computational formula for $SS_{w.\,cell}$. The computational symbols at the bottom of Table 7.15 are used to partition the error variation for each of the error terms into parts which may be checked for homogeneity by means of an F_{max} test.

The analysis of variance is summarized in Table 7.16. If a model which includes interactions with subjects is appropriate for this experiment, the expected values for the mean squares are those shown in Table 7.11 and the structure of F ratios is determined by these expected values. However, should the existence of interactions with subjects be open to question, preliminary tests on the model are appropriate. In this case such interactions have relatively few degrees of freedom. A check on the homogeneity of such interactions is carried out in Table 7.17, by use of Bartlett's test. Since the

TABLE 7.17 **Test for homogeneity of interactions with subjects**

SS	MS	df	log MS	1/df
234.89	29.36	8	1.468	0.125
105.56	13.20	6	1.121	0.125
127.11	7.94	16	0.900	0.062
$\sum SS = 467.56$		$\sum df = 32$		$\sum (1/df) = 0.312$

$$MS_{pooled} = \left(\sum SS\right) \Big/ \sum df = 467.56/32 = 14.61$$

$$A = \sum [(df)_i \log MS_i] = 8(1.468) + 8(1.121) + 16(0.900) \qquad = 35.112$$

$$B = \left(\sum df\right) \log MS_{pooled} = 32(1.165) \qquad = 37.280$$

$$C = 1 + \frac{1}{3(k-1)}\left[\sum (1/df) - \left(1\Big/\sum df\right)\right] = 1 + \tfrac{1}{6}[0.312 - 0.031] \quad = 1.047$$

$$\chi^2 = \frac{2.303(B-A)}{C} = \frac{2.303(37.280 - 35.112)}{1.047} = 4.77$$

$$k = \text{number of } MS_i \qquad \chi^2_{0.80}(k-1) = \chi^2_{0.80}(2) = 3.22$$

observed chi square (4.77) exceeds the critical value (3.22) for a test with $\alpha = 0.20$, the test indicates that the interactions should not be pooled. Equivalently, the test indicates that interactions with subjects should not be dropped from the model.

Thus tests on B and AB use $MS_{\text{error }(b)}$ as a denominator for F ratios; tests on C and AC use $MS_{\text{error }(c)}$ as a denominator; tests on BC and ABC use $MS_{\text{error }(bc)}$ as a denominator. The main effect of A is tested with $MS_{\text{error }(a)}$. By using $\alpha = 0.05$ for all tests, the main effects for factors B (periods) and C (dials) are found to be statistically significant. Inspection of the totals for levels b_1, b_2, and b_3 indicates decreasing accuracy scores for the consecutive time periods. Inspection of the totals for the dials indicates that dial c_3 is monitored with the greatest accuracy and dial c_1 monitored with the least accuracy.

The AB interaction is also noted to be statistically significant. The profiles of means corresponding to the cell totals in the AB summary table are plotted in Fig. 7-1. The profiles indicate a difference in the rate of decline in the accuracy scores in the three periods, the group working under noise level a_1 showing a slower decline rate than the group working under a_2. Differences between corresponding points on these profiles have the form

$$\overline{AB}_{1j} - \overline{AB}_{2j}.$$

FIGURE 7-1

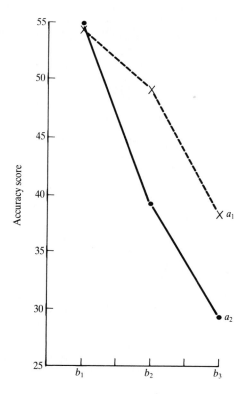

The standard error of the difference between these two means is estimated by

$$\sqrt{\frac{2(SS_{\text{subj w. groups}} + SS_{B \times \text{subj w. groups}})}{nr[p(n-1) + p(n-1)(q-1)]}} = \sqrt{\frac{2(2491.11 + 234.89)}{9(12)}}$$

$$= \sqrt{50.48} = 7.10.$$

By way of contrast, the standard error of the difference between two means of the following form,

$$\overline{AB}_{i1} - \overline{AB}_{i2},$$

is estimated by

$$\sqrt{2MS_{\text{error }(b)}/nr} = \sqrt{2(29.36)/9} = 2.55.$$

The latter standard error is considerably smaller than that computed in the last paragraph. A difference of the form $\overline{AB}_{1j} - \overline{AB}_{2j}$ is in part confounded with between-group effects, whereas a difference of the form $\overline{AB}_{i1} - \overline{AB}_{i2}$ is entirely a within-subject effect.

Assumptions

It was pointed out earlier that the analysis of this design partitions the within-cell variation of a $p \times q \times r$ completely-randomized design into the components of variation associated with subjects. Each of these components may be checked for homogeneity, one of the assumptions made when the computed F ratio is considered to be distributed in the form of the F distribution.

It is appropriate to test for homogeneity of the p components of the between-subject variation,

Subj w. groups	$p(n-1)$
Subj w. groups G_1	$n-1$
. . .	. . .
Subj w. groups G_p	$n-1$

An $F_{\max}$ test for the homogeneity of the parts has the critical value $F_{\max(1-\alpha)}(p, n-1)$. It is also possible to use $F_{\max}$ to check the homogeneity of the p components of each of the three within-subject sources of variation. For example,

$BC \times$ Subj w. groups	$p(n-1)(q-1)(r-1)$
$BC \times$ Subj w. groups G_1	$(n-1)(q-1)(r-1)$
. . .	. . .
$BC \times$ Subj w. groups G_p	$(n-1)(q-1)(r-1)$

An $F_{\max}$ test in this last case is, in part, a check on whether or not mean covariances of a set of variance–covariance matrices are equal. The critical value for this test is $F_{\max(1-\alpha)}[p, (n-1)(q-1)(r-1)]$. However, it is important to stress that the test on homogeneity of the within-subject components of variation provides only a partial check on the assumptions. More appropriate tests are generalizations of those given in Sec. 7.2 concerning the homogeneity and form of the covariance matrices.

For this design with repeated measures on two factors, there are three sets of $p = 2$ covariance matrices which may be constructed. One set is obtained from the $B \times$ subj w. groups G_i summary tables:

$$B_{a_1} = \begin{bmatrix} 459.11 & 418.77 & 244.11 \\ & 385.44 & 220.28 \\ & & 131.44 \end{bmatrix}; \quad B_{a_2} = \begin{bmatrix} 224.77 & 122.78 & 105.78 \\ & 75.11 & 75.11 \\ & & 87.11 \end{bmatrix};$$

$$B_{\text{pooled}} = \begin{bmatrix} 341.94 & 270.78 & 174.94 \\ & 230.28 & 147.70 \\ & & 109.28 \end{bmatrix}.$$

$\text{MS}_{B \times \text{subj w. groups}}$ may be obtained from B_{pooled}, as

$$\overline{\text{var}} - \overline{\text{cov}} = 227.17 - 197.81 = 29.36.$$

It is important to note that the test on σ_β^2 and $\sigma_{\alpha\beta}^2$ use this MS as a denominator. This involves the assumptions that the population covariance matrices estimated by B_{a_1} and B_{a_2} are homogeneous and that B_{pooled} is circular. Precisely, one assumes

$$M_B^{*\prime}\Sigma_{a_1}M^* = M_B^{*\prime}\Sigma_{a_2}M_B^* = \cdots = M_B^{*\prime}\Sigma_{a_p}M^* = M^{*\prime}\Sigma M^* = \lambda I$$

From the $C \times$ subj w. groups G_i summary tables, another set of $p = 2$ covariance matrices may be obtained.

$$C_{a_1} = \begin{bmatrix} 398.77 & 312.45 & 327.27 \\ & 263.11 & 264.45 \\ & & 272.11 \end{bmatrix}; \quad C_{a_2} = \begin{bmatrix} 133.00 & 81.50 & 146.50 \\ & 50.33 & 87.00 \\ & & 181.00 \end{bmatrix};$$

$$C_{\text{pooled}} = \begin{bmatrix} 265.88 & 196.98 & 236.88 \\ & 156.72 & 175.72 \\ & & 226.56 \end{bmatrix}.$$

From C_{pooled}, one notes that

$$\text{MS}_{C \times \text{subj w. groups}} = \overline{\text{var}} - \overline{\text{cov}} = 216.39 - 203.19 = 13.20.$$

The validity of the F statistics using $\text{MS}_{C \times \text{subj w. groups}}$ as the denominator, namely those to test σ_γ^2 and $\sigma_{\alpha\gamma}^2$, depends upon the homogeneity and circularity of these matrices:

$$M_c^{*\prime}\Sigma_{a_1}M_c^* = M_c^{*\prime}\Sigma_{a_2}M_c^* = M_c^{*\prime}\Sigma M_c^* = \lambda I.$$

A third set of matrices may be obtained from the basic data as given in

Table 7.13. That set of covariance matrices is also defined separately for levels a_1 and a_2 of factor A. Schematically, those matrices are the 9×9 matrices,

$$
BC_{a_1} = \begin{array}{c} \\ abc_{111} \\ abc_{112} \\ \vdots \\ abc_{133} \end{array}
\begin{array}{cccc}
abc_{111} & abc_{112} & \cdots & abc_{133} \\
s^2 & \text{cov} & \cdots & \text{cov} \\
 & s^2 & \cdots & \text{cov} \\
 & & & \vdots \\
 & & & s^2
\end{array}
$$

$$
BC_{a_2} = \begin{array}{c} \\ abc_{211} \\ abc_{212} \\ \vdots \\ abc_{233} \end{array}
\begin{array}{cccc}
abc_{211} & abc_{212} & \cdots & abc_{233} \\
s^2 & \text{cov} & \cdots & \text{cov} \\
 & s^2 & \cdots & \text{cov} \\
 & & & \vdots \\
 & & & s^2
\end{array}
$$

$$
BC_{\text{pooled}} = \begin{array}{c} \\ abc_{.11} \\ abc_{.12} \\ \vdots \\ abc_{.33} \end{array}
\begin{array}{cccc}
abc_{.11} & abc_{.12} & \cdots & abc_{.33} \\
\bar{s}^2 & \overline{\text{cov}} & \cdots & \overline{\text{cov}} \\
 & \bar{s}^2 & \cdots & \overline{\text{cov}} \\
 & & & \vdots \\
 & & & \bar{s}^2
\end{array}
$$

From these matrices, it will be found that $32(\overline{\text{var}} - \overline{\text{cov}}) = SS_{B \times \text{subj w. groups}} + SS_{C \times \text{subj w. groups}} + SS_{BC \times \text{subj w. groups}}$.

Each of these sets of covariance matrices may be tested for homogeneity and circularity using the methods discussed in Sec. 7.2. Alternatively, if there is reason to suspect that the assumptions have not been met, the conservative test proposed by Greenhouse and Geisser may be used. They are summarized for this design in the following table:

F ratio	Critical values	
	Usual test	**Conservative test**
$\dfrac{MS_b}{MS_{B \times \text{subj w. group}}}$	$F_{1-\alpha}[(q-1), p(n-1)(q-1)]$	$F_{1-\alpha}[1, p(n-1)]$
$\dfrac{MS_{ab}}{MS_{B \times \text{subj w. group}}}$	$F_{1-\alpha}[(p-1)(q-1), p(n-1)(q-1)]$	$F_{1-\alpha}[(p-1), p(n-1)]$
$\dfrac{MS_c}{MS_{C \times \text{subj w. group}}}$	$F_{1-\alpha}[(r-1), p(n-1)(r-1)]$	$F_{1-\alpha}[1, p(n-1)]$
$\dfrac{MS_{ac}}{MS_{C \times \text{subj w. group}}}$	$F_{1-\alpha}[(p-1)(r-1), p(n-1)(r-1)]$	$F_{1-\alpha}[(p-1), p(n-1)]$
$\dfrac{MS_{bc}}{MS_{BC \times \text{subj w. group}}}$	$F_{1-\alpha}[(q-1)(r-1), p(n-1)(q-1)(r-1)]$	$F_{1-\alpha}[1, p(n-1)]$
$\dfrac{MS_{abc}}{MS_{BC \times \text{subj w. group}}}$	$F_{1-\alpha}[(p-1)(q-1)(r-1), p(n-1)(q-1)(r-1)]$	$F_{1-\alpha}[(p-1), p(n-1)]$

For most covariance matrices encountered in practice, indications are that the conservative test is very conservative, particularly when n, p, q, and r are small. Accordingly, when the usual degrees of freedom lead to rejection of an hypothesis but the conservative test leads to non-rejection, the experimenter may want to compute $\hat{\varepsilon}$ and adjust the degrees of freedom using that estimate of ε.

General Expected Values for the Mean Squares

The expected values for the mean squares given in Table 7.11 are for the special case in which A, B, and C are fixed factors. In that table, $D_p = D_q = D_r = 0$, and the results can only be generalized to the population of subjects from which those in the experiment were randomly selected. The advantage of this special case is that the F tests have maximum power if the assumptions are met. The general case is given in Table 7.18;

$$D_p = 1 - \frac{p}{P}, \qquad D_q = 1 - \frac{q}{Q}, \qquad D_r = 1 - \frac{r}{R}.$$

Thus, D_p, D_q, and D_r are either 0 or 1, depending upon whether factors A, B, and C are fixed or random, respectively.

As an example of another special case, if $D_p = 1$, $D_q = 0$ and $D_r = 0$, then the special case given in Table 7.19 is obtained.

It is obvious that when A is a random factor and B and C are fixed, there is very little statistical power for testing the B and C main effects and BC

TABLE 7.18 General expected values for mean squares

Effect	i	j	k	m	o	E(MS)
α_i	D_p	q	r	n	1	$\sigma_\varepsilon^2 + D_q D_r \sigma_{\beta\gamma\pi}^2 + n D_q D_r \sigma_{\alpha\beta\gamma}^2 + q D_r \sigma_{\gamma\pi}^2 + n q D_r \sigma_{\alpha\gamma}^2 + r D_q \sigma_{\beta\pi}^2 + n r D_q \sigma_{\alpha\beta}^2 + q r \sigma_\pi^2 + n q r \sigma_\alpha^2$
$\pi_{m(i)}$	1	q	r	1	1	$\sigma_\varepsilon^2 + D_q D_r \sigma_{\beta\gamma\pi}^2 + q D_r \sigma_{\gamma\pi}^2 + r D_q \sigma_{\beta\pi}^2 + q r \sigma_\pi^2$
β_j	p	D_q	r	n	1	$\sigma_\varepsilon^2 + D_r \sigma_{\beta\gamma\pi}^2 + n D_p D_r \sigma_{\alpha\beta\gamma}^2 + n p D_r \sigma_{\beta\gamma}^2 + r \sigma_{\beta\pi}^2 + n r D_p \sigma_{\alpha\beta}^2 + n p r \sigma_\beta^2$
$\alpha\beta_{ij}$	D_p	D_q	r	n	1	$\sigma_\varepsilon^2 + D_r \sigma_{\beta\gamma\pi}^2 + n D_r \sigma_{\alpha\beta\gamma}^2 + r \sigma_{\beta\pi}^2 + n r \sigma_{\alpha\beta}^2$
$\beta\pi_{jm(i)}$	1	D_q	r	1	1	$\sigma_\varepsilon^2 + D_r \sigma_{\beta\gamma\pi}^2 + r \sigma_{\beta\pi}^2$
γ_k	p	q	D_r	n	1	$\sigma_\varepsilon^2 + D_q \sigma_{\beta\gamma\pi}^2 + n D_p D_q \sigma_{\alpha\beta\gamma}^2 + n p D_q \sigma_{\beta\gamma}^2 + q \sigma_{\gamma\pi}^2 + n q D_p \sigma_{\alpha\gamma}^2 + n p q \sigma_\gamma^2$
$\alpha\gamma_{ik}$	D_p	q	D_r	n	1	$\sigma_\varepsilon^2 + D_q \sigma_{\beta\gamma\pi}^2 + n D_q \sigma_{\alpha\beta\gamma}^2 + q \sigma_{\gamma\pi}^2 + n q \sigma_{\alpha\gamma}^2$
$\gamma\pi_{km(i)}$	1	q	D_r	1	1	$\sigma_\varepsilon^2 + D_q \sigma_{\beta\gamma\pi}^2 + q \sigma_{\gamma\pi}^2$
$\beta\gamma_{jk}$	p	D_q	D_r	n	1	$\sigma_\varepsilon^2 + \sigma_{\beta\gamma\pi}^2 + n D_p \sigma_{\alpha\beta\gamma}^2 + n p \sigma_{\beta\gamma}^2$
$\alpha\beta\gamma_{ijk}$	D_p	D_q	D_r	n	1	$\sigma_\varepsilon^2 + \sigma_{\beta\gamma\pi}^2 + n \sigma_{\alpha\beta\gamma}^2$
$\beta\gamma\pi_{jkm(i)}$	1	D_q	D_r	1	1	$\sigma_\varepsilon^2 + \sigma_{\beta\gamma\pi}^2$
$\varepsilon_{o(ijkm)}$	1	1	1	1	1	σ_ε^2

TABLE 7.19 **Expected values of mean squares for the case in which factor A is random and factors B and C are fixed**

Source	E(MS)
Between subjects	
A	$\sigma_\varepsilon^2 + qr\sigma_\pi^2 + nqr\sigma_\alpha^2$
Subj w. groups	$\sigma_\varepsilon^2 + qr\sigma_\pi^2$
Within subjects	
B	$\sigma_\varepsilon^2 + r\sigma_{\beta\pi}^2 + nr\sigma_{\alpha\beta}^2 + npr\sigma_\beta^2$
AB	$\sigma_\varepsilon^2 + r\sigma_{\beta\pi}^2 + nr\sigma_{\alpha\beta}^2$
$B \times$ subj w. groups	$\sigma_\varepsilon^2 + r\sigma_{\beta\pi}^2$
C	$\sigma_\varepsilon^2 + q\sigma_{\gamma\pi}^2 + nq\sigma_{\alpha\gamma}^2 + npq\sigma_\gamma^2$
AC	$\sigma_\varepsilon^2 + q\sigma_{\gamma\pi}^2 + nq\sigma_{\alpha\gamma}^2$
$C \times$ subj w. groups	$\sigma_\varepsilon^2 + q\sigma_{\gamma\pi}^2$
BC	$\sigma_\varepsilon^2 + \sigma_{\beta\gamma\pi}^2 + n\sigma_{\alpha\beta\gamma}^2 + np\sigma_{\beta\gamma}^2$
ABC	$\sigma_\varepsilon^2 + \sigma_{\beta\gamma\pi}^2 + n\sigma_{\alpha\beta\gamma}^2$
$BC \times$ subj w. groups	$\sigma_\varepsilon^2 + \sigma_{\beta\gamma\pi}^2$

interaction. It is likely that the experimenter would want to draw on background information to consider dropping the interactions with A from the model. In the absence of such information, preliminary tests on the model may be made in order to check the desirability of pooling interactions with the random factor.

7.4 THREE-FACTOR EXPERIMENT WITH REPEATED MEASURES (CASE II)

In the last section the case in which there are repeated measures on two of the three factors was considered. In this section the case in which there are repeated measures on only one of the three factors will be considered. This case may be represented schematically as follows:

		c_1	c_2	$\cdots$	c_r
	b_1	G_{11}	G_{11}	$\cdots$	G_{11}
a_1	$\vdots$	$\vdots$	$\vdots$		$\vdots$
	b_q	G_{1q}	G_{1q}	$\cdots$	G_{1q}
	$\vdots$				
	b_1	G_{p1}	G_{p1}	$\cdots$	G_{p1}
a_p	$\vdots$	$\vdots$	$\vdots$		$\vdots$
	b_q	G_{pq}	G_{pq}	$\cdots$	G_{pq}

Each of the groups is observed under all levels of factor C, but each group is assigned to only one combination of factors A and B. The notation G_{ij} denotes the group of subjects assigned to treatment combination ab_{ij}. A subject within group G_{ij} is identified by the subscript $m(ij)$. This notation indicates that the subject effect is nested under both factors A and B.

The observations for individual subjects in group G_{ij} have the form:

	Subject	c_1	$\cdots$	c_k	$\cdots$	c_r	Total
	$1(ij)$	X_{ij11}	$\cdots$	X_{ijk1}	$\cdots$	X_{ijr1}	$P_{1(ij)}$
	$2(ij)$	X_{ij12}	$\cdots$	X_{ijk2}	$\cdots$	X_{ijr2}	$P_{2(ij)}$
a_ib_j	$m(ij)$	X_{ij1m}	$\cdots$	X_{ijkm}	$\cdots$	X_{ijrm}	$P_{m(ij)}$
	$n(ij)$	X_{ij1n}	$\cdots$	X_{ijkn}	$\cdots$	X_{ijrn}	$P_{n(ij)}$

The structural model on which the following analysis is based has the following form:

$$X_{ijkm} = \mu + \alpha_i + \beta_j + \alpha\beta_{ij} + \pi_{m(ij)}$$
$$+ \gamma_k + \alpha\gamma_{ik} + \beta\gamma_{jk} + \alpha\beta\gamma_{ijk} + \gamma\pi_{km(ij)} + \varepsilon_{0(ijkm)}$$

Since the subject factor is nested under both factors A and B, there can be no interaction between these factors and the subject factor. This model has implicit homogeneity assumptions on variance–covariance matrices associated with the repeated measures. The analysis of variance for this plan takes the form given in Table 7.20. The expected values in this table are for the special

TABLE 7.20 Summary of analysis of variance

Source of variation	df	E(MS)†
Between subjects	$npq - 1$	
A	$p - 1$	$\sigma_\varepsilon^2 + r\sigma_\pi^2 + nqr\sigma_\alpha^2$
B	$q - 1$	$\sigma_\varepsilon^2 + r\sigma_\pi^2 + npr\sigma_\beta^2$
AB	$(p-1)(q-1)$	$\sigma_\varepsilon^2 + r\sigma_\pi^2 + nr\sigma_{\alpha\beta}^2$
Subj w. groups [error (between)]	$pq(n-1)$	$\sigma_\varepsilon^2 + r\sigma_\pi^2$
Within subjects	$npq(r-1)$	
C	$r - 1$	$\sigma_\varepsilon^2 + \sigma_{\gamma\pi}^2 + npq\sigma_\gamma^2$
AC	$(p-1)(r-1)$	$\sigma_\varepsilon^2 + \sigma_{\gamma\pi}^2 + nq\sigma_{\alpha\gamma}^2$
BC	$(q-1)(r-1)$	$\sigma_\varepsilon^2 + \sigma_{\gamma\pi}^2 + np\sigma_{\beta\gamma}^2$
ABC	$(p-1)(q-1)(r-1)$	$\sigma_\varepsilon^2 + \sigma_{\gamma\pi}^2 + n\sigma_{\alpha\beta\gamma}^2$
$C \times$ subj w. groups [error (within)]	$pq(n-1)(r-1)$	$\sigma_\varepsilon^2 + \sigma_{\gamma\pi}^2$

† Assumes A, B, and C fixed factors.

case in which A, B, and C are considered fixed factors. The general case as obtained from the Cornfield-Tukey algorithm is given in Table 7.26.

An alternative partition of the total variation permits a comparison

Source	df
Total	$npqr - 1$
Between cells	$pqr - 1$
Within cells	$pqr(n - 1)$
Subj w. groups	$pq(n - 1)$
$C \times$ subj w. groups	$pq(n - 1)(r - 1)$

between this plan and a $p \times q \times r$ factorial experiment in which there are no repeated measures, but n observations per cell. The main effects and all interactions of factors A, B, and C are part of the between-cell variation whether or not there are repeated measures. The partition of the between-cell variation is identical in the two cases. When there are repeated measures on factor C, the within-cell variation is subdivided into two parts. One of these parts is

$$SS_{\text{subj w. groups}} = r \sum \sum \sum (\bar{P}_{m(ij)} - \overline{AB}_{ij})^2$$

$$= \frac{\sum \sum \sum P^2_{m(ij)}}{r} - \frac{\sum \sum (AB_{ij})^2}{nr}.$$

(The symbol $\sum \sum \sum P^2_{m(ij)}$ represents the sum of the squared totals from each subject. Each total is based upon r observations.) This source of variation is a measure of the extent to which the mean of a subject differs from the mean of the group in which the subject is located. The other part of the within-cell variation is

$$SS_{C \times \text{subj w. groups}} = SS_{\text{w. cell}} - SS_{\text{subj w. groups}},$$

where

$$SS_{\text{w. cell}} = \sum \sum \sum \sum (X_{ijkm} - \overline{ABC}_{ijk})^2$$

$$= \sum \sum \sum \sum X^2_{ijkm} - \frac{\sum (ABC_{ijk})^2}{n}.$$

Because of the structure of the F ratio for this plan (when A, B, and C are fixed factors), the following notation is sometimes used:

$$SS_{\text{subj w. groups}} = SS_{\text{error (between)}},$$

$$SS_{C \times \text{subj w. groups}} = SS_{\text{error (within)}}.$$

Each of these error terms may be subdivided and tested for homogeneity by means of $F_{\max}$ tests (see following).

TABLE 7.21 **Denominator of F ratio for simple effects**

Simple effect		Denominator of F ratio
A at b_j	$\overline{AB}_{1j} - \overline{AB}_{2j}$	$\left.\right\}$ $\text{MS}_{\text{error (between)}}$
B at a_i	$\overline{AB}_{i1} - \overline{AB}_{i2}$	
C at a_i	$\overline{AC}_{i1} - \overline{AC}_{i2}$	$\left.\right\}$ $\text{MS}_{\text{error (within)}}$
C at b_j	$\overline{BC}_{j1} - \overline{BC}_{j2}$	
C at ab_{ij}	$\overline{ABC}_{ij1} - \overline{ABC}_{ij2}$	
A at c_k	$\overline{AC}_{1k} - \overline{AC}_{2k}$	$\left.\right\}$ $[\text{MS}_{\text{error (between)}} + (r-1)\text{MS}_{\text{error (within)}}]/r$
B at c_k	$\overline{BC}_{1k} - \overline{BC}_{2k}$	
AB at c_k	$\overline{ABC}_{12k} - \overline{ABC}_{34k}$	

In making tests on simple main effects and applying t, F, or q statistics to examine differences among means, denominators appropriate for F ratios are indicated in Table 7.21. Recall that variation associated with simple main effects (and comparisons involving those differences) is a mixture of effects due to main effects and interactions.

In cases where the main effects and interaction effects have different error terms, a compromise error term is constructed. The latter is a weighted average of the different error terms, the weights being the respective degrees of freedom. Because of this pooling of heterogeneous sources of variation, the resulting F tests are potentially subject to bias and the experimenter may want to adjust the degrees of freedom to reduce bias (see Sec. 7.3).

Assumptions

With regard to the between-subject effects, the variation due to differences among subjects may be partitioned into the following parts:

Source	df
Subj w. G_{11}	$n - 1$
Subj w. G_{12}	$n - 1$
$\cdots$	$\cdots$
Subj w. G_{pq}	$n - 1$

There will be pq terms, each having the general form

$$\text{SS}_{\text{subj w. } G_{ij}} = r \sum_m (\bar{P}_{m(ij)} - \overline{AB}_{ij})^2.$$

The assumption that these components are homogeneous may be tested with an $F_{\max}$ statistic; the critical value for the test would be $F_{\max (1-\alpha)}(pq, n-1)$.

The assumptions concerning the within-subject effects can be partially evaluated by testing for homogeneity of the following components of variation:

Source	df
$C \times$ Subj w. G_{11}	$(n-1)(r-1)$
$C \times$ Subj w. g_{12}	$(n-1)(r-1)$
$\cdots$	$\cdots$
$C \times$ Subj w. G_{pq}	$(n-1)(r-1)$

There will be pq terms; each has the general form

$$\mathrm{SS}_{C \times \text{subj w. } G_{ij}} = \sum_m \sum_k (X_{ijkm} - \bar{P}_{m(ij)} - \overline{ABC}_{ijk} + \overline{AB}_{ij})^2.$$

The critical value for an $F_{\max}$ test in this case would be

$$F_{\max (1-\alpha)}[pq, (n-1)(r-1)].$$

Should either of these two error terms prove to be heterogeneous in terms of the criterion scale of measurement being used, the experimenter should consider a transformation on the scale of measurement in terms of which the analysis of variance may be carried out.

The assumptions regarding the within-subject variation are concerned with the homogeneity and structure of the covariance matrices computed over the levels of factor C. There are pq such matrices, one for each group of subjects. For group G_{ij}, the matrix has the form

		c_1	c_2	$\cdots$	c_r
	c_1	var_{11}	cov_{12}	$\cdots$	cov_{1r}
$C_{ab_{ij}} =$	c_2		var_{22}	$\cdots$	cov_{2r}
	$\vdots$				$\vdots$
	c_r			$\cdots$	var_{rr}

The overall assumption is that in the population these pq matrices are homogeneous and their pooled common matrix is circular, i.e.,

$$M_c^{*\prime} \Sigma_{ab_{11}} M_c^* = M_c^{*\prime} \Sigma_{ab_{12}} M_c^* = \cdots = M_c^{*\prime} \Sigma_{ab_{pq}} M_c^* = M_c^{*\prime} \Sigma M_c^* = \lambda I.$$

When these assumptions are questionable, it may be desirable to use critical values of the conservative tests, which values involving factor C have the form

$$F_{1-\alpha}[1, pq(n-1)] \quad \text{instead of} \quad F_{1-\alpha}[(r-1), pq(n-1)(r-1)],$$

and

$$F_{1-\alpha}[(p-1), pq(n-1)] \quad \text{instead of} \quad F_{1-\alpha}[(p-1)(r-1), pq(n-1)(r-1)].$$

That is, the degrees of freedom for numerator and denominator are each divided by $r-1$.

Computational Procedures

A numerical example will be used to illustrate the computational procedures. (This example is a modified version of an experiment actually conducted by Meyer and Noble [1958].) Suppose that an experimenter is interested in evaluating the effect of anxiety (factor A) and muscular tension (factor B) on a learning task. Subjects who score extremely low on a scale measuring manifest anxiety are assigned to level a_1; subjects who score extremely high are assigned to level a_2. The tension factor is defined by pressure exerted on a dynamometer. One half of the subjects at level a_1 are assigned at random to tension condition b_1; the other half are assigned to level b_2. The subjects at level a_2 are divided in a similar manner. Subjects are given four blocks of trials (factor C). The criterion is the number of errors in each block of trials. Suppose that the observed data are those given in Table 7.22.

In this table subjects 1, 2, and 3 form group G_{11}; subjects 4, 5, and 6 form group G_{12}; etc. Subject 6 is represented symbolically as $P_{3(12)}$, that is, the third subject in G_{12}. This plan may be classified as a $2 \times 2 \times 4$ factorial experiment with repeated measures on the last factor, $n = 3$. Summary data obtained from the basic observations are given in Table 7.23. All these summary tables are identical to those that would be obtained for a $2 \times 2 \times 4$ factorial experiment having no repeated measures.

Computational symbols are defined and evaluated in Table 7.24. Symbol (10) is the only one unique to a repeated-measure design. The data for the latter symbol are obtained from the total column in Table 7.22.

The analysis of variance is summarized in Table 7.25. Suppose that the 0.05 level of significance is used in all tests. The main effect for factor C (trials)

TABLE 7.22 Basic data for numerical example

		Subjects	c_1	c_2	c_3	c_4	Total
				Blocks of trials			
a_1	b_1	1	18	14	12	6	50
		2	19	12	8	4	43
		3	14	10	6	2	32
	b_2	4	16	12	10	4	42
		5	12	8	6	2	28
		6	18	10	5	1	34
a_2	b_1	7	16	10	8	4	38
		8	18	8	4	1	31
		9	16	12	6	2	36
	b_2	10	19	16	10	8	53
		11	16	14	10	9	49
		12	16	12	8	8	44

TABLE 7.23   Summary table for numerical example

ABC summary table

		c_1	c_2	c_3	c_4	Total
a_1	b_1	51	36	26	12	125
	b_2	46	30	21	7	104
a_2	b_1	50	30	18	7	105
	b_2	51	42	28	25	146
Total		198	138	93	51	480

AB summary table

	b_1	b_2	Total
a_1	125	104	229
a_2	105	146	251
Total	230	250	480

AC summary table

	c_1	c_2	c_3	c_4	Total
a_1	97	66	47	19	229
a_2	101	72	46	32	251
Total	198	138	93	51	480

BC summary table

	c_1	c_2	c_3	c_4	Total
b_1	101	66	44	19	230
b_2	97	72	49	32	250
Total	198	138	93	51	480

TABLE 7.24   Definitions and numerical values of computational symbols

$$(1) = G^2/npqr \qquad = (480)^2/48 \qquad = 4800.00$$

$$(2) = \sum X^2 \qquad = 18^2 + 14^2 + \cdots + 8^2 + 8^2 \qquad = 6058$$

$$(3) = \left(\sum A_i^2\right)\Big/ nqr \qquad = (229^2 + 251^2)/24 \qquad = 4810.08$$

$$(4) = \left(\sum B_j^2\right)\Big/ npr \qquad = (230^2 + 250^2)/24 \qquad = 4808.33$$

$$(5) = \left(\sum C_k^2\right)\Big/ npq \qquad = (198^2 + 138^2 + 93^2 + 51^2)/12 \qquad = 5791.50$$

$$(6) = \left[\sum (AB_{ij}^2)\right]\Big/ nr \qquad = (125^2 + 104^2 + 105^2 + 146^2)/12 \quad = 4898.50$$

$$(7) = \left[\sum (AC_{ik}^2)\right]\Big/ nq \qquad = (97^2 + 66^2 + \cdots + 46^2 + 32^2)/6 \;= 5810.00$$

$$(8) = \left[\sum (BC_{jk}^2)\right]/np \qquad = [101^2 + 66^2 + \cdots + 49^2 + 32^2)/6 = 5812.00$$

$$(9) = \left[\sum (ABC_{ijk}^2)\right]\Big/ n \qquad = (51^2 + 36^2 + \cdots + 28^2 + 25^2)/3 \;= 5923.33$$

$$(10) = \left(\sum P_m^2\right)\Big/ r \qquad = (50^2 + 43^2 + \cdots + 49^2 + 44^2)/4 \;= 4981.00$$

TABLE 7.25   **Summary of analysis of variance**

Source of variation	Computational formula	SS	df	MS	F
Between subjects	$(10) - (1)$	181.00	11		
A (anxiety)	$(3) - (1)$	10.08	1	10.08	
B (tension)	$(4) - (1)$	8.33	1	8.33	
AB	$(6) - (3) - (4) + (1)$	80.09	1	80.09	7.77*
Subj w. groups [error (between)]	$(10) - (6)$	82.50	8	10.31	
Within subjects	$(2) - (10)$	1077.00	36		
C (trials)	$(5) - (1)$	991.50	3	330.50	152.30*
AC	$(7) - (3) - (5) + (1)$	8.42	3	2.81	1.29
BC	$(8) - (4) - (5) + (1)$	12.17	3	4.06	1.87
ABC	$(9) - (6) - (7) - (8) + (3) + (4) + (5) - (1)$	12.74	3	4.25	1.96
$C \times$ subj w. groups [error (within)]	$(2) - (9) - (10) + (6)$	52.17	24	2.17	

is found to be statistically significant. This indicates that the average number of errors differ in the four blocks of trials. Inspection of the totals for the blocks indicates a decreasing number of errors from c_1 to c_4. The anxiety $\times$ tension interaction is also statistically significant. This indicates that the pattern of the number of errors in the two anxiety groups depends upon the level of muscular tension. The profiles corresponding to this interaction effect are shown in Fig. 7-2. These profiles indicate that the effect of muscular tension upon number of

FIGURE 7-2

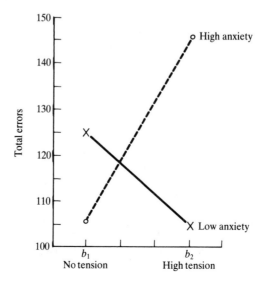

errors differs—high- and low-anxiety-level groups perform in different ways. A test on the difference between mean number of errors between the two anxiety levels under the no-tension condition (b_1) is given by

$$F = \frac{(AB_{11} - AB_{21})^2}{2nr\text{MS}_{\text{error(between)}}} = \frac{(125 - 105)^2}{2(12)(10.31)} = 1.62.$$

The critical value for this test is

$$F_{0.95}(1, 8) = 5.32.$$

Thus, the data indicate no statistically significant difference between the high- and low-anxiety groups under the condition of no tension. A test on the difference between the high- and low-anxiety groups under the high-tension condition is given by

$$F = \frac{(AB_{12} - AB_{22})^2}{2nr\text{MS}_{\text{error(between)}}} = \frac{(104 - 146)^2}{2(12)(10.31)} = 7.13.$$

The critical value for this test is also 5.32. Hence, the data indicate a statistically significant difference in the performance of the high- and low-anxiety groups under the high-tension conditions; the high-anxiety group tends to make significantly more errors than does the low-anxiety group.

None of the interactions with factor C is statistically significant. Hence, the data indicate that the shapes of the learning curves are essentially identical under each of the treatment combinations.

VARIANCE–COVARIANCE MATRICES ASSOCIATED WITH NUMERICAL EXAMPLE. Apart from the homogeneity assumptions required for the validity of the usual F tests, the variance–covariance matrices provide information which is of use in its own right in describing processes operating in the experiment. The variance–covariance matrices associated with the data in Table 7.22 are given below:

	Level ab_{11}					Level ab_{12}			
	c_1	c_2	c_3	c_4		c_1	c_2	c_3	c_4
c_1	7.00	4.00	5.00	4.00	c_1	9.33	4.00	0.00	−0.66
c_2		4.00	6.00	4.00	c_2		4.00	4.00	2.00
c_3			9.33	6.00	c_3			7.00	4.00
c_4				4.00	c_4				2.34

Level ab_{21}

	c_1	c_2	c_3	c_4
c_1	1.33	−2.00	−2.00	−1.34
c_2		4.00	2.00	1.00
c_3			4.00	3.00
c_4				2.34

Level ab_{22}

	c_1	c_2	c_3	c_4
c_1	3.00	3.00	1.00	−0.50
c_2		4.00	2.00	0.00
c_3			1.33	0.33
c_4				0.33

The variance–covariance matrix obtained by averaging corresponding entries in each of the above matrices is given below:

Pooled variances and covariances

	c_1	c_2	c_3	c_4
c_1	5.16	2.25	1.00	0.38
c_2		4.00	3.50	1.75
c_3			5.42	3.33
c_4				2.25

In this experiment, the levels of factor C represent successive blocks of trials in a learning experiment. Typically in this kind of experiment the variances tend to decrease as the learning increases. In the pooled variance–covariance matrix this trend is not clearly shown (5.16, 4.00, 5.42, 2.25). Further, the covariances between neighboring blocks of trials tend to be relatively higher than covariances between blocks which are further apart. This trend is clearly shown in the pooled variance–covariance matrix. The pattern assumptions on the pooled variance–covariance matrix required for the strict validity of the usual F test do not in general hold for learning experiments. (Use of Hotelling's T^2 statistic will, however, provide an exact test even if the pattern assumptions do not hold.)

From the pooled covariance matrix, the average of the entries along the main diagonal defines $\overline{\text{var}}$, and the average of the entries off the main diagonal defines $\overline{\text{cov}}$. In this case, $\overline{\text{var}} = 4.21$, and $\overline{\text{cov}} = 2.04$. In terms of the latter quantities,

$$\text{MS}_{\text{error(between)}} = \overline{\text{var}} + (r - 1)\overline{\text{cov}} = 10.33,$$
$$\text{MS}_{\text{error(within)}} = \overline{\text{var}} - \overline{\text{cov}} = 2.17.$$

Within rounding error, these values are equal to those obtained for the corresponding mean squares in Table 7.25.

General Expected Values for Mean Squares

The expected values for the mean squares given in Table 7.20 are a special case of those given in Table 7.26. Depending upon the experimental design,

TABLE 7.26 **General expected values for means squares**

Effect	i	j	k	m	o	E(MS)
α_i	D_p	q	r	n	1	$\sigma_\varepsilon^2 + D_r\sigma_{\gamma\pi}^2 + nD_qD_r\sigma_{\alpha\beta\gamma}^2 + nqD_r\sigma_{\alpha\gamma}^2 + r\sigma_\pi^2 + nrD_q\sigma_{\alpha\beta}^2 + nqr\sigma_\alpha^2$
β_j	p	D_q	r	n	1	$\sigma_\varepsilon^2 + D_r\sigma_{\gamma\pi}^2 + nD_pD_r\sigma_{\alpha\beta\gamma}^2 + npD_r\sigma_{\beta\gamma}^2 + r\sigma_\pi^2 + nrD_p\sigma_{\alpha\beta}^2 + npr\sigma_\beta^2$
$\alpha\beta_{ij}$	D_p	D_q	r	n	1	$\sigma_\varepsilon^2 + D_r\sigma_{\gamma\pi}^2 + nD_r\sigma_{\alpha\beta\gamma}^2 + r\sigma_\pi^2 + nr\sigma_{\alpha\beta}^2$
$\pi_{m(ij)}$	1	1	r	1	1	$\sigma_\varepsilon^2 + D_r\sigma_{\gamma\pi}^2 + r\sigma_\pi^2$
γ_k	p	q	D_r	n	1	$\sigma_\varepsilon^2 + \sigma_{\gamma\pi}^2 + nD_pD_q\sigma_{\alpha\beta\gamma}^2 + npD_q\sigma_{\beta\gamma}^2 + nqD_p\sigma_{\alpha\gamma}^2 + npq\sigma_\gamma^2$
$\alpha\gamma_{ik}$	D_p	q	D_r	n	1	$\sigma_\varepsilon^2 + \sigma_{\gamma\pi}^2 + nD_q\sigma_{\alpha\beta\gamma}^2 + nq\sigma_{\alpha\gamma}^2$
$\beta\gamma_{jk}$	p	D_q	D_r	n	1	$\sigma_\varepsilon^2 + \sigma_{\gamma\pi}^2 + nD_p\sigma_{\alpha\beta\gamma}^2 + np\sigma_{\beta\gamma}^2$
$\alpha\beta\gamma_{ijk}$	D_p	D_q	D_r	n	1	$\sigma_\varepsilon^2 + \sigma_{\gamma\pi}^2 + n\sigma_{\alpha\beta\gamma}^2$
$\gamma\pi_{km(ij)}$	1	1	D_r	1	1	$\sigma_\varepsilon^2 + \sigma_{\gamma\pi}^2$
$\varepsilon_{o(ijkm)}$	1	1	1	1	1	σ_ε^2

D_p, D_q, and D_r are either zero or unity. The expected values in Table 7.20 are obtained from those in Table 7.26 by assuming that each of these D's is zero, i.e., that factors A, B, and c are fixed.

7.5 OTHER MULTIFACTOR REPEATED-MEASURE PLANS

The plans considered in this chapter have the following general form:

	v_1	v_2	$\cdots$	v_h	
u_1	G_1	G_1	$\cdots$	G_1	
u_2	G_2	G_2	$\cdots$	G_2	n subjects per group
$\vdots$	$\vdots$	$\vdots$		$\vdots$	
u_g	G_g	G_g	$\cdots$	G_g	

The analysis of this general form may be outlined as follows:

Source	df
Between subjects	$ng - 1$
U	$g - 1$
Subjects w. groups	$g(n - 1)$
Within subjects	$ng(h - 1)$
V	$h - 1$
UV	$(g - 1)(h - 1)$
$V \times$ subj w. groups	$g(n - 1)(h - 1)$

The levels of factor U may, for example, constitute the pq treatment combinations in a $p \times q$ factorial set. In this case the following subdivisions are possible:

Source	df	Source	df
U	$g-1$	UV	$(g-1)(h-1)$
A	$p-1$	AV	$(p-1)(h-1)$
B	$q-1$	BV	$(q-1)(h-1)$
AB	$(p-1)(q-1)$	ABV	$(p-1)(q-1)(h-1)$

Alternatively, U may define the levels of factor A, and V may define the treatment combinations in a $q \times r$ factorial set. In this case the following subdivisions are possible:

Source	df	Source	df
V	$h-1$	UV	$(g-1)(h-1)$
B	$q-1$	AB	$(p-1)(q-1)$
C	$r-1$	AC	$(p-1)(r-1)$
BC	$(q-1)(r-1)$	ABC	$(p-1)(q-1)(r-1)$

Source	df
$V \times$ subj w. groups	$g(n-1)(h-1)$
$B \times$ subj w. groups	$p(n-1)(q-1)$
$C \times$ subj w. groups	$p(n-1)(r-1)$
$BC \times$ subj w. groups	$p(n-1)(q-1)(r-1)$

As a third case, the levels of factor U may constitute pq treatment combinations in a $p \times q$ factorial set, and the levels of factor V may constitute the rs combinations in an $r \times s$ factorial set. In this case the general form specializes to the analysis summarized in Table 7.27. In this table, terms have been rearranged to indicate denominators for F ratios. The expected values given in this table are derived under the assumption that factors A, B, C, and D are fixed.

To illustrate the subdivision of the UV interaction for this case, one may first subdivide the U factor as follows:

Source	df
UV	$(g-1)(h-1)$
AV	$(p-1)(h-1)$
BV	$(q-1)(h-1)$
ABV	$(p-1)(q-1)(h-1)$

TABLE 7.27 **Summary of analysis of variance**

Source of variation	df	E(MS)
Between subjects	$npq - 1$	
A	$p - 1$	$\sigma_\varepsilon^2 + rs\sigma_\pi^2 + nqrs\sigma_\alpha^2$
B	$q - 1$	$\sigma_\varepsilon^2 + rs\sigma_\pi^2 + nprs\sigma_\beta^2$
AB	$(p - 1)(q - 1)$	$\sigma_\varepsilon^2 + rs\sigma_\pi^2 + nrs\sigma_{\alpha\beta}^2$
Subjects w. groups	$pq(n - 1)$	$\sigma_\varepsilon^2 + rs\sigma_\pi^2$
Within subjects	$npq(rs - 1)$	
C	$r - 1$	$\sigma_\varepsilon^2 + s\sigma_{\gamma\pi}^2 + npqs\sigma_\gamma^2$
AC	$(p - 1)(r - 1)$	$\sigma_\varepsilon^2 + s\sigma_{\gamma\pi}^2 + nqs\sigma_{\alpha\gamma}^2$
BC	$(q - 1)(r - 1)$	$\sigma_\varepsilon^2 + s\sigma_{\gamma\pi}^2 + nps\sigma_{\beta\gamma}^2$
ABC	$(p - 1)(q - 1)(r - 1)$	$\sigma_\varepsilon^2 + s\sigma_{\gamma\pi}^2 + ns\sigma_{\alpha\beta\gamma}^2$
$C \times$ subj w. groups	$pq(n - 1)(r - 1)$	$\sigma_\varepsilon^2 + s\sigma_{\gamma\pi}^2$
D	$s - 1$	$\sigma_\varepsilon^2 + r\sigma_{\delta\pi}^2 + npqr\sigma_\delta^2$
AD	$(p - 1)(s - 1)$	$\sigma_\varepsilon^2 + r\sigma_{\delta\pi}^2 + nqr\sigma_{\alpha\delta}^2$
BD	$(q - 1)(s - 1)$	$\sigma_\varepsilon^2 + r\sigma_{\delta\pi}^2 + npr\sigma_{\beta\delta}^2$
ABD	$(p - 1)(q - 1)(s - 1)$	$\sigma_\varepsilon^2 + r\sigma_{\delta\pi}^2 + nr\sigma_{\alpha\beta\delta}^2$
$D \times$ subj w. groups	$pq(n - 1)(s - 1)$	$\sigma_\varepsilon^2 + r\sigma_{\delta\pi}^2$
CD	$(r - 1)(s - 1)$	$\sigma_\varepsilon^2 + \sigma_{\gamma\delta\pi}^2 + npq\sigma_{\gamma\delta}^2$
ACD	$(p - 1)(r - 1)(s - 1)$	$\sigma_\varepsilon^2 + \sigma_{\gamma\delta\pi}^2 + nq\sigma_{\alpha\gamma\delta}^2$
BCD	$(q - 1)(r - 1)(s - 1)$	$\sigma_\varepsilon^2 + \sigma_{\gamma\delta\pi}^2 + np\sigma_{\beta\gamma\delta}^2$
ABCD	$(p - 1)(q - 1)(r - 1)(s - 1)$	$\sigma_\varepsilon^2 + \sigma_{\gamma\delta\pi}^2 + n\sigma_{\alpha\beta\gamma\delta}^2$
$CD \times$ subj w. groups	$pq(n - 1)(r - 1)(s - 1)$	$\sigma_\varepsilon^2 + \sigma_{\gamma\delta\pi}^2$

Then each of the interactions with factor V may be subdivided. For example, the AV interaction may be subdivided into the following parts:

Source	df
AV	$(p - 1)(h - 1)$
AC	$(p - 1)(r - 1)$
AD	$(p - 1)(s - 1)$
ACD	$(p - 1)(r - 1)(s - 1)$

Analogous partitions may be made for the BV and ABV interactions.

Computational procedures for all treatment effects in the analysis summarized in Table 7.27 follow the usual procedures for a four-factor factorial experiment. Variation due to subjects within groups is part of the within-cell variation. The latter is given by

$$SS_{\text{w.cell}} = \sum X^2 - \frac{\sum (ABCD_{ijko})^2}{n}.$$

Variation due to main effects of subjects within groups is given by

$$SS_{\text{subj w. groups}} = \frac{\Sigma\, P_m^2}{rs} - \frac{\Sigma\, (AB_{ij})^2}{nrs}$$

The pooled interaction of treatment effects with subject effects is given by

$$SS_{\text{pooled int w. groups}} = SS_{\text{w. cell}} - SS_{\text{subj w. groups}}.$$

This pooled interaction corresponds to the $V \times$ subjects within groups interaction in the general form of this plan. The $C \times$ subjects within groups part of this pooled interaction is given by

$$SS_{C \times \text{subj w. groups}} = \frac{\Sigma\, (CP_{km})^2}{s} - \frac{\Sigma\, (ABC_{ijk})^2}{ns} - SS_{\text{subj w. groups}}.$$

Still another special case of the design given at the beginning of this section is one that may be sketched as follows:

$$u_1 \quad \frac{v_1 \quad v_2 \quad \cdots \quad v_h}{G_1 \quad G_1 \quad \cdots \quad G_1} \quad n \text{ subjects per group.}$$

One convenient analysis of variance for this design may be outlined as follows:

Source	df
Between subjects	$n - 1$
Subjects w. groups	$n - 1$
Within subjects	$n(h - 1)$
V	$h - 1$
$V \times$ subj w. groups	$(h - 1)(n - 1)$

If the levels of factor V define the $h = pq$ factorial combinations of factors A and B, the analysis of variance given above takes the following form:

Source			df	
Between subjects				$n - 1$
Subjects w. groups				$n - 1$
Within subjects				$n(h - 1)$
V	A	$h - 1$		$p - 1$
	B			$q - 1$
	AB			$(p - 1)(q - 1)$
$V \times$ subj w. groups	$A \times$ subj w. groups	$(h - 1)(n - 1)$		$(p - 1)(q - 1)$
	$B \times$ subj w. groups			$(q - 1)(n - 1)$
	$AB \times$ subj w. groups			$(p - 1)(q - 1)(n - 1)$

If both factors A and B are fixed, then the within-subject variation may be subdivided as follows:

Source	df
Within subjects	$n(h-1)$
A	$p-1$
Error $(a) = A \times$ subj w. groups	$(p-1)(n-1)$
B	$q-1$
Error $(b) = B \times$ subj w. groups	$(q-1)(n-1)$
AB	$(p-1)(q-1)$
Error $(ab) = AB \times$ subj w. groups	$(p-1)(q-1)(n-1)$

F ratios for this design have the form

$$F = \frac{MS_a}{MS_{\text{error }(a)}}, \qquad F = \frac{MS_b}{MS_{\text{error }(b)}}, \qquad F = \frac{MS_{ab}}{MS_{\text{error }(ab)}}.$$

The sampling distributions of these F ratios may be approximated by the appropriate F distribution provided the pattern assumptions on the relevant covariance matrices are met.

Controlling Sequence Effects

For the plans that have been discussed in this chapter, in cases where the sequence of administration of the treatments was not dictated by the nature of the experimental variables, it was suggested that order be randomized independently for each subject. A partial control of sequence effects is provided by the use of the Latin-square principle; this principle is discussed in Chapter 9. A variety of repeated-measure designs using this principle is also discussed in Chapter 9. A more complete control of sequence effects (but one which is more costly in terms of experimental effort) is available. This more complete control is achieved by building what may be called a sequence factor into the design.

Consider a $p \times r$ factorial experiment in which there are to be repeated measures on the factor having r levels. The number of different sequences or arrangements of r levels is $r! = r(r-1)(r-2)(r-3) \cdots (1)$. For example, if r is 3, the number of possible sequences is $3! = 3 \cdot 2 \cdot 1 = 6$; if r is 5, the number of possible sequences is $5! = 5 \cdot 4 \cdot 3 \cdot 2 \cdot 1 = 120$. Each of the possible sequences may define a level of factor B in which $q = r!$. Thus, instead of the original $p \times r$ factorial experiment one has a $p \times q \times r$ factorial experiment.

The analysis of the latter experiment would have the following form:

Source	df
Between subjects	$npq - 1$
A	$p - 1$
B (sequence of C)	$q - 1 = r! - 1$
AB	$(p - 1)(q - 1)$
Subjects within groups	$pq(n - 1)$
Within subjects	$npq(r - 1)$
C	$r - 1$
AC	$(p - 1)(r - 1)$
BC	$(q - 1)(r - 1)$
ABC	$(p - 1)(q - 1)(r - 1)$
$C \times$ subj w. groups	$pq(n - 1)(r - 1)$

This kind of sequence factor may be constructed in connection with any repeated-measure design in which the sequence can logically be varied. However, for designs in which the number of levels of the factor on which there are repeated measures is five or more the required number of levels of the sequence factor becomes prohibitively large.

One possible method of reducing this number is to select deliberately representative sequences from among the total possible sequences. A different approach might be to take a stratified random sample of all possible sequences, where the strata are constructed so as to assure a partial balance with respect to the order in which each of the levels appears within sequences which are used in the experiment. This kind of stratification may be achieved by using a Latin square.

7.6 TESTS ON TRENDS

Consider a $p \times q$ factorial experiment in which the levels of factor B define steps along an underlying continuum, i.e., intensity of light, dosage, blocks of trials in a learning experiment. The magnitude of the AB interaction in this kind of experiment may be regarded as a measure of global differences in the patterns or shapes of the profiles for the simple main effect of factor B. It is often of interest to study more specific aspects of such differences in patterns. Toward this end it is necessary to define dimensions in terms of which relatively irregular, experimentally determined profiles may be described. There are different methods whereby descriptive categories for this purpose may be established. In this section such categories will be defined in terms of polynomials of varying degree. Other functions, such as logarithmic or exponential, rather than polynomials, may be more appropriate for some profiles. The latter functional forms are not so readily handled as polynomials. However, polynomials may be used as first approximations to the latter forms.

Given the set of means $\overline{AB}_{i1}, \overline{AB}_{i2}, \ldots, \overline{AB}_{iq}$ in a $p \times q$ factorial experiment. The line joining these means (the profile of a simple main effect of factor B at level a_i) may have an irregular shape. As a first approximation to a quantitative description of the shape of a profile, one may obtain the best-fitting linear function (straight line). The slope of this best-fitting straight line defines the linear trend of the profile. As a second approximation to the pattern of the experimentally determined set of points, one may fit a second-degree (quadratic) function. The increase in goodness of fit over the linear fit defines what is known as the quadratic trend of the profile. As a third approximation to the pattern, one may obtain the best-fitting third-degree (cubic) function. The increase in goodness of fit of the latter function over both the linear and quadratic functions defines the cubic trend of the profile.

This process of fitting polynomial functions of increasingly higher degree can be continued up to a function of degree $q - 1$, where q is the number of points in the profile. A polynomial of degree $q - 1$ will always provide an exact fit to q points, since statistically there are only $q - 1$ degrees of freedom in this set of points. In most practical applications of the procedures to be described here, the degree of the polynomial is seldom carried beyond 3.

Global differences between shapes of profiles for simple main effects of factor B give rise to the AB interaction. Differences between the linear trends of such profiles define the part of the AB interaction which is called AB (linear). Thus the AB (linear) interaction represents a specific part of the overall AB interaction. Differences between quadratic trends in the profiles of the simple main effects define the AB (quadratic) variation. In general, the overall variation due to AB interaction may be divided into nonoverlapping, additive parts. These parts arise from specific kinds of differences in the shapes of profiles—differences in linear trends, differences in quadratic trends, etc. Symbolically, the AB interaction may be partitioned into the following parts:

Source of variation	df
AB	$(p-1)(q-1)$
AB (linear)	$p-1$
AB (quadratic)	$p-1$
$\cdots$	
AB (degree $q-1$)	$p-1$

These parts will sum to the overall AB variation.

The expected value of the mean square due to differences in linear trends has the following form:

$$\mathrm{E(MS}_{ab\,(\mathrm{lin})}) = \sigma_\varepsilon^2 + n\sigma_{\alpha\beta\,(\mathrm{lin})}^2.$$

A test on differences in linear trends involves the hypothesis that $\sigma_{\alpha\beta\,(\mathrm{lin})}^2 = 0$. This is equivalent to a test on the hypothesis that the profiles of the simple main effects have equal slopes, i.e., that the best-fitting linear functions are parallel.

The expected value of the mean square due to differences in quadratic trends has the following general form:

$$E(MS_{ab(\text{quad})}) = \sigma_\varepsilon^2 + n\sigma_{\alpha\beta(\text{quad})}^2.$$

A test on differences in these trends indicates whether or not the experimental data support the hypothesis that the profiles have equal quadratic trends.

Computational Procedures

Computational procedures will be described for the case of a $p \times q \times r$ factorial experiment in which there are repeated measures on factor C and n subjects in each group. This experimental plan has the form:

		c_1	c_2	$\cdots$	c_k	$\cdots$	c_r
a_1	b_1	G_{11}	G_{11}	$\cdots$	G_{11}	$\cdots$	G_{11}
	$\vdots$	$\vdots$	$\vdots$		$\vdots$		$\vdots$
	b_q	G_{1q}	G_{1q}	$\cdots$	G_{1q}	$\cdots$	G_{1q}
	$\vdots$	$\vdots$	$\vdots$		$\vdots$		$\vdots$
a_p	b_1	G_{p1}	G_{p1}	$\cdots$	G_{p1}	$\cdots$	G_{p1}
	$\vdots$	$\vdots$	$\vdots$		$\vdots$		$\vdots$
	b_q	G_{pq}	G_{pq}	$\cdots$	G_{pq}	$\cdots$	G_{pq}

Suppose that the levels of factor C represent equal steps along an underlying continuum. For example, suppose that the levels of factor C are r consecutive blocks of trials in a learning experiment. Under these conditions best-fitting linear, quadratic, cubic, etc., functions are most readily obtained by using the coefficients of orthogonal polynomials associated with r levels of an independent variable. Such coefficients are given in Table D.10.

The coefficients associated with the linear function will be designated

$$u_1, u_2, \ldots, u_k, \ldots, u_r.$$

For example, for the case in which $r = 4$, the respective coefficients are

$$-3, \quad -1, \quad 1, \quad 3.$$

The coefficients associated with the quadratic function having r experimentally determined points will be designated

$$v_1, v_2, \ldots, v_k, \ldots, v_r.$$

For the case $r = 4$, the respective coefficients are

$$1, \quad -1, \quad -1, \quad 1.$$

Note that the sum of the coefficients in each case is zero. Hence these coefficients define a comparison or contrast among the r points. The coefficients associated with the cubic function will be designated

$$w_1, w_2, \ldots, w_k, \ldots, w_r.$$

In an experiment of this kind there are three sets of interactions that may be divided into parts associated with differences between trends—the AC, the BC, and the ABC interactions. Procedures for obtaining the variation due to differences in linear trends within each of these interactions will be outlined. Higher-order trends will be found to follow the same general pattern. It will also be convenient to indicate procedures for obtaining the variation due to linear and higher-order trends for the main effect of factor C. The latter indicate the goodness of fit polynomials of varying degree to the profile corresponding to the main effect of factor C.

The notation to be used in obtaining the linear part of the variation in interactions with factor C as well as the variation in the linear part of the variation in the main effect of factor C is summarized in part i of Table 7.28. The symbol $X'_{m(ij)}$ is a weighted sum of the r observations on subject $m(ij)$, the weights being the respective linear coefficients of the appropriate polynomial. The analysis of linear trends for this case reduces to what is essentially an analysis of variance of a $p \times q$ factorial experiment with n observations per cell, an observation being an $X'_{m(ij)}$.

Other symbols defined in part i are also weighted sums. To illustrate, ABC'_{ij} is a weighted sum of terms appearing in a row of an ABC summary table. For example, the row which corresponds to level a_1 and level b_1 has the form

$$ABC_{111} \quad ABC_{112} \quad \cdots \quad ABC_{11k} \quad \cdots \quad ABC_{11r}.$$

Each of these totals is the sum of n observations. From these totals,

$$ABC'_{11} = u_1(ABC_{111}) + u_2(ABC_{112}) + \cdots + u_r(ABC_{11r}).$$

An equivalent expression for ABC'_{ij} is

$$ABC'_{ij} = X'_{1(ij)} + X'_{2(ij)} + \cdots + X'_{n(ij)} = \sum_m X'_{m(ij)}.$$

One expression serves as a computational check on the other.

Computational symbols convenient for use in the computation of the linear sources of variation are given in part ii. In the denominator of all symbols is the term $\sum u_k^2$. The other term in the denominators is the number of observations that go into an element which is weighted in the weighted sum. For example, there are n observations in ABC_{ijk}; there are nq observations in AC_{ik}; there are np observations in BC_{jk}. Actual computational formulas are

TABLE 7.28 **Notation for analysis of linear trend**

Coefficients for linear comparison:

$$u_1, u_2, \ldots, u_k, \ldots, u_r$$

(i)

$$X'_{m(ij)} = \sum_k u_k(X_{ijkm})$$

$$ABC'_{ij} = \sum_k u_k(ABC_{ijk}) \qquad = \sum_m X'_{m(ij)}$$

$$AC'_i = \sum_k u_k(AC_{ik}) \qquad = \sum_j ABC'_{ij}$$

$$BC'_j = \sum_k u_k(BC_{jk}) \qquad = \sum_i ABC'_{ij}$$

$$C' = \sum_k u_k C_k \qquad = \sum_i \sum_j ABC'_{ij} = \sum_i \sum_j \sum_m X'_{m(ij)}$$

(ii)

$$(1') = (C')^2/npq\left(\sum u_k^2\right) \qquad (3') = \sum (AC'_i)^2/nq\left(\sum u_k^2\right)$$

$$(2') = \sum (X'_{m(ij)})^2 / \left(\sum u_k^2\right) \qquad (4') = \sum (BC'_j)^2/np\left(\sum u_k^2\right)$$

$$(5') = \sum (ABC'_{ij})^2/n\left(\sum u_k^2\right)$$

(iii)

Source	Computational formula	df
Within subjects (linear)	(2')	npq
C(linear)	(1')	1
AC (linear)	(3') − (1')	$p-1$
BC (linear)	(4') − (1')	$q-1$
ABC (linear)	(5') − (3') − (4') + (1')	$(p-1)(q-1)$
$C \times$ subj w. groups (linear)	(2') − (5')	$pq(n-1)$

summarized in part iii. The mean square due to AC (linear) estimates an expression of the form

$$\sum_i (\beta_i - \beta)^2,$$

where the β_i's represent regression coefficients for linear profiles corresponding to simple main effects of factor C at each of the levels of factor A, and where β represents a pooled regression coefficient for all linear profiles in the set.

Computational procedures for the quadratic trend are summarized in Table 7.29. Each of the entries in this table has a corresponding entry in Table 7.28, with v_k replacing corresponding u_k throughout. The symbol $X''_{m(ij)}$ is used to distinguish a weighted sum in terms of quadratic weights from the corresponding sum in terms of linear weights, designated by the symbol $X'_{m(ij)}$. Higher-order trends follow the same pattern, with the appropriate coefficients

TABLE 7.29 **Notation for analysis of quadratic trend**

Coefficients for quadratic comparison:

$$v_1, v_2, \ldots, v_k, \ldots, v_r$$

(i)

$$X''_{m(ij)} = \sum_k v_k(X_{ijkm})$$

$$ABC''_{ij} = \sum_k v_k(ABC_{ijk}) \qquad = \sum_m X''_{m(ij)}$$

$$AC''_i = \sum_k v_k(AC_{ik}) \qquad = \sum_j ABC''_{ij}$$

$$BC''_j = \sum_k v_k(BC_{jk}) \qquad = \sum_i ABC''_{ij}$$

$$C'' = \sum_k v_k C_k \qquad = \sum_i \sum_j ABC''_{ij} = \sum_i \sum_j \sum_m X''_{m(ij)}$$

(ii)

$$(1'') = (C'')^2/npq\left(\sum v_k^2\right) \qquad (3'') = \sum (AC''_i)^2/nq\left(\sum v_k^2\right)$$

$$(2'') = \sum (X''_{m(ij)})^2 \Big/ \left(\sum v_k^2\right) \qquad (4'') = \sum (BC''_j)^2/np\left(\sum v_k^2\right)$$

$$(5'') = \sum (ABC''_{ij})^2/n\left(\sum v_k^2\right)$$

Source	Computational formula
Within subjects (quadratic)	$(2'')$
C (quadratic)	$(1'')$
AC (quadratic)	$(3'') - (1'')$
(iii) BC (quadratic)	$(4'') - (1'')$
ABC (quadratic)	$(5'') - (3'') - (4'') + (1'')$
$C \times$ subj w. groups (quadratic)	$(2'') - (5'')$

serving as the weights. If, for example, $r = 4$, it will be found that

$$SS_c = SS_{c(\text{lin})} + SS_{c(\text{quad})} + SS_{c(\text{cubic})}.$$

Similarly,
$$SS_{ac} = SS_{ac(\text{lin})} + SS_{ac(\text{quad})} + SS_{ac(\text{cubic})}.$$

Numerical Example

The numerical data in part i of Table 7.30 will be used to illustrate the computational procedures. These data represent a $2 \times 2 \times 4$ factorial experiment with repeated measures on factor C, three observations in each group. Suppose that factor C represents equally spaced blocks of trials in a learning experiment. For example, subject 1 is assigned to treatment combination ab_{11} and has scores of 1, 6, 5, and 7, respectively, on a series of four blocks of trials.

Since factor C has four levels, coefficients for the case in which there are

TABLE 7.30 **Analysis of linear trend—numerical example**

Linear coefficients: $\quad -3 \quad -1 \quad 1 \quad 3 \quad \sum u_k^2 = 20$

<table>
<tr><th></th><th></th><th>Subject</th><th>c_1</th><th>c_2</th><th>c_3</th><th>c_4</th><th>$X'_{m(ij)}$</th><th>ABC'_{ij}</th></tr>
<tr><td rowspan="6">a_1</td><td rowspan="3">b_1</td><td>1</td><td>1</td><td>6</td><td>5</td><td>7</td><td>17</td><td></td></tr>
<tr><td>2</td><td>0</td><td>6</td><td>7</td><td>9</td><td>28</td><td></td></tr>
<tr><td>3</td><td>3</td><td>8</td><td>8</td><td>9</td><td>18</td><td>63</td></tr>
<tr><td rowspan="3">b_2</td><td>4</td><td>2</td><td>7</td><td>12</td><td>15</td><td>44</td><td></td></tr>
<tr><td>5</td><td>1</td><td>6</td><td>8</td><td>9</td><td>26</td><td></td></tr>
<tr><td>6</td><td>3</td><td>7</td><td>10</td><td>11</td><td>27</td><td>97</td></tr>
<tr><td rowspan="6">a_2</td><td rowspan="3">b_1</td><td>7</td><td>1</td><td>2</td><td>7</td><td>12</td><td>38</td><td></td></tr>
<tr><td>8</td><td>1</td><td>1</td><td>4</td><td>10</td><td>30</td><td></td></tr>
<tr><td>9</td><td>1</td><td>1</td><td>4</td><td>8</td><td>24</td><td>92</td></tr>
<tr><td rowspan="3">b_2</td><td>10</td><td>2</td><td>2</td><td>8</td><td>12</td><td>36</td><td></td></tr>
<tr><td>11</td><td>3</td><td>2</td><td>10</td><td>15</td><td>44</td><td></td></tr>
<tr><td>12</td><td>2</td><td>2</td><td>7</td><td>13</td><td>38</td><td>118</td></tr>
<tr><td></td><td></td><td></td><td>20</td><td>50</td><td>90</td><td>130</td><td>370</td><td>370</td></tr>
</table>

(i)

<table>
<tr><th></th><th></th><th>c_1</th><th>c_2</th><th>c_3</th><th>c_4</th><th>ABC'_{ij}</th><th>AC'_i</th></tr>
<tr><td rowspan="2">a_1</td><td>b_1</td><td>4</td><td>20</td><td>20</td><td>25</td><td>63</td><td></td></tr>
<tr><td>b_2</td><td>6</td><td>20</td><td>30</td><td>35</td><td>97</td><td>160</td></tr>
<tr><td rowspan="2">a_2</td><td>b_1</td><td>3</td><td>4</td><td>15</td><td>30</td><td>92</td><td></td></tr>
<tr><td>b_2</td><td>7</td><td>6</td><td>25</td><td>40</td><td>· 118</td><td>210</td></tr>
<tr><td></td><td></td><td>20</td><td>50</td><td>90</td><td>130</td><td>370</td><td>370</td></tr>
</table>

(ii)

<table>
<tr><th></th><th>c_1</th><th>c_2</th><th>c_3</th><th>c_4</th><th>AC'_i</th><th>C'</th></tr>
<tr><td>a_1</td><td>10</td><td>40</td><td>50</td><td>60</td><td>160</td><td></td></tr>
<tr><td>a_2</td><td>10</td><td>10</td><td>40</td><td>70</td><td>210</td><td>370</td></tr>
<tr><td></td><td>20</td><td>50</td><td>90</td><td>130</td><td>370</td><td></td></tr>
</table>

(iii)

<table>
<tr><th></th><th>c_1</th><th>c_2</th><th>c_3</th><th>c_4</th><th>BC'_j</th><th>C'</th></tr>
<tr><td>b_1</td><td>7</td><td>24</td><td>35</td><td>55</td><td>155</td><td></td></tr>
<tr><td>b_2</td><td>13</td><td>26</td><td>55</td><td>75</td><td>215</td><td>370</td></tr>
<tr><td></td><td>20</td><td>50</td><td>90</td><td>130</td><td>370</td><td></td></tr>
</table>

(iv)

four points to be fitted are appropriate. From Table D.10 the linear coefficients are

$$-3, \quad -1, \quad 1, \quad 3.$$

These coefficients appear at the top of part i. From the data on subject 1 one obtains

$$X'_{1(11)} = (-3)(1) + (-1)(6) + (1)(5) + (3)(7) = 17,$$

the weighted sum of the observations on subject 1, the weights being the linear coefficients. Other entries in the column headed $X'_{m(ij)}$ are obtained in an analogous manner. For example,

$$X'_{4(12)} = (-3)(2) + (-1)(7) + (1)(12) + (3)(15) = 44.$$

The entries in the column headed ABC'_{ij} are obtained as follows:

$$ABC'_{11} = X'_{1(11)} + X'_{2(11)} + X'_{3(11)} = 17 + 28 + 18 = 63.$$
$$ABC'_{12} = X'_{4(12)} + X'_{5(12)} + X'_{6(12)} = 44 + 26 + 27 = 97.$$

The left-hand side of part ii represents an ABC summary table obtained in the usual manner from data on the left-hand side of part i. From the first row of the ABC summary table one obtains

$$ABC'_{11} = (-3)(4) + (-1)(20) + (1)(20) + (3)(25) = 63.$$

This entry provides a check on the entry ABC'_{11} computed in part i. The second row of the ABC summary table is used to obtain ABC'_{12}. A corresponding entry is available from part i.

The left-hand side of part iii represents an AC summary table. The entries in the column headed AC'_i are weighted sums of the entries in the corresponding rows. Checks on these entries may be obtained from part ii. Checks on entries in part iv may also be obtained from the ABC'_{ij} column of part ii. For example,

$$BC'_1 = ABC'_{11} + ABC'_{21} = 63 + 92 = 155;$$
$$BC'_2 = ABC'_{12} + ABC'_{22} = 97 + 118 = 215.$$

All the totals required in the analysis of linear trend may be obtained from the $X'_{m(ij)}$ column of part i of Table 7.30. Hence parts ii to iv are not actually required. In practice, however, part ii should be computed to serve as a check on the $X'_{m(ij)}$ column. Additional checks are provided by parts iii and iv.

Computational symbols defined in part ii of Table 7.28 are obtained in part i of Table 7.31. For the case in which there are four points in each profile, $\sum u_k^2 = 20$. Each total C_k is the sum of $npq = 12$ observations. Hence the denominator for symbol $(1')$ is $12(20)$. Since each total AC_{ik} is the sum of $nq = 6$ observations, the denominator for the symbol $(3')$ is $6(20)$.

The analysis of variance for the linear trend of the within-subject effects is summarized in part ii of Table 7.31. For the basic data in part i of Table 7.30, there are $npq = 12$ subjects and $r = 4$ observations on each subject.

TABLE 7.31 **Analysis of linear trend—numerical example**

$$(1') = (370)^2/12(20) = 570.42$$
$$(2') = (17^2 + 28^2 + \cdots + 44^2 + 38^2)/20 = 616.70$$
$$(3') = (160^2 + 210^2)/6(20) = 580.83$$
$$(4') = (155^2 + 215^2)/6(20) = 585.42$$
$$(5') = (63^2 + 97^2 + 92^2 + 118^2)/3(20) = 596.10$$

Source of variation	SS	df	MS	F
Within subjects (linear)	$(2') = 616.70$	12		
C (linear)	$(1') = 570.42$	1	570.42	221.09*
AC linear)	$(3') - (1') = 10.41$	1	10.41	4.03
BC (linear)	$(4') - (1') = 15.00$	1	15.00	5.81*
ABC (linear)	$(5') - (3') - (4') + (1') = 0.27$	1	0.27	
$C \times$ subj w. groups (linear)	$(2') - (5') = 20.60$	8	2.58	

Hence the total degrees of freedom for within-subject effects are $npq(r - 1) = 36$. In the analysis of variance of trend, these 36 degrees of freedom are partitioned as follows:

Within subjects	36	$npq(r - 1)$
Within subjects (linear)	12	npq
Within subjects (quadratic)	12	npq
Within subjects (cubic)	12	npq

The 12 degrees of freedom for the linear trend of the within-subject effects are analyzed in part ii of Table 7.31.

A test on linear trend in the main effect of factor C has the form

$$F = \frac{\text{MS}_{c(\text{lin})}}{\text{MS}_{C \times \text{subj w. groups(lin)}}} = 221.09.$$

At the 0.05 level of significance, this test indicates that the best-fitting straight line to the profile of the C main effects has a slope which is significantly different from zero. In terms of the expected values of the mean squares, this F ratio has the structure

$$\frac{\text{E(numerator)}}{\text{E(denominator)}} = \frac{\sigma_\varepsilon^2 + \sigma_{\pi\gamma(\text{lin})}^2 + npq\sigma_{\gamma(\text{lin})}^2}{\sigma_\varepsilon^2 + \sigma_{\pi\gamma(\text{lin})}^2}.$$

The profile corresponding to the C main effects (in terms of treatment means) is shown in Fig. 7-3.

The profiles corresponding to the simple effects of factor C at levels b_1 and b_2 are also shown in this figure. Inspection of these profiles suggests that

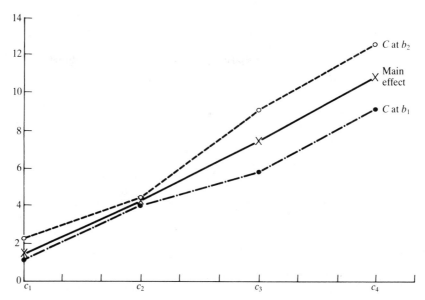

FIGURE 7-3   Profiles of BC interaction and C main effect.

the best-fitting line to the profile for b_2 would have a different slope from the best-fitting line to the profile for b_1, that is, that these lines would not be parallel. A test of the hypothesis that there is no difference in these slopes (no difference in linear trend) has the form

$$F = \frac{MS_{bc\text{(lin)}}}{MS_{C \times \text{subj w. groups(lin)}}} = 5.81.$$

At the 0.05 level of significance, this test indicates that the linear trends of the BC profiles cannot be considered to be equal.

Profiles corresponding to the AC interaction are shown in Fig. 7-4. Inspection indicates that these profiles differ in shape but that the best-fitting straight lines might be parallel. The test of the latter hypothesis is given by

$$F = \frac{MS_{ac\text{(lin)}}}{MS_{C \times \text{subj w. groups(lin)}}} = 4.03.$$

The value does not exceed the critical value for a 0.05-level test. Hence the experimental evidence does not reject the hypothesis that the linear trends are equal. Thus differences in shapes of these profiles, if there are statistically significant differences, must be due to quadratic or high-order trends.

A summary of the analysis of variance for the quadratic trend is given in Tables 7.32 and 7.33. This analysis follows the same general procedures as those used in the analysis of the linear trend; in this case the quadratic

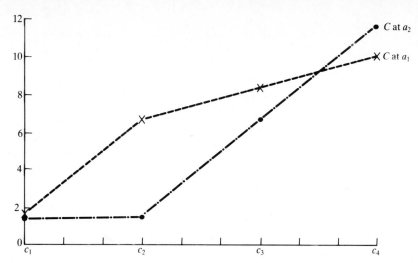

FIGURE 7-4   Profiles of *AC* interaction.

TABLE 7.32   Analysis of quadratic trend—numerical example

Quadratic coefficients   1   −1   −1   1 $\sum v_k^2 = 4$

		Subject	c_1	c_2	c_3	c_4	$X''_{m(ij)}$	ABC''_{ij}
a_1	b_1	1	1	6	5	7	−3	
		2	0	6	7	9	−4	
		3	3	8	8	9	−4	−11
	b_2	4	2	7	12	15	−2	
		5	1	6	8	9	−4	
		6	3	7	10	11	−3	−9
a_2	b_1	7	1	2	7	12	4	
		8	1	1	4	10	6	
		9	1	1	4	8	4	14
	b_2	10	2	2	8	12	4	
		11	3	2	10	15	6	
		12	2	2	7	13	6	16
			20	50	90	130	10	10

(i)

		c_1	c_2	c_3	c_4	ABC''_{ij}	AC'_i
a_1	b_1	4	20	20	25	−11	
	b_2	6	20	30	35	−9	−20
a_2	b_1	3	4	15	30	14	
	b_2	7	6	25	40	16	30
		20	50	90	130	10	10

(ii)

572

TABLE 7.33   **Analysis of quadratic trend—numerical example**

(i)

$$(1'') = (10)^2/12(4) = 2.08$$
$$(2'') = (-3)^2 + (-4)^2 + \cdots + 6^2 + 6^2 = 56.50$$
$$(3'') = [(-20)^2 + 30^2]/6(4) = 54.17$$
$$(4'') = [3^2 + 7^2]/6(4) = 2.42$$
$$(5'') = [(-11)^2 + (-9)^2 + 14^2 + 16^2]/3(4) = 54.50$$

(ii)

Source of variation	SS	df	MS	F
Within subjects (quadratic)	$(2') = 56.51$	12		
C (quadratic)	$(1'') = 2.08$	1	2.08	8.32*
AC (quadratic)	$(3'') - (1'') = 52.09$	1	52.09	208.36*
BC (quadratic)	$(4'') - (1'') = 0.34$	1	0.34	
ABC (quadratic)	$(5'') - (3'') - (4'') + (1'') = 0.00$	1	0.00	
$C \times$ subj w. groups (quadratic)	$(2'') - (5'') = 2.00$	8	0.25	

coefficients replace the linear coefficients as weights. The test of differences in the quadratic trends of the AC profiles is given by

$$F = \frac{MS_{ac(\text{quad})}}{MS_{C \times \text{subj w. groups(quad)}}} = 208.36.$$

Hence the data tend to reject the hypothesis that there is no difference in the quadratic trends of the AC profiles. Inspection of Fig. 7-4 indicates that the profile at a_1 clearly has a different curvature from the profile at a_2. The significant F ratio for the main effect in Table 7.33 indicates that the quadratic trend in the profile of the C main effect is different from zero. The analysis of variance for the cubic trend is summarized in Table 7.34.

In general, the analysis of differences in trends for interaction terms is not made unless there is evidence to show that some difference in shapes exists. This evidence is provided by the usual overall tests on interactions, which indicate the presence or absence of global differences in the shapes of profiles. The overall analysis of variance for the within-subject effects is summarized in Table 7.35. This analysis is made by means of the usual

TABLE 7.34   **Analysis of cubic trend—numerical example**

Source of variation	SS	df	MS	F
Within subject (cubic)	20.30	12		
C (cubic)	0.42	1	0.42	
AC (cubic)	10.42	1	10.42	30.64*
BC (cubic)	6.66	1	6.66	19.59*
ABC cubic)	0.07	1	0.07	
$C \times$ subj w. groups (cubic)	2.73	8	0.34	

TABLE 7.35 **Overall analysis of variance for within subjects effects—numerical example**

Source of variation	SS	df	MS	F
Within subjects	693.50	36		
C	572.92	3	190.97	180.16*
AC	72.92	3	24.30	22.92*
BC	22.00	3	7.33	6.92*
ABC	0.33	3	0.11	
C × subj w. groups	25.34	24	1.06	

computational procedures for a $p \times q \times r$ factorial experiment having repeated measures on factor C. The basic observational data in part i of Table 7.30 and the summary tables at the left of parts ii to iv are used in the overall analysis of variance. The significant AC and BC interactions indicate that there are global differences in the trends of the corresponding profiles. The nature of such differences is explored in the analysis of the linear, quadratic, and cubic trends.

It is of interest to compare the overall analysis with the analysis of the individual trends. It will be noted that:

	SS	df
Within subjects (overall)	693.50	36
Within subjects (linear)	616.70	12
Within subjects (quadratic)	56.51	12
Within subjects (cubic)	20.30	12

It will also be noted that:

	SS
AC (overall)	72.92
AC (linear)	10.41
AC (quadratic)	52.09
AC (cubic)	10.42

In each case the sum of the parts will be numerically equal to the corresponding overall variation.

It is of particular interest to look at the parts of terms that go into the denominator of the F ratios. In this case:

	SS	MS
$C \times$ subj w. groups (overall)	25.34	1.06
$C \times$ subj w. groups (linear)	20.60	2.58
$C \times$ subj w. groups (quadratic)	2.00	0.25
$C \times$ subj w. groups (cubic)	2.73	0.34

The parts of the overall variation of this interaction need not be homogeneous; each of these parts does not estimate the same source of variation. The parts measure the deviation of a weighted sum about the mean of the weighted sums; the weights are different for each of the parts. The expected values of the mean squares of the parts are to a degree dependent upon the weights; the latter in turn determine the shape of the curve that is being fitted to the experimental data. Different structural models underlie the analysis of variance for linear, quadratic, and cubic trends.

7.7 UNEQUAL GROUP SIZE

Consider the following design:

	b_1	$\cdots$	b_1	Group size
a_1	G_1	$\cdots$	G_1	n_1
a_2	G_2	$\cdots$	G_2	n_2
$\vdots$	$\vdots$		$\vdots$	$\vdots$
a_p	G_p	$\cdots$	G_p	n_p

Total number of subjects $= N$

If the levels of factor A represent different strata within a specified population, then the n_i may be proportional to the number of individuals actually in each of these strata in the population. In this case, a least-squares solution for the effects and the sums of squares is appropriate. However, if the original plan for an experiment calls for equal group size, but the completed experiment does not have equal group size because of conditions unrelated to the treatments per se, then an unweighted-means solution is the more appropriate. Both types of solution are considered in this section.

Because the cell frequencies will be proportional by columns, the least-squares solution can be obtained quite simply. The case of proportional cell frequencies is discussed in Sec. 5.20. What simplifies the computational procedures is the orthogonality of SS_a and SS_b. If one defines

$$SS_{ab} = SS_{b.\ cell} - SS_a - SS_b,$$

one will have the following additivity:

$$SS_{b.\ cell} = SS_a + SS_b + SS_{ab}.$$

This type of additivity holds for equal cell frequencies as well as proportional cell frequencies. In general, for unequal cell frequencies

$$SS_{a+b} \neq SS_a + SS_b;$$

however, for proportional cell frequencies

$$SS_{a+b} = SS_a + SS_b.$$

Computational symbols for this case are defined in Table 7.36. The sums of squares are obtained by the relations given in Table 7.16, using the symbols as defined in Table 7.36. The degrees of freedom for the sums of squares are obtained from those given in Table 7.11 by replacing np with N throughout, where $N = \Sigma n_i$. For example,

$$p(n-1) \qquad \text{becomes} \qquad N-p,$$
$$p(n-1)(q-1) \qquad \text{becomes} \qquad (N-p)(q-1).$$

The starting point for an unweighted-means solution is an ABC' summary table in which a cell entry is a mean; that is,

$$ABC'_{ijk} = \frac{ABC_{ijk}}{n_i}.$$

From this summary table, AB' and AC' summaries are computed in the usual

TABLE 7.36   **Unequal group size—least-squares solution**

$(1) = \dfrac{G^2}{Nqr}$	$(6) = \dfrac{\Sigma\,[(AB_{ij})^2/n_i]}{r}$
$(2) = \Sigma\,X^2$	$(7) = \dfrac{\Sigma\,[(AC_{ik})^2/n_i]}{q}$
$(3) = \dfrac{\Sigma\,(A_i^2/n_i)}{qr}$	$(8) = \dfrac{\Sigma\,(BC_{jk})^2}{N}$
$(4) = \dfrac{\Sigma\,B_j^2}{NR}$	$(9) = \Sigma\left[\dfrac{(ABC_{ijk})^2}{n_i}\right]$
$(5) = \dfrac{\Sigma\,C_k^2}{NQ}$	$(10) = \dfrac{\Sigma\,P_m^2}{qr}$

TABLE 7.37 **Unequal group size—unweighted means solution**

$$(1') = G'^2/pqr \qquad\qquad (6') = \left[\sum (AB'_{ij})^2\right]\Big/r$$

$$(3') = \left(\sum A_i'^2\right)\Big/qr \qquad (7') = \left[\sum (AC'_{ik})^2\right]\Big/q$$

$$(4') = \left(\sum B_j'^2\right)\Big/pr \qquad (8') = \left[\sum (BC'_{jk})^2\right]\Big/p$$

$$(5') = \left(\sum C_k'^2\right)\Big/pq \qquad (9') = \sum (ABC'_{ijk})^2$$

$$SS_a = \bar{n}[(3') - (1')] \qquad SS_{ab} = \bar{n}[(6') - (3') - (4') + (1')]$$
$$SS_b = \bar{n}[(4') - (1')] \qquad SS_{ac} = \bar{n}[(7') - (3') - (5') + (1')]$$
$$SS_c = \bar{n}[(5') - (1')] \qquad SS_{bc} = \bar{n}[(8') - (4') - (5') + (1')]$$
$$SS_{abc} = \bar{n}[(9') - (6') - (7') - (8') + (3') + (4') + (5') - (1')]$$

manner; that is,

$$AB'_{ij} = \sum_k ABC'_{ijk},$$

$$A'_1 = \sum_j AB'_{ij}.$$

Computational symbols appropriate for this case are given in Table 7.37. Only those sums of squares which do not involve the subject factor are given here. Sums of squares which do involve the subject factor are identical with those in a least-squares analysis.

In a least-squares solution,

$$SS_{total} = SS_{b.\ cell} + SS_{w.\ cell}.$$

This relationship, however, does not hold for an unweighted-means solution. If the n_i do not differ markedly, both types of solution lead to numerically similar final products.

The computational procedures that have been discussed above can be specialized to the case of a $p \times q$ factorial experiment with repeated measures on factor B. This is done by setting $r = 1$ and dropping all terms involving factor C. The starting point for an unweighted-means analysis in this case is a summary table in which

$$AB'_{ij} = \frac{AB_{ij}}{n_i}.$$

A numerical example of this case is given in Table 7.38.

A summary of the computational steps in obtaining both the least-squares and the unweighted-means solutions appears in Table 7.39. Symbols associated with the least-squares solution appear at the left. The unweighted-means

TABLE 7.38 **Numerical example**

	Subject	b_1	b_2	b_3	Total	
a_1	1	3	6	9	18	
	2	6	10	14	30	$n_1 = 3$
	3	10	15	18	43	
a_2	4	8	12	16	36	
	5	3	5	8	16	
	6	1	3	8	12	$n_2 = 5$
	7	12	18	26	56	
	8	9	10	18	37	
a_3	9	10	22	16	48	
	10	3	15	8	26	
	11	7	16	10	33	$n_3 = 4$
	12	5	20	12	37	
	Total	77	152	163	392	$N = 12$

TABLE 7.39 **Computational procedures**

	AB summary table					AB' summary table			
		b_1	b_2	b_3	Total		b_1	b_2	b_3	Total
(i)	a_1	19	31	41	91	a_1	6.33	10.33	13.67	30.33
	a_2	33	48	76	157	a_2	6.60	9.60	15.20	31.40
	a_3	25	73	46	144	a_2	6.25	18.25	11.50	36.00
	Total	77	152	163	392	Total	19.18	38.18	40.37	97.73

(ii)

$(1) = G^2/Nq \qquad = 4268.44$

$(2) = \sum X^2 \qquad = 5504.00$

$(3) = \sum (A_i^2/n_i q) \qquad = 4291.38$

$(4) = \left(\sum B_j^2\right)\big/N \qquad = 4633.50$

$(5) = \sum [(AB_{ij})^2/n_i] = 4852.30$

$(6) = \left(\sum P_m^2\right)\big/q \qquad = 4904.00$

$(1') = G'^2/pq \qquad = 1061.24$

$(3') = \left(\sum A_i'^2\right)\big/q \; = 1067.29$

$(4') = \left(\sum B_j'^2\right)\big/p \; = 1151.77$

$(5') = \sum (AB_{ij}')^2 \qquad = 1204.78$

(iii)

$$\bar{n} = \frac{p}{\sum (1/n_i)} = \frac{3}{(1/3) + (1/5) + (1/4)} = 3.830$$

TABLE 7.40   **Analysis of variance for numerical example—unweighted-means solution**

Source of variation	Computational formula	SS	df	MS	F
Between subjects			11		
A	$\bar{n}[(3') - (1')]$	23.17	2	11.29	
Subjects w. groups	$(6) - (3)$	612.62	9	68.06	
Within subjects			24		
B	$\bar{n}[(4') - (1')]$	346.73	2	173.36	79.89
AB	$\bar{n}[(5') - (3') - (4') + (1')]$	179.86	4	44.97	20.72
B × subjects w. groups.	$(2) - (5) - (6) + (3)$	39.08	18	2.17	

analysis is summarized in Table 7.40. The two solutions are compared in Table 7.41.

Individual comparisons for the case of a $p \times q$ factorial experiment having repeated measures on factor B will be outlined in what follows. For the case of the least-squares solution,

$$\bar{A}_i = \frac{A_i}{n_i q} \quad \text{and} \quad \bar{B}_j = \frac{B_j}{N}.$$

F ratios in tests on individual comparisons take the form

$$F = \frac{(\bar{A}_i - \bar{A}_{i'})^2}{\text{MS}_{\text{subj w. groups}}[(1/n_i q) + (1/n_{i'} q)]},$$

$$F = \frac{(\bar{B}_j - \bar{B}_{j'})^2}{\text{MS}_{B \times \text{subj w. groups}}(2/N)}.$$

For the case of the unweighted-means solution,

$$\bar{A}_i = \frac{A_i'}{q} \quad \text{and} \quad \bar{B}_j = \frac{B_j'}{p}.$$

F ratios in tests on individual comparisons take the form

$$F = \frac{(\bar{A}_i - \bar{A}_{i'})^2}{\text{MS}_{\text{subj w. groups}}[(1/n_i q) + (1/n_{i'} q)]},$$

$$F = \frac{(\bar{B}_j - \bar{B}_{j'})^2}{\text{MS}_{B \times \text{subj w. groups}}(2/\bar{n} p)}.$$

TABLE 7.41   **Comparison of solutions**

Source	Unweighted means	Least squares
A	23.17	22.94
B	346.73	365.06
AB	179.86	195.86

7.8 MEASURES OF ASSOCIATION AND STATISTICAL POWER

Earlier in this chapter it was emphasized that there are numerous ways to design a factorial experiment with repeated measures on one or more of the factors. In the instance of a three-factor design, for example, there are seven possibilities. When considering variance components or treatment effect magnitudes for purposes of estimating statistical power or measures of strength of association, the number of alternatives is increased because one must take into account whether each factor (other than subjects) is fixed or random. With a three-factor design, this creates seven combinations. Hence, there are 49 possible design-model combinations! Finally, one may assume either an additive or nonadditive structural model for *each* interaction involving subjects. Clearly, this increases the possibilities enormously. For these and other reasons, one rarely encounters a detailed discussion of the topic of statistical power for multifactor designs involving repeated measures.

Given the large number of possibilities, there is little point to beginning to list their properties. Vaughan and Corballis (1969) list some of the general properties of estimates of variance components and Dodd and Schultz (1975) provide computational formulas for measures of association for selected repeated-measures designs with fixed and random factors. The interested reader is encouraged to study their presentations.

7.9 EXERCISES

1. How many subjects would be needed for each of the following designs (the factors with repeated measures are denoted with a bar. For example, $p \times q \times \bar{r}$ is a three-factor factorial design with repeated measures on factor C) if there are to be 10 subjects per nested group?
   (a) $p \times \bar{q} = 2 \times \bar{3}$.
   (b) $p \times \bar{q} \times r = 2 \times \bar{4} \times 3$.
   (c) $\bar{p} \times \bar{q} \times \bar{r} = \bar{3} \times \bar{2} \times \bar{2}$,
   (d) $p \times \bar{q} \times \bar{r} = 4 \times \bar{2} \times \bar{2}$,

2. What are the expected values of the mean squares for each of the following designs? Random factors are denoted with a small letter, fixed factors are denoted with capital letters, and repeated measures are denoted with a bar. For example, $Ab\bar{C}$ denotes factors A and C are fixed, factor b is random and there are repeated measures on factor C.
   (a) $A\bar{B}$
   (b) $a\bar{b}$
   (c) $A\bar{B}\bar{C}$
   (d) $A\bar{b}c$
   (e) $\bar{a}\bar{b}\bar{c}$.

3. The following data are from an experiment wherein two groups of subjects were formed ($a_1 = $ Low, $a_2 = $ High) based upon their measured anxiety scores. Subjects were observed under three stress conditions with the order of presentation

independently randomized for each subject. The dependent variable was a measure of eye-hand coordination. The following data were obtained.

	Subject	b_1	b_2	b_3
	1	6	9	4
	2	5	7	3
	3	9	11	8
a_1	4	8	8	4
	5	7	7	3
	6	7	7	4
	7	8	9	5
	8	10	4	7
	9	6	3	3
	10	8	5	6
a_2	11	11	7	4
	12	9	3	3
	13	8	5	6
	14	11	7	5

(a) Assuming factors A and B are both fixed, what are the expected values of the mean squares?

(b) Plot the $\overline{AB}_{ij}$ values. What appears to be the outcome of the study? Does increasing stress have the same effect upon low-anxiety as upon high-anxiety subjects in this task?

(c) Complete an analysis of variance and test

$$H_0: \mu_{1.} = \mu_{2.}, \qquad H_0: \mu_{.1} = \mu_{.2} = \mu_{.3}, \qquad H_0: \sigma^2_{\alpha\beta} = 0$$

(use $\alpha = 0.05$ for all tests).

(d) Carry out appropriate analyses of simple main effects for each group of subjects and for each stress condition ($\alpha = 0.05$).

(e) Assume that the stress conditions were developed to represent equally-spaced conditions. Complete a trend analysis for the total stress condition means ($\bar{B}_j$) and for each group separately ($\overline{AB}_{1j}$ and $\overline{AB}_{2j}$ for a_1 and a_2, respectively).

(f) Compute S_1, S_2, S_{pooled}, and S_0.

(1) Using the χ^2 statistic (7.4), evaluate the hypothesis that S_1 and S_2 both estimate a common population matrix Σ ($\alpha = 0.05$).

(2) Compute $\hat{\varepsilon}$ from S_{pooled}. What does the numerical value of $\hat{\varepsilon}$ tell you about the degree of departure of S_{pooled} from circularity?

(3) Use the χ^2 statistic of (7.8) to test the hypothesis $H_0: M_B^{*'}\Sigma M_B^* = \lambda I$ ($\alpha = 0.05$).

(4) Show numerically that

$$MS_{b \times \text{sub}} = \overline{\text{Var}} - \overline{\text{Cov}} \text{ from } S_0$$

$$MS_{b \times \text{sub w } a_1} = \overline{\text{Var}} - \overline{\text{Cov}} \text{ from } S_1$$

$$MS_{b \times \text{sub w } a_2} = \overline{\text{Var}} - \overline{\text{Cov}} \text{ from } S_2.$$

4. The following data are from a three-factor experiment wherein factors A and B are fixed and factor C is random.

	Subjects	b_1			b_2			b_3		
		c_1	c_2	c_3	c_1	c_2	c_3	c_1	c_2	c_3
a_1	1	25	43	50	30	42	47	18	27	36
	2	15	31	40	20	27	37	15	22	31
	3	50	55	65	48	44	60	30	37	40
a_2	4	40	38	51	15	24	41	16	13	25
	5	32	35	45	20	27	33	12	17	27
	6	46	50	67	30	29	47	21	19	36

(a) What are the expected values of the mean squares?

(b) Carry out an appropriate analysis of variance and test all effects ($\alpha = 0.05$).

(c) Plot the $\overline{ABC}_{ijk}$'s separately for each level of factor C. Did factor C influence the outcome with regard to the effects of A and B?

(d) Complete an appropriate analysis of simple main effects for comparing A for each level of factor B and comparing B for each level of factor C ($\alpha = 0.05$).

(e) Test the following set of *a priori* hypotheses ($\alpha = 0.05$) using F statistics with appropriate $MS_{denominator}$

$$H_0: \mu_{..1} = \mu_{..2}$$

$$H_0: \frac{\mu_{..1} + \mu_{..2}}{2} = \mu_{..3}$$

$$H_0: \mu_{11.} = \mu_{21.}$$

(f) Use the Newman–Keuls procedure to compare all B means ($\alpha = 0.05$).

(g) Compute the variance–covariance matrices associated with the B × subjects within group effects (B_{a_1}, B_{a_2}, B_{pooled}). Are B_{a_1} and B_{a_2} homogeneous? Is B_{pooled} circular?

CHAPTER 8

FACTORIAL EXPERIMENTS IN WHICH SOME OF THE INTERACTIONS ARE CONFOUNDED

8.1 GENERAL PURPOSE

At this point, it is well to briefly reconsider the treatment of factorial designs with repeated measures on subjects with a new emphasis, the emphasis being upon controlling block sizes and the cost of that control in confounding of effects. Those designs are special cases of designs from agriculture which used blocking to reduce error. When all factorial conditions appear in each block, the randomized-block factorial design has as one specialized equivalent a repeated measures design in which each subject is observed under all treatment conditions. Illustrated in terms of a 2×3 factorial design,

	Randomized block								Repeated measures					
	a_1			a_2					a_1			a_2		
	b_1	b_2	b_3	b_1	b_2	b_3			b_1	b_2	b_3	b_1	b_2	b_3
Block_1								Subject_1	$\longrightarrow$					
Block_2	G_1	G_1	G_1	G_1	G_1	G_1	=	Subject_2	$\longrightarrow$					
$\vdots$								$\vdots$			$\vdots$			
Block_n								Subject_n	$\longrightarrow$					

This illustration emphasizes that there is a single group of subjects (G_1) which is observed under all treatments. As was seen earlier, this design has the advantage of removing between-subject (Block) effects from error, but at the expense of requiring highly-restrictive assumptions on tests of factorial effects (A, B, AB interaction), all of which are within-subject effects. The other disadvantage is the block size. All subjects are observed under all treatment conditions, requiring a block size of pq treatments in a two-factor design, pqr in a three-factor design, etc.

When repeated measures are taken upon some, but not all, treatment conditions, the block size is reduced but the cost is confounding of some effects. These designs with repeated measures on the same subjects are special cases of split-plot factorial designs developed to control error in agricultural work by systematically "splitting" plots of land. For example, consider the 2×3 factorial design,

Split-plot factorial					Repeated measures design			
	b_1	b_2	b_3			b_1	b_2	b_3
$\text{Block}_{1(1)}$					$\text{Subject}_{1(1)}$	$\longrightarrow$		
$\text{Block}_{2(1)}$					$\text{Subject}_{2(1)}$	$\longrightarrow$		
a_1 $\quad\vdots$	G_1	G_1	G_1	a_1	$\vdots$		$\vdots$	
$\text{Block}_{n(1)}$					$\text{Subject}_{n(1)}$	$\longrightarrow$		
				$=$				
$\text{Block}_{1(2)}$					$\text{Subject}_{1(2)}$	$\longrightarrow$		
$\text{Block}_{2(2)}$					$\text{Subject}_{2(2)}$	$\longrightarrow$		
a_2 $\quad\vdots$	G_2	G_2	G_2	a_2	$\vdots$		$\vdots$	
$\text{Block}_{n(2)}$					$\text{Subject}_{n(2)}$	$\longrightarrow$		

wherein levels of factor A are assigned to groups of subjects (G_1 and G_2), the members of which are observed under only one level of factor A, but under all levels of factor B.

The levels of factor A (more generally, the variables on which there are *not* repeated measures) represent nuisance variables included to reduce error, classification variables which are included because they are of interest in their own right or because they are being treated as nuisance variables, or experimental variables to which levels were assigned. These designs allow partitioning of between- and within-subject effects. They provide increased precision with regard to within-subject effects (B, AB), but at the expense of restrictive assumptions regarding the structure of covariance matrices. Here, the emphasis is upon the fact that the block size has been reduced. Each subject is observed under only q, not pq, treatment conditions. In more general terms, the size of the block wherein homogeneity of conditions must be maintained has been reduced. There is a cost, however, since the main effect of factor A is inextricably confounded with the group effects, whatever may define the groups. The results are possible ambiguity regarding the nature of the A main effects and less power with regard to tests of significance on the A main effect. More generally, this would be true for all between-subject effects.

It would be desirable to be able to reduce block sizes without confounding any effects. That is not possible (with the exception of the completely randomized design in which each subject is only observed once). When blocking is used to reduce errors, confounding of some effects with differences between blocks always occurs for the between-block portion of the design. What *is* possible, however, is that designs may be structured so that block sizes are reduced and the confounding is with interactions, or components of interactions. In this chapter, two general classes of such designs will be considered.

One class of designs is one wherein a relatively small number of the possible treatment conditions of a factorial design are assigned to each block, the assignment being accomplished in such a way as to control the variation which is confounded with between-block differences.

In this context, a block may be a person, a group of people, a period of time, a geographical location, a source of experimental material, etc. Small block size in this context is equivalent to homogeneity of the conditions under which the treatment effects are measured. There can be considerable variation among blocks; this source of variation does not affect the precision of the within-block information. When practical working conditions rule against having a complete replication within a single block while still maintaining homogeneity of the uncontrolled sources of error, then balanced incomplete-block designs provide the next best alternative.

These plans use all the treatment combinations required for the complete factorial experiment, but within any one block only a fraction of all possible treatment combinations appear. The number of treatment combinations per block will be called the block size. The primary purpose of these plans is to control experimental error (1) by keeping the block size small and (2) by eliminating block differences from experimental error. The cost of this added control on experimental error will be the loss of some information on higher-order interactions. Differences between blocks will form a part of some interaction; hence components of such interactions will be confounded with the block effects. Whether or not the sacrifice of information on components of higher-order interactions is worth the added control depends upon the magnitude of the block effects.

Admittedly there is some danger in using designs in which any effect is confounded. This is particularly true in exploratory studies. However, the potential advantage of these designs—increased precision with respect to effects of primary interest—provides the experimenter with a potent source of motivation for their use.

A second class of designs is included in this chapter because the same principles of confounding are used for their structure. Fractional factorial designs are designs in which not all of the treatment conditions of a factorial design are examined. The number of treatment combinations in a factorial design can become quite large (256 treatment conditions in a 2^8 factorial design; 65,536 in a 2^{16} factorial design). When some interactions, usually higher-order interactions, can be considered negligible relative to main effects and lower-order interactions, one need include only a selected fraction of the complete factorial set in the experiment. The cost to the experimenter is that selected higher-order interactions will be confounded with main effects and lower-order interactions.

Latin squares may be considered a special case of such designs and are discussed in Chapter 9.

8.2 ASSIGNING TREATMENTS TO BLOCKS

Modular Arithmetic

Construction of the designs to be presented in this chapter depends upon techniques for analyzing interaction terms into component parts and for assigning treatments to blocks in such a way that there is balance with regard to the effects which are not to be confounded with differences between blocks. These procedures are simplified through the use of modular arithmetic.

By definition, an integer I modulus an integer m is the remainder obtained by dividing I by m. For example, the integer 18 to the modulus 5 is 3, since the remainder when 18 is divided by 5 is 3. This result is usually written

$$18 \, (\text{mod} \, 5) = 3$$

and is read "18 modulo 5 is 3." Other examples are:

$$20 \, (\text{mod} \, 5) = 0,$$

$$7 \, (\text{mod} \, 5) = 2,$$

$$3 \, (\text{mod} \, 5) = 3.$$

Thus, I is any integer of interest, m is the modulus and is any positive integer, q is the quotient obtained by dividing I by m, and r is the remainder, and

$$I = qm + r.$$

The remainder r is the integer of interest.

When two values of I have the same remainder when divided by the same modulus, they are said to be *congruent* relative to that modulus. For example, from above

$$3 \, (\text{mod} \, 5) = 3$$

$$18 \, (\text{mod} \, 5) = 3;$$

3 is congruent to 18 modulo 5. In general any value of I is congruent to its remainder r. Also, in general all integers are congruent to some value of r between 0 and $m - 1$ for any modulus. Thus, if the modulus 3 is used, all integers are congruent to 0, 1, or 2. For the modulus 3,

$$18 \, (\text{mod} \, 3) = 0$$

$$7 \, (\text{mod} \, 3) = 1,$$

$$20 \, (\text{mod} \, 3) = 2.$$

All integers are congruent to one of the integers, 0 or 1 modulus 2; all integers are congruent to one of the integers 0, 1, 2, 3, or 4, modulus 5, etc. For purposes of the work in the following sections, the moduli will be limited to prime numbers, i.e., numbers divisible by no numbers smaller than themselves except unity. For example, 1, 2, 3, 5, 7, 11, etc., are prime numbers.

In order to construct designs, only two operations with modular arithmetic will be used, addition and multiplication.

The operation of modular addition is shown in the following examples:

$$2 + 1 = 0 \,(\mathrm{mod}\,3),$$
$$0 + 2 = 2 \,(\mathrm{mod}\,3),$$
$$2 + 2 = 1 \,(\mathrm{mod}\,3);$$
$$2 + 2 = 4 \,(\mathrm{mod}\,5),$$
$$4 + 4 = 3 \,(\mathrm{mod}\,5),$$
$$1 + 4 = 0 \,(\mathrm{mod}\,5).$$

To add two integers, one obtains the ordinary sum, and then one expresses this sum in terms of the modulus. For example, $4 + 4 = 8$; $8 \,(\mathrm{mod}\,5) = 3$. Hence, $4 + 4 = 3 \,(\mathrm{mod}\,5)$. Unless the modulus is understood from the context, it is written after the operation as $(\mathrm{mod}\,m)$.

The operation of multiplication is illustrated by the following examples.

$$2 \cdot 2 = 1 \,(\mathrm{mod}\,3),$$
$$2 \cdot 0 = 0 \,(\mathrm{mod}\,3);$$
$$4 \cdot 2 = 3 \,(\mathrm{mod}\,5),$$
$$3 \cdot 3 = 4 \,(\mathrm{mod}\,5).$$

The product of two numbers is formed as in ordinary multiplication, and is expressed in terms of the modulus.

Algebraic equations may be solved in terms of a modular system. For example, by using the modulus 3, the equation

$$2x = 1 \,(\mathrm{mod}\,3)$$

has the solution $x = 2$. To obtain the solution, both sides of this equation are multiplied by a number which will make the coefficient of x equal to unity, modulus 3. Thus

$$2 \cdot 2x = 2 \,(\mathrm{mod}\,3).$$

Since $2 \cdot 2 = 1 \,(\mathrm{mod}\,3)$, the last equation becomes $x = 2$. As another example, the equation

$$4x = 3 \,(\mathrm{mod}\,5)$$

has the solution $x = 2$. To obtain this solution, both sides of the equation are multiplied by an integer that will make the coefficient of x equal to unity. If both sides of this equation are multiplied by 4,

$$4 \cdot 4x = 4 \cdot 3 \,(\text{mod } 5).$$

Expressing the respective products to the modulus 5, one has

$$16x = 12 \quad \text{or} \quad x = 2 \,(\text{mod } 5).$$

Equations of the form $ax_1 + bx_2 = c \,(\text{mod } m)$ may always be reduced to the form $x_1 + dx_2 = k \,(\text{mod } m)$. For example, the equation

$$2x_1 + x_2 = 1 \,(\text{mod } 3)$$

becomes, after multiplying both sides by 2,

$$x_1 + 2x_2 = 2 \,(\text{mod } 3).$$

As another example,

$$2x_1 + 4x_2 = 2 \,(\text{mod } 5)$$

becomes, after multiplying both sides by 3,

$$x_1 + 2x_2 = 1 \,(\text{mod } 5).$$

The equation $2x_1 + 4x_2 = 2 \,(\text{mod } 5)$ and the equation $x_1 + 2x_2 = 1 \,(\text{mod } 5)$ have the same roots. It may be verified that when $x_1 = 0$, $x_2 = 3$; hence one pair of roots for these equations is $(0, 3)$. Other roots are $(1, 0)$ and $(2, 2)$. To show that $(2, 2)$ is a root of the equation $x_1 + 2x_2 = 1 \,(\text{mod } 5)$, substituting $x_1 = 2$ and $x_2 = 2$ in this equation yields

$$2 + 2(2) = 1 \,(\text{mod } 5).$$

The numerical value of the left-hand side of the equation is 6, which to the modulus 5 is 1.

Revised Notation for Factorial Experiments

The introduction of a modified notation for the treatment combinations in a factorial experiment will permit more convenient application of modular arithmetic. This revised notation is illustrated for the case of a $3 \times 3 \times 2$ factorial experiment in Table 8.1. The three levels of factor A are designated

TABLE 8.1 **Notation for a $3 \times 3 \times 2$ factorial experiment**

	c_0			c_1		
	b_0	b_1	b_2	b_0	b_1	b_2
a_0	(000)	(010)	(020)	(001)	(011)	(021)
a_1	(100)	(110)	(120)	(101)	(111)	(121)
a_2	(200)	(210)	(220)	(201)	(211)	(221)

by the subscripts 0, 1, and 2. The treatment combination consisting of level a_1, level b_0, and level c_1 is designated by the symbol (101). The digit in the first position indicates the level of factor A, the digit in the third position indicates the level of factor C. Thus, the symbol (ijk) represents the treatment combination abc_{ijk}.

Assigning Treatments

To illustrate how modular arithmetic may be used in conjunction with this new notation system, consider a 2×2 factorial design. There are four treatment conditions, ab_{00}, ab_{01}, ab_{10} and ab_{11} (00, 01, 10, 11). All of the treatment conditions in this experiment may be expressed in the form (ij) by suitable choice of i and j. Let x_1 stand for the digit in the first position of this symbol, and let x_2 stand for the digit in the second position. The relation $x_1 + x_2 = 0 \,(\text{mod}\, 2)$ is satisfied by the symbols (00), (11). To show this

$$x_1 + x_2 = 0 = 0 + 0 = 0 \,(\text{mod}\, 2)$$

$$x_1 + x_2 = 0 = 1 + 1 = 0 \,(\text{mod}\, 2).$$

The relation $x_1 + x_2 = 0$ is said to define or generate the set of treatment combinations (00), (11). By similar reasoning, the relation $x_1 + x_2 = 1 \,(\text{mod}\, 2)$ generates the set of treatments (01), (10). In summary, then, for a 2×2 factorial design, one may divide the total set of four treatment conditions into two balanced sets of two each:

$x_1 + x_2 = 0 \,(\text{mod}\, 2)$	$x_1 + x_2 = 1 \,(\text{mod}\, 2)$
(00)	(10)
(11)	(01)

Balance here refers to the main effects. Note that a_0 appears once and only once in each set. Similarly, a_1, b_0, and b_2 each appear once and only once in each set. Thus, there is balance with respect to the main effects of both factors A and B; any difference between the means of the two sets is *not* a function of the main effects, but rather a function of the AB interaction. This is true only if factors A and B are fixed; the blocks (sets of treatments) are assumed to be random. Consider that the sets of treatments are assigned to blocks. Hence, the between-block differences are free of main effects, but are confounded with the two-factor interaction.

This same basic concept underlies the construction of designs of any size of the form p^k where p is the number of levels of each factor and is a prime number. Thus, one may construct balanced sets of treatments for the p^2 series, 2×2, 3×3, 5×5, 7×7, etc, two-factor factorial designs. The same is true of p^3 designs, $2 \times 2 \times 2$, $3 \times 3 \times 3$, $5 \times 5 \times 5$, etc.

To generalize for p^2 designs, all treatment conditions satisfying the relation

$$x_i + x_j = r \,(\text{mod}\, p)$$

are assigned to a single group of treatments, with a different group being formed for each value of r. Thus, in a 3×3 factorial design with nine treatment conditions, there are three balanced sets of three treatments each defined by

$x_1 + x_2 = 0 \pmod 3$	$x_1 + x_2 = 1 \pmod 3$	$x_1 + x_2 = 2 \pmod 3$
(00)	(01)	(11)
(12)	(10)	(20)
(21)	(22)	(02).

These are also balanced sets with regard to main effects, but information concerning the $A \times B$ interaction is (partially) confounded with between-blocks differences. (More will be said of partial confounding in the next section.)

One may also generalize in the other direction for different values of k. Consider the three-factor design $2^3 = 2 \times 2 \times 2$. One may establish balanced sets of treatment conditions which confound the three-factor interaction with block differences, but are balanced with regard to both the main effects and two-factor interactions. The relation

$$x_i + x_j + x_k = r \pmod 2 \qquad\qquad r = 0, 1$$

may be used to form the two groups of four treatments each:

$x_1 + x_2 + x_3 = 0 \pmod 2$	$x_1 + x_2 + x_3 = 1 \pmod 2$
(000)	(001)
(011)	(100)
(101)	(010)
(110)	(111)

Note that each level of each factor occurs an equal number of times within a set. Note also that all possible pairs of treatments occur once and only once with each set. Hence, each set is balanced with respect to the A, B, and C main effects as well as AB, AC, and BC interactions. Therefore, the difference between the sum of all observations in the two sets is a function of the ABC interaction.

8.3 METHODS FOR OBTAINING AND CONFOUNDING INTERACTION COMPONENTS

All of the designs considered in this chapter involve isolating and confounding interactions, or components of interactions, with between-block effects. It is desirable, therefore, to illustrate general procedures for this purpose. The methods of partitioning interactions presented here apply only to factorial experiments of the p^k series, where p is the number of levels of k factors and is a prime number.

In the simplest factorial design, a 2×2 design, the $A \times B$ interaction has a single degree of freedom which may be associated with a single component of interaction variance, an AB component. It has been shown that the defining relation

$$x_1 + x_2 = r \ (\text{mod} \ 2) \qquad\qquad r = 0, 1$$

can be used to partition the four treatment conditions into two sets of two treatments each,

Block 1	Block 2
$x_1 + x_2 = 0$	$x_1 + x_2 = 1$
(00)	(01)
(11)	(10)
$(AB)_0$	$(AB)_1$

with the sets being balanced with regard to the main effects. The interaction is completely confounded with the difference between the two blocks. That is, the difference between the two block totals, $(AB)_0$ and $(AB)_1$, is identical to the interaction comparison.

A 3×3 factorial design has an $A \times B$ interaction with four degrees of freedom which may be partitioned into two orthogonal components, each with two degrees of freedom.

The first component is the AB component (what Kempthorne (1952) has called the $AB(J)$ component) and is isolated by using the defining relation

$$x_1 + x_2 = r \ (\text{mod} \ 3) \qquad\qquad r = 0, 1, 2$$

to define three sets of three treatments each:

Block 1	Block 2	Block 3
$x_1 + x_2 = 0$	$x_1 + x_2 = 1$	$x_1 + x_2 = 2$
(00)	(01)	(11)
(12)	(10)	(20)
(21)	(22)	(02)
$(AB)_0$	$(AB)_1$	$(AB)_2$

The symbol $(AB)_r$ designates the sum of the observations for the treatment conditions in that block. As noted in Sec. 8.2, main effects are balanced within blocks; between blocks there are no main effects, but the AB component of the $A \times B$ interaction is identical to the difference between blocks with two degrees of freedom. (This, and other components of interactions, have no meaning except in terms of defining these blocks.)

To illustrate what is meant by balance in this context, assume that the following linear model holds:

$$X_{ij} = \mu + \alpha_i + \beta_j + (\alpha\beta)_{ij} + \varepsilon_{ij},$$

where $\sum_i \alpha_i = 0$, $\sum_j \beta_j = 0$, and $\sum_i (\alpha\beta)_{ij} = \sum_j (\alpha\beta)_{ij} = 0$. When A and B are fixed factors, these restrictions on the parameters in the model follow from the definition of the effects. An observation made on a treatment combination on the left-hand side of the following equations estimates the sum of the parameters indicated on the right-hand side:

$$(00) = \mu + \alpha_0 + \beta_0 + (\alpha\beta)_{00} + \varepsilon_{00},$$
$$(12) = \mu + \alpha_1 + \beta_2 + (\alpha\beta)_{12} + \varepsilon_{12},$$
$$(21) = \mu + \alpha_2 + \beta_1 + (\alpha\beta)_{21} + \varepsilon_{21}.$$

The sum of the observations on this set of treatments will not contain effects associated with either of the main effects, since $\alpha_0 + \alpha_1 + \alpha_2 = 0$ and $\beta_0 + \beta_1 + \beta_2 = 0$. The sum of the observations in this set of treatments will, however, involve an interaction effect, since $(\alpha\beta)_{00} + (\alpha\beta)_{12} + (\alpha\beta)_{21} \neq 0$. Thus the set (00), (12), (21), which is defined by the relation $x_1 + x_2 = 0 \pmod 3$, is said to be balanced with respect to both main effects but not balanced with respect to the interaction effect. The sets defined by the relations $x_1 + x_2 = 1$ and $x_1 + x_2 = 2$ are also balanced with respect to both main effects but unbalanced with respect to the interaction effect.

There is a second component of the $A \times B$ interaction which also has two degrees of freedom and which can be confounded with the between-block main effects. That component, the AB^2 or $AB(I)$ [Kempthorne, (1952)] component is defined by the relation

$$x_1 + 2x_2 = r \pmod 3.$$

Thus, block assignments are defined as

Block 1	Block 2	Block 3
$x_1 + 2x_2 = 0$	$x_1 + 2x_2 = 1$	$x_1 + 2x_2 = 2$
(00)	(02)	(01)
(11)	(10)	(12)
(22)	(21)	(20)
$(AB^2)_0$	$(AB^2)_1$	$(AB^2)_2$

These sets, too, are balanced with regard to main effects, but differences among the block totals, $(AB^2)_0$, $(AB^2)_1$, and $(AB^2)_2$, are identical to the AB^2 component of the $A \times B$ variation and degrees of freedom.

This example illustrates partial confounding. In the first case, the AB component is confounded between blocks, but there is information regarding the AB^2 component from within the blocks. Note that the differences among treatments (00), (12), and (21) occur *within* block 1 in the first instance, but *between* blocks 1, 2, and 3 in the second case. In the second case the $A \times B$ interaction is also only partially confounded, the confounding being of the AB^2 component. The numerical example in Table 8.2 illustrates the computation of

TABLE 8.2 **Computation of components of interaction in 3×3 factorial experiment having four observations per cell**

(i)

	b_0	b_1	b_2	Total
a_0	45	20	20	$85 = A_0$
a_1	25	50	20	$95 = A_1$ $(n = 4)$
a_2	20	50	80	$150 = A_2$
Total	90	120	120	$330 = G$
	B_0	B_1	B_2	

(ii)

$$SS_{ab} = \frac{45^2 + 20^2 + \cdots + 50^2 + 80^2}{4} - \frac{85^2 + 95^2 + 150^2}{12}$$

$$- \frac{90^2 + 120^2 + 120^2}{12} + \frac{330^2}{36}$$

$$= 633.33$$

(iii)

$x_1 + x_2 = 0$	$x_1 + x_2 = 1$	$x_1 + x_2 = 2$
$(00) = 45$	$(01) = 20$	$(02) = 20$
$(12) = 20$	$(10) = 25$	$(11) = 50$
$(21) = 50$	$(22) = 80$	$(20) = 20$
$(AB)_0 = 115$	$(AB)_1 = 125$	$(AB)_2 = 90$

$$SS_{AB} = \frac{115^2 + 125^2 + 90^2}{12} - \frac{330^2}{36}$$

$$= 54.17$$

(iv)

$x_1 + 2x_2 = 0$	$x_1 + 2x_2 = 1$	$x_1 + 2x_2 = 2$
$(00) = 45$	$(02) = 20$	$(01) = 20$
$(11) = 50$	$(10) = 25$	$(12) = 20$
$(22) = 80$	$(21) = 50$	$(20) = 20$
$(AB^2)_0 = 175$	$(AB^2)_1 = 95$	$(AB^2)_2 = 60$

$$SS_{AB^2} = \frac{175^2 + 95^2 + 60^2}{12} - \frac{330^2}{36}$$

$$= 579.17$$

the AB component of the interaction. The entries in the cells of part i of this table are assumed to be the sums over four observations: i.e., the data in part i represent a summary of a 3×3 factorial experiment in which there are four observations per cell.

The sum of squares for the overall $A \times B$ interaction, which has four degrees of freedom, is computed in part ii. The sum of squares for the AB component, which has two degrees of freedom, is computed in part iii. The sum of all observations in the set of treatment combinations defined by the relation $x_1 + x_2 = 0$ is denoted by the symbol $(AB)_0$. Similarly, the sum of all observations in the set defined by $x_1 + x_2 = 1$ is denoted by the symbol $(AB)_1$.

The sum of squares corresponding to the AB component is given by

$$SS_{AB} = \frac{(AB)_0^2 + (AB)_1^2 + (AB)_2^2}{3n} - \frac{G^2}{9n},$$

where n is the number of observations in each of the cell entries in part i. For the data in part i, $SS_{AB} = 54.17$. The sum of squares for the AB^2 component is given by

$$SS_{AB^2} = \frac{(AB^2)_0^2 + (AB^2)_1^2 + (AB^2)_2^2}{3n} - \frac{G^2}{9n}.$$

The numerical value for this sum of squares is 579.17.

The partition of the overall interaction may be summarized as follows:

Source	SS	df
$A \times B$	633.33	4
AB	54.17	2
AB^2	579.17	2

Within rounding error $SS_{ab} = SS_{AB} + SS_{AB^2}$. In this case the AB^2 component of the interaction is considerably larger than the AB component. Inspection of part i of Table 8.2 indicates that the large totals are on the diagonal running from upper left to lower right. The treatment totals on this diagonal are in the same set for the AB^2 component but in different sets for the AB component. Hence, the AB^2 component is large relative to the AB component.

The computation of the components of the $A \times B$ interaction may be simplified by use of the procedure illustrated in Table 8.3. The cell entries at the top of this table are the same as those in part i of Table 8.2, with rows a_0 and a_1 appearing twice. Totals of the form $(AB)_i$ are obtained by summing the entries on diagonals running from upper right to lower left; totals of the form $(AB^2)_i$ are obtained by summing entries on diagonals running from upper left to lower right. From these totals the components of the interaction are computed by the same formulas as those used in Table 8.2. The treatment

TABLE 8.3   Simplified computation of the components of the $A \times B$ interaction

combinations falling along these diagonals actually form the balanced sets defined by modular relations.

These procedures are easily generalized to p^2 designs of any size. In the case of $5^2 = 5 \times 5$ factorial designs, there are 25 treatment conditions. The $A \times B$ interaction has 16 degrees of freedom and may be partitioned as follows:

Source	df	Defining relation
$A \times B$	16	
AB	4	$x_1 + x_2 = r \pmod 5$
AB^2	4	$x_1 + 2x_2 = r \pmod 5$
AB^3	4	$x_1 + 3x_2 = r \pmod 5$
AB^4	4	$x_1 + 4x_2 = r \pmod 5$

Hence, one may confound the AB component with four degrees of freedom between five blocks, with the treatment conditions for the five blocks being assigned by $x_1 + x_2 = 0$, 1, 2, 3, and 4, respectively. Within blocks there will be information regarding the AB^2, AB^3, and AB^4 components of variation, but not the AB component. Alternatively, one may confound any of the other components using the appropriate relation. For example, the balanced sets of treatment combinations from which the AB^3 component of the interaction is obtained are defined by the following relations, all with respect to the modulus 5.

Block 1	Block 2	Block 3
$x_1 + 3x_2 = 0$	$x_1 + 3x_2 = 1$	$x_1 + 3x_2 = 2$
(00)	(02)	(04)
(13)	(10)	(12)
(21)	(23)	(20)
(34)	(31)	(33)
(42)	(44)	(41)

Block 4	Block 5
$x_1 + 3x_2 = 3$	$x_1 + 3x_2 = 4$
(01)	(03)
(14)	(11)
(22)	(24)
(30)	(32)
(43)	(40)

Each of these sets is balanced with respect to both main effects.

TABLE 8.4 **Computation of components of interaction in a 5×5 factorial experiment**

	b_0	b_1	b_2	b_3	b_4
a_0	5	10	15	20	25
a_1	10	15	20	25	30
a_2	15	15	15	15	20
a_3	20	15	10	10	5

(i)

$(AB)_4 = 110$ —a_4— 30	20	5	5	5	— — 50 $= (AB^4)_0$
$(AB)_0 = 80$ —a_0— 5	10	15	20	25	— — 65 $= (AB^4)_1$
$(AB)_1 = 55$ —a_1— 10	15	20	25	30	— — 85 $= (AB^4)_2$
$(AB)_2 = 55$ —a_2— 15	15	15	15	20	— —100 $= (AB^4)_3$
$(AB)_3 = 80$ —a_3— 20	15	10	10	5	— — 80 $= (AB^4)_4$

$$\overline{380} \qquad\qquad\qquad\qquad \overline{380}$$

	b_0	b_2	b_4	b_1	b_3
a_0	5	15	25	10	20
a_1	10	20	30	15	25
a_2	15	15	20	15	15
a_3	20	10	5	15	10

(ii)

$(AB^3)_4 = 95$ —a_4— 30	5	5	20	5	— — 65 $= (AB^2)_0$
$(AB^3)_0 = 55$ —a_0— 5	15	25	10	20	— — 70 $= (AB^2)_1$
$(AB^3)_1 = 60$ —a_1— 10	20	30	15	25	— — 65 $= (AB^2)_2$
$(AB^3)_2 = 90$ —a_2— 15	15	20	15	15	— — 80 $= (AB^2)_3$
$(AB^3)_3 = 80$ —a_3— 20	10	5	15	10	— —100 $= (AB^2)_4$

$$\overline{380} \qquad\qquad\qquad\qquad \overline{380}$$

The computation of the components of the $A \times B$ interaction in a 5×5 factorial experiment may be carried out by an extension of the method used in Table 8.3. This extension is illustrated using the data in Table 8.4. In part i, the totals required for the computation of the AB component appear at the left, and the totals required for the AB^4 component appear at the right. In part ii, totals required for the AB^2 and the AB^3 components are obtained. The arrangement of the b's in part ii is given by multiplying subscripts to b's in part i by 2 and then reducing the resulting numbers to the modulus 5. By performing this operation, the sequence b_0, b_1, b_2, b_3, b_4, becomes the sequence b_0, b_2, b_4, b_1, b_3; the latter sequence appears in part ii. The AB^2 component of the interaction is obtained from the totals in the lower right of part ii. Assuming one observation per cell,

$$\text{SS}_{AB^2} = \frac{65^2 + 70^2 + 65^2 + 80^2 + 100^2}{5} - \frac{380^2}{25} = 174.00.$$

Other components are obtained in an analogous manner. The numerical values of the components of the interaction for the data in Table 8.4 are as follows:

Source	SS	df
$A \times B$	1136.00	16
AB	414.00	4
AB^2	174.00	4
AB^3	254.00	4
AB^4	294.00	4

The general case for defining the components of p^2 designs is given by using defining relationships,

$$c_1 x_1 + c_2 x_2 = r \pmod{p}$$

the coefficients of which correspond to all powers of A and B between 1 and r, modulus p. For the 2×2 design, $r = 0$ and 1 modulus 2. Only $r = 1$ may be used as powers of A and B and

$$A^1 B^1 = AB$$

is the only component of the $A \times B$ interaction. The defining relation has $c_1 = c_2 = 1$, and is, therefore

$$x_1 + x_2 = r \pmod{2}.$$

The 3×3 design uses coefficients equal to 1 or 2 as powers of A and B. Thus, one has as components of the $A \times B$ interaction,

$A \times B$ component	Defining relations
$A^1B^1 = AB$	$x_1 + x_2 = r \pmod 3$
$A^1B^2 = AB^2$	$x_1 + 2x_2 = r \pmod 3$
$A^2B^1 = AB^2$	$2x_1 + x_2 = r \pmod 3$
$A^2B^2 = AB$	$2x_1 + 2x_2 = r \pmod 3$

But we have already seen that there are only two unique components of the $A \times B$ interaction, AB and AB^2. That is because the potential components A^2B^1 and A^2B^2 define exactly the same treatment conditions as do AB and AB^2 respectively. The relation,

$$2x_1 + x_2 = r \pmod 3$$

defines the same set of treatment combinations as

$$2(2)x_1 + 2x_2 = 2r \pmod 3$$

$$x_1 + 2x_2 = 2r \pmod 3.$$

Multiplying both sides of a defining relation by a constant is algebraically equivalent to raising the symbol for the corresponding component to a power equal to that constant. In this example, the constant is 2. Hence,

$$(A^2B)^2 = A^4B^2 = AB^2,$$

and

$$(A^2B^2)^2 = A^4B^4 = AB.$$

Thus, there are only two unique defining relations, the convention being to select those for which the power of A is 1.

The general case for p^3 designs is to use the defining relations

$$x_1 + c_2x_2 + c_3x_3 = r \pmod p$$

to define and confound the components of the three-factor interactions, where c_2 and c_3 take values between 1 and $p - 1$ and x_1 always has a coefficient of 1. For example, in a $3 \times 3 \times 3$ factorial experiment, the three-factor interaction may be partitioned into the following components:

Source	df	Defining relations for 3 blocks each
$A \times B \times C$	8	
ABC	2	$x_1 + x_2 + x_3 = 0, 1, 2$
ABC^2	2	$x_1 + x_2 + 2x_3 = 0, 1, 2$
AB^2C	2	$x_1 + 2x_2 + x_3 = 0, 1, 2$
AB^2C^2	2	$x_1 + 2x_2 + 2x_3 = 0, 1, 2.$

In a $5 \times 5 \times 5$ experiment, the 75 treatment conditions can be blocked into 5 blocks of 15 treatments each by confounding any of 16 unique components of the $A \times B \times C$ interaction, each with four degrees of freedom:

16 components

Source	df	Defining relations for 5 blocks each
$A \times B \times C$	64	
ABC	4	$x_1 + x_2 + x_3 = 0, 1, 2, 3, 4$
ABC^2	4	$x_1 + x_2 + 2x_3 = 0, 1, 2, 3, 4$
ABC^3	4	$x_1 + x_2 + 3x_3 = 0, 1, 2, 3, 4$
ABC^4	4	$x_1 + x_2 + 4x_3 = 0, 1, 2, 3, 4$
AB^2C^1	4	$x_1 + 2x_2 + x_3 = 0, 1, 2, 3, 4$
$\vdots$	$\vdots$	$\vdots$
AB^4C^4	4	$x_1 + 4x_2 + 4x_3 = 0, 1, 2, 3, 4.$

Returning to the $3 \times 3 \times 3$ design, as an example, the sets of treatment combinations from which the AB^2C^2 component is computed are defined by the following relations:

$x_1 + 2x_2 = 2x_3 = 0 \pmod 3$	$x_1 + 2x_2 + 2x_3 = 1 \pmod 3$
(000)	(002)
(012)	(011)
(021)	(020)
(101)	(100)
(110)	(112)
(122)	(121)
(202)	(201)
(211)	(210)
(220)	(222)

$$x_1 + 2x_2 + 2x_3 = 2 \pmod 3$$

(001)
(010)
(022)
(102)
(111)
(120)
(200)
(212)
(221)

The sum of the observations within each of these sets is balanced with respect to all the main effects and all the two-factor interactions. There is no balance for the three-factor interaction. Hence differences between sums over the sets form one of the components of the three-factor interaction, in this case the AB^2C^2 component. Treatment combinations from which the AB^2C component is computed are defined by relations of the form $x_1 + 2x_2 + x_3 = r \pmod 3$.

The computation of the components of the three-factor interaction is illustrated in Table 8.5. In part i summary data for observations made at level c_0 are given. Summary data for levels c_1 and c_2 appear in parts ii and iii, respectively. Totals corresponding to the AB component for level c_0 appear at the left in part i. These totals also appear in part iv under the column headed c_0. The totals at the left of parts ii and iii make up the columns c_1 and c_2 in part iv. The ABC component of the three-factor interaction is computed from totals at the left of part iv; the ABC^2 component is obtained from the totals at the right of part iv. For example, if there are n observations in each cell of a

TABLE 8.5 **Computation of the components of a three-factor interaction in a $3 \times 3 \times 3$ factorial experiment**

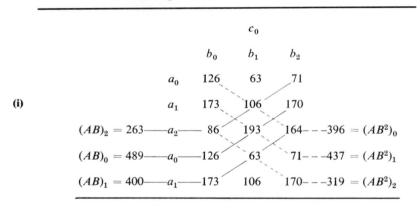

TABLE 8.5   *(Continued)*

c_2

	b_0	b_1	b_2
a_0	103	80	54
a_1	123	52	109

(iii)

$(AB)_2 = 198$——a_2—— 92   101   60 – – –$215 = (AB^2)_0$

$(AB)_0 = 313$——a_0——103   80   54 – – –$278 = (AB^2)_1$

$(AB)_1 = 263$——a_1——123   52   109 – – –$281 = (AB^2)_2$

	c_0	c_1	c_2
$(AB)_0$	489	389	313
$(AB)_1$	400	342	263

(iv)

$(ABC)_2 = 918$——$(AB)_2$——263   307   198 – – –$1029 = (ABC^2)_0$

$(ABC)_0 = 1059$——$(AB)_0$——489   389   313 – – –$1020 = (ABC^2)_1$

$(ABC)_1 = \dfrac{987}{2964}$——$(AB)_1$——400   342   263 – – – $\dfrac{915}{2964} = (ABC^2)_2$

	c_0	c_1	c_2
$(AB^2)_0$	396	340	215
$(AB^2)_1$	437	325	278

(v)

$(AB^2C)_2 = 859$——$(AB^2)_2$——319   373   281 – – –$1002 = (AB^2C^2)_0$

$(AB^2C)_0 = 1047$——$(AB^2)_0$——396   340   215 – – –$1025 = (AB^2C^2)_1$

$(AB^2C)_1 = 1058$——$(AB^2)_1$——437   325   278 – – – $937 = (AB^2C^2)_2$

$3 \times 3 \times 3$ factorial experiment, the ABC component is given by

$$\text{SS}_{ABC} = \frac{918^2 + 1059^2 + 987^2}{9n} - \frac{2964^2}{27n}.$$

In part v of the table, the entries under column c_0 are obtained from the totals at the right of part i. The entries in columns c_1 and c_2 are obtained, respectively, from the totals to the right of parts ii and iii. Totals at the left of part v are used to obtain the AB^2C component of the three-factor interaction; totals at the right are used to obtain the AB^2C^2 component.

The treatment combinations that are summed to obtain the total $(AB^2C^2)_0$ in part v may be shown to be those belonging to set $x_1 + 2x_2 + 2x_3 = 0$. Similarly, the total $(AB^2C^2)_1$ is the sum of all observations on the treatment set $x_1 + 2x_2 + 2x_3 = 1$. The scheme presented in Table 8.5 provides a convenient method for obtaining the sum over balanced sets. In general the symbol $(AB^iC^j)_k$ represents the sum of all treatment combinations satisfying the relation

$$x_1 + ix_2 + jx_3 = k \text{ (mod 3)}.$$

Rather than using the scheme presented in Table 8.5, it is sometimes more convenient to form the sets of treatment combinations by means of their defining relations and obtain the sums directly from the sets.

In the notation system used by Yates as well as Cochran and Cox, the following components of the three-factor interaction in a $3 \times 3 \times 3$ factorial experiment are equivalent:

Modular notation	Yates notation
ABC	$ABC(Z)$
ABC^2	$ABC(Y)$
AB^2C	$ABC(X)$
AB^2C^2	$ABC(W)$

The modular-notation system is the more convenient and lends itself to generalization beyond the $3 \times 3 \times 3$ factorial experiment. For example, in a $5 \times 5 \times 5$ factorial experiment, the three-factor interaction may be partitioned into the following parts:

Source	df
$A \times B \times C$	64
ABC	4
ABC^2	4
ABC^3	4
ABC^4	4
AB^2C	4
$\cdots$	$\cdots$
AB^4C^4	4

There are 16 components in all, each having four degrees of freedom. The balanced sets used to obtain the AB^4C^4 component are defined by the relations $x_1 + 4x_2 + 4x_3 = 0, 1, 2, 3, 4 \text{ (mod 5)}$. For example, the sum $(AB^4C^4)_2$ is obtained from the treatment combinations belonging to the set defined by the relation $x_1 + 4x_2 + 4x_3 = 2$; there will be 25 treatment combinations in this set.

With designs involving three (or more) factors, it is possible to structure blocks of treatment conditions based upon confounding components of any of the interactions. For example, in a three-factor design one could confound the AC, AB, or BC interactions. Typically, however, the block structure is based upon the highest order interaction in the absence of information whether that interaction is likely to be large and of special interest to the experimenter. Later in this chapter, it will be shown that one can also construct blocks on the basis of more than one interaction in the same study.

8.4 SIMPLIFIED COMPUTATIONAL PROCEDURES FOR 2^k FACTORIAL EXPERIMENTS

Designs in which $p = 2$ for all factors, 2^k factorial experiments, offer the simplest cases wherein confounding of interactions can be incorporated into the designs. Because all effects invoke only a single degree of freedom in 2^k designs, all computational procedures reduce to those developed for comparisons, making it possible to use simplified computational procedures for all analyses.

Computational procedures for 2×2, $2 \times 2 \times 2$, $2 \times 2 \times 2 \times 2$, etc., factorial experiments may be simplified by use of the device employed in forming balanced sets. The simplified computational procedures will be illustrated by the numerical example given in Table 8.6. Cell totals in part i are the sum of five observations. The sums of squares obtained by the procedures to be outlined are the *unadjusted* sums of squares if the experiment involves any confounding.

The patterns of the algebraic signs in part ii are determined as follows (the x's refer to digits in the treatment combinations at the top of each column; all addition is modulo 2):

$$G: \qquad\qquad\qquad\qquad \text{All positive}$$
$$A: \quad - \text{ if } x_1 \qquad = 0, \qquad + \text{ if } x_1 \qquad = 1$$
$$B: \quad - \text{ if } x_2 \qquad = 0, \qquad + \text{ if } x_2 \qquad = 1$$
$$C: \quad - \text{ if } x_3 \qquad = 0, \qquad + \text{ if } x_3 \qquad = 1$$
$$AB: \quad + \text{ if } x_1 + x_2 \qquad = 0, \qquad - \text{ if } x_1 + x_2 \qquad = 1$$
$$AC: \quad + \text{ if } x_1 + x_3 \qquad = 0, \qquad - \text{ if } x_1 + x_3 \qquad = 1$$
$$BC: \quad + \text{ if } x_2 + x_3 \qquad = 0, \qquad - \text{ if } x_2 + x_3 \qquad = 1$$
$$ABC: \quad - \text{ if } x_1 + x_2 + x_3 = 0, \qquad + \text{ if } x_1 + x_2 + x_3 = 1$$

In general, if the number of factors which are interacting is even, then the zero modular sum receives the positive sign; if the number of factors interacting is odd, then the zero modular sum receives a negative sign. In this context main effects are classified with the interaction of an odd number of factors.

The entry at the right of each row in part ii is a weighted sum of the cell totals at the top of each column, the weights being ±1 as determined by the pattern of signs in each row. For example, the entry at the right of row A is given by

$$-5 - 10 - 15 - 15 + 10 + 20 + 20 + 5 = 10.$$

TABLE 8.6 $2 \times 2 \times 2$ **Factorial experiment with five observations per cell**

(i)

		b_0		b_1		
		c_0	c_1	c_0	c_1	Total
	a_0	5	10	15	15	45
	a_1	10	20	20	5	55
		15	30	35	20	100

(ii)

	Treat comb:	(000)	(001)	(010)	(011)	(100)	(101)	(110)	(111)	Comparison
	Cell total:	5	10	15	15	10	20	20	5	100
G		+	+	+	+	+	+	+	+	100
A		−	−	−	−	+	+	+	+	10
B		−	−	+	+	−	−	+	+	10
C		−	+	−	+	−	+	−	+	0
AB		+	+	−	−	−	−	+	+	−20
AC		+	−	+	−	−	+	−	+	−10
BC		+	−	−	+	+	−	−	+	−30
ABC		−	+	+	−	+	−	−	+	−20

(iii)

$$\text{SS}_a = \frac{(10)^2}{5(8)} = 2.50 \qquad \text{SS}_{ac} = \frac{(-10)^2}{5(8)} = 2.50$$

$$\text{SS}_b = \frac{(10)^2}{5(8)} = 2.50 \qquad \text{SS}_{bc} = \frac{(-30)^2}{5(8)} = 22.50$$

$$\text{SS}_c = 0 \qquad \text{SS}_{abc} = \frac{(-20)^2}{5(8)} = 10.00$$

$$\text{SS}_{ab} = \frac{(-20)^2}{5(8)} = 10.00$$

As another example, the entry at the right of row ABC is given by

$$-5 + 10 + 15 - 15 + 10 - 20 - 20 + 5 = -20.$$

The pattern of the signs in the last expression is that in row ABC. The weighted sum of the cell totals for row ABC actually corresponds to the difference $(ABC)_1 - (ABC)_0$, where $(ABC)_1$ represents the sum of all observations on treatment combinations which satisfy the relation

$$x_1 + x_2 + x_3 = 1 \;(\text{mod } 2).$$

Alternatively, the totals at the right of the rows represent the comparisons corresponding to the effects at the left of the rows. The general form of a comparison (assuming the same number of observations in each cell total) is

$$\text{Comparison} = c_1 T_1 + c_2 T_2 + \cdots + c_k T_k, \qquad \sum c_j = 0,$$

where the T's represent cell totals. The sum of squares corresponding to a comparison is given by

$$SS_{comparison} = \frac{(comparison)^2}{n \sum c^2},$$

where n is the number of observations summed to obtain the cell totals. The c's in part ii are either $+1$ or -1, depending upon the sign; for each of the rows $\sum c^2 = 8$. The sums of squares for comparisons corresponding to main effects and interactions are computed in part iii. In this example, n is assumed to be equal to 5.

The extension of these computational procedures to any factorial experiment of the form 2^k is direct. Once the pattern of signs corresponding to a row in part ii is determined, the weighted sum of the cell totals corresponding to a row gives the number value of the comparison. For any comparison determined in this manner, $\sum c^2 = 2^k$.

In 2^k factorial experiments a specialized notation is frequently used to designate the treatment combinations. This specialized notation for a $2 \times 2 \times 2$ factorial experiment is as follows:

	b_0		b_1	
	c_0	c_1	c_0	c_1
a_0	(1)	c	b	bc
a_1	a	ac	ab	abc

The relationship between the notation system used thus far in this chapter and the specialized notation system is as follows:

Treatment combination	(000)	(010)	(001)	(011)	(100)	(110)	(101)	(111)
Specialized notation	(1)	b	c	bc	a	ab	ac	abc

In the specialized notation system, the symbol for a treatment combination contains only those letters for which the factor is at level 1. Conversely, if a factor is at level 0 in a treatment combination, then the letter corresponding to that factor does not appear in the symbol.

In terms of the latter notation system, sign patterns for the comparisons may be determined by a relatively simple rule. In the sign pattern for an interaction of the form XY, a symbol receives a positive sign if it contains both of the letters X and Y or neither of these letters; a symbol receives a negative sign otherwise. In the sign pattern for an interaction of the form XYZ, a symbol receives a positive sign if it contains either all three of the letters X, Y, and Z or just one of the three letters; a symbol receives a negative sign otherwise. For the general case, in the interaction of an *even* number of factors, a symbol receives a positive sign if it contains an even number of the interacting factors (zero being considered an even number); otherwise it receives a negative sign. In the interaction of an *odd* number of factors, a symbol receives a positive sign if it contains an odd number of the interacting factors; otherwise the symbol receives a minus sign. A main effect may be considered included under the latter case. The following example illustrates the general case:

Symbols:	(1)	b	c	bc	a	ab	ac	abc
A	−	−	−	−	+	+	+	+
C	−	−	+	+	−	−	+	+
AC	+	+	−	−	−	−	+	+

For the case of 2^4 factorial experiments, the sign patterns for some of the comparisons are illustrated below:

	(1)	a	b	ab	c	ac	bc	abc	d	ad	bd	abd	cd	acd	bcd	abcd
A	−	+	−	+	−	+	−	+	−	+	−	+	−	+	−	+
AB	+	−	−	+	+	−	−	+	+	−	−	+	+	−	−	+
ABC	−	+	+	−	+	−	−	+	−	+	+	−	+	−	−	+
ABCD	+	−	−	+	−	+	+	−	−	+	+	−	+	−	−	+

Given the pattern of signs corresponding to a comparison, the sum of squares for that comparison is readily obtained from the treatment totals.

A systematic computing scheme for obtaining the comparisons corresponding to main effects and interactions is illustrated in Table 8.7. This scheme is quite useful when the number of factors is large. The basic data in

TABLE 8.7 **Simplified computational procedures**

Effect:

Treatment combination	Total	(1)	(2)	(3)	Comparison
(1)	5	15	50	100	G
a	10	35	50	10	A
b	15	30	10	10	B
ab	20	20	0	−20	AB
c	10	5	20	0	C
ac	20	5	−10	−10	AC
bc	15	10	0	−30	BC
abc	5	−10	−20	−20	ABC
Upper half	⋯	100	110	100	
Lower half	⋯	10	−10	−60	
Odds	45	60	80		
Evens	55	50	20		

(ii)

Table 8.7 are obtained from part i of Table 8.6. The treatment combinations must be arranged in the order given in this table. (If a fourth factor were present, the order for the treatment combinations having this factor at level 1 would be *d, ad, bd, abd, cd, acd, bcd, abcd.*)

The entries in the total column are the cell totals obtained from part i of Table 8.6. The entries in the upper half of column 1 are the sums of successive pairs of the entries in the total column, i.e., $5 + 10 = 15$, $15 + 20 = 35$, $10 + 20 = 30$, and $15 + 5 = 20$. The entries in the lower half of column 1 are differences between successive pairs in the total column, i.e., $10 - 5 = 5$, $20 - 15 = 5$, $20 - 10 = 10$, and $5 - 15 = -10$.

The entries in the upper half of column 2 are the sums of successive pairs of entries in column 1, that is, $15 + 35 = 50$, $30 + 20 = 50$. The entries in the lower half of column 2 are the differences between successive pairs of entries in column 1, that is, $35 - 15 = 20$, $20 - 30 = -10$.

The entries in column 3 are obtained from the entries in column 2 by a procedure analogous to that by which the entries in column 2 were obtained from column 1. This procedure is continued until column k is reached, where k is the number of factors. In this example $k = 3$; hence the procedure is terminated at column 3. The entries in column 3 give the numerical values of the comparisons corresponding to the treatment effects to the left of each row. These values are identical to those obtained in part ii of Table 8.6.

Checks on the numerical work are given in part ii of Table 8.7. The respective sums for the upper and lower halves for each of the columns are obtained. One then obtains the sum of every other entry in each column, starting with the first entry, i.e., the sum of odd-numbered entries. One also obtains the sum of the even-numbered entries in each of the columns. These sums are shown in part ii. The sum of the upper half of column 1 is checked by the sum of the odds and evens under the total column; the sum of the lower half of column 1 is checked by the difference between the evens and odds in the total column. The sum of the upper half of column 2 is checked by the sum of the odds and the evens under column 1; the sum of the lower half of column 2 is checked by the difference between evens and odds for column 1. Analogous checks are made for column 3.

8.5 DESIGNS FOR 2^k EXPERIMENTS

In general, the number of ways in which components of interactions can be confounded is very large when all possibilities can be considered. Because of that, only selected cases can be considered in this chapter. Kirk (1982, Chapter 12) has provided a useful summary of references wherein a detailed discussion of various design alternatives has been presented.

Designs wherein each factor has only two levels, 2^k factorial experiments, represent the simplest cases for constructing designs with interactions confounded, but provide information which can be generalized to more complex designs.

The 2^2 Experiment

The simplest of all designs is the 2×2 factorial, wherein it has already been demonstrated that the four treatment conditions may be assigned to two groups of two treatments each, using the defining relation $x_1 + x_2 = 0, 1 \pmod 2$. Thus, the result is

Block 1	Block 2
(00)	(01)
(11)	(10)

One useful way to use this information would be to assign groups of subjects to the two blocks and have repeated measures on the two treatments within each block. Thus, the design is

Treatment Conditions (ab_{ij})

	Subject$_{1(1)}$	00	11
Group$_1$	Subject$_{2(1)}$	00	11
($x_1 + x_2 = 0$)	⋮	⋮	⋮
	Subject$_{n(1)}$	00	11
	Subject$_{1(2)}$	01	10
Group$_2$	Subject$_{2(2)}$	01	10
($x_1 + x_2 = 1$)	⋮	⋮	⋮
	Subject$_{n(1)}$	01	10

The advantage of this design over a design with repeated measures on all four treatment conditions is that the block size is reduced from four to two. The advantage over a design in which there are repeated measures on only one factor is that group effects are confounded with the $A \times B$ interaction, not the A or B main effects. Herein, both main effects are completely within-block effects, but the $A \times B$ interaction is totally confounded with the group main effects. With only a single degree of freedom, there is only one component of the $A \times B$ interaction, the AB component. The structural model for this design can be expressed as:

$$X_{ijkm} = \mu + \alpha_i + \beta_j + \pi_{m(k)} + (\alpha\beta_{ij} \text{ or } \gamma_k) + \alpha\beta\pi_{ijm(k)} + \varepsilon_{ijkm},$$

where α_i = the main effect of a_i. A is fixed, therefore $\sum_i \alpha_i = 0$.
β_j = the b_j main effect. B is fixed; $\sum_j \beta_j = 0$

$\pi_{m(k)}$ = the subject main effect, nested in group k. Subjects are random; $\pi_{m(k)} = N(0, \sigma_\pi^2)$.

$\alpha\beta_{ij}$ = the interaction of A and B. It is totally confounded with the group main effect γ_k.

3LE 8.8   Analysis of 2×2 factorial experiment in blocks of size 2

Source of variation		General df†	Specialized df	E(MS)
ween subjects		$nr - 1$	$2n - 1$	
roups (or AB)		$r - 1$	1	$\sigma_\varepsilon^2 + l\sigma_\pi^2 + nl\sigma_\gamma^2$
ooled subj. w. groups		$r(n - 1)$	$2(n - 1)$	$\sigma_\varepsilon^2 + l\sigma_\pi^2$
Subj. w. g_1	$n - 1$			
Subj. w. g_2	$n - 1$			
ain subjects		$nr(l - 1)$	$2n$	
		$p - 1$	1	$\sigma_\varepsilon^2 + \sigma_{\alpha\beta\pi}^2 + nr\sigma_\alpha^2$
		$q - 1$	1	$\sigma_\varepsilon^2 + \sigma_{\alpha\beta\pi}^2 + nr\sigma_\beta^2$
ooled $AB \times$ subj. w. groups		$r(n - 1)(l - 1)$	$2(n - 1)$	$\sigma_\varepsilon^2 + \sigma_{\alpha\beta\pi}^2$
$AB \times$ subj. w. g_1	$(n - 1)(l - 1)$			
$AB \times$ subj. w. g_2	$(n - 1)(l - 1)$			
l		$nrl - 1$	$4n - 1$	

number of treatments in a block; herein, $l = 2$.

number of groups; herein, $r = 2$.

γ_k = the group main effect totally confounded with the AB interaction. Groups are fixed. Hence, $\sum\limits_{k} \gamma = 0$.

$\alpha\beta\pi_{ijm(k)}$ = the interaction of A and B with subjects.

ε_{ijkm} = a random error component. It cannot be estimated directly.

An analysis of variance summary table is provided in Table 8.8, assuming there are n subjects in each group.

The computational procedures offer no new challenges. Since all factors are at two levels, the simplified procedures described in Sec. 8.4 may be used for computations. The variation of the confounded AB interaction is obtained when the group main effect is computed in the usual fashion.

It is apparent from the E(MS) that with these assumptions, the two main-effects tests on A and B utilize the within-block interaction with subjects as a denominator; the group main effect or AB interaction test utilizes the between-subject MS as its denominator. Since both of these involve pooling information from within the two groups, the only assumption is that the sources are homogeneous with regard to the two groups. Since with two treatments there is only one covariance, there are no other assumptions regarding the structure of the covariance matrices.

Designs for $2 \times 2 \times 2$ Factorial Experiments (in Blocks of Size 4)

A $2 \times 2 \times 2$ factorial experiment offers a number of design alternatives with regard to confounding interactions to reduce block size. Perhaps the most reasonable of those is based upon dividing the eight treatment conditions into two balanced sets of four treatments each in such a way that all main effects and two-factor interactions are balanced within each set. This can be accomplished by confounding on the basis of the three-factor interaction using the defining relation $x_1 + x_2 + x_3 = 0$ (mod 2) and $x_1 + x_2 + x_3 = 1$ (mod 2) for assigning treatments to blocks 1 and 2, respectively. Those sets are

$x_1 + x_2 + x_3 = 0$ (mod 2)	$x_1 + x_2 + x_3 = 1$ (mod 2)
Block 1	Block 2
(000)	(001)
(011)	(010)
(101)	(100)
(110)	(111)

An experiment designed around this allocation of treatments to blocks provides no within-block information regarding the three-factor interaction. The single component of the $A \times B \times C$ interaction, the ABC component with 1 degree of freedom, is identical to the between-block main effect. However, it is possible to replicate the experiment in such a way that within-block information is provided on the three-factor interaction as well as on all of the two-factor interactions. A minimum of eight blocks, four replications, is required to achieve the required balance, with confounding of the AB, AC, BC, or ABC interactions between pairs of blocks within each replication.

The plan shown in Table 8.9 provides within-Block information on the AB, AC, BC, and ABC interactions, the information for each being from three of the four replications. In the first replication, AB is confounded with differences between blocks 1 and 2. However, within-block information on AB is available from all other replications. The treatment combinations in block 1 satisfy the relation $x_1 + x_2 = 0$ (mod 2); the treatment combinations in block 2 satisfy the relation $x_1 + x_2 = 1$ (mod 2). Since within-block information on AB is available from six of the eight blocks, the relative within-block information on the AB interaction is $\frac{6}{8} = \frac{3}{4}$.

TABLE 8.9 **Balanced design with partial within-block information on all interactions**

Rep 1		Rep 2		Rep 3		Rep 4	
Block 1	Block 2	Block 3	Block 4	Block 5	Block 6	Block 7	Block 8
(000)	(010)	(000)	(001)	(000)	(001)	(000)	(001)
(001)	(011)	(010)	(011)	(011)	(010)	(011)	(010)
(110)	(100)	(101)	(100)	(100)	(101)	(101)	(100)
(111)	(101)	(111)	(110)	(111)	(110)	(110)	(111)
AB		AC		BC		ABC	

To show that block 3, for example, provides within-block information on *AB,* two of the four treatment combinations in this block satisfy the relation $x_1 + x_2 = 0$ and hence belong to what will be called the set J_0—that is, (000) and (111). The other two treatment combinations in block 3 belong to the set J_1, that is, they satisfy the relation $x_1 + x_2 = 1$. The difference between the totals for the J_0 set and the J_1 set provides information on the *AB* component, which is free of block effects. In addition to block 3, each of blocks 4 through 8 contains two treatment combinations belonging to set J_0 and two belonging to set J_1.

The *AC* interaction is completely confounded with the difference between blocks 3 and 4, but within-block information on *AC* is available from all other blocks. Hence, the relative within-block information on *AC* is $\frac{6}{8}$ or $\frac{3}{4}$. In block 3, the treatment combinations satisfy the relation $x_1 + x_3 = 0 \, (\text{mod } 2)$; in block 4 the treatment combinations satisfy the relation $x_1 + x_3 = 1 \, (\text{mod } 2)$.

The *BC* interaction is completely confounded with the difference between blocks 5 and 6, those treatments having been assigned by blocks by the relations $x_2 + x_3 = 0 \, (\text{mod } 2)$ and $x_2 + x_3 = 1 \, (\text{mod } 2)$, respectively. Like the other interactions, there is $\frac{3}{4}$ within-block information on the *BC* interaction from all blocks except 5 and 6.

Blocks 7 and 8 in Table 8.9 are identical to blocks 1 and 2 defined earlier in terms of the three-factor interactions. In the latter design, no within-block information is available on the *ABC* interaction; the design in Table 8.9 provides $\frac{3}{4}$ relative within-block information on *ABC*, such information being available from blocks 1 through 6.

One could view the design in Table 8.9 as providing five possible alternative ways to carry out a $2 \times 2 \times 2$ factorial experiment. Each replication offers a way to carry out the experiment in which there is no within-block information on one of the interactions, but there is information on all other interactions. For the researcher who has no interest in either a particular interaction or in a domain in which that particular interaction is known not to exist, one replication provides a reasonable design alternative. Where all interactions are of interest, the entire set of four replications may be incorporated into the design, providing a common amount of within-block information on all interactions. Regardless of which of the five design possibilities are pursued, the block size is only four. The total design in Table 8.9 is an example of a design with balanced partial confounding, meaning that all effects of the same order (in this case, two-factor interactions) were confounded with blocks an equal number of times. In the case of unbalanced partial confounding, that is not the case.

The analysis of the total design (4 reps) in Table 8.9 takes the form given in Table 8.10, based upon one observation per treatment condition ($m =$ number of replications = 4; $n =$ number of blocks = 2; $l =$ block size = 4).

In this analysis, the symbol $(AB)'$ indicates that only partial within-block information is available for *AB*. In the computation of $(AB)'$, only information from blocks 3 through 8 is used. The *AB* comparison given by the

TABLE 8.10 **Analysis of balanced design**

Source of variation	df	E(MS)	
Between blocks	$nm - 1 = 7$		
Replications	$m - 1 = 3$		
Blocks within reps	$m(n - 1) = 4$		
AB	1		
AC	1		
BC	1		
ABC	1		
Within Blocks	$nm(l - 1) = 24$		
A	$(p - 1) = 1$	$\sigma_\varepsilon^2 + 4m\sigma_\alpha^2$	$= \sigma_\varepsilon^2 + 16\sigma_\alpha^2$
B	$(q - 1) = 1$	$\sigma_\varepsilon^2 + 4m\sigma_\beta^2$	$= \sigma_\varepsilon^2 + 16\sigma_\beta^2$
C	$(r - 1) = 1$	$\sigma_\varepsilon^2 + 4m\sigma_\gamma^2$	$= \sigma_\varepsilon^2 + 16\sigma_\gamma^2$
$(AB)'$	$= 1$	$\sigma_\varepsilon^2 + 2m(\frac{3}{4})\sigma_{\alpha\beta}^2$	$= \sigma_\varepsilon^2 + (\frac{3}{4})8\sigma_{\alpha\beta}^2$
$(AC)'$	$= 1$	$\sigma_\varepsilon^2 + 2m(\frac{3}{4})\sigma_{\alpha\gamma}^2$	$= \sigma_\varepsilon^2 + (\frac{3}{4})8\sigma_{\alpha\gamma}^2$
$(BC)'$	$= 1$	$\sigma_\varepsilon^2 + 2m(\frac{3}{4})\sigma_{\beta\gamma}^2$	$= \sigma_\varepsilon^2 + (\frac{3}{4})8\sigma_{\beta\gamma}^2$
$(ABC)'$	$= 1$	$\sigma_\varepsilon^2 + 2m(\frac{3}{4})\sigma_{\alpha\beta\gamma}^2$	$= \sigma_\varepsilon^2 + (\frac{3}{4})4\sigma_{\alpha\beta\gamma}^2$
Residual	$= 17$	σ_ε^2	
Total	$(nml - 1) = 31$		

difference between block 1 and block 2 is confounded by differences between these blocks; this comparison represents one of the four degrees of freedom for blocks within replications. In computing $(AC)'$, only information from blocks 1, 2, and 5 through 8 is used. Similarly, $(ABC)'$ is based upon information from blocks 1 through 6. The difference between the total for block 7 and the total for block 8 gives rise to the between-block component of ABC.

Each of the main effects is determined from data obtained from all four replications; the within-block information on the interactions is based upon data obtained in each case from three of the four replications. Hence there are three *effective* replications for the interactions, but four *effective* replications for the main effects. The degrees of freedom for the within-block residual are made up of the following parts:

Residual	<u>17</u>
$A \times$ reps	3
$B \times$ reps	3
$C \times$ reps	3
$(AB)' \times$ reps	2
$(AC)' \times$ reps	2
$(BC)' \times$ reps	2
$(ABC)' \times$ reps	2

Since each interaction has only three effective replications, each interaction with replications has only two degrees of freedom.

The presentation in Table 8.10 is based upon a single observation per treatment condition. A reasonable way to use the design summarized in Table 8.9 would involve assigning groups of n subjects at random to one of the eight blocks and observing each subject under each of the four treatment conditions in the block to which that group is assigned. Thus, schematically, the design is (with repeated measures over 1 block of $l = 4$ treatments for subjects in each group):

Treatment conditions

Group	Subjects				
Group$_1$ $x_1 + x_2 = 0$	$S_{1(1)}$ $S_{2(1)}$ $\vdots$ $S_{n(1)}$	(000)	(001)	(110)	(111)
Group$_2$ $x_1 + x_2 = 1$	$S_{1(2)}$ $S_{2(2)}$ $\vdots$ $S_{n(2)}$	(010)	(011)	(100)	(101)
Group$_3$ $x_1 + x_3 = 0$	$S_{1(3)}$ $S_{2(3)}$ $\vdots$ $S_{n(3)}$	(000)	(010)	(101)	(111)
Group$_4$ $x_1 + x_3 = 1$	$S_{1(4)}$ $S_{2(4)}$ $\vdots$ $S_{n(4)}$	(001)	(011)	(100)	(110)
Group$_5$ $x_2 + x_3 = 0$	$S_{1(5)}$ $S_{2(5)}$ $\vdots$ $S_{n(5)}$	(000)	(011)	(100)	(111)
Group$_6$ $x_2 + x_3 = 1$	$S_{1(6)}$ $S_{2(6)}$ $\vdots$ $S_{n(6)}$	(001)	(010)	(101)	(110)
Group$_7$ $x_1 + x_2 + x_3 = 0$	$S_{1(7)}$ $S_{2(7)}$ $\vdots$ $S_{n(7)}$	(000)	(011)	(101)	(110)
Group$_8$ $x_1 + x_2 + x_3 = 1$	$S_{1(8)}$ $S_{2(8)}$ $\vdots$ $S_{n(8)}$	(001)	(010)	(100)	(111)

TABLE 8.11   **Analysis of balanced design with repeated measures**

Source of variation	df	E(MS)
Between subjects	$8n - 1$	
Groups	7	
Reps	3	
AB	1	$\sigma_\varepsilon^2 + 4\sigma_{\text{people}}^2 + 2n\sigma_{\alpha\beta}^2$
AC	1	$\sigma_\varepsilon^2 + 4\sigma_{\text{people}}^2 + 2n\sigma_{\alpha\gamma}^2$
BC	1	$\sigma_\varepsilon^2 + 4\sigma_{\text{people}}^2 + 2n\sigma_{\beta\gamma}^2$
ABC	1	$\sigma_\varepsilon^2 + 4\sigma_{\text{people}}^2 + n\sigma_{\alpha\beta\gamma}^2$
Subjects within groups	$8(n-1)$	$\sigma_\varepsilon^2 + 4\sigma_{\text{people}}^2$
Within subjects	$24n$	
A	1	$\sigma_\varepsilon^2 + 16n\sigma_\alpha^2$
B	1	$\sigma_\varepsilon^2 + 16n\sigma_\beta^2$
C	1	$\sigma_\varepsilon^2 + 16n\sigma_\gamma^2$
$(AB)'$	1	$\sigma_\varepsilon^2 + (\frac{3}{4})8n\sigma_{\alpha\beta}^2$
$(AC)'$	1	$\sigma_\varepsilon^2 + (\frac{3}{4})8n\sigma_{\alpha\gamma}^2$
$(BC)'$	1	$\sigma_\varepsilon^2 + (\frac{3}{4})8n\sigma_{\beta\gamma}^2$
$(ABC)'$	1	$\sigma_\varepsilon^2 + (\frac{3}{4})4n\sigma_{\alpha\beta\gamma}^2$
Residual	$24n - 7$	σ_ε^2

Assume the order of presentation of the four treatments is independently randomized for each subject. Assume further that all interactions with subjects are zero. Under these assumptions the analysis takes the form given in Table 8.11. In this analysis the individual subject is considered the experimental unit. Tests on main effects and interactions use the residual mean square in the denominator of the F ratio. There is usually no interest in a test on differences between blocks or the components of such differences. In some cases, between-block estimates of the interactions may be combined with the corresponding within-block estimates. Such pooled estimates are given by a weighted sum of the between-subject and within-subject components, the weights being the respective reciprocals of the between- and within-person residuals. F tests on such combined estimates require a weighted pooling of the respective residuals.

The cell totals for the design in Table 8.9 may be designated by the following notation:

	b_0		b_1	
	c_0	c_1	c_0	c_1
a_0	$X_{000.}$	$X_{001.}$	$X_{010.}$	$X_{011.}$
a_1	$X_{100.}$	$X_{101.}$	$X_{110.}$	$X_{111.}$

Each of these totals will be based upon four observations. Since all the treatment combinations do not appear in all the blocks, means based upon these totals will not be free of block effects. If, for example, the cell total for treatment combination (101) were free of block effects, it would estimate

$$X_{101.} = 4\mu + 4\alpha_1 + 4\beta_0 + 4\gamma_1 + 4(\alpha\beta)_{10} + 4(\alpha\gamma)_{11}$$

$$+ 4(\beta\gamma)_{01} + 4(\alpha\beta\gamma)_{101}$$

$$+ \text{(sum of all block effects)}.$$

In this last expression, the sum of all block effects would be a constant (under the assumptions made); hence differences between any two X's would be free of block effects. It is readily verified that the following quantity will estimate the sum of the parameters on the right-hand side of the last expression:

$$X'_{101} = \frac{A_1 + B_0 + C_1}{4} + \frac{(AB)'_1 + (AC)'_0 + (BC)'_1 + (ABC)'_0}{3} - \frac{3G}{4},$$

where $(AB)'_1 = $ total of all treatment combinations which satisfy the relation $x_1 + x_2 = 1 \pmod{2}$ and appear in blocks 3 through 8; similarly $(AC)'_0 = $ total of all treatment combinations which satisfy the relation $x_1 + x_3 = 0 \pmod{2}$ and appear in blocks 1, 2, 4 through 8. The quantity $X'_{101.}$ is called an adjusted cell total. The adjusted cell mean for treatment combination (101) is

$$\bar{X}'_{101} = \frac{X'_{101.}}{4}.$$

For the general case, an adjusted cell total for the design in Table 8.9 has the form

$$X'_{ijk.} = \frac{A_i + B_j + C_k}{4} + \frac{(AB)'_{i+j} + (AC)'_{i+k} + (BC)'_{j+k}}{3}$$

$$+ \frac{(ABC)'_{i+j+k}}{3} - \frac{3G}{4},$$

where $(AB)'_{i+j} = $ sum of all treatment combinations which satisfy the relation $x_1 + x_2 = (i + j)\pmod{2}$ and which appear in blocks providing within-block information on AB. Similarly $(ABC)'_{i+j+k} = $ sum of all treatment combinations which satisfy the relation $x_1 + x_2 + x_3 = (i + j + k)\pmod{2}$ and which appear in blocks providing within-block information on ABC.

Adjusted totals having the form $X'_{ij..}$ are obtained from the relation

$$X'_{ij..} = X'_{ij0.} + X'_{ij1.}.$$

Similarly
$$X'_{i.k.} = X'_{i0k.} + X'_{i1k.}.$$

Individual comparisons among the treatment combinations use the adjusted cell totals. The effective number of observations in the adjusted cell total $X'_{ijk.}$ is actually somewhat less than four since there is only $\frac{3}{4}$ relative within-block information on the interaction effects. For most practical purposes a comparison between two adjusted cell totals is given by

$$F = \frac{(X'_{ijk.} - X'_{pqr.})^2}{8 \, \mathrm{MS}_{\mathrm{res}}}.$$

$$F = \frac{(X'_{ij..} - X'_{pq..})^2}{16 \, \mathrm{MS}_{\mathrm{res}}}.$$

The squared standard error of a difference between two adjusted cell means which takes into account the effective number of replications is readily obtained. For the design given in Table 8.9 consider the difference

$$\overline{ABC}'_{011} - \overline{ABC}'_{111} = [\bar{A}_0 - \bar{A}_1] + [\overline{(AB)}'_1 - \overline{(AB)}'_0] + [\overline{(AC)}'_1 - \overline{(AC)}'_0]$$
$$+ [\overline{(ABC)}'_0 - \overline{(ABC)}'_1].$$

Since there is complete information on each $\bar{A}_i$, there are 16 basic observations contributing to this mean. Since there is only $\frac{3}{4}$ information on each of the interactions, there are only 12 basic observations contributing to each of the other means on the right. Hence, the squared standard errors of the terms in brackets are, respectively,

$$\frac{2\,\mathrm{MS}_{\mathrm{res}}}{16}, \quad \frac{2\,\mathrm{MS}_{\mathrm{res}}}{12}, \quad \frac{2\,\mathrm{MS}_{\mathrm{res}}}{12}, \quad \frac{2\,\mathrm{MS}_{\mathrm{res}}}{12}.$$

Since the terms in brackets on the right are distributed independently, the squared standard error of the difference between the adjusted cell means is given by

$$\hat{\sigma}^2_{(\overline{ABC}'_{011} - \overline{ABC}'_{111})} = \frac{2\,\mathrm{MS}_{\mathrm{res}}}{16} + \frac{3(2\,\mathrm{MS}_{\mathrm{res}})}{12} = \frac{5\,\mathrm{MS}_{\mathrm{res}}}{8}.$$

If there were no confounding,

$$\hat{\sigma}^2_{(\overline{ABC}'_{011} - \overline{ABC}'_{111})} = \frac{8\,\mathrm{MS}_{\mathrm{res}}}{16} = \frac{\mathrm{MS}_{\mathrm{res}}}{2}.$$

The *relative* effective number of replications on the comparison in question is given by

$$\frac{\frac{1}{2}\,\mathrm{MS}_{\mathrm{res}}}{\frac{5}{8}\,\mathrm{MS}_{\mathrm{res}}} = \frac{4}{5}.$$

NUMERICAL EXAMPLE OF $2 \times 2 \times 2$ **FACTORIAL EXPERIMENT IN BLOCKS OF SIZE 4.** The purpose of this hypothetical experiment was to evaluate the effects of various treatment combinations upon the progress of mental patients in specified diagnostic categories. The treatments and their levels are given in Table 8.12. It was desired to have 10 patients in each cell of a factorial experiment, necessitating a total of 80 patients for the experiment. However, no more than 20 patients meeting specifications were available from a single

TABLE 8.12   **Definition of factors**

Factor	Level	Definition
Drug A	a_0	No drug A
	a_1	Drug A administered
Drug B	b_0	No drug B
	b_1	Drug B administered
Psychotherapy	c_0	No psychotherapy
	c_1	Psychotherapy administered

hospital, but four hospitals were available for the study. It was anticipated that there would be large differences among hospitals. In order to prevent such differences from confounding main effects and two-factor interactions, the design in Table 8.13 was used.

In the construction of this design, the relation $x_1 + x_2 + x_3 = r \pmod 2$ was used to divide the eight treatment combinations into blocks of size 4. Hospitals were assigned at random to blocks. Hospitals 1 and 2 make up one replication; hospitals 3 and 4 make up the second replication. Within each replication, the ABC interaction is completely confounded with between-hospital differences. From each hospital, 20 patients meeting the specifications were selected and assigned at random to subgroups of five patients each. The subgroups were then assigned at random to one of the treatment conditions allocated to the hospital to which the subgroup belonged.

Each patient was rated by a panel of judges both before and after the treatment combinations were administered. The difference between these two ratings was taken as the criterion of progress. Since some of the treatments were administered to the subgroups as a unit, the subgroup of five patients was considered to be the experimental unit, rather than the individual patient. The mean criterion score for each subgroup is given in Table 8.13 to the right of the

TABLE 8.13   **Design and data for numerical example**

Rep 1		Rep 2	
Hospital 1	**Hospital 2**	**Hospital 3**	**Hospital 4**
(100) 6	(000) 2	(100) 14	(000) 3
(010) 10	(110) 4	(010) 15	(110) 6
(001) 6	(101) 15	(001) 9	(101) 25
(111) 8	(011) 18	(111) 12	(011) 22
30	39	50	56

$$\Sigma \Sigma X^2 = 2605$$

TABLE 8.14   **Summary of numerical analysis**

		b_0		b_1		
		c_0	c_1	c_0	c_1	Total
(i)	a_0	5	15	25	40	85
	a_1	20	40	10	20	90
		25	55	35	60	175

	Treatment combinations	Total	(1)	(2)	(3)	
	(1)	5	25	60	175	G
	a	20	35	115	5	$A = A_1 - A_0$
	b	25	55	0	15	$B = B_1 - B_0$
	ab	10	60	5	-75	AB
(ii)						
	c	15	15	10	55	$C = C_1 = C_0$
	ac	40	-15	5	5	AC
	bc	40	25	-30	-5	BC
	abc	20	-20	-45	-15	ABC

(iii)

$$SS_a = (5)^2/16 \quad\ = \ 1.57 \qquad SS_{ac} = (5)^2/16 \ \ \ \ = \ 1.57$$
$$SS_b = (15)^2/16 \ \ = \ 14.06 \qquad SS_{bc} = (-5)^2/16 \ = \ 1.57$$
$$SS_c = (55)^2/16 \ \ = 189.06 \qquad SS_{abc} = (-15)^2/16 = 14.06$$
$$SS_{ab} = (-75)^2/16 \ = 351.57$$
$$SS_{\text{hospitals}} = (30^2 + 39^2 + 50^2 + 56^2)/4 - (175)^2/16 = 100.19$$
$$SS_{\text{total}} = 2605 - (175)^2/16 \qquad\qquad\qquad = 690.94$$

corresponding symbol for the treatment combination. Each of these means is considered a single observation for purposes of the analysis of variance.

Summary tables and details of the computations are given in Table 8.14. Cell totals for the treatment combinations appear in part i; these totals are obtained by combining the data from the two replications. Each of these cell totals is the sum of two observations. The numerical values for individual comparisons corresponding to the main effects and the interactions are computed in part ii. Here the entries in the upper half of column 1 are obtained from the total column by summing successive pairs of values in the total column; the entries in the lower half of column 1 are obtained by taking the difference between successive pairs of values in the total column. Column 2 is obtained from column 1 by an analogous procedure, and similarly column 3 is obtained from column 2. The entries in column 3 are the values of the comparisons. The corresponding sums of squares are given in part iii. The sum of squares for the main effect of factor A has the general definition

$$SS_a = \frac{C_a^2}{2^k r},$$

where C_a = comparison corresponding to main effect of factor A,
k = number of factors,
r = number of replications.

In this case C_a is the entry in column 3 in row a, which is 5. For this case $r = 2$, and $k = 3$; hence

$$SS_a = \frac{(5)^2}{2^k(2)} = \frac{25}{16} = 1.57.$$

The analysis of variance for these data is given in Table 8.15. The within-hospital sum of squares is obtained by subtracting the between-hospital sum of squares from the total sum of squares. The within-hospital residual is obtained from the relation

$$SS_{res(w)} = SS_{w. \text{ hospital}} - (\text{sum of main effects and two-factor interactions})$$
$$= 590.75 - 559.40 = 31.35.$$

Although the ABC interaction is completely confounded with between-hospital differences within a single replication, by including information from the two replications the ABC component may be estimated.

The within-hospital residual mean square is used as the denominator for all tests on within-hospital effects. The F tests show no significant interactions involving factor C (psychotherapy), but a significant main effect. It may be concluded from this information that the effect of psychotherapy is independent of the effect of the drugs; further, the groups given psychotherapy showed significantly greater improvement than did groups which were not given psychotherapy.

The interaction between the drugs is seen to be highly significant. The following summary data obtained from part i of Table 8.14 are useful in the

TABLE 8.15   **Analysis of variance**

Source	SS	df	MS	F
Between hospitals	100.19	3		
Replications	85.56	1		
Residual (b)	14.63	2		
Within hospitals	590.75	12		
A Drug A	1.57	1	1.57	—
B Drug B	14.06	1	14.06	2.69
C Psychotherapy	189.06	1	189.06	36.22**
AB	351.57	1	351.57	67.35**
AC	1.57	1	1.57	—
BC	1.57	1	1.57	—
Residual (w)	31.35	6	5.22	

$$**F_{0.99}(1, 6) = 13.74$$

interpretation of this interaction:

	b_0	b_1
a_0	20	65
a_1	60	30

These data indicate that the use of both drugs simultaneously is not better than the use of either drug alone. The test on the comparison between the levels of drug B in the absence of drug A is given by

$$F = \frac{(AB_{00} - AB_{01})^2}{2nr\mathrm{MS}_{\mathrm{res}(w)}} = \frac{(20 - 65)^2}{2(4)(5.22)} = 48.49.$$

If this comparison is considered to belong in the *a priori* category, the critical value for a 0.05-level test is $F_{0.95}(1, 6) = 5.99$. If this comparison is considered to belong in the *a posteriori* category, the critical value for a 0.05-level test is, as given by Scheffé, $3F_{0.95}(3, 6) = 3(4.76) = 14.28$. (In the present context this test would belong in the *a priori* category.) In either instance, it may be concluded that drug B has a significant effect upon progress in the absence of drug A.

A test on the effect of drug A in the absence of drug B is given by

$$F = \frac{(20 - 60)^2}{2(4)(5.22)} = 38.31.$$

Clearly, drug A has a significant effect upon progress in the absence of drug B. To compare the relative effectiveness of the two drugs when each is used in the absence of the other,

$$F = \frac{(60 - 65)^2}{2(4)(5.22)} = 0.60.$$

Thus, the data indicate that drug A and drug B are equally effective.

The denominator of the three preceding F tests has the general form $nr(\sum c^2)(\mathrm{MS}_{\mathrm{error}})$; nr is the number of experimental units summed to obtain the total in the comparison, $\sum c^2$ is the sum of the squares of the coefficients in the comparison, and $\mathrm{MS}_{\mathrm{error}}$ is the appropriate error term for the comparison.

In Table 8.15 the within-hospital residual sum of squares was obtained by subtraction. This term is actually the pooled interaction of treatment effects (with the exception of ABC) with the hospitals receiving the same set of treatment combinations. Direct computation of the residual sum of squares is illustrated in Table 8.16. Since hospitals 1 and 3 had the same set of treatment conditions, the data at the left in part i provide three of the six degrees of freedom of the residual term. If the four treatment combinations common to hospitals 1 and 3 are considered as four levels of a single factor, then the interaction of the levels of this factor with the hospital factor (defined by hospitals 1 and 3) is part of the sum of squares for residuals. This interaction is

TABLE 8.16   **Computation of the components of the residual (w)**

	Treat	Hosp. 1	Hosp. 3	Total	Treat	Hosp. 2	Hosp. 4	Total
	a	6	14	20	(1)	2	3	5
	b	10	15	25	ab	4	6	10
(i)	c	6	9	15	ac	15	25	40
	abc	8	12	20	bc	18	22	40
		30	50	80		39	56	95

(ii)	Treat × hosp. interaction $= (6^2 \times 10^2 + \cdots + 9^2 + 12^2)$ $- (20^2 + \cdots + 20^2)/2 - (30^2 + 50^2)/4$ $+ 80^2/8 = 7.00$	Treat × hosp. interaction $= (2^2 \times 4^2 + \cdots + 25^2 + 22^2)$ $- (5^2 + \cdots + 40^2)/2 - (39^2 + 56^2)/4$ $+ 95^2/8 = 24.37$

(iii) $\qquad\qquad\qquad\qquad\qquad SS_{res} = 7.00 + 24.37 = 31.37$

computed at the left in part ii. An analogous interaction term is obtained from the data at the right in part i.

NUMERICAL EXAMPLE OF $2 \times 2 \times 2$ **FACTORIAL EXPERIMENT IN BLOCKS OF SIZE 4 (REPEATED MEASURES).** The purpose of this experiment was to evaluate the preferences for advertisements made up by varying the size (factor A), the style of type (factor B), and the color (factor C). The definitions of the levels of these three factors are given in Table 8.17.

The experimenter desired to have within-subject estimates on all main effects and interactions; however, the task of having each subject judge all eight combinations was not considered experimentally feasible. Loss of interest on the part of the subjects and excessive time demands (as indicated by a pilot study) ruled against the procedure of having each subject judge all combinations. The experimenter was willing to sacrifice precision with respect to the three-factor interaction in order to keep the number of judgments an individual had to make down to four. The plan outlined in Table 8.18 was chosen for use.

TABLE 8.17   **Definition of factors**

Factor	Level	Definition
Size (A)	a_0	Small
	a_1	Large
Style (B)	b_0	Gothic
	b_1	Roman
Color (C)	c_0	Green
	c_1	Blue

TABLE 8.18   Outline of plan and basic data

		Group I						Group II			
Person	**(100)**	**(010)**	**(001)**	**(111)**	**Total**	**Person**	**(000)**	**(110)**	**(101)**	**(011)**	**Total**
1	16	8	2	8	34	4	10	12	8	3	33
2	10	4	3	7	24	5	11	16	10	5	42
3	9	3	0	5	17	6	4	7	7	2	20
Total	35	15	5	20	75	Total	25	35	25	10	95

(i) marks the upper block.

	Treat comb.: Cell totals:	(100) 35	(010) 15	(001) 5	(111) 20	(000) 25	(110) 35	(101) 25	(011) 10	Comparison
G		+	+	+	+	+	+	+	+	170
A		+	−	−	+	−	+	+	−	60
B		−	+	−	+	−	+	−	+	−10
C		−	−	+	+	−	−	+	+	−50
AB		−	−	+	+	+	+	−	−	0
AC		−	+	−	+	+	−	+	−	0
BC		+	−	−	+	+	−	−	+	10
ABC		+	+	+	+	−	−	−	−	−20

(ii) marks the middle block.

(iii):

$$SS_a = (60)^2/24 = 150.00 \qquad\qquad SS_{ab} = 0 \qquad SS_{bc} = (10)^2/24$$

$$SS_b = (-10)^2/24 = 4.17 \qquad\qquad SS_{ac} = 0 \qquad\qquad = 4.17$$

$$SS_c = (-50)^2/24 = 104.17 \qquad SS_{abc} = (-20)^2/24 = 16.67$$

$$SS_{subj} = (34^2 + 24^2 + 17^2 + 33^2 + 42^2 + 20^2)/4 - (170)^2/24 = 114.33$$

$$SS_{total} = (16^2 + 8^2 + \cdots + 7^2 + 2^2) - (170)^2/24 = 409.83$$

In order to keep this illustrative example simple, it will be assumed that a sample of six subjects was used in the experiment. (In practice, this sample size would be too small.) The subjects were divided at random into two groups. Individuals within each group judged only four of the eight different make-ups. The combinations of factors judged by group I satisfied the relation $x_1 + x_2 + x_3 = 1 \pmod 2$, and the combinations judged by group II satisfied the relation $x_1 + x_2 + x_3 = 0 \pmod 2$. In this design the ABC comparison is completely confounded with differences between groups; within-subject estimates are available on all other factorial effects.

The order in which a subject judged a particular combination was randomized independently for each subject. Order could, however, have been controlled by means of a Latin square. (Plan 7 in Sec. 9.7 utilizes the Latin-square principle with what is essentially the design given in Table 8.8. The number of subjects per group would have to be a multiple of 4 in order to use the Latin square.)

The comparisons corresponding to the main effects and interactions of the factors are obtained at the right in part ii of Table 8.18. The method by which the ABC comparison is obtained shows clearly that this comparison is

TABLE 8.19 **Summary of analysis**

Source of variation	SS	df	MS	F
Between subjects	114.33	5		
ABC (groups)	16.67	1	16.67	
Subjects within groups	97.67	4	24.42	
Within subjects	295.50	18		
A Size	150.00	1	150.00	54.54**
B Type style	4.17	1	4.17	1.51
C Color	104.17	1	104.17	37.88**
AB	0	1	0	
AC	0	1	0	
BC	4.17	1	4.17	1.51
Residual	32.99	12	2.75	

$$**F_{0.99}(1, 12) = 9.33$$

completely confounded with differences between the two groups. The sums of squares corresponding to the factorial effects, between-subject variation, and total variation are computed in part iii. The overall analysis of variance is summarized in Table 8.19.

The sum of squares due to the within-subject variation is obtained from the relation

$$SS_{\text{w. subj}} = SS_{\text{total}} - SS_{\text{b. subj}}$$
$$= 409.83 - 114.33 = 295.50.$$

The residual sum of squares is given by

$$SS_{\text{res}} = SS_{\text{w. subj}} - (\text{sum of main effects and 2-factor interactions})$$
$$= 295.50 - 262.51 = 32.99.$$

Assuming that factors *A*, *B*, and *C* are fixed, the residual term is the proper denominator for all within-subject effects. The proper denominator for between-subject effects is the mean square for subjects within groups. In this design the *ABC* interaction is a between-subject effect—but this interaction is completely confounded with differences among groups. Generally there would be little interest in testing the *ABC* interaction. (In this case the *F* ratio would be less than 1.)

For the within-subject data in Table 8.19, none of the interactions is statistically significant. This result implies that the main effects (if any) operate independently; i.e., the main effects are additive. The tests made in Table 8.19 indicate that the size and color main effects are statistically significant. Inspection of the summary data in Table 8.18 indicates that large size (a_1) is preferred no matter which of the styles or colors is used. Similarly, green (c_0) is preferred over blue no matter which size or style of type is used. There is no statistically significant difference between the two styles of type used in the experiment; there is however, a slight preference for the Gothic (b_0). If one were to make an overall recommendation with respect to the most preferred make-up of the advertising copy, the large size in the green color would be the best combination.

Returning to structural considerations underlying the analysis of the design, the residual term in the analysis consists of the following pooled interactions:

Subject × treatments (within group I)	6
Subject × treatments (within group II)	6
Residual	12

The residual terms in Table 8.19 may be computed directly from the interaction terms given above. The four treatment combinations assigned to the subjects within group I are considered to be four levels of a single factor; the subject by treatment interaction is computed by the usual computational formulas for a two-factor interaction.

The analysis of the general case of a $2 \times 2 \times 2$ factorial experiment in blocks of size 4 with repeated measures is outlined in Table 8.20. In this analysis there are n subjects in each group, and the experiment is replicated r times. The analysis of the design in Table 8.18 is a special case of the more general design in Table 8.20. In the special case $n = 3$, and $r = 1$. In a design having more than one replication, the ABC interaction may be tested by using the subjects within groups in the denominator of an F ratio. This test will generally be considerably less sensitive than tests on the main effects and two-factor interactions.

TABLE 8.20   Analysis of general case of design in Table 8.18

Source of variation		df
Between subjects		$2nr - 1$
Replications		$r - 1$
Groups within replications		r
ABC	1	
Residual (groups)	$r - 1$	
Subjects within groups		$2r(n - 1)$
Within subjects		$6nr$
A		1
B		1
C		1
AB		1
AC		1
BC		1
Residual (within subject)		$6(nr - 1)$

8.6 DESIGNS FOR 3^k EXPERIMENTS

In all 2^k designs, each interaction has only a single degree of freedom and, therefore, only a single component which may be confounded. With 3^k experiments, interactions have more components providing a wider variety of options for confounding.

Designs for 3×3 Factorial Experiments

A 3×3 factorial design has only a single $A \times B$ interaction to provide the basis for confounding. However, that interaction has four degrees of freedom and may, therefore, be partitioned into two components, each with two degrees of freedom. Accordingly, the nine treatment combinations in this experiment may be partitioned into three sets in such a way that differences between sets form one of the components of the $A \times B$ interaction. The design outlined in Table 8.21 gives two such partitions. In replication 1, the AB (or J) component is used to define the sets (blocks); in replication 2, the AB^2 (or I) component is used to define the sets (blocks).

The treatment combinations in block 1 satisfy the relation $x_1 + x_2 = 0 \,(\mathrm{mod}\,3)$; the treatment combinations in blocks 2 and 3 satisfy the respective relations $x_1 + x_2 = 1 \,(\mathrm{mod}\,3)$ and $x_1 + x_2 = 2 \,(\mathrm{mod}\,3)$. Hence differences between blocks within replication 1 are completely confounded with the AB (or J) component of $A \times B$. That is, a difference between two block totals in replication 1 is simultaneously an estimate of block differences as well as differences which form part of the AB component. (A formal proof of this is given later in this section.)

In replication 2, each of the blocks contains treatment combinations which satisfy the relation $x_1 + 2x_2 = i \,(\mathrm{mod}\,3)$. For example, the treatment combinations in block 6 all satisfy the relation $x_1 + 2x_2 = 2 \,(\mathrm{mod}\,3)$. Hence, differences between blocks within replication 2 are completely confounded with the AB^2 (or I) component of $A \times B$.

The design in Table 8.21 may be considered useful for carrying out an experiment in any one of three ways. Each of the two replications could be an

TABLE 8.21 3×3 **factorial experiment in blocks of size 3**

	Replication 1			Replication 2		
	Block 1	Block 2	Block 3	Block 4	Block 5	Block 6
	(00)	(01)	(02)	(00)	(02)	(01)
	(12)	(10)	(20)	(11)	(10)	(12)
	(21)	(22)	(11)	(22)	(21)	(20)
Component confounded		AB (or J)			AB^2 (or I)	

TABLE 8.22   **Analysis of design in Table 8.21**

Source	df		E(MS)
Between blocks	5		
Replications	1		
AB (from rep 1)	2		
AB^2 (from rep 2)	2		
Within blocks	12		
A	2		$\sigma_\varepsilon^2 + 6\sigma_\alpha^2$
B	2		$\sigma_\varepsilon^2 + 6\sigma_\beta^2$
$A \times B$	4		
AB (from rep 2)		2	$\sigma_\varepsilon^2 + (\frac{1}{2})(2)\sigma_{\alpha\beta_J}^2$
AB^2 (from rep 1)		2	$\sigma_\varepsilon^2 + (\frac{1}{2})(2)\sigma_{\alpha\beta_I}^2$
Residual	4		σ_ε^2
$A \times$ rep		2	
$B \times$ rep		2	

experiment wherein the researcher simply loses within-block information about one of the components of the $A \times B$ interaction. Alternatively, an experiment might involve both replications and over the two replications an equal amount of information is provided regarding both components of the $A \times B$ interaction.

Assuming one observation per cell, the analysis takes the form given in Table 8.22. Within-block information on the main effects is available from both replications. Within-block information on the AB (or J) component is available only from replication 2; within-block information on the AB^2 (or I) component is available only from replication 1. Since within-block information on the components of $A \times B$ is available from only one of the two replications, the relative within-block information on $A \times B$ is said to be $\frac{1}{2}$. For main effects, however, the relative within-block information is $\frac{2}{2} = 1$, since both replications provide within-block information on the main effects. The design in Table 8.21 is balanced in the sense that the same amount of relative within-block information is provided on each of the components of $A \times B$.

The denominator of F ratios for within-block effects is the pooled interaction of the main effects with the replications. The two components of the $A \times B$ interaction are generally combined, and the combined interaction (with four degrees of freedom) is tested as a unit. If, however, the individual components are meaningful in terms of the experimental variables, separate tests on the components may be made. In most cases the components of $A \times B$ that are confounded with block effects are not tested. There are, however, techniques for combining the between-block information on the interaction with the within-block information to obtain an overall estimate of the interaction. Such techniques are said to recover the between-block information on the interaction effects. These techniques will not be considered in this section.

The block in this design may be an individual subject—in this case each subject is observed under all treatment combinations assigned to a given block. The block may be a group of three subjects—in this case each subject is observed under one of the three treatment combinations assigned to the block. The block may be a group of n subjects—in this case the n subjects may be observed under all treatment combinations within a given block. The analysis of this design takes the form given in Table 8.23.

The expected values of the mean squares have the same general form as those given in Table 8.22. The residual again provides an estimate of the within-block experimental error. The $12n - 8$ degrees of freedom for the residual is the pooled interaction of the main effects with the replications and the interaction of the main effects with the subjects within groups. The breakdown of these degrees of freedom is as follows:

Residual	$12n - 8$
$A \times$ rep	2
$B \times$ rep	2
Treat $\times$ subj w. group	$12n - 12$

A formal algebraic proof will now be outlined to demonstrate that the AB component in the design in Table 8.21 is confounded with block effects within replication 1 but is free of such confounding within replication 2. This proof assumes that an observation under treatment combination ab_{ij} in block k provides an estimate (disregarding the experimental error) of the sum of the parameters on the right-hand side of the following expression,

$$X_{ijk} \doteq \mu + \alpha_i + \beta_j + (\alpha\beta)_{ij} + \pi_k,$$

TABLE 8.23   **Analysis of 3×3 factorial experiment in blocks of size 3 (repeated measurements)**

Source	df
Between subjects	$6n - 1$
Groups	5
Replications	1
AB (from rep 1)	2
AB^2 (from rep 2)	2
Subjects within groups	$6(n - 1)$
Within subjects	$12n$
A	2
B	2
AB (from rep 2)	2
AB^2 (from rep 1)	2
Residual	$12n - 8$

where the symbol π_k designates the effect of block k. Assuming that factors A and B are fixed, $\sum \alpha_i = 0$, $\sum \beta_j = 0$, $\sum_i (\alpha\beta)_{ij} = 0$, and $\sum_j (\alpha\beta)_{ij} = 0$. These restrictions on the above model follow directly from the basic definition of treatment effects. Interactions with block effects do not appear on the right-hand side of the model; hence the implicit assumption that such effects either do not exist or that such effects are negligible relative to the magnitude of the other effects.

The set of treatment combinations which satisfy the relation $x_1 + x_2 = i$ define the set J_i. It will be convenient to define the sum of the interaction effects in the set J_0 by the symbol $3(\alpha\beta)_{j_0}$. Thus

$$3(\alpha\beta)_{J_0} = (\alpha\beta)_{00} + (\alpha\beta)_{12} + (\alpha\beta)_{21}.$$

Similarly, by definition,

$$3(\alpha\beta)_{J_1} = (\alpha\beta)_{01} + (\alpha\beta)_{10} + (\alpha\beta)_{22},$$
$$3(\alpha\beta)_{J_2} = (\alpha\beta)_{02} + (\alpha\beta)_{11} + (\alpha\beta)_{20}.$$

In terms of the basic model and the specialized definitions, for observations on treatment combinations in the set J_0 in replication 1 of the design in Table 8.21,

$$
\begin{aligned}
X_{00} &\doteq \mu + \alpha_0 + \beta_0 + (\alpha\beta)_{00} + \pi_1 \\
X_{12} &\doteq \mu + \alpha_1 + \beta_2 + (\alpha\beta)_{12} + \pi_1 \\
X_{21} &\doteq \mu + \alpha_2 + \beta_1 + (\alpha\beta)_{21} + \pi_1 \\
\hline
J_{0.} &\doteq 3\mu + 3(\alpha\beta)_{J_0} + 3\pi_1
\end{aligned}
$$

The symbol $J_{0.}$ is used to designate the sum of all observations on treatment combinations in the set J_0. Similarly

$$J_{1.} \doteq 3\mu + 3(\alpha\beta)_{J_1} + 3\pi_2,$$
$$J_{2.} \doteq 3\mu + 3(\alpha\beta)_{J_2} + 3\pi_3.$$

The sum of squares for the AB component of $A \times B$ is obtained from differences between these J totals. For example,

$$J_{0.} - J_{1.} \doteq 3(\alpha\beta)_{J_0} - 3(\alpha\beta)_{J_1} + 3\pi_1 - 3\pi_2.$$

Each of the other possible comparisons among the J's also includes block effects. Hence, from the data in replication 1, SS_{AB} is completely confounded with differences among blocks.

In contrast, for replication 2,

$$
\begin{aligned}
X_{00} &\doteq \mu + \alpha_0 + \beta_0 + (\alpha\beta)_{00} + \pi_4 \\
X_{12} &\doteq \mu + \alpha_1 + \beta_2 + (\alpha\beta)_{12} + \pi_6 \\
X_{21} &\doteq \mu + \alpha_2 + \beta_1 + (\alpha\beta)_{21} + \pi_5 \\
\hline
J_{0.} &\doteq 3\mu + 3(\alpha\beta)_{J_0} + \pi_4 + \pi_5 + \pi_6.
\end{aligned}
$$

Similarly, for replication 2,

$$J_{1.} \doteq 3\mu + 3(\alpha\beta)_{J_1} + \pi_4 + \pi_5 + \pi_6,$$
$$J_{2.} \doteq 3\mu + 3(\alpha\beta)_{J_2} + \pi_4 + \pi_5 + \pi_6.$$

Differences between J totals in replication 2 are free of block effects. For example,

$$J_{0.} - J_{1.} \doteq 3(\alpha\beta)_{J_0} - 3(\alpha\beta)_{J_1}.$$

Hence, within-block information on the AB components of $A \times B$ may be obtained from replication 2.

To show that replication 1 provides within-block information on the AB^2 (or I) component of $A \times B$,

$$
\begin{aligned}
X_{00} &\doteq \mu + \alpha_0 + \beta_0 + (\alpha\beta)_{00} + \pi_1 \\
X_{11} &\doteq \mu + \alpha_1 + \beta_1 + (\alpha\beta)_{11} + \pi_3 \\
X_{22} &\doteq \mu + \alpha_2 + \beta_2 + (\alpha\beta)_{22} + \pi_2 \\
\hline
I_{0.} &\doteq 3\mu + 3(\alpha\beta)_{I_0} + \pi_1 + \pi_2 + \pi_3.
\end{aligned}
$$

Similarly, for replication 1,

$$I_{1.} \doteq 3\mu + 3(\alpha\beta)_{I_1} + \pi_1 + \pi_2 + \pi_3,$$
$$I_{2.} \doteq 3\mu + 3(\alpha\beta)_{I_2} + \pi_1 + \pi_2 + \pi_3.$$

Since each I total contains the same block effects, differences between these totals will be free of block effects. Hence, information on the I component of $A \times B$ obtained from replication 1 will not be confounded with block effects.

For the general case of a design having r replications (one observation per cell) of the design in Table 8.21, with $r/2$ replications of the form of replication 1 and $r/2$ of the form of replication 2, the sum of squares for the J component of $A \times B$ is

$$SS'_{AB(J)} = \frac{\sum J_{i.}^2}{3(r/2)} - \frac{(\sum J_{i.})^2}{9(r/2)},$$

where J totals are restricted to the replications in which the J component of $A \times B$ is free of block effects. Similarly, the sum of squares for the I components of $A \times B$ is given by

$$SS'_{AB(I)} = \frac{\sum I_{i.}^2}{3(r/2)} - \frac{(\sum I_{i.})^2}{9(r/2)},$$

where the I totals are restricted to replications in which the I component of $A \times B$ is free of block effects.

If the symbol AB_{ij} represents the sum of all observations on treatment combination ab_{ij}, then this sum will not be free of block effects, since all treatment combinations do not appear in each of the blocks. An adjusted sum which is free of block effects is given by

$$AB'_{ij} = \frac{A_i + B_j}{3} + \frac{J_{(i+j).} + I_{(i+2j).}}{\frac{3}{2}} - \frac{G}{3},$$

where A_i = sum of all observations at level a_i,

$\quad\ \ B_j$ = sum of all observations at level b_j,

$\quad J_{(i+j).}$ = sum of all observations on treatment combinations which satisfy the relation $x_1 + x_2 = i + j \pmod 3$ in replications in which differences between J's are free of block effects,

$I_{(i+2j).}$ = sum of all observations on treatment combinations which satisfy the relation $x_1 + 2x_2 = i + 2j \pmod 3$ in replications in which differences between I's are free of block effects.

For example, the adjusted total for all observations made under treatment combination ab_{02} is

$$AB'_{02} = \frac{A_0 + B_2}{3} + \frac{J_{2.} + I_{1.}}{\frac{3}{2}} - \frac{G}{3}.$$

In terms of the general linear model, this last expression estimates the parameters on the right-hand side of the following expression:

$$AB'_{02} \doteq r\mu + r\alpha_0 + r\beta_2 + r(\alpha\beta)_{J_2} + r(\alpha\beta)_{I_1}$$
$$+ \frac{\text{sum of all block effects}}{3}.$$

Since all adjusted totals will contain this last term, differences between the adjusted totals will be free of block effects. To demonstrate that AB'_{02} actually does estimate the parameters on the right-hand side,

$$\frac{A_0}{3} \doteq r\mu + r\alpha_0 + \tfrac{1}{3}(\text{sum of all block effects})$$

$$\frac{B_2}{3} \doteq r\mu + r\beta_2 + \tfrac{1}{3}(\text{sum of all block effects})$$

$$\frac{J_{2.}}{\frac{3}{2}} \doteq r\mu + r(\alpha\beta)_{J_2} + \tfrac{2}{3}(\text{sum of blocks in which } J \text{ is free of block effects})$$

$$\frac{I_{1.}}{\frac{3}{2}} \doteq r\mu + r(\alpha\beta)_{I_1} + \tfrac{2}{3}(\text{sum of blocks in which } I \text{ is free of block effects})$$

$$\frac{-G}{3} \doteq -3r\mu - (\text{sum of all block effects})$$

$$\rule{11cm}{0.4pt}$$

$$AB'_{02} \doteq r\mu + r\alpha_0 + r\beta_2 + r(\alpha\beta)_{J_2} + r(\alpha\beta)_{I_1} + \frac{\text{sum of all block effects}}{3}.$$

In general it can be shown that

$$(\bar{J}_{(i+j).} - \bar{G}) + (\bar{I}_{(i+2j).} - \bar{G}) = \widehat{\alpha\beta}_{ij}$$

or

$$(\widehat{\alpha\beta})_{J_{i+j}} + (\widehat{\alpha\beta})_{I_{i+2j}} = \widehat{\alpha\beta}_{ij}.$$

For example, if $i = 0$ and $j = 2$,

$$3\bar{J}_{2.} = \overline{AB}_{02} + \overline{AB}_{11} + \overline{AB}_{20}$$
$$3\bar{I}_{1.} = \overline{AB}_{02} + \overline{AB}_{10} + \overline{AB}_{21}$$
$$0 = \overline{AB}_{02} + \overline{AB}_{12} + \overline{AB}_{22} - (\overline{AB}_{02} + \overline{AB}_{12} + \overline{AB}_{22})$$

$$3(\bar{J}_{2.} + \bar{I}_{1.}) = 3\overline{AB}_{02} + 3\bar{A}_1 + 3\bar{A}_2 - 3\bar{B}_2$$
$$= 3\overline{AB}_{02} + 3\bar{G} - 3\bar{A}_0 - 3\bar{B}_2.$$

Hence

$$(\bar{J}_{2.} - \bar{G}) + (\bar{I}_{1.} + \bar{G}) = \overline{AB}_{02} + \bar{A}_0 - \bar{B}_2 + \bar{G}$$
$$= \widehat{\alpha\beta}_{02}.$$

Similarly, if $i = 1$ and $j = 1$, then

$$(\bar{J}_{2.} - \bar{G}) + (\bar{I}_{0.} - \bar{G}) = \overline{AB}_{11} - \bar{A}_1 - \bar{B}_1 + \bar{G}$$
$$= \widehat{\alpha\beta}_{11}.$$

In making comparisons among the means of treatment combinations, one uses the adjusted totals to obtain the means. The effective number of observations in each of these adjusted means is less than r, since information on the I and J components of the $A \times B$ interaction is obtained from only one-half of the replications. The number of *effective* replications in the adjusted total is given by

$$\frac{1 + 1 + 1 + 1 + 1}{1 + 1 + (1/\frac{1}{2}) + (1/\frac{1}{2}) + 1} r = \tfrac{5}{7}r.$$

The terms in the numerator of this expression represent the relative information in each of the totals entering into AB'_{ij}, assuming there was no confounding. The terms in the denominator are the reciprocals of the relative information in each of the totals actually given by the design.

For most practical purposes, however, the adjusted cell means may be handled as if they were based upon r replications. The adjusted mean for cell ab_{ij} is

$$\overline{AB'_{ij}} = \frac{AB'_{ij}}{r}.$$

If this design had r replications with n observations per cell, AB'_{ij} would have the definition given above but

$$\overline{AB'_{ij}} = \frac{AB'_{ij}}{nr}.$$

If there were no confounding in a design having r replications,

$$\sigma_{AB}^2 = \frac{\sigma_\varepsilon^2}{r}.$$

For the design given in Table 8.21, in which one has only $\frac{1}{2}$ information on the interaction,

$$\sigma_{AB'}^2 = \frac{\sigma_\varepsilon^2}{(\frac{5}{7})r} = \frac{7\sigma_\varepsilon^2}{5r} = \frac{\sigma_\varepsilon^2}{r_{\text{effective}}}.$$

When the effective number of replications is close to the actual number of replications, the latter is often used in place of $r_{\text{effective}}$ in the denominator.

NUMERICAL EXAMPLE OF 3×3 **FACTORIAL EXPERIMENT IN BLOCKS OF SIZE 3.** In the experiment to be described the object was to obtain within-subject information on all factorial effects in a 3×3 factorial experiment. However, it was not experimentally feasible to observe each subject under each of the nine treatment combinations. Each person could be observed under three treatment combinations. The design outlined in Table 8.24 was selected for use.

The experimenter wished to have two observations under each treatment combination. A random sample of 12 subjects was obtained from a specified population and was divided at random into six groups of 2 subjects each. The groups were then assigned at random to the blocks in Table 8.24. The 2 subjects within each group were observed under each of the three treatment combinations in the assigned block. The order in which a subject was observed under a treatment condition was randomized for each subject. The data obtained from this experiment are summarized in Table 8.24.

In the row having person 1 at the left, the entries 14, 7, and 15 are the respective observations (with order randomized) on person 1 under treatment combinations (00), (12), and (21). The sum of these three observations on person 1 is denoted by the symbol P_1. The symbols G_i denote the totals for the six observations made within a group (block). The symbols R_j denote the totals of the 18 observations made within a single replication. Additional data required for the computation of the sums of squares in the analysis are given in Table 8.25.

The sums of squares for all effects except the $A \times B$ interaction are computed in the same manner as that used in any factorial experiment having repeated measures. Data required for computation of all effects except the components of $A \times B$ are summarized in parts ii and iii of Table 8.25. From the data in part iii, the between-subject sum of squares is given by

$$\frac{\sum P^2}{3} - \frac{G^2}{36} = 3815.33 - 3025.00 = 790.33.$$

TABLE 8.24 Summary of observed data

Block	Person				Total	
		(00)	(12)	(21)		
1	1	14	7	15	$36 = P_1$	
	2	6	3	5	$14 = P_2$	$50 = G_1$
		(01)	(10)	(22)		
2	3	3	4	10	$17 = P_3$	
	4	7	6	30	$43 = P_4$	$60 = G_2$
		(02)	(11)	(20)		
3	5	5	15	7	$27 = P_5$	
	6	5	5	3	$13 = P_6$	$40 = G_3$
						$150 = R_1$
		(00)	(11)	(22)		
4	7	10	10	15	$35 = P_7$	
	8	15	20	25	$60 = P_8$	$95 = G_4$
		(02)	(10)	(21)		
5	9	3	5	12	$20 = P_9$	
	10	7	10	18	$35 = P_{10}$	$55 = G_5$
		(01)	(12)	(20)		
6	11	6	7	5	$18 = P_{11}$	
	12	4	3	5	$12 = P_{12}$	$30 = G_6$
						$180 = R_2$

TABLE 8.25 Summary data required for analysis

(i)

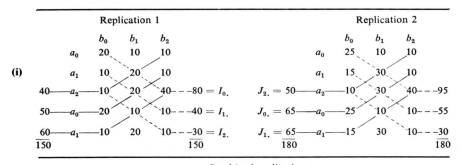

Replication 1

	b_0	b_1	b_2	
a_0	20	10	10	
a_1	10	20	10	
40 —— a_2 —10	20	40 - -80 $= I_0.$		
50 —— a_0 —20	10	10 - -40 $= I_1.$		
60 —— a_1 —10	20	10 - -30 $= I_2.$		
150		150		

Replication 2

	b_0	b_1	b_2	
a_0	25	10	10	
a_1	15	30	10	
$J_2. = 50$ —— a_2 —10	30	40 - -95		
$J_0. = 65$ —— a_0 25	10	10 - -55		
$J_1. = 65$ —— a_1 —15	30	10 - -30		
180		180		

Combined replications

(ii)

	b_0	b_1	b_2	Total
a_0	45	20	20	$85 = A_0$
a_1	25	50	20	$95 = A_1$
a_2	20	50	80	$150 = A_2$
Total	90	120	120	$330 = G$
	B_0	B_1	B_2	

(iii)

$$G^2/9nr = 3025.00$$
$$\Sigma\Sigma X^2 = 4494$$
$$(\Sigma A^2)/3nr = 3229.17$$
$$(\Sigma B^2)/3nr = 3075.00$$

$$(\Sigma P^2)/3 = 3815.33$$
$$(\Sigma G_i^2)/3n = 3441.67$$
$$(\Sigma R^2)/9n = 3050.00$$

The within-subject sum of squares is given by

$$\sum \sum X^2 - \frac{\sum P^2}{3} = 4494 - 3815.33 = 678.67.$$

Data required for the sums of squares for groups, replications, and the main effects of factors A and B are also given in part iii.

From the data in part i, both the between- and within-subject components of the $A \times B$ interaction may be computed. From the totals at the right of replication 1, the within-subject information on the I component of $A \times B$ is given by

$$SS_{AB(I)} = SS_{AB^2} = \frac{\sum I_{i.}^2}{3n} - \frac{(\sum I_{i.})^2}{9n}$$

$$= \frac{80^2 + 40^2 + 30^2}{3(2)} - \frac{(150)^2}{18} = 233.33.$$

From the totals at the left of replication 2, the within-subject information on the J component of $A \times B$ is given by

$$SS_{AB(J)} = SS_{AB} = \frac{\sum J_{i.}^2}{3n} - \frac{(\sum J_{i.})^2}{9n}$$

$$= \frac{50^2 + 65^2 + 65^2}{6} - \frac{(180)^2}{18} = 25.00.$$

Thus within-subject information on the components of the $A \times B$ interaction is obtained separately from each of the replications—one component from replication 1, the other from replication 2.

The between-subject information on the J component of $A \times B$ is obtained from the totals at the left of replication 1.

$$SS_{AB(J)} = SS_{AB} = \frac{40^2 + 50^2 + 60^2}{6} - \frac{(150)^2}{18} = 33.33.$$

The between-subject information on the I component of $A \times B$ is obtained from the totals to the right of replication 2.

$$SS_{AB(I)} = SS_{AB^2} = \frac{95^2 + 55^2 + 30^2}{6} - \frac{(180)^2}{18} = 358.33.$$

The residual sum of squares in Table 8.26 is obtained from the relation

$$SS_{res} = SS_{w. \, subj} - SS_a - SS_b - SS_{AB}(within) - SS_{AB^2}(within).$$

The residual sum of squares may also be computed directly from the interactions of factor A and B with the replications and subjects within groups.

Unless there is an *a priori* reason for handling the components of the $A \times B$ interaction separately, a single test is made on the combined within-subject components of this interaction. (In cases in which the large cell values in a two-way summary table fall along the diagonal running from upper left to lower right, the AB^2 component will be large relative to the AB component.) In this numerical example the $A \times B$ interaction is statistically significant. The simple effects for both factor A and factor B are between-subject effects;

TABLE 8.26 **Summary of analysis**

Source	SS	SS	df	MS	F
Between subjects		790.33	11		
Groups (blocks)		416.67	5		
Replications	25.00		1		
AB (from rep 1)	33.33		2		
AB^2 (from rep 2)	358.33		2		
Subjects within groups		373.66	6	62.28	
Within subjects		678.67	24		
A		204.17	2	102.08	9.82**
B		50.00	2	25.00	2.41
$A \times B$ (adjusted)		258.33	4	64.58	6.22**
AB (from rep 2)	25.00		2		
AB^2 (from rep 1)	233.33		2		
Residual		166.17	16	10.39	

$$**F_{0.99}(2, 16) = 6.23; \quad F_{0.99}(4, 16) = 4.77$$

however, approximations to tests on simple effects may be obtained by working with the adjusted cell totals. Differences among the latter totals may be considered to be within-subject effects.

To illustrate the computation of the adjusted cell totals, for treatment combination ab_{02},

$$AB'_{02} = \frac{A_0 + B_2}{3} + \frac{I_{1.} + J_{2.}}{\frac{3}{2}} - \frac{G}{3}$$

$$= \frac{85 + 120}{3} + \frac{40 + 50}{\frac{3}{2}} - \frac{330}{3} = 18.33.$$

(Note that in part i of Table 8.25 cell ab_{02} contributes to the $I_{1.}$ total in replication 1 and to the $J_{2.}$ total in replication 2.) The unadjusted cell total is 20. As another example, the adjusted total for cell ab_{11} has the form

$$AB'_{11} = \frac{A_1 + B_1}{3} + \frac{I_{0.} + J_{2.}}{\frac{3}{2}} - \frac{G}{3}.$$

Comparisons among the adjusted cell totals use the within-subject residual mean square as an error term. For approximate tests, the number of effective observations in each cell is considered to be $nr = 4$.

To illustrate the procedures for tests on adjusted cell totals,

$$F = \frac{(AB'_{02} - AB'_{22})^2}{2nr \, \text{MS}_{\text{res}}}.$$

The adjusted total AB'_{02} was found to be 18.33. The adjusted total AB'_{22} is given by

$$AB'_{22} = \frac{A_2 + B_2}{3} + \frac{I_{0.} + J_{1.}}{\frac{3}{2}} - \frac{G}{3}.$$

(Note that ab_{22} contributes to the $I_{0.}$ total in replication 1 and to the $J_{1.}$ total in replication 2.)

$$AB'_{22} = \frac{150 + 120}{3} + \frac{80 + 65}{\frac{3}{2}} - \frac{330}{3}$$

$$= 76.57.$$

Thus
$$F = \frac{(18.33 - 76.67)^2}{2(2)(2)(10.39)} = 40.95.$$

The critical value for a 0.05-level (*a priori*) test is $F_{0.95}(1, 16) = 4.49$.

Designs for $3 \times 3 \times 3$ Factorial Experiments

The 27 treatment conditions of a $3 \times 3 \times 3$ factorial experiment may be divided into sets in numerous ways and balance will still be maintained with respect to main effects and two-factor interactions. One may achieve balance with blocks of size 9, or if it is required that block sizes be even smaller, with block sizes of 3 treatment combinations using double confounding (to be introduced later in this section).

In a $3 \times 3 \times 3$ design, the $A \times B \times C$ interaction with eight degrees of freedom may be partitioned into four unique components, each with two degrees of freedom:

	df
$A \times B \times C$	8
ABC	2
ABC^2	2
AB^2C	2
AB^2C^2	2

Any one of those components may be used to define three balanced sets of nine treatments each. For example, the sets formed by using the ABC component are as follows:

$x_1 + x_2 + x_3 = 0 \pmod 3$	$x_1 + x_2 + x_3 = 1 \pmod 3$
(000)	(001)
(012)	(010)
(021)	(022)
(102)	(100)
(111)	(112)
(120)	(121)
(201)	(202)
(210)	(211)
(222)	(220)

$$x_1 + x_2 + x_3 = 2 \pmod 3$$

(002)
(011)
(020)
(101)
(110)
(122)
(200)
(212)
(221)

A design consisting of these three blocks would provide within-block information on all effects except the ABC component of the three-factor interaction. With only a single replication (assuming only one observation per cell) no estimate of experimental error is available.

If the experiment were to be replicated by using the same block structure as that given above, the design would lack balance with respect to the components of the three-factor interaction. That is, within-block information would be available on three of the four components of this interaction, but no within-block information would be available on the ABC component. A design which has balance with respect to the components of the three-factor interaction may be constructed by means of the scheme outlined in Table 8.27. A minimum of four replications is required for balance. The blocks within each of the replications are constructed by means of relations associated with a component of the three-factor interaction; each of the replications involves a different component. Hence, within-block information on all the three-factor components is available from some three of the four replications.

The structure of the blocks defined by the design in Table 8.27 is given in Table 8.28. Blocks in replication 1 are balanced with respect to all main effects and all two-factor interactions. These blocks are also balanced with respect to all components of the three-factor interaction except the ABC component. To illustrate the balance with respect to the ABC^2 component within block 1, the nine treatment combinations in this block may be divided into the following sets:

$(ABC^2)_0$	$(ABC^2)_1$	$(ABC^2)_2$
(000)	(021)	(012)
(120)	(111)	(102)
(210)	(201)	(222)

TABLE 8.27 **Construction of blocks of size 9**

Replication	Block	Component confounded	Defining relation (mod 3)
1	1	$(ABC)_0$	$x_1 + x_2 + x_3 = 0$
	2	$(ABC)_1$	$x_1 + x_2 + x_3 = 1$
	3	$(ABC)_2$	$x_1 + x_2 + x_3 = 2$
2	4	$(ABC^2)_0$	$x_1 + x_2 + 2x_3 = 0$
	5	$(ABC^2)_1$	$x_1 + x_2 + 2x_3 = 1$
	6	$(ABC^2)_2$	$x_1 + x_2 + 2x_3 = 2$
3	7	$(AB^2C)_0$	$x_1 + 2x_2 + x_3 = 0$
	8	$(AB^2C)_1$	$x_1 + 2x_2 + x_3 = 1$
	9	$(AB^2C)_2$	$x_1 + 2x_2 + x_3 = 2$
4	10	$(AB^2C^2)_0$	$x_1 + 2x_2 + 2x_3 = 0$
	11	$(AB^2C^2)_1$	$x_1 + 2x_2 + 2x_3 = 1$
	12	$(AB^2C^2)_2$	$x_1 + 2x_2 + 2x_3 = 2$

TABLE 8.28   **Design corresponding to Table 8.27**

Replication 1			Replication 2		
Block 1	**Block 2**	**Block 3**	**Block 4**	**Block 5**	**Block 6**
(000)	(001)	(002)	(000)	(002)	(001)
(012)	(010)	(011)	(011)	(010)	(012)
(021)	(022)	(020)	(022)	(021)	(020)
(102)	(100)	(101)	(101)	(100)	(102)
(111)	(112)	(110)	(112)	(111)	(110)
(120)	(121)	(122)	(120)	(122)	(121)
(201)	(202)	(200)	(202)	(201)	(200)
(210)	(211)	(212)	(210)	(212)	(211)
(222)	(220)	(221)	(221)	(220)	(222)
	ABC			ABC^2	

Replication 3			Replication 4		
Block 7	**Block 8**	**Block 9**	**Block 10**	**Block 11**	**Block 12**
(000)	(001)	(002)	(000)	(002)	(001)
(011)	(012)	(010)	(012)	(011)	(010)
(022)	(020)	(021)	(021)	(020)	(022)
(102)	(100)	(101)	(101)	(100)	(102)
(110)	(111)	(112)	(110)	(112)	(111)
(121)	(122)	(120)	(122)	(121)	(120)
(201)	(202)	(200)	(202)	(201)	(200)
(212)	(210)	(211)	(211)	(210)	(212)
(220)	(221)	(222)	(220)	(222)	(221)
	AB^2C			AB^2C^2	

Differences between the totals for these sets form part of the ABC^2 component.

Assuming one observation per cell, the analysis of this design has the form given in Table 8.29. The computation of the sums of squares for main effects and two-factor interactions follows the same rules as those of the replicated factorial experiment. In computing the within-block components of $A \times B \times C$, data from replications in which a component is confounded with block effects are not used. For example, to compute the within-block component of ABC^2, data from all replications except replication 2 are combined to form a three-way summary table. From this summary table one obtains the totals $(ABC^2)'_0$, $(ABC^2)'_1$, and $(ABC^2)'_2$, where $(ABC^2)'_i$ represents the sum of observations in all cells which satisfy the relation $x_1 + x_2 + 2x_3 = i \pmod 3$. Then

$$\text{SS}'_{ABC^2} = \frac{\sum (ABC^2)'^2_i}{27} - \frac{[\sum (ABC^2)'_i]^2}{81}.$$

TABLE 8.29   **Analysis of design having block size 9 (one observation per cell)**

Source of variation	df	E(MS)
Between blocks	$\overline{11}$	
Replications	$\overline{3}$	
Blocks within reps	8	
ABC (from rep 1)	2	
ABC^2 (from rep 2)	2	
AB^2C (from rep 3)	2	
AB^2C^2 (from rep 4)	2	
Within blocks	$\overline{96}$	
A	$\overline{2}$	$\sigma_\varepsilon^2 + 36\sigma_\alpha^2$
B	2	$\sigma_\varepsilon^2 + 36\sigma_\beta^2$
C	2	$\sigma_\varepsilon^2 + 36\sigma_\gamma^2$
$A \times B$	4	$\sigma_\varepsilon^2 + 12\sigma_{\alpha\beta}^2$
$A \times C$	4	$\sigma_\varepsilon^2 + 12\sigma_{\alpha\gamma}^2$
$B \times C$	4	$\sigma_\varepsilon^2 + 12\sigma_{\beta\gamma}^2$
$(A \times B \times C)'$ $(\frac{3}{4})$	8	$\sigma_\varepsilon^2 + (\frac{3}{4})(4)\sigma_{\alpha\beta\gamma}^2$
ABC (omit rep 1)	2	
ABC^2 (omit rep 2)	2	
AB^2C (omit rep 3)	2	
AB^2C^2 (omit rep 4)	2	
Residual	70	σ_ε^2
Main effects × reps	18	
2-factor int × reps	36	
3-factor int × reps	16	

As a partial check on the numerical work, $\sum (ABC^2)'_i$ is equal to the sum of all observations in replications 1, 3, and 4.

The within-cell residual is most conveniently obtained by subtracting the within-cell treatment effects from the total within-cell variation. The sources of variation which are pooled to form the residual term are shown in Table 8.29. These sources may be computed separately. In this design there are only three effective replications on each of the components of the three-factor interaction; thus the $ABC \times$ replications interaction, for example, has four degrees of freedom. Hence the three-factor × replications interaction has a total of 16 degrees of freedom—4 degrees of freedom for each of the four components of the three-factor interaction.

In making tests on differences between adjusted cell means, adjusted cell totals are required. Such totals are given by

$$9ABC'_{ijk} = A_i + B_j + C_k + (AB)_{i+j} + (AC)_{i+k} + (BC)_{j+k} + (AB^2)_{i+2j}$$
$$+ (AC^2)_{i+2k} + (BC^2)_{j+2k} + \tfrac{4}{3}[(ABC)'_{i+j+k} + (ABC^2)'_{i+j+2k}$$
$$+ (AB^2C)'_{i+2j+k} + (AB^2C^2)'_{i+2j+2k}] - 4G,$$

where the symbol $(ABC)'_{i+j+k}$ represents a total obtained from those replications in which this part of the three-factor interaction is not confounded with block totals. For example,

$$9ABC'_{012} = A_0 + B_1 + C_2 + (AB)_1 + (AC)_2 + (BC)_0 + (AB^2)_2$$
$$+ (AC^2)_1 + (BC^2)_2 + \tfrac{4}{3}[(ABC)'_0 + (ABC^2)'_2 + (AB^2C)'_1$$
$$+ (AB^2C^2)'_0] - 4G,$$

$$9ABC'_{001} = A_0 + B_0 + C_1 + (AB)_0 + (AC)_1 + (BC)_1 + (AB^2)_0$$
$$+ (AC^2)_2 + (BC^2)_2 + \tfrac{4}{3}[(ABC)'_1 + (ABC^2)'_2$$
$$+ (AB^2C)'_1 + (AB^2C^2)'_2] - 4G.$$

The difference between the means corresponding to these adjusted totals is given by

$$\overline{ABC}'_{012} - \overline{ABC}'_{001} = (\bar{B}_1 - \bar{B}_0) + (\bar{C}_2 - \bar{C}_1) + [\overline{(AB)}_1 - \overline{(AB)}_0]$$
$$+ [\overline{(AC)}_2 - \overline{(AC)}_1] + [\overline{(BC)}_0 - \overline{(BC)}_1]$$
$$+ [\overline{(AB^2)}_2 - \overline{(AB^2)}_0] + [\overline{(AC^2)}_1 - \overline{(AC^2)}_2]$$
$$= \tfrac{4}{3}[\overline{(ABC)}'_0 - \overline{(ABC)}'_1] + \tfrac{4}{3}[\overline{(AB^2C^2)}'_0 - \overline{(AB^2C^2)}'_2].$$

The effective information in this difference relative to a design in which there is no confounding is given by

$$\frac{9}{7 + 2(4/3)} = \frac{27}{29}.$$

Since the two-factor interactions in the design given in Table 8.28 are not confounded with block effects, no adjustments are required for cell totals in two-way summary tables. Differences between means computed from such totals will be free of block effects.

BLOCK SIZE = 3. In dividing the 27 treatment combinations into blocks of size 9, a relation of the general form

$$u = x_1 + u_2 x_2 + u_3 x_3 = i \; (\text{mod } 3)$$

was used for each of the replications. The relation u corresponded to some component of the three-factor interaction. In the analysis of the resulting design, the u component was confounded with block effects within the replication having blocks defined by the u relation. The 27 treatment combinations in a $3 \times 3 \times 3$ factorial experiment may be divided into blocks of size 3 by requiring that the treatment combinations within a given block simultaneously satisfy the two relations

$$u = i \; (\text{mod } 3),$$
$$v = j \; (\text{mod } 3),$$

where v is some relation other than u.

In the analysis of a replication having blocks formed in this way, the components corresponding to u and v will both be confounded with differences between blocks. In addition the components corresponding to the relations $u + v$ and $u + 2v$ will also be confounded with block effects. The latter components are known as the *generalized interactions*, or *aliases*, of the components corresponding to u and v. To illustrate, suppose that the blocks within a replication are defined by the relations

$$u = x_1 + x_2 + 2x_3 = i \pmod 3,$$
$$v = x_1 + 2x_2 \quad = j \pmod 3.$$

These relations correspond, respectively, to the ABC^2 and the AB^2 components. One of the generalized interactions, or aliases, is given by

$$u + v = 2x_1 + 3x_2 + 2x_3 = (i + j) \pmod 3$$
$$= 2x_1 + 2x_3 = (i + j) \pmod 3$$
$$= x_1 + x_3 = 2(i + j) \pmod 3.$$

(The last line is obtained from the one above by multiplying both sides of the equation by 2 and then reducing coefficients to the modulus 3.) This last relation corresponds to the AC component. The second generalized interaction of u and v is given by

$$u + 2v = 3x_1 + 5x_2 + 2x_3 = (i + 2j) \pmod 3$$
$$= 2x_2 + 2x_3 = (i + 2j) \pmod 3$$
$$= x_2 + x_3 = 2(i + 2j) \pmod 3.$$

This last relation corresponds to the BC component.

To summarize this illustrative example, blocks are defined by relations corresponding to the ABC^2 and AB^2 components. The generalized interactions, or aliases, of these components are the AC and BC components. Hence, in a replication defined by these relations, the analysis would have the following form:

Between blocks	8
AB^2	2
AC	2
BC	2
ABC^2	2
Within blocks	18
A, B, C	2 each
AB, AC^2, BC^2	2 each
ABC, AB^2C, AB^2C^2	2 each

The defining relations in this example may be symbolized by $(ABC^2)_i$ and $(AB^2)_j$; the aliases may be symbolized by $(AC)_{2(i+j)}$ and $(BC)_{2(i+2j)}$. The block defined by $(ABC^2)_0$ and $(AB^2)_1$ is

$$(022), \qquad (101), \qquad (210).$$

It may be verified that each of the treatment combinations in the blocks also satisfies the relations $(AC)_{2(0+1)} = (AC)_2$ and $(BC)_{2(0+2)} = (BC)_1$.

In general, if two relations are used simultaneously to define blocks, one needs to know the generalized interactions of the components corresponding to these relations in order to carry out the analysis. There is a relatively simple rule for determining the aliases of any two components. Given two components having the general form W and X, their aliases will have the general forms WX and WX^2. To illustrate the use of this rule, given

$$W = ABC^2 \quad \text{and} \quad X = AB^2,$$

one alias has the form

$$WX = (ABC^2)(AB^2) = A^2B^3C^2 = A^2C^2 = AC,$$

upon reduction of the exponents to the modulus 3. The second alias has the form

$$WX^2 = (ABC^2)(AB^2)^2 = (ABC^2)(A^2B^4) = A^3B^5C^2 = B^2C^2 = BC.$$

It is immaterial which of the components is designated W and which is designated X, since the aliases are also given by the general forms W^2X and WX. As another example, the aliases of the components AB and AC are

$$WX = (AB)(AC) = A^2BC = AB^2C^2,$$
$$WX^2 = (AB)(AC)^2 = A^3BC^2 = BC^2.$$

To construct a design having within-block information on all components of the interactions, yet providing complete information on all main effects, the scheme presented in Table 8.30 may be used. The aliases associated with the pairs of defining relations are indicated. The design represented by this scheme will provide some within-block information with respect to all interaction components. For example, the AB^2 component is confounded with block effects in replications 1 and 2 but is free of block effects in replications 3 and 4. Hence, the relative within-block information on this component is $\frac{1}{2}$. The AC^2 component is confounded in replications 1 and 3 but is not confounded in blocks 2 and 4. It will be found that all the components of two-factor

TABLE 8.30 **Construction of blocks of size 3**

Replication	Defining relations	Aliases
1	ABC, AB^2	AC^2, BC^2
2	ABC^2, AB^2	AB, BC
3	AB^2C, AB	AC^2, BC
4	AB^2C^2, AB	AC, BC^2

interactions are confounded with blocks in two of the four replications but are free of such confounding in two of the four replications. Each of the components of the three-factor interaction is confounded with block effects in one of the replications but is free of block effects in three of the four replications. Hence, the relative information on the components of the three-factor interaction is $\frac{3}{4}$.

The blocks corresponding to the design outlined in Table 8.30 are obtained by subdividing the blocks in Table 8.28. Block 1 in the latter table is subdivided as follows:

$(AB^2)_0$	$(AB^2)_1$	$(AB^2)_2$
(000)	(021)	(012)
(111)	(102)	(120)
(222)	(210)	(201)

Each of the treatment combinations within a block satisfies the relation $(ABC)_0$ as well as the relation heading the block. Block 2 in Table 8.28 is subdivided as follows:

$(AB^2)_0$	$(AB^2)_1$	$(AB^2)_2$
(001)	(022)	(010)
(112)	(100)	(121)
(220)	(211)	(202)

Block 3 in Table 8.28 is subdivided as follows:

$(AB^2)_0$	$(AB^2)_1$	$(AB^2)_2$
(002)	(020)	(011)
(110)	(101)	(122)
(221)	(212)	(200)

The nine blocks of size 3 that have just been constructed form replication 1 of the design in Table 8.30.

The overall analysis of the design takes the form given in Table 8.31.

TABLE 8.31   **Analysis of design in Table 8.30**

Source of variation	df	
Between blocks	35	
Replications	3	
Blocks within reps	32	
Within blocks	72	
Main effects: A, B, C	6	(2 each)
Two-factor interaction:		
AB, AB^2 ($\frac{1}{2}$ information)	4	(2 each)
AC, AC^2 ($\frac{1}{2}$ information)	4	(2 each)
BC, BC^2 ($\frac{1}{2}$ information)	4	(2 each)
Three-factor interaction:		
$ABC, ABC^2, AB^2C, AB^2C^2$ ($\frac{3}{4}$ information)	8	(2 each)
Residual	46	

Within-block information on the main effects is complete; hence no special computational procedures are required.

In computing the AB component, only information from blocks in which this component is not confounded is used. Blocks of this kind are in replications 1 and 2; the blocks in replications 3 and 4 do not provide within-block information on AB. All within-block information on AB^2 is obtained from replications 3 and 4. Hence, the sum of squares for AB^2 is computed from a summary table prepared from replications 3 and 4. Given this summary table,

$$SS'_{AB^2} = \frac{(AB^2)_0'^2 + (AB^2)_1'^2 + (AB^2)_2'^2}{18} - \frac{[\sum (AB^2)_i']^2}{54},$$

where $(AB^2)_i'$ is the sum of observations on all treatment combinations in replications 3 and 4 which satisfy the relation $x_1 + 2x_2 = i \pmod 3$. As a partial check on the numerical work $\sum (AB^2)_i'$ is equal to the sum of all observations in replications 3 and 4.

Other components of the two-factor interactions are computed in an analogous manner. The within-block information on AC is obtained from replications 1 and 3; similar information on AC^2 is obtained from replications 2 and 4.

Within-block information on three-factor interaction components is obtained from some three of the four replications. For example, information from replications 2, 3, and 4 is combined to obtain the ABC component. Given a summary table of observations from these three replications,

$$SS'_{ABC} = \frac{(ABC)_0'^2 + (ABC)_1'^2 + (ABC)_2'^2 + (ABC)_3'^2}{27} - \frac{[\sum (ABC)_i']^2}{81},$$

where $(ABC)_i'$ is the sum of observations in replications 2, 3, and 4 satisfying the relation $x_1 + x_2 + x_3 = i \pmod 3$. The other components of the three-factor interaction are computed in an analogous manner, the ABC^2 component, for example, being obtained from replications 1, 3, and 4. Since components of both two-factor and three-factor interactions are partially confounded with block effects, estimates of cell means require adjustment for block effects. The latter adjustment is most readily made by adjusting cell totals. Adjusted cell totals are given by

$$\begin{aligned}
ABC'_{ijk} = {} & \tfrac{1}{9}(A_i + B_j + C_k) + \tfrac{2}{9}[(AB)'_{i+j} + (AB^2)'_{i+2j} + (AC)'_{i+k} \\
& + (AC^2)'_{i+2k} + (BC)'_{j+k} + (BC^2)'_{j+2k}] \\
& + \tfrac{4}{27}[(ABC)'_{i+j+k} + (ABC^2)'_{i+j+2k} \\
& + (AB^2C)'_{i+2j+k} + (AB^2C^2)'_{i+2j+2k}] - \tfrac{4}{9}G.
\end{aligned}$$

The primes indicate that summations are restricted to replications in which a component is not confounded with block effects. The sums required for obtaining an adjusted cell total are obtained in the course of computing the within-block components of the interactions. In terms of the basic linear model, it may be shown that

$$ABC'_{ijk} \doteq 4[\mu + \alpha_i + \beta_j + \gamma_k + (\alpha\beta)_{ij} + (\alpha\gamma)_{ik} + (\beta\gamma)_{jk}$$
$$+ (\alpha\beta\gamma)_{ijk}] + 4(\text{sum of all block effects}).$$

The right-hand side of this last expression represents the parameters that would be estimated by a cell total if each block contained all treatment combinations. Differences between two adjusted totals will be free of block effects, since the last term on the right-hand side is a constant for all cells. With the exception of the block effects, each of the parameters on the right-hand side is estimated independently of all others. Estimates of the parameters associated with main effects are each based upon four effective replications. However, estimates of parameters of two-factor interactions are based upon two effective replications, and estimates of parameters for three-factor interactions are based upon three effective replications. In making comparisons among adjusted cell totals in the three-way table, for most practical purposes one may consider each of these adjusted cell totals as being based upon four replications. Exact methods for taking into account the difference in the effective number of replications for the separate parts of the adjusted cell totals are, however, available (cf. Federer [1955, chap. 9]).

An adjusted total for a cell in a two-way summary table, the cell ab_{ij}, for example, has the form

$$AB'_{ij} = \tfrac{1}{3}(A_i + B_j) + \tfrac{2}{3}[(AB)'_{i+j} + (AB^2)'_{i+2j}] - \tfrac{1}{3}G.$$

Similarly an adjusted total for the cell ac_{ik} has the form

$$AC'_{ik} = \tfrac{1}{3}(A_i + C_k) + \tfrac{2}{3}[(AC)'_{i+k} + (AC^2)'_{i+2k}] - \tfrac{1}{3}G.$$

For comparisons among adjusted totals in a two-way summary table, the effective number of observations in a total varies as a function of the nature of the comparison. The difference between adjusted totals which are in the same row or column of a two-way summary table is based upon $(\tfrac{3}{5})(12)$ effective observations, whereas the difference between adjusted totals which are not in the same row or column is based upon $(\tfrac{2}{3})(12)$ effective observations. Comparisons involving mixtures of these two kinds of differences have effective numbers of observations which may be determined by the general expression for the variance of a linear combination of independent terms.

Thus far the design outlined in Table 8.30 has been considered for the case in which there is one observation per cell. Several variations on this basic design are possible. One variation is to have the block represent a group of n subjects. Each of the groups would be assigned at random to the blocks, and each of the n subjects within a group would be observed, in a random order, under each of the treatment combinations within a given block. The analysis of the resulting design would have the form shown in Table 8.32. Thus, with only three observations per subject, within-subject estimates of all factorial effects are available.

TABLE 8.32 **Analysis of design in Table 8.30 with repeated measures**

Source of variation	df	
Between subjects	$\overline{36n - 1}$	
Groups	$\overline{35}$	
Subjects within groups	$36(n - 1)$	
Within subjects	$\overline{72n}$	
Main effects: A, B, C	$\overline{6}$	(2 each)
Two-factor interaction:		
AB, AB^2 ($\frac{1}{2}$ information)	4	(2 each)
AC, AC^2 ($\frac{1}{2}$ information)	4	(2 each)
BC, BC^2 ($\frac{1}{2}$ information)	4	(2 each)
Three-factor interaction:		
ABC, ABC^2, AB^2C, AB^2C^2 ($\frac{3}{4}$ information)	8	(2 each)
Residual	$72n - 26$	

To summarize the principles underlying the construction of designs for $3 \times 3 \times 3$ factorial experiments, blocks of size 9 may be constructed by utilizing relations corresponding to three-factor interactions. If this is done, components of three-factor interactions are either completely or partially confounded with block effects. To construct blocks of size 3, the blocks of size 9 are subdivided by means of relations corresponding to two-factor interactions. In this case, in addition to the interaction corresponding to the defining relations, the aliases also become confounded with block effects.

The principles developed in this section may be extended to include factorial experiments of the form $p \times p \times p$, where p is a prime number. Use of components of the three-factor interaction reduces the block size to p^2. Then blocks of size p^2 are reduced to size p through use of relations corresponding to the components of two-factor interactions. For example, in a $5 \times 5 \times 5$ factorial experiment, the relations u and v may be used to obtain blocks of size 5. In addition to components corresponding to the relations u and v, components corresponding to the following relations will also be confounded with block effects:

$$u + v, \quad u + 2v, \quad u + 3v, \quad u + 4v.$$

For a single replication with block size 5, the number of blocks required would be 25. Hence the degrees of freedom for blocks within a single replication would be 24. Within a single replication, six components of interactions are confounded with block effects; each component has 4 degrees of freedom. Hence 24 degrees of freedom corresponding to the six components of interactions are confounded with differences between blocks, the latter differences also having 24 degrees of freedom.

In terms of the multiplicative scheme, the aliases of the components W and X in a $5 \times 5 \times 5$ factorial experiment have the general form

$$WX, \quad WX^2, \quad WX^3, \quad WX^4.$$

To make the notation system unique, the exponent of the first letter in an interaction term is made unity by raising the whole term to an appropriate power and then reducing exponents modulo 5. It is not difficult to show that WX^k and $(WX^k)^n$, where n is any number modulo 5, correspond to equivalent relations. For example, the following relations are equivalent in the sense that they define the same set of treatment combinations:

$$AC^2: \quad x_1 + 2x_3 = i \;(\text{mod } 5),$$
$$A^2C^4: \quad 2x_1 + 4x_3 = 2i \;(\text{mod } 5).$$

8.7 MIXED DESIGNS

Designs wherein the number of levels of each factor are not all equal are labeled *mixed* designs. Thus, a $3 \times 2 \times 2$ design is a mixed design as is a $2 \times 3 \times 2$ design. In order to avoid confounding any particular interaction effect between blocks, it is necessary for the block size to be a multiple of the number of treatment conditions needed to define the effect. Thus, in a 2×2 design, four treatment conditions define the $A \times B$ interaction and a larger design which involves two levels of A and two levels of B would confound the AB interaction were block sizes not a multiple of four. In a $3 \times 2 \times 2$ design, block sizes must be a multiple of six to avoid confounding the $A \times B$ interaction, a multiple of six for the $A \times C$ interaction, and a multiple of four to avoid confounding the $B \times C$ interaction. This restricts the number of design possibilities for mixed designs.

Balanced $3 \times 2 \times 2$ Factorial Experiment in Blocks of Size 6

It is possible to construct a balanced design for a $3 \times 2 \times 2$ factorial experiment in blocks of size 6 by partially confounding the BC and ABC interactions. A minimum of the three replications is required for balance; in this balanced design the relative information on BC is $\frac{8}{9}$, and the relative information on ABC is $\frac{5}{9}$. The balanced design is given in schematic form in Table 8.33a. In Table 8.33a the symbol K_0 designates the set of treatment combinations satisfying the relation $x_2 + x_3 = 0 \;(\text{mod } 2)$, and the symbol K_1 designates the set of treatment combinations satisfying the relation $x_2 + x_3 = 1 \;(\text{mod } 2)$. In terms of the symbols for individual treatment combinations, the design is given in Table 8.33b. The spacings within the blocks designate treatment combinations belonging to different K sets.

TABLE 8.33a

Level of A	Rep 1		Rep 2		Rep 3	
	Block 1	Block 2	Block 3	Block 4	Block 5	Block 6
a_0	K_0	K_1	K_1	K_0	K_1	K_0
a_1	K_1	K_0	K_0	K_1	K_1	K_0
a_2	K_1	K_0	K_1	K_0	K_0	K_1

TABLE 8.33b

	Rep 1		Rep 2		Rep 3	
	Block 1	**Block 2**	**Block 3**	**Block 4**	**Block 5**	**Block 6**
	(000)	(001)	(001)	(000)	(001)	(000)
	(011)	(010)	(010)	(011)	(010)	(011)
	(101)	(100)	(100)	(101)	(101)	(100)
	(110)	(111)	(111)	(110)	(110)	(111)
	(201)	(200)	(201)	(200)	(200)	(201)
	(210)	(211)	(210)	(211)	(211)	(210)

The computational procedures for all factorial effects, except the BC and ABC interactions, are identical to those for a factorial experiment in which there is no confounding. The BC and ABC interactions require adjustment for block effects. A simplified procedure for computing the BC interaction will be outlined for the case in which there is no confounding. The adjustments required for the partial confounding with block effects will then be obtained.

Assuming that the BC interaction were not confounded with blocks, the total of all observations in the set K_0, which will be designated by the symbol $K_{0.}$, may be shown to be an estimate of the following parameters of the linear model (assuming one observation per cell):

$$K_{0.} \doteq 18\mu + 18(\beta\gamma)_{K_0}.$$

The symbol $(\beta\gamma)_{K_0}$ denotes the K_0 component of the BC interaction. Similarly the total of all observations in set K_1, designated by the symbol $K_{1.}$, may be shown to estimate

$$K_{1.} \doteq 18\mu + 18(\beta\gamma)_{K_1}.$$

Hence the difference between these two totals provides an estimate of

$$K_{0.} - K_{1.} \doteq 18(\beta\gamma)_{K_0} - 18(\beta\gamma)_{K_1}.$$

Since the BC interaction has only these two components,

$$(\beta\gamma)_{K_0} + (\beta\gamma)_{K_1} = 0, \quad \text{and hence} \quad (\beta\gamma)_{K_0} = -(\beta\gamma)_{K_1}.$$

(The sum of all components of an interaction term in the general linear model is assumed to be zero, since these terms are measured in deviation units about the grand mean.)

Suppose that the symbol $(\beta\gamma)$ is used to denote $(\beta\gamma)_{K_0}$. Then

$$-(\beta\gamma) = (\beta\gamma)_{K_1}.$$

Hence $$K_{0.} - K_{1.} \doteq 18(\beta\gamma) - [-18(\beta\gamma)] = 36(\beta\gamma).$$

Thus, if there were no confounding with blocks, the difference between the sum of all observations in set K_0 and all observations in set K_1 estimates a parameter which is equal in absolute value to the difference between the K

components of the BC interaction. Since the BC interaction has only one degree of freedom, there is only one independent parameter associated with it. In terms of the parameters of the model, disregarding the experimental error, the sum of squares for the BC interaction would be

$$\text{SS}_{bc} \doteq 18(\beta\gamma)_{K_0}^2 + 18(\beta\gamma)_{K_1}^2 = 36(\beta\gamma)^2.$$

Thus a computational formula for the BC interaction, if there were no confounding with blocks, would be

$$\text{SS}_{bc} = \frac{(K_{0.} - K_{1.})^2}{36} \doteq 36(\beta\gamma)^2.$$

In the design in Table 8.33a, however, the BC interaction is partially confounded with block effects. The difference between the total of all observations in the set K_0 and all observations in the set K_1 actually estimates a mixture of $(\beta\gamma)$ and block effects, i.e.,

$$K_{0.} - K_{1.} \doteq 36(\beta\gamma) + 2(\pi_2 + \pi_4 + \pi_6 - \pi_1 - \pi_3 - \pi_5),$$

where the π's represent block effects. If P_i represents the total of all observations in block i,

$$(\tfrac{1}{3})(P_2 + P_4 + P_6 - P_1 - P_3 - P_5) \doteq 4(\beta\gamma) + 2(\pi_2 + \pi_4 + \pi_6 - \pi_1 - \pi_3 - \pi_5).$$

The quantity on the left-hand side of this last equation may be used to adjust the difference $K_{0.} - K_{1.}$ for block effects. The adjusted difference takes the form

$$Q = K_{0.} - K_{1.} - (\tfrac{1}{3})(P_2 + P_4 + P_6 - P_1 - P_3 - P_5)$$
$$\doteq 32(\beta\gamma).$$

Thus the adjusted difference between the K totals provides 32 effective observations in the estimation of $(\beta\gamma)$; but if there were no confounding with blocks, the unadjusted difference between the K totals would provide 36 effective observations. Hence the relative effective information on BC is $\frac{32}{36}$, or $\frac{8}{9}$. The adjusted sum of squares for BC takes the form

$$\text{SS}_{bc}' = \frac{Q^2}{32} \doteq 32(\beta\gamma)^2.$$

The problem of finding the appropriate adjustment for the ABC interaction follows the same general pattern as that which has just been indicated for the BC interaction. A simplified procedure for finding the ABC interaction will first be outlined for the case in which there is no confounding. The symbol K_{0i} will be used to designate the subset of all treatment combinations in the set K_0 which are at level a_i; similarly the symbol K_{1i} will be used to designate the subset of treatment combinations in the set K_1 which are at level a_i. The totals for all observations in the respective subsets will be denoted by the symbols $K_{0i.}$ and $K_{1i.}$. If the symbol $(\alpha\beta\gamma)_{K_{0i}}$ denotes an effect associated with the ABC interaction,

$$K_{0i.} - K_{1i.} \doteq 6(\alpha\beta\gamma)_{K_{1i}} - 6(\alpha\beta\gamma)_{K_{1i}} + 12(\beta\gamma).$$

Since the sum of the components of an interaction at a fixed level of one of the factors is zero,

$$(\alpha\beta\gamma)_{K_{0i}} + (\alpha\beta\gamma)_{K_{1i}} = 0; \quad \text{hence} \quad (\alpha\beta\gamma)_{K_{0i}} = -(\alpha\beta\gamma)_{K_{1i}}.$$

If the symbol $(\alpha\beta\gamma)_i$ designates either $(\alpha\beta\gamma)_{K_{0i}}$ or $-(\alpha\beta\gamma)_{K_{1i}}$, assuming there were no confounding with blocks,

$$K_{0i.} - K_{1i.} \doteq 12(\alpha\beta\gamma)_i + 12(\beta\gamma).$$

Specifically, for each level of factor A,

$$K_{00.} - K_{10.} \doteq 12(\alpha\beta\gamma)_0 + 12(\beta\gamma),$$
$$K_{01.} - K_{11.} \doteq 12(\alpha\beta\gamma)_1 + 12(\beta\gamma),$$
$$K_{02.} - K_{12.} \doteq 12(\alpha\beta\gamma)_2 + 12(\beta\gamma).$$

Thus, if no confounding were present,

$$\frac{\Sigma (K_{0i.} - K_{1i.})^2}{12} \doteq 12(\alpha\beta\gamma)_0^2 + 12(\alpha\beta\gamma)_1^2 + 12(\alpha\beta\gamma)_2^2 + 36(\beta\gamma)^2.$$

The sum of the first three terms on the right-hand side of the last equation defines SS_{ABC} in terms of the parameters of the model; the last term defines SS_{BC}. (In both cases the error component has not been included.) Hence

$$\frac{\Sigma (K_{0i.} - K_{1i.})^2}{12} = SS_{abc} + SS_{bc}.$$

Thus, if there were no confounding, a computational formula for SS_{ABC} would be given by

$$SS_{abc} = \frac{\Sigma (K_{0i.} - K_{1i.})^2}{12} - \frac{(K_{0.} - K_{1.})^2}{36}.$$

In words, the ABC sum of squares is obtained by summing the BC interaction at each level of factor A and then subtracting the overall BC interaction.

$$SS_{abc} = \sum SS_{bc \text{ at } a_i} - SS_{bc}.$$

For factorial experiments in which some of the factors are at two levels, this general computational procedure is simpler than direct calculation of the three-factor interaction.

In the design under consideration the difference $K_{00} - K_{10}$ is not free of block effects. For this design

$$K_{00} - K_{10} \doteq 12(\alpha\beta\gamma)_0 + 12(\beta\gamma) + 2(\pi_1 + \pi_4 + \pi_6 - \pi_2 - \pi_3 - \pi_5).$$

The blocks in which K_0 appears at level a_0 have positive signs; the blocks in which K_1 appears at level a_0 have negative signs. In obtaining the adjustment for block effects it is more convenient to work with the expression

$$3(K_{00} - K_{10}) \doteq 36(\alpha\beta\gamma)_0 + 36(\beta\gamma) + 6(\pi_1 + \pi_4 + \pi_6 - \pi_2 - \pi_3 - \pi_5).$$

The adjustment for block effects requires the term

$$(\text{adj } a_0) = P_1 + P_4 + P_6 - P_2 - P_3 - P_5$$
$$\doteq 16(\alpha\beta\gamma)_0 + 4(\beta\gamma) + 6(\pi_1 + \pi_4 + \pi_6 - \pi_2 - \pi_3 - \pi_5).$$

The adjusted difference used to obtain the sum of squares for the three-factor interaction is

$$3R_0 = 3(K_{00.} - K_{10.}) - (\text{adj } a_0) - Q \doteq 20(\alpha\beta\gamma)_0,$$

where Q is the quantity used in the computation of SS'_{bc}. Other adjustments for the levels of factor A are

$$(\text{adj } a_1) = P_2 + P_3 + P_6 - P_1 - P_4 - P_5,$$
$$(\text{adj } a_2) = P_2 + P_4 + P_5 - P_1 - P_3 - P_6.$$

The adjusted differences used in the computation of SS'_{ABC} are

$$3R_1 = 3(K_{01.} - K_{11.}) - (\text{adj } a_1) - Q \doteq 20(\alpha\beta\gamma)_1.$$
$$3R_2 = 3(K_{02.} - K_{12.}) - (\text{adj } a_2) - Q \doteq 20(\alpha\beta\gamma)_2.$$

An adjusted difference of the form $3R_i$ provides 20 effective observations in the estimation of the parameter $(\alpha\beta\gamma)_i$, whereas the corresponding unadjusted difference provides 36 effective observations. Hence the relative information for the ABC interaction in this design is $\frac{20}{36} = \frac{5}{9}$. A computational formula for the adjusted sum of squares for the ABC interaction is given by

$$\text{SS}'_{abc} = \frac{\sum (3R_i)^2}{9(\frac{20}{3})} \doteq (\tfrac{20}{3})[(\alpha\beta\gamma)_0^2 + (\alpha\beta\gamma)_1^2 + (\alpha\beta\gamma)_2^2].$$

If there were no confounding with blocks,

$$\text{SS}_{abc} \doteq 12[(\alpha\beta\gamma)_0^2 + (\alpha\beta\gamma)_1^2 + (\alpha\beta\gamma)_2^2],$$

where the error component has been disregarded. The ratio $(\frac{20}{3})/12 = \frac{5}{9}$, the relative information for ABC. The overall analysis of the balanced design in Table 8.33 is given in Table 8.34. In the underlying model, all factors are assumed to be fixed, blocks are assumed to be random, and the block $\times$ treatment interactions are assumed to be zero or negligible. Only under these stringent assumptions are the adjustments for block effects valid. In making F tests on all factorial effects, MS_{res} forms the denominator of all F ratios. In making comparisons between adjusted cell means, the effective number of observations on the component parts should be taken into account.

The adjustment for $\overline{BC}_{00}$ is obtained by considering the parameters actually estimated by the total of all observations under treatment combination

TABLE 8.34 **Analysis of design in Table 8.33**

Source of variation	SS	df	MS	E(MS)
Between blocks		5		
Replications		2		
Blocks within reps		3		
Within blocks		30		
A		2		$\sigma_\varepsilon^2 + nqr\sigma_\alpha^2$
B		1		$\sigma_\varepsilon^2 + npr\sigma_\beta^2$
C		1		$\sigma_\varepsilon^2 + npq\sigma_\gamma^2$
AB		2		$\sigma_\varepsilon^2 + nr\sigma_{\alpha\beta}^2$
AC		2		$\sigma_\varepsilon^2 + nq\sigma_{\alpha\gamma}^2$
(BC)'		1		$\sigma_\varepsilon^2 + (\frac{8}{9})np\sigma_{\beta\gamma}^2$
(ABC)'		2		$\sigma_\varepsilon^2 + (\frac{5}{9})n\sigma_{\alpha\beta\gamma}^2$
Residual		19		σ_ε^2

bc_{00}, the levels of factor A being disregarded. There are nine such observations.

$$BC_{00} \doteq 9\mu + 9\beta_0 + 9\gamma_0 + 9(\beta\gamma)_{00} + (\pi_1 + \pi_3 + \pi_5)$$
$$+ 2(\pi_2 + \pi_4 + \pi_6).$$

To obtain an adjustment for BC_{00}, one must construct an expression which estimates the block effects on the right-hand side of this last equation. This expression is given by

$$(\text{adj } BC_{00}) = (\tfrac{1}{6})(P_1 + P_3 + P_5) + (\tfrac{1}{3})(P_2 + P_4 + P_6) - (\tfrac{1}{32})Q - (\tfrac{1}{4})G$$
$$\doteq (\pi_1 + \pi_3 + \pi_5) + 2(\pi_2 + \pi_4 + \pi_6).$$

The adjusted total for the cell bc_{00} is thus

$$BC_{00}' = BC_{00} - (\text{adj } BC_{00}) \doteq 9\mu + 9\beta_0 + 9\gamma_0 + 9(\beta\gamma)_{00}.$$

The adjusted mean for cell bc_{00} is given by

$$\overline{BC_{00}'} = \frac{BC_{00}'}{9} \doteq \mu + \beta_0 + \gamma_0 + (\beta\gamma)_{00}.$$

Since the treatment combination bc_{00} and bc_{11} both belong to the set K_0, and since the design is symmetrical with respect to the parts of K_0, the adjustment for $\overline{BC_{11}}$ is the same as that used for $\overline{BC_{00}}$.

By similar arguments and use of the relation that $(\beta\gamma)_{K_0} = -(\beta\gamma)_{K_1}$, the adjustment for both $\overline{BC_{01}}$ and $\overline{BC_{10}}$ may be shown to be

$$(\text{adj } BC_{01}) = (\text{adj } BC_{10}) = (\tfrac{1}{3})(P_1 + P_3 + P_5)$$
$$+ (\tfrac{1}{6})(P_2 + P_4 + P_6) + (\tfrac{1}{32})Q - (\tfrac{1}{4})G.$$

In the arguments that have been used in the course of arriving at various adjustments, certain assumptions about restrictions on the parameters in the

TABLE 8.35 **Restrictions on parameters in model**

	c_0		c_1				b_0	b_1
	b_0	b_1	b_0	b_1				
a_0	$(\alpha\beta\gamma)_0$	$-(\alpha\beta\gamma)_0$	$-(\alpha\beta\gamma)_0$	$(\alpha\beta\gamma)_0$	c_0		$(\beta\gamma)$	$-(\beta\gamma)$
a_1	$(\alpha\beta\gamma)_1$	$-(\alpha\beta\gamma)_1$	$-(\alpha\beta\gamma)_1$	$(\alpha\beta\gamma)_1$	c_1		$-(\beta\gamma)$	$(\beta\gamma)$
a_2	$(\alpha\beta\gamma)_2$	$-(\alpha\beta\gamma)_2$	$-(\alpha\beta\gamma)_2$	$(\alpha\beta\gamma)_2$				
					Sum		0	0
Sum	0	0	0	0				

general linear model have been invoked. These restrictions are made explicit in Table 8.35.

NUMERICAL EXAMPLE OF $3 \times 2 \times 2$ **FACTORIAL EXPERIMENT IN BLOCKS OF SIZE 6.** Data for this type of design will generally take the form given in Table 8.36. The observation is given opposite the symbol for the treatment combination. The make-up of the blocks is that given in Table 8.33. In the behavioral sciences the blocks may correspond to an individual or to a group of individuals.

Summary data for the factorial effects are given in Table 8.37. From part iv of this table one obtains $K_{0.}$ and $K_{1.}$:

$$K_{0.} = 60 + 50 = 110,$$
$$K_{1.} = 90 + 100 = 190.$$

From the block totals in Table 8.36, one finds

$$P_2 + P_4 + P_6 - P_1 - P_3 - P_b = -56.$$

Hence

$$Q = K_{0.} - K_{1.} - \frac{P_2 + P_4 + P_6 - P_1 - P_3 - P_5}{3}$$
$$= 110 - 190 - \frac{(-56)}{3}$$
$$= -61.33.$$

TABLE 8.36 **Data for design in Table 8.33**

Rep 1		Rep 2		Rep 3		
Block 1	Block 2	Block 3	Block 4	Block 5	Block 6	
(000) 4	(001) 10	(001) 5	(000) 3	(001) 5	(000) 3	
(011) 5	(010) 20	(010) 10	(011) 4	(010) 10	(011) 1	
(101) 15	(100) 5	(100) 15	(101) 5	(101) 10	(100) 0	
(110) 20	(111) 10	(111) 15	(110) 5	(110) 5	(111) 5	
(201) 20	(200) 10	(201) 10	(200) 10	(200) 10	(201) 20	
(210) 10	(211) 1	(210) 5	(211) 5	(211) 4	(210) 5	
$P_1 = 74$	$P_2 = 56$	$P_3 = 60$	$P_4 = 32$	$P_5 = 44$	$P_6 = 34$	$G = 300$

TABLE 8.37 **Summary data for Table 8.36**

(i)

		b_0		b_1		
		c_0	c_1	c_0	c_1	Total
	a_0	10	20	40	10	80
	a_1	20	30	30	30	110
	a_2	30	50	20	10	110
	Total	60	100	90	50	300

(ii)

	b_0	b_1
a_0	30	50
a_1	50	60
a_2	80	30
Total	160	140

(iii)

	c_0	c_1
a_0	50	30
a_1	50	60
a_2	50	60
Total	150	150

(iv)

	c_0	c_1
b_0	60	100
b_1	90	50
Total	150	150

Having the numerical value of Q, one obtains the adjusted sum of squares for BC from the relation

$$\text{SS}'_{bc} = \frac{Q^2}{32} = \frac{(-61.33)^2}{32} = 117.54.$$

Expressions of the form $3(K_{0i.} - K_{1i.})$ are obtained from part i of Table 8.37.

$$3(K_{00.} - K_{10.}) = 3[(10 + 10) - (20 + 40)] = -120,$$
$$3(K_{01.} - K_{11.}) = 3[(20 + 30) - (30 + 30)] = -30,$$
$$3(K_{02.} - K_{12.}) = 3[(30 + 10) - (50 + 20)] = -90.$$

Adjustments for the above expressions are, respectively,

$$(\text{adj } a_0) = P_1 + P_4 + P_6 - P_2 - P_3 - P_5 = -20$$
$$(\text{adj } a_1) = P_2 + P_3 + P_6 - P_1 - P_4 - P_5 = 0$$
$$\underline{(\text{adj } a_2) = P_2 + P_4 + P_5 - P_1 - P_3 - P_6 = -36}$$
$$\text{Sum} = P_2 + P_4 + P_6 - P_1 - P_3 - P_5 = -56$$

The R's required for computing SS'_{abc} are given by

$$3R_0 = 3(K_{00.} - K_{10.}) - (\text{adj } a_0) - Q = -38.67$$
$$3R_1 = 3(K_{01.} - K_{11.}) - (\text{adj } a_1) - Q = 31.33$$
$$\underline{3R_2 = 3(K_{02.} - K_{12.}) - (\text{adj } a_2) - Q = 7.33}$$
$$\Sigma (3R) = 3(-80) - (-56) - 3(-61.33) = -0.01$$

Within rounding error, $\Sigma (3R) = 0$.

The adjusted sum of squares for ABC is

$$SS'_{abc} = \frac{\Sigma (3R_i)^2}{60} = 42.18.$$

A summary of the computation of all sums of squares required in the analysis of variance is given in Table 8.38. The residual terms in this analysis may be obtained either by subtracting the total of the adjusted treatment sums of squares from $SS_{w. block}$ or by the method indicated in the table.

The relative efficiency of a design involving small block size as compared with a completely randomized design depends in large part upon the relative magnitudes of $MS_{block\,w,\,rep}$ and MS_{res} (adj). For the data under consideration these mean squares are, respectively, 33.55 and 20.37. The smaller the latter mean square relative to the former, the more efficient the design involving the smaller block size.

To illustrate the computation of the adjustments for the BC means,

$$
\begin{aligned}
(\text{adj } BC_{00}) &= (\tfrac{1}{6})(P_1 + P_3 + P_5) + (\tfrac{1}{3})(P_2 + P_4 + P_6) - (\tfrac{1}{32})Q - (\tfrac{1}{4})G \\
&= (\tfrac{1}{6})(178) + (\tfrac{1}{3})(122) - (-1.92) - 75 \\
&= 29.67 + 40.67 + 1.92 - 75 = -2.74.
\end{aligned}
$$

TABLE 8.38 **Computation of SS for Table 8.37**

$(1) = G^2/36$ $\quad = 2500$	$(7) = [\Sigma\,(AC)^2]/6$ $\quad = 2600.00$	
$(2) = \Sigma\,X^2$ $\quad = 3618$	$(8) = [\Sigma\,(BC)^2]/9$ $\quad = 2688.89$	
$(3) = (\Sigma\,A^2)/12$ $\quad = 2550.00$	$(9) = [\Sigma\,(ABC)^2]/3 = 3066.67$	
$(4) = (\Sigma\,B^2)/18$ $\quad = 2511.11$	$(10) = (\Sigma\,P^2)/6$ $\quad = 2721.33$	
$(5) = (\Sigma\,C^2)/18$ $\quad = 2500.00$	$(11) = (\Sigma\,\text{Rep}^2)/12$ $\quad = 2620.67$	
$(6) = [\Sigma\,(AB)^2]/6 = 2800.00$		

SS_{blocks}	$= (10) - (1)$	$= 221.33$

SS_{reps}	$= (11) - (1)$	$= 120.67$
$SS_{blocks\,w.\,rep}$	$= (10) - (11)$	$= 100.66$
$SS_{w.\,block}$	$= (2) - (10)$	$= 896.67$

SS_a	$= (3) - (1)$	$=\quad 50.00$
SS_b	$= (4) - (1)$	$=\quad 11.11$
SS_c	$= (5) - (1)$	$=\quad 0$
SS_{ab}	$= (6) - (3) - (4) + (1)$	$=\quad 238.89$
SS_{ac}	$= (7) - (3) - (5) + (1)$	$=\quad 50.00$
$SS_{bc}(\text{unadj})$	$= (8) - (4) - (5) + (1)$	$=\quad 177.78$
$SS_{bc}(\text{adj})$	$= SS'_{bc}$	$= (117.54)$
$SS_{abc}(\text{unadj})$	$= (9) - (6) - (7) - (8) + (3) + (4) + (5) - (1)$	$=\quad 38.89$
$SS_{abc}(\text{adj})$	$= SS'_{abc}$	$= (42.18)$
$SS_{res}(\text{unadj})$	$= (2) - (9) - (10) + (1)$	$=\quad 330.00$
$SS_{res}(\text{adj})$	$= SS_{res}(\text{unadj}) + SS_{bc}(\text{unadj}) + SS_{abc}(\text{unadj})$ $- SS_{bc}(\text{adj}) - SS_{abc}(\text{adj})$	$=\quad 386.95$

The adjusted mean is

$$\overline{BC'_{00}} = \overline{BC_{00}} - \frac{(-2.74)}{9} = 6.67 - \frac{(-2.74)}{9} = 6.97.$$

The adjustment for $\overline{BC_{01}}$ will be numerically equal but opposite in sign to the adjustment for $\overline{BC_{00}}$. Thus

$$\overline{BC'_{01}} = \overline{BC_{01}} - \frac{2.74}{9} = 11.11 - \frac{2.74}{9} = 10.81.$$

The restrictions on the parameters underlying the linear model for a $3 \times 2 \times 2$ factorial experiment as shown in Table 8.35 may be illustrated numerically through use of the data in Table 8.37. These restrictions also hold for estimates of these parameters. For example, assuming no confounding,

$$(\alpha\beta\gamma)_{000} \doteq \frac{ABC_{000}}{3} - \frac{AB_{00}}{6} - \frac{AC_{00}}{6} - \frac{BC_{00}}{9} + \frac{A_0}{12} + \frac{B_0}{18} + \frac{C_0}{18} - \frac{G}{36}$$

$$\doteq -1.11.$$

According to Table 8.36, $(\alpha\beta\gamma)_{000} = -(\alpha\beta\gamma)_{001}$. The latter parameter is estimated by

$$(\alpha\beta\gamma)_{001} \doteq \frac{ABC_{001}}{3} - \frac{AB_{00}}{6} - \frac{AC_{01}}{6} - \frac{BC_{01}}{9} + \frac{A_0}{12} + \frac{B_0}{18} + \frac{C_1}{18} - \frac{G}{36}$$

$$\doteq 1.11.$$

Thus $\qquad (\alpha\beta\gamma)_{000} = -(\alpha\beta\gamma)_{001} = (\alpha\beta\gamma)_0 \doteq -1.11.$

(Partially Balanced) $3 \times 3 \times 3 \times 2$ Factorial Experiment in Blocks of Size 6

The principles used in the construction of the $3 \times 2 \times 2$ factorial design for block size 6 may be extended to cover a $3 \times 3 \times 3 \times 2$ factorial experiment with block size 6. To illustrate the construction of this design, the following notation will be used:

L_{ij} = set of all treatment combinations satisfying
both the relations

$$x_1 + x_2 = i \pmod 3 \quad \text{and} \quad x_1 + x_3 = j \pmod 3.$$

For example, the fourth factor being disregarded, the treatment combinations in the set L_{00} have the form (000–), (122–), and (211–). As another example, the treatment combinations in the set L_{12} have the form (012–), (101–), and (220–). For each of the treatment combinations in the set L_{12} the relations $x_1 + x_2 = 1 \pmod 3$ and $x_1 + x_3 = 2 \pmod 3$ are satisfied. Each of the sets L_{ij} consists of three treatment combinations at level d_0 and three at level d_1.

TABLE 8.39 **Partially balanced** $3 \times 3 \times 3 \times 2$ **design**

Level of D	Block:	1	2	3	4	5	6	7	8	9
d_0		L_{00}	L_{01}	L_{02}	L_{10}	L_{11}	L_{12}	L_{20}	L_{21}	L_{22}
d_1		L_{12}	L_{22}	L_{11}	L_{01}	L_{20}	L_{21}	L_{02}	L_{00}	L_{10}

The design in Table 8.39 represents a partially balanced design. The actual treatment combinations in this design are given in Table 8.40. A minimum of four replications is required for complete balance. To construct the latter, the defining relations for i and j may be changed; i.e., the relations

$$x_1 + x_2 = i \ (\text{mod } 3), \qquad x_1 + 2x_3 = j \ (\text{mod } 3)$$

will define sets of L's which could make up a second replication. The assignment of the L's defined in this manner would be identical to that shown in Table 8.39.

The design given in this table has the following restrictions imposed upon the assignment of the L's to the blocks: (1) All the possible L's occur once and only once at each level of factor D. (2) Within each block a subscript does not occur twice in the same position; that is, L_{01} and L_{02} cannot occur within the same block, since the subscript zero would be repeated within the same position within the same block. (3) The sum of the subscripts (modulo 3) for L's within the same block must be equal. For example, in block 9 one finds L_{22} and L_{10} in the same block; the sum of the subscripts for L_{22} is $2 + 2 = 1 \ (\text{mod } 3)$, and the sum of the subscripts for L_{10} is $1 + 0 \ (\text{mod } 3)$.

In the original definition of L_{ij}, the relations used correspond to the AB and AC components of the $A \times B$ and $A \times C$ interactions, respectively. The relative information on these components is $\frac{3}{4}$. The generalized interactions of the AB and AC components are BC^2 and AB^2C^2. The relative information on BC^2 is $\frac{3}{4}$, but there is no within-block information on the AB^2C^2 component. The ABC, ACD, and B^2C^2D components are also partially confounded with block effects; the relative within-block information on each of these components is $\frac{1}{4}$. However, the AB^2C^2D component is not confounded with block effects.

TABLE 8.40 **Partially balanced** $3 \times 3 \times 3 \times 2$ **design**

Block:	1	2	3	4	5	6	7	8	9
	(0000)	(0010)	(0020)	(0100)	(0110)	(0120)	(0200)	(0210)	(0220)
	(1220)	(1200)	(1210)	(1020)	(1000)	(1010)	(1120)	(1100)	(1110)
	(2110)	(2120)	(2100)	(2210)	(2220)	(2200)	(2010)	(2020)	(2000)
	(0121)	(0221)	(0111)	(0011)	(0201)	(0211)	(0021)	(0001)	(0101)
	(1011)	(1111)	(1001)	(1201)	(1121)	(1101)	(1211)	(1221)	(1021)
	(2201)	(2001)	(2221)	(2121)	(2011)	(2021)	(2101)	(2111)	(2211)

To show that the design in Table 8.40 provides no within-block information on the AB^2C^2 component, it is necessary to show that no comparisons which belong to this component can be obtained from information provided by a single block. The treatment combinations defining the AB^2C^2 sets are located in the following blocks:

	Blocks
$x_1 + 2x_2 + 2x_3 = 0 \pmod 3$	1, 6, 8
$x_1 + 2x_2 + 2x_3 = 1 \pmod 3$	3, 5, 7
$x_1 + 2x_2 + 2x_3 = 2 \pmod 3$	2, 4, 9

Thus no single block contains treatment combinations which belong to more than one of the AB^2C^2 sets. Hence any comparison between such sets will involve differences between blocks.

The picture with respect to the AB^2C^2 component may be contrasted with that presented by the AB component, for which there is $\frac{3}{4}$ relative within-block information. The blocks which contain treatment combinations belonging to the AB sets are the following:

		Blocks
J_0:	$x_1 + x_2 = 0 \pmod 3$	1, 2, 3, 4, 7, 8
J_1:	$x_1 + x_2 = 1 \pmod 3$	1, 3, 4, 5, 6, 9
J_2:	$x_1 + x_2 = 2 \pmod 3$	2, 5, 6, 7, 8, 9

Thus within-block information on the AB component is available on the following comparisons in the blocks indicated:

	Blocks
J_0 versus J_1	1, 3, 4
J_0 versus J_2	2, 7, 8
J_1 versus J_2	5, 6, 9

In the design given in Table 8.40 each J set occurs in the same block with each of the other J sets three times.

Procedures for obtaining the adjusted sums of squares for the two-factor interactions which are partially confounded with block effects will be illustrated by working with the AB (or J) component. The symbol J_0 will be used to represent the set of treatment combinations which satisfy the relation $x_1 + x_2 = 0 \pmod 3$. For the design in Table 8.39, these treatment combinations occur in cells of the form L_{0j}, that is, cells in which the first subscript of an L is zero. The symbol $J_0.$ will be used to designate the sum of all treatment combinations in the set $J_0.$. In terms of the parameters of the general linear model,

$$2J_{0.} = 2\sum_j L_{0j} \doteq 36\mu + 36(\alpha\beta)_{J_0} + 6(\pi_1 + \pi_2 + \pi_3 + \pi_4 + \pi_7 + \pi_8).$$

In words, the right-hand side of the last expression indicates that the total J_0 is partially confounded with block effects. The symbol $\sum P_{L_{0j}}$ will be used to designate the sum of totals for blocks in which treatment combinations belonging to J_0 are located. Thus

$$\sum P_{L_{0j}} = P_1 + P_2 + P_3 + P_4 + P_7 + P_8.$$

In terms of the parameters of the general linear model,

$$\sum P_{L_{0j}} \doteq 36\mu + 9(\alpha\beta)_{J_0} + 6(\pi_1 + \pi_2 + \pi_3 + \pi_4 + \pi_7 + \pi_8).$$

A quantity convenient for use in obtaining the adjusted sum of squares for the J component of $A \times B$ is

$$2Q_{J_0} = 2J_{0.} - \sum P_{L_{0j}} \doteq 27(\alpha\beta)_{J_0}.$$

The coefficient of $(\alpha\beta)_{J_0}$ is 36 in the $2J_{0.}$ total and 27 in the $2Q_{J_0}$ total. The ratio $\frac{27}{36} = \frac{3}{4}$ gives the relative within-block information for the AB component.
    The other quantities required for the computation of the adjusted sum of squares for the AB component are

$$2Q_{J_1} = 2J_{1.} - \sum P_{L_{1j}} \doteq 27(\alpha\beta)_{J_1},$$

where $P_{L_{1j}}$ represents a total for a block containing treatment combinations belonging to the set J_1, and

$$2Q_{J_2} = 2J_{2.} - \sum P_{L_{2j}} \doteq 27(\alpha\beta)_{J_2}.$$

The adjusted sum of squares for the AB component is given by

$$\text{SS}'_{J(AB)} = \frac{\sum (2Q_{J_i})^2}{108} = \left(\frac{27}{2}\right) \sum (\alpha\beta)_{J_i}^2.$$

(The error component has been disregarded in this last expression.) If the AB component were not partially confounded with block effects, the sum of squares for this component would be given by

$$\text{SS}_{J(AB)} = \frac{\sum (2J_{i.})^2}{144} - \frac{[\sum (2J_i)]^2}{432} \doteq 18 \sum (\alpha\beta)_{J_i}^2.$$

[The ratio of the coefficients of $\sum (\alpha\beta)^2$ provides the formal definition of relative within-block information. In this case the ratio is $(\frac{27}{2})/18 = \frac{3}{4}$.]
    Adjustments for the AC component of $A \times C$ are obtained in an analogous manner. If K_j designates the set of treatment combinations which satisfy the relation $x_1 + x_3 = j \pmod 3$, and if $K_{j.}$ designates the sum of all

observations on treatment combinations belonging to the set K_j, then

$$2Q_{K_j} = 2K_{j.} - \sum_i P_{L_{ij}} \doteq 27(\alpha\beta)_{K_j}.$$

For example,

$$2Q_{K_0} = 2K_{0.} - \sum_i P_{L_{i0}} \doteq 27(\alpha\gamma)_{K_0}.$$

The adjusted sum of squares for the AC component is

$$SS'_{K(AC)} = \frac{\sum (2Q_{K_j})^2}{108} \doteq \left(\frac{27}{2}\right) \sum (\alpha\gamma)^2_{K_j}.$$

Adjustments for the BC^2 component may be cast in the following form:

$$2Q_{(BC^2)_m} = 2(BC^2)_{m.} + \sum P_{(BC^2)_m} \doteq 27(\beta\gamma^2)_m.$$

In this expression $(BC^2)_{m.}$ designates the sum of all observations on treatment combinations which satisfy the relation $x_2 + 2x_3 = m \pmod 3$, and $P_{(BC^2)_m}$ designates a total for a block containing treatment combinations which belong to the set $(BC^2)_m$. Blocks which have treatment combinations in the latter set are those containing L_{ij}'s which satisfy the relation $i + 2j = m \pmod 3$. For example, treatment combinations in the set $(BC^2)_0$ are included in L_{00}, L_{22}, and L_{11}; these L's are located in blocks 1, 2, 3, 5, 8, and 9. Hence

$$\sum P_{(BC^2)_0} = P_1 + P_2 + P_3 + P_5 + P_8 + P_9.$$

The process of obtaining the adjustments for the three-factor interactions which are partially confounded with block effects is simplified by utilizing the following restrictions on the underlying parameters,

$$(\alpha\beta\delta)_{J_0 \text{ at } d_0} + (\alpha\beta\delta)_{J_0 \text{ at } d_1} = 0,$$

and hence

$$(\alpha\beta\delta)_{J_0 \text{ at } d_0} = -(\alpha\beta\delta)_{J_0 \text{ at } d_1} = (\alpha\beta\delta)_{J_0}.$$

Analogous restrictions hold for J_1 and J_2.

$$(\alpha\beta\delta)_{J_1 \text{ at } d_0} = -(\alpha\beta\delta)_{J_1 \text{ at } d_1} = (\alpha\beta\delta)_{J_1},$$
$$(\alpha\beta\delta)_{J_2 \text{ at } d_0} = -(\alpha\beta\delta)_{J_2 \text{ at } d_1} = (\alpha\beta\delta)_{J_2}.$$

If there were no confounding with blocks, the difference between the totals $J_{0. \text{ at } d_0}$ and $J_{0. \text{ at } d_1}$ would be a function only of the term $(\alpha\beta\delta)_{J_0}$. This result follows from the basic definition of a three-factor interaction; in this case the ABD interaction is a measure of the difference between AB profiles at the two levels of factor D. Since the AB component is partially confounded with block effects, the $AB \times D$ component will also be partially confounded with block effects.

$$2J_{0. \text{ at } d_0} - 2J_{0. \text{ at } d_1} \doteq 36(\alpha\beta\delta)_{J_0} + 6(\pi_1 + \pi_2 + \pi_3 - \pi_4 - \pi_7 - \pi_8).$$

The last term in the above expression represents the block effects with which the three-factor interaction is confounded. Blocks containing L_{0j} at level d_0

appear with positive signs; blocks containing L_{0j} at level d_1 appear with negative signs. To adjust for block effects,

$$\sum P_{L_{0j} \text{ at } d_0} - \sum P_{L_{0j} \text{ at level } d_1} \doteq 27(\alpha\beta\delta)_{J_0} + 6(\pi_1 + \pi_2 + \pi_3 - \pi_4 - \pi_7 - \pi_8).$$

The expression $\sum P_{L_{0j} \text{ at } d_0}$ denotes the sum of totals for all blocks which contain L_{0j} at level d_0. The right-hand side of the above expression makes use of the fact that $(\alpha\beta\delta)_{J_0} + (\alpha\beta\delta)_{J_1} + (\alpha\beta\delta)_{J_2} = 0$. An estimate of $(\alpha\beta\delta)_{J_0}$, which is free of block effects, is given by

$$2R_{j_0} = 2J_{0. \text{ at } d_0} - 2J_{0. \text{ at } d_1} - \left(\sum P_{L_{0j} \text{ at } d_0} - \sum P_{L_{0j} \text{ at } d_1}\right)$$

$$\doteq 9(\alpha\beta\delta)_{J_0}.$$

If there were no confounding with blocks, the coefficient of $(\alpha\beta\delta)_{J_0}$ would be 36. The ratio $\frac{9}{36} = \frac{1}{4}$ gives the relative within-block information on the $AB \times D$ component of the $A \times B \times D$ interaction. Other quantities required in order to compute $SS'_{AB \times D}$ are

$$2R_{J_1} = 2J_{1. \text{ at } d_0} - 2J_{1. \text{ at } d_1} - \left(\sum P_{L_{1j} \text{ at } d_0} + \sum P_{L_{1j} \text{ at } d_1}\right)$$

$$\doteq 9(\alpha\beta\delta)_{J_1},$$

$$2R_{J_2} = 2J_{2. \text{ at } d_0} - 2J_{2. \text{ at } d_1} - \left(\sum P_{L_{2j} \text{ at } d_0} + \sum P_{L_{2j} \text{ at } d_1}\right)$$

$$\doteq 9(\alpha\beta\delta)_{J_2}.$$

The adjusted sum of squares for $AB \times D$ is

$$SS'_{AB \times D} = \frac{\sum 2R_{J_i}^2}{36} \doteq 9 \sum (\alpha\beta\delta)_{J_i}^2.$$

Quantities required for the adjusted sum of squares for the $AC \times D$ component have the form

$$2R_{K_j} = 2K_{j. \text{ at } d_0} - 2K_{j. \text{ at } d_1} - \left(\sum_i P_{L_{ij} \text{ at } d_0} + \sum_i P_{L_{ij} \text{ at } d_1}\right)$$

$$\doteq 9(\alpha\beta\delta)_{K_j}.$$

The corresponding quantities for the $BC^2 \times D$ component have the form

$$2R_{(BC^2)_m} = (BC^2)_{m \text{ at } d_0} - (BC^2)_{m \text{ at } d_1}$$

$$- \left(\sum P_{(BC^2)_m \text{ at } d_0} + \sum P_{(BC^2)_m \text{ at } d_1}\right)$$

$$\doteq 9(\beta\gamma^2\delta)_m.$$

8.8 FRACTIONAL REPLICATIONS

Designs have already been considered wherein main effects or interactions were confounded with group differences. In all those designs, all of the possible treatment combinations in the factorial set were included in the actual experiment. This results in the experimenter being able to estimate all factorial effects, albeit in some cases those were wholly or partially confounded with block differences. What remains to be considered are designs wherein all of the treatment combinations are *not* included in the experiment. This may have value because the number of treatment combinations in a complete factorial set becomes quite large as the number of factors increases. For example, a 2^8 factorial design requires a total of 256 treatment combinations; a 2^{16} factorial experiment requires 65,536 treatment combinations!

Fractional replication designs, or fractional factorial designs, are those designs wherein only a fraction of the total set of treatment conditions is included in the experiment. Primarily limited to designs of the p^k series, where p is a prime number, such designs can be quite useful as a way to reduce experimental effort, but this is true under highly restrictive circumstances. Those circumstances are that the experimenter must have solid empirical or theoretical knowledge of the interactions prior to designing the study, since some effects are always confounded with each other. In some cases, each sum of squares may have numerous alternative interpretations. Hence, only when the experimenter knows that some of the effects do not exist from theory or prior experimentation is it possible to give unambiguous interpretation to those effects. This is probably the primary reason that fractional replication has been used very little in the social and behavioral sciences. As the name "fractional replication" implies, however, one might replicate a fraction. That is, one may carry out $\frac{1}{3}$ or $\frac{1}{2}$ of a factorial design and, in the presence of an ambiguous outcome, elect to replicate an additional $\frac{1}{3}$ or $\frac{1}{2}$ of the total factorial design to reduce the ambiguity. Thus, over a series of fractional replications, the choice of successive fractions being determined by the results of the preceding fractions, ambiguity of results might be eliminated. Sequential design strategies do create difficulties associated with interpreting levels of significance since the design sequence depends upon the outcome of the previous analyses.

The principles for selecting the set of treatments which will provide maximum information on main effects and lower-order interactions are essentially those followed in assigning treatments to blocks in a complete factorial experiment. In general, a single defining relation will select a $\frac{1}{2}$ replication of a 2^k series experiment. Thus, either $x_1 + x_2 + x_3 = 0 \pmod{2}$, or $x_1 + x_2 + x_3 = 1 \pmod{2}$ can be used to select four of the treatment conditions of a $2 \times 2 \times 2$ factorial set. When a $\frac{1}{2}$ replication of a 2^k series experiment is carried out, all effects have two *aliases*, aliases being effects which cannot be distinguished, (i.e., are totally confounded with each other). If a further reduction in size is required, say a $\frac{1}{4}$ replication of a $2 \times 2 \times 2$ design, a second defining relation is required and all effects will have four aliases. Similarly, for experiments in the 3^k series, a $\frac{1}{3}$ replication is selected with a single defining relation and all effects will have three aliases; a $\frac{1}{9}$ replication is selected by two defining relations and all effects will have nine aliases.

To illustrate the kind of confounding which arises in a fractional replication, consider a one-half replication of a 2^3 factorial experiment. Suppose that the treatments in this one-half replication correspond to the treatments in the set $(ABC)_0$, which are (000), (011), (101), and (110). Comparisons corresponding to the main effects and interactions may be indicated schematically as follows (the columns indicate the weights for a comparison):

	A	B	C	AB	AC	BC	ABC
$(000) = (1)$	$-$	$-$	$-$	$-$	$-$	$-$	$-$
$(011) = bc$	$-$	$+$	$+$	$+$	$+$	$-$	$-$
$(101) = ac$	$+$	$-$	$+$	$+$	$-$	$+$	$-$
$(110) = ab$	$+$	$+$	$-$	$-$	$+$	$+$	$-$

Note that the pattern of the comparison corresponding to the main effect of A (the column headed A) and the pattern of the comparison corresponding to the BC interaction (the column headed BC) are identical. (These two patterns would not continue to be identical if the remaining treatments in the complete factorial were added.) Hence, if only information on these four treatment combinations is available, variation due to the main effect of A is completely confounded with variation due to the BC interaction. Similarly, by using information from the one-half replication given above, B and AC are completely confounded; C and AB are also completely confounded. The sign pattern of ABC is not that of a comparison; it will be found that variation due to ABC cannot be estimated.

The effects which cannot be distinguished in a fractional replication, aliases, may be determined by means of a relatively simple rule. Consider a one-half replication of a 2^4 factorial experiment defined by the relation $(ABCD)_0$. The alias of the main effect of A is given by

$$A \times ABCD = A^2BCD = BCD.$$

BCD is the generalized interaction of A and $ABCD$; it is also the alias of A in a one-half replication defined by $(ABCD)_0$ or $(ABCD)_1$. The alias of AB is

$$AB \times ABCD = A^2B^2CD = CD.$$

The alias of ABC is the generalized interaction of ABC and the defining relation, i.e.,

$$ABC \times ABCD = D.$$

In general, the alias of an effect in a fractional replication is the generalized interaction of that effect with the defining relation or relations, should there be more than one.

The analysis of variance for one-half replication of a 2^4 factorial experiment, by using $(ABCD)_0$ or $(ABCD)_1$ as the defining relation, is given in Table 8.41. The aliases are indicated. (It will be noted that, if BCD is the generalized interaction of A and $ABCD$, then A will be the generalized

TABLE 8.41 **One-half replication of a 2^k factorial experiment**

Source	df
A (BCD)	1
B (ACD)	1
C (ABD)	1
D (ABC)	1
AB (CD)	1
AC (BD)	1
AD (BC)	1
Within cell	$8(n-1)$
Total	$8n-1$

interaction of BCD and $ABCD$.) Main effects are aliased with three-factor interactions, and two-factor interactions are aliased with other two-factor interactions. The four-factor interaction cannot be estimated. If three-factor and higher-order interactions may be considered negligible, then estimates of the variance due to the main effects are given by this fractional replication. There is considerable ambiguity about what interpretation should be made if two-factor interactions should prove to be significant, since pairs of two-factor interactions are completely confounded.

By way of contrast, consider a one-half replication of a 2^5 factorial experiment. Suppose that the treatments are selected through use of the relation $(ABCDE)_0$ or $(ABCDE)_1$. The analysis of variance may be outlined as indicated below (aliases are indicated in parentheses):

Source	df
Main effects (4-factor interactions)	5
Two-factor interactions (3-factor interactions)	10
Within cell	$16(n-1)$
Total	$16n-1$

If three-factor and higher-order interactions are negligible, this fractional replication provides information for tests on main effects as well as two-factor interactions.

A single defining relation for a 2^4 factorial experiment will select a one-half replication. If k is large, it is desirable to have a one-quarter or even a one-eighth replication. In order to select a one-fourth replication, the treatments are required to satisfy, simultaneously, two defining relations. Suppose that these defining relations are designated U and V. The aliases of an effect E will have the form

$$E \times U, \quad E \times V, \quad E \times (U \times V).$$

In words, the aliases of an effect in a one-fourth replication are the generalized interactions of that effect with each of the defining relations as well as the generalized interaction of the effect with the interaction of the defining relations.

For example, consider a one-fourth replication of a 2^6 factorial experiment. Suppose that the defining relations are $(ABCE)_0$ and $(ABDF)_0$. The generalized interaction of these two relations is $(CDEF)_0$. A partial list of the aliases is as follows:

Effect	Aliases
A	$BCE, BDF, ACDEF$
B	$ACE, ADF, BCDEF$
AB	$CE, DF, ABCDEF$
CD	$ABED, ABCF, EF$

In this case, main effects are aliased with three-factor and higher-order interactions; two-factor interactions are aliased with other two-factor as well as higher-order interactions.

As another example, consider a one-fourth replication of a 2^7 factorial experiment. Suppose that the defining relations for the selected treatments are $(ABCDE)_0$ and $(ABCFG)_0$. The generalized interaction of these relations is $(DEFG)_0$. A partial listing of the aliases is as follows:

Effect	Aliases
A	$BCDE, BCFG, ADEFG$
B	$ACDE, ACFG, BDEFG$
AB	$CDE, CFG, ABDEFG$
DE	$ABC, ABCDEFG, FG$

In this design main effects are aliased with four-factor and higher-order interactions. With the exception of $DE = FG$, $DG = EF$, $DF = EG$, all other two-factor interactions are aliased with three-factor or higher-order interactions. The two-factor interactions which are equated are aliased. This design yields unbiased tests on main effects and several of the two-factor interactions provided that three-factor and higher-order interactions are negligible.

For a one-eighth replication of a 2^6 factorial experiment, three defining relations are required to select the set of treatments. If these relations are designated U, V, and W, the aliases of an effect E are given by the following interactions:

$$E \times U, \quad E \times V, \quad E \times W;$$

$$E \times (U \times V), \quad E \times (U \times W), \quad E \times (V \times W), \quad E \times (U \times V \times W).$$

In general, if m is the number of defining relations, then the number of aliases of an effect is

$$m + \binom{m}{2} + \binom{m}{3} + \cdots + \binom{m}{m}.$$

For example, when $m = 3$,

$$3 + \binom{3}{2} + \binom{3}{3} = 3 + 3 + 1 = 7.$$

Fractional Replication in Blocks

To illustrate the general method for arranging the treatments in a fractional replication into blocks, consider a 2^6 factorial experiment. Suppose that a one-half replication of 64 treatments is selected by means of the relation $(ABCDEF)_0$. Now suppose that the resulting 32 treatments are subdivided into two sets of 16 treatments by means of the relation ABC, one set being $(ABC)_0$ and the other $(ABC)_1$. The resulting sets of 16 treatments are given in part i of Table 8.42. Suppose that the latter sets define the blocks. In the analysis of the resulting experiment, main effects will be aliased with five-factor interactions. Two-factor interactions will be aliased with four-factor interactions. Three-factor interactions will be aliased in pairs as follows:

Effect	Alias
ABC	DEF
ABD	CEF
ABE	CDF

The pair $ABC = DEF$ is confounded with differences between blocks.

TABLE 8.42 **One-half replication of 2^6 factorial (defining relation: $[ABCDEF]_0$)**

	Block 1 $(ABC)_0$				Block 2 $(ABC)_1$			
(i)	(1)	ab	ac	bc	ae	af	ad	bd
	abef	ef	de	df	bf	be	ce	cf
	acde	acdf	abdf	acef	cd	abcd	abcf	abce
	bcdf	bcde	bcef	abde	abcdef	cdef	bdef	adef

	Block 1′ $(ABD)_0$		Block 1″ $(ABD)_1$		Block 2′ $(ABD)_1$		Block 2″ $(ABD)_0$	
(ii)	(1)	ab	ac	bc	ae	af	ad	bd
	abef	ef	de	df	bf	be	ce	cf
	acde	acdf	abdf	acef	cf	abcd	abcf	abce
	bcdf	bcde	bcef	abde	abcdef	cdef	bdef	adef

Suppose that the blocks of 16 are further subdivided into blocks of size 8 by means of the relations $(ABD)_0$ and $(ABD)_1$. The resulting blocks are given in part ii of the table. The aliases remain the same as in the previous analysis, but now there is additional confounding with blocks. The three degrees of freedom confounded with between-block differences are

$$ABC = DEF, \qquad ABD = CEF,$$

as well as
$$ABC \times ABD = CD.$$

Note that the generalized interaction of DEF and CEF is also CD.

Thus in a one-half replication of a 2^6 factorial experiment in blocks of size 8, if three-factor and higher-order interactions are negligible, main effects and all two-factor interactions except CD may be tested. Some of the three-factor interactions as well as CD are confounded with block effects, but other pairs of three-factor interactions are clear of block effects, provided that the appropriate model is strictly additive with respect to block effects.

Computational Procedures

Computational procedures for a one-half replication of a 2^k factorial experiment are identical to those of a complete replication of a 2^{k-1} factorial experiment. For example, the eight treatments in a one-half replication of a 2^4 factorial experiment actually form a complete replication of a 2^3 factorial experiment if the levels of one of the factors are disregarded. If the one-half replication is defined by the relation $(ABCD)_0$, the treatments are

$$(1), ab, ac, ad, bc, bd, cd, abcd.$$

If the levels of factor D are disregarded, the treatments are

$$(1), ab, ac, a, bc, b, c, abc;$$

these are the eight treatment combinations in a 2^3 factorial experiment. Corresponding effects in the three-factor and four-factor experiments are given below:

Three-factor experiment	Four-factor experiment (one-half rep)
A	$A = BCD$
B	$B = ACD$
C	$C = ABD$
AB	$AB = CD$
AC	$AC = BD$
BC	$BC = AD$
ABC	$ABC = D$

Suppose that a one-quarter replication of a 2^5 factorial experiment is defined by the relations $(ABE)_0$ and $(CDE)_0$. The treatments in this fractional replication are

$$(1), ab, cd, ace, bce, ade, bde, abcde.$$

If factors D and E are disregarded, the treatments are

$$(1), ab, c, ac, bc, a, b, abc;$$

these are the treatments in a complete replication of a 2^3 factorial experiment. The aliases of these effects are their generalized interactions with ABE, CDE, and $ABE \times CDE = ABCD$. Thus there is the following correspondence between this 2^3 factorial experiment and the one-quarter replication of a 2^5 factorial experiment:

Five-factor experiment (one-quarter rep)
$A = BE,\ ACDE,\ BCD$
$B = AE,\ BCDE,\ ACD$
$C = ABCE,\ DE,\ ABD$
$AB = E,\ ABCDE,\ CD$
$AC = BCE,\ ADE,\ BD$
$BC = ACE,\ BDE,\ AD$
$ABC = CE,\ ABDE,\ D$

That is, if a one-quarter replication of a 2^5 factorial is analyzed as if it were a complete replication of a 2^3 factorial, the corresponding effects are indicated—thus the analysis reduces to the analysis of a complete factorial having two fewer factors.

Extensive tables of fractional replications of experiments in the 2^k series are given in Cochran and Cox (1957, pp. 276–289). The plans in these tables permit the arrangement of the treatments into blocks of various sizes. To avoid having main effects and two-factor interactions aliased with lower-order interactions, care must be taken in selecting the defining relations for fractional replications and blocks. The plans tabulated in Cochran and Cox are those which tend to minimize undesirable aliases.

Fractional Replication for Designs in the 3^k Series

Principles used in the 2^k series may be generalized to factorial experiments in the p^k series, where p is a prime number. In a 3^3 factorial experiment, a one-third replication may be constructed by any of the components of the three-factor interaction: ABC, ABC^2, AB^2C, or AB^2C^2. Each of these components will subdivide the 27 treatments in a 3^3 factorial set into three sets of 9 treatments each. If one of the sets is defined by $(ABC)_i$, where $i = 0$, 1, or 2, the aliases of the main effect of factor A are

$$A \times ABC = A^2BC = AB^2C^2,$$
$$A^2 \times ABC = BC.$$

The aliases of AB^2 are

$$AB^2 \times ABD = A^2B^3C = AC^2,$$

$$(AB^2)^2 \times ABC = A^3B^5C = B^2C = BC^2.$$

In general, if the defining relation for a one-third replication in a 3^k experiment is R, then the aliases of an effect E are

$$E \times R \quad \text{and} \quad E^2 \times R.$$

The following correspondence may be established between a one-third replication of a 3^3 factorial and a complete replication of a 3^2 factorial; assume that the defining relation is $(ABC)_i$:

3^2 factorial experiment	3^3 factorial experiment (one-third rep)
A	$A = AB^2C^2 = BC$
B	$B = AB^2C = AC$
AB	$AB = ABC^2 = C$
AB^2	$AB^2 = AC^2 = BC^2$

From the point of view of computational procedures, a one-third replication of a 3^3 factorial is equivalent to a complete replication of a 3^2 factorial experiment. Since two-factor interactions are aliased with main effects, this plan is of little practical use unless it can be assumed that all interactions are negligible.

A one-third replication of a 3^4 factorial experiment may be constructed from any one of the components of the four-factor interaction. If one of the sets of 27 treatments defined by $(ABDE)_i$ is used, then the correspondence given in Table 8.43 may be established between the fractional replication of a 3^4 factorial and a complete replication of a 3^3 factorial. Main effects are aliased with three-factor and higher-order interactions. Some of the two-factor interactions are also aliased with other two-factor interactions. If, however, the two-factor interactions with factor D are negligible, then the other two-factor interactions are clear of two-factor aliases.

Assignment of treatments to blocks follows the same general principles as those given in earlier sections of this chapter. Plans for fractional replications in the 3^k series are given in Cochran and Cox (1957, pp. 290–291). The following notation systems are equivalent:

$$AB(I) = AB^2, \quad ABC(W) = AB^2C^2, \quad ABC(Y) = ABC^2,$$

$$AB(J) = AB, \quad ABC(X) = AB^2C, \quad ABC(Z) = ABC.$$

TABLE 8.43 **One-third replication of a 3^4 factorial experiment (defining relation: $ABCD$)**

Source	df
$A = AB^2CD^2 = BCD$	2
$B = AB^2CD = ACD$	2
$C = ABC^2D = ABD$	2
$AB = ABC^2D^2 = CD$	2
$AB^2 = AC^2D^2 = BC^2D^2$	2
$AC = AB^2CD^2 = BD$	2
$AC^2 = AB^2D^2 = BC^2D$	2
$BC = AB^2C^2D = AD$	2
$BC^2 = AB^2D = AC^2D$	2
$ABC = ABCD^2 = D$	2
$ABC^2 = ABD^2 = CD^2$	2
$AB^2C = ACD^2 = BD^2$	2
$AB^2C^2 = AD^2 = BCD^2$	2
Within cell	$27(n-1)$
Total	$27n - 1$

OTHER FRACTIONAL-REPLICATION DESIGNS. Latin squares and Greco-Latin squares may be considered fractional replications of factorial experiments. Experimental designs in these categories will be considered in Chapter 9. A number of references for mixed fractional designs are provided by Kirk (1982, p. 681).

8.9 EXERCISES

1. The construction of both balanced incomplete block and fractional factorial designs utilizes modular arithmetic to describe and select treatment conditions.

(*a*) Express the integers 21, 7, 8, 12, 42, 61, and 114 in terms of mod 5, mod 3, and mod 2.

(*b*) Add:

(Mod 3)		(Mod 7)	
$3 + 4$	$14 + 2$	$2 + 1$	$14 + 7$
$6 + 8$	$12 + 1$	$3 + 6$	$11 + 9$
$2 + 12$	$3 + 8$	$4 + 12$	$21 + 46$

(*c*) Solve the equations for x.

$$2x = 3 \ (\text{mod } 5)$$
$$4x = 32 \ (\text{mod } 3)$$
$$12x = 6 \ (\text{mod } 7)$$
$$11x = 41 \ (\text{mod } 2)$$

(*d*) Using modular notation, describe each of the following treatment conditions from a factorial design.

$$abc_{111} \qquad ab_{21}$$
$$abcd_{2123} \qquad abc_{213}$$
$$ab_{32} \qquad abcde_{23142}$$

2. For two-factor designs of dimension p^2, one may design experiments which confound all of the two-factor interaction between blocks in the case of a 2×2 design or parts of the two-factor interaction when $p > 2$. For p^3 designs, one may confound all the three-factor interaction in a $2 \times 2 \times 2$ design or parts of the three-factor interaction when $p > 2$. Construct blocks as indicated by the designated confounding.

	Design size	Between-block confounding
(a)	3×3	AB^2
(b)	$\times 5$	AB^4
(c)	$3 \times 3 \times 3$	AB^2C^2
(d)	$5 \times 5 \times 5$	AB^3C^4
(e)	$2 \times 2 \times 2$	ABC

3. An experimenter was interested in evaluating the impact of three dimensions of advertising upon consumer behavior:

Factor A	Viewing Frequency	$p = 2,$
Factor B	Viewing Duration	$q = 2,$
Factor C	Message Complexity	$r = 2.$

Prototype messages were developed for each of the $2 \times 2 \times 2 = 8$ treatment conditions. Because of the nature of the tasks, (s)he decided that the same subjects could be tested under at most four conditions. Design experiments as follows:

Total subjects available	No. of blocks	Block size	Between-block confounding
20	2	4	ABC
20	2	4	AC
20	2	4	AC

(*a*) For each design, write the structural model.
(*b*) For each design, list the treatment conditions for each block.
(*c*) For each design prepare an analysis of variance summary table showing sources of variation and numerical values for df.

4. An experimenter interested in a $2 \times 2 \times 2$ factorial experiment did *not* expect a three-factor interaction. With only ten subjects available, (s)he decided to observe each subject under only four treatment conditions and to confound the ABC interactions with differences between two groups of five subjects each. (S)he

obtained:

	Subject	\multicolumn{4}{c}{Treatments}			
	Subject	(100)	(010)	(001)	(111)
	1	18	10	4	10
Block 1 = Group 1	2	12	6	5	9
	3	11	5	2	7
	4	9	3	2	7
	5	14	8	7	11

	Subject	\multicolumn{4}{c}{Treatments}			
	Subject	(000)	(110)	(101)	(011)
	6	12	14	10	5
Block 2 = Group 2	7	13	18	12	7
	8	6	9	9	4
	9	15	20	14	9
	10	11	16	10	5

(*a*) What is the structural model for this design?
(*b*) Complete the analysis of variance.

5. Design experiments as follows:

	Factorial design size	Between-block confounding
(a)	3×3	AB
(b)	3×3	AB^2
(c)	$3 \times 3 \times 3$	ABC
(d)	$3 \times 3 \times 3$	AB^2C^2
(e)	5×5	AB^3
(f)	$5 \times 5 \times 5$	AB^3C^4

Assume that repeated measures are taken on subjects, a group of 10 subjects is assigned at random to each block of treatments, and the treatments in that block are administered to each subject in an independent random order.
(1) Show each design schematically listing treatments in each block.
(2) Write the analysis of variance summary table for each design. Show numerical values for df and show E(MS) assuming all factors are fixed except for subjects.

6. In a $3 \times 3 \times 3$ design, there are 27 treatment conditions. With a block size of nine, one may construct three blocks of nine treatments each by confounding one of the components of the three-factor interaction between blocks. To further reduce block size, one may confound another interaction component between blocks. Double confounding generates confounding with regard to *generalized interactions* or *aliases* of the confounding relations. For each design, generate the relevant blocks of three treatment conditions each and list aliases of the defining relations.

Block Size = 9	Block Size = 3
ABC	AB^2
ABC^2	AC
AB^2C^2	AC^2
AC	ABC^2
ABC	AC

CHAPTER 9

LATIN SQUARES AND RELATED DESIGNS

9.1 DEFINITION AND ENUMERATION OF LATIN SQUARE

A Latin square is a balanced two-way classification scheme. By way of definition, consider the following 3×3 arrangement:

$$
\begin{array}{ccc}
a & b & c \\
b & c & a \\
c & a & b
\end{array}
$$

In this arrangement, each letter occurs just once in each row and just once in each column. The following arrangement also exhibits this kind of balance:

$$
\begin{array}{ccc}
b & c & a \\
a & b & c \\
c & a & b
\end{array}
$$

The latter arrangement was obtained from the first by interchanging the first and second rows.

Two Latin squares are *orthogonal* if, when they are combined, the same pair of symbols occurs no more than once in the composite square. For example, consider the following 3×3 Latin squares:

$$
\begin{array}{ccc}
(1) & (2) & (3) \\
\begin{array}{ccc} a_1 & a_2 & a_3 \\ a_2 & a_3 & a_1 \\ a_3 & a_1 & a_2 \end{array} &
\begin{array}{ccc} b_2 & b_3 & b_1 \\ b_3 & b_1 & b_2 \\ b_1 & b_2 & b_3 \end{array} &
\begin{array}{ccc} c_1 & c_2 & c_3 \\ c_3 & c_1 & c_2 \\ c_2 & c_3 & c_1 \end{array}
\end{array}
$$

674

Combining squares (1) and (2) yields the composite square

$$a_1b_2 \quad a_2b_3 \quad a_3b_1$$
$$a_2b_3 \quad a_3b_1 \quad a_1b_2$$
$$a_3b_1 \quad a_1b_2 \quad a_2b_3$$

In this composite the treatment combination a_1b_2 occurs more than once; hence squares (1) and (2) are not orthogonal.

Combining squares (1) and (3) yields the following composite:

$$a_1c_1 \quad a_2c_2 \quad a_3c_3$$
$$a_2c_3 \quad a_3c_1 \quad a_1c_2$$
$$a_3c_2 \quad a_1c_3 \quad a_2c_1$$

In this composite no treatment combination is repeated. There are nine possible treatment combinations that may be formed from three levels of factor A and three levels of factor C. Each of these possibilities appears in the composite. Hence squares (1) and (3) are orthogonal.

Extensive tables of sets of orthogonal Latin squares are given in Fisher and Yates (1953) and Cochran and Cox (1957). The composite square obtained by combining two orthogonal Latin squares is called a Greco-Latin square. The 3×3 Greco-Latin square obtained by combining squares (1) and (3) above may be represented schematically as follows:

$$11 \quad 22 \quad 33$$
$$23 \quad 31 \quad 12$$
$$32 \quad 13 \quad 21$$

This representation uses only the subscripts that appear with the a's and c's. Interchanging any two rows of a Greco-Latin square will still yield a Greco-Latin square. For example, interchanging the first and third rows of the above square yields the following Greco-Latin square:

$$32 \quad 13 \quad 21$$
$$23 \quad 31 \quad 12$$
$$11 \quad 22 \quad 33$$

Any two columns of a Greco-Latin square may also be interchanged without affecting the required balance.

A collection of $p - 1$ Latin squares of size $p \times p$ is said to form a *complete set* if each square in the collection is orthogonal to every other square. There can be at most $p - 1$ squares in a complete set. For the case of 4×4 squares, the following collection defines a complete set:

$$
\begin{array}{cccc\quad cccc\quad cccc}
1 & 2 & 3 & 4 & 1 & 2 & 3 & 4 & 1 & 2 & 3 & 4 \\
2 & 1 & 4 & 3 & 3 & 4 & 1 & 2 & 4 & 3 & 2 & 1 \\
3 & 4 & 1 & 2 & 4 & 3 & 2 & 1 & 2 & 1 & 4 & 3 \\
4 & 3 & 2 & 1 & 2 & 1 & 4 & 3 & 3 & 4 & 1 & 2
\end{array}
$$

There are many such sets for 4×4 squares. However, each set cannot contain more than three squares.

It is not always possible to find a Latin square orthogonal to a given Latin square. For example, no orthogonal squares exist for 6×6 squares. If the dimension of a square is capable of being expressed in the form (prime number)^n, where n is any integer, then a complete set of squares exists. For example, complete sets exist for squares of the following dimensions.

$$3 = 3^1, \qquad 4 = 2^2, \qquad 5 = 5^1, \qquad 8 = 2^3, \qquad 9 = 3^2.$$

In addition, there are cases in which complete sets exist even though the dimension of the square is not of the form (prime number)^n, particularly when the dimension is divisible by 4. For example, a complete set may be constructed for squares of dimension 12×12.

The *standard form* of a Latin square is, by definition, that square obtained by rearranging the rows and columns until the letters in the first row and the letters in the first column are in alphabetical order. For example, the square

$$
\begin{array}{ccc}
b & a & c \\
c & b & a \\
a & c & b
\end{array}
\tag{9.1}
$$

has the standard form

$$
\begin{array}{ccc}
a & b & c \\
b & c & a \\
c & a & b.
\end{array}
\tag{9.2}
$$

The standard form (2) is obtained from (1) by interchanging columns 1 and 2. All 3×3 Latin squares may be reduced to this standard form. From this standard form $(3!) \cdot (2!) - 1 = (3 \cdot 2 \cdot 1)(2 \cdot 1) - 1 = 11$ different nonstandard 3×3 Latin squares may be constructed. Hence, including the standard form, there are 12 different 3×3 Latin squares.

For 4×4 Latin squares there are four different standard forms. One of these four is given in (3).

$$
\begin{array}{cccc}
a & b & c & d \\
b & a & d & c \\
c & d & b & a \\
d & c & a & b
\end{array}
\tag{9.3}
$$

A second standard form is given by (4).

$$
\begin{array}{cccc}
a & b & c & d \\
b & c & d & a \\
c & d & a & b \\
d & a & b & c
\end{array}
\tag{9.4}
$$

From each of these standard forms $(4!)(3!) - 1 = 143$ different non-standard 4×4 Latin squares may be constructed by the process of interchanging rows and columns. Nonstandard squares constructed from standard form (3) will be different from nonstandard squares constructed from standard form (4). Thus (3) potentially represents 144 Latin squares (143 nonstandard squares plus 1 standard square). Standard form (4) also represents potentially 144 different 4×4 Latin squares. Since there are 4 different standard forms, the potential number of different 4×4 Latin squares is $4(144) = 576$.

The number of possible standard forms of a Latin square increases quite rapidly as the dimension of the square increases. For example, a 6×6 Latin square has 9408 standard forms. Each of these forms represents potentially $(6!)(5!) = 86,400$ different squares. The total number of different 6×6 Latin squares that may be constructed is

$$(9408)(86,400) = 812,851,200.$$

In general, one may generate $p!(p - 1)! - 1$ Latin squares from each standard form.

In most tables, only standard forms of Latin squares are given. To obtain a Latin square for use in an experimental design, one of the standard squares of suitable dimension should be selected at random. The rows and columns of the selected square are then randomized independently. The levels of the factorial effects are then assigned at random to the rows, columns, and Latin letters of the square, respectively. To illustrate the procedure for randomizing the rows and columns of a 4×4 Latin square, suppose that square (9.3) is obtained from a table of Latin squares. Two random sequences of digits 1 through 4 are then obtained from tables of random sequences. Suppose that the sequences obtained are $(2, 4, 1, 3)$ and $(3, 4, 1, 2)$. The columns of square (9.3) are now rearranged in accordance with the first sequence. That is, column 2 is moved into the first position, column 4 into the second position, column 1 into the third position, and column 3 into the fourth position. The resulting square is

$$
\begin{array}{cccc}
b & d & a & c \\
a & c & b & d \\
d & a & c & b \\
c & b & d & a \\
\end{array}
$$

The rows of the resulting squares are now rearranged in accordance with the second random sequence. That is, row 3 is moved to the first position, row 4 moved to the second position, row 1 moved to the third position, and row 2 moved to the fourth position. After these moves have been made, the resulting square is

$$
\begin{array}{cccc}
d & a & c & b \\
c & b & d & a \\
b & d & a & c \\
a & c & b & d \\
\end{array}
$$

This last square represents a random rearrangement of the rows and columns of the original 4×4 standard form. This last square may be considered as a random choice from among the 144 squares represented by the standard form (9.3). Since (9.3) was chosen at random from the standard forms, the square that has just been constructed may be considered a random choice from the 576 possible different 4×4 Latin squares.

Some additional definitions of types of Latin squares will be helpful in using tables. The *conjugate* of a Latin square is obtained by interchanging the rows and columns. For example, the following squares are conjugates:

$$
\begin{array}{ccc}
a & b & c \\
c & a & b \\
b & c & a
\end{array}
\qquad
\begin{array}{ccc}
a & c & b \\
b & a & c \\
c & b & a
\end{array}
$$

The square on the right is obtained from the square on the left by writing the columns as rows. That is, the first column of the square on the left is the first row of the square on the right, the second column of the square on the left is the second row of the square on the right, etc. Conversely, the square on the left may be obtained from the square on the right by writing the rows of the latter as columns.

A one-step *cyclic permutation* of a sequence of letters is one which moves the first letter in the sequence to the extreme right, simultaneously moving all other letters in one position to the left. For example, given the sequence *abcd*, a one-step cyclic permutation yields *bcda*; a second cyclic permutation yields *cdab*; a third cyclic permutation yields *dabc*; and a fourth cyclic permutation yields *abcd*—the latter is the starting sequence. Given a sequence of p letters, a $p \times p$ Latin square may be constructed by $p - 1$ one-step cyclic permutations of these letters. In the case of the sequence *abcd,* the Latin square formed by cyclic permutations is

$$
\begin{array}{cccc}
a & b & c & d \\
b & c & d & a \\
c & d & a & b \\
d & a & b & c.
\end{array}
$$

A *balanced set* of Latin squares is a collection in which each letter appears in each possible position once and only once. For a $p \times p$ square, there will be p squares in a balanced set. Given any $p \times p$ square, a balanced set may be constructed by cyclic permutations of the columns. For example, the squares given below form a balanced set:

$$
\begin{array}{ccccccccc}
\mathbf{I} & & & \mathbf{II} & & & \mathbf{III} & & \\
a & b & c & b & a & c & c & a & b \\
c & a & b & a & b & c & b & c & a \\
b & c & a & c & a & b & a & b & c
\end{array}
$$

Square II is obtained from square I by moving the first column of square I to the extreme right. Square III is obtained from square II by moving the first column of square II to the extreme right. The resulting set is balanced in the sense that each of the nine positions within the squares contains any given letter once and only once.

One square may be obtained from another by substitution of one letter for another. For example, given the following square:

$$a \quad b \quad c \quad d$$
$$b \quad a \quad d \quad c$$
$$c \quad d \quad b \quad a$$
$$d \quad c \quad a \quad b$$

Suppose that each of the a's is replaced by a b, each of the b's replaced by a c, each of the c's by an a, and each of the d's is not changed. This kind of replacement procedure is called a *one-to-one transformation*. The square resulting from this transformation is given below:

$$b \quad c \quad a \quad d$$
$$c \quad b \quad d \quad a$$
$$a \quad d \quad c \quad b$$
$$d \quad a \quad b \quad c.$$

This last square has the standard form given below:

$$a \quad b \quad c \quad d$$
$$b \quad d \quad a \quad c$$
$$c \quad a \quad d \quad b$$
$$d \quad c \quad b \quad a.$$

Since this latter square has a different standard form from that of the original square, the one-to-one transformation yields a square which is different from any square which can be constructed by permutation of the rows or columns of the original square.

9.2 USES OF LATIN SQUARES

Latin squares have essentially four related uses in research design in the social and behavioral sciences. They are typically used to control two or more nuisance variables, to counterbalance order effects in repeated-measures designs, to confound treatment conditions with group main effects, or as balanced fractional replications from a complete factorial design.

Control of Nuisance Variables

In the original application of Latin square designs in agricultural experimentation, the cells of a $p \times p$ Latin square define p^2 experimental units. For example, the cells may be plots of land in a field. The selection of the Latin square defines the manner in which the levels of a single factor are assigned to the experimental units. That is, the procedure in selecting the Latin square specifies the randomization procedure necessary for the validity of statistical tests made in subsequent analyses. In its classic agricultural setting, the Latin-square design represents a single-factor experiment with restricted randomization with respect to row and column effects associated with the experimental units. In this design it is assumed that treatment effects do not interact with the row and column effects. Fisher (1951) and Wilk and Kempthorne (1957) carefully distinguish between the use of a Latin square to provide the design for the randomization procedure and the use of a Latin square for other purposes.

The generalization of this classical application is to any research environment wherein two nuisance variables may be assigned to the rows and columns, respectively, of a Latin square and p levels of a single treatment factor are assigned to the cells of the Latin square. In applications in the social, behavioral or biological sciences, the row and column variables are typically organismic variables and the Latin square provides a method for controlling individual differences among experimental units. For example, suppose that it is desired to control differences among litters as well as differences among sizes within litters for animals assigned to given treatment conditions. If there are four treatments, and if the size of the litter is four, then a 4×4 Latin square may be used to obtain the required balance. Use of this plan provides the experimenter with a dual balance. That is, the experimental units under any treatment are balanced with respect to both litter and size within litter.

	Size within litter			
Litter	1	2	3	4
1	t_2	t_1	t_4	t_3
2	t_3	t_4	t_1	t_2
3	t_1	t_2	t_3	t_4
4	t_4	t_3	t_2	t_1

This plan may be replicated as many times as is required. An alternative plan, not having this dual balance, would assign the experimental units at random to the treatment conditions. This plan is to be preferred to the balanced plan when the variables under control by restricted randomization do not in fact reduce the experimental error sufficiently to offset the loss in the degrees of freedom for estimating the experimental error. That is, the benefit of the Latin square depends upon the size of row and column effects, which effects are removed from the experimental error of a completely randomized design.

The principle of controlling nuisance variables may be extended to three variables by using a Greco-Latin square, and to four or more variables with a hyper-Greco-Latin square. We have seen that a Greco-Latin square design is formed when two orthogonal Latin squares are superimposed, the name coming from assigning Greek letters to the cells of one square and Latin letters to the other. Thus, the two Latin squares

$$
\begin{array}{ccc}
a & b & c \\
b & c & a \\
c & a & b
\end{array}
\quad \text{and} \quad
\begin{array}{ccc}
\alpha & \beta & \gamma \\
\gamma & \alpha & \beta \\
\beta & \gamma & \alpha
\end{array}
$$

form the Greco-Latin square

$$
\begin{array}{ccc}
a\alpha & b\beta & c\gamma \\
b\gamma & c\alpha & a\beta \\
c\beta & a\gamma & b\alpha.
\end{array}
$$

This Greco-Latin square forms the experimental design,

$$
\begin{array}{cccc}
 & b_1 & b_2 & b_3 \\
a_1 & cd_{11} & cd_{22} & cd_{33} \\
a_2 & cd_{23} & cd_{31} & cd_{12} \\
a_3 & cd_{32} & cd_{13} & cd_{21}
\end{array}
$$

when levels of factors A, B, and C are nuisance variables and levels of factor D are the treatment levels.

This approach can, in principle, be extended further. A hyper-Greco-Latin square is formed when one or more additional orthogonal Latin squares is superimposed upon a Greco-Latin square, providing for the control of a fourth, fifth, etc., nuisance variable. In practice, however, this application is limited by three considerations. First, for reasons to be explained later, it is necessary to assume that all interactions among the variables included in the design are zero. Second, there is a limited number of orthogonal Latin squares with which to work; because of the limited number of degrees of freedom, one can only combine 3 orthogonal 4×4 squares, 4 orthogonal 5×5 squares, etc. There are no more than $p - 1$ mutually orthogonal squares in any single complete set. Finally, as seen earlier there are not always orthogonal Latin squares from which to form Greco- or hyper-Greco-Latin squares.

Counterbalancing Order Effects

Another important use of the Latin square in the area of the behavioral sciences is to counterbalance order effects in plans calling for repeated measures. For example, consider the following experimental plan:

	Order 1	Order 2	Order 3	Order 4
Group 1	a_3	a_1	a_2	a_4
Group 2	a_2	a_3	a_4	a_1
Group 3	a_4	a_2	a_1	a_3
Group 4	a_1	a_4	a_3	a_2

Suppose that each of the groups represents a random subsample from a larger random sample. Each of the subjects within group 1 is given treatments a_1 through a_4 in the order indicated by the columns of the Latin square. Upon completion of the experiment, each of the levels of factor A will be administered once in each of the orders. Hence there is a kind of balance with respect to the order effect. If an order effect exists, it is "controlled" in the weak sense that each treatment appears equally often in each of the orders. Implicit in this type of "control" are the assumptions of a strictly additive model with respect to the order factor. That is, the order factor is assumed to be additive with respect to the treatment and group factors; also order is assumed not to interact with the latter factors. (Further, the homogeneity-of-covariance assumptions underlying a repeated-measure design are still required for the validity of the final tests.)

In another sense, however, order effects are not under control. Consider the administration of a_2 under order 3. For the plan given above, a_2 is preceded by a_3 and a_1 in that order. Should the sequence in which a_1 and a_3 precede a_2 have any appreciable effect, this plan would not provide an adequate control on such sequence (carry-over) effects. (The term *sequence effect* will be used to indicate differential effects associated with the order in which treatments precede other treatments.) Differences among the groups in this plan essentially represent differences among the four sequences called for by this plan.

Confounding Main Effects with Groups

A modification of the plan that has just been considered leads to another important use of the Latin square: its use as a confounded factorial design wherein there are two treatments, one of which is confounded with between-group differences.

Suppose that each of the groups is assigned to a different level of factor B. The result is:

	Order 1	Order 2	Order 3	Order 4
b_1 (Group 1)	a_3	a_1	a_2	a_4
b_2 (Group 2)	a_2	a_3	a_4	a_1
b_3 (Group 3)	a_4	a_2	a_1	a_3
b_4 (Group 4)	a_1	a_4	a_3	a_2

Obviously, differences between groups and sequence effects are both totally confounded with the B main effects. However, if the sequence effects are negligible relative to the effects of factor B, differences among the groups measure the effects due to factor B. In this design, the order main effects are confounded with the AB interaction, but if interactions with order effects are negligible, then partial information with respect to the AB interaction may be obtained. Assuming n subjects in each of the groups, the analysis of this plan takes the following form:

Source of variation	df
Between subjects	$4n - 1$
Groups (B)	3
Subjects within groups	$4(n - 1)$
Within subjects	$12n$
Order	3
A	3
$(AB)'$ (partial information)	6
Residual	$12n - 12$

Balanced Fractional Replication

When treatments are assigned to all three dimensions, rows, columns, and cells, of a Latin square, the Latin square provides a convenient way to select a balanced fractional replication from a complete factorial experiment. Greco-Latin squares and hyper-Greco-Latin squares may be used in the same manner. In general, a Latin square may be viewed as a $1/p$ fractional replication of a $p \times p \times p$ factorial experiment, a Greco-Latin square provides a $1/p^2$ fractional replication of a $p \times p \times p \times p$ factorial design and a hyper-Greco-Latin square provides a $1/p^3$ fractional replication of a $p \times p \times p \times p \times p$ design. Thus, for example, in the 3^k series of factorial designs, a Latin square provides $\frac{1}{3}$, (9 of the 27 factorial conditions), a Greco-Latin square provides $\frac{1}{9}$, (9 of the 81 factorial conditions of the four-factor design), and a hyper-Greco-Latin square defines the 9 treatment conditions which provide $\frac{1}{27}$ of the 243 treatment conditions of a 3^5 factorial design.

The principles will be illustrated through the interesting structural relation between a $p \times p \times p$ factorial design and a $p \times p$ Latin square. In particular, they will be illustrated by a $3 \times 3 \times 3$ factorial design and a 3×3 Latin square, wherein it will be shown that the factorial design may be partitioned into a balanced set of 3, 3×3 Latin squares. In the following representation of a $3 \times 3 \times 3$ factorial experiment, those treatment combinations marked X form one Latin square, those marked Y form a second, and those marked Z form a third. The set of three squares formed in this manner constitutes a balanced set:

	c_1			c_2			c_3		
	b_1	b_2	b_3	b_1	b_2	b_3	b_1	b_2	b_3
a_1	X	Y	Z	Z	X	Y	Y	Z	X
a_2	Z	X	Y	Y	Z	X	X	Y	Z
a_3	Y	Z	X	X	Y	Z	Z	X	Y

The treatment combinations marked X may be grouped as follows:

$$abc_{111} \quad abc_{122} \quad abc_{133}$$
$$abc_{221} \quad abc_{232} \quad abc_{213}$$
$$abc_{331} \quad abc_{312} \quad abc_{323}.$$

This set of treatment combinations may also be represented in the following schematic form:

	(X)		
	b_1	b_2	b_3
a_1	c_1	c_2	c_3
a_2	c_3	c_1	c_2
a_3	c_2	c_3	c_1

In this latter arrangement the c's form a Latin square.

The treatment combinations marked Y and Z in the factorial experiment may be represented by the following Latin squares:

	(Y)				(Z)		
	b_1	b_2	b_3		b_1	b_2	b_3
a_1	c_3	c_1	c_2	a_1	c_2	c_3	c_1
a_2	c_2	c_3	c_1	a_2	c_1	c_2	c_3
a_3	c_1	c_2	c_3	a_3	c_3	c_1	c_2

The correspondence between the p, $p \times p$ Latin squares and the $p \times p \times p$ factorial experiment illustrated above can best be understood in terms of the modular relations used in Chapter 8. In general, the Latin squares defined as fractional replications are those which correspond to defining relations associated with the components of the $A \times B \times C$ interaction. In a $3 \times 3 \times 3$ design the $A \times B \times C$ interaction has the four unique components ABC, ABC^2, AB^2C, and AB^2C^2, each of which has the three defining relations associated with mod 3 arithmetic. Thus, one has

$$(ABC)_0 \quad (ABC^2)_0 \quad (AB^2C)_0 \quad (AB^2C^2)_0$$
$$(ABC)_1 \quad (ABC^2)_1 \quad (AB^2C)_1 \quad (AB^2C^2)_1$$
$$(ABC)_2 \quad (ABC^2)_2 \quad (AB^2C)_2 \quad (AB^2C^2)_2$$

as the total of twelve defining relations. Each of these four sets of three can be used to reduce a $3 \times 3 \times 3$ design to a set of 3, 3×3 Latin squares. (There are 12, 3×3 Latin squares.)

In the example illustrated above, the AB^2C component of the $A \times B \times C$ interaction was used and the correspondence between the Latin square fractions of the $3 \times 3 \times 3$ factorial given above and the components of the

$A \times B \times C$ interaction is

Latin square	Component of $A \times B \times C$
(X)	$(AB^2C)_0$
(Y)	$(AB^2C)_2$
(Z)	$(AB^2C)_1$

That is, if one were to express the levels of the factors as a_0, a_1, a_2, etc., then the Latin square given by (X) consists of those treatment combinations which satisfy the relation

$$x_1 + 2x_2 + x_3 = 0 \;(\mathrm{mod}\; 3).$$

As presented in Chapter 8, fractional replications always involve confounding of effects. In a complete factorial experiment there is balance in the sense that treatment a_i occurs in combination with each b_j and each c_k as well as in combination with all possible pairs bc_{jk}. In a Latin square there is only partial balance; each a_i occurs in combination with each b_j and each c_k, but each a_i does not occur in combination with all possible pairs bc_{jk}. For example, in square (Y) only the following combinations of bc occur with level a_1:

$$bc_{13} \quad bc_{21} \quad bc_{32}.$$

The following combinations of bc do *not* occur with level a_1:

$$bc_{11} \quad bc_{12} \quad bc_{22} \quad bc_{23} \quad bc_{31} \quad bc_{33}.$$

A Latin square is balanced with respect to main effects but only partially balanced with respect to two-factor interactions.

It is of interest to note the parameters estimated by the sum of all observations at level a_1 in Latin square (Y). Assume for the moment that the cell means have the following form:

$$\overline{ABC}_{113} = \mu + \alpha_1 + \beta_1 + \gamma_3 + \varepsilon_{113} + \alpha\beta_{11} + \alpha\gamma_{13} + \beta\gamma_{13}$$

$$\overline{ABC}_{121} = \mu + \alpha_1 + \beta_2 + \gamma_1 + \varepsilon_{121} + \alpha\beta_{12} + \alpha\gamma_{11} + \beta\gamma_{21}$$

$$\overline{ABC}_{132} = \mu + \alpha_1 + \beta_3 + \gamma_2 + \varepsilon_{132} + \alpha\beta_{13} + \alpha\gamma_{12} + \beta\gamma_{32}$$
$$\bar{A}_1 = \mu + \alpha_1 + 0 \;\; + 0 \;\; + \bar{\varepsilon}_1 \;\; + 0 \;\;\;\;\; + 0 \;\;\;\;\; + \overline{\beta\gamma}_{\alpha_1}.$$

Assuming further that factors A, B, and C are fixed, it follows that

$$\sum_j \beta_j = 0, \qquad \sum_k \gamma_k = 0, \qquad \sum_j \alpha\beta_{1j} = 0, \qquad \sum_k \alpha\gamma_{1k} = 0.$$

However,
$$\beta\gamma_{13} + \beta\gamma_{21} + \beta\gamma_{32} \neq 0.$$

Thus, in addition to sources of variation due to α and $\bar{\varepsilon}$, $\bar{A}$ includes a source of variation due to $\beta\gamma$. Unless $\sigma^2_{\beta\gamma} = 0$, the main effect due to factor A will be confounded with the BC interaction.

In general, when Latin squares are used, the interactions among variables assigned to rows, columns, and cells of the square must be zero if main effects are to be interpretable. This is because main effects always have as aliases components of two-factor interactions. The components of two-factor interactions which are not confounded with main effects are, themselves, aliases. In Chapter 8, it was pointed out that in a $\frac{1}{3}$ replication of a 3^k experiment the aliases were defined as

$$E \times R \quad \text{and} \quad E^2 \times R,$$

where E is an effect and R is the defining relation. Thus, when $(ABC)_i$ is the defining relation in a $\frac{1}{3}$ rep of a $3 \times 3 \times 3$ design, the aliases for main effects are (mod 3)

$$A = A \times ABC = A^2BC = (A^2BC)^2 = AB^2C^2$$
$$A^2 \times ABC = A^3BC = BC.$$

Thus, $A = AB^2C^2 = BC$. For all effects:

$$A = AB^2C^2 = BC$$
$$B = AB^2C = AC$$
$$C = ABC^2 = AB$$
$$AB^2 = AC^2 = BC^2.$$

Note that every main effect is confounded with a component of the two-factor interaction of the other two variables.

These notions may be generalized. For example, in the case of a $2 \times 2 \times 2$ factorial design, a 2×2 Latin square is a $\frac{1}{2}$ replication, wherein the four treatment conditions which define each of the two possible Latin squares may be selected by either the $(ABC)_0$ or $(ABC)_1$ relation. Thus, the outcome is:

Defining relation	Treatment conditions	Latin square			
$x_1 + x_2 + x_3 = 0 \,(\text{mod } 2)$	(000), (011), (101), (110)			b_0	b_1
			a_0	c_0	c_1
			a_1	c_1	c_0
$x_1 + x_2 + x_3 = 1 \,(\text{mod } 2)$	(001), (010), (100), (111)			b_0	b_1
			a_0	c_1	c_0
			a_1	c_0	c_1

In both Latin squares, main effects are confounded with the two-factor interaction between the other two variables (i.e., $A = BC$, $B = AC$, $C = AB$).

When Greco-Latin squares or hyper-Greco-Latin squares are used as a $1/p^2$ or $1/p^3$ replication of a p^4 or p^5 design it is well to keep in mind that a large number of interactions must be assumed to be zero if main effects are to have meaning. In the absence of strong data or theory to that effect, such designs should probably be avoided.

It is possible to use Latin squares in all of the ways discussed as building blocks within more comprehensive designs. Accordingly, there are many possible design configurations. What is presented here is a sample of those possibilities.

9.3 ANALYSIS OF LATIN-SQUARE DESIGNS—NO REPEATED MEASURES

PLAN 1. Consider the following 3×3 Latin square as a fractional replication of a $3 \times 3 \times 3$ factorial experiment:

	b_1	b_2	b_3
a_1	c_2	c_1	c_3
a_2	c_3	c_2	c_1
a_3	c_1	c_3	c_2

Assume there are n observations in each cell. Assume further that two-factor and three-factor interactions are negligible relative to main effects. The model for an observation made in cell ijk may be expressed as

$$X_{ijkm} = \mu + \alpha_{i(s)} + \beta_{j(s)} + \gamma_{k(s)} + \text{res}_{(s)} + \varepsilon_{m(ijk)}.$$

The subscript (s) is used to indicate that the effect in question is estimated from data obtained from a Latin square. The term $\text{res}_{(s)}$ includes all sources of variation due to treatment effects which are not predictable from the sum of the main effects. Under this model, the analysis and the expected values of the mean square are outlined below:

Source of variation	df	df for general case	E(MS)
A	2	$p-1$	$\sigma_\varepsilon^2 + np\sigma_\alpha^2$
B	2	$p-1$	$\sigma_\varepsilon^2 + np\sigma_\beta^2$
C	2	$p-1$	$\sigma_\varepsilon^2 + np\sigma_\gamma^2$
Residual	2	$(p-1)(p-2)$	$\sigma_\varepsilon^2 + \sigma_{\text{res}}^2$
Within cell	$9(n-1)$	$p^2(n-1)$	σ_ε^2

If, indeed, interactions are negligible, the variance due to the residual sources should not differ appreciably from the variance due to experimental error. According to the expected values of the mean squares, when $\sigma_{\text{res}}^2 = 0$, the expected values for the residual and the within-cell variances are both estimates of variance due to experimental error. A partial test on the appropriateness of the model is therefore given by the F ratio

$$F = \frac{\text{MS}_{\text{res}}}{\text{MS}_{\text{w. cell}}}.$$

The magnitude of this F ratio indicates the extent to which the observed data conform to the model (which postulates no interactions). However, a test of this kind is somewhat unsatisfactory. Decisions as to the appropriateness of the model should, in general, be based upon evidence independent of that obtained in the actual experiment. Pilot studies, guided by subject-matter knowledge, should, wherever possible, serve as the basis for formulating the model under which the analysis is to be made.

Granting the appropriateness of the model, tests on main effects can readily be carried out. If interaction is present, some of the tests on main effects will no longer be possible. If, for example, all interactions with factor A may be considered negligible but the BC interaction not negligible, then the main effect of factor A will no longer be clear of interaction effects. However, main effects of B and C will be clear of interaction effects; i.e., tests on these latter main effects can be carried out.

Numerical example. Computational procedures for the plan to be described are similar to those used in a two-factor factorial experiment. The data in Table 9.1 will be used for illustrative purposes. Suppose that an experimenter

TABLE 9.1 **Numerical example**

(i)

Design:	b_1	b_3	b_2
a_2	c_3	c_2	c_1
a_1	c_2	c_1	c_3
a_3	c_1	c_3	c_2

Observed data:	b_1	b_3	b_2
a_2	6, 8, 12, 7	0, 0, 1, 4	0, 2, 2, 5
a_1	2, 5, 3, 1	2, 2, 4, 6	9, 10, 12, 12
a_3	0, 1, 1, 4	2, 1, 1, 5	0, 1, 1, 4

Cell totals

(ii)

	b_1	b_3	b_2	Total	
a_2	33	5	9	$47 = A_2$	
a_1	11	14	43	$68 = A_1$	$n = 4$
a_3	6	9	6	$21 = A_3$	$p = 3$
Total	50	28	58	$136 = G$	
	B_1	B_3	B_2		
	29	22	85		
	C_1	C_2	C_3		

(iii)

$$(1) = G^2/np^2 = 513.78 \qquad (4) = \sum B^2/np = 554.00$$
$$(2) = \sum X^2 = 978.00 \qquad (5) = \sum C^2/np = 712.50$$
$$(3) = \sum A^2/np = 606.17 \qquad (6) = \sum (ABC)^2/n = 878.50$$

$$SS_a = (3) - (1) = 92.39 \qquad SS_{b.\ cells} = (6) - (1) = 364.72$$
$$SS_b = (4) - (1) = 40.22 \qquad SS_{w.\ cells} = (2) - (6) = 99.50$$
$$SS_c = (5) - (1) = 198.72$$

$$SS_{res} = (6) - (3) - (4) - (5) + 2(1) = 33.39$$

is interested in evaluating the relative effectiveness of three drugs (factor B) on three categories (factor C) of patients. Patients for the experiment are obtained from three different hospitals (factor A).

The experimenter obtains 12 patients from each of the hospitals. Of these 12 patients, 4 belong to category c_1, 4 to category c_2, and 4 to category c_3. The total number of patients in the experiment is 36; the total number of patients in any one category is 12.

The design for the experiment is the Latin square given at the left of part i. The first row of this Latin square indicates the manner in which the 12 patients from hospital a_2 are assigned to the drugs. The four patients in category c_3 are given drug b_1; the four patients in category c_2 are given drug b_3; the four patients in category c_1 are given drug b_2. The criterion scores for these three sets of four patients are given in the first row of the table of observed data.

In part ii are the cell totals for the four observations within each cell of the design. The entry in row a_2, column b_1, which is 33, is the sum of the criterion scores for the four patients in category c_3 from hospital a_2—these four patients were given drug b_1. This total will be designated by the symbol ABC_{213}. Similarly, the entry in row a_1, column b_2, which is 43, will be designated by the symbol ABC_{123}—this total is the sum of the four observations under treatment conditions abc_{123}. Row totals and column totals in part ii define, respectively, the A_i's and the B_j's. The C_k's are also obtained from the cell totals. From the design, one locates cells at specified levels of factor C; thus

$$C_1 = 9 + 14 + 6 = 29,$$
$$C_2 = 5 + 11 + 6 = 22,$$
$$C_3 = 33 + 43 + 9 = 85.$$

Computational symbols are defined in part iii. In terms of the symbols, the variation due to the main effect of factor A is estimated by

$$SS_a = np \sum (\bar{A}_i - \bar{G})^2 = (3) - (1) = 92.39.$$

The variation due to the main effect of factor B is estimated by

$$SS_b = np \sum (\bar{B}_j - \bar{G})^2 = (4) - (1) = 40.22.$$

Similarly the variation due to the main effect of factor C is estimated by

$$SS_c = np \sum (\bar{C}_k - G)^2 = (5) - (1) = 198.72.$$

The residual sum of squares is computed in a somewhat indirect manner. The variation between the nine cells in the Latin square is

$$SS_{b.\ cells} = n \sum (\overline{ABC_{ijk}} - \bar{G})^2 = (6) - (1) = 364.72.$$

This source of variation represents a composite of all factorial effects, main effects as well as interactions. There are $8 = p^2 - 1$ degrees of freedom in this source of variation. The residual variation is given by

$$SS_{res} = SS_{b.\ cells} - SS_a - SS_b - SS_c$$
$$= (6) - (3) - (4) - (5) + 2(1) = 33.39.$$

From this point of view, the residual is that part of the between-cell variation which cannot be accounted for by additivity of the three main effects. If no interactions exist, this source of variation provides an estimate of experimental error. If interactions do exist, the residual variation is, in part, an estimate of these interactions.

The within-cell variation is estimated by

$$SS_{w.\ cell} = \sum_m (X_{ijkm} - \overline{ABC}_{ijk})^2 = (2) - (6) = 99.50.$$

A summary of the analysis of variance is given in Table 9.2.

A partial test of the hypothesis that all interactions are negligible is given by

$$F = \frac{MS_{res}}{MS_{w.\ cell}} = \frac{16.70}{3.69} = 4.53.$$

For a 0.05-level test, the critical value is $F_{0.95}(2, 27) = 3.35$. Hence the experimental data tend to contradict the hypothesis that the interactions are negligible. Under these conditions, the adequacy of the Latin-square design is questionable—estimates of the main effects will be confounded by interaction terms.

If all interactions with the hospital factor are negligible, then the variation due to the residual represents partial information on the drug by category interaction. Under this latter assumption, the main effects of the drug factor and category factor will not be confounded with interaction effects. If the assumption is made that all interactions with the hospital factor are

TABLE 9.2 **Analysis of variance for numerical example**

Source of variation	SS	df	MS	F
Hospitals (A)	92.39	2	46.20	12.52*
Drugs (B)	40.22	2	20.11	5.45*
Categories (C)	198.72	2	99.36	26.93*
Residual	33.39	2	16.70	4.53*
Within cell	99.50	27	3.69	
Total	464.22	35		

*$F_{0.95}(2, 27) = 3.35$

negligible, the experimental data indicate that the drug by category interaction is statistically significant. Tests on main effects for drugs and categories also indicate statistically significant variation. The test on the main effects due to hospitals cannot adequately be made since this source of variation is partially confounded with the drug by category interaction. If the hospital factor is a random factor, there will ordinarily be little intrinsic interest in this test.

The experimental data do indicate statistically significant differences between the relative effectiveness of the drugs; however, in view of the presence of drugs by category interaction, the interpretation of these differences requires an analysis of the simple effects. Information for this latter type of analysis is not readily obtained from a Latin-square design. Had the existence of an interaction effect been anticipated, a complete factorial experiment with respect to the interacting factors would have been the more adequate design.

To show the relationship between the analysis of variance for a Latin square and the analysis for a two-factor factorial experiment, suppose factor A in Table 9.1 is disregarded. Then the analysis of variance is as follows:

Source	SS	df
B	$(4) - (1) = 40.22$	2
C	$(5) - (1) = 198.72$	2
BC	$\dfrac{\Sigma (BC)^2}{n} - (4) - (5) + (1) = 125.78$	4
Within cell	$(2) - (6) = 99.50$	27

The two degrees of freedom for the main effect of factor A are part of the BC interaction of the two-factor factorial experiment. Thus in a Latin square the interaction term is partitioned as follows:

BC	SS		df
A		92.39	2
Residual	$SS_{bc} - SS_a =$	33.39	2
		125.78	4

PLAN 2. Use of a Latin square as part of a larger design is illustrated in the following plan:

		b_1	b_2	b_3			b_1	b_2	b_3
	a_1	c_3	c_2	c_1		a_1	c_1	c_3	c_2
d_1	a_2	c_1	c_3	c_2	d_2	a_2	c_2	c_1	c_3
	a_3	c_2	c_1	c_3		a_3	c_3	c_2	c_1

Assume that there are n independent observations within each cell. All observations in a single square are made at the same level of factor D. The separate squares are at different levels of factor D. In some plans it is desirable to choose a balanced set of squares, in others use of the same square throughout is to be preferred, while in still other plans independent randomization of the squares is to be preferred. Guides in choosing the squares will be discussed after the analysis has been outlined.

A model for which this plan provides adequate data is the following:

$$E(X_{ijkmo}) = \mu + \alpha_{i(s)} + \beta_{j(s)} + \gamma_{k(s)} + \delta_m$$
$$+ \alpha\delta_{i(s)m} + \beta\delta_{j(s)m} + \gamma\delta_{k(s)m} + \text{res}_{(s)}.$$

The subscript (s) indicates that an effect forms one of the dimensions of the square. It will be noted that no interactions are assumed to exist between factors that form part of the same Latin square (i.e., factors A, B, and C). However, interactions between the factor assigned to the whole square (factor D) and the factors that form the parts are included in the model.

Assuming that all factors are fixed and that there are n observations in each cell, the appropriate analysis and expected values for the mean squares (as obtained from the above model) are outlined in Table 9.3. A partial check on the appropriateness of the model is provided by the F ratio

$$F = \frac{MS_{\text{res}}}{MS_{\text{w. cell}}}.$$

When the model is appropriate, this ratio should not differ appreciably from 1.00.

Use of this experimental plan requires a highly restrictive set of assumptions with respect to some of the interactions. Should these assumptions be violated, main effects will be partially confounded with interaction effects. If, for example, it may be assumed that interactions with factor A are negligible, but that the BC interaction cannot be considered negligible, then

TABLE 9.3   Analysis of Plan 2

Source of variation	df	df for general case	E(MS)
A	2	$p - 1$	$\sigma_\varepsilon^2 + npq\sigma_\alpha^2$
B	2	$p - 1$	$\sigma_\varepsilon^2 + npq\sigma_\beta^2$
C	2	$p - 1$	$\sigma_\varepsilon^2 + npq\sigma_\gamma^2$
D	1	$q - 1$	$\sigma_\varepsilon^2 + np^2\sigma_\delta^2$
AD	2	$(p-1)(q-1)$	$\sigma_\varepsilon^2 + np\sigma_{\alpha\delta}^2$
BD	2	$(p-1)(q-1)$	$\sigma_\varepsilon^2 + np\sigma_{\beta\delta}^2$
CD	2	$(p-1)(q-1)$	$\sigma_\varepsilon^2 + np\sigma_{\gamma\delta}^2$
Residual	4	$q(p-1)(p-2)$	$\sigma_\varepsilon^2 + n\sigma_{\text{res}}^2$
Within cell	$18(n-1)$	$p^2q(n-1)$	σ_ε^2

the main effect of factor A will be confounded with the BC interaction. However, main effects of factors B and C will not be confounded. When interactions with factor A are negligible, partial information on the BC interaction is available from the within-square residuals. When such information is to be used to make inferences about the BC interaction, it is generally advisable (if the design permits) to work with a balanced set of Latin squares rather than to work with independently randomized squares. Use of a balanced set of squares will provide partial information on all the components of the interaction term. Use of the same square throughout is to be avoided in this context, since information on only a limited number of the interaction components will be available.

Computational procedures for Plan 2. The computational procedures assume that there are q levels of factor D and n observations in each cell of the $p \times p$ Latin squares included in the plan. The observed data will consist of q squares, one for each level of factor D; each square will contain np^2 observations. Hence the total number of observations in the experiment is np^2q. From the observed data, a summary table of the following form may be prepared (for illustrative purposes, assume that $p = 3$ and $q = 2$):

	d_1	d_2	Total
a_1	AD_{11}	AD_{12}	A_1
a_2	AD_{21}	AD_{22}	A_2
a_3	AD_{31}	AD_{32}	A_3
Total	D_1	D_2	G

Each of the AD_{im}'s in this summary table is the sum of the np observations in the experiment which were made under treatment combination ad_{im}. From this summary table, one may compute the following sums of squares:

$$SS_a = \frac{\sum A_i^2}{npq} - \frac{G^2}{np^2q},$$

$$SS_d = \frac{\sum D_m^2}{np^2} - \frac{G^2}{np^2q},$$

$$SS_{ad} = \frac{\sum (AD_{im})^2}{np} - \frac{\sum A_i^2}{npq} - \frac{\sum D_m^2}{np^2} + \frac{G^2}{np^2q}.$$

In a manner analogous to that by which the AD summary table is constructed, one may construct a BD summary table. From this latter table one computes SS_b and SS_{bd}. From a CD summary table one can compute SS_d and SS_{cd}.

To obtain the variation due to the residual sources, one proceeds as follows: The Latin square assigned to level d_m will be called square m. The residual variation within square m is given by

$$SS_{res(m)} = \frac{\sum\limits_{(m)} (\text{cell totals})^2}{n} - \frac{\sum\limits_{(m)} A_i^2}{np} - \frac{\sum\limits_{(m)} B_j^2}{np} - \frac{\sum\limits_{(m)} C_k^2}{np} + \frac{2G_m^2}{np^2}.$$

The notation $\sum\limits_{(m)}$ indicates that the summation is restricted to square m. The degrees of freedom for residual variation within square m are

$$(p-1)(p-2).$$

The residual variation for the whole experiment is

$$SS_{res} = \sum SS_{res(m)}.$$

The degrees of freedom for SS_{res} are

$$df_{res} = \sum (p-1)(p-2) = q(p-1)(p-2).$$

As a partial check on the assumptions underlying the analysis, the within-square residuals for each of the squares should be homogeneous. One may use an F_{max} test for this purpose.

The within-cell variation is given by

$$SS_{w.\,cell} = \sum X^2 - \frac{\sum (\text{cell total})^2}{n},$$

where the summation is over the entire experiment. To check the assumption of homogeneity of error variation, the summation in the last expression may be restricted to the individual cells. The qp^2 sums of squares obtained in this manner may then be checked for homogeneity by means of an F_{max} test.

As an additional check on the assumption of no interactions between the factors which form the dimensions of the squares, one has the F ratio

$$F = \frac{MS_{res}}{MS_{w.\,cell}}.$$

When $\sigma_{res}^2 = 0$, this F ratio should be approximately unity. The residual variation is sometimes pooled with the within-cell variation to provide a pooled estimate of the experimental error, i.e.,

$$SS_{pooled\,error} = SS_{res} + SS_{w.\,cell}.$$

The degrees of freedom for $SS_{pooled\,error}$ is the sum of the degrees of freedom for the parts.

PLAN 3 resembles Plan 2 in form, but the assumptions underlying it are quite different. Here the treatment combinations in a $p \times p \times p$ factorial experiment are divided into a balanced set of $p \times p$ Latin squares. The levels of factors A,

B, and C are then assigned at random to the symbols defining the Latin square. Then the levels of factor D are assigned at random to the whole squares. Hence the number of levels for each factor must be p. An illustration in terms of a balanced set of 3×3 Latin squares is given below:

		b_1	b_2	b_3
	a_1	c_1	c_3	c_2
d_1	a_2	c_3	c_2	c_1
	a_3	c_2	c_1	c_3

		b_1	b_2	b_3
	a_1	c_2	c_1	c_3
d_2	a_2	c_1	c_3	c_2
	a_3	c_3	c_2	c_1

		b_1	b_2	b_3
	a_1	c_3	c_2	c_1
d_3	a_2	c_2	c_1	c_3
	a_3	c_1	c_3	c_2

For the special case in which p is a prime number, a balanced set of squares may be constructed by means of the modular arithmetic discussed in Chapter 8. The squares given above correspond to the relationship

$$x_1 + x_2 + x_3 = 0, 1, 2 \,(\text{mod } 3)$$

when one expresses the levels of the factors in terms of the subscripts 0, 1, 2, that is, when a_1, a_2, a_3 are replaced by a_0, a_1, a_2, etc. If p is not a prime number, one may obtain a balanced set of squares by means of a series of one-step cyclic permutations.

In this plan all the 27 possible combinations of the factors A, B, and C are present. However, only one-third of the 81 possible combinations of the factors A, B, C, and D that would be present in the complete four-factor factorial experiment are present in the above plan. If interactions with factor D are negligible, then this plan will provide complete information with respect to the main effects of factors A, B, and C, as well as all two-factor interactions between these factors. The main effect of factor D will be partially confounded with the ABC interaction; however, partial information with respect to the ABC interaction may be obtained.

This design is particularly useful when the experimenter is interested primarily in a three-factor factorial experiment in which control with respect to the main effects of a fourth factor is deemed desirable. The model appropriate for this plan is the following:

$$\mathrm{E}(X_{ijkmo}) = \mu + \alpha_i + \beta_j + \gamma_k + \alpha\beta_{ij} + \alpha\gamma_{ik} + \beta\gamma_{jk} + \delta_m + \alpha\beta\gamma'_{ijk}.$$

The prime symbol on the three-factor interaction indicates only partial information. (This plan can perhaps be more accurately classified as a balanced incomplete-block design.) Note that no interactions with factor D are included in the model; should such interactions exist, estimates of the variation due to factors A, B, C, and their two-factor interactions will be confounded with interactions with factor D.

TABLE 9.4   Analysis of Plan 3

Source of variation	df	df for general case	E(MS)
A	2	$p - 1$	$\sigma_\varepsilon^2 + np^2\sigma_\alpha^2$
B	2	$p - 1$	$\sigma_\varepsilon^2 + np^2\sigma_\beta^2$
C	2	$p - 1$	$\sigma_\varepsilon^2 + np^2\sigma_\gamma^2$
AB	4	$(p - 1)^2$	$\sigma_\varepsilon^2 + np\sigma_{\alpha\beta}^2$
AC	4	$(p - 1)^2$	$\sigma_\varepsilon^2 + np\sigma_{\alpha\gamma}^2$
BC	4	$(p - 1)^2$	$\sigma_\varepsilon^2 + np\sigma_{\beta\gamma}^2$
D	2	$(p - 1)$	$\sigma_\varepsilon^2 + np^2\sigma_\delta^2$
$(ABC)'$	6	$(p - 1)^3 - (p - 1)$	$\sigma_\varepsilon^2 + n\sigma_{\alpha\beta\gamma}^2$
Within cell	$27(n - 1)$	$p^3(n - 1)$	σ_ε^2

Assuming (1) that the model is appropriate for the experiment data, (2) that there are n observations in each of the p^3 cells in the experiment, and (3) that A, B, and C are fixed factors, an outline of the analysis and the expected values of the mean squares is given in Table 9.4.

Computational procedures for Plan 3. Because Plan 3 includes a balanced set of Latin squares, one may construct an ABC summary table of the following form:

	b_1			b_2			b_3		
	c_1	c_2	c_3	c_1	c_2	c_3	c_1	c_2	c_3
a_1	ABC_{111}			ABC_{121}			ABC_{131}		
a_2									
a_3									

Each total of the form ABC_{ijk} is based upon n observations. By means of the usual computational formulas for a three-factor factorial experiment having n observations per cell, one may obtain the sums of squares for all the factorial effects, including SS_{abc}. For example,

$$SS_a = \frac{\sum A_i^2}{np^2} - \frac{G^2}{np^3}.$$

The sum of squares due to the three-factor interaction, SS_{abc}, includes the variation due to the main effect of factor D. The adjusted sum of squares for this three-factor interaction is given by

$$SS'_{abc} = SS_{abc} - \left(\frac{\sum D_m^2}{np^2} - \frac{G^2}{np^3}\right).$$

SS'_{abc} includes that part of the ABC interaction which is not confounded with the main effect due to factor D. The degrees of freedom for SS'_{abc} are

$$df_{SS'_{abc}} = df_{SS_{abc}} - df_{SS_d}$$
$$= (p-1)^3 - (p-1).$$

The within-cell variation is given by

$$SS_{w.\ cell} = \sum X^2 - \frac{\sum (cell\ total)^2}{n},$$

where the notation (cell total) represents the sum of the n observations in the experiment made under a unique combination of factors A, B, C, and D. The summation is over all cells in the experiment.

PLAN 4 uses the treatment combinations making up a factorial set as one or more dimensions of a Latin square. From many points of view, Plan 4 may be regarded as a special case of Plan 1. A square of dimension $p^2 \times p^2$ is required for this plan. It will be illustrated by the following 4×4 square:

	cd_{11}	cd_{12}	cd_{21}	cd_{22}
ab_{11}	t_2	t_1	t_3	t_4
ab_{12}	t_3	t_2	t_4	t_1
ab_{21}	t_1	t_4	t_2	t_3
ab_{22}	t_4	t_3	t_1	t_2

The treatment combinations along the rows are those forming a 2×2 factorial experiment; the treatment combinations across the columns also form a 2×2 factorial experiment. The letters in the square may or may not form a factorial set. For illustrative purposes suppose that they do not. Assume that there are n observations in each cell. If the treatment sets which define the dimensions of the Latin square do not interact, then an appropriate analysis is given in Table 9.5. The expected values of the mean squares assume that A, B, C, and D are

TABLE 9.5   Analysis of Plan 4

Source of variation	df	df for general case	E(MS)
Row effects	3	$p^2 - 1$	
A	1	$p - 1$	$\sigma_\varepsilon^2 + np^2\sigma_\alpha^2$
B	1	$p - 1$	$\sigma_\varepsilon^2 + np^2\sigma_\beta^2$
AB	1	$(p-1)^2$	$\sigma_\varepsilon^2 + np\sigma_{\alpha\beta}^2$
Column effects	3	$p^2 - 1$	
C	1	$p - 1$	$\sigma_\varepsilon^2 + np^2\sigma_\gamma^2$
D	1	$p - 1$	$\sigma_\varepsilon^2 + np^2\sigma_\delta^2$
CD	1	$(p-1)^2$	$\sigma_\varepsilon^2 + np\sigma_{\gamma\delta}^2$
Letters in cells	3	$p^2 - 1$	
T	3	$p^2 - 1$	$\sigma_\varepsilon^2 + np^2\sigma_\tau^2$
Residual	6	$(p^2-1)(p^2-2)$	$\sigma_\varepsilon^2 + n\sigma_{res}^2$
Within cell	$16(n-1)$	$p^4(n-1)$	σ_ε^2

fixed factors. (Note that the factors within a dimension of the Latin square may interact.)

Computational procedures for Plan 4. To obtain SS_a and SS_{ab}, the p^2 row totals are arranged in the form of an AB summary table.

	b_1	b_2	Total
a_1	AB_{11}	AB_{12}	A_1
a_2	AB_{21}	AB_{22}	A_2
Total	B_1	B_2	G

Each AB_{ij} is the sum of np^2 observations. Hence each A_i total is based upon np^3 observations. The variation due to the main effects of factor A is

$$SS_a = \frac{\sum A_i^2}{np^3} - \frac{G^2}{np^4}.$$

The variation due to the AB interaction is

$$SS_{ab} = \frac{\sum (AB_{ij})^2}{np^2} - \frac{\sum A_i^2}{np^3} - \frac{\sum B_j^2}{np^3} + \frac{G^2}{np^4}.$$

The sums of squares SS_c, SS_d, and SS_{cd} are computed in an analogous manner from the column totals.

If the sum of the np^2 observations at level t_0 is designated by the symbol T_0, then the variation due to the treatments assigned to the letters of the square is

$$SS_t = \frac{\sum T_0^2}{np^2} - \frac{G^2}{np^4}.$$

The variation due to residual sources is

$$SS_{res} = \frac{\sum (\text{cell total})^2}{n} - \frac{\sum (AB_{ij})^2}{np^2} - \frac{\sum (CD_{km})^2}{np^2} - \frac{\sum T_0^2}{np^2} + \frac{2G^2}{np^4}.$$

The within-cell variation is

$$SS_{w.\,cell} = \sum X^2 - \frac{\sum (\text{cell total})^2}{n},$$

where the summation is over all cells in the experiment.

Summary of plans in Sec. 9.3

Plan 1   **Plan 2**

	b_1	b_2	b_3
a_1	c_2	c_1	c_3
a_2	c_3	c_2	c_1
a_3	c_1	c_3	c_2

d_1		b_1	b_2	b_3
	a_1	c_3	c_2	c_1
	a_2	c_1	c_3	c_2
	a_3	c_2	c_1	c_3

d_2		b_1	b_2	b_3
	a_1	c_1	c_3	c_2
	a_2	c_2	c_1	c_3
	a_3	c_3	c_2	c_1

Plan 3

d_1		b_1	b_2	b_3
	a_1	c_1	c_2	c_3
	a_2	c_2	c_3	c_1
	a_3	c_3	c_1	c_2

d_2		b_1	b_2	b_3
	a_1	c_2	c_3	c_1
	a_2	c_3	c_1	c_2
	a_3	c_1	c_2	c_3

d_3		b_1	b_2	b_3
	a_1	c_3	c_1	c_2
	a_2	c_1	c_2	c_3
	a_3	c_2	c_3	c_1

Plan 4

	cd_{11}	cd_{12}	cd_{21}	cd_{22}
ab_{11}	t_2	t_1	t_3	t_4
ab_{12}	t_3	t_2	t_4	t_1
ab_{21}	t_1	t_4	t_2	t_3
ab_{22}	t_4	t_3	t_1	t_2

9.4 ANALYSIS OF GRECO-LATIN SQUARES

In its classic context, a Latin-square arrangement permits a two-way control in variation of the experimental units, i.e., control of row and column effects. In a similar context, a Greco-Latin square permits a three-way control in the variation of the experimental units, i.e., row effects, column effects, and "layer" effects. Thus, a Greco-Latin square defines a restricted randomization procedure whereby p treatments are assigned to p^2 experimental units so as to obtain balance along three dimensions.

From the point of view of construction, a Greco-Latin square is a composite of two orthogonal Latin squares. (Independent randomization of rows and columns is required before the resulting composite square is used in practice.) In order to maintain the identity of the squares which are combined to form the composite, the cells of one square are often designated by Latin letters, and the cells of the second square by Greek letters. This procedure is demonstrated for two 3×3 squares.

	I			**II**			**Composite**	
a	b	c	α	β	γ	$a\alpha$	$b\beta$	$c\gamma$
b	c	a	γ	α	β	$b\gamma$	$c\alpha$	$a\beta$
c	a	b	β	γ	α	$c\beta$	$a\gamma$	$b\alpha$

An equivalent representation in terms of numbers rather than letters is given below. In the resulting composite square the first digit in a pair represents the level of one effect, and the second digit the level of a second effect.

I			**II**			**Composite**		
1	2	3	1	2	3	11	22	33
2	3	1	3	1	2	23	31	12
3	1	2	2	3	1	32	13	21 .

In a Greco-Latin square, there are in reality four variables—namely, row, column, Latin-letter, and Greek-letter variables. From this point of view, a Greco-Latin square may be regarded as a kind of four-factor experiment. There are p^2 cells in this square; hence there are p^2 treatment combinations. In a four-factor factorial experiment in which each factor has p levels, there are p^4 treatment combinations. A Greco-Latin square may also be regarded as a p^2/p^4 or $1/p^2$ fractional replication of a $p \times p \times p \times p$ factorial experiment.

In terms of the modular notation introduced in Chapter 8, a Greco-Latin square is a balanced fraction of a p^4 factorial experiment, if p is a prime number. For example, when $p = 3$, the nine treatment combinations which simultaneously satisfy the relations

$$x_2 + x_3 + x_4 = 0 \,(\text{mod } 3),$$
$$x_1 + x_2 + 2x_3 = 0 \,(\text{mod } 3),$$

are the following:

$$(0\ 0\ 0\ 0) \quad (0\ 1\ 1\ 1) \quad (0\ 2\ 2\ 2)$$
$$(1\ 0\ 1\ 2) \quad (1\ 1\ 2\ 0) \quad (1\ 2\ 0\ 1)$$
$$(2\ 0\ 2\ 1) \quad (2\ 1\ 0\ 2) \quad (2\ 2\ 1\ 0) .$$

These nine treatments may be arranged as follows:

	b_0	b_1	b_2
a_0	00	11	22
a_1	12	20	01
a_2	21	02	10

The entries in the table represent the levels of factor C and D. The modular condition given above may be expressed in the form

$$BCD = 0, \qquad ABC^2 = 0.$$

The generalized interaction is

$$AB^2D = 0, \qquad ACD^2 = 0.$$

For the Greco-Latin square given above one has

$$ABC^2 = AB^2D = ACD^2 = BCD = I,$$

where I represents what is called an identity element. That is, in this

Greco-Latin square, considered as a fraction of a 3^4 factorial experiment, the components of the interactions corresponding to the symbols given above are completely confounded.

As a fractional replication of a factorial experiment, main effects of each of the factors will be confounded with two-factor and higher-order interaction effects. For example, the main effects of factor A will be confounded with the *BC, CD,* and *BCD* interactions. In general, the utility of a single Greco-Latin square is limited to experimental situations in which the four dimensions of the square have negligible interactions. However, Greco-Latin squares may be used to good advantage as part of more inclusive designs. The latter are illustrated in Sec. 9.7. If all interactions between factors defining the dimensions of a Greco-Latin square are negligible, then the analysis of variance takes the form given in Table 9.6. This analysis assumes that there are n independent observations in each of the cells. The specific degrees of freedom are for the case of a 3×3 square. For this special case, the degrees of freedom of the residual variation are zero; only for the case $p > 3$ will the residual variation be estimable. A partial check on the assumptions made about negligible interactions is given by

$$F = \frac{\text{MS}_{\text{res}}}{\text{MS}_{\text{w. cell}}}.$$

Depending upon the outcome of this test, the residual sum of squares is sometimes pooled with the within-cell variation to provide an overall estimate of the variation due to experimental error.

A summary of the computational procedures is given in Table 9.7. These procedures differ only slightly from those appropriate for the Latin square. The residual variation is obtained from the relation

$$\text{SS}_{\text{res}} = \text{SS}_{\text{b. cells}} - \text{SS}_a - \text{SS}_b - \text{SS}_c - \text{SS}_d.$$

Residual variation includes interaction terms if these are not negligible. Otherwise the residual variation provides an estimate of experimental error.

TABLE 9.6   Analysis of variance for Greco-Latin square

Source of variation	df	df for general case	E(MS)
A (rows)	2	$p-1$	$\sigma_\varepsilon^2 + np\sigma_\alpha^2$
B (columns)	2	$p-1$	$\sigma_\varepsilon^2 + np\sigma_\beta^2$
C (Latin letters)	2	$p-1$	$\sigma_\varepsilon^2 + np\sigma_\gamma^2$
D (Greek letters)	2	$p-1$	$\sigma_\varepsilon^2 + np\sigma_\delta^2$
Residual	0	$(p-1)(p-3)$	$\sigma_\varepsilon^2 + n\sigma_{\text{res}}^2$
Within cell	$9(n-)$	$p^2(n-1)$	σ_ε^2
Total	$9n-1$	np^2-1	

TABLE 9.7 **Computational procedures for Greco-Latin square**

(i)

$(1) = G^2/np^2$	$(5) = (\sum C_k^2)/np$
$(2) = \sum X^2$	$(6) = (\sum D_m^2)/np$
$(3) = (\sum A_i^2)/np$	$(7) = [\sum (\text{cell total})^2]/n$
$(4) = (\sum B_j^2)/np$	

(ii)

A	$(3) - (1)$
B	$(4) - (1)$
C	$(5) - (1)$
D	$(6) - (1)$
Residual	$(7) - (3) - (4) - (5) - (6) + 3(1)$
Within cell	$(2) - (7)$
Total	$(2) - (1)$

9.5 ANALYSIS OF LATIN SQUARES—REPEATED MEASURES

In the plans that are discussed in this section, all the restrictions on the model underlying a repeated-measure design for a factorial experiment are necessary in order that the final F tests be valid. These restrictions were discussed in Chapters 4 and 7. Special attention should be given to the possible presence of nonadditive sequence effects in experiments which do not involve learning. In particular, a repeated-measure design assumes that all pairs of observations on the same subjects have a constant correlation. If this assumption is violated, resulting tests on within-subject effects tend to be biased in the direction of yielding too many significant results.

The equivalent of the conservative test proposed by Box (1954) and by Greenhouse and Geisser (1959) can be adapted for use in connection with the designs that follow. For example, if the test for a within-subject main effect (as indicated by the model requiring the homogeneity-of-correlation condition) requires the critical value

$$F_{1-\alpha}[(p - 1), p(n - 1)(p - 1)],$$

then the corresponding critical value under the conservative test procedure is

$$F_{1-\alpha}[1, p(n - 1)].$$

In principle, the degrees of freedom for the numerator and denominator of the F distribution required in the usual test (as given by the expected values of the mean squares obtained from the restricted model) are divided by the degrees of freedom for the factor on which there are repeated measures.

PLAN 5. Consider the following 3×3 Latin square in which groups of n

subjects are assigned at random to the rows:

	a_1	a_2	a_3
G_1	b_3	b_1	b_2
G_2	b_1	b_2	b_3
G_3	b_2	b_3	b_1

In this plan each of the n subjects in G_1 is observed under all treatment combinations in row 1, that is, ab_{13}, ab_{21}, ab_{32}. For example, the levels of factor A may represent three kinds of targets, and the levels of factor B may represent three distances. There are nine possible treatment combinations in the complete 3×3 factorial experiment; each of these nine appears in the Latin square. However, the individuals within any one group are observed only under three of the nine possibilities. Suppose the order in which a subject is observed under each treatment combination is randomized independently for each subject.

If the interactions with the group factor are negligible, the following model will be appropriate for the analysis (this assumption is reasonable if the groups represent random subsamples from a common population):

$$E(X_{ijkm}) = \mu + \delta_k + \pi_{m(k)} + \alpha_i + \beta_j + \alpha\beta'_{ij}.$$

In this model δ_k represents effects associated with the groups and $\pi_{m(k)}$ effects associated with subjects within the groups. The symbol $\alpha\beta'_{ij}$ indicates that only partial information is available on this source of variation. Assuming that factors A and B are fixed factors, the analysis and the expected values of the mean squares are given in Table 9.8.

In this analysis, only $(p-1)(p-2)$ degrees of freedom for the AB interaction appear as within-subject effects. The missing $p-1$ degrees of freedom define the variation among the groups. Since differences among the groups, in part, reflect differences due to the effects of various combinations of A and B (which are balanced with respect to the main effects), such differences

TABLE 9.8 Analysis of Plan 5

Source of variation	df	df for general case	E(MS)
Between subjects	$3n - 1$	$np - 1$	
Groups	2	$p - 1$	$\sigma_\varepsilon^2 + p\sigma_\pi^2 + np\sigma_\delta^2$
Subjects within groups	$3(n-1)$	$p(n-1)$	$\sigma_\varepsilon^2 + p\sigma_\pi^2$
Within subjects	$6n$	$np(p-1)$	
A	2	$p - 1$	$\sigma_\varepsilon^2 + np\sigma_\alpha^2$
B	2	$p - 1$	$\sigma_\varepsilon^2 + np\sigma_\beta^2$
$(AB)'$	2	$(p-1)(p-2)$	$\sigma_\varepsilon^2 + n\sigma_{\alpha\beta}^2$
Error (within)	$6n - 6$	$p(n-1)(p-1)$	σ_ε^2

define part of the AB interaction. It is readily shown that

$$\mathrm{SS}_{ab} = \mathrm{SS}_{\mathrm{groups}} + \mathrm{SS}'_{ab},$$

where SS_{ab} is the variation due to the AB interaction as computed in a two-factor factorial experiment. From some points of view $\mathrm{SS}_{\mathrm{groups}}$ may be regarded as the between-subject component of the AB interaction. For most practical purposes, only SS'_{ab} (the within-subject component) is tested; tests on the latter component will generally be the more powerful.

The appropriateness of the model should be given serious consideration before this plan is used for an experiment. A possible alternative plan, which requires the same amount of experimental effort but does not utilize the Latin-square principle, is the following:

	a_1	a_2	a_3
G_1	b_1	b_1	b_1
G_2	b_2	b_2	b_2
G_3	b_3	b_3	b_3

Again the groups are assumed to be random samples of size n from a common population. In this plan each of the n subjects in group 1 is observed under the treatment combinations ab_{11}, ab_{21}, and ab_{31}. Assume that the order in which subjects are observed under each treatment combination is randomized independently for each subject. In this plan there are repeated measures on factor A but no repeated measures on factor B. A model appropriate for estimation and tests under this plan is

$$E(X_{ijkm}) = \mu + \beta_j + \pi_{k(j)} + \alpha_i + \alpha\beta_{ij} + \alpha\pi_{ik(j)}.$$

For this model, assuming that factors A and B are fixed, the analysis is outlined in Table 9.9. In contrast to Plan 5, under this plan the AB interaction is not confounded with between-group differences; however, all components of the main effect of factor B are between-subject components. That is, differences between levels of factor B are simultaneously differences between

TABLE 9.9   Analysis of alternative to Plan 5

Source of variation	df	df for general case	E(MS)
Between subjects	$3n - 1$	$np - 1$	
B	2	$p - 1$	$\sigma_\varepsilon^2 + p\sigma_\pi^2 + np\sigma_\beta^2$
Subjects within groups	$3(n - 1)$	$p(n - 1)$	$\sigma_\varepsilon^2 + p\sigma_\pi^2$
Within subjects	$6n$	$np(p - 1)$	
A	2	$p - 1$	$\sigma_\varepsilon^2 + \sigma_{\alpha\pi}^2 + np\sigma_\alpha^2$
AB	4	$(p - 1)(p - 1)$	$\sigma_\varepsilon^2 + \sigma_{\alpha\pi}^2 + n\sigma_{\alpha\beta}^2$
$A \times$ subjects within groups	$6n - 6$	$p(n - 1)(p - 1)$	$\sigma_\varepsilon^2 + \sigma_{\alpha\pi}^2$

groups of people. Hence use of the Latin square permits a more sensitive test on the main effects of factor B, provided that the model under which the analysis is made is appropriate. In general the $A \times$ subjects-within-groups interaction under the alternative plan will be of the same order of magnitude as the error (within) term in Plan 5.

If the experimenter's primary interest is in factor A and its interaction with factor B, and if there is little interest in the main effects of factor B, use of the Latin-square plan is not recommended. However, if the main effects of factor B are also of primary interest to the experimenter, use of the Latin square has much to recommend it. By suitable replication, some within-subject information may be obtained on all components of the AB interaction. Plan 5 forms a building block out of which other plans may be constructed.

Computational procedures for Plan 5. Computational procedures for Plan 5 are similar to those given for Plan 1. The sources of variation SS_a, SS_b, and SS_{groups} are computed in a manner analogous to those used in Plan 1 for corresponding effects. The variation due to the within-subject components of the AB interaction is given by

$$SS'_{ab} = SS_{ab} - SS_{\text{groups}},$$

where SS_{ab} is computed from an AB summary table by means of the usual computational formulas for this interaction.

The variation due to subjects within groups is given by

$$SS_{\text{subj w. groups}} = \frac{\sum P^2_{m(k)}}{p} - \frac{\sum G^2_k}{np},$$

where $P_{m(k)}$ represents the sum of the p observations on person m in group k, and where G_k represents the sum of the np observations in group k. The summation is over the whole experiment. If the summation is limited to a single group, one obtains $SS_{\text{subj w. group } k}$. There will be p such sources of variation. It is readily shown that

$$SS_{\text{subj w. groups}} = \sum SS_{\text{subj w. group } k}.$$

That is, the sum of squares on the left represents a pooling of the sources of variation on the right; the latter may be checked for homogeneity by means of an $F_{\max}$ test.

It is convenient to compute $SS_{\text{error(within)}}$ from $SS_{\text{w. cell}}$. The latter is given by

$$SS_{\text{w. cell}} = \sum X^2 - \frac{\sum (AB_{ij})^2}{n},$$

where AB_{ij} represents a cell total. The summation is over the whole experiment. From this source of variation,

$$SS_{\text{error(within)}} = SS_{\text{w. cell}} - SS_{\text{subj w. groups}}.$$

A somewhat modified computational procedure provides the parts of the error term that may be checked for homogeneity. One first computes

$$SS_{\text{w. cell for } G_k} = \sum X^2 - \frac{\sum (AB_{ij})^2}{n},$$

where the summation is limited to those cells in which group k participates. The degrees of freedom for this source of variation are $p(n-1)$. Then

$$SS_{\text{error(within) for } G_k} = SS_{\text{w. cell for } G_k} - SS_{\text{subj w. } G_k}.$$

Degrees of freedom for this source of variation are $p(n-1)-(n-1)$, which is equal to $(n-1)(p-1)$. It is readily shown that

$$SS_{\text{error(within)}} = \sum SS_{\text{error(within) for } G_k};$$

that is, the variation on the left is a pooling of the sources of variation on the right. The degrees of freedom for the pooled error (within) and the degrees of freedom of the parts are related as follows:

$$df_{\text{error(within)}} = \sum_k (n-1)(p-1) = p(n-1)(p-1).$$

Thus error (within) is partitioned into p parts; each of the parts has $(n-1)(p-1)$ degrees of freedom.

PLAN 6. In Plan 5, the groups assigned to the rows of the Latin square form a quasi factor. Essentially, Plan 5 may be regarded as one complete replication of a two-factor factorial experiment arranged in incomplete blocks. From this point of view, the plan to be discussed in this section may be regarded as a fractional replication of a three-factor factorial experiment arranged in incomplete blocks.

In this plan each subject within G_1 is assigned to the treatment combinations abc_{111}, abc_{231}, and abc_{321}. Thus each subject in G_1 is observed under all levels of factor A and B but under only one level of factor C. For each subject there is balance with respect to the main effects of factors A and B, but there is no balance with respect to any of the interactions. Similarly, each subject in G_2 is assigned to the treatment combinations abc_{122}, abc_{212}, and abc_{332}. Again there is balance with respect to the main effects of factors A and B, but there is no balance with respect to interactions.

		a_1	a_2	a_3
G_1	c_1	b_1	b_3	b_2
G_2	c_2	b_2	b_1	b_3
G_3	c_3	b_3	b_2	b_1

If all interactions are negligible relative to main effects (a highly restrictive assumption), the following model is appropriate for making esti-

TABLE 9.10   **Analysis of Plan 6**

Source of variation	df	df for general case	E(MS)
Between subjects	$3n-1$	$np-1$	
C	2	$p-1$	$\sigma_\varepsilon^2 + p\sigma_\pi^2 + np\sigma_\gamma^2$
Subjects within groups	$3(n-1)$	$p(n-1)$	$\sigma_\varepsilon^2 + p\sigma_\pi^2$
Within subjects	$6n$	$np(p-1)$	
A	2	$p-1$	$\sigma_\varepsilon^2 + np\sigma_\alpha^2$
B	2	$p-1$	$\sigma_\varepsilon^2 + np\sigma_\beta^2$
Residual	2	$(p-1)(p-2)$	$\sigma_\varepsilon^2 + n\sigma_{\text{res}}^2$
Error (within)	$6n-6$	$p(n-1)(p-1)$	σ_ε^2

mates and tests in the analysis of variance:

$$E(X_{ijkm}) = \mu + \gamma_{k(s)} + \pi_{m(k)} + \alpha_{i(s)} + \beta_{j(s)} + \text{res}_{(s)}.$$

The analysis of variance and the expected values of the mean squares are summarized in Table 9.10.

The analysis of Plan 6 is quite similar to the analysis of Plan 5. Differences among groups in the latter plan correspond to differences due to the main effects of factor C in the present plan; what was part of the AB interaction in Plan 5 is a residual term in the present plan. It is of interest to note the relationship between the analysis of a two-factor factorial experiment which does not have repeated measures and the analysis of Plan 6. The total number of observations in Plan 6 is the same as that of a two-factor factorial experiment in which there are n observations per cell. The Latin-square arrangement in Plan 6 permits the partition of what is formally a two-factor interaction into a main effect and a residual effect. The latter is a mixture of interaction effects if these exist. The fact that there are repeated measures in Plan 6 permits the within-cell variation to be partitioned into one part involving differences between subjects and one part which does not involve differences between subjects, provided of course that homogeneity of covariances exists.

Two-factor experiment		Plan 6	
df	Source of variation	Source of variation	df
$p-1$	A	A	$p-1$
$p-1$	B	B	$p-1$
$(p-1)(p-1)$	AB	$\left\{\begin{array}{l} C \\[1em] \text{Residual} \end{array}\right.$	$p-1$
			$(p-1)(p-2)$
$p^2(n-1)$	Within cell	$\left\{\begin{array}{l} \text{Subj w. gp} \\[1em] \text{Error (within)} \end{array}\right.$	$p(p-1)$
			$p(n-1)(p-1)$

TABLE 9.11 **Complete factorial analog of Plan 6**

		a_1	a_2	a_3	a_1	a_2	a_3	a_1	a_2	a_3
G_1	c_1	b_1	b_1	b_1	b_2	b_2	b_2	b_3	b_3	b_3
G_2	c_2	b_1	b_1	b_1	b_2	b_2	b_2	b_3	b_3	b_3
G_3	c_3	b_1	b_1	b_1	b_2	b_2	b_2	b_3	b_3	b_3

Because of the highly restrictive assumptions with respect to the interactions, use of Plan 6 is appropriate only when experience has shown that such interactions are negligible. A partial check on this assumption is given by the ratio

$$F = \frac{\text{MS}_{\text{res}}}{\text{MS}_{\text{error(within)}}}.$$

According to the model under which the analysis of variance is made, σ^2_{res} should be zero when the assumptions with respect to the interactions are satisfied. In cases in which one of the factors, say A, is the experimental variable of primary interest and factors B and C are of the nature of control factors (i.e., replications or order of presentation) this plan is potentially quite useful. With this type of experimental design interactions can frequently be assumed to be negligible relative to main effects.

In exploratory studies in which interaction effects may be of primary interest to the experimenter, there is generally no substitute for the complete factorial experiment. The complete factorial analog of Plan 6 is represented schematically in Table 9.11. In order to have complete within-subject information on the main effects of factors A and B as well as complete within-subject information on all interactions, including interactions with factor C, p^2 observations on each subject are required. In Plan 6, only p observations are made on each of the subjects. Use of Plan 6 reduces the overall cost of the experiment in terms of experimental effort—at the possible cost, however, of inconclusive results. Should the experimenter find evidence of interaction effects which invalidate the analysis of Plan 6, he may, if his work is planned properly, enlarge the experiment into Plan 8a. It will be noted that the latter may be constructed from a series of plans having the form of Plan 6. The assumptions in Plan 8a are less restrictive with respect to interactions than are those underlying Plan 6.

Computational procedures for Plan 6. Computational procedures for Plan 6 are identical to those outlined for Plan 5. Here $\text{SS}_c = \text{SS}_{\text{groups}}$ and $\text{SS}'_{ab} = \text{SS}_{\text{res}}$. All other sums of squares are identical. Tests for homogeneity of error variance are also identical.

PLAN 7 is related to Plan 5 as well as to Plan 6. Plan 7 may be regarded as being formed from Plan 5 by superimposing an orthogonal Latin square. This plan may also be viewed as a modification of Plan 6 in which the C factor is converted into a within-subject effect. The combinations of factors B and C which appear in the cells of the following plan are defined by a Greco-Latin square:

	a_1	a_2	a_3
G_1	bc_{11}	bc_{23}	bc_{32}
G_2	bc_{22}	bc_{31}	bc_{13}
G_3	bc_{33}	bc_{12}	bc_{21}

The groups of subjects are assigned at random to the rows of the square; the levels of factor A are also assigned at random to the columns of the square. The subjects within G_1 are observed under treatment combinations abc_{111}, abc_{223}, and abc_{332}. (Assume that the order in which a subject is observed under a particular treatment combination is randomized independently for each subject.) Provided that all interactions are negligible, unbiased estimates of the differential main effects of factors A, B, and C can be obtained. Further, the expected values of the mean squares for these main effects will not involve a between-subject component. The model under which the analysis of Plan 7 can be carried out is

$$E(X_{ijkmo}) = \mu + \delta_{m(s)} + \pi_{o(m)} + \alpha_{i(s)} + \beta_{j(s)} + \gamma_{k(s)}.$$

The symbol $\delta_{m(s)}$ designates the effect of group m, and the symbol $\pi_{o(m)}$ designates the additive effect of person o within group m.

An outline of the analysis, assuming that the model is appropriate, is given in Table 9.12. For a 3×3 square, the variation due to the residual cannot be estimated, since there are zero degrees of freedom for this source of variation. However, for squares of higher dimension a residual term will be estimable. The latter represents the variation due to interactions, if these exist. The variation between groups may also be regarded as part of the interaction variation.

If the levels of factor C define the order in which subjects are observed under combinations of factors A and B, then Plan 7 becomes a special case of

TABLE 9.12   **Analysis of Plan 7**

Source of variation	df	df for general case	E(MS)
Between subjects	$3n-1$	$np-1$	
Groups	2	$p-1$	$\sigma_\varepsilon^2 + p\sigma_\pi^2 + np\sigma_\delta^2$
Subjects within groups	$3(n-1)$	$p(n-1)$	$\sigma_\varepsilon^2 + p\sigma_\pi^2$
Within subjects	$6n$	$np(p-1)$	
A	2	$p-1$	$\sigma_\varepsilon^2 + np\sigma_\alpha^2$
B	2	$p-1$	$\sigma_\varepsilon^2 + np\sigma_\beta^2$
C	2	$p-1$	$\sigma_\varepsilon^2 + np\sigma_\gamma^2$
Residual	0	$(p-1)(p-3)$	$\sigma_\varepsilon^2 + n\sigma_{\text{res}}^2$
Error (within)	$6n-6$	$p(n-1)(p-1)$	σ_ε^2

Plan 5. In terms of factor C as an order factor, the schematic representation of Plan 7 given earlier in this section may be reorganized as follows:

	Order 1	Order 2	Order 3
G_1	ab_{11}	ab_{33}	ab_{22}
G_2	ab_{23}	ab_{12}	ab_{31}
G_3	ab_{32}	ab_{21}	ab_{13}

Thus the subjects within G_1 are observed under treatment combinations ab_{11}, ab_{33}, and ab_{22} in that order. With one of the factors representing an order factor, the variation between groups may be regarded as representing a sequence effect; this latter source of variation may also be regarded as part of the confounded interaction effects.

Computational procedures for Plan 7. The computational procedures for Plan 7 do not differ appreciably from those of the Greco-Latin square. Following the computational procedures for the latter, one obtains SS_a, SS_b, SS_c, and SS_{groups}. The between-cell variation is given by

$$SS_{\text{b. cells}} = \frac{\Sigma\,(\text{cell total})^2}{n} - \frac{G^2}{np^2}.$$

From this sum of squares one obtains

$$SS_{res} = SS_{\text{b. cells}} - (SS_a + SS_b + SS_c + SS_{groups}).$$

From this last relationship, the degrees of freedom for the residual source of variation are

$$df_{res} = (p^2 - 1) - 4(p - 1) = (p - 1)(p + 1 - 4)$$
$$= (p - 1)(p - 3).$$

The variation due to subjects within groups is

$$SS_{\text{subj w. groups}} = \frac{\Sigma\,P_{m(k)}^2}{p} - \frac{\Sigma\,G_k^2}{np},$$

where $P_{m(k)}$ is the sum of the p observations on person m in group k, and where G_k is the sum of the np observations in group k. The error (within) variation is obtained indirectly from the within-cell variation. The latter is given by

$$SS_{\text{w. cell}} = \Sigma\,X^2 - \frac{\Sigma\,(\text{cell total})^2}{n},$$

where the summation is over the whole experiment. From this one obtains

$$SS_{error(within)} = SS_{\text{w. cell}} - SS_{\text{subj w. groups}}.$$

This method of computing this source of variation shows that the degrees of freedom for error (within) are

$$\mathrm{df}_{\mathrm{error(within)}} = p^2(n-1) - p(n-1)$$
$$= p(n-1)(p-1).$$

The sum of squares for error (within) may be partitioned by the procedures given under Plan 5. That is, by limiting the summations for $SS_{\mathrm{w.\ cells}}$ and $SS_{\mathrm{subj\ w.\ groups}}$ to single groups, one may obtain p terms each of the general form $SS_{\mathrm{error(within)\ for\ }G_k}$. The degrees of freedom for each of these terms are $(n-1)(p-1)$.

PLAN 8 uses Plan 5 as a building block. Disregarding the repeated-measure aspect, this plan also resembles Plan 2. A schematic representation of Plan 8 is given below:

		Square I					Square II		
		a_1	a_2	a_3			a_1	a_2	a_3
c_1	G_1	b_1	b_2	b_3	c_2	G_4	b_2	b_3	b_1
	G_2	b_2	b_3	b_1		G_5	b_1	b_2	b_3
	G_3	b_3	b_1	b_2		B_6	b_3	b_1	b_2

In general there will be q squares, one for each level of factor C. Different squares are used for each level of factor C. In square I, all observations are at level c_1; in square II, all observations are at level c_2. There is no restriction on the number of levels of factor C.

Depending upon what can be assumed about the interactions, different analyses are possible. If the interactions between factors A, B, and groups (the dimensions of the squares) are negligible, then unbiased tests can be made on all main effects and the two-factor interactions with factor C. The model under which the latter analysis is made is the following:

$$\mathrm{E}(X_{ijkmo}) = \mu + \gamma_k + \delta_{m(k)} + \pi_{o(km)} + \alpha_{i(s)} + \beta_{j(s)} + \alpha\gamma_{ik} + \beta\gamma_{jk}.$$

The analysis outlined in Table 9.13 follows from this model; the expected values for the mean squares assume that factor C is fixed. It is also assumed that the order of administration of the treatment combinations is randomized independently for each subject.

The assumptions underlying Plan 8, which lead to the analysis summarized in Table 9.13, are different from the assumptions used in the analysis of Plan 5. A set of assumptions, consistent with those in Plan 5, leads to the analysis for Plan 8a. The latter plan has the same schematic representation as Plan 8. However, in Plan 8a only the interactions involving the group factor are assumed to be negligible. Under these latter assumptions, the appropriate model is the following:

$$\mathrm{E}(X_{ijkmo}) = \mu + \gamma_k + \delta_{m(k)} + \pi_{o(km)} + \alpha_i + \beta_j + \alpha\beta'_{ij} + \alpha\gamma_{ik} + \beta\gamma_{jk}.$$

TABLE 9.13 **Analysis of Plan 8**

Source of variation	df	df for general case	E(MS)
Between subjects	$6n - 1$	$npq - 1$	
C	1	$q - 1$	$\sigma_\varepsilon^2 + p\sigma_\pi^2 + np\sigma_\delta^2 + np^2\sigma_\gamma^2$
Groups within C	4	$q(p - 1)$	$\sigma_\varepsilon^2 + p\sigma_\pi^2 + np\sigma_\delta^2$
Subjects within groups	$6(n - 1)$	$pq(n - 1)$	$\sigma_\varepsilon^2 + p\sigma_\pi^2$
Within subjects	$12n$	$npq(p - 1)$	
A	2	$p - 1$	$\sigma_\varepsilon^2 + npq\sigma_\alpha^2$
B	2	$p - 1$	$\sigma_\varepsilon^2 + npq\sigma_\beta^2$
AC	2	$(p - 1)(q - 1)$	$\sigma_\varepsilon^2 + np\sigma_{\alpha\gamma}^2$
BC	2	$(p - 1)(q - 1)$	$\sigma_\varepsilon^2 + np\sigma_{\beta\gamma}^2$
Residual	4	$q(p - 1)(p - 2)$	$\sigma_\varepsilon^2 + n\sigma_{\text{res}}^2$
Error (within)	$12n - 12$	$pq(n - 1)(p - 1)$	σ_ε^2

The analysis resulting from this model, assuming factors A and B fixed, is outlined in Table 9.14.

If the number of levels of factor C is equal to p, and if a balanced set of squares is used, then the components of the AB interaction which are confounded will be balanced. However, if the same Latin square is used for each of the levels of factor C, the same set of $p - 1$ degrees of freedom of the AB interaction is confounded in each square. It is of interest to compare the partition of the total degrees of freedom in a $3 \times 3 \times 3$ factorial experiment with the partition made under Plan 8a, assuming that a balanced set of squares is used in the construction of the design. These partitions are presented in Table 9.15.

TABLE 9.14 **Analysis of Plan 8a**

Source of variation	df	df for general case	E(MS)
Between subjects	$6n - 1$	$npq - 1$	
C	1	$q - 1$	$\sigma_\varepsilon^2 + p\sigma_\pi^2 + np\sigma_\delta^2 + np^2\sigma_\gamma^2$
Groups within C	4	$q(p - 1)$	$\sigma_\varepsilon^2 + p\sigma_\pi^2 + np\sigma_\delta^2$
Subjects within groups	$6(n - 1)$	$pq(n - 1)$	$\sigma_\varepsilon^2 + p\sigma_\pi^2$
Within subjects	$12n$	$npq(p - 1)$	
A	2	$p - 1$	$\sigma_\varepsilon^2 + npq\sigma_\alpha^2$
B	2	$p - 1$	$\sigma_\varepsilon^2 + npq\sigma_\beta^2$
AC	2	$(p - 1)(q - 1)$	$\sigma_\varepsilon^2 + np\sigma_{\alpha\gamma}^2$
BC	2	$(p - 1)(q - 1)$	$\sigma_\varepsilon^2 + np\sigma_{\beta\gamma}^2$
AB' from square I	2	$(p - 1)(p - 2)$	$\sigma_\varepsilon^2 + n\sigma_{\alpha\beta}^2$
AB' from square II	2	$(p - 1)(p - 2)$	$\sigma_\varepsilon^2 + n\sigma_{\alpha\beta}^2$
Error (within)	$12n - 12$	$pq(n - 1)(p - 1)$	σ_ε^2

TABLE 9.15 **Partitions in Plan 8a and** $3 \times 3 \times 3$ **factorial experiment**

3 × 3 × 3 factorial		Plan 8a	
df	Source of variation	Source of variation	df
2	A	A	2
2	B	B	2
2	C	C	2
4	AC	AC	4
4	BC	BC	4
4	AB ⎱	⎰ Groups within C	6
8	ABC ⎰	⎱ Σ (AB' for each square)	6
27(n − 1)	Within cell	⎰ Subjects within groups	9(n − 1)
		⎱ Error (within)	18(n − 1)

The 12 degrees of freedom corresponding to the AB and ABC interactions in the factorial experiment appear in Plan 8a as the sum of 6 degrees of freedom for groups within C and 6 degrees of freedom for what is partial information on the simple interaction of AB at each level of c_k. In the general case, the relationship is as follows:

$$
\begin{array}{llll}
\text{df} & & & \text{df} \\
(p-1)^2 & AB \;\rbrace & \begin{cases} \text{Groups within } C \\ \sum (AB' \text{ for each square}) \end{cases} & \begin{array}{l} p(p-1) \\ p(p-1)(p-2) \end{array} \\
\overline{p(p-1)^2} & ABC & & \overline{p(p-1)^2}
\end{array}
$$

In order to have complete within-subject information on all effects, except the main effects of factor C, p^2 observations on each subject are required. In Plan 8a (constructed with a balanced set of squares) only p observations are required on each subject. What is lost in reducing the number of observations per subject from p^2 to p is partial information on the AB and ABC interactions, specifically $p(p-1)$ of these degrees of freedom. This loss in information is, in many cases, a small price to pay for the potential saving in experimental feasibility and effort.

In Plan 8a, the source of variation SS'_{ab}, which is actually part of the simple AB interaction for each of the levels of factor C, may be tested separately or as a sum. As a sum, this source of variation is a mixture of the AB and ABC interactions.

Computational procedures for Plan 8. Computational procedures for Plan 8 are summarized in Table 9.16. These procedures may also be followed for Plan 8a. In the latter plan, SS_{res} becomes $\sum SS'_{ab}$ for each square.

In part i of this table symbols convenient for use in the computational formulas are defined. Computational formulas are given in part ii. The order in which the sums of squares are given in part ii corresponds to the order in Table 9.13. For purposes of checking homogeneity of the parts $SS_{error(within)}$, this

TABLE 9.16 **Summary of computational procedures for Plan 8**

(i)

$$(1) = G^2/np^2q \qquad (6) = [\sum (AC_{ik})^2]/np$$
$$(2) = \sum X^2 \qquad (7) = [\sum (BC_{jk})^2]/np$$
$$(3) = (\sum A_i^2)/npq \qquad (8) = \sum (P_{o(m)}^2)/p$$
$$(4) = (\sum B_j^2)/npq \qquad (9) = [\sum (\text{cell total})^2]/n$$
$$(5) = (\sum C_k^2)/np^2 \qquad (10) = (\sum G_m^2)/np$$

(In each case the summation is over the whole experiment.)

(ii)

$$SS_{\text{b. subjects}} = (8) - (1)$$
$$SS_c = (5) - (1)$$
$$SS_{\text{groups w. } C} = (10) - (5)$$
$$SS_{\text{subj w. groups}} = (8) - (10)$$
$$SS_{\text{w. subj}} = (2) - (8)$$
$$SS_a = (3) - (1)$$
$$SS_b = (4) - (1)$$
$$SS_{ac} = (6) - (3) - (5) + (1)$$
$$SS_{bc} = (7) - (4) - (5) + (1)$$
$$SS_{\text{res}} = (9) - (10) - (6) - (7) + 2(5)$$
$$SS_{\text{error(within)}} = (2) - (9) - (8) + (10)$$

source of variation may be partitioned into pq nonoverlapping parts—one part for each of the pq groups in the experiment. The part corresponding to G_m is

$$SS_{\text{error(within) for } G_m} = (2g_m) - (9g_m) - (8g_m) + (10g_m).$$

where $(2g_m)$ designates the numerical value of (2) if the summation in the latter is restricted to G_m. Analogous definitions hold for the other computational symbols containing g_m. It is readily shown that

$$SS_{\text{error(within)}} = \sum SS_{\text{error(within) for } G_m}.$$

The $F_{\max}$ statistic may be used to check on the homogeneity of the parts that are pooled to provide the overall error term for the within-subject effects. It is readily verified that

$$\sum (2g_m) = (2), \qquad \sum (9g_m) = (9), \quad \text{etc.}$$

The variation due to subjects within groups may also be checked for homogeneity. The sum of squares $SS_{\text{subj w. groups}}$ may be partitioned into pq parts, one part for each group. Each part has the general form

$$SS_{\text{subj w. } G_m} = (8g_m) - (10g_m),$$

where $(8g_m)$ is the numerical value of (8) if the summation is restricted to group m.

If a balanced set of squares is used in the construction of Plan 8a, the computational procedures may be simplified. One may use the regular computational procedures for a three-factor factorial experiment having n observations per cell as the starting point. In addition one computes $SS_{\text{groups w. }C}$ and $SS_{\text{subj w. groups}}$ by means of the procedures given for Plan 8. Then

$$\sum (SS'_{ab \text{ for each square}}) = SS_{ab} + SS_{abc} - SS_{\text{groups w. }C},$$

$$SS_{\text{error(within)}} = SS_{\text{w. cell}} - SS_{\text{subj w. groups}}.$$

PLAN 9 may be viewed as a special case of Plan 8a in which the same square is used for all levels of factor C. Hence the same components of the AB interaction are confounded within each of the squares, and the same components of the ABC interaction are confounded in differences between squares. Full information will be available on some components of both the AB and ABC interactions. The number of levels of factors A and B must be equal; there is no restriction on the number of levels of factor C. Factors A, B, and C are considered to be fixed; interactions with the group factor are assumed to be negligible. A schematic representation of this plan for the case in which $p = 3$ and $q = 3$ is given below:

		I					**II**					**III**		
		a_1	a_2	a_3			a_1	a_2	a_3			a_1	a_2	a_3
	G_1	b_2	b_3	b_1		G_4	b_2	b_3	b_1		G_7	b_2	b_3	b_1
c_1	G_2	b_1	b_2	b_3	c_2	G_5	b_1	b_2	b_3	c_3	G_8	b_1	b_2	b_3
	G_3	b_3	b_1	b_2		G_6	b_3	b_1	b_2		G_9	b_3	b_1	b_2

It is of considerable interest to indicate the manner in which the AB and ABC interactions are confounded. A given row in each of the above squares represents the same combination of treatments A and B. For example, the first row in each square involves ab_{12}, ab_{23}, and ab_{31}. A summary table of the following form will be shown to have special meaning in the interpretation of the AB and ABC interactions:

Row	c_1	c_2	c_3	**Total**
1	G_1	G_4	G_7	R_1
2	G_2	G_5	G_8	R_2
3	G_3	G_6	G_9	R_3
Total	C_1	C_2	C_3	Grand total

In this summary table each G designates the sum of the np observations made within a group.

The total R_1 represents the sum of the npq observations in row 1 of all squares; this sum is also $G_1 + G_4 + G_7$. This total is balanced with respect to the main effects of factors A, B, and C; it is also balanced with respect to the ABC interaction. The latter balance follows from the fact that sums of the form

$$\alpha\beta\gamma_{121} + \alpha\beta\gamma_{122} + \alpha\beta\gamma_{123} = 0,$$
$$\alpha\beta\gamma_{231} + \alpha\beta\gamma_{232} + \alpha\beta\gamma_{233} = 0.$$

However, the total R_1 is not balanced with respect to the AB interaction, since

$$\alpha\beta_{12} + \alpha\beta_{23} + \alpha\beta_{31} \neq 0.$$

By similar reasoning each of the other R's may be shown to be balanced with respect to all main effects as well as the ABC interaction; however, each of the other R's is not balanced with respect to the AB interaction. Thus variation due to differences between the R's represents two of the four degrees of freedom of the AB interaction. In general such differences represent $p - 1$ of the $(p - 1)^2$ degrees of freedom of the AB interaction.

Since differences between the rows define $p - 1$ degrees of freedom of the AB interaction, the row $\times C$ interaction will define $(p - 1)(q - 1)$ degrees of freedom of the $AB \times C$ interaction. The latter interaction is equivalent to the ABC interaction. Hence $(p - 1)(q - 1)$ of the $(p - 1)(p - 1)(q - 1)$ degrees of freedom for the ABC interaction are confounded with row effects. The remaining degrees of freedom are not confounded with row effects; that is, $(p - 1)(p - 2)(q - 1)$ degrees of freedom of the ABC interaction are within-subject effects.

In some texts the following notation has been used:

$$\text{SS}_{\text{rows}} = \text{SS}_{ab(\text{between})},$$
$$\text{SS}_{\text{row}\times C} = \text{SS}_{abc(\text{between})}.$$

In terms of this notation,

$$\text{SS}_{ab} = \text{SS}_{ab(\text{between})} + \text{SS}_{ab(\text{within})}.$$

The corresponding degrees of freedom are

$$(p - 1)(p - 1) = (p - 1) + (p - 1)(p - 2).$$

The three-factor interaction takes the following form:

$$\text{SS}_{abc} = \text{SS}_{abc(\text{between})} + \text{SS}_{abc(\text{within})},$$
$$(p - 1)(p - 1)(q - 1) = (p - 1)(q - 1) + (p - 1)(p - 2)(q - 1).$$

In each case the "between" component is part of the between-subject variation, and the "within" component is part of the within-subject effects.

The model under which the analysis of variance for this plan may be carried out is

$$E(X_{ijkmo}) = \mu + \gamma_k + (\text{row})_m + (\gamma \times \text{row})_{km}$$
$$+ \pi_{o(m)} + \alpha_i + \beta_j + \alpha\beta'_{ij} + \alpha\gamma_{ik} + \beta\gamma_{jk} + \alpha\beta\gamma'_{ijk}.$$

The analysis corresponding to this model is summarized in Table 9.17. The expected values of the mean squares in this table are derived under the

TABLE 9.17 **Analysis of Plan 9**

Source of variation	df	df for general case	E(MS)
Between subjects	$9n - 1$	$npq - 1$	
C	2	$q - 1$	$\sigma_\varepsilon^2 + p\sigma_\pi^2 + np^2\sigma_\gamma^2$
Rows [AB (between)]	2	$p - 1$	$\sigma_\varepsilon^2 + p\sigma_\pi^2 + nq\sigma_{\alpha\beta}^2$
$C \times$ row [ABC (between)]	4	$(p - 1)(q - 1)$	$\sigma_\varepsilon^2 + p\sigma_\pi^2 + n\sigma_{\alpha\beta\gamma}^2$
Subjects w. groups	$9(n - 1)$	$pq(n - 1)$	$\sigma_\varepsilon^2 + p\sigma_\pi^2$
Within subjects	$18n$	$npq(p - 1)$	
A	2	$p - 1$	$\sigma_\varepsilon^2 + npq\sigma_\alpha^2$
B	2	$p - 1$	$\sigma_\varepsilon^2 + npq\sigma_\beta^2$
AC	4	$(p - 1)(q - 1)$	$\sigma_\varepsilon^2 + np\sigma_{\alpha\gamma}^2$
BC	4	$(p - 1)(q - 1)$	$\sigma_\varepsilon^2 + np\sigma_{\beta\gamma}^2$
$(AB)'$	2	$(p - 1)(p - 2)$	$\sigma_\varepsilon^2 + nq\sigma_{\alpha\beta}^2$
$(ABC)'$	4	$(p - 1)(p - 2)(q - 1)$	$\sigma_\varepsilon^2 + n\sigma_{\alpha\beta\gamma}^2$
Error (within)	$18n - 18$	$pq(p - 1)(n - 1)$	σ_ε^2

assumptions that factors A, B, and C are fixed; the group factor and subjects within groups are considered random. All interactions with the group and subject effects are considered negligible.

The analysis given in this table indicates that Plan 9 may be considered as a special case of a $p \times p \times q$ factorial experiment arranged in blocks of size p, the groups having the role of blocks. The differences between the groups may be partitioned as follows:

Between groups	$pq - 1$
C	$q - 1$
Groups within C	$q(p - 1)$
Rows	$p - 1$
$C \times$ rows	$(p - 1)(q - 1)$

What corresponds to the within-cell variation in a $p \times p \times q$ factorial experiment having n observations per cell is partitioned as follows in Plan 9.

Within cell	$p^2q(n - 1)$
Subjects w. groups	$pq(n - 1)$
Error (within)	$pq(n - 1)(p - 1)$

Numerical example of Plan 9. Suppose that a research worker is interested in evaluating the relative effectiveness of three variables in the design of a package. The variables to be studied are kinds of material, style of printing to be used, and color of the material. Each variable constitutes a factor; there are three levels under each factor. That is, there are three kinds of material, three styles of printing, and three colors. A total of $3 \times 3 \times 3 = 27$ different packages can be constructed. Suppose that all 27 packages are constructed.

If the research worker selects Plan 9 for use, each subject is required to judge only 3 of the 27 packages. Under the conditions of the study, this number is considered to be the largest number feasible for any one subject. One of the main effects in Plan 9 (that of factor C) is wholly a between-subject effect, but within-subject information is available with respect to the interactions with that factor. Anticipating interactions with the color factor, and desiring within-subject information on interactions with the color factor, the research worker decides to let color correspond to factor C in Plan 9. This plan is symmetrical with respect to factors A and B; hence there is no difference whether the material factor corresponds to factor A or B. Suppose that the material factor is made to correspond to factor A.

The number of subjects to be used in each of the groups depends upon the precision that is desired. In related studies of this kind a minimum of 10 to 20 subjects per group is generally required to obtain a satisfactory power. Depending upon the degree of variability of the judgments, a larger or smaller number of subjects will be required. For purposes of illustrating the computational procedures, suppose that there are only two subjects in each group. The basic observational data for this illustration are given in Table 9.18. The design is that given earlier in this section; the data have been rearranged for computational convenience.

The subjects are asked to rate the packages assigned to them on a 15-point criterion scale. Subjects are assigned at random to the groups; the order in which a subject judges a set of packages is randomized independently for each subject. Subjects in groups 1, 4, and 7 each judge combinations ab_{12}, ab_{23}, and ab_{31}. However, these combinations appear in a different color (factor C) for each of the three groups. Person 1 made the ratings 2, 2, and 3 for the respective combinations, all of which are at color c_1. Person 6 made the ratings 7, 5, and 9 for the respective combinations—these combinations are in color c_3. The assignment of the treatment combinations to the groups follows the schematic representation of Plan 9 given earlier in this section. For ease in computation the data in Table 9.18 have been arranged. In addition to the basic observed data, totals needed in the analysis of variance are given at its right.

Summary data obtained from Table 9.18 appear in parts i and ii of Table 9.19. An ABC summary table appears in part i. Entries in part i have the general symbol ABC_{ijk} and are each based upon two observations. For example, the entry ABC_{111} is the sum of all observations made under treatment combination abc_{111}. Only subjects 7 and 8 are observed under this treatment combination. Hence as

$$ABC_{111} = 5 + 8 = 13.$$

As another example, only subjects 11 and 12 are observed under treatment combination abc_{333}; hence as

$$ABC_{333} = 8 + 9 = 17.$$

TABLE 9.18   **Numerical example of Plan 9**

	Group	Person	a_1	a_2	a_3	Person total	Group total	Row total
			b_2	b_3	b_1			
c_1	G_1	1	2	2	3	$7 = P_1$		
		2	1	1	7	9	$16 = G_1$	
c_2	G_4	3	5	8	1	14		
		4	9	12	7	28	42	
c_3	G_7	5	5	4	6	15		
		6	7	5	9	21	36	$94 = R_1$
			b_1	b_2	b_3			
c_1	G_2	7	5	4	7	16		
		8	8	5	8	21	37	
c_2	G_5	9	8	10	4	22		
		10	10	14	6	30	52	
c_3	G_8	11	10	10	8	28		
		12	7	3	9	19	47	136
			b_3	b_1	b_2			
c_1	G_3	13	3	2	5	10		
		14	6	4	9	19	29	
c_2	G_6	15	8	9	6	23		
		16	10	10	5	25	48	
c_3	G_9	17	12	6	10	28		
		18	8	8	2	18	46	123
	Total		124	117	112	$353 = G$	353	353

From the data in part i, *AB, AC,* and *BC* summary tables may be prepared; these appear in part ii. Data for the $C \times$ row summary table in part ii are obtained from the column headed Group total in Table 9.18. Computational symbols convenient for use in obtaining the required sums of squares are defined in part iii. The numerical values of these symbols for the data are also given.

The analysis of variance is summarized in Table 9.20. Factors *A, B,* and *C* are considered to be fixed. Tests on the between-subject effects use $MS_{\text{subj w. groups}}$ in the denominator of F ratios. Tests on within-subject effects use $MS_{\text{error(within)}}$. It will be noted that the denominator for the within-subject effects (3.22) is considerably smaller than the denominator for the between-subject effects (10.94).

TABLE 9.19 Summary data for numerical example

(i)

		c_1			c_2			c_3			
		a_1	a_2	a_3	a_1	a_2	a_3	a_1	a_2	a_3	Total
	b_1	13	6	10	18	19	8	17	14	15	120
	b_2	3	9	14	14	24	11	12	13	12	112
	b_3	9	3	15	18	20	10	20	9	17	121
											353

	a_1	a_2	a_3	Total		a_1	a_2	a_3	Total
b_1	48	39	33	120	c_1	25	18	39	82
b_2	29	46	37	112	c_2	50	63	29	142
b_3	47	32	42	121	c_3	49	36	44	129
Total	124	117	112	353	Total	124	117	112	353

(ii)

	b_1	b_2	b_3	Total		Row 1	Row 2	Row 3	Group total
c_1	29	26	27	82	c_1	16	37	29	82
c_2	45	49	48	142	c_2	42	52	48	142
c_3	46	37	46	129	c_3	36	47	46	129
Total	120	112	121	353	Total	94	136	123	353

(iii)

$(1) = G^2/np^2q = 2307.57$

$(2) = \sum X^2 = 2811$

$(3) = (\sum A_i^2)/npq = 2311.61$

$(4) = (\sum B_j^2)/npq = 2310.28$

$(5) = (\sum C_k^2)/np^2 = 2418.28$

$(6) = [\sum (AB_{ij})^2]/nq = 2372.83$

$(7) = [\sum (AC_{ik})^2]/np = 2568.83$

$(8) = [\sum (BC_{jk})^2]/np = 2429.50$

$(9) = [\sum (ABC_{ijk})^2]/n = 2654.50$

$(10) = (\sum P_o^2)/p = 2575.00$

$(11) = (\sum G_m^2)/np = 2476.50$

$(12) = (\sum R_s^2)/npq = 2358.94$

TABLE 9.20 Analysis of variance for numerical example

Source of variation	Computational formula	SS	df	MS	F
Between subjects	$(10) - (1)$	267.43	17		
C (color)	$(5) - (1)$	110.71	2	55.36	5.06*
Rows	$(12) - (1)$	51.37	2	25.68	2.35
C × row	$(11) - (5) - (12) + (1)$	6.85	4	1.71	
Subjects within group	$(10) - (11)$	98.50	9	10.94	
Within subjects	$(2) - (10)$	236.00	36		
A (material)	$(3) - (1)$	4.04	2	2.02	
B (printing)	$(4) - (1)$	2.71	2	1.36	
AC	$(7) - (3) - (5) + (1)$	146.51	4	36.63	11.38**
BC	$(8) - (4) - (5) + (1)$	8.51	4	2.13	
AB'	$[(6) - (3) - (4) + (1)] - [(12) - (1)]$	7.14	2	3.57	
ABC'	$[(9) - (6) - (7) - (8) + (3) + (4) + (5) - (1)]$ $- [(11) - (5) - (12) + (1)]$	9.09	4	2.27	
Error (within)	$(2) - (10) - (9) + (11)$	58.00	18	3.22	

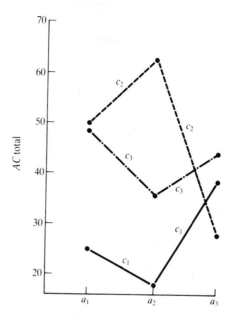

FIGURE 9-1

The F tests indicate a highly significant AC interaction. To help interpret this interaction effect, the profiles for simple main effects of factor A (materials) at the various levels of factor C (colors) are given in Fig. 9-1. These profiles were prepared from the AC summary table in part ii of Table 9.19. Although color c_2 has the highest overall average rating, c_2 in combination with material a_3 has one of the lower average ratings. Material a_2 in combination with color c_2 has the highest average rating. An analysis of the simple main effects of factor A for the levels of factor C will permit statistical tests of the differences among the set of points in the same profile. These tests are summarized in Table 9.21.

Differences between the points on the profile for c_2 are statistically significant ($F = 15.24$). A test on the difference between a_1 and a_2 at level c_2 is

TABLE 9.21 **Analysis of simple effects for factor A**

Source of variation	Computational formula	SS	df	MS	F
A at level c_1	$(3c_1) - (1c_1)$	38.11	2	19.06	5.92*
A at level c_2	$(3c_2) - (1c_2)$	98.11	2	49.06	15.24**
A at level c_3	$(3c_3) - (1c_3)$	14.33	2	7.16	2.22
Error (within)	(From Table 9.20)	58.00	18	3.22	

given by

$$F = \frac{(AC_{12} - AC_{22})^2}{2np\,\text{MS}_{\text{error(within)}}}$$
$$= \frac{(50 - 63)^2}{2(6)(3.22)} = 4.37.$$

If the latter test is considered as being in the post hoc category for differences between the levels of factor A at c_2, the 0.05-level Scheffé critical value is

$$(p - 1)F_{0.95}(p - 1, \text{df}_{\text{error(within)}}) = 2F_{0.95}(2, 18)$$
$$= 2(3.55) = 7.10.$$

However, if this test is considered as a single comparison in the post hoc partition of A and AC, then the 0.05-level Scheffé critical value is

$$[(p - 1) + (p - 1)(q - 1)]F_{0.95}[(p - 1) + (p - 1)(q - 1), \text{df}_{\text{error(within)}}]$$
$$= 6F_{0.95}(6, 18) = 6(2.66) = 15.96.$$

Tests on simple main effects are generally made along the dimension of greatest interest to the experimenter. This dimension, by design, is most frequently the within-subject dimension. However, should the experimenter desire to make tests on the simple main effects of what corresponds to factor C, the denominator of such tests is not $\text{MS}_{\text{subj w. groups}}$. Rather the denominator is $\text{MS}_{\text{w. cell}}$ for the appropriate level of the simple main effect. For example, in making tests on the simple main effects of factor C at level a_2, the appropriate denominator is $\text{MS}_{\text{w. cell (for } a_2)}$. Computationally,

$$\text{MS}_{\text{w. cell (for } a_2)} = \frac{(2a_2) - (9a_2)}{pq(n - 1)}.$$

PLAN 10 is essentially an extension of Plan 6; more explicitly, Plan 6 is the building block from which Plan 10 is constructed. The latter is a series of such building blocks, each at a different level of factor D. Alternatively, Plan 10 may be viewed as a fractional replication of a $p \times p \times p \times q$ factorial experiment. As an illustration, a $3 \times 3 \times 3 \times 2$ factorial experiment will be used. A schematic representation of this plan is given below:

			a_1	a_2	a_3				a_1	a_2	a_3
	G_1	c_1	b_3	b_1	b_2		G_4	c_1	b_2	b_1	b_3
d_1	G_2	c_2	b_2	b_3	b_1	d_2	G_5	c_2	b_1	b_3	b_2
	G_3	c_3	b_1	b_2	b_3		G_6	c_3	b_3	b_2	b_1

As shown above, a different square is used for the two levels of factor D. In cases where partial information on confounded interactions is to be recovered, it is desirable to use the same square for each level of factor D.

TABLE 9.22   **Analysis of Plan 10**

Source of variation	df	df for general case	E(MS)
Between subjects	$6n-1$	$npq-1$	
$C(AB')$	2	$p-1$	$\sigma_\varepsilon^2 + p\sigma_\pi^2 + npq\sigma_\gamma^2$
D	1	$q-1$	$\sigma_\varepsilon^2 + p\sigma_\pi^2 + np^2\sigma_\delta^2$
$CD\ (AB' \times D)$	2	$(p-1)(q-1)$	$\sigma_\varepsilon^2 + p\sigma_\pi^2 + np\sigma_{\gamma\delta}^2$
Subjects within groups	$6(n-1)$	$pq(n-1)$	$\sigma_\varepsilon^2 + p\sigma_\pi^2$
Within subjects	$12n$	$npq(p-1)$	
A	2	$p-1$	$\sigma_\varepsilon^2 + npq\sigma_\alpha^2$
B	2	$p-1$	$\sigma_\varepsilon^2 + npq\sigma_\beta^2$
AD	2	$(p-1)(q-1)$	$\sigma_\varepsilon^2 + np\sigma_{\alpha\delta}^2$
BD	2	$(p-1)(q-1)$	$\sigma_\varepsilon^2 + np\sigma_{\beta\delta}^2$
$(AB)''$ $\Big\}$ residual	$\Big\{$ 2	$(p-1)(p-2)$	$\sigma_\varepsilon^2 + nq\sigma_{\alpha\beta}^2$
$(AB)'' \times D$	2	$(p-1)(p-2)(q-1)$	$\sigma_\varepsilon^2 + n\sigma_{\alpha\beta\delta}^2$
Error (within)	$12n-12$	$pq(n-1)(p-1)$	σ_ε^2

The complete factorial experiment for the illustrative example includes $3 \times 3 \times 3 \times 2 = 54$ treatment combinations. Only 18 treatment combinations appear in the above plan (i.e., one-third of the total). If the factors forming the dimensions of the square (factors A, B, and C) do not interact with each other (these dimensions may, however, interact with factor D), then an outline of the analysis of variance is given in Table 9.22. The expected values given in this table are derived under the assumption that factors A, B, C, and D are fixed. Groups and subjects within groups are considered random.

If, for example, the AB interaction were not negligible, then the main effects of factor C and the CD interaction would be confounded with this interaction. A partial check on the assumption that dimensions of the Latin square do not interact with each other is provided by the F ratio

$$F = \frac{MS_{res}}{MS_{error(within)}}.$$

A somewhat better check on these assumptions is obtained by computing the residual and error (within) separately for each level of factor D as well as the corresponding pooled terms. Individual tests are made for the separate levels as well as for the pooled terms.

Relative to what would be the case in a complete factorial experiment, the within-cell variation is partitioned as follows:

Within cell	$p^2q(n-1)$
Subjects w. groups	$pq(n-1)$
Error (within)	$pq(n-1)(p-1)$

All other sources of variation are part of the between-cell variation; the degrees of freedom for the latter are $p^2q - 1$.

Plan 10 is useful in situations illustrated by the following example: Suppose that a research worker is interested in evaluating the effectiveness of q different methods of training (factor D) on marksmanship. There are p different kinds of targets (factor B) to be used in the evaluation process. Each target is to be placed at p different distances (factor C). Subjects are to fire at each of the p targets, but subjects are assigned to only one distance. The order (factor A) in which subjects fire at the targets is balanced by means of a Latin square. In this kind of experiment, primary interest is generally in the main effects of factor D and the interactions with factor D, particularly the BD and CD interactions. The BD interaction is a within-subject effect; the CD interaction is a between-subject effect. If the experimenter has the choice of what variables are assigned as factors B and C, factor B should be the one on which the more precise information is desired. The experimenter may not always have his choice in such matters—the dictates of experimental feasibility frequently force a decision of this kind in a given direction.

Computational procedures. Computational procedures for this plan are summarized in Table 9.23. Since all treatment combinations in the factorial experiment involving factors C and D appear in this plan, a CD summary table may be prepared. From the latter summary table one may compute sums of squares of the main effects of C and D as well as the sum of squares for their interaction. One may also prepare AD and BD summary tables, since all the treatment combinations in corresponding two-factor factorial experiments occur for these two sets of variables.

TABLE 9.23   **Computational procedures for Plan 10**

$(1) = G^2/np^2q$	$(7) = [\sum (AD_{im})^2]/np$
$(2) = \sum X^2$	$(8) = [\sum (BD_{jm})^2]/np$
$(3) = (\sum A_i^2)/npq$	$(9) = [\sum (CD_{km})^2]/np$
$(4) = (\sum B_j^2)/npq$	$(10) = (\sum P_o^2)/p$
$(5) = (\sum C_k^2)/npq$	$(11) = [\sum (\text{cell total})^2]/n$
$(6) = (\sum D_m^2)/np^2$	

Between subjects	$(10) - (1)$
C	$(5) - (1)$
D	$(6) - (1)$
CD	$(9) - (5) - (6) + (1)$
Subjects within groups	$(10) - (9)$
(ii) Within subjects	$(2) - (10)$
A	$(3) - (1)$
B	$(4) - (1)$
AD	$(7) - (3) - (6) + (1)$
BD	$(8) - (4) - (6) + (1)$
Residual	$(11) - (7) - (8) - (9) + 2(6)$
Error (within)	$(2) - (10) - (11) + (9)$

For the basic observations one may obtain each of the P_o, where the latter symbol denotes the sum of the p observations on an individual subject. The expression (cell total) used in computational symbol (11) denotes the sum of the n observations made under a specified treatment combination. Another symbol for this total is $ABCD_{ijkm}$.

The residual variation is that part of the variation between cells remaining after (presumably) all the unconfounded sources of variation due to treatment effects have been taken into account. In symbols,

$$SS_{res} = SS_{b.\ cells} - (SS_a + SS_b + SS_c + SS_d + SS_{cd} + SS_{ad} + SS_{bd}).$$

The homogeneity of the residual variation may be checked by computing separate residual terms for each Latin square. Since each of the Latin squares represents a different level of factor D, the latter procedure is equivalent to computing a separate residual term for each level of factor D.

$$SS_{res\ for\ level\ d_m} = (11d_m) - (7d_m) - (8d_m) - (9d_m) + 2(6d_m),$$

where the symbol $(11d_m)$ is (11) with the summation restricted to level d_m.

The variation due to error (within) is that part of the within-cell variation which remains after variation due to differences between subjects within cells is removed. In symbols,

$$SS_{error(within)} = SS_{w.\ cell} - SS_{subj\ w.\ groups}.$$

The latter term may be checked for homogeneity by computing a separate $SS_{error(within)}$ for each group. Computationally,

$$SS_{error(within)\ for\ G_r} = 2(g_r) - (10g_r) - (11g_r) + (9g_r).$$

PLAN 11. In Plan 7 only a fraction of the treatment combinations in a $p \times p \times p$ factorial experiment actually appears in the experiment. However, in Plan 11 all the treatment combinations in this factorial experiment are used. The primary purpose of this plan is to obtain complete within-subject information on all main effects, as well as partial within-subject information on all interaction effects in a $p \times p \times p$ factorial experiment. Yet only p observations on each subject are required.

The construction of this plan will be illustrated by means of a $3 \times 3 \times 3$ factorial experiment. The starting point for this plan is a balanced set of 3×3 Latin squares.

I			II			III		
1	3	2	3	2	1	2	1	3
3	2	1	2	1	3	1	3	2
2	1	3	1	3	2	3	2	1

It is noted that square II is obtained from square I by means of a one-step cyclic permutation of the rows. Similarly, square III is obtained from square II

TABLE 9.24   Schematic representation of Plan 11

		a_1	a_2	a_3			a_1	a_2	a_3			a_1	a_2	a_3
(i)	G_1	bc_{12}	bc_{31}	bc_{23}		G_4	bc_{32}	bc_{21}	bc_{13}		G_7	bc_{22}	bc_{11}	bc_{33}
	G_2	bc_{33}	bc_{22}	bc_{11}		G_5	bc_{23}	bc_{12}	bc_{31}		G_8	bc_{13}	bc_{32}	bc_{21}
	G_3	bc_{21}	bc_{13}	bc_{32}		G_6	bc_{11}	bc_{33}	bc_{22}		G_9	bc_{31}	bc_{23}	bc_{12}
(ii)	G_1	(112)	(231)	(323)		G_4	(132)	(221)	(313)		G_7	(122)	(211)	(333)
	G_2	(133)	(222)	(311)		G_5	(123)	(212)	(331)		G_8	(113)	(232)	(321)
	G_3	(121)	(213)	(332)		G_6	(111)	(233)	(322)		G_9	(131)	(223)	(312)

by a one-step cyclic permutation. One now constructs a square orthogonal to square I. The following square has this property:

$$\mathbf{I'}$$

$$\begin{matrix} 2 & 1 & 3 \\ 3 & 2 & 1 \\ 1 & 3 & 2 \end{matrix}$$

This square is also orthogonal to squares II and III.

In the design given in part i of Table 9.24, the subscripts for factor B are determined by the corresponding numbers in squares I, II, and III. The subscripts for factor C are determined by the numbers in square I'. A different notation system is used in part ii of this table—the numbers in parentheses represent the respective subscripts for the treatment combinations.

The n subjects in each group are observed under the treatment combinations in each of the rows. These sets are balanced with respect to main effects but only partially balanced with respect to interaction effects. For purposes of illustrating the manner in which the AB interaction is partially confounded with differences between groups, consider the sets of treatment combinations assigned to the following groups:

$$\begin{matrix} G_1 & (112) & (231) & (323) \\ G_6 & (111) & (233) & (322) \\ G_8 & (113) & (232) & (321) \end{matrix}$$

Within each of these groups there are repeated measures on the same set of combinations of factor A and B, namely, ab_{11}, ab_{23}, and ab_{32}. There is balance with respect to main effects as well as the AC, BC, and ABC interactions when the sum of all observations in the three groups is obtained. If all factors are fixed, it may be shown by direct substitution in the basic linear model that

$$E(G_{1+6+8}) = 9n\mu + 3n(\alpha\beta_{11} + \alpha\beta_{23} + \alpha\beta_{32}) + 3n(\delta_1 + \delta_6 + \delta_8).$$

The symbol G_{1+6+8} denotes the sum of the $9n$ observations in these three groups. The effects δ_1, δ_6, and δ_8 designate group effects. Since G_2, G_4, and

G_9 are each observed under the set of treatment combinations ab_{13}, ab_{22}, and ab_{31}, and since there is balance with respect to the main effects as well as the AC and BC interactions,

$$\mathrm{E}(G_{2+4+9}) = 9n\mu + 3n(\alpha\beta_{13} + \alpha\beta_{22} + \alpha\beta_{31}) + 3n(\delta_2 + \delta_4 + \delta_9).$$

It may also be shown that

$$\mathrm{E}(G_{3+5+7}) = 9n\mu + 3n(\alpha\beta_{12} + \alpha\beta_{21} + \alpha\beta_{33}) + 3n(\delta_3 + \delta_5 + \delta_7).$$

Thus differences between the three totals G_{1+6+8}, G_{2+4+9}, and G_{3+5+7} are in part due to the AB interaction and in part due to group effects. Hence two of the four degrees of freedom of the AB interaction are partially confounded with differences between groups.

In Plan 11, as constructed in Table 9.24, two-factor interactions are partially confounded with the sets of group totals given below:

Interaction	Sets of group totals		
AB	G_{1+6+8},	G_{2+4+9},	G_{3+5+7}
AC	G_{1+4+7},	G_{2+5+8},	G_{3+6+9}
BC	G_{1+5+9},	G_{2+6+7},	G_{3+4+8}

In each case two of the four degrees of freedom for the respective two-factor interactions are confounded with differences between groups. The remaining degrees of freedom for the variation due to differences between groups are confounded with the three-factor interaction. The totals involved in the latter are G_{1+2+3}, G_{4+5+6}, and G_{7+8+9}. An outline of the analysis of variance appears in Table 9.25.

This plan may be improved by constructing a replication in which different components of the interactions are confounded with group effects. This replication may be obtained from a second set of balanced squares. The following balanced set is different from the original set:

I			II			III		
1	2	3	2	3	1	3	1	2
2	3	1	3	1	2	1	2	3
3	1	2	1	2	3	2	3	1

The following square is orthogonal to square I:

I'		
1	2	3
3	1	2
2	3	1

A plan constructed from this set of squares is given in Table 9.26.

TABLE 9.25   **Analysis of Plan 11**

Source of variation	df	df for general case	E(MS)
Between subjects	$9n - 1$	$\dfrac{np^2 - 1}{p^2 - 1}$	
Groups	8		
$\quad (AB)'$	2	$p - 1$	
$\quad (AC)'$	2	$p - 1$	
$\quad (BC)'$	2	$p - 1$	
$\quad (ABC)'$	2	$(p - 1)(p - 2)$	
$\quad$ Subjects within groups	$9n - 9$	$p^2(n - 1)$	
Within subjects	$18n$	$np^2(p - 1)$	
$\quad A$	2	$p - 1$	$\sigma_\varepsilon^2 + np^2\sigma_\alpha^2$
$\quad B$	2	$p - 1$	$\sigma_\varepsilon^2 + np^2\sigma_\beta^2$
$\quad C$	2	$p - 1$	$\sigma_\varepsilon^2 + np^2\sigma_\gamma^2$
$\quad (AB)''$	2	$(p - 1)(p - 2)$	$\sigma_\varepsilon^2 + np\sigma_{\alpha\beta}^2$
$\quad (AC)''$	2	$(p - 1)(p - 2)$	$\sigma_\varepsilon^2 + np\sigma_{\alpha\gamma}^2$
$\quad (BC)''$	2	$(p - 1)(p - 2)$	$\sigma_\varepsilon^2 + np\sigma_{\beta\gamma}^2$
$\quad (ABC)''$	6	$(p - 1)^3 - (p - 1)(p - 2)$	$\sigma_\varepsilon^2 + n\sigma_{\alpha\beta\gamma}^2$
$\quad$ Error (within)	$18n - 18$	$p^2(p - 1)(n - 1)$	σ_ε^2

For this replication, it may be shown that

$$\mathrm{E}(G_{1+6+8}) = 9n + 3n(\alpha\beta_{11} + \alpha\beta_{22} + \alpha\beta_{33}) + 3n(\delta_1 + \delta_6 + \delta_8).$$

The set of $\alpha\beta$'s included in this expected value is different from that included in the original plan. For this replication it may be shown that variation among the totals

$$G_{1+6+8}, \qquad G_{2+4+9}, \quad \text{and} \quad G_{3+5+7}$$

represents two of the four degrees of freedom of the AB interaction; however, the two degrees of freedom that are confounded here are not identical with those confounded in the original plan.

In terms of the notation of Chapter 8 on components of interaction, in the original plan the AB^2 components of the $A \times B$ interaction are confounded with group effects; in the replication the AB components are confounded with group effects. Hence the original plan provided within-subject information on the AB^2 components, and the replication provides within-subject information on the AB components. Similarly, in the original plan the AC components of $A \times C$ are confounded with group effects; in the replication the AC^2

TABLE 9.26   **Replication of Plan 11**

G_1	(111)	(222)	(333)	G_4	(121)	(232)	(313)	G_7	(131)	(212)	(323)
G_2	(123)	(231)	(312)	G_5	(133)	(211)	(322)	G_8	(113)	(221)	(332)
G_3	(132)	(213)	(321)	G_6	(112)	(223)	(331)	G_9	(122)	(233)	(311)

components are confounded. A comparable condition holds for the $B \times C$ interaction. Use of the replication will provide some within-subject information on all components of the two-factor interactions. However, additional replications are required to obtain within-subject information on all components of the three-factor interaction. The original plan provides within-subject information on the AB^2C^2 component; the replication provides within-subject information on the ABC component. No within-subject information is available on the ABC^2 or the AB^2C^2 components.

Computational procedures for Plan 11. Computational procedures here are similar to those used in a $p \times p \times p$ factorial experiment in which there are n observations per cell. The first steps actually duplicate the latter procedures. The nonreplicated version of Plan 11 will be considered first; the replicated plan will be considered later.

Since all the treatment combinations in a $p \times p \times p$ factorial experiment appear in Plan 11, an ABC summary table may be prepared from the basic observations. From the latter summary table one obtains AB, AC, and BC summary tables. Most of the computational symbols in part i of Table 9.27 are obtained from these summary tables. Symbol (10) involves the totals P_o; the latter are the sums of the set of observations on an individual subject. The computational symbols in part ii require special comment.

The symbol G_m denotes the sum of the np observations in group m. The symbol G_{ab} is the sum of those G_m's which are assigned to the same set of ab_{ij}. For assignments made in accordance with the principles given in the last section, in a $3 \times 3 \times 3$ experiment the G_{ab}'s are

$$G_{1+6+8}, \qquad G_{2+4+9} \quad \text{and} \quad G_{3+5+7},$$

where $G_{1+6+8} = G_1 + G_6 + G_8$. In general there will be np^2 observations in each of such totals. the G_{ac}'s are made up of the following totals:

$$G_{1+4+7}, \qquad G_{2+5+8}, \quad \text{and} \quad G_{3+6+9}.$$

Each of the latter G_m's which are combined into a single total is assigned to the same set of ac_{ik}. For example, inspection of Table 9.24 indicates that groups 1,

TABLE 9.27   **Definition of computational symbols**

(i)

$(1) = G^2/np^3$	$(6) = [\sum (AB_{ij})^2]/np$
$(2) = \sum X^2$	$(7) = [\sum (AC_{ik})^2]/np$
$(3) = (\sum A_i^2)/np^2$	$(8) = [\sum (BC_{jk})^2]/np$
$(4) = (\sum B_j^2)/np^2$	$(9) = [\sum (ABC_{ijk})^2]/n$
$(5) = (\sum C_k^2)/np^2$	$(10) = (\sum P_o^2)/p$

(ii)

$(11) = (\sum G_m^2)/np$
$(12) = (\sum G_{ab}^2)/np^2 = (G_{1+6+8}^2 + G_{2+4+9}^2 + G_{3+5+7}^2)/np^2$
$(13) = (\sum G_{ac}^2)/np^2 = (G_{1+4+7}^2 + G_{2+5+8}^2 + G_{3+6+9}^2)/np^2$
$(14) = (\sum G_{bc}^2)/np^2 = (G_{1+5+9}^2 + G_{2+6+7}^2 + G_{3+4+8}^2)/np^2$

TABLE 9.28 **Computational formulas**

Between subjects	$(10) - (1)$
Between groups	$(11) - (1)$
AB'	$(12) - (1)$
AC'	$(13) - (1)$
BC'	$(14) - (1)$
ABC'	$(11) - (12) - (13) - (14) + 2(1)$
Subjects within groups	$(10) - (11)$
Within subjects	$(2) - (10)$
A	$(3) - (1)$
B	$(4) - (1)$
C	$(5) - (1)$
AB''	$[(6) - (3) - (4) + (1)] - [(12) - (1)]$
AC''	$[(7) - (3) - (5) + (1)] - [(13) - (1)]$
BC''	$[(8) - (4) - (5) + (1)] - [(14) - (1)]$
ABC''	$[(9) - (6) - (7) - (8) + (3) + (4) + (5)$ $- (1)] - [(11) - (12) - (13) - (14) + 2(1)]$
Error (within)	$[(2) - (9)] - [(10) - (11)]$

4, and 7 are assigned to the sets ac_{12}, ac_{21}, and ac_{33}. The level of factor B changes for the different groups, but the set of ac_{ik} remains the same.

Computational formulas for the sum of squares are summarized in Table 9.28. The parts of $SS_{error(within)}$ may be checked for homogeneity by computing a separate sum of squares for each of the groups. Thus

$$SS_{\text{error (within) for } G_m} = [(2g_m) - (9g_m)] - [(10g_m) - (11g_m)],$$

where the symbol $(2g_m)$ represents the symbol (2), in which the summation is restricted to G_m.

If Plan 11 is replicated, it is generally wise to carry out separate computations for each replication; those terms which are homogeneous may then be combined. Since different components of the two-factor interactions are estimated in each of the two replications, the two-factor interactions are in a sense nested within the replications. Thus,

$$SS''_{ab} = SS''_{ab \text{ from rep 1}} + SS''_{ab \text{ for rep 2}}.$$

Similar relationships hold for other two-factor interactions as well as the three-factor interaction. The error (within) term for the combined replications is given by

$$SS_{\text{error (within)}} = SS_{\text{error (within) from rep 1}} + SS_{\text{error (within) from rep 2}}.$$

In a sense, the error (within) effects are also nested within each replication.

Main effects, however, are not nested within replications. The latter are computed by obtaining $A \times$ replication, $B \times$ replication, and $C \times$ replication summary tables from the basic data. From such tables main effects and corresponding interactions may be computed. The latter interactions are pooled with error (within) if the components prove to be homogeneous with error (within).

PLAN 12 resembles Plan 5 as well as Plan 8 but yet has features that neither of the latter designs has. A schematic representation of Plan 12 is given below:

	c_1			c_2		
	b_1	b_2	b_3	b_1	b_2	b_3
G_1	a_2	a_1	a_3	a_2	a_1	a_3
G_2	a_3	a_2	a_1	a_3	a_2	a_1
G_3	a_1	a_3	a_2	a_1	a_3	a_2

In general, there will be p levels of factor A and p levels of factor B. The same $p \times p$ Latin square is used at each of the q levels of factor C. Plan 12 may be regarded as a fractional replication of a $p \times p \times q$ factorial experiment. If the interaction with the group factor is negligible, complete within-subject information is available for the main effects of factors A, B, and C. Complete within-subject information is also available on the AC and BC interactions; partial within-subject information is available on the AB and ABC interactions.

The analysis of variance is outlined in Table 9.29. In obtaining the expected values of the mean squares it is assumed that factors A, B, and C are

TABLE 9.29 **Analysis of Plan 12**

Source	df	E(MS)
Between subjects	$np - 1$	
Groups	$p - 1$	
Subj w. groups	$p(n - 1)$	
Within subjects	$np(pq - 1)$	
A	$p - 1$	$\sigma_\varepsilon^2 + \sigma_u^2 + npq\sigma_\alpha^2$
B	$p - 1$	$\sigma_\varepsilon^2 + \sigma_u^2 + npq\sigma_\beta^2$
$(AB)'$	$(p - 1)(p - 2)$	$\sigma_\varepsilon^2 + \sigma_u^2 + np\sigma_{\alpha\beta'}^2$
Residual (1)	$p(n - 1)(p - 1)$	$\sigma_\varepsilon^2 + \sigma_u^2$
C	$q - 1$	$\sigma_\varepsilon^2 + \sigma_v^2 + np^2\sigma_\gamma^2$
$C \times$ groups	$(p - 1)(q - 1)$	$\sigma_\varepsilon^2 + \sigma_v^2 + np\sigma_{\gamma\delta}^2$
Residual (2)	$p(n - 1)(q - 1)$	$\sigma_\varepsilon^2 + \sigma_v^2$
AC	$(p - 1)(q - 1)$	$\sigma_\varepsilon^2 + \sigma_w^2 + np\sigma_{\alpha\gamma}^2$
BC	$(p - 1)(q - 1)$	$\sigma_\varepsilon^2 + \sigma_w^2 + np\sigma_{\beta\gamma}^2$
$(AB)'C$	$(p - 1)(p - 2)(q - 1)$	$\sigma_\varepsilon^2 + \sigma_w^2 + n\sigma_{\alpha\beta'\gamma}^2$
Residual (3)	$p(n - 1)(p - 1)(q - 1)$	$\sigma_\varepsilon^2 + \sigma_w^2$

Pooled error = residual (1) + residual (2) + residual (3)
$$\text{df}_{\text{pooled error}} = p(n - 1)(pq - 1)$$

fixed; subjects within the groups define a random variable. The terms σ_u^2, σ_v^2, and σ_w^2, appearing in the expected values, represent interactions with subject effects. Because factors A and B are dimensions of a Latin square, the $A \times$ subject within group interaction cannot be distinguished from the $B \times$ subject within group interaction. However, the $C \times$ subject within group interaction can be distinguished from the others, since factor C is not one of the dimensions of the Latin square. In general, the three residual terms should be pooled into a single error term if there is neither *a priori* nor experimental evidence for heterogeneity of these components.

The computational procedures for this plan are simplified if the analysis of variance is carried out in two stages. In the first stage one of the dimensions of the Latin square, say factor A, is disregarded. Then the plan reduces to a $p \times q$ factorial experiment with repeated measures on both factors. The analysis of variance for the first stage is outlined in Table 9.30. The detailed computational procedures given in Sec. 7.3 may be adapted for use to obtain the first stage of the analysis.

In the second stage of the analysis, the presence of factor A as a dimension of the Latin square is taken into account. The $B \times$ group interaction is partitioned as follows:

$$\begin{array}{cc} B \times \text{group} & (p-1)^2 \\ \hline A & p-1 \\ AB' & (p-1)(p-2) \,. \end{array}$$

The latter interaction term may be obtained by subtraction or by the relation

$$\mathrm{SS}_{ab'} = \mathrm{SS}_{ab} - \mathrm{SS}_{\text{groups}},$$

where SS_{ab} is obtained from an AB summary table for the combined levels of

TABLE 9.30   **First stage in the analysis of Plan 12**

Source	df
Between subjects	$np - 1$
Groups	$p - 1$
Subjects w. group	$p(n - 1)$
Within subjects	$np(pq - 1)$
B	$p - 1$
$B \times$ group	$(p - 1)^2$
$B \times$ subj w. group	$p(n - 1)(p - 1)$
C	$(q - 1)$
$C \times$ group	$(p - 1)(q - 1)$
$C \times$ subj w. group	$p(n - 1)(q - 1)$
BC	$(p - 1)(q - 1)$
$BC \times$ group	$(p - 1)^2(q - 1)$
$BC \times$ subj w. group	$p(n - 1)(p - 1)(q - 1)$

factor C. The $BC \times$ group interaction is partitioned as follows:

$$
\begin{array}{ll}
BC \times \text{group} & (p-1)^2(q-1) \\
AC & (p-1)(q-1) \\
AB'C & (p-1)(p-2)(q-1)
\end{array}
$$

The latter interaction term may be obtained by subtraction from the following relation,

$$\text{SS}_{ab'c} = \text{SS}_{abc} - \text{SS}_{c \times \text{group}},$$

where SS_{abc} is obtained from an ABC summary table.

The residual terms in Table 9.29 are equivalent to the following interactions:

$$\text{SS}_{\text{res}(1)} = \text{SS}_{b \times \text{subj w. group}},$$

$$\text{SS}_{\text{res}(2)} = \text{SS}_{c \times \text{subj w. group}},$$

$$\text{SS}_{\text{res}(3)} = \text{SS}_{bc \times \text{subj w. group}}.$$

If only the pooled error is obtained, the latter is given by

$$\text{SS}_{\text{pooled error}} = \text{SS}_{\text{w. cell}} - \text{SS}_{\text{subj w. group}}.$$

PLAN 13 resembles Plan 9; in this case, however, a Greco-Latin square replaces the Latin square. A schematic representation of Plan 13 is given below:

		c_1	c_2	c_3				c_1	c_2	c_3
	G_1	ab_{12}	ab_{31}	ab_{23}			G_4	ab_{12}	ab_{31}	ab_{23}
d_1	G_2	ab_{33}	ab_{22}	ab_{11}		d_2	G_5	ab_{33}	ab_{22}	ab_{11}
	G_3	ab_{21}	ab_{13}	ab_{32}			G_6	ab_{21}	ab_{13}	ab_{32}

The same Greco-Latin square is used for each level of factor D.

The analysis of variance for this plan is most easily understood if it is made in two stages. In the first stage, two of the four dimensions of the Greco-Latin square are disregarded. Suppose that factors A and B are disregarded. The resulting plan may be considered as a $q \times p \times p$ factorial experiment with repeated measures on one of the factors. The analysis of variance for the first stage appears in the upper part of Table 9.31.

In the second stage, the interactions which involve two dimensions of the square (C and rows) are partitioned into main effects and interactions associated with factors A and B. This stage of the analysis is shown in the lower part of Table 9.31. It should be noted that $(AB)'$ cannot be distinguished from $(AC)'$ or $(BC)'$. This latter source of variation is sometimes called the uniqueness of the Greco-Latin square. In the partition of the $CD \times$ row interaction, $(AB)'D$ cannot be distinguished from $(AC)'D$ or $(BC)'D$.

If all factors are fixed, all within-subject effects are tested by means of F ratios having $C \times$ subjects within group as a denominator. If interactions between the dimensions of the square are negligible, $(AB)'$ and $(AB)'D$ may be pooled with the experimental error. The F ratios for between-subject effects have subjects within groups as a denominator.

TABLE 9.31   **Analysis of variance for Plan 13**

	Source	df
	Between subjects	$npq - 1$
	Rows	$p - 1$
	D	$q - 1$
	$D \times$ rows	$(p - 1)(q - 1)$
	Subjects within groups	$pq(n - 1)$
(i)	Within subjects	$npq(p - 1)$
	C	$p - 1$
	$C \times$ rows	$(p - 1)^2$
	CD	$(p - 1)(q - 1)$
	$CD \times$ rows	$(p - 1)^2(q - 1)$
	$C \times$ subj w. group (Error)	$pq(n - 1)(p - 1)$
	$C \times$ rows	$(p - 1)^2$
	A	$p - 1$
	B	$p - 1$
	$(AB)'$	$(p - 1)(p - 3)$
(ii)	$CD \times$ rows	$(p - 1)^2(q - 1)$
	AD	$(p - 1)(q - 1)$
	BD	$(p - 1)(q - 1)$
	$(AB)'D$	$(p - 1)(p - 3)(q - 1)$

Summary of Plans in Sec. 9.5

Plan 5

	a_1	a_2	a_3
G_1	b_3	b_1	b_2
G_2	b_1	b_2	b_3
G_3	b_2	b_3	b_1

Plan 6

		a_1	a_2	a_3
G_1	c_1	b_1	b_3	b_2
G_2	c_2	b_2	b_1	b_3
G_3	c_3	b_3	b_2	b_1

Plan 7

	a_1	a_2	a_3
G_1	bc_{11}	bc_{23}	bc_{32}
G_2	bc_{22}	bc_{31}	bc_{13}
G_3	bc_{33}	bc_{12}	bc_{21}

Plan 8

		a_1	a_2	a_3
	G_1	b_1	b_2	b_3
c_1	G_2	b_2	b_3	b_1
	G_3	b_3	b_1	b_2

		a_1	a_2	a_3
	G_4	b_2	b_3	b_1
c_2	G_5	b_1	b_2	b_3
	G_6	b_3	b_1	b_2

Plan 9

		a_1	a_2	a_3
	G_1	b_2	b_3	b_1
c_1	G_2	b_1	b_2	b_3
	G_3	b_3	b_1	b_2

		a_1	a_2	a_3
	G_4	b_2	b_3	b_1
c_2	G_5	b_1	b_2	b_3
	G_6	b_3	b_1	b_2

		a_1	a_2	a_3
	G_7	b_2	b_3	b_1
c_3	G_8	b_1	b_2	b_3
	G_9	b_3	b_1	b_2

Plan 10

			a_1	a_2	a_3
	G_1	c_1	b_3	b_1	b_2
d_1	G_2	c_2	b_2	b_3	b_1
	G_3	c_3	b_1	b_2	b_3

			a_1	a_2	a_3
	G_4	c_1	b_2	b_1	b_3
d_2	G_5	c_2	b_1	b_3	b_2
	G_6	c_3	b_3	b_2	b_1

Summary of Plans in Sec. 9.5—(*Continued*)

Plan 11

	a_1	a_2	a_3
G_1	bc_{12}	bc_{31}	bc_{23}
G_2	bc_{33}	bc_{22}	bc_{11}
G_3	bc_{21}	bc_{13}	bc_{32}

	a_1	a_2	a_3
G_4	bc_{32}	bc_{21}	bc_{13}
G_5	bc_{23}	bc_{12}	bc_{31}
G_6	bc_{11}	bc_{33}	bc_{22}

	a_1	a_2	a_3
G_7	bc_{22}	bc_{11}	bc_{33}
G_8	bc_{13}	bc_{32}	bc_{21}
G_9	bc_{31}	bc_{23}	bc_{12}

Plan 12

	c_1			c_2		
	b_1	b_2	b_3	b_1	b_2	b_3
G_1	a_2	a_1	a_3	a_2	a_1	a_3
G_2	a_3	a_2	a_1	a_3	a_2	a_1
G_3	a_1	a_3	a_2	a_1	a_3	a_2

Plan 13

		c_1	c_2	c_3
	G_1	ab_{12}	ab_{31}	ab_{23}
d_1	G_2	ab_{33}	ab_{22}	ab_{11}
	G_3	ab_{21}	ab_{13}	ab_{32}

		c_1	c_2	c_3
	G_4	ab_{12}	ab_{31}	ab_{23}
d_2	G_5	ab_{33}	ab_{22}	ab_{11}
	G_6	ab_{21}	ab_{13}	ab_{32}

9.6 EXERCISES

1. Write Latin squares in standard form for each of the following:
   (*a*) 3×3
   (*b*) 4×4
   (*c*) 5×5

2. How many are there?
   (*a*) 4×4 Latin squares
   (*b*) 6×6 Latin squares.

3. Construct a randomly selected 4×4 Latin square.

4. Using the Latin square from (3), construct a balanced set of Latin squares.

5. Starting with any 3×3 Latin square,
   (*a*) Write that Latin square in standard form,
   (*b*) Transform that square through a one-to-one transformation, and
   (*c*) Write the transformed Latin square in standard form.

6. Form a 3×3 Greco-Latin square. Show how that square can be used to design an experiment with two treatment conditions ($p = 3$, $q = 3$) and two nuisance variables, each at three levels.

7. An experimenter was interested in designing a study with two factors, factor A with $p = 2$ levels and factor B with $q = 4$ levels. It was necessary to have repeated measures on factor B, but factor A represented a between-group difference.

(a) How many possible sequences are there for the levels of factor B?

(b) Show schematically how the experimenter could use a total of $n = 96$ subjects and, with a between-subject sequence factor, control for order effects for the repeated-measures factor B.

(c) Show how Latin square(s) can be used to accomplish the same kind of control over order effects. What are the advantages of this control? Disadvantages?

(d) In (c) if these groups of subjects are *not* randomly selected, how may one interpret the "sequence main effect"? If groups are randomly formed, how may one interpret the "sequence main effect"?

8. How many orthogonal Latin squares would be required to construct a balanced fractional replication of:

(a) a $3 \times 3 \times 3 \times 3$ factorial design?

(b) a $5 \times 5 \times 5 \times 5 \times 5$ factorial design?

9. Use the following defining relations to reduce a $3 \times 3 \times 3$ factorial design to a set of 3, 3×3 Latin squares by selecting appropriate treatment conditions to define the fractional replication represented by the Latin square:

(a) ABC^2

(b) AB^2C^2

10. What are the aliases for the main effects of factor A in 9(a) and 9(b) above?

11. In general, what are the main effects confounded with when a Latin square is used as a balanced fractional replication of a complete factorial experiment?

12. A 3×3 Latin square was used to form a fractional replication of a $3 \times 3 \times 3$ factorial design using the defining relation $(AB^2C)_0$ to select the treatment conditions. Hence, the treatment conditions are:

$$
\begin{array}{ccc}
 & b_0 \quad b_1 \quad b_2 \\
a_0 & c_0 \quad c_1 \quad c_2 \\
a_1 & c_2 \quad c_0 \quad c_1 \\
a_2 & c_1 \quad c_2 \quad c_0
\end{array}
\quad = \quad
\begin{array}{ccc}
 & b_1 \quad b_2 \quad b_3 \\
a_1 & c_1 \quad c_2 \quad c_3 \\
a_2 & c_3 \quad c_1 \quad c_2 \\
a_3 & c_2 \quad c_3 \quad c_1
\end{array}
$$

An independent random sample of $n = 6$ subjects was observed under each of the nine treatment conditions. The data were:

	b_1	b_2	b_3
a_1	8, 10, 14, 9, 7, 9	2, 2, 3, 6, 1, 1	2, 4, 4, 7, 1, 3
a_2	4, 7, 5, 3, 3, 6	4, 4, 6, 8, 3, 3	11, 12, 14, 14, 10, 11
a_3	2, 3, 3, 6, 0, 0	4, 3, 3, 7, 3, 2	2, 3, 3, 6, 1, 2

(a) What are the aliases for the A, B, and C main effects?

(b) Assuming no interactions, what is the structural model for this design?

(c) If, in fact, there is a real BC interaction, how can the experimenter interpret the A main effect?

(d) Carry out the appropriate analysis of variance and test the hypotheses, $\sigma_\alpha^2 = 0$, $\sigma_\beta^2 = 0$, $\sigma_\gamma^2 = 0$ ($\alpha = 0.05$). Assume all factors are fixed.

13. Use Latin squares to design an experiment in which it is assumed that there are no interactions between factors A, B, and C, but that any of those factors may interact with a factor D. There are $p = q = r = 3$ levels of factors A, B, and C. There are $s = 2$ levels of factor D.

14. Use a 4×4 Latin square to design an experiment in which there are repeated measures on ab_{ij} treatment conditions and between-group differences are confounded with part of the AB interaction. In this design, there are $p = q = 4$ levels of factors A and B. There are four groups of $n = 10$ subjects each. Each group is observed under only four of the sixteen possible ab_{ij} treatment conditions.

(a) Show the design schematically.

(b) Discuss the limitations of this design.

(c) Maintaining the restriction that any one group of subjects may be observed under only four treatment conditions, what alternative design is possible?

(d) Provide an ANOV summary table for the design showing all sources of variation and providing numerical values for all degrees of freedom.

15. Latin squares were used to control sequence effects in the following manner wherein 8 of the possible 24 sequences for administering the levels of factor B were included in the experiment. Subjects were selected and assigned at random to levels of factor A and to sequences. Schematically, the design is:

	Sequences	Subjects	Order 1	2	3	4
		1				
	1	2	b_1	b_2	b_3	b_4
		3				
	2	4	b_2	b_1	b_4	b_3
a_1		5				
	3	6	b_3	b_4	b_1	b_2
		7				
	4	8	b_4	b_3	b_2	b_1
		9				
	5	10	b_3	b_1	b_2	b_4
		11				
	6	12	b_4	b_2	b_1	b_3
a_2		13				
	7	14	b_1	b_3	b_4	b_2
		15				
	8	16	b_2	b_4	b_3	b_1

The corresponding observed data were:

	Sequences	Subjects	Order 1	2	3	4
		1	0	0	5	3
	1	2	3	1	5	4
		3	4	3	6	2
	2	4	1	1	6	4
a_1		5	4	2	6	5
	3	6	5	4	7	3
		7	2	0	4	3
	4	8	3	2	5	1
		9	4	2	7	8
	5	10	5	4	6	6
		11	7	5	8	9
	6	12	5	3	8	9
a_2		13	6	5	7	7
	7	14	8	6	9	10
		15	4	3	5	5
	8	16	6	4	7	8

(a) Write a structural model assuming there are no pre-existing group effects confounded with A or sequence main effects and that there is no real interaction between order and subjects within sequences.

(b) Carry out the analysis of variance making tests of significance on A, B and sequence main effects, and on the AB interaction ($\alpha = 0.05$). Assume all effects are fixed except subjects.

(c) Plot the $\overline{AB}_{ij}$.

(d) Does the sequence in which levels of factor B occur have an effect?

(e) If there were such an interaction, what interaction would make it impossible to interpret the B main effect?

CHAPTER 10

ANALYSIS OF COVARIANCE

10.1 GENERAL PURPOSE

There are two general methods for controlling variability due to experimental error—direct and statistical. Direct control includes such methods as grouping the experimental units into homogeneous strata or blocks, increasing the uniformity of the conditions under which the experiment is run, and increasing the accuracy of the measurements. Replicated experiments, randomized block designs, repeated-measure designs, split-plot designs, incomplete-block designs—these designs use the direct-control principle to increase the precision of the experiment.

In this chapter, designs which use an indirect, or statistical, control (1) to increase the precision of the experiment and (2) to remove potential sources of bias in the experiment will be discussed. The latter objective is one that is particularly important in situations where the experimenter cannot assign individual units at random to the experimental conditions. Statistical control is achieved by measuring one or more concomitant variates in addition to the variate of primary interest. The latter variate will be termed the criterion, or simply the variate; the concomitant variates will be called covariates. Measurements on the covariates are made for the purpose of adjusting the measurements on the variate.

For example, the purpose may be to evaluate the effectiveness of different methods of teaching. The covariate may be a measure of aptitude; the variate is a measure of achievement after the teaching is complete. If the experimenter is forced to work with intact classes when the teaching methods are assigned to groups of subjects, it is possible, indeed likely, that the classes would vary in aptitude. The analysis of covariance can be used to adjust achievement for those differences in aptitude. As another example, suppose that the purpose of an experiment is to determine the relative effectiveness of methods of extinction upon a learned response. The variate in this experiment may be a measure of extinction; the covariate may be a measure associated with the degree of learning at the start of the extinction trials. In this type of design one often will have intact groups in the sense that each group may have learned a specified performance under a different method before the start of the extinction phase. As still another example, suppose that the purpose of an experiment is to measure the relative effectiveness of various stress situations upon blood pressure. In this case a measure of blood pressure under a condition of no stress may be the covariate. As another example, suppose that the purpose of an experiment is to evaluate the effect of electrical stimulation on the weight of denervated muscle. The weight of the corresponding normal muscle may be a useful covariate. In general, the analysis of covariance is potentially useful in any situation wherein subjects assigned to treatments are not equated with regard to some variable(s) which are correlated with the dependent variable, but are unaffected by the treatments.

Considerable care is needed in using the analysis of covariance in "adjusting" for initial or final differences between groups of experiment units. Lord (1969) gives some good examples of how this type of adjustment may result in highly misleading interpretations. Interpretations and possible misinterpretations of adjusted means are discussed later in this chapter. The intrinsic nature of the concomitance between the variate and the covariate requires examination. If this concomitance is predominantly due to a dimension along which an adjustment is desired, such an adjustment may be made. However, should this concomitance be due largely to factors which are not those for which control is wanted, then making an adjustment for the covariate may lead to relatively meaningless results.

The analysis of covariance should be viewed as only one of numerous ways to control for the effects of a covariate upon the variate. Moreover, direct experimental design control of the types discussed throughout this book may be used simultaneously with statistical control within the same experiment. One or more factors may be under direct control; one or more factors may be under statistical control.

To illustrate some statistical control possibilities, suppose that the means on the variate in a single-factor experiment are denoted

$$\bar{Y}_1, \bar{Y}_2, \ldots, \bar{Y}_k,$$

and the means on the covariate are denoted

$$\bar{X}_1, \bar{X}_2, \ldots, \bar{X}_k.$$

Primary interest lies in differences among the $\bar{Y}_j$. Suppose that differences in the $\bar{X}_j$ are due to sources of variation related to the $\bar{Y}_j$ but not directly related to the treatment effects. If this is the case, then more precise information on the treatment effects may be obtained by adjusting the $\bar{Y}_j$ for the association with the $\bar{X}_j$. Suppose the adjusted variate means are denoted

$$\bar{Y}_1', \bar{Y}_2', \ldots, \bar{Y}_k'.$$

There may be several different ways of making the adjustment. In some cases, the adjustment may take the form of a simple difference between variate and covariate; that is,

$$\bar{Y}_j' = \bar{Y}_j - \bar{X}_j.$$

In other cases, the adjusted mean may take the form

$$\bar{Y}_j' = \bar{Y}_j / \bar{X}_j.$$

The appropriate form of the adjustment is usually determined from prior knowledge about the interrelationship between variate and covariate.

When analysis of covariance is used for the adjustment, it essentially combines regression analysis procedures with analysis of variance procedures. The regression analysis component adjusts the variate for the effects of the covariate; the analysis of variance assesses treatment effects on the adjusted variate. However, it should be emphasized that analysis of covariance is *not* simply the analysis of variance of residual scores from a regression analysis (Maxwell, et al., 1985). Although the form of the regression need not be linear, only the linear case will be considered in this chapter. In terms of a linear adjustment procedure, an adjusted treatment mean in the analysis of covariance takes the form

$$\bar{Y}_{j'} = \bar{Y}_j - b(\bar{X}_j - \bar{X}),$$

where

$$\bar{X} = \frac{\sum \bar{X}_j}{k},$$

and where b is the coefficient in the appropriate regression.

In many cases, more important than the adjustment of the treatment means is the reduction in the experimental error due to the regression of the variate on the covariate. The higher the within-treatment correlation (say ρ) between X and Y the smaller the variance due to the experimental error in the analysis of covariance relative to the corresponding experimental error in the analysis of variance. If the latter is denoted σ_ε^2, then the experimental error in the analysis of covariance, say $\sigma_{\varepsilon'}^2$, will be

$$\sigma_{\varepsilon'}^2 = \sigma_\varepsilon^2(1 - \rho^2)\frac{f_\varepsilon}{f_\varepsilon - 1},$$

where f_ε is the degrees of freedom for estimating σ_ε^2.

This point is illustrated in Fig. 10.1. In Fig. 10.1a, the correlation ρ between X and Y is larger than is the correlation shown in Fig. 10.1b, as evidenced by less variance of Y about the regression lines in 10.1a. The

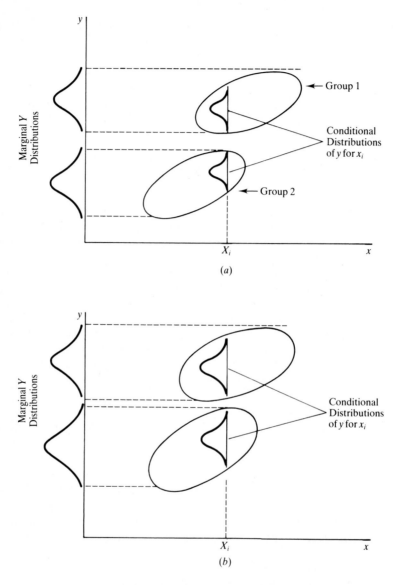

FIGURE 10-1 The reduction of error in the dependent variable due to correlation with the covariate.

marginal distributions of Y illustrate the error variance in Y which would obtain in an analysis of variance wherein the covariate is not considered. The variance of the conditional distributions of Y, given some value of X, reflect the error variance in Y when the covariate is considered. Obviously, this variance decreases as ρ increases as illustrated by comparing Panel (a) with

Panel (b). When $\rho = 0$, the error variance is that of the marginal distributions and there is no advantage to measuring the covariate.

If, instead of using analysis of covariance for adjusting Y, the covariate is used to form blocks which are homogeneous with respect to the covariate, and if the relationship between X and Y is linear, then the effect of this kind of blocking is to reduce the experimental error from

$$\sigma_\varepsilon^2 \qquad \text{to} \qquad \sigma_\varepsilon^2(1 - \rho^2).$$

Thus, when the regression is linear, covariance adjustment is approximately as effective as stratification with respect to the covariate. However, if the regression is not linear, and a linear adjustment is used, then stratification will generally provide greater reduction in the experimental error. In a real sense, stratification is a function-free regression scheme. Stratification with respect to the covariate converts the covariate into a factor—a single-factor experiment is converted into a two-factor experiment, the factors being the treatment and the covariate.

When the covariate is actually affected by the treatment, the adjustment process removes more than what can be considered an error component from the variate. It also may remove part of the treatment effect on Y. If the measurements on both the variate and the covariate are made after the administration of the treatment, it is possible that the covariate may have been affected by the treatment. An analysis of variance on the covariate may throw some light on this issue. In some experimental work where both the variate and covariate are affected by the treatments, the purpose of such experiments has been to investigate the underlying process by which the treatment actually affects the variate. It may be that the treatment has its effect on Y through its effect on X. There are some difficulties that are encountered in the interpretation of the results of such experiments. These difficulties are not that the model breaks down but rather that the adjusted data may not correspond to any situation that could actually be realized experimentally.

If the measurements on the covariate are made before the treatments are administered, the covariate cannot be affected by the treatments. When an experimenter is forced by the nature of the real world to work with intact groups, the covariate means under treatments j and j', denoted $\bar{X}_j$ and $\bar{X}_{j'}$, may differ. The adjusted difference between the variate means, using a linear adjustment, takes the form

$$\bar{Y}_j' - \bar{Y}_{j'}' = \bar{Y}_j - \bar{Y}_{j'} - b(\bar{X}_j - \bar{X}_{j'}).$$

If one defines the difference

$$\tau_j - \tau_{j'} = \mu_{y_j} - \mu_{y_{j'}} - \beta(\bar{X}_j - \bar{X}_{j'}),$$

then

$$E(\bar{Y}_j' - \bar{Y}_{j'}') = E(\bar{Y}_j - \bar{Y}_{j'}) - E[b(\bar{X}_j - \bar{X}_{j'})]$$

$$= \mu_{y_j} - \mu_{y_{j'}} - \beta(\bar{X}_j - \bar{X}_{j'})$$

$$= \tau_j - \tau_{j'}.$$

That is, the expected value of the difference between the adjusted means is an unbiased estimator of the corresponding difference between the treatment effects. The expected value of the difference between the unadjusted treatment means is

$$E(\bar{Y}_j - \bar{Y}_{j'}) = \mu_{y_j} - \mu_{y_{j'}} = \tau_j - \tau_{j'} + \beta(\bar{X}_j - \bar{X}_{j'});$$

that is, this difference will be biased as an estimate of the corresponding treatment effects by a factor that depends upon β and the magnitude of $\bar{X}_j - \bar{X}_{j'}$. When this latter difference is relatively large, the standard error of the adjusted difference will tend to be quite large. At best, covariance adjustment for large initial biases on the covariate are poor substitutes for direct control. A more complete discussion of this point is given by Cochran (1957).

Analysis of covariance was originally presented by Fisher (Fisher, 1932). An excellent as well as quite readable summary of the wide variety of uses of the analysis of covariance is contained in a special issue of *Biometrics* (1957, **13**, no. 3), which is devoted entirely to this topic. In this issue is a rather lengthy discussion by H. F. Smith on the interpretation of the adjusted treatment means, particularly for the case in which the treatment affects the covariate. A more recent presentation of analysis of covariance and its applications which is very useful has been presented by Cox and McCullough (1982).

10.2 SINGLE-FACTOR EXPERIMENT

Notation

The notation system for the analysis of covariance differs somewhat from author to author. The notation that will be used in this chapter is that used by Cochran (1957). The notation system used by Scheffé (1959, pp. 192–213) is more readily generalized but is unnecessarily complicated for the limited coverage that is included in this chapter.

The observations for individual i under treatment j will be denoted

$$X_{ij}, Y_{ij}, \quad \begin{array}{l} i = 1, 2, \ldots, n, \\ j = 1, 2, \ldots, k, \end{array}$$

where X_{ij} is the measure on the covariate and Y_{ij} is the observation of the dependent variable after the administration of treatment j. Thus under treatment j there are n pairs of observations. These n pairs of observations are symbolized in Table 10.1. There will be k treatments ($j = 1, 2, \ldots, k$).

In the analysis of covariance, it is necessary to consider three sets of numbers, the variation of the variate, the variation of the covariate, and the covariation of the variate and covariate, for all sources of variation associated with an analysis of variance of the same design. When this notation is applied to a single factor experiment, T will be used for treatment effects, E for within-treatment or error effects, and S for total (sum) effects. Thus, the following variations and covariations are the basic ingredients for the analysis of covariance:

Source	Variation variate	Variation covariate	Covariation variate–covariate
Treatments	T_{yy}	T_{xx}	T_{xy}
Error	E_{yy}	E_{xx}	E_{xy}
Total	S_{yy}	S_{xx}	S_{xy}

The notation is provided in Table 10.1 in detail for the single-factor, completely randomized design.

TABLE 10.1 **Notation for the analysis of covariance**

	Treatment 1		$\cdots$	Treatment j		$\cdots$	Treatment k		
	Y_{11} $\quad$ X_{11}			Y_{1j} $\quad$ X_{1j}			Y_{1k} $\quad$ X_{1k}		
	Y_{21} $\quad$ X_{21}			Y_{2j} $\quad$ X_{2j}			Y_{2k} $\quad$ X_{2k}		
	$\vdots$ $\quad$ $\vdots$			$\vdots$ $\quad$ $\vdots$			$\vdots$ $\quad$ $\vdots$		
	Y_{n1} $\quad$ X_{n1}			Y_{nj} $\quad$ X_{nj}			Y_{nk} $\quad$ X_{nk}		
Sum	T_{y_1} $\quad$ T_{x_1}		$\cdots$	T_{y_j} $\quad$ T_{x_j}		$\cdots$	T_{y_k} $\quad$ T_{x_k}	$\sum T_{y_j} = G_y$ $\sum T_{x_j} = G_x$	
Mean	$\bar{Y}_1$ $\quad$ $\bar{X}_1$		$\cdots$	$\bar{Y}_j$ $\quad$ $\bar{X}_j$		$\cdots$	$\bar{Y}_k$ $\quad$ $\bar{X}_k$	$\bar{Y}$ $\quad$ $\bar{X}$	

$$(1x) = G_x^2/kn \qquad (1xy) = G_x G_y/kn \qquad (1y) = G_y^2/kn$$

$$(2x) = \sum X^2 \qquad (2xy) = \sum XY \qquad (2y) = \sum Y^2$$

$$(3x) = \left(\sum T_{x_j}^2\right)\Big/n \qquad (3xy) = \left(\sum T_{x_j}T_{y_j}\right)\Big/n \qquad (3y) = \left(\sum T_{y_j}^2\right)\Big/n$$

Sources of variation and covariation:

Treatments:	$T_{xx} = n \sum (\bar{X}_j - \bar{X})^2$	$T_{xy} = n \sum (\bar{X}_j - \bar{X})(\bar{Y}_j - \bar{Y})$	$T_{yy} = n \sum (\bar{Y}_j - \bar{Y})^2$
	$= (3x) - (1x)$	$= (3xy) - (1xy)$	$= (3y) - (1y)$
Error:	$E_{xx} = \sum\sum (X_{ij} - \bar{X}_j)^2$	$E_{xy} = \sum\sum (X_{ij} - \bar{X}_j)(Y_{ij} - \bar{Y}_j)$	$E_{yy} = \sum\sum (Y_{ij} - \bar{Y}_j)^2$
	$= (2x) - (3x)$	$= (2xy) - (3xy)$	$= (2y) - (3y)$
Total	$S_{xx} = \sum\sum (X_{ij} - \bar{X})^2$	$S_{xy} = \sum\sum (X_{ij} - \bar{X})(Y_{ij} - \bar{Y})$	$S_{yy} = \sum\sum (Y_{ij} - \bar{Y})^2$
	$= (2x) - (1x)$	$= (2xy) - (1xy)$	$= (2y) - (1y)$

In Table 10.1,

$\bar{Y}_j$ = mean of measurements on variate under treatment j.
E_{xx_j} = variation on covariate under treatment j.
E_{yy_j} = variation on variate under treatment j.
E_{xy_j} = covariation between variate and covariate under treatment j.
$E_{xx} = \Sigma E_{xx_j}$, $E_{yy} = \Sigma E_{yy_j}$, $E_{xy} = \Sigma E_{xy_j}$.
T_{xx} = between-treatment variation on covariate.
T_{yy} = between-treatment variation on variate.
T_{xy} = between-treatment covariation.
S_{xx} = overall variation on covariate = $T_{xx} + E_{xx}$.
S_{yy} = overall variation on variate = $T_{yy} + E_{yy}$.
S_{xy} = overall covariation = $T_{xy} + E_{xy}$.

Least-Squares Estimators of Parameters in Analysis of Covariance Model

For the analysis of covariance to be useful, the dependent variable must be a function of treatment effects *and* regression on the covariate. Thus, the model for an observation on the variate Y_{ij} on unit i under treatment j is assumed to have the form

$$Y_{ij} = \mu + \tau_j + \beta(X_{ij} - \bar{X}) + \varepsilon_{ij} \quad (i = 1, 2, \ldots, n; j = 1, 2, \ldots, k), \quad (10.1)$$

where treatments are fixed and only ε_{ij} is a random variable. Thus,

$$\varepsilon_{ij}: N(0, \sigma_\varepsilon^2) \text{ for all } j.$$

The following constraint on the τ_j is assumed to be part of the model:

$$\sum \tau_j = 0.$$

Additional assumptions about the regression part of the model will be made explicit later in this section.

If one ignores the τ_j in (10.1), the model takes the form of the linear regression model as in (10.2).

$$Y_{ij} = \mu_y + \beta(X_{ij} - \bar{X}) + \varepsilon_{ij}. \quad (10.2)$$

On the other hand if one ignores β in (10.1), the model takes the form of the usual analysis of variance model as in (10.3).

$$Y_{ij} = \mu_y + \tau_j + \varepsilon_{ij} \quad \left(\sum \tau_j = 0\right). \quad (10.3)$$

One may also rewrite the model in (10.1) in the form

$$Y'_{ij} = Y_{ij} - \beta(X_{ij} - \bar{X}) = \mu_y + \tau_j + \varepsilon_{ij}. \quad (10.4)$$

In (10.4) Y'_{ij} is a residual from the regression of Y on X. Y'_{ij} represents that part of Y_{ij} "adjusted for" the linear effect of the covariate, or that part of the variate with the effect of the covariate "partialled out." This model (10.4) may be regarded as the model for the analysis of covariance. In the analysis of covariance, one essentially carries out an analysis of variance on the Y'_{ij}, after one takes into account the fact that the Y'_{ij} will not be statistically independent. To obtain the least-squares estimators of the parameters in model (10.4), one may obtain the corresponding estimators in model (10.1). The parameters to be estimated are

$$\mu, \tau_1, \tau_2, \ldots, \tau_k, \beta, \sigma_\varepsilon^2.$$

The corresponding least-squares estimators will be denoted

$$\hat{\mu}, \hat{\tau}_1, \hat{\tau}_2, \ldots, \hat{\tau}_k, \hat{\beta}, \hat{\sigma}_\varepsilon^2.$$

The constraint

$$\sum \hat{\tau}_j = 0$$

will be imposed upon the estimators of the τ_j. To obtain the least-squares estimators, one minimizes the quantity

$$\phi = \sum \hat{\varepsilon}_{ij}^2 = \sum \sum [Y_{ij} - \hat{\mu} - \hat{\tau}_j - \hat{\beta}(X_{ij} - \bar{X})]^2. \tag{10.5}$$

Taking the partial derivative of (10.2) with respect to $\hat{\mu}$ and setting the result equal to zero yields the normal equation for $\hat{\mu}$,

$$-2 \sum_i \sum_j [Y_{ij} - \hat{\mu} - \hat{\tau}_j - \hat{\beta}(X_{ij} - \bar{X})] = 0.$$

Using the constraints and after some rearrangement, this equation reduces to

$$kn\hat{\mu} = G_y. \tag{10.6}$$

Hence

$$\hat{\mu} = \frac{G_y}{kn} = \bar{Y}.$$

The normal equation for $\hat{\tau}_j$, the treatment effects, is

$$-2 \sum_i [X_{ij} - \hat{\mu} - \hat{\tau}_j - \hat{\beta}(X_{ij} - \bar{X})] = 0 \quad (j = 1, 2, \ldots, k).$$

Using the estimator of μ obtained from (10.6), one may write the normal equation from τ_j in the form

$$n\bar{Y} + n\hat{\tau}_j + \hat{\beta}(T_{x_j} - n\bar{X}) = T_{y_j} \quad (j = 1, 2, \ldots, k). \tag{10.7}$$

Solving (10.7) for $\hat{\tau}_j$ gives

$$\hat{\tau}_j = \bar{Y}_j - \bar{Y} - \hat{\beta}(\bar{X}_j - \bar{X}) \quad (j = 1, 2, \ldots, k).$$

In words, the estimator of treatment effects is the analysis of variance estimator of treatment effects, $\bar{Y}_j - \bar{Y}$, adjusted for linear regression on the covariance means, $\hat{\beta}(\bar{X}_j - \bar{X})$. Note that the least-squares estimator of τ_j in the analysis of variance is that special case where $\hat{\beta} = 0$.

The normal equation for estimating β is

$$-2 \sum_i \sum_j [Y_{ij} - \hat{\mu} - \hat{\tau}_j - \hat{\beta}(X_{ij} - \bar{X})](X_{ij} - \bar{X}) = 0,$$

which may be written in the form

$$\sum_i \sum_j (Y_{ij} - \bar{Y})(X_{ij} - \bar{X}) - \sum_i \sum_j (\bar{Y}_j - \bar{Y})(X_{ij} - \bar{X})$$

$$+ \sum_i \sum_j \hat{\beta}(\bar{X}_j - \bar{X})(X_{ij} - \bar{X}) - \sum_i \sum_j \hat{\beta}(X_{ij} - \bar{X})^2 = 0.$$

One notes that

$$\sum_i \sum_j (Y_{ij} - \bar{Y})(X_{ij} - \bar{X}) = S_{xy},$$

$$\sum_i \sum_j (\bar{Y}_j - \bar{Y})(X_{ij} - \bar{X}) = T_{xy},$$

$$\sum_i \sum_j (\bar{X}_j - \bar{X})(X_{ij} - \bar{X}) = T_{xx},$$

$$\sum_i \sum_j (X_{ij} - \bar{X})^2 = S_{xx}.$$

Using these relations, the normal equation for β may be rewritten in the simplified form

$$S_{xy} - T_{xy} + \hat{\beta}T_{xx} - \hat{\beta}S_{xx} = 0.$$

Hence

$$\hat{\beta}(S_{xx} - T_{xx}) = S_{xy} - T_{xy}.$$

Thus the least-squares estimator of β is

$$\hat{\beta} = b_E = \frac{S_{xy} - T_{xy}}{S_{xx} - T_{xx}} = \frac{E_{xy}}{E_{xx}}.$$

Thus b_E, the estimator of $\hat{\beta}$, is the ratio of the pooled within-class covariation to the pooled within-class variation on the covariate.

The minimum value of $\sum \hat{\varepsilon}_{ij}^2$ may be obtained from (10.5) by replacing the parameters by their least-squares estimators. After some algebraic manipulations, one finds that

$$\text{minimum} \sum \hat{\varepsilon}_{ij}^2 = E_{yy}' = E_{YY} - b_E E_{xy} = E_{yy} - (E_{xy}^2 / E_{xx}).$$

It is important to note that E_{yy} is the error estimate appropriate for the analysis of variance. Thus, the error estimate in the analysis of covariance, E_{yy}'

is reduced by

$$E_{xy}^2/E_{xx} = b_E E_{xy}.$$

Alternatively, one may view E_{xy}^2/E_{xx} as the increase in predictability over the analysis of variance due to including the covariate in the model equation.

This same result may be obtained from a somewhat different approach using results which follow from the general linear model. In matrix form the normal equations developed above may be represented as

$$
\begin{bmatrix}
kn & n & n & \cdots & n & 0 \\
n & n & 0 & \cdots & 0 & T_{x_1} - \bar{X} \\
n & n & 0 & \cdots & 0 & T_{x_2} - \bar{X} \\
\vdots & \vdots & \vdots & \vdots & \vdots & \vdots \\
n & n & 0 & \cdots & n & \bar{T}_{x_k} - \bar{X} \\
0 & X_{ij} - \bar{X} & X_{ij} - \bar{X} & \cdots & X_{ij} - \bar{X} & S_{xx}
\end{bmatrix}
\begin{bmatrix}
\hat{\mu} \\
\hat{\tau}_1 \\
\hat{\tau}_2 \\
\vdots \\
\hat{\tau}_k \\
\hat{\beta}
\end{bmatrix}
=
\begin{bmatrix}
G_y \\
T_{y_1} \\
T_{y_2} \\
\vdots \\
T_{y_k} \\
S_{xy}
\end{bmatrix}
$$

If one drops the first row of this set of equations, the predictable variation due to treatments and regression on the covariate $R(\tau, \beta \mid \mu)$ is given by

$$
\begin{aligned}
R(\tau, \beta \mid \mu) &= \sum \hat{\tau}_j T_{y_j} + \hat{\beta} S_{xy} \\
&= \sum_i \sum_j [\bar{Y}_j - \bar{Y} - \hat{\beta}(\bar{X}_j - \bar{X})] T_{y_j} + \hat{\beta}(T_{xy} + E_{xy}) \\
&= T_{yy} - \hat{\beta} T_{xy} + \hat{\beta} T_{xy} + \hat{\beta} E_{xy} \\
&= T_{yy} + \hat{\beta} E_{xy} = T_{yy} + b_E E_{xy} = T_{yy} + (E_{xy}^2/E_{xx}).
\end{aligned}
$$

This end product may be rationalized as follows: The predictable variation is in part due to differences among the treatment means $\bar{Y}_j$, which is T_{yy}, and in part due to the within-class regression of Y on X, which is E_{xy}^2/E_{xx}. Hence the variation due to error is

$$
\begin{aligned}
S_{yy} - R(\tau, \beta \mid \mu) &= S_{yy} - T_{yy} - (E_{xy}^2/E_{xx}) \\
&= E_{yy} - (E_{xy}^2/E_{xx}) = E_{yy} - b_E E_{xy} = E_{yy}'.
\end{aligned}
$$

This is the minimum value for $\sum \hat{\varepsilon}_{ij}^2$. The unbiased estimate of σ_ε^2 is given by

$$\hat{\sigma}_\varepsilon^2 = \frac{E_{yy}'}{k(n-1) - 1}.$$

The degrees of freedom for $\hat{\sigma}_\varepsilon^2$ are obtained as follows: E_{yy} is based upon $k(n-1)$ degrees of freedom; one loses an additional degree of freedom when β is replaced by the estimator b_E.

Complete and Various Reduced Models

Four models for the observations are summarized in Table 10.2. The complete analysis of covariance model, Model (d), includes both the treatment effects, τ_j, and regression of Y on X, β.

TABLE 10.2   Complete and reduced models in the ANOCOV

Model	
(a) $Y_{ij} = \mu + \varepsilon_{ij}$	(ignores both treatments and covariate)
(b) $Y_{ij} = \mu + \tau_j + \varepsilon_{ij}$	(ignores covariate)
(c) $Y_{ij} = \mu + \beta(X_{ij} - \bar{X}) + \varepsilon_{ij}$	(ignores treatments)
(d) $Y_{ij} = \mu + \beta(X_{ij} - \bar{X}) + \tau_j + \varepsilon_{ij}$	(complete model)

Model	Predictable variation	Error variation
(a)	$R(\mu) = \left(\sum Y\right)^2 \Big/ kn$	$S_{yy} = \sum Y^2 - \left(\sum Y\right)^2 \Big/ kn$
(b)	$R(\tau \mid \mu) = T_{yy}$	$E_{yy} = S_{yy} - T_{yy}$
(c)	$R(\beta \mid \mu) = b_s S_{xy}$	$S'_{yy} = S_{yy} - b_s S_{xy}$
	$\quad\quad = S_{xy}^2 / S_{xx}$	$\quad\quad = S_{yy} - (S_{xy}^2 / S_{xx})$
	where $b_S = S_{xy}/S_{xx}$	
(d)	$R(\beta, \tau \mid \mu) = S_{yy} - E'_{yy}$	$E'_{yy} = E_{yy} - b_E E_{xy}$
	$\quad\quad = T_{yy} + (E_{xy}^2 / E_{xx})$	$\quad\quad = E_{yy} - (E_{xy}^2 / E_{xx})$

$$R(\tau \mid \mu, \beta) = R(\beta, \tau \mid \mu) - R(\beta \mid \mu)$$
$$= T_{yy} + (E_{xy}^2 / E_{xx}) - (S_{xy}^2 / S_{xx})$$
$$= T_{yy} + b_E E_{xy} - b_S S_{xy}$$
$$= T_{yy_R}$$

Model (a) is of interest only in terms of specifying error variance when there are neither treatment effects nor regression of Y on X. Under this model, the least-squares estimator of μ is

$$\hat{\mu} = G_y/kn = \bar{Y}.$$

The variation due to $\hat{\mu}$ is given by

$$R(\mu) = \hat{\mu} G_y = kn\bar{Y}^2 = \left(\sum Y^2\right)\Big/kn.$$

The error variation associated with Model (a) is

$$S_{yy} = \sum_{} Y_{ij}^2 - \left(\sum Y_{ij}\right)^2 \Big/ kn = \sum Y_{ij}^2 - R(\mu),$$

which is the overall variation on the variate. That is, the total variation in the dependent variable is due to error when there are neither treatment effects nor regression of Y on X in the model.

Model (b) is the usual model for the analysis of variance. In this case the predictable variation is

$$R(\tau \mid \mu) = R(\tau, \mu) - R(\mu)$$
$$= T_{yy} + R(\mu) - R(\mu) = T_{yy}$$

and the error variation is

$$E_{yy} = S_{yy} - T_{yy},$$

where T_{yy} is the between-treatment variation of the analysis of variance. Hence, the error of Model (a) is reduced by the magnitude of the treatment variation T_{yy} when treatment effects are included in the model.

Model (c) is the model for the regression of Y on X disregarding all treatment effects. The predictable variation under this model is

$$R(\beta/\mu) = b_S S_{xy} = S_{xy}^2/S_{xx}$$

where

$$b_S = S_{xy}/S_{xx},$$

and b_s is called the overall regression coefficient. The variation due to error under model (c) is

$$S_{yy}' = S_{yy} - b_s S_{xy} = S_{yy} - (S_{xy}^2/S_{xx}).$$

Under Model (c), then, error is reduced to the extent that there is (linear) regression of Y on X when treatments are disregarded.

Model (d) is the complete model for the analysis of covariance. It has been shown that the predictable variation associated with this model is

$$R(\beta, \tau \mid \mu) = T_{yy} + \frac{E_{xy}^2}{E_{xx}} = T_{yy} + b_E E_{xy}.$$

Thus, the increase in predictability of Model (d) over Model (b) is a function only of the within-class regression b_E. Since $T_{yy} = S_{yy} - E_{yy}$, the predictable variation under Model (d) can also be written

$$R(\beta, \tau \mid \mu) = S_{yy} - \left[E_{yy} - \frac{E_{xy}^2}{E_{xx}} \right].$$

Hence the term in brackets represents variation due to error under Model (d). This variation due to error may be written as

$$E_{yy}' = S_{yy} - R(\beta, \tau \mid \mu) = S_{yy} - T_{yy} - b_E E_{xy}$$
$$= E_{yy} - b_E E_{xy}.$$

It is this difference in error between Model (b) and Model (d) which is of primary interest in the analysis of covariance since it is that difference which reflects the decrease in error (increase in predictability) associated with adding the regression of the dependent variable on the covariate to the analysis of variance treatment effects. That difference has been shown to be

$$E_{xy}^2/E_{xx} = b_E E_{xy}.$$

That part of the predictable variation associated with the analysis of covariance (Model d) which cannot be predicted from the regression of Y on X (Model c) is also of interest. This difference represents the contribution of the treatment effects above and beyond the linear regression of the variate on the covariate. This source of variation represents what is called the *reduced variation due to treatments* and is denoted by the symbol T_{yyR}. Thus,

$$T_{yyR} = R(\tau \mid \mu, \beta) = R(\beta, \tau \mid \mu) - R(\beta \mid \mu)$$

$$= S_{yy} - \left[E_{yy} - \frac{E_{xy}^2}{E_{xx}} \right] - \frac{S_{xy}^2}{S_{xx}}$$

$$= \left[S_{yy} - \frac{S_{xy}^2}{S_{xx}} \right] - \left[E_{yy} - \frac{E_{xy}^2}{E_{xx}} \right]$$

$$= S'_{yy} - E'_{yy}.$$

Since $T_{yy} = S_{yy} - E_{yy}$, this expression may also be written in the form

$$T_{yyR} = S_{yy} - E_{yy} + \frac{E_{xy}^2}{E_{xx}} - \frac{S_{xy}^2}{S_{xx}}$$

$$= T_{yy} + \frac{E_{xy}^2}{E_{xx}} - \frac{S_{xy}^2}{S_{xx}}$$

$$= T_{yy} + b_E E_{xy} - b_S S_{xy}.$$

Since T_{yyR} represents the unique contribution of the τ_j above and beyond β in the complete model, *it will be T_{yyR} which will be involved in testing the hypothesis that all τ_j are equal to zero in the analysis of covariance model.*

External (Between-Class) Regression

There are actually three regression coefficients which can be of interest to the experimenter: the internal or within-treatment regression coefficient, b_E; the total or overall regression coefficient, b_s, which would be obtained by ignoring the treatments (Model c); and b_T, the external or between-class regression coefficient.

To consider b_T, consider the pairs of means

$$(\bar{X}_1, \bar{Y}_1), (\bar{X}_2, \bar{Y}_2), \ldots, (\bar{X}_k, \bar{Y}_k).$$

From these pairs of means one may compute

$$T_{xx} = n \sum (\bar{X}_j - \bar{X})^2,$$

$$T_{xy} = n \sum (\bar{X}_j - \bar{X})(\bar{Y}_j - \bar{Y}),$$

$$T_{yy} = n \sum (\bar{Y}_j - \bar{Y})^2.$$

The regression of $\bar{Y}_j$ on $\bar{X}_j$ takes the form

$$\hat{\bar{Y}}_j - \bar{Y} = b_T(\bar{X}_j - \bar{X})$$

where

$$b_T = T_{xy}/T_{xx}.$$

This regression is called the between-class (or external) regression, and b_T is called the between-class (or external) regression coefficient. The regression function in question is simply the line of dependent-variable means ($\bar{Y}_j$) regressing on the covariate means ($\bar{X}_j$). The total variation of the dependent variable which is of interest, therefore, is T_{yy}, and that part of T_{yy} which can be predicted from the between-class regression is

$$b_T T_{xy} = b_T^2 T_{xx} = \frac{T_{xy}^2}{T_{xx}}.$$

The corresponding error variation is the deviation of the $\bar{Y}_j$ about the between-class regression line and is that part of T_{yy} which cannot be predicted from the between-class regression. The variation is

$$T'_{yy} = T_{yy} - b_T T_{xy} = T_{yy} - \frac{T_{xy}^2}{T_{xx}}.$$

In general, b_T, and thus, T'_{yy}, does not enter directly into the analysis of covariance. In cases where the T_j are not directly related to the covariate, the external regression need not have any meaning which is relevant to the analysis of covariance. Hence the external regression is often disregarded. However, it may be shown that

$$T_{yyR} = T'_{yy} + (b_E - b_T)^2 \frac{T_{xx} E_{xx}}{T_{xy} + E_{xy}}$$

where T_{yyR} is that variation which *is* directly involved in the analysis of covariance. Thus the reduced variation due to treatments may be partitioned into two parts. One part (T'_{yy}), having $k - 2$ degrees of freedom, measures the variation due to the residuals of the treatment means about the between-treatment regression line. The second part, having one degree of freedom, measures the variation due to the difference between b_T and b_E. If

$$b_T = b_E \quad \text{then} \quad T_{yyR} = T'_{yy};$$

if

$$b_T \neq b_E \quad \text{then} \quad T_{yyR} > T'_{yy}.$$

It is noted that if $b_T = b_E$, then it must be that $b_T = b_E = b_S$. This follows from the fact that

$$b_S = \frac{T_{xy} + E_{xy}}{T_{xx} + E_{xx}} = \frac{S_{xy}}{S_{xx}}.$$

Adjusted Treatment Means

Although it is somewhat counter to intuition, b_E, not b_T, is involved when one adjusts treatment means for the covariate. An unbiased estimate of β in Model

(d) which will not be influenced by the magnitude of the between-class covariation between the covariate and the variate is given by the within-class regression coefficient b_E. If one replaces β in that model by its least-squares estimator, the model for the analysis for covariance may be written

$$Y_{ij} = \mu + b_E(X_{ij} - \bar{X}) + \tau_j + \varepsilon_{ij}.$$

Moving the term $b_E(X_{ij} - \bar{X})$ to the left-hand side, this last equation becomes

$$Y'_{ij} = Y_{ij} - b_E(X_{ij} - \bar{X}) = \mu + \tau_j + \varepsilon_{ij}.$$

Y'_{ij} is a residual from the within-class regression of Y on X; the model for this residual is the usual model for the analysis of variance. Hence the analysis of covariance may be regarded as an analysis of variance on the residuals from the internal regression of Y on X. Y'_{ij} may be regarded as an *adjusted* observation on element i under treatment j—the adjustment is for the linear regression of Y on X. In this sense the effect of the covariate has been "partialed out" of the variate.

Within treatment j, the mean of the Y'_{ij} is

$$\bar{Y}'_j = \sum_i \frac{1}{n}[Y_{ij} - b_E(X_{ij} - \bar{X})] = \mu + \tau_j + \bar{\varepsilon}_j.$$

Hence

$$\bar{Y}'_j = \bar{Y}_j - b_E(X_j - \bar{X}) = \mu + \tau_j + \bar{\varepsilon}_j.$$

$\bar{Y}'_j$ is called the adjusted mean for treatment j. The adjustment "removes" or "partials out" from $\bar{Y}_j$ that part which may be considered a linear function of $\bar{X}_j$. Thus, if the model for a treatment mean is

$$\bar{Y}_j = \mu + \beta(\bar{X}_j - \bar{X}) + \tau_j + \bar{\varepsilon}_j,$$

then

$$\bar{Y}'_j = \bar{Y}_j - \beta(\bar{X}_j - \bar{X}) = \mu + \tau_j + \bar{\varepsilon}_j.$$

Replacing β by its estimator b_E,

$$\bar{Y}'_j = \bar{Y}_j - b_E(\bar{X}_j - \bar{X}) = \mu + \tau_j + \bar{\varepsilon}'_j,$$

where $\bar{\varepsilon}'_j$ includes a part which is a function of the sampling error of the estimator b_E. Since

$$\hat{\tau}_j = \bar{Y}_j - \bar{Y} - b_E(\bar{X}_j - \bar{X}),$$

one has

$$\bar{Y}'_j = \hat{\tau}_j + \bar{Y}.$$

The variation due to the adjusted treatment means for the variate is defined by

$$T_{yyA} = n \sum (\bar{Y}'_j - \bar{Y})^2.$$

There are $k - 2$ degrees of freedom associated with this source of variation. The $\bar{Y}'_j$ are not independent because b_E is used in all of the adjustments. Because of this, T_{yyA} is not involved in the overall test in the analysis of covariance. Rather, T_{yyR}, the reduced treatment variation, is used. The reduced treatment variation is related to the variation of the adjusted treatment means as follows:

$$T_{yyR} = T_{yyA} - (b_T - b_E)^2 \frac{T_{xx}^2}{T_{xx} + E_{xx}} .$$

Thus, if $\quad\quad\quad\quad b_T = b_E, \quad$ then $\quad T_{yyR} = T_{yyA};$

if $\quad\quad\quad\quad\quad b_T \neq b_E, \quad$ then $\quad T_{yyR} < T_{yyA}.$

In terms of Model (d) it may be shown that

$$b_T - b_E = \frac{\sum (\bar{X}_j - \bar{X})\tau_j}{\sum (\bar{X}_j - \bar{X})^2} + f(\varepsilon),$$

where $f(\varepsilon)$ is a term that is a function of ε. The expected value of this term is zero. If the covariate is uncorrelated with the τ_j, then

$$E\left[\sum (\bar{X}_j - \bar{X})\tau_j\right] = 0.$$

Hence $\quad\quad\quad\quad\quad\quad\quad E(b_T - b_E) = 0.$

Since $\bar{Y}'$, the adjusted mean, has the form

$$\bar{Y}'_j = \bar{Y} - b_E(\bar{X}_j - \bar{X}),$$

its interpretation is somewhat ambiguous. It looks as if the adjusted mean were obtained from the regression of $\bar{Y}$ on $\bar{X}$ with the regression coefficient b_T replaced by b_E. An alternative approach to obtaining $\bar{Y}'_j$ will help to clarify this apparent paradox. The internal regression for treatment j, replacing b_{E_j} by b_E, is

$$\hat{Y}_{ij} = \bar{Y}_j + b_E(X_{ij} - \bar{X}_j).$$

If one lets

$$X_{ij} = \bar{X},$$

then $\quad\quad\quad \hat{Y}_{\bar{X}} = \bar{Y}_j + b_E(\bar{X} - \bar{X}_j) = \bar{Y}_j - b_E(\bar{X}_j - \bar{X}).$

The expression on the extreme right is that for $\bar{Y}'_j$. Thus $\bar{Y}'_j$ may be interpreted as a regression estimate of Y_{ij} when $X_{ij} = \bar{X}, j = 1, 2, \ldots, k$. Since b_E is used in place of b_{E_j}, the assumption is that the within-treatment regressions are homogeneous, i.e.,

$$\beta_{E_1} = \beta_{E_2} = \cdots = \beta_{E_k} = \beta.$$

From general principles of regression analysis, the variance of the adjusted means is

$$\sigma_{\bar{Y}_j}^2 = \sigma_\varepsilon^2 \left[\frac{1}{n} + \frac{(\bar{X}_j - \bar{X})^2}{E_{xx}}\right],$$

and the covariance between $\bar{Y}'_j$ and $\bar{Y}'_{j'}$ is

$$\sigma_{\bar{Y}'_j, \bar{Y}'_{j'}} = \frac{\sigma_\varepsilon^2 (\bar{X}_j - \bar{X})(\bar{X}_{j'} - \bar{X})}{E_{xx}}.$$

If one takes the covariance between the $\bar{Y}'_j$ into account in computing the variation due to the adjusted means, the result is

$$T_{yyR} = \sum a_{jj'}(\bar{Y}'_j - \bar{Y})(\bar{Y}'_{j'} - \bar{Y})$$

where

$$a_{jj} = n\left[1 - \frac{n(\bar{X}_j - \bar{X})^2}{T_{xx} + E_{xx}}\right]$$

$$a_{jj'} = \frac{n^2(\bar{X}_j - \bar{X})(\bar{X}_{j'} - \bar{X})}{T_{xx} + E_{xx}} \quad (j \neq j').$$

T_{yyR} in this case represents a quadratic form in the adjusted treatment means. The $a_{jj'}$ turn out to be the elements of the inverse of the covariance matrix (deleting the factor σ_ε^2) of the $\bar{Y}'_j$.

The squared standard error of the difference between two adjusted treatment means is given by

$$\sigma_{\bar{Y}'_j - \bar{Y}'_{j'}}^2 = \sigma_{Y'_j}^2 + \sigma_{Y'_{j'}}^2 - 2\sigma_{\bar{Y}'_j, \bar{Y}'_{j'}}$$

$$= \sigma_\varepsilon^2 \left[\frac{2}{n} - \frac{(\bar{X}_j - \bar{X}_{j'})^2}{E_{xx}}\right].$$

To obtain the estimator of this squared standard error, σ_ε^2 is replaced by $\hat{\sigma}_\varepsilon^2$ which is

$$\hat{\sigma}_\varepsilon^2 = \frac{E_{yy} - b_E E_{xy}}{k(n-1) - 1}$$

$$= \frac{E'_{yy}}{k(n-1) - 1}$$

$$= MS'_{error},$$

the error estimate of the analysis of covariance.

Summary and Interrelation Between Sources of Variation

Three regression coefficients have been discussed. The internal regression coefficient is defined by

$$b_E = \frac{E_{xy}}{E_{xx}}.$$

If one restricted the internal regression to the information within treatment j

one would obtain

$$b_{E_j} = \frac{E_{xy_j}}{E_{xx_j}} :$$

b_E is related to the b_{E_j} as follows:

$$b_E = \frac{\sum E_{xy_j}}{\sum E_{xx_j}} .$$

Thus b_E is the ratio of the pooled numerators of the b_{E_j} to the pooled denominators.

A second regression coefficient is the external regression coefficient, the regression of the $\bar{Y}_j$ on the $\bar{X}_j$, given by

$$b_T = \frac{T_{xy}}{T_{xx}} .$$

It has been indicated that under some circumstances this coefficient may have no meaning in the analysis.

The third regression coefficient is the overall regression coefficient given by

$$b_S = \frac{S_{xy}}{S_{xx}} .$$

This regression coefficient is the one that is obtained if the set of *kn* observations is regarded as a single sample, i.e., if the treatments are ignored.

The relevant "total" variation and that part of this relevant variation which is predictable just from linear regression on the covariate is summarized for each of those regression coefficients as follows:

Regression	"Total" variation	Predictable variation	Error variation
Overall: $b_S = \dfrac{S_{xy}}{S_{xx}}$	S_{yy}	$b_S S_{xy}$	$S'_{yy} = S_{yy} - b_S S_{xy} = S_{yy} - \left(\dfrac{S_{xy}^2}{S_{xx}}\right)$
External: $b_T = \dfrac{T_{xy}}{T_{xx}}$	T_{yy}	$b_T T_{xy}$	$T'_{yy} = T_{yy} - b_T T_{xy} = T_{yy} - \left(\dfrac{T_{xy}^2}{T_{xx}}\right)$
Internal: $b_E = \dfrac{E_{xy}}{E_{xx}}$	E_{yy}	$b_E E_{xy}$	$E'_{yy} = E_{yy} - b_E E_{xy} = E_{yy} - \left(\dfrac{E_{xy}^2}{E_{xx}}\right)$

In general,

$$S'_{yy} \neq T'_{yy} + E'_{yy}.$$

That is, the variation of the residuals about the overall regression line is not the sum of the variation about the between-treatment (external) regression line and the variation about the pooled within-treatment (internal) regression line (unless $b_E = b_T$). Rather

$$S'_{yy} = E'_{yy} + T'_{yy} + (b_T - b_E)^2 \frac{T_{xx} E_{xx}}{T_{xx} + E_{xx}}$$

$$= E'_{yy} + T_{yyR}.$$

The total residual variation about the overall regression line is partitioned into three parts, one of which is a function of $(b_T - b_E)^2$ which depends upon covariation between the covariate and treatment effects in the data; the expected value of this covariation is assumed to be zero. Alternatively, S'_{yy} may be viewed as the sum of two parts, E'_{yy} and T_{yyR}. It is the sum

$$S'_{yy} = E'_{yy} + T_{yyR}$$

which is involved in the basic hypothesis test of the analysis of covariance.[1]

The variation due to prediction in the analysis of covariance model is

$$R(\beta, \tau \mid \mu) = T_{yy} + b_E E_{xy}.$$

In words, the predictable variation is that due to the treatments normally associated with an analysis of variance (T_{yy}) plus a component associated with the regression of Y on X ($b_E E_{xy}$). If one disregarded the treatments in the analysis of covariance model, the variation due to prediction would be

$$R(\beta \mid \mu) = b_S S_{xy}.$$

Hence that part of the variation in the analysis of covariance model due to treatments which is orthogonal to the variation due to the linear regression of X and Y is

$$R(\tau \mid \mu, \beta) = R(\beta, \tau \mid \mu) - R(\beta \mid \mu)$$

$$= T_{yy} + b_E E_{xy} - b_S S_{xy}.$$

One notes that this source of variation is not obtained from a single regression equation—rather it is obtained from the difference between the predictable variation associated with two different regression equations. One may obtain

---

[1] Alternative expressions for the reduced treatment variation:

$$T_{yyR} = T_{yy} + b_E E_{xy} - b_S S_{xy} = T_{yy} + \frac{E_{xy}^2}{E_{xx}} - \frac{S_{xy}^2}{S_{xx}}$$

$$= T'_{yy} + (b_T - b_E)^2 \frac{T_{xx} E_{xx}}{T_{xx} + E_{xx}}$$

$$= T_{yyA} - (b_T - b_E)^2 \frac{T_{xx}^2}{T_{xx} + E_{xx}}.$$

this last result in the following equivalent way:

$$\begin{bmatrix} \text{Error associated with model} \\ Y_{ij} = \mu + \beta(X_{ij} - \bar{X}) + \varepsilon_{ij} \end{bmatrix} - \begin{bmatrix} \text{Error associated with model} \\ Y_{ij} = \mu + \beta(X_{ij} - \bar{X}) + \tau_j + \varepsilon_{ij} \end{bmatrix}$$

$$= [S_{yy} - b_S S_{xy}] - [E_{yy} - b_E E_{xy}]$$

$$= T_{yy} - b_S S_{xy} + b_E E_{xy}.$$

Other relationships involving b_E and b_T are summarized in Table 10.3. From this table one notes that

$$T_{yyR} = T_{yyA} = T'_{yy} \quad \text{when} \quad b_E = b_T.$$

If the units are assigned at random to the treatments and if the treatment has

TABLE 10.3 Interrelationship between T_{yyR}, T_{yyA}, and T'_{yy}

$$T_{yyR} = T_{yy} - b_S S_{xy} + b_E E_{xy} = T_{yy} - (S_{xy}^2/S_{xx}) + (E_{xy}^2/E_{xx})$$

$$T_{yyA} = n \sum (\bar{Y}'_j - \bar{Y})^2 = n \sum \hat{\tau}_j^2$$

$$T'_{yy} = T_{yy} - b_T T_{xy} = T_{yy} - (T_{xy}^2/T_{xx})$$

$$T_{yyA} = n \sum \hat{\tau}_j^2$$

$$= n \sum [\bar{Y}_j - \bar{Y} - b_E(\bar{X}_j - \bar{X})]^2$$

$$= n \sum (\bar{Y}_j - \bar{Y})^2 + nb_E^2 \sum (\bar{X}_j - \bar{X})^2 - 2n \sum b_E(\bar{X}_j - \bar{X})(\bar{Y}_j - \bar{Y})$$

$$= T_{yy} + b_E^2 T_{xx} - 2b_E T_{xy}$$

$$= T_{yy} + b_E^2 T_{xx} - 2b_E(b_T T_{xx})$$

$$= T_{yy} - b_T^2 T_{xx} + b_T^2 T_{xx} + b_E^2 T_{xx} - 2b_E b_T T_{xx}$$

$$= T_{yy} - (T_{xy}^2/T_{xx}) + (b_T - b_E)^2 T_{xx}$$

$$= T'_{yy} + (b_T - b_E)^2 T_{xx}$$

$$= T_{yyR} + \frac{(b_T - b_E)^2 T_{xx}^2}{T_{xx} + E_{xx}} \quad \text{Note: If } T_{yyA} = 0, \text{ then } T_{yyR} = 0.$$

$$T_{yyR} = \sum \sum a_{jj'}(\bar{Y}'_j - \bar{Y})(\bar{Y}'_{j'} - \bar{Y}) \quad \text{where} \quad \begin{cases} a_{jj} = n\left[1 - \dfrac{n(\bar{X}_j - \bar{X})^2}{T_{xx} + E_{xx}}\right] \\ a_{jj'} = -\dfrac{(\bar{X}_j - \bar{X}_{j'})^2}{T_{xx} + E_{xx}} \end{cases}, \quad j \neq j'$$

$$= T_{yyA} - \frac{(b_T - b_E)^2 T_{xx}^2}{T_{xx} + E_{xx}} = Y_{yyA} - \frac{n^2 \sum (\bar{X}_j - \bar{X})(\bar{Y}'_j - Y)}{T_{xx} + E_{xx}}$$

$$= T'_{yy} + \frac{(b_T - b_E)^2 T_{xx} E_{xx}}{T_{xx} + E_{xx}}$$

$$T'_{yy} = T_{yyA} - (b_T - b_E)^2 T_{xx} = \frac{(b_T - b_E)^2 T_{xx} E_{xx}}{T_{xx} + E_{xx}} = b_T T_{xy} + b_E E_{xy} - b_S S_{xy}$$

$$= T_{yyR} - \frac{(b_T - b_E)^2 T_{xx} E_{xx}}{T_{xx} + E_{xx}}$$

no effect upon the covariate, it is reasonable to expect that

$$E(b_E) = E(b_T).$$

However, the standard errors of these two regression coefficients are quite different and in any applied problem these two estimators may be quite different from each other. (In general, b_E will have the smaller standard error.)

From this table one also notes that

$$T_{yyA} - T_{yyR} = \frac{(b_T - b_E)^2 T_{xx}^2}{T_{xx} + E_{xx}}.$$

The within-class correlation coefficient is defined by

$$r_{\text{w. class}} = \frac{E_{xy}}{\sqrt{E_{xx}} \sqrt{E_{yy}}}.$$

Similarly the between-class correlation coefficient is defined by

$$r_{\text{b. class}} = \frac{T_{xy}}{\sqrt{T_{xx}} \sqrt{T_{yy}}}.$$

Thus

$$b_E = \frac{E_{xy}}{E_{xx}} = r_{\text{w. class}} \frac{\sqrt{E_{yy}}}{\sqrt{E_{xx}}}.$$

Also

$$b_T = \frac{T_{xy}}{T_{xx}} = r_{\text{b. class}} \frac{\sqrt{T_{yy}}}{\sqrt{T_{xx}}}.$$

Hence

$$E'_{yy} = E_{yy} - b_E E_{xy} = E_{yy} - r_{\text{w. class}} \frac{E_{xy} \sqrt{E_{yy}}}{\sqrt{E_{xx}}}$$

$$= (E_{yy} - r^2_{\text{w. class}}) E_{yy}$$

$$= (1 - r^2_{\text{w. class}}) E_{yy}.$$

Also, by the same reasoning,

$$T'_{yy} = (1 - r^2_{\text{b. class}}) T_{yy}.$$

Test Procedures

Testing the hypothesis of no treatment effects in the analysis of covariance follows standard procedures for tests in multiple regression. The complete model in the analysis of covariance is

$$Y_{ij} = \mu + \beta(X_{ij} - \bar{X}) + \tau_j + \varepsilon_{ij}.$$

Under the hypothesis that all $\tau_j = 0$, the complete model reduces to the regression model,

$$Y_{ij} = \mu + \beta(X_{ij} - \bar{X}) + \varepsilon_{ij}.$$

The variation due to error under the reduced model is

$$Q_1 = S'_{yy} = S_{yy} - b_S S_{xy} = S_{yy} - \frac{S_{xy}^2}{S_{xx}}.$$

The degrees of freedom for Q_1 are

$$f_1 = kn - 2.$$

The variation due to error under the complete model is

$$Q_2 = E'_{yy} = E_{yy} - b_E E_{xy} = E_{yy} - \frac{E_{xy}^2}{E_{xx}}.$$

The degrees of freedom for Q_2 are

$$f_2 = k(n - 1) - 1.$$

The variation due to deviation from the hypothesis that all $\tau_j = 0$ is

$$\begin{aligned} Q_1 - Q_2 &= (S_{yy} - b_S S_{xy}) - (E_{yy} - b_E E_{xy}) \\ &= S_{yy} - E_{yy} - b_S S_{xy} + b_E E_{xy} \\ &= T_{yy} - b_S S_{xy} + b_E E_{xy} = T_{yyR}. \end{aligned}$$

The degrees of freedom for $Q_1 - Q_2$ are

$$\begin{aligned} f_1 - f_2 &= kn - 2 - [k(n - 1) - 1] \\ &= k - 1. \end{aligned}$$

The sampling distribution of the quadratic form Q_2 may be shown to be

$$\chi^2(f_2).$$

The sampling distribution of $Q_1 - Q_2$ is independently distributed of Q_2 as

$$\chi^2(f_1 - f_2) \text{ when all } \tau_j = 0;$$

$Q_1 - Q_2$ is distributed as the noncentral chi-square

$$\chi^2\left(f_1 - f_2; \lambda = \frac{n \sum \tau_j^2}{\sigma_\varepsilon^2}\right)$$

when the hypothesis that all $\tau_j = 0$ is not true. Hence when all $\tau_j = 0$,

$$\begin{aligned} F &= \frac{(Q_1 - Q_2)/(f_1 - f_2)}{Q_2/f_2} \\ &= \frac{T_{yyR}/(k - 1)}{(E_{yy} - b_E E_{xy})/[k(n - 1) - 1]} \\ &= \frac{T_{yyR}/(k - 1)}{E'_{yy}/[k(n - 1) - 1]} \end{aligned}$$

is distributed as, $F[k - 1, k(n - 1) - 1]$.

TABLE 10.4   **Comparison of analysis of variance and analysis of covariance**

	Analysis of variance			
Source of variation	**SS**	**df**	**MS**	**E(MS)**
(i) Treatments	T_{yy}	$k-1$	MS_{treat}	$\sigma_\varepsilon^2 + n\sigma_\tau^2$
Error	E_{yy}	$k(n-1)$	MS_{error}	σ_ε^2
Total	S_{yy}	$kn-1$		
	Analysis of covariance			
(ii) Treatments	T_{yyR}	$k-1$	$MS_{treat\,(R)}$	$\sigma_{\varepsilon\mid\beta}^2 + n\sigma_{\tau\mid\beta}^2$
Error	E'_{yy}	$k(n-1)-1$	MS'_{error}	$\sigma_{\varepsilon\mid\beta}^2$
Total	S'_{yy}	$kn-2$		

A comparison of the analysis of variance and the analysis of covariance is presented in Table 10.4. If one ignores the data on the covariate, one obtains the analysis of variance given in part i. Here the error variance, σ_ε^2, is estimated from the within-cell variation. In the analysis of covariance, the error of variance, $\sigma_{\varepsilon'}^2 = \sigma_{\varepsilon\mid\beta}^2$, is estimated from the within-cell variation less that part of the within-cell variation which is a function of the covariate.

In the analysis of variance, the variation due to treatments is considered to be all the between-class variation. However, in the analysis of covariance, the reduced treatment variation is used. To differentiate between the case in which the covariate is ignored and the case in which adjustment is made for the covariate, the notation σ_τ^2 and $\sigma_{\tau\mid\beta}^2$ is used. The structure of the F ratio is indicated by the expected value of the mean squares.

In terms of the regression lines in Fig. 10-2, the test procedure is equivalent to testing the hypothesis that the overall regression line with slope b_S fits the data as well as the within-class regression lines with slope b_E. The numerator of F is

$$\frac{\begin{bmatrix}\text{Variation due to residuals}\\ \text{about overall regression}\\ \text{lines}\end{bmatrix} - \begin{bmatrix}\text{Variation due to residuals about}\\ \text{regression lines with common slope}\\ b_E \text{ fitted through each of the}\\ \text{class means}\end{bmatrix}}{k-1}$$

Equivalently, this numerator has the form

$$\frac{Q_1 - Q_2}{(kn-1) - k(n-1)},$$

where Q_1 = variation due to error assuming H_0 is true (i.e., no difference due to treatments)

$= S_{yy} - (S_{xy}^2/S_{xx})$,

Q_2 = variation due to error with no restriction other than homogeneity of within-class regression

$= E_{yy} - (E_{xy}^2/E_{xx})$.

TESTING SUB-HYPOTHESES. *A priori* comparisons among adjusted means may be carried out using t or F statistics. For simple differences between two adjusted means, the (two-tailed) hypothesis takes the form

$$H_0: \sum c_j \tau_j = 0 = \tau_j - \tau_{j'} = 0.$$

The estimate of $\tau_j - \tau_{j'}$ is $\bar{Y}'_j - \bar{Y}'_{j'} = \bar{Y}_j - \bar{Y}_{j'} - b_E(\bar{X}_j - \bar{X}_{j'})$. The squared standard error of the difference between these adjusted means is

$$s_{\bar{Y}'_j - \bar{Y}'_{j'}}^2 = \text{MS}'_{\text{error}} \left[\frac{2}{n} + \frac{(\bar{X}_j - \bar{X}_{j'})^2}{E_{xx}} \right].$$

One may use either a t-test or an equivalent F-test in the decision rule. The t statistic is given by

$$t_{\text{obs}} = \frac{\bar{Y}'_j - \bar{Y}'_{j'}}{s_{\bar{Y}_j - \bar{Y}_{j'}}}.$$

The decision rule in this case is

Reject H_0 if $t_{\text{obs}} < t_{\alpha/2}[k(n-1)-1]$

or if $t_{\text{obs}} > t_{1-\alpha/2}[k(n-1)-1]$.

Equivalently one may use the statistic,

$$t_{\text{obs}}^2 = F_{\text{obs}} = \frac{(\bar{Y}'_j - \bar{Y}'_{j'})^2}{s_{\bar{Y}'_j - \bar{Y}'_{j'}}^2}.$$

The decision rule in this case is reject H_0 if

$$F_{\text{obs}} > F_{1-\alpha}[1, k(n-1)-1].$$

In general, hypotheses about *a priori* comparisons take the two-tailed form

$$H_0: \sum c_j \tau_j = 0 \qquad H_1: \sum c_j \tau_j \neq 0$$

where the c_j are known constants defining a comparison. In the general case one may use the test statistic

$$F_{\text{obs}} = \frac{(\sum c_j \bar{Y}'_j)^2}{\text{MS}'_{\text{error}} \left(\sum \dfrac{c_j^2}{n_j} + \dfrac{\sum [c_j(\bar{X}_j - \bar{X})]^2}{E_{xx}} \right)}.$$

The decision rule is:

$$\text{Reject } H_0 \text{ if } F_{\text{obs}} > F_{1-\alpha}[1, k(n-1)-1].$$

In making approximate Newman–Keuls tests on the differences between all possible pairs of ordered adjusted means, an approximation to the standard error of a single adjusted mean is

$$s_{\bar{Y}'} = \sqrt{\frac{\text{MS}'_{\text{error}}}{n}\left[1 + \frac{T_{xx}/(k-1)}{E_{xx}}\right]}.$$

This approximation averages over all pairs of covariate means. Consider an ordered difference between two adjusted means of the form

$$\bar{Y}'_j - \bar{Y}'_{j'}$$

where

$$j' - j + 1 = r,$$

and r is the number of ordered steps between the two adjusted means.

Under the Newman–Keuls procedure, the decision rules for the approximate tests are as follows:

Reject the hypothesis of no difference if

$$\bar{Y}'_j - \bar{Y}'_{j'} > s_{\bar{Y}'} q_{1-\alpha}[r, k(n-1)-1],$$

where $q_{0.99}[r, k(n-1)-1]$ is the 99 percentile point on the studentized range distribution, provided the proper sequential conditions on the Newman–Keuls tests are followed.

If one were to use the Scheffé procedure in testing differences between all pairs of adjusted means, one would compute statistics of the form

$$F_{\text{obs}} = \frac{(\bar{Y}'_j - \bar{Y}'_{j'})^2}{\text{MS}'_{\text{error}}\left[\dfrac{2}{n} + \dfrac{(\bar{X}_j - \bar{X}_{j'})^2}{E_{xx}}\right]}.$$

The decision rules would be as follows:

Reject the hypothesis of no difference if

$$F_{\text{obs}} > (k-1)F_{1-\alpha}[k-1, k(n-1)-1].$$

Summary of Assumptions and Test for Homogeneity of Internal Regression

From the various models given in Table 10.2, it follows that there is only a single regression coefficient. This implies that the within-class regression coefficients are homogeneous, that is,

$$\beta_{E_1} = \beta_{E_2} = \cdots = \beta_{E_k} = \beta_E.$$

Further, the implication is that

$$\beta_E = \beta_T = \beta_S.$$

Implicit also in the model is that the correct form of the relationship between the variate and the covariate is linear.

In addition to these assumptions about the regression part of the model are the usual assumptions about the analysis-of-variance part of the model: namely, that the ε_{ij} are distributed independently as $N(0, \sigma_\varepsilon^2)$ within each of the treatment classes.

Upon combining the regression model with the analysis-of-variance model to obtain the complete analysis-of-covariance model, an assumption with respect to additivity of treatment and regression effects is implied. Further, the error term in the complete model is assumed to be $N(0, \sigma_{\varepsilon'}^2)$ within each of the treatment classes, where

$$\hat{\varepsilon}_{ij}' = Y_{ij} - \hat{\mu} - \hat{\beta}(X_{ij} - \bar{X}) - \hat{\tau}_j$$
$$= Y_{ij} - \bar{Y} - b_E(X_{ij} - \bar{X}) - [\bar{Y}_j - \bar{Y} - b_E(\bar{X}_j - \bar{X})]$$
$$= (Y_{ij} - \bar{Y}_j) - b_E(X_{ij} - \bar{X}_j).$$

With regard to the homogeneity of the within-class regression coefficients, if assignment of units to treatments is random and the treatments do not affect the covariate, one expects that assumption to be met. If intact groups are assigned to the treatments, there may possibly be heterogeneity of internal regression. If this heterogeneity cannot be considered part of random error, the analysis of covariance model breaks down and the usual test procedures will no longer lead to appropriate conclusions. The test for homogeneity of internal regression takes the form

$$H_0: \beta_{E_1} = \beta_{E_2} = \cdots = \beta_{E_k} = \beta_E$$
$$H_1: \text{not } H_0$$

where

$$\beta_{E_j} = \frac{\sigma_{xy_j}}{\sigma_{xx_j}} \quad \text{and} \quad \beta_E = \frac{\Sigma \sigma_{xy_j}}{\Sigma \sigma_{xx_j}}.$$

A test of the assumption of homogeneity of within-class regressions is put in the perspective of the total analysis of covariance by the summary in Table 10.5 where the total residual variation about the overall regression line with slope b_S, S_{yy}', is partitioned into residual variation about the common within-class regression coefficient b_E, E_{yy}', and the reduced treatment variation T_{yyR}. Thus

$$S_{yy}' = E_{yy}' + T_{yyR}.$$

In the upper half of the table, E_{yy}' is partitioned as a basis for testing the hypothesis of homogeneity of within-class slopes.

$$E_{yy}' = S_1 + S_2,$$

TABLE 10.5 **Partition of residual variation about overall regression**

Source of variation	SS	df
Within-class residual	$E'_{yy} = E_{yy} - (E^2_{xy}/E_{xx}) = E_{yy} - b_E E_{xy}$	$k(n-1)-1$
Residual w. class variation using individual w. class regression	$S_1 = E_{yy} - \sum b_{E_j} E_{xy_j}$	$k(n-1)-k$
Difference between the b_{E_j} and b_E	$S_2 = [E_{yy} - b_E E_{xy}] - \left[E_{yy} - \sum b_{E_j} E_{xy_j}\right]$ $= \sum b_{E_j} E_{xy_j} - b_E E_{xy}$	$k-1$
Reduced treatment	$T_{yyR} = T_{yy} + b_E E_{xy} - b_S S_{xy}$	$k-1$
Residual b. class variation using b. class regression	$S_3 = T_{yy} - b_T T_{xy} = T'_{yy}$	$k-2$
Difference between b_T and b_E	$S_4 = [S_{yy} - b_S S_{xy}] - [S_{yy} - (b_T T_{xy} + b_E E_{xy})]$ $= b_T T_{xy} + b_E E_{xy} - b_S S_{xy}$	1
Total	$S'_{yy} = S_{yy} - b_S S_{xy}$	$kn-2$

where

$S_1 =$ variation due to residuals about w. class regression lines with slopes b_{E_j},

$$S_2 = \begin{bmatrix} \text{variation due to residuals} \\ \text{about w. class regression} \\ \text{lines with common slope } b_E \end{bmatrix} - S_1.$$

S_1 arises when one does not assume homogeneity of internal regressions and does not, therefore, pool regressions into a common slope b_E. From the data within each treatment one may compute

$$E_{xx_j} = \sum_i (X_{ij} - \bar{X}_j)^2,$$

$$E_{xy_j} = \sum_i (X_{ij} - \bar{X}_j)(Y_{ij} - \bar{Y}_j),$$

$$E_{yy_j} = \sum_i (Y_{ij} - \bar{Y}_j)^2.$$

Further, based upon the data from within treatment j one may compute

$$b_{E_j} = \frac{E_{xy_j}}{E_{xx_j}}.$$

The predictable variation from the linear regression based upon data from within only treatment j is

$$b_{E_j} E_{xy_j} = \frac{E^2_{xy_j}}{E_{xx_j}}.$$

The corresponding residual (error) variation is

$$E_{yy_j} - \frac{E^2_{xy_j}}{E_{xx_j}}.$$

S_1 is a measure of error variation which is based upon these k, separate, within-treatment regression coefficients. Hence,

$$S_1 = E_{yy} - \sum b_{E_j} E_{xy_j} = \sum (E_{yy_j} - E_{xy_j}/E_{xx_j}).$$

The degrees of freedom are $k(n - 1) - k$.

A measure of heterogeneity of the internal regressions (i.e., deviation from the hypothesis of homogeneity of slopes) is

$$S_2 = E'_{yy} - S_1$$

$$= (E_{yy} - b_E E_{xy}) - \left(E_{yy} - \sum b_{E_j} E_{xy_j} \right)$$

$$= \sum b_{E_j} E_{xy_j} - b_E E_{xy}.$$

This source of variation is based upon the degrees of freedom

$$[k(n - 1) - 1] - [k(n - 1) - k] = k - 1.$$

In summary, then, S_1 measures the variation due to residuals about the k individual within-treatment regression lines. E'_{yy} measures variation about the one common regression line; S_2 measures variation due to the difference between the k individual regression coefficients and the single within-treatment regression coefficient. Thus, S_2 provides a measure of deviation from the hypothesis of homogeneity of regressions.

To test the hypothesis of homogeneity of the within-class regression coefficients, one uses the F ratio:

$$F = \frac{(E'_{yy} - S_1)/(k - 1)}{S_1/[k(n - 1) - k]}$$

$$= \frac{S_2/(k - 1)}{S_1/[k(n - 1) - k]}.$$

Under the hypothesis of homogeneity of the within-class regressions, the sampling distribution of this statistic is given by the F distribution having $k - 1$ and $k(n - 1) - k$ degrees of freedom. When H_0 is true, numerator and denominator may be shown to be distributed as independent chi squares.

When H_0 is not true, the numerator is distributed as a noncentral chi square with a noncentrality parameter which is a function of the degree of heterogeneity of the internal regressions. Thus the F distribution $F[k-1, k(n-1)-1]$ is used in formulating the decision rule for this test.

If the units have been assigned at random to the treatments and the treatments have no effect upon the covariate, then making this test is not necessary. On the other hand, as part of the data analysis it may be of some interest to know the degree to which there is heterogeneity of the internal regressions.

COMPARING INTERNAL AND EXTERNAL REGRESSIONS. The lower half of Table 10.5 is relevant to evaluating the between-class regression coefficient b_T. Suppose that the primary purpose of the analysis of covariance is to reduce the error variance by using the covariate to reduce the within-treatment variance. Assume further that the covariate is not affected by the treatments. In this case the external regression need have no meaning in the data analysis. In this type of design, the units are generally assigned at random to the treatments. In this case the external regression is generally due to chance alone since the expectation of each $\bar{X}_j$ is μ_X for all treatments and, thus, $E(b_T) = 0$. It also follows that the adjusted means $\bar{Y}'_j$ will differ only slightly from the corresponding $\bar{Y}_j$.

On the other hand, suppose that intact groups are assigned to the treatments and that the $\bar{X}_j$ do differ by an amount that cannot be considered as being due to chance alone. Thus because of difference due to the covariate, the statistic

$$\bar{Y}_j - \bar{Y}_{j'}$$

is a biased estimator of

$$\tau_j - \tau_{j'}.$$

If this bias is a linear function of $\bar{X}_j - \bar{X}_{j'}$, it may be that this bias may be removed by using the estimator

$$\bar{Y}_j - \bar{Y}_{j'} - b_E(\bar{X}_j - \bar{X}_{j'}).$$

But if b_T and b_E differ markedly, there is some question about just what type of "bias" is being removed by this type of estimator. A question arises about whether the regression of $\bar{Y}$ on $\bar{X}$ may or may not be relevant to adjusting for bias in the estimator. Does the treatment have the same effect on $\bar{Y}$ when $\bar{X}_j$ varies from treatment to treatment? The answer to this question is relevant to the interpretation of the estimator of $\tau_j - \tau_{j'}$. There is no single answer to this question. Contingencies in data analysis which arise from circumstances which are not built into the design of an experiment usually do not have a unique or efficient answer—they may not have even a good approximate answer. Such is the case if the external regression is relevant and differs markedly from the internal regression. A good discussion of this point will be found in Smith, H. F. (*Biometrics*, 1957, pp. 295–302).

A procedure does exist for testing whether or not the internal regression and external regression are equal. This test should be restricted to the case where it can be assumed that the external regression has meaning in the analysis of the data. The hypothesis has the form

$$H_0: \beta_E = \beta_T \qquad H_1: \beta_E \neq \beta_T.$$

In the lower half of Table 10.5, one has the following partition of the reduced treatment variation:

$$T_{yyR} = S_3 + S_4,$$

where $S_3 = T'_{yy} = $ variation of residuals about b. class regression line,

$S_4 = $ variation related to difference between b_T and b_E

$$= (b_T - b_E)^2 \frac{T_{xx} + E_{xx}}{T_{xx} E_{xx}}.$$

One notes that

$$(b_T - b_E)^2 \frac{T_{xx} E_{xx}}{T_{xx} + E_{xx}} = \frac{1}{S_{xx}} \left[\frac{E_{xx} T_{xy}^2}{T_{xx}} + \frac{T_{xx} E_{xy}^2}{E_{xx}} - 2 T_{xy} E_{xy} \right].$$

The term on the right may be written

$$\frac{1}{S_{xx}} \left[\frac{E_{xx} T_{xy}^2 + T_{xx} T_{xy}^2}{T_{xx}} + \frac{T_{xx} E_{xy}^2 + E_{xx} E_{xy}^2}{E_{xx}} - T_{xy}^2 - E_{xy}^2 - 2 T_{xy} E_{xy} \right]$$

$$= \frac{T_{xy}^2}{T_{xx}} + \frac{E_{xy}^2}{E_{xx}} - \frac{(T_{xy} + E_{xy})^2}{S_{xx}} = S_4.$$

Under the hypothesis that the between class regression is linear, E'_{yy} and S_3 would both be estimates of variation due to experimental error. Hence the statistic

$$F_3 = \frac{S_3/(k-2)}{E'_{yy}/[k(n-1)-1]}$$

is distributed as the F distribution with degrees of freedom $k - 2$ and $k(n - 1) - 1$, when the hypothesis of linearity of regression is true (assuming homogeneity of the within-class regression).

Unless k, the number of treatments, is relatively large, the estimate of b_T, which is based upon the k pairs $(\bar{X}_j, \bar{Y}_j)$, will be relatively unstable. A test for the equality of β_T and β_E is somewhat more complex than the tests which have just been described. The term $[S_{yy} - (b_T T_{xy} + b_E E_{xy})]$ in S_4 is not the variation due to residuals about any single regression line. Hence the appropriate F ratio does not have a simple form.

An estimate of $(\beta_T - \beta_E)^2$ is given by

$$(b_T - b_E)^2 = S_4 \frac{T_{xx} + E_{xx}}{T_{xx} E_{xx}}.$$

An estimate of the square of the standard error of $b_T - b_E$ is given by

$$s^2_{b_T - b_E} = s^2_{b_T} + s^2_{b_E}$$

$$= \frac{v_T}{T_{xx}} + \frac{v_E}{E_{xx}} = \frac{v_T E_{xx} + v_E T_{xx}}{T_{xx} E_{xx}},$$

where
$$v_T = \frac{T'_{yy}}{k-2}, \qquad v_E = \frac{E'_{yy}}{k(n-1)-1}.$$

Hence, to test the hypothesis that $\beta_T = \beta_E$, one may use the F' statistic

$$F' = \frac{S_4(T_{xx} + E_{xx})/T_{xx} E_{xx}}{s^2_{b_T - b_E}} = \frac{S_4(T_{xx} + E_{xx})}{v_T E_{xx} + v_E T_{xx}}.$$

The sampling distribution of this F' statistic may be approximated by an F distribution having one degree of freedom for the numerator, and the degrees of freedom for the denominator, as given by the Satterthwaite approximation, are

$$\text{df}_{\text{denom}} = \frac{(v_T E_{xx} + v_E T_{xx})^2}{[(v_T E_{xx})^2/(k-2)] + \{(v_E T_{xx})^2/[k(n-1)-1]\}}.$$

Bivariate Normal Model

The analysis of covariance need not be restricted to the case in which X is a fixed variable. Suppose that the pairs of potential observations under treatment j are denoted

$$(X_{ij}, Y_{ij}).$$

Suppose that these potential observations define treatment population j. Assume that the joint distribution of X and Y within treatment population j is bivariate normal with parameters

$$\mu_{x_j}, \mu_{y_j}, \sigma^2_x, \sigma^2_y, \sigma_{xy} \quad (j = 1, 2, \ldots, k).$$

Note that σ^2_x, σ^2_y, and σ_{xy} do not depend upon j. The regression of Y on X within treatment population j is

$$Y = \alpha_j + \beta X$$

where
$$\beta = \frac{\sigma_{xy}}{\sigma^2_x} \qquad \text{and} \qquad \alpha_j = \mu_{y_j} - \beta \mu_x.$$

Since all of the potential populations have the same regression coefficient, β, the regression lines will be parallel.

These regression lines would be identical if

$$\alpha_j = \alpha_{j'} \qquad \text{for} \qquad j \neq j'.$$

From the definitions of α_j and $\alpha_{j'}$, if $\alpha_j = \alpha_{j'}$ then

$$\mu_{y_j} - \beta\mu_{x_j} = \mu_{y_{j'}} - \beta\mu_{x_{j'}}.$$

From the definitions of τ_j and $\tau_{j'}$ in the analysis of covariance model,

$$\tau_j = \mu_{y_j} - \mu_y - \beta(\mu_{x_j} - \mu_x),$$
$$\tau_{j'} = \mu_{y_{j'}} - \mu_y - \beta(\mu_{x_{j'}} - \mu_x).$$

Hence
$$\tau_j - \tau_{j'} = \mu_{y_j} - \mu_{y_{j'}} - \beta(\mu_{x_j} - \mu_{x_{j'}}).$$

One notes that

$$\alpha_j - \alpha_{j'} = (\mu_{y_j} - \mu_{y_{j'}}) - \beta(\mu_{x_j} - \mu_{x_{j'}}).$$

Hence
$$\alpha_j - \alpha_{j'} = \tau_j - \tau_{j'} \qquad \text{for all} \qquad j \neq j'.$$

Thus, testing the hypothesis that all $\tau_j = 0$ in the analysis of covariance model is equivalent to testing the hypothesis that all of the within-treatment class regression lines are identical. Since the regression lines were assumed to be parallel to begin with, one is really testing the hypothesis that the regression constants (the α_j's) are all equal. This point is illustrated geometrically in the next section.

Nothing has been said in this development about whether or not the covariate is influenced by the treatments. As long as the model holds, statistically rigorous tests can be made. However, if the treatments do influence the magnitude of the covariate, the hypothesis that is tested may have little or no meaning in terms of an empirical experiment. That is, it may not be possible, experimentally, to vary Y when X is held constant.

Geometric Representation

In Fig. 10-2, the data points for an experiment having $k = 3$ treatments and $n = 7$ observations under each treatment are shown.

The within-treatment regression lines

$$Y_{ij} = \bar{Y}_j + b_{E_j}(X_{ij} - \bar{X}_j) \quad (j = 1, 2, 3)$$

where
$$b_{E_j} = \frac{E_{xy_j}}{E_{xx_j}}$$

are shown. For treatment class j, the point $(\bar{X}_j, \bar{Y}_j)$ is on the regression line. Inspection of these lines indicates that they are not parallel. The regression line for treatment 2 has a somewhat steeper slope than do the other two regression lines.

The overall regression line, obtained by disregarding the treatment classes, is also shown. It is noted that the overall regression line does not provide a good fit to the data points since the $\bar{Y}_j$ tend to fall relatively far from this line.

In Fig. 10-3, the lines with common slope b_E are drawn through the points $(\bar{X}_j, \bar{Y}_j)$. These lines may be considered to define the within-class

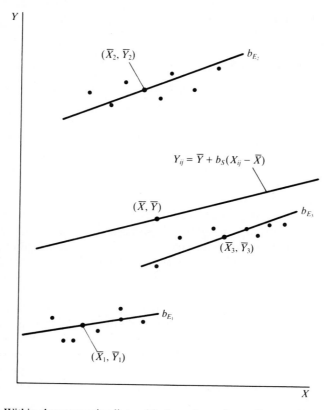

FIGURE 10-2   Within-class regression lines with slopes b_{E_j} and overall regression line with slope b_s.

regression under the assumption of homogeneous regression. The between-class line is also shown in this figure. Since this line is drawn parallel to the within-class regression lines, implicit is the assumption that $b_T = b_E$. (If this equality holds then $b_E = b_S$.)

The adjusted treatment means are shown in Fig. 10-4. The adjusted means are obtained from the intersection of the within-class regression lines with common slope b_E and the line $X = \bar{X}$.

In Fig. 10-4 lines with common slope

$$b_E = \frac{E_{xy}}{E_{xx}}$$

are drawn through the treatment means $(\bar{X}_j, \bar{Y}_j)$. Since the three lines in Fig. 10-4 have the same slope, they are parallel. The equation of the line passing through the point $(\bar{X}_j, \bar{Y}_j)$ is

$$\hat{Y}_{ij} = \bar{Y}_j + b_E(X_{ij} - \bar{X}_j).$$

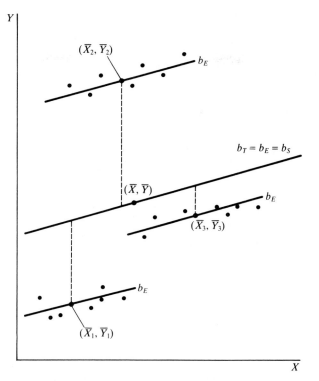

FIGURE 10-3 Within-class regression lines each with slope b_E and between-class regression line with slope $b_T = b_E$.

If one lets

$$X_{ij} = \bar{X},$$

then

$$\hat{Y}_{ij} = \bar{Y}_j + b_E(\bar{X} - \bar{X}_j) = \bar{Y}_j - b_E(\bar{X}_j - \bar{X}).$$

But the expression on the right defines $\bar{Y}'_j$, the adjusted mean for treatment j. Thus the latter may be interpreted as a regression estimate of Y_{ij} when $X_{ij} = \bar{X}$.

Geometrically the $\bar{Y}'_j$ are the values of $\hat{Y}_{ij}$ corresponding to the points at which the vertical line

$$X = \bar{X}$$

intersects the three parallel lines. If the three parallel lines in Fig. 10-2 were actually identical then all $\bar{Y}'_j$ would be equal. Since the analysis of covariance

$$\hat{\tau}_j = \bar{Y}_j - \bar{Y} - b_E(\bar{X}_j - \bar{X})$$
$$= \bar{Y}'_j - \bar{Y},$$

if all $\bar{Y}'_j$ are equal, then all $\hat{\tau}_j$ will be equal. Further if all $\hat{\tau}_j$ are equal, then T_{yyR} will be zero.

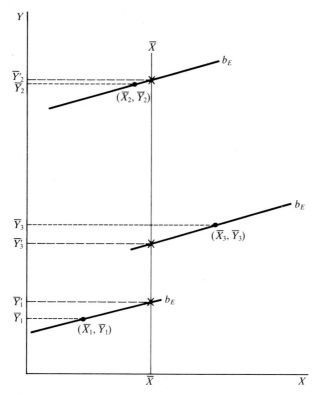

FIGURE 10-4   Adjusted treatment means, $\hat{Y}_j = \bar{Y}_j - b_E(\bar{X}_j - \bar{X})$.

Numerical Example of Single-Factor Experiment

Computational symbols that will be used in the numerical example are summarized in Table 10.6. The symbols in parts i and ii are required only if tests on the assumptions underlying the analysis of covariance are made. Symbols required for the overall analysis of covariance are summarized in parts iii and iv.

A small numerical example of the analysis of covariance is presented in Table 10.7. In this example, random samples of $n = 7$ elements were assigned to the $k = 3$ treatments. The treatments represent different methods of teaching a course; the dependent variable Y is a measure of achievement after completion of the course and the covariate X is an aptitude measure obtained prior to administering the treatments. Clearly, if X is measured prior to the treatments it cannot be affected by the treatments. Further, since the samples are randomly selected, any differences due to the covariate means are random differences.

The basic observations are given in part (i) of the table. In this same part

TABLE 10.6   **Computational formulas for analysis of covariance**

(i)
$$(2x_j) = \sum_i X_{ij}^2 \qquad (2xy_j) = \sum_i X_{ij}Y_{ij} \qquad (2y_j) = \sum_i Y_{ij}^2$$
$$(3x_j) = T_{x_j}^2/n \qquad (3xy_j) = T_{x_j}T_{y_j}/n \qquad (3y_j) = T_{y_j}^2/n$$

(ii)
$$E_{xx_1} = (2x_1) - (3x_1) \qquad E_{xy_1} = (2xy_1) - (3xy_1) \qquad E_{yy_1} = (2y_1) - (3y_1)$$
$$\cdots \qquad\qquad \cdots \qquad\qquad \cdots$$
$$E_{xx_k} = (2x_k) - (3x_k) \qquad E_{xy_k} = (2xy_k) - (3xy_k) \qquad E_{yy_k} = (2y_k) - (3y_k)$$

(iii)
$$(1x) = G_x^2/kn \qquad (1xy) = G_xG_y/kn \qquad (1y) = G_y^2/kn$$
$$(2x) = \sum (2x_j) \qquad (2xy) = \sum (2xy_j) \qquad (2y) = \sum (2y_j)$$
$$= \sum X^2 \qquad\qquad = \sum XY \qquad\qquad = \sum Y^2$$
$$(3x) = \sum (3x_j) \qquad (3xy) = \sum (3xy_j) \qquad (3y) = \sum (3y_j)$$
$$= \left(\sum T_{x_j}^2\right)\Big/n \qquad = \left(\sum T_{x_j}T_{y_j}\right)\Big/n \qquad = \left(\sum T_{y_j}^2\right)\!n$$

(iv)
$$S_{xx} = (2x) - (1x) \qquad S_{xy} = (2xy) - (1xy) \qquad S_{yy} = (2y) - (1y)$$
$$E_{xx} = (2x) - (3x) \qquad E_{xy} = (2xy) - (3xy) \qquad E_{yy} = (2y) - (3y)$$
$$T_{xx} = (3x) - (1x) \qquad T_{xy} = (3xy) - (1xy) \qquad T_{yy} = (3y) - (1y)$$

(v)
$$S_{yy}' = S_{yy} - (S_{xy}^2/S_{xx})$$
$$E_{yy}' = E_{yy} - (E_{xy}^2/E_{xx})$$
$$T_{yyR} = S_{yy}' - E_{yy}'$$

of the table, the entries under treatment 1 are as follows:

$$\sum_i X_{i1} = 66 \qquad \sum_i Y_{i1} = 100$$
$$\sum_i X_{i1}^2 = 736 \qquad \sum_i Y_{i1}^2 = 1528$$
$$\sum_i X_{i1}Y_{i1} = 1046.$$

In words, these entries are the sum, the sum of the squares, and the sum of the products of the pairs of observations under treatment 1. The totals to the right of part i are as follows:

$$G_x = \sum_j \left(\sum_i X_{ij}\right) = 179 \qquad G_y = \sum_j \left(\sum_i Y_{ij}\right) = 322$$
$$\sum_j \left(\sum_i X_{ij}^2\right) = 1911 \qquad\qquad \sum_j \left(\sum_i Y_{ij}^2\right) = 5468$$
$$\sum_j \left(\sum_i X_{ij}Y_{ij}\right) = 3096.$$

TABLE 10.7   **Numerical example of analysis of covariance**

	Treatment 1		Treatment 2		Treatment 3			
	X	Y	X	Y	X	Y		
(i)	3	8	13	18	14	26	$k = 3$	
	7	12	17	22	10	22	$n = 7$	
	10	16	10	16	8	20		
	8	14	9	14	4	16		
	15	20	4	8	2	14		
	8	12	6	10	8	18		
	15	18	2	6	6	12		Totals

	$\sum(\ )$:	66	100	61	94	52	128	$G_x = 179$	$G_y = 322$
	$\sum(\ )^2$:	736	1528	695	1460	480	2480	$\sum X^2 = 1911$	$\sum Y^2 = 5468$
	$\sum XY$:	1046		998		1052		$\sum XY = 3096$	

(ii)

$$(1x) = 1525.76 \qquad (1xy) = 2744.67 \qquad (1y) = 4937.33$$
$$(2x) = 1911 \qquad (2xy) = 3096 \qquad (2y) = 5468$$
$$(3x) = 1540.14 \qquad (3xy) = 2712.86 \qquad (3y) = 5031.43$$

(iii)

$$T_{xx} = (3x) - (1x) = 14.38 \qquad T_{xy} = (3xy) - (1xy) = -31.81 \qquad T_{yy} = (3y) - (1y) = 94.10$$
$$E_{xx} = (2x) - (3x) = 370.86 \qquad E_{xy} = (2xy) - (3xy) = 383.14 \qquad E_{yy} = (2y) - (3y) = 436.57$$
$$S_{xx} = (2x) - (1x) = 385.24 \qquad S_{xy} = (2xy) - (1xy) = 351.33 \qquad S_{yy} = (2y) - (1y) = 530.67$$

(iv)

$$T_{yyR} = T_{yy} + \frac{E_{xy}^2}{E_{xx}} - \frac{S_{xy}^2}{S_{xx}} = S'_{yy} - E'_{yy}$$
$$= 94.10 + 395.83 - 320.40 = 169.53$$

$$E'_{yy} = E_{yy} - \frac{E_{xy}^2}{E_{xx}} = 436.57 - 395.83 = 40.74$$

$$S'_{yy} = S_{yy} - \frac{S_{xy}^2}{S_{xx}} = 530.67 - 320.40 = 210.27$$

These entries are the sums of the corresponding entries under the treatment headings.

The entries in part ii are the computational symbols used in the overall analyses. These symbols are defined in Table 10.6, part iii. Thus, for example,

$$(1x) = G_{x/kn}^2 = (179)^2/(3)(7) = 1525.76$$

$$(2x) = \sum (2x_j) = \sum_j \left(\sum_i X_{ij}^2 \right) = 1911$$

$$(3x) = \sum (3x_j) = \left(\sum T_{x_j}^2 \right) n = 1540.14.$$

From these computational symbols, the basic ingredients for the analyses are computed in part iii (and defined in part iv) of Table 10.6. These values provide all of the numbers needed to carry out an analysis of variance of the dependent variable Y, an analysis of variance of the covariate X or an analysis of covariance. Thus, for example

$$T_{xy} = (3xy) - (1xy) = -31.81$$
$$E_{xy} = (2xy) - (1xy) = 383.14$$
$$S_{xy} = (2xy) - (1xy) = 351.33.$$

Note that covariations, symbols having subscripts xy, may be either positive or negative, while symbols with subscripts xx or yy are variations and can only be positive. In all cases,

$$T + E = S.$$

Terms which enter directly into the analysis of covariance are computed in part iv, all entries being obtained from part iii. T_{yyR}, E'_{yy}, and S'_{yy} will all be positive and, further,

$$S'_{yy} = T_{yyR} + E'_{yy},$$

where S'_{yy} is the "total" variation in the analysis of covariance. It is the variation due to the residuals from the regression equation

$$Y_{ij} = \bar{Y} - b_S(X_{ij} - \bar{X}),$$

where
$$b_S = S_{xy}/S_{xx}.$$

It is reasonable to carry out an analysis of variance of the dependent variable Y, disregarding the covariate X. That analysis is summarized in Table 10.8. The overall F ratio ($F = 1.94$) indicates no statistical differences among the treatments. In this analysis all of the variation within the treatments is considered as being due to error. One notes that the correlation ratio in this analysis is

$$\frac{T_{yy}}{S_{yy}} = \frac{94.10}{436.57} = 0.21,$$

TABLE 10.8 **Analysis of variance for example in Table 10.7**

Source	SS	df	MS	F
Treatments	$T_{yy} = 94.10$	2	47.05	1.94
Error	$E_{yy} = 436.47$	18	24.25	
Total	$S_{yy} = 530.67$	20		

$$**F_{0.99}(2, 18) = 6.01$$

which indicates that 21 percent of the total variation in Y is due to differences between treatments, whereas 79 percent is due to within-treatment variation or error. The purpose of the analysis of covariance in this case is to remove or partial out of the error variation that part of Y which is a linear function of X. If the analysis of covariance is successful, the 79 percent due to error will be reduced.

Prior to carrying out an analysis of covariance, it may be instructive to evaluate the assumption of homogeneity of within-treatment regression coefficients. Parts i and ii of Table 10.6 define the values needed to compute the within-treatment regression coefficients and Table 10.9 provides the data for the numerical example.

The within-treatment regression coefficients are defined by

$$b_{E_j} = \frac{E_{xy_j}}{E_{xx_j}} \quad (j = 1, 2, 3).$$

Thus, for example

$$E_{xx_1} = \sum X_1^2 - \frac{(\sum X_1)^2}{n} = 736 - \frac{(66)^2}{7} = 113.71,$$

$$E_{xy_1} = \sum X_1 Y_1 - \frac{(\sum X_1)(\sum Y_1)}{n} = 1046 - \frac{(66)(100)}{7} = 103.14,$$

$$E_{yy_1} = \sum Y_1^2 - \frac{(\sum Y_1)^2}{n} = 1528 - \frac{(100)^2}{7} = 99.43,$$

and the within-treatment regression coefficient for treatment 1 is

$$b_{E_1} = \frac{E_{xy_1}}{E_{xx_1}} = \frac{103.14}{113.71} = 0.907.$$

To test for homogeneity of regressions, one needs

$$\sum \frac{E_{xy_j}^2}{E_{xx_j}} = 398.47.$$

The variation of the individual observations about the unpooled within-class

TABLE 10.9 Within-treatment regression coefficients

	Treatment 1	Treatment 2	Treatment 3	Total
E_{xx_j}	113.71	163.42	93.71	$370.86 = E_{xx}$
E_{xy_j}	103.14	178.86	101.14	$383.14 = E_{xy}$
E_{yy_j}	99.43	197.71	139.43	$436.57 = E_{yy}$
b_{E_j}	0.907	1.054	1.075	$b_E = 1.033$
$E_{xy_j}^2/E_{xx_j}$	93.55	195.76	139.43	$\sum (E_{xy_j}^2/E_{xx_j}) = 398.47$

regression lines is

$$S_1 = E_{yy} - \sum \frac{E^2_{xy_j}}{E_{xx_j}} = 436.57 - 398.47 = 38.10.$$

The variation of the individual within-class regression coefficients about the pooled within-class regression coefficient is

$$S_2 = \sum \frac{E^2_{xy_j}}{E_{xx_j}} - \frac{E^2_{xy}}{E_{xx}} = 398.47 - \frac{(383.14)^2}{370.84}$$

$$= 398.47 - 395.85 = 2.62.$$

The statistic used in the test of homogeneity of within-class regression is

$$F = \frac{[\sum (E^2_{xy_j}/E_{xx_j}) - E^2_{xy}/E_{xx}]/(k-1)}{[E_{yy} - \sum (E^2_{xy_j}/E_{xx_j})]/[k(n-1)-k]}$$

$$= \frac{(398.47 - 395.85)/2}{(436.57 - 398.47)/15} = 0.52.$$

This may also be written as

$$F = \frac{S_2/(k-1)}{S_1/k(n-2)} = \frac{(2.62)/2}{(38.10)/15} = 0.52.$$

The numerator of this F ratio is a measure of deviation from the hypothesis of homogeneity of within-treatment regression; the denominator is the mean square due to residuals about the individual within-treatment regression lines. For this example, the F ratio indicates that there are no statistically significant deviations from homogeneity. The critical value for this test is

$$F_{1-\alpha}[k-1, k(n-1)-k].$$

An analysis of covariance based upon the values in Table 10.7 is summarized in Table 10.10. The overall F ratio ($F = 35.32$) indicates that there are highly significant differences due to the treatments if the variate is adjusted for the covariate. This is in contrast to the analysis of variance wherein there were no differences in achievement (Y) due to the different teaching methods when aptitude was not taken into account. What accounts for this difference?

TABLE 10.10 **Analysis of covariance for example in Table 10.7**

Source	SS	df	MS	F
Treatments	$T_{yyR} = 169.53$	2	84.77	35.22**
Error	$E'_{yy} = 40.74$	17	2.40	
Total	$S'_{yy} = 210.27$	19		

$**F_{0.99}(2, 17) = 6.11$

The difference between the outcome of the analysis of variance and the analysis of covariance can be simply expressed in terms of the correlation ratio. For the analysis of variance, only 21 percent of the Y variation was due to the treatments, while 79 percent was error. In the analysis of covariance,

$$\frac{T_{yyR}}{S'_{yy}} = \frac{169.53}{210.27} = 0.81,$$

meaning that only 19 percent of the variation of Y is due to error and 81 percent is associated with treatments when the linear dependence of Y on X is partialed out.

The difference in magnitudes of the two F ratios is in part due to the reduction in the denominators, i.e., the estimates of σ_ε^2. In the analysis of variance

$$\hat{\sigma}_\varepsilon^2 = MS_{error} = 24.25;$$

In the analysis of covariance,

$$\hat{\sigma}_\varepsilon^2 = MS'_{error} = 2.40.$$

The difference in these two estimates is a function of the size of the squared overall within-treatment correlation. One may examine the magnitude of the individual within-class correlations. The squares of those correlations (from Table 10.9) are:

$$r_{E_1}^2 = \frac{E_{xy_1}^2}{E_{xx_1}E_{yy_1}} = \frac{103.14^2}{(113.71)(99.43)} = 0.94$$

$$r_{E_2}^2 = \frac{E_{xy_2}^2}{E_{xx_2}E_{yy_2}} = \frac{178.86^2}{(163.42)(197.71)} = 0.99$$

$$r_{E_3}^2 = \frac{E_{xy_3}^2}{E_{xx_3}E_{yy_3}} = \frac{101.14^2}{(93.71)(139.43)} = 0.78.$$

The squared pooled within-treatment correlation is

$$r_E^2 = \frac{E_{xy}^2}{E_{xx}E_{yy}} = \frac{383.14^2}{(370.84)(436.57)} = 0.9067$$

and

$$MS'_{error} = MS_{error}(1 - r_E^2)\left[\frac{k(n-1)}{k(n-1)-1}\right]$$

$$= (24.25)(0.0933)\left(\frac{18}{17}\right) = 2.40.$$

Thus, the larger r_E^2, the smaller MS'_{error} relative to MS_{error}.

Another reason that the F ratio may change in the analysis of covariance relative to the analysis of variance depends upon the relative magnitude of the numerators. In this example, in the analysis of variance

$$MS_{treat} = 47.05$$

whereas in the analysis of covariance

$$MS'_{treat} = 84.77.$$

The reduced sums of squares for treatments, T_{yyR}, depends in part upon r_E^2 and in part upon the magnitude of the squared between-class correlation (from Table 10.7)

$$r_T^2 = \frac{T_{xy}^2}{T_{xx}T_{yy}} = \frac{(-31.81)^2}{(14.38)(94.10)} = 0.75.$$

When r_T is large relative to r_E, the reduction in the treatment variation can be relatively larger than the reduction in the error variation. When this occurs, the F ratio in the analysis of covariance will actually be smaller than the corresponding F ratio in the analysis of variance. The latter finding would generally indicate that bias due to the covariate had inflated the F ratio in the original analysis of variance.

When r_T is negative and r_E is positive, T_{yyA} will always be larger than T_{yy}. The reduced sum of squares, T_{yyR}, may in this case also be larger than T_{yy}. When this happens, the F ratio in the original analysis of variance is deflated because of the bias due to the covariate.

One can also look at the relative magnitude of the analysis of variance and analysis of covariance treatment effects in terms of the relation,

$$MS'_{treat} = \frac{1}{k-1}\left(E_{yy} + \frac{E_{xy}^2}{E_{xx}} - \frac{S_{xy}^2}{S_{xx}}\right)$$

$$= MS_{treat} + \frac{1}{k-1}\left(\frac{E_{xy}^2}{E_{xx}} - \frac{S_{xy}^2}{S_{xx}}\right).$$

MS'_{treat} will be larger than MS_{treat} whenever

$$\frac{E_{xy}^2}{E_{xx}} > \frac{S_{xy}^2}{S_{xx}} \qquad \text{or} \qquad b_E E_{xy} > b_S S_{xy}.$$

For the numerical example under consideration

$$\frac{E_{xy}^2}{E_{xx}} = 395.88 \qquad \text{whereas} \qquad \frac{S_{xy}^2}{S_{xx}} = 320.40.$$

Hence $MS'_{treat} > MS_{treat}$.

In general

$$T_{yyR} > T_{yy}$$

when T_{xy} is negative and E_{xy} is positive. In this case

$$T_{xy} = -31.81 \qquad \text{and} \qquad E_{xy} = 383.14.$$

TABLE 10.11   **Analysis of variance on covariate in Table 10.7**

Source	SS	df	MS	F
Treatments	$T_{xx} = 14.38$	2	7.19	0.35
Error	$E_{xx} = 370.86$	18	20.60	
Total	$S_{xx} = 385.24$	20		

A negative value for T_{xy} implies a negative value for the between-treatment correlation, which for this example is

$$r_T = \frac{T_{xy}}{\sqrt{T_{xx}}\sqrt{T_{yy}}} = -0.8647.$$

Even though r_T is large for this example, with $k = 3$ there are only three pairs of points on which r_T is based. Hence this estimate of ρ_T will have a very large standard error. In this case a confidence interval on ρ_T will include zero.

Although in this case there is no reason to expect differences between aptitude means for the treatments (since subjects were assigned at random), in general it may be of interest to do an analysis of variance of the covariate. That analysis is summarized in Table 10.11. The overall F test indicates that there are no statistically significant differences among the covariate means. If the experimental units were assigned at random to the treatment conditions and the treatments did not affect the covariate, any differences among the covariate means would be due to chance. If the experimental units could not be assigned to the treatment conditions at random and the covariate was not affected by the treatments, differences among the covariate means, if there were such, could be a function of the sampling bias.

The outcome of the analysis of covariance indicates that it may be of interest to explore differences among the treatment means of the variate, adjusted for the effects of the covariate.

If individual comparisons are desired, such comparisons are made in terms of the adjusted treatment means. The latter are shown in Table 10.12.

One may use adjusted means to evaluate planned or post mortem

TABLE 10.12   **Adjusted treatment means**

	Treatment 1	Treatment 2	Treatment 6	Mean
$\bar{Y}_j$	14.825	13.429	18.286	$\bar{Y} = 15.333$
$\bar{X}_j$	9.429	8.714	7.349	$\bar{X} = 8.524$
$\bar{Y}'_j = \bar{Y}_j - b_E(\bar{X}_j - \bar{X})$	13.350	13.233	19.417	$\bar{Y}' = 15.333$

$$T_{yyA} = n \sum (\bar{Y}'_j - \bar{Y})^2 = 7[(-1.983)^2 + (-2.100)^2 + (4.084)^2] = 175.207$$

comparisons using an appropriate F, t, or q statistic and applying any of the techniques discussed in Chap. 3 for evaluating differences among treatment means. For this purpose, one uses MS'_{error} from the analysis of covariance as an error estimate,

$$\hat{\sigma}_\varepsilon^2 = MS'_{error} = \frac{E_{yy} - b_E E_{xy}}{k(n-1) - 1}.$$

It will be assumed that the covariate is random and that there may be differences among covariate means which are not due to error, such as may occur when intact groups are used. An F statistic which may be used to evaluate any comparison

$$C_{\bar{Y}'} = \sum c_j \bar{Y}'_j \qquad \sum c_j = 0$$

among adjusted means is given by

$$F = \frac{C_{\bar{Y}'}^2}{MS'_{error}\left\{ \sum \frac{c_j^2}{n_j} + \frac{\sum [c_j(\bar{X}_j - \bar{X})]^2}{E_{xx}} \right\}}.$$

This F with degrees of freedom equal to 1 and $k(n-1) - 1$ is useful for *a priori* comparisons or for using the Scheffé procedure with $k - 1$ and $k(n-1) - 1$ degrees of freedom.

Equivalently, one may compute a t statistic with $k(n-1) - 1$ degrees of freedom as $\sqrt{F}$. Thus,

$$t = \frac{C_{\bar{Y}'}}{\sqrt{MS'_{error}\left\{ \sum \frac{c_j^2}{n_j} + \frac{\sum [c_j(\bar{X}_j - \bar{X})]^2}{E_{xx}} \right\}}}$$

may be used for such procedures as the Dunn–Bonferroni procedure for evaluating multiple *a priori* comparisons.

Techniques which use the q statistic, such as the Tukey and Newman–Keuls procedures, may be extended to the analysis of covariance by utilizing a sampling distribution presented by Bryant and Paulson (1976). The distribution for q is called the generalized studentized range statistic. Under the conditions cited herein, the statistic

$$q_p = \frac{\bar{Y}'_j - \bar{Y}'_{j'}}{\sqrt{MS'_{error}\left[\frac{2}{n} + (\bar{X}_j - \bar{X}_{j'})^2 / E_{xx} \right] \big/ 2}}$$

may be used to evaluate any difference between pairs of means. Tables of this statistic are provided in Appendix D. Tabled values are determined by three parameters, the degrees of freedom for MS'_{error}, $v = k(n-1) - 1$, the number of treatment levels k, and the number of covariates p. The studentized range statistic applied to the analysis of variance is the special case of the generalized studentized range statistic where $p = 0$. Thus, decisions about the differences among adjusted means may be made in terms of the tabled values, $q_{\alpha; p, k, v}$ (see Appendix D).

As an example of these applications, suppose that one desired to test the hypothesis

$$H_0: \psi = 2\tau_3 - \tau_1 - \tau_2 = 0.$$

An estimate of ψ is

$$\hat{\psi} = C = 2\bar{Y}'_3 - \bar{Y}'_1 - \bar{Y}'_2$$
$$= (2)(19.417) - 13.350 - 13.233 = 12.251.$$

The F statistic is

$$F = \frac{(12.251)^2}{2.40\left[\dfrac{6}{7} + \dfrac{[2(-1.034) - (0.905) - (0.190)]^2}{370.86}\right]}$$

$$= 70.66.$$

If this is considered to be a test of an *a priori* hypothesis, then the critical value for this F statistic is

$$F_{0.99}(1, 17) = 8.40$$

for a level of significance of 0.01. Thus, the data indicate that this hypothesis may be rejected. As another example, to test the hypothesis

$$H_0: \tau_1 - \tau_2 = 0,$$

the observed comparison is

$$C = \bar{Y}'_1 - \bar{Y}'_2 = 13.350 - 13.233 = 0.117.$$

In this case,

$$F = \frac{C^2}{MS'_{error}\left[\dfrac{2}{n} + \dfrac{(\bar{X}_1 - \bar{X}_2)^2}{E_{xx}}\right]} = \frac{(0.117)^2}{0.6939} = 0.02,$$

and the decision is to not reject the null hypothesis of the 0.01 level of significance.

This same F may be used for other procedures, such as the Scheffé procedure, in which case the decision rule would be to reject the null hypothesis if F_{obs} exceeds $(k - 1)F_{1-\alpha}[k - 1, k(n - 1) - 1]$.

In general, when considering tests on differences between adjusted means, if the covariate is affected by the treatment, extreme care is needed in interpreting adjusted treatment means. The latter may not correspond to anything that can be realized experimentally. The adjustment process may also remove part of the effect of the treatment on the variate. It may also be the case that the treatment can have no effect on the variate except as mediated through the covariate. The nature of the relationship between the covariate and the variate is vital in attempting to interpret adjusted treatment means when the covariate is potentially affected by the treatment. In this latter case the between-treatment regression is also highly relevant in obtaining any kind of meaningful adjustment. As mentioned earlier, Smith (1957) has an excellent discussion of some of the problems encountered in working with adjusted treatment means.

It is of interest to carry out an analysis of variance of the residuals

$$Y'_{ij} = Y_{ij} - b_E(X_{ij} - \bar{X})$$

to illustrate directly that this procedure is essentially identical to the analysis of covariance. An analysis of variance of the residuals is summarized in Table 10.13. The basic data are those in Table 10.7. Several decimal places are carried here in order to illustrate certain relationships between the direct analysis of variance of the residuals and the usual analysis of covariance. Usually the two analyses will yield almost identical results.

The individual residuals are given in part i. From Table 10.7, the first pair of values under treatment 1 is

$$X_{i1} = 3 \qquad Y_{i1} = 8.$$

The first residual in Table 10.13 is

$$Y'_{i1} = 8 - 1.0331(3 - 8.52383) = 13.707.$$

Other entries in part i are obtained in an analogous manner. Column sums and column sum of squares are obtained in the lower half of part i. The column means are identical with the adjusted means computed in Table 10.12. Thus the adjusted means are the means of the columns of residuals.

The computational symbols that would be computed in an ordinary analysis of variance are obtained in part ii. The analysis of variance of the residuals is summarized in part iii. One notes that the variation due to the treatments (175.17) is actually equal to T_{yyA} as computed from the adjusted treatment means in Table 10.12. The relationship between T_{yyR} which appears in the analysis of covariance and T_{yyA} is given in part iv. As long as $b_T \neq b_E$,

$$T_{yyR} > T_{yyA}.$$

In this example, T_{yyA} and T_{yyR} do not differ markedly. (Such is generally the case.) T_{yyA} is larger than T_{yyR} because the $\bar{Y}'_j$ are correlated. The covariance between $\bar{Y}'_j$ and $\bar{Y}'_{j'}$ is shown in part v.

The within-treatment variation of the residuals is actually equal to E'_{yy} in the analysis of covariance. Thus E'_{yy} in the analysis of covariance is equivalent to the within-treatment variation of the residuals

$$Y'_{ij} = Y_{ij} - b_E(X_{ij} - \bar{X}).$$

These residuals are scaled so that their mean is equal to $\bar{Y}$.

TABLE 10.13   **Analysis of variance of residuals**

$$Y'_{ij} = Y_{ij} - b_E(X_{ij} - \bar{X})$$
$$= Y_{ij} - 1.0331(X_{ij} - 8.52383)$$

	Y'_{i1}	Y'_{i2}	Y'_{i3}	
	13.707	13.376	20.343	
	13.574	13.243	10.475	
	14.475	14.475	20.541	
	14.541	13.508	20.674	
	13.309	12.674	20.740	
(i)	12.541	12.607	18.541	
	11.309	12.740	14.607	
				Total
$\sum_i Y'_{ij}$:	93.456	92.623	135.921	322.000
$\sum_i Y'^2_{ij}$:	1255.401	1228.160	2669.691	5153.252
$\bar{Y}'_j$:	13.351	13.232	19.417	

(ii) $(1y') = G^2_{y'}/kn = 4937.333$ $(2y') = \sum\left(\sum Y'^2_{ij}\right) = 5153.252$ $(3y') = \sum (T^2_{y'})/n = 5112.509$

(iii)
$$T_{yyA} = (3y') - (1y') = 175.17$$
$$E'_{yy} = (2y') - (3y') = 40.74$$
$$\overline{}$$
$$(2y') - (1y') = 215.91$$

(iv)
$$Y_{yyR} = T_{yyA} - \frac{(b_T - b_E)^2 T^2_{xx}}{S_{xx}}$$
$$= 175.17 - \frac{(-2.2121 - 1.0331)^2(14.38)^2}{385.24}$$
$$= 169.52$$

(v)
$$\text{Cov}(\bar{Y}'_j, \bar{Y}'_{j'}) = \frac{\text{MS}'_{\text{error}}(\bar{X}_j - \bar{X})(\bar{X}_{j'} - \bar{X})}{E_{xx}}$$

Unequal Cell Frequencies

Suppose that the sample sizes under each of the treatments are as follows:

Treatment 1	Treatment 2	$\cdots$	Treatment k	Total
n_1	n_2		n_k	$N = \sum n_j$

If a least-squares solution is desired, then the computational symbols are given by

$$(1x) = G^2_x/N \qquad (1xy) = G_X G_y/N \qquad (1y) = G^2_y/N$$

$$(2x) = \sum X^2 \qquad (2xy) = \sum XY \qquad (2y) = \sum Y^2$$

$$(3x) = \sum (T^2_{x_j}/n_j) \qquad (3xy) = \sum (T_{x_j} T_{y_j}/n_j) \qquad (3y) = \sum (T^2_{y_j}/n_j)$$

With these changes in the computations symbols, computational procedures for obtaining the basic sources of variation are identical with those used in the case of equal sample sizes. The analysis of covariance takes the following form:

Source of Variation	SS	df	MS
Treatments	T_{yyR}	$k-1$	MS'_{treat}
Error	E'_{yy}	$N-k-1$	MS'_{error}

Use of Covariate as a Factor

Rather than using a covariance analysis, the experimenter might have used the covariate as a classification factor, thus creating a two-factor experiment. The goal of such an analysis is to remove the effects of the covariate from error. Stratification may be viewed as a function-free regression plan relating the dependent variable to the stratified covariate.

Consider, for example, the following data for an analysis of covariance:

Treatment 1		Treatment 2		Treatment 3	
X	Y	X	Y	X	Y
1	3	1	8	1	14
1	5	1	10	1	10
2	8	1	9	2	18
2	10	2	14	3	22
3	10	2	16	3	20
4	16	2	18	4	26
4	18	4	22	4	24
4	14	4	24	2	28

Suppose that X represents a characteristic of the experimental unit measured before the administration of the treatment. If one lets X define a classification factor, then the basic data given above may be cast in the form of the following two-factor experiment.

	Treatment 1	Treatment 2	Treatment 3
$X=1$	3, 5	8, 10, 9	14, 10
$X=2$	8, 10	14, 16, 18	18
$X=3$	10	—	22, 20
$X=4$	16, 18, 20	22, 24	26, 34, 28

When the number of units per treatment is relatively large, each cell in the resulting factorial may have an adequately large (say five or more) number of entries. When the number of units per treatment is relatively small, the resulting frequencies per cell will be relatively small and some cells may have no entries. Such is the case of the example given on p. 787. In this latter case, one would be ill-advised to convert to a factorial design.

There are both advantages and disadvantages of converting from a covariance analysis to a factorial design, using the covariate to define a classification factor. One disadvantage is the resulting unequal cell frequencies. Another disadvantage results if the covariate is considered to define a random factor, in which case the denominator for the F ratio in the test on the treatment factor is the interaction term (if the latter cannot be pooled with the within-cell variance).

The advantage to the factorial approach resides primarily in the fact that the assumptions are less restrictive. The analysis of covariance requires the assumption of homogeneity of within-treatment regression coefficients. Moreover, for simplicity one typically assumes that the regression is linear in analysis of covariance whereas the factorial analysis is function free. Another advantage of the factorial approach is that one is able to evaluate the complete interaction effect between the treatment and the stratified covariate. The linear part of that interaction effect is measured by the within-treatment correlation in the analysis of covariance. Thus, when the regressions are, indeed, linear, the two approaches essentially lead to the same result with regard to reducing error.

10.3 MULTIPLE COVARIATES

A single-factor design (no repeated measures) with two covariates will be used to illustrate the principles underlying the use of multiple covariates. All of the assumptions underlying the use of a single covariate extend to the use of multiple covariates.

The notation system as well as the approach used to handle the two covariates will be such that extension to p covariates is quite direct. The notation for two covariates in a single-factor design is as follows:

	Treatment j		
	X_1	X_2	Y
	X_{11j}	X_{21j}	Y_{1j}
	X_{12j}	X_{22j}	Y_{2j}
	$\vdots$	$\vdots$	$\vdots$
	X_{1nj}	X_{2nj}	Y_{nj}
Total	T_{x1j}	T_{x2j}	T_{yj}

The computational symbols have the following general form:

$$(1x_1x_2) = \frac{G_{x_1}G_{x_2}}{kn} \qquad (2x_1x_2) = \sum X_1X_2 \qquad (3x_1x_2) = \frac{\sum T_{x1_j}T_{x2_j}}{n}$$

$$(1x_1y) = \frac{G_{x_1}G_y}{kn} \qquad (2x_1y) = \sum X_1Y \qquad (3x_1y) = \frac{\sum T_{x1_j}T_{y_j}}{n}$$

The basic variations and covariations that enter into the analysis of covariance will be denoted as follows:

Treatments:	T_{11}	T_{22}	T_{12}	T_{1y}	T_{2y}	T_{yy}
Error:	E_{11}	E_{22}	E_{12}	E_{1y}	E_{2y}	E_{yy}
Total:	S_{11}	S_{22}	S_{12}	S_{1y}	S_{2y}	S_{yy}

For example, covariations are given by

$$T_{12} = (3x_1x_2) - (1x_1x_2) \qquad T_{1y} = (3x_1y) - (1x_1y)$$

$$E_{12} = (2x_1x_2) - (3x_1x_2) \qquad E_{1y} = (2x_1y) - (3x_1y)$$

$$S_{12} = (2x_1x_2) - (1x_1x_2) \qquad S_{1y} = (2x_1y) - (1x_1y)$$

In the analysis of multiple covariance, the data on the variate Y are adjusted for the linear effects of the covariates through the use of a multiple regression equation. If separate regression equations were to be computed from within each treatment, the adjusted Y for treatment j would take the form

$$Y'_{ij} = Y_{ij} - b_{y \cdot x1_j}(X_{1_{ij}} - \bar{X}_{1_j}) - b_{y \cdot x2_j}(X_{2_{ij}} - \bar{X}_{2_j}),$$

where $b_{y \cdot x1_j}$ and $b_{y \cdot x2_j}$ are partial regression coefficients for predicting the dependent variable Y from covariates X_1 and X_2, respectively, within treatment class j. If the within-treatment regressions are homogeneous, the adjusted Y in terms of the pooled within-treatment regression coefficients takes the form

$$Y'_{ij} = Y_{ij} - b_{y \cdot x_1}(X_{1_{ij}} - \bar{X}_1) - b_{y \cdot x_2}(X_{2_{ij}} - \bar{X}_2).$$

The complete model for the case of two covariates is

$$Y'_{ij} = Y_{ij} - \beta_{y \cdot x_1}(X_{1_{ij}} - \bar{X}_1) - \beta_{y \cdot x_2}(X_{2_{ij}} - \bar{X}_2) = \mu + \tau_j + \varepsilon_{ij}.$$

That is, the model for an adjusted observation is the model for an observation in the usual analysis of variance. Thus, the analysis of covariance is an analysis of variance of Y'_{ij}.

To obtain the least-squares estimates of the regression coefficients in the complete model, the normal equations have the form

$$\begin{bmatrix} E_{11} & E_{12} \\ E_{21} & E_{22} \end{bmatrix} \begin{bmatrix} b_{E_1} \\ b_{E_2} \end{bmatrix} = \begin{bmatrix} E_{1y} \\ E_{2y} \end{bmatrix},$$

where

$$E = \begin{bmatrix} E_{11} & E_{12} \\ E_{21} & E_{22} \end{bmatrix}$$

is the matrix of pooled within-treatment variations and covariations for X_1 and X_2,

$$\mathbf{e} = \begin{bmatrix} E_{1y} \\ E_{2y} \end{bmatrix}$$

is the vector of covariations between the covariates X_1, and X_2 and the dependent variable Y, and

$$\mathbf{b}_E = \begin{bmatrix} b_{E_1} \\ b_{E_2} \end{bmatrix}$$

is the vector of unknown partial regression coefficients. (The complete notation for which is $b_{E_y \cdot x_1}$ and $b_{E_y \cdot x_2}$). Thus, in matrix format, the normal equation for obtaining the within-treatment regression coefficients is

$$E\mathbf{b}_E = \mathbf{e},$$

from which one obtains (provided E is nonsingular)

$$b_E = E^{-1}\mathbf{e}.$$

If one lets

$$\begin{bmatrix} E_{11} & E_{12} \\ E_{21} & E_{22} \end{bmatrix}^{-1} = \begin{bmatrix} E^{11} & E^{12} \\ E^{21} & E^{22} \end{bmatrix},$$

then the solution to the normal equations has the general form

$$\begin{bmatrix} b_{E_1} \\ b_{E_2} \end{bmatrix} = \begin{bmatrix} E^{11} & E^{12} \\ E^{21} & E^{22} \end{bmatrix} \begin{bmatrix} E_{1y} \\ E_{2y} \end{bmatrix} = \begin{bmatrix} E^{11}E_{1y} + E^{12}E_{2y} \\ E^{21}E_{1y} + E^{22}E_{2y} \end{bmatrix}.$$

For the special case of a 2×2 matrix,

$$E^{11} = \frac{E_{22}}{E_{11}E_{22} - E_{12}^2} \qquad E^{12} = \frac{-E_{12}}{E_{11}E_{22} - E_{12}^2}$$

$$E^{21} = \frac{-E_{21}}{E_{11}E_{22} - E_{12}^2} \qquad E^{22} = \frac{E_{11}}{E_{11}E_{22} - E_{12}^2}.$$

For this case an explicit solution for the regression coefficients is

$$b_{Ey \cdot x_1} = b_{E_1} = \frac{E_{22}E_{1y} - E_{12}E_{2y}}{E_{11}E_{22} - E_{12}^2},$$

$$b_{Ey \cdot x_2} = b_{E_2} = \frac{E_{11}E_{2y} - E_{21}E_{1y}}{E_{11}E_{22} - E_{12}^2}.$$

The variation due to error under the complete model is

$$E'_{yy} = E_{yy} - (b_{E_1}E_{1y} + b_{E_2}E_{2y}).$$

The degrees of freedom are

$$f_{E'} = k(n - 1) - p,$$

where p is the number of covariates.

Under the restriction on the complete model that all treatment effects are 0 ($\tau_j = 0$), the reduced model for the analysis of covariance is the regression model

$$Y_{ij} = \mu + \beta_1(X_{1_{ij}} - \bar{X}_1) + \beta_2(X_{2_{ij}} - \bar{X}_2) + \varepsilon_{ij}.$$

The appropriate regression of Y on X_1 and X_2 in this case is the total regression, b_s, disregarding treatment classes. The normal equations for estimating the regression coefficients in this case are

$$\begin{bmatrix} S_{11} & S_{12} \\ S_{21} & S_{22} \end{bmatrix} \begin{bmatrix} b_{s_1} \\ b_{s_2} \end{bmatrix} = \begin{bmatrix} S_{1y} \\ S_{2y} \end{bmatrix}$$

$$S \cdot \mathbf{b}_s = \mathbf{s}$$

If one lets

$$\begin{bmatrix} S_{11} & S_{12} \\ S_{21} & S_{22} \end{bmatrix}^{-1} = \begin{bmatrix} S^{11} & S^{12} \\ S^{21} & S^{22} \end{bmatrix}$$

then the solution of the regression coefficients takes the form

$$\begin{bmatrix} b_{s_1} \\ b_{s_2} \end{bmatrix} = \begin{bmatrix} S^{11} & S^{12} \\ S^{21} & S^{22} \end{bmatrix} \begin{bmatrix} S_{1y} \\ S_{2y} \end{bmatrix} = \begin{bmatrix} S^{11}S_{1y} + S^{12}S_{2y} \\ S^{21}S_{1y} + S^{22}S_{2y} \end{bmatrix}.$$

In explicit form the regression coefficients under the reduced model are

$$b_{s_y \cdot x_1} = b_{s_1} = \frac{S_{22}S_{1y} - S_{12}S_{2y}}{S_{11}S_{22} - S_{12}^2},$$

$$b_{s_y \cdot x_2} = b_{s_2} = \frac{S_{11}S_{2y} - S_{21}S_{1y}}{S_{11}S_{22} - S_{12}^2}.$$

Hence the variation due to error under the reduced model is

$$S'_{yy} = S_{yy} - (b_{s_1}S_{1y} + b_{s_2}S_{2y}).$$

This variation is the variation of the residuals about the overall regression line with degrees of freedom equal to

$$f_{S'} = kn - 1 - p.$$

The measure of deviation from the hypothesis of no treatment effects is the variation due to treatments adjusted for the covariates,

$$
\begin{aligned}
T_{yyR} &= S'_{yy} - E'_{yy} \\
&= [S_{yy} - (b_{S_1}S_{1y} + b_{S_2}S_{2y})] - [E_{yy} - (b_{E_1}E_{1y} + b_{E_2}E_{2y})] \\
&= T_{yy} - [(b_{S_1}S_{1y} + b_{S_2}S_{2y}) + (b_{E_1}E_{1y} + b_{E_2}E_{2y})].
\end{aligned}
$$

The degrees of freedom for this source of variation are

$$ f_{S'} = f_{E'} = k - 1. $$

Putting all of this information together, a summary of the analysis of covariance is given in Table 10.14.

The evaluation of differences among means is carried out with adjusted means where an adjusted treatment mean takes the form

$$ \bar{Y}'_j = \bar{Y}_j - b_{E_1}(\bar{X}_{1_j} - \bar{X}_1) - b_{E_2}(\bar{X}_{2_j} - \bar{X}_2). $$

The variance (squared standard error) of the difference between two adjusted treatment means is

$$ \operatorname{var}(\bar{Y}'_j - \bar{Y}'_{j'}) = \mathrm{MS}'_{error}\left[\frac{2}{n} + d_1^2 E^{11} + d_2^2 E^{22} + 2d_1 d_2 E^{12}\right] $$

where

$$ d_1 = \bar{X}_{1_j} - \bar{X}_{1_{j'}} \qquad \text{and} \qquad d_2 = \bar{X}_{2_j} - \bar{X}_{2_{j'}}. $$

The average squared standard error, averaged over all pairs of differences of the adjusted treatment means, is

$$ \frac{\mathrm{MS}'_{error}}{n}\left[1 + \frac{T_{11}E^{11} + T_{22}E^{22} + 2T_{12}E^{12}}{k - 1}\right]. $$

This value is useful for procedures such as the Newman–Keuls procedure wherein the goal is to make multiple comparisons with a common standard error.

For the general case of p covariates, expressions for the regression coefficients and the variation of the residuals are most readily written in matrix notation. Suppose that the variate is denoted X_0 and that the covariates are denoted

$$ X_1, X_2, \ldots, X_p. $$

TABLE 10.14 Analysis of covariance for case of two covariates

Source	SS	df	MS	F
Treatments	$T_{yyR} = S'_{yy} - E'_{yy}$	$k - 1$	MS'_{treat}	$\mathrm{MS}'_{treat}/\mathrm{MS}'_{treat}$
Error	E'_{yy}	$k(n-1) - 2$	MS'_{error}	
Total	S'_{yy}	$kn - 3$		

Let

$$E = \begin{bmatrix} E_{11} & E_{12} & \cdots & E_{1p} \\ E_{21} & E_{22} & \cdots & E_{2p} \\ \vdots & & & \vdots \\ E_{p1} & E_{p2} & \cdots & E_{pp} \end{bmatrix}; \quad \mathbf{b}_E = \begin{bmatrix} b_{E_1} \\ b_{E_2} \\ \vdots \\ b_{E_p} \end{bmatrix}; \quad \mathbf{e}_o = \begin{bmatrix} E_{01} \\ E_{02} \\ \vdots \\ E_{0p} \end{bmatrix}$$

be the within-treatment information, where E contains the variations and covariations involving the p covariates, $\mathbf{e}_0$ is the vector of covariations between the dependent variable X_0 and the covariates, and $\mathbf{b}_E$ is the vector of within-class partial regression coefficients. Then,

$$\mathbf{b}_E = E^{-1} \mathbf{e}_0,$$

and the residual or error variation is

$$E'_{00} = E_{00} - \mathbf{b}'_E \mathbf{e}_0.$$

The corresponding overall matrices, ignoring treatments, may be denoted

$$S = \begin{bmatrix} S_{11} & S_{12} & \cdots & S_{1p} \\ S_{21} & S_{22} & \cdots & S_{2p} \\ \vdots & & & \vdots \\ S_{p1} & S_{p2} & \cdots & S_{pp} \end{bmatrix}; \quad \mathbf{b}_S = \begin{bmatrix} b_{S_1} \\ b_{S_2} \\ \vdots \\ b_{S_p} \end{bmatrix}; \quad \mathbf{s}_0 = \begin{bmatrix} S_{01} \\ S_{02} \\ \vdots \\ S_{0p} \end{bmatrix}.$$

The overall partial regression coefficients are

$$\mathbf{b}_S = S^{-1} \mathbf{s}_0,$$

and the error variation taken about the total regression surface is

$$S'_{00} = S_{00} - \mathbf{b}'_s \mathbf{s}_0.$$

Combining the within-treatment information with the total regression information, the reduced variation due to treatments is

$$T_{00R} = S'_{00} - E'_{00}.$$

Assuming n observation under each of the k treatments, the analysis of covariance takes the following form:

TABLE 10.15   Analysis of covariance with p covariates

Source	SS	df
Treatments	$T_{00R} = S'_{00} - E'_{00}$	$k - 1$
Error	$E'_{00} = E_{00} - \mathbf{b}'_E \mathbf{e}_0$	$k(n - 1) - p$
Total	S'_{00}	$kn - p - 1$

An adjusted treatment mean has the form

$$\bar{Y}'_j = \bar{Y}_j - \sum_{r=1}^{p} b_{E_r}(\bar{X}_{r_j} - \bar{X}_r).$$

Define the vector **d** as

$$\mathbf{d} = \begin{bmatrix} \bar{X}_{1_j} - \bar{X}_{1_{j'}} \\ \bar{X}_{2_j} - \bar{X}_{2_{j'}} \\ \vdots \\ \bar{X}_{p_j} - \bar{X}_{p_{j'}} \end{bmatrix}.$$

Then the variance between two adjusted treatment means is

$$\text{var}(\bar{Y}_j - \bar{Y}_{j'}) = \text{MS}'_{\text{error}}\left[\frac{2}{n} + \mathbf{d}'E^{-1}\mathbf{d}\right].$$

Numerical Example for Case of Two Covariates

A numerical example for the case of $p = 2$ covariates with $n = 12$ independent units under each treatment is illustrated in Table 10.16. The basic observations are given in the upper part of the table.

TABLE 10.16   **Numerical example—analysis of covariance with two covariates** ($k = 2$, $n = 12$)

	Treatment 1			Treatment 2					
	X_1	X_2	Y	X_1	X_2	Y			
	1	3	18	4	3	26			
	1	5	24	5	4	33			
	3	7	33	6	5	42			
	5	1	20	3	4	30			
	2	6	34	2	3	29			
	2	2	16	1	3	19			
	4	1	12	2	1	15			
	3	3	26	3	5	34			
	2	6	34	5	2	26			
	5	1	20	3	4	34			
	6	1	22	1	6	33			
	7	3	35	5	2	20			
$\sum(\ )$:	41	39	294	40	42	341	$\sum X_1 = 81$	$\sum X_2 = 81$	$\sum Y = 635$
$\sum(\ )^2$:	183	181	7886	164	170	10,333	$\sum X_1^2 = 347$	$\sum X_2^2 = 351$	$\sum Y^2 = 18{,}219$

Cross-products for treat 1					Cross-products for treat 2			
	X_1	X_2	Y			X_1	X_2	Y
X_1	183	107	1012		X_1	164	138	1185
X_2		181	1102		X_2		170	1295
Y			7886		Y			10333

TABLE 10.16   (*Continued*)

	Combined cross-products		
	X_1	X_2	Y
X_1	347	245	2197
X_2		351	2397
Y			18219

$(1x_1) = 273.375$	$(1x_2) = 273.375$	$(1y) = 16{,}801.04$
$(2x_1) = 347$	$(2x_2) = 351$	$(2y) = 18{,}219$
$(3x_1) = 273.417$	$(3x_2) = 273.75$	$(3y) = 16{,}893.08$
$(1x_1x_2) = 273.375$	$(1x_1 y) = 2143.12$	$(1x_2 y) = 2143.12$
$(2x_1x_2) = 245$	$(2x_1 y) = 2197$	$(2x_2 y) = 2397$
$(3x_1x_2) = 273.250$	$(3x_1 y) = 2141.17$	$(3x_2 y) = 2149.00$

	X_1	X_2	X_1X_2	X_1Y	X_2Y	Y
$T = (3) - (1)$	0.042	0.375	-0.125	-1.95	5.88	92.08
$E = (2) - (3)$	73.583	77.25	-28.250	55.83	248.00	1325.92
$S = (2) - (1)$	73.625	77.625	-28.375	53.88	253.88	1418.00

Normal equations for within-treatment regression:

$$\begin{bmatrix} 73.583 & -28.25 \\ -28.25 & 77.25 \end{bmatrix} \begin{bmatrix} b_{E_{y \cdot x_1}} \\ b_{E_{y \cdot x_2}} \end{bmatrix} = \begin{bmatrix} 55.83 \\ 248.00 \end{bmatrix}$$

$$\quad E \qquad\qquad \mathbf{b}_E \qquad\quad \mathbf{e}$$

Solution to normal equations for within-treatment regression:

$$\begin{bmatrix} 0.01581 & 0.005782 \\ 0.005782 & 0.01506 \end{bmatrix} \begin{bmatrix} 55.83 \\ 248.00 \end{bmatrix} = \begin{bmatrix} 2.3166 \\ 4.0577 \end{bmatrix}$$

$$\quad E^{-1} \qquad\qquad \mathbf{e} \qquad\quad \mathbf{b}_E$$

Predictable variation from within-treatment regression:

$$\mathbf{b}'_E\mathbf{e} = 1135.65$$

Normal equations for overall regression:

$$\begin{bmatrix} 76.625 & -28.375 \\ -28.375 & 77.625 \end{bmatrix} \begin{bmatrix} b_{S_{y \cdot x_1}} \\ b_{S_{y \cdot x_2}} \end{bmatrix} = \begin{bmatrix} 53.88 \\ 253.88 \end{bmatrix}$$

$$\quad S \qquad\qquad \mathbf{b}_s \qquad\quad \mathbf{s}$$

Solution to normal equation for overall regression:

$$\begin{bmatrix} 0.01581 & 0.005779 \\ 0.005779 & 0.014995 \end{bmatrix} \begin{bmatrix} 53.88 \\ 253.88 \end{bmatrix} = \begin{bmatrix} 2.3190 \\ 4.1183 \end{bmatrix}$$

$$\quad S^{-1} \qquad\qquad \mathbf{s} \qquad\quad \mathbf{b}_s$$

Predictable variation from overall regression:

$$\mathbf{b}'_s\mathbf{s} = 1170.50$$

The computational symbols in the lower third of the table are direct generalizations of those used in the analysis of covariance having only a single covariate. For example,

$$(1x_1x_2) = G_{x_1}G_{x_2}/kn = (81)(81)/24 = 273.375$$

$$(2x_1x_2) = \sum X_1X_2 = 245$$

$$(3x_1x_2) = \left[\left(\sum X_{1_1}\right)\left(\sum X_{2_1}\right) + \left(\sum X_{1_2}\right)\left(\sum X_{2_2}\right)\right]\Big/n$$

$$= [(41)(39) + (40)(42)]/12 = 273.250.$$

The basic ingredients for the analysis of covariance are given at the top of Table 10.16. For example,

$$T_{x_1x_2} = (3x_1x_2) - (1x_1x_2) = 273.250 - 273.375 = -0.125$$

$$E_{x_1x_2} = (2x_1x_2) - (3x_1x_2) = 245.00 - 273.250 = -28.250$$

$$S_{x_1x_2} = (2x_1x_2) - (1x_1x_2) = 245.000 - 273.250 = -28.375.$$

$$E \qquad \mathbf{b}_E = \mathbf{e}.$$

The normal equations for the within-treatment regression weights are given in the middle of Table 10.16. The solution is also given. For example, in non-matrix form

$$b_{E_{y \cdot x_1}} = \frac{E_{22}E_{1y} - E_{12}E_{2y}}{E_{11}E_{22} - E_{12}^2}$$

$$= \frac{(77.25)(55.83) - (-28.250)(248.000)}{(73.583)(77.25) - (-28.25)^2}$$

$$= 2.3166.$$

The vector of overall regression weights is obtained at the bottom of Table 10.6. Thus,

$$\mathbf{b}_S = S^{-1}\mathbf{s},$$

and has

$$\mathbf{b}_S = \begin{bmatrix} 2.3190 \\ 4.1196 \end{bmatrix}.$$

In non-matrix form

$$b_{S_{y \cdot x_1}} = \frac{S_{22}S_{1y} - S_{12}S_{2y}}{S_{11}S_{22} - S_{12}^2}$$

$$= \frac{(77.625)(53.88) - (-28.375)(253.88)}{(73.625)(77.625) - (-28.375)^2}$$

$$= 2.3190,$$

$$b_{S_{y \cdot x_2}} = \frac{-S_{11}S_{2y} + S_{21}S_{1y}}{S_{11}S_{22} - S_{12}^2}$$

$$= \frac{-(-28.375)(53.88) + (73.625)(253.88)}{4910.00}$$

$$= 4.1183.$$

The predictable variation due to within-treatment regression is

$$\mathbf{b}_E'\mathbf{e} = (2.3166)(55.83) + (4.0577)(248.00)$$

$$= 1135.65.$$

Hence the residual variation associated with the within-treatment regression is

$$E_{yy}' = E_{yy} - \mathbf{b}_E'\mathbf{e} = 1325.92 - 1135.65 = 190.27.$$

The predictable variation due to overall regression is

$$\mathbf{b}_S'\mathbf{s} = (2.3190)(53.88) + (4.1183)(253.88) = 1170.50.$$

Hence the corresponding error variation is

$$S_{yy}' = S_{yy} - \mathbf{b}_S'\mathbf{s} = 1418.00 - 1170.50 = 247.50.$$

Thus the reduced variation due to treatments is

$$T_{yyR}' = S_{yy}' - E_{yy}' = 247.50 - 190.27 = 57.23.$$

A summary of the analysis of variance is given in Table 10.17. One notes that the treatment effects are not statistically significant. A summary of the analysis of covariance is given in Table 10.18. In the analysis of covariance, the treatments are significant at the 0.05 level. The mean square due to error in

TABLE 10.17   **Analysis of variance of data in Table 10.16**

Source	SS	df	MS	F
Treatments	$T_{yy} = 92.08$	1	92.08	1.53
Error	$E_{yy} = 1325.92$	22	60.27	
Total	$S_{yy} = 1418.00$	21		

TABLE 10.18   **Analysis of covariance of data in Table 10.16**

Source	SS	df	MS	F
Treatments	$T_{yyR} = 57.23$	1	57.23	6.02
Error	$E'_{yy} = 190.27$	20	9.51	
Total	$S'_{yy} = 247.50$	21		

the analysis of covariance is 9.51 compared to 60.27 in the analysis of variance. The reduction in the mean square error is a function of the squared multiple correlation $r^2_{E_{y(x_1 x_2)}}$ which is

$$r^2_{E_{y(x_1 x_2)}} = \frac{\mathbf{b}'_E \mathbf{e}}{S_{yy}} = \frac{1135.56}{1325.92} = 0.8565.$$

One has

$$\text{MS}'_{\text{error}} = (1 - r^2_{E_{y(x_1 x_2)}})\text{MS}_{\text{error}} \frac{22}{20}$$

$$= (0.1435)(60.27)\frac{22}{20} = 9.51.$$

The difference between the adjusted treatment means is

$$\bar{Y}'_1 - \bar{Y}'_2 = (\bar{Y}_1 - \bar{Y}_2) - b_{E_y \cdot x_1}(\bar{X}_{1_1} - \bar{X}_{1_2}) - b_{E_y \cdot x_2}(\bar{X}_{2_1} - \bar{X}_{2_2})$$

$$= (-3.9167) - 2.3166(0.08333) - 4.0577(-0.2500)$$

$$= -3.096.$$

For this numerical example, the difference between the unadjusted means (-3.917) differs very little from the difference in the adjusted means (-3.096).

To obtain the square of the standard error of the difference between the adjusted treatment means, one proceeds in a manner which is very similar to that used in the usual multiple regression. Suppose one lets

$$E^{-1} = \begin{bmatrix} 0.015810 & 0.005782 \\ 0.005782 & 0.015060 \end{bmatrix} = \begin{bmatrix} E^{11} & E^{12} \\ E^{21} & E^{22} \end{bmatrix}.$$

The squared standard error of $\bar{Y}'_1 - \bar{Y}'_2$ is given by

$$\text{var}\,(\bar{Y}'_1 - \bar{Y}'_2) = \text{MS}'_{\text{error}}\left[\frac{2}{n} + (\bar{X}_{1_1} - \bar{X}_{1_2})^2 E^{11}\right.$$

$$\left. + 2(\bar{X}_{1_1} - \bar{X}_{1_2})(\bar{X}_{2_1} - \bar{X}_{2_2})E^{12} + (\bar{X}_{2_1} - \bar{X}_{2_2})^2 E^{22}\right]$$

$$= 9.51\left[\frac{2}{12} + (0.006944)(0.01581)\right.$$

$$\left. + 2(-0.02083)(0.005782) + (0.0625)(0.01506)\right]$$

$$= 9.51[0.1667 + 0.0008] = 1.593.$$

Since there are only $k = 2$ treatments in this numerical example, the overall F statistic in the analysis of covariance is equivalent to

$$F = \frac{(\bar{Y}_1' - \bar{Y}_2')^2}{\text{var}\,(\bar{Y}_1' - \bar{Y}_2')} = \frac{(-3.096)^2}{1.593} = 6.02.$$

The critical value for this F statistic is

$$F_{1-\alpha}[1, k(n-1) - p] = F[1, 20],$$

where p is the number of covariates. This F statistic will differ from the overall F statistic only by rounding error.

It is instructive to look at the actual residual values of the dependent variable with the linear effects of X and X_2 removed. The within-treatment regression equation for the numerical example has the form

$$\hat{Y}_{ij} = \bar{Y} + b_{E_{y \cdot x_1}}(X_{1_{ij}} - \bar{X}_1) + b_{E_{y \cdot x_2}}X_{2_{ij}} - \bar{X}_2)$$
$$= b_{E_{y \cdot x_1}}X_{1_{ij}} + b_{E_{y \cdot x_2}}X_{2_{ij}} + (\bar{Y} - b_{E_{y \cdot x_1}}\bar{X}_1 - b_{E_{y \cdot x_2}}\bar{X}_2).$$

TABLE 10.19 **Analysis of residuals from within-treatment regression**

$$Y'' = Y - 2.3166X_1 - 4.0577X_2$$

	Treatment 1	Treatment 2	
	3.510	4.561	
	1.395	5.186	
	−2.354	7.812	
	4.359	6.819	
	5.021	12.194	
	3.251	4.510	
	−1.324	6.309	
	6.877	6.762	
	5.021	6.302	
	4.359	10.819	
	4.043	6.337	
	6.611	0.302	
			Total
$\sum Y_j'$:	40.769	77.913	118.68
$\sum Y_j'^2$:	227.90	606.80	834.70

(1) = 586.89	(2) = 834.70	(3) = 644.70

Source	SS	df	MS	F
Treatments	$T_{yyA} = 57.49$	1	57.49	6.04*
Error	$E_{yy}' = 109.32$	20	9.52	

$$T_{yyA} = (3) - (1) \qquad E_{yy}' = (2) - (3)$$

The term in parentheses at the extreme right is a constant and will have no effect on variances. Define the residuals

$$Y_{ij}'' = Y_{ij} - b_{E_y \cdot x_1} X_{1_{ij}} - b_{E_y \cdot x_2} X_{2_{ij}}.$$

These residuals differ from the residuals from the within-treatment regression equation only by the constant in the within-treatment regression equation. The Y_{ij}'' corresponding to the basic data in Table 10.16 are given in Table 10.19.

An approximation to the analysis of covariance is obtained by carrying out an analysis of variance on the Y''. In Table 10.19 the term E_{yy}' will differ from the corresponding term in the analysis of covariance only because of rounding error. The term T_{yyA} in this table is the variation due to the adjusted treatment means. For this numerical example, T_{yyA} differs very little from T_{yyR}.

The means of the Y'' are

$$\bar{Y}_1'' = 3.397 \qquad \bar{Y}_2'' = 6.492.$$

To get back to the original scale of measurement, an adjusted mean is

$$\bar{Y}_1' = \bar{Y}_1'' + 2.3166\bar{X}_1 + 4.0577\bar{X}_2$$
$$= 3.397 + 2.3166(3.3750) + 4.0577(3.3750)$$
$$= 24.910.$$
$$\bar{Y}_2' = 6.492 + 2.3166(3.3750) + 4.0577(3.3750)$$
$$= 28.005.$$

The direct computation of the adjusted treatment means is obtained from

$$\bar{Y}_1' = \bar{Y}_1 - 2.3166(\bar{X}_{1_1} - \bar{X}) - 4.0577(\bar{X}_{2_1} - \bar{X}_2)$$
$$= 24.500 - 2.3166(0.04167) - 4.0577(-0.1250)$$
$$= 24.911.$$
$$\bar{Y}_2' = \bar{Y}_2 - 2.3166(-0.04167) - 4.0577(0.1250)$$
$$= 28.417 - 0.4107$$
$$= 28.006.$$

10.4   FACTORIAL EXPERIMENT

The analysis of covariance for a factorial experiment is a direct generalization of the corresponding analysis for a single-factor experiment. Assuming a $p \times q$ factorial experiment having n observations in each cell, the model is as follows:

$$Y_{ijk}' = Y_{ijk} - \beta(X_{ijk} - \bar{X}) = \mu + \alpha_j + \beta_k + \alpha\beta_{jk} + \varepsilon_{ijk}.$$

One notes that the regression coefficient β does not depend upon j or k. This demands that the regression of Y on X is homogeneous within all treatment conditions, i.e., $\beta_{E_{jk}} - \beta_E$ for all pq cells. That is, an observation, adjusted for the effect of the covariate, estimates the parameters in the usual analysis of variance. If the covariate is ignored, its effect augments variation due to experimental error; the latter includes all uncontrolled sources of variation. It will be assumed throughout this section that A and B represent fixed factors. Thus, $\sum \alpha_j = \sum \beta_j = \sum_i \alpha\beta_{ij} = \sum_j \alpha\beta_{ij} = 0$.

The observations on the covariate and the criterion with cell ab_{jk} of the experiment are represented as follows:

$$
\begin{array}{cc}
X & Y \\
X_{1jk} & Y_{1jk} \\
X_{2jk} & Y_{2jk} \\
\cdots & \cdots \\
X_{njk} & Y_{njk}
\end{array}
$$

In each of the pq cells in the experiment there are n pairs of observations. The following notation denotes the various sums needed in the analysis:

$AB_{x_{jk}}$ = sum of covariate measures in cell ab_{jk}.
$AB_{y_{jk}}$ = sum of criterion measures in cell ab_{jk}.
A_{x_j} = sum of all covariate measures at level a_j.
A_{y_j} = sum of all criterion measures at level a_j.
B_{x_k} = sum of all covariate measures at level b_k.
B_{y_k} = sum of all criterion measures at level b_k.
G_x = sum of all covariate measures.
G_y = sum of all criterion measures.

The means corresponding to the sets of sums defined above are obtained by dividing the respective sums by the number of experimental units over which the sum is taken. For example,

$$
\overline{AB}_{x_{jk}} = \frac{AB_{x_{jk}}}{n}, \qquad \bar{A}_{y_j} = \frac{A_{y_j}}{nq}, \qquad \bar{G}_y = \frac{G_y}{npq}.
$$

The variation due to main effects and interactions is defined as follows. For the variate:

$$
A_{yy} = nq \sum (\bar{A}_{y_j} - \bar{G}_y)^2,
$$

$$
B_{yy} = np \sum (\bar{B}_{y_k} - \bar{G}_y)^2,
$$

$$
AB_{yy} = n \sum (\overline{AB}_{y_{jk}} - \bar{A}_{y_j} - \bar{B}_{y_k} + \bar{G}_y)^2.
$$

For the covariate:

$$
A_{xx} = nq \sum (\bar{A}_{x_j} - \bar{G}_x)^2,
$$

$$
B_{xx} = np \sum (\bar{B}_{x_k} - \bar{G}_x)^2,
$$

$$
AB_{xx} = n \sum (\overline{AB}_{x_{jk}} - \bar{A}_{x_j} - \bar{B}_{x_k} + \bar{G}_x)^2.
$$

For the cross-products:

$$A_{xy} = nq \sum (\bar{A}_{x_j} - \bar{G}_x)(\bar{A}_{y_j} - \bar{G}_y),$$

$$B_{xy} = np \sum (\bar{B}_{x_k} - \bar{G}_x)(\bar{B}_{y_k} - \bar{G}_y),$$

$$AB_{xy} = n \sum (\overline{AB}_{x_{jk}} - \bar{A}_{x_j} - \bar{B}_{x_k} + \bar{G}_x)(\overline{AB}_{y_{jk}} - \bar{A}_{y_j} - \bar{B}_{y_k} + \bar{G}_y).$$

The variation of the covariate within cell ab_{jk} is

$$E_{xx_{jk}} = \sum_i (X_{ijk} - \overline{AB}_{x_{jk}})^2.$$

The variation of the variate within this cell is

$$E_{yy_{jk}} = \sum_i (Y_{ijk} - \overline{AB}_{y_{jk}})^2.$$

The covariation for this cell is

$$E_{xy_{jk}} = \sum_i (X_{ijk} - \overline{AB}_{x_{jk}})(Y_{ijk} - \overline{AB}_{y_{jk}}).$$

The pooled within-cell variations are given by

$$E_{xx} = \sum E_{xx_{jk}}, \qquad E_{yy} = \sum E_{yy_{jk}}, \qquad E_{xy} = \sum E_{xy_{jk}}.$$

From the data within cell ab_{jk}, the regression coefficient for the regression of Y on X is

$$b_{E_{jk}} = \frac{E_{xy_{jk}}}{E_{xx_{jk}}}.$$

The residual about this regression line within cell ab_{jk} is

$$E'_{yy_{jk}} = E_{yy_{jk}} - \frac{E^2_{xy_{jk}}}{E_{xx_{jk}}}.$$

Under the hypothesis that

$$\beta_{E_{11}} = \beta_{E_{12}} = \cdots = \beta_{E_{pq}} = \beta_E,$$

that is, homogeneity of the within-cell regressions, an estimate of β_E is

$$b_E = \frac{E_{xy}}{E_{xx}}.$$

The within-class regression lines, based upon the pooled within-class estimate of the regression coefficient, have the form

$$\hat{Y}_{ijk} = b_E(X_{ijk} - \overline{AB}_x) + \overline{AB}_{y_{jk}}.$$

The variation of the residuals about these lines is

$$D = E'_{yy} = E_{yy} - b_E E_{xy} = E_{yy} - \frac{E_{xy}^2}{E_{xx}}.$$

If factors A and B are fixed, this source of variation is an estimate of experimental error in the analysis of covariance; its form is identical to the corresponding term in a single-factor experiment.

Equivalently, E'_{yy} is the error variation associated with the model

$$Y_{ijk} = (\alpha + \beta X_{ijk}) + \tau_{jk} + \varepsilon_{ijk},$$

where

$$\tau_{jk} = \alpha_j + \beta_k + \alpha\beta_{jk}.$$

If one restricts this model to the case in which

$$\alpha_j = 0, \qquad\qquad j = 1, 2, \ldots, p,$$

then the variation due to error in the restricted model may be shown to be

$$D'_a = (A_{yy} + E_{yy}) - \frac{(A_{xy} + E_{xy})^2}{A_{xx} + E_{xx}}.$$

The restricted model is the one which corresponds to the hypothesis that all $\alpha_j = 0$. A measure of deviation from hypothesis is given by

$$A'_{yy} = D'_a - D = A_{yy} - \frac{(A_{xy} + E_{xy})^2}{A_{xx} + E_{xx}} + \frac{E_{xy}^2}{E_{xx}}.$$

In terms of the notation system used for a single-factor experiment,

$$A'_{yy} = A_{yyR}.$$

The "prime" symbol will be used throughout this section and those that follow on factorial experiments to imply the reduced variation.

If one restricts the model in the preceding paragraph so that $\beta_k = 0$ (for all k), then the variation due to error is

$$D'_b = (B_{yy} + E_{yy}) - \frac{(B_{xy} + E_{xy})^2}{B_{xx} + E_{xx}}.$$

A measure of deviation from the hypothesis that $\beta_k = 0$ is thus

$$B'_{yy} = D'_b - D = B_{yy} - \frac{(B_{xy} + E_{xy})^2}{B_{xx} + E_{xx}} + \frac{E_{xy}^2}{E_{xx}}.$$

Similarly, if the model is restricted to the case in which all $\alpha\beta_{jk}$ are set equal to zero, the variation due to error is

$$D'_{ab} = (AB_{yy} + E_{yy}) - \frac{(AB_{xy} + E_{xy})^2}{AB_{xx} + E_{xx}}.$$

A measure of deviation from hypothesis with respect to the interaction effects is

$$AB'_{yy} = D'_{ab} - D = AB_{yy} - \frac{(AB_{xy} + E_{xy})^2}{AB_{xx} + E_{xx}} + \frac{E_{xy}^2}{E_{xx}}.$$

Each of the variations due to deviation from hypothesis has the general form

$$S_\omega - S_\Omega,$$

where S_ω = variation due to error under model restricted to correspond to case in which a specified hypothesis is true,

S_Ω = variation due to error under no restrictions on model.

The analysis of variance is contrasted with the analysis of covariance in Table 10.20. Assuming all factors fixed, MS'_{error} is the proper denominator for F tests on main effects and interaction. An approximation to the reduced sum of squares for main effects and interactions is

$$A''_{yy} = A_{yy} - 2b_E A_{xy} + b_E^2 A_{xx},$$

$$B''_{yy} = B_{yy} - 2b_E B_{xy} + b_E^2 B_{xx},$$

$$AB''_{yy} = AB_{yy} - 2b_E AB_{xy} + b_E^2 AB_{xx}.$$

In cases where the treatments do not affect the covariate and the bias in the treatment means associated with the covariate is not large, these approximations will be quite close.

The analysis of covariance model for a single observation on the variate is

$$Y_{ijk} = \mu + \beta(X_{ijk} - \bar{X}) + \alpha_j + \beta_k + \alpha\beta_{jk} + \varepsilon_{ijk}.$$

Hence the model for a cell mean in a two-factor factorial design with n units per cell is

$$\overline{AB}_{y_{jk}} = \mu + \beta(\overline{AB}_{x_{jk}} - \bar{X}) + \alpha_j + \beta_k + \alpha\beta_{jk} + \bar{\varepsilon}_{jk}.$$

One may rewrite this model in the form

$$\overline{AB}_{y_{jk}} - \beta(\overline{AB}_{x_{jk}} - \bar{X}) = \mu + \alpha_j + \beta_k + \alpha\beta_{jk} + \bar{\varepsilon}_{jk}.$$

The right-hand side of this last expression is the model for a cell mean in the analysis of variance. The left-hand side represents a residual obtained by

TABLE 10.20   **Summary of analysis of variance and analysis of covariance**

Source	Analysis of variance			Analysis of covariance		
	SS	df	MS	SS	df	MS
A	A_{yy}	$p-1$	MS_a	A'_{yy}	$p-1$	MS'_a
B	B_{yy}	$q-1$	MS_b	B'_{yy}	$q-1$	MS'_b
AB	AB_{yy}	$(p-1)(q-1)$	MS_{ab}	AB'_{yy}	$(p-1)(q-1)$	MS'_{ab}
Error	E_{yy}	$pq(n-1)$	MS_{error}	E'_{yy}	$pq(n-1)-1$	MS'_{error}

partialling out the linear effect of the covariate. An estimate of this residual is given by

$$\overline{AB}'_{y_{jk}} = \overline{AB}_{y_{jk}} - b_E(\overline{AB}_{x_{jk}} - \bar{X}).$$

Equivalently, if

$$Y'_{ijk} = Y_{ijk} - b_E(X_{ijk} - \bar{X}),$$

then

$$\overline{AB}'_{y_{jk}} = \frac{\sum_i Y'_{ijk}}{n}.$$

$\overline{AB}'_{jk}$ is called the adjusted cell mean. It is seen to be the mean of the residuals in cell ab_{jk}, where the residuals have the form Y'_{ijk}.

An adjusted marginal mean is defined as follows:

$$\bar{A}'_{y_j} = \bar{A}_{y_j} - b_E(\bar{A}_{x_j} - \bar{X}) = \frac{\sum_k \overline{AB}'_{y_{jk}}}{q}.$$

Thus $\bar{A}'_{y_j}$ may be obtained by adjusting $\bar{A}_{y_j}$ or by taking the mean of the adjusted cell means at level a_j. Similarly,

$$\bar{B}'_{y_k} = \bar{B}_{y_k} - b_E(\bar{B}_{x_k} - \bar{X}) = \frac{\sum_j \overline{AB}'_{y_{ik}}}{p}.$$

In terms of the model for a cell mean one has

$$E(\overline{AB}'_{y_{jk}}) = E[\overline{AB}_{y_{jk}} - b_E(\overline{AB}_{x_{jk}} - \bar{X})] = \mu + \alpha_j + \beta_k + \alpha\beta_{jk}$$

since $E(\bar{\varepsilon}_{jk}) = 0$. Similarly,

$$E(\bar{A}'_{y_j}) = E[\bar{A}_{y_j} - b_E(\bar{A}_{x_j} - \bar{X})] = \mu + \alpha_j,$$

$$E(\bar{B}'_{y_k}) = \mu + \beta_j,$$

$$E(\overline{AB}'_{y_{jk}} - \bar{A}'_{y_j} - \bar{B}'_{y_k} + \bar{Y}) = \alpha\beta_{jk}.$$

If one wishes to examine the variations of the adjusted variates, then let

$$A''_{yy} = nq \sum (\bar{A}_{y_j} - \bar{Y})^2$$

$$= nq \sum [\bar{A}_y - \bar{Y} - b_E(A_{x_j} - \bar{X})^2]$$

$$= A_{yy} + b_E^2 A_{xx} - 2b_E A_{xy}.$$

A''_{yy} corresponds to T_{yyA} in a single-factor design. A''_{yy} will always be larger than

A'_{yy}; however, when the differences between the covariate means are small, A''_{yy} will be quite close to A'_{yy}. By analogy,

$$B''_{yy} = np \sum (\bar{B}'_{yk} - \bar{Y})^2 = B_{yy} + b_E^2 B_{xx} - 2b_E B_{xy}$$

$$AB''_{yy} = AB_{yy} + b_E^2 AB_{xx} - 2b_E AB_{xy}$$

$$E''_{yy} = E_{yy} + b_E^2 E_{xx} - 2b_E E_{xy}$$

$$= E_{yy} + \frac{E_{xy}^2}{E_{xx}} - 2\frac{E_{xy}^2}{E_{xx}}$$

$$= E_{yy} - \frac{E_{xy}^2}{E_{xx}} = E'_{yy}.$$

One also notes that

$$A''_{yy} + B''_{yy} + AB''_{yy} + E''_{yy} = S_{yy} + b_E^2 S_{xx} - 2b_E S_{xy},$$

where

$$S_{yy} = \sum (Y_{ijk} - \bar{Y})^2$$

$$S_{xy} = \sum (Y_{ijk} - \bar{Y})(X_{ijk} - \bar{X})$$

$$S_{xx} = \sum (X_{ijk} - \bar{X})^2.$$

A comparison among the adjusted cell means has the form

$$\hat{\psi} = \sum \sum c_{jk} \overline{AB}'_{y_{jk}} \qquad \left(\sum \sum c_{jk} = 0 \right).$$

The estimate of the squared standard error of this comparison is

$$s_{\hat{\psi}}^2 = \mathrm{MS}'_{\mathrm{error}} \left[\frac{\sum \sum c_{jk}^2}{n} + \frac{(\sum \sum c_{jk} \overline{AB}_{x_{jk}})^2}{E_{xx}} \right].$$

For the special case of a simple comparison of the form

$$\hat{\psi}_1 = \overline{AB}'_{y_{jk}} - \overline{AB}'_{y_{j'k'}}.$$

the squared standard error reduces to

$$s_{\hat{\psi}_1}^2 = \mathrm{MS}'_{\mathrm{error}} \left[\frac{2}{n} + \frac{(\overline{AB}_{x_{jk}} - \overline{AB}_{x_{j'k'}})^2}{E_{xx}} \right].$$

Another comparison of special interest is one between adjusted A means,

$$\hat{\psi}_2 = \bar{A}'_{y_j} - \bar{A}'_{y_{j'}} = \frac{1}{q} \sum_k \overline{AB}'_{y_{jk}} - \frac{1}{q} \sum_k \overline{AB}'_{y_{j'k}}.$$

The squared standard error for this type of comparison reduces to

$$s_{\hat{\psi}_2}^2 = \mathrm{MS}'_{\mathrm{error}} \left[\frac{2}{nq} + \frac{(\bar{A}_{x_j} - \bar{A}_{x_{j'}})^2}{E_{xx}} \right].$$

More generally, if the comparison has the form

$$\hat{\psi} = \sum c_j \bar{A}'_{y_j},$$

then the squared standard error is equal to

$$s^2_{\hat{\psi}} = MS'_{error}\left[\frac{\sum c_j^2}{nq} + \frac{(\sum c_j \bar{A}'_{x_j})^2}{E_{xx}}\right].$$

For a comparison among the adjusted B means,

$$\hat{\psi} = \sum c_k \bar{B}'_{y_k},$$

and

$$s^2_{\hat{\psi}} = MS'_{error}\left[\frac{\sum c_k^2}{np} + \frac{(\sum c_k \bar{B}'_{x_k})^2}{E_{xx}}\right].$$

For the special case of a simple comparison,

$$\hat{\psi}_3 = \bar{B}'_{y_k} - \bar{B}'_{y_{k'}},$$

and the squared standard error reduces to

$$s^2_{\psi_3} = MS'_{error}\left[\frac{2}{np} - \frac{(\bar{B}'_{x_k} - \bar{B}'_{x_{k'}})^2}{E_{xx}}\right].$$

The variances of comparisons may all be used to construct t or F statistics to be used for procedures to test hypotheses concerning adjusted cell, A or B means. For such purposes,

$$F = \frac{\hat{\psi}^2}{s^2_{\hat{\psi}}}$$

is an F distribution with degrees of freedom equal to 1 and the degrees of freedom of MS'_{error}, $pq(n-1) - 1$. Since $t^2 = F$ when F has a single degree of freedom in the numerator,

$$t = \frac{\hat{\psi}}{\sqrt{s^2_{\hat{\psi}}}} = t[pq(n-1) - 1].$$

For example, to test the *a priori* hypothesis,

$$H_0: \sum c_j \alpha_j = 0, \quad \left(\sum c_j = 0\right),$$

the appropriate test statistic is

$$F = \frac{(\sum c_j \bar{A}'_{y_j})^2}{s^2_{\hat{\psi}}}.$$

When the hypothesis being tested is true, this F statistic is distributed as

$$F[1, pq(n-1) - 1],$$

provided the distribution assumptions underlying the model hold.

As an example, consider the following hypothesis in a 3×2 factorial analysis of covariance:

$$H_0: \psi = 2\alpha_3 - \alpha_1 - \alpha_2 = 0.$$

An estimate of ψ is given by

$$\hat{\psi} = 2\bar{A}'_{y_3} - \bar{A}'_{y_1} - \bar{A}'_{y_2}.$$

In terms of the adjusted cell means

$$\hat{\psi} = 2\frac{(\overline{AB}'_{y_{31}} + \overline{AB}'_{y_{32}})}{2} - \frac{(\overline{AB}'_{y_{11}} + \overline{AB}'_{y_{12}})}{2} - \frac{(\overline{AB}'_{y_{21}} + \overline{AB}'_{y_{22}})}{2}.$$

The estimate of the squared standard error of this comparison is

$$s_{\hat{\psi}}^2 = MS'_{error}\left[\frac{6}{2n} + \frac{(2\bar{A}'_{x_3} - \bar{A}'_{x_1} - \bar{A}'_{x_2})^2}{E_{xx}}\right].$$

Note that $\sum c_j^2 = 4 + 1 + 1 = 6$. The number of basic observations in $\bar{A}_y$ is $nq = 2n$. Hence the F statistic in this test is

$$F = \frac{(2\bar{A}'_{y_3} - \bar{A}'_{y_1} - \bar{A}'_{y_2})^2}{MS'_{error}\left[\frac{6}{2n} + \frac{(2\bar{A}'_{x_3} - \bar{A}'_{x_1} - \bar{A}'_{x_2})^2}{E_{xx}}\right]}.$$

For purposes of applying techniques for making multiple comparisons among differences of the form $\bar{A}'_{y_j} - \bar{A}'_{y_{j'}}$ one may use the squared error averaged over all values of $\bar{A}_{x_j} - \bar{A}_{x_{j'}}$ which is given by

$$\frac{2MS'_{error}}{nq}\left[1 + \frac{A_{xx}/(p-1)}{E_{xx}}\right].$$

For multiple comparisons among pairs of $\bar{B}'_{y_k}$ or $\overline{AB}'_{y_{jk}}$, the squared standard errors would be

$$\frac{2MS'_{error}}{np}\left[1 + \frac{B_{xx}/q-1}{E_{xx}}\right],$$

and

$$\frac{2MS'_{error}}{n}\left[1 + \frac{AB_{xx}/(p-1)(q-1)}{E_{xx}}\right],$$

respectively.

For procedures which use the q statistic, such as the Tukey and Newman–Keuls procedures, the squared standard errors of a single $\bar{A}'_{y_j}$, $\bar{B}'_{y_k}$, or $\overline{AB}'_{y_{jk}}$ averaged over all $\bar{A}_{x_j}$, $\bar{B}_{x_j}$, or $\overline{AB}_{x_{jk}}$, are

$$\frac{MS'_{error}}{nq}\left[1 + \frac{A_{xx}/p-1}{E_{xx}}\right],$$

$$\frac{MS'_{error}}{np}\left[1 + \frac{B_{xx}/q-1}{E_{xx}}\right],$$

and

$$\frac{\text{MS}'_{\text{error}}}{n}\left[1 + \frac{AB_{xx}/(p-1)(q-1)}{E_{xx}}\right],$$

respectively.

Test for Homogeneity of Internal Regressions

In the factorial design, the pooled within-class regression coefficient is used to obtain $\bar{A}'_y$, $\bar{B}'_y$, and $\overline{AB}'_y$. Implicit in this adjustment process is the assumption that b_E is the appropriate regression coefficient for all of these adjustments.

The test for homogeneity of the within-class regression coefficients in a factorial design is quite similar to the corresponding test in a single-factor design. In making a test for homogeneity of within-cell regression, the error term may be partitioned as follows:

Source	df
$E'_{yy} = E_{yy} - (E^2_{xy}/E_{xx})$	$pq(n-1) - 1$
$S_1 = E_{yy} - \sum\sum (E^2_{xy_{jk}}/E_{xx_{jk}})$	$pq(n-2)$
$S_2 = \sum\sum (E^2_{xy_{jk}}/E_{xx_{jk}}) - (E^2_{xy}/E_{xx})$	$pq - 1$

In this partition, E'_{yy} represents the variation due to error in a model which assumes homogeneity of regressions. It is the variation of individual observations about that common regression line. S_1 represents variation due to error in a model which does not assume homogeneity of the within-cell regressions. It is the variation of the observations about the pq individual within-cell regression lines. S_2 is a measure of the deviation from the hypothesis of homogeneity of regressions, $E_{yy} - S_1$. It is the variation of the individual within-cell regression coefficients about the pooled within-class regression coefficient b_E. The degrees of freedom are

$$[pq(n-1) - 1] - [pq(n-2)] = pq - 1.$$

The test for homogeneity of within-class regression uses the statistic

$$F = \frac{S_2/(pq-1)}{S_1/pq(n-2)}$$

$$= \frac{(\sum\sum b_{E_{jk}}E_{xy_{jk}} - b_E E_{xy})/(pq-1)}{(E_{yy} - \sum\sum b_{E_{jk}}E_{xy_{jk}})/[pq(n-2)]}.$$

When the hypothesis of homogeneity of internal regressions is true this F statistic is distributed as

$$F[pq - 1, pq(n-2)].$$

In most experimental situations in the behavioral sciences, the underlying model is probably much more complex than is implied by this model. Caution in the use of covariates in a factorial design is advised. The model for the analysis outlined in this section is a highly restrictive one. One should be aware of the existence of such designs but one should also be aware of their weaknesses as well as their strengths.

Computational Procedures for Factorial Experiment

Computational procedures for the analysis of covariance for a $p \times q$ factorial experiment having n observations per cell will be considered first. The case of unequal cell frequencies is considered later in this section, where the equivalent of an unweighted-means analysis is outlined. Procedures in this latter case require relatively small changes from those to be given for the case of equal cell frequencies.

Assuming n pairs of observations in each of the pq cells, computational formulas for the sums of squares needed in the analysis of covariance are given in Table 10.21. In each case, the range of summation is over all possible values of the total that are squared and summed. Symbols $(1x)$ through $(5x)$ are those

TABLE 10.21 Computational formulas for the analysis of covariance in a factorial experiment

(i)

$$(1x) = G_x^2/npq \qquad (1xy) = G_x G_y/npq \qquad (1y) = G_y^2/npq$$

$$(2x) = \sum X^2 \qquad (2xy) = \sum XY \qquad (2y) = \sum Y^2$$

$$(3x) = \left(\sum A_x^2\right)/nq \qquad (3xy) = \left(\sum A_x A_y\right)/nq \qquad (3y) = \left(\sum A_y^2\right)/nq$$

$$(4x) = \left(\sum B_x^2\right)/np \qquad (4xy) = \left(\sum B_x B_y\right)/np \qquad (4y) = \left(\sum B_y^2\right)/np$$

$$(5x) = \left(\sum AB_x^2\right)/n \qquad (5xy) = \left(\sum AB_x AB_y\right)/n \qquad (5y) = \left(\sum AB_y^2\right)/n$$

(ii)

$$A_{xx} = (3x) - (1x) \qquad A_{xy} = (3xy) - (1xy) \qquad A_{yy} = (3y) - (1y)$$

$$B_{xx} = (4x) - (1x) \qquad B_{xy} = (4xy) - (1xy) \qquad B_{yy} = (4y) - (1y)$$

$$AB_{xx} = (5x) - (3x) \qquad AB_{xy} = (5xy) - (3xy) \qquad AB_{yy} = (5y) - (3y)$$

$$\qquad - (4x) + (1x) \qquad \qquad - (4xy) + (1xy) \qquad \qquad - (4y) + (1y)$$

$$E_{xx} = (2x) - (5x) \qquad E_{xy} = (2xy) - (5xy) \qquad E_{yy} = (2y) - (5y)$$

(iii)

$$E'_{yy} = E_{yy} - (E_{xy}^2/E_{xx})$$

$$(A + E)'_{yy} = (A_{yy} + E_{yy}) - \frac{(A_{xy} + E_{xy})^2}{A_{xx} + E_{xx}}, \qquad A'_{yy} = (A + E)'_{yy} - E'_{yy}$$

$$(B + E)'_{yy} = (B_{yy} + E_{yy}) - \frac{(B_{xy} + E_{xy})^2}{B_{xx} + E_{xx}}, \qquad B'_{yy} = (B + E)'_{yy} - E'_{yy}$$

$$(AB + E)'_{yy} = (AB_{yy} + E_{yy}) - \frac{(AB_{xy} + E_{xy})^2}{(AB_{xx} + E_{xx})}, \qquad AB'_{yy} = (AB + E)'_{yy} - E'_{yy}$$

used in an analysis of variance on the covariate. Symbols $(1y)$ through $(5y)$ are those used in the usual analysis of variance on the criterion. Symbols $(1xy)$ through $(5xy)$ are used to estimate the covariances needed in the adjustment process.

A 2×3 factorial experiment having $n = 5$ observations per cell will be used to illustrate the computational procedures. Suppose that the $p = 2$ levels of factor A represent methods of instructing in teaching map reading, and suppose that the $q = 3$ levels of factor B represent three instructors. For purposes of the present analysis, both factors are considered to be fixed. The covariate measure in this experiment is the score on an achievement test on map reading prior to the training; the criterion measure is the score on a comparable form of the achievement test after training is completed. Assume that intact groups of $n = 5$ subjects each are assigned at random to the cells of the experiment. Suppose that data obtained from this experiment are those given in the upper part of Table 10.22.

TABLE 10.22 **Numerical example**

Method	b_1 Instr. 1		b_2 Instr. 2		b_2 Instr. 3	
	X	Y	X	Y	X	Y
	40	95	30	85	50	90
	35	80	40	100	40	85
a_1	40	95	45	85	40	90
	50	105	40	90	30	80
	45	100	40	90	40	85
	50	100	50	100	45	95
	30	95	30	90	30	85
a_2	35	95	40	95	25	75
	45	110	45	90	50	105
	30	88	40	95	35	85

AB summary:

	b_1		b_2		b_3		Total	
	X	Y	X	Y	X	Y	X	Y
a_1	210	475	195	450	200	430	605	1355
a_2	190	488	205	470	185	445	580	1403
Total	400	963	400	920	385	875	1185	2758

$$
\begin{aligned}
&(1x) = 46{,}808 && (1xy) = 108{,}941 && (1y) = 253{,}552 \\
&(2x) = 48{,}325 && (2xy) = 110{,}065 && (2y) = 255{,}444 \\
&(3x) = 46{,}828 && (3xy) = 108{,}901 && (3y) = 253{,}629 \\
&(4x) = 46{,}822 && (4xy) = 109{,}008 && (4y) = 253{,}939 \\
&(5x) = 46{,}895 && (5xy) = 108{,}979 && (5y) = 254{,}019
\end{aligned}
$$

In this table, for example, the first subject under method a_1 and b_2 has scores of 30 and 85, respectively, on the covariate and the criterion.

In symbols,

$$X_{121} = 30, \qquad Y_{121} = 85.$$

An AB summary table appears under the observed data. There are two entries in each cell of this table—one represents the sum of the observations on the covariate, the other the sum for the criterion. For example, the sum of the $n = 5$ observations on the covariate under treatment combination ab_{12} is

$$AB_{x_{12}} = 30 + 40 + 45 + 40 + 40 = 195.$$

The corresponding sum for the criterion data is

$$AB_{y_{12}} = 85 + 100 + 85 + 90 + 90 = 450.$$

The entries in the total columns at the right of the AB summary table are the sums of corresponding entries in the rows. For example,

$$A_{x_1} = \sum_k AB_{x_{1k}} = 210 + 195 + 200 = 605.$$

The corresponding sum for the criterion data is

$$A_{y_1} = \sum_k AB_{y_{1k}} = 475 + 450 + 430 = 1355.$$

The total of the first column in the summary table is

$$B_{x_1} = \sum_j AB_{x_{j1}} = 210 + 190 = 400.$$

The corresponding sum for the criterion is

$$B_{y_1} = \sum_j AB_{y_{j1}} = 475 + 488 = 963.$$

The grand totals for the covariate and the criterion are

$$G_x = \sum A_{x_j} = \sum B_{x_k} = 1185,$$
$$G_y = \sum A_{y_j} = \sum B_{y_k} = 2758.$$

The computational symbols in the lower part of Table 10.22 are defined in part i of Table 10.21. The only symbols requiring special comment are those in the center column. These entries are obtained as follows:

$$(1xy) = \frac{(1185)(2758)}{30},$$

$$(2xy) = (40)(95) + (35)(80) + \cdots + (50)(105) + (35)(85),$$

$$(3xy) = \frac{(605)(1355) + (580)(1403)}{15},$$

$$(4xy) = \frac{(400)(963) + (400)(920) + (385)(875)}{10},$$

$$(5xy) = \frac{(210)(475) + (190)(488) + \cdots + (185)(445)}{5}$$

TABLE 10.23   **Summary data for numerical example**

$A_{xx} = 21$	$A_{xy} = -40$	$A_{yy} = 77$
$B_{xx} = 15$	$B_{xy} = 67$	$B_{yy} = 387$
$AB_{xx} = 52$	$AB_{xy} = 11$	$AB_{yy} = 3$
$E_{xx} = 1430$	$E_{xy} = 1086$	$E_{yy} = 1425$
1518	1124	1892

$$E'_{yy} = 1425 - (1086^2/1430)$$
$$= 600$$

$(A + E)'_{yy} = 748$	$A'_{yy} = 748 - 600 = 148$
$(B + E)'_{yy} = 892$	$B'_{yy} = 892 - 600 = 292$
$(AB + E)'_{yy} = 616$	$AB'_{yy} = 616 - 600 = 16$

The basic data for all these symbols except $(2xy)$ are obtained from the AB summary table.

Sums of squares and sums of products are given in Table 10.23. Computational formulas for these terms are given in parts ii and iii of Table 10.21. Note that it is possible for the entries that are used to obtain covariances to be either positive or negative. In this case the between-class covariation of the totals corresponding to the main effects of factor A is negative (-40). Inspection of the total columns at the right of the AB summary in Table 10.22 indicates that the higher criterion total is paired with the lower covariate total; hence the negative covariation.

The analysis of variance for the criterion data is summarized in Table 10.24. This analysis disregards the presence of the covariate. Differences between the methods of training are tested by means of the statistic

$$F = \frac{77}{59.4} = 1.30.$$

(The instructor factor is considered to be fixed.) This test indicates no statistically significant difference between the methods insofar as the mean of the groups is concerned.

The analysis of covariance is summarized in Table 10.25. Note that the error mean square in this case is 26.1, compared with 59.4 in the case of the

TABLE 10.24   **Analysis of variance**

Source	SS	df	MS	F
A Methods	$A_{yy} = 77$	1	77	1.30
B Instructors	$B_{yy} = 387$	2	193.5	3.26
AB	$AB_{yy} = 3$	2	1.5	
Error	$E_{yy} = 1425$	24	59.4	
Total	1892	29		

$$F_{0.95}(2, 24) = 3.40$$

TABLE 10.25 **Analysis of covariance**

Source	SS	df	MS	F
A Methods	$A'_{yy} = 148$	1	148.0	5.67
B Instructors	$B'_{yy} = 292$	2	146.0	5.59
AB	$AB'_{yy} = 16$	2	8.0	
Error	$E'_{yy} = 600$	23	26.1	
		28		

$$F_{0.95}(1, 23) = 4.28; \ F_{0.95}(2, 23) = 3.44$$

analysis of variance. Further note that the adjusted method mean square is 148, compared with 77 in the analysis of variance. This increase in the adjusted method variance is a function of the negative covariance for the between-method totals. A 0.05-level test on the methods in the analysis of covariance indicates statistically significant differences between the criterion means. Thus, when a linear adjustment is made for the effect of variation due to differences in prior experience in map reading, as measured by the covariate, there are statistically significant differences between the training methods.

An estimate of the square of the within-cell correlation is

$$r^2_{\text{within}} = \frac{E^2_{xy}/E_{xx}}{E_{yy}} = \frac{(1086)^2/1430}{1425} = 0.5788.$$

The mean square due to experimental error in the analysis of covariance is

$$\text{MS}'_{\text{error}} = \text{MS}_{\text{error}}(1 - r^2_{\text{within}}) \frac{pq(n - 1)}{pq(n - 1) - 1}$$
$$= 59.375(0.4212)(24/23) = 26.10.$$

The adjusted cell and marginal means are given in Table 10.26. Since the cell and marginal means on X do not vary appreciably, the adjusted means on Y differ relatively little from the unadjusted means. In the table the adjusted marginal means are obtained by taking the mean of the corresponding adjusted cell means. For example,

$$\bar{A}'_{y_1} = \frac{\sum \overline{AB}'_{y_{1k}}}{3} = 89.70.$$

This adjusted marginal mean is also given by

$$\bar{A}'_{y_1} = \bar{A}_{y_1} - b_E(\bar{A}_{x_1} - \bar{X})$$
$$= 90.33 - (0.7594)(40.33 - 39.50)$$
$$= 89.70.$$

Since the analysis of covariance indicates that the interaction is negligible

TABLE 10.26   **Adjusted cell and marginal means**

$$\overline{AB}'_{y_{jk}} = \overline{AB}_{y_{jk}} - b_E(\overline{AB}_{x_{jk}} - \bar{G}_x)$$
$$= \overline{AB}_{y_{jk}} - 0.7549(\overline{AB}_{x_{jk}} - 39.50)$$

	b_1	b_2	b_3	
a_1	$\overline{AB}_{x_{11}} = 42.00$ $\overline{AB}_{y_{11}} = 95.00$ $\overline{AB}'_{y_{11}} = 93.10$	$\overline{AB}_{x_{12}} = 39.00$ $\overline{AB}_{y_{12}} = 90.00$ $\overline{AB}'_{y_{12}} = 90.38$	$\overline{AB}_{x_{13}} = 40.00$ $\overline{AB}_{y_{13}} = 86.00$ $\overline{AB}'_{y_{13}} = 85.62$	$\bar{A}_{x_1} = 40.33$ $\bar{A}_{y_1} = 90.33$ $\bar{A}'_{y_1} = 89.70$
a_2	$\overline{AB}_{x_{21}} = 38.00$ $\overline{AB}_{y_{21}} = 97.60$ $\overline{AB}'_{y_{21}} = 98.74$	$\overline{AB}_{x_{22}} = 41.00$ $\overline{AB}_{y_{22}} = 94.00$ $\overline{AB}'_{y_{22}} = 92.86$	$\overline{AB}_{x_{23}} = 37.00$ $\overline{AB}_{y_{23}} = 89.00$ $\overline{AB}'_{y_{23}} = 93.94$	$\bar{A}_{x_2} = 38.67$ $\bar{A}_{y_2} = 93.53$ $\bar{A}'_{y_2} = 94.16$
	$\bar{B}_{x_1} = 40.00$ $\bar{B}_{y_1} = 96.30$ $\bar{B}'_{y_1} = 95.92$	$\bar{B}_{x_2} = 40.00$ $\bar{B}_{y_2} = 92.00$ $\bar{B}'_{y_2} = 91.62$	$\bar{B}_{x_2} = 38.50$ $\bar{B}_{y_3} = 87.50$ $\bar{B}'_{y_3} = 88.26$	$\bar{G}_x = 39.50$ $\bar{G}_y = 91.93$ $\bar{G}'_y = 91.93$

$(F = 0.28)$, one may restrict attention to the marginal means. To illustrate procedures for testing an *a priori* comparison, suppose one wanted to test the following statistical hypothesis:

$$H_0: \psi = 2\beta_1 - \beta_2 - \beta_3 = 0 \qquad H_1: \psi \neq 0 \qquad \alpha = 0.05.$$

An estimate of ψ is given by

$$\hat{\psi} = 2\bar{B}'_{y_1} - \bar{B}'_{y_2} - \bar{B}'_{y_3}$$
$$= 2(95.92) - 91.62 - 88.26 = 11.96.$$

An estimate of the squared standard error of this comparison is

$$s_{\hat{\psi}}^2 = MS'_{error}\left[\frac{\sum c_k^2}{np} + \frac{(2\bar{B}_{x_1} - \bar{B}_{x_2} - \bar{B}_{x_3})^2}{E_{xx}}\right]$$
$$= 26.11\left[\frac{6}{10} + \frac{(80.00 - 40.00 - 38.50)^2}{1430.00}\right]$$
$$= 26.11[0.60 + 0.16]$$
$$= 19.84.$$

The test statistic is

$$F = \frac{\hat{\psi}^2}{s_{\hat{\psi}}^2} = \frac{(11.96)^2}{19.84} = 7.21.$$

The critical value in this case is

$$F_{0.95}(1, 23) = 4.28.$$

Hence the experimental data contradict the hypothesis that the comparison in H_0 is equal to zero.

If one were to use the Tukey (a) procedure for testing the difference between the largest and smallest of the adjusted treatment means for factor B, the test statistic would be

$$q = \frac{95.92 - 88.26}{\sqrt{MS'_{error}\left[\frac{2}{10} + \frac{(40.00 - 38.50)^2}{E_{xx}}\right]\Big/2}}$$

$$= \frac{7.66}{\sqrt{26.11[0.20 + 0.002]/2}} = \frac{7.66}{1.62} = 4.73.$$

The critical value in this case is

$$q_{0.95}(r = 3, 23) = 3.56.$$

If one were to use the Scheffé procedure for making the same test as in the last paragraph, the test statistic would be

$$F = \frac{(95.92 - 88.26)^2}{MS'_{error}\left[\frac{2}{10} + \frac{(40.00 - 38.50)^2}{1430.00}\right]}$$

$$= \frac{(7.66)^2}{26.11[0.20 + 0.002]} = \frac{(7.66)^2}{5.27} = 11.12.$$

The critical value in this case is

$$2F_{0.95}[2, 23] = 2(3.42) = 6.84.$$

To put the Tukey (a) and the Scheffé procedures in terms of comparable units, the Tukey (a) decision rule may be cast in the form

Reject H_0 if

$$95.92 - 88.26 = 7.66 > (1.62)(3.56) = 5.77.$$

The Scheffé decision rule for this example takes the form

Reject H_0 if

$$95.92 - 88.26 = 7.66 > \sqrt{(5.27)(6.84)} = 6.00.$$

As is usually the case with simple comparisons, the Scheffé procedure gives the larger critical value.

If one were to use the Newman–Keuls procedure for testing all ordered differences among the adjusted treatment means for levels of factor B, the approximate critical values would be

$$q_{1-\alpha}(r, 23)\sqrt{\frac{MS'_{error}}{np}\left[1 + \frac{B_{xx}/(q-1)}{E_{xx}}\right]}.$$

TABLE 10.27 **Approximate analysis of covariance**

	Approximation	Approximate SS	Exact SS
	$A''_{yy} = A_{yy} + b_E^2 A_{xx} - 2b_E A_{xy}$	149.56	147.42
	$B''_{yy} = B_{yy} + b_E^2 B_{xx} - 2b_E B_{xy}$	294.92	292.81
	$AB''_{yy} = AB_{yy} + b_E^2 AB_{xx} - 2b_E AB_{xy}$	14.93	14.41
	$E'_{yy} = E_{yy} + b_E^2 E_{xx} - 2b_E E_{xy}$	600.45	600.45

The approximate analysis of covariance is compared with the usual analysis of covariance in Table 10.27. Since there is relatively little variation among the cell means on the covariate, the approximation and the usual method of analysis yield almost identical results. E'_{yy} will always be identical in both analyses.

Unequal Cell Frequencies—Unweighted-Means Analysis

Under the conditions for which the unweighted-means analysis is appropriate in a factorial design which does not include a covariate, there is an equivalent unweighted-means analysis for the analysis of covariance. The computational

TABLE 10.28 **Computational formulas (unequal cell frequencies)**

Notation:			b_1		b_2		b_3		Total	
$\overline{AB}_{x_{jk}} = AB_{x_{jk}}/n_{jk}$	a_1		$\overline{AB}_{x_{11}}$	$\overline{AB}_{y_{11}}$	$\overline{AB}_{x_{12}}$	$\overline{AB}_{y_{12}}$	$\overline{AB}_{x_{13}}$	$\overline{AB}_{y_{13}}$	A_{x_1}	A_{y_1}
$\overline{AB}_{y_{jk}} = AB_{y_{jk}}/n_{jk}$	a_2		$\overline{AB}_{x_{21}}$	$\overline{AB}_{y_{21}}$	$\overline{AB}_{x_{22}}$	$\overline{AB}_{y_{22}}$	$\overline{AB}_{x_{23}}$	$\overline{AB}_{y_{23}}$	A_{x_2}	A_{y_2}
		Total	B_{x_1}	B_{y_1}	B_{x_2}	B_{y_2}	B_{x_3}	B_{y_3}	G_x	G_y

(i)	$(1x) = \tilde{n}G_x^2/pq$	$(1xy) = \tilde{n}G_xG_y/pq$	$(1y) = \tilde{n}G_y^2/pq$
	$(2x) = \sum X^2$	$(2xy) = \sum XY$	$(2y) = \sum Y^2$
	$(3x) = \tilde{n} \sum (A_x^2)/q$	$(3xy) = \tilde{n} \sum (A_xA_y)/q$	$(3y) = \tilde{n} \sum (A_y^2)/q$
	$(4x) = \tilde{n} \sum (B_x^2)/p$	$(4xy) = \tilde{n} \sum (B_xB_y)/p$	$(4y) = \tilde{n} \sum (B_y^2)/p$
	$(5x) = \tilde{n} \sum (\overline{AB}_x^2)$	$(5xy) = \tilde{n} \sum (\overline{AB}_x\overline{AB}_y)$	$(5y) = \tilde{n} \sum (\overline{AB}_y^2)$
	$(5'x) = \sum (AB_{x_{jk}}^2/n_{jk})$	$(5'xy) = \sum (AB_{x_{jk}}AB_{y_{jk}}/n_{jk})$	$(5'y) = \sum (AB_{y_{jk}}^2/n_{jk})$

(ii)	$A_{xx} = (3x) - (1x)$	$A_{xy} = (3xy) - (1xy)$	$A_{yy} = (3y) - (1y)$
	$B_{xx} = (4x) - (1x)$	$B_{xy} = (4xy) - (1xy)$	$B_{yy} = (4y) - (1y)$
	$AB_{xx} = (5x) - (3x)$	$AB_{xy} = (5xy) - (3xy)$	$AB_{yy} = (5y) - (3y)$
	$\quad - (4x) + (1x)$	$\quad - (4xy) + (1xy)$	$\quad - (4y) + (1y)$
	$E_{xx} = (2x) - (5'x)$	$E_{xy} = (2xy) - (5'xy)$	$E_{yy} = (2y) - (5'y)$

(iii)	Same as part iii of Table 10.21

procedures for a two-factor factorial experiment having one covariate are outlined in Table 10.28. These procedures are readily generalized to higher-order factorial experiments having one covariate.

If one considers the variate separately from the covariate, the procedures in Table 10.28 will produce an unweighted-means analysis of variance.

TABLE 10.29   **Unequal cell frequencies—numerical example**

(i)

		b_1		b_2		b_3	
		X	Y	X	Y	X	Y
		3	8	2	14	3	16
		5	16	1	11	2	10
a_1		1	10	8	20	1	14
		9	24	7	15	2	14
				4	12	6	22
						2	16
		7	18	0	8	0	10
		0	7	4	16	1	15
		4	10	8	20	9	26
a_2		6	15	5	18	4	18
		9	23			4	18
						7	26
						8	24

(ii)

n_{jk}:	b_1	b_2	b_3
a_1	4	5	6
a_2	5	4	7
$\bar{n} = 4.961$			

AB_{jk}:	b_1		b_2		b_3		Total	
	X	Y	X	Y	X	Y	X	Y
a_1	18	58	22	72	16	92	56	222
a_2	26	73	17	62	33	137	76	272
Total	44	131	39	134	49	229	132	494

$\overline{AB_{jk}}$:	b_1		b_2		b_3		Total	
	X	Y	X	Y	X	Y	X	Y
a_1	4.50	14.50	4.40	14.40	2.67	15.33	11.57	44.23
a_2	5.20	14.60	4.25	15.50	4.71	19.57	14.16	49.67
Total	9.70	29.10	8.65	29.90	7.38	34.90	25.73	93.90

(iii)

$(1x) = 547.39$	$(1xy) = 1997.67$	$(1y) = 7290.36$
$(2x) = 822$	$(2xy) = 2500$	$(2y) = 8742$
$(3x) = 552.94$	$(3xy) = 2009.32$	$(3y) = 7314.83$
$(4x) = 554.09$	$(4xy) = 1980.60$	$(4y) = 7339.38$
$(5x) = 565.68$	$(5xy) = 2001.82$	$(5y) = 7387.00$
$(5'x) = 583.49$	$(5'xy) = 2112.09$	$(5'y) = 7996.55$

Similarly, if the covariate were considered separately, one would have an unweighted-means analysis on the covariate.

The cell means for the variate and the covariate are given at the top of Table 10.28. The row and column totals for these cell means are also given. For example,

$$A_{x_1} = \sum_k \overline{AB}_{x_{1k}}, \qquad A_{y_1} = \sum_k \overline{AB}_{y_{1k}}.$$

The computational symbols are defined in part i. Here

$$\bar{n} = \frac{pq}{\sum (1/n_{ij})} = \text{harmonic mean of cell frequencies.}$$

The sums of squares and sums of products needed in the analysis of covariance are defined in terms of the computational symbols in part ii. Part ii in Table 10.28 is the same as part iii in Table 10.21.

A numerical example is worked in Table 10.29. In part i of this table are the basic data. The cell frequencies and the harmonic mean of the cell frequencies are given in part ii. The cell totals are also given in part ii. In the lower half of part ii are the cell means and the marginal totals for the cell means. It is from this part of the table that one computes most of the computational symbols defined in part i of Table 10.28. The numerical values of these symbols for the data in part i of Table 10.29 appear in part iii. For

TABLE 10.30 **Unequal cell frequencies—numerical example**

(i)

$A_{xx} = 5.55$	$A_{xy} = 11.65$	$A_{yy} = 24.47$
$B_{xx} = 6.70$	$B_{xy} = -17.07$	$B_{yy} = 49.02$
$AB_{xx} = 6.04$	$AB_{xy} = 9.57$	$AB_{yy} = 23.15$
$E_{xx} = 238.51$	$E_{xy} = 387.91$	$E_{yy} = 745.45$

(ii)

$$E'_{yy} = 745.45 - \frac{(387.91)^2}{238.51} = 114.56$$

$$(A+E)'_{yy} = 769.92 - \frac{(399.56)^2}{244.06} = 115.78 \qquad A'_{yy} = 1.22$$

$$(B+E)'_{yy} = 794.47 - \frac{(370.84)^2}{245.21} = 233.64 \qquad B'_{yy} = 119.08$$

$$(AB+E)'_{yy} = 768.60 - \frac{(397.48)^2}{244.55} = 122.55 \qquad AB'_{yy} = 7.99$$

(iii)

Source of variation	Analysis of variance				Analysis of covariance			
	SS	df	MS	F	SS	df	MS	F
A	24.47	1	24.47	0.82	1.22	1	1.22	0.26
B	49.02	2	24.51	0.82	119.08	2	59.54	12.48**
AB	23.15	2	11.58	0.39	7.99	2	4.00	0.84
Within cell	745.45	25	29.82		114.56	24	4.77	

example,

$$(1x) = \frac{\bar{n}G_x^2}{pq} = \frac{4.961(25.73)^2}{2(3)} = 547.39,$$

$$(1xy) = \frac{\bar{n}G_xG_y}{pq} = \frac{4.961(25.73)(93.90)}{2(3)} = 1997.67.$$

The analysis of covariance is summarized in Table 10.30. Part i of this table follows from part ii of Table 10.28. Part ii follows from part iii of Table 10.28. The resulting analysis of variance and analysis of covariance are summarized in part iii. The large increase in the F ratio for the main effects of factor B is due to the relatively large negative between-class covariance between the variate and covariate means for the levels of factor B.

10.5   ANALYSIS OF COVARIANCE—REPEATED MEASURES

The design to be considered in this section is the analog of the split-plot design in agricultural research. In the behavioral sciences area the covariance matrix for the repeated measures is very likely to be more complicated than the corresponding covariance structure assumed for the usual split-plot design. All of the assumptions for the usual repeated-measure design plus the added assumptions for the use of covariates underlie this design. In essence one has two separate covariance analyses—one for the between-subject effects, the other for the within-subject effects. The model for this design may be written in the form

$$Y'_{ijk} = Y_{ijk} - \beta_p(\overline{AB}_{x_{jk}} - \bar{G}_x) - \beta_w(X_{ijk} - \overline{AB}_{x_{jk}})$$
$$= \mu + \alpha_j + \pi_{i(j)} + \beta_k + \alpha\beta_{jk} + \beta\pi_{i(j)k} + \varepsilon_{ijk},$$

where β_p = between-subject regression coefficient,

β_w = within-subject regression coefficient.

In the special case when

$$\beta_p = \beta_w = \beta$$

then the model becomes

$$Y'_{ijk} = Y_{ijk} - \beta(X_{ijk} - \bar{G}_x) = \mu + \alpha_j + \pi_{i(j)} + \beta_k + \alpha\beta_{jk} + \beta\pi_{i(j)k} + \varepsilon_{ijk}.$$

The design may be represented schematically as shown at the left of Table 10.31. Assume that there are n subjects in each of the groups. The usual analysis of variance is summarized at the right, but the notation that is used in the analysis of covariance is incorporated into the summary. Adjustment procedures depend upon whether or not the between- and within-subject regression coefficients can be considered homogeneous. In the first part of the discussion that follows these regression coefficients are not assumed homogeneous.

TABLE 10.31   Factorial experiment, repeated measures

					Source	SS	df
					Between subjects		$np - 1$
	b_1	b_2	$\cdots$	b_q	A	A_{yy}	$p - 1$
					Subj w. gp	P_{yy}	$p(n - 1)$
a_1	G_1	G_1	$\cdots$	G_1	Within subjects		$np(q - 1)$
a_2	G_2	G_2	$\cdots$	G_2			
$\vdots$	$\vdots$		$\cdots$	$\vdots$	B	B_{yy}	$q - 1$
a_p	G_p	G_p		G_p	AB	AB_{yy}	$(p - 1)(q - 1)$
					Residual	E_{yy}	$p(q - 1)(n - 1)$
							$npq - 1$

For a two-factor design with repeated measures on factor B, there are two special cases. In case (1), a single covariate measure is associated with all Y measures on a single individual. In this case the observations on individual i at level a_j may be represented as follows:

	Individual		b_1	b_2	$\cdots$	b_q	Total
a_j	i	X_{ij}	Y_{ij1}	Y_{ij2}		Y_{ijq}	$P_{y_{ij}}$

Here the covariate score X_i is a measure taken before the administration of any of the treatments. Hence the same X_i is paired with all criterion scores on subject i. In contrast, for case (2) the covariate measure is taken just before, just after, or simultaneously with the criterion measure. The data for subject i in this case may be represented as follows:

	Individual	b_1	b_2	$\cdots$	b_q	Total
a_j	i	$X_{ij1}Y_{ij1}$	$X_{ij2}Y_{ij2}$	$\cdots$	$X_{ijq}Y_{ijq}$	$P_{x_{ij}}P_{y_{ij}}$

Thus for case (2) each criterion measure on subject i is paired with a unique covariate measure. Case (1) may be considered as a special case of case (2) in which all the X_{ij}'s for subject i are equal. Hence computational procedures for case (2) may be used for case (1).

Under case (2), both the between-subject (whole-plot) comparisons and the within-subject (split-plot) comparisons are adjusted for the effect of the covariate. Under case (1), only the between-subject (whole-plot) comparisons are adjusted for the effect of the covariate—the within-subject (split-plot) comparisons are adjusted for the effect of the covariate—the within-subject (split-plot) comparisons will all have adjustments which are numerically equal to zero.

The notation that will be used is essentially that defined in Sec. 10.4. Two additional symbols are required.

$P_{x_{i(j)}}$ = sum of the q observations on the covariate subject i in group G_j,

$P_{y_{i(j)}}$ = sum of the q observations on the criterion for subject i in group G_j.

The following variations and covariations are associated with differences between subjects within the groups:

$$P_{xx} = q \sum \sum (\bar{P}_{x_{i(j)}} - \bar{A}_{x_j})^2$$

$$P_{xy} = q \sum \sum (\bar{P}_{x_{i(j)}} - \bar{A}_{x_j})(\bar{P}_{y_{i(j)}} - \bar{A}_{y_j}),$$

$$P_{yy} = q \sum \sum (\bar{P}_{y_{i(j)}} - \bar{A}_{y_j})^2.$$

The basic data for the between-subjects part of the analysis in both cases may be represented as follows:

	a_1		$\cdots$	a_p			
	X	Y		X	Y		
	$P_{x_{11}}$	$P_{y_{11}}$		$P_{x_{1p}}$	$P_{y_{1p}}$		
	$P_{x_{21}}$	$P_{y_{21}}$		$P_{x_{2p}}$	$P_{y_{2p}}$		
	$\vdots$	$\vdots$		$\vdots$	$\vdots$		
	$P_{x_{n1}}$	$P_{y_{n1}}$		$P_{x_{np}}$	$P_{y_{np}}$		
Total	A_{x_1}	A_{y_1}	$\cdots$	A_{x_p}	A_{y_p}	G_x	G_y

From this part of the data, one may compute the following computational symbols:

$$(1x) = G_x^2/npq \qquad (1xy) = G_x G_y/npq \qquad (1y) = G_y^2/npq$$

$$(3x) = \left(\sum A_{x_j}^2\right)\Big/nq \quad (3xy) = \left(\sum A_{x_j}A_{y_j}\right)\Big/nq \quad (3y) = \left(\sum A_{y_j}^2\right)\Big/nq$$

$$(6x) = \left(\sum P_{x_{i(j)}}^2\right)\Big/q \quad (6xy) = \left(\sum P_{x_{i(j)}}P_{y_{i(j)}}\right)\Big/q \quad (6y) = \left(\sum P_{y_{i(j)}}^2\right)\Big/q$$

One may now carry out the equivalent of a single-factor analysis of covariance corresponding to the between-subject part of the repeated-measure design. Toward this objective one has

$$A_{xx} = (3x) - (1x) \qquad A_{yy} = (3y) - (1y)$$

$$P_{xx} = (6x) - (3x) \qquad P_{yy} = (6y) - (3y)$$

$$A_{xy} = (3xy) - (1xy)$$

$$P_{xy} = (6xy) - (3xy).$$

The linear regression for the subjects-within-group data has the following form:

$$\bar{P}_{y_{i(j)}} = b_p(\bar{P}_{x_{i(j)}} - \bar{A}_{x_j}) + \bar{A}_{y_j},$$

where b_p, the internal regression coefficient for the between-subject part of the design, is

$$b_p = \frac{P_{xy}}{P_{xx}}.$$

The adjusted variation due to between-subject error, the variation of residuals about this regression line, is

$$P'_{yy} = P_{yy} - \frac{P_{xy}^2}{P_{xx}} = P_{yy} - b_p P_{xy}.$$

This source of variation has degrees of freedom

$$p(n - 1) - 1.$$

The mean square corresponding to this latter variation is the adjusted error for between-subject effects. The reduced variation due to the other between-subject source, the reduced variation due to the main effects of factor A, is

$$A'_{yy} = (A_{yy} + P_{yy}) - \frac{(A_{xy} + P_{xy})^2}{A_{xx} + P_{xx}} - P'_{yy}.$$

This source of variation has $p - 1$ degrees of freedom.

For the within-subject part of the analysis, from the basic data and the AB summary data, one computes the following computational symbols:

$$(2x) = \sum X^2 \qquad\qquad (2y) = \sum Y^2$$

$$(4x) = \left(\sum B_{x_k}^2\right)\Big/ np \qquad (4y) = \left(\sum B_{y_k}^2\right)\Big/ np$$

$$(5x) = \left(\sum AB_{x_{jk}}^2\right)\Big/ n \qquad (5y) = \left(\sum AB_{y_{jk}}^2\right)\Big/ n$$

$$(2xy) = \sum XY$$

$$(4xy) = \left(\sum B_{x_k} B_{y_k}\right)\Big/ np$$

$$(5xy) = \left(\sum AB_{x_{jk}} AB_{y_{jk}}\right)\Big/ n$$

From these symbols and those obtained earlier, one computes the terms that enter into the within-subject part of the analysis of covariance.

$$B_{xx} = (4x) - (1x) \qquad\qquad B_{yy} = (4y) - (1y)$$
$$AB_{xx} = (5x) - (3x) - (4x) + (1x) \qquad AB_{yy} = (5y) - (3y) - (4y) + (1y)$$
$$E_{xx} = (2x) - (5x) \qquad\qquad E_{yy} = (2y) - (5y)$$
$$B_{xy} = (4xy) - (1xy)$$
$$AB_{xy} = (5xy) - (3xy) - (4xy) + (1xy)$$
$$E_{xy} = (2xy) - (5xy).$$

The within-subject error components in this design have the following general form:

$$\text{Residual } (X) = \text{within cell } (X) - P_{xx}.$$

Thus, one computes the within-cell values

$$W_{xx} = E_{xx} - P_{xx} = \sum\sum (X_{ijk} - \overline{AB}_{x_{jk}}) - P_{xx}$$
$$W_{yy} = E_{yy} - P_{yy} = \sum\sum (Y_{ijk} - \overline{AB}_{y_{jk}}) - P_{yy}$$
$$W_{xy} = E_{xy} - P_{xy} = \sum\sum [X_{ijk}Y_{ijk} - (\overline{AB}_{x_{jk}})(\overline{AB}_{y_{jk}})] - P_{xy}.$$

The variation due to error for the within-subject part of the analysis of covariance is

$$W'_{yy} = W_{yy} - \frac{W_{xy}^2}{W_{xx}} = W_{yy} - b_w W_{xy},$$

where the regression coefficient for the within-subject effects is

$$b_w = \frac{W_{xy}}{W_{xx}}.$$

Hence, W'_{yy} is the variation of residuals about the within-subject regression line. This source of variation has $p(n-1)(q-1) - 1$ degrees of freedom.

In an analysis of variance without repeated measures,

$$E_{yy} = SS_{\text{w. cell}}$$

with degrees of freedom

$$pq(n-1).$$

In an analysis of variance with repeated measures,

$$W_{yy} = E_{yy} - P_{yy} = SS_{B \times \text{Subj w. } a}$$

with degrees of freedom

$$pq(n-1) - p(n-1) = p(n-1)(q-1).$$

In the fixed model,

$$E(\text{MS}_{B \times \text{subj w. } a}) = \sigma_{\varepsilon}^2.$$

The other variations in the within-subject part of the analysis of covariance are:

$$B'_{yy} = (B_{yy} + W_{yy}) - \frac{(B_{xy} + W_{xy})^2}{B_{xx} + W_{xx}} - W'_{yy}$$

$$AB'_{yy} = (AB_{yy} + W_{yy}) - \frac{(AB_{xy} + W_{xy})^2}{AB_{xx} + W_{xx}} - W'_{yy}.$$

The analysis of covariance is summarized in Table 10.32. The mean square due to error for the between-subject part of the analysis is

$$s_p^2 = \text{MS}_{\text{Subj w. } a} = \frac{P'_{yy}}{p(n-1)-1} = \frac{P_{yy} - (P_{xy}^2/P_{xx})}{p(n-1)-1}.$$

For the within-subject part of the analysis, the mean square due to error is

$$s_w^2 = \text{MS}_{\text{res}} = \frac{W'_{yy}}{p(n-1)(q-1)-1} = \frac{W_{yy} - (W_{xy}^2/W_{xx})}{p(n-1)(q-1)-1}.$$

The adjusted mean for level a_j is given by

$$\bar{A}'_{y_j} = \bar{A}_{y_j} - b_p(\bar{A}_{x_j} - \bar{G}_X).$$

The estimate of the squared error of a difference of the form

$$\bar{A}'_{y_j} - \bar{A}'_{y_{j'}}.$$

TABLE 10.32   **Analysis of covariance for design in Table 10.31**

Source	X^2	XY	Y^2	Adjusted variation	df	MS
A	A_{xx}	A_{xy}	A_{yy}	$A'_{yy} = (A_{yy} + P_{yy}) - \dfrac{(A_{xy} + P_{xy})^2}{A_{xx} + P_{xx}} - P'_{yy}$	$p - 1$	
Subj w. a	P_{xx}	P_{xy}	P_{yy}	$P'_{yy} = P_{yy} - \dfrac{P_{xy}^2}{P_{xx}}$	$p(n-1)-1$	s_p^2
B	B_{xx}	B_{xy}	B_{yy}	$B'_{yy} = (B_{yy} + W_{yy}) - \dfrac{(B_{xy} + W_{xy})^2}{B_{xx} + W_{xx}} - W'_{yy}$	$q - 1$	
AB	AB_{xx}	AB_{xy}	AB_{yy}	$AB'_{yy} = (AB_{yy} + W_{yy}) - \dfrac{(AB_{xy} + W_{xy})^2}{AB_{xx} + W_{xx}} - W'_{yy}$	$(p-1)(q-1)$	
Residual	W_{xx}	W_{xy}	W_{yy}	$W'_{yy} = W_{yy} - \dfrac{W_{xy}^2}{W_{xx}}$	$p(n-1)(q-1)-1$	s_w^2

Note: If a single X is associated with all Y on a given subject, the following sums of squares will be zero:

$B_{xx}, B_{xy}, AB_{xx}, AB_{xy}, W_{xx}, W_{xy}.$

is

$$\text{var}\,(\bar{A}'_j - \bar{A}'_{j'}) = s_p^2 \left[\frac{2}{nq} + \frac{(\bar{A}_{x_j} - \bar{A}_{x_{j'}})^2}{P_{xx}} \right].$$

A comparison among the adjusted means for the levels of factor A is given by

$$\hat{\psi} = \sum c_j \bar{A}'_{y_j}.$$

The variance of this estimator is

$$\text{var}\,(\hat{\psi}) = s_p^2 \left[\frac{\sum c_j^2}{nq} + \frac{(\sum c_j \bar{A}_{x_j})^2}{P_{xx}} \right].$$

The adjusted mean for level b_k is given by

$$\bar{B}'_{y_k} = \bar{B}_{y_k} - b_w(\bar{B}_{x_k} - G_x).$$

The estimate of the squared standard error of a comparison of the form

$$\bar{B}'_{y_k} - \bar{B}'_{y_{k'}}$$

is

$$\text{var}\,(\bar{B}'_{y_k} - \bar{B}'_{y_{k'}}) = s_w^2 \left[\frac{2}{np} + \frac{(\bar{B}_{x_k} - \bar{B}_{x_{k'}})^2}{W_{xx}} \right].$$

An adjusted cell mean is given by

$$\overline{AB}'_{y_{jk}} = \overline{AB}_{y_{jk}} - b_p(\bar{A}_{x_j} - \bar{A}_{x_j}) - b_w(\overline{AB}_{x_{jk}} - \bar{A}_{x_j}).$$

The difference between two adjusted cell means at the same level of factor A has the form

$$\overline{AB}'_{y_{jk}} - \overline{AB}'_{y_{jk'}} = \overline{AB}_{y_{jk}} - \overline{AB}_{y_{jk'}} - b_w(\overline{AB}_{x_{jk}} - \overline{AB}_{x_{jk'}}).$$

Thus only b_w enters into this type of difference. The variance of this comparison is

$$\text{var}\,(\overline{AB}'_{y_{jk}} - \overline{AB}'_{y_{jk'}}) = s_w^2 \left[\frac{2}{n} + \frac{(\overline{AB}_{x_{jk}} - \overline{AB}_{x_{jk'}})^2}{W_{xx}} \right].$$

The difference between two adjusted cell means at the same level of factor b has the form

$$\overline{AB}'_{y_{jk}} - \overline{AB}'_{y_{j'k}} = \overline{AB}_{y_{jk}} - \overline{AB}_{y_{j'k}} - b_p(\bar{A}_{x_j} - \bar{A}_{x_{j'}}) - b_w(\overline{AB}_{x_{jk}} - \overline{AB}_{x_{j'k}} - \bar{A}_{x_j} + \bar{A}_{x_{j'}}).$$

One notes that this comparison involves both b_p and b_w. Hence the variance of this type of comparison has a relatively more complicated form:

$$\frac{2}{n} \frac{s_p^2 + (q-1)s_w^2}{q} + \frac{s_p^2(\bar{A}_{x_j} - \bar{A}_{x_{j'}})^2}{P_{xx}} + \frac{s_w^2(\overline{AB}_{x_{jk}} - \overline{AB}_{x_{j'k}} - \bar{A}_{x_j} + \bar{A}_{x_{j'}})^2}{W_{xx}}$$

It will be recalled that in the analysis of variance this type of comparison also has a squared standard error which is also a mixture of the mean squares due to error for the between and within subjects parts. Adjustments for comparisons among the cell means which belong to the AB interaction will involve only the regression coefficient b_w. Hence the variation of such comparisons will involve only b_w.

If it can be assumed that the regression coefficients in the between-subject and the within-subject parts of the analysis are equal, i.e., that $\beta_p = \beta_w$, then the indications are that b_w can be used in making all adjustments on the means. A test on the hypothesis that $\beta_p = \beta_w$ is given by

$$t' = \frac{b_p - b_w}{\sqrt{s_1^2 + s_2^2}},$$

where $s_1^2 = s_p^2/P_{xx}$ and $s_2^2 = s_w^2/E_{xx}$. s_1^2 and s_2^2 are the respective error variances for b_p and b_w. Since the variances in the denominator of this t' statistic will not in general be homogeneous, the sampling distribution of t' is not that of the usual t statistic. If the degrees of freedom for s_p^2 and s_w^2 are both larger than 20, the normal distribution $N(0, 1)$ may be used to approximate the sampling distribution of t'. In other cases the sampling distribution of t' may be approximated by the usual t distribution with degrees of freedom f,

$$f = \frac{(s_1^2 + s_2^2)^2}{(s_1^4/f_p) + (s_2^4/f_w)},$$

where f_p and f_w are the respective degrees of freedom for s_p^2 and s_w^2.

When it can be assumed that $\beta_p = \beta_w$, the analysis of covariance has the form given in Table 10.33. All the adjustments for within-subject effects are identical to those given in Table 10.32. The adjustment procedures for the between-subject effects are, however, different. For purposes of making

TABLE 10.33   **Covariance analysis when $\beta_p - \beta_w$**

Source	Adjusted variation	df	MS
A	$A'_{yy} = (A_{yy} + E_{yy}) - \dfrac{(A_{xy} + E_{xy})^2}{A_{xx} + E_{xx}} - E'_{yy}$	$p - 1$	
Subj w. gp	$P'_{yy} = (P_{yy} + E_{yy}) - \dfrac{(P_{xy} + E_{xy})^2}{P_{xx} + E_{xx}} - E'_{yy}$	$p(n-1)$	s_p^2
B	$B'_{yy} = (B_{yy} + E_{yy}) - \dfrac{(B_{xy} + E_{xy})^2}{(B_{xx} + E_{xx})} - E'_{yy}$	$q - 1$	
AB	$AB'_{yy} = (AB_{yy} + E_{yy}) - \dfrac{(AB_{xy} + E_{xy})^2}{(AB_{xx} + E_{xx})} - E'_{yy}$	$(p-1)(q-1)$	
Residual	$E'_{yy} = E_{yy} - (E_{xy}^2/E_{xx})$	$p(q-1)(n-1) - 1$	s_w^2
A (adj.)	$A''_{yy} = A_{yy} - 2b_w A_{xy} + b_w^2 A_{xx}$	$p - 1$	
Subj w. A (adj.)	$P''_{yy} = P_{yy} - 2b_w P_{xy} + b_w^2 P_{xx}$	$p(n-1)$	$s_p'^2$

overall tests, there is some indication that the adjustments for between-subject effects given at the bottom of this table are to be preferred to those indicated at the top. The two adjustment procedures are not algebraically equivalent.

Adjusted means for within-subject effects are identical to those given earlier in this section. The adjusted mean for level a_j now has the form

$$\bar{A}'_{y_j} = \bar{A}_{y_j} - b_w(\bar{A}_{x_j} - \bar{G}_x).$$

The error variance for the difference between $\bar{A}'_{y_j}$ and $\bar{A}'_{y_{j'}}$ in this case is approximately

$$s'^2_p\left[\frac{2}{nq} + \frac{(\bar{A}_{x_j} - \bar{A}_{x_{j'}})^2}{W_{xx}}\right].$$

An adjusted cell mean in this case is

$$\overline{AB}'_{y_{jk}} = \overline{AB}_{y_{jk}} - b_w(\overline{AB}_{x_{jk}} - \bar{G}_x).$$

The error variance for the difference between two adjusted cell means which are at the same level of factor A is identical to that given earlier in this section—this difference is a within-subject cell effect. The error variance for the difference between two adjusted cell means which are not at the same level of A is approximately

$$\frac{2[s'^2_p + (q-1)s^2_w]}{nq} + \frac{(\overline{AB}_{x_{jk}} - \overline{AB}_{x_{j'k}})^2 s^2_w}{W_{xx}}.$$

Numerical Example—Single Covariate Measure for Each Individual

Computational procedures for case (1) of the analysis of covariance are illustrated in Table 10.34. Here one has a 2×2 factorial design with $n = 4$ and repeated measures on factor B. The observations on individual 1 assigned to level a_1 are represented as follows:

	Individual	b_1	b_2
a_1	1	$X_{11} = 3$ $Y_{111} = 5$	$X_{11} = 3$ $Y_{112} = 8$

Note that the covariate measure is a constant for all Y on individual i. The basic data for the analysis appear in part (i).

In part (ii) there is the AB summary table. The cell totals are

$$18 = AB_{x_{11}} \qquad 57 = AB_{y_{11}} \qquad 18 = AB_{x_{12}} \qquad 40 = AB_{y_{12}}$$
$$21 = AB_{x_{21}} \qquad 75 = AB_{y_{21}} \qquad 21 = AB_{x_{22}} \qquad 55 = AB_{y_{22}}$$

TABLE 10.34 **Numerical example—single covariate for all observations on an individual**

	Individual	b_1 X	b_1 Y	b_2 X	b_2 Y	Total P_x	Total P_y
	1	3	5	3	8	6	18
	2	5	15	5	12	10	27
a_1	3	8	20	8	14	16	34
	4	2	12	2	6	4	18
	5	1	15	1	10	2	25
	6	8	25	8	20	16	45
a_2	7	10	20	10	15	20	35
	8	2	15	2	10	4	25
	Total	39	132	39	95	78	227
		B_{x_1}	B_{y_1}	B_{x_2}	B_{y_2}	G_x	G_y

(i)

	b_1 X	b_1 Y	b_2 X	b_2 Y	Total X	Total Y
a_1	18	57	18	40	36	97
a_2	21	75	21	55	42	130
Total	39	132	39	95	78	227

(ii)

(iii)

$(1x) = 380.25$	$(1xy) = 1106.62$	$(1y) = 3220.5625$
$(2x) = 542$	$(2xy) = 1282$	$(2y) = 3609$
$(3x) = 382.50$	$(3xy) = 1282$	$(3y) = 3288.625$
$(4x) = 380.25$	$(4xy) = 1106.62$	$(4y) = 3306.12$
$(5x) = 382.50$	$(5xy) = 1119.00$	$(5y) = 3374.75$
$(6x) = 542.00$	$(6xy) = 1282.00$	$(6y) = 3516.50$

(iv)

$A_{xx} = 2.25$	$A_{xy} = 12.38$	$A_{yy} = 68.06$
$B_{xx} = 0$	$B_{xy} = 0$	$B_{yy} = 85.58$
$AB_{xx} = 0$	$AB_{xy} = 0$	$AB_{yy} = 0.57$
$E_{xx} = 159.50$	$E_{xy} = 163.00$	$E_{yy} = 234.25$
$P_{xx} = 159.50$	$P_{xy} = 163.00$	$P_{yy} = 227.88$

The marginal totals are

$$A_{x_1} = 36 \qquad A_{y_1} = 97 \qquad V_{x_1} = 39 \qquad B_{y_1} = 132$$

$$A_{x_2} = 42 \qquad A_{y_2} = 130 \qquad B_{x_2} = 39 \qquad B_{y_2} = 95.$$

Computational symbols, which were defined earlier in this section, are computed in part (iii). With the exception of (2) and (6), information for these symbols is contained in the AB summary table. Symbols (2) and (6) are obtained from the data in part (i). For example,

$$(1xy) = \frac{G_x G_y}{npq} = \frac{(78)(227)}{16} = 1106.62$$

$$(2xy) = \sum XY = (3)(5) + (5)(15) + \cdots + (2)(10) = 1282$$

$$(3xy) = \frac{\sum A_{x_j} A_{y_j}}{nq} = \frac{(36)(97) + (42)(130)}{8} = 1119.00$$

$$(6xy) = \frac{\sum P_{x_{i(j)}} P_{y_{i(j)}}}{q} = \frac{(6)(18) + (1)(27) + \cdots + (4)(25)}{2}$$

$$= 1282.00.$$

The basic ingredients for the analysis of covariance are computed in part (iv). The computational formulas for these sources of variation have been given earlier in this section. For example,

$$A_{xy} = (3xy) - (1xy) = 12.38$$
$$B_{xy} = (3xy) - (1xy) = 0$$
$$AB_{xy} = (5xy) - (3xy) - (4xy) + (1xy) = 0$$
$$E_{xy} = (2xy) - (5xy) = 163.00$$
$$P_{xy} = (6xy) - (3xy) = 163.00.$$

In case (1) it will always be that

$$B_{xy} = 0, \qquad AB_{xy} = 0, \qquad E_{xy} = P_{xy}.$$

The analysis of variance for the numerical example is summarized in part (i) of Table 10.35. As is usually the case for repeated-measure design, the

TABLE 10.35 **Analysis of variance and covariance for numerical example in Table 10.34**

	Source of variation	SS	df	MS	F
	Between subjects				
	A	$A_{yy} = 68.06$	1	68.06	1.79
	Subj w. a	$P_{yy} = 227.88$	6	37.98	
(i)					
	Within subjects				
	B	$B_{yy} = 85.06$	1	85.06	80.72**
	AB	$AB_{yy} = 0.57$	1	0.57	0.54
	Residual	$W_{yy} = 6.37$	6	1.06	
(ii)					
	Between subjects				
	A (adj)	$A'_{yy} = 44.481$	1	44.481	3.628
	Subj w. a (adj)	$P'_{yy} = 61.300$	5	12.260	

mean square for error for the within-subject part (1.06) is considerably smaller than the mean square for error in the between-subject part (37.98). Under case (1) only the between-subject part of the analysis can be adjusted for the covariate. The within-subject part of the analysis of covariance remains identical with the corresponding part of the analysis of variance.

The analysis of covariance for the between-subject part is summarized in part (ii) of Table 10.35. One notes that the error mean square in part (ii) is 12.260 compared with 37.98 in part (i). Hence the covariate has reduced the error to about one-third of its original magnitude. The square of the correlation between X and Y for the between-subject part of the analysis is

$$r_p^2 = \frac{P_{xy}^2}{P_{xx}P_{yy}} = 0.731.$$

To test for the main effect of A in the analysis of covariance

$$F_a = \frac{44.48}{12.26} = 3.628.$$

The critical value in this case is

$$F_{0.95}(1, 5) = 6.61.$$

Thus the indications are that there are no statistically significant differences due to the main effect of A, even after adjustment has been made for the linear effect of the covariate. One notes that the adjustment process reduced the variation due to the main effects of A from 68.06 to 44.48. However, the reduction in the error was proportionately greater.

Since the F statistic in part (ii) has only one degree of freedom, it will be of interest to demonstrate numerically that this F is identical numerically with the F that one obtains in testing the following hypothesis:

$$H_0: \alpha_1 - \alpha_2 = 0 \qquad H_1: \alpha_1 - \alpha_2 \neq 0.$$

This hypothesis will be tested by the general principles for testing hypotheses about comparisons in terms of the adjusted means. In this case the adjusted means for factor A are

$$\bar{A}'_{y_j} = \bar{A}_{y_j} - b_p(\bar{A}_{x_j} - \bar{G}_x)$$

where

$$b_p = \frac{P_{xy}}{P_{xx}} = \frac{163.00}{159.50} = 1.0219.$$

Hence

$$\bar{A}'_{y_1} = 12.1250 - 1.0219(4.5000 - 4.8750)$$
$$= 12.5082.$$
$$\bar{A}'_{y_2} = 16.2500 - 1.0219(5.2500 - 4.8750)$$
$$= 15.8668.$$

The squared standard error of the differences between these two adjusted means is given by

$$s_p^2\left[\frac{2}{nq}+\frac{(\bar{A}_{x_1}-\bar{A}_{x_2})^2}{P_{xx}}\right]=12.26\left[\frac{2}{8}+\frac{(4.5000-5.2500)^2}{159.50}\right]=3.1082.$$

The test statistic is thus

$$F=\frac{(\bar{A}'_{y_1}-\bar{A}'_{y_2})^2}{3.1082}=\frac{(-3.3586)^2}{3.1082}=3.629.$$

In the analysis of covariance $F=3.628$. The difference is due to rounding error.

When the covariate means do not differ markedly, a close approximation to A''_{yy} is given by

$$A''_{yy}=A_{yy}+b_p^2 A_{xx}-2b_p A_{xy}.$$

For this numerical example

$$A''_{yy}=68.06+(1.0219)^2(2.25)-2(1.0219)(12.38)=45.11.$$

In the analysis of covariance table

$$A'_{yy}=44.481.$$

A''_{yy} will always be larger than A'_{yy}.

Numerical Example—Distinct X for each Y

Suppose that the covariate is a measure of blood pressure. Suppose further that the covariate measure is taken immediately before each of the q treatments is administered. In this case there will be a distinct X measure associated with each Y. Computational procedures are actually identical with those discussed for case (1) in which there was only a single X measure associated with all of the Y measures on an individual.

A numerical example of case (2) is given in Table 10.36. The AB summary table has been incorporated with the basic data in part (i). The design is a 3×2 factorial with repeated measures on factor B. There are $n=3$ individuals assigned at random to each level of factor A. The computational symbols are given in part (ii). For example,

$$(1xy)=\frac{G_x G_y}{npq}=\frac{(135)(237)}{18}=1777.50.$$

$$(3xy)=\frac{\sum A_{x_j}A_{y_j}}{nq}=\frac{(46)(89)+(39)(59)+(50)(89)}{6}=1807.50.$$

$$(5xy)=\frac{\sum AB_{x_{jk}}AB_{y_{jk}}}{n}$$

$$=\frac{(19)(35)+(27)(54)+(20)(27)+(19)(32)+(24)(39)+(26)(50)}{3}$$

$$=1835.67$$

$$(6xy)=\frac{\sum P_{x_{i(j)}}P_{y_{i(j)}}}{q}=\frac{(7)(22)+(14)(29)+\cdots+(21)(37)}{2}=1964.00.$$

TABLE 10.36   **Numerical example for case (2)**

	Individual	b_1 X	b_1 Y	b_2 X	b_2 Y	Total X	Total Y
	1	3	8	4	14	7	22
a_1	2	5	11	9	18	14	29
	3	11	16	14	22	25	38
	Total	19	35	27	54	46	89
	4	2	6	1	8	3	14
a_2	5	8	12	9	14	17	26
	6	10	9	9	10	19	19
	Total	20	27	19	32	39	59
	7	7	10	4	10	11	20
a_3	8	8	14	10	18	18	32
	9	9	15	12	22	21	37
	Total	24	39	26	50	50	89
	Column total	63	101	72	136	135	237

(i)

(ii)

$(1x) = 1012.50$	$(1xy) = 1777.50$	$(1y) = 3120.50$
$(2x) = 1233$	$(2xy) = 2004$	$(2y) = 3495$
$(3x) = 1022.83$	$(3xy) = 1807.50$	$(3y) = 3220.50$
$(4x) = 1017.00$	$(4xy) = 1795.00$	$(4y) = 3188.556$
$(5x) = 1034.33$	$(5xy) = 1835.67$	$(5y) = 3305.00$
$(6x) = 1207.50$	$(6xy) = 1964.00$	$(6y) = 3397.50$

(iii)

$A_{xx} = 10.33$	$A_{xy} = 30.00$	$A_{yy} = 100.00$
$B_{xx} = 4.50$	$B_{xy} = 17.50$	$B_{yy} = 68.56$
$AB_{xx} = 7.00$	$AB_{xy} = 10.67$	$AB_{yy} = 16.44$
$E_{xx} = 198.67$	$E_{xy} = 168.33$	$E_{yy} = 190.00$
$P_{xx} = 184.67$	$P_{xy} = 156.50$	$P_{yy} = 177.00$
$W_{xx} = 4.00$	$W_{xy} = 11.83$	$W_{yy} = 13.00$

The basic ingredients for both the analysis of variance and the analysis of covariance are summarized in part (iii). For example,

$$A_{xy} = (3xy) - (1xy) = 30.00.$$
$$AB_{xy} = (5xy) - (3xy) - (4xy) + (1xy) = 10.67.$$
$$E_{xy} = (2xy) - (5xy) = 168.33.$$
$$P_{xy} = (6xy) - (3xy) = 156.50.$$
$$W_{xy} = E_{xy} - P_{xy} = 11.83.$$

The analysis of variance for these data is summarized in Table 10.37. Note that the mean square due to error for the between-subject part of the

TABLE 10.37 **Analysis of variance for example in Table 10.36**

Source	SS	df	MS	F
Between subjects				
A	$A_{yy} = 100.00$	2	50.00	1.69
Subj w. a	$P_{yy} = 177.00$	6	29.50	
Within subjects				
B	$B_{yy} = 68.06$	1	68.06	31.36**
AB	$AB_{yy} = 16.44$	2	8.22	3.78
Residual	$W_{yy} = 13.00$	6	2.17	

$$F_{0.95}(1, 6) = 5.09$$
$$F_{0.99}(1, 6) = 13.7$$
$$F_{0.95}(2, 6) = 5.14$$

analysis is

$$\frac{P_{yy}}{p(n-1)} = 29.50.$$

The mean square due to error for the within-subject part of the analysis is

$$\frac{W_{yy}}{p(n-1)(q-1)} = \frac{13.00}{6} = 2.17.$$

As is usually the case in a repeated-measure design, the within-subject error is considerably smaller than the between-subject error. In the analysis of variance the only statistically significant source of variation is that due to the main effect of factor B.

The analysis of covariance is summarized in Table 10.38. The adjusted

TABLE 10.38 **Analysis of covariance for example in Table 10.37**

Source	SS	df	MS	F
Between subjects				
A (adj)	$A'_{yy} = 54.26$	2	27.13	3.06
Subj w. a (adj)	$P'_{yy} = 44.37$	5	$s_p'^2 = 8.87$	
Within subjects				
B (adj)	$B'_{yy} = 31.55$	1	31.55	52.58**
AB (adj)	$AB'_{yy} = 2.33$	2	1.16	1.93
Residual	$W'_{yy} = 3.00$	5	$s_w'^2 = 0.60$	

variations are obtained from the formulas given in Table 10.32. For example,

$$A'_{yy} = (A_{yy} + P_{yy}) - \frac{(A_{xy} + P_{xy})^2}{A_{xx} + P_{xx}} - P'_{yy}$$

$$= A_{yy} - \frac{(A_{xy} + P_{xy})^2}{A_{xx} + P_{xx}} + \frac{P_{xy}^2}{E_{xx}}$$

$$= 100.00 - \frac{(30.00 + 156.50)^2}{10.33 + 184.67} + \frac{(156.50)^2}{184.67} = 54.26.$$

$$P'_{yy} = P_{yy} - \frac{P_{xy}^2}{P_{xx}} = 177.00 - \frac{(156.50)^2}{184.67} = 44.37.$$

The regression coefficient for the between-subject part of the analysis is

$$b_p = \frac{P_{xy}}{P_{xx}} = \frac{156.50}{184.67} = 0.847.$$

For the within-subject part of the analysis

$$b_w = \frac{W_{xy}}{W_{xx}} = \frac{11.83}{14.00} = 0.8450.$$

For this numerical example, the two regression coefficients are almost identical. Since the degrees of freedom associated with both regressions are, in this case, the same, there is no need to use b_w in place of b_p in adjusting the cell and marginal means.

Adjusting the error terms for the covariate reduces the between-subject error from 29.50 to 8.87. The corresponding adjustment reduces the within-subject error from 2.17 to 0.60. In both cases the adjusted error is about 30 percent of the unadjusted error. The relevant squared correlations are

$$r_p^2 = \frac{P_{xy}^2}{P_{xx}P_{yy}} = 0.75, \qquad r_w^2 = \frac{W_{xy}^2}{W_{xx}W_{yy}} = 0.77.$$

Since the test on the main effects of factor B has just one degree of freedom in the numerator, it will again be demonstrated numerically that this test is equivalent to the test on the difference between corresponding adjusted treatment means. One has

$$\bar{B}'_{y_j} = \bar{B}_{y_j} - b_w(\bar{B}_{x_j} - \bar{G}_x).$$

Thus
$$\bar{B}'_{y_1} = \bar{B}_{y_1} - 0.845(\bar{B}_{x_1} - 7.500)$$

$$= 11.222 - 0.845(7.000 - 7.500)$$

$$= 11.645.$$

$$B'_{y_2} = 15.111 - 0.845(8.000 - 7.500) = 14.689.$$

The variance of the difference between these adjusted means is

$$\text{var}\,(\bar{B}'_{y_1} - \bar{B}'_{y_2}) = s_w^2 \left[\frac{2}{np} + \frac{(\bar{B}_{x_1} - \bar{B}_{x_2})^2}{W_{xx}} \right]$$

$$= 0.600 \left[\frac{2}{9} + \frac{(7.000 - 8.000)^2}{14.00} \right].$$

$$= 0.176.$$

To test the statistical hypothesis

$$H_0: \beta_1 - \beta_2 = 0 \qquad H_1: \beta_1 - \beta_2 \neq 0$$

the appropriate test statistic is

$$F = \frac{(\bar{B}'_{y_1} - \bar{B}'_{y_2})^2}{\text{var}\,(\bar{B}'_{y_1} - \bar{B}'_{y_2})} = \frac{(11.645 - 14.689)^2}{0.176} = 52.58.$$

The corresponding F statistic in the analysis of covariance table is 52.58.

Although the F test on the main effects of A is not statistically significant, the procedures for testing the following statistical hypothesis will be illustrated.

$$H_0: \alpha_1 - \alpha_2 = 0 \qquad H_1: \alpha_1 - \alpha_2 \neq 0.$$

In practice this test would be made only if it were in the *a priori* category. The adjusted treatment means are given by

$$\bar{A}'_{y_1} = \bar{A}_{y_1} - b_p(\bar{A}_{x_1} - \bar{G}_x)$$
$$= 14.83 - 0.847(7.67 - 7.50) = 14.69.$$
$$\bar{A}'_{y_2} = 9.83 - 0.847(6.50 - 7.50) = 10.68.$$

The estimate of the variance of the difference between adjusted means in this case is

$$\text{var}\,(\bar{A}'_{y_1} - \bar{A}'_{y_2}) = s_p^2 \left[\frac{2}{nq} + \frac{(\bar{A}_{x_1} - \bar{A}_{x_2})^2}{P_{xx}} \right]$$

$$= 8.87 \left[\frac{2}{6} + \frac{(14.69 - 10.68)^2}{184.67} \right]$$

$$= 3.02.$$

The appropriate test statistic in this case is

$$F = \frac{(\bar{A}'_{y_1} - \bar{A}'_{y_2})^2}{\text{var}\,(\bar{A}'_{y_1} - \bar{A}'_{y_2})} = \frac{(14.69 - 10.68)^2}{3.02}$$

$$= 5.32.$$

The critical value for an *a priori* test is

$$F_{0.95}[1,\,5] = 6.61.$$

Hence the data do not contradict the hypothesis of no difference between α_1 and α_2.

10.6 EXERCISES

1. In the following studies, list five possible covariates which may increase the precision with which estimation occurs in studies designed to evaluate.
(*a*) The impact of training procedures upon the accuracy of clinical judgments.
(*b*) The effects of motivation upon the acquisition of mathematical skills.
(*c*) The relation between educational level and religious attitudes.
(*d*) The degree to which communication is related to organizational management style.

2. An experimenter studied the effects of expectation upon reactions to TV commercials. Three different product expectations were generated through different sets of instructions and a set of five commercials was administered to seven subjects under each of the three conditions. Each subject evaluated product desirability on a 100-point scale for all five commercials and the mean rating (rounded) was recorded as each subject's reaction. A covariate, attitude towards the industry represented by the commercials, was measured prior to the treatments. The data were:

			Expectations		
	1		**2**		**3**
X	**Y**	**X**	**Y**	**X**	**Y**
53	58	63	68	64	76
73	62	67	62	60	72
60	66	60	66	58	70
58	64	59	64	54	66
65	70	54	58	52	54
58	62	56	60	58	68
65	68	52	56	56	62

(*a*) What is the estimate of variation due to error given each of the following structural models for the dependent variable:
1. $Y_{ij} = \mu + \varepsilon_{ij}$,
2. $Y_{ij} = \mu + \tau_j + \varepsilon_{ij}$,
3. $Y_{ij} = \mu + \beta(X_{ij} - \bar{X}) + \varepsilon_{ij}$,
4. $Y_{ij} = \mu + \beta(X_{ij} - \bar{X}) + \tau_j + \varepsilon_{ij}$?

(*b*) From (a), what is the increase in predictability (reduction of SS_{error}) associated with the analysis of variance model, the regression model, and the analysis of covariance model, as compared to $Y_{ij} = \mu + \varepsilon_{ij}$?

(*c*) Compute and interpret the between-class regression coefficient. Compute the variation which is predictable from the regression function using the between-class regression coefficient.

(*d*) Compute and interpret the within-class regression coefficients (b_{E_j}) for each treatment condition and the overall internal regression coefficient (b_E). Compute the predictable variation and error variation due to including internal regression in the equation for Y_{ij}.

(*e*) Compute the overall regression coefficient (b_s). What is the numerical value of predictable and error variation from a model using b_s as a regression coefficient? How is this function to be interpreted?

(f) Carry out the analysis of covariance, present the analysis of covariance summary table, and test the analysis of covariance hypothesis, $H_0: \sigma^2_{\tau \mid \beta} = 0$, ($\alpha = 0.05$).

(g) Show numerically that the error variation from the analysis of covariance can be expressed as the error variation computed about the overall regression function (S'_{yy}) minus the reduced treatment variation (T_{yyR}),

$$E'_{yy} = S'_{yy} - T_{yyR}.$$

(h) Show numerically that the predictable variation in the analysis of covariance is the variation due to treatments of the analysis of variance plus the predictable variation due to the internal regression of Y on X minus the total regression,

$$T_{yyR} = T_{yy} + b_E E_{xy} - b_s S_{xy}.$$

(i) Complete an analysis of variance. Summarize the ANOV and test the analysis of variance hypothesis, $H_0: \sigma^2_\tau = 0$, ($\alpha = 0.05$).

(j) Compare the ANOV and ANOCov outcomes:

(1) Show numerically that the error variation of the analysis of variance is reduced in direct proportion to the square of the within-class correlation coefficient in the analysis of covariance. That is,

$$E'_{yy} = (1 - \tau^2_{\text{w. class}})E_{yy}.$$

(2) Show numerically the relationship between MS'_{error} of the analysis of covariance and MS_{error} of the analysis of variance as a function of the square of the within-class correlation coefficient.

(k) Compute the adjusted means $\bar{Y}'_1$, $\bar{Y}'_2$, $\bar{Y}'_3$, and $\bar{Y}'$.

(l) Use the Newman–Keuls procedure to compare all unique pairs of adjusted means ($\alpha = 0.05$) using the generalized studentized range statistic.

3. An experimenter obtained the following data on $n = 8$ subjects under each of three treatment conditions:

		Treatments			
	1		2		3
X	Y	X	Y	X	Y
6	15	4	15	3	15
3	4	4	19	6	27
3	6	3	10	3	11
6	19	6	23	5	23
5	11	4	17	4	29
6	17	6	25	4	19
4	9	3	10	6	25
4	11	3	11	5	21

(a) Complete an analysis of variance of Y (Y fixed).

(b) Complete an analysis of covariance (Y fixed).

(c) Reanalyze the data as a two-factor experiment using the X values to define levels of a fixed factor.

(d) Compare the outcomes of the three analyses.

4. An experimenter was interested in evaluating the effects of environmental enrichment upon intellectual development. (S)he manipulated two levels of an environmental complexity variable (A), and three levels of an age variable (B). Randomly sampled groups of rats were exposed to either a_1 or a_2 at three ages (b_1, b_2, and b_3, respectively). As adults, they were tested in a discrimination learning task (Y). (S)he was concerned that alertness to visual stimulation might be a covariate of influence in the learning task. Hence, a measure of visual attentiveness was taken prior to treatment. The following data were obtained:

	Age					
	b_1		b_2		b_3	
Complexity	X	Y	X	Y	X	Y
	45	100	35	90	55	95
	40	85	45	105	45	90
a_1	45	100	50	90	45	95
	55	110	45	95	35	85
	50	105	45	95	45	90
	55	105	55	105	50	100
	35	100	35	95	35	90
a_2	40	100	45	100	30	80
	50	115	50	95	55	110
	35	90	45	100	40	90

(a) Compute $b_{E_{jk}}$ for all treatment conditions and test the hypothesis that all regression coefficients are homogeneous.

(b) Carry out an analysis of variance of Y (A and B fixed).

(c) Carry out an analysis of covariance of Y (A and B fixed).

(d) Compare the outcome of the analysis of variance and analysis of covariance using r_{within}^2 and the relationship between MS_{error} and MS'_{error} as the basis for the comparison.

(e) Compute all adjusted marginal and treatment means.

(f) Using adjusted means, test the hypotheses ($\alpha = 0.05$):

$$H_0: \psi_1 = \beta_1 - \beta_2 = 0$$
$$H_0: \psi_2 = \alpha_1 - \alpha_2 = 0$$
$$H_0: \psi_3 = 2\beta_1 - \beta_2 - \beta_3 = 0.$$

RANDOM VARIABLES

The concept of a *random* variable is basic in modern statistics. In mathematics, a function of a variable is usually a rule whereby one or more values (usually numbers) are associated with different values of the variable. For example, consider the function

$$f(x) = 2x + 5.$$

When

$$x = 0, \qquad f(x) = 5;$$
$$x = 1, \qquad f(x) = 7;$$
$$x = 2, \qquad f(x) = 9.$$

If x is a random variable (or *variate*), the probability density function on x, say $f(x)$, gives the probability that the variate assumes the value x. That is,

$$f(x) = \Pr(x).$$

If one distinguishes between the name of the variate (x) and the values (say x') that the variate can assume, then

$$f(x = x') = \Pr(x = x').$$

In some contexts, $f(x)$ represents a model for the relative frequency (in a series of experiments) with which the variate x will assume specified values. For example, if $x = 0$, 1, or 2, but no other values, a probability density function may be formulated as follows:

$$f(x = 0) = 0.50 = p_0,$$
$$f(x = 1) = 0.20 = p_1,$$
$$f(x = 2) = 0.30 = p_2.$$

If this density function is an appropriate model for a series of n independent experiments, the expected frequencies of the outcomes are as indicated below.

Outcome	Expected frequency
$x = 0$	$np_0 = 0.50n$
$x = 1$	$np_1 = 0.20n$
$x = 2$	$np_2 = 0.30n$

One of the basic problems in statistics is to evaluate the goodness of fit of various models to experimental data.

A.1 RANDOM VARIABLES AND PROBABILITY DISTRIBUTIONS

Associated with a *random* variable is a probability distribution. If the symbol x denotes a random variable, then the symbol $f(x)$ will denote the *probability density* for x. For example, the probability that the random variable x assumes the specific value x_j is given by

$$\Pr(x = x_j) = f(x_j).$$

A probability *measure* on the random variable x is defined by a function having the following properties:

(i) $0 \le \Pr(x \le x_j) \le 1.$
(ii) $\Pr(-\infty \le x \le \infty) = 1.$
(iii) For $x_k > x_j$, $\Pr(x_j \le x \le x_k) = \Pr(x \le x_k) - \Pr(x \le x_j).$

The *distribution function* for a random variable x will be denoted by the symbol $F(x)$. The distribution function, as a probability law, is interpreted as follows:

$$\Pr(x \le x_j) = F(x_j) = \int_{-\infty}^{x_j} f(x)\, dx.$$

That is, the distribution function of a random variable x represents a cumulative probability. In some contexts the "product" $f(x)\, dx$, which can be considered to define the area of a rectangle with height $f(x)$ and width dx, is called the *probability element*.

Any nonnegative function, whose integral over the entire range of the variable in the function is unity, will define a probability density. Conversely, a random variable x is said to have a density function $f(x)$ if

$$\int_{-\infty}^{x_j} f(x)\, dx = \Pr(x \le x_j).$$

The term *distribution* is used rather loosely to refer either to the probability density or the distribution function. The context will generally make it clear which one is implied. The distribution which defines a random variable is called its probability *law*.

It is convenient to define the range of a random variable to be from $-\infty$ to $+\infty$. If, for example, the density function is zero for all values of $x \leq 0$, the probability density may be defined as

$$\Pr(x) = f(x), \qquad\qquad x > 0,$$
$$= 0, \qquad\qquad x \leq 0.$$

As another example, if the random variable x has zero probability outside the interval 0 to 1,

$$\Pr(x) = f(x), \qquad\qquad 0 < x < 1,$$
$$= 0, \qquad\qquad \text{otherwise.}$$

A random variable may be either continuous or discrete. Only continuous variables are considered in this section. Associated with the distribution of a random variable are one or more *parameters*. The latter are constants which determine certain characteristics of the distribution. For example, suppose

$$f(x) = \gamma e^{-\gamma x}, \qquad\qquad x > 0, \gamma > 0,$$
$$= 0, \qquad\qquad \text{otherwise.}$$

For this probability density, the random variable is x, and the parameter is γ. To make explicit the distinction between the variable and the parameter one may write

$$f(x \mid \gamma) = \gamma e^{-\gamma x}, \qquad\qquad x > 0, \gamma > 0.$$

For $\gamma = 1$, the probability density takes the form

$$f(x \mid \gamma = 1) = e^{-x}, \qquad\qquad x > 0,$$
$$= 0, \qquad\qquad \text{otherwise.}$$

This probability law is shown geometrically in Fig. A-1. This example defines what is called the exponential probability law or the exponential distribution for a random variable x. The random variable defined by this density is called an "exponential variable." The exponential distribution is actually a family of distributions—a member of the family is specified by assigning a numerical value to the parameter γ. The distribution function for an exponential variable has the form

$$\Pr(x \leq x_j) = \int_0^{x_j} f(x)\,dx = \int_0^{x_j} \gamma e^{-\gamma x}\,dx.$$

It is sometimes convenient to introduce a dummy variable, say t, and represent

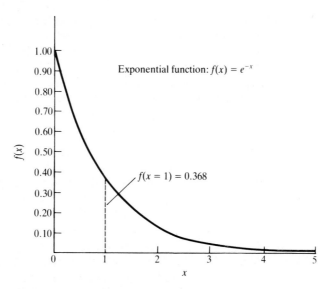

FIGURE A-1 Exponential probability law when $\gamma = 1$.

the distribution function in the form

$$F(x) = \Pr\,(t \le x) = \int_0^x f(t)\,dt = \int_0^x \gamma e^{-\gamma t}\,dt.$$

The dummy variable t is called the variable of integration. This notation makes explicit the fact that the value of this integral depends upon the upper limit.

If a probability density for a random variable x contains the parameters $\theta_1, \ldots, \theta_p$, the following alternative notation systems are used:

$$f(x \mid \theta_1, \ldots, \theta_p), \qquad f_x(\theta_1, \ldots, \theta_p), \qquad f(\theta_1, \ldots, \theta_p).$$

or simply $f(x)$.

The random variable itself is called the argument of the function. Which one of the notation systems is used depends upon what the context is trying to emphasize. The corresponding distribution is written in the alternative forms

$$F(X \mid \theta_1, \ldots, \theta_p), \qquad F_x(\theta_1, \ldots, \theta_p), \qquad F(x).$$

Expected Value

Let $F(x)$ be the distribution function for a random variable x. Let $g(x)$ be an arbitrary function on x. If the Riemann–Stieltjes integral

$$\int_{-\infty}^{\infty} g(x)\,dF(x)$$

exists, its value is said to be the *expected value* of $g(x)$. That is,

$$E[g(x)] = \int_{-\infty}^{\infty} g(x) \, dF(x).$$

The existence of this expected value requires that $g(x)$ be integrable with respect to $F(x)$. Under additional regularity assumptions with respect to $F(x)$, $E[g(x)]$ may be expressed in terms of the density function. Thus,

$$E[g(x)] = \int_{-\infty}^{\infty} g(x) f(x) \, dx.$$

If the random variable x is discrete, then the Riemann–Stieltjes integral becomes the sum of products. A requirement for the existence of the expected value is that

$$\int_{-\infty}^{\infty} |g(x)| \, dF(x) < \infty.$$

The *expected value* of a random variable (or, equivalently, the first *moment* of a probability distribution) is, by definition,

$$\alpha_1 = \mu_1 = E(x) = \int_{-\infty}^{\infty} x f(x) \, dx.$$

The *m*th *noncentral* (or raw) moment of a probability distribution is

$$\alpha_m = E(x^m) = \int_{-\infty}^{\infty} x^m f(x) \, dx, \qquad\qquad m \geq 1.$$

(m is usually an integer). The *m*th *central* moment is

$$\mu_m = E[x - E(x)]^m = \int_{-\infty}^{\infty} [x - E(x)]^m f(x) \, dx, \qquad\qquad m > 1.$$

The second central moment is the variance of the distribution.
For example, if

$$f(x) = \gamma e^{-\gamma x},$$

it can be shown that

$$\mu_1 = E(x) = \int_{-\infty}^{\infty} x f(x) \, dx = \frac{1}{\gamma}.$$

The second central moment is

$$\mu_2 = E\left[x - \frac{1}{\gamma}\right]^2 = \int_{-\infty}^{\infty} \left[x - \frac{1}{\gamma}\right]^2 f(x) \, dx = \frac{1}{\gamma^2}.$$

For many probability densities, the first and second moments are either equal to corresponding parameters of the distribution or are some relatively simple function of the parameters of the distribution. In general, the parameters of a probability density determine its moments. Vice versa, a distribution is uniquely determined by its moments. In practice the parameters of a distribution are estimated from the moments of an empirical distribution. If a distribution is symmetric about $E(x)$, then all odd moments will be zero.

Associated with some probability distributions is what is called a *moment-generating* function. The latter, if it exists, is given by

$$M_x(t) = E(e^{tx}) = \int_{-\infty}^{\infty} e^{tx} f(x) \, dx,$$

where $f(x)$ is the density function for the random variable x. If $M_x(t)$ is finite for $|t| \le T$ for some $T > 0$, then $M_x(t)$ may be expressed in the following form (valid for $|t| < T$):

$$M_x(t) = 1 + E(x)t + E(x^2)\frac{t^2}{2!} + \cdots + E(x^m)\frac{t^m}{m!} + \cdots.$$

Thus the mth raw moment is the coefficient of t^m in the series expansion of $M_x(t)$. Equivalently,

$$E(x^m) = M_x^{(m)}(t = 0), \qquad \text{where} \qquad M_x^{(m)}(t = 0)$$

is the mth derivative of $M_x(t)$ with respect to t, evaluated for $t = 0$. It will be found that

$$M_x^{(1)}(t) = E(xe^{tx}) \qquad \text{which, for } t = 0, \text{ is } E(x),$$
$$M_x^{(2)}(t) = E(x^2 e^{tx}) \qquad \text{which, for } t = 0, \text{ is } E(x^2),$$
$$M_x^{(3)}(t) = E(x^3 e^{tx}) \qquad \text{which, for } t = 0, \text{ is } E(x^3).$$

For example, the moment-generating function for the exponential distribution has the relatively simple form

$$g(t) = \left(1 - \frac{t}{\gamma}\right)^{-1}.$$

The first derivative of this function is

$$\frac{dg}{dt} = \frac{1}{\gamma}\left(1 - \frac{t}{\gamma}\right)^{-2}.$$

For $t = 0$,

$$\frac{dg}{dt} = \frac{1}{\gamma} = E(x).$$

The second derivative of $g(t)$ is

$$\frac{d^2g}{dt} = \frac{2}{\gamma^2}\left(1 - \frac{t}{\gamma}\right)^{-3}.$$

For $t = 0$,

$$\frac{d^2g}{dt^2} = \frac{2}{\gamma^2} = E(x^2) = \alpha_2.$$

To obtain the second central moment,

$$\mu_2 = E[x - E(x)]^2 = E[x - \mu_1]^2 = E(x^2) - \mu_1^2$$

$$= \frac{2}{\gamma^2} - \frac{1}{\gamma^2} = \frac{1}{\gamma^2}.$$

The mathematical principle underlying the moment-generating function is a relatively simple one. For suitable choice of t and x, one has the following converging power series:

$$e^{tx} = 1 + \frac{(tx)}{1!} + \frac{(tx)^2}{2!} + \cdots + \frac{(tx)^m}{m!} + \cdots .$$

Hence

$$M_x(t) = \int_{-\infty}^{\infty} e^{tx} f(x) \, dx$$

$$= 1 \int_{-\infty}^{\infty} f(x) \, dx + \frac{t}{1!} \int_{-\infty}^{\infty} x f(x) \, dx + \frac{t^2}{2!} \int_{-\infty}^{\infty} x^2 f(x) \, dx$$

$$+ \cdots + \frac{t^m}{m!} \int_{-\infty}^{\infty} x^m f(x) \, dx + \cdots$$

$$= 1 + \frac{t}{1!} E(x) + \frac{t^2}{2!} E(x^2) + \cdots + \frac{t^m}{m} E(x^m) + \cdots$$

$$= \sum_{j=0}^{\infty} \frac{t^j}{j!} \alpha_j, \qquad \text{where} \qquad \alpha_j = E(x^j).$$

For discrete (in contrast to continuous) variables it is convenient to work with the *probability-generating function* rather than with the moment-generating function. For a discrete distribution in which $x = 0, 1, 2, \ldots$, the probability-generating function is defined to be

$$P(t) = \sum_{j=0}^{\infty} t^j f(x_j)$$

$$= t^0 f(0) + t^1 f(1) + t^2 f(2) + t^3 f(3) + \cdots .$$

If one takes the first and second derivatives of $P(t)$ with respect to t one has

$$\frac{dP}{dt} = f(1) + 2tf(2) + 3t^2 f(3) + 4t^3 f(4) + \cdots ,$$

$$\frac{d^2 P}{dt^2} = 2f(2) + 6tf(3) + 12t^2 f(4) + \cdots .$$

If one sets $t = 1$ in the expressions given above and defines ϕ_1 and ϕ_2 as indicated below, one has

$$\phi_1 = \frac{dP}{dt}\bigg|_{t=1} = f(1) + 2f(2) + 3f(3) + 4f(4) + \cdots,$$

$$\phi_2 = \frac{d^2P}{dt^2}\bigg|_{t=1} = 2f(2) + 6f(3) + 12f(4) + 20f(5) + \cdots.$$

One notes that

$$\phi_1 = \mathrm{E}(x) \qquad \text{and} \qquad \phi_2 = \mathrm{E}[x(x-1)].$$

In general, the *m*th *factorial* moment of a distribution is

$$\phi_m = \mathrm{E}[x(x-1)(x-2)\cdots(x-m+1)] = \frac{d^mP}{dt^m}\bigg|_{t=1}.$$

The factorial moments are related to the raw moments as follows:

$$\phi_1 = \alpha_1, \qquad \phi_2 = \alpha_2 - \alpha_1, \qquad \phi_3 = \alpha_3 - 3\alpha_2 + 2\alpha_1,$$
$$\phi_4 = \alpha_4 - 6\alpha_3 + 11\alpha_2 - 6\alpha_1.$$

Rather than working with the moment-generating function, it is often convenient to work with the *characteristic function,* which is defined by

$$g(t) = \mathrm{E}(e^{itx}) = \int_{-\infty}^{\infty} e^{itx}f(x)\,dx.$$

The integral on the right exists for all distribution functions. If $\mathrm{E}(x^m)$ exists, then $g(t)$ may be expanded in terms of a Taylor series as follows:

$$g(t) = \sum_{j=0}^{m} \alpha_j \frac{(it)^j}{j!} + 0(t^m) \qquad\qquad \text{as } t \to 0.$$

The *m*th derivative (with respect to t) of $g(t)$ may be shown to be

$$\frac{d^mg}{dt^m} = i^m \int_{-\infty}^{\infty} e^{itx}x^mf(x)\,dx.$$

If one sets $t = 0$ in this derivative one has

$$\frac{d^mg}{dt^m} = i^m \int_{-\infty}^{\infty} x^mf(x)\,dx = i^m\mathrm{E}(x^m).$$

Hence it follows that

$$\mathrm{E}(x^m) = \alpha_m,$$

where α_m is the coefficient of $(it)^m/m!$ in the Taylor series expansion of $g(t)$. Thus the function $g(t)$ may be considered a special case of a moment-generating function.

In addition to the moments, there is another set of parameters which are useful in characterizing a distribution function; the latter set are called *cumulants*. The cumulants are obtained from the log of the characteristic function. Let

$$h(t) = \ln g(t).$$

The function $h(t)$ is called the second characteristic of the random variable x. If $E(x^m)$ exists, then $h(x)$ may be expanded in a Taylor series as follows:

$$h(t) = \sum_{j=0}^{m} \kappa_j \frac{(it)^j}{j!} + 0(t^m) \qquad \text{as } t \to 0.$$

κ_j in this series is the jth cumulant of the distribution. Alternatively, the mth cumulant may be obtained from

$$\left. \frac{d^m h}{dt^m} \right|_{t=0} = \kappa_m.$$

Lower-order cumulants, raw moments, and central moments are related as follows:

$$\kappa_1 = \alpha_1 = \mu_1,$$
$$\kappa_2 = \alpha_2 - \alpha_2^2 = \mu_2,$$
$$\kappa_3 = \alpha_3 - 3\alpha_1\alpha_2 + 2\alpha_1^3 = \mu_3,$$
$$\kappa_4 = \alpha_4 - 3\alpha_2^2 - 4\alpha_1\alpha_3 + 12\alpha_1^2\alpha_2 - 6\alpha_1^4 = \mu_4 - 3\mu_2^2.$$

The *skewness* of a distribution is measured by

$$\sqrt{\beta_1} = \frac{\mu_3}{\mu_2^{3/2}} = \frac{\kappa_3}{\kappa_2^{3/2}}.$$

The *kurtosis* of a distribution is measured by

$$\beta_2 = \frac{\mu_4}{\mu_2^2} = \frac{\kappa_4}{\kappa_3^2} + 3.$$

Independent Random Variables

Consider two random variables x and y. The *joint* probability density of x and y gives

$$\text{Pr}(x, y) = f(x, y).$$

The joint distribution function gives

$$\text{Pr}(x \leq x_i, y \leq y_j) = \int_{-\infty}^{x_i} \int_{-\infty}^{y_j} f(x, y) \, dx \, dy.$$

The probability density function of the random variable x considered by itself (or the marginal density for x) is

$$\text{Pr}(x) = \int_{-\infty}^{\infty} f(x, y) \, dy = g(x).$$

Similarly the probability density function for the random variable y considered by itself is

$$\Pr(y) = \int_{-\infty}^{\infty} f(x, y)\, dx = h(y).$$

If the joint probability density of x and y is the product of the marginal densities, i.e., if

$$f(x, y) = g(x)h(y),$$

then the random variables x and y are said to be *independent*. Equivalently, the random variables x and y are said to be independently distributed. For example, if the joint density of x and y is

$$f(x, y) = kme^{x+y},$$

and if the marginal densities are

$$g(x) = ke^x \qquad \text{and} \qquad h(x) = me^y,$$

then

$$f(x, y) = g(x)h(y) = (ke^x)(me^y) = kme^{x+y}.$$

For this example, x and y are distributed independently.

A.2 NORMAL DISTRIBUTION

A random variable x has a normal distribution with parameters μ and σ^2 [symbolized $N(\mu, \sigma^2)$] if its density function is given by

$$f(x) = \frac{1}{\sqrt{2\pi}\,\sigma} \exp\left[-\frac{(x - \mu)^2}{2\sigma^2} \right].$$

The distribution function is given by

$$\Pr(x \le x_j) = F(x_j) = \int_{-\infty}^{x_j} f(x)\, dx.$$

The density function and its relationship to the distribution function are illustrated in Fig. A-2.

The density function $f(x_j)$ defines the height of the curve at the point $x = x_j$. The distribution function $F(x_j)$ gives the area under the curve from $-\infty$ to x_j. Area in this case corresponds to probability. Thus

$$\Pr(x \le x_j) = F(x_j).$$

In Fig. A-3, the density at the point $x = x_i$ is given by the height $f(x_i)$. The density at the point $x = x_j$ is given by $f(x_j)$. The area under the curve between the points x_i and x_j corresponds to the probability

$$\Pr(x_i \le x \le x_j) = F(x_j) - F(x_i),$$

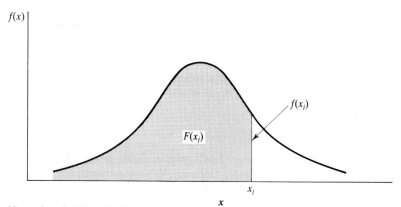

FIGURE A-2   Normal probability distribution.

that is, the difference between the areas under the curve from $-\infty$ to x_j and from $-\infty$ to x_i.

The expected value of the random variable x is

$$E(x) = \mu.$$

Thus the parameter μ of the normal distribution is the expected value of the distribution. The variance of the random variable x is

$$E(x - \mu)^2 = \sigma^2.$$

Thus the parameter σ^2 in the normal distribution is actually the variance of the distribution.

One also has

$$E(x - \mu)^3 = 0.$$

FIGURE A-3   Normal probability distribution.

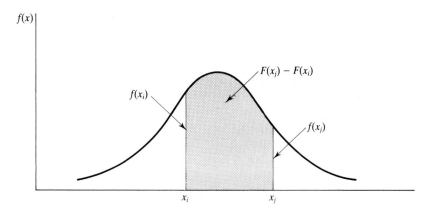

All odd central moments will be zero. Further

$$E(x - \mu)^4 = 3\sigma^4.$$

All even central moments may be expressed as functions of σ^2.

The normal distribution has the following reproductive property. If $x_1, \ldots, x_n$ are independently distributed as $N(\mu_i, \sigma_i^2)$, $i = 1, \ldots, n$, then the random variable

$$y = x_1 + \cdots + x_n$$

is distributed as $N(\mu = \Sigma\mu_i, \sigma^2 = \Sigma\sigma_i^2)$. That is, the random variable y is normally distributed with parameters $\Sigma\mu_i$ and $\Sigma\sigma_i^2$. This reproductive property of the normal distribution has important consequences. In particular, if $x_1, \ldots, x_n$ are independently, identically, and normally distributed as $N(\mu, \sigma^2)$, then the random variable

$$y = \frac{x_1 + \cdots + x_n}{n}$$

is distributed as

$$N\left(\mu, \frac{\Sigma\sigma^2}{n^2}\right) = N\left(\mu, \frac{n\sigma^2}{n^2}\right) = N\left(\mu, \frac{\sigma^2}{n}\right).$$

Variables which are Normal and Independent, with Identical Distributions, are said to be NIID variables. In this case, the mean of the distribution of the random variable y is

$$E(y) = \mu,$$

and the variance of the random variable y is

$$E(y - \mu)^2 = \sigma_y^2 = \frac{\sigma^2}{n}.$$

A.3 GAMMA AND CHI-SQUARE DISTRIBUTIONS

A random variable x has a *gamma* distribution if its density function has the form

$$g(\alpha, p) = \frac{\alpha^p}{\Gamma(p)} e^{-\alpha x} x^{p-1}, \qquad x, \alpha, p > 0, \tag{1}$$

where α and p are parameters of the distribution. The corresponding distribution function is

$$G(\alpha, p) = \int_0^x g(\alpha, p) \, dx. \tag{2}$$

A random variable having this distribution function is called a gamma variable.

The expected value of a gamma variable is

$$E(x) = \mu = \frac{p}{\alpha};$$

its variance is

$$\sigma^2 = \frac{p}{\alpha^2}.$$

A geometric representation of the gamma probability law is shown in Fig. A-4. For each of the three densities shown in this figure, $\alpha = \frac{1}{2}$. In this case, the larger p is, the flatter the appearance of the density function. Also, the larger the value of the parameter p, the larger is the mean. In all cases the total area under the curve is unity.

The gamma distribution has the following *reproductive* property. If the random variables $x_1, \ldots, x_k$ are each independently distributed as gamma variables with parameters α, p_i, then the random variable y, defined by

$$y = \Sigma x_i,$$

is a gamma variable with parameters α, Σp_i. That is, the probability density of the random variable y has the form

$$f(y) = g(\alpha, \Sigma p_i).$$

The chi-square distribution is that special case of the gamma distribution

FIGURE A-4   Gamma probability distribution.

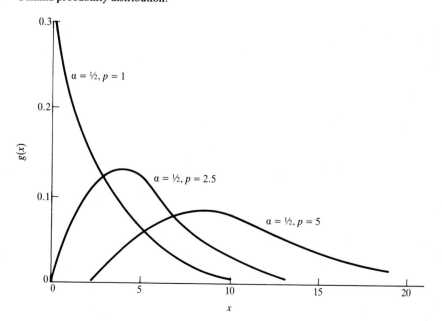

for which the parameters are

$$\alpha = \frac{1}{2} \quad \text{and} \quad p = \frac{k}{2}.$$

Thus a random variable x is distributed as chi square if the density function has the form

$$g\left(\frac{1}{2}, \frac{k}{2}\right) = \frac{(\frac{1}{2})^{k/2}}{\Gamma(k/2)} e^{-x/2} x^{(k/2)-1}.$$

The density function corresponding to this special case of a gamma variable is denoted

$$\chi^2(k) = g\left(\frac{1}{2}, \frac{k}{2}\right).$$

The parameter k is called the degrees of freedom of the chi-square distribution. The expected value of a chi-square variable is

$$\mu = \mathrm{E}(x) = \frac{p}{\alpha} = \frac{k/2}{\frac{1}{2}} = k.$$

The variance of a chi-square variable is

$$\sigma^2 = \frac{p}{\alpha^2} = \frac{k/2}{(\frac{1}{2})^2} = 2k.$$

A chi-square variable has the same sort of reproductive property as a gamma variable. If $x_1, \ldots, x_p$ are independent chi-square variables distributed as $\chi^2(k_1), \ldots, \chi^2(k_p)$, then the random variable

$$y = x_1 + \cdots + x_p$$

has the density function given by $\chi^2(k = \Sigma k_i)$.

A chi-square variable is related to a normally distributed variable. If x is a random variable with the distribution $N(0, 1)$, then the random variable $y = x^2$ is distributed as chi square with one degree of freedom; symbolically, y is $\chi^2(1)$. Further, if the random variables $x_1, \ldots, x_k$ are independently distributed as $N(0, 1)$, then the random variable y defined by

$$y = x_1^2 + \cdots + x_k^2$$

will be distributed as chi square with k degrees of freedom. Symbolically,

$$y: \chi^2(k).$$

This last statement is read: y is distributed as chi square with k degrees of freedom.

If $x_1, \ldots, x_k$ are independently distributed as $N(\mu_i, \sigma^2)$, where $i = 1, \ldots, k$, then the random variable y defined by

$$y = \frac{x_1^2 + \cdots + x_k^2}{\sigma^2}$$

will be distributed as a *noncentral* chi-square variable with degrees of freedom equal to k and noncentrality parameter λ given by

$$\lambda = \frac{\mu_1^2 + \cdots + \mu_k^2}{\sigma^2} = \frac{\mu^2}{\sigma^2}, \quad \text{where} \quad \mu = \Sigma \mu_i^2.$$

[Scheffé (1959) defines the noncentrality parameter as

$$\delta^2 = \frac{\Sigma \mu_i^2}{\sigma^2} \quad \text{or} \quad \delta = \sqrt{\frac{\Sigma \mu_i^2}{\sigma^2}}.$$

Rao (1965) defines the noncentrality parameter as

$$\lambda_R = \frac{\Sigma \mu_i^2}{\sigma^2}.$$

Graybill (1961) defines the noncentrality parameter as

$$\lambda_G = \frac{\Sigma \mu_i^2}{2\sigma^2}.$$

The notation system adopted by Rao is the one followed here.]

If $x_1, \ldots, x_k$ are independently distributed as $N(\mu_i, \sigma^2/n)$, then the random variable

$$y = \frac{x_1^2 + \cdots + x_k^2}{\sigma^2/n} = \frac{n\Sigma x_i^2}{\sigma^2}$$

will be distributed as a noncentral chi square with noncentrality parameter

$$\lambda = \frac{n\Sigma \mu_i^2}{\sigma^2}.$$

This is the form of the noncentrality parameter that one encounters in the analysis of variance. Each x_i in this case corresponds to a mean based upon n observations. It should be noted that the noncentrality parameter as defined here is obtained by replacing each x_i in y by $E(x_i)$.

The noncentral chi-square distribution is denoted by the symbol $\chi^2(k; \lambda)$. The density function for this distribution has the form

$$\chi^2(k; \lambda) = e^{-\lambda/2} \sum_{r=0}^{\infty} \frac{1}{r!} \left(\frac{\lambda}{2}\right)^r g\left(\frac{1}{2}, r + \frac{k}{2}\right).$$

When $\lambda = 0$, the only nonzero term in this summation is that corresponding to $r = 0$. Hence, when $\lambda = 0$,

$$\chi^2(k; 0) = g\left(\frac{1}{2}, \frac{k}{2}\right) = \chi^2(k).$$

The chi-square distribution is that special case of the noncentral chi-square distribution corresponding to $\lambda = 0$. To distinguish between the former and the latter distributions, the former is sometimes called the *central* chi-square distribution. When the term "chi-square distribution" is used, it is the central distribution that is implied unless otherwise indicated.

The expected value of a variate having a noncentral chi-square distribution is

$$E[\chi^2(k; \lambda)] = k + \lambda.$$

The variance of a noncentral chi-square variate is

$$2k + 4\lambda.$$

The noncentral chi-square distribution has the same kind of additive properties as does the central chi-square distribution. If u_1 is distributed as $\chi^2(k_1; \lambda_1)$ and u_2 is independently distributed as $\chi^2(k_2; \lambda_2)$, then the random variable $u_1 + u_2$ is distributed as

$$\chi^2(k_1 + k_2; \lambda_1 + \lambda_2).$$

The noncentral chi square may be approximated by a central chi-square distribution as follows:

$$\chi^2_{1-\alpha}(k; \lambda) = c\chi^2_{1-\alpha}(k'),$$

where c and k' are determined from the following relationships:

$$ck' = k + \lambda,$$
$$c^2k' = k + 2\lambda.$$

These relationships equate the means and variances of the central and noncentral chi-square distributions. For example, if $k = 10$ and $\lambda = 2$,

$$c = 1.17 \quad \text{and} \quad k' = 10.29.$$

A.4 BETA AND *F* DISTRIBUTIONS

Let x_1 and x_2 be independently distributed random variables with

$$x_1: g(\alpha, p_1) \quad \text{and} \quad x_2: g(\alpha, p_2).$$

Thus x_1 and x_2 are independent gamma variables. Let the random variable y be defined as

$$y = \frac{x_1}{x_1 + x_2} = \frac{x_1/x_2}{(x_1/x_2) + 1}.$$

The density function for y is given by what is called a beta distribution having parameters p_1 and p_2 and denoted $b(p_1, p_2)$. Thus

$$y: b(p_1, p_2) = \frac{\Gamma(p_1 + p_2)}{\Gamma(p_1)\Gamma(p_2)} y^{p_1 - 1}(1 - y)^{p_2 - 1}$$

$$= \frac{1}{\beta(p_1, p_2)} y^{p_1 - 1}(1 - y)^{p_2 - 1}, \qquad 0 < y < 1.$$

The expected value of a beta variable is

$$\mu = \mathrm{E}(y) = \frac{p_1}{p_1 + p_2}.$$

The variance of a beta variable is

$$\sigma^2 = \frac{p_1 p_2}{(p_1 + p_2)^2 (p_1 + p_2 + 1)}.$$

The form of the density function for various values of the parameters is shown in Fig. A-5.

There is a quasi-symmetry to the beta distribution in the sense that

$$\int_0^{y_i} b(p_1, p_2) \, dy = 1 - \int_0^{1-y_i} b(p_2, p_1) \, dy,$$

or equivalently,

$$\int_{y_i}^1 b(p_1, p_2) \, dy = \int_0^{1-y_i} b(p_2, p_1) \, dy.$$

This quasi-symmetry is illustrated in Fig. A-6.

FIGURE A-5   Beta probability distribution.

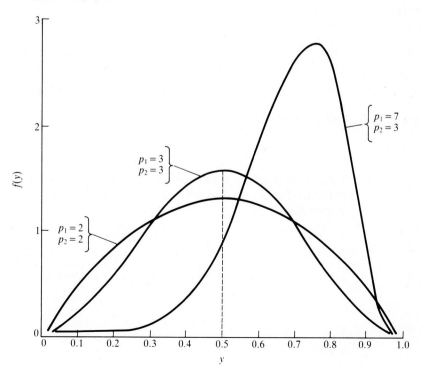

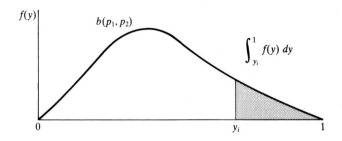

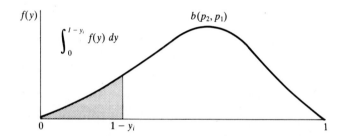

FIGURE A-6   Quasi-symmetry of beta distribution.

Consider now the independent random variables

$$x_1: \chi^2(k_1) \qquad \text{and} \qquad x_2: \chi^2(k_2).$$

Define the random variable F as

$$F = \frac{x_1/k_1}{x_2/k_2}.$$

Thus F is the ratio of two independent chi-square variables. The density function for F is that of the F distribution with parameters k_1 and k_2. Symbolically,

$$F: F(k_1, k_2) = \frac{(k_1/k_2)^{k_1/2}}{\beta(k_1/2, \, k_2/2)} \frac{F^{(k_1/2)-1}}{[1 + (k_1/k_2)F]^{(k_1+k_2)/2}}.$$

The variable y, which was defined above, may be cast in the form

$$y = \frac{x_1}{x_1 + x_2} = \frac{x_1/x_2}{(x_1/x_2) + 1} = \frac{(k_1/k_2)F}{(k_1/k_2)F + 1} = \frac{k_1 F}{k_1 F + k_2},$$

where

$$F = \frac{x_1/k_1}{x_2/k_2}.$$

Solving this last equation for F gives

$$F = \frac{k_2}{k_1} \frac{y}{1-y}.$$

Thus the random variable F is a transformed beta variable. The relationship between the F and beta distributions may be expressed as follows:

$$\int_{y_i}^{1} b\left(\frac{k_1}{2}, \frac{k_2}{2}\right) dy = 1 - \int_{0}^{y_i} b\left(\frac{k_1}{2}, \frac{k_2}{2}\right) dy = \int_{F_i}^{\infty} F(k_1, k_2) \, dF,$$

where

$$y_i = \frac{k_1 F_i}{k_1 F_i + k_2} \quad \text{or} \quad F_i = \frac{k_2}{k_1} \frac{y_i}{1 - y_i}.$$

Thus

$$\Pr(y \geq y_i) = \Pr(F \geq F_i).$$

Note that

$$1 - y_i = \frac{k_2}{k_2 + k_1 F_i} = \frac{1}{1 + (k_1/k_2) F_i}.$$

Tables of the F distribution are actually computed from tables of the beta distribution. The relationship between probabilities (areas) of the beta and F distributions is illustrated in Fig. A-7.

The first moment of the F distribution is

$$E(F) = \frac{k_2}{k_2 - 2}, \qquad\qquad k_2 > 2.$$

The mode of the F distribution, for $k_1 > 2$, is at the point

$$\frac{k_1 - 2}{k_1} \frac{k_2}{k_2 + 2}.$$

The second central moment of the F distribution is

$$E[F - E(F)]^2 = \frac{2k_2^2(k_1 + k_2 - 2)}{k_1(k_2 - 2)^2(k_2 - 4)}, \qquad\qquad k_2 > 4.$$

Consider now the independent random variables

$$x_1: \chi^2(k_1; \lambda) \qquad \text{and} \qquad x_2: \chi^2(k_2).$$

That is, x_1 is distributed as noncentral chi square, and x_2 is distributed as central chi square. Let the random variable F be defined as

$$F = \frac{x_1/k_1}{x_2/k_2}.$$

This random variable has a *noncentral* F distribution with noncentrality parameter λ. The symbol $F(k_1, k_2; \lambda)$ is used to denote the noncentral F distribution. The noncentral F is closely related to the noncentral beta

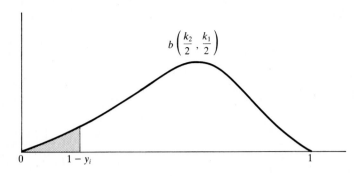

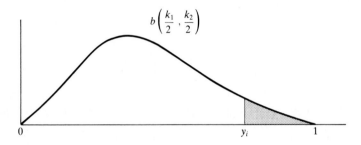

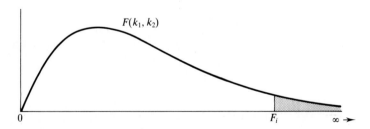

FIGURE A-7 Relationship between probabilities obtained from beta and F distributions.

distribution; the latter has the probability density

$$b\left(\frac{k_1}{2}, \frac{k_2}{2}; \lambda\right) = e^{-\lambda/2} \sum_{r=0}^{\infty} \left(\frac{\lambda}{2}\right)^r \left(\frac{1}{r!}\right) b\left(\frac{k_1}{2} + r, \frac{k_2}{2}\right).$$

When $\lambda = 0$, the only nonzero term in this summation is that corresponding to $r = 0$. In this case, the term corresponding to $r = 0$ is

$$b\left(\frac{k_1}{2}, \frac{k_2}{2}; 0\right) = b\left(\frac{k_1}{2}, \frac{k_2}{2}\right).$$

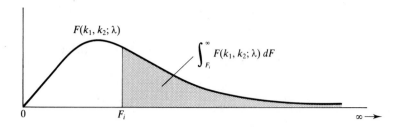

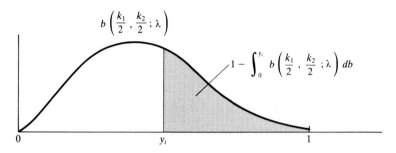

FIGURE A-8   Relationship between noncentral F and noncentral beta.

Thus the ordinary (or central) beta distribution is that special case of the noncentral beta in which the noncentrality parameter is zero. (See Fig. A-8.)

The expected value of the noncentral F distribution is

$$\frac{k_2(k_1 + \lambda)}{(k_2 - 2)k_1} = \frac{k_2}{k_2 - 2}\left(1 + \frac{\lambda}{k_1}\right), \qquad k_2 > 2.$$

The second raw moment is

$$\frac{k_2^2}{(k_2 - 2)(k_2 - 4)k_1^2}[(k_1 + \lambda)^2 + 2(k_2 + 2\lambda)], \qquad k_2 > 4.$$

The relationship between the noncentral F and the noncentral beta distributions is the same as the corresponding relationship between the central distributions. Tables of the noncentral beta distribution as prepared by Tang appear in Graybill (1961, pp. 444–459). In terms of the noncentrality parameter as defined here, the noncentrality parameter as used in these tables is

$$\phi = \sqrt{\frac{\lambda}{k_1 + 1}}.$$

From the tables as constructed by Tang,

$$1 - \int_0^{y_i} b\left(\frac{k_1}{2}, \frac{k_2}{2}; \phi\right) dy = \int_{F_i}^{\infty} F(k_1, k_2; \lambda) \, dF,$$

where

$$y_i = \frac{k_1 F_i}{k_1 F_i + k_2}.$$

A portion of the tables of the noncentral F constructed by Tiku (1967) appears in Table D.14.

Explicitly the probability density for the noncentral F is

$$F(k_1, k_2; \lambda) = e^{(-\lambda/2)} \sum_{r=0}^{\infty} \frac{(\lambda/2)^r (k_1/k_2)^{f_r}}{\beta(f_r, k_2/2)} \frac{F^{f_r - 1}}{[1 + (k_1/k_2)F]^{f_r + (k_2/2)}},$$

where

$$f_r = \frac{k_1}{2} + r.$$

The noncentral F distribution may be approximated quite well by a central F distribution as follows:

$$\int_{F_{1-\alpha}}^{\infty} F(k_1, k_2; \lambda) \, dF \doteq \int_{(1/c)F_{1-\alpha}}^{\infty} F(k_1', k_2) \, dF,$$

where

$$F_{1-\alpha} = F_{1-\alpha}(k_1, k_2), \qquad c = \frac{k_1 + \lambda}{k_1}, \qquad k_1' = \frac{(k_1 + \lambda)^2}{k_1 + 2\lambda}.$$

For example, if

$$\alpha = 0.01, \qquad k_1 = 4, \qquad k_2 = 6, \qquad \text{and} \qquad \lambda = 16.2,$$

then

$$F_{0.99}(4, 6) = 9.15.$$

From tables of the noncentral F distribution one will find that

$$\int_{9.15}^{\infty} F(4, 6; 16.2) = 0.24.$$

$$\left(\text{Note:} \quad \phi = \sqrt{\frac{16.2}{5}} = 1.80.\right)$$

To use the approximation by means of the central F distribution,

$$c = \frac{4 + 16.2}{4} = 5.05, \qquad k_1' = \frac{(4 + 16.2)^2}{4 + 2(16.2)} = 8.99,$$

$$\frac{1}{c} F_{0.99}(4, 6) = \frac{1}{5.05}(9.15) = 1.81.$$

By interpolation in tables of the central F distribution,

$$\int_{1.81}^{\infty} F(8.99, 6) \, dF = 0.24.$$

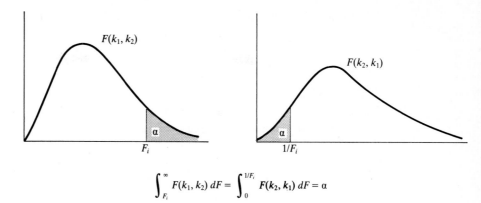

$$\int_{F_i}^{\infty} F(k_1, k_2)\, dF = \int_0^{1/F_i} F(k_2, k_1)\, dF = \alpha$$

FIGURE A-9   Quasi-symmetry of F distribution.

Relatively extensive tables of the noncentral F have been prepared by Tiku (1967).

The F distribution has a quasi-symmetry which is similar to that of the beta distribution. This symmetry is illustrated for the case of the central F distribution in Fig. A-9. From this relationship one may compute left-hand areas of $F(k_2, k_1)$ from right-hand areas of $F(k_1, k_2)$. The latter areas are found in tables of the central F distribution.

A.5   STUDENT'S t DISTRIBUTION

Let the random variables x and y be independently distributed as

$$x: N(0, 1), \qquad y: \chi^2(k).$$

That is, x is a unit normal variate, and y is a chi-square variate. Define the random variable t as

$$t = \frac{x}{\sqrt{y/k}}.$$

The random variable t will be distributed as Student's t with parameter k. Symbolically,

$$t: t(k).$$

The probability density function for Student's t distribution has the form

$$f(t) = \frac{\Gamma[\frac{1}{2} + (k/2)]}{\sqrt{k}\,\Gamma(\frac{1}{2})\Gamma(k/2)} \left(1 + \frac{t^2}{k}\right)^{-(k+1)/2}$$

$$= \frac{1}{\sqrt{k}\beta(\frac{1}{2}, k/2)} \left(1 + \frac{t^2}{k}\right)^{-(k+1)/2}.$$

Student's t distribution is symmetric about $E(t)$, which is

$$E(t) = 0.$$

The second moment of the t distribution is

$$E(t^2) = \sigma_t^2 = \frac{k}{k-2}.$$

In general, since the t distribution is symmetric about zero, all odd moments will be zero. For even moments, if $m < k$, the mth moment is given by

$$\mu_m = \frac{1(3)(5) \cdots (m-1)k^{m/2}}{(k-2)(k-4) \cdots (k-m)}.$$

In particular, if $m = 2$,

$$\mu_2 = E(t^2) = \frac{k}{k-2}.$$

Student's t distribution is closely related to the F distribution. Specifically, if one defines the random variable $v = t^2$, where $t: t(k)$, then the distribution of the random variable v is $F(1, k)$. This relationship follows from the fact that

$$t^2 = \frac{x^2}{y/k} = \frac{\chi^2(1)}{\chi^2(k)/k} = F(1, k).$$

One notes that

$$E(t^2) = \sigma_t^2 = E[F(1, k)] = \frac{k}{k-2}.$$

That is, the variance of the t distribution is the mean of the F distribution that corresponds to the t distribution.

Consider now the independently distributed random variables

$$x: N(\mu, \sigma^2) \qquad \text{and} \qquad \frac{y}{\sigma^2} = \chi^2(k).$$

Let

$$\sqrt{\lambda} = \sqrt{\frac{\mu^2}{\sigma^2}} \qquad \text{and} \qquad t = \frac{x/\sigma}{\sqrt{y/k\sigma^2}} = \frac{x}{\sqrt{y/k}}.$$

The random variable defined above has a *noncentral* t distribution with noncentrality parameter $\sqrt{\lambda}$. The density function for the noncentral t distribution has the form

$$t(k; \sqrt{\lambda}) = \frac{k^{k/2}}{\Gamma(k/2)} \frac{e^{-\lambda/2}}{(k+t^2)^{(k+1)/2}} h(t),$$

where

$$h(t) = \sum_{s=0}^{\infty} \Gamma\left(\frac{k+s+1}{2}\right) \left(\frac{\lambda^{s/2}}{s!}\right) \left(\frac{2t^2}{k+t^2}\right)^{s/2}.$$

When $\sqrt{\lambda} = 0$, the only nonzero term in the summation is that corresponding to $s = 0$. It will be found that $t(k; 0)$ reduces to the ordinary (or central) Student's t distribution.

The noncentral t distribution may be approximated by

$$\Pr\left(t \leq u\right) = \Pr\left[z \leq (u - \sqrt{\lambda})\left(1 + \frac{u^2}{2k}\right)^{-\frac{1}{2}}\right],$$

where z is $N(0, 1)$. When $\sqrt{\lambda} = 0$, one has an approximation to the central t distribution. For example, if $k = 20$ and $\lambda = 0$, from tables of the central t distribution one has

$$\Pr\left(t \leq 1.32\right) = 0.90.$$

The approximation gives

$$\Pr\left(t \leq 1.32\right) \doteq \Pr\left\{z \leq 1.32\left[1 + \frac{(1.32)^2}{20}\right]^{-\frac{1}{2}}\right\} = \Pr\left(z \leq 1.29\right)$$

$$= 0.90.$$

Just as the square of a central t variate is a central F variate, so the square of a noncentral t variate will be a noncentral F variate. Thus, $t^2(k; \sqrt{\lambda}) = F(1, k; \lambda)$. Hence one may also use the method outlined under the noncentral F to approximate the noncentral t.

A.6   BIVARIATE NORMAL DISTRIBUTION

If one is considering, simultaneously, two random variables, say x and y, the joint distribution function has the general form

$$F(x', y') = \Pr\left(x \leq x', y \leq y'\right) = \int_{-\infty}^{x'} \int_{-\infty}^{y'} f(x, y)\, dx\, dy,$$

where $f(x, y)$ is the joint density function. Geometrically, the probability element $f(x, y)\, dx\, dy$ represents the volume of a solid rectangle having a base area equal to $dx\, dy$ and height equal to $f(x, y)$.

The bivariate normal distribution has the density function

$$f(x, y) = ke^{-Q^2/2},$$

where

$$Q^2 = \frac{1}{1 - \rho^2}\left[\frac{(x - \mu_x)^2}{\sigma_x^2} + \frac{(y - \mu_y)^2}{\sigma_y^2} - \frac{2\rho(x - \mu_x)(y - \mu_y)}{\sigma_x \sigma_y}\right],$$

$$k = \frac{1}{2\pi\sigma_x\sigma_y\sqrt{1 - \rho^2}}.$$

To make the parameters of this distribution explicit, the density function may be written in the form

$$f(x, y; \mu_x, \mu_y, \sigma_x^2, \sigma_y^2, \rho).$$

The bivariate normal distribution may also be represented in an alternative form. Let

$$\mathbf{u} = \begin{bmatrix} x \\ y \end{bmatrix}, \qquad \mathbf{\mu} = \begin{bmatrix} \mu_x \\ \mu_y \end{bmatrix}, \qquad \Sigma = \begin{bmatrix} \sigma_x^2 & \rho\sigma_x\sigma_y \\ \rho\sigma_x\sigma_y & \sigma_y^2 \end{bmatrix}, \qquad |\Sigma| = \sigma_x^2\sigma_y^2(1 - \rho^2).$$

The density function for the bivariate normal is

$$f(\mathbf{u}) = k \exp\left[-\tfrac{1}{2}(\mathbf{u} - \mathbf{\mu})'\Sigma^{-1}(\mathbf{u} - \mathbf{\mu})\right],$$

where

$$k = \frac{1}{2\pi \, |\Sigma|^{\frac{1}{2}}}.$$

Associated with a bivariate distribution is a set of marginal distributions. The marginal distribution of the y variable is

$$f_1(y) = \int_{-\infty}^{\infty} f(x, y) \, dx.$$

For the bivariate normal distribution, this marginal distribution is the univariate normal distribution with parameters μ_y and σ_y^2. The marginal distribution for the x variable is

$$f_2(x) = \int_{-\infty}^{\infty} f(x, y) \, dy.$$

For the bivariate normal distribution, this marginal distribution is the univariate normal distribution with parameters μ_x and σ_x^2. Thus the parameters μ_x, μ_y, σ_x^2, σ_y^2 of the bivariate distribution are the parameters of the corresponding univariate marginal distributions.

Also associated with a bivariate distribution is a set of conditional distributions, that is, the distribution of one variate for a fixed value of the second variate. The conditional probability density of y for fixed x is denoted by the symbol $f(y \mid x)$. This conditional density is related to the joint and marginal densities as follows:

$$f(y \mid x) = \frac{f(x, y)}{f_2(x)}.$$

In terms of probabilities,

$$\Pr(y \mid x) = \frac{\Pr(x, y)}{\Pr(x)} \qquad \text{or} \qquad \Pr(x, y) = \Pr(y \mid x) \Pr(x).$$

That is, the joint probability of x and y is the product of the conditional probability of y given x and the probability of x. The distribution function for a conditional distribution has the form

$$F(y = y' \mid x = x') = \int_{-\infty}^{y'} f(y \mid x = x') \, dy = \int_{-\infty}^{y'} \frac{f(x', y)}{f_2(x')} \, dy.$$

For the bivariate normal distribution, the probability density $f(y \mid x)$ is the univariate normal distribution with parameters

$$\mu_{y \mid x} = \alpha_{yx} + \beta_{yx} x \qquad \text{and} \qquad \sigma^2_{y \mid x} = \sigma^2_y (1 - \rho^2),$$

where $\qquad \beta_{yx} = \rho \left(\dfrac{\sigma_y}{\sigma_x} \right) \qquad$ and $\qquad \alpha_{yx} = \mu_y - \beta_{yx} \mu_x.$

The parameter ρ is defined by

$$\rho = \frac{\sigma_{xy}}{\sigma_x \sigma_y}, \qquad \text{where } \sigma_{xy} = \text{covariance between } x \text{ and } y.$$

One notes that the conditional variance $\sigma^2_{y \mid x}$ does not depend upon x.

In general, the conditional distribution of x for fixed y is given by

$$f(x \mid y) = \frac{f(x, y)}{f_1(y)}.$$

For the special case of the bivariate normal distribution, the probability density $f(x \mid y)$ is the univariate normal with parameters

$$\mu_{x \mid y} = \alpha_{xy} + \beta_{xy} y \qquad \text{and} \qquad \sigma^2_{x \mid y} = \sigma^2_x (1 - \rho^2),$$

where $\qquad \beta_{xy} = \rho \left(\dfrac{\sigma_x}{\sigma_y} \right) \qquad$ and $\qquad \alpha_{xy} = \mu_x - \beta_{xy} \mu_y.$

One notes that the conditional variance $\sigma_{x \mid y}$ does not depend upon y.

In general, the r, s joint central moment of a bivariate distribution is defined by

$$\mu_{r,s} = E[(x - \mu_x)^r (y - \mu_y)^s] = \int_{-\infty}^{\infty} \int_{-\infty}^{\infty} (x - \mu_x)^r (y - \mu_y)^s f(x, y) \, dx \, dy.$$

For the special case of the bivariate normal distribution,

$$\mu_{10} = \mu_x \qquad \text{and} \qquad \mu_{01} = \mu_y.$$

Thus μ_x and μ_y, which are moments of the marginal distributions, are also the indicated moments of the joint distribution. One also has

$$\mu_{20} = \sigma^2_x \qquad \text{and} \qquad \mu_{02} = \sigma^2_y.$$

It may also be shown that (for the special case of the bivariate normal)

$$\mu_{11} = \sigma_{xy} = \rho \sigma_x \sigma_y.$$

Thus the covariance between x and y, σ_{xy}, is a moment of the joint distribution. In terms of the joint-moment notation, the parameter ρ has the form

$$\rho = \frac{\mu_{11}}{\sqrt{\mu_{10}\mu_{01}}} \, .$$

Other joint moments of the bivariate normal distribution are as follows:

$$\mu_{30} = \mu_{12} = \mu_{21} = 0,$$
$$\mu_{40} = 3\sigma_x^4, \qquad \mu_{31} = 3\rho\sigma_x^3\sigma_y, \qquad \mu_{22} = (1 + 2\rho^2)\sigma_x^2\sigma_y^2,$$
$$\mu_{04} = 3\sigma_y^4, \qquad \mu_{13} = 3\rho\sigma_x\sigma_y^3.$$

A.7 MULTIVARIATE NORMAL DISTRIBUTION

Let

$$\mathbf{x}' = [x_1 \ x_2 \ \cdots \ x_p]$$

be a vector of random variables whose joint probability density function is

$$f(\mathbf{x}) = \frac{1}{(2\pi)^{p/2} \, |\Sigma|^{\frac{1}{2}}} \exp \left[-\tfrac{1}{2}(\mathbf{x} - \boldsymbol{\mu})'\Sigma^{-1}(\mathbf{x} - \boldsymbol{\mu})\right],$$

where

$$\underset{p,1}{\boldsymbol{\mu}} = \begin{bmatrix} \mu_1 \\ \mu_2 \\ \vdots \\ \mu_p \end{bmatrix}, \qquad \underset{p,p}{\Sigma} = \begin{bmatrix} \sigma_1^2 & \sigma_{12} & \cdots & \sigma_{1p} \\ \sigma_{21} & \sigma_2^2 & \cdots & \sigma_{2p} \\ \vdots & \vdots & & \vdots \\ \sigma_{p1} & \sigma_{p2} & \cdots & \sigma_p^2 \end{bmatrix}, \qquad \text{rank}(\Sigma) = p.$$

A vector random variable $\mathbf{x}$ having this density function is said to be distributed as a p-variate normal distribution with parameters $\boldsymbol{\mu}$ and Σ. In symbols,

$$\mathbf{x}: N_p(\boldsymbol{\mu}, \Sigma).$$

The parameter Σ is called the *dispersion* (or covariance) matrix for the vector variable $\mathbf{x}$. The distribution function $F(\mathbf{x}_j)$ represents

$$F(\mathbf{x}_j) = \text{Pr}(\mathbf{x} \le \mathbf{x}_j), \qquad \text{where} \qquad \mathbf{x}_j' = [x_{1j} \ x_{2j} \ \cdots \ x_{pj}].$$

The marginal distribution for each of the component variables x_i can be shown to be

$$x_i: N(\mu_i, \sigma_i^2), \qquad\qquad i = 1, 2, \ldots, p.$$

That is, each x_i is univariate normal with the parameters indicated. For the special case in which

$$\Sigma = \begin{bmatrix} \sigma_1^2 & 0 & \cdots & 0 \\ 0 & \sigma_2^2 & \cdots & 0 \\ \vdots & \vdots & & \vdots \\ 0 & 0 & \cdots & \sigma_p^2 \end{bmatrix},$$

the joint density function becomes

$$f(\mathbf{x}) = f_1(x_1)f_2(x_2) \cdots f_p(x_p),$$

where $f_i(x_i)$ is the univariate density $N(\mu_i, \sigma_i^2)$. Thus, for a multivariate normal distribution, if the dispersion matrix is diagonal, the component variables are *statistically independent*; that is, the joint distribution is the product of the marginal distributions.

Let the random variable u be defined by

$$u = \underset{1,p}{\mathbf{k}'} \underset{p,1}{\mathbf{x}},$$

where $\mathbf{k}$ is a vector of known constants. The random variable u will be distributed as a univariate normal with parameters

$$\mu_u = \mathbf{k}'\boldsymbol{\mu} \qquad \text{and} \qquad \sigma_u^2 = \mathbf{k}'\Sigma\mathbf{k}.$$

In general, any linear function of the components of $\mathbf{x}$ will be normally distributed.

Let the vector variable $\mathbf{x}$ be partitioned as follows:

$$\underset{p,1}{\mathbf{x}} = \begin{bmatrix} x_1 \\ \vdots \\ x_{p-1} \\ \hline x_p \end{bmatrix} = \begin{matrix} p-1 \\ 1 \end{matrix}\begin{bmatrix} \mathbf{x}_{p-1} \\ x_p \end{bmatrix}.$$

Also let

$$\underset{p,1}{\boldsymbol{\mu}} = \begin{matrix} p-1 \\ 1 \end{matrix}\begin{bmatrix} \boldsymbol{\mu}_{p-1} \\ \mu_p \end{bmatrix}, \qquad \underset{p,p}{\Sigma} = \begin{matrix} p-1 \\ 1 \end{matrix}\overset{\begin{matrix} p-1 & 1 \end{matrix}}{\begin{bmatrix} \Sigma_{p-1} & \boldsymbol{\sigma}_{p-1} \\ \boldsymbol{\sigma}'_{p-1} & \sigma_p^2 \end{bmatrix}},$$

where

$$\boldsymbol{\sigma}_{p-1} = \begin{bmatrix} \sigma_{1p} \\ \sigma_{2p} \\ \vdots \\ \sigma_{p-1,p} \end{bmatrix}.$$

Thus the random variable $\mathbf{x}_{p-1}$ consists of the first $p-1$ components of the vector $\mathbf{x}$. Hence,

$$\mathbf{x}_{p-1}: N_{p-1}(\boldsymbol{\mu}_{p-1}, \Sigma_{p-1}), \qquad x_p: N_1(\mu_p, \sigma_p^2).$$

The conditional distribution of x_p for a fixed set of values for $\mathbf{x}_{p-1}$, say $\mathbf{x}_{p-1,j}$, will be univariate normal in form with mean

$$\mu_p \mid \mathbf{x}_{p-1,j} = \alpha + \boldsymbol{\beta}'\mathbf{x}_{p-1,j},$$

where $\qquad \boldsymbol{\beta} = \Sigma_{p-1}^{-1}\boldsymbol{\sigma}_{p-1} \qquad \text{and} \qquad \alpha = \mu_p - \boldsymbol{\beta}'\boldsymbol{\mu}_{p-1}.$

The variance of this conditional distribution is

$$\sigma_p^2 \mid \mathbf{x}_{p-1,j} = \sigma_p^2 - \boldsymbol{\beta}' \Sigma_{p-1} \boldsymbol{\beta}$$
$$= \sigma_p^2 - \boldsymbol{\sigma}'_{p-1} \Sigma_{p-1}^{-1} \boldsymbol{\sigma}_{p-1}.$$

The last line follows from the one above by replacing $\boldsymbol{\beta}$ with $\Sigma_{p-1}^{-1} \boldsymbol{\sigma}_{p-1}$. One notes that the conditional variance does not depend upon $\mathbf{x}_{p-1,j}$. One also notes that the conditional means are linear functions of the components of $\mathbf{x}_{p-1}$. When

$$\Sigma_{p-1} = \text{diagonal matrix,}$$

that is, when the components of $\mathbf{x}_{p-1}$ are statistically independent, then

$$\beta_j = \frac{\sigma_{jp}}{\sigma_j^2}, \qquad\qquad j = 1, \ldots, p-1.$$

The square of the correlation between x_p and a linear function of the components of $\mathbf{x}_{p-1}$, say $m = \mathbf{k}' \mathbf{x}_{p-1}$, is given by

$$\rho_{x_p m}^2 = \frac{\text{cov}^2 (x_p, m)}{\text{var}(x_p)\,\text{var}(m)} = \frac{(\mathbf{k}' \boldsymbol{\sigma}_{p-1})^2}{\sigma_p^2 (\mathbf{k}' \Sigma_{p-1} \mathbf{k})}.$$

The numerator follows from the relationship

$$\text{cov}(x_p, \mathbf{k}' \mathbf{x}_{p-1}) = \sum_{j=1}^{p-1} k_j \sigma_{jp} = \mathbf{k}' \boldsymbol{\sigma}_{p-1}.$$

The maximum possible squared correlation is attained when

$$\mathbf{k} = c\boldsymbol{\beta} \qquad \text{or} \qquad m = c\boldsymbol{\beta}' \mathbf{x}_{p-1},$$

where
$$c = \text{arbitrary constant,}$$
$$\boldsymbol{\beta} = \Sigma_{p-1}^{-1} \boldsymbol{\sigma}_{p-1}.$$

For this choice of the vector $\mathbf{k}$ one has

$$\rho_{x_p m}^2 = \frac{(c\boldsymbol{\beta}' \boldsymbol{\sigma}_{p-1})^2}{\sigma_p^2 (c^2 \boldsymbol{\beta}' \Sigma_{p-1} \boldsymbol{\beta})}$$
$$= \frac{(\boldsymbol{\beta}' \boldsymbol{\sigma}_{p-1})^2}{\sigma_p^2 (\boldsymbol{\beta}' \Sigma_{p-1} \Sigma_{p-1}^{-1} \boldsymbol{\sigma}_{p-1})}$$
$$= \frac{(\boldsymbol{\beta}' \boldsymbol{\sigma}_{p-1})^2}{\sigma_p^2 (\boldsymbol{\beta}' \boldsymbol{\sigma}_{p-1})} = \frac{\boldsymbol{\beta}' \boldsymbol{\sigma}_{p-1}}{\sigma_p^2}.$$

This maximum correlation is called the *multiple correlation*. $\rho_{x_p m}$ is taken to be $+\sqrt{\rho_{x_p m}^2}$.

If one drops the arbitrary constant c and lets

$$m = \boldsymbol{\beta}' \mathbf{x}_{p-1},$$

then the random variable m is univariate normal with expected value

$$E(m) = \boldsymbol{\beta}'\boldsymbol{\mu}_{p-1}$$

and variance

$$\sigma_m^2 = \boldsymbol{\beta}'\Sigma_{p-1}\boldsymbol{\beta} = \boldsymbol{\sigma}_{p-1}'\Sigma_{p-1}^{-1}\boldsymbol{\sigma}_{p-1} = \boldsymbol{\beta}'\boldsymbol{\sigma}_{p-1}.$$

Let the vector $\mathbf{x}$ now be partitioned as follows:

$$\mathbf{x} = \begin{bmatrix} x_1 \\ \vdots \\ x_k \\ \hline x_{k+1} \\ \vdots \\ x_p \end{bmatrix} = \begin{bmatrix} \mathbf{x}_1 \\ \mathbf{x}_2 \end{bmatrix},$$

where $\mathbf{x}_1$ contains the first k components of $\mathbf{x}$, and $\mathbf{x}_2$ contains the last $p - k$ components of $\mathbf{x}$. Let $\boldsymbol{\mu}$ and Σ be partitioned in a similar manner.

$$\boldsymbol{\mu} = \begin{matrix} k \\ p-k \end{matrix} \begin{bmatrix} \boldsymbol{\mu}_1 \\ \boldsymbol{\mu}_2 \end{bmatrix}, \qquad \Sigma = \begin{matrix} \\ k \\ p-k \end{matrix} \begin{matrix} k \quad\;\; p-k \\ \begin{bmatrix} \Sigma_{11} & \Sigma_{12} \\ \Sigma_{21} & \Sigma_{22} \end{bmatrix} \end{matrix},$$

where $\Sigma_{11} =$ dispersion matrix of $\mathbf{x}_1$,
$\Sigma_{22} =$ dispersion matrix of $\mathbf{x}_2$,
$\Sigma_{12} =$ covariance matrix between $\mathbf{x}_1$ and $\mathbf{x}_2$.

The vector variables $\mathbf{x}_1$ and $\mathbf{x}_2$ are distributed as follows:

$$\mathbf{x}_1: N_k(\boldsymbol{\mu}_1, \Sigma_{11}), \qquad \mathbf{x}_2: N_{p-k}(\boldsymbol{\mu}_2, \Sigma_{22}).$$

The joint conditional distribution of the vector variable $\mathbf{x}_1$, given that $\mathbf{x}_2$ is equal to some fixed value, say $\mathbf{x}_{2j}$, will be

$$f(\mathbf{x}_1 \mid \mathbf{x}_2 = \mathbf{x}_{2j}) = N_k(\boldsymbol{\mu}_{1\mid 2j}, \Sigma_{1\mid 2}),$$

where
$$\Sigma_{1\mid 2} = \Sigma_{11} - B'\Sigma_{22}B,$$
$$B = \Sigma_{22}^{-1}\Sigma_{21}.$$

An alternative expression for $\Sigma_{1\mid 2}$, the matrix of conditional variances and covariances, is obtained if B is replaced by its definition:

$$\Sigma_{1\mid 2} = \Sigma_{11} - \Sigma_{12}\Sigma_{22}^{-1}\Sigma_{21}.$$

A typical diagonal element in this matrix is

$$\sigma^2(x_j \mid \mathbf{x}_2) = \sigma_{x_j}^2 - \boldsymbol{\beta}_j'\Sigma_{22}\boldsymbol{\beta}_j, \qquad\qquad j = 1, 2, \ldots, k,$$

where
$$\boldsymbol{\beta}_j = j\text{th column of } B.$$

$\sigma^2(x_j \mid \mathbf{x}_2)$ is called the conditional variance of x_j given that $\mathbf{x}_2$ is some fixed value. A typical off-diagonal element in the matrix $\Sigma_{1|2}$ has the form

$$\sigma(x_i, x_j \mid \mathbf{x}_2) = \sigma_{x_i x_j} - \boldsymbol{\beta}_i'\Sigma_{22}\boldsymbol{\beta}_j,$$

where
$$\boldsymbol{\beta}_i = i\text{th column of } B,$$
$$\boldsymbol{\beta}_j = j\text{th column of } B.$$

The expected value of this joint conditional distribution is

$$E(\mathbf{x}_1 \mid \mathbf{x}_{2j}) = \boldsymbol{\alpha} + B'\mathbf{x}_{2j},$$

where
$$\underset{p-k,k}{B} = \Sigma_{22}^{-1}\Sigma_{21}$$

$$\underset{k,1}{\boldsymbol{\alpha}} = \boldsymbol{\mu}_1 - B'\boldsymbol{\mu}_2.$$

Consider now two populations of elements. In both populations the random variable is $\mathbf{x}$. Assume that in population 1 the distribution of $\mathbf{x}$ is $N_p(\boldsymbol{\mu}_1, \Sigma)$; in population 2, assume that the distribution of $\mathbf{x}$ is $N_p(\boldsymbol{\mu}_2, \Sigma)$. Note that Σ is the same for both distributions. The ratio of the two probability densities for the vector $\mathbf{x}$ is

$$\lambda(\mathbf{x}) = \frac{\exp\left[-\tfrac{1}{2}(\mathbf{x} - \boldsymbol{\mu}_1)'\Sigma^{-1}(\mathbf{x} - \boldsymbol{\mu}_1)\right]}{\exp\left[-\tfrac{1}{2}(\mathbf{x} - \boldsymbol{\mu}_2)'\Sigma^{-1}(\mathbf{x} - \boldsymbol{\mu}_2)\right]}.$$

If one lets

$$y = L(\mathbf{x}) = \ln \lambda(\mathbf{x}),$$

then

$$y = L(\mathbf{x}) = \left[-\tfrac{1}{2}(\mathbf{x} - \boldsymbol{\mu}_1)'\Sigma^{-1}(\mathbf{x} - \boldsymbol{\mu}_1)\right] - \left[-\tfrac{1}{2}(\mathbf{x} - \boldsymbol{\mu}_2)'\Sigma^{-1}(\mathbf{x} - \boldsymbol{\mu}_2)\right]$$
$$= (\boldsymbol{\mu}_1' - \boldsymbol{\mu}_2')\Sigma^{-1}\mathbf{x} - \tfrac{1}{2}(\boldsymbol{\mu}_1'\Sigma^{-1}\boldsymbol{\mu}_1 - \boldsymbol{\mu}_2'\Sigma^{-1}\boldsymbol{\mu}_2)$$
$$= \boldsymbol{\beta}'\mathbf{x} - c,$$

where
$$\boldsymbol{\beta} = \Sigma^{-1}(\boldsymbol{\mu}_1 - \boldsymbol{\mu}_2), \qquad c = \tfrac{1}{2}(\boldsymbol{\mu}_1'\Sigma^{-1}\boldsymbol{\mu}_1 - \boldsymbol{\mu}_2'\Sigma^{-1}\boldsymbol{\mu}_2).$$

$\lambda(\mathbf{x})$ is called the likelihood ratio. $L(x)$ is called the linear discriminant function. Thus the linear discriminant function is the natural logarithm of the likelihood ratio.

The random variable y defined in the preceding paragraph is a linear function of the components of $\mathbf{x}$. Hence y is normally distributed. One has

$$L(\boldsymbol{\mu}_1) = \boldsymbol{\beta}'\boldsymbol{\mu}_1 - c,$$
$$L(\boldsymbol{\mu}_2) = \boldsymbol{\beta}'\boldsymbol{\mu}_2 - c.$$

Hence
$$L(\boldsymbol{\mu}_1) - L(\boldsymbol{\mu}_2) = \boldsymbol{\beta}'(\boldsymbol{\mu}_1 - \boldsymbol{\mu}_2) = (\boldsymbol{\mu}_1' - \boldsymbol{\mu}_2')\Sigma^{-1}(\boldsymbol{\mu}_1 - \boldsymbol{\mu}_2)$$
$$= \boldsymbol{\beta}'\Sigma\boldsymbol{\beta}.$$

From the definition of $L(\mathbf{x})$, it follows that

$$\sigma_y^2 = \boldsymbol{\beta}'\Sigma\boldsymbol{\beta} = L(\boldsymbol{\mu}_1) - L(\boldsymbol{\mu}_2).$$

$L(\boldsymbol{\mu}_1) - L(\boldsymbol{\mu}_2)$ is sometimes called the *distance* between two multivariate normal populations. One notes that this distance is actually the variance of the random variable y.

   If the parameters in the preceding paragraph are replaced by their unbiased maximum-likelihood estimators, one obtains what is known as the Mahalanobis D^2 statistic. Thus

$$D^2 = L(\hat{\boldsymbol{\mu}}_1) - L(\hat{\boldsymbol{\mu}}_2) = (\hat{\boldsymbol{\mu}}_1' - \hat{\boldsymbol{\mu}}_2')\hat{\Sigma}^{-1}(\hat{\boldsymbol{\mu}}_1 - \hat{\boldsymbol{\mu}}_2).$$

Under random sampling with sizes n_1 and n_2, respectively, from populations 1 and 2, under the hypothesis that $\boldsymbol{\mu}_1 = \boldsymbol{\mu}_2$, the statistic

$$F = \frac{n_1 + n_2 - p - 1}{p} \frac{n_1 n_2}{(n_1 + n_2)(n_1 + n_2 - 2)} D^2$$

is distributed as $F(p, n_1 + n_2 - p - 1)$. This test using the D^2 statistic is equivalent to a corresponding test using Hotelling's T^2 statistic.

A.8 DISTRIBUTION OF QUADRATIC FORMS

Let

$$\underset{n,1}{\mathbf{y}} = \text{vector of random variables},$$

$$\underset{n,n}{A} = \text{symmetric matrix of known constants}.$$

A *quadratic form* is an expression of the structure

$$Q = \mathbf{y}'A\mathbf{y}.$$

The distribution of quadratic forms has an important role in interval estimation and hypothesis testing for those areas in which an underlying linear model is assumed.

   Suppose

$$\mathbf{y} = N_n(\boldsymbol{\mu}, \Sigma).$$

That is, the vector variable has an n-variate normal distribution. A basic theorem on the distribution of quadratic forms states that

$$Q = \mathbf{y}'A\mathbf{y}$$

will be distributed as

$$\chi^2(k; \lambda), \qquad\qquad\qquad k \leq n,$$

if and only if the matrix $(A\Sigma)$ is idempotent and has rank equal to k. Here the noncentrality parameter is

$$\lambda = \boldsymbol{\mu}'A\boldsymbol{\mu}.$$

That is, Q is distributed as a noncentral chi square with parameters k and λ.

Some special cases of this theorem are of considerable interest. If

$$\mathbf{y}: N_n(\mathbf{0}, \Sigma), \qquad \text{then} \qquad Q = \mathbf{y}'A\mathbf{y}: \chi^2(k), \qquad \text{where } k = \text{rank } (A).$$

In particular, if $A = \Sigma^{-1}$ the theorem holds. As another special case, if

$$\mathbf{y}: N_n(\boldsymbol{\mu}, \sigma^2 I), \qquad \text{then} \qquad Q = \frac{\mathbf{y}'\mathbf{y}}{\sigma^2}: \chi^2(n; \lambda),$$

where

$$\lambda = \frac{\boldsymbol{\mu}'\boldsymbol{\mu}}{\sigma^2}.$$

If $\qquad \mathbf{y}: N_n(\boldsymbol{\mu}, I), \qquad$ then $\qquad Q = \mathbf{y}'I\mathbf{y}: \chi^2(n; \lambda),$

where $\qquad \lambda = \boldsymbol{\mu}'\boldsymbol{\mu}.$

If $\qquad \mathbf{y}: N_n(\boldsymbol{\mu}, I), \qquad$ then $\qquad Q = \mathbf{y}'A\mathbf{y}: \chi^2(k; \lambda),$

where $\qquad \lambda = \boldsymbol{\mu}'A\boldsymbol{\mu} \qquad$ and $\qquad A$ is idempotent of rank k.

Consider the two quadratic forms

$$Q_1 = \mathbf{y}'P\mathbf{y} \qquad \text{and} \qquad Q_2 = \mathbf{y}'M\mathbf{y},$$

where $\qquad \mathbf{y}: N_n(\mathbf{0}, 1).$

A necessary and sufficient condition for the distributions of Q_1 and Q_2 to be independent is that

$$PM = 0.$$

In particular, if Q_1 and Q_2 are chi-square variates (either central or non-central), then the joint density of Q_1 and Q_2 is the product of the separate densities.

An important theorem underlying the analysis of variance is the following: Suppose $\mathbf{y}: N_n(\boldsymbol{\mu}, I)$ and

$$\mathbf{y}'\mathbf{y} = \mathbf{y}'P_1\mathbf{y} + \mathbf{y}'P_2\mathbf{y} + \cdots + \mathbf{y}'P_m\mathbf{y}$$
$$= Q_1 + Q_2 + \cdots + Q_m.$$

1. A necessary and sufficient condition that

$$\mathbf{y}'P_j\mathbf{y}: \chi^2(k_j; \lambda_j), \qquad \text{where} \qquad \lambda_j = \boldsymbol{\mu}'P_j\boldsymbol{\mu},$$

is that P_j be idempotent of rank k_j.

2. A necessary and sufficient condition that the Q_j $(j = 1, \ldots, m)$ be jointly independent is that

$$\Sigma(\text{rank } P_j) = \text{rank } (\Sigma P_j) = \text{rank } (I).$$

Equivalently, the Q_j will be jointly independent if

$$P_j P_{j'} = 0 \qquad \text{for all } j \neq j'.$$

Actually a necessary and sufficient condition for both (1) and (2) to hold is that any *one* of the following be true:

(i) P_j be idempotent, $j = 1, \ldots, m.$

(ii) $P_j P_{j'} = 0,$ $j \neq j',$

(iii) $\text{rank}(\Sigma P_j) = \Sigma(\text{rank } P_j).$

An example of the application of this last theorem is as follows: Suppose

$$Q_j: \chi^2(k_j; \lambda_j) \quad \text{where } \lambda_j = \mu' P_j \mu,$$

$$Q_{j'}: \chi^2(k_{j'}; 0) \quad \text{where } \mu' P_{j'} \mu = 0, \ P_j P_{j\cdot} = 0.$$

Then $F = \dfrac{Q_j/k_j}{Q_{j'}/k_{j'}}$ is distributed as $F(k_j, k_{j'}; \lambda_j).$

VECTOR AND MATRIX
ALGEBRA

With univariate statistics one usually expresses relations in terms of scalar mathematics, the mathematics of real numbers. With multiple independent or dependent variables, it is usually more convenient to express relations in terms of vectors and matrices, collections of scalars. Thus, matrix algebra is relevant to the various cases of the general linear model such as analysis of variance, analysis of covariance, and multiple linear regression problems. Good introductions to vector and matrix algebra are provided by Searle (1966) and Horst (1963), and in most introductory multivariate analysis texts such as those of Timm (1975) and Lunneborg and Abbott (1983).

B.1 VECTORS AND MATRICES

Vectors

Vectors will be denoted by bold lower-case letters (**a**). A vector is a collection of ordered scalars (real numbers), the entries of which are its elements. In the usual, or "natural," arrangement for vectors, the scalars are written as a column. Thus,

$$\underset{(3 \times 1)}{\mathbf{a}} = \begin{bmatrix} 2 \\ 4 \\ 1 \end{bmatrix}$$

is a *column vector* with three elements arranged in a single column. Its *order* is 3×1 (read, "three by one"), the first number signifying the number of rows and the second number the single column. The vector

$$\underset{(2 \times 1)}{\mathbf{b}} = \begin{bmatrix} b_1 \\ b_2 \end{bmatrix}$$

is of order "2×1."

In this volume, the notation which has also been used is a *row vector*—a vector written as a row. It is denoted with a prime and called the *transpose* of a column vector. Thus, "**a** transpose" is the row vector

$$\underset{(1 \times 3)}{\mathbf{a}'} = [2, 4, 1], \quad \text{and}$$

$$\underset{(1 \times 2)}{\mathbf{b}'} = [b_1, b_2].$$

The orders (1×3) and (1×2) for vectors $\mathbf{a}'$ and $\mathbf{b}'$, respectively, indicate that the scalars are written in a single row with 3 entries in $\mathbf{a}'$ and 2 entries in $\mathbf{b}'$. If one wishes to convey that a row vector has been changed to a column vector, one may transpose the row vector. Thus, $(\mathbf{a}')' = \mathbf{a}$. Whenever possible, vectors will be illustrated as transposes in this presentation in order to save printing space.

In the social and behavioral sciences, vectors are often used to write the observations on a dependent variable for n subjects. Hence,

$$\underset{(1 \times n)}{\mathbf{x}'} = [X_1, X_2, \ldots, X_n] \quad \text{or}$$

$$\underset{(1 \times n)}{\mathbf{y}'} = [Y_1, Y_2, \ldots, Y_n]$$

will represent such data vectors. When the illustration is more abstract, the general vector will be of order $(p \times 1)$ and its transpose will be of order $(1 \times p)$.

Scalars convey information only about magnitudes above and below zero. Vectors contain information about both magnitude and direction. This is best appreciated by representing a vector geometrically; the information in a vector of order $(p \times 1)$ may be represented in a p-dimensional space. For example, the vector

$$\underset{(2 \times 1)}{\mathbf{x}} = \begin{bmatrix} 2 \\ 4 \end{bmatrix}$$

can be represented as a point in a two-dimensional space (Fig. B-1a). As another example, the vector

$$\underset{(3 \times 1)}{\mathbf{y}} = \begin{bmatrix} 4 \\ 2 \\ 5 \end{bmatrix}$$

can be represented in a three-dimensional space (Fig. B-1b).

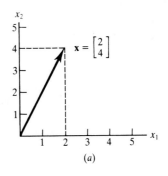

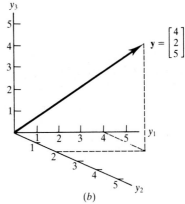

FIGURE B-1   Vectors in 2(B-1a) and 3(B-1b) dimensions.

Matrices

Matrices are doubly-ordered sets of scalars having both rows and columns. Matrices will be denoted by capital letters; the scalars which are the elements will be denoted by small letters with subscripts for both rows and columns. For example,

$$\underset{(2 \times 2)}{A} = \begin{bmatrix} a_{11} & a_{12} \\ a_{21} & a_{22} \end{bmatrix} = \begin{bmatrix} 2 & 1 \\ 8 & 6 \end{bmatrix}$$

is a matrix of order (2×2) with four elements arranged in two rows and two columns. In general, matrices will have p rows $(i = 1, 2, \ldots, p)$ and q columns $(j = 1, 2, \ldots, q)$. Hence,

$$\underset{(p \times q)}{A} = \begin{bmatrix} a_{11} & a_{12} & \cdots & a_{1j} & \cdots & a_{1q} \\ a_{21} & a_{22} & \cdots & a_{2j} & \cdots & a_{2q} \\ \vdots & \vdots & \vdots & \vdots & \vdots & \vdots \\ a_{i1} & a_{i2} & \cdots & a_{ij} & \cdots & a_{iq} \\ \vdots & \vdots & \vdots & \vdots & \vdots & \vdots \\ a_{p1} & a_{p2} & \cdots & a_{pj} & \cdots & a_{pq} \end{bmatrix}.$$

A shorthand notation is

$$\underset{(p \times q)}{A} = [a_{ij}].$$

Matrices may be viewed as collections of vectors, or vectors may be viewed as "degenerate matrices" with only a single column or, in the case of transposes, with a single row. Similarly, scalars may be treated as matrices of order (1×1).

Viewed as a collection of vectors, a matrix may be presented as follows:

$\mathbf{a}_{.j}$ = column j of the matrix A as a column vector

$\mathbf{a}'_{.j}$ = column j of the matrix A as a row vector

$\mathbf{a}_{i.}$ = row i of the matrix A as a column vector

$\mathbf{a}'_{i.}$ = row i of the matrix A as a row vector.

This notation allows one to distinguish rows and columns from a matrix written either as vectors or as transposes. Using this notation, a matrix may be presented as a row of columns,

$$\underset{(p \times q)}{A} = [\mathbf{a}_{.1}, \mathbf{a}_{.2}, \ldots, \mathbf{a}_{.j}, \ldots, \mathbf{a}_{.p}], \quad \text{or}$$

as a column of rows,

$$\underset{(p \times q)}{A} = \begin{bmatrix} \mathbf{a}'_{1.} \\ \mathbf{a}'_{2.} \\ \vdots \\ \mathbf{a}'_{i.} \\ \vdots \\ \mathbf{a}'_{p.} \end{bmatrix}.$$

Some Kinds of Vectors and Matrices

In the social and behavioral sciences, the matrix of central attention is usually a *data matrix* which contains information about n subjects, each measured with regard to k attributes or under k conditions or upon k occasions. Consequently, this matrix X is of order $(n \times k)$ with subjects assigned to rows and treatment conditions, or attributes, assigned to columns. The typical element of the matrix is x_{ij}.

Since the number of subjects (rows) exceeds the number of conditions of measurement (columns), X is a *vertical matrix,* the number of rows of which exceeds the number of columns. The transpose, X', is a *horizontal matrix,* a matrix wherein the number of columns exceeds the number of rows. When the number of rows equals the number of columns, the matrix is a *square matrix.*

Statistical analyses involve various algebraic manipulations and transformations of the data matrix. The manipulations involve utilizing various special vectors and matrices, and the transformations of X may yield matrices with special properties. Some of those special cases are discussed here.

A *null vector* or *null matrix* is a vector or matrix with all elements equal to zero. As a vector, it will be denoted $\mathbf{o}$; as a matrix, it will be $O = [o_{ij}]$. The null vector and null matrix operate as does zero in scalar algebra.

A *unit vector* is a vector in which all entries equal 1. It will be written $\mathbf{1}$. It will be noted later that the product of the unit vector and its transpose, $\mathbf{1}\,\mathbf{1}'$, generates a matrix with all elements equal to 1. The unit vector is a special case of a *scalar vector,* which is any vector the entries of which are all a constant. Hence,

$$\mathbf{2}' = [2, 2, 2], \quad \text{and}$$
$$\mathbf{3}' = [3, 3, 3].$$

The matrix, which operates as does one in scalar algebra multiplication, is called an *identity matrix.* It is a square matrix in which the main diagonal elements are all equal to unity and the off-diagonal elements are all zero. Hence,

$$\underset{(3 \times 3)}{I} = \begin{bmatrix} 1 & 0 & 0 \\ 0 & 1 & 0 \\ 0 & 0 & 1 \end{bmatrix}.$$

Multiplying any matrix by the identity matrix leaves the matrix unchanged.

The identity matrix is a special case of a *scalar matrix,* which is any square matrix wherein all entries on the diagonal are equal to any constant scalar and all off-diagonal entries are zero. For example,

$$A = \begin{bmatrix} 4 & 0 \\ 0 & 4 \end{bmatrix}$$

is a scalar matrix.

The identity matrix and scalar matrix are both special cases of a *diagonal matrix,* a square matrix with all off-diagonal elements equal to zero. The elements on the diagonal may be zero and need not be equal. The matrix

$$D = \begin{bmatrix} 2 & 0 & 0 \\ 0 & 6 & 0 \\ 0 & 0 & 4 \end{bmatrix}$$

is an example of a diagonal matrix. A diagonal matrix is often denoted D with subscripts indicating what is contained on the diagonal.

A *symmetric matrix* is a square matrix which is equal to its transpose. That is, entries above the diagonal are equal to corresponding entries below the diagonal. For example,

$$A = \begin{bmatrix} 1 & 2 & 3 \\ 2 & 4 & 5 \\ 3 & 5 & 6 \end{bmatrix} = A'$$

is a symmetric matrix. Symmetric matrices play a large role in multivariate statistics, since both variance–covariance matrices and correlation matrices are symmetric matrices and, to a large degree, multivariate statistical procedures involve analyzing those values.

B.2 VECTOR AND MATRIX EQUALITY

Two vectors or two matrices are equal if all corresponding entries are equal. Clearly, for this to be the case, they must be of the same order.

B.3 MATRIX TRANSPOSITION

It has already been stated that a column of scalars written as a row would be the transpose of a vector. For matrices, taking the transpose consists of writing the columns of the matrix as rows. The columns of A are the rows of A'. For example, if

$$\underset{(3 \times 2)}{A} = \begin{bmatrix} 1 & 8 \\ 2 & 1 \\ 4 & 3 \end{bmatrix},$$

$$\underset{(2 \times 3)}{A'} = \begin{bmatrix} 1 & 2 & 4 \\ 8 & 1 & 3 \end{bmatrix}.$$

Transposes have certain useful properties. One of these is that transposes "undo each other." That is

$$(A')' = A.$$

Another is that the transpose of a sum of matrices is the sum of the transposes

$$(A + B + C)' = A' + B' + C',$$

but the transpose of a product is the product of the transposes taken in reverse order,

$$(ABC)' = C'B'A'.$$

In a later section, inverses will be presented. If A^{-1} is the regular inverse of A, then the transpose of the inverse is equal to the inverse of the transpose,

$$(A^{-1})' = (A')^{-1}.$$

Finally, the products of a matrix and its own transpose are interesting and useful. The minor product of A with its transpose $A'A$ is a symmetric matrix the diagonal elements of which are the sums of squares of the columns of A and the off-diagonal elements of which are sums of products between column entries. The major product of A and its transpose AA' is also a symmetric matrix. The values on the main diagonal are sums of squares over rows of A and the off-diagonal entries are sums of products between rows.

B.4 VECTOR AND MATRIX ADDITION AND SUBTRACTION

Any scalars may be added or subtracted, but two vectors or matrices may be added or subtracted only if they are of the same order. When they are of the same order, they are said to have *additive conformability*. To add or subtract vectors or matrices, one simply adds or subtracts corresponding elements. Thus, for vectors,

$$\underset{(2\times 1)}{\mathbf{c}} = \underset{(2\times 1)}{\mathbf{a}} + \underset{(2\times 1)}{\mathbf{b}} = \begin{bmatrix} 2 \\ 4 \end{bmatrix} + \begin{bmatrix} 1 \\ 3 \end{bmatrix} = \begin{bmatrix} 3 \\ 7 \end{bmatrix}, \quad \text{or}$$

$$\underset{(2\times 1)}{\mathbf{c}} = \underset{(2\times 1)}{\mathbf{a}} - \underset{(2\times 1)}{\mathbf{b}} = \begin{bmatrix} 2 \\ 4 \end{bmatrix} - \begin{bmatrix} 1 \\ 3 \end{bmatrix} = \begin{bmatrix} 1 \\ 1 \end{bmatrix}.$$

For matrices,

$$\underset{(2\times 2)}{A} + \underset{(2\times 2)}{B} = \begin{bmatrix} a_{11} & a_{12} \\ a_{21} & a_{22} \end{bmatrix} + \begin{bmatrix} b_{11} & b_{12} \\ b_{21} & b_{22} \end{bmatrix} = \begin{bmatrix} a_{11}+b_{11} & a_{12}+b_{12} \\ a_{21}+b_{21} & a_{22}+b_{22} \end{bmatrix}.$$

Geometrically, addition of two vectors is represented as the diagonal of a parallelogram, as follows in Fig. B-2:

$$\underset{(2\times 1)}{\mathbf{c}} = \underset{(2\times 1)}{\mathbf{a}} + \underset{(2\times 1)}{\mathbf{b}} = \begin{bmatrix} 3 \\ 1 \end{bmatrix} + \begin{bmatrix} 1 \\ 3 \end{bmatrix} = \begin{bmatrix} 4 \\ 4 \end{bmatrix}.$$

FIGURE B-2   Vector addition: $\begin{bmatrix} 3 \\ 1 \end{bmatrix} + \begin{bmatrix} 1 \\ 3 \end{bmatrix} = \begin{bmatrix} 4 \\ 4 \end{bmatrix}$.

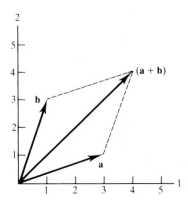

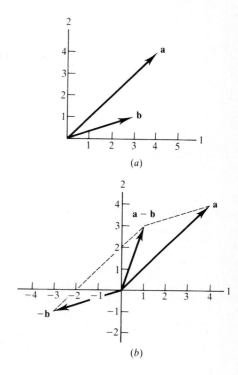

FIGURE B-3   Vector subtraction as a parallelogram.   (b)

Vector subtraction also follows the parallelogram rule of vector addition. To see this, consider subtracting the two vectors,

$$\mathbf{a} = \begin{bmatrix} 4 \\ 4 \end{bmatrix}, \qquad \mathbf{b} = \begin{bmatrix} 3 \\ 1 \end{bmatrix},$$

plotted in Fig. B-3a. The subtraction $\mathbf{a} - \mathbf{b}$ can be conceptualized as the addition of $\mathbf{a}$ and $-\mathbf{b}$. Thus, in Fig. B-3b, the addition of $\mathbf{a}$ and $-\mathbf{b}$, $\mathbf{a} - \mathbf{b}$, defines the diagonal of a parallelogram.

B.5   VECTOR AND MATRIX MULTIPLICATION

There are numerous ways to multiply vectors and matrices. These include multiplying a vector or matrix by a scalar, multiplying vectors, multiplying matrices, and multiplying matrices by vectors.

When vectors or matrices are multiplied, order is important. In any multiplication, the first vector or matrix is called the *premultiplier*, or *prefactor*, and the second is called the *postmultiplier*, or *postfactor*. For example, in the product

$$\mathbf{a}'\mathbf{b} = \mathbf{c},$$

$\mathbf{a}'$ is the premultiplier and $\mathbf{b}$ is the postmultiplier. The product is said to result from the premultiplication of $\mathbf{b}$ by $\mathbf{a}'$ or from the postmultiplication of $\mathbf{a}'$ by $\mathbf{b}$. As another example, in the matrix product

$$AB = C,$$

A is the prefactor and B is the postfactor.

Conformability for Multiplication

Given these definitions, *conformability for multiplication requires that the number of columns of the prefactor equal the number of rows of the postfactor. The product will always have the number of rows of the prefactor and the number of columns of the postfactor.* Thus, the following products exist:

1. $\underset{(1 \times p)(p \times 1)}{\mathbf{a}' \quad \mathbf{b}} = \underset{(1 \times 1)}{c}$

A row vector may be multiplied by a column vector and the product will always be a scalar. Both vectors must have the same number of elements (p). A row vector *cannot* be multiplied by a row vector.

2. $\underset{(p \times 1)(1 \times q)}{\mathbf{a} \quad \mathbf{b}'} = \underset{(p \times q)}{C}$

A column vector may be multiplied by a row vector. The vectors need not be of the same size and the product will always be a matrix with the number of rows of the prefactor and columns of the postfactor. A column vector may *not* be multiplied by a column vector.

3. $\underset{(1 \times p)(p \times q)}{\mathbf{a}' \quad B} = \underset{(1 \times q)}{c'}$

A matrix may be premultiplied by a row vector of the right size. The product is a row vector. A matrix may *not* be premultiplied by a column vector.

4. $\underset{(p \times q)(q \times 1)}{A \quad \mathbf{b}} = \underset{(p \times 1)}{c}$

A matrix may be postmultiplied by a column vector of the right size. The result is a column vector with the number of elements equal to the number of rows of the matrix. A matrix may *not* be postmultiplied by a row vector.

5. $\underset{(p \times q)(q \times m)}{A \quad B} = \underset{(p \times m)}{C}$

Two matrices may be multiplied when they are conformable for multiplication. The product has the number of rows of the prefactor and the number of columns of the postfactor.

Vector and Matrix Multiplication by a Constant

In order to multiply either a vector or a matrix by a scalar constant, one multiplies all elements of the vector or matrix by the constant. Thus,

$$\underset{(p \times 1)}{c\mathbf{a}} = c\begin{bmatrix} a_1 \\ a_2 \\ \vdots \\ a_p \end{bmatrix} = \begin{bmatrix} ca_1 \\ ca_2 \\ \vdots \\ ca_p \end{bmatrix}, \quad \text{and}$$

$$2\begin{bmatrix} 4 \\ 2 \end{bmatrix} = \begin{bmatrix} 8 \\ 4 \end{bmatrix}.$$

Also,

$$cA = c\begin{bmatrix} a_{11} & a_{12} \\ a_{21} & a_{22} \end{bmatrix} = \begin{bmatrix} ca_{11} & ca_{12} \\ ca_{21} & ca_{21} \end{bmatrix}.$$

Geometrically, multiplying a vector by a scalar changes the length of the vector. For example,

$$c\mathbf{a} = (2)\begin{bmatrix} 2 \\ 2 \end{bmatrix} = \begin{bmatrix} 4 \\ 4 \end{bmatrix}$$

is illustrated in Fig. B-4.

LINEAR COMBINATIONS OF VECTORS. *Linear combinations* of vectors may be formed by combining vector addition and multiplication by a scalar. This is of importance in statistical analyses because researchers very often transform or combine dependent variable information by forming linear combinations of the observations. This is the case, for example, when one adds item scores to obtain a total test score for each subject, or when one computes the mean score for each subject over a set of items or sessions. Consider the simple case

FIGURE B-4   Scalar multiplication: $a = \begin{bmatrix} 2 \\ 2 \end{bmatrix}$, $2\begin{bmatrix} 2 \\ 2 \end{bmatrix} = \begin{bmatrix} 4 \\ 4 \end{bmatrix}$.

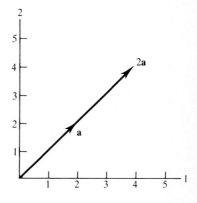

of three subjects measured on two items or occasions:

	Items	
Subject	**1**	**2**
1	X_{11}	X_{12}
2	X_{21}	X_{22}
3	X_{31}	X_{32}

These results may be viewed as two data vectors,

$$\underset{(n \times 1)}{\mathbf{x}_1} = \begin{bmatrix} X_{11} \\ X_{21} \\ X_{31} \end{bmatrix} \quad \text{and} \quad \underset{(n \times 1)}{\mathbf{x}_2} = \begin{bmatrix} X_{12} \\ X_{22} \\ X_{32} \end{bmatrix}.$$

If a sum is obtained for each subject, the result can be represented as the linear combination,

$$c_1 \mathbf{x}_1 + c_2 \mathbf{x}_2 = 1\mathbf{x}_1 + 1\mathbf{x}_2 = 1 \begin{bmatrix} X_{11} \\ X_{21} \\ X_{31} \end{bmatrix} + 1 \begin{bmatrix} X_{12} \\ X_{22} \\ X_{32} \end{bmatrix} = \begin{bmatrix} X_{11} + X_{12} \\ X_{21} + X_{22} \\ X_{31} + X_{32} \end{bmatrix}.$$

As another example, suppose the researcher wants to obtain a mean for the two items for each subject. This can be accomplished as

$$c_1 \mathbf{x}_1 + c_2 \mathbf{x}_2 = \tfrac{1}{2}\mathbf{x}_1 + \tfrac{1}{2}\mathbf{x}_2 = \frac{1}{2} \begin{bmatrix} X_{11} \\ X_{21} \\ X_{31} \end{bmatrix} + \frac{1}{2} \begin{bmatrix} X_{12} \\ X_{22} \\ X_{32} \end{bmatrix} = \begin{bmatrix} (X_{11} + X_{12})/2 \\ (X_{21} + X_{22})/2 \\ (X_{31} + X_{32})/2 \end{bmatrix}.$$

Both of these examples are special cases of obtaining a linear combination or weighted sum of vectors. In general,

$$\mathbf{x}_c = c_1 \mathbf{x}_1 + c_2 \mathbf{x}_2 + \cdots + c_k \mathbf{x}_k$$

is a linear combination of the vectors $\mathbf{x}_1$ through $\mathbf{x}_k$ and c_1 through c_k are any scalars which may be of interest to the researcher or which are inherent in the algebraic manipulations being carried out as, for example, when summing or computing a mean.

Consideration of linear combinations of vectors leads to the consideration of vectors which can or cannot be expressed as linear combinations of other vectors. When vectors can be combined such that

$$c_1 \mathbf{x}_1 + c_2 \mathbf{x}_2 + \cdots + c_k \mathbf{x}_k = \mathbf{0},$$

where c_1 through c_k are any scalars which are not all zero and $\mathbf{o}$ is a null vector, the vectors are *linearly dependent*. When all of the scalars must be zero for this equation to hold, the vectors are *linearly independent*.

Vector by Vector Multiplication

There are two ways in which one may form a vector product: row by column, and column by row multiplication. The first of these is referred to as the *inner, scalar, minor,* or *dot product.* The second, column by row multiplication, is called the *outer product, major product,* or *matrix product.*

INNER PRODUCT. The product of a row vector and a column vector (*inner product, scalar product, minor product,* or *dot product*) is always a scalar. A row vector is multiplied by a column vector by taking the sum of products of corresponding elements. Thus,

$$\underset{(1 \times p)(p \times 1)}{\mathbf{a}' \quad \mathbf{b}} = [a_1, a_2, \ldots, a_p] \begin{bmatrix} b_1 \\ b_2 \\ \vdots \\ b_p \end{bmatrix} = a_1 b_1 + a_2 b_2 + \cdots a_p b_p.$$

For example,

$$[2, 4, 6] \begin{bmatrix} 1 \\ 3 \\ 1 \end{bmatrix} = (2)(1) + (4)(3) + (6)(1) = 20.$$

In this product, the row vector is the premultiplier; the column vector is the postmultiplier. It should be apparent that for vectors to be conformable for multiplication both must have the same number of elements. That is, the number of columns of the premultiplier must be equal to the number of rows of the postmultiplier.

From the point of view of statistical operations, there are a number of interesting results which follow from this definition of the inner product of two vectors. These include:

1 Sums
2 Sum of squares
3 Vector length
4 Normalized vectors
5 Distance between vectors
6 Orthogonal vectors.

1. Sums. Summation of a set of numbers can be accomplished as the product of a row vector with 1 as each element and a column vector, the entries of which are the numbers to be summed. Define the *unit vector* or *sum vector* as

$$\underset{(1 \times n)}{\mathbf{1}'} = [1, 1, \ldots, 1_n], \quad \text{and}$$

a vector of numbers to be summed as

$$\underset{(n \times 1)}{\mathbf{x}} = \begin{bmatrix} X_1 \\ X_2 \\ \vdots \\ X_n \end{bmatrix}.$$

Then,

$$\underset{(1 \times n)(n \times 1)}{\mathbf{1'} \quad \mathbf{x}} = [1, 1, \ldots, 1_n] \begin{bmatrix} X_1 \\ X_2 \\ \vdots \\ X_n \end{bmatrix}$$

$$= (1)X_1 + (1)X_2 + \cdots + (1)X_n = \sum_{i=1}^{n} X_i.$$

2. Sum of the squares. For statistical operations, the sum of squares of a set of dependent variable measures on n subjects is often required. This value, $\sum X_i^2$, may be obtained as the inner product of the data vector. Thus,

$$\underset{(1 \times n)(n \times 1)}{\mathbf{x'} \quad \mathbf{x}} = [X_1, X_2, \ldots, X_n] \begin{bmatrix} X_1 \\ X_2 \\ \vdots \\ X_n \end{bmatrix} = X_1^2 + X_2^2 + \cdots + X_n^2 = \sum_{i=1}^{n} X_i^2.$$

3. Vector length. The length, or *norm*, of a vector is the square root of its inner product;

$$\|a\| = (\mathbf{a'a})^{\frac{1}{2}} = \sqrt{\sum_{i=1}^{p} a_i^2}.$$

Geometrically, the norm can be represented as in Fig. B-5, where the norm for

FIGURE B-5 Norm of a vector.

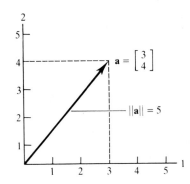

the vector $\mathbf{a} = \begin{bmatrix} 3 \\ 4 \end{bmatrix}$ is illustrated. Numerically,

$$\|a\| = (\mathbf{a}'\mathbf{a})^{\frac{1}{2}} = \left([3, 4] \begin{bmatrix} 3 \\ 4 \end{bmatrix} \right)^{\frac{1}{2}} = (25)^{\frac{1}{2}} = 5.$$

This result follows from the Pythagorean theorem. Note that $\|a\|$ is simply the hypotenuse of a right triangle, the length of the sides of which are defined by the numerical values of a_1 and a_2.

4. Normalized vectors. A *normalized,* or standardized, vector is a vector of unit length. If

$$\mathbf{a}^* = \begin{bmatrix} a_1^* \\ a_2^* \\ \vdots \\ a_p^* \end{bmatrix}$$

is a normalized vector, then $\|\mathbf{a}^*\| = 1.0$. To normalize a vector, each element is divided by the norm of the vector. Thus,

$$\mathbf{a}^* = \frac{1}{\|a\|}\mathbf{a}.$$

For example, if $\mathbf{a} = \begin{bmatrix} 1 \\ 2 \\ 3 \end{bmatrix}$, then $\|a\| = (\mathbf{a}'\mathbf{a})^{\frac{1}{2}} = \sqrt{14}$. Consequently,

$$\mathbf{a}^* = \frac{1}{\sqrt{14}} \begin{bmatrix} 1 \\ 2 \\ 3 \end{bmatrix} = \begin{bmatrix} 1/\sqrt{14} \\ 2/\sqrt{14} \\ 3/\sqrt{14} \end{bmatrix}, \quad \text{and}$$

$$\|\mathbf{a}^*\| = \left[[1/\sqrt{14}, 2/\sqrt{14}, 3/\sqrt{14}] \begin{bmatrix} 1/\sqrt{14} \\ 2/\sqrt{14} \\ 3/\sqrt{14} \end{bmatrix} \right]^{\frac{1}{2}}$$

$$= \left[\frac{1}{14} + \frac{2}{14} + \frac{9}{14} = \frac{14}{14} \right]^{\frac{1}{2}} = 1.0.$$

5. Distance between vectors. The Euclidean distance between two vectors can also be obtained from the Pythagorean theorem. If $\mathbf{a}$ and $\mathbf{b}$ are two vectors, then the distance between them is denoted $\|\mathbf{a} - \mathbf{b}\|$ and is the square root of the sum of squares of differences between the elements of the two vectors. That is,

$$\|\mathbf{a} - \mathbf{b}\| = \{[\mathbf{a} - \mathbf{b}]'[\mathbf{a} - \mathbf{b}]\}^{\frac{1}{2}} = \left[\sum_{i=1}^{p} (a_i - b_i)^2 \right]^{\frac{1}{2}}.$$

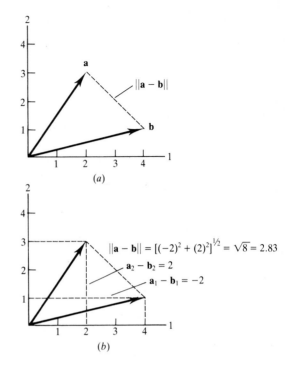

FIGURE B-6 Distance between vectors.

For example, the distance between $\mathbf{a} = \begin{bmatrix} 2 \\ 3 \end{bmatrix}$ and $\mathbf{b} = \begin{bmatrix} 4 \\ 1 \end{bmatrix}$ is shown in Fig. B-6a, and the distance computations are illustrated in Fig. B-6b, where

$$\|\mathbf{a} - \mathbf{b}\| = [(a_1 - b_1)^2 + (a_2 - b_2)^2]^{\frac{1}{2}}$$
$$= [(2 - 4)^2 + (3 - 1)^2]^{\frac{1}{2}}$$
$$= [(-2)^2 + (2)^2]^{\frac{1}{2}} = 8^{\frac{1}{2}} = 2.83.$$

6. Orthogonal vectors. Vectors are *orthogonal* when the sum of products of their corresponding entries is zero. Equivalently, their inner product is zero. This relation between vectors is denoted $\mathbf{a} \perp \mathbf{b}$. For example, the vectors $\mathbf{a}' = [2, -2, 0]$ and $\mathbf{b}' = [0, 0, 2]$ are orthogonal, since

$$\mathbf{a}'\mathbf{b} = (2)(0) + (-2)(0) + (0)(2) = 0.$$

Geometrically, orthogonal vectors form a right interior angle. This is illustrated in Fig. B-7 for the vectors $\mathbf{a}' = [2, 3]$ and $\mathbf{b}' = [3, -2]$.

A *mutually orthogonal set* of vectors is defined when all vectors in the set are orthogonal relative to each other.

Orthonormal vectors are vectors which are orthogonal and are also of unit length (normalized).

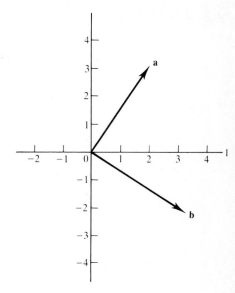

FIGURE B-7   Orthogonal vectors.

OUTER PRODUCT. The product of a *column* vector and row vector is called the *outer product, major product,* or *matrix product.* It is column by row multiplication and yields a matrix rather than a scalar. As is the case with row by column multiplication, vectors must have the same number of entries for the outer product to be formed and the result will be a square matrix. Hence,

$$\underset{(p \times 1)(1 \times p)}{\mathbf{a} \quad \mathbf{b}'} = \underset{(p \times p)'}{C}$$

where C is a product matrix. C is actually obtained by carrying out row by column multiplication of $\mathbf{a}$ and $\mathbf{b}'$. For example, if $\mathbf{a} = \begin{bmatrix} 1 \\ 3 \end{bmatrix}$ and $\mathbf{b} = \begin{bmatrix} 2 \\ 4 \end{bmatrix}$,

$$\mathbf{ab}' = \begin{bmatrix} 1 \\ 3 \end{bmatrix} [2, 4] = \begin{bmatrix} c_{11} & c_{12} \\ c_{21} & c_{22} \end{bmatrix} = \begin{bmatrix} 2 & 4 \\ 6 & 12 \end{bmatrix}.$$

To obtain the entries in the product matrix c_{ij}, one multiplies row_i from $\mathbf{a}$ by column_j from $\mathbf{b}$. Thus,

$$c_{11} = \text{row}_1 \times \text{column}_1 = (1)(2) = 2$$
$$c_{12} = \text{row}_1 \times \text{column}_2 = (1)(4) = 4$$
$$c_{21} = \text{row}_2 \times \text{column}_1 = (3)(2) = 6$$
$$c_{22} = \text{row}_2 \times \text{column}_2 = (3)(4) = 12.$$

Vector by Matrix Multiplications

Earlier, it was pointed out that because of the rules of conformability, a matrix may only be premultiplied by a row vector or postmultiplied by a column vector. Thus, both of the following products exist:

$$\underset{(1 \times p)}{\mathbf{a}'} \underset{(p \times q)}{B} = \underset{(1 \times q)}{\mathbf{c}'},$$

$$\underset{(p \times q)}{B} \underset{(q \times 1)}{\mathbf{a}} = \underset{(p \times 1)}{\mathbf{c}}.$$

In the first case, premultiplying a matrix by a row vector, one proceeds by carrying out row (the vector) by column (columns of the matrix) multiplication of vectors. In the example

$$\underset{(1 \times 3)}{[2, 1, 4]} \underset{(3 \times 3)}{\begin{bmatrix} 1 & 3 & 6 \\ 2 & 4 & 2 \\ 5 & 1 & 3 \end{bmatrix}} = [c_1, c_2, c_3] = [24, 14, 26],$$

$$c_1 = \mathbf{a}'\mathbf{b}_{.1} = (2)(1) + (1)(2) + (4)(5) = 24,$$
$$c_2 = \mathbf{a}'\mathbf{b}_{.2} = (2)(3) + (1)(4) + (4)(1) = 14, \quad \text{and}$$
$$c_3 = \mathbf{a}'\mathbf{b}_{.3} = (2)(6) + (1)(2) + (4)(3) = 26.$$

Postmultiplying a matrix by a column vector proceeds in the same general fashion. The rows of the matrix are each multiplied by the column vector to obtain the elements of the product. Hence, in the product

$$\underset{(3 \times 2)}{B} \underset{(2 \times 1)}{\mathbf{a}} = \underset{(3 \times 1)}{\mathbf{c}}$$

$$\begin{bmatrix} 1 & 3 & 6 \\ 2 & 4 & 2 \\ 5 & 1 & 3 \end{bmatrix} \begin{bmatrix} 2 \\ 1 \\ 4 \end{bmatrix} = \begin{bmatrix} c_1 \\ c_2 \\ c_3 \end{bmatrix} = \begin{bmatrix} 29 \\ 16 \\ 23 \end{bmatrix},$$

$$c_1 = \mathbf{b}'_{1.}\mathbf{a} = (1)(2) + (3)(1) + (6)(4) = 29$$
$$c_2 = \mathbf{b}'_{2.}\mathbf{a} = (2)(2) + (4)(1) + (2)(4) = 16, \quad \text{and}$$
$$c_3 = \mathbf{b}'_{3.}\mathbf{a} = (5)(2) + (1)(1) + (3)(4) = 23.$$

Matrix by Matrix Multiplication

Two matrices may also be multiplied by the rules of row by column multiplication of vectors. Conformability for multiplication requires that the number of columns of the prefactor equal the number of rows of the postfactor. Hence, the product

$$\underset{(p \times q)}{A} \underset{(q \times m)}{B} = \underset{(p \times m)}{C}$$

TABLE B.1 Summary of properties of vector addition and multiplication

Operations	Associative law	Identity law	Inverse law	Commutative law	Distributive law (vectors and matrices)	Distributive law (scalars)
Addition	$(a+b)+c = a+(b+c)$ $(A+B)+C = A+(B+C)$	$a+o=a$ $A+0=A$	$a+(-a)=0$ $A+(-A)=0$	$a+b=b+a$ $A+B=B+A$	$l(a+b)=la+lb$ $l(A+B)=lA+lB$	— —
Scalar Multiplication	$l(wa)=(lw)a$ $l(wA)=lwA$	— —	— —	$la=al$ $lA=Al$	— —	$(l+w)a=la+wa$ $(l+w)A=lA+wA$
Inner Products (Vectors)	$(a')(wb)=lw(a'b)$	—	—	$a'b=b'a$	$a'(b+c)=a'b+a'c$	—
Matrix Products	$(AB)C=A(BC)$ $l(AB)=(lA)B$	— —	— —	— —	$X(Y+Z)=XY+XZ$ $(X+Y)Z=XZ+YZ$	— —

exists. Note that the product has the number of rows of the premultiplier and columns of the postmultiplier. Given these constraints, the elements of the product matrix c_{ij} are each obtained through row (row_i) by column ($column_j$) multiplication,

$$c_{ij} = \mathbf{a}'_{i.}\mathbf{b}_{.j}.$$

In the numerical example,

$$\begin{bmatrix} 2 & 4 \\ 1 & 8 \end{bmatrix}\begin{bmatrix} 6 & 3 \\ 5 & 4 \end{bmatrix} = \begin{bmatrix} c_{11} & c_{12} \\ c_{21} & c_{22} \end{bmatrix} = \begin{bmatrix} 32 & 22 \\ 46 & 35 \end{bmatrix},$$

$$c_{11} = \mathbf{a}'_{1.}\mathbf{b}_{.1} = (2)(6) + (4)(5) = 32,$$
$$c_{12} = \mathbf{a}'_{1.}\mathbf{b}_{.2} = (2)(3) + (4)(4) = 22,$$
$$c_{21} = \mathbf{a}'_{2.}\mathbf{b}_{.1} = (1)(6) + (8)(5) = 46, \quad \text{and}$$
$$c_{22} = \mathbf{a}'_{2.}\mathbf{b}_{.2} = (1)(3) + (8)(4) = 35.$$

The fact that the product AB exists does not imply that the product BA exists, as is the case with scalars. The two products AB and BA both exist only when p equals m. In general, when AB and BA both exist, the two products will not be equal.

Multiplication Summary

In summary, then, all products of vectors and matrices may be viewed as special cases of row by column multiplication and follow two rules. The first rule is that the number of columns of the premultiplier must equal the number of rows of the postmultiplier. The second is that the product will have as its order the number of rows of the premultipler and the number of columns of the postmultiplier.

The properties that vector and matrix addition and multiplication exhibit are summarized in Table B.1.

B.6 MATRIX INVERSION

The reciprocal of a scalar, x, is written as $1/x$ or x^{-1}. For any nonzero scalar, the reciprocal is that number which, when multiplied by the number of which it is the reciprocal, yields 1. That is,

$$x\left(\frac{1}{x}\right) = xx^{-1} = 1.$$

Division with scalars is the same as multiplication by the reciprocal. For example,

$$\frac{y}{x} = \left(\frac{1}{x}\right)y = x^{-1}y.$$

Moreover, these relations are useful for solving scalar equations. Consider, for example, the following

$$5x = 35.$$

$$x = \frac{35}{5} = 7,$$

wherein solving for x can be accomplished by multiplying both sides of the equation by the reciprocal of 5. Hence

$$5x = 35$$

$$\left(\frac{1}{5}\right)5x = \left(\frac{1}{5}\right)35$$

$$x = 7.$$

In general,

$$ax = b$$

$$\left(\frac{1}{a}\right)ax = \left(\frac{1}{a}\right)b$$

$$x = b/a, \quad \text{or}$$

$$x = a^{-1}b,$$

is a solution to the equation for the unknown x.

In matrix algebra, the functions of a reciprocal are carried out with the matrix equivalent of a reciprocal, the *inverse* of a matrix. The inverse *is* that matrix which functions with a matrix as does the corresponding reciprocal with its scalar. Thus, in the relation

$$AA^{-1} = A^{-1}A = I, \tag{B.1}$$

A^{-1} is the *regular inverse* of the square matrix A and I is an identity matrix. All nonzero scalars have a reciprocal. However, all matrices do not have an inverse which satisfies (B.1). In general, only *square basic matrices* have regular inverses wherein (B.1) is satisfied. When A^{-1} does exist, it is of the same order as A. When a matrix has a unique inverse, it is said to be *nonsingular*; *a singular* matrix does not have a regular inverse.

Regular inverses have certain properties which are of interest. We have already seen that an inverse, by definition, commutes with the matrix of which it is the inverse. That is,

$$AA^{-1} = A^{-1}A = I.$$

It is also useful to know that inverses "undo" themselves, that is

$$(A^{-1})^{-1} = A,$$

that the inverse of a symmetric matrix is, itself, symmetric,

$$\text{if} \quad A' = A, \quad \text{then} \quad (A^{-1})' = A^{-1}, \quad \text{and}$$

that the transpose of an inverse is the inverse of the transpose

$$(A^{-1})' = (A')^{-1}.$$

There is a useful relation involving the product of basic matrices. If A, B, and C are square basic matrices, then A^{-1}, B^{-1}, and C^{-1} exist. If they are of the same order, then the product ABC also exists and the inverse of the product is the product of the inverses taken in reverse order:

$$(ABC)^{-1} = C^{-1}B^{-1}A^{-1}.$$

Finally, the inverse of a matrix multiplied by a scalar is equal to the reciprocal of the scalar multiplied by the inverse:

$$(cA)^{-1} = \left(\frac{1}{c}\right)A^{-1}.$$

Whether or not a matrix is singular depends upon its *rank* [written, $r(A)$ for the matrix A]. The rank of a matrix refers to the amount of independent, or nonredundant, information in a matrix. For a null matrix the rank is zero, otherwise the rank is the number of independent rows or columns, whichever is smaller. Recall that vectors are linearly independent when they cannot be expressed as a linear combination of other vectors in a specified set. That is, they are not proportional to each other. Hence, when none of the rows or columns can be expressed as a linear combination of the other rows or columns, the matrix is said to be of *full rank*; it is a nonsingular, or basic matrix, and its rank is equal to the smaller of the number of its rows or columns. If the rank is less than the smaller of the dimensions, the matrix is ranked deficient and singular.

Certain properties of rank are of importance for transformations of matrices. One of these is that transposition does not change the rank of a matrix. That is,

$$r(A) = r(A').$$

This makes intuitive sense since rearranging rows and columns of a matrix should not change the amount of information in the matrix.

When matrices are summed, the rank of the sum lies between the absolute value of the difference in their ranks and the sum of their ranks. That is,

$$|r(A) - r(B)| \le r(A + B) \le r(A) + r(B).$$

When matrices are multiplied, the rank of the product is always less than or equal to the smaller of the ranks of the two matrices which are multiplied and is always greater than the sum of the ranks of the two matrices which are multiplied less their common order. That is,

$$r(A) + r(B) - \text{Common Order} \le r(AB) \le \text{minimum of } r(A) \text{ and } r(B).$$

This leads to the conclusion that premultiplying or postmultiplying a matrix by a nonsingular matrix does not change the rank of a matrix. That is, if B is a square basic matrix,

$$r(A) = r(AB) = r(BA).$$

Other consequences are that one may rescale a matrix, rearrange its rows or columns, or rotate a matrix without changing its rank since those operations are carried out by pre- or postmultiplying by an appropriate matrix (see Lunneborg and Abbott, 1983, Chapter 3, for a more complete discussion of these points).

   Although in multivariate statistics the regular inverse is usually of greatest interest, there are other inverses which may prove to be of interest in the solution of matrix equations. For any matrix, square or rectangular, singular or nonsingular, there is an inverse called the *generalized inverse* or g-inverse (g for generalized). It is not necessarily unique. The generalized inverse, A^-, is a matrix which satisfies the properties,

$$A(A^-A) = (AA^-)A = A, \quad \text{and}$$

$$A^-(AA^-) = (A^-A)A^- = A^-.$$

If A is singular, A^- is not unique; if A is a square basic matrix, A^- is A^{-1}. There are special cases of the g-inverse, the *Penrose inverse* and *least squares inverse,* which are also useful.

Finding Inverses

In general, the best way to compute the regular inverse is to use a computer. For large matrices, the amount of computational labor is extensive. In some cases, however, the inverse is easy to obtain. It is simple to obtain the regular inverse of a permutation matrix, a diagonal matrix, or small matrices.

   A permutation matrix is a matrix with one and only one nonzero entry in each row and column and that entry is one. It is useful to rearrange rows (by premultiplication) or columns (by postmultiplication) of a matrix. A permutation matrix has as its inverse its own transpose. For example, if the permutation matrix is

$$P = \begin{bmatrix} 0 & 1 \\ 1 & 0 \end{bmatrix},$$

then
$$PP' = P'P = I$$

meets the requirements for $P' = P^{-1}$.

   Diagonal matrices have inverses which are simple to obtain. The regular inverse of a diagonal matrix is another diagonal matrix, the diagonal entries of which are the reciprocals of the diagonal elements of the original matrix. In the simple case, for example,

$$
\begin{bmatrix} a_{11} & 0 \\ 0 & a_{22} \end{bmatrix}
\begin{bmatrix} \dfrac{1}{a_{11}} & 0 \\ 0 & \dfrac{1}{a_{22}} \end{bmatrix}
= \begin{bmatrix} 1 & 0 \\ 0 & 1 \end{bmatrix}.
$$

$\qquad\qquad A \qquad\qquad\quad A^{-1} \qquad\qquad\quad I$

For any 2×2 nonsingular square matrix, one may obtain the inverse rather simply by using the *determinant* of the matrix. For the matrix

$$
A = \begin{bmatrix} a_{11} & a_{12} \\ a_{21} & a_{22} \end{bmatrix} = \begin{bmatrix} 2 & 4 \\ 3 & 1 \end{bmatrix},
$$

the determinant $|A|$ is computed as

$$
\begin{aligned}
|A| &= a_{11}a_{22} - a_{12}a_{21} \\
&= (2)(1) - (4)(3) = -10.
\end{aligned}
$$

From $|A|$, the inverse is

$$
A^{-1} = \begin{bmatrix} \dfrac{a_{22}}{|A|} & \dfrac{-a_{12}}{|A|} \\ \dfrac{-a_{21}}{|A|} & \dfrac{a_{11}}{|A|} \end{bmatrix}
= \begin{bmatrix} \dfrac{1}{-10} & \dfrac{-4}{-10} \\ \dfrac{-3}{-10} & \dfrac{2}{-10} \end{bmatrix}
= \begin{bmatrix} -0.10 & 0.40 \\ 0.30 & -0.20 \end{bmatrix}.
$$

To verify the values for A^{-1}, one has

$$
AA^{-1} = A^{-1}A = I
$$

$$
\begin{bmatrix} 2 & 4 \\ 3 & 1 \end{bmatrix}
\begin{bmatrix} -0.10 & 0.40 \\ 0.30 & -0.20 \end{bmatrix}
= \begin{bmatrix} -0.10 & 0.40 \\ 0.30 & -0.20 \end{bmatrix}
\begin{bmatrix} 2 & 4 \\ 3 & 1 \end{bmatrix}
= \begin{bmatrix} 1 & 0 \\ 0 & 1 \end{bmatrix}.
$$

In multivariate statistics one often wants the inverse of a correlation matrix. For that special case of a 2×2 correlation matrix R, the inverse, is

$$
R^{-1} = \begin{bmatrix} \dfrac{1}{1 - r_{12}^2} & \dfrac{-r_{12}}{1 - r_{12}^2} \\ \dfrac{-r_{12}}{1 - r_{12}^2} & \dfrac{1}{1 - r_{12}^2} \end{bmatrix},
$$

since the determinant $|R| = 1 - r_{12}^2$.

For larger matrices, if one is stranded without a computer or moderately useful hand calculator, one may compute the regular inverse by using one of a number of standard algorithms. Those are usually illustrated in introductory matrix algebra or multivariate statistics texts. One algorithm suggested by Dwyer (among others) is readily adapted to the desk calculator.

Let M be a symmetric nonsingular matrix. This matrix may be factored into two triangular matrices

$$M = TT',$$

where T is a lower triangular matrix. (A lower triangular matrix is a square matrix having zeros everywhere above the main diagonal.) The inverse of the matrix M may be expressed in the form

$$M^{-1} = (TT')^{-1} = (T')^{-1}T^{-1}$$
$$= U'U, \quad \text{where} \quad U = T^{-1}.$$

The inverse of the matrix T is relatively easy to obtain. The Dwyer algorithm obtains the T and U matrices simultaneously. The inverse of a lower triangular matrix will be a lower triangular matrix.

Before going into details of the algorithm, consider the problem of finding the matrix T for the case in which M is a 2×2 matrix. For this case,

$$\underset{T}{\begin{bmatrix} t_{11} & 0 \\ t_{21} & t_{22} \end{bmatrix}} \underset{T'}{\begin{bmatrix} t_{11} & t_{21} \\ 0 & t_{22} \end{bmatrix}} = \underset{M}{\begin{bmatrix} m_{11} & m_{12} \\ m_{21} & m_{22} \end{bmatrix}}.$$

Hence

$$t_{11}^2 + 0 = m_{11} \quad \text{or} \quad t_{11} = \sqrt{m_{11}},$$

$$t_{11}t_{21} + 0 = m_{12} \quad \text{or} \quad t_{21} = \frac{m_{12}}{t_{11}},$$

$$t_{21}^2 + t_{22}^2 = m_{22} \quad \text{or} \quad t_{22} = \sqrt{m_{22} - t_{21}^2}.$$

To find U, the inverse of T,

$$\underset{T}{\begin{bmatrix} t_{11} & 0 \\ t_{21} & t_{22} \end{bmatrix}} \underset{U}{\begin{bmatrix} u_{11} & u_{12} \\ u_{21} & u_{22} \end{bmatrix}} = \underset{I}{\begin{bmatrix} 1 & 0 \\ 0 & 1 \end{bmatrix}}.$$

Hence

$$t_{11}u_{11} = 1 \quad \text{or} \quad u_{11} = \frac{1}{t_{11}},$$

$$t_{11}u_{12} = 0 \quad \text{or} \quad u_{12} = 0,$$

$$t_{21}u_{11} + t_{22}u_{21} = 0 \quad \text{or} \quad u_{21} = \frac{-t_{21}u_{11}}{t_{22}},$$

$$t_{21}u_{12} + t_{22}u_{22} = 1 \quad \text{or} \quad u_{22} = \frac{1}{t_{22}}.$$

Details in the computations are given in Table B.2. A numerical example for the case of a 3×3 matrix appears in Table B.3. At the left of part i of Table B.3 is the upper half of the entries in a 3×3 symmetric matrix. At the right of part i is an identity matrix of the same order as M; only the lower half

TABLE B.2 **Dwyer algorithm for the inverse of a symmetric matrix**

	M	I
(i)	T'	U
		$M^{-1} = U'U$

(ii)

	m_{11}	m_{12}	m_{13}	d_{11}			Check
		m_{22}	m_{23}	d_{21}	d_{22}		
			m_{33}	d_{31}	d_{32}	d_{33}	
t_1	t_{11}	t_{12}	t_{13}	u_{11}			$m_{11}u_{11} = t_{11}$
$t_{2.1}$		t_{22}	t_{23}	u_{21}	u_{22}		$m_{11}u_{21} + m_{12}u_{22} = 0$
$t_{3.12}$			t_{33}	u_{31}	u_{32}	u_{33}	$m_{11}u_{31} + m_{12}u_{32} + m_{13}u_{33} = 0$

(iii)

$$t_{11} = \sqrt{m_{11}}; \qquad t_{1j} = m_{1j}/t_{11}; \quad u_{11} = d_{11}/t_{11} \qquad j = 2, 3$$

$$t_{22} = \sqrt{m_{22} - t_{12}^2}; \qquad t_{2j} = (m_{2j} - t_{12}t_{1j})/t_{22}; \qquad j = 3$$
$$u_{2k} = (d_{2k} - t_{12}u_{2k})/t_{22} \qquad k = 1, 2$$

$$t_{33} = \sqrt{m_{33} - t_{13}^2 - t_{23}^2}; \qquad u_{3k} = (d_{3k} - t_{13}u_{1k} - t_{23}u_{2k})/t_{33} \qquad k = 1, 2, 3$$

(iv)

$$t_{pp} = \sqrt{m_{pp} - t_{1p}^2 - t_{2p}^2 - \cdots - t_{(p-1)p}^2}$$

$$t_{pj} = (m_{pj} - t_{1p}t_{1j} - t_{2p}t_{2j} - \cdots - t_{(p-1)p}t_{(p-1)j})/t_{pp} \qquad j > p$$

$$u_{pk} = (d_{pk} - t_{1p}u_{1k} - t_{2p}u_{2k} - \cdots - t_{(p-1)p}u_{(p-1)k})/t_{pp} \qquad k \leq p$$

of this identity matrix is recorded. The computational formulas for obtaining the entries in the T matrix in part ii of Table B.3 are given in part iii of Table B.2. Thus,

$$t_{11} = \sqrt{m_{11}} = \sqrt{16} = 4.0000,$$

$$t_{12} = \frac{m_{12}}{t_{11}} = \frac{8}{4.0000} = 2.0000,$$

$$t_{13} = \frac{m_{13}}{t_{11}} = \frac{4}{4.0000} = 1.0000.$$

TABLE B.3 **Numerical example of Dwyer algorithm**

		1	2	3	1	2	3	
(i)	M	16	8	4	1			
			29	12	0	1		
				86	0	0	1	Check
(ii)	T'	4.0000	2.0000	1.0000	0.2500			4.0000
			5.0000	2.0000	−0.1000	0.2000		0.0000
				9.0000	−0.005555	−0.04444	0.1111	0.0000
(iii)					0.07253	−0.01975	−0.0006173	1.0000
					−0.01975	0.041975	−0.004938	0.0000
					−0.0006173	−0.004938	0.012346	0.0000

The first entry in the U matrix (at the right of part ii) is

$$u_{11} = \frac{d_{11}}{t_{11}} = \frac{1}{4} = 0.2500.$$

The entries in the second row of the matrices in part ii of Table B.3 are given by

$$t_{22} = \sqrt{m_{22} - t_{12}^2} = \sqrt{29 - (2.0000)^2} = \sqrt{25.0000} = 5.0000,$$

$$t_{23} = \frac{m_{23} - t_{12}t_{13}}{t_{22}} = \frac{12 - (2.0000)(1.0000)}{5.000} = 2.0000,$$

$$u_{21} = \frac{d_{21} - t_{12}u_{13}}{t_{22}} = \frac{0 - (2.0000)(0.2500)}{5.0000} = -0.1000,$$

$$u_{22} = \frac{1}{t_{22}} = \frac{1}{5.0000} = 0.2000.$$

As a partial check on the computations,

$$m_{11}u_{21} + m_{12}u_{22} = 16(-0.1000) + 8(0.2000) = 0.0000 \text{ (within rounding error).}$$

The entries in the third row of part ii of Table B.3 are obtained as follows:

$$t_{33} = \sqrt{m_{33} - t_{13}^2 - t_{23}^2} = \sqrt{86 - (1)^2 - (2)^2} = 9.0000,$$

$$u_{31} = \frac{d_{31} - t_{13}u_{11} - t_{23}u_{21}}{t_{33}}$$

$$= \frac{0 - (1)(0.2500) - (2)(-1.000)}{9} = -0.005555,$$

$$u_{32} = \frac{d_{32} - t_{13}u_{12} - t_{23}u_{22}}{t_{33}}$$

$$= \frac{0 - (1)(0) - (2)(0.2000)}{9} = -0.04444,$$

$$u_{33} = \frac{1}{t_{33}} = 0.1111.$$

It is noted that an entry of the form u_{kk} will always be $1/t_{kk}$. Again as a partial check on the computations,

$$m_{11}u_{31} + m_{12}u_{32} + m_{13}m_{33} = 0 \quad \text{(within rounding error).}$$

As another computational check, the sum of the squares of the entries in each column of the T matrix should be the entry in the corresponding main diagonal of the matrix M. For example,

$$(2.0000) + (5.0000)^2 = 29,$$

$$(1.0000)^2 + (2.0000)^2 + (9.0000)^2 = 86.$$

The inverse of the matrix M is shown in part iii of Table B.3. It is obtained by premultiplying the matrix at the right of part ii by its transpose. This can be done conveniently as a column-by-column multiplication. For example, column 1 times itself is

$$(0.2500)^2 + (-0.1000)^2 + (-0.005555)^2 = 0.07253.$$

Column 1 times column 2 is

$$(-0.1000)(0.2000) + (-0.005555)(-0.04444) = -0.01975.$$

A final check is given by

$$M^{-1}M = 1 \quad \text{(within rounding error)}.$$

The general computational formula for any diagonal element of the T matrix appears in the first row of part iv in Table B.2. A similar formula for any off-diagonal element of the T matrix appears in the second row. The third row contains the general formula for any element in the U matrix. With regard to the latter formula, it may be noted that

$$d_{pk} = 0 \quad \text{if} \quad p \neq k,$$
$$d_{pk} = 1 \quad \text{if} \quad p = k,$$
$$u_{jk} = 0 \quad \text{if} \quad j < k.$$

Further u_{kk} will always have the form $1/t_{kk}$.

It should be noted that rounding error cumulates very rapidly in this type of computation. If four-significant-digit accuracy is wanted in the inverse, at least six significant digits should be carried at all intermediate states of the calculations. It should also be noted that, if the matrix M is singular, a diagonal entry of the T matrix will become zero. Hence, the algorithm will collapse since it requires division by such diagonal elements.

If the matrix M is a covariation matrix, the elements of the matrix T will turn out to be of interest in their own right—quite apart from being a step along the way to getting the inverse matrix. The elements on the main diagonal of the T matrix will be found to be partial variations, and the elements of the main diagonal will be related to partial covariations. If the matrix M is a correlation matrix, the elements of T will be related to partial correlations.

B.7   LINEAR TRANSFORMATIONS AND SOLVING LINEAR EQUATIONS

Linear relations among sets of variables are encountered often because they provide a relatively simple and intuitively appealing model for relating independent variables and dependent variables. The most general statement of such models is, indeed, called the *general linear model*. The analysis of variance structural models for various experimental designs, the linear regression model, the analysis of covariance model, the model for discriminant function analysis, and the principal components analysis models are all cases in point. The linear regression model and analysis of variance models will be presented in Appendix C in terms of the general linear model. For present purposes, the point is simply to illustrate how systems of simultaneous linear equations can be solved using the regular or generalized inverse.

Consider the statement

$$\underset{(n \times k)}{X} \underset{(k \times 1)}{\mathbf{c}} = \underset{(n \times 1)}{\mathbf{y}}. \tag{B.2}$$

In (B.2), X is a data matrix—a matrix of observations on n subjects taken on k attributes, on k occasions, or under k treatment conditions; $\mathbf{c}$ is a set of k weights or coefficients for combining the attributes linearly; and $\mathbf{y}$ is a set of n scores which are a linear combination of the variables represented by the k columns of X. For example, if $n = 4$ and $k = 3$, the single matrix equation given by (B.2) is

$$\begin{bmatrix} X_{11} & X_{12} & X_{13} \\ X_{21} & X_{22} & X_{23} \\ X_{31} & X_{32} & X_{33} \\ X_{41} & X_{42} & X_{43} \end{bmatrix} \begin{bmatrix} c_1 \\ c_2 \\ c_3 \end{bmatrix} = \begin{bmatrix} Y_1 \\ Y_2 \\ Y_3 \\ Y_4 \end{bmatrix},$$

which is a succinct way to express multiple scalar equations, each of which expresses the Y variable for one subject as a weighted sum of the X variables,

$$Y_1 = c_1 X_{11} + c_2 X_{12} + c_3 X_{13}$$
$$Y_2 = c_1 X_{21} + c_2 X_{22} + c_3 X_{23}$$
$$Y_3 = c_1 X_{31} + c_2 X_{32} + c_3 X_{33}$$
$$Y_4 = c_1 X_{41} + c_2 X_{42} + c_3 X_{43}.$$

When the weights $\mathbf{c}$ are known, there is no problem posed by (B.2); $\mathbf{y}$ is simply a known linear transformation of the column variables of X. For example, an instructor may want to base a final grade upon a weighted sum of three exams, with the first exam being weighted half as much as the midterm and the final exam being weighted twice as much as the midterm. Hence, any individual's final grade is based upon the score

$$Y_i = 0.5 X_{i1} + 1.0 X_{i2} + 2 X_{i3},$$

and the transformation for all n students in the class is

$$\underset{(n \times 1)}{\mathbf{y}} = \underset{(n \times 3)}{X} \underset{(3 \times 1)}{\mathbf{c}}.$$

Knowing the weights in $\mathbf{c}$ makes it possible to take advantage of well-known relations involving linear transformations. For example, the mean of a linear transformation is the same linear transformation applied to the means of the X variables. That is,

$$\bar{Y} = \mathbf{c}'\bar{\mathbf{x}}$$

$$= (c_1 \quad c_2 \quad c_3) \begin{bmatrix} \bar{X}_1 \\ \bar{X}_2 \\ \bar{X}_3 \end{bmatrix}$$

$$= c_1\bar{X}_1 + c_2\bar{X}_2 + c_3\bar{X}_3.$$

The variance of Y, s_y^2, is given by

$$s_y^2 = \mathbf{c}'S_x\mathbf{c},$$

where S_x is the variance-covariance matrix for the X variables. In scalar terms

$$s_y^2 = \sum_{j=1}^{k} c_j^2 s_j^2 + 2 \sum c_j c_{j'} s_{jj'} \qquad j < j'$$

$$= c_1^2 s_1^2 + c_2^2 s_2^2 + c_3^2 s_3^2 + 2c_1 c_2 s_{12} + 2c_1 c_3 s_{13} + 2c_2 c_3 s_{23}.$$

If multiple linear transformations of X are desired, they can be achieved with a matrix C, the columns of which are the coefficients of m transformations. Hence

$$\underset{(n \times k)}{X} \underset{(k \times m)}{C} = \underset{(n \times m)}{Y}.$$

In this latter case,

$$C'\bar{\mathbf{x}} = \bar{\mathbf{y}}$$

is the vector of means of the m, y variables and

$$C'S_x C = Sy$$

is the variance–covariance matrix for the m linear combinations $\mathbf{y}$.

The interesting problem associated with (B.2) arises when the weights in $\mathbf{c}$ are *not* known. To obtain values for the coefficients, one must solve a system of simultaneous linear equations. Using matrix procedures, this involves use of the inverse. Earlier, the point was made that the reciprocal of scalar algebra functions as does the inverse of matrix algebra. To solve the scalar equation $ax = b$ for the unknown x, one multiplies by the reciprocal of a,

$$ax = b$$

$$\left(\frac{1}{a}\right)ax = \left(\frac{1}{a}\right)b = a^{-1}b$$

$$(1)x = \frac{b}{a}.$$

To solve the matrix equation $A\mathbf{x} = b$ for the unknown entries in the vector x, one multiplies by the inverse of A,

$$A\mathbf{x} = \mathbf{b}$$
$$A^{-1}A\mathbf{x} = A^{-1}\mathbf{b}$$
$$I\mathbf{x} = A^{-1}\mathbf{b}$$
$$\mathbf{x} = A^{-1}\mathbf{b}.$$

This result, $\mathbf{x} = A^{-1}\mathbf{b}$, is a solution to a set of linear scalar equations and provides the weights needed to express the columns of A as the linear combination $\mathbf{b}$. For example, in the matrix equation

$$
\underset{(3\times 3)}{A} \underset{(3\times 1)}{\mathbf{x}} = \underset{(3\times 1)}{\mathbf{b}}
$$

$$
\begin{bmatrix} a_{11} & a_{12} & a_{13} \\ a_{21} & a_{22} & a_{23} \\ a_{31} & a_{32} & a_{33} \end{bmatrix} \begin{bmatrix} X_1 \\ X_2 \\ X_3 \end{bmatrix} = \begin{bmatrix} b_1 \\ b_2 \\ b_3 \end{bmatrix},
$$

the elements of $\mathbf{x}$ are unknown. Hence, in the set of simultaneous linear scalar equations

$$a_{11}X_1 + a_{12}X_2 + a_{13}X_3 = b_1$$
$$a_{21}X_1 + a_{22}X_2 + a_{23}X_3 = b_2$$
$$a_{31}X_1 + a_{32}X_2 + a_{33}X_3 = b_3,$$

a solution for the unknowns of $\mathbf{x}$ is provided by

$$
\underset{(3\times 1)}{\mathbf{x}} = \underset{(3\times 3)}{A^{-1}} \underset{(3\times 1)}{\mathbf{b}}.
$$

This assumes that A^{-1} exists. By the same reasoning, for the matrices A, X, and B, a solution for X is provided by

$$AX = B$$
$$A^{-1}AX = A^{-1}B$$
$$IX = A^{-1}B$$
$$X = A^{-1}B$$

as long as conformability for multiplication is maintained and A^{-1} exists. A unique solution exists when A is nonsingular. A solution which is not unique exists, using the g-inverse of A, A^-, when A is singular.

This requirement to use the inverse to solve sets of linear equations arises in the various specializations of the general linear model. Consider the equation

$$
\underset{(n\times 1)}{\mathbf{y}} = \underset{[n\times(k+1)]}{X} \underset{[(k+1)\times 1]}{\beta}
$$

which is a population linear model for a dependent variable Y for n subjects, expressing Y as a weighted sum of the k independent variables X. The vector $\boldsymbol{\beta}$ is a set of weights for the independent variables which is unknown but is estimated from experimental data. The same equation for a sample of n subjects which can be used to compute $\mathbf{b}$ as an estimate of $\boldsymbol{\beta}$ is given by

$$\underset{(n \times 1)}{\mathbf{y}} = \underset{[n \times (k+1)]}{X} \underset{[(k+1) \times 1]}{\mathbf{b}}$$

$$\begin{bmatrix} Y_1 \\ Y_2 \\ \vdots \\ Y_i \\ \vdots \\ Y_n \end{bmatrix} = \begin{bmatrix} 1 & X_{11} & X_{12} & \cdots & X_{1k} \\ 1 & X_{21} & X_{22} & \cdots & X_{2k} \\ \vdots & \vdots & \vdots & & \vdots \\ 1 & X_{n1} & X_{n2} & \cdots & X_{nk} \end{bmatrix} \begin{bmatrix} b_0 \\ b_1 \\ b_2 \\ \vdots \\ b_k \end{bmatrix}$$

In scalar terms, the set of simultaneous linear equations is

$$Y_1 = b_0 + b_1 X_{11} + b_2 X_{12} + \cdots + b_k X_{1k}$$
$$Y_2 = b_0 + b_1 X_{21} + b_2 X_{22} + \cdots + b_k X_{2k}$$
$$\vdots$$
$$Y_n = b_0 + b_1 X_{n1} + b_2 X_{n2} + \cdots + b_k X_{nk}.$$

The solution of interest is for the unknown vector of weights $\mathbf{b}$. It is that problem which defines a large portion of univariate and multivariate statistics. In general, the solution is given by

$$\mathbf{b} = X^{-1}\mathbf{y},$$

when X is a square basic matrix. Otherwise, the solution resides in working with some transformation of X which meets that requirement. Details will be presented in Appendix C.

B.8 BASIC STATISTICAL OPERATIONS

Expressing relations in vector or matrix terms provides no increase in efficiency in the univariate case. However, since one can generalize to any number of variables, it is helpful to examine basic operations in vector and matrix terms.
Let

$$\underset{(1 \times n)}{\mathbf{1}'} = [1, 1, \ldots, 1]$$

$$\underset{(n \times 1)(1 \times n)}{\mathbf{1} \; \mathbf{1}'} = \underset{(n \times n)}{J} = \begin{bmatrix} 1 & 1 & \cdots & 1 \\ 1 & 1 & \cdots & 1 \\ \vdots & \vdots & & \vdots \\ 1 & 1 & \cdots & 1 \end{bmatrix}$$

$$\underset{(1 \times n)}{\mathbf{x}'} = [X_1, X_2, \ldots, X_n] \qquad \mathbf{y}' = [Y_1 Y_2 \cdots Y_n]$$

$$\underset{(n \times k)}{X} = \begin{bmatrix} X_{11} & X_{12} & \cdots & X_{1k} \\ X_{21} & X_{22} & \cdots & X_{2k} \\ \vdots & \vdots & & \vdots \\ X_{n1} & X_{n2} & \cdots & X_{nk} \end{bmatrix}$$

$$\underset{(n \times p)}{Y} = \begin{bmatrix} Y_{11} & Y_{12} & \cdots & Y_{1p} \\ Y_{21} & Y_{22} & \cdots & Y_{2p} \\ \vdots & \vdots & & \vdots \\ Y_{n1} & Y_{n2} & \cdots & Y_{np} \end{bmatrix}$$

$$\underset{[n \times (k+p)]}{M} = [X : Y]$$

$$= \begin{bmatrix} X_{11} & X_{12} & \cdots & X_{1k} & Y_{11} & Y_{12} & \cdots & Y_{1p} \\ X_{21} & X_{22} & \cdots & X_{2k} & Y_{21} & Y_{22} & \cdots & Y_{2p} \\ \vdots & \vdots & & \vdots & \vdots & \vdots & & \vdots \\ X_{n1} & X_{n2} & \cdots & X_{nk} & Y_{n1} & Y_{n2} & \cdots & Y_{np} \end{bmatrix}.$$

1. *Sums*: Any number of variables (matrix columns) may be summed by premultiplying by a unit vector:

$$\mathbf{1}'\mathbf{x} = [1, 1, \ldots, 1] \begin{bmatrix} X_1 \\ X_2 \\ \vdots \\ X_n \end{bmatrix}$$

$$= (1)X_1 + (1)X_2 + \cdots + (1)X_n = \sum_{i=1}^{n} X_i.$$

$$\mathbf{1}'X = [1, 1, \ldots, 1] \begin{bmatrix} X_{11} & X_{12} & \cdots & X_{1n} \\ X_{21} & X_{22} & \cdots & X_{2k} \\ \vdots & \vdots & & \vdots \\ X_{n1} & X_{n2} & \cdots & X_{nk} \end{bmatrix}$$

$$= [\sum X_{.1}, \sum X_{.2}, \ldots, \sum X_{.k}].$$

$$\mathbf{1}'M = [1, 1, \ldots, 1] \begin{bmatrix} X_{11} & X_{12} & \cdots & X_{1n} & Y_{11} & Y_{12} & \cdots & Y_{1p} \\ X_{21} & X_{22} & \cdots & X_{2k} & Y_{21} & Y_{22} & \cdots & Y_{2p} \\ \vdots & \vdots & & \vdots & \vdots & \vdots & & \vdots \\ X_{n1} & X_{n2} & \cdots & X_{nk} & Y_{n1} & Y_{n2} & \cdots & Y_{np} \end{bmatrix}$$

$$= [\sum X_{.1}, \sum X_{.2}, \ldots, \sum X_{.k} \mid \sum Y_{.1} \sum Y_{.2} \cdots \sum Y_{.p}].$$

2. *Means*:

$$\frac{1}{n}\mathbf{1}'\mathbf{x} = \sum_{i=1}^{n} X_i/n = \bar{X}.$$

$$\frac{1}{n}\mathbf{1}'X = [\bar{X}_{.1}, \bar{X}_{.2}, \ldots, \bar{X}_{.k}].$$

$$\frac{1}{n}\mathbf{1}'M = [\bar{X}_{.1}, \bar{X}_{.2}, \ldots, \bar{X}_{.k} \mid \bar{Y}_{.1}, \bar{Y}_{.2}, \ldots, \bar{Y}_{.p}].$$

3. *Sums of squares and sums of products*: The minor product of a vector provides the sums of squares of the entries. The minor product of a matrix is a square symmetric matrix of order $(k \times k)$ with the sums of squares of column variables on the main diagonal and sums of products between columns off the diagonal. The major product provides the same result for row variables in a square symmetric matrix of order $(n \times n)$.

$$\mathbf{x}'\mathbf{x} = [X_1, X_2, \ldots, X_n]\begin{bmatrix} X_1 \\ X_2 \\ \vdots \\ X_n \end{bmatrix} = \sum_{i=1}^{n} X_i^2.$$

$$\begin{matrix} X' & X \\ (k \times n)(n \times k) \end{matrix} = \begin{bmatrix} \sum X_{.1}^2 & \sum X_{.1}X_{.2} & \cdots & \sum X_{.1}X_{.k} \\ & \sum X_{.2}^2 & \cdots & \sum X_{.2}X_{.k} \\ & & & \vdots \\ & & & \sum X_{.k}^2 \end{bmatrix}$$

$$M'M = \begin{bmatrix} X'X & X'Y \\ Y'X & Y'Y \end{bmatrix}$$

$$XX' = \begin{bmatrix} \sum X_{1.}^2 & \sum X_{1.}X_{2.} & \cdots & \sum X_{1.}X_{n.} \\ & \sum X_{2.}^2 & \cdots & \sum X_{2.}X_{n.} \\ & & & \vdots \\ & & & \sum X_{n.}^2 \end{bmatrix}$$

$$MM' = \begin{bmatrix} XX' & XY' \\ YX' & YY' \end{bmatrix}.$$

4. *Variation and covariation*: The variation of (SS) and covariation (SP) among any number of variables may be obtained from the generalizations of the formulas for sums of squares and sums:

$$\text{SS}_X = \sum_{i=1}^{n} X_i^2 - \left(\sum_{i=1}^{n} X_i\right)\bigg/n$$

$$= \mathbf{x}'\mathbf{x} - \left(\frac{1}{n}\right)\mathbf{1}'\mathbf{x}\mathbf{1}'\mathbf{x}$$

$$= \mathbf{x}'\mathbf{x} - \left(\frac{1}{n}\right)\mathbf{x}'J\mathbf{x}.$$

$$\text{SP}_{xy} = \mathbf{x}'\mathbf{y} - \left(\frac{1}{n}\right)\mathbf{x}'J\mathbf{y}$$

$$V_X = X'X - \left(\frac{1}{n}\right)X'JX = \begin{bmatrix} \text{SS}_{X_1} & \text{SP}_{X_1X_2} & \cdots & \text{SP}_{X_1X_k} \\ & \text{SS}_{X_2} & \cdots & \text{SP}_{X_2X_k} \\ & & & \vdots \\ & & & \text{SS}_{X_k} \end{bmatrix}$$

$$V_M = M'M - \left(\frac{1}{n}\right)M'JM = \begin{bmatrix} V_X & V_{XY} \\ V_{YX} & V_Y \end{bmatrix}.$$

5. *Variances and Covariances*:

$$s_X^2 = \frac{1}{n-1}\,\text{SS}_X = \frac{1}{n-1}\left[\mathbf{x}'\mathbf{x} - \left(\frac{1}{n}\right)\mathbf{x}'J\mathbf{x}\right]$$

$$S_X = \frac{1}{n-1}\,V_X = \frac{1}{n-1}\left[X'X - \left(\frac{1}{n}\right)X'JX\right]$$

$$= \begin{bmatrix} s_{X_1}^2 & \text{cov}_{X_1X_2} & \cdots & \text{cov}_{X_1X_k} \\ & s_{X_2}^2 & \cdots & \text{cov}_{X_2X_k} \\ & & & \vdots \\ & & & s_{X_k}^2 \end{bmatrix}$$

$$S_M = \frac{1}{n-1}\,V_m = \frac{1}{n-1}\left[M'M - \left(\frac{1}{n}\right)M'JM\right]$$

$$= \begin{bmatrix} S_X & S_{XY} \\ S_{YX} & S_Y \end{bmatrix}.$$

6. *Correlations*: The product normal correlation may be easily computed from variations and covariations

$$r_{xy} = \frac{\text{SP}_{xy}}{\sqrt{(\text{SS}_x)(\text{SS}_y)}}$$

$$= \frac{\mathbf{x}'\mathbf{y} - \left(\frac{1}{n}\right)\mathbf{x}'J\mathbf{y}}{\sqrt{\left[\mathbf{x}'\mathbf{x} - \left(\frac{1}{n}\right)\mathbf{x}'J\mathbf{x}\right]\left[\mathbf{y}'\mathbf{y} - \left(\frac{1}{n}\right)\mathbf{y}'J\mathbf{y}\right]}}.$$

Let

$$D_V^{-1} = \begin{bmatrix} \dfrac{1}{\sqrt{\text{SS}_{x_1}}} & 0 \\ & \dfrac{1}{\sqrt{\text{SS}_{x_2}}} \end{bmatrix}.$$

Then, $r_{xy} = D_V^{-1} V_x D_V^{-1} = \begin{bmatrix} \dfrac{1}{\sqrt{\text{SS}_x}} & 0 \\ 0 & \dfrac{1}{\sqrt{\text{SS}_y}} \end{bmatrix}\begin{bmatrix} \text{SS}_x & \text{SP}_{xy} \\ & \text{SS}_y \end{bmatrix}\begin{bmatrix} \dfrac{1}{\sqrt{\text{SS}_x}} & 0 \\ 0 & \dfrac{1}{\sqrt{\text{SS}_y}} \end{bmatrix}.$

Hence, if
$$D_{V_X}^{-1} = \begin{bmatrix} \dfrac{1}{\sqrt{SS_{x_1}}} & 0 & \cdots & 0 \\[2ex] & \dfrac{1}{\sqrt{SS_{x_2}}} & \cdots & 0 \\[2ex] & & & \dfrac{1}{\sqrt{SS_{x_k}}} \end{bmatrix},$$

and
$$D_{V_M}^{-1} = \begin{bmatrix} \dfrac{1}{\sqrt{SS_{x_1}}} & 0 & \cdots & 0 & \cdots & 0 \\[2ex] & \dfrac{1}{\sqrt{SS_{x_2}}} & \cdots & 0 & \cdots & 0 \\[1ex] & \vdots & & \vdots & & \vdots \\[1ex] & & & \dfrac{1}{\sqrt{SS_{y_1}}} & \cdots & 0 \\[1ex] & & & \vdots & & \vdots \\[1ex] & & & & & \sqrt{SS_{y_p}} \end{bmatrix},$$

then
$$R_{XX} = D_{V_X}^{-1} V_X D_{V_X}^{-1} = \begin{bmatrix} 1.00 & r_{X_1 X_2} & \cdots & r_{X_1 X_k} \\ & 1.00 & \cdots & r_{X_2 X_k} \\ & & & \vdots \\ & & & 1.00 \end{bmatrix}$$

$$R_M = D_{V_M}^{-1} V_M D_{V_M}^{-1} = \begin{bmatrix} R_{XX} & R_{XY} \\ R_{YX} & R_{YY} \end{bmatrix}.$$

APPENDIX C

LINEAR MODELS: REGRESSION AND THE ANALYSIS OF VARIANCE

In Chapter 1, it was stated that science is concerned with understanding variability in nature. It is the purpose of science to discover patterns in variability which simplify and permit accurate prediction. Both regression analysis and analysis of variance are concerned with that goal. They seek to establish the nature and degree of relations between multiple independent variables and a dependent variable. In both cases, one is interested in combining information about subjects contained in independent variables in order to predict a dependent variable. Independent and dependent variables may be quantitative or qualitative in nature. In the case of regression analysis, the quantitative information in the independent variables is used for prediction if it exists, the experimenter specifies a particular relation between the independent and dependent variables, and the relations among independent variables are taken into account. In the case of analysis of variance, independent variables are treated qualitatively even when magnitude information exists, relations among independent variables are not taken into account, and it is not necessary to specify the nature of the function which relates the independent and dependent variables.

Underlying the statistical aspects of both regression analysis and analysis of variance is a series of linear models plus a set of distribution assumptions about the random variables in those models. In classic analysis of variance and analysis of regression, the basic independent variables are considered fixed. In more general applications of the analysis of variance, the independent variables may be fixed, random, or some mixture of fixed and random variables. If the variables are all random, the model is called the *variance-component model*. If the variables are a mixture of fixed and random variables, the model is called a *mixed model*. There is no probability density associated with a fixed variable. Given the outcome of an experiment, if a specified treatment has been administered, the value of a fixed variable is an unknown constant associated with that treatment. On the other hand, associated with a random variable is a probability density having one or more parameters. The outcome of an experiment involving one or more random variables is a function of the form of the probability density and the values of the parameters.

The term *regression model* is used in two different senses. In the more classic sense, the basic variables are considered fixed. In this sense, the analysis-of-variance model for fixed variables is a special case of the regression model. In some statistical literature (see Graybill, 1961), the term regression model refers to the case in which variables are random (usually having a multivariate normal distribution).

C.1 LINEAR RELATIONS: LEAST-SQUARES PROCEDURES

If one is interested only in describing relations among samples of data but not in inferences about the populations from which the samples were drawn, it is not necessary to make assumptions about the population distributions of the variables of interest. For example, one may wish to describe the linear relation which exists in a data set consisting of observations on a single independent variable X and a single dependent variable Y. This would be the simple linear regression problem in the univariate case. In the more complex case, one may want to describe a data set involving multiple independent variables and a single dependent variable. This is a problem in multiple regression.

Univariate Case

Let the data in a sample from a specified population be represented as follows:

Sample element	X	Y
1	X_1	Y_1
2	X_2	Y_2
$\vdots$	$\vdots$	$\vdots$
n	X_n	Y_n

Let

$$\bar{X} = \frac{\sum X}{n} = \text{mean for } X; \qquad \bar{Y} = \frac{\sum Y}{n} = \text{mean for } Y;$$

$$\text{SS}_X = \sum (X - \bar{X})^2 = \sum X^2 - \frac{(\sum X)^2}{n} = \text{variation of } X;$$

$$SS_Y = \sum (Y - \bar{Y})^2 = \sum Y^2 - \frac{(\sum Y)^2}{n} = \text{variation of } Y;$$

$$SP_{XY} = \sum (X - \bar{X})(Y - \bar{Y})$$

$$= \sum XY - \frac{(\sum X)(\sum Y)}{n} = \text{covariation between } X \text{ and } Y.$$

Suppose it is desired to build a prediction system of the form

$$\hat{Y} = b_0 + b_1 X, \tag{C.1}$$

where b_0 and b_1 are to be determined in a way which optimizes the prediction of Y in the sample. One optimizing principle is the *least-squares* criterion, which optimizes in the sense that it minimizes the sum of the squares of the errors of prediction. That is, if Y_i is the observed dependent variable for an element and $\hat{Y}_i$ is the predicted value, then the difference $Y_i - \hat{Y}_i$ may be viewed as an error of prediction and

$$\sum (Y - \hat{Y})^2 = \text{minimum for the sample data.} \tag{C.2}$$

Expression (C.2) represents the *least-squares* optimization criterion wherein b_0 and b_1 determined in such a way as to satisfy (C.2) are the least-squares definitions of b_0 and b_1.

Expression (C.2) may be written in the form

$$\sum (Y - b_0 - b_1 X)^2 = \sum Y^2 + n b_0^2 + b_1^2 \left(\sum X^2\right) - 2b_0 \left(\sum Y\right) - 2b_1 \left(\sum XY\right)$$

$$+ 2b_0 b_1 \left(\sum X\right) = \text{minimum.} \tag{C.3}$$

Expression (C.3) may be minimized by taking the partial derivations with respect to b_0 and b_1 and then setting the results equal to zero. The end product defines the set of *normal equations*. They are

$$n b_0 + b_1 \left(\sum X\right) - \sum Y = 0,$$

$$b_1 \left(\sum X^2\right) - \sum (XY) + b_0 \left(\sum X\right) = 0. \tag{C.4}$$

Solving the first equation for b_0 in terms of b_1 gives

$$b_0 = \bar{Y} - b_1 \bar{X}. \tag{C.5}$$

Substituting the expression for b_0 given in (C.5) into the second equation in (C.4) yields, after some manipulation,

$$b_1(SS_X) = SP_{XY} \quad \text{or} \quad b_1 = \frac{SP_{XY}}{SS_X}. \tag{C.6}$$

Thus, the prediction equation (C.1),

$$\hat{Y}_i = b_0 + b_1 X_i,$$

may be rewritten with b_0 and b_1 defined by the least-squares criterion as

$$\hat{Y} = (\bar{Y} - b_1 \bar{X}) + b_1 X \qquad \text{or} \qquad \hat{Y} - \bar{Y} = b_1(X - \bar{X}). \qquad \text{(C.7)}$$

If one sums both sides of the equation at the right over all sample elements, one obtains

$$\sum (\hat{Y} - \bar{Y}) = b_1 \sum (X - \bar{X}) = 0,$$

since $\sum (X - \bar{X}) = 0$. Hence

$$\sum \bar{Y} = \sum Y \qquad \text{or} \qquad \bar{\hat{Y}} = \bar{Y}. \qquad \text{(C.8)}$$

The following properties of variations are readily established. If K is the linear transformation of X,

$$K = c_0 + c_1 X, \quad \text{then} \quad SS_K = c_1^2 SS_X.$$

If $\qquad\qquad U = V - W, \quad \text{then} \quad SS_U = SS_V + SS_W - 2SP_{VW}.$

Since $\qquad\qquad\qquad \hat{Y} = b_0 + b_1 X,$

it follows that

$$SS_{\hat{Y}} = b_1^2 SS_X = \frac{SP_{XY}^2}{SS_X^2} SS_X = \frac{SP_{XY}^2}{SS_X} = b_1 SP_{XY}. \qquad \text{(C.9)}$$

Also $\qquad\qquad\qquad SS_{Y-\hat{Y}} = SS_Y + SS_{\hat{Y}} - 2SP_{Y\hat{Y}}.$

But $\qquad SP_{Y\hat{Y}} = \sum Y\hat{Y} - \frac{(\sum Y)(\sum \hat{Y})}{n} = \sum Y\hat{Y} - \frac{(\sum Y)^2}{n}$

$$= \sum Y(\bar{Y} - b_1\bar{X} + b_1 X) - \frac{(\sum Y)^2}{n}$$

$$= b_1 \left[\sum XY - \frac{(\sum X)(\sum Y)}{n} \right] + \frac{(\sum Y)^2}{n} - \frac{(\sum Y)^2}{n}$$

$$= b_1 SP_{XY} = SS_{\hat{Y}}.$$

Hence

$$SS_{Y-\hat{Y}} = SS_Y + SS_{\hat{Y}} - 2SS_{\hat{Y}} = SS_Y - SS_{\hat{Y}}. \qquad \text{(C.10)}$$

Rearranging the terms in (C.10) one has

$$SS_y = SS_{\hat{Y}} + SS_{Y-\hat{Y}}. \qquad \text{(C.11)}$$

Before going on, it may be worthwhile to summarize in words what has been illustrated by expressions (C.1) through (C.11). Expression (C.1) is a linear equation, the equation for a straight line in a plane. If one defines an error of prediction as the difference between the observed value of Y and the predicted value of Y, $\hat{Y}$, then errors of prediction are

$$e_i = Y_i - \hat{Y}_i$$

and geometrically represent distances above and below the linear function defined by the $\hat{Y}_i$. Hence, one may write the identity,

$$\begin{aligned} Y_i &= \hat{Y}_i + (Y_i - \hat{Y}_i) \\ &= \hat{Y}_i + e_i. \end{aligned}$$

This serves to emphasize that the dependent variable may be viewed as the sum of two components: $\hat{Y}_i$, which is linearly dependent upon the independent variable, and the errors, which are errors in the sense that they cannot be linearly predicted from the dependent variable ($e_i = Y_i - \hat{Y}_i$).

When the least-squares criterion is used to obtain b_0 (C.5) and b_1 (C.6), the average predicted value which lies on the straight line of best fit, $\bar{\hat{Y}}$, is equal to the average value of Y, $\bar{Y}$ (C.8); hence, the average error is zero ($\bar{e} = \bar{Y} - \bar{\hat{Y}} = 0$).

Just as Y_i may be decomposed into $\hat{Y}_i$ and e_i, the total variation of Y may be decomposed into two additive components (C.11), one of which is linearly dependent upon the independent variable ($SS_{\hat{Y}}$) and a second, which is due to error in the sense of not being linearly dependent upon $X(SS_{Y-\hat{Y}})$.

Since,

$$SS_Y = SS_{\hat{Y}} + SS_{Y-\hat{Y}},$$

and since the least-squares solution minimizes $SS_{Y-\hat{Y}}$, it should be obvious that for any given set of data $SS_{\hat{Y}}$ is maximized. It should also be obvious that it is desirable for $SS_{\hat{Y}}$ to be as large as possible and for $SS_{Y-\hat{Y}}$ to be as small as possible. When $SS_Y = SS_{\hat{Y}}$, there are no errors of prediction; $SS_{Y-\hat{Y}} = 0$, and all of the observed values of Y fall exactly on a straight line. Under those conditions, Y is totally predictable from X with a linear equation. At the other extreme, when $SS_Y = SS_{Y-\hat{Y}}$ and there is no predictable variation in Y from X with a linear equation, $SS_{\hat{Y}} = 0$. When this occurs, the regression line has no slope and $b_1 = 0$. Hence

$$\begin{aligned} \hat{Y}_i &= b_0 + b_1 X_i \\ &= b_0 \\ &= \bar{Y} - b_1 \bar{X} \\ &= \bar{Y}. \end{aligned}$$

That is, for all values of X, one predicts $\bar{Y}$.

From these results, one might correctly conclude that the proportion of SS_Y which is related to X, $SS_{\hat{Y}}$, might provide a useful index of goodness of fit of the least-squares line to the observed data. Indeed, that is the case. Let the product–moment correlation between X and Y, r_{XY}, be defined as

$$r_{XY} = \frac{SP_{XY}}{\sqrt{SS_X SS_Y}}. \tag{C.12}$$

Then,

$$r_{XY}^2 = \frac{SP_{XY}^2}{SS_X SS_Y} = \frac{b_1 SP_{XY}}{SS_Y} = \frac{SS_{\hat{Y}}}{SS_Y}. \tag{C.13}$$

That is, the square of the product–moment correlation between X and Y is the proportion of variation in Y in the sample which can be predicted from X with a linear equation in which b_0 and b_1 are defined by the least-squares criterion. Since $SS_{\hat{Y}}$ is maximized and $SS_{Y-\hat{Y}}$ is minimized, r_{XY}^2 is maximized and $(1 - r_{XY}^2)$ is minimized. In terms of r_{XY}^2,

$$SS_{\hat{Y}} = r_{XY}^2 SS_Y, \quad \text{and}$$
$$SS_{Y-\hat{Y}} = SS_Y - SS_{\hat{Y}} = (1 - r_{XY}^2) SS_Y. \tag{C.14}$$

Hence,

$$SS_Y = r_{XY}^2 SS_Y + (1 - r_{XY}^2) SS_Y. \tag{C.15}$$

A numerical example to illustrate the material discussed so far in this section is given in Table C.1. The sample data are given at the left in part i. To the right of part i various summary statistics are computed. The sample values of b_0 and b_1 as defined by the least-squares criterion are obtained in part ii. The numerical value for r_{XY}^2 is also computed in part ii. For this sample $r_{XY}^2 = 0.980$, indicating that 98 percent of the total variation in Y can be predicted.

The prediction equation is given in part iii of the table. The predicted scores, $\hat{Y}$, as obtained from this prediction equation, are given in part iv. For example, for element 1, $X = 3$,

$$\hat{Y}_1 = 5.853 + 1.683(3) = 10.902.$$

The error (or residual) associated with element 1 is

$$Y_1 - \hat{Y}_1 = 10 - 10.902 = -0.902.$$

A relationship that will be established in a later section is the following:

$$\sum \hat{Y}^2 = b_0 \sum Y + b_1 \sum XY$$

$$= 5.853(105) + 1.683(1157) = 2561.80.$$

As computed in part iv, $\sum \hat{Y}^2 = 2561.89$. The difference in the two numerical results is due to rounding error. The variation associated with the predicted Y scores, computed in four different (but equivalent) ways, is given in the bottom part of part iv. The computations agree to three significant digits. The residual or error variation is computed by two different methods in part v. Again, the differences are due to rounding error.

TABLE C.1 **Numerical example of construction of prediction system for sample data**

Sample data:

(i)

Element	X	Y
1	3	10
2	5	14
3	8	20
4	12	28
$n = 5$	17	33
$\sum (\ )$	45	105
$\sum (\ )^2$	531	2569
$\sum XY$	1157	

$$\bar{X} = \frac{\sum X}{n} = 9 \qquad \bar{Y} = \frac{\sum Y}{n} = 21$$

$$SS_X = \sum X^2 - \frac{(\sum X)^2}{n} = 531 - 405 = 126$$

$$SS_Y = \sum Y^2 - \frac{(\sum Y)^2}{n} = 2569 - 2205 = 364$$

$$SP_{XY} = \sum XY - \frac{(\sum X)(\sum Y)}{n} = 1157 - 945 = 212$$

(ii)

$$b_1 = \frac{SP_{XY}}{SS_X} = \frac{212}{126} = 1.683 \qquad b_0 = \bar{Y} - b_1\bar{X} = 5.853$$

$$r_{XY}^2 = \frac{SP_{XY}^2}{SS_X SS_Y} = \frac{(212)^2}{(126)(364)}$$
$$= 0.980$$

(iii)

$$\hat{Y} = b_0 + b_1 X = 5.853 + 1.683X$$

Element	Y	$\hat{Y}$	$Y - \hat{Y}$
1	10	10.902	−0.902
2	14	14.268	−0.268
3	20	19.317	0.683
4	28	26.049	1.951
5	33	34.464	−1.464
$\sum (\ )$	105	105.000	0.000
$\sum (\ )^2$	2569	2561.89	7.30

(iv)

$$SS_{\hat{Y}} = \sum \hat{Y}^2 - \frac{(\sum \hat{Y})^2}{n} = 2561.89 - 2205.00 = 356.89$$

$$= b_1 SP_{XY} = 1.683(212) \qquad\qquad = 356.80$$

$$= \frac{SP_{XY}^2}{SS_X} = \frac{(212)^2}{126} \qquad\qquad = 356.70$$

$$= r_{XY}^2 SS_Y = 0.980(364) \qquad\qquad = 356.72$$

(v)

$$SS_{Y-\hat{Y}} = \sum (Y - \hat{Y})^2 = 7.30 \qquad SS_{Y-\hat{Y}} = (1 - r_{XY}^2)SS_Y = 0.020(364) = 7.28$$

UNIVARIATE CASE—MATRIX NOTATION. Although using matrix notation provides no advantage in the univariate case, to generalize to the multivariate case it will be helpful to cast this material in matrix notation.

To introduce greater symmetry into the solution for b_0 and b_1 it is convenient to introduce a dummy variable $X_0 = 1$ for all sample elements. The sample data may now be represented as follows:

Sample element	X_0	X_1	Y	
1	1	X_{11}	Y_1	
2	1	X_{21}	Y_1	$(n > 2)$
$\vdots$	$\vdots$	$\vdots$	$\vdots$	
n	1	X_{n1}	Y_n	

Define

$$\underset{(n \times 1)}{\mathbf{y}} = \begin{bmatrix} Y_1 \\ \vdots \\ Y_n \end{bmatrix} \quad \underset{(n \times 2)}{X} = \begin{bmatrix} 1 & X_{11} \\ \vdots & \vdots \\ 1 & X_{n1} \end{bmatrix} \quad \underset{(2 \times 1)}{\mathbf{b}} = \begin{bmatrix} b_0 \\ b_1 \end{bmatrix} \quad \underset{(n \times 1)}{\hat{\mathbf{y}}} = \begin{bmatrix} \hat{Y}_1 \\ \vdots \\ \hat{Y}_n \end{bmatrix}.$$

In terms of these definitions, the prediction equation (C.1) takes the form

$$\hat{\mathbf{y}} = X\mathbf{b}. \tag{C.16}$$

The errors (residuals) are given by

$$\mathbf{e} = \mathbf{y} - \hat{\mathbf{y}} = \mathbf{y} - X\mathbf{b}. \tag{C.17}$$

The least-squares criterion for goodness of fit of the prediction system minimizes the sum of squares of the residuals

$$\sum e^2 = \mathbf{e'e} =$$
$$= (\mathbf{y} - \hat{\mathbf{y}})'(\mathbf{y} - \hat{\mathbf{y}})$$
$$= (\mathbf{y} - X\mathbf{b})'(\mathbf{y} - X\mathbf{b})$$
$$= \mathbf{y'y} - \mathbf{y'}X\mathbf{b} - \mathbf{b'}X'\mathbf{y} + \mathbf{b'}X'X\mathbf{b}$$
$$= \mathbf{y'y} + \mathbf{b'}X'X\mathbf{b} - 2\mathbf{b}X'\mathbf{y}. \tag{C.18}$$

This last step follows from the fact that both $\mathbf{y'}X\mathbf{b}$ and $\mathbf{b'}X'\mathbf{y}$ are scalars and are equal. Differentiation of (C.18) with respect to $\mathbf{b}$ and setting the result equal to zero yields the set of normal equations

$$(X'X)\mathbf{b} = X'\mathbf{y}. \tag{C.19}$$

The normal equations are collectively the set of equations which result from the least-squares solution and are used to obtain the regression coefficients of $\mathbf{b}$.

For the univariate case, $X'X$ will always be nonsingular. Hence, the solution of **b** is obtained by multiplying both sides of the normal equations by $(X'X)^{-1}$.

$$(X'X)^{-1}(X'X)\mathbf{b} = (X'X)^{-1}X'\mathbf{y}$$
$$I\mathbf{b} = (X'X)^{-1}X'\mathbf{y}$$
$$\mathbf{b} = (X'X)^{-1}X'\mathbf{y}. \tag{C.20}$$

For the multivariate case, $X'X$ may be singular, in which the solution for **b** is not unique.

Since the prediction equation in (C.1) takes the form of (C.16), it follows from the solution to the normal equations that the prediction equation may be rewritten as

$$\hat{\mathbf{y}} = X\mathbf{b}$$
$$= X(X'X)^{-1}X'\mathbf{y}. \tag{C.21}$$

From this result it also follows that the vector of residuals may be expressed as

$$\mathbf{e} = \mathbf{y} - \hat{\mathbf{y}}$$
$$= \mathbf{y} - X(X'X)^{-1}X'\mathbf{y}$$
$$= [I - X(X'X)^{-1}X']\mathbf{y}. \tag{C.22}$$

It is of special interest to obtain expressions for the sum of the squares of residual scores and predicted scores and for the sum of cross products between observed and predicted values of the dependent variable.

For the residuals,

$$\sum e^2 = \mathbf{e}'\mathbf{e}$$
$$= \mathbf{y}'[I - X(X'X)^{-1}X']'[I - X(X'X)^{-1}X']\mathbf{y}$$
$$= \mathbf{y}'[I - X(X'X)^{-1}X']\mathbf{y}. \tag{C.23}$$

The last expression follows from the fact that $I - X(X'X)^{-1}X'$ is idempotent.[1]

---

[1] The matrices $X(X'X)^{-1}X'$ and $I - X(X'X)^{-1}X'$ have some interesting properties. Let

$$P = X(X'X)^{-1}X'$$
$$M = I - X(X'X)^{-1}X'.$$

The matrices P and M are:
(a) *symmetric*—$P = P'$ and $M = M'$.
(b) *idempotent*—$PP = P$ and $MM = M$.
(c) *orthogonal*—$PM = P(1 - P) = P - P = 0.$
$$MP = (I - P)P = 0.$$
(d) *complementary*—$P + M = P + (I - P) = I.$

Additional properties are that

$$PX = X(X'X)^{-1}X'X = X$$
$$MX = (I - P)X = X - X = 0.$$

Finally, $\mathbf{1}P = \mathbf{1}'$ and $\mathbf{1}'M = \mathbf{0}'$ indicates that each column of P sums to unity and each column of M sums to zero.

It is also possible to express $\sum e^2$ in other ways which are computationally useful:

$$\mathbf{e'e} = \mathbf{y'y} - \mathbf{y'}X(X'X)^{-1}X'\mathbf{y}$$

$$= \mathbf{y'y} - \mathbf{y'}X\mathbf{b} \tag{C.24}$$

follows from (C.23) and the solution to the normal equations, $\mathbf{b} = (X'X)^{-1}X'\mathbf{y}$.

A simple expression is:

$$\mathbf{e'e} = \mathbf{y'y} - \mathbf{y'}\hat{\mathbf{y}}$$

$$= \mathbf{y'}(\mathbf{y} - \hat{\mathbf{y}})$$

$$= \mathbf{y'e}. \tag{C.25}$$

The sum of the squares of predicted scores may also be obtained in various ways. Basically,

$$\sum \hat{Y}^2 = \hat{\mathbf{y}}'\hat{\mathbf{y}}$$

$$= (X\mathbf{b})'X\mathbf{b}$$

$$= \mathbf{y'}[X(X'X)^{-1}X'][X(X'X)^{-1}X']\mathbf{y}$$

$$= \mathbf{y'}[X(X'X)^{-1}X']\mathbf{y}. \tag{C.26}$$

In this development the last step follows from the fact that $X(X'X)^{-1}X'$ is idempotent.

It is also possible to express (C.26) simply as

$$\sum \hat{Y}^2 = \mathbf{b'}X'\mathbf{y}. \tag{C.27}$$

This result follows from (C.26) and the solution to the normal equations. By (C.27) one sees that the sum of the squares of the predicted scores can be easily obtained by premultiplying the vector on the right-hand side of the normal equations $(X'\mathbf{y})$ by the transpose of the vector $\mathbf{b}$.

An expression for the sum of the cross products between Y and $\hat{Y}$ shows that $\sum Y\hat{Y}$ is actually equal to $\sum \hat{Y}^2$:

$$\sum Y\hat{Y} = \mathbf{y'}\hat{\mathbf{y}}$$

$$= \mathbf{y'}X\mathbf{b}$$

$$= \mathbf{y'}X(X'X)^{-1}X'\mathbf{y}$$

$$= \sum \hat{Y}^2. \tag{C.28}$$

This result leads to a useful alternative approach to the relationship for $\sum e^2$ in (C.23),

$$\sum e^2 = \sum (Y - \hat{Y})^2$$

$$= \sum Y^2 + \sum \hat{Y}^2 - 2 \sum Y\hat{Y}$$

$$= \sum Y^2 + \sum \hat{Y}^2 - 2 \sum \hat{Y}^2$$

$$= \sum Y^2 - \sum \hat{Y}^2. \tag{C.29}$$

In matrix terms,

$$\sum e^2 = \sum Y^2 - \sum \hat{Y}^2$$

$$= \mathbf{y'y} - \mathbf{y'}X(X'X)^{-1}X'\mathbf{y}$$

$$= \mathbf{y'}[I - X(X'X)^{-1}X']\mathbf{y}$$

$$= (\text{C.23}).$$

It is also very useful to rearrange (C.29) to show that

$$\sum Y^2 = \sum \hat{Y}^2 + \sum e^2. \tag{C.30}$$

That is, one can decompose the total sum of the squares of the dependent variable into two orthogonal components, the sum of the squares of the predicted scores plus the sum of the squares of the errors. Since the least-squares solution minimizes $\sum e^2$, it follows that for any given data set $\sum \hat{Y}^2$ is maximized. Since $\sum \hat{Y}^2 = \sum Y\hat{Y}$, it also follows that $\sum Y\hat{Y}$ is maximized.

It is simple and useful to use (C.30) to show that SS_Y, the total variation of the dependent variable, can also be decomposed into two orthogonal parts, the variation of predicted scores plus the variation of error scores,

$$SS_Y = SS_{\hat{Y}} + SS_e. \tag{C.31}$$

This result follows from noting that $\bar{Y} = \bar{\hat{Y}}$, $\bar{e} = 0$ and $\hat{Y}$ and e are independent. Most simply, if one subtracts $(\sum Y)^2/n$ from both sides of (C.30), one obtains:

$$\sum Y^2 - \left(\sum Y\right)^2 \bigg/ n = \sum \hat{Y}^2 - \frac{\sum Y^2}{n} + \sum e^2$$

$$\sum (Y - \bar{Y})^2 = \sum (\hat{Y} - \bar{\hat{Y}})^2 + \sum (e - 0)^2$$

$$SS_Y = SS_{\hat{Y}} + SS_e.$$

Hence, the least-squares solution minimizes error variation and maximizes variation of predicted scores.

It is also important to develop an expression for r_{XY}^2, the square of the linear correlation between the independent and dependent variables, in terms of the least-squares solution. That development is based upon the demonstration that $\sum Y\hat{Y} = \sum \hat{Y}^2$ in (C.28).

Since

$$\hat{Y} = b_0 + b_1 X_1,$$

it follows that

$$SS_{\hat{Y}} = b_1^2 SS_X.$$

Using, in addition, the fact that $b_1 = SP_{XY}/SS_X$, one can write

$$
\begin{aligned}
SS_{\hat{Y}} &= b_1^2 SS_X \\
&= \frac{SP_{XY}^2}{SS_X^2} SS_X \\
&= \frac{SP_{XY}^2}{SS_X}.
\end{aligned}
\tag{C.32}
$$

From this, an important result follows:

$$r_{XY}^2 = \frac{SP_{XY}^2}{SS_X SS_Y} = \frac{SP_{XY}^2/SS_X}{SS_Y} = \frac{SS_{\hat{Y}}}{SS_Y}. \tag{C.33}$$

In words, the squared correlation between the independent and dependent variables may be expressed as the proportion of SS_Y which is linearly related to the independent variable X, since $SS_{\hat{Y}}$ is the variation of the points on the least-squares line of best fit to the observed data. Hence, $SS_{\hat{Y}}$ is maximized and r_{XY}^2 is a measure of goodness of fit of the least-squares solution to the observed data.

Finally, since from (C.32) $SS_Y = SS_{\hat{Y}} + SS_e$, and from rearranging (C.33) $SS_{\hat{Y}} = r_{XY}^2 SS_Y$, it follows that one may also write SS_e in terms of r_{XY}^2 as:

$$
\begin{aligned}
SS_e &= SS_Y - SS_{\hat{Y}} \\
&= SS_Y - r_{XY}^2 SS_Y \\
&= (1 - r_{XY}^2) SS_Y.
\end{aligned}
\tag{C.34}
$$

Rearranging (C.34) so that $(1 - r_{XY}^2) = \dfrac{SS_e}{SS_Y}$ makes it explicit that $(1 - r_{XY}^2)$ is the proportion of the variation in the dependent variable which is *not* predictable with the linear function using the least-squares solution. It also follows that one can express the decomposition of SS_Y into error variation and predictable variation in terms of r_{XY}^2:

$$
\begin{aligned}
SS_Y &= SS_{\hat{Y}} + SS_e \\
&= r_{XY}^2 SS_Y + (1 - r_{XY}^2) SS_Y
\end{aligned}
$$

$$\left(\begin{array}{c} \text{Variation} \\ \text{predictable from } X \end{array} \right) + \left(\begin{array}{c} \text{Variation not} \\ \text{predictable from } X \end{array} \right). \tag{C.35}$$

Hence, if one knows r_{XY}^2 and SS_Y, one can evaluate goodness of fit of the least-squares solution.

It is worthwhile to make one additional point. Since $\hat{Y}$ is simply the linear transformation of the independent variable, $\hat{Y} = b_0 + b_1 X_1$, and since the linear correlation r_{XY} is invariant under linear transformations on either X or Y, it follows that $r_{XY}^2 = r_{Y\hat{Y}}^2$, a measure of the extent to which a straight line fits the relation between $\hat{Y}$ and Y. This point can be developed by analogy with (C.33):

$$r_{Y\hat{Y}}^2 = \frac{SP_{Y\hat{Y}}^2}{SS_Y SS_{\hat{Y}}} = \frac{SS_{\hat{Y}}^2}{SS_Y SS_{\hat{Y}}} = \frac{SS_{\hat{Y}}}{SS_Y} = r_{XY}^2. \tag{C.36}$$

All the relationships developed in (C.16) through (C.36) can be generalized to the case in which the matrix X contains any number of variables, provided $X'X$ is nonsingular. None of the relationships has any constraint upon the size of the X matrix. However, if the number of rows of X is less than the number of columns, or if any of the X variables are linearly dependent, the matrix $X'X$ will be singular.

The numerical example in Table C.1 is presented in matrix format in Table C.2. The data matrix X is combined with the vector $\mathbf{y}$ in an augmented data matrix in Part (i). For some purposes it is desirable to work with $X'_{aug}X_{aug}$ rather than $X'X$. Part (i) also presents $X'X$ and $X'\mathbf{y}$, the elements of the normal equations, $X'X\mathbf{b} = X'\mathbf{y}$.

TABLE C.2   Numerical example

(i)

$$\text{Data matrix } X_{aug} = \begin{bmatrix} X_0 & X_1 & Y \\ 1 & 3 & 10 \\ 1 & 5 & 14 \\ 1 & 8 & 20 \\ 1 & 12 & 28 \\ 1 & 17 & 33 \end{bmatrix}; \quad X'X = \begin{bmatrix} 5 & 45 \\ 45 & 531 \end{bmatrix}; \quad X'\mathbf{y} = \begin{bmatrix} 105 \\ 1157 \end{bmatrix}$$

(ii)

$$(X'X)^{-1} = \begin{bmatrix} 0.8429 & -0.07143 \\ -0.07143 & 0.007937 \end{bmatrix}; \quad \mathbf{b} = (X'X)^{-1}(X'\mathbf{y}) = \begin{bmatrix} 5.860 \\ 1.683 \end{bmatrix}$$

(iii)

$$X'_{aug}X_{aug} = \begin{bmatrix} X_0 & X_1 & Y \\ 5 & 45 & 105 \\ 45 & 531 & 1157 \\ 105 & 1157 & 2569 \end{bmatrix}; \quad (X'_{aug}X_{aug})^{-1} = \begin{bmatrix} X_0 & X_1 & Y \\ 5.5392 & 1.2778 & -0.8019 \\ 1.2778 & 0.3956 & -0.2304 \\ -0.8019 & -0.2304 & 0.1369 \end{bmatrix}$$

(iv)

$$b_0 = -p^{X_0 Y}/p^{YY} = -(-0.8019)/0.1369 = 5.856$$
$$b_1 = -p^{X_1 Y}/p^{YY} = -(-0.2304)/0.1369 = 1.683$$
$$r_{XY}^2 = 1 - [1/(p^{YY}SS_Y)] = 1 - [1/(0.1369)(364.00)] = 1 - (1/49.83) = 0.97994$$

For this simple regression problem,

$$X'X = \begin{bmatrix} n & \sum X \\ \sum X & \sum X^2 \end{bmatrix} = \begin{bmatrix} 5 & 45 \\ 45 & 531 \end{bmatrix}$$

$$X'\mathbf{y} = \begin{bmatrix} \sum X \\ \sum Y^2 \end{bmatrix} = \begin{bmatrix} 105 \\ 1157 \end{bmatrix}.$$

Hence, the normal equations

$$X'X\mathbf{b} = X'\mathbf{y}$$

are in scalar form

$$nb_0 + \sum X b_1 = \sum Y$$

$$\sum X b_1 + \sum X^2 b_2 = \sum Y^2.$$

The solution for $\mathbf{b}$ in terms of $X'X$ and $X'\mathbf{y}$ as presented in Part (ii) is

$$\mathbf{b} = (X'X)^{-1}X'\mathbf{y}.$$

The linear equation for the least-squares fit to these data is, then,

$$\hat{Y}_i = 1.683X_i + 5.860.$$

Within rounding error, the numerical values for b_0 and b_1 agree with those given in Table C.1.

The data are presented in terms of X_{aug} in Part iii of Table C.2, wherein $X'_{\text{aug}}X_{\text{aug}}$ contains both $X'X$ and $X'\mathbf{y}$. From the inverse of $X'_{\text{aug}}X_{\text{aug}}$, it is simple to obtain both $\mathbf{b}$ and r_{XY}^2. This is shown in Part iv. Let an element of $X'_{\text{aug}}X_{\text{aug}}$ be denoted p^{ij}. Then the components of the vector $\mathbf{b}$ may be obtained as indicated in Part iv. These relationships between the components of $\mathbf{b}$ and the elements in row (or column) Y of $(X'_{\text{aug}}X_{\text{aug}})^{-1}$ follow quite directly from the relationship between $(X'X)^{-1}$ and $(X'_{\text{aug}}X_{\text{aug}})^{-1}$. The elements of row Y of the latter inverse are proportional to $(X'X)^{-1}(X'\mathbf{y})$.

The square of the correlation between X and Y may also be found from the element p^{YY} as indicated in part iv. The relationship follows from the fact that

$$\frac{1}{p^{YY}} = \text{SS}_{Y-\hat{Y}}.$$

Hence

$$1 - \frac{1}{p^{YY}\text{SS}_Y} = 1 - \frac{\text{SS}_{Y-\hat{Y}}}{\text{SS}_Y} = r_{XY}^2.$$

Multivariate Case

In the multivariate case, there are p independent variables and a single dependent variable measured on each of n subjects. Hence, the sample data may be represented as:

Sample element	X_0	X_1	$\cdots$	X_p	Y
1	1	X_{11}	$\cdots$	X_{1p}	Y_1
2	1	X_{21}	$\cdots$	X_{2p}	Y_2
$\vdots$	$\vdots$	$\vdots$		$\vdots$	$\vdots$
n	1	X_{n1}	$\cdots$	X_{np}	Y_n

There are $p + 1$ X variables, including a dummy variable X_0. Let

$$\frac{X}{(n \times p + 1)} = \text{matrix of observations on } X_0, X_1, \ldots, X_p;$$

$$\frac{\mathbf{y}}{n \times 1} = \text{vector of observations on } Y;$$

$$\frac{\hat{\mathbf{y}}}{n \times 1} = \text{vector of predicted scores on } Y;$$

$$\mathbf{e} = \mathbf{y} - \hat{\mathbf{y}} = \text{vector of errors or residuals.}$$

The prediction system is to be linear in $X_0, X_1, \ldots, X_p$. That is,

$$\hat{Y} = b_0 X_0 + b_1 X_1 + \cdots + b_p X_p.$$

These weights in the prediction system have different interpretations in different contexts. In the case of multiple linear regression, the elements of

$$\mathbf{b} = \begin{bmatrix} b_0 \\ b_1 \\ \vdots \\ b_p \end{bmatrix}$$

are partial regression coefficients. In the univariate case, geometrically the regression equation is the equation for a straight line in a two space (X, Y). The coefficients b_0 and b_1 are, respectively, the intercept and slope of that line. In the limiting multivariate case wherein there are two predictors, the regression equation defines points on a plane in a three space $(X_1, X_2 Y)$. In that space, b_0 represents the intercept of the Y axis by the plane and b_1 and b_2 are *partial regression coefficients*. They represent the slope of the plane with regard to the X_1 and X_2 axes, respectively. The coefficients may be viewed as the regression of Y on that variable with the other variable held constant (partialed out). In general, with p predictors, the equation is that of a hyperplane in a $p + 1$ space.

In some applications, a more complete notation system for the weights in the prediction system is needed. A widely used notation is one given below.

$$\hat{Y} = b_{Y0.12\ldots p} X_0 + b_{Y1.02\ldots p} X_1 + b_{Y2.01\ldots p} X_2 + \cdots + b_{Yp.01\ldots(p-1)} X_p.$$

If, for example, $p = 3$, the prediction system in this notation has the form

$$\hat{Y} = b_{Y0.123} X_0 + b_{Y1.023} X_1 + b_{Y2.013} X_2 + b_{Y3.012} X_3.$$

Where the context makes apparent just what predictors are in the system, the more complete notation will not be used. Where, however, one is using the complete set of predictors as well as subsets of the complete system, the more complete notation system will be needed.

One may represent the observed Y in the form

$$Y = \hat{Y} + e \quad \text{or} \quad e = Y - \hat{Y}.$$

Thus $\hat{Y}$ represents that part of Y which is a linear function of X, and e represents that part of Y which is *not* a linear function of X. In matrix notation,

$$\hat{\mathbf{y}} = X\mathbf{b}, \qquad \mathbf{y} = \hat{\mathbf{y}} + \mathbf{e},$$

where $\mathbf{b}' = [b_0 \ b_1 \ \cdots \ b_p]$.

The normal equations, the solution to the normal equations, and other important relations were presented earlier in (C.16) through (C.36) in terms of X and $\mathbf{y}$, the independent variables and dependent variables in their untransformed format for the univariate case. All of those relations hold for the multivariate case and are not repeated here. However, in the multivariate case, for some purposes it is desirable and simpler to present the variables in deviation score form, the result of which is that the components of $\mathbf{b}$ are expressed in terms of the variations and covariations of the variables.

Toward that end, suppose that the scale of measurement of the X variables is changed so that each variable has a mean of zero. That is, suppose $\bar{X}_j$ is subtracted from each X_{ij}. Hence,

$$x_{ij} = X_{ij} - \bar{X}_j,$$

and X stated in deviation score form is:

$$X_D = \quad
\begin{array}{c|cccc}
\text{Sample} & & & & \\
\text{element} & x_0 & x_1 & \cdots & x_p \\
\hline
1 & 1 & x_{11} & \cdots & x_{1p} \\
2 & 1 & x_{21} & \cdots & x_{2p} \\
\vdots & \vdots & \vdots & & \vdots \\
n & 1 & x_{n1} & \cdots & x_{np}
\end{array}$$

Since all transformed variables in X_D sum to zero, $X_D'X_D$ takes the form

$$X_D'X_D =
\begin{bmatrix}
n & 0 & \cdots & 0 \\
0 & SS_{X_1} & \cdots & SP_{X_1 X_p} \\
\vdots & \vdots & & \vdots \\
0 & SP_{X_p X_1} & \cdots & SS_{X_p}
\end{bmatrix}
=
\begin{bmatrix}
n & 0 & \cdots & 0 \\
0 & & & \\
\vdots & & V_{XX} & \\
0 & & &
\end{bmatrix}
=
\begin{bmatrix}
n & \mathbf{0}' \\
\mathbf{0} & V_{XX}
\end{bmatrix},$$

where V_{XX} is the variation–covariation matrix for the variables $X_1, \ldots, X_p$.

If a similar transformation is made on the components of the vector $\mathbf{y}$, one has

$$X_D'\mathbf{y}_D =
\begin{bmatrix}
\Sigma Y \\
SP_{X_1 Y} \\
\vdots \\
SP_{X_p Y}
\end{bmatrix}
=
\begin{bmatrix}
0 \\
\mathbf{v}_{XY}
\end{bmatrix},$$

where $\mathbf{v}_{XY}$ = vector of covariations between Y and $X_1, \ldots, X_p$ and $\sum Y_D = \sum (Y_i - \bar{Y}) = 0$.

In terms of the transformed variables, the prediction equation becomes

$$\hat{\mathbf{y}}_D = X_D \mathbf{b}. \tag{C.37}$$

That is, one is predicting for each subject the dependent variable in deviation score form,

$$\hat{y}_i = b_1 x_{i1} + b_2 x_{i2} + \cdots + b_p x_{ip}.$$

Note that in deviation form $b_0 = 0$ since $\mathbf{b}_0 = \bar{Y} - b_1 \bar{X}_1 - b_2 \bar{X}_2 - \cdots - b_p \bar{X}_p$, and all means are zero. To return to the original units of Y, one need only add $\bar{Y}$, since $\hat{\bar{Y}} = \bar{Y}$. Hence,

$$\hat{Y}_i = \hat{y}_i + \bar{Y}.$$

The normal equations take the matrix form

$$(X_D' X_D) \mathbf{b} = X_D' \mathbf{y}_D \tag{C.38}$$

and the scalar form

$$b_1 SS_{X_1} + b_2 SP_{X_1 X_2} + \cdots + b_p SP_{X_1 X_p} = SP_{X_1 Y}$$
$$b_1 SP_{X_1 X_2} + b_2 SS_{X_2} + \cdots + b_p SP_{X_2 X_p} = SP_{X_2 Y}$$
$$\vdots \quad \vdots \quad \vdots \quad \vdots \quad \vdots$$
$$b_1 SP_{X_1 X_p} + b_2 SP_{X_2 X_p} + \cdots + b_p SS_{X_p} = SP_{X_p Y}.$$

The solution to the normal equations in deviation score form is

$$\mathbf{b} = (X_D' X_D)^{-1} X_D' \mathbf{y}_D$$
$$= V_{XX}^{-1} \mathbf{v}_{XY}. \tag{C.39}$$

The variation of both the predicted scores and residuals are simple to obtain from this solution. Using the relation (C.27) one obtains from the deviation score format the special case,

$$SS_{\hat{Y}} = \mathbf{b}' X_D' \mathbf{y}_D$$
$$= \mathbf{v}_{XY}' V_{XX}^{-1} \mathbf{v}_{XY}$$
$$= \mathbf{b}' \mathbf{v}_{XY} \quad \text{where } \mathbf{b}' = (b_1 \cdots b_p). \tag{C.40}$$

The variation of the residuals is provided by

$$SS_{\text{error}} = SS_Y - SS_{\hat{Y}}$$
$$= SS_Y - \mathbf{b}' \mathbf{v}_{XY}. \tag{C.41}$$

The square of the correlation between Y and $\hat{Y}$ from (C.36) is given by

$$r_{Y\hat{Y}}^2 = \frac{SS_{\hat{Y}}}{SS_Y} = \frac{\mathbf{b}' \mathbf{v}_{XY}}{SS_Y}. \tag{C.42}$$

Equivalently, using the relationship $SS_{\hat{Y}} = SS_Y - SS_{\text{error}}$,

$$r_{Y\hat{Y}}^2 = \frac{SS_Y - SS_{\text{error}}}{SS_Y} = 1 - \frac{SS_{\text{error}}}{SS_Y}. \tag{C.43}$$

The squared correlation for the case of multiple predictors is denoted by

$$r_{Y\hat{Y}}^2 = r_{Y(X_1 X_2 \cdots X_p)}^2 = r_{Y(12 \cdots p)}^2, \tag{C.44}$$

and is called the *squared multiple correlation*. It is important to note the meaning of $r^2_{Y\hat{Y}}$ for the multivariate case. In the univariate case, it was shown that $r^2_{Y\hat{Y}} = r^2_{XY}$, the squared zero-order correlation between the independent and dependent variables. In the multivariate case, $r^2_{Y\hat{Y}}$, the squared multiple correlation, represents the proportion of the total variation of Y in the sample that can be predicted from the least-squares linear function of $X_1, X_2, \ldots, X_p$ (b_0 has no effect on the correlation, its only role being to determine $\hat{Y}$).

The squared multiple correlation plays the same role in the multivariate case as does r^2_{XY} in the univariate case as a measure of goodness of fit. It may also be used, as in the univariate case, to express the decomposition of SS_Y:

$$SS_Y = SS_{\hat{Y}} + SS_{error}$$
$$= r^2_{Y(12\ldots p)}SS_Y + (1 - r^2_{Y(12\ldots p)})SS_Y. \tag{C.45}$$

Standard score solution. The regression weights in **b** are not in comparable units of measurement. To compare the magnitude of the partial regression coefficients, one must express the regression problem in *standard score* form. That is, all variables have the same variance. Consider a convenient transformation of X and **y** wherein all variables have been standardized so that the means are zero and the variances are unity:

$$y_i^* = \frac{Y_i - \bar{Y}}{s_y}$$

$$x_{ij}^* = \frac{X_{ij} - \bar{X}_j}{s_{X_j}}.$$

Then,

$$X^* = \begin{array}{c|ccccc} \text{Sample element} & x_0 & x_1^* & \cdots & x_p^* \\ \hline 1 & 1 & x_{11}^* & \cdots & x_{1p}^* \\ 2 & 1 & x_{21}^* & \cdots & x_{2p}^* \\ \vdots & \vdots & \vdots & & \vdots \\ n & 1 & x_{n1}^* & \cdots & x_{np}^* \end{array}$$

and

$$\mathbf{y}^* = \begin{bmatrix} y_1^* \\ y_2^* \\ \vdots \\ y_n^* \end{bmatrix}.$$

Under this transformation, the variations of all of the standardized variables are $n - 1$, the variances are 1.0, and the correlations among standardized variables are all equal to the covariances. That is,

$$X^{*\prime}X^* = \begin{bmatrix} n & 0 & \cdots & 0 \\ 0 & n-1 & \cdots & SP_{x_1^* x_p^*} \\ \vdots & \vdots & & \vdots \\ 0 & SP_{x_p^* x_1^*} & \cdots & n-1 \end{bmatrix} = \begin{bmatrix} n & \mathbf{0}' \\ \mathbf{0} & V_{x^* x^*} \end{bmatrix},$$

and

$$\frac{1}{n-1} V_{X^*X^*} = \begin{bmatrix} 1 & \text{Cov}_{x_1^* x_2^*} & \cdots & \text{Cov}_{x_1^* x_p^*} \\ \text{Cov}_{x_2^* x_1^*} & 1 & \cdots & \text{Cov}_{x_2^* x_p^*} \\ \vdots & \vdots & & \vdots \\ \text{Cov}_{x_p^* x_1^*} & \cdots & \cdots & 1 \end{bmatrix}$$

$$= \begin{bmatrix} 1 & r_{X_1 X_2} & \cdots & r_{X_1 X_p} \\ r_{X_2 X_1} & 1 & \cdots & r_{X_2 X_p} \\ \vdots & \vdots & & \vdots \\ r_{X_p X_1} & \cdots & \cdots & 1 \end{bmatrix} = R_{XX}$$

R_{XX} is the $p \times p$ matrix of intercorrelations among the predictor variables.

Similarly, for the relation $X^{*\prime} \mathbf{y}^*$ one has

$$X^{*\prime} \mathbf{y}^* = \begin{bmatrix} \Sigma \, y^* \\ \text{SP}_{x_1^* y^*} \\ \vdots \\ \text{SP}_{x_p^* y^*} \end{bmatrix} = \begin{bmatrix} 0 \\ \mathbf{v}_{x^* y^*} \end{bmatrix},$$

and

$$\frac{1}{n-1} X^* \mathbf{y}^* = \begin{bmatrix} 0 \\ \text{Cov}_{x_1^* y^*} \\ \vdots \\ \text{Cov}_{x_p^* y^*} \end{bmatrix} = \begin{bmatrix} 0 \\ r_{X_1 Y} \\ r_{X_2 Y} \\ \vdots \\ r_{X_p Y} \end{bmatrix} = \mathbf{r}_{XY}.$$

The vector $\mathbf{r}_{XY}$, which contains the correlations between each of the predictors and Y, is sometimes called the *validity vector*.

In terms of these standardized variables, the prediction equation becomes

$$\hat{\mathbf{y}}^* = X^* \mathbf{b}^*. \tag{C.46}$$

This expresses the dependent variable in standard score form for each subject as

$$y_i^* = b_1^* x_{i1}^* + b_2^* x_{i2}^* + \cdots + b_p^* x_{ip}^*.$$

In standard score form, $b_0^* = 0$ and the b_j^* are *standardized partial regression coefficients*. Some authors use the notation β_j and refer to the standardized weights as *beta weights*. However, herein Greek letters will be reserved for the parameters β_j and β_j^*, of which b_j and b_j^* are the respective estimates.

The relation between the "raw score," or unstandardized weights, and the standardized weights is

$$b_j^* = b_j \frac{s_{X_j}}{s_Y}, \quad \text{or}$$

$$b_j = b_j^* \frac{s_Y}{s_{X_j}}. \tag{C.47}$$

From (C.47) it is obvious that when the variables are standardized to any common variance, $b_j = b_j^*$. In matrix terms,

$$\mathbf{b} = s_Y D_{S_X}^{-1} \mathbf{b}^*, \tag{C.48}$$

where D_{S_X} is the diagonal matrix with standard deviations of the predictors on the main diagonal, s_Y is the scalar standard deviation of Y, and $\mathbf{b}^*$ is the vector of standardized weights.

The normal equations in standard score form express the unknown weights $\mathbf{b}^*$ as a function of correlations among the variables. That is, when

$$(X^{*\prime} X^*)\mathbf{b}^* = X^{*\prime} \mathbf{y}^*$$

is multiplied by $1/(n-1)$, one obtains

$$R_{XX}\mathbf{b}^* = \mathbf{r}_{XY}, \tag{C.49}$$

which expresses the b_j^* in scalar terms as

$$b_1^* + b_2^* r_{X_1 X_2} + \cdots + b_p^* r_{X_1 X_p} = r_{X_1 Y}$$
$$b_1^* r_{X_2 X_1} + b_2^* + \cdots + b_p^* r_{X_2 X_p} = r_{X_2 Y}$$
$$\vdots \qquad \qquad \vdots$$
$$b_1^* r_{X_p X_1} + b_2^* r_{X_p X_2} + \cdots + b_p^* = r_{X_p Y}.$$

The solution to (C.49) in terms of the correlation matrix and the validity vector is, then,

$$\mathbf{b}^* = R_{XX}^{-1} \mathbf{r}_{XY}. \tag{C.50}$$

One advantage to obtaining $\mathbf{b}^*$ is that the square of the multiple correlation may be easily obtained as

$$r_{Y(12 \cdots p)}^2 = \mathbf{r}_{XY}' \mathbf{b}^*, \tag{C.51}$$

a special case of (C.42). This is particularly useful because it shows that the proportion of variation in the dependent variable which is predictable from the least-squares equations, $r_{Y(12 \cdots p)}^2$, is a weighted sum of the validities where the weights are the b_j^*. That is,

$$r_{Y(12 \cdots p)}^2 = r_{Y1} b_1^* + r_{Y2} b_2^* + \cdots + r_{Yp} b_p^*.$$

Substituting the solution to the normal equations (C.50) for $\mathbf{b}^*$ in (C.51), one can also express the squared multiple correlation as

$$r_{Y(12 \cdots p)}^2 = \mathbf{r}_{XY}' R_{XX}^{-1} \mathbf{r}_{XY}. \tag{C.52}$$

A numerical example in which $p = 2$ and $n = 6$ appears in Table C.3. The basic data are provided in Part i. Part ii displays the solution to the normal equations in terms of "raw scores," providing numerical values for b_0, $b_{Y1.2}$, and $b_{Y2.1}$ in the equation:

$$\hat{Y}_i = 2.8759 X_{i1} + 0.2362 X_{i2} - 3.9233.$$

TABLE C.3 **Numerical example**

(i)

Sample element	X_0	X_1	X_2	Y
1	1	3	6	10
2	1	5	1	5
3	1	7	2	15
4	1	7	10	20
5	1	9	7	40
6	1	9	10	10

$$SS_Y = 783.33$$

$$\mathbf{v}_{XY} = \begin{bmatrix} 83.33 \\ 75.00 \end{bmatrix}$$

(ii)

$$X'X = \begin{bmatrix} n & \sum X_1 & \sum X_2 \\ \sum X_1 & \sum X_1^2 & \sum X_1 X_2 \\ \sum X_2 & \sum X_2 X_1 & \sum X_2^2 \end{bmatrix} = \begin{bmatrix} 6 & 40 & 36 \\ 40 & 294 & 260 \\ 36 & 260 & 290 \end{bmatrix}$$

$$X'\mathbf{y} = \begin{bmatrix} \sum Y \\ \sum X_1 Y \\ \sum X_2 Y \end{bmatrix} = \begin{bmatrix} 100 \\ 750 \\ 675 \end{bmatrix}$$

$$\mathbf{b} = (X'X)^{-1}X'\mathbf{y} = \begin{bmatrix} 1.813750 & -0.230060 & -0.018900 \\ -0.230060 & 0.045604 & -0.012325 \\ -0.018900 & -0.012325 & 0.016845 \end{bmatrix}\begin{bmatrix} 100 \\ 750 \\ 675 \end{bmatrix} = \begin{bmatrix} -3.92326 \\ 2.87588 \\ 0.23622 \end{bmatrix}$$

(iii)

$$X'_D X_D = V_{XX} = \begin{bmatrix} SS_{X_1} & SP_{X_1 X_2} \\ SP_{X_2 X_1} & SS_{X_2} \end{bmatrix} = \begin{bmatrix} 27.3333 & 20.0000 \\ 20.0000 & 74.0000 \end{bmatrix}$$

$$X'_D \mathbf{y}_D = \mathbf{v}_{XY} = \begin{bmatrix} SP_{X_1 Y} \\ SP_{X_2 Y} \end{bmatrix} = \begin{bmatrix} 83.3333 \\ 75.000 \end{bmatrix}$$

$$\mathbf{b} = (X'_D X_D)^{-1} X'_D \mathbf{y}_D = V_{XX}^{-1}\mathbf{v}_{XY} = \begin{bmatrix} 0.04560 & -0.01232 \\ -0.01232 & 0.01684 \end{bmatrix}\begin{bmatrix} 83.3333 \\ 75.0000 \end{bmatrix}$$

$$= \begin{bmatrix} 2.8759 \\ 0.2362 \end{bmatrix} = \begin{bmatrix} b_{Y_{1.2}} \\ b_{Y_{2.1}} \end{bmatrix}$$

(iv)

$$\sum \hat{Y}_i^2 = \mathbf{y}X(X'X)^{-1}X'\mathbf{y}$$

$$= \mathbf{b}X'\mathbf{y} = [-3.92326 \quad 2.87588 \quad 0.23622]\begin{bmatrix} 100 \\ 750 \\ 675 \end{bmatrix} = 1924.03$$

$$\sum (Y - \hat{Y})^2 = \sum Y^2 + \sum \hat{Y}^2 - 2\sum Y\hat{Y}.$$

But

$$\sum Y\hat{Y} = \mathbf{y}'X\mathbf{b} = \mathbf{y}'X(X'X)^{-1}X'\mathbf{y} = \sum \hat{Y}^2.$$

Hence

$$\sum (Y - \hat{Y})^2 = \sum Y^2 - \sum \hat{Y}^2$$

$$= 2450.00 - 1924.03 = 525.97.$$

$$SS_{\hat{Y}} = [b_1 \quad b_2]\mathbf{r}_{XY}$$

$$= [2.87588 \quad 0.23622]\begin{bmatrix} 83.33 \\ 75.00 \end{bmatrix} = 257.36$$

$$= r_{Y(12)}^2 SS_Y = (0.3285)(783.3333) = 257.36.$$

$$SS_{Y-\hat{Y}} = \sum (Y - \hat{Y})^2 = 525.97$$

$$= (1 - r_{Y(12)}^2)SS_Y$$

$$= (1 - 0.3285)(783.3333) = 525.97.$$

TABLE C.3 (*Continued*)

(v)

$$\frac{1}{n-1} X'^* X^* = R_{XX} = \begin{bmatrix} 1.00 & r_{12} \\ r_{12} & 1.00 \end{bmatrix} = \begin{bmatrix} 1.0000 & 0.4447 \\ 0.4447 & 1.0000 \end{bmatrix}$$

$$\mathbf{r}_{XY} = \begin{bmatrix} r_{Y1} \\ r_{Y2} \end{bmatrix} = \begin{bmatrix} 0.5695 \\ 0.3115 \end{bmatrix}$$

$$\mathbf{b}^* = R_{XX}^{-1} \mathbf{r}_{XY} = \begin{bmatrix} 1.3279 & -0.5906 \\ -0.5906 & 1.3279 \end{bmatrix} \begin{bmatrix} 0.5695 \\ 0.3115 \end{bmatrix} = \begin{bmatrix} b_{Y1.2}^* \\ b_{Y2.1}^* \end{bmatrix} = \begin{bmatrix} 0.5372 \\ 0.0726 \end{bmatrix}$$

(vi)

$$r_{Y(12)}^2 = \frac{SS_{\hat{Y}}}{SS_Y} = \frac{[b_1 b_2] \mathbf{v}_{XY}}{SS_Y} = 0.3285$$

$$= \mathbf{b}^{*'} \mathbf{r}_{XY} = [0.5372 \quad 0.0726] \begin{bmatrix} 0.5695 \\ 0.3115 \end{bmatrix} = 0.3285.$$

Part iii presents the solution in terms of deviation scores. That is, the solution to the normal equations provides numerical values for b_1 and b_2 in terms of the variation–covariation matrix V_{XX} and the vector $\mathbf{v}_{XY}$. The resulting prediction equation is:

$$\hat{y}_i = 2.8759 x_{i1} + 0.2362 x_{i2}.$$

To provide the total equation in raw score form one may obtain b_0 as

$$b_0 = \bar{Y} - b_1 \bar{X}_1 - b_2 \bar{X}_2.$$

The standard-score solution, based upon R_{XX} and $\mathbf{r}_{XY}$, is provided in Part iv. For the standard-score equation,

$$\hat{y}_i^* = 0.5372 x_{i1}^* + 0.0726 x_{i2}^*$$

and the standardized partial regression coefficients may be compared. It is also possible to obtain the standardized partial regression coefficients as:

$$b_j^* = b_j \frac{s_{X_j}}{s_Y}.$$

Hence,

$$b_{Y1.2}^* = b_{Y1.2} \frac{s_{X_1}}{s_Y} = 2.8759 \left(\frac{2.3381}{12.5166} \right) = 0.5372,$$

$$b_{Y2.1}^* = b_{Y2.1} \frac{s_{X_2}}{s_Y} = 0.2362 \left(\frac{3.8471}{12.5166} \right) = 0.0726.$$

Part v presents SS_Y and $SS_{\hat{Y}}$ obtained in several ways; Part vi provides various computations for the squared-multiple correlation.

In Table C.4, computations are done through use of X_{aug}, where X_{aug} is X augmented by the Y column, $\mathbf{y}$. Let p^{ij} denote the element in row i and column j of $(X'_{\text{aug}} X_{\text{aug}})^{-1}$. The components of $\mathbf{b}$ are obtained as indicated in Part ii; the square of the multiple correlation is also obtained in Part ii. Other squared multiple correlations are computed in Part iii.

TABLE C.4   **Numerical example in terms of X_{aug}**

(i)

$$X'_{aug}X_{aug} = \begin{array}{cccc} X_0 & X_1 & X_2 & Y \end{array}$$

$$X'_{aug}X_{aug} = \begin{bmatrix} 6 & 40 & 36 & 100 \\ 40 & 294 & 260 & 750 \\ 36 & 260 & 290 & 675 \\ 100 & 750 & 675 & 2450 \end{bmatrix}$$

$$(X'_{aug}X_{aug})^{-1} = \begin{array}{cccc} X_0 & X_1 & X_2 & Y \end{array}$$

$$(X'_{aug}X_{aug})^{-1} = \begin{bmatrix} 1.84309 & -0.25152 & -0.020659 & 0.0074593 \\ -0.25152 & 0.061328 & -0.011034 & -0.00546786 \\ -0.020659 & -0.011034 & 0.016951 & -0.00044913 \\ 0.0074593 & -0.00546786 & -0.00044913 & 0.00190128 \end{bmatrix}$$

(ii)

$$b_0 = \frac{-p^{Y0}}{p^{YY}} = \frac{-0.0074593}{0.00190128} = -3.92326$$

$$b_1 = \frac{-p^{Y1}}{p^{YY}} = \frac{-(-0.00546786)}{0.00190128} = 2.87588$$

$$b_2 = \frac{-p^{Y2}}{p^{YY}} = \frac{-(-0.00044913)}{0.00190128} = 0.23622$$

$$r^2_{Y(12)} = 1 - \frac{1}{p^{YY}SS_Y} = 1 - \frac{1}{(0.00190128)(783.33)} = 0.3286$$

(iii)

$$r^2_{1(Y2)} = 1 - \frac{1}{p^{11}SS_1} = 1 - \frac{1}{(0.061328)(27.33)} = 0.4034$$

$$r^2_{2(Y1)} = 1 - \frac{1}{p^{22}SS_2} = 1 - \frac{1}{(0.016951)(74.00)} = 0.2028$$

Correlations: Multiple, Semipartial, and Partial

The square of the multiple correlation has already been discussed as a measure of goodness of fit. As the proportion of variation of the dependent variable which is predictable from the least-squares solution, $r^2_{Y(12\cdots p)}$ provides a convenient measure of goodness of fit of the observed dependent variable to the predicted dependent variable.

Beyond this interpretation, the squared multiple correlation provides a foundation for discussing the incremental increase in $SS_{\hat{Y}}$ or, equivalently, the incremental decrease in $SS_{Y-\hat{Y}}$, associated with adding new independent variables to a prediction equation. Consider the simplest case wherein all independent variables are linearly independent. Under those circumstances,

$$R_{XX} = I.$$

Hence, from equation (C.50),

$$\mathbf{b}^* = R^{-1}\mathbf{r}_{XY}$$

$$= \mathbf{r}_{XY}.$$

That is, when the independent variables are uncorrelated, the standardized partial regression coefficients are the corresponding correlations with the dependent variable $\mathbf{r}_{XY}$. From this, it follows that

$$r^2_{Y(12\cdots p)} = \mathbf{b}'\mathbf{r}_{XY}$$
$$= \mathbf{r}'_{XY}\mathbf{r}_{XY}$$
$$= r^2_{Y1} + r^2_{Y2} + \cdots + r^2_{Y_p}.$$

The square of the multiple correlation is simply the sum of the squares of the validities. Each squared validity coefficient expresses the proportion of variation in Y which could be predicted by an equation with only that particular independent variable. That is, r^2_{Y1} assesses goodness of fit for the equation $\hat{Y}_i = b_1 X_{i1} + b_0$; r^2_{Y2} assesses for the equation $\hat{Y}_i = b_2 X_{i2} + b_0$, etc. Hence, when $R_{XX} = I$, the incremental value of adding, or loss from deleting, variables in prediction equations is the squared validity of that variable; total prediction is the sum of the independent parts.

When the independent variables are themselves correlated ($R_{XX} \neq I$), the situation becomes more complex. Consider the numerical example summarized in Table C.3. For those data,

$$R_{XX} = \begin{bmatrix} 1 & 0.4447 \\ & 1 \end{bmatrix}$$

$$\mathbf{r}_{XY} = \begin{bmatrix} 0.5695 \\ 0.3115 \end{bmatrix}$$

$$r^2_{Y(12)} = 0.3285.$$

If one were to write the equation $\hat{Y}_i = b_1 X_{i1} + b_0$, $r^2_{Y1} = 0.5695^2 = 0.3243$ expresses the fact that one can predict 32 percent of the variation in Y from this equation. With the equation $\hat{Y}_i = b_2 X_{i2} + b_0$, $r^2_{Y2} = 0.3115^2 = 0.0970$ asserts that 9.7 percent of SS_Y can be "accounted for" by the second independent variable when used alone. However,

$$r^2_{Y(12)} < (r^2_{Y1} + r^2_{Y2}) = (0.3243 + 0.0973)$$

because X_1 and X_2 are correlated to the extent of 0.4447. That is, X_1 and X_2 share $r^2_{X_1 X_2} = 0.4447^2 = 0.1976$ common variance. When X_2 is added to an equation which already contains X_1, the incremental increase in $SS_{\hat{Y}}$ is less than $r^2_{Y2} SS_Y$ because part of X_2 is linearly identical to X_1. Likewise, when X_1 is added to an equation which already predicts Y from X_2, the incremental change is less than $r^2_{Y1} SS_Y$ because the part of X_1 which is linearly dependent upon X_2 is already in the prediction equation.

To assess the value of adding predictors to an equation when the predictors are correlated, the solution is to create new independent variables which are uncorrelated among themselves so that the squared multiple correlation may be expressed as the sum of additive parts. These new variables are *partial* or *part scores*. Partial variables are simply residual variables or errors from a regression equation. Given $\hat{Y}_i = bX + b_0$, then $e_i = Y - \hat{Y}_i$ is the component of the Y variable which does *not* depend linearly upon X. The effects of the variable X may be said to have been "partialed out" of the variable Y. The resulting error score is called a partial score, and it is linearly independent of X; $r_{Xe} = 0$.

Partial variables may be viewed as statistically controlled variables. Chapters 1 and 10 stress that control of supplementary variables (concomitant variables, covariates) is fundamental to increasing precision in assessing the effects of independent variables upon dependent variables. Control may be direct, through experimental manipulation, or indirect, through statistical manipulation. Partial variables are variables which are created statistically to model experimental control. That is, partial variables estimate the values of a variable for a population in which the subjects are homogeneous with regard to the concomitant variables, the effects of which have been partialed out or held constant.

Partial scores have been expressed in matrix terms in (C.22) as

$$\mathbf{e} = \mathbf{y} - X\mathbf{b}$$
$$= \mathbf{y} - X(X'X)^{-1}X'\mathbf{y}$$
$$= [I - X(X'X)^{-1}X']\mathbf{y}.$$

Many properties of partial variables have been presented earlier or are easily inferred logically. For the least-squares solution, it has already been shown that the sum and mean of the errors are zero and the variation is $(1 - r^2_{Y(12\cdots p)})\mathrm{SS}_Y$. Since the square of the multiple correlation is

$$r^2_{Y(12\cdots p)} = r^2_{Y\hat{Y}},$$

and since $\hat{Y}$ is independent of the error scores, $Y - \hat{Y}$, the square of the correlation between the dependent variable and the partial scores is

$$r^2_{Ye} = (1 - r^2_{Y(12\cdots p)}).$$

Finally, the correlations between the partial scores and any of the X variables, $r_{X_j e}$, is zero, since the partial scores are, by definition, the part of the Y variable which is linearly independent of the X variables.

A simple notation for partial variables is,

$$e = (Y \cdot 12 \cdots p),$$

indicating that the effects of variables X_1 through X_p have been partialed out of variable Y. When multiple sets of variables are involved, a more complex notation is required. For example, if there are p variables, k of which are in one subset and the remainder in another, one could designate partial scores as

$$e = (Y \cdot 12 \cdots p)$$

for the entire set, and

$$e = (Y \cdot 12 \cdots k), \text{ and}$$
$$e = (Y \cdot k + 1 \cdots p)$$

for the two subsets.

SEMIPARTIAL CORRELATIONS. A *semipartial* or *part* correlation coefficient is the correlation between a "whole" score and a partial score. For example, $r_{Y(2.1)}$ is the correlation between the whole (unpartialed) dependent variable Y and the partial variable $(X_2 \cdot X_1)$. The latter partial variable is the part of X_2 which has the effects of X_1 partialed out. It is the part of X_2 which cannot be predicted from X_1. It is the error in X_2 which results when X_2 is predicted from X_1 with a linear equation. It is an estimate of the correlation between Y and X_2 when X_2 is measured for a population in which X_1 is homogeneous.

Semipartial correlations may be of interest in their own right or as a tool to assess a multiple regression solution. In the first instance, for example, a therapist may have an interest in assessing the relation between progress in therapy (Y) and verbal facility (X_1) when the linear effects of intelligence (X_2) have been removed from verbal facility, $r_{Y(1.2)}$.

First-order semipartial correlations are computed simply from zero-order correlations.[2] For any three variables,

$$r_{1(2.3)} = \frac{r_{12} - r_{13}r_{23}}{\sqrt{1 - r_{23}^2}} \qquad (C.53)$$

is the semipartial correlation between the whole variable X_1 and the part of variable X_2 which is not linearly dependent upon X_3. When more than three variables are involved, it is simpler to compute squared semipartial correlations from squared multiple correlations.

Squared semipartial correlations are very useful for expressing the incremental reduction of SS_{error} which results from adding variables to regression equations. Consider two regression equations,

$$\hat{Y}_i = b_0 + b_1 X_{i1}$$

versus
$$\hat{Y}_i = b_0 + b_{Y1.2}X_{i1} + b_{Y2.1}X_{i2},$$

where it is of interest to assess the value of adding predictor X_2 to an equation which predicts Y with only X_1 in the equation. In the case of the first equation,

$$r_{Y1}^2 = \frac{SS_{\hat{Y}}}{SS_Y} = 1 - \frac{SS_{Y-\hat{Y}}}{SS_Y}$$

is the proportion of variation in Y predictable with only X_1. When both variables are in the equation, the squared multiple correlation

$$r_{Y(12)}^2 = \frac{SS_{\hat{Y}}}{SS_Y} = 1 - \frac{SS_{Y-\hat{Y}}}{SS_Y}$$

---

[2] It is possible to partial the effects of any number of variables. In this context, correlations among unpartialed scores are *zero-order correlations*. Semipartial correlations with one variable partialed are *first-order semipartial correlations* (e.g. $r_{Y(2.1)}$); semipartials with the effects of two variables partialed out are *second-order semipartial correlations,* etc.

expresses the proportion of predictable variation. Hence,

$$r^2_{Y(12)} - r^2_{Y1}$$

provides the proportion of total variation in the dependent variable predictable when X_2 is added to an equation containing X_1. Moreover, this difference is the squared semipartial correlation of interest,

$$r^2_{Y(2.1)} = r^2_{Y(12)} = r^2_{Y1}.$$

Rearranging

$$r^2_{Y(12)} = r^2_{Y1} - r^2_{Y(2.1)}$$

makes it clear that total prediction with X_1 and X_2 can be viewed as prediction with variable $X_1(r^2_{Y1})$ plus the effect of adding the part of X_2 which is not related to $X_1[r^2_{Y(2.1)}]$. Variables X_1 and $(X_2 \cdot X_1)$ are uncorrelated.

Consider the two-predictor numerical example summarized in Table C.3. For that example,

$$r^2_{Y(2.1)} = \frac{(r_{Y2} - r_{Y1}r_{12})^2}{1 - r^2_{12}} = 0.0042.$$

Hence,

$$r^2_{Y(12)} = r^2_{Y1} + r^2_{Y(2.1)} = 0.3243 + 0.0042 = 0.3285.$$

The conclusion is that one can predict 32.85 percent of the total variation in the dependent variable with an equation in which both X_1 and X_2 are predictors $[r^2_{Y(12)} = 0.3285]$. Of this total, 32.43 percent can be predicted with an equation utilizing $X_1(r^2_{Y1} = 0.3243)$ only; adding predictor X_2 to the equation increases the predictable variation by only 0.42 percent $[r^2_{Y(2.1)} = 0.0042]$.

With this same example, one can contemplate adding predictor X_1 to an equation which contains predictor X_2. Hence

$$r^2_{Y(1.2)} = \frac{(r_{Y1} - r_{Y2}r_{12})^2}{1 - r^2_{12}} = 0.2315,$$

and

$$r^2_{Y(12)} = r^2_{Y2} + r^2_{Y(1.2)} = 0.0970 + 0.2315 = 0.3285.$$

Adding predictor X_1 to an equation with X_2 as a predictor increments $SS_{\hat{Y}}$ (reduces $SS_{Y-\hat{Y}}$) by 23.15 percent.

The squared multiple correlation, then, may be viewed as the sum of a series of squared semipartial correlations, each of which expresses the utility of adding a particular variable with the effects of all previous variables partialed out. The squared multiple correlation is sometimes referred to as the *coefficient of multiple determination*, whereas the squared semipartial correlation is the *coefficient of partial determination*.

Equivalently, the same relations can be expressed in terms of additive predicted variation. For example,

$$r^2_{Y(12)} = r^2_{Y1} + r^2_{Y(2.1)}$$

multiplied by SS_Y yields

$$r^2_{Y(12)}SS_Y = r^2_{Y1}SS_Y + r^2_{Y(2.1)}SS_Y$$
$$SS_{\hat{Y}(12)} = SS_{\hat{Y}(1)} + SS_{\hat{Y}(2.1)}.$$

That is, the variation which is predictable with both X_1 and $X_2[SS_{\hat{Y}(12)}]$ is the variation predictable with only $X_1[SS_{\hat{Y}(1)}]$ plus the variation which is predictable when X_2 is added $[SS_{\hat{Y}(2.1)}]$. This relation also makes it clear that the squared semipartial correlation expresses the increment in prediction as a proportion of the total variation in Y,

$$r^2_{Y(2.1)} = \frac{SS_{\hat{Y}(2.1)}}{SS_Y}.$$

In general, there are $p!$ sequences for considering predictors. For example, with three predictors there are $3! = 6$ sequences wherein each squared semipartial represents an incremental increase in predictable variation:

$$\begin{aligned} r^2_{Y(123)} &= r^2_{Y1} + r^2_{Y(2.1)} + r^2_{Y(3.12)} \\ &= r^2_{Y1} + r^2_{Y(3.1)} + r^2_{Y(2.13)} \\ &= r^2_{Y2} + r^2_{Y(1.2)} + r^2_{Y(3.12)} \\ &= r^2_{Y2} + r^2_{Y(3.2)} + r^2_{Y(1.23)} \\ &= r^2_{Y3} + r^2_{Y(1.3)} + r^2_{Y(2.13)} \\ &= r^2_{Y3} + r^2_{Y(2.3)} + r^2_{Y(1.23)}. \end{aligned} \tag{C.54}$$

The experimenter should, of course, consider the particular sequence which is sensible in terms of relevant theory or practice.

These sequences make it apparent that one may obtain any particular semipartial as either the difference between two squared multiple correlations or as the difference between a squared multiple correlation and a squared zero-order correlation coefficient. Consider, for example, the following:

$$r^2_{Y(12)} = r^2_{Y1} + r^2_{Y(2.1)}$$
$$r^2_{Y(123)} = r^2_{Y1} + r^2_{Y(2.1)} + r^2_{Y(3.12)}$$
$$r^2_{Y(1234)} = r^2_{Y1} + r^2_{Y(2.1)} + r^2_{Y(3.12)} + r^2_{Y(4.123)}.$$

Hence,

$$r^2_{Y(2.1)} = r^2_{Y(12)} - r^2_{Y1}$$
$$r^2_{Y(3.12)} = r^2_{Y(123)} - r^2_{Y12}$$
$$r^2_{Y(4.123)} = r^2_{Y(1234)} - r^2_{Y(123)}.$$

In general, if a total set of p, X variables is divided into two subsets with k variables in set X_a and $(k + 1 \cdots p)$ predictors in set X_b, then

$$r^2_{Y(X_a \cdot X_b)} = r^2_{Y(12 \cdots p)} - r^2_{Y(k+1 \cdots p)}. \tag{C.55}$$

Finally, it is also possible to compute *squared multiple semipartial correlations* as the difference between squared multiple correlations or squared multiple and zero-order correlations. For example,

$$r^2_{Y(23.1)} = r^2_{Y(123)} - r^2_{Y1}, \quad \text{and}$$
$$R^2_{Y(23.45)} = r^2_{Y(2345)} - r^2_{Y(45)}.$$

The first relation assesses the increment in prediction when *both* X_2 and X_3 are used to predict Y for an equation which contains X_1. Equivalently, it is an estimate of the correlation when X_2 and X_3 are used to predict Y for a population with constant X_1 scores. In general, squared multiple semipartials assess the impact of adding multiple variables while controlling one or more additional variables.

PARTIAL CORRELATIONS. *Partial correlations* are correlations between *two* partial scores. Consider, for example, that one may want to evaluate the correlation between progress in therapy (Y) and verbal facility (X_1) with the effects of intelligence (X_2) partialed out of both therapy *and* verbal factility. Hence, $r_{(Y.2)(1.2)}$ is of interest where both ($Y.2$) and (1.2) are error variables with regard to linear dependence upon intelligence.

First-order partial correlations may be computed from zero-order correlations. For example, for any three variables, X_1, X_2, and X_3,

$$r_{(1.3)(2.3)} = \frac{r_{12} - r_{13}r_{23}}{\sqrt{1 - r^2_{13}} \sqrt{1 - r^2_{23}}} \tag{C.56}$$

is the correlation between the part of X_1 which is linearly independent of X_3 and the part of X_2 which is linearly independent of X_3.

Higher-order partial correlations may be obtained by generalizing from the formula for $r_{(1.3)(2.3)}$ and substituting lower-order partial correlations for zero-order correlations.[3]

Like squared semipartial correlations, squared partial correlations may be of interest in evaluating regression solutions and are typically computed from squared multiple correlation coefficients or, in the case of first-order partial correlations, from squared multiple and squared zero-order correlations coefficients.

Earlier, it was emphasized that squared semipartial correlation coefficients express the proportion of the total variation in Y, SS_Y, which can be predicted by adding variables to a prediction equation. In contrast, the squared partial correlation coefficient expresses the proportion by which the *residual variation* may be predicted by adding new variables to the equation.

---

[3] For example, the second-order partial correlation, $r_{(1.34)(2.34)}$ may be obtained as

$$r_{(1.34)(2.34)} = \frac{r_{(1.3)(2.3)} - r_{(1.3)(4.3)}r_{(2.3)(4.3)}}{\sqrt{1 - r^2_{(1.3)(4.3)}}\sqrt{1 - r^2_{(2.3)(4.3)}}}$$

Consider the squared partial correlation coefficient

$$r^2_{(Y.1)(2.1)} = \frac{r^2_{Y(12)} - r^2_{Y1}}{1 - r^2_{Y1}} = \frac{r^2_{Y(2.1)}}{1 - r^2_{Y1}}.$$

In this case, one might consider X_1 a control variable and $r_{(Y.1)(2.1)}$ the correlation between Y and X_2 with predictor X_1 controlled. In this equation, the numerator is the squared semipartial correlation, $r^2_{Y(2.1)}$. It expresses the increment in predictable variation associated with adding predictor X_2 to an equation containing X_1. The denominator is the proportion of residual variation associated with an equation with only X_1 as a predictor. Hence, $r^2_{(Y.1)(2.1)}$ expresses the increment in predicted variation relative to the residual variation without that predictor. This point is perhaps best appreciated by multiplying both the numerator and denominator by SS_Y. One obtains

$$\frac{SS_{\hat{Y}(12)} - SS_{\hat{Y}(1)}}{SS_Y - SS_{\hat{Y}(1)}} = \frac{SS_{\hat{Y}(2.1)}}{SS_Y - SS_{\hat{Y}(1)}} = \frac{\text{Increase in } SS_{\hat{Y}} \text{ by adding } X_2}{\text{Residual variation without } X_2}.$$

As another example,

$$r_{(Y.12)(3.12)} = \frac{r^2_{Y(123)} - r^2_{Y(12)}}{1 - r^2_{Y(12)}} = \frac{r^2_{Y(3.12)}}{1 - r^2_{Y(12)}}$$

expresses the increment in $SS_{\hat{Y}}$ associated with adding X_3 as a predictor relative to the residual variation with only X_1 and X_2 in the equation. Likewise, it is an estimate of the squared correlation between Y and X_3 with populations in which both X_1 and X_2 are homogeneous.

A general expression for a squared partial correlation may be used to express the effects of adding one set of one or more variables to a prediction equation already containing one or more additional independent variables. If there are p independent variables, k of which are in one subset and $k + 1 \cdots p$ in another, then

$$r^2_{(Y.12 \cdots k)(k+1 \cdots p.12 \cdots k)} = \frac{r^2_{Y(12 \cdots p)} - r^2_{Y(12 \cdots k)}}{1 - r^2_{Y(12 \cdots k)}} \tag{C.57}$$

expresses the increase in predictable variation associated with adding the set of independent variables $k + 1 \cdots p$ to a prediction equation which already contains X_1 through X_k as predictors. This increase is relative to the residual variation associated with the variables X_1 through X_k. As examples,

$$r^2_{(Y.12)(3.12)} = \frac{r^2_{Y(123)} - r^2_{Y(12)}}{1 - r^2_{Y(12)}} = \frac{r^2_{Y(3.12)}}{1 - r^2_{Y(12)}},$$

and

$$r^2_{(Y.12)(34.12)} = \frac{r^2_{Y(1234)} - r^2_{Y(12)}}{1 - r^2_{Y(12)}} = \frac{r^2_{Y(34.12)}}{1 - r^2_{Y(12)}}.$$

This latter example, $r^2_{(Y.12)(34.12)}$, is an example of a squared *multiple partial correlation coefficient*.

C.2 THE GENERAL LINEAR MODEL

To this point the discussion of the regression problem has been limited to descriptive statistics derived from the observed sample data. No attempt has been made to specify population parameters or to derive sampling distributions for statistics which are estimators of those parameters. These steps are required when developing tests of significance and establishing interval estimates of the parameters. Assumptions about how data were sampled, about the nature of the populations from which the data were sampled, and about the model which relates observations to the parameters of the model are required. The *general linear model* provides that framework.

The general linear model is quite simple, but is widely useful. It is, for example, the model which underlies simple and multiple regression, analysis of variance, and analysis of covariance. In its "classic form" it states that for fixed values of one or more independent variables, one may express the dependent variable(s) as a linear combination of the set of independent variables. The assumptions which completely establish the nature of sampling distributions are that for each set of fixed values of the independent variables, the dependent variable is normally distributed and the variance is constant, but the means of the dependent variable are expected to vary as the independent variables vary. It is also assumed that all elements are selected independently.

Consider a population of elements in which the following model holds.

$$Y = \beta_0 + \beta_1 X_1 + \cdots + \beta_p X_p + \varepsilon$$
$$= X\boldsymbol{\beta} + \boldsymbol{\varepsilon}. \tag{C.58}$$

For a specific element i,

$$X' = \mathbf{x}_i' = [1 \quad X_{i1} \quad \cdots \quad X_{ip}], \quad \text{and} \quad \boldsymbol{\beta} = \begin{bmatrix} \beta_0 \\ \beta_1 \\ \vdots \\ \beta_p \end{bmatrix}.$$

and the model takes the form

$$Y_i = \mathbf{x}_i'\boldsymbol{\beta} + \varepsilon_i = \beta_0 + X_{i1}\beta_1 + X_{i2}\beta_2 + \cdots + X_{ip}\beta_p + \varepsilon_i.$$

The components of the vector $\mathbf{x}_i'$ are a set of fixed constants associated with the element i. The error ε_i is a random variable.

Let the data, given by a random sample of n elements from a population in which model (C.58) holds, be denoted

$$\begin{bmatrix} Y_1 & 1 & X_{11} & \cdots & X_{1p} \\ \vdots & \vdots & \vdots & & \vdots \\ Y_i & 1 & X_{i1} & \cdots & X_{ip} \\ \vdots & \vdots & \vdots & & \vdots \\ Y_n & 1 & X_{n1} & \cdots & X_{np} \end{bmatrix} = \begin{bmatrix} \mathbf{y} & X \\ (n \times 1) & [n \times (p+1)] \end{bmatrix}.$$

The model for the sample has the form

$$\underset{(n \times 1)}{\mathbf{y}} = \underset{[n \times (p+1)]}{X} \underset{[(p+1) \times 1]}{\boldsymbol{\beta}} + \underset{(n \times 1)}{\boldsymbol{\varepsilon}}. \tag{C.59}$$

As part of the model, it is assumed that $E(\boldsymbol{\varepsilon}) = 0$. Hence, the regression equation for $E(\mathbf{y})$ is

$$E(\mathbf{y}) = X\boldsymbol{\beta}. \tag{C.60}$$

By this model, then, one expects the means of the dependent variable to be a linear function of the fixed X values used in the experiment and the regression parameters of $\boldsymbol{\beta}$. The interpretation of the components of $\boldsymbol{\beta}$ varies with the nature of the X variables. In the regression context, the independent variables are typically quantitative, β_0 is the Y intercept and the other elements of $\boldsymbol{\beta}$ are partial regression coefficients. When the X variables are qualitative as they typically are, for example, in the analysis of variance, the elements of $\boldsymbol{\beta}$ are interpreted in terms of means. More will be said of that in Sec. C.3.

Estimation and Properties of Estimators: X Fixed, ε Normally Distributed

If one assumes for the model in (C.59) that the columns of X represent fixed variables and the errors are independently and identically distributed, then the covariance matrix for the error vector is

$$E(\boldsymbol{\varepsilon}'\boldsymbol{\varepsilon}) = \underset{(n \times n)}{\sigma_\varepsilon^2 I} = \begin{bmatrix} \sigma_\varepsilon^2 & 0 & \cdots & 0 \\ 0 & \sigma_\varepsilon^2 & & \vdots \\ \vdots & \vdots & & \vdots \\ 0 & 0 & \cdots & \sigma_\varepsilon^2 \end{bmatrix}. \tag{C.61}$$

That is, the covariances are zero and the variances are identical for all fixed sets of X values.

The right-hand side of (C.59) contains only one random variable, namely ε. Hence, the least-squares principle may be used to obtain estimates of the parameters $\boldsymbol{\beta}$ and σ_ε^2. The model represents precisely the set of conditions under which the Gauss–Markov theorem holds. This theorem states that the least-squares estimators have minimum sampling variance in the class of all unbiased estimators which are linear functions of $\mathbf{y}$. To obtain the least-squares estimators, one first notes that

$$\boldsymbol{\varepsilon} = \mathbf{y} - X\boldsymbol{\beta}. \tag{C.62}$$

Hence, one minimizes

$$\sum_{i=1}^{n} \varepsilon_i^2 = \boldsymbol{\varepsilon}'\boldsymbol{\varepsilon} \qquad \text{with respect to } \boldsymbol{\beta}. \tag{C.63}$$

The resulting normal equations are identical in form to those given earlier in

(C.19). That is,

$$(X'X)\mathbf{b} = X'\mathbf{y}, \tag{C.64}$$

and the solution for the estimates of $\boldsymbol{\beta}$ is given by

$$\underset{[(p+1) \times 1]}{\mathbf{b}} = (X'X)^{-1}X'\mathbf{y}, \tag{C.65}$$

provided that $(X'X)$ is nonsingular.

All of the developments made in Sec. C.1 generalize to the present case. Thus,

$$\hat{\mathbf{y}} = X\mathbf{b},$$
$$= X(X'X)^{-1}X'\mathbf{y}, \tag{C.66}$$

and

$$\mathbf{y} - \hat{\mathbf{y}} = \mathbf{y} - X(X'X)^{-1}X'\mathbf{y}$$
$$= [I - X(X'X)^{-1}X']\mathbf{y}. \tag{C.67}$$

One also has as the sum of the squares of the predicted and error scores, respectively,

$$\sum \hat{Y}^2 = \hat{\mathbf{y}}'\hat{\mathbf{y}}$$
$$= (X\mathbf{b})'(X\mathbf{b})$$
$$= \mathbf{b}'X'X\mathbf{b}$$
$$= \mathbf{y}'[X(X'X)^{-1}X']\mathbf{y}$$
$$= \mathbf{b}'X'\mathbf{y} \quad (\text{since } X'X\mathbf{b} = X'y), \tag{C.68}$$

and

$$\sum e^2 = \mathbf{e}'\mathbf{e}$$
$$= (\mathbf{y} - \hat{\mathbf{y}})(\mathbf{y} - \hat{\mathbf{y}})$$
$$= \mathbf{y}'\mathbf{y} - \mathbf{y}'[X(X'X)^{-1}X']\mathbf{y}$$
$$= \mathbf{y}'[I - X(X'X)^{-1}X']\mathbf{y}. \tag{C.69}$$

Typically, the general linear model includes the assumption that the errors, the components of $\boldsymbol{\varepsilon}$, are normally distributed. The estimators of $\boldsymbol{\beta}$ and σ_ε^2 are not affected by the form of the distribution specified for $\boldsymbol{\varepsilon}$. However, if one assumes that X is fixed and that $\boldsymbol{\varepsilon}$ is multivariate normal, then the form of the sampling distributions of the estimators, under random sampling, is also specified. If one adds to the model in (C.59) the normality assumption, then the maximum-likelihood principle may be used to obtain estimates of the parameters of the linear model. These estimators (adjusted for bias) are identical to the least-squares estimators.

Under the normality assumption on $\boldsymbol{\varepsilon}$, the conditional distribution of Y

for $\mathbf{x}_i = [1\ X_{i1} X_{i2} \cdots X_{ip}]$ will be univariate normal with

$$E(Y_i) = E(\mathbf{x}_i'\mathbf{b}) = \mathbf{x}_i'\boldsymbol{\beta}, \tag{C.70}$$

and with
$$\sigma_{Y_i}^2 = \sigma_\varepsilon^2. \tag{C.71}$$

If the errors are normally distributed, Y_i is also normally distributed. Hence, the distribution of Y_i is totally specified.

The parameters to be estimated are the $p + 1$ elements of $\boldsymbol{\beta}$ and the unknown, but constant, variance σ_ε^2.

An unbiased estimate of σ_ε^2 is

$$\hat{\sigma}_\varepsilon^2 = \frac{\sum e_i^2}{n - p - 1} = \frac{\mathbf{y}'\mathbf{y} - \mathbf{b}'X'\mathbf{y}}{n - p - 1}. \tag{C.72}$$

The least-squares, or maximum-likelihood, estimate of $\boldsymbol{\beta}$ is

$$\hat{\boldsymbol{\beta}} = \mathbf{b} = (X'X)^{-1}X'\mathbf{y}.$$

It is important to note that the elements of the vector $\mathbf{b}$ are each linear functions of $\mathbf{y}$, since $(X'X)^{-1}X'$ is a constant for any given experiment. Hence, all properties of the sampling distribution of the regression coefficients can be deduced from the properties of the distribution of $\mathbf{y}$. As discussed, $\mathbf{y}$ is a vector, the elements of which are normally distributed; $E(\mathbf{y})$ is a vector for which $E(\mathbf{y}) = X\boldsymbol{\beta}$ and which is estimated by $X\mathbf{b} = X(X'X)^{-1}X'\mathbf{y}$. The variance–covariance matrix for $\mathbf{y}$ is an $(n \times n)$ matrix with σ_ε^2 on the main diagonal and zero elsewhere.

What, then, are the properties of the sampling distribution of the elements of $\mathbf{b}$?

First, the estimators of the elements of $\mathbf{b}$ are unbiased:

$$\begin{aligned}
E(\mathbf{b}) &= E[(X'X)^{-1}X'\mathbf{y}] \\
&= [(X'X)^{-1}X']E(\mathbf{y}) \\
&= [(X'X)^{-1}X']X\boldsymbol{\beta} \quad \text{since } E(\mathbf{y}) = X\boldsymbol{\beta} \\
&= \boldsymbol{\beta} \tag{C.73}
\end{aligned}$$

since X and, therefore, $(X'X)^{-1}X'X$ is fixed for any given experiment.

Second, the elements of $\mathbf{b}$ are normally distributed. This follows directly from the assumption that $\boldsymbol{\varepsilon}$ is normally distributed and, consequently, $\mathbf{y}$ is normally distributed. Hence, since $\mathbf{b}$ is a linear function of y, the elements of $\mathbf{b}$ are univariate normal.

Third, the variance–covariance matrix of the elements of $\mathbf{b}$ can be obtained from the variance–covariance matrix for $\mathbf{y}$. Recall that for Y, the covariance matrix is $\sigma^2 I$. The covariance matrix for the sampling distribution of the vector $\mathbf{b}$ can be obtained from the general principle that the covariance matrix of any vector variable $\mathbf{v}$ defined by

$$\mathbf{v} = A\mathbf{z}$$

(where A is a matrix of known values and $\mathbf{z}$ is a vector variable having covariance matrix V) has the form

$$\operatorname{cov}(\mathbf{v}) = AVA'.$$

Since $\mathbf{b} = (X'X)^{-1}X'\mathbf{y}$,

$$
\begin{aligned}
E[\operatorname{cov}(b)] &= E(\operatorname{cov}[(X'X)^{-1}X'\mathbf{y}]) \\
&= (X'X)^{-1}X'E[\operatorname{cov}(\mathbf{y})]X(X'X)^{-1} \\
&= [(X'X)^{-1}X']\sigma_\varepsilon^2 I[X(X'X)^{-1}] \\
&= \sigma_\varepsilon^2[(X'X)^{-1}X'][X(X'X)^{-1}] \\
&= \sigma_\varepsilon^2(X'X)^{-1}
\end{aligned}
\tag{C.74}
$$

since $\quad (X'X)^{-1}X'[X(X'X)^{-1}] = (X'X)^{-1}.$

Since

$$\hat{\sigma}_\varepsilon^2 = \frac{\sum e_i^2}{n - p - 1},$$

one obtains an estimate of the covariance matrix for $\mathbf{b}$ as

$$\operatorname{est}\operatorname{cov}(\mathbf{b}) = \hat{\sigma}_\varepsilon^2(X'X)^{-1}. \tag{C.75}$$

The matrix est cov (b) is a $p \times p$ matrix, the diagonal elements of which are observed estimates of the variances of each of the regression coefficients. The off-diagonal elements are covariances between the components of $\mathbf{b}$. The diagonal elements, the variances for the individual regression coefficients, can be obtained as

$$\hat{\sigma}_{b_j}^2 = \hat{\sigma}_\varepsilon^2 c^{jj}, \tag{C.76}$$

where c^{jj} is a diagonal element from $(X'X)^{-1}$.

In summary, then, the elements of $\mathbf{b}$ are normally distributed with $E(\mathbf{b}) = \boldsymbol{\beta}$ and $E[\operatorname{cov}(b)] = \sigma_\varepsilon^2(X'X)^{-1}$. Estimates of $E[\operatorname{cov}(b)]$ are given by $\hat{\sigma}_\varepsilon^2(X'X)^{-1}$. From this information, it is possible to develop tests of significance for the elements of $\boldsymbol{\beta}$.

It may also be of interest to specify the sampling distribution of differences between regression coefficients $b_j - b_{j'}$. These too are normally distributed when each of the b_j is normally distributed, with $E(b_j - b_{j'}) = \beta_j - \beta_{j'}$, and having estimated variance equal to

$$\hat{\sigma}_{b_j - b_{j'}}^2 = \hat{\sigma}_\varepsilon^2(c^{jj} + c^{j'j'} - 2c^{jj'}), \tag{C.77}$$

where c_{jj}, $c_{j'j'}$ and $c_{jj'}$ are all elements from $(X'X)^{-1}$. More generally, if $\mathbf{c}'\boldsymbol{\beta}$ represents any linear function of the components of $\boldsymbol{\beta}$, the sampling distribution of the statistic $\mathbf{c}'\mathbf{b}$ will be univariate normal with

$$E(\mathbf{c}'\mathbf{b}) = \mathbf{c}'\beta, \text{ and with variance,} \tag{C.78}$$

$$
\begin{aligned}
\sigma_{\mathbf{c}'\mathbf{b}}^2 &= \mathbf{c}'E[\operatorname{cov}(b)]\mathbf{c} \\
&= \sigma_\varepsilon^2 \mathbf{c}'(X'X)^{-1}\mathbf{c}.
\end{aligned}
\tag{C.79}
$$

The variance of $\mathbf{c}'\mathbf{b}$ is estimated by substituting $\hat{\sigma}_\varepsilon^2$ for σ_ε^2 in (C.79).

It is also possible to develop variance formulas for predicted values of Y corresponding to a specified set of X values and for differences between observed and predicted Y values.

If

$$\hat{Y}_i = \mathbf{x}_i' \mathbf{b}, \qquad \text{where} \qquad \mathbf{x}_i' = [1 \quad X_{i1} \quad X_{i2} \quad \cdots \quad X_{1p}],$$

then it is clear that $\hat{Y}_i$ is a linear function of $\mathbf{b}$. Hence, the variance of $\hat{Y}_i$ is

$$
\begin{aligned}
\sigma_{\hat{Y}_i}^2 &= E[\mathrm{var}\,(\hat{Y}_i)] \\
&= \mathbf{x}_i' E[\mathrm{cov}(b)] \mathbf{x}_i \\
&= \sigma_\varepsilon^2 \mathbf{x}_i' (X'X)^{-1} \mathbf{x}_i.
\end{aligned}
\tag{C.80}
$$

For an error score estimate, $Y_i - \hat{Y}_i$, the variance is given by

$$
\begin{aligned}
E[\mathrm{var}\,(Y_i - \hat{Y}_i)] &= \sigma_{Y_i}^2 + \sigma_{\hat{Y}_i}^2 \\
&= \sigma_\varepsilon^2 + \sigma_\varepsilon^2 \mathbf{x}_i' (X'X)^{-1} \mathbf{x}_i \\
&= \sigma_\varepsilon^2 [I - \mathbf{x}_i' (X'X)^{-1} \mathbf{x}_i].
\end{aligned}
$$

One notes that since for fixed $\mathbf{x}_i$, Y_i and $\hat{Y}_i$ are uncorrelated, the variance of the sampling distribution of $Y_i - \hat{Y}_i$ is the sum of the conditional variance of Y for fixed X and the variance of $\hat{Y}_i$. Both $\hat{Y}_i$ and $Y_i - \hat{Y}_i$ have univariate normal distributions when $\boldsymbol{\varepsilon}$ and, therefore, Y have normal distributions.

Testing Statistical Hypotheses

Under the assumptions of the general linear model, it is possible to specify the nature of the sampling distributions of the regression statistics, $\hat{\sigma}_\varepsilon^2$ and $\mathbf{b}$.

One may be interested in testing particular hypotheses regarding σ_ε^2. For that purpose, the statistic

$$\hat{\sigma}_\varepsilon^2 = \sum_{i=1}^n e_i^2 / n - p - 1 = \frac{\mathbf{y}'\mathbf{y} - \mathbf{b}'X\mathbf{y}}{n - p - 1}$$

is an unbiased estimate of σ_ε^2 and the statistic

$$(n - p - 1)\hat{\sigma}_\varepsilon^2 / \sigma_\varepsilon^2 \tag{C.81}$$

is distributed as chi square with $n - p - 1$ degrees of freedom.

From (C.81), it also follows that the statistic

$$t = \frac{Y_i - \mathbf{x}_i \boldsymbol{\beta}}{\hat{\sigma}_{\hat{Y}_i}} \tag{C.82}$$

is distributed as Student's t with $n - p - 1$ degrees of freedom, where $\hat{\sigma}_{\hat{Y}_i}$ is obtained from (C.80) by substituting $\hat{\sigma}_\varepsilon^2$ for σ_ε^2.

Earlier, it was shown that $\hat{\sigma}_{b_j}^2 = \hat{\sigma}_\varepsilon^2 c^{jj}$ (C.75) and that $\hat{\sigma}_{b_j - b_{j'}}^2 = \hat{\sigma}_\varepsilon^2 (c^{jj} + c^{j'j'} - 2c^{jj'})$ (C.77). From this information and the assumptions of the general linear model, one concludes that hypotheses regarding individual regression coefficients may be evaluated using the statistic

$$t = \frac{\mathbf{b}_j - \boldsymbol{\beta}_j}{\hat{\sigma}_{b_j}} \tag{C.83}$$

which is distributed as Student's t with $n - p - 1$ degrees of freedom.
    The statistic

$$t = \frac{(b_j - b_{j'}) - (\beta_j - \beta_{j'})}{\hat{\sigma}_{b_j - b_{j'}}} \tag{C.84}$$

is distributed as Student's t with $n - p - 1$ degrees of freedom and may be used to evaluate differences between pairs of regression coefficients. Indeed, if $c'\boldsymbol{\beta}$ represents *any* linear combination of the elements of $\boldsymbol{\beta}$, then sampling distribution of $\mathbf{c}'\mathbf{b}$ will be univariate normal with $E(\mathbf{c}'\mathbf{b}) = \mathbf{c}'\boldsymbol{\beta}$ and with variance

$$\sigma_{\mathbf{c}'\mathbf{b}}^2 = \mathbf{c}'E[\text{cov}\,(b)]\mathbf{c} = \sigma_\varepsilon^2 \mathbf{c}'(X'X)^{-1}\mathbf{c}.$$

Hence, the statistic

$$t = \frac{\mathbf{c}'(\mathbf{b} - \boldsymbol{\beta})}{\hat{\sigma}_{\mathbf{c}'\mathbf{b}}} \tag{C.85}$$

is distributed as Student's t with parameter $n - p - 1$. In (C.85), $\hat{\sigma}_{\mathbf{c}'\mathbf{b}}$ is obtained by replacing σ_ε^2 by $\hat{\sigma}_\varepsilon^2$.
    In general, one is interested in hypotheses regarding the elements of $\boldsymbol{\beta}$. A general approach in which one can test hypotheses about all of the elements of $\boldsymbol{\beta}$ or any subset of the elements of $\boldsymbol{\beta}$ is desirable. Since the variation associated with partitioning the total variation of Y by some regression model may result in statistics with chi square distributions, hypotheses regarding the elements of $\boldsymbol{\beta}$ may be evaluated with statistics with F distributions.

FIXED MODEL: TESTING THE HYPOTHESIS $\boldsymbol{\beta} = \boldsymbol{\beta}^*$. Assume the fixed model

$$\mathbf{y} = X\boldsymbol{\beta} + \boldsymbol{\varepsilon},$$

where $\boldsymbol{\varepsilon}: N(\mathbf{0}, \sigma_\varepsilon^2 I)$. An hypothesis of general interest is that a model used to generate particular values for the elements of $\boldsymbol{\beta}$ is tenable. Let $\boldsymbol{\beta}^*$ be a vector of regression weights which is generated by the model. This includes any values for $\boldsymbol{\beta}$, but a special case which is often of interest is that in which $\boldsymbol{\beta}^* = \mathbf{0}$.
    The residual variation associated with the least-squares solution in which $\boldsymbol{\beta}$ is estimated by $\mathbf{b}$ is given by (C.23). Let that variation, then, be

$$Q_0 = \sum (Y - \hat{Y})^2 = \mathbf{y}'\mathbf{y} - \mathbf{y}'X(X'X)^{-1}X'\mathbf{y}.$$

Under the hypothesis that $\boldsymbol{\beta} = \boldsymbol{\beta}^*$, where $\boldsymbol{\beta}^*$ is any specified vector, the estimate of variation due to error is

$$Q_1 = \sum (y - X\boldsymbol{\beta}^*) = (\mathbf{y} - X\boldsymbol{\beta}^*)'(\mathbf{y} - X\boldsymbol{\beta}^*)$$

$$= \mathbf{y}'\mathbf{y} - 2\boldsymbol{\beta}^{*\prime}X'\mathbf{y} + \boldsymbol{\beta}^{*\prime}(X'X)\boldsymbol{\beta}^*.$$

A measure of deviation from the hypothesis, then, is given by

$$Q_2 = Q_1 - Q_0 = \boldsymbol{\beta}^{*\prime}(X'X)\boldsymbol{\beta}^* - 2\boldsymbol{\beta}^{*\prime}X'\mathbf{y} + \mathbf{y}X(X'X)^{-1}X'\mathbf{y}$$

$$= (\mathbf{y} - X\boldsymbol{\beta}^*)'X(X'X)^{-1}X'(\mathbf{y} - X\boldsymbol{\beta}^*).$$

The last line in the above expression follows from the line above by rearrangement of the terms.

It may be shown that both Q_2 and Q_0 are independently distributed as chi square with degrees of freedom $n - (n-p) = p$ and $n - p$, respectively. Hence, the ratio

$$F = \frac{(Q_1 - Q_0)/p}{Q_0/(n-p)} \qquad \text{(C.86)}$$

is distributed as $F(p, n-p)$ when the hypothesis that $\boldsymbol{\beta} = \boldsymbol{\beta}^*$ is true. The test procedure is summarized in Table C.5.

The special case wherein $\boldsymbol{\beta}^* = 0$ is often of interest. For this case, one has the following:

$$Q_1 = \sum Y^2 = \mathbf{y}'\mathbf{y}$$

$$Q_0 = \sum (Y - \hat{Y})^2 = \mathbf{y}'\mathbf{y} - \mathbf{y}'X(X'X)^{-1}X'\mathbf{y}$$

$$Q_2 = Q_1 - Q_0 = \mathbf{y}'X(X'X)^{-1}X'\mathbf{y}.$$

Hence,

$$F = \frac{(Q_1 - Q_0)/p}{Q_0/(n-p)} = \frac{\mathbf{y}'X(X'X)^{-1}X'\mathbf{y}/p}{\mathbf{y}'\mathbf{y} - \mathbf{y}'X(X'X)^{-1}X'\mathbf{y}/(n-p)}. \qquad \text{(C.87)}$$

TABLE C.5   **Testing the hypothesis $\boldsymbol{\beta} = \boldsymbol{\beta}^*$**

Source of variation	SS	df	MS
Residual assuming $\boldsymbol{\beta} = \boldsymbol{\beta}^*$	Q_1	n	
Residual if $\boldsymbol{\beta}$ is estimated by $\mathbf{b}$	Q_0	$n - p$	$Q_0/(n-p)$
Deviation from hypothesis	$Q_2 = Q_1 - Q_0$	p	$(Q_1 - Q_0)/p$

$$F = \frac{(Q_1 - Q_0)/p}{Q_0/(n-p)}$$

TESTING THE HYPOTHESIS $\boldsymbol{\beta}_j = \mathbf{0}$. It is often useful to evaluate whether a particular subset of a larger set of regression coefficients is zero, $\boldsymbol{\beta}_j = \mathbf{0}$. Suppose that it is meaningful to partition a total set of p predictors into two subsets, one with k predictors and one with $(p - k)$ predictors. The total matrix of independent variable measures on n subjects is then

$$\underset{(n \times p)}{X} = \underset{(n \times k)}{[X_1} \quad \underset{n \times (p - k)}{X_2]} \qquad \text{where} \qquad k < p.$$

Consider the model with all predictors

$$\mathbf{y} = X\boldsymbol{\beta} + \boldsymbol{\varepsilon}_\beta, \tag{C.88}$$

when $X_1 \cdots X_p$ are fixed variables and $\boldsymbol{\varepsilon}_\beta = N(\mathbf{0}, \sigma^2_{\varepsilon_b} I)$. If one partitions the X variables into two subsets, one with k predictors and one with $p - k$ predictors, then

$$\boldsymbol{\beta} = \underset{p - k}{\overset{k}{\begin{bmatrix} \boldsymbol{\beta}_1 \\ \boldsymbol{\beta}_2 \end{bmatrix}}}, \qquad \text{and (C.88) takes the form}$$

$$\mathbf{y} = X_1\boldsymbol{\beta}_1 + X_2\boldsymbol{\beta}_2 + \boldsymbol{\varepsilon}_\beta.$$

Consider two submodels,

$$\mathbf{Y} = X_1\boldsymbol{\alpha}_1 + \boldsymbol{\varepsilon}_{\alpha_1}, \qquad \text{where} \qquad \boldsymbol{\varepsilon}_{\alpha_1} : N(\mathbf{0}, \sigma^2_{\varepsilon_{\alpha_1}} I); \tag{C.89}$$

$$\mathbf{Y} = X_2\boldsymbol{\alpha}_2 + \boldsymbol{\varepsilon}_{\alpha_2}, \qquad \text{where} \qquad \boldsymbol{\varepsilon}_{\alpha_2} : N(\mathbf{0}, \sigma^2_{\varepsilon_{\alpha_2}} I). \tag{C.90}$$

Using least-squares estimation procedures, the variation due to error under models (C.88) through (C.90) is summarized in part i of Table C.6. Thus, Q_β is

TABLE C.6   **Testing the hypothesis $\boldsymbol{\beta}_j = 0$**

	Source of variation	df
(i)	(C.88) $Q_\beta = \mathbf{y'y} - \mathbf{y'}P_\beta\mathbf{y} = \sum Y^2 - \hat{\boldsymbol{\beta}}'X'\mathbf{y}$	$n - p$
	(C.89) $Q_{\alpha_1} = \mathbf{y'y} - \mathbf{y'}P_{\alpha_1}\mathbf{y} = \sum Y^2 - \hat{\boldsymbol{\alpha}}'_1 X'_1\mathbf{y}$	$n - k$
	(C.90) $Q_{\alpha_2} = \mathbf{y'y} - \mathbf{y'}P_{\alpha_2}\mathbf{y} = \sum Y^2 - \hat{\boldsymbol{\alpha}}'_2 X'_2\mathbf{y}$	$n - (p - k)$
(ii)	$\begin{aligned} Q_{\alpha_2} - Q_\beta &= \mathbf{y'}P_\beta\mathbf{y} - \mathbf{y'}P_{\alpha_2}\mathbf{y} \\ &= R(\boldsymbol{\beta}) - R(\boldsymbol{\alpha}_2) \\ &= R(\boldsymbol{\beta}_1 \mid \boldsymbol{\beta}_2) \end{aligned}$	$n - (p - k) - (n - p) = k$
	$\begin{aligned} Q_{\alpha_1} - Q_\beta &= \mathbf{y'}P_\beta\mathbf{y} - \mathbf{y'}P_{\alpha_1}\mathbf{y} \\ &= R(\boldsymbol{\beta}) - R(\boldsymbol{\alpha}_1) \\ &= R(\boldsymbol{\beta}_2 \mid \boldsymbol{\beta}_1) \end{aligned}$	$n - k - (n - p) = p - k$
(iii)	$F_{\beta_1 \mid \beta_2} = \dfrac{(Q_{\alpha_2} - Q_\beta)/k}{Q_\beta/(n - p)} \qquad F_{\beta_2 \mid \beta_1} = \dfrac{(Q_{\alpha_1} - Q_\beta)/(p - k)}{Q_\beta/(n - p)}$	

the variation due to error as obtained under model (C.88). In the expression Q_β,

$$P_\beta = X(X'X)^{-1}X'.$$

Similarly,

$$P_{\alpha_1} = X_1(X_1'X_1)^{-1}X_1' \quad \text{and} \quad P_{\alpha_2} = X_2(X_2'X_2)^{-1}X_2'$$

in Q_{α_1} and Q_{α_2}.

The difference between Q_{α_2} and Q_β may be expressed in the following form:

$$Q_{\alpha_2} - Q_\beta = (y'y - y'P_{\alpha_2}y) - (y'y - y'P_\beta y)$$

$$= y'P_\beta y - y'P_{\alpha_2}y$$

$$= R(\beta) - R(\alpha_2) = R(\beta_1 \mid \beta_2),$$

where $R(\beta)$ is that part of the total sum of squares for Y that can be predicted under model (C.88), and $R(\alpha_2)$ is that part of the total sum of squares for Y that can be predicted under model (C.89). $R(\beta_1 \mid \beta_2)$ represents that part of the variation due to β_1 that is orthogonal to β_2.

The difference

$$Q_{\alpha_1} - Q_\beta = y'P_\beta y - y'P_{\alpha_1}y$$

$$= R(\beta) - R(\alpha_1) = R(\beta_2 \mid \beta_1)$$

represents that part of the variation due to β_2 which is orthogonal to β_1. Hence one has the following relationships:

$$R(\beta) = R(\beta_1 \mid \beta_2) + R(\alpha_2)$$

$$= R(\beta_2 \mid \beta_1) + R(\alpha_1).$$

Under the hypothesis that $\beta_2 = 0$, a measure of deviation from hypothesis is given by

$$Q_{\alpha_1} - Q_\beta = R(\beta_2 \mid \beta_1).$$

When the hypothesis that $\beta_2 = 0$ is true,

$$E[R(\beta_2 \mid \beta_1)] = (p - k)\sigma_\varepsilon^2,$$

$$E(Q_\beta) = (n - p)\sigma_\varepsilon^2.$$

Further, $Q_{\alpha_1} - Q_\beta$ and Q_β are independently distributed as chi square with respective degrees of freedom $p - k$ and $n - p$. Hence the appropriate F ratio for testing the hypothesis that $\beta_2 = 0$ is

$$\frac{(Q_{\alpha_1} - Q_\beta)/(p - k)}{Q_\beta/(n - p)} = \frac{R(\beta_2 \mid \beta_1)/(p - k)}{Q_\beta/(n - p)}.$$

By analogy, to test the hypothesis that $\boldsymbol{\beta}_1 = \mathbf{0}$

$$\frac{(Q_{\alpha_2} - Q_\beta)/k}{Q_\beta/(n-p)} = \frac{R(\boldsymbol{\beta}_1 \mid \boldsymbol{\beta}_2)/k}{Q_\beta/(n-p)}.$$

When $\boldsymbol{\beta}_1 = \mathbf{0}$, the sampling distribution of the latter ratio is $F(k, n-p)$.

Consider the special case wherein the variables in X_1 do not covary with the variables in X_2. That is, $X_1'X_2 = 0$ and

$$X'X = \begin{bmatrix} X_1'X_1 & 0 \\ 0 & X_2'X_2 \end{bmatrix}.$$

For this special case

$$P_\beta = X(X'X)^{-1}X' = [X_1 \quad X_2]\begin{bmatrix} (X_1'X_1)^{-1} & 0 \\ 0 & (X_2'X_2)^{-1} \end{bmatrix}\begin{bmatrix} X_1' \\ X_2' \end{bmatrix}$$

$$= X_1(X_1'X_1)^{-1}X_1' + X_2(X_2'X_2)^{-1}X_2'$$

$$= P_{\alpha 1} + P_{\alpha 2}.$$

Hence

$$\mathbf{y}'P_\beta\mathbf{y} = \mathbf{y}'(P_{\alpha_1} + P_{\alpha_2})\mathbf{y} = \mathbf{y}'P_{\alpha_1}\mathbf{y}' + \mathbf{y}'P_{\alpha_2}\mathbf{y}.$$

Thus

$$R(\boldsymbol{\beta}) = R(\boldsymbol{\alpha}_1) + R(\boldsymbol{\alpha}_2).$$

That is, the total predictable variation from (C.88) is the sum of the predictable variation from the two components in model (C.89) and (C.90). It also follows that

$$R(\boldsymbol{\beta}_1 \mid \boldsymbol{\beta}_2) = R(\boldsymbol{\alpha}_1) = R(\boldsymbol{\beta}_1),$$

$$R(\boldsymbol{\beta}_2 \mid \boldsymbol{\beta}_1) = R(\boldsymbol{\alpha}_2) = R(\boldsymbol{\beta}_2).$$

For this special case it also follows that

$$\boldsymbol{\beta}_1 = \boldsymbol{\alpha}_1 \qquad \text{and} \qquad \boldsymbol{\beta}_2 = \boldsymbol{\alpha}_2.$$

In general, one would not expect the variables in X_1 and X_2 to be independent. Where $X_1'X_2 \neq 0$, one may may partition the inverse of $X'X$ as follows:

$$(X'X)^{-1} = \begin{array}{c} \\ k \\ p-k \end{array}\begin{matrix} k & p-k \\ \begin{bmatrix} C_{11} & C_{12} \\ C_{21} & C_{22} \end{bmatrix} \end{matrix}$$

where

$$C_{11} = [X_1'X_1 - X_1'P_{\alpha_2}X_1]^{-1},$$

$$C_{22} = [X_2'X_2 - X_2'P_{\alpha_1}X_2]^{-1},$$

$$C_{12} = C_{21}' = -(X_1'X_1)^{-1}X_1'X_2[X_2'X_2 - X_2'P_{\alpha_1}X_2]^{-1}.$$

Hence,

$$\boldsymbol{\beta} = (X'X)^{-1}X'\mathbf{y} = (X'X)^{-1}\begin{bmatrix} X_1' \\ X_2' \end{bmatrix}\mathbf{y} = (X'X)^{-1}\begin{bmatrix} X_1'\mathbf{y} \\ X_2'\mathbf{y} \end{bmatrix}$$

$$= \begin{bmatrix} C_{11} & C_{12} \\ C_{21} & C_{22} \end{bmatrix}\begin{bmatrix} X_1'\mathbf{y} \\ X_2'\mathbf{y} \end{bmatrix}$$

$$= \begin{bmatrix} C_{11}X_1'\mathbf{y} + C_{12}X_2'\mathbf{y} \\ C_{21}X_1'\mathbf{y} + C_{22}X_2'\mathbf{y} \end{bmatrix} = \begin{bmatrix} \hat{\boldsymbol{\beta}}_1 \\ \hat{\boldsymbol{\beta}}_2 \end{bmatrix}.$$

This last relationship indicates that $\hat{\boldsymbol{\beta}}_1$ is in part a function of the variables in X_2 as well as the variables in X_1. However, when $X_1'X_2 = 0$, $C_{12} = 0$, and $C_{11} = (X_1'X_1)^{-1}$; hence $\hat{\boldsymbol{\beta}}_1$ in this special case will be a function of only those variables in X_1.

Another special case of considerable interest is that wherein one does not wish to consider β_0 as part of the hypothesis. Interest resides only in the regression coefficients for the predictors. In the present framework this is the case wherein $k = 1$ and X_1 is a vector with $X = 1$ for all elements. For this case,

$$X_1'X_1 = n,$$

$$P_{\alpha_1} = X_1(X_1'X_1)^{-1}X_1' = \frac{1}{n}\underset{(n \times n)}{U},$$

where U is a matrix of unities. Further,

$$\mathbf{y}'P_{\alpha_1}\mathbf{y} = \frac{1}{n}\left(\sum Y\right)^2$$

Hence, $$Q_{\alpha_1} = \mathbf{y}'\mathbf{y} - \mathbf{y}'P_{\alpha_1}\mathbf{y} = \sum Y^2 - \frac{1}{n}\left(\sum Y\right)^2 = \text{SS}_Y.$$

In this case, to test the hypothesis that $\boldsymbol{\beta}_2 = \mathbf{0}$, one has

$$R(\boldsymbol{\beta}_2 \mid \boldsymbol{\beta}_1) = Q_{\alpha_1} - Q_\beta$$
$$= \text{SS}_Y - \text{SS}_{Y-\hat{Y}}$$
$$= \text{SS}_{\hat{Y}}.$$

Hence the F ratio takes the form

$$F = \frac{\text{SS}_{\hat{Y}}/(p-1)}{\text{SS}_{Y-\hat{Y}}/(n-p)}.$$

When $\boldsymbol{\beta}_2 = \mathbf{0}$, this F ratio is distributed as $F(p-1, n-p)$. This is a test of the hypothesis that $\boldsymbol{\beta} = 0$ where $\boldsymbol{\beta}$ does not contain β_0.

As an application of the general case of the test procedure, consider the numerical example in Table C.3. In this example, the X variables are X_0, X_1,

X_2, and

$$n = 6 \quad \text{and} \quad p = 3.$$

The numerical value of Q_β as obtained from part iv of Table C.3 is

$$Q_\beta = \sum (Y - \hat{Y})^2 = 525.96.$$

Let

$$\frac{X}{6 \times 3} = [\mathbf{X}_0 \quad \mathbf{X}_1 \mid \mathbf{X}_2] = \frac{[X_1 \quad X_2]}{6 \times 2 \; 6 \times 1}.$$

That is,

$$X_1 = [\mathbf{X}_0 \quad \mathbf{X}_1] \quad \text{and} \quad X_2 = [\mathbf{X}_2].$$

One finds that

$$Q_{\alpha_1} = 529.27.$$

Hence,

$$R(\beta_2 \mid \beta_0, \beta_1) = Q_{\alpha_1} - Q_\beta = 3.29.$$

That is, that part of reduction in the sum of squares due to β_2, which is orthogonal to both β_0 and β_1, is 3.29. Under the hypothesis that $\beta_2 = 0$, $R(\beta_2 \mid \beta_0, \beta_1)$ measures the deviation from hypothesis. To test the hypothesis that $\beta_2 = 0$, the appropriate F ratio is

$$F = \frac{(Q_{\alpha_1} - Q_\beta)/1}{Q_\beta/3} = \frac{3.29}{525.96/3} = 0.0189.$$

The critical value for a 0.05-level test is $F_{0.95}(1, 3) = 10.1$. Hence, these data do not contradict the hypothesis that $\beta_2 = 0$. The power of this test is extremely low since the degrees of freedom for the denominator of the F ratio are so small.

As another application of the general test procedure, one may test the hypothesis that

$$\begin{bmatrix} \beta_1 \\ \beta_2 \end{bmatrix} = \begin{bmatrix} 0 \\ 0 \end{bmatrix}.$$

From part ii and part iv of Table C.3,

$$Q_{\alpha_1} = 783.33,$$
$$Q_\beta = 525.96.$$

Hence, the measure of deviation from hypothesis is

$$R(\beta_1, \beta_2 \mid \beta_0) = Q_{\alpha_1} - Q_\beta = 257.37.$$

In this case the appropriate F ratio is

$$F = \frac{257.37/2}{525.96/3} = 0.73.$$

For a 0.05-level test, $F_{0.95}(2, 3) = 9.55$. Again, because of the very small number of degrees of freedom for the denominator of the F ratio, this test has extremely low power.

C.3 THE GENERAL LINEAR MODEL AND THE ANALYSIS OF VARIANCE

Within the context of experimental design, what one knows about each element are the values of the dependent variable and the particular treatment condition under which observation occurred. The fixed-effects analysis of variance, then, may be viewed as a special case of the general linear model wherein regression procedures may be utilized with qualitative independent variables—the treatment classifications—to predict a quantitative dependent variable. The assumptions of the general linear model establish the nature of sampling distributions and justify tests of significance on parameters.

Some authors have emphasized the regression approach to analysis of variance computations (e.g., Cohen and Cohen, 1975) and Kirk (1982) has presented appropriate regression analyses for each of the experimental designs which he discusses. The advantage of such an approach is that it emphasizes the underlying identity of regression analysis and analysis of variance and also relates those topics to multivariate procedures within a single context. In general, however, the "usual" analysis of variance computational formulas for the various sources of variation are simple, special cases of the corresponding regression analysis computations, wherein the simplification results from the nature of the experimental designs. For that reason, the more traditional approach is used in this volume. For illustrative purposes, the completely randomized design will be presented here in a regression format. Generalization to more complex designs is readily accomplished.

Completely Randomized Design

In the completely randomized single-factor design considered in detail in Chapter 3, nk elements are sampled from some population of interest, n of which are assigned at random to each of the k treatment conditions. The assumptions of the general linear model are used to justify tests of significance and to establish the nature of sampling distributions. That is, it is assumed the observations are independent, the observations are normally distributed in all populations and all treatment populations have a common variance. Treatment population means are assumed to be linearly related to predictors.

The structural model for the observations in (3.18) is

$$X_{ij} = \mu + \tau_j + \varepsilon_{ij},$$

where μ = the grand mean of the treatment populations,
$\tau_j = \mu_j - \mu$ = effect of treatment j
$\varepsilon_{ij} = X_{ij} - \mu_j$ = random error.

From this, it is simple to express the observations in terms of treatment condition means. That is,

$$X_{ij} = \mu + \tau_j + \varepsilon_{ij}$$

$$= \mu + (\mu_j - \mu) + \varepsilon_{ij}$$

$$= \mu_j + \varepsilon_{ij} \tag{C.91}$$

Hence, the analysis of variance can be conceptualized in terms of treatment means rather than in terms of the parameters, μ and τ_j. The model in (C.91) is sometimes referred to as the full-rank experimental design model.

One may easily reconceptualize the structural model in (C.91) in regression terms. Let the matrix X be a *design matrix* or *structural matrix* which provides information about the assignment of elements to treatment conditions. For (C.91),

	Treatments	Elements	Predictors X_1	X_2	$\cdots$	X_j	$\cdots$	X_k	
		1(1)	1	0	$\cdots$	0	$\cdots$	0	$Y_{1(1)}$
		2(1)	1	0	$\cdots$	0	$\cdots$	0	$Y_{2(1)}$
	1	3(1)	1	0	$\cdots$	0	$\cdots$	0	$Y_{3(1)}$
		$\vdots$	$\vdots$	$\vdots$		$\vdots$		$\vdots$	$\vdots$
		$n(1)$	1	0	$\cdots$	0	$\cdots$	0	$Y_{n(1)}$
		1(2)	0	1	$\cdots$	0	$\cdots$	0	$Y_{1(2)}$
		2(2)	0	1	$\cdots$	0	$\cdots$	0	$Y_{2(2)}$
	2	3(2)	0	1	$\cdots$	0	$\cdots$	0	$Y_{3(2)}$
		$\vdots$	$\vdots$	$\vdots$		$\vdots$		$\vdots$	$\vdots$
X		$n(2)$	0	1	$\cdots$	0	$\cdots$	0	$Y_{n(2)}$
$(nk \times k) =$	$\vdots$	$\vdots$	$\vdots$	$\vdots$		$\vdots$		$\vdots$	$\mathbf{y}$
		1(j)	0	0	$\cdots$	1	$\cdots$	0	$(nk \times 1) = Y_{1(j)}$
		2(j)	0	0	$\cdots$	1	$\cdots$	0	$Y_{2(j)}$
	j	3(j)	0	0	$\cdots$	1	$\cdots$	0	$Y_{3(j)}$
		$\vdots$	$\vdots$	$\vdots$		$\vdots$		$\vdots$	$\vdots$
		$n(j)$	0	0	$\cdots$	1	$\cdots$	0	$Y_{n(j)}$
	$\vdots$	$\vdots$	$\vdots$	$\vdots$		$\vdots$		$\vdots$	$\vdots$
		1(k)	0	0	$\cdots$	0	$\cdots$	1	$Y_{1(k)}$
		2(k)	0	0	$\cdots$	0	$\cdots$	1	$Y_{2(k)}$
	k	3(k)	0	0	$\cdots$	0	$\cdots$	1	$Y_{3(k)}$
		$\vdots$	$\vdots$	$\vdots$		$\vdots$		$\vdots$	$\vdots$
		$n(k)$	0	0	$\cdots$	0	$\cdots$	1	$Y_{n(k)}$

In the structural matrix, each column represents an independent variable which takes 0–1 values; 1 is assigned if an element belongs to a particular treatment condition and 0 is assigned otherwise. For example, when $n = 2$ and

$k = 3,$

$$\underset{(6 \times 3)}{X} = \begin{bmatrix} 1 & 0 & 0 \\ 1 & 0 & 0 \\ 0 & 1 & 0 \\ 0 & 1 & 0 \\ 0 & 0 & 1 \\ 0 & 0 & 1 \end{bmatrix}.$$

In the notation of regression analysis, $\mathbf{y}$ is the vector of dependent variable values. When $n = 2$ and $k = 3,$

$$\underset{(6 \times 1)}{\mathbf{y}} = \begin{bmatrix} Y_{1(1)} \\ Y_{2(1)} \\ Y_{1(2)} \\ Y_{2(2)} \\ Y_{1(3)} \\ Y_{2(3)} \end{bmatrix}.$$

With these two definitions, then, the individual observations may be expressed as the linear equation,

$$\underset{(nk \times 1)}{\mathbf{y}} = \underset{(nk \times k)}{X} \underset{(k \times 1)}{\boldsymbol{\beta}} + \underset{(nk \times 1)}{\boldsymbol{\varepsilon}},$$

where the elements of $\boldsymbol{\beta}$ are the unknown regression parameters. This equation expresses the observations as a linear transformation of the regression parameters of $\boldsymbol{\beta}$ plus a random error component. Since $E(\boldsymbol{\varepsilon}) = \mathbf{0}$ over an entire population,

$$E(\mathbf{y}) = X\boldsymbol{\beta} = \begin{bmatrix} \mu_1 \\ \mu_2 \\ \vdots \\ \mu_k \end{bmatrix}.$$

In order to estimate those parameters from least-squares procedures, the normal equations are

$$(X'X)\hat{\boldsymbol{\beta}} = X'\mathbf{y}.$$

It is instructive to examine these equations in scalar terms. The product $(X'X)$ is a diagonal matrix with the treatment-group sample sizes as the entries:

$$(X'X) = \begin{bmatrix} n_1 & 0 & 0 & \cdots & 0 \\ 0 & n_2 & 0 & \cdots & 0 \\ 0 & 0 & n_3 & \cdots & 0 \\ \vdots & \vdots & \vdots & & \vdots \\ 0 & 0 & 0 & \cdots & n_k \end{bmatrix}$$

The product $X'\mathbf{y}$ is a vector of order $(k \times 1)$ which contains the sums of the dependent variable for each treatment condition. That is,

$$X'\mathbf{y} = \begin{bmatrix} \sum Y_1 \\ \sum Y_2 \\ \vdots \\ \sum Y_k \end{bmatrix}.$$

Hence, the k normal equations in scalar terms are:

$$n_1\hat{\beta}_1 - 0\hat{\beta}_2 + 0\hat{\beta}_3 + \cdots + 0\hat{\beta}_k = \sum Y_1$$

$$0\hat{\beta}_1 + n_2\hat{\beta}_2 + 0\hat{\beta}_3 + \cdots + 0\hat{\beta}_k = \sum Y_2$$

$$0\hat{\beta}_1 + 0\hat{\beta}_2 + n_3\hat{\beta}_3 + \cdots + 0\hat{\beta}_k = \sum Y_3$$

$$\vdots \qquad \vdots \qquad \vdots \qquad \qquad \vdots \qquad \vdots$$

$$0\hat{\beta}_1 + 0\hat{\beta}_2 + 0\hat{\beta}_3 + \cdots + n_k\hat{\beta}_k = \sum Y_k.$$

When X is nonsingular, as in (C.91), the solution to the normal equations is

$$\hat{\boldsymbol{\beta}} = (X'X)^{-1}X'\mathbf{y}.$$

In this equation, since X is a diagonal matrix with the elements on the main diagonal equal to the treatment sample sizes, $(X'X)^{-1}$ is a diagonal matrix with $1/n_j$ on the main diagonal, and

$$\hat{\boldsymbol{\beta}} = \begin{bmatrix} \dfrac{1}{n_1} & 0 & \cdots & 0 \\ & \dfrac{1}{n_2} & \cdots & 0 \\ & & \vdots & \\ & & & \dfrac{1}{n_k} \end{bmatrix} \begin{bmatrix} \sum Y_1 \\ \sum Y_2 \\ \vdots \\ \sum Y_k \end{bmatrix} = \begin{bmatrix} \bar{Y}_1 \\ \bar{Y}_2 \\ \vdots \\ \bar{Y}_k \end{bmatrix}.$$

The simple conclusion is that each treatment population mean in (C.91) has as its least-squares estimator the corresponding observed treatment mean:

$$\boldsymbol{\beta} = \begin{bmatrix} \mu_1 \\ \mu_2 \\ \vdots \\ \mu_k \end{bmatrix}, \quad \text{and} \quad \hat{\boldsymbol{\beta}} = \begin{bmatrix} \bar{Y}_1 \\ \bar{Y}_2 \\ \vdots \\ \bar{Y}_k \end{bmatrix}.$$

The predicted scores for each element,

$$\hat{\mathbf{y}} = X\boldsymbol{\beta},$$

are, then, the respective treatment condition means. Hence, the regression function involved is the "line of means." When the treatment conditions are qualitative in nature, no particular relation among these means may be specified; one may consider the representation of predicted scores to be a "function-free" regression system. Predicted values are the treatment means, and error is defined as the deviation of each individual observation from the line of means:

$$\hat{Y}_{ij} = \bar{Y}_j, \quad \text{and}$$

$$e_{ij} = Y_{ij} - \hat{Y}_{ij}$$

$$= Y_{ij} - \bar{Y}_j.$$

The analysis of variance sums of squares follow from these results. Total variation of the individual observations about the grand mean is

$$SS_{total} = \mathbf{y'y} - \mathbf{y'1}\left(\frac{1}{nk}\right)\mathbf{1'y}$$

$$= \sum \sum Y_{ij}^2 - \left(\sum \sum Y_{ij}\right)^2 \bigg/ nk. \tag{C.92}$$

In the analysis of variance notation of Chapter 3, total variation of the dependent variable was given in (3.9) as

$$SS_{total} = \sum \sum (X_{ij} - \bar{G})^2$$

$$= \sum \sum X_{ij}^2 - G^2/nk.$$

Equations (C.92) and (3.9) are identical.

The analysis of variance within-treatment variation, $SS_{\text{within treatment}}$, is the variation of the individual observations about their respective treatment means. In regression terms this was given in (C.24) as

$$\mathbf{e'e} = \mathbf{y'y} - \mathbf{y'}X\hat{\beta}.$$

Since

$$e = (Y_{ij} - \bar{Y}_j),$$

in the case of analysis of variance notation

$$SS_{\text{within}} = \sum \sum (X_{ij} - \bar{T}_j)^2$$

is algebraically identical to (C.24).

Finally, the variation of predicted scores is the variation of treatment means. In analysis of variance notation,

$$\text{SS}_{\text{between treatments}} = n \sum (\bar{T}_j - \bar{G})^2.$$

This source of variation may be viewed as the decrease in error variation associated with the fact that the means are not all equal. Equivalently, it may be viewed as the increase in error variation associated with the constraint that all means are equal (except for random error). In terms of the discussion in Sec. C.2, which is summarized in Table C.5, $\text{SS}_{\text{between treatments}}$ is the equivalent of $Q_2 = Q_1 - Q_0$. The constraint that all means are equal is equivalent to assuming that $\beta = \beta^*$ and the analysis of variance F testing the hypothesis of equal treatment means is equivalent to the F provided in Table C.5.

Representation in terms of (C.91) is not the usual presentation of the analysis of variance as a special case of the general linear model. Rather, the "usual presentation" is in terms of (3.18),

$$X_{ij} = \mu + \tau_j + \varepsilon_{ij},$$

wherein the population means are expressed in terms of the overall mean μ and the treatment effects τ_j. In this context, (3.18) may be characterized as being overparameterized. As will be seen, this creates difficulties in estimating β because the X matrix which represents this model directly is rank deficient.

The regression model has the form

$$Y_{ij} = \beta_0 X_0 + \beta_1 X_{i1} + \beta_2 X_{i2} + \cdots + \beta_k X_{ik} + \varepsilon_{ij}. \tag{C.93}$$

In this notation system,

Y_{ij} = observation on element i under treatment j

$X_0 = 1$ for all elements

$$X_{i1} = \begin{array}{l} 1 \text{ if } j = 1 \\ 0 \text{ if } j \neq 1 \end{array}$$

$\vdots$

$$X_{ik} = \begin{array}{l} 1 \text{ if } j = k \\ 0 \text{ if } j \neq k \end{array}$$

ε_{ij} is a random variable distributed as $N(0, \sigma_\varepsilon^2)$,

$\beta_0, \beta_1, \ldots, \beta_k$ are parameters to be estimated.

In general,

$$\underset{(nk \times 1)}{\mathbf{y}} = \underset{[nk \times (k+1)]}{X} \underset{[(k+1) \times 1]}{\beta} + \underset{(nk \times 1)}{\varepsilon}.$$

The design matrix in detail, then, is

Treatments	Elements	Predictors X_0	X_1	X_2	$\cdots$	X_k
	1(1)	1	1	0	$\cdots$	0
	2(1)	1	1	0	$\cdots$	0
1	$\vdots$	$\vdots$	$\vdots$	$\vdots$		$\vdots$
	$n(1)$	1	1	0	$\cdots$	0
	1(2)	1	0	1	$\cdots$	0
	2(2)	1	0	1	$\cdots$	0
2	$\vdots$	$\vdots$	$\vdots$	$\vdots$		$\vdots$
	$n(2)$	1	0	1	$\cdots$	0
$\vdots$	$\vdots$	$\vdots$	$\vdots$	$\vdots$		$\vdots$
	1(k)	1	0	0	$\cdots$	1
	2(k)	1	0	0	$\cdots$	1
k	$\vdots$	$\vdots$	$\vdots$	$\vdots$		$\vdots$
	$n(k)$	1	0	0	$\cdots$	1

In the normal equations, $X'X\hat{\boldsymbol{\beta}} = X'\mathbf{y}$, with this X matrix $X'X$ becomes

$$X'X = \begin{bmatrix} n_k & n_1 & n_2 & \cdots & n_k \\ n_1 & n_1 & 0 & \cdots & 0 \\ n_2 & 0 & n_2 & \cdots & 0 \\ \vdots & & & & \\ n_k & 0 & 0 & \cdots & n_k \end{bmatrix}.$$

The product $X'X$ is singular since the first column of $X'X$ is equal to the sum of the remaining columns. Hence, the components of $\hat{\beta}$ will not be unique.

A general solution for $\hat{\beta}$ has the form

$$\boldsymbol{\beta} = \begin{bmatrix} 0 + z \\ \bar{Y}_1 - z \\ \vdots \\ \bar{Y}_k - z \end{bmatrix} \tag{C.94}$$

where z is any real number. From (C.94) one notes that $\hat{\beta}_0 + \hat{\beta}_j = \bar{Y}_j$ for all possible choices of z. Hence, for any solution for $\boldsymbol{\beta}$, $\bar{Y}_j$ is constant. One also notes that $\beta_j - \beta_{j'}$ does not depend upon the choice of z. In general, any function of the elements of $\boldsymbol{\beta}$ of the form $\sum c_j\beta_j$ is said to be estimable if the corresponding function $\sum c_j\hat{\beta}_j$ does not depend upon the choice of z. Estimability in this sense requires that

$$c_0 = \sum_{j=1}^{k} c_j \quad \text{or} \quad c_0 - \sum_{j=1}^{k} c_j = 0.$$

In the general case, $\beta_0 + \beta_j$ will be estimable and any comparison among the β_j will be estimable; that is

$$c_1\beta_1 + c_2\beta_2 + \cdots + c_k\beta_k, \quad \text{where} \quad \sum c_j = 0$$

is estimable.

The analysis of variance model for fixed variables is the special case of (C.94) wherein $z = \bar{Y}$. When $z = \bar{Y}$

$$\hat{\beta} = \begin{bmatrix} 0 + z \\ \bar{Y}_1 - z \\ \bar{Y}_2 - z \\ \vdots \\ \bar{Y}_k - z \end{bmatrix} = \begin{bmatrix} \bar{Y} \\ \bar{Y}_1 - \bar{Y} \\ \bar{Y}_2 - \bar{Y} \\ \vdots \\ \bar{Y}_k - \bar{Y} \end{bmatrix}.$$

That is,

$$\beta = \begin{bmatrix} \beta_0 \\ \beta_1 \\ \vdots \\ \beta_k \end{bmatrix} = \begin{bmatrix} \mu \\ \tau_1 = \mu_1 - \mu \\ \vdots \\ \tau_k = \mu_k - \mu \end{bmatrix}, \qquad \text{and}$$

$$\hat{\beta} = \begin{bmatrix} \bar{Y} \\ \bar{Y}_1 - \bar{Y} \\ \vdots \\ \bar{Y}_k - \bar{Y} \end{bmatrix}.$$

In the notation of Chapter 3,

$$\hat{\beta} = \begin{bmatrix} \bar{Y} \\ \bar{Y}_1 - \bar{Y} \\ \bar{Y}_2 - \bar{Y} \\ \vdots \\ Y_k - \bar{Y} \end{bmatrix} = \begin{bmatrix} \bar{G} \\ \bar{T}_1 - \bar{G} \\ \bar{T}_2 - \bar{G} \\ \vdots \\ \bar{T}_k - \bar{G} \end{bmatrix}.$$

The regression coefficients are equal to the grand mean and the analysis of variance treatment effects as defined in (3.18). This is equivalent to stating that the analysis of variance model for fixed variables is generally the special case of (C.93) which includes the side condition that $\sum n_j \beta_j = 0$ (or, when n_j is constant, $\sum \beta_j = 0$). When this condition is part of the model, the analysis of variance parameters of (3.18), μ and τ_j, are the elements of $\hat{\beta}$. This is the solution to the estimation problem given in Chapter 3.

To realize this solution, one may use an X matrix for the design matrix which is labeled "effect coding." This label arises because the elements of $\hat{\beta}$ are estimates of the analysis of variance model, μ, and τ_j, the treatment effects.

For effect coding, X has the form:

Treatments	Elements	X_0	X_1	X_2	$\cdots$	X_{k-1}
	1(1)	1	1	0	$\cdots$	0
	2(1)	1	1	0	$\cdots$	0
1	3(1)	1	1	0	$\cdots$	0
	$\vdots$	$\vdots$	$\vdots$	$\vdots$		$\vdots$
	$n(1)$	1	1	0	$\cdots$	0

Continued

(Continued)

Treatments	Elements	X_0	X_1	X_2	$\cdots$	X_{k-1}
	1(2)	1	0	1	$\cdots$	0
	2(2)	1	0	1	$\cdots$	0
2	3(2)	1	0	1	$\cdots$	0
	$\vdots$	$\vdots$	$\vdots$	$\vdots$		$\vdots$
	$n(2)$	1	0	1	$\cdots$	0
$\vdots$						
	1(j)	1	0	0	$\cdots$	0
	2(j)	1	0	0	$\cdots$	0
j	3(j)	1	0	0	$\cdots$	0
	$\vdots$	$\vdots$	$\vdots$	$\vdots$		$\vdots$
	$n(j)$	1	0	0	$\cdots$	0
$\vdots$						
	1(k)	1	-1	-1	$\cdots$	-1
	2(k)	1	-1	-1	$\cdots$	-1
k	3(k)	1	-1	-1	$\cdots$	-1
	$\vdots$	$\vdots$	$\vdots$	$\vdots$		$\vdots$
	$n(k)$	1	-1	-1	$\cdots$	-1

Note that there are only k columns in X, the first of which provides information about β_0. There are only $k-1$ columns needed to code information about membership in the k groups. This conclusion is intuitively appealing; if one knows the group membership of subjects in $k-1$ groups, one knows that the group membership of the remaining subjects must be group k.

Stated otherwise, since $\Sigma \beta_j = 0$, $\beta_k = -\sum_{j=1}^{k} \beta_j$.

To illustrate these points in numerical form, the example used in Chapter 3 and summarized in Tables 3.1 and 3.2 is presented in terms of effect coding in Table C.7. Part (i) presents the basic data ($\mathbf{y}$ and X) in regression format. The solution for $\hat{\beta}$ is provided in Part (ii). The partition of variation in terms of regression and residual is provided in Part (iii). One may observe that the partition of the variation is identical to the analysis of variance partition presented in Table 3.2.

TABLE C.7 **Numerical example**

	Treatments	Elements	X_0	X_1	X_2	Y	
		1(1)	1	1	0	3	$n = 8$
		2(1)	1	1	0	5	$k = 3$
		3(1)	1	1	0	2	
	1	4(1)	1	1	0	4	
		5(1)	1	1	0	8	
		6(1)	1	1	0	4	
		7(1)	1	1	0	3	
		8(1)	1	1	0	9	
		1(2)	1	0	1	4	
		2(2)	1	0	1	4	
		3(2)	1	0	1	3	
(i)	2	4(2)	1	0	1	8	
		5(2)	1	0	1	7	
		6(2)	1	0	1	4	
		7(2)	1	0	1	2	
		8(2)	1	0	1	5	

Continued

TABLE C.7   (*Continued*)

Treatments	Elements	X_0	X_1	X_2	Y
	1(3)	1	−1	−1	6
	2(3)	1	−1	−1	7
	3(3)	1	−1	−1	8
	4(3)	1	−1	−1	6
3	5(3)	1	−1	−1	7
	6(3)	1	−1	−1	9
	7(3)	1	−1	−1	10
	8(3)	1	−1	−1	9

(ii)

$$X'X = \begin{bmatrix} nk & 0 & 0 \\ 0 & 2n & n \\ 0 & & 2n \end{bmatrix} = \begin{bmatrix} 24 & 0 & 0 \\ 0 & 16 & 8 \\ 0 & 8 & 16 \end{bmatrix}$$

$$X'y = \begin{bmatrix} \sum Y \\ \sum Y_1 - \sum Y_3 \\ \sum Y_2 - \sum Y_3 \end{bmatrix} = \begin{bmatrix} 137 \\ 38 - 62 = -24 \\ 37 - 62 = -25 \end{bmatrix}$$

$$\hat{\boldsymbol{\beta}} = (X'X)^{-1}X'y = \begin{bmatrix} 0.0417 & 0 & 0 \\ 0 & 0.0833 & -0.0415 \\ 0 & -0.0415 & 0.0833 \end{bmatrix} \begin{bmatrix} 137 \\ -24 \\ -25 \end{bmatrix}$$

$$= \begin{bmatrix} \hat{\beta}_0 \\ \hat{\beta}_1 \\ \hat{\beta}_2 \end{bmatrix} = \begin{bmatrix} 5.71 \\ -0.96 \\ -1.09 \end{bmatrix} = \begin{bmatrix} \bar{G} \\ \bar{T}_1 - \bar{G} \\ \bar{T}_2 - \bar{G} \end{bmatrix}$$

$$\hat{\beta}_3 = -(\hat{\beta}_1 + \hat{\beta}_2) = 2.05 = \bar{T}_3 - \bar{G}.$$

$$y'y = \sum \sum Y_{i(j)}^2 = 919$$

$$\hat{\boldsymbol{\beta}}X'y = 832.12$$

$$\left(\sum \sum Y \right)^2 \Big/ nk = 782.04$$

(iii)

$$SS_{regression} = \hat{\boldsymbol{\beta}}'X'y - \left(\sum \sum Y_{i(j)} \right)^2 \Big/ nk = 832.12 - 782.04 = 50.08$$

$$SS_{error} = y'y - \hat{\boldsymbol{\beta}}'X'y = 919.00 - 832.12 = 86.88$$

$$SS_{total} = y'y - \left(\sum \sum Y_{i(j)} \right)^2 \Big/ nk = 919 - 782.04 = 136.96$$

There are other X matrices which may be used to resolve the rank problem posed by (C.91). The effect coding approach was presented here because the elements of $\hat{\boldsymbol{\beta}}$ are the same as the analysis of variance structural model parameters. The choice of a particular X matrix has no effect upon the breakdown of total variation and, hence, upon hypothesis tests. That is, even though the solution for **b** is not unique when $X'X$ is singular, $\sum (Y - \hat{Y})^2 = \sum Y^2 - \hat{\boldsymbol{\beta}}'X'y$ will be unique since the normal equations represent both necessary and sufficient conditions for minimizing error variation. Different X matrices do result in different elements for $\hat{\boldsymbol{\beta}}$. Numerous authors emphasize two alternative coding schemes: *dummy coding* and *orthogonal coding*. One such author is Kirk (1982) who presents a detailed explanation containing numerical examples for all of the designs which he considers.

TABLES

TABLE D.1   **Unit normal distribution**†

$$[P(z \le z_{1-\alpha}) = 1 - \alpha]$$

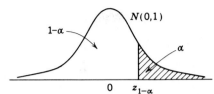

$z_{1-\alpha}$	$1 - \alpha$	$z_{1-\alpha}$	$1 - \alpha$	$z_{1-\alpha}$	$1 - \alpha$	$z_{1-\alpha}$	$1 - \alpha$
.00	.500	.35	.637	.70	.758	1.05	.853
.01	.504	.36	.641	.71	.761	1.06	.855
.02	.508	.37	.644	.72	.764	1.07	.858
.03	.512	.38	.648	.73	.767	1.08	.860
.04	.516	.39	.652	.74	.770	1.09	.862
.05	.520	.40	.655	.75	.773	1.10	.864
.06	.524	.41	.659	.76	.776	1.11	.867
.07	.528	.42	.663	.77	.779	1.12	.869
.08	.532	.43	.666	.78	.782	1.13	.871
.09	.536	.44	.670	.79	.785	1.14	.873
.10	.540	.45	.674	.80	.788	1.15	.875
.11	.544	.46	.677	.81	.791	1.16	.877
.12	.548	.47	.681	.82	.794	1.17	.879
.13	.552	.48	.684	.83	.797	1.18	.881
.14	.556	.49	.688	.84	.800	1.19	.883
.15	.560	.50	.691	.85	.802	1.20	.885
.16	.564	.51	.695	.86	.805	1.21	.887
.17	.567	.52	.698	.87	.808	1.22	.889
.18	.571	.53	.702	.88	.811	1.23	.891
.19	.575	.54	.705	.89	.813	1.24	.893
.20	.579	.55	.709	.90	.816	1.25	.894
.21	.583	.56	.712	.91	.819	1.26	.896
.22	.587	.57	.716	.92	.821	1.27	.898
.23	.591	.58	.719	.93	.824	1.28	.900
.24	.595	.59	.722	.94	.826	1.29	.901
.25	.599	.60	.726	.95	.829	1.30	.903
.26	.603	.61	.729	.96	.831	1.31	.905
.27	.606	.62	.732	.97	.834	1.32	.907
.28	.610	.63	.736	.98	.836	1.33	.908
.29	.614	.64	.739	.99	.839	1.34	.910
.30	.618	.65	.742	1.00	.841	1.35	.911
.31	.622	.66	.745	1.01	.844	1.36	.913
.32	.626	.67	.749	1.02	.846	1.37	.915
.33	.629	.68	.752	1.03	.848	1.38	.916
.34	.633	.69	.755	1.04	.851	1.39	.918

TABLE D.1 (*Continued*)

$$[P(z \leq z_{1-\alpha}) = 1 - \alpha]$$

$z_{1-\alpha}$	$1 - \alpha$	$z_{1-\alpha}$	$1 - \alpha$	$z_{1-\alpha}$	$1 - \alpha$	$z_{1-\alpha}$	$1 - \alpha$
1.40	.919	1.75	.960	2.10	.982	2.45	.993
1.41	.921	1.76	.961	2.11	.983	2.46	.993
1.42	.922	1.77	.962	2.12	.983	2.47	.993
1.43	.924	1.78	.962	2.13	.983	2.48	.993
1.44	.925	1.79	.963	2.14	.984	2.49	.994
1.45	.926	1.80	.964	2.15	.984	2.50	.994
1.46	.928	1.81	.965	2.16	.985	2.51	.994
1.47	.929	1.82	.966	2.17	.985	2.52	.994
1.48	.931	1.83	.966	2.18	.985	2.53	.994
1.49	.932	1.84	.967	2.19	.986	2.54	.994
1.50	.933	1.85	.968	2.20	.986	2.55	.995
1.51	.934	1.86	.969	2.21	.986	2.56	.995
1.52	.936	1.87	.969	2.22	.987	2.57	.995
1.53	.937	1.88	.970	2.23	.987	2.58	.995
1.54	.938	1.89	.971	2.24	.987	2.59	.995
1.55	.939	1.90	.971	2.25	.988		
1.56	.941	1.91	.972	2.26	.988	2.60	.9953
1.57	.942	1.92	.973	2.27	.988		
1.58	.943	1.93	.973	2.28	.989	2.70	.9965
1.59	.944	1.94	.974	2.29	.989		
						2.80	.9974
1.60	.945	1.95	.974	2.30	.989		
1.61	.946	1.96	.975	2.31	.990	2.90	.9981
1.62	.947	1.97	.976	2.32	.990		
1.63	.948	1.98	.976	2.33	.990	3.00	.9987
1.64	.949	1.99	.977	2.34	.990		
						3.20	.9993
1.65	.951	2.00	.977	2.35	.991		
1.66	.952	2.01	.978	2.36	.991	3.40	.9997
1.67	.953	2.02	.978	2.37	.991		
1.68	.954	2.03	.979	2.38	.991	3.60	.9998
1.69	.954	2.04	.979	2.39	.992		
						3.80	.99993
1.70	.955	2.05	.980	2.40	.992		
1.71	.956	2.06	.980	2.41	.992	4.00	.999968
1.72	.957	2.07	.981	2.42	.992		
1.73	.958	2.08	.981	2.43	.992	4.50	.999997
1.74	.959	2.09	.982	2.44	.993	5.00	.9999997
						5.50	.9999999
1.645	.950	2.326	.990	3.090	.999	3.891	.99995
1.960	.975	2.576	.995	3.291	.9995	4.417	.999995

TABLE D.2 **Student's *t* distribution**

df	Percentile point								
	70	75	80	87.5	90	95	97.5	99	99.5
1	.73	1.00	1.38	2.41	3.08	6.31	12.71	31.82	63.66
2	.62	.81	1.06	1.60	1.89	2.92	4.30	6.96	9.92
3	.58	.79	.98	1.42	1.64	2.35	3.18	4.54	5.84
4	.57	.77	.94	1.34	1.53	2.13	2.78	3.75	4.60
5	.56	.75	.92	1.30	1.48	2.02	2.57	3.36	4.03
6	.55	.74	.91	1.27	1.44	1.94	2.45	3.14	3.71
7	.55	.73	.90	1.25	1.42	1.89	2.36	3.00	3.50
8	.55	.72	.89	1.24	1.40	1.86	2.31	2.90	3.36
9	.54	.71	.88	1.23	1.38	1.83	2.26	2.82	3.25
10	.54	.70	.88	1.22	1.37	1.81	2.23	2.76	3.17
11	.54	.70	.88	1.21	1.36	1.80	2.20	2.72	3.11
12	.54	.69	.87	1.21	1.36	1.78	2.18	2.68	3.05
13	.54	.69	.87	1.21	1.35	1.77	2.16	2.65	3.01
14	.54	.69	.87	1.20	1.34	1.76	2.14	2.62	2.98
15	.54	.69	.87	1.20	1.34	1.75	2.13	2.60	2.95
16	.54	.69	.86	1.20	1.34	1.75	2.12	2.58	2.92
17	.53	.69	.86	1.19	1.33	1.74	2.11	2.57	2.90
18	.53	.69	.86	1.19	1.33	1.73	2.10	2.55	2.88
19	.53	.69	.86	1.19	1.33	1.73	2.09	2.54	2.86
20	.53	.69	.86	1.18	1.32	1.72	2.09	2.53	2.85
21	.53	.69	.86	1.18	1.32	1.72	2.08	2.52	2.83
22	.53	.69	.86	1.18	1.32	1.72	2.07	2.51	2.82
23	.53	.68	.86	1.18	1.32	1.71	2.07	2.50	2.81
24	.53	.68	.86	1.18	1.32	1.71	2.06	2.49	2.80
25	.53	.68	.86	1.18	1.32	1.71	2.06	2.49	2.79
26	.53	.68	.86	1.18	1.32	1.71	2.06	2.48	2.78
27	.53	.68	.86	1.18	1.31	1.70	2.05	2.47	2.77
28	.53	.68	.86	1.17	1.31	1.70	2.05	2.47	2.76
29	.53	.68	.85	1.17	1.31	1.70	2.05	2.46	2.76
30	.53	68	.85	1.17	1.31	1.70	2.04	2.46	2.75
40	.53	.68	.85	1.17	1.30	1.68	2.02	2.42	2.70
50	.53	.67	.85	1.16	1.30	1.68	2.01	2.40	2.68
60	.53	.67	.85	1.16	1.30	1.67	2.00	2.39	2.66
80	.53	.67	.85	1.16	1.29	1.66	1.99	2.37	2.64
100	.53	.67	.84	1.16	1.29	1.66	1.98	2.36	2.63
200	.52	.67	.84	1.15	1.29	1.65	1.97	2.35	2.60
500	.52	.67	.84	1.15	1.28	1.65	1.96	2.33	2.59
∞	.52	.67	.84	1.15	1.28	1.64	1.96	2.33	2.58

TABLE D.3 *F* distribution†

| df for denom. | $1 - \alpha$ | \multicolumn{12}{c}{df for numerator} |
		1	2	3	4	5	6	7	8	9	10	11	12
1	.75	5.83	7.50	8.20	8.58	8.82	8.98	9.10	9.19	9.26	9.32	9.36	9.41
	.90	39.9	49.5	53.6	55.8	57.2	58.2	58.9	59.4	59.9	60.2	60.5	60.7
	.95	161	200	216	225	230	234	237	239	241	242	243	244
2	.75	2.57	3.00	3.15	3.23	3.28	3.31	3.34	3.35	3.37	3.38	3.39	3.39
	.90	8.53	9.00	9.16	9.24	9.29	9.33	9.35	9.37	9.38	9.39	9.40	9.41
	.95	18.5	19.0	19.2	19.2	19.3	19.3	19.4	19.4	19.4	19.4	19.4	19.4
	.99	98.5	99.0	99.2	99.2	99.3	99.3	99.4	99.4	99.4	99.4	99.4	99.4
3	.75	2.02	2.28	2.36	2.39	2.41	2.42	2.43	2.44	2.44	2.44	2.45	2.45
	.90	5.54	5.46	5.39	5.34	5.31	5.28	5.27	5.25	5.24	5.23	5.22	5.22
	.95	10.1	9.55	9.28	9.12	9.10	8.94	8.89	8.85	8.81	8.79	8.76	8.74
	.99	34.1	30.8	29.5	28.7	28.2	27.9	27.7	27.5	27.3	27.2	27.1	27.1
4	.75	1.81	2.00	2.05	2.06	2.07	2.08	2.08	2.08	2.08	2.08	2.08	2.08
	.90	4.54	4.32	4.19	4.11	4.05	4.01	3.98	3.95	3.94	3.92	3.91	3.90
	.95	7.71	6.94	6.59	6.39	6.26	6.16	6.09	6.04	6.00	5.96	5.94	5.91
	.99	21.2	18.0	16.7	16.0	15.5	15.2	15.0	14.8	14.7	14.5	14.4	14.4
5	.75	1.69	1.85	1.88	1.89	1.89	1.89	1.89	1.89	1.89	1.89	1.89	1.89
	.90	4.06	3.78	3.62	3.52	3.45	3.40	3.37	3.34	3.32	3.30	3.28	3.27
	.95	6.61	5.79	5.41	5.19	5.05	4.95	4.88	4.82	4.77	4.74	4.71	4.68
	.99	16.3	13.3	12.1	11.4	11.0	10.7	10.5	10.3	10.2	10.1	9.96	9.89
6	.75	1.62	1.76	1.78	1.79	1.79	1.78	1.78	1.77	1.77	1.77	1.77	1.77
	.90	3.78	3.46	3.29	3.18	3.11	3.05	3.01	2.98	2.96	2.94	2.92	2.90
	.95	5.99	5.14	4.76	4.53	4.39	4.28	4.21	4.15	4.10	4.06	4.03	4.00
	.99	13.7	10.9	9.78	9.15	8.75	8.47	8.26	8.10	7.98	7.87	7.79	7.72
7	.75	1.57	1.70	1.72	1.72	1.71	1.71	1.70	1.70	1.69	1.69	1.69	1.68
	.90	3.59	3.26	3.07	2.96	2.88	2.83	2.78	2.75	2.72	2.70	2.68	2.67
	.95	5.59	4.74	4.35	4.12	3.97	3.87	3.79	3.73	3.68	3.64	3.60	3.57
	.99	12.2	9.55	8.45	7.85	7.46	7.19	6.99	6.84	6.72	6.62	6.54	6.47
8	.75	1.54	1.66	1.67	1.66	1.66	1.65	1.64	1.64	1.64	1.63	1.63	1.62
	.90	3.46	3.11	2.92	2.81	2.73	2.67	2.62	2.59	2.56	2.54	2.52	2.50
	95	5.32	4.46	4.07	3.84	3.69	3.58	3.50	3.44	3.39	3.35	3.31	3.28
	.99	11.3	8.65	7.59	7.01	6.63	6.37	6.18	6.03	5.91	5.81	5.73	5.67
9	.75	1.51	1.62	1.63	1.63	1.62	1.61	1.60	1.60	1.59	1.59	1.58	1.58
	.90	3.36	3.01	2.81	2.69	2.61	2.55	2.51	2.47	2.44	2.42	2.40	2.38
	.95	5.12	4.26	3.86	3.63	3.48	3.37	3.29	3.23	3.18	3.14	3.10	3.07
	.99	10.6	8.02	6.99	6.42	6.06	5.80	5.61	5.47	5.35	5.26	5.18	5.11
10	.75	1.49	1.60	1.60	1.59	1.59	1.58	1.57	1.56	1.56	1.55	1.55	1.54
	.90	3.28	2.92	2.73	2.61	2.52	2.46	2.41	2.38	2.35	2.32	2.30	2.28
	.95	4.96	4.10	3.71	3.48	3.33	3.22	3.14	3.07	3.02	2.98	2.94	2.91
	.99	10.0	7.56	6.55	5.99	5.64	5.39	5.20	5.06	4.94	4.85	4.77	4.71
11	.75	1.47	1.58	1.58	1.57	1.56	1.55	1.54	1.53	1.53	1.52	1.52	1.51
	.90	3.23	2.86	2.66	2.54	2.45	2.39	2.34	2.30	2.27	2.25	2.23	2.21
	.95	4.84	3.98	3.59	3.36	3.20	3.09	3.01	2.95	2.90	2.85	2.82	2.79
	.99	9.65	7.21	6.22	5.67	5.32	5.07	4.89	4.74	4.63	4.54	4.46	4.40
12	.75	1.46	1.56	1.56	1.55	1.54	1.53	1.52	1.51	1.51	1.50	1.50	1.49
	.90	3.18	2.81	2.61	2.48	2.39	2.33	2.28	2.24	2.21	2.19	2.17	2.15
	.95	4.75	3.89	3.49	3.26	3.11	3.00	2.91	2.85	2.80	2.75	2.72	2.69
	.99	9.33	6.93	5.95	5.41	5.06	4.82	4.64	4.50	4.39	4.30	4.22	4.16

TABLE D.3 (*Continued*)

	df for numerator												$1-\alpha$	df for denom.
15	20	24	30	40	50	60	100	120	200	500	∞		
9.49	9.58	9.63	9.67	9.71	9.74	9.76	9.78	9.80	9.82	9.84	9.85	.75	
61.2	61.7	62.0	62.3	62.5	62.7	62.8	63.0	63.1	63.2	63.3	63.3	.90	1
246	248	249	250	251	252	252	253	253	254	254	254	.95	
3.41	3.43	3.43	3.44	3.45	3.45	3.46	3.47	3.47	3.48	3.48	3.48	.75	
9.42	9.44	9.45	9.46	9.47	9.47	9.47	9.48	9.48	9.49	9.49	9.49	.90	2
19.4	19.4	19.5	19.5	19.5	19.5	19.5	19.5	19.5	19.5	19.5	19.5	.95	
99.4	99.4	99.5	99.5	99.5	99.5	99.5	99.5	99.5	99.5	99.5	99.5	.99	
2.46	2.46	2.46	2.47	2.47	2.47	2.47	2.47	2.47	2.47	2.47	2.47	.75	
5.20	5.18	5.18	5.17	5.16	5.15	5.15	5.14	5.14	5.14	5.14	5.13	.90	3
8.70	8.66	8.64	8.62	8.59	8.58	8.57	8.55	8.55	8.54	8.53	8.53	.95	
26.9	26.7	26.6	26.5	26.4	26.4	26.3	26.2	26.2	26.2	26.1	26.1	.99	
2.08	2.08	2.08	2.08	2.08	2.08	2.08	2.08	2.08	2.08	2.08	2.08	.75	
3.87	3.84	3.83	3.82	3.80	3.80	3.79	3.78	3.78	3.77	3.76	3.76	.90	
5.86	5.80	5.77	5.75	5.72	5.70	5.69	5.66	5.66	5.65	5.64	5.63	.95	4
14.2	14.0	13.9	13.8	13.7	13.7	13.7	13.6	13.6	13.5	13.5	13.5	.99	
1.89	1.88	1.88	1.88	1.88	1.88	1.87	1.87	1.87	1.87	1.87	1.87	.75	
3.24	3.21	3.19	3.17	3.16	3.15	3.14	3.13	3.12	3.12	3.11	3.10	.90	5
4.62	4.56	4.53	4.50	4.46	4.44	4.43	4.41	4.40	4.39	4.37	4.36	.95	
9.72	9.55	9.47	9.38	9.29	9.24	9.20	9.13	9.11	9.08	9.04	9.02	.99	
1.76	1.76	1.75	1.75	1.75	1.75	1.74	1.74	1.74	1.74	1.74	1.74	.75	
2.87	2.84	2.82	2.80	2.78	2.77	2.76	2.75	2.74	2.73	2.73	2.72	.90	6
3.94	3.87	3.84	3.81	3.77	3.75	3.74	3.71	3.70	3.69	3.68	3.67	.95	
7.56	7.40	7.31	7.23	7.14	7.09	7.06	6.99	6.97	6.93	6.90	6.88	.99	
1.68	1.67	1.67	1.66	1.66	1.66	1.65	1.65	1.65	1.65	1.65	1.65	.75	
2.63	2.59	2.58	2.56	2.54	2.52	2.51	2.50	2.49	2.48	2.48	2.47	.90	7
3.51	3.44	3.41	3.38	3.34	3.32	3.30	3.27	3.27	3.25	3.24	3.23	.95	
6.31	6.16	6.07	5.99	5.91	5.86	5.82	5.75	5.74	5.70	5.67	5.65	.99	
1.62	1.61	1.60	1.60	1.59	1.59	1.59	1.58	1.58	1.58	1.58	1.58	.75	
2.46	2.42	2.40	2.38	2.36	2.35	2.34	2.32	2.32	2.31	2.30	2.29	.90	8
3.22	3.15	3.12	3.08	3.04	3.02	3.01	2.97	2.97	2.95	2.94	2.93	.95	
5.52	5.36	5.28	5.20	5.12	5.07	5.03	4.96	4.95	4.91	4.88	4.86	.99	
1.57	1.56	1.56	1.55	1.55	1.54	1.54	1.53	1.53	1.53	1.53	1.53	.75	
2.34	2.30	2.28	2.25	2.23	2.22	2.21	2.19	2.18	2.17	2.17	2.16	.90	9
3.01	2.94	2.90	2.86	2.83	2.80	2.79	2.76	2.75	2.73	2.72	2.71	.95	
4.96	4.81	4.73	4.65	4.57	4.52	4.48	4.42	4.40	4.36	4.33	4.31	.99	
1.53	1.52	1.52	1.51	1.51	1.50	1.50	1.49	1.49	1.49	1.48	1.48	.75	
2.24	2.20	2.18	2.16	2.13	2.12	2.11	2.09	2.08	2.07	2.06	2.06	.90	10
2.85	2.77	2.74	2.70	2.66	2.64	2.62	2.59	2.58	2.56	2.55	2.54	.95	
4.56	4.41	4.33	4.25	4.17	4.12	4.08	4.01	4.00	3.96	3.93	3.91	.99	
1.50	1.49	1.49	1.48	1.47	1.47	1.47	1.46	1.46	1.46	1.45	1.45	.75	
2.17	2.12	2.10	2.08	2.05	2.04	2.03	2.00	2.00	1.99	1.98	1.97	.90	11
2.72	2.65	2.61	2.57	2.53	2.51	2.49	2.46	2.45	2.43	2.42	2.40	.95	
4.25	4.10	4.02	3.94	3.86	3.81	3.78	3.71	3.69	3.66	3.62	3.60	.99	
1.48	1.47	1.46	1.45	1.45	1.44	1.44	1.43	1.43	1.43	1.42	1.42	.75	
2.10	2.06	2.04	2.01	1.99	1.97	1.96	1.94	1.93	1.92	1.91	1.90	.90	12
2.62	2.54	2.51	2.47	2.43	2.40	2.38	2.35	2.34	2.32	2.31	2.30	.95	
4.01	3.86	3.78	3.70	3.62	3.57	3.54	3.47	3.45	3.41	3.38	3.36	.99	

TABLE D.3 (*Continued*)

df for denom.	$1 - \alpha$	1	2	3	4	5	6	7	8	9	10	11	12
		\multicolumn{12}{c}{df for numerator}
13	.75	1.45	1.54	1.54	1.53	1.52	1.51	1.50	1.49	1.49	1.48	1.47	1.47
	.90	3.14	2.76	2.56	2.43	2.35	2.28	2.23	2.20	2.16	2.14	2.12	2.10
	.95	4.67	3.81	3.41	3.18	3.03	2.92	2.83	2.7.	2.71	2.67	2.63	2.60
	.99	9.07	6.70	5.74	5.21	4.86	4.62	4.44	4.30	4.19	4.10	4.02	3.96
14	.75	1.44	1.53	1.53	1.52	1.51	1.50	1.48	1.48	1.47	1.46	1.46	1.45
	.90	3.10	2.73	2.52	2.39	2.31	2.24	2.19	2.15	2.12	2.10	2.08	2.05
	.95	4.60	3.74	3.34	3.11	2.96	2.85	2.76	2.70	2.65	2.60	2.57	2.53
	.99	8.86	6.51	5.56	5.04	4.69	4.46	4.28	4.14	4.03	3.94	3.86	3.80
15	.75	1.43	1.52	1.52	1.51	1.49	1.48	1.47	1.46	1.46	1.45	1.44	1.44
	.90	3.07	2.70	2.49	2.36	2.27	2.21	2.16	2.12	2.09	2.06	2.04	2.02
	.95	4.54	3.68	3.29	3.06	2.90	2.79	2.71	2.64	2.59	2.54	2.51	2.48
	.99	8.68	6.36	5.42	4.89	4.56	4.32	4.14	4.00	3.89	3.80	3.73	3.67
16	.75	1.42	1.51	1.51	1.50	1.48	1.48	1.47	1.46	1.45	1.45	1.44	1.44
	.90	3.05	2.67	2.46	2.33	2.24	2.18	2.13	2.09	2.06	2.03	2.01	1.99
	.95	4.49	3.63	3.24	3.01	2.85	2.74	2.66	2.59	2.54	2.49	2.46	2.42
	.99	8.53	6.23	5.29	4.77	4.44	4.20	4.03	3.89	3.78	3.69	3.62	3.55
17	.75	1.42	1.51	1.50	1.49	1.47	1.46	1.45	1.44	1.43	1.43	1.42	1.41
	.90	3.03	2.64	2.44	2.31	2.22	2.15	2.10	2.06	2.03	2.00	1.98	1.96
	.95	4.45	3.59	3.20	2.96	2.81	2.70	2.61	2.55	2.49	2.45	2.41	2.38
	.99	8.40	6.11	5.18	4.67	4.34	4.10	3.93	3.79	3.68	3.59	3.52	3.46
18	.75	1.41	1.50	1.49	1.48	1.46	1.45	1.44	1.43	1.42	1.42	1.41	1.40
	.90	3.01	2.62	2.42	2.29	2.20	2.13	2.08	2.04	2.00	1.98	1.96	1.93
	.95	4.41	3.55	3.16	2.93	2.77	2.66	2.58	2.51	2.46	2.41	2.37	2.34
	.99	8.29	6.01	5.09	4.58	4.25	4.01	3.84	3.71	3.60	3.51	3.43	3.37
19	.75	1.41	1.49	1.49	1.47	1.46	1.44	1.43	1.42	1.41	1.41	1.40	1.40
	.90	2.99	2.61	2.40	2.27	2.18	2.11	2.06	2.02	1.98	1.96	1.94	1.91
	.95	4.38	3.52	3.13	2.90	2.74	2.63	2.54	2.48	2.42	2.38	2.34	2.31
	.99	8.18	5.93	5.01	4.50	4.17	3.94	3.77	3.63	3.52	3.43	3.36	3.30
20	.75	1.40	1.49	1.48	1.46	1.45	1.44	1.42	1.42	1.41	1.40	1.39	1.39
	.90	2.97	2.59	2.38	2.25	2.16	2.09	2.04	2.00	1.96	1.94	1.92	1.89
	.95	4.35	3.49	3.10	2.87	2.71	2.60	2.51	2.45	2.39	2.35	2.31	2.28
	.99	8.10	5.85	4.94	4.43	4.10	3.87	3.70	3.56	3.46	3.37	3.29	3.23
22	.75	1.40	1.48	1.47	1.45	1.44	1.42	1.41	1.40	1.39	1.39	1.38	1.37
	.90	2.95	2.56	2.35	2.22	2.13	2.06	2.01	1.97	1.93	1.90	1.88	1.86
	.95	4.30	3.44	3.05	2.82	2.66	2.55	2.46	2.40	2.34	2.30	2.26	2.23
	.99	7.95	5.72	4.82	4.31	3.99	3.76	3.59	3.45	3.35	3.26	3.18	3.12
24	.75	1.39	1.47	1.46	1.44	1.43	1.41	1.40	1.39	1.38	1.38	1.37	1.36
	.90	2.93	2.54	2.33	2.19	2.10	2.04	1.98	1.94	1.91	1.88	1.85	1.83
	.95	4.26	3.40	3.01	2.78	2.62	2.51	2.42	2.36	2.30	2.25	2.21	2.18
	.99	7.82	5.61	4.72	4.22	3.90	3.67	3.50	3.36	3.26	3.17	3.09	3.03
26	.75	1.38	1.46	1.45	1.44	1.42	1.41	1.40	1.39	1.37	1.37	1.36	1.35
	.90	2.91	2.52	2.31	2.17	2.08	2.01	1.96	1.92	1.88	1.86	1.84	1.81
	.95	4.23	3.37	2.98	2.74	2.59	2.47	2.39	2.32	2.27	2.22	2.18	2.15
	.99	7.72	5.53	4.64	4.14	3.82	3.59	3.42	3.29	3.18	3.09	3.02	2.96
28	.75	1.38	1.46	1.45	1.43	1.41	1.40	1.39	1.38	1.37	1.36	1.35	1.34
	.90	2.89	2.50	2.29	2.16	2.06	2.00	1.94	1.90	1.87	1.84	1.81	1.79
	.95	4.20	3.34	2.95	2.71	2.56	2.45	2.36	2.29	2.24	2.19	2.15	2.12
	.99	7.64	5.45	4.57	4.07	3.75	3.53	3.36	3.23	3.12	3.03	2.96	2.90

TABLE D.3 (*Continued*)

15	20	24	30	40	50	60	100	120	200	500	∞	1 − α	df for denom.
1.46	1.45	1.44	1.43	1.42	1.42	1.42	1.41	1.41	1.40	1.40	1.40	.75	
2.05	2.01	1.98	1.96	1.93	1.92	1.90	1.88	1.88	1.86	1.85	1.85	.90	13
2.53	2.46	2.42	2.38	2.34	2.31	2.30	2.26	2.25	2.23	2.22	2.21	.95	
3.82	3.66	3.59	3.51	3.43	3.38	3.34	3.27	3.25	3.22	3.19	3.17	.99	
1.44	1.43	1.42	1.41	1.41	1.40	1.40	1.39	1.39	1.39	1.38	1.38	.75	
2.01	1.96	1.94	1.91	1.89	1.87	1.86	1.83	1.83	1.82	1.80	1.80	.90	
2.46	2.39	2.35	2.31	2.27	2.24	2.22	2.19	2.18	2.16	2.14	2.13	.95	14
3.66	3.51	3.43	3.35	3.27	3.22	3.18	3.11	3.09	3.06	3.03	3.00	.99	
1.43	1.41	1.41	1.40	1.39	1.39	1.38	1.38	1.37	1.37	1.36	1.36	.75	
1.97	1.92	1.90	1.87	1.85	1.83	1.82	1.79	1.79	1.77	1.76	1.76	.90	15
2.40	2.33	2.29	2.25	2.20	2.18	2.16	2.12	2.11	2.10	2.08	2.07	.95	
3.52	3.37	3.29	3.21	3.13	3.08	3.05	2.98	2.96	2.92	2.89	2.87	.99	
1.41	1.40	1.39	1.38	1.37	1.37	1.36	1.36	1.35	1.35	1.34	1.34	.75	
1.94	1.89	1.87	1.84	1.81	1.79	1.78	1.76	1.75	1.74	1.73	1.72	.90	16
2.35	2.28	2.24	2.19	2.15	2.12	2.11	2.07	2.06	2.04	2.02	2.01	.95	
3.41	3.26	3.18	3.10	3.02	2.97	2.93	2.86	2.84	2.81	2.78	2.75	.99	
1.40	1.39	1.38	1.37	1.36	1.35	1.35	1.34	1.34	1.34	1.33	1.33	.75	
1.91	1.86	1.84	1.81	1.78	1.76	1.75	1.73	1.72	1.71	1.69	1.69	.90	17
2.31	2.23	2.19	2.15	2.10	2.08	2.06	2.02	2.01	1.99	1.97	1.96	.95	
3.31	3.16	3.08	3.00	2.92	2.87	2.83	2.76	2.75	2.71	2.68	2.65	.99	
1.39	1.38	1.37	1.36	1.35	1.34	1.34	1.33	1.33	1.32	1.32	1.32	.75	
1.89	1.84	1.81	1.78	1.75	1.74	1.72	1.70	1.69	1.68	1.67	1.66	.90	18
2.27	2.19	2.15	2.11	2.06	2.04	2.02	1.98	1.97	1.95	1.93	1.92	.95	
3.23	3.08	3.00	2.92	2.84	2.78	2.75	2.68	2.66	2.62	2.59	2.57	.99	
1.38	1.37	1.36	1.35	1.34	1.33	1.33	1.32	1.32	1.31	1.31	1.30	.75	
1.86	1.81	1.79	1.76	1.73	1.71	1.70	1.67	1.67	1.65	1.64	1.63	.90	19
2.23	2.16	2.11	2.07	2.03	2.00	1.98	1.94	1.93	1.91	1.89	1.88	.95	
3.15	3.00	2.92	2.84	2.76	2.71	2.67	2.60	2.58	2.55	2.51	2.49	.99	
1.37	1.36	1.35	1.34	1.33	1.33	1.32	1.31	1.31	1.30	1.30	1.29	.75	
1.84	1.79	1.77	1.74	1.71	1.69	1.68	1.65	1.64	1.63	1.62	1.61	.90	20
2.20	2.12	2.08	2.04	1.99	1.97	1.95	1.91	1.90	1.88	1.86	1.84	.95	
3.09	2.94	2.86	2.78	2.69	2.64	2.61	2.54	2.52	2.48	2.44	2.42	.99	
1.36	1.34	1.33	1.32	1.31	1.31	1.30	1.30	1.30	1.29	1.29	1.28	.75	
1.81	1.76	1.73	1.70	1.67	1.65	1.64	1.61	1.60	1.59	1.58	1.57	.90	22
2.15	2.07	2.03	1.98	1.94	1.91	1.89	1.85	1.84	1.82	1.80	1.78	.95	
2.98	2.83	2.75	2.67	2.58	2.53	2.50	2.42	2.40	2.36	2.33	2.31	.99	
1.35	1.33	1.32	1.31	1.30	1.29	1.29	1.28	1.28	1.27	1.27	1.26	.75	
1.78	1.73	1.70	1.67	1.64	1.62	1.61	1.58	1.57	1.56	1.54	1.53	.90	24
2.11	2.03	1.98	1.94	1.89	1.86	1.84	1.80	1.79	1.77	1.75	1.73	.95	
2.89	2.74	2.66	2.58	2.49	2.44	2.40	2.33	2.31	2.27	2.24	2.21	.99	
1.34	1.32	1.31	1.30	1.29	1.28	1.28	1.26	1.26	1.26	1.25	1.25	.75	
1.76	1.71	1.68	1.65	1.61	1.59	1.58	1.55	1.54	1.53	1.51	1.50	.90	26
2.07	1.99	1.95	1.90	1.85	1.82	1.80	1.76	1.75	1.73	1.71	1.69	.95	
2.81	2.66	2.58	2.50	2.42	2.36	2.33	2.25	2.23	2.19	2.16	2.13	.99	
1.33	1.31	1.30	1.29	1.28	1.27	1.27	1.26	1.25	1.25	1.24	1.24	.75	
1.74	1.69	1.66	1.63	1.59	1.57	1.56	1.53	1.52	1.50	1.49	1.48	.90	28
2.04	1.96	1.91	1.87	1.82	1.79	1.77	1.73	1.71	1.69	1.67	1.65	.95	
2.75	2.60	2.52	2.44	2.35	2.30	2.26	2.19	2.17	2.13	2.09	2.06	.99	

df for numerator (column span over 15 through ∞)

TABLE D.3 (*Continued*)

df for denom.	$1 - \alpha$	df for numerator											
		1	2	3	4	5	6	7	8	9	10	11	12
30	.75	1.38	1.45	1.44	1.42	1.41	1.39	1.38	1.37	1.36	1.35	1.35	1.34
	.90	2.88	2.49	2.28	2.14	2.05	1.98	1.93	1.88	1.85	1.82	1.79	1.77
	.95	4.17	3.32	2.92	2.69	2.53	2.42	2.33	2.27	2.21	2.16	2.13	2.09
	.99	7.56	5.39	4.51	4.02	3.70	3.47	3.30	3.17	3.07	2.98	2.91	2.84
40	.75	1.36	1.44	1.42	1.40	1.39	1.37	1.36	1.35	1.34	1.33	1.32	1.31
	.90	2.84	2.44	2.23	2.09	2.00	1.93	1.87	1.83	1.79	1.76	1.73	1.71
	.95	4.08	3.23	2.84	2.61	2.45	2.34	2.25	2.18	2.12	2.08	2.04	2.00
	.99	7.31	5.18	4.31	3.83	3.51	3.29	3.12	2.99	2.89	2.80	2.73	2.66
60	.75	1.35	1.42	1.41	1.38	1.37	1.35	1.33	1.32	1.31	1.30	1.29	1.29
	.90	2.79	2.39	2.18	2.04	1.95	1.87	1.82	1.77	1.74	1.71	1.68	1.66
	.95	4.00	3.15	2.76	2.53	2.37	2.25	2.17	2.10	2.04	1.99	1.95	1.92
	.99	7.08	4.98	4.13	3.65	3.34	3.12	2.95	2.82	2.72	2.63	2.56	2.50
120	.75	1.34	1.40	1.39	1.37	1.35	1.33	1.31	1.30	1.29	1.28	1.27	1.26
	.90	2.75	2.35	2.13	1.99	1.90	1.82	1.77	1.72	1.68	1.65	1.62	1.60
	.95	3.92	3.07	2.68	2.45	2.29	2.17	2.09	2.02	1.96	1.91	1.87	1.83
	.99	6.85	4.79	3.95	3.48	3.17	2.96	2.79	2.66	2.56	2.47	2.40	2.34
200	.75	1.33	1.39	1.38	1.36	1.34	1.32	1.31	1.29	1.28	1.27	1.26	1.25
	.90	2.73	2.33	2.11	1.97	1.88	1.80	1.75	1.70	1.66	1.63	1.60	1.57
	.95	3.89	3.04	2.65	2.42	2.26	2.14	2.06	1.98	1.93	1.88	1.84	1.80
	.99	6.76	4.71	3.88	3.41	3.11	2.89	2.73	2.60	2.50	2.41	2.34	2.27
∞	.75	1.32	1.39	1.37	1.35	1.33	1.31	1.29	1.28	1.27	1.25	1.24	1.24
	.90	2.71	2.30	2.08	1.94	1.85	1.77	1.72	1.67	1.63	1.60	1.57	1.55
	.95	3.84	3.00	2.60	2.37	2.21	2.10	2.01	1.94	1.88	1.83	1.79	1.75
	.99	6.63	4.61	3.78	3.32	3.02	2.80	2.64	2.51	2.41	2.32	2.25	2.18

TABLE D.3a *F* **distribution (supplement)**

df for denom.	$1 - \alpha$	df for numerator									
		1	2	3	4	5	6	7	8	9	10
2	.995	198.5	199.0	199.2	199.2	199.3	199.3	199.4	199.4	199.4	199.4
	.999	998.5	999.0	999.2	999.2	999.3	999.3	999.4	999.4	999.4	999.4
3	.995	55.55	49.80	47.47	46.20	45.39	44.84	44.43	44.13	43.88	43.69
	.999	167.0	148.5	141.1	137.1	134.6	132.8	131.6	130.6	129.9	129.2
4	.995	31.33	26.28	24.26	23.16	22.46	21.98	21.62	21.35	21.14	20.97
	.999	74.14	61.25	56.18	53.44	51.71	50.52	49.66	49.00	48.48	48.05
5	.995	22.79	18.31	16.53	15.56	14.94	14.51	14.20	13.96	13.77	13.62
	.999	47.18	37.12	33.20	31.08	29.75	28.83	28.16	27.65	27.24	26.92
6	.995	18.64	14.54	12.92	12.03	11.46	11.07	10.79	10.57	10.39	10.15
	.999	35.51	27.00	23.70	21.92	20.80	20.03	19.46	19.03	18.69	18.41
7	.995	16.24	12.40	10.88	10.05	9.52	9.16	8.89	8.68	8.51	8.38
	.999	29.25	21.69	18.77	17.20	16.21	15.52	15.02	14.63	14.33	14.28
8	.995	14.69	11.04	9.60	8.81	8.30	7.95	7.69	7.50	7.34	7.21
	.999	25.42	18.49	15.83	14.39	13.48	12.86	12.40	12.05	11.77	11.54

F distribution (Continued)†

15	20	24	30	40	50	60	100	120	200	500	∞	1 − α	df for denom.
					df for numerator								
1.32	1.30	1.29	1.28	1.27	1.26	1.26	1.25	1.24	1.24	1.23	1.23	.75	
1.72	1.67	1.64	1.61	1.57	1.55	1.54	1.51	1.50	1.48	1.47	1.46	.90	30
2.01	1.93	1.89	1.84	1.79	1.76	1.74	1.70	1.68	1.66	1.64	1.62	.95	
2.70	2.55	2.47	2.39	2.30	2.25	2.21	2.13	2.11	2.07	2.03	2.01	.99	
1.30	1.28	1.26	1.25	1.24	1.23	1.22	1.21	1.21	1.20	1.19	1.19	.75	
1.66	1.61	1.57	1.54	1.51	1.48	1.47	1.43	1.42	1.41	1.39	1.38	.90	40
1.92	1.84	1.79	1.74	1.69	1.66	1.64	1.59	1.58	1.55	1.53	1.51	.95	
2.52	2.37	2.29	2.20	2.11	2.06	2.02	1.94	1.92	1.87	1.83	1.80	.99	
1.27	1.25	1.24	1.22	1.21	1.20	1.19	1.17	1.17	1.16	1.15	1.15	.75	
1.60	1.54	1.51	1.48	1.44	1.41	1.40	1.36	1.35	1.33	1.31	1.29	.90	60
1.84	1.75	1.70	1.65	1.59	1.56	1.53	1.48	1.47	1.44	1.41	1.39	.95	
2.35	2.20	2.12	2.03	1.94	1.88	1.84	1.75	1.73	1.68	1.63	1.60	.99	
1.24	1.22	1.21	1.19	1.18	1.17	1.16	1.14	1.13	1.12	1.11	1.10	.75	
1.55	1.48	1.45	1.41	1.37	1.34	1.32	1.27	1.26	1.24	1.21	1.19	.90	120
1.75	1.66	1.61	1.55	1.50	1.46	1.43	1.37	1.35	1.32	1.28	1.25	.95	
2.19	2.03	1.95	1.86	1.76	1.70	1.66	1.56	1.53	1.48	1.42	1.38	.99	
1.23	1.21	1.20	1.18	1.16	1.14	1.12	1.11	1.10	1.09	1.08	1.06	.75	
1.52	1.46	1.42	1.38	1.34	1.31	1.28	1.24	1.22	1.20	1.17	1.14	.90	200
1.72	1.62	1.57	1.52	1.46	1.41	1.39	1.32	1.29	1.26	1.22	1.19	.95	
2.13	1.97	1.89	1.79	1.69	1.63	1.58	1.48	1.44	1.39	1.33	1.28	.99	
1.22	1.19	1.18	1.16	1.14	1.13	1.12	1.09	1.08	1.07	1.04	1.00	.75	
1.49	1.42	1.38	1.34	1.30	1.26	1.24	1.18	1.17	1.13	1.08	1.00	.90	∞
1.67	1.57	1.52	1.46	1.39	1.35	1.32	1.24	1.22	1.17	1.11	1.00	.95	
2.04	1.88	1.79	1.70	1.59	1.52	1.47	1.36	1.32	1.25	1.15	1.00	.99	

TABLE D.3a ### F distribution (supplement)

df for denom.	1 − α	df for numerator									
		1	2	3	4	5	6	7	8	9	10
9	.995	13.61	10.11	8.72	7.96	7.47	7.13	6.88	6.69	6.54	6.42
	.999	22.86	16.39	13.90	12.56	11.71	11.13	10.70	10.37	10.11	9.89
10	.995	12.83	9.43	8.08	7.34	6.87	6.54	6.30	6.12	5.97	5.85
	.999	21.04	14.91	12.56	11.28	10.48	9.93	9.52	9.20	8.96	8.75
12	.995	11.75	8.51	7.23	6.52	6.07	5.76	5.52	5.35	5.20	5.09
	.999	18.64	12.97	10.80	9.63	8.89	8.38	8.00	7.71	7.48	7.29
20	.995	9.94	6.99	5.82	5.17	4.76	4.47	4.26	4.09	3.96	3.85
	.999	14.82	9.53	8.10	7.10	6.46	6.02	5.69	5.44	5.24	5.08
40	.995	8.83	6.07	4.98	4.37	3.99	3.71	3.51	3.35	3.22	3.12
	.999	12.61	8.25	6.59	5.70	5.13	4.73	4.44	4.21	4.02	3.87
60	.995	8.49	5.80	4.73	4.14	3.76	3.49	3.29	3.13	3.01	2.90
	.999	11.97	7.77	6.17	5.31	4.76	4.37	4.09	3.86	3.69	3.54
120	·995	8.18	5.54	4.50	3.92	3.55	3.28	3.09	2.93	2.81	2.71
	.999	11.38	7.32	5.78	4.95	4.42	4.04	3.77	3.55	3.38	3.24

TABLE D.4 Distribution of the studentized range statistic†

| df for $s_{\bar{X}}$ | $1-\alpha$ | \multicolumn{14}{c}{r = number of steps between ordered means} |
		2	3	4	5	6	7	8	9	10	11	12	13	14	15
1	.95	18.0	27.0	32.8	37.1	40.4	43.1	45.4	47.4	49.1	50.6	52.0	53.2	54.3	55.4
	.99	90.0	135	164	186	202	216	227	237	246	253	260	266	272	277
2	.95	6.09	8.3	9.8	10.9	11.7	12.4	13.0	13.5	14.0	14.4	14.7	15.1	15.4	15.7
	.99	14.0	19.0	22.3	24.7	26.6	28.2	29.5	30.7	31.7	32.6	33.4	34.1	34.8	35.4
3	.95	4.50	5.91	6.82	7.50	8.04	8.48	8.85	9.18	9.46	9.72	9.95	10.2	10.4	10.5
	.99	8.26	10.6	12.2	13.3	14.2	15.0	15.6	16.2	16.7	17.1	17.5	17.9	18.2	18.5
4	.95	3.93	5.04	5.76	6.29	6.71	7.05	7.35	7.60	7.83	8.03	8.21	8.37	8.52	8.66
	.99	6.51	8.12	9.17	9.96	10.6	11.1	11.5	11.9	12.3	12.6	12.8	13.1	13.3	13.5
5	.95	3.64	4.60	5.22	5.67	6.03	6.33	6.58	6.80	6.99	7.17	7.32	7.47	7.60	7.72
	.99	5.70	6.97	7.80	8.42	8.91	9.32	9.67	9.97	10.2	10.5	10.7	10.9	11.1	11.2
6	.95	3.46	4.34	4.90	5.31	5.63	5.89	6.12	6.32	6.49	6.65	6.79	6.92	7.03	7.14
	.99	5.24	6.33	7.03	7.56	7.97	8.32	8.61	8.87	9.10	9.30	9.49	9.65	9.81	9.95
7	.95	3.34	4.16	4.69	5.06	5.36	5.61	5.82	6.00	6.16	6.30	6.43	6.55	6.66	6.76
	.99	4.95	5.92	6.54	7.01	7.37	7.68	7.94	8.17	8.37	8.55	8.71	8.86	9.00	9.12
8	.95	3.26	4.04	4.53	4.89	5.17	5.40	5.60	5.77	5.92	6.05	6.18	6.29	6.39	6.48
	.99	4.74	5.63	6.20	6.63	6.96	7.24	7.47	7.68	7.87	8.03	8.18	8.31	8.44	8.55
9	.95	3.20	3.95	4.42	4.76	5.02	5.24	5.43	5.60	5.74	5.87	5.98	6.09	6.19	6.28
	.99	4.60	5.43	5.96	6.35	6.66	6.91	7.13	7.32	7.49	7.65	7.78	7.91	8.03	8.13
10	.95	3.15	3.88	4.33	4.65	4.91	5.12	5.30	5.46	5.60	5.72	5.83	5.93	6.03	6.11
	.99	4.48	5.27	5.77	6.14	6.43	6.67	6.87	7.05	7.21	7.36	7.48	7.60	7.71	7.81
11	.95	3.11	3.82	4.26	4.57	4.82	5.03	5.20	5.35	5.49	5.61	5.71	5.81	5.90	5.99
	.99	4.39	5.14	5.62	5.97	6.25	6.48	6.67	6.84	6.99	7.13	7.26	7.36	7.46	7.56
12	.95	3.08	3.77	4.20	4.51	4.75	4.95	5.12	5.27	5.40	5.51	5.62	5.71	5.80	5.88
	.99	4.32	5.04	5.50	5.84	6.10	6.32	6.51	6.67	6.81	6.94	7.06	7.17	7.26	7.36

TABLE D.4   *(Continued)*

r = number of steps between ordered means

df for $s_{\bar{X}}$	1 − α	2	3	4	5	6	7	8	9	10	11	12	13	14	15
13	.95	3.06	3.73	4.15	4.45	4.69	4.88	5.05	5.19	5.32	5.43	5.53	5.63	5.71	5.79
	.99	4.26	4.96	5.40	5.73	5.98	6.19	6.37	6.53	6.67	6.79	6.90	7.01	7.10	7.19
14	.95	3.03	3.70	4.11	4.41	4.64	4.83	4.99	5.13	5.25	5.36	5.46	5.55	5.64	5.72
	.99	4.21	4.89	5.32	5.63	5.88	6.08	6.26	6.41	6.54	6.66	6.77	6.87	6.96	7.05
16	.95	3.00	3.65	4.05	4.33	4.56	4.74	4.90	5.03	5.15	5.26	5.35	5.44	5.52	5.59
	.99	4.13	4.78	5.19	5.49	5.72	5.92	6.08	6.22	6.35	6.46	6.56	6.66	6.74	6.82
18	.95	2.97	3.61	4.00	4.28	4.49	4.67	4.82	4.96	5.07	5.17	5.27	5.35	5.43	5.50
	.99	4.07	4.70	5.09	5.38	5.60	5.79	5.94	6.08	6.20	6.31	6.41	6.50	6.58	6.65
20	.95	2.95	3.58	3.96	4.23	4.45	4.62	4.77	4.90	5.01	5.11	5.20	5.28	5.36	5.43
	.99	4.02	4.64	5.02	5.29	5.51	5.69	5.84	5.97	6.09	6.19	6.29	6.37	6.45	6.52
24	.95	2.92	3.53	3.90	4.17	4.37	4.54	4.68	4.81	4.92	5.01	5.10	5.18	5.25	5.32
	.99	3.96	4.54	4.91	5.17	5.37	5.54	5.69	5.81	5.92	6.02	6.11	6.19	6.26	6.33
30	.95	2.89	3.49	3.84	4.10	4.30	4.46	4.60	4.72	4.83	4.92	5.00	5.08	5.15	5.21
	.99	3.89	4.45	4.80	5.05	5.24	5.40	5.54	5.56	5.76	5.85	5.93	6.01	6.08	6.14
40	.95	2.86	3.44	3.79	4.04	4.23	4.39	4.52	4.63	4.74	4.82	4.91	4.98	5.05	5.11
	.99	3.82	4.37	4.70	4.93	5.11	5.27	5.39	5.50	5.60	5.69	5.77	5.84	5.90	5.96
60	.95	2.83	3.40	3.74	3.98	4.16	4.31	4.44	4.55	4.65	4.73	4.81	4.88	4.94	5.00
	.99	3.76	4.28	4.60	4.82	4.99	5.13	5.25	5.36	5.45	5.53	5.60	5.67	5.73	5.79
120	.95	2.80	3.36	3.69	3.92	4.10	4.24	4.36	4.48	4.56	4.64	4.72	4.78	4.84	4.90
	.99	3.70	4.20	4.50	4.71	4.87	5.01	5.12	5.21	5.30	5.38	5.44	5.51	5.56	5.61
∞	.95	2.77	3.31	3.63	3.86	4.03	4.17	4.29	4.39	4.47	4.55	4.62	4.68	4.74	4.80
	.99	3.64	4.12	4.40	4.60	4.76	4.88	4.99	5.08	5.16	5.23	5.29	5.35	5.40	5.45

† This table is abridged from Table II.2 in *The Probability Integrals of the Range and of the Studentized Range*, prepared by H. Leon Harter, Donald S. Clemm, and Eugene H. Guthrie. These tables are published in WADC tech. Rep. 58–484, vol. 2, 1959, Wright Air Development Center, and are reproduced with the kind permission of the authors.

TABLE D.5 **Arcsin transformation ($\phi = 2 \arcsin \sqrt{X}$)**

X	ϕ	X	ϕ	X	ϕ	X	ϕ	X	ϕ
.001	.0633	.041	.4078	.36	1.2870	.76	2.1177	.971	2.7993
.002	.0895	.042	.4128	.37	1.3078	.77	2.1412	.972	2.8053
.003	.1096	.043	.4178	.38	1.3284	.78	2.1652	.973	2.8115
.004	.1266	.044	.4227	.39	1.3490	.79	2.1895	.974	2.8177
.005	.1415	.045	.4275	.40	1.3694	.80	2.2143	.975	2.8240
.006	.1551	.046	.4323	.41	1.3898	.81	2.2395	.976	2.8305
.007	.1675	.047	.4371	.42	1.4101	.82	2.2653	.977	2.8371
.008	.1791	.048	.4418	.43	1.4303	.83	2.2916	.978	2.8438
.009	.1900	.049	.4464	.44	1.4505	.84	2.3186	.979	2.8507
.010	.2003	.050	.4510	.45	1.4706	.85	2.3462	.980	2.8578
.011	.2101	.06	.4949	.46	1.4907	.86	2.3746	.981	2.8650
.012	.2195	.07	.5355	.47	1.5108	.87	2.4039	.982	2.8725
.013	.2285	.08	.5735	.48	1.5308	.88	2.4341	.983	2.8801
.014	.2372	.09	.6094	.49	1.5508	.89	2.4655	.984	2.8879
.015	.2456	.10	.6435	.50	1.5708	.90	2.4981	.985	2.8960
.016	.2537	.11	.6761	.51	1.5908	.91	2.5322	.986	2.9044
.017	.2615	.12	.7075	.52	1.6108	.92	2.5681	.987	2.9131
.018	.2691	.13	.7377	.53	1.6308	.93	2.6062	.988	2.9221
.019	.2766	.14	.7670	.54	1.6509	.94	2.6467	.989	2.9315
.020	.2838	.15	.7954	.55	1.6710	.95	2.6906	.990	2.9413
.021	.2909	.16	.8230	.56	1.6911	.951	2.6952	.991	2.9516
.022	.2978	.17	.8500	.57	1.7113	.952	2.6998	.992	2.9625
.023	.3045	.18	.8763	.58	1.7315	.953	2.7045	.993	2.9741
.024	.3111	.19	.9021	.59	1.7518	.954	2.7093	.994	2.9865
.025	.3176	.20	.9273	.60	1.7722	.955	2.7141	.995	3.0001
.026	.3239	.21	.9521	.61	1.7926	.956	2.7189	.996	3.0150
.027	.3301	.22	.9764	.62	1.8132	.957	2.7238	.997	3.0320
.028	.3363	.23	1.0004	.63	1.8338	.958	2.7288	.998	3.0521
.029	.3423	.24	1.0239	.64	1.8546	.959	2.7338	.999	3.0783
.030	.3482	.25	1.0472	.65	1.8755	.960	2.7389		
.031	.3540	.26	1.0701	.66	1.8965	.961	2.7440		
.032	.3597	.27	1.0928	.67	1.9177	.962	2.7492		
.033	.3654	.28	1.1152	.68	1.9391	.963	2.7545		
.034	.3709	.29	1.1374	.69	1.9606	.964	2.7598		
.035	.3764	.30	1.1593	.70	1.9823	.965	2.7652		
.036	.3818	.31	1.1810	.71	2.0042	.966	2.7707		
.037	.3871	.32	1.2025	.72	2.0264	.967	2.7762		
.038	.3924	.33	1.2239	.73	2.0488	.968	2.7819		
.039	.3976	.34	1.2451	.74	2.0715	.969	2.7876		
.040	.4027	.35	1.2661	.75	2.0944	.970	2.7934		

TABLE D.6 **Distribution of t statistic in comparing treatment means with a control†‡**

df for MS$_{error}$	$1 - \alpha$	k = number of means (including control)								
		2	3	4	5	6	7	8	9	10
5	.95	2.02	2.44	2.68	2.85	2.98	3.08	3.16	3.24	3.30
	.975	2.57	3.03	3.29	3.48	3.62	3.73	3.82	3.90	3.97
	.99	3.36	3.90	4.21	4.43	4.60	4.73	4.85	4.94	5.03
	.995	4.03	4.63	4.98	5.22	5.41	5.56	5.69	5.80	5.89
6	.95	1.94	2.34	2.56	2.71	2.83	2.92	3.00	3.07	3.12
	.975	2.45	2.86	3.10	3.26	3.39	3.49	3.57	3.64	3.71
	.99	3.14	3.61	3.88	4.07	4.21	4.33	4.43	4.51	4.59
	.995	3.71	4.21	4.51	4.71	4.87	5.00	5.10	5.20	5.28
7	.95	1.89	2.27	2.48	2.62	2.73	2.82	2.89	2.95	3.01
	.975	2.36	2.75	2.97	3.12	3.24	3.33	3.41	3.47	3.53
	.99	3.00	3.42	3.66	3.83	3.96	4.07	4.15	4.23	4.30
	.995	3.50	3.95	4.21	4.39	4.53	4.64	4.74	4.82	4.89
8	.95	1.86	2.22	2.42	2.55	2.66	2.74	2.81	2.87	2.92
	.975	2.31	2.67	2.88	3.02	3.13	3.22	3.29	3.35	3.41
	.99	2.90	3.29	3.51	3.67	3.79	3.88	3.96	4.03	4.09
	.995	3.36	3.77	4.00	4.17	4.29	4.40	4.48	4.56	4.62
9	.95	1.83	2.18	2.37	2.50	2.60	2.68	2.75	2.81	2.86
	.975	2.26	2.61	2.81	2.95	3.05	3.14	3.20	3.26	3.32
	.99	2.82	3.19	3.40	3.55	3.66	3.75	3.82	3.89	3.94
	.995	3.25	3.63	3.85	4.01	4.12	4.22	4.30	4.37	4.43
10	.95	1.81	2.15	2.34	2.47	2.56	2.64	2.70	2.76	2.81
	.975	2.23	2.57	2.76	2.89	2.99	3.07	3.14	3.19	3.24
	.99	2.76	3.11	3.31	3.45	3.56	3.64	3.71	3.78	3.83
	.995	3.17	3.53	3.74	3.88	3.99	4.08	4.16	4.22	4.28
11	.95	1.80	2.13	2.31	2.44	2.53	2.60	2.67	2.72	2.77
	.975	2.20	2.53	2.72	2.84	2.94	3.02	3.08	3.14	3.19
	.99	2.72	3.06	3.25	3.38	3.48	3.56	3.63	3.69	3.74
	.995	3.11	3.45	3.65	3.79	3.89	3.98	4.05	4.11	4.16
12	.95	1.78	2.11	2.29	2.41	2.50	2.58	2.64	2.69	2.74
	.975	2.18	2.50	2.68	2.81	2.90	2.98	3.04	3.09	3.14
	.99	2.68	3.01	3.19	3.32	3.42	3.50	3.56	3.62	3.67
	.995	3.05	3.39	3.58	3.71	3.81	3.89	3.96	4.02	4.07
13	.95	1.77	2.09	2.27	2.39	2.48	2.55	2.61	2.66	2.71
	.975	2.16	2.48	2.65	2.78	2.87	2.94	3.00	3.06	3.10
	.99	2.65	2.97	3.15	3.27	3.37	3.44	3.51	3.56	3.61
	.995	3.01	3.33	3.52	3.65	3.74	3.82	3.89	3.94	3.99
14	.95	1.76	2.08	2.25	2.37	2.46	2.53	2.59	2.64	2.69
	.975	2.14	2.46	2.63	2.75	2.84	2.91	2.97	3.02	3.07
	.99	2.62	2.94	3.11	3.23	3.32	3.40	3.46	3.51	3.56
	.995	2.98	3.29	3.47	3.59	3.69	3.76	3.83	3.88	3.93

TABLE D.6 (*Continued*)†‡

df for MS_{error}	$1 - \alpha$	k = number of means (including control)								
		2	3	4	5	6	7	8	9	10
16	.95	1.75	2.06	2.23	2.34	2.43	2.50	2.56	2.61	2.65
	.975	2.12	2.42	2.59	2.71	2.80	2.87	2.92	2.97	3.02
	.99	2.58	2.88	3.05	3.17	3.26	3.33	3.39	3.44	3.48
	.995	2.92	3.22	3.39	3.51	3.60	3.67	3.73	3.78	3.83
18	.95	1.73	2.04	2.21	2.32	2.41	2.48	2.53	2.58	2.62
	.975	2.10	2.40	2.56	2.68	2.76	2.83	2.89	2.94	2.98
	.99	2.55	2.84	3.01	3.12	3.21	3.27	3.33	3.38	3.42
	.995	2.88	3.17	3.33	3.44	3.53	3.60	3.66	3.71	3.75
20	.95	1.72	2.03	2.19	2.30	2.39	2.46	2.51	2.56	2.60
	.975	2.09	2.38	2.54	2.65	2.73	2.80	2.86	2.90	2.95
	.99	2.53	2.81	2.97	3.08	3.17	3.23	3.29	3.34	3.38
	.995	2.85	3.13	3.29	3.40	3.48	3.55	3.60	3.65	3.69
24	.95	1.71	2.01	2.17	2.28	2.36	2.43	2.48	2.53	2.57
	.975	2.06	2.35	2.51	2.61	2.70	2.76	2.81	2.86	2.90
	.99	2.49	2.77	2.92	3.03	3.11	3.17	3.22	3.27	3.31
	.995	2.80	3.07	3.22	3.32	3.40	3.47	3.52	3.57	3.61
30	.95	1.70	1.99	2.15	2.25	2.33	2.40	2.45	2.50	2.54
	.975	2.04	2.32	2.47	2.58	2.66	2.72	2.77	2.82	2.86
	.99	2.46	2.72	2.87	2.97	3.05	3.11	3.16	3.21	3.24
	.995	2.75	3.01	3.15	3.25	3.33	3.39	3.44	3.49	3.52
40	.95	1.68	1.97	2.13	2.23	2.31	2.37	2.42	2.47	2.51
	.975	2.02	2.29	2.44	2.54	2.62	2.68	2.73	2.77	2.81
	.99	2.42	2.68	2.82	2.92	2.99	3.05	3.10	3.14	3.18
	.995	2.70	2.95	3.09	3.19	3.26	3.32	3.37	3.41	3.44
60	.95	1.67	1.95	2.10	2.21	2.28	2.35	2.39	2.44	2.48
	.975	2.00	2.27	2.41	2.51	2.58	2.64	2.69	2.73	2.77
	.99	2.39	2.64	2.78	2.87	2.94	3.00	3.04	3.08	3.12
	.995	2.66	2.90	3.03	3.12	3.19	3.25	3.29	3.33	3.37
120	.95	1.66	1.93	2.08	2.18	2.26	2.32	2.37	2.41	2.45
	.975	1.98	2.24	2.38	2.47	2.55	2.60	2.65	2.69	2.73
	.99	2.36	2.60	2.73	2.82	2.89	2.94	2.99	3.03	3.06
	.995	2.62	2.85	2.97	3.06	3.12	3.18	3.22	3.26	3.29
∞	.95	1.64	1.92	2.06	2.16	2.23	2.29	2.34	2.38	2.42
	.975	1.96	2.21	2.35	2.44	2.51	2.57	2.61	2.65	2.69
	.99	2.33	2.56	2.68	2.77	2.84	2.89	2.93	2.97	3.00
	.995	2.58	2.79	2.92	3.00	3.06	3.11	3.15	3.19	3.22

† Entries in rows .975 and .995 are for two-sided simultaneous confidence intervals with α = .05 and .01, respectively. Entries in rows .95 and .99 are for one-sided confidence simultaneous intervals with α = .05 and 0.01, respectively.

‡ This table is reproduced from: A multiple comparison procedure for comparing several treatments with a control. *Journal of the American Statistical Association*, 1955, **50**, 1096–1121, and New tables for multiple comparisons with a control. *Biometrics*, 1964, **20**, 482–491, with the permission of the author, C. W. Dunnett, and the editors.

TABLE D.7 **Distribution of $F_{\max}$ statistic†**

df for s_X^2	$1 - \alpha$	k = number of variances								
		2	3	4	5	6	7	8	9	10
4	.95	9.60	15.5	20.6	25.2	29.5	33.6	37.5	41.4	44.6
	.99	23.2	37.	49.	59.	69.	79.	89.	97.	106.
5	.95	7.15	10.8	13.7	16.3	18.7	20.8	22.9	24.7	26.5
	.99	14.9	22.	28.	33.	38.	42.	46.	50.	54.
6	.95	5.82	8.38	10.4	12.1	13.7	15.0	16.3	17.5	18.6
	.99	11.1	15.5	19.1	22.	25.	27.	30.	32.	34.
7	.95	4.99	6.94	8.44	9.70	10.8	11.8	12.7	13.5	14.3
	.99	8.89	12.1	14.5	16.5	18.4	20.	22.	23.	24.
8	.95	4.43	6.00	7.18	8.12	9.03	9.78	10.5	11.1	11.7
	.99	7.50	9.9	11.7	13.2	14.5	15.8	16.9	17.9	18.9
9	.95	4.03	5.34	6.31	7.11	7.80	8.41	8.95	9.45	9.91
	.99	6.54	8.5	9.9	11.1	12.1	13.1	13.9	14.7	15.3
10	.95	3.72	4.85	5.67	6.34	6.92	7.42	7.87	8.28	8.66
	.99	5.85	7.4	8.6	9.6	10.4	11.1	11.8	12.4	12.9
12	.95	3.28	4.16	4.79	5.30	5.72	6.09	6.42	6.72	7.00
	.99	4.91	6.1	6.9	7.6	8.2	8.7	9.1	9.5	9.9
15	.95	2.86	3.54	4.01	4.37	4.68	4.95	5.19	5.40	5.59
	.99	4.07	4.9	5.5	6.0	6.4	6.7	7.1	7.3	7.5
20	.95	2.46	2.95	3.29	3.54	3.76	3.94	4.10	4.24	4.37
	.99	3.32	3.8	4.3	4.6	4.9	5.1	5.3	5.5	5.6
30	.95	2.07	2.40	2.61	2.78	2.91	3.02	3.12	3.21	3.29
	.99	2.63	3.0	3.3	3.4	3.6	3.7	3.8	3.9	4.0
60	.95	1.67	1.85	1.96	2.04	2.11	2.17	2.22	2.26	2.30
	.99	1.96	2.2	2.3	2.4	2.4	2.5	2.5	2.6	2.6
∞	.95	1.00	1.00	1.00	1.00	1.00	1.00	1.00	1.00	1.00
	.99	1.00	1.00	1.00	1.00	1.00	1.00	1.00	1.00	1.00

† This table is abridged from Table 31 in *Biometrika Tables for Statisticians*, vol. 1. (2d ed.) New York: Cambridge, 1958. Edited by E. S. Pearson and H. O. Hartley. Reproduced with the kind permission of E. S. Pearson and the trustees of *Biometrika*.

TABLE D.8   Critical values for Cochran's test for homogeneity of variance†

$$C = (\text{largest } s^2)/(\sum s_j^2)$$

df for s_j^2	$1 - \alpha$	$k = $ number of variances										
		2	3	4	5	6	7	8	9	10	15	20
1	.95	.9985	.9669	.9065	.8412	.7808	.7271	.6798	.6385	.6020	.4709	.3894
	.99	.9999	.9933	.9676	.9279	.8828	.8376	.7945	.7544	.7175	.5747	.4799
2	.95	.9750	.8709	.7679	.6838	.6161	.5612	.5157	.4775	.4450	.3346	.2705
	.99	.9950	.9423	.8643	.7885	.7218	.6644	.6152	.5727	.5358	.4069	.3297
3	.95	.9392	.7977	.6841	.5981	.5321	.4800	.4377	.4027	.3733	.2758	.2205
	.99	.9794	.8831	.7814	.6957	.6258	.5685	.5209	.4810	.4469	.3317	.2654
4	.95	.9057	.7457	.6287	.5441	.4803	.4307	.3910	.3584	.3311	.2419	.1921
	.99	.9586	.8335	.7212	.6329	.5635	.5080	.4627	.4251	.3934	.2882	.2288
5	.95	.8772	.7071	.5895	.5065	.4447	.3974	.3595	.3286	.3029	.2195	.1735
	.99	.9373	.7933	.6761	.5875	.5195	.4659	.4226	.3870	.3572	.2593	.2048
6	.95	.8534	.6771	.5598	.4783	.4184	.3726	.3362	.3067	.2823	.2034	.1602
	.99	.9172	.7606	.6410	.5531	.4866	.4347	.3932	.3592	.3308	.2386	.1877
7	.95	.8332	.6530	.5365	.4564	.3980	.3535	.3185	.2901	.2666	.1911	.1501
	.99	.8988	.7335	.6129	.5259	.4608	.4105	.3704	.3378	.3106	.2228	.1748
8	.95	.8159	.6333	.5175	.4387	.3817	.3384	.3043	.2768	.2541	.1815	.1422
	.99	.8823	.7107	.5897	.5037	.4401	.3911	.3522	.3207	.2945	.2104	.1646
9	.95	.8010	.6167	.5017	.4241	.3682	.3259	.2926	.2659	.2439	.1736	.1357
	.99	.8674	.6912	.5702	.4854	.4229	.3751	.3373	.3067	.2813	.2002	.1567
16	.95	.7341	.5466	.4366	.3645	.3135	.2756	.2462	.2226	.2032	.1429	.1108
	.99	.7949	.6059	.4884	.4094	.3529	.3105	.2779	.2514	.2297	.1612	.1248
36	.95	.6602	.4748	.3720	.3066	.2612	.2278	.2022	.1820	.1655	.1144	.0879
	.99	.7067	.5153	.4057	.3351	.2858	.2494	.2214	.1992	.1811	.1251	.0960
144	.95	.5813	.4031	.3093	.2513	.2119	.1833	.1616	.1446	.1308	.0889	.0675
	.99	.6062	.4230	.3251	.2644	.2229	.1929	.1700	.1521	.1376	.0934	.0709

† Reproduced with permission from C. Eisenhart, M. W. Hastay, and W. A. Wallis, *Techniques of Statistical Analysis*, chap. 15. New York: McGraw-Hill, 1947.

TABLE D.9 **Chi-square distribution†**

df	Percentile point						
	50	75	90	95	97.5	99	99.5
1	.46	1.3	2.7	3.8	5.0	6.6	7.9
2	1.4	2.8	4.6	6.0	7.4	9.2	10.6
3	2.4	4.1	6.3	7.8	9.4	11.3	12.8
4	3.4	5.4	7.8	9.5	11.1	13.3	14.9
5	4.4	6.6	9.2	11.1	12.8	15.1	16.7
6	5.4	7.8	10.6	12.6	14.4	16.8	18.5
7	6.4	9.0	12.0	14.1	16.0	18.5	20.3
8	7.3	10.2	13.4	15.5	17.5	20.1	22.0
9	8.3	11.4	14.7	16.9	19.0	21.7	23.6
10	9.3	12.5	16.0	18.3	20.5	23.2	25.2
11	10.3	13.7	17.3	19.7	21.9	24.7	26.8
12	11.3	14.8	18.5	21.0	23.3	26.2	28.3
13	12.3	16.0	19.8	22.4	24.7	27.7	29.8
14	13.3	17.1	21.1	23.7	26.1	29.1	31.3
15	14.3	18.2	22.3	25.0	27.5	30.6	32.8
16	15.3	19.4	23.5	26.3	28.8	32.0	34.3
17	16.3	20.5	24.8	27.6	30.2	33.4	35.7
18	17.3	21.6	26.0	28.9	31.5	34.8	37.2
19	18.3	22.7	27.2	30.1	32.9	36.2	38.6
20	19.3	23.8	28.4	31.4	34.2	37.6	40.0
21	20.3	24.9	29.6	32.7	35.5	38.9	41.4
22	21.3	26.0	30.8	33.9	36.8	40.3	42.8
23	22.3	27.1	32.0	35.2	38.1	41.6	44.2
24	23.3	28.2	33.2	36.4	39.4	43.0	45.6
25	24.3	29.3	34.4	37.7	40.6	44.3	46.9
26	25.3	30.4	35.6	38.9	41.9	45.6	48.3
27	26.3	31.5	36.7	40.1	43.2	47.0	49.6
28	27.3	32.6	37.9	41.3	44.5	48.3	51.0
29	28.3	33.7	39.1	42.6	45.7	49.6	52.3
30	29.3	34.8	40.3	43.8	47.0	50.9	53.7
40	39.3	45.6	51.8	55.8	59.3	63.7	66.8
60	59.3	67.0	74.4	79.1	83.3	88.4	92.0
100	99.3	109.1	118.5	124.3	129.6	135.8	140.2

For df > 30, $\chi^2_{1-\alpha} \doteq [\sqrt{2(\mathrm{df}) - 1} + z_{1-\alpha}]^2/2$.
For example, when df $= 60$,

$$\chi^2_{.95} = [\sqrt{2(60) - 1} + 1.645]^2/2 = 79.$$

† This table is abridged from Table 8 in *Biometrika Tables for Statisticians*, vol. 1. (2d ed.) New York: Cambridge, 1958. Edited by E. S. Pearson and H. O. Hartley. Reproduced with the kind permission of E. S. Pearson and the trustees of *Biometrika*.

TABLE D.10 **Coefficients of orthogonal polynomials**

k	Polynomial	$X = 1$	2	3	4	5	6	7	8	9	10	$\Sigma \xi'^2$	λ
3	Linear	−1	0	1								2	1
	Quadratic	1	−2	1								6	3
	Linear	−3	−1	1	3							20	2
4	Quadratic	1	−1	−1	1							4	1
	Cubic	−1	3	−3	1							20	$10/3$
	Linear	−2	−1	0	1	2						10	1
5	Quadratic	2	−1	−2	−1	2						14	1
	Cubic	−1	2	0	−2	1						10	$5/6$
	Quartic	1	−4	6	−4	1						70	$35/12$
	Linear	−5	−3	−1	1	3	5					70	2
6	Quadratic	5	−1	−4	−4	−1	5					84	$3/2$
	Cubic	−5	7	4	−4	−7	5					180	$5/3$
	Quartic	1	−3	2	2	−3	1					28	$7/12$
	Linear	−3	−2	−1	0	1	2	3				28	1
7	Quadratic	5	0	−3	−4	−3	0	5				84	1
	Cubic	−1	1	1	0	−1	−1	1				6	$1/6$
	Quartic	3	−7	1	6	1	−7	3				154	$7/12$
	Linear	−7	−5	−3	−1	1	3	5	7			168	2
	Quadratic	7	1	−3	−5	−5	−3	1	7			168	1
8	Cubic	−7	5	7	3	−3	−7	−5	7			264	$2/3$
	Quartic	7	−13	−3	9	9	−3	−13	7			616	$7/12$
	Quintic	−7	23	−17	−15	15	17	−23	7			2184	$7/10$
	Linear	−4	−3	−2	−1	0	1	2	3	4		60	1
	Quadratic	28	7	−8	−17	−20	−17	−8	7	28		2772	3
9	Cubic	−14	7	13	9	0	−9	−13	−7	14		990	$5/6$
	Quartic	14	−21	−11	9	18	9	−11	−21	14		2002	$7/12$
	Quintic	−4	11	−4	−9	0	9	4	−11	4		468	$3/20$
	Linear	−9	−7	−5	−3	−1	1	3	5	7	9	330	2
	Quadratic	6	2	−1	−3	−4	−4	−3	−1	2	6	132	$1/2$
10	Cubic	−42	14	35	31	12	−12	−31	−35	−14	42	8580	$5/3$
	Quartic	18	−22	−17	3	18	18	3	−17	−22	18	2860	$5/12$
	Quintic	−6	14	−1	−11	−6	6	11	1	−14	6	780	$1/10$

TABLE D.11   Curves of constant power for tests on main effects†

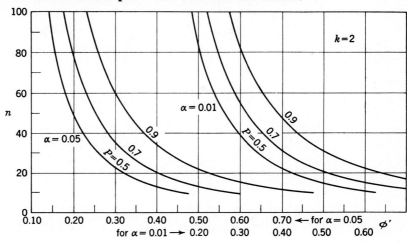

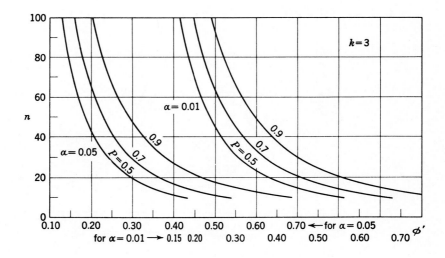

TABLE D.11 **Curves of constant power for tests on main effects** (*Continued*)†

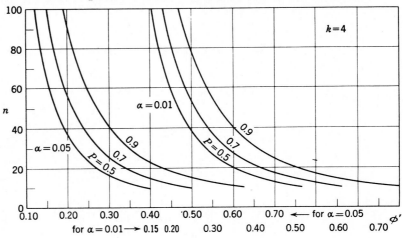

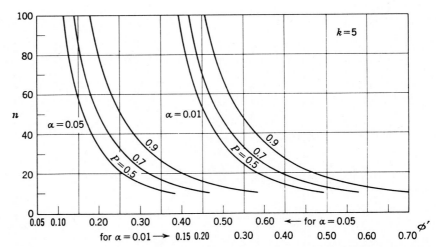

† Reproduced from L. S. Feldt and M. W. Mahmoud, Power function charts for specification of sample size in analysis of variance. *Psychometrika*, 1958, 23, 201–210, with permission of the editor.

TABLE D.12 Random permutations of 16 numbers

12	11	16	11	7	4	13	7	16	16	14	15	7	13	13	3
5	9	9	3	1	2	5	6	3	5	11	7	13	16	7	16
13	15	2	5	6	8	2	11	6	10	13	8	2	9	15	10
16	4	5	16	9	11	12	13	4	8	15	5	8	12	3	5
10	12	10	7	14	15	14	10	12	3	5	14	7	3	9	4
8	14	15	14	12	7	1	7	13	5	3	12	5	14	11	7
3	16	3	6	16	6	8	3	9	11	7	10	6	2	6	6
1	1	8	9	2	16	10	14	14	2	4	16	2	1	15	5
15	3	12	8	3	10	11	8	2	14	10	4	15	4	11	8
4	10	4	4	15	13	15	1	6	1	15	6	13	16	12	15
7	8	7	15	10	3	15	2	1	12	9	3	10	4	8	4
14	13	6	12	5	12	4	16	4	9	12	14	4	3	10	1
11	5	14	2	14	14	6	15	10	8	16	11	1	2	10	2
9	7	11	13	8	1	7	12	13	6	2	13	11	7	16	9

TABLE D.12   Random permutations of 16 numbers (*Continued*)

```
 12 13 16   6 12   10  5 12   1 10    4  6   6  1  4    7 13   2 10    8 16   1 13 16   11 15   9  2 12    4 10  10  1  9    6 15  15  1 13    1 16   2
  6  1 13   2  7   12 16 10  11 13    8  2  15  7  8   16  1  14  3    6  1   2  5 14   12 11   5  7  4    7 12   8  6 10   12  7   6 16  7   16 12  12
 10 14 11  12  4   15 13 16   3 11    7 16  11  8  6   16  4  15  4    3 12  11 14  9    8 10  13  5  1    7  9   5  9 14   10  3  16  6  7   10 16   7
  7  7  2  10  8   16 13 15   9  4   11  3   8 16  4    9  2  16 14    4  4  15  8  4    4  4  11 10  9    8 15  12 13 11    5 14  14 15  8    8  7   5
  2 16 10   8 11   14  4  3   6  1   14  9   2 16  9   11  7   9  3   11 10  12 12 10   16 16  14 15 12    9  7   8  4 15   13 12  12 10 14    3 16  14
 11  3  6   4 15    1  3  6   4 13   13  8  14 11  1    6  5   1  8   15  8  10  6  3    2  1   1 14  6   10 14   4 13 11    7  4   5  3 10    4  4  13
  9 11  1   3  6    2 14 11   7  4    9 11   7  3 13    4  9   3  7    7 11   4  4 13    9  3   3 11  2   16  3  11 14 12    3 11   4 10 16    9 14   6
 16 15  3   7 16    4 15 14   2  2    6  4  16  2  7    1  8   8 11   10 10   8  5 14   10 15  15 16 14    4  1   9 11 15   13  6   9 11 16    1  7  14
 13 10  7   9  3    3 16 12   5 16   16 15   4 10  3   14 13   6  1    8 15   9  3  7    6  4   6  1  3   11 15  15 11  7   16  9   3 14 10    7 11  15
  4 12 12   5 16    5  7 10  12  5    1  2   3 13 12    5 10   2  3    2 16   1  7 12    3  8   7 16  8    1 13  16  4  8    2  9   5 12  6   14  5  16
  5  9  5  11  6    9  8 14   8  3   11 12   5 14 16    2 16  13 15    9  8   7 15 11    5 12   2 13 16   14  4   8  3  6    9  7  10  9  2    6 12   1
 15  6  9  13  5   13 11  2   9 13    3  5  11  6  5   16 12  12  2   15  5  14 11  5   13  9   4  8 11    8  8   2  1 13    2 16   9  7 11    5  3  10
  3  4 15  11 13    8 14  8   4 15   15  7   8  4  2   13 13   5 13    6 11   3 13 12   15 11  10  3  5   12 10  13 15  9   16 11  11  5 14    8  5   9
  1  2 13   6  1   14  4  5  15  7   12  9   2  5  7    3 12  14  6   11 16  16  9  4    7 15   5  2  9    5  6   3 10  3   15  2  14 11 13    4 13   4
 14  8  2   2  1    9  7  5  16  2    5 11   7 10 15    5 15  11  5    1  7  13  1  2   14  8  16  9 13   16  5   6 12 10    2  3   4 14 15    7 14   4
  8  5  5   1  2    7 10  1   9 13    4  7  10  9  6    8  3   7  2   11  6   7 13 10    4 14   4 13 10    6  4  12 11  6   11  7  13 10  4   13  4   4
```

TABLE D.13 **Noncentral t distribution†**

Values of the noncentrality parameter for a one-sided test with $\alpha = 0.050$

f	β = type 2 error										
	.01	.05	.10	.20	.30	.40	.50	.60	.70	.80	.90
1	16.47	12.53	10.51	8.19	6.63	5.38	4.31	3.35	2.46	1.60	.64
2	6.88	5.52	4.81	3.98	3.40	2.92	2.49	2.07	1.63	1.15	.50
3	5.47	4.46	3.93	3.30	2.85	2.48	2.13	1.79	1.43	1.02	.46
4	4.95	4.07	3.60	3.04	2.64	2.30	1.99	1.67	1.34	.96	.43
5	4.70	3.87	3.43	2.90	2.53	2.21	1.91	1.61	1.29	.92	.42
6	4.55	3.75	3.33	2.82	2.46	2.15	1.86	1.57	1.26	.90	.41
7	4.45	3.67	3.26	2.77	2.41	2.11	1.82	1.54	1.24	.89	.40
8	4.38	3.62	3.21	2.73	2.38	2.08	1.80	1.52	1.22	.88	.40
9	4.32	3.58	3.18	2.70	2.35	2.06	1.78	1.51	1.21	.87	.39
10	4.28	3.54	3.15	2.67	2.33	2.04	1.77	1.49	1.20	.86	.39
11	4.25	3.52	3.13	2.65	2.31	2.02	1.75	1.48	1.19	.86	.39
12	4.22	3.50	3.11	2.64	2.30	2.01	1.74	1.47	1.19	.85	.38
13	4.20	3.48	3.09	2.63	2.29	2.00	1.74	1.47	1.18	.85	.38
14	4.18	3.46	3.08	2.62	2.28	2.00	1.73	1.46	1.18	.84	.38
15	4.17	3.45	3.07	2.61	2.27	1.99	1.72	1.46	1.17	.84	.38
16	4.16	3.44	3.06	2.60	2.27	1.98	1.72	1.45	1.17	.84	.38
17	4.14	3.43	3.05	2.59	2.26	1.98	1.71	1.45	1.17	.84	.38
18	4.13	3.42	3.04	2.59	2.26	1.97	1.71	1.45	1.16	.83	.38
19	4.12	3.41	3.04	2.58	2.25	1.97	1.71	1.44	1.16	.83	.38
20	4.12	3.41	3.03	2.58	2.25	1.97	1.70	1.44	1.16	.83	.38
21	4.11	3.40	3.03	2.57	2.24	1.96	1.70	1.44	1.16	.83	.38
22	4.10	3.40	3.02	2.57	2.24	1.96	1.70	1.44	1.16	.83	.37
23	4.10	3.39	3.02	2.56	2.24	1.96	1.69	1.43	1.15	.83	.37
24	4.09	3.39	3.01	2.56	2.23	1.95	1.69	1.43	1.15	.83	.37
25	4.09	3.38	3.01	2.56	2.23	1.95	1.69	1.43	1.15	.83	.37
26	4.08	3.38	3.01	2.55	2.23	1.95	1.69	1.43	1.15	.82	.37
27	4.08	3.38	3.00	2.55	2.23	1.95	1.69	1.43	1.15	.82	.37
28	4.07	3.37	3.00	2.55	2.22	1.95	1.69	1.43	1.15	.82	.37
29	4.07	3.37	3.00	2.55	2.22	1.94	1.68	1.42	1.15	.82	.37
30	4.07	3.37	3.00	2.54	2.22	1.94	1.68	1.42	1.15	.82	.37
40	4.04	3.35	2.98	2.53	2.21	1.93	1.67	1.42	1.14	.82	.37
60	4.02	3.33	2.96	2.52	2.19	1.92	1.66	1.41	1.13	.81	.37
100	4.00	3.31	2.95	2.50	2.18	1.91	1.66	1.40	1.13	.81	.37
∞	3.97	3.29	2.93	2.49	2.17	1.90	1.64	1.39	1.12	.80	.36

$$\Pr\left[\text{noncentral } t > t_{1-\alpha} \mid \delta = (\mu_1 - \mu_0)(\sqrt{n}/\sigma)\right] = 1 - \beta.$$

† This table is reproduced from: The power of Student's t test. *Journal of the American Statistical Association*, 1965, **60,** 320–333, with the permission of the author, D. B. Owen, and the editors.

TABLE D.13 (*Continued*)

Values of the noncentrality parameter for a one-sided test with $\alpha = 0.025$

f	β = type 2 error										
	.01	.05	.10	.20	.30	.40	.50	.60	.70	.80	.90
1	32.83	24.98	20.96	16.33	13.21	10.73	8.60	6.68	4.91	3.22	1.58
2	9.67	7.77	6.80	5.65	4.86	4.21	3.63	3.07	2.50	1.88	1.09
3	6.88	5.65	5.01	4.26	3.72	3.28	2.87	2.47	2.05	1.57	.94
4	5.94	4.93	4.40	3.76	3.31	2.93	2.58	2.23	1.86	1.44	.87
5	5.49	4.57	4.09	3.51	3.10	2.75	2.43	2.11	1.76	1.37	.82
6	5.22	4.37	3.91	3.37	2.98	2.64	2.34	2.03	1.70	1.32	.80
7	5.06	4.23	3.80	3.27	2.89	2.57	2.27	1.98	1.66	1.29	.78
8	4.94	4.14	3.71	3.20	2.83	2.52	2.23	1.94	1.63	1.27	.77
9	4.85	4.07	3.65	3.15	2.79	2.48	2.20	1.91	1.60	1.25	.76
10	4.78	4.01	3.60	3.11	2.75	2.45	2.17	1.89	1.59	1.23	.75
11	4.73	3.97	3.57	3.08	2.73	2.43	2.15	1.87	1.57	1.22	.74
12	4.69	3.93	3.54	3.05	2.70	2.41	2.13	1.85	1.56	1.21	.74
13	4.65	3.91	3.51	3.03	2.69	2.39	2.12	1.84	1.55	1.21	.73
14	4.62	3.88	3.49	3.01	2.67	2.38	2.11	1.83	1.54	1.20	.73
15	4.60	3.86	3.47	3.00	2.66	2.37	2.09	1.82	1.53	1.19	.72
16	4.58	3.84	3.46	2.98	2.65	2.36	2.09	1.81	1.53	1.19	.72
17	4.56	3.83	3.44	2.97	2.64	2.35	2.08	1.81	1.52	1.18	.72
18	4.54	3.82	3.43	2.96	2.63	2.34	2.07	1.80	1.52	1.18	.72
19	4.52	3.80	3.42	2.95	2.61	2.33	2.06	1.80	1.51	1.17	.71
20	4.51	3.79	3.41	2.95	2.61	2.33	2.06	1.79	1.51	1.17	.71
21	4.50	3.78	3.40	2.93	2.60	2.32	2.05	1.79	1.50	1.17	.71
22	4.49	3.77	3.39	2.93	2.60	2.32	2.05	1.78	1.50	1.17	.71
23	4.48	3.77	3.39	2.93	2.59	2.31	2.05	1.78	1.50	1.17	.71
24	4.47	3.76	3.38	2.92	2.59	2.31	2.04	1.78	1.50	1.16	.71
25	4.46	3.75	3.37	2.92	2.58	2.30	2.04	1.77	1.49	1.16	.71
26	4.46	3.75	3.37	2.92	2.58	2.30	2.04	1.77	1.49	1.16	.70
27	4.45	3.74	3.36	2.91	2.58	2.30	2.03	1.77	1.49	1.16	.70
28	4.44	3.73	3.36	2.90	2.57	2.29	2.03	1.77	1.49	1.16	.70
29	4.44	3.73	3.35	2.90	2.57	2.29	2.03	1.77	1.48	1.16	.70
30	4.43	3.73	3.35	2.90	2.57	2.29	2.02	1.76	1.48	1.16	.70
40	4.39	3.69	3.32	2.87	2.55	2.27	2.01	1.75	1.47	1.15	.69
60	4.36	3.66	3.29	2.85	2.53	2.25	1.99	1.73	1.46	1.14	.69
100	4.33	3.64	3.27	2.83	2.51	2.23	1.98	1.73	1.45	1.12	.68
∞	4.29	3.60	3.24	2.80	2.48	2.21	1.96	1.71	1.44	1.12	.68

$$\Pr[\text{noncentral } t > t_{1-\alpha} \mid \delta = (\mu_1 - \mu_0)(\sqrt{n}/\sigma)] = 1 - \beta.$$

TABLE D.13   (*Continued*)
Values of the noncentrality parameter for a one-sided test with $\alpha = 0.010$

f	β = type 2 error										
	.01	.05	.10	.20	.30	.40	.50	.60	.70	.80	.90
1	82.00	62.40	52.37	40.80	33.00	26.79	21.47	16.69	12.27	8.07	4.00
2	15.22	12.26	10.74	8.96	7.73	6.73	5.83	4.98	4.12	3.20	2.08
3	9.34	7.71	6.86	5.87	5.17	4.59	4.07	3.56	3.03	2.44	1.66
4	7.52	6.28	5.64	4.88	4.34	3.88	3.47	3.06	2.63	2.14	1.48
5	6.68	5.62	5.07	4.40	3.93	3.54	3.17	2.81	2.42	1.98	1.38
6	6.21	5.25	4.74	4.13	3.70	3.33	2.99	2.66	2.30	1.88	1.32
7	5.91	5.01	4.53	3.96	3.55	3.20	2.88	2.56	2.22	1.82	1.27
8	5.71	4.85	4.39	3.84	3.44	3.11	2.80	2.49	2.16	1.77	1.24
9	5.56	4.72	4.28	3.75	3.37	3.04	2.74	2.43	2.11	1.74	1.22
10	5.45	4.63	4.20	3.68	3.31	2.99	2.69	2.39	2.08	1.71	1.20
11	5.36	4.56	4.14	3.63	3.26	2.94	2.65	2.36	2.05	1.69	1.18
12	5.29	4.50	4.09	3.58	3.22	2.91	2.62	2.33	2.03	1.67	1.17
13	5.23	4.46	4.04	3.55	3.19	2.88	2.60	2.31	2.01	1.65	1.16
14	5.18	4.42	4.01	3.51	3.16	2.86	2.57	2.29	1.99	1.64	1.15
15	5.14	4.38	3.98	3.49	3.14	2.84	2.56	2.28	1.98	1.63	1.14
16	5.11	4.35	3.95	3.47	3.12	2.82	2.54	2.26	1.97	1.62	1.14
17	5.08	4.33	3.93	3.45	3.10	2.80	2.53	2.25	1.96	1.61	1.13
18	5.05	4.31	3.91	3.43	3.09	2.79	2.52	2.24	1.95	1.60	1.13
19	5.03	4.29	3.89	3.42	3.07	2.78	2.50	2.23	1.94	1.60	1.12
20	5.01	4.27	3.88	3.40	3.06	2.77	2.50	2.22	1.93	1.59	1.12
21	4.99	4.25	3.86	3.39	3.05	2.76	2.49	2.22	1.92	1.59	1.11
22	4.97	4.24	3.85	3.38	3.04	2.75	2.48	2.21	1.92	1.58	1.11
23	4.96	4.23	3.84	3.37	3.03	2.74	2.47	2.20	1.91	1.58	1.11
24	4.94	4.22	3.83	3.36	3.02	2.73	2.47	2.20	1.91	1.57	1.11
25	4.93	4.20	3.82	3.35	3.02	2.73	2.46	2.19	1.90	1.57	1.10
26	4.92	4.19	3.81	3.34	3.01	2.72	2.45	2.19	1.90	1.57	1.10
27	4.91	4.19	3.80	3.34	3.00	2.72	2.45	2.18	1.90	1.56	1.10
28	4.90	4.18	3.79	3.33	3.00	2.71	2.44	2.18	1.89	1.56	1.10
29	4.89	4.17	3.79	3.32	2.99	2.71	2.44	2.17	1.89	1.56	1.10
30	4.88	4.16	3.78	3.32	2.99	2.70	2.44	2.17	1.89	1.55	1.09
40	4.82	4.11	3.74	3.28	2.95	2.67	2.41	2.15	1.86	1.54	1.08
60	4.76	4.06	3.69	3.24	2.92	2.64	2.38	2.12	1.84	1.52	1.07
100	4.72	4.03	3.66	3.21	2.89	2.62	2.36	2.10	1.83	1.51	1.06
∞	4.65	3.97	3.61	3.17	2.85	2.58	2.33	2.07	1.80	1.48	1.04

$$\Pr\left[\text{noncentral } t > t_{1-\alpha} \mid \delta = (\mu_1 - \mu_0)(\sqrt{n}/\sigma)\right] = 1 - \beta.$$

TABLE D.14 **Noncentral F distribution†**

Tabled entries are $\Pr\left[F(f_1, f_2; \phi) < F_{1-\alpha}(f_1, f_2)\right]$

Power = 1 − (tabled entry)

f_2	$1-\alpha$	.50	1.0	1.2	1.4	1.6	ϕ 1.8	2.0	2.2	2.6	3.0	4.0
							$f_1 = 1$					
2	.95	.93	.86	.83	.78	.74	.69	.64	.59	.49	.40	.20
	.99	.99	.97	.96	.95	.94	.93	.91	.90	.87	.83	.72
4	.95	.91	.80	.74	.67	.59	.51	.43	.35	.22	.12	.02
	.99	.98	.95	.94	.92	.89	.86	.82	.78	.67	.56	.23
6	.95	.91	.78	.70	.62	.52	.43	.34	.26	.14	.06	.00
	.99	.98	.93	.90	.86	.81	.75	.69	.61	.46	.31	.08
8	.95	.90	.76	.68	.59	.49	.39	.30	.22	.11	.04	.00
	.99	.98	.92	.89	.84	.78	.70	.62	.54	.37	.22	.03
10	.95	.90	.75	.66	.57	.47	.37	.28	.20	.09	.03	.00
	.99	.98	.92	.87	.82	.75	.67	.58	.49	.31	.17	.02
12	.95	.90	.74	.65	.56	.45	.35	.26	.19	.08	.03	
	.99	.97	.91	.87	.81	.73	.65	.55	.46	.28	.14	
16	.95	.90	.74	.64	.54	.43	.33	.24	.17	.07	.02	
	.99	.97	.90	.85	.79	.71	.61	.52	.42	.24	.11	
20	.95	.90	.73	.63	.53	.42	.32	.23	.16	.06	.02	
	.99	.97	.90	.85	.78	.69	.59	.49	.39	.21	.10	
30	.95	.89	.72	.62	.52	.40	.31	.22	.15	.06	.02	
	.99	.97	.89	.83	.76	.67	.57	.46	.36	.19	.08	
∞	.95	.89	.71	.70	.49	.38	.28	.19	.12	.04	.01	
	.99	.97	.88	.81	.72	.62	.51	.40	.30	.14	.05	

f_2	$1-\alpha$	.50	1.0	1.2	1.4	1.6	1.8	2.0	2.2	2.6	3.0	4.0
							$f_1 = 2$					
2	.95	.93	.88	.85	.82	.78	.75	.70	.66	.57	.48	.29
	.99	.99	.98	.97	.96	.95	.94	.93	.92	.89	.86	.78
4	.95	.92	.82	.77	.70	.62	.54	.46	.38	.24	.14	.02
	.99	.98	.96	.94	.92	.89	.85	.81	.76	.66	.54	.27
6	.95	.91	.79	.71	.63	.53	.43	.34	.26	.13	.05	.00
	.99	.98	.94	.91	.87	.82	.76	.70	.62	.46	.31	.07
8	.95	.91	.77	.68	.58	.48	.37	.28	.20	.08	.03	.00
	.99	.98	.93	.89	.84	.78	.70	.61	.52	.34	.19	.02
10	.95	.91	.75	.66	.55	.44	.34	.24	.16	.06	.02	.00
	.99	.98	.92	.88	.82	.74	.65	.55	.45	.26	.13	.01
12	.95	.90	.74	.64	.53	.42	.31	.22	.14	.05	.01	
	.99	.98	.91	.86	.80	.71	.61	.51	.40	.22	.09	
16	.95	.90	.73	.62	.51	.39	.28	.19	.12	.04	.01	
	.99	.97	.90	.84	.77	.67	.57	.45	.34	.16	.06	
20	.95	.90	.72	.61	.49	.37	.26	.17	.11	.03	.01	
	.99	.97	.90	.83	.75	.65	.53	.42	.31	.14	.04	
30	.95	.90	.71	.59	.47	.35	.24	.15	.09	.02	.00	
	.99	.97	.88	.82	.72	.61	.49	.37	.26	.10	.03	
∞	.95	.89	.68	.56	.43	.30	.20	.12	.06	.01	.00	
	.99	.97	.86	.77	.66	.53	.40	.28	.18	.05	.01	

† This table is abridged from: Tables of the power of the F test. *Journal of the American Statistical Association*, 1967, **62**, 525–539, with the permission of the author, M. L. Tiku, and the editors.

TABLE D.14 (*Continued*)

f_2	$1 - \alpha$	.50	1.0	1.2	1.4	1.6	ϕ 1.8	2.0	2.2	2.6	3.0	4.0
							$f_1 = 3$					
2	.95	.93	.89	.86	.83	.80	.76	.73	.69	.60	.52	.32
	.99	.99	.98	.97	.96	.96	.95	.94	.93	.90	.88	.80
4	.95	.92	.83	.77	.71	.63	.55	.47	.39	.25	.14	.02
	.99	.98	.96	.94	.92	.89	.86	.82	.77	.67	.55	.28
6	.95	.91	.79	.71	.62	.52	.42	.33	.24	.11	.04	.00
	.99	.98	.94	.91	.87	.82	.76	.69	.61	.44	.29	.06
8	.95	.91	.76	.67	.57	.46	.35	.25	.17	.06	.02	.00
	.99	.98	.93	.89	.84	.77	.68	.59	.49	.30	.16	.01
10	.95	.91	.75	.65	.53	.41	.30	.21	.13	.04	.01	
	.99	.98	.92	.87	.80	.72	.62	.52	.41	.22	.09	
12	.95	.90	.73	.62	.51	.38	.27	.18	.11	.03	.01	
	.99	.98	.91	.85	.78	.69	.58	.46	.35	.17	.06	
16	.95	.90	.71	.60	.47	.34	.23	.14	.08	.02	.00	
	.99	.97	.90	.83	.74	.64	.51	.39	.28	.11	.03	
20	.95	.90	.70	.58	.45	.32	.21	.13	.07	.01	.00	
	.99	.97	.89	.82	.72	.60	.47	.35	.24	.08	.02	
30	.95	.89	.68	.55	.42	.29	.18	.10	.05	.01	.00	
	.99	.97	.87	.79	.68	.55	.42	.29	.18	.05	.01	
∞	.95	.88	.64	.50	.36	.23	.13	.07	.03	.00	.00	
	.99	.97	.84	.73	.59	.44	.30	.18	.10	.02	.00	

f_2	$1 - \alpha$						$f_1 = 4$					
2	.95	.94	.89	.87	.84	.81	.77	.74	.70	.62	.54	.34
	.99	.99	.98	.97	.97	.96	.95	.94	.93	.91	.88	.81
4	.95	.92	.83	.78	.71	.64	.55	.47	.39	.25	.14	.02
	.99	.98	.96	.94	.92	.89	.86	.82	.78	.67	.56	.28
6	.95	.92	.79	.71	.62	.52	.41	.31	.23	.10	.04	.00
	.99	.98	.94	.91	.87	.82	.76	.68	.60	.43	.28	.05
8	.95	.91	.76	.66	.55	.44	.33	.23	.15	.05	.01	.00
	.99	.98	.93	.89	.83	.76	.67	.57	.47	.28	.14	.01
10	.95	.91	.74	.63	.51	.39	.27	.18	.11	.03	.01	
	.99	.98	.92	.87	.79	.70	.60	.49	.37	.19	.07	
12	.95	.90	.72	.61	.48	.35	.24	.15	.08	.02	.00	
	.99	.98	.91	.85	.76	.66	.55	.42	.31	.13	.04	
16	.95	.90	.70	.57	.44	.31	.19	.11	.06	.01	.00	
	.99	.97	.89	.82	.72	.60	.47	.34	.23	.08	.02	
20	.95	.89	.68	.55	.41	.28	.17	.09	.04	.01	.00	
	.99	.97	.88	.80	.69	.56	.42	.29	.18	.05	.01	
30	.95	.89	.66	.52	.37	.24	.14	.07	.03	.00	.00	
	.99	.97	.86	.77	.64	.50	.35	.22	.13	.03	.00	
∞	.95	.88	.60	.45	.29	.17	.08	.04	.01	.00	.00	
	.99	.96	.81	.68	.53	.36	.22	.11	.05	.01	.00	

TABLE D.15 **Bonferroni t statistic†**

$$\alpha_{Bon} = 0.05$$

$$\alpha_{ind} = 0.05/m$$

		Number of comparisons (m)									
		1	**2**	**3**	**4**	**5**	**6**	**7**	**8**	**9**	**10**
Error df (f)	**100α/m:**	**5.0000**	**2.5000**	**1.6667**	**1.2500**	**1.0000**	**0.8333**	**0.7143**	**0.6250**	**0.5556**	**0.5000**
2		4.3027	6.2053	7.6488	8.8602	9.9248	10.8859	11.7687	12.5897	13.3604	14.0890
3		3.1824	4.1765	4.8567	5.3919	5.8409	6.2315	6.5797	6.8952	7.1849	7.4533
4		2.7764	3.4954	3.9608	4.3147	4.6041	4.8510	5.0675	5.2611	5.4366	5.5976
5		2.5706	3.1634	3.5341	3.8100	4.0321	4.2193	4.3818	4.5257	4.6553	4.7733
6		2.4469	2.9687	3.2875	3.5212	3.7074	3.8630	3.9971	4.1152	4.2209	4.3168
7		2.3646	2.8412	3.1276	3.3353	3.4995	3.6358	3.7527	3.8552	3.9467	4.0293
8		2.3060	2.7515	3.0158	3.2060	3.3554	3.4789	3.5844	3.6766	3.7586	3.8325
9		2.2622	2.6850	2.9333	3.1109	3.2498	3.3642	3.4616	3.5465	3.6219	3.6897
10		2.2281	2.6338	2.8701	3.0382	3.1693	3.2768	3.3682	3.4477	3.5182	3.5814
11		2.2010	2.5931	2.8200	2.9809	3.1058	3.2081	3.2949	3.3702	3.4368	3.4966
12		2.1788	2.5600	2.7795	2.9345	3.0545	3.1527	3.2357	3.3078	3.3714	3.4284
13		2.1604	2.5326	2.7459	2.8961	3.0123	3.1070	3.1871	3.2565	3.3177	3.3725
14		2.1448	2.5096	2.7178	2.8640	2.9768	3.0688	3.1464	3.2135	3.2727	3.3257
15		2.1314	2.4899	2.6937	2.8366	2.9467	3.0363	3.1118	3.1771	3.2346	3.2860
16		2.1199	2.4729	2.6730	2.8131	2.9208	3.0083	3.0821	3.1458	3.2019	3.2520
17		2.1098	2.4581	2.6550	2.7925	2.8982	2.9840	3.0563	3.1186	3.1735	3.2224
18		2.1009	2.4450	2.6391	2.7745	2.8784	2.9627	3.0336	3.0948	3.1486	3.1966
19		2.0930	2.4334	2.6251	2.7586	2.8609	2.9439	3.0136	3.0738	3.1266	3.1737
20		2.0860	2.4231	2.6126	2.7444	2.8453	2.9271	2.9958	3.0550	3.1070	3.1534
21		2.0796	2.4138	2.6013	2.7316	2.8314	2.9121	2.9799	3.0382	3.0895	3.1352
22		2.0739	2.4055	2.5912	2.7201	2.8188	2.8985	2.9655	3.0231	3.0737	3.1188
23		2.0687	2.3979	2.5820	2.7079	2.8073	2.8863	2.9525	3.0095	3.0595	3.1040
24		2.0639	2.3909	2.5736	2.7002	2.7969	2.8751	2.9406	2.9970	3.0465	3.0905
25		2.0595	2.3846	2.5660	2.6916	2.7874	2.8649	2.9298	2.9856	3.0346	3.0782
26		2.0555	2.3788	2.5589	2.6836	2.7787	2.8555	2.9199	2.9752	3.0237	3.0669
27		2.0518	2.3734	2.5525	2.6763	2.7707	2.8469	2.9107	2.9656	3.0137	3.0565
28		2.0484	2.3685	2.5465	2.6695	2.7633	2.8389	2.9023	2.9567	3.0045	3.0469
29		2.0452	2.3638	2.5409	2.6632	2.7564	2.8316	2.8945	2.9485	3.9959	3.0380
30		2.0423	2.3596	2.5357	2.6574	2.7500	2.8247	2.8872	2.9409	3.9880	3.0298
35		2.0301	2.3420	2.5145	2.6334	2.7238	2.7966	2.8575	2.9097	2.9554	2.9960
40		2.0211	2.3289	2.4989	2.6157	2.7045	2.7759	2.8355	2.8867	2.9314	2.9712
45		2.0141	2.3189	2.4868	2.6021	2.6896	2.7599	2.8187	2.8690	2.9130	2.9521
50		2.0086	2.3109	2.4772	2.5913	2.6778	2.7473	2.8053	2.8550	2.8984	2.9370
55		2.0040	2.3044	2.4694	2.5825	2.6682	2.7370	2.7944	2.8436	2.8866	2.9247
60		2.0003	2.2990	2.4630	2.5752	2.6603	2.7286	2.7855	2.8342	2.8768	2.9146
70		1.9944	2.2906	2.4529	2.5639	2.6479	2.7153	2.7715	2.8195	2.8615	2.8987
80		1.9901	2.2844	2.4454	2.5554	2.6387	2.7054	2.7610	2.8086	2.8502	2.8870
90		1.9867	2.2795	2.4395	2.5489	2.6316	2.6978	2.7530	2.8002	2.8414	2.8779
100		1.9840	2.2757	2.4349	2.5437	2.6259	2.6918	2.7466	2.7935	2.8344	2.8707
110		1.9818	2.2725	2.4311	2.5394	2.6213	2.6868	2.7414	2.7880	2.8287	2.8648
120		1.9799	2.2699	2.4280	2.5359	2.6174	2.6827	2.7370	2.7835	2.8240	2.8599
250		1.9695	2.2550	2.4102	2.5159	2.5956	2.6594	2.7124	2.7577	2.7972	2.8322
500		1.9647	2.2482	2.4021	2.5068	2.5857	2.6488	2.7012	2.7460	2.7850	2.8195
1000		1.9623	2.2448	2.3980	2.5022	2.5808	2.6435	2.6957	2.7402	2.7790	2.8133
∞		1.9600	2.2414	2.3940	2.4977	2.5758	2.6383	2.6901	2.7344	2.7729	2.8070

† Table reproduced from B. J. R. Bailey, Tables of the Bonferroni t Statistic, *Journal of the American Statistical Association*, 1977, 72, 469–478, with permission of the editor.

TABLE D.15   (*Continued*)

$$\alpha_{\text{Bon}} = 0.05$$

$$\alpha_{\text{ind}} = 0.05/m$$

		\multicolumn{10}{c}{Number of comparisons (m)}								
		15	**20**	**28**	**36**	**45**	**55**	**78**	**91**	**120**	**190**
Error df (f)	**100α/m:**	**0.3333**	**0.2500**	**0.1786**	**0.1389**	**0.1111**	**0.0909**	**0.0641**	**0.0549**	**0.0417**	**0.0263**
2		17.2772	19.9625	23.6326	26.8049	29.9750	33.1436	39.4778	42.6439	48.9745	61.6320
3		8.5752	9.4649	10.6166	11.5632	12.4715	13.3471	15.0165	15.8165	17.3582	20.2528
4		6.2541	6.7583	7.3924	7.8998	8.3763	8.8271	9.6655	10.0585	10.8016	12.1519
5		5.2474	5.6042	6.0447	6.3914	6.7126	7.0128	7.5625	7.8166	8.2913	9.1365
6		4.6979	4.9807	5.3255	5.5937	5.8399	6.0680	6.4813	6.6705	7.0210	7.6363
7		4.3553	4.5946	4.8839	5.1068	5.3101	5.4973	5.8339	5.9868	6.2684	6.7577
8		4.1224	4.3335	4.5869	4.7810	4.9570	5.1183	5.4065	5.5368	5.7755	6.1869
9		3.9542	4.1458	4.3744	4.5485	4.7058	4.8494	5.1048	5.2197	5.4295	5.7888
10		3.8273	4.0045	4.2150	4.3747	4.5184	4.6492	4.8810	4.9849	5.1740	5.4963
11		3.7283	3.8945	4.0913	4.2400	4.3735	4.4947	4.7087	4.8044	4.9781	5.2729
12		3.6489	3.8065	3.9925	4.1327	4.2582	4.3719	4.5722	4.6615	4.8233	5.0969
13		3.5838	3.7345	3.9118	4.0452	4.1643	4.2721	4.4614	4.5457	4.6981	4.9549
14		3.5296	3.6746	3.8448	3.9725	4.0865	4.1894	4.3698	4.4500	4.5947	4.8379
15		3.4837	3.6239	3.7882	3.9113	4.0209	4.1198	4.2928	4.3695	4.5079	4.7400
16		3.4443	3.5805	3.7398	3.8589	3.9649	4.0604	4.2272	4.3011	4.4341	4.6568
17		3.4102	3.5429	3.6980	3.8137	3.9165	4.0091	4.1706	4.2421	4.3706	4.5853
18		3.3804	3.5101	3.6614	3.7742	3.8744	3.9644	4.1214	4.1907	4.3154	4.5232
19		3.3540	3.4812	3.6292	3.7395	3.8373	3.9251	4.0781	4.1456	4.2669	4.4688
20		3.3306	3.4554	3.6006	3.7087	3.8044	3.8903	4.0398	4.1057	4.2240	4.4208
21		3.3097	3.4325	3.5751	3.6812	3.7750	3.8593	4.0056	4.0701	4.1858	4.3780
22		3.2909	3.4118	3.5522	3.6564	3.7487	3.8314	3.9750	4.0382	4.1516	4.3397
23		3.2739	3.3931	3.5314	3.6341	3.7249	3.8062	3.9474	4.0095	4.1207	4.3052
24		3.2584	3.3761	3.5126	3.6139	3.7033	3.7834	3.9223	3.9834	4.0928	4.2739
25		3.2443	3.3606	3.4955	3.5954	3.6836	3.7626	3.8995	3.9597	4.0674	4.2455
26		3.2313	3.3464	3.4797	3.5785	3.6656	3.7436	3.8787	3.9380	4.0441	4.2196
27		3.2194	3.3334	3.4653	3.5629	3.6491	3.7261	3.8595	3.9181	4.0228	4.1958
28		3.2084	3.3214	3.4520	3.5486	3.6338	3.7101	3.8419	3.8997	4.0032	4.1739
29		3.1982	3.3102	3.4397	3.5354	3.6198	3.6952	3.8256	3.8828	3.9850	4.1537
30		3.1888	3.2999	3.4282	3.5231	3.6067	3.6814	3.8105	3.8671	3.9682	4.1350
35		3.1502	3.2577	3.3816	3.4730	3.5534	3.6252	3.7490	3.8032	3.8999	4.0590
40		3.1218	3.2266	3.3473	3.4362	3.5143	3.5840	3.7040	3.7564	3.8499	4.0035
45		3.1000	3.2028	3.3211	3.4081	3.4845	3.5525	3.6696	3.7208	3.8118	3.9612
50		3.0828	3.1840	3.3003	3.3858	3.4609	3.5277	3.6425	3.6926	3.7818	3.9279
55		3.0688	3.1688	3.2836	3.3679	3.4418	3.5076	3.6206	3.6699	3.7576	3.9010
60		3.0573	3.1562	3.2697	3.3530	3.4260	3.4910	3.6025	3.6511	3.7376	3.8789
70		3.0393	3.1366	3.2481	3.3299	3.4015	3.4652	3.5744	3.6220	3.7065	3.8445
80		3.0259	3.1220	3.2321	3.3127	3.3833	3.4460	3.5536	3.6004	3.6835	3.8191
90		3.0156	3.1108	3.2197	3.2995	3.3693	3.4313	3.5375	3.5837	3.6658	3.7995
100		3.0073	3.1018	3.2099	3.2890	3.3582	3.4196	3.5248	3.5705	3.6517	3.7840
110		3.0007	3.0945	3.2018	3.2804	3.3491	3.4100	3.5144	3.5598	3.6403	3.7714
120		2.9951	3.0885	3.1952	3.2733	3.3416	3.4021	3.5058	3.5509	3.6308	3.7609
250		2.9637	3.0543	3.1577	3.2332	3.2991	3.3575	3.4573	3.5007	3.5774	3.7020
500		2.9494	3.0387	3.1406	3.2150	3.2798	3.3373	3.4354	3.4779	3.5532	3.6754
1000		2.9423	3.0310	3.1322	3.2059	3.2703	3.3272	3.4245	3.4666	3.5412	3.6622
∞		2.9352	3.0233	3.1237	3.1970	3.2608	3.3172	3.4136	3.4554	3.5293	3.6491

TABLE D.15 (*Continued*)

$$\alpha_{Bon} = 0.01$$

$$\alpha_{ind} = 0.01/m$$

Error df (f)	100α/m:	1 1.0000	2 0.5000	3 0.3333	4 0.2500	5 0.2000	6 0.1667	7 0.1429	8 0.1250	9 0.1111	10 0.1000
2		9.9248	14.0890	17.2772	19.9625	22.3271	24.4643	26.4292	28.2577	29.9750	31.5991
3		5.8409	7.4533	8.5752	9.4649	10.2145	10.8668	11.4532	11.9838	12.4715	12.9240
4		4.6041	5.5976	6.2541	6.7583	7.1732	7.5287	7.8414	8.1216	8.3763	8.6103
5		4.0321	4.7733	5.2474	5.6042	5.8934	6.1384	6.3518	6.5414	6.7126	6.8688
6		3.7074	4.3168	4.6979	4.9807	5.2076	5.3982	5.5632	5.7090	5.8399	5.9588
7		3.4995	4.0293	4.3553	4.5946	4.7853	4.9445	5.0815	5.2022	5.3101	5.4079
8		3.3554	3.8325	4.1224	4.3335	4.5008	4.6398	4.7590	4.8636	4.9570	5.0413
9		3.2498	3.6897	3.9542	4.1458	4.2968	4.4219	4.5288	4.6224	4.7058	4.7809
10		3.1693	3.5814	3.8273	4.0045	4.1437	4.2586	4.3567	4.4423	4.5184	4.5869
11		3.1058	3.4966	3.7283	3.8945	4.0247	4.1319	4.2232	4.3028	4.3735	4.4370
12		3.0545	3.4284	3.6489	3.8065	3.9296	4.0308	4.1169	4.1918	4.2582	4.3178
13		3.0123	3.3725	3.5838	3.7345	3.8520	3.9484	4.0302	4.1013	4.1643	4.2208
14		2.9768	3.3257	3.5296	3.6746	3.7874	3.8798	3.9582	4.0263	4.0865	4.1405
15		2.9467	3.2860	3.4837	3.6239	3.7328	3.8220	3.8975	3.9630	4.0209	4.0728
16		2.9208	3.2520	3.4443	3.5805	3.6862	3.7725	3.8456	3.9089	3.9649	4.0150
17		2.8982	3.2224	3.4102	3.5429	3.6458	3.7297	3.8007	3.8623	3.9165	3.9651
18		2.8784	3.1966	3.3804	3.5101	3.6105	3.6924	3.7616	3.8215	3.8744	3.9216
19		2.8609	3.1737	3.3540	3.4812	3.5794	3.6595	3.7271	3.7857	3.8373	3.8834
20		2.8453	3.1534	3.3306	3.4554	3.5518	3.6303	3.6966	3.7539	3.8044	3.8495
21		2.8314	3.1352	3.3097	3.4325	3.5272	3.6043	3.6693	3.7255	3.7750	3.8193
22		2.8188	3.1188	3.2909	3.4118	3.5050	3.5808	3.6448	3.7000	3.7487	3.7921
23		2.8073	3.1040	3.2739	3.3931	3.4850	3.5597	3.6226	3.6770	3.7249	3.7676
24		2.7969	3.0905	3.2584	3.3761	3.4668	3.5405	3.6025	3.6561	3.7033	3.7454
25		2.7874	3.0782	3.2443	3.3606	3.4502	3.5230	3.5842	3.6371	3.6836	3.7251
26		2.7787	3.0669	3.2313	3.3464	3.4350	3.5069	3.5674	3.6197	3.6656	3.7066
27		2.7707	3.0565	3.2194	3.3334	3.4210	3.4922	3.5520	3.6037	3.6491	3.6896
28		2.7633	3.0469	3.2084	3.3214	3.4082	3.4786	3.5378	3.5889	3.6338	3.6739
29		2.7564	3.0380	3.1982	3.3102	3.3962	3.4660	3.5247	3.5753	3.6198	3.6594
30		2.7500	3.0298	3.1888	3.2999	3.3852	3.4544	3.5125	3.5626	3.6067	3.6460
35		2.7238	2.9960	3.1502	3.2577	3.3400	3.4068	3.4628	3.5110	3.5534	3.5911
40		2.7045	2.9712	3.1218	3.2266	3.3069	3.3718	3.4263	3.4732	3.5143	3.5510
45		2.6896	2.9521	3.1000	3.2028	3.2815	3.3451	3.3984	3.4442	3.4845	3.5203
50		2.6778	2.9370	3.0828	3.1840	3.2614	3.3239	3.3763	3.4214	3.4609	3.4960
55		2.6682	2.9247	3.0688	3.1688	3.2451	3.3068	3.3585	3.4029	3.4418	3.4764
60		2.6603	2.9146	3.0573	3.1562	3.2317	3.2927	3.3437	3.3876	3.4260	3.4602
70		2.6479	2.8987	3.0393	3.1366	3.2108	3.2707	3.3208	3.3638	3.4015	3.4350
80		2.6387	2.8870	3.0259	3.1220	3.1953	3.2543	3.3037	3.3462	3.3833	3.4163
90		2.6316	2.8779	3.0156	3.1108	3.1833	3.2417	3.2906	3.3326	3.3693	3.4019
100		2.6259	2.8707	3.0073	3.1018	3.1737	3.2317	3.2802	3.3218	3.3582	3.3905
110		2.6213	2.8648	3.0007	3.0945	3.1660	3.2235	3.2717	3.3130	3.3491	3.3812
120		2.6174	2.8599	2.9951	3.0885	3.1595	3.2168	3.2646	3.3057	3.3416	3.3735
250		2.5956	2.8322	2.9637	3.0543	3.1232	3.1785	3.2248	3.2644	3.2991	3.3299
500		2.5857	2.8195	2.9494	3.0387	3.1066	3.1612	3.2067	3.2457	3.2798	3.3101
1000		2.5808	2.8133	2.9423	3.0310	3.0984	3.1526	3.1977	3.2365	3.2703	3.3003
∞		2.5758	2.8070	2.9352	3.0233	3.0902	3.1440	3.1888	3.2272	3.2608	3.2905

TABLE D.15   (*Continued*)

$$\alpha_{Bon} = 0.01$$
$$\alpha_{ind} = 0.01/m$$

Error df (f)	100α/m:	15 0.0667	20 0.0500	28 0.0357	36 0.0278	45 0.0222	55 0.0182	78 0.0128	91 0.0110	120 0.0083	190 0.0053
						Number of comparisons (m)					
2		38.7105	44.7046	52.9009	59.9875	67.0709	74.1519	88.3091	95.3861	109.5377	137.8350
3		14.8194	16.3263	18.2806	19.8889	21.4337	22.9239	25.7675	27.1309	29.7598	34.6984
4		9.5679	10.3063	11.2378	11.9851	12.6881	13.3540	14.5946	15.1768	16.2788	18.2841
5		7.4990	7.9757	8.5667	9.0332	9.4665	9.8722	10.6168	10.9616	11.6067	12.7578
6		6.4338	6.7883	7.2226	7.5617	7.8737	8.1636	8.6901	8.9317	9.3800	10.1692
7		5.7954	6.0818	6.4295	6.6987	6.9448	7.1721	7.5819	7.7685	8.1130	8.7132
8		5.3737	5.6174	5.9114	6.1375	6.3432	6.5323	6.8712	7.0248	7.3069	7.7947
9		5.0757	5.2907	5.5484	5.7458	5.9245	6.0883	6.3803	6.5121	6.7533	7.1679
10		4.8547	5.0490	5.2810	5.4578	5.6175	5.7634	6.0225	6.1391	6.3517	6.7154
11		4.6845	4.8633	5.0761	5.2378	5.3833	5.5160	5.7509	5.8562	6.0480	6.3745
12		4.5496	4.7165	4.9144	5.0644	5.1991	5.3216	5.5380	5.6348	5.8107	6.1091
13		4.4401	4.5975	4.7837	4.9244	5.0506	5.1651	5.3670	5.4571	5.6204	5.8969
14		4.3495	4.4992	4.6759	4.8091	4.9284	5.0364	5.2266	5.3113	5.4647	5.7235
15		4.2733	4.4166	4.5854	4.7125	4.8261	4.9289	5.1094	5.1897	5.3350	5.5794
16		4.2084	4.3463	4.5086	4.6305	4.7393	4.8377	5.0102	5.0868	5.2252	5.4578
17		4.1525	4.2858	4.4425	4.5600	4.6648	4.7594	4.9251	4.9986	5.1313	5.3538
18		4.1037	4.2332	4.3850	4.4987	4.6001	4.6915	4.8514	4.9222	5.0500	5.2639
19		4.0609	4.1869	4.3345	4.4450	4.5434	4.6320	4.7868	4.8554	4.9789	5.1854
20		4.0230	4.1460	4.2900	4.3976	4.4933	4.5795	4.7299	4.7965	4.9163	5.1163
21		3.9892	4.1096	4.2503	4.3554	4.4487	4.5328	4.6794	4.7442	4.8607	5.0551
22		3.9589	4.0769	4.2147	4.3175	4.4089	4.4910	4.6342	4.6974	4.8111	5.0004
23		3.9316	4.0474	4.1826	4.2835	4.3730	4.4534	4.5935	4.6553	4.7664	4.9513
24		3.9068	4.0207	4.1536	4.2527	4.3405	4.4194	4.5567	4.6173	4.7261	4.9070
25		3.8842	3.9964	4.1272	4.2246	4.3109	4.3885	4.5233	4.5828	4.6894	4.8667
26		3.8635	3.9742	4.1031	4.1990	4.2840	4.3602	4.4928	4.5513	4.6560	4.8300
27		3.8446	3.9538	4.0809	4.1755	4.2592	4.3344	4.4649	4.5224	4.6255	4.7965
28		3.8271	3.9351	4.0606	4.1539	4.2365	4.3108	4.4392	4.4959	4.5974	4.7657
29		3.8110	3.9177	4.0418	4.1339	4.2155	4.2886	4.4155	4.4714	4.5714	4.7372
30		3.7961	3.9016	4.0243	4.1154	4.1960	4.2683	4.3936	4.4487	4.5475	4.7110
35		3.7352	3.8362	3.9534	4.0403	4.1170	4.1857	4.3047	4.3569	4.4503	4.6047
40		3.6906	3.7884	3.9017	3.9855	4.0594	4.1256	4.2399	4.2901	4.3797	4.5275
45		3.6565	3.7519	3.8622	3.9437	4.0156	4.0798	4.1907	4.2393	4.3261	4.4689
50		3.6297	3.7231	3.8311	3.9108	3.9611	4.0438	4.1520	4.1994	4.2840	4.4230
55		3.6080	3.6999	3.8060	3.8843	3.9532	4.0147	4.1208	4.1672	4.2500	4.3860
60		3.5901	3.6807	3.7853	3.8624	3.9303	3.9908	4.0951	4.1408	4.2221	4.3556
70		3.5622	3.6509	3.7531	3.8284	3.8946	3.9537	4.0553	4.0997	4.1788	4.3085
80		3.5416	3.6288	3.7293	3.8033	3.8683	3.9262	4.0259	4.0694	4.1469	4.2738
90		3.5257	3.6118	3.7110	3.7839	3.8480	3.9051	4.0032	4.0461	4.1223	4.2471
100		3.5131	3.5983	3.6964	3.7686	3.8319	3.8883	3.9853	4.0276	4.1028	4.2260
110		3.5028	3.5874	3.6846	3.7561	3.8189	3.8747	3.9707	4.0126	4.0870	4.2088
120		3.4943	3.5783	3.6748	3.7458	3.0808	3.8634	3.9586	4.0001	4.0739	4.1946
250		3.4462	3.5270	3.6196	3.6875	3.7471	3.8000	3.8907	3.9303	4.0004	4.1149
500		3.4245	3.5037	3.5946	3.6612	3.7195	3.7713	3.8601	3.8987	3.9673	4.0790
1000		3.4137	3.4922	3.5822	3.6481	3.7059	3.7571	3.8449	3.8831	3.9509	4.0612
∞		3.4029	3.4808	3.5699	3.6352	3.6923	3.7430	3.8299	3.8676	3.9346	4.0436

TABLE D.16 **Two-sides t based on Šidák's multiplicative inequality†**

Error df (f)	α‡	2	3	4	5	6	7	8	9	10	15	20	25	30	35	40	45	50
2	0.01	14.071	17.248	19.925	22.282	24.413	26.372	28.196	29.908	31.528	38.620	44.598	49.865	54.626	59.004	63.079	66.906	70.526
	0.05	6.164	7.582	8.774	9.823	10.769	11.639	12.449	13.208	13.927	17.072	19.721	22.054	24.163	26.103	27.908	29.603	31.206
	0.10	4.243	5.243	6.081	6.816	7.480	8.090	8.656	9.188	9.691	11.890	13.741	15.371	16.845	18.199	19.459	20.642	21.761
	0.20	2.828	3.531	4.116	4.628	5.089	5.512	5.904	6.272	6.620	8.138	9.414	10.537	11.552	12.484	13.351	14.166	14.936
3	0.01	7.447	8.565	9.453	10.201	10.853	11.436	11.966	12.453	12.904	14.796	16.300	17.569	18.678	19.670	20.570	21.398	22.167
	0.05	4.156	4.626	5.355	5.799	6.185	6.529	6.842	7.128	7.394	8.505	9.387	10.129	10.778	11.357	11.883	12.366	12.815
	0.10	3.149	3.690	4.115	4.471	4.780	5.055	5.304	5.532	5.744	6.627	7.326	7.914	8.427	8.886	9.301	9.683	10.038
	0.20	2.294	2.734	3.077	3.363	3.610	3.829	4.028	4.209	4.377	5.076	5.628	6.091	6.495	6.855	7.181	7.481	7.759
4	0.01	5.594	6.248	6.751	7.166	7.520	7.832	8.112	8.367	8.600	9.556	10.294	10.902	11.424	11.884	12.297	12.672	13.017
	0.05	3.481	3.941	4.290	4.577	4.822	5.036	5.228	5.402	5.562	6.214	6.714	7.127	7.480	7.790	8.069	8.322	8.554
	0.10	2.751	3.150	3.452	3.699	3.909	4.093	4.257	4.406	4.542	5.097	5.521	5.870	6.169	6.432	6.667	6.880	7.076
	0.20	2.084	2.434	2.697	2.911	3.092	3.250	3.391	3.518	3.635	4.107	4.468	4.763	5.015	5.237	5.435	5.614	5.779
5	0.01	4.771	5.243	5.599	5.888	6.133	6.346	6.535	6.706	6.862	7.491	7.968	8.355	8.684	8.971	9.226	9.457	9.668
	0.05	3.152	3.518	3.791	4.012	4.197	4.358	4.501	4.630	4.747	5.219	5.573	5.861	6.105	6.317	6.506	6.676	6.831
	0.10	2.549	2.882	3.129	3.327	3.493	3.638	3.765	3.880	3.985	4.403	4.718	4.972	5.187	5.374	5.540	5.689	5.826
	0.20	1.973	2.278	2.503	2.683	2.834	2.964	3.079	3.182	3.275	3.649	3.928	4.153	4.343	4.508	4.654	4.786	4.906
6	0.01	4.315	4.695	4.977	5.203	5.394	5.559	5.704	5.835	5.954	6.428	6.782	7.068	7.308	7.516	7.701	7.867	8.018
	0.05	2.959	3.274	3.505	3.690	3.845	3.978	4.095	4.200	4.296	4.675	4.956	5.182	5.372	5.536	5.682	5.812	5.930
	0.10	2.428	2.723	2.939	3.110	3.253	3.376	3.484	3.580	3.668	4.015	4.272	4.477	4.649	4.798	4.930	5.048	5.155
	0.20	1.904	2.184	2.387	2.547	2.681	2.795	2.895	2.985	3.066	3.385	3.620	3.808	3.965	4.100	4.220	4.327	4.424
7	0.01	4.027	4.353	4.591	4.782	4.941	5.078	5.198	5.306	5.404	5.791	6.077	6.306	6.497	6.663	6.809	6.939	7.058
	0.05	2.832	3.115	3.321	3.484	3.620	3.736	3.838	3.929	4.011	4.336	4.574	4.764	4.923	5.059	5.180	5.287	5.385
	0.10	2.347	2.618	2.814	2.969	3.097	3.206	3.302	3.388	3.465	3.768	3.990	4.167	4.314	4.441	4.552	4.651	4.741
	0.20	1.858	2.120	2.309	2.457	2.579	2.684	2.775	2.856	2.929	3.214	3.423	3.588	3.725	3.842	3.946	4.038	4.121
8	0.01	3.831	4.120	4.331	4.498	4.637	4.756	4.860	4.953	5.038	5.370	5.613	5.807	5.969	6.107	6.230	6.339	6.437
	0.05	2.743	3.005	3.193	3.342	3.464	3.569	3.661	3.743	3.816	4.105	4.316	4.482	4.621	4.740	4.844	4.937	5.021
	0.10	2.289	2.544	2.726	2.869	2.987	3.088	3.176	3.254	3.324	3.598	3.798	3.955	4.086	4.198	4.296	4.383	4.462
	0.20	1.824	2.075	2.254	2.393	2.508	2.605	2.690	2.765	2.832	3.095	3.286	3.435	3.559	3.665	3.758	3.840	3.914
9	0.01	3.688	3.952	4.143	4.294	4.419	4.526	4.619	4.703	4.778	5.072	5.287	5.457	5.598	5.720	5.826	5.921	6.006
	0.05	2.677	2.923	3.099	3.237	3.351	3.448	3.532	3.607	3.675	3.938	4.129	4.280	4.405	4.512	4.605	4.688	4.763
	0.10	2.246	2.488	2.661	2.796	2.907	3.001	3.083	3.155	3.221	3.474	3.658	3.802	3.921	4.023	4.112	4.191	4.262
	0.20	1.799	2.041	2.212	2.345	2.454	2.546	2.627	2.698	2.761	3.008	3.185	3.324	3.438	3.536	3.621	3.697	3.765
10	0.01	3.580	3.825	4.002	4.141	4.256	4.354	4.439	4.515	4.584	4.852	5.046	5.199	5.326	5.434	5.529	5.614	5.690
	0.05	2.626	2.860	3.027	3.157	3.264	3.355	3.434	3.505	3.568	3.813	3.989	4.128	4.243	4.341	4.426	4.502	4.571
	0.10	2.213	2.446	2.611	2.739	2.845	2.934	3.012	3.080	3.142	3.380	3.552	3.686	3.796	3.891	3.973	4.046	4.112
	0.20	1.799	2.014	2.180	2.308	2.413	2.501	2.578	2.646	2.706	2.941	3.108	3.239	3.346	3.438	3.517	3.588	3.651

Number of comparisons (m)

Number of comparisons (m)

Error df (f)	α‡	2	3	4	5	6	7	8	9	10	15	20	25	30	35	40	45	50
11	0.01	3.495	3.726	3.892	4.022	4.129	4.221	4.300	4.371	4.434	4.682	4.860	5.001	5.117	5.216	5.303	5.380	5.450
	0.05	2.586	2.811	2.970	3.094	3.196	3.283	3.358	3.424	3.484	3.715	3.880	4.010	4.117	4.208	4.288	4.353	4.422
	0.10	2.186	2.412	2.571	2.695	2.796	2.881	2.955	3.021	3.079	3.306	3.468	3.595	3.699	3.788	3.865	3.933	3.995
	0.20	1.763	1.993	2.154	2.279	2.380	2.465	2.539	2.605	2.663	2.888	3.048	3.172	3.274	3.361	3.436	3.503	3.583
12	0.01	3.427	3.647	3.804	3.927	4.029	4.114	4.189	4.256	4.315	4.547	4.714	4.845	4.953	5.045	5.125	5.196	5.260
	0.05	2.553	2.770	2.924	3.044	3.141	3.224	3.296	3.359	3.416	3.636	3.793	3.916	4.017	4.103	4.178	4.244	4.304
	0.10	2.164	2.384	2.539	2.658	2.756	2.838	2.910	2.973	3.029	3.247	3.402	3.522	3.621	3.705	3.779	3.843	3.901
	0.20	1.750	1.975	2.133	2.254	2.353	2.436	2.508	2.571	2.628	2.845	2.999	3.118	3.216	3.299	3.371	3.434	3.491
13	0.01	3.371	3.582	3.733	3.850	3.946	4.028	4.099	4.162	4.218	4.438	4.595	4.718	4.819	4.906	4.981	5.048	5.108
	0.05	2.526	2.737	2.886	3.002	3.096	3.176	3.245	3.306	3.361	3.571	3.722	3.839	3.935	4.017	4.088	4.151	4.207
	0.10	2.146	2.361	2.512	2.628	2.723	2.803	2.872	2.933	2.988	3.198	3.347	3.463	3.557	3.638	3.708	3.770	3.825
	0.20	1.739	1.961	2.116	2.234	2.331	2.412	2.482	2.544	2.599	2.809	2.958	3.074	3.168	3.248	3.317	3.378	3.433
14	0.01	3.324	3.528	3.673	3.785	3.878	3.956	4.024	4.084	4.138	4.347	4.497	4.614	4.710	4.792	4.863	4.926	4.982
	0.05	2.503	2.709	2.854	2.967	3.058	3.135	3.202	3.261	3.314	3.518	3.662	3.775	3.867	3.946	4.014	4.074	4.128
	0.10	2.131	2.342	2.489	2.603	2.696	2.774	2.841	2.900	2.953	3.157	3.301	3.413	3.504	3.582	3.649	3.708	3.761
	0.20	1.730	1.949	2.101	2.217	2.312	2.392	2.460	2.520	2.574	2.779	2.924	3.036	3.128	3.205	3.272	3.331	3.384
15	0.01	3.285	3.482	3.622	3.731	3.820	3.895	3.961	4.019	4.071	4.271	4.414	4.526	4.618	4.696	4.764	4.824	4.877
	0.05	2.483	2.685	2.827	2.937	3.026	3.101	3.166	3.224	3.275	3.472	3.612	3.721	3.810	3.885	3.951	4.009	4.060
	0.10	2.118	2.325	2.470	2.582	2.672	2.748	2.814	2.872	2.924	3.122	3.262	3.370	3.459	3.534	3.599	3.656	3.708
	0.20	1.722	1.938	2.088	2.203	2.296	2.374	2.441	2.500	2.553	2.754	2.896	3.005	3.094	3.169	3.234	3.291	3.343
16	0.01	3.251	3.443	3.579	3.684	3.771	3.844	3.907	3.963	4.013	4.206	4.344	4.451	4.540	4.614	4.679	4.737	4.788
	0.05	2.467	2.665	2.804	2.911	2.998	3.072	3.135	3.191	3.241	3.433	3.569	3.675	3.761	3.834	3.897	3.953	4.003
	0.10	2.106	2.311	2.453	2.563	2.652	2.726	2.791	2.848	2.898	3.092	3.228	3.334	3.420	3.493	3.556	3.612	3.662
	0.20	1.715	1.929	2.077	2.190	2.282	2.359	2.425	2.483	2.535	2.732	2.871	2.978	3.064	3.138	3.201	3.257	3.307
17	0.01	3.221	3.409	3.541	3.664	3.728	3.799	3.860	3.914	3.963	4.150	4.284	4.387	4.472	4.544	4.607	4.662	4.712
	0.05	2.452	2.647	2.783	2.889	2.974	3.046	3.108	3.163	3.212	3.399	3.532	3.634	3.718	3.789	3.851	3.905	3.954
	0.10	2.096	2.298	2.439	2.547	2.634	2.708	2.771	2.826	2.876	3.066	3.199	3.303	3.387	3.458	3.519	3.574	3.622
	0.20	1.709	1.921	2.068	2.179	2.270	2.346	2.411	2.468	2.519	2.713	2.849	2.954	3.039	3.111	3.173	3.227	3.276
18	0.01	3.195	3.379	3.508	3.609	3.691	3.760	3.820	3.872	3.920	4.102	4.231	4.332	4.414	4.484	4.544	4.598	4.646
	0.05	2.439	2.631	2.766	2.869	2.953	3.024	3.085	3.138	3.186	3.370	3.499	3.599	3.681	3.750	3.810	3.863	3.910
	0.10	2.088	2.287	2.426	2.532	2.619	2.691	2.753	2.808	2.857	3.043	3.174	3.275	3.358	3.427	3.487	3.540	3.587
	0.20	1.704	1.914	2.059	2.170	2.259	2.334	2.399	2.455	2.505	2.696	2.830	2.933	3.017	3.087	3.148	3.201	3.249
19	0.01	3.173	3.353	3.479	3.578	3.658	3.725	3.784	3.835	3.881	4.059	4.185	4.283	4.363	4.430	4.489	4.541	4.588
	0.05	2.427	2.617	2.750	2.852	2.934	3.004	3.064	3.116	3.163	3.343	3.470	3.569	3.649	3.716	3.775	3.826	3.872
	0.10	2.080	2.277	2.415	2.520	2.605	2.676	2.738	2.791	2.839	3.023	3.152	3.251	3.332	3.400	3.459	3.511	3.557
	0.20	1.699	1.908	2.052	2.161	2.250	2.324	2.388	2.443	2.493	2.682	2.813	2.915	2.997	3.066	3.126	3.179	3.225

TABLE D.16 (Continued)

Number of comparisons (m)

Error df (f)	α‡	2	3	4	5	6	7	8	9	10	15	20	25	30	35	40	45	50
20	0.01	3.152	3.329	3.454	3.550	3.629	3.695	3.752	3.802	3.848	4.021	4.144	4.239	4.317	4.383	4.441	4.491	4.536
	0.05	2.417	2.605	2.736	2.836	2.918	2.986	3.045	3.097	3.143	3.320	3.445	3.541	3.620	3.686	3.743	3.794	3.839
	0.10	2.073	2.269	2.405	2.508	2.593	2.663	2.724	2.777	2.824	3.005	3.132	3.229	3.309	3.376	3.433	3.484	3.530
	0.20	1.695	1.902	2.045	2.154	2.241	2.315	2.378	2.433	2.482	2.668	2.798	2.898	2.979	3.048	3.106	3.158	3.204
21	0.01	3.134	3.308	3.431	3.525	3.602	3.667	3.724	3.773	3.817	3.987	4.108	4.201	4.277	4.342	4.397	4.447	4.491
	0.05	2.408	2.594	2.723	2.822	2.903	2.970	3.028	3.080	3.125	3.300	3.422	3.517	3.594	3.659	3.715	3.765	3.809
	0.10	2.067	2.261	2.396	2.498	2.581	2.651	2.711	2.764	2.810	2.989	3.114	3.210	3.288	3.354	3.411	3.461	3.505
	0.20	1.691	1.897	2.039	2.147	2.234	2.306	2.369	2.424	2.472	2.656	2.785	2.884	2.964	3.031	3.089	3.140	3.185
22	0.01	3.118	3.289	3.410	3.503	3.579	3.643	3.698	3.747	3.790	3.957	4.075	4.166	4.241	4.304	4.359	4.407	4.450
	0.05	2.400	2.584	2.712	2.810	2.889	2.956	3.014	3.064	3.109	3.281	3.402	3.495	3.571	3.634	3.690	3.738	3.782
	0.10	2.061	2.254	2.387	2.489	2.572	2.641	2.700	2.752	2.798	2.974	3.098	3.193	3.270	3.334	3.390	3.440	3.484
	0.20	1.688	1.892	2.033	2.141	2.227	2.299	2.361	2.415	2.463	2.646	2.773	2.871	2.950	3.016	3.073	3.123	3.168
23	0.01	3.103	3.272	3.392	3.483	3.558	3.621	3.675	3.723	3.766	3.930	4.046	4.135	4.208	4.270	4.324	4.371	4.413
	0.05	2.392	2.574	2.701	2.798	2.877	2.943	3.000	3.050	3.094	3.264	3.383	3.475	3.550	3.613	3.667	3.715	3.757
	0.10	2.056	2.247	2.380	2.481	2.563	2.631	2.690	2.741	2.787	2.961	3.083	3.177	3.253	3.317	3.372	3.421	3.464
	0.20	1.685	1.888	2.028	2.135	2.221	2.292	2.354	2.407	2.455	2.636	2.762	2.859	2.937	3.002	3.059	3.109	3.153
24	0.01	3.089	3.257	3.375	3.465	3.539	3.601	3.654	3.702	3.744	3.905	4.019	4.107	4.179	4.240	4.292	4.339	4.380
	0.05	2.385	2.566	2.692	2.788	2.866	2.931	2.988	3.037	3.081	3.249	3.366	3.457	3.531	3.593	3.646	3.693	3.735
	0.10	2.051	2.241	2.373	2.473	2.554	2.622	2.680	2.731	2.777	2.949	3.070	3.162	3.238	3.301	3.355	3.403	3.446
	0.20	1.682	1.884	2.024	2.130	2.215	2.286	2.347	2.400	2.448	2.627	2.752	2.848	2.925	2.990	3.046	3.095	3.139
25	0.01	3.077	3.243	3.359	3.449	3.521	3.583	3.635	3.682	3.723	3.882	3.995	4.081	4.152	4.212	4.263	4.309	4.350
	0.05	2.379	2.558	2.683	2.779	2.856	2.921	2.976	3.025	3.069	3.235	3.351	3.440	3.513	3.574	3.627	3.674	3.715
	0.10	2.047	2.236	2.367	2.466	2.547	2.614	2.672	2.722	2.767	2.938	3.058	3.149	3.224	3.286	3.340	3.387	3.430
	0.20	1.679	1.881	2.020	2.125	2.210	2.280	2.341	2.394	2.441	2.619	2.743	2.838	2.914	2.979	3.034	3.083	3.126
26	0.01	3.066	3.230	3.345	3.433	3.505	3.566	3.618	3.664	3.705	3.862	3.972	4.058	4.128	4.186	4.237	4.282	4.322
	0.05	2.373	2.551	2.675	2.770	2.847	2.911	2.966	3.014	3.058	3.222	3.337	3.425	3.497	3.558	3.610	3.656	3.697
	0.10	2.043	2.231	2.361	2.460	2.540	2.607	2.664	2.714	2.759	2.928	3.047	3.137	3.211	3.273	3.326	3.373	3.415
	0.20	1.677	1.878	2.012	2.121	2.205	2.275	2.335	2.388	2.435	2.612	2.735	2.829	2.905	2.968	3.023	3.071	3.114
27	0.01	3.056	3.218	3.332	3.419	3.491	3.550	3.602	3.647	3.688	3.843	3.952	4.036	4.105	4.163	4.213	4.257	4.297
	0.05	2.368	2.545	2.668	2.762	2.838	2.902	2.956	3.004	3.047	3.210	3.324	3.411	3.483	3.542	3.594	3.639	3.680
	0.10	2.039	2.227	2.356	2.454	2.534	2.600	2.657	2.707	2.751	2.919	3.036	3.126	3.199	3.261	3.313	3.360	3.401
	0.20	1.675	1.875	2.012	2.117	2.201	2.270	2.330	2.383	2.429	2.605	2.727	2.820	2.896	2.959	3.013	3.061	3.103

TABLE D.16 (*Continued*)

Number of comparisons (m)

Error df (f)	α‡	2	3	4	5	6	7	8	9	10	15	20	25	30	35	40	45	50
28	0.01	3.046	3.207	3.320	3.407	3.477	3.536	3.587	3.632	3.672	3.825	3.933	4.017	4.084	4.142	4.191	4.235	4.274
	0.05	2.363	2.539	2.661	2.755	2.830	2.893	2.948	2.995	3.038	3.199	3.312	3.399	3.469	3.528	3.579	3.624	3.664
	0.10	2.036	2.222	2.351	2.449	2.528	2.594	2.650	2.700	2.744	2.911	3.027	3.116	3.188	3.249	3.301	3.347	3.388
	0.20	1.672	1.872	2.009	2.113	2.196	2.266	2.326	2.378	2.424	2.599	2.720	2.812	2.887	2.950	3.004	3.051	3.093
29	0.01	3.037	3.197	3.309	3.395	3.464	3.523	3.574	3.618	3.658	3.809	3.916	3.998	4.065	4.122	4.171	4.214	4.252
	0.05	2.358	2.534	2.655	2.748	2.823	2.886	2.940	2.987	3.029	3.189	3.301	3.387	3.457	3.515	3.566	3.610	3.650
	0.10	2.033	2.218	2.346	2.444	2.522	2.588	2.644	2.693	2.737	2.903	3.018	3.107	3.178	3.239	3.291	3.336	3.377
	0.20	1.671	1.869	2.006	2.110	2.193	2.262	2.321	2.373	2.419	2.593	2.713	2.805	2.880	2.942	2.995	3.042	3.084
30	0.01	3.029	3.188	3.298	3.384	3.453	3.511	3.561	3.605	3.644	3.794	3.900	3.981	4.048	4.103	4.152	4.194	4.232
	0.05	2.354	2.528	2.649	2.742	2.816	2.878	2.932	2.979	3.021	3.180	3.291	3.376	3.445	3.503	3.553	3.597	3.637
	0.10	2.030	2.215	2.342	2.439	2.517	2.582	2.638	2.687	2.731	2.895	3.010	3.098	3.169	3.229	3.280	3.325	3.366
	0.20	1.669	1.867	2.003	2.106	2.189	2.258	2.317	2.369	2.414	2.587	2.707	2.798	2.872	2.934	2.987	3.034	3.076
40	0.01	2.970	3.121	3.225	3.305	3.370	3.425	3.472	3.513	3.549	3.689	3.787	3.862	3.923	3.975	4.019	4.058	4.093
	0.05	2.323	2.492	2.608	2.696	2.768	2.827	2.878	2.923	2.963	3.113	3.218	3.298	3.363	3.418	3.464	3.506	3.542
	0.10	2.009	2.189	2.312	2.406	2.481	2.544	2.597	2.644	2.686	2.843	2.952	3.036	3.103	3.160	3.208	3.251	3.289
	0.20	1.656	1.850	1.983	2.083	2.164	2.231	2.288	2.338	2.382	2.548	2.663	2.751	2.821	2.880	2.931	2.975	3.015
60	0.01	2.914	3.056	3.155	3.230	3.291	3.342	3.386	3.425	3.459	3.589	3.679	3.749	3.805	3.852	3.893	3.929	3.961
	0.05	2.294	2.456	2.568	2.653	2.721	2.777	2.826	2.869	2.906	3.049	3.148	3.223	3.284	3.336	3.379	3.418	3.452
	0.10	1.989	2.163	2.283	2.373	2.446	2.506	2.558	2.603	2.643	2.793	2.897	2.976	3.040	3.093	3.139	3.179	3.214
	0.20	1.643	1.834	1.963	2.061	2.139	2.204	2.259	2.308	2.350	2.511	2.621	2.705	2.772	2.828	2.876	2.918	2.956
120	0.01	2.859	2.994	3.087	3.158	3.215	3.263	3.304	3.340	3.372	3.493	3.577	3.641	3.693	3.736	3.774	3.807	3.836
	0.05	2.265	2.422	2.529	2.610	2.675	2.729	2.776	2.816	2.852	2.987	3.081	3.152	3.209	3.257	3.298	3.334	3.366
	0.10	1.968	2.138	2.254	2.342	2.411	2.469	2.519	2.562	2.600	2.744	2.843	2.918	2.978	3.029	3.072	3.110	3.143
	0.20	1.631	1.817	1.944	2.039	2.115	2.178	2.231	2.278	2.319	2.474	2.580	2.660	2.724	2.778	2.824	2.864	2.899
∞	0.01	2.806	2.934	3.022	3.089	3.143	3.188	3.226	3.260	3.289	3.402	3.480	3.539	3.587	3.627	3.661	3.691	3.718
	0.05	2.237	2.388	2.491	2.569	2.631	2.683	2.727	2.766	2.800	2.928	3.016	3.083	3.137	3.182	3.220	3.254	3.284
	0.10	1.949	2.114	2.226	2.311	2.378	2.434	2.482	2.523	2.560	2.697	2.791	2.862	2.920	2.967	3.008	3.044	3.075
	0.20	1.618	1.801	1.925	2.018	2.091	2.152	2.204	2.249	2.289	2.438	2.540	2.617	2.678	2.729	2.773	2.811	2.844

† Table reproduced from P. A. Games, An improved *t* table for simultaneous control on *g* contrasts. *Journal of the American Statistical Association*, 1977, 72, 531–534, with permission of the editor.

‡ $\alpha_{expw} = 1 - (1 - \alpha_{ind})^m$, where α_{ind} is the probability of a type 1 error on each contrast, and *m* is the number of contrasts.

TABLE D.17 Studentized maximum modulus (two-tailed)†

Error df (f)	α	Number of comparisons (m) 2	3	4	5	6	7	8	9	10	11	12	13	14	15	16
2	0.10	3.83	4.38	4.77	5.06	5.30	5.50	5.67	5.82	5.96	6.08	6.18	6.28	6.37	6.45	6.53
	0.05	5.57	6.34	6.89	7.31	7.65	7.93	8.17	8.38	8.57	8.74	8.89	9.03	9.16	9.28	9.39
	0.01	12.73	14.44	15.65	16.59	17.35	17.99	18.53	19.01	19.43	19.81	20.15	20.46	20.75	21.02	21.26
3	0.10	2.99	3.37	3.64	3.84	4.01	4.15	4.27	4.38	4.47	4.55	4.63	4.70	4.76	4.82	4.88
	0.05	3.96	4.43	4.76	5.02	5.23	5.41	5.56	5.69	5.81	5.92	6.01	6.10	6.18	6.26	6.33
	0.01	7.13	7.91	8.48	8.92	9.28	9.58	9.84	10.06	10.27	10.45	10.61	10.76	10.90	11.03	11.15
4	0.10	2.66	2.98	3.20	3.37	3.51	3.62	3.72	3.81	3.89	3.96	4.02	4.08	4.13	4.18	4.23
	0.05	3.38	3.74	4.00	4.20	4.37	4.50	4.62	4.72	4.82	4.90	4.98	5.04	5.11	5.17	5.22
	0.01	5.46	5.99	6.36	6.66	6.90	7.10	7.27	7.43	7.57	7.69	7.80	7.91	8.00	8.09	8.17
5	0.10	2.49	2.77	2.96	3.12	3.24	3.34	3.43	3.51	3.58	3.64	3.69	3.75	3.79	3.84	3.88
	0.05	3.09	3.40	3.62	3.79	3.93	4.04	4.14	4.23	4.31	4.38	4.45	4.51	4.56	4.61	4.66
	0.01	4.70	5.11	5.40	5.63	5.81	5.97	6.11	6.23	6.33	6.43	6.52	6.60	6.67	6.74	6.81
6	0.10	2.39	2.64	2.82	2.96	3.07	3.17	3.25	3.32	3.38	3.44	3.49	3.54	3.58	3.62	3.66
	0.05	2.92	3.19	3.39	3.54	3.66	3.77	3.86	3.94	4.01	4.07	4.13	4.18	4.23	4.28	4.32
	0.01	4.27	4.61	4.86	5.05	5.20	5.33	5.45	5.55	5.64	5.72	5.80	5.86	5.93	5.99	6.04
7	0.10	2.31	2.56	2.73	2.86	2.96	3.05	3.13	3.19	3.25	3.31	3.35	3.40	3.44	3.48	3.51
	0.05	2.80	3.06	3.24	3.38	3.49	3.59	3.67	3.74	3.80	3.86	3.92	3.96	4.01	4.05	4.09
	0.01	4.00	4.30	4.51	4.68	4.81	4.93	5.03	5.12	5.20	5.27	5.33	5.39	5.45	5.50	5.55
8	0.10	2.26	2.49	2.66	2.78	2.88	2.97	3.04	3.10	3.16	3.21	3.26	3.30	3.34	3.37	3.41
	0.05	2.72	2.96	3.13	3.26	3.36	3.45	3.53	3.60	3.66	3.71	3.76	3.81	3.85	3.89	3.93
	0.01	3.81	4.08	4.27	4.42	4.55	4.65	4.74	4.82	4.89	4.96	5.02	5.07	5.12	5.17	5.21
9	0.10	2.22	2.45	2.60	2.72	2.82	2.90	2.97	3.03	3.09	3.13	3.18	3.22	3.26	3.29	3.32
	0.05	2.66	2.89	3.05	3.17	3.27	3.36	3.43	3.49	3.55	3.60	3.65	3.69	3.73	3.77	3.80
	0.01	3.67	3.92	4.10	4.24	4.35	4.45	4.53	4.61	4.67	4.73	4.79	4.84	4.88	4.92	4.96
10	0.10	2.19	2.41	2.56	2.68	2.77	2.85	2.92	2.98	3.03	3.08	3.12	3.16	3.20	3.23	3.26
	0.05	2.61	2.83	2.98	3.10	3.20	3.28	3.35	3.41	3.47	3.52	3.56	3.60	3.64	3.68	3.71
	0.01	3.57	3.80	3.97	4.10	4.20	4.29	4.37	4.44	4.50	4.56	4.61	4.66	4.70	4.74	4.78
11	0.10	2.17	2.38	2.53	2.64	2.73	2.81	2.88	2.93	2.98	3.03	3.07	3.11	3.15	3.18	3.21
	0.05	2.57	2.78	2.93	3.05	3.14	3.22	3.29	3.35	3.40	3.45	3.49	3.53	3.57	3.60	3.63
	0.01	3.48	3.71	3.87	3.99	4.09	4.17	4.25	4.31	4.37	4.42	4.47	4.51	4.55	4.59	4.63

TABLE D.17 *(Continued)*

		Number of comparisons (m)														
Error df (f)	α	2	3	4	5	6	7	8	9	10	11	12	13	14	15	16
12	0.10	2.15	2.36	2.50	2.61	2.70	2.78	2.84	2.90	2.95	2.99	3.03	3.07	3.10	3.14	3.17
	0.05	2.54	2.75	2.89	3.00	3.09	3.17	3.24	3.29	3.34	3.39	3.43	3.47	3.51	3.54	3.57
	0.01	3.42	3.63	3.78	3.90	4.00	4.08	4.15	4.21	4.26	4.31	4.36	4.40	4.44	4.48	4.51
14	0.10	2.12	2.32	2.46	2.57	2.65	2.72	2.79	2.84	2.89	2.93	2.97	3.01	3.04	3.07	3.10
	0.05	2.49	2.69	2.83	2.94	3.02	3.09	3.16	3.21	3.26	3.30	3.34	3.38	3.41	3.45	3.48
	0.01	3.32	3.52	3.66	3.77	3.85	3.93	3.99	4.05	4.10	4.15	4.19	4.23	4.26	4.30	4.33
16	0.10	2.10	2.29	2.43	2.53	2.62	2.69	2.75	2.80	2.85	2.89	2.93	2.96	2.99	3.02	3.05
	0.05	2.46	2.65	2.78	2.89	2.97	3.04	3.10	3.15	3.20	3.24	3.28	3.31	3.35	3.38	3.40
	0.01	3.25	3.43	3.57	3.67	3.75	3.82	3.88	3.94	3.99	4.03	4.07	4.11	4.14	4.17	4.20
18	0.10	2.08	2.27	2.41	2.51	2.59	2.66	2.72	2.77	2.81	2.85	2.89	2.92	2.96	2.99	3.01
	0.05	2.43	2.62	2.75	2.85	2.93	3.00	3.05	3.11	3.15	3.19	3.23	3.26	3.29	3.32	3.35
	0.01	3.19	3.37	3.50	3.60	3.68	3.74	3.80	3.85	3.90	3.94	3.98	4.01	4.04	4.07	4.10
20	0.10	2.07	2.26	2.39	2.49	2.57	2.63	2.69	2.74	2.79	2.83	2.86	2.90	2.93	2.96	2.98
	0.05	2.41	2.59	2.72	2.82	2.90	2.96	3.02	3.07	3.11	3.15	3.19	3.22	3.25	3.28	3.31
	0.01	3.15	3.32	3.45	3.54	3.62	3.68	3.74	3.79	3.83	3.87	3.91	3.94	3.97	4.00	4.03
24	0.10	2.05	2.23	2.36	2.46	2.53	2.60	2.66	2.70	2.75	2.79	2.82	2.85	2.88	2.91	2.94
	0.05	2.38	2.56	2.68	2.77	2.85	2.91	2.97	3.02	3.06	3.10	3.13	3.16	3.19	3.22	3.25
	0.01	3.09	3.25	3.37	3.46	3.53	3.59	3.64	3.69	3.73	3.77	3.80	3.83	3.86	3.89	3.91
30	0.10	2.03	2.21	2.33	2.43	2.50	2.57	2.62	2.67	2.71	2.75	2.78	2.81	2.84	2.87	2.89
	0.05	2.35	2.52	2.64	2.73	2.80	2.87	2.92	2.96	3.00	3.04	3.07	3.11	3.13	3.16	3.18
	0.01	3.03	3.18	3.29	3.38	3.45	3.51	3.55	3.60	3.64	3.67	3.70	3.73	3.76	3.78	3.81
40	0.10	2.01	2.18	2.30	2.40	2.47	2.53	2.58	2.63	2.67	2.71	2.74	2.77	2.80	2.82	2.85
	0.05	2.32	2.49	2.60	2.69	2.76	2.82	2.87	2.91	2.95	2.99	3.02	3.05	3.08	3.10	3.12
	0.01	2.97	3.12	3.22	3.30	3.37	3.42	3.47	3.51	3.54	3.58	3.61	3.63	3.66	3.68	3.71
60	0.10	1.99	2.16	2.28	2.37	2.44	2.50	2.55	2.59	2.63	2.67	2.70	2.73	2.76	2.78	2.80
	0.05	2.29	2.45	2.56	2.65	2.72	2.77	2.82	2.86	2.90	2.93	2.96	2.99	3.02	3.04	3.06
	0.01	2.91	3.05	3.15	3.23	3.29	3.34	3.38	3.42	3.46	3.49	3.51	3.54	3.56	3.59	3.61
∞	0.10	1.95	2.11	2.23	2.31	2.38	2.43	2.48	2.52	2.56	2.59	2.62	2.65	2.67	2.70	2.72
	0.05	2.24	2.39	2.49	2.57	2.63	2.68	2.73	2.77	2.80	2.83	2.86	2.88	2.91	2.93	2.95
	0.01	2.81	2.93	3.02	3.09	3.14	3.19	3.23	3.26	3.29	3.32	3.34	3.36	3.38	3.40	3.42

TABLE D.17 (*Continued*)

Error df (f)	α	Number of comparisons (m) 17	18	19	20	21	22	23	24	25	26	27	28	29	30	31	32
2	0.10	6.60	6.67	6.74	6.80	6.85	6.91	6.96	7.01	7.05	7.10	7.14	7.18	7.22	7.26	7.30	7.33
	0.05	9.49	9.59	9.68	9.77	9.85	9.92	10.00	10.07	10.13	10.20	10.26	10.32	10.37	10.43	10.48	10.53
	0.01	21.49	21.71	21.91	22.11	22.29	22.46	22.63	22.78	22.93	23.08	23.21	23.35	23.47	23.59	23.71	23.83
3	0.10	4.93	4.98	5.02	5.07	5.11	5.15	5.18	5.22	5.25	5.28	5.31	5.34	5.37	5.40	5.42	5.45
	0.05	6.39	6.45	6.51	6.57	6.62	6.67	6.71	6.76	6.80	6.84	6.88	6.92	6.95	6.99	7.02	7.05
	0.01	11.27	11.37	11.47	11.56	11.65	11.74	11.82	11.89	11.97	12.04	12.11	12.17	12.23	12.29	12.35	12.41
4	0.10	4.27	4.31	4.35	4.38	4.42	4.45	4.48	4.51	4.54	4.56	4.59	4.61	4.64	4.66	4.68	4.70
	0.05	5.27	5.32	5.37	5.41	5.45	5.49	5.52	5.56	5.59	5.63	5.66	5.69	5.71	5.74	5.77	5.79
	0.01	8.25	8.32	8.39	8.45	8.51	8.57	8.63	8.68	8.73	8.78	8.83	8.87	8.92	8.96	9.00	9.04
5	0.10	3.92	3.95	3.99	4.02	4.05	4.08	4.10	4.13	4.16	4.18	4.20	4.22	4.25	4.27	4.29	4.30
	0.05	4.70	4.74	4.78	4.82	4.85	4.89	4.92	4.95	4.98	5.00	5.03	5.06	5.08	5.11	5.13	5.15
	0.01	6.87	6.93	6.98	7.03	7.08	7.13	7.17	7.21	7.25	7.29	7.33	7.36	7.40	7.43	7.46	7.49
6	0.10	3.70	3.73	3.76	3.79	3.82	3.84	3.87	3.89	3.92	3.94	3.96	3.98	4.00	4.02	4.04	4.06
	0.05	4.36	4.39	4.43	4.46	4.49	4.52	4.55	4.58	4.60	4.63	4.65	4.68	4.70	4.72	4.74	4.76
	0.01	6.09	6.14	6.18	6.23	6.27	6.31	6.34	6.38	6.41	6.45	6.48	6.51	6.54	6.57	6.59	6.62
7	0.10	3.55	3.58	3.61	3.63	3.66	3.69	3.71	3.73	3.75	3.78	3.80	3.81	3.83	3.85	3.87	3.88
	0.05	4.13	4.16	4.19	4.22	4.25	4.28	4.31	4.33	4.35	4.38	4.40	4.42	4.44	4.46	4.48	4.50
	0.01	5.59	5.64	5.68	5.72	5.75	5.79	5.82	5.85	5.88	5.91	5.94	5.96	5.99	6.01	6.04	6.06
8	0.10	3.44	3.47	3.50	3.52	3.55	3.57	3.59	3.61	3.64	3.66	3.67	3.69	3.71	3.73	3.74	3.76
	0.05	3.96	3.99	4.02	4.05	4.08	4.10	4.13	4.15	4.18	4.20	4.22	4.24	4.26	4.28	4.29	4.31
	0.01	5.25	5.29	5.33	5.36	5.39	5.43	5.45	5.48	5.51	5.54	5.56	5.59	5.61	5.63	5.65	5.67
9	0.10	3.35	3.38	3.41	3.44	3.46	3.48	3.50	3.53	3.55	3.56	3.58	3.60	3.62	3.63	3.65	3.66
	0.05	3.84	3.87	3.90	3.92	3.95	3.97	4.00	4.02	4.04	4.06	4.08	4.10	4.12	4.14	4.15	4.17
	0.01	5.00	5.04	5.07	5.10	5.13	5.16	5.19	5.21	5.24	5.26	5.29	5.31	5.33	5.35	5.37	5.39
10	0.10	3.29	3.32	3.34	3.37	3.39	3.41	3.43	3.45	3.47	3.49	3.51	3.53	3.54	3.56	3.57	3.59
	0.05	3.74	3.77	3.80	3.82	3.85	3.87	3.89	3.91	3.94	3.95	3.97	3.99	4.01	4.03	4.04	4.06
	0.01	4.81	4.84	4.88	4.91	4.93	4.96	4.99	5.01	5.03	5.06	5.08	5.10	5.12	5.14	5.16	5.18
11	0.10	3.24	3.26	3.29	3.31	3.34	3.36	3.38	3.40	3.42	3.43	3.45	3.47	3.48	3.50	3.51	3.53
	0.05	3.66	3.69	3.72	3.74	3.77	3.79	3.81	3.83	3.85	3.87	3.89	3.91	3.92	3.94	3.95	3.97
	0.01	4.66	4.69	4.72	4.75	4.78	4.80	4.83	4.85	4.87	4.89	4.91	4.93	4.95	4.97	4.99	5.01
12	0.10	3.19	3.22	3.24	3.27	3.29	3.31	3.33	3.35	3.37	3.39	3.40	3.42	3.43	3.45	3.46	3.48
	0.05	3.60	3.63	3.65	3.68	3.70	3.72	3.74	3.76	3.78	3.80	3.82	3.83	3.85	3.87	3.88	3.90
	0.01	4.54	4.57	4.60	4.63	4.65	4.67	4.70	4.72	4.74	4.76	4.78	4.80	4.82	4.83	4.85	4.87

TABLE D.17 *(Continued)*

		Number of comparisons (m)														
Error df (f)	α	17	18	19	20	21	22	23	24	25	26	27	28	29	30	31	32
14	0.10	3.13	3.15	3.18	3.20	3.22	3.24	3.26	3.28	3.29	3.31	3.33	3.34	3.36	3.37	3.39	3.40
	0.05	3.50	3.53	3.55	3.58	3.60	3.62	3.64	3.66	3.68	3.69	3.71	3.73	3.74	3.76	3.77	3.78
	0.01	4.36	4.39	4.41	4.44	4.46	4.48	4.50	4.52	4.54	4.56	4.58	4.60	4.61	4.63	4.65	4.66
16	0.10	3.08	3.10	3.12	3.15	3.17	3.19	3.20	3.22	3.24	3.26	3.27	3.29	3.30	3.31	3.33	3.34
	0.05	3.43	3.46	3.48	3.50	3.52	3.54	3.56	3.58	3.60	3.61	3.63	3.64	3.66	3.67	3.69	3.70
	0.01	4.23	4.25	4.28	4.30	4.32	4.34	4.36	4.38	4.40	4.42	4.43	4.45	4.47	4.48	4.50	4.51
18	0.10	3.04	3.06	3.08	3.11	3.13	3.14	3.16	3.18	3.20	3.21	3.23	3.24	3.26	3.27	3.28	3.30
	0.05	3.38	3.40	3.42	3.44	3.46	3.48	3.50	3.52	3.54	3.55	3.57	3.58	3.60	3.61	3.62	3.64
	0.01	4.13	4.15	4.18	4.20	4.22	4.24	4.26	4.27	4.29	4.31	4.33	4.34	4.36	4.37	4.38	4.40
20	0.10	3.01	3.03	3.05	3.07	3.09	3.11	3.13	3.15	3.16	3.18	3.19	3.21	3.22	3.23	3.25	3.26
	0.05	3.33	3.36	3.38	3.40	3.42	3.44	3.46	3.47	3.49	3.50	3.52	3.53	3.55	3.56	3.57	3.59
	0.01	4.05	4.07	4.10	4.12	4.14	4.16	4.17	4.19	4.21	4.22	4.24	4.25	4.27	4.28	4.30	4.31
24	0.10	2.96	2.98	3.01	3.03	3.04	3.06	3.08	3.10	3.11	3.13	3.14	3.16	3.17	3.18	3.19	3.21
	0.05	3.27	3.29	3.31	3.33	3.35	3.37	3.39	3.40	3.42	3.43	3.45	3.46	3.48	3.49	3.50	3.51
	0.01	3.94	3.96	3.98	4.00	4.02	4.04	4.05	4.07	4.09	4.10	4.12	4.13	4.14	4.16	4.17	4.18
30	0.10	2.92	2.94	2.96	2.98	3.00	3.01	3.03	3.05	3.06	3.08	3.09	3.10	3.12	3.13	3.14	3.15
	0.05	3.21	3.23	3.25	3.27	3.29	3.30	3.32	3.33	3.35	3.36	3.38	3.39	3.40	3.42	3.43	3.44
	0.01	3.83	3.85	3.87	3.89	3.91	3.92	3.94	3.95	3.97	3.98	4.00	4.01	4.02	4.03	4.04	4.06
40	0.10	2.87	2.89	2.91	2.93	2.95	2.97	2.98	3.00	3.01	3.03	3.04	3.05	3.06	3.08	3.09	3.10
	0.05	3.14	3.17	3.18	3.20	3.22	3.24	3.25	3.27	3.28	3.29	3.31	3.32	3.33	3.34	3.36	3.37
	0.01	3.73	3.74	3.76	3.78	3.80	3.81	3.83	3.84	3.85	3.87	3.88	3.89	3.90	3.91	3.93	3.94
60	0.10	2.83	2.85	2.87	2.88	2.90	2.92	2.93	2.95	2.96	2.98	2.99	3.00	3.01	3.02	3.04	3.05
	0.05	3.08	3.10	3.12	3.14	3.16	3.17	3.19	3.20	3.21	3.23	3.24	3.25	3.26	3.27	3.28	3.30
	0.01	3.63	3.64	3.66	3.68	3.69	3.71	3.72	3.73	3.75	3.76	3.77	3.78	3.79	3.80	3.81	3.82
∞	0.10	2.74	2.76	2.77	2.79	2.81	2.82	2.84	2.85	2.86	2.87	2.89	2.90	2.91	2.92	2.93	2.94
	0.05	2.97	2.98	3.00	3.02	3.03	3.04	3.06	3.07	3.08	3.09	3.11	3.12	3.13	3.13	3.15	3.16
	0.01	3.44	3.45	3.47	3.48	3.49	3.50	3.52	3.53	3.54	3.55	3.56	3.57	3.58	3.59	3.60	3.60

† Table reproduced from R. E. Bechhofer and C. W. Dunnett, Multiple Comparisons for Orthogonal Contrasts: Examples and Tables. *Technometrics*, 1982, 24, 213–222, with permission of the editor.

TABLE D.18   **Imhof F†**

$$F_{0.95}(h,\ hm)‡$$

h \ m	2	3	4	5	6	7	8
1.00	18.513	10.128	7.709	6.608	5.987	5.591	5.318
1.05	16.936	9.554	7.366	6.358	5.785	5.418	5.163
1.10	15.613	9.053	7.062	6.133	5.603	5.261	5.023
1.15	14.488	8.613	6.790	5.931	5.436	5.117	4.893
1.20	13.523	8.223	6.545	5.746	5.284	4.984	4.774
1.25	12.687	7.875	6.323	5.578	5.145	4.862	4.664
1.30	11.957	7.563	6.121	5.424	5.016	4.749	4.562
1.35	11.314	7.281	5.937	5.282	4.879	4.644	4.466
1.40	10.744	7.025	5.768	5.150	4.786	4.547	4.377
1.45	10.236	6.792	5.612	5.029	4.683	4.455	4.294
1.50	9.780	6.579	5.468	4.915	4.587	4.370	4.216
1.60	8.997	6.202	5.210	4.711	4.413	4.214	4.073
1.70	8.350	5.880	4.986	4.532	4.258	4.076	3.946
1.80	7.806	5.602	4.789	4.373	4.121	3.952	3.831
1.90	7.343	5.358	4.615	4.231	3.997	3.840	3.728
2.00	6.944	5.143	4.459	4.103	3.885	3.379	3.634
2.10	6.597	4.952	4.319	3.987	3.784	3.646	3.548
2.20	6.293	4.781	4.192	3.882	3.691	3.562	3.469
2.30	6.024	4.627	4.077	3.786	3.606	3.484	3.396
2.40	5.784	4.487	3.972	3.697	3.527	3.412	3.328
2.50	5.568	4.360	3.875	3.616	3.455	3.345	3.266
2.60	5.374	4.244	3.786	3.541	3.387	3.283	3.207
2.70	5.198	4.137	3.704	3.471	3.325	3.225	3.153
2.80	5.038	4.038	3.628	3.405	3.266	3.171	3.102
2.90	4.892	3.947	3.557	3.344	3.211	3.120	3.054
3.00	4.757	3.863	3.490	3.287	3.160	3.073	3.009
3.20	4.518	3.710	3.370	3.183	3.066	2.985	2.926
3.40	4.313	3.577	3.264	3.091	2.982	2.907	2.852
3.60	4.134	3.459	3.169	3.008	2.907	2.836	2.785
3.80	3.977	3.354	3.084	2.934	2.838	2.772	2.724
4.00	3.838	3.259	3.007	2.866	2.776	2.714	2.668
4.20	3.714	3.174	2.937	2.804	2.720	2.661	2.618
4.40	3.602	3.096	2.873	2.748	2.667	2.612	2.571
4.60	3.501	3.026	2.815	2.696	2.619	2.566	2.527
4.80	3.410	2.961	2.761	2.648	2.575	2.524	2.487
5.00	3.326	2.901	2.711	2.603	2.534	2.485	2.450
5.20	3.249	2.846	2.665	2.561	2.495	2.449	2.414
5.40	3.178	2.795	2.621	2.523	2.459	2.415	2.382
5.60	3.113	2.747	2.581	2.487	2.425	2.382	2.351
5.80	3.052	2.703	2.544	2.452	2.394	2.352	2.322

† This table is reproduced from J. P. Imhof: Testing the hypothesis of no fixed main-effects in Scheffé's mixed model. *Annals of Mathematical Statistics*, 1962, 33, 1085–1095. By permission of the Institute of Mathematical Statistics.

‡ $F_{0.95}[(k-1)\hat{\varepsilon},\ (k-1)(n-1)\hat{\varepsilon}] = F_{0.95}(h,\ hm),\ h = (k-1)\hat{\varepsilon}$

$$m = n - 1$$

TABLE D.18 (*Continued*)

$$F_{0.99}h, hm$$

h \ m	2	3	4	5	6	7	8
1.00	98.503	34.116	21.198	16.258	13.745	12.246	11.259
1.05	83.954	30.786	19.606	15.236	12.985	11.631	10.733
1.10	72.597	28.025	18.247	14.349	12.317	11.086	10.265
1.15	63.570	25.706	17.075	13.571	11.726	10.600	9.846
1.20	56.278	23.736	16.054	12.884	11.199	10.164	9.467
1.25	50.303	22.045	15.159	12.274	10.726	9.770	9.124
1.30	45.345	20.581	14.367	11.727	10.299	9.413	8.812
1.35	41.183	19.302	13.662	11.236	9.913	9.088	8.526
1.40	37.655	18.178	13.032	10.791	9.561	8.790	8.264
1.45	34.635	17.183	12.464	10.387	9.239	8.516	8.022
1.50	32.029	16.296	11.950	10.017	8.943	8.264	7.798
1.60	27.779	14.788	11.058	9.368	8.419	7.814	7.397
1.70	24.481	13.554	10.310	8.815	7.968	7.425	7.048
1.80	21.862	12.528	9.673	8.339	7.576	7.084	6.741
1.90	19.743	11.663	9.125	7.924	7.231	6.783	6.469
2.00	18.000	10.925	8.649	7.559	6.927	6.515	6.226
2.10	16.545	10.287	8.231	7.236	6.655	6.275	6.008
2.20	15.314	9.732	7.861	6.948	6.411	6.059	5.810
2.30	14.262	9.243	7.532	6.689	6.191	5.863	5.631
2.40	13.354	8.811	7.237	6.455	5.991	5.684	5.467
2.50	12.563	8.425	6.970	6.242	5.808	5.521	5.317
2.60	11.869	8.079	6.729	6.049	5.641	5.371	5.178
2.70	11.255	7.768	6.509	5.871	5.487	5.232	5.050
2.80	10.709	7.485	6.308	5.708	5.345	5.104	4.932
2.90	10.220	7.227	6.123	5.557	5.214	4.985	4.821
3.00	9.780	6.992	5.953	5.417	5.092	4.874	4.718
3.20	9.020	6.577	5.649	5.166	4.872	4.674	4.531
3.40	8.389	6.222	5.386	4.948	4.679	4.497	4.367
3.60	7.856	5.915	5.156	4.755	4.508	4.340	4.220
3.80	7.400	5.648	4.953	4.584	4.355	4.200	4.088
4.00	7.006	5.412	4.773	4.431	4.218	4.074	3.969
4.20	6.662	5.203	4.611	4.293	4.095	3.960	3.862
4.40	6.360	5.015	4.465	4.168	3.982	3.856	3.763
4.60	6.091	4.847	4.333	4.054	3.880	3.760	3.673
4.80	5.852	4.694	4.213	3.950	3.786	3.673	3.590
5.00	5.636	4.556	4.103	3.855	3.699	3.592	3.514
5.20	5.442	4.429	4.001	3.767	3.619	3.517	3.443
5.40	5.265	4.313	3.908	3.685	3.545	3.448	3.377
5.60	5.104	4.205	3.822	3.610	3.476	3.383	3.315
5.80	4.956	4.106	3.741	3.539	3.411	3.322	3.258

TABLE D.19 **Sphericity criterion W† (1% points)**

	k = Number of treatments						
N = Sample size	4	5	6	7	8	9	10
5	$0.0^5 3665$						
6	$0.0^3 6904$	$0.0^6 9837$					
7	$0.0^2 5031$	$0.0^3 2184$	$0.0^6 2970$				
8	0.01503	$0.0^2 1828$	$0.0^4 7187$	$0.0^7 8604$			
9	0.03046	$0.0^2 6123$	$0.0^3 6758$	$0.0^4 2424$	$0.0^7 2760$		
10	0.05010	0.01361	$0.0^2 2498$	$0.0^3 2520$	$0.0^5 8306$	$0.0^8 9216$	
11	0.07258	0.02416	$0.0^2 6033$	$0.0^2 1017$	$0.0^4 9438$	$0.0^5 2879$	$0.0^8 3573$
12	0.09679	0.03730	0.01148	$0.0^2 2646$	$0.0^3 4120$	$0.0^4 3544$	$0.0^5 1004$
13	0.1218	0.05248	0.01880	$0.0^2 5369$	$0.0^2 1149$	$0.0^3 1663$	$0.0^4 1332$
14	0.1471	0.06915	0.02782	$0.0^2 9296$	$0.0^2 2476$	$0.0^3 4943$	$0.0^4 6681$
15	0.1721	0.08685	0.03830	0.01444	$0.0^2 4516$	$0.0^2 1126$	$0.0^3 2108$
16	0.1966	0.10518	0.04998	0.02073	$0.0^2 7343$	$0.0^2 2160$	$0.0^3 5065$
17	0.2204	0.1239	0.06261	0.02807	0.01098	$0.0^2 3669$	$0.0^2 1018$
18	0.2434	0.1426	0.07595	0.03635	0.01542	$0.0^2 5707$	$0.0^2 1804$
19	0.2655	0.1613	0.08982	0.04541	0.02062	$0.0^2 8300$	$0.0^2 2914$
20	0.2867	0.1797	0.1040	0.05514	0.02652	0.01146	$0.0^2 4386$
22	0.3264	0.2156	0.1330	0.07612	0.04017	0.01940	$0.0^2 8498$
24	0.3626	0.2497	0.1620	0.09845	0.05580	0.02933	0.01421
26	0.3956	0.2819	0.1904	0.1215	0.07287	0.04095	0.02145
28	0.4257	0.3120	0.2180	0.1447	0.09092	0.05392	0.03007
30	0.4531	0.3402	0.2445	0.1677	0.1096	0.06795	0.03989
34	0.5013	0.3910	0.2940	0.2125	0.1475	0.09805	0.06231
42	0.5769	0.4741	0.3789	0.2939	0.2211	0.1611	0.1136
50	0.6331	0.5383	0.4475	0.3632	0.2876	0.2221	0.1671
60	0.6856	0.6001	0.5157	0.4348	0.3594	0.2912	0.2311
80	0.7558	0.6852	0.6129	0.5408	0.4705	0.4034	0.3411
100	0.8006	0.7407	0.6782	0.6144	0.5505	0.4879	0.4275
140	0.8541	0.8085	0.7598	0.7088	0.6562	0.6028	0.5495
200	0.8961	0.8626	0.8262	0.7874	0.7465	0.7040	0.6605
300	0.9297	0.9066	0.8811	0.8535	0.8239	0.7927	0.7600

TABLE D.19 (*Continued*)
Sphericity criterion W (5% points)

	k = Number of means						
N = Sample size	4	5	6	7	8	9	10
5	$0.0^4 9528$						
6	$0.0^2 3866$	$0.0^4 2578$					
7	0.01687	$0.0^2 1262$	$0.0^5 7479$				
8	0.03866	$0.0^2 6400$	$0.0^3 4267$	$0.0^5 2284$			
9	0.06640	0.01650	$0.0^2 2553$	$0.0^3 1473$	$0.0^6 7219$		
10	0.09739	0.03110	$0.0^2 7004$	$0.0^3 9434$	$0.0^4 5149$	$0.0^6 2326$	
11	0.1297	0.04919	0.01435	$0.0^2 2950$	$0.0^3 3631$	$0.0^4 1817$	$0.0^7 7722$
12	0.1621	0.06970	0.02433	$0.0^2 6524$	$0.0^2 1233$	$0.0^3 1397$	$0.0^5 6455$
13	0.1938	0.09174	0.03653	0.01179	$0.0^2 2924$	$0.0^3 5114$	$0.0^4 5370$
14	0.2244	0.1146	0.05051	0.01870	$0.0^2 5613$	$0.0^2 1295$	$0.0^3 2107$
15	0.2535	0.1378	0.06583	0.02712	$0.0^2 9379$	$0.0^2 2629$	$0.0^3 5667$
16	0.2812	0.1608	0.08210	0.03682	0.01423	$0.0^2 4616$	$0.0^2 1214$
17	0.3074	0.1835	0.09900	0.04761	0.02011	$0.0^2 7314$	$0.0^2 2235$
18	0.3321	0.2058	0.1163	0.05927	0.02693	0.01074	$0.0^2 3692$
19	0.3533	0.2273	0.1337	0.07161	0.03460	0.01489	$0.0^2 5630$
20	0.3772	0.2482	0.1511	0.08446	0.04299	0.01973	$0.0^2 8071$
22	0.4173	0.2876	0.1854	0.1111	0.06154	0.03129	0.01448
24	0.4530	0.3240	0.2185	0.1383	0.08178	0.04494	0.02282
26	0.4848	0.3575	0.2501	0.1654	0.1030	0.06022	0.03287
28	0.5134	0.3882	0.2800	0.1920	0.1248	0.07667	0.04435
30	0.5390	0.4164	0.3081	0.2178	0.1467	0.09392	0.05698
34	0.5833	0.4663	0.3594	0.2665	0.1898	0.1296	0.08468
42	0.6508	0.5453	0.4442	0.3515	0.2697	0.2006	0.1444
50	0.6998	0.6046	0.5106	0.4211	0.3389	0.2660	0.2035
60	0.7447	0.6603	0.5749	0.4910	0.4112	0.3376	0.2715
80	0.8037	0.7354	0.6641	0.5916	0.5196	0.4499	0.3840
100	0.8406	0.7835	0.7228	0.6597	0.5955	0.5317	0.4694
140	0.8842	0.8413	0.7948	0.7453	0.6935	0.6405	0.5870
200	0.9179	0.8868	0.8525	0.8153	0.7757	0.7342	0.6913
300	0.9447	0.9234	0.8996	0.8734	0.8452	0.8151	0.7833

† Entries are far left-handed side of the distribution of W ($0 \le W \le 1$).
This table is reproduced from B. N. Nagarsenker and K. C. S. Pillai: The distribution of the sphericity test criterion. *Journal of Multivariate Analysis,* 1973, 3, 226–235, with the permission of the editor.

TABLE D.20   **Bryant-Paulson generalized studentized range (upper 0.05 points)†**

Error df (f)	Number of means (k)										
	2	3	4	5	6	7	8	10	12	16	20
	$p = 1$ Covariate										
2	7.96	11.00	12.99	14.46	15.61	16.56	17.36	18.65	19.68	21.23	22.40
3	5.42	7.18	8.32	9.17	9.84	10.39	10.86	11.62	12.22	13.14	13.83
4	4.51	5.84	6.69	7.32	7.82	8.23	8.58	9.15	9.61	10.30	10.82
5	4.06	5.17	5.88	6.40	6.82	7.16	7.45	7.93	8.30	8.88	9.32
6	3.79	4.78	5.40	5.86	6.23	6.53	6.78	7.20	7.53	8.04	8.43
7	3.62	4.52	5.09	5.51	5.84	6.11	6.34	6.72	7.03	7.49	7.84
8	3.49	4.34	4.87	5.26	5.57	5.82	6.03	6.39	6.67	7.10	7.43
10	3.32	4.10	4.58	4.93	5.21	5.43	5.63	5.94	6.19	6.58	6.87
12	3.22	3.95	4.40	4.73	4.98	5.19	5.37	5.67	5.90	6.26	6.53
14	3.15	3.85	4.28	4.59	4.83	5.03	5.20	5.48	5.70	6.03	6.29
16	3.10	3.77	4.19	4.49	4.72	4.91	5.07	5.34	5.55	5.87	6.12
18	3.06	3.72	4.12	4.41	4.63	4.82	4.98	5.23	5.44	5.75	5.98
20	3.03	3.67	4.07	4.35	4.57	4.75	4.90	5.15	5.35	5.65	5.88
24	2.98	3.61	3.99	4.26	4.47	4.65	4.79	5.03	5.22	5.51	5.73
30	2.94	3.55	3.91	4.18	4.38	4.54	4.69	4.91	5.09	5.37	5.58
40	2.89	3.49	3.84	4.09	4.29	4.45	4.58	4.80	4.97	5.23	5.43
60	2.85	3.43	3.77	4.01	4.20	4.35	4.48	4.69	4.85	5.10	5.29
120	2.81	3.37	3.70	3.93	4.11	4.26	4.38	4.58	4.73	4.97	5.15
	$p = 2$ Covariates										
2	9.50	13.18	15.59	17.36	18.75	19.89	20.86	22.42	23.66	25.54	26.94
3	6.21	8.27	9.60	10.59	11.37	21.01	12.56	13.44	14.15	15.22	16.02
4	5.04	6.54	7.51	8.23	8.80	9.26	9.66	10.31	10.83	11.61	12.21
5	4.45	5.68	6.48	7.06	7.52	7.90	8.23	8.76	9.18	9.83	10.31
6	4.10	5.18	5.87	6.37	6.77	7.10	7.38	7.84	8.21	8.77	9.20
7	3.87	4.85	5.47	5.92	6.28	6.58	6.83	7.24	7.57	8.08	8.46
8	3.70	4.61	5.19	5.61	5.94	6.21	6.44	6.82	7.12	7.59	7.94
10	3.49	4.31	4.82	5.19	5.49	5.73	5.93	6.27	6.54	6.95	7.26
12	3.35	4.12	4.59	4.93	5.20	5.43	5.62	5.92	6.17	6.55	6.83
14	3.26	3.99	4.44	4.76	5.01	5.22	5.40	5.69	5.92	6.27	6.54
16	3.19	3.90	4.32	4.63	4.88	5.07	5.24	5.52	5.74	6.07	6.33
18	3.14	3.82	4.24	4.54	4.77	4.96	5.13	5.39	5.60	5.92	6.17
20	3.10	3.77	4.17	4.46	4.69	4.88	5.03	5.29	5.49	5.81	6.04
24	3.04	3.69	4.08	4.35	4.57	4.75	4.90	5.14	5.34	5.63	5.86
30	2.99	3.61	3.98	4.25	4.46	4.62	4.77	5.00	5.18	5.46	5.68
40	2.93	3.53	3.89	4.15	4.34	4.50	4.64	4.86	5.04	5.30	5.50
60	2.88	3.46	3.80	4.05	4.24	4.39	4.52	4.73	4.89	5.14	5.33
120	2.82	3.38	3.72	3.95	4.13	4.28	4.40	4.60	4.75	4.99	5.17

TABLE D.20   (*Continued*)

Error					Number of means (*k*)						
df (f)	2	3	4	5	6	7	8	10	12	16	20

upper 0.05 *points*

p = 3 Covariates

	2	3	4	5	6	7	8	10	12	16	20
2	10.83	15.06	17.82	19.85	21.45	22.76	23.86	25.66	27.08	29.23	30.83
3	6.92	9.23	10.73	11.84	12.72	13.44	14.06	15.05	15.84	17.05	17.95
4	5.51	7.18	8.25	9.05	9.67	10.19	10.63	11.35	11.92	12.79	13.45
5	4.81	6.16	7.02	7.66	8.17	8.58	8.94	9.52	9.98	10.69	11.22
6	4.38	5.55	6.30	6.84	7.28	7.64	7.94	8.44	8.83	9.44	9.90
7	4.11	5.16	5.82	6.31	6.70	7.01	7.29	7.73	8.08	8.63	9.03
8	3.91	4.88	5.49	5.93	6.29	6.58	6.83	7.23	7.55	8.05	8.42
10	3.65	4.51	5.05	5.44	5.75	6.01	6.22	6.58	6.86	7.29	7.62
12	3.48	4.28	4.78	5.14	5.42	5.65	5.85	6.17	6.43	6.82	7.12
14	3.37	4.13	4.59	4.93	5.19	5.41	5.59	5.89	6.13	6.50	6.78
16	3.29	4.01	4.46	4.78	5.03	5.23	5.41	5.69	5.92	6.27	6.53
18	3.23	3.93	4.35	4.66	4.90	5.10	5.27	5.54	5.76	6.09	6.34
20	3.18	3.86	4.28	4.57	4.81	5.00	5.16	5.42	5.63	5.96	6.20
24	3.11	3.76	4.16	4.44	4.67	4.85	5.00	5.25	5.45	5.75	5.98
30	3.04	3.67	4.05	4.32	4.53	4.70	4.85	5.08	5.27	5.56	5.78
40	2.97	3.57	3.94	4.20	4.40	4.56	4.70	4.92	5.10	5.37	5.57
60	2.90	3.49	3.83	4.08	4.27	4.43	4.56	4.77	4.93	5.19	5.38
120	2.84	3.40	3.73	3.97	4.15	4.30	4.42	4.62	4.77	5.01	5.19

upper 0.01 *points*

p = 1 Covariate

	2	3	4	5	6	7	8	10	12	16	20
2	19.09	26.02	30.57	33.93	36.58	38.76	40.60	43.59	45.95	49.55	52.24
3	10.28	13.32	15.32	16.80	17.98	18.95	19.77	21.12	22.19	23.82	25.05
4	7.68	9.64	10.93	11.89	12.65	13.28	13.82	14.70	15.40	16.48	17.29
5	6.49	7.99	8.97	9.70	10.28	10.76	11.17	11.84	12.38	13.20	13.83
6	5.83	7.08	7.88	8.48	8.96	9.36	9.70	10.25	10.70	11.38	11.90
7	5.41	6.50	7.20	7.72	8.14	8.48	8.77	9.26	9.64	10.24	10.69
8	5.12	6.11	6.74	7.20	7.58	7.88	8.15	8.58	8.92	9.46	9.87
10	4.76	5.61	6.15	6.55	6.86	7.13	7.35	7.72	8.01	8.47	8.82
12	4.54	5.31	5.79	6.15	6.43	6.67	6.87	7.20	7.46	7.87	8.18
14	4.39	5.11	5.56	5.89	6.15	6.36	6.55	6.85	7.09	7.47	7.75
16	4.28	4.96	5.39	5.70	5.95	6.15	6.32	6.60	6.83	7.18	7.45
18	4.20	4.86	5.26	5.56	5.79	5.99	6.15	6.42	6.63	6.96	7.22
20	4.14	4.77	5.17	5.45	5.68	5.86	6.02	6.27	6.48	6.80	7.04
24	4.05	4.65	5.02	5.29	5.50	5.68	5.83	6.07	6.26	6.56	6.78
30	3.96	4.54	4.89	5.14	5.34	5.50	5.64	5.87	6.05	6.32	6.53
40	3.88	4.43	4.76	5.00	5.19	5.34	5.47	5.68	5.85	6.10	6.30
60	3.79	4.32	4.64	4.86	5.04	5.18	5.30	5.50	5.65	5.89	6.07
120	3.72	4.22	4.52	4.73	4.89	5.03	5.14	5.32	5.47	5.69	5.85

TABLE D.20 (*Continued*)

					Number of means (k)						
Error df (f)	2	3	4	5	6	7	8	10	12	16	20

upper 0.01 *points*

$p = 2$ Covariates

Error df (f)	2	3	4	5	6	7	8	10	12	16	20
2	23.11	31.55	37.09	41.19	44.41	47.06	49.31	52.94	55.82	60.20	63.47
3	11.97	15.56	17.91	19.66	21.05	22.19	23.16	24.75	26.01	27.93	29.38
4	8.69	10.95	12.43	13.54	14.41	15.14	15.76	16.77	17.58	18.81	19.74
5	7.20	8.89	9.99	10.81	11.47	12.01	12.47	13.23	13.84	14.77	15.47
6	6.36	7.75	8.64	9.31	9.85	10.29	10.66	11.28	11.77	12.54	13.11
7	5.84	7.03	7.80	8.37	8.83	9.21	9.53	10.06	10.49	11.14	11.64
8	5.48	6.54	7.23	7.74	8.14	8.48	8.76	9.23	9.61	10.19	10.63
10	5.02	5.93	6.51	6.93	7.27	7.55	7.79	8.19	8.50	8.99	9.36
12	4.74	5.56	6.07	6.45	6.75	7.00	7.21	7.56	7.84	8.27	8.60
14	4.56	5.31	5.78	6.13	6.40	6.63	6.82	7.14	7.40	7.79	8.09
16	4.42	5.14	5.58	5.90	6.16	6.37	6.55	6.85	7.08	7.45	7.73
18	4.32	5.00	5.43	5.73	5.98	6.18	6.35	6.63	6.85	7.19	7.46
20	4.25	4.90	5.31	5.60	5.84	6.03	6.19	6.46	6.67	7.00	7.25
24	4.14	4.76	5.14	5.42	5.63	5.81	5.96	6.21	6.41	6.71	6.95
30	4.03	4.62	4.98	5.24	5.44	5.61	5.75	5.98	6.16	6.44	6.66
40	3.93	4.48	4.82	5.07	5.26	5.41	5.54	5.76	5.93	6.19	6.38
60	3.83	4.36	4.68	4.90	5.08	5.22	5.35	5.54	5.70	5.94	6.12
120	3.73	4.24	4.54	4.75	4.91	5.05	5.16	5.35	5.49	5.71	5.88

$p = 3$ Covariates

Error df (f)	2	3	4	5	6	7	8	10	12	16	20
2	26.54	36.26	42.64	47.36	51.07	54.13	56.71	60.90	64.21	69.25	73.01
3	13.45	17.51	20.17	22.15	23.72	25.01	26.11	27.90	29.32	31.50	33.13
4	9.59	12.11	13.77	15.00	15.98	16.79	17.47	18.60	19.50	20.87	21.91
5	7.83	9.70	10.92	11.82	12.54	13.14	13.65	14.48	15.15	16.17	16.95
6	6.85	8.36	9.34	10.07	10.65	11.13	11.54	12.22	12.75	13.59	14.21
7	6.23	7.52	8.36	8.98	9.47	9.88	10.23	10.80	11.26	11.97	12.51
8	5.81	6.95	7.69	8.23	8.67	9.03	9.33	9.84	10.24	10.87	11.34
10	5.27	6.23	6.84	7.30	7.66	7.96	8.21	8.63	8.96	9.48	9.88
12	4.94	5.80	6.34	6.74	7.05	7.31	7.54	7.90	8.20	8.65	9.00
14	4.72	5.51	6.00	6.36	6.65	6.89	7.09	7.42	7.69	8.10	8.41
16	4.56	5.30	5.76	6.10	6.37	6.59	6.77	7.08	7.33	7.71	8.00
18	4.44	5.15	5.59	5.90	6.16	6.36	6.54	6.83	7.06	7.42	7.69
20	4.35	5.03	5.45	5.75	5.99	6.19	6.36	6.63	6.85	7.19	7.45
24	4.22	4.86	5.25	5.54	5.76	5.94	6.10	6.35	6.55	6.87	7.11
30	4.10	4.70	5.06	5.33	5.54	5.71	5.85	6.08	6.27	6.56	6.78
40	3.98	4.54	4.88	5.13	5.32	5.48	5.61	5.83	6.00	6.27	6.47
60	3.86	4.39	4.72	4.95	5.12	5.27	5.39	5.59	5.75	6.00	6.18
120	3.75	4.25	4.55	4.77	4.94	5.07	5.18	5.37	5.51	5.74	5.90

APPENDIX E

TOPICS CLOSELY RELATED TO THE ANALYSIS OF VARIANCE

A large set of topics is related to the analysis of variance. What is presented here is a subset of those topics which may be particularly useful to the researcher.

E.1 USE OF ANALYSIS OF VARIANCE TO ESTIMATE RELIABILITY OF MEASUREMENTS.

In Chapter 4, it was pointed out that the variance-component model of the analysis of variance may be used to estimate reliability of measurements.

Given a person possessing a magnitude π of a specified characteristic, in appraising this characteristic with some measuring device, the observed score may have the magnitude $\pi + \eta$. The quantity η is the error of measurement; all measurement has some of this kind of error. The latter is due in part to the measuring device itself and in part to the conditions surrounding the measurement. In the development that follows, it will be assumed that the magnitude of the error of measurement is uncorrelated with π. A measurement on person i with measuring instrument j may be represented as

$$X_{ij} = \pi_i + \eta_{ij}, \tag{E.1}$$

where X_{ij} = observed measurement,
π_i = true magnitude of characteristic being measured,
η_{ij} = error of measurement.

Upon repeated measurement with the same or comparable instruments, π_i is

TABLE E.1 **Estimation of reliability**

| Person | \multicolumn{5}{c}{Comparable measurements} | Total | Mean |
	1	2	$\cdots$	j	$\cdots$	k		
1	X_{11}	X_{12}		X_{1j}		X_{1k}	P_1	$\bar{P}_1$
2	X_{21}	X_{22}		X_{2j}		X_{2k}	P_2	$\bar{P}_2$
$\vdots$	$\vdots$	$\vdots$	$\vdots$	$\vdots$	$\vdots$	$\vdots$	$\vdots$	$\vdots$
i	X_{i1}	X_{i2}		X_{ij}		X_{ik}	P_i	$\bar{P}_i$
$\vdots$	$\vdots$	$\vdots$	$\vdots$	$\vdots$	$\vdots$	$\vdots$	$\vdots$	$\vdots$
n	X_{n1}	X_{n2}		X_{nj}		X_{nk}	P_n	$\bar{P}_n$
Total	T_1	T_2	$\cdots$	T_j	$\cdots$	T_k	G	

assumed to remain constant, whereas η_{ij} is assumed to vary. The mean of k such repeated measures may be represented as

$$\frac{\sum_j X_{ij}}{k} = \bar{P}_i = \pi_i + \bar{\eta}_i. \tag{E.2}$$

A schematic representation of a random sample of k measurements on the same or comparable measuring instruments is shown in Table E.1. If π_i remains constant for such measurement, the variance within person i is due to error of measurement, and the pooled within-person variance also estimates variance due to error of measurement. On the other hand, the variance in the $\bar{P}$'s is in part due to differences between the true magnitudes of the characteristic possessed by the n people and in part due to differences in the average error of measurement for each person. The analysis of variance and the expected values for the mean squares for data of the type shown in Table E.1 are given in Table E.2. $\mathrm{MS}_{\text{b. people}}$ is defined as

$$\mathrm{MS}_{\text{b. people}} = \frac{k \sum (\bar{P}_i - \bar{G})^2}{n - 1},$$

whereas the variance of the $\bar{P}$'s is given by

$$s_{\bar{P}}^2 = \frac{\sum (\bar{P}_i - \bar{G})^2}{n - 1}.$$

TABLE E.2 **Analysis of variance for model in (E.1)**

Source of variation	MS	E(MS)
Between people	$\mathrm{MS}_{\text{b. people}}$	$\sigma_\eta^2 + k\sigma_\pi^2$
Within people	$\mathrm{MS}_{\text{w. people}}$	σ_η^2

Thus
$$\text{MS}_{\text{b. people}} = k s_{\bar{P}}^2.$$

In terms of (E.2), the expected value of the variance of the $\bar{P}$'s is

$$E(s_{\bar{P}}^2) = \sigma_{\bar{\eta}}^2 + \sigma_{\pi}^2.$$

The quantity σ_{π}^2 is the variance of the true measures in the population of which the n people in the study represent a random sample. From the relationship between $\text{MS}_{\text{b. people}}$ and $s_{\bar{P}}^2$,

$$E(\text{MS}_{\text{b. people}}) = k\sigma_{\bar{\eta}}^2 + k\sigma_{\pi}^2 = \sigma_{\eta}^2 + k\sigma_{\pi}^2,$$

since
$$k\sigma_{\bar{\eta}}^2 = \sigma_{\eta}^2.$$

The reliability of $\bar{P}_i$, the mean of k measurements, is defined as

$$\rho_k = \frac{\sigma_{\pi}^2}{\sigma_{\pi}^2 + \sigma_{\bar{\eta}}^2} = \frac{\sigma_{\pi}^2}{\sigma_{\pi}^2 + (\sigma_{\eta}^2/k)} . \tag{E.3}$$

In words, the reliability of the mean of k measurements is the variance due to true scores divided by the sum of the variance due to true scores and the variance due to the mean of the errors of measurement. If one defines

$$\theta = \frac{\sigma_{\pi}^2}{\sigma_{\eta}^2},$$

then the expression for ρ_k may be cast in the form

$$\begin{aligned}
\rho_k &= \frac{\sigma_{\pi}^2}{\sigma_{\pi}^2 + (\sigma_{\eta}^2/k)} = \frac{\sigma_{\pi}^2/\sigma_{\eta}^2}{(\sigma_{\pi}^2/\sigma_{\eta}^2) + (\sigma_{\eta}^2/k\sigma_{\eta}^2)} \\
&= \frac{k(\sigma_{\pi}^2/\sigma_{\eta}^2)}{1 + k(\sigma_{\pi}^2/\sigma_{\eta}^2)} \\
&= \frac{k\theta}{1 + k\theta} .
\end{aligned} \tag{E.4}$$

When $k = 1$, (E.4) becomes

$$\rho_1 = \frac{\theta}{1 + \theta} = \frac{\sigma_{\pi}^2}{\sigma_{\pi}^2 + \sigma_{\eta}^2}, \tag{E.5}$$

which, by definition, is the reliability of a single measurement. Within the context of the variance-component model of the analysis of variance, (E.5) represents the *intraclass* correlation.

The reliability of the mean of k measurements, ρ_k, may be expressed in terms of the reliability of a single measurement, ρ_1, as follows:

$$\rho_k = \frac{k\rho_1}{1 + (k - 1)\rho_1} . \tag{E.6}$$

To establish (E.6), replace ρ_1 in (E.6) by the expression for ρ_1 in (E.5). Thus,

$$\rho_k = \frac{k[\theta/(1+\theta)]}{1+(k-1)[\theta/(1+\theta)]} = \frac{k\theta}{1+k\theta}.$$

Hence the expression on the right-hand side of (E.6) is identical to the expression on the right-hand side of the expression given in (E.4).

In the psychometric literature, (E.6) is known as the Spearman–Brown prediction formula. The assumptions underlying this formula are those underlying the model in (E.1), namely, that the error of measurement is uncorrelated with the true score, that the sample of n people on whom the observations are made is a random sample from a population of people to which inferences are to be made, that the sample of k measuring instruments used is a random sample from a population of comparable measuring instruments, and that the within-person variance may be pooled to provide an estimate of σ_η^2.

The expected values of the mean squares associated with the model in (E.1) are given in Table E.2. From these expected values one has the following estimator for σ_η^2:

$$\hat{\sigma}_\eta^2 = MS_{w.\,people}.$$

If one equates $MS_{b.\,people}$ to its expectation and then replaces parameters by their estimators, one has

$$MS_{b.\,people} = \hat{\sigma}_\eta^2 + k\hat{\sigma}_\pi^2$$
$$= MS_{w.\,people} + k\hat{\sigma}_\pi^2.$$

Hence an estimate of the variance component σ_π^2 is given by

$$\hat{\sigma}_\pi^2 = \frac{MS_{b.\,people} - MS_{w.\,people}}{k}.$$

Under the assumption that the random variables π and η in (E.1) are independently and normally distributed, the estimators for $\hat{\sigma}_\pi^2$ and $\hat{\sigma}_\eta^2$ can be shown to be the unbiased maximum-likelihood estimators.

From these estimators, one logical estimate for θ would seem to be

$$\hat{\theta} = \frac{\hat{\sigma}_\pi^2}{\hat{\sigma}_\eta^2} = \frac{MS_{b.\,people} - MS_{w.\,people}}{kMS_{w.\,people}}.$$

This estimator will, however, be biased. In general, the ratio of two unbiased estimators will provide a biased estimator of the ratio. In terms of this estimator of θ, an estimate of the reliability, ρ_k, is given by

$$\begin{aligned} r_k = \hat{\rho}_k &= \frac{k\hat{\theta}}{1+k\hat{\theta}} = \frac{(MS_{b.\,people} - MS_{w.\,people})/MS_{w.\,people}}{1+[(MS_{b.\,people} - MS_{w.\,people})/MS_{w.\,people}]} \\ &= \frac{MS_{b.\,people} - MS_{w.\,people}}{MS_{b.\,people}} \\ &= 1 - \frac{MS_{w.\,people}}{MS_{b.\,people}} = \frac{F-1}{F}, \end{aligned} \tag{E.7}$$

where $F = MS_{\text{b. people}}/MS_{\text{w. people}}$. The reliability of a single measurement is estimated by

$$r_1 = \hat{\rho}_1 = \frac{\hat{\theta}}{1 + \hat{\theta}} = \frac{MS_{\text{b. people}} - MS_{\text{w. people}}}{MS_{\text{b. people}} + (k-1)MS_{\text{w. people}}}. \tag{E.8}$$

It is possible to obtain an unbiased estimator of θ; indeed, the unbiased estimator of θ was obtained in Sec. 3.5. In terms of the notation used in this section, the unbiased estimator obtained in Sec. 3.5 is given by

$$\hat{\theta}' = \frac{MS_{\text{b. people}} - \{n(k-1)/[n(k-1)-2]\}MS_{\text{w. people}}}{\{kn(k-1)/[n(k-1)-2]\}MS_{\text{w. people}}}.$$

$$= \frac{MS_{\text{b. people}} - mMS_{\text{w. people}}}{km MS_{\text{w. people}}} \tag{E.9}$$

where $m = \dfrac{n(k-1)}{n(k-1)-2}$.

In terms of the estimator in (E.1), the estimator of the reliability of the mean of k measurements is

$$r_k' = \frac{k\hat{\theta}'}{1 + k\hat{\theta}'}. \tag{E.10}$$

In general $\qquad\qquad \hat{\theta}' < \hat{\theta}.$

Hence $\qquad\qquad r_k' < r_k.$

Numerical Example

To illustrate the material that has been discussed up to this point, a numerical example is given in Table E.3. In this example $n = 6$ people are rated by $k = 4$ judges on a specified characteristic. The data in the columns represent the rating given by the individual judges. The data within a row represent the rating received by a person. For example, person 1 received the ratings 2, 4, 3, and 3. The row totals are designated by the symbols P_i; the column totals are designated by the symbols T_j. In the computational work in parts ii and iii, the judges play the role that treatments had in earlier sections.

A summary of the analysis of variance appears in Table E.4. Only the between- and within-subject mean squares are needed to estimate the reliability as given by (E.7). The additional mean squares given in Table E.4 will be used in connection with an alternative definition of reliability, which will be discussed later in this section.

From the data in Table E.4, the estimate of θ is

$$\hat{\theta} = \frac{MS_{\text{b. people}} - MS_{\text{w. people}}}{kMS_{\text{w. people}}} = \frac{24.50 - 2.00}{4(2.00)} = 2.8125.$$

Hence the estimate of the reliability of the mean of the $k = 4$ judges, as

TABLE E.3 **Numerical example**

	Person	Judge 1	Judge 2	Judge 3	Judge 4	Total
	1	2	4	3	3	$12 = P_1$
	2	5	7	5	6	$23 = P_2$
	3	1	3	1	2	$7 = P_3$
(i)	4	7	9	9	8	$33 = P_4$
	5	2	4	6	1	$13 = P_5$
	6	6	8	8	4	$26 = P_6$
	Total	23	35	32	24	$114 = G$
		T_1	T_2	T_3	T_4	

(ii) $$(1) = \frac{G^2}{kn} = 541.50 \quad (2) = \sum \left(\sum X^2 \right) = 700 \quad (3) = \frac{\sum T_j^2}{n} = 559.00 \quad (4) = \frac{\sum P_i^2}{k} = 664.00$$

(iii)

$$\begin{aligned} SS_{b.people} &= (4) - (1) & = 122.50 \\ SS_{w.people} &= (2) - (4) & = 36.00 \\ SS_{b.judges} &= (3) - (1) & = 17.50 \\ SS_{res} &= (2) - (3) - (4) + (1) = & 18.50 \\ SS_{total} &= (2) - (1) & = 158.50 \end{aligned}$$

obtained from (E.7), is

$$r_4 = \frac{4\hat{\theta}}{1 + 4\hat{\theta}} = \frac{4(2.8125)}{1 + 4(2.8125)} = 0.9184.$$

The estimate of the reliability of a single judge, as obtained from (E.8), is

$$r_1 = \frac{\hat{\theta}}{1 + \hat{\theta}} = \frac{2.8125}{1 + 2.8125} = 0.7377.$$

To illustrate the application of the Spearman–Brown prophecy formula, one may obtain r_4 from the relationship

$$r_4 = \frac{4r_1}{1 + 3r_1} = \frac{4(0.7377)}{1 + 3(0.7377)} = 0.9184.$$

The unbiased estimator of θ as obtained from the data in Table E.4, as

TABLE E.4 **Analysis of variance**

Source of variation	SS		df	MS
Between people		122.50	5	24.50
Within people		36.00	18	2.00
Between judges	17.50		3	5.83
Residual	18.50		15	1.23
Total		158.50	23	

obtained from (E.9), is

$$\hat{\theta}' = \frac{24.50 - \{6(3)/[6(3)-2]\}(2.00)}{\{4(6)(3)/6(3)-2]\}(2.00)} = 2.4722.$$

In terms of this estimator, the reliability of the mean of $k = 4$ judges, as obtained from (E.10), is

$$r_4' = \frac{4\hat{\theta}'}{1+4\hat{\theta}'} = \frac{4(2.4722)}{1+4(2.4722)} = 0.9082.$$

Alternative Model—Adjustment for Anchor Points

A more general (in one sense) model than that used in (E.1) has the form

$$X_{ij} = \pi_i + \alpha_j + \eta_{ij} \quad \begin{cases} i = 1, \ldots, n, \\ j = 1, \ldots, k. \end{cases} \tag{E.11}$$

where X_{ij} = observed measurement,
π_i = true magnitude of characteristic measured,
α_j = anchor point (main effect) of measuring instrument,
η_{ij} = error of measurement.

In terms of the representation in Table E.1, differences due to anchor points are due to differences in the T_j.

Under the model in (E.11), the analysis of variance has the form given in Table E.5. One should note that the term η_{ij} in the model represented by (E.1) includes the term α_j that appears in model (E.11). That is, the term η_{ij} in model (E.1) is more inclusive than the corresponding term in model (E.11).

In terms of the model in (E.11), the reliability of the mean of k observations is defined by

$$\rho_k = \frac{k\theta}{1+k\theta}, \qquad \text{where} \qquad \theta = \frac{\sigma_\pi^2}{\sigma_\eta^2}. \tag{E.12}$$

In form, (E.12) is identical to that given earlier in this section; however, the

TABLE E.5 **Analysis of variance for model in (E.11)**

Source of variation	SS		df	MS	E(MS)
Between people	$SS_{\text{b. people}}$		$n-1$	$MS_{\text{b. people}}$	$\sigma_\eta^2 + k\sigma_\pi^2$
Within people	$SS_{\text{w. people}}$		$n(k-1)$		
Judges (anchor points)	SS_{judges}		$k-1$	MS_{judges}	$\sigma_\eta^2 + n\sigma_\alpha^2$
Residual	SS_{res}		$(n-1)(k-1)$	MS_{res}	σ_η^2

model on which (E.12) is based is different from the earlier model. From the E(MS) in Table E.5,

$$\hat{\sigma}_\eta^2 = MS_{res}.$$

(From the model used earlier in this section, $\hat{\sigma}_\eta^2 = MS_{w.\ people}.$) Also

$$\hat{\sigma}_\pi^2 = \frac{MS_{b.\ people} - MS_{res}}{k}.$$

Hence

$$\hat{\theta} = \frac{\hat{\sigma}_\pi^2}{\hat{\sigma}_\eta^2} = \frac{MS_{b.\ people} - MS_{res}}{kMS_{res}}.$$

The unbiased estimate of θ is given by

$$\hat{\theta}' = \frac{MS_{b.\ people} - \{(n-1)(k-1)/[(n-1)(k-1)-2]\}MS_{res}}{\{k(n-1)(k-1)/[(n-1)(k-1)-2]\}MS_{res}}$$

$$= \frac{MS_{b.\ people} - m'MS_{res}}{km'MS_{res}}$$

where $m' = \dfrac{(n-1)(k-1)}{(n-1)(k-1)-2}.$

In terms of the numerical example summarized in Table E.4,

$$\hat{\theta} = \frac{24.500 - 1.233}{4(1.233)} = 4.7176,$$

$$\hat{\theta}' = \frac{24.500 - \{5(3)/[5(3)-2]\}(1.233)}{\{4(5)(3)/[5(3)-2]\}(1.233)} = 4.0552.$$

Thus, when differences due to anchor points are not considered part of the error of measurement, the estimate of reliability of the mean of $k = 4$ observations, using $\hat{\theta}$, is

$$r_4 = \frac{4\hat{\theta}}{1+4\hat{\theta}} = \frac{18.8704}{19.8704} = 0.9497,$$

$$r_1 = \frac{\hat{\theta}}{1+\hat{\theta}} = \frac{4.7176}{5.7176} = 0.8251.$$

The corresponding estimate using $\hat{\theta}'$ is

$$r_4' = \frac{4\hat{\theta}'}{1+4\hat{\theta}'} = \frac{16.2208}{17.2208} = 0.9419.$$

In terms of the $k \times k$ variance–covariance matrix of the measuring instruments, it will be found that

$$r_1 = \frac{\overline{cov}}{\overline{var}}; \tag{E.13}$$

that is, the estimate of reliability for a single measurement, when differences due to anchor points are not considered part of error of measurement, is the average covariance among the measurements divided by the average variance. The relationship in (E.13) follows from the fact that

$$MS_{b. \text{ people}} = \overline{\text{var}} + (k-1)\,\overline{\text{cov}},$$

$$MS_{res} = \overline{\text{var}} - \overline{\text{cov}}.$$

Hence
$$\hat{\theta} = \frac{[\overline{\text{var}} + (k-1)\,\overline{\text{cov}}] - [\overline{\text{var}} - \overline{\text{cov}}]}{k(\overline{\text{var}} - \overline{\text{cov}})}$$

$$= \frac{\overline{\text{cov}}}{\overline{\text{var}} - \overline{\text{cov}}}.$$

Thus
$$r_1 = \frac{\hat{\theta}}{1+\hat{\theta}} = \frac{\overline{\text{cov}}/(\overline{\text{var}} - \overline{\text{cov}})}{1 + \overline{\text{cov}}/(\overline{\text{var}} - \overline{\text{cov}})},$$

$$= \frac{\overline{\text{cov}}}{\overline{\text{var}}}.$$

To illustrate the relationship in (E.13) the variance–covariance matrix for the numerical data given in Table E.3 is given in Table E.6. For this matrix the mean of the entries on the main diagonal is

$$\overline{\text{var}} = \frac{6.1660 + 6.1660 + 9.0660 + 6.800}{4} = 7.0495.$$

The mean of the entries off the main diagonal is

$$\overline{\text{cov}} = 5.8163.$$

Hence
$$r_1 = \frac{\overline{\text{cov}}}{\overline{\text{var}}} = \frac{5.8163}{7.0495} = 0.8251.$$

Since neither the variance within a judge nor the covariance between any two judges depends upon the anchor points, any correlational measure for reliability will not depend upon differences due to anchor points.

TABLE E.6 **Variance–covariance matrix for numerical example in Table E.3**

	Judge 1	Judge 2	Judge 3	Judge 4
Judge 1	6.1660	6.1660	6.4660	5.6000
Judge 2		6.1660	6.4660	5.6000
Judge 3			9.0660	4.6000
Judge 4				6.8000

Direct Adjustment for Anchor Points—Numerical Example

Consider the numerical data in Table E.3. The totals and means for each of the columns (judges) are as follows:

	Judge 1	Judge 2	Judge 3	Judge 4	
Total	23	35	32	24	114
Mean	3.83	5.83	5.33	4.00	$4.75 = \bar{G}$

The anchor points for the judges are given by

$$\hat{\alpha}_1 = \bar{T}_1 - \bar{G} = -0.99, \qquad \hat{\alpha}_3 = \bar{T}_3 - \bar{G} = 0.59,$$
$$\hat{\alpha}_2 = \bar{T}_2 - \bar{G} = 1.08, \qquad \hat{\alpha}_4 = \bar{T}_4 - \bar{G} = -0.75.$$

To adjust the data obtained from judge j for his anchor point, one subtracts $\hat{\alpha}_j$ from his ratings. For example, the adjusted data for judge 1 is obtained by subtracting $\hat{\alpha}_1 = -0.99$ from all entries in the first column of the data in part i of Table E.3. If similar adjustments are made for the other columns, the data in part i of Table E.7 will be obtained. The model for the adjusted data may be represented as follows:

$$X'_{ij} = X_{ij} - \hat{\alpha}_j = \pi_i + \eta_{ij}. \tag{E.14}$$

Note that the adjustment process has no effect upon the row totals. The

TABLE E.7 **Numerical example (adjusted data)**

	Person	Judge 1	Judge 2	Judge 3	Judge 4	Total
	1	2.92	2.92	2.41	3.75	12
	2	5.92	5.92	4.41	6.75	23
	3	1.92	1.92	0.41	2.75	7
(i)	4	7.92	7.92	8.41	8.75	33
	5	2.92	2.92	5.41	1.75	13
	6	6.92	6.92	7.41	4.75	26
	Total	28.52	28.52	28.46	28.50	114

(ii)

$$(1) = \frac{G^2}{kn} = 541.50 \qquad (2) = \sum \sum X^2 = 682.50 \qquad (3) = \frac{\sum T_j^2}{n} = 541.50$$

$$(4) = \frac{\sum P_i^2}{k} = 664.00$$

(iii)

$$
\begin{aligned}
SS_{b.\ people} &= (4) - (1) & &= 122.50 \\
SS_{w.\ people} &= (2) - (4) & &= 18.50 \\
SS_{b.\ judges} &= (3) - (1) & &= 0.00 \\
SS_{res} &= (2) - (3) - (4) + (1) = 18.50 \\
SS_{total} &= (2) - (1) & &= 141.00
\end{aligned}
$$

TABLE E.8 **Analysis of variance (adjusted data)**

Source of variation	SS	df	MS
Between people	122.50	5	24.500
Within people (adj.)	18.50	15	1.233
Total	141.00	20	

adjustment process does, however, make all the column totals equal, within rounding error.

In parts ii and iii of Table E.7 the sums of squares for the various sources of variation are computed by means of the usual computational formulas. A summary of the analysis of variance is given in Table E.8. Since $k - 1$ independent parameters are estimated in order to obtain the adjustments, the degrees of freedom associated with $SS_{w.\ people}$ (adjusted) are

$$n(k - 1) - (k - 1) = (n - 1)(k - 1) \quad \text{rather than} \quad n(k - 1).$$

One notes that $MS_{w.\ people}$(adjusted) in this analysis is equal numerically to MS_{res} in the analysis-of-variance Table E.4. Thus replacing $MS_{w.\ people}$ by $MS_{w.\ people}$(adjusted) is equivalent to replacing $MS_{w.\ people}$ by MS_{res}. In essence, this is what was done in the preceding subsection.

The right-hand side of the model in (E.14) has the same form as the model in (E.1), but in (E.1) η_{ij} includes differences due to anchor points. The assumptions underlying the model in (E.1) also apply to the model in (E.14). However, in estimating the parameters in the model, under the model in (E.14) $MS_{w.\ people}$(adjusted) replaces $MS_{w.\ people}$. For example, under the model in (E.14), the (biased) estimator of θ is given by

$$\hat{\theta} = \frac{MS_{b.\ people} - MS_{w.\ people}(\text{adjusted})}{k MS_{w.\ people}(\text{adjusted})}$$

$$= \frac{MS_{b.\ people} - MS_{res}}{k MS_{res}}.$$

Reliability of a Test of k Items

Table E.9 represents data that would be obtained from the administration of a test of k items. The totals $P_1, P_2, \ldots, P_n$ represent the test scores for the people taking the tests, provided that the score on the test is obtained by summing the scores on the individual items. An estimate of the reliability of the test may be obtained from (E.12). The reliability of a total is the same as that of a mean score. The computational procedures used in Sec. 4.2, with the test items having the role of the treatments, will provide the quantities required in (E.12). If the test items are scored 1 for correct and 0 for incorrect, the only information required to obtain an estimate of the reliability of the test

TABLE E.9 **Representation of test scores**

Person	Item 1	Item 2	$\cdots$	Item k	Test score
1	X_{11}	X_{12}		X_{1k}	P_1
2	X_{21}	X_{22}		X_{2k}	P_2
$\vdots$	$\vdots$	$\vdots$		$\vdots$	$\vdots$
n	X_{n1}	X_{n2}		X_{nk}	P_n
	T_1	T_2	$\cdots$	T_k	G

are the scores on the tests and the number of correct responses to each item. (In cases where the observed data consist of 0's and 1's, $\sum X = \sum X^2$.) The error of measurement in this case may be interpreted (in part) as a measure of the extent to which people having the same test scores do not have identical profiles of correct responses. For person 1, the profile of responses is $X_{11}, X_{12}, \ldots, X_{1k}$.

TABLE E.10 **Reliability of a test of $k = 5$ dichotomous items**

			Items				
Person	1	2	3	4	5		
1	1	1	1	1	1	$5 = P_1$	
2	1	1	1	1	0	$4 = P_2$	
3	1	1	1	0	1	4	
4	1	1	0	1	0	3	$k = 5$
5	1	1	1	0	0	3	$n = 10$
6	1	1	0	0	1	3	
7	1	1	0	0	0	2	
8	0	1	1	0	0	2	
9	1	0	1	0	0	2	
10	1	0	0	0	0	1	
Total	9	8	6	3	3	$29 = G$	

$$(1) = G^2/kn = 16.82 \qquad (3) = \sum T^2/n = 19.90$$

$$(2) = \sum X^2 = 29 \qquad (4) = \sum P^2/k = 19.40$$

$$\text{SS}_{\text{b. people}} = (4) - (1) = 2.58 \qquad \text{MS}_{\text{b. people}} = 0.2867$$

$$\text{SS}_{\text{res}} = (2) - (3) - (4) + (1) = 6.52 \qquad \text{MS}_{\text{res}} = 0.1811$$

$$\hat{\theta} = \frac{\text{MS}_{\text{b. people}} - \text{MS}_{\text{res}}}{k\text{MS}_{\text{res}}} = 0.1166$$

$$r_5 = \frac{5\hat{\theta}}{1 + 5\hat{\theta}} = \frac{0.5831}{1.5831} = 0.3683$$

TABLE E.11   **Variance–covariance matrix for items in Table E.10**

	1	2	3	4	5
1	0.1000	−0.0222	−0.0444	0.0333	0.0333
2		0.1778	0.0222	0.0667	0.0667
3			0.2667	0.0222	0.0667
4				0.2333	0.0111
5					0.2333

(i) rows 1–5

(ii)

$$\overline{\mathrm{var}} = 0.0201 \qquad \overline{\mathrm{cov}} = 0.0211$$

$$r_1 = \frac{\overline{\mathrm{cov}}}{\overline{\mathrm{var}}} = 0.1044$$

$$r_5 = \frac{5r_1}{1 + 4r_1} = 0.3682$$

Two numerical examples using dichotomous items are given in this subsection. In both examples the distribution of the test scores is the same. However, in the second example individuals having the same scores have identical profiles. In Table E.10, the steps in the computation of the reliability are given in detail. The reliability for the test is $r_5 = 0.3683$.

The covariance matrix for the items is given in Table E.11. From $\overline{\mathrm{var}}$ and $\overline{\mathrm{cov}}$ in this table one obtains r_1. From the latter, by means of the Spearman–Brown relationship, one may compute r_5. Within rounding error, r_5 obtained here is the same as r_5 obtained in Table E.10.

TABLE E.12   **Reliability of a test of $k = 5$ dichotomous items—comparable profiles**

	Items					
Person	**1**	**2**	**3**	**4**	**5**	**Total**
1	1	1	1	1	1	5
2	1	1	1	1	0	4
3	1	1	1	1	0	4
4	1	1	1	0	0	3
5	1	1	1	0	0	3
6	1	1	1	0	0	3
7	1	1	0	0	0	2
8	1	1	0	0	0	2
9	1	1	0	0	0	2
10	1	0	0	0	0	1
Total	10	9	6	3	1	29

$$\mathrm{MS_{b.\,people}} = 0.2867 \qquad \mathrm{MS_{res}} = 0.1033$$

$$\hat{\theta} = 0.1033 \qquad r_5 = \frac{5\hat{\theta}}{1 + 5\hat{\theta}} = 0.6397$$

In Table E.12, the row totals are the same as those in Table E.10. However, in Table E.12 individuals having the same row totals have the same row profiles. MS_{res} in this table is reduced from 0.1811 (in Table E.10) to 0.1033. The resulting reliability is raised from 0.3683 to 0.6397. One notes that, in spite of the fact that all individuals having the same score have identical row profiles, the reliability is not unity.

Under this method of defining reliability, MS_{res} is a measure of what is called the subject by item interaction. As long as $MS_{b.\,people} > 0$, with dichotomous items $MS_{res} > 0$. Hence the reliability cannot reach unity.

Summary

One additional point about the model underlying reliability should be made explicit and emphasized. Just as in the basic model for correlated observations discussed in Chap. 4, one assumes that the π_i's are constant under all measurements made. This assumption implies that the correlation between the judges (tests, items) be constant. In particular the analysis-of-variance model cannot be used to estimate reliability when the true score changes irregularly from one measurement to the next, as, for example, when practice effects are present in some nonsystematic manner. If, however, changes in the underlying true score are systematic and constant for all subjects, then adjustments for this change may be made by eliminating variation due to change from the within-subject variation.

E.2 ANALYSIS OF VARIANCE FOR RANKED DATA

Suppose that an experimenter is interested in determining whether or not there is any difference between various methods of packaging a product. In an experiment, subjects are asked to rank the methods in order of preference. A numerical example of this kind of experiment is given in Table E.13. Person 1, for example, assigned rank 1 to method 3, rank 2 to method 2, rank 3 to method 1, and rank 4 to method 4.

The computational formulas in Sec. 4.2 may be used to obtain sums of squares required for the analysis of variance. $SS_{b.\,people}$ will always be zero. Upon replicating the experiment with random samples of subjects, SS_{total} will remain constant provided that no tied ranks are permitted. Rather than an F statistic, the chi-square statistic

$$\chi^2_{ranks} = \frac{SS_{methods}}{(SS_{methods} + SS_{res})/n(k-1)} = \frac{SS_{methods}}{MS_{w.\,people}}$$

$$= \frac{n(k-1)SS_{methods}}{SS_{w.\,people}} \tag{E.13}$$

is used to test the hypothesis of no difference in mean rank for the methods.

TABLE E.13 **Numerical example**

Person	Method 1	Method 2	Method 3	Method 4	Total
1	3	2	1	4	10
2	4	3	1	2	10
3	2	4	1	3	10
4	1	3	2	4	10
5	2	3	1	4	10
6	1	4	2	3	10
7	2	3	1	4	10
$n = 8$	1	4	2	3	10
Total	16	26	11	27	80

$$(1) = \frac{G^2}{kn} = 200.00 \qquad (2) = \sum\sum X^2 = 240 \qquad (3) = \frac{\sum T_j^2}{n} = \frac{1782}{8} = 222.75$$

$$(4) = \frac{\sum P_i^2}{k} = \frac{800}{4} = 200.00$$

$$\begin{aligned}
\text{SS}_{\text{methods}} &= (3) - (1) && = 22.75 \\
\text{SS}_{\text{res}} &= (2) - (3) - (4) + (1) &&= 17.25 \\
\text{SS}_{\text{w. people}} &= (2) - (4) && = 40.00
\end{aligned}$$

The higher the agreement between people in ranking the methods, the larger $\text{SS}_{\text{methods}}$ will be. For the data in Table E.13,

$$\chi^2_{\text{ranks}} = \frac{8(3)(22.75)}{40.00} = 13.65.$$

The critical value of this statistic for a 0.01-level test is

$$\chi^2_{0.99}(k-1) = \chi^2_{0.99}(3) = 11.3.$$

Since the observed χ^2 exceeds the critical value, the data contradict the hypothesis of no difference between the mean ranks for the different methods of packaging. Inspection of Table E.13 indicates that methods 1 and 3 have the smaller means and methods 2 and 4 the larger means.

When no tied ranks are permitted,

$$\text{SS}_{\text{w. people}} = \frac{nk(k^2 - 1)}{12},$$

and the χ^2 statistic becomes

$$\chi^2_{\text{ranks}} = \frac{12}{nk(k+1)} \left(\sum T_j^2\right) - 3n(k+1). \qquad (E.14)$$

The expression for χ^2 in (E.14) is algebraically equivalent to (E.13) when no ties are permitted; (E.13) may be used whether or not ties are present. For the data in Table E.13, expression (E.14) gives

$$\chi^2_{\text{ranks}} = \frac{12}{8(4)(5)}(1782) - 3(8)(5)$$
$$= 13.65.$$

Use of this statistic in testing the hypothesis on the mean ranks defines what is called the Friedman test.

The rationale underlying the use of the chi-square distribution rather than an F distribution for making this type of test is (nonrigorously) as follows: If no ties are permitted, upon replication of the experiment, $MS_{\text{w. subj}}$ is not subject to sampling variation. Hence $MS_{\text{w. subj}}$ may be regarded as a parameter rather than as a statistic. Thus

$$\chi^2_{\text{ranks}} = \frac{SS_{\text{methods}}}{MS_{\text{w. subj}}} = \frac{SS_{\text{methods}}}{\sigma^2_{\text{w. subj}}}.$$

Under the hypothesis of no differences among the methods

$$\chi^2_{\text{ranks}} \quad \text{is distributed as} \quad \chi^2(k-1).$$

An index of the extent to which people agree in their preferences is given by the coefficient of concordance, which is defined as

$$W = \frac{SS_{\text{methods}}}{SS_{\text{total}}}. \tag{E.15}$$

This coefficient is related to the average intercorrelation between the rankings assigned by the people; this relationship is

$$\bar{r} = \frac{nW - 1}{n - 1}. \tag{E.16}$$

The test in (E.13) may be regarded as a test of the hypothesis that the coefficient of concordance in the population of people is zero. For the data in Table E.13,

$$W = \frac{22.75}{40.00} = 0.569.$$

The average intercorrelation between the people is

$$\bar{r} = \frac{8(0.569) - 1}{8 - 1} = 0.507.$$

The index W corresponds to a correlation ratio, whereas $\bar{r}$ corresponds to a product-moment correlation (or equivalently a rank-difference correlation).

The average intercorrelation between the people may also be computed through use of what is equivalent to the model in (E.11). In this case

$$\hat{\theta} = \frac{\hat{\sigma}^2_{\text{methods}}}{\hat{\sigma}^2_{\text{res}}} = \frac{(\text{MS}_{\text{methods}} - \text{MS}_{\text{res}})/n}{\text{MS}_{\text{res}}}$$

$$= \frac{[(22.75/3) - (17.25/21)]/8}{17.25/21} = 1.0290.$$

Thus
$$\bar{r} = \frac{\hat{\theta}}{1 + \hat{\theta}} = \frac{1.0290}{2.0290} = 0.507.$$

Alternatively,

$$\bar{r} = \frac{\hat{\sigma}^2_{\text{methods}}}{\hat{\sigma}^2_{\text{res}} + \hat{\sigma}^2_{\text{methods}}} = \frac{\hat{\theta}}{1 + \hat{\theta}},$$

which is a biased estimator of the intraclass correlation.

E.3 DICHOTOMOUS DATA

Observed data may in some cases be classified into one of two classes; for example, a characteristic may be present or absent, a response is either yes or no, a drug is either fatal or it is not. Such data are said to be dichotomous. One of the two dichotomies may conveniently be designated by a 0, the other by a 1. Which category is assigned the zero is arbitrary.

Consider an experiment designed to study the effects of an advertising campaign upon the attitude of a potential population of buyers toward a product. The data may take the form given in Table E.14. In this table a 0 is used to indicate an unfavorable attitude, and a 1 is used to indicate a favorable attitude. Suppose that a random sample of 10 subjects is selected for the study. Each subject is interviewed at the end of five different time periods. For example, subject 1 was not favorable at any time; subject 5 was not favorable on the first four interviews but was favorable on the fifth interview.

To test the hypothesis of no change in the percentage of favorable replies over the time periods, the statistic

$$Q = \frac{n(k-1)\text{SS}_{\text{time}}}{\text{SS}_{\text{w. people}}} \tag{E.17}$$

may be used. The Q statistic has the same form as χ^2_{ranks}, which was used in Sec. E.2. Under the hypothesis of no change in the percentage of favorable replies, Cochran (1950) has shown that the sampling distribution of the Q statistic is approximated by a chi-square distribution with $k-1$ degrees of freedom, when n is reasonably large. For an α-level test the critical value for the Q statistic is $x^2_{1-\alpha}(k-1)$.

For the data in Table E.14,

$$Q = \frac{10(5-1)(2.08)}{7.60} = 10.95.$$

TABLE E.14 **Numerical example**

Subject	Time 1	Time 2	Time 3	Time 4	Time 5	Total
1	0	0	0	0	0	$0 = P_1$
2	0	0	1	1	0	$2 = P_2$
3	0	0	1	1	1	3
4	0	1	1	1	1	4
5	0	0	0	0	1	1
6	0	1	0	1	1	3
7	0	0	1	1	1	3
8	1	0	0	1	1	3
9	1	1	1	1	1	5
10	1	1	1	1	1	5
Total	3	4	6	8	8	29

$$(1) = \frac{G^2}{kn} = \frac{29^2}{50} = 16.82 \qquad (2) = \sum \sum X^2 = 29 \qquad (3) = \frac{\sum T_j^2}{n} = \frac{189}{10} = 18.90$$

$$(4) = \frac{\sum P_i^2}{k} = \frac{107}{5} = 21.40$$

			df	
$SS_{b.people}$	$= (4) - (1)$	$= 4.58$		
$SS_{w.people}$	$= (2) - (4)$	$= 7.60$		
SS_{time}	$= (3) - (1)$	$= 2.08$	4	$MS_{time} = 0.520$
SS_{res}	$= (2) - (3) - (4) + (1) = 5.52$		36	$MS_{res} = 0.153$
SS_{total}	$= (2) - (1)$	$= 12.18$		

The critical value for a 0.05-level test is $\chi^2_{0.95}(5 - 1) = 9.5$. Hence the experimental data contradict the hypothesis of no change in the percentage of favorable replies. Examination of the data indicates a systematic increase in the percentage of favorable replies. Cochran (1950) has indicated that the F statistic computed by treating the data as if the measurements were normally distributed variables will yield probability statements which are relatively close to those obtained by use of the Q statistic. For the data in Table E.14,

$$F = \frac{MS_{time}}{MS_{res}} = \frac{0.520}{0.153} = 3.40.$$

For a 0.05-level test the critical value for the F statistic is $F_{0.95}(4, 36) = 2.63$. Thus the use of the F statistic also leads to the rejection of the hypothesis of no change in the percentage of favorable replies.

E.4 KRUSKAL–WALLIS H TEST

Analogous to a single classification analysis of variance in which there are no repeated measures is the analysis of variance for ranked data. Suppose that there are k treatment classes having n_j observations in each class. Suppose further that the observations are in the form of ranks. That is, the criterion scores are ranks assigned irrespective of the treatment class to which an observation belongs. The data given below illustrate what is meant:

Treatment 1	Treatment 2	Treatment 3
1	3	6
2	5	9
4	8	12
7	10	13
	11	14

To test the hypothesis that the ranks within the treatment classes are a random sample from a common population of ranks, the following statistic may be used:

$$H = \frac{SS_{treat}}{MS_{total}}.$$

Numerator and denominator of the H statistic have the usual analysis-of-variance definitions.

When the hypothesis being tested is true, and when each n_j is larger than 5, the sampling distribution of this statistic may be approximated by a chi-square distribution having $k - 1$ degrees of freedom. For small values of n_j and k, special tables for the H statistic are available. Computational procedures for this test duplicate the procedures for a single classification analysis of variance. The latter procedures correct for tied ranks, whereas the specialized formulas for the H statistic require corrections for tied ranks, if these occur.

Wallace (1959) compared various methods of approximating the exact sampling distribution of the H statistic for the special case of $k = 3$ and each $n_j < 6$. When all $n_j = 5$, the chi-square approximation gave results which differed only in the third decimal place from the exact probability. A typical example is the following: When the exact probability was 0.0094, the chi-square approximation was 0.0089.

The Mann–Whitney U statistic is closely related to the H statistic when $k = 2$. Extensive tables for the U statistic for small n_j are available [see Siegel (1956, pp. 271–277)]. Individual comparisons between two treatments following an overall H test may be made by means of the U statistic. An application of this procedure will be found in Lewis and Cotton (1958). If one of the treatments represents a control group, the nonparameteric analog of the Dunnett procedure is described in Sec. E.6 of this appendix.

A different approach for handling data which are in terms of ranks is to transform the ranks into normalized scores. Tables for doing this are given in Walker and Lev (1953, p. 480). More extensive tables of expected values of normal order statistics are in Harter (1960). In the latter form the data may be handled by means of the usual analysis of variance. The latter approach may lead to somewhat different conclusions. If the population to which inferences are to be made is considered to be one in which the criterion scores are normally distributed, then the analysis of variance in terms of the transformed scores is the more appropriate. On the other hand, if inferences are limited to ordinal measurement on the criterion scale, then the Kruskal–Wallis H statistic provides the more appropriate type of analysis.

E.5 CONTINGENCY TABLE WITH REPEATED MEASURES

Consider an experiment in which n judges are asked to assign ranks to r products. Data obtained from this experiment may be summarized as follows:

	Rank						
Product	**1**	**2**	$\cdots$	j	$\cdots$	r	**Total**
1	n_{11}	n_{12}	$\cdots$	n_{1j}	$\cdots$	n_{1r}	n
2	n_{21}	n_{22}	$\cdots$	n_{2j}	$\cdots$	n_{2r}	n
$\vdots$	$\vdots$	$\vdots$		$\vdots$		$\vdots$	$\vdots$
i	n_{i1}	n_{i2}	$\cdots$	n_{ij}	$\cdots$	n_{ir}	n
$\vdots$	$\vdots$	$\vdots$		$\vdots$		$\vdots$	$\vdots$
r	n_{r1}	n_{r2}	$\cdots$	n_{rj}	$\cdots$	n_{rr}	n
Total	n	n	$\cdots$	n	$\cdots$	n	nr

In this summary, n_{ij} represents the number of times product i receives a rank of j. (The sampling distributions to be discussed in this section are obtained by limiting procedures which assume n to be large. The approximations have been shown to be reasonably close for $nr = 30$ and larger. In similar limiting procedures, $n = 5$ and larger provide adequate approximations.)

To test the hypothesis of no differences between the products with respect to the frequency with which the products receive the rank of j, the statistic

$$Q_{j.}^2 = \frac{r \sum_i [n_{ij} - (n/r)]^2}{n} = \frac{\left(r \sum_i n_{ij}^2\right) - n^2}{n}$$

may be used. When there are no differences between the frequencies in column j, except those due to sampling error, Q_j has a sampling distribution which is approximated by a chi-square distribution having $r - 1$ degrees of freedom.

To test the overall hypothesis of no differences between the ranks of the products, the statistic

$$Q^2 = \sum Q_j^2$$

may be used. Under the hypothesis of no difference between the ranks assigned to the products, Anderson (1959) has shown that the statistic

$$\frac{(r-1)Q^2}{r} \doteq \chi^2 \qquad \text{with} \qquad \text{df} = (r-1)^2.$$

If the statistic $(r-1)Q^2/r$ exceeds the critical value for a test having level of significance α, as determined from the appropriate sampling distribution, the hypothesis of no difference between the frequencies within the columns is rejected.

Anderson (1959) has shown that the Friedman statistic discussed in Sec. E.2 provides a test on $r-1$ components of the overall chi square. The latter may be partitioned into individual comparisons, or contrasts, each having a single degree of freedom. In making tests on such comparisons, one uses the following estimates of the variances and covariances for the cell frequencies:

$$\text{var}\,(n_{ij}) = \frac{n(r-1)}{r^2},$$

$$\text{cov}\,(n_{ij}, n_{ik}) = \frac{-n}{r^2},$$

where n_{ij} and n_{ik} are two frequencies in the same row,

$$\text{cov}\,(n_{ij}, n_{kj}) = \frac{-n}{r^2},$$

where n_{ij} and n_{kj} are two frequencies in the same column, and

$$\text{cov}\,(n_{ij}, n_{km}) = \frac{n}{r^2(r-1)},$$

where n_{ij} and n_{km} are two frequencies in different rows and columns.

A 3×3 contingency table will be used for illustrative purposes. The cell frequencies are the column headings.

	n_{11}	n_{12}	n_{13}	n_{21}	n_{22}	n_{23}	n_{31}	n_{32}	n_{33}
C_1	0	0	0	−1	0	1	0	0	0
C_2	1	0	0	0	0	0	−1	0	0
C_3	1	0	−1	0	0	0	−1	0	1

The coefficients in row C_1 represent a linear comparison among the ranks assigned to product 2. The numerical value of the chi-square statistic corresponding to this comparison is

$$\chi^2_{C_1} = \frac{(n_{23} - n_{21})^2}{\text{var}\,(n_{23} - n_{21})}.$$

The denominator of this statistic is

$$\text{var}\,(n_{23} - n_{21}) = \text{var}\,(n_{23}) + \text{var}\,(n_{21}) - 2\,\text{cov}\,(n_{23}, n_{21})$$

$$= \frac{n(r-1)}{r^2} + \frac{n(r-1)}{r^2} - \frac{2(-n)}{r^2}$$

$$= \frac{2n}{r}.$$

The above chi-square statistic has one degree of freedom. Should this statistic exceed the critical value for an α-level test, the data would indicate a statistically significant difference between the rankings assigned to product 2.

The coefficients in row C_2 represent a linear comparison among the products for rank 1. (This comparison is not orthogonal to C_1). The chi-square statistic corresponding to this comparison is

$$\chi^2_{C_2} = \frac{(n_{11} - n_{31})^2}{\text{var}\,(n_{11} - n_{31})} = \frac{(n_{11} - n_{31})^2}{2n/r}$$

$$= \frac{r(n_{11} - n_{31})^2}{2n}.$$

This chi-square statistic has one degree of freedom.

The coefficients in row C_3 represent a comparison between the differences in linear rankings for products 1 and 3. (Comparison C_3 is orthogonal to comparison C_1.) The chi-square statistic corresponding to this comparison is

$$\chi^2_{C_3} = \frac{(n_{11} - n_{13} + n_{33} - n_{31})^2}{\text{var}\,(n_{11} - n_{13} + n_{33} - n_{31})}.$$

The individual variances and covariances required to obtain the term in the denominator are given by

$$\text{var}\,(n_{11} - n_{13} + n_{33} - n_{31}) = 4\,\text{var}\,(n_{ij}) - 4\,\text{cov}\,(n_{ij}, n_{ik})$$

$$- 4\,\text{cov}\,(n_{ij}, n_{kj}) + 4\,\text{cov}\,(n_{ij}, n_{km})$$

$$= \frac{4n}{r-1}.$$

Thus

$$\chi^2_{C_3} = \frac{(r-1)(n_{11} - n_{13} + n_{33} - n_{31})^2}{4n}.$$

The chi-square statistic used in the Friedman test is equivalent to the sum of $r - 1$ orthogonal comparisons among the products. For the case of a 3×3 contingency table, C_1 and C_3 are orthogonal comparisons of this kind. Hence

$$\chi^2_{C_1} + \chi^2_{C_3} = \chi^2_{\text{ranks}} \equiv \frac{\text{SS}_{\text{products}}}{\text{MS}_{\text{w. judge}}},$$

where the last term on the right is the statistic used in the Friedman test.

TABLE E.15   Numerical example

Judge	Product a	b	c	Total
1	2	1	3	$6 = P_1$
2	1	2	3	6
3	1	3	2	6
4	1	2	3	6
5	2	1	3	6
6	1	2	3	6
7	1	3	2	6
8	1	2	3	6
$T_a = 10$	16	22		48

(i)

$$G^2/nr = (48^2)/8(3) = 96.00 \qquad \left(\sum T_j^2\right)\Big/n = 105.00$$

$$\sum X^2 = 112 \qquad \left(\sum P_i^2\right)\Big/r = 96.00$$

$$SS_{products} = 105 - 96.00 = 9.00$$

$$SS_{w.\,judge} = 112 - 96.00 = 16.00 \qquad MS_{w.\,judge} = 16.00/16 = 1.00$$

$$\chi^2_{ranks} = \frac{SS_{products}}{MS_{w.\,judge}} = 9.00$$

Product	Rank 1	2	3	Total
a	6	2	0	8
b	2	4	2	8
c	0	2	6	8
	8	8	8	

(ii)

$$\chi^2_{C_1} = 3(2-2)^2/2(8) = 0$$

$$\chi^2_{C_3} = 2(6-0+6-0)/4(8) = 9$$

$$\chi^2_{C_1} + \chi^2_{C_3} = 9$$

The numerical example given in Table E.15 illustrates this last relationship. Basic data are given in part i. There are $n = 8$ judges and $r = 3$ products. The rankings assigned by each judge are shown. The variations obtained in part i are defined as follows:

$$SS_{products} = \frac{\sum T_j^2}{n} - \frac{G^2}{nr},$$

$$SS_{w.\,judge} = \sum X^2 - \frac{\sum P_i^2}{r}.$$

Computation of this latter source of variation may be simplified when no tied ranks are permitted. The critical value for a 0.05-level test is $\chi^2_{0.95}(2) = 6.00$. Hence the test in part i indicates that the differences in ranks assigned to the products are statistically significant.

Data from part i are rearranged to form a contingency table in part ii. The comparison C_1, which was defined earlier in this section, indicates no difference in the linear ranking for product b. The critical value associated with a 0.05-level test on C_3 is $\chi^2_{0.95}(1) = 3.8$. Hence the data indicate that there is a statistically significant difference between the linear rankings for products a and c. Note that

$$\chi^2_{C_1} + \chi^2_{C_3} = \chi^2_{\text{ranks}}.$$

E.6 COMPARING TREATMENT EFFECTS WITH A CONTROL

Procedures for comparing all treatments with a control were discussed in Sec. 3.11. A nonparametric analog of these procedures has been developed by Steel (1959). A numerical example will be used to illustrate the procedures for comparing all treatments with a control when data are in terms of ranks. In a sense, these comparisons are part of the overall hypothesis tested by the Kruskal–Wallis H statistic.

The basic data for this numerical example are given in part i of Table E.16. Suppose that only the rank order of these measurements is considered meaningful. The data in part ii are in terms of ranks. To obtain these ranks,

TABLE E.16   Numerical example

Control			Treatment a	Treatment b	Treatment c
45			35	58	75
50			40	62	78
60	$n=5$		45	70	80
62			48	78	80
75			50	80	84

Control			Treatment a	Treatment b	Treatment c
a	b	c			
3.5	1	1	1	3	5.5
6.5	2	2	2	6	7
8	4	3	3.5	8	8.5
9	5	4	5	9	8.5
10	7	5.5	6.5	10	10
37.0	19.0	15.5	18.0	36.0	29.5
T'_a	T'_b	T'_c	T_a	T_b	T_c

the control scores and the treatment a scores are combined; then ranks 1 to $2n$ are assigned to the combined set of scores. In case of ties, the mean of the tied ranks is used. The combined sets of scores for the control and treatment a groups are as follows:

Scores ...	35	40	45	45	48	50	50	60	62	75
Ranks ...	1	2	3.5	3.5	5	6.5	6.5	8	9	10

Data from the control conditions are underscored. The combined sets of scores from the control and treatment c conditions are as follows:

Scores ...	45	50	60	62	75	75	78	80	80	84
Ranks ...	1	2	3	4	5.5	5.5	7	8.5	8.5	10

The sum of the ranks for the control group and each of the treatment groups is then computed. T'_a represents the sum of ranks for the control condition when the scores are ranked with reference to treatment a. The test statistic used in the decision rule about the difference between treatment a and the control condition is $\min(T'_a, T_a)$, that is, the smaller of T'_a and T_a. In this case,

$$\min(T'_a, T_a) = \min(37, 18) = 18.$$

As a partial check on the numerical work,

$$T'_i + T_i = n(2n + 1).$$

Steel (1959) constructed tables of the sampling distribution of the statistic $\min(T'_i, T_i)$. Probabilities in these tables are in terms of an experimentwise error rate. By definition, the latter is the ratio of the number of experiments with one or more false significance statements to the total number of experiments. For the case $n = 5$ and $k = 3$, where k is the number of treatments (excluding the control), the critical value for the rank sum statistic for a two-tailed test with error rate 0.05 is 16. The decision is made to reject the hypothesis of no difference between treatment i and the control if

$$\min(T'_i, T_i) \leq 16.$$

For the data in Table E.16, treatment c is statistically different from the control, but none of the other differences between the treatments and the control is statistically significant, with a 0.05-level experimentwise error rate. Had the direction of the differences between the control and the experimental groups been predicted prior to the experiment, one-tailed rather than two-tailed tests would be appropriate. The critical value for a 0.05-level one-tailed test in which $n = 5$ and $k = 3$ is 18.

E.7   GENERAL PARTITION OF DEGREES OF FREEDOM IN A CONTINGENCY TABLE

To illustrate the procedures to be discussed in this section, consider the three-dimensional contingency table having the following form (all observations are assumed to be independent):

	c_1		c_2	
	b_1	b_2	b_1	b_2
a_1	n_{111}	n_{121}	n_{112}	n_{122}
a_2	n_{211}	n_{221}	n_{212}	n_{222}
a_3	n_{311}	n_{321}	n_{312}	n_{322}

In general there will be p classes for category A, q classes for category B, and r classes for category C. The frequency in cell abc_{ijk} will be designated by the symbol n_{ijk}.

If the B category in the above contingency table is disregarded, the resulting AC summary table will have the following form:

	c_1	c_2	Total
a_1	$n_{1.1}$	$n_{1.2}$	$n_{1..}$
a_2	$n_{2.1}$	$n_{2.2}$	$n_{2..}$
a_3	$n_{3.1}$	$n_{3.2}$	$n_{3..}$
Total	$n_{..1}$	$n_{..2}$	$n_{...}$

In general the following notation will be used:

$$\sum_i n_{ijk} = n_{.jk}, \qquad \sum_j n_{ijk} = n_{i.k}, \qquad \sum_k n_{ijk} = n_{ij.};$$

$$\sum_i \sum_j n_{ijk} = \sum_i n_{i.k} = n_{..k}, \qquad \sum_i \sum_k n_{ijk} = \sum_i n_{ij.} = n_{.j.};$$

$$\sum_i \sum_j \sum_k n_{ijk} = \sum_i \sum_j n_{ij.} = \sum_i n_{i..} = n_{....}$$

If sampling is random with respect to all categories, $pqr - 1$ parameters are necessary to specify the population from which the sample of size $n_{...}$ was drawn. These parameters may be specified in terms of the following proportions:

$$P_{ijk} = \text{proportion of population frequency in cell } abc_{ijk}.$$

The expected frequency in cell abc_{ijk}, which will be designated by the symbol n'_{ijk}, is

$$n_{ijk} = P_{ijk} n_{....}$$

The expected frequencies for the marginal totals of category A would be

$$n'_{i..} = \sum_j \sum_k n'_{ijk};$$

alternatively,

$$n'_{i..} = \sum_j \sum_k P_{ijk} n_{...} = P_{i..} n_{...}.$$

The symbol $P_{i..}$ designates the population proportion for the category a_i. The other expected marginal frequencies are

$$n'_{.j.} = P_{.j.} n_{...},$$

$$n'_{..k} = P_{..k} n_{...}.$$

The expected frequency for a cell in the AB summary table is given by

$$n'_{ij.} = \sum_k n'_{ijk}$$

$$= \sum_k P_{ijk} n_{...} = P_{ij.} n_{...}.$$

Other expected frequencies for two-way summary tables are

$$n'_{i.k} = P_{i.k} n_{...},$$

$$n'_{.jk} = P_{.jk} n_{...}.$$

If all the $pqr - 1$ parameters in the population are specified by an *a priori* model, and if the sampling is random with respect to all categories, then the total chi square indicated in Table E.17 may be partitioned in the manner shown in this table. This partition bears a marked resemblance to an analysis-of-variance table.

TABLE E.17   **Partition of chi square**

Source	Chi square	df
Total	$\chi^2_{\text{total}} = \sum \sum \sum [(n_{ijk} - n'_{ijk})^2 / n'_{ijk}]$	$pqr - 1$
A	$\chi^2_a = \sum [(n_{i..} - n'_{i..})^2 / n'_{i..}]$	$p - 1$
B	$\chi^2_b = \sum [(n_{.j.} - n'_{.j.})^2 / n'_{.j.}]$	$q - 1$
C	$\chi^2_c = \sum [(n_{..k} - n'_{..k})^2 / n'_{..k}]$	$r - 1$
AB	$\chi^2_{ab} = \sum \sum [(n_{ij.} - n'_{ij.})^2 / n'_{ij.}] - \chi^2_a - \chi^2_b$	$(p - 1)(q - 1)$
AC	$\chi^2_{ac} = \sum \sum [(n_{i.k} - n'_{i.k})^2 / n'_{i.k}] - \chi^2_a - \chi^2_c$	$(p - 1)(r - 1)$
BC	$\chi^2_{bc} = \sum \sum [(n_{.jk} - n'_{.jk})^2 / n'_{.jk}] - \chi^2_b - \chi^2_c$	$(q - 1)(r - 1)$
ABC	$\chi^2_{abc} = \chi^2_{\text{total}} - \chi^2_a - \chi^2_b - \chi^2_c - \chi^2_{ab} - \chi^2_{ac} - \chi^2_{bc}$	$(p - 1)(q - 1)(r - 1)$

Tests with respect to conformity with the specified model may be made, provided that the sampling distributions for the statistics indicated may be approximated by chi-square distributions. If each of the expected cell frequencies is greater than 5, the chi-square distributions will provide good approximations. If a relatively small number of expected frequencies are less than 5, the chi-square approximations will still be good.

A review of some of the work done on the partition of chi square in contingency tables appears in Sutcliffe (1957). A comprehensive review of methods for testing interactions is summarized in Goodman (1970). If the model for the population can be completely specified on *a priori* grounds, and if the sampling is random with respect to all categories, then the method of partition indicated in Table E.17 may be carried out quite readily. In practice, however, certain of the parameters in the model are often estimated from the observed data. For example, the parameters $P_{i..}$, $P_{.j.}$, and $P_{..k}$ may be estimated from the marginal frequencies of the sample data. Under the hypothesis of no interactions of any order (i.e., no two-category or no three-category interactions), the expected proportion for cell abc_{ijk} is

$$P_{ijk} = P_{i..} P_{.j.} P_{..k},$$

and the expected frequency in cell abc_{ijk} is

$$n'_{ijk} = P_{ijk} n_{....}.$$

Under this method for specifying the model for the population, the total chi square may be partitioned as shown in Table E.18. In this case, note that the degrees of freedom for the total chi square are

$$(pqr - 1) - (p - 1) - (q - 1) - (r - 1) = pqr - p - q - r + 2.$$

Should the three-factor interaction be statistically significant in this type of analysis, the two-way summary tables should be studied separately within a fixed level of the third category. In these latter tables, the marginal totals may be used in some cases to estimate the cell frequencies. For example, if the AB

TABLE E.18 **Partition of chi square when probabilities are estimated from marginal totals**

Source	Chi square	df
Total	$\chi^2_{\text{total}} = \sum \sum \sum [(n_{ijk} - n'_{ijk})^2 / n'_{ijk}]$	$(pqr - 1) - (p - 1) - (q - 1) - (r - 1)$
AB	$\chi^2_{ab} = \sum \sum [(n_{ij.} - n'_{ij.})^2 / n'_{ij.}]$	$(p - 1)(q - 1)$
AC	$\chi^2_{ac} = \sum \sum [(n_{i.k} - n'_{i.k})^2 / n'_{i.k}]$	$(p - 1)(r - 1)$
BC	$\chi^2_{bc} = \sum \sum [(n_{.jk} - n'_{.jk})^2 / n'_{.jk}]$	$(q - 1)(r - 1)$
ABC	$\chi^2_{abc} = \chi^2_{\text{total}} - \chi^2_{ab} - \chi^2_{ac} - \chi^2_{bc}$	$(p - 1)(q - 1)(r - 1)$

data for level c_1 are being studied under the hypothesis of no interaction between categories A and B for level c_1,

$$n'_{ij1} \doteq \frac{n_{i.1} n_{.j1}}{n_{..1}} .$$

This expected value for cell $ij1$ will not in general be the same as that obtained under the hypothesis of no interactions of any order.

Another case which arises in practice is one in which the sampling is restricted with respect to the number of observations in each of the cells of the form ab_{ij} but random with respect to the category C. If the marginal totals are used in the estimation of $P_{..k}$, then

$$P_{..k} = \frac{n_{..k}}{n_{...}} , \qquad P_{ij.} = \frac{n_{ij.}}{n_{...}} .$$

Under the hypothesis of no interactions,

$$n'_{ijk} = P_{ij.} P_{..k} n_{...} .$$

In this case, chi square may be partitioned in the following manner:

Source	df
Total	$(pq - 1)(r - 1)$
AC	$(p - 1)(r - 1)$
BC	$(q - 1)(r - 1)$
ABC	$(p - 1)(q - 1)(r - 1)$

Should the three-factor interaction prove to be statistically significant in this case, it is advisable to study the equivalent of simple effects for category C at each of the separate levels of factors A and B.

In analyzing contingency tables into main effects and interactions of various orders, Goodman (1970) defines such effects in terms of $\ln P_{ijk}$, $\ln P_{ij.}$, $\ln P_{i..}$, etc. Distribution problems associated with tests of hypotheses are more readily handled in terms of this transformation.

REFERENCES

Abu Libdeh, O. (1984). *Strength of association in the simple general linear model: a comparative study of Hays' omega-squared.* Doctoral dissertation, University of Chicago.

Anderson, R. L. (1959). Use of contingency tables in the analysis of consumer preference studies. *Biometrics, 15,* 582–590.

Anderson, R. L., and E. E. Houseman (1942). Tables of orthogonal polynomial values extended to N = 104. *Research Bulletin 297,* Ames, Iowa.

Anderson, R. L., and T. A. Bancroft (1952). *Statistical theory in research.* New York: McGraw-Hill.

Anderson, T. W. (1958). *Introduction to multivariate statistical analysis.* New York: Wiley.

Aspin, A. A. (1949). Tables for use in comparisons whose accuracy involves two variances separately estimated. *Biometrika, 36,* 290–293.

Bailey, B. J. R. (1977). Tables of the Bonferroni *t* statistics. *Journal of the American Statistical Association, 72,* 469–478.

Barcikowski, R. S. (1973). Optimum sample size and number of levels in a one-way random effects analysis of variance. *The Journal of Experimental Education,* 41, **4,** 10–16.

Bartlett, M. S. (1937). Some examples of statistical methods of research in agriculture and applied biology. *Journal of the Royal Statistical Society Supplement, 4,* 137–170.

Bechhofer, R. E., and C. W. Dunnett (1982). Multiple comparisons for orthogonal contrasts: examples and tables. *Technometrics, 24,* 213–222.

Behrens, W. U. (1929). Ein Beitrug zur Fehlerberechnung bei wenigan Bechachtungen. *Land. Jb., 68,* 807–837.

Bennett, C. A., and N. L. Franklin (1954). *Statistical analysis in chemistry and the chemical industry.* New York: Wiley.

Bishop, T. A. (1976). Heteroscedastic ANOVA, MANOVA, and multiple comparisons. Unpublished PhD thesis, Ohio State University.

Boik, R. J. (1979). Interactions, partial interactions, and interaction contrasts in the analysis of variance. *Psychological Bulletin, 86,* 1084–1089.

Box, G. E. P. (1950). Problems in the analysis of growth and wear curves. *Biometrics, 6,* 362–389.

Box, G. E. P. (1953). Non-normality and tests on variance. *Biometrika, 40,* 318–335.

Box, G. E. P. (1954a). Some theorems on quadrative forms applied in the study of analysis of variance problems; I: Effect of inequality of variance in the one-way classification. *Annals of Mathematical Statistics, 25,* 290–302.

Box, G. E. P. (1954b). Some theorems on quadrative forms applied in the study of analysis of variance problems; II: Effects of inequality of variance and of correlation between errors in a two-way classification. *Annals of Mathematical Statistics, 25,* 484–498.

Bozivich, H., T. A. Bancroft, and H. O. Hartley (1956). Power of analysis of variance procedures for certain incompletely specified models. *Annals of Mathematical Statistics, 27,* 1017–1043.

Bratcher, T. L., A. M. Moran, and W. J. Zimmer (1970). Tables of sample sizes in the analysis of variance. *Journal of Quality Technology, 2,* 156–164.

Brown, M. B., and A. B. Forsythe (1974). The ANOV and multiple comparisons for data with heterogeneous variances. *Biometrics, 30,* 719–724.

Bryant, J. L., and A. S. Paulson (1976). An extension of Tukey's method of multiple comparisons to experimental designs with random concomitant variables. *Biometrika, 63,* 631–638.

Busemeyer, J. R. (1980). Importance of measurement theory, error theory, and experimental design for testing the significance of interactions. *Psychological Bulletin, 88,* 237–244.

Cleveland, W. S. (1985). *The elements of graphing data.* Belmont, CA: Wadsworth.

Cochran, W. G. (1941). The distribution of the largest of a set of estimated variances as a fraction of their total. *Annals of Eugenics, 11,* 47–52.

Cochran, W. G. (1947). Some consequences when assumptions for the analysis of variance are not satisfied. *Biometrics, 3,* 22–38.

Cochran, W. G. (1950). The comparison of percentages in matched samples. *Biometrika, 37,* 256–266.

Cochran, W. G. (1951). Testing a linear relation among variances. *Biometrics, 7,* 17–32.

Cochran, W. G. (1957). Analysis of covariance: its nature and use. *Biometrics, 13,* 261–281.

Cochran, W. G., and G. M. Cox (1957). *Experimental designs.* 2nd ed. New York: Wiley.

Cohen, J. (1977). *Statistical power analysis for the behavioral sciences.* Rev. ed. New York: Academic Press.

Cohen, J. (1988). *Statistical power analysis for the behavioral sciences.* 2nd ed. Hillsdale, N.J.: Lawrence Erlbaum Associates.

Cohen, J., and P. Cohen (1983). *Applied multiple regression/correlation analysis for the behavioral sciences, 2d ed.* Hillsdale, N.J.: Lawrence Erlbaum Associates, Publishers.

Collier, R. O., Jr., and F. B. Baker (1963). The randomization distribution of *F*-ratios for the split-plot design—an empirical investigation. *Biometrika, 50,* 431–438.

Collier, R. O., Jr., F. B. Baker, G. K. Mandeville, and H. T. Hayes (1967). Estimates of test size for several test procedures based on variance ratios in the repeated measures design. *Psychometrika, 32,* 339–353.

Conover, W. J., M. E. Johnson, and M. M. Johnson (1981). A comparative study of tests for homogeneity of variances with applications to the outer continental shelf bidding data. *Technometrics, 23,* 357–361.

Cook, T. D., and D. T. Campbell, (1979). *Quasi experimentation: design and analysis issues for field settings.* Boston: Houghton Mifflin.

Cornfield, J., and J. W. Tukey (1956). Average values of mean squares in factorials. *Annals of Mathematical Statistics, 27,* 907–949.

Cox, D. R. (1958). *Planning of experiments.* New York: Wiley.

Cox, D. R., and P. McCullogh (1982). Some aspects of analysis of covariance. *Biometrics, 38,* 541–561.

Crump, S. L. (1951). The present status of variance component analysis. *Biometrics, 7,* 1–16.

Dixon, W. J. and J. W. Tukey (1968). Approximate behavior of the distribution of winsorized *t* trimming/winsorization 2. *Technometrics, 10,* 83–98.

Dodd, D. H., and R. F., Schultz, Jr. (1973). Computational procedures for estimating magnitude of effect for some analysis of variance designs. *Psychological Bulletin,* 79, **6,** 391–395.

Durcan, D. B. (1955). Multiple range and multiple *F* tests. *Biometrics, 11,* 1–42.

Duncan, D. B. (1957). Multiple range tests for correlated and heteroscedastic means. *Biometrics,* **13,** 164–176.

Dunn, O. J. (1961). Multiple comparisons among means. *Journal of the American Statistical Association,* **56,** 52–64.

Dunn, O. J. (1974). On multiple tests and confidence intervals. *Communication in Statistics,* **3,** 101–103.

Dunnett, C. W. (1955). A multiple comparison procedure for comparing several treatments with a control. *Journal of the American Statistical Association,* **50,** 1096–1121.

Dunnett, C. W. (1964). New tables for multiple comparisons with a control. *Biometrics,* **20,** 482–491.

Dwyer, P. S. (1951). *Linear computations.* New York: Wiley.

Eisenhart, C. (1947). The assumptions underlying the analysis of variance. *Biometrics,* **3,** 1–21.

Eisenhart, C., M. W. Hastay, and W. A. Wallis (1947). *Techniques of statistical analysis,* ch. 15. New York: McGraw Hill.

Federer, W. T. (1955). *Experimental design.* New York: Macmillan.

Federer, W. T. (1963). Relationships between a three-way classification disproportionate numbers analysis of variance and several two-way classification and nested analyses. *Biometrics,* **19,** 629–637.

Feldt, L. S. and M. W. Mahmoud (1958). Power function charts for specification of sample size in analysis of variance. *Psychometrika,* **23,** 201–210.

Fisher, R. A. (1932). *Statistical methods for research workers.* Edinburgh: Oliver & Boyd.

Fisher, R. A. (1951). *The design of experiments.* 6th ed. Edinburgh: Oliver & Boyd.

Fisher, R. A. and F. Yates (1953). *Statistical tables for biological, agricultural, and medical research.* 4th ed. Edinburgh: Oliver & Boyd.

Fleiss, J. L. (1969). Estimating the magnitude of experimental effects. *Psychological Bulletin,* **72,** 273–276.

Gabriel, K. R., J. Putter, and Y. Wax (1973). Simultaneous confidence intervals for product-type interaction contrasts. *Journal of the Royal Statistical Society (B),* **35,** pp. 234–244.

Gaito, J. (1965). Unequal intervals and unequal *n* in trend analysis. *Psychological Bulletin,* **63,** 125–127.

Games, P. A. (1977). An improved *t* table for simultaneous control on *g* contrasts. *Journal of the American Statistical Association,* **72,** 531–534.

Gayen, A. K. (1949). The distribution of Student's *t* in random samples of any size drawn from non-normal universes. *Biometrika,* **36,** 353–369.

Gaylor, D. W., and F. N. Hopper (1969). Estimating the degrees of freedom for linear combinations of mean squares by Satterthwaite's formula. *Technometrics,* **11,** 691–706.

Geisser, S. (1959). A method for testing treatment effects in the presence of learning. *Biometrics,* **15,** 389–395.

Geisser, S., and S. W. Greenhouse (1958). An extension of Box's results on the use of the *F* distribution in multivariate analysis. *Annals of Mathematical Statistics,* **29,** 885–891.

Glass, G. V. (1976). Primary, secondary, and meta-analysis of research. *Educational Researcher,* **5,** 3–8.

Glass, G. V., P. D. Peckham, and J. R. Sanders (1972). Consequences of failure to meet assumptions underlying analysis of variance and covariance. *Review of Educational Research,* 412, **3,** 237–288.

Goodman, L. A. (1970). The multivariate analysis of qualitative data: interactions among multiple classifications. *Journal of the American Statistical Association,* **65,** 226–256.

Gosslee, G. D., and H. L. Lucas (1965). Analysis of variance of disproportionate data when interaction is present. *Biometrics,* **21,** 115–133.

Grandage, A. (1958). Orthogonal coefficients for unequal intervals. *Biometrics,* **14,** 287–289.

Graybill, F. A. (1961). *An introduction to linear statistical models.* Vol. I. New York: McGraw-Hill.

Green, B. F., and J. Tukey (1960). Complex analysis of variance: general problems. *Psychometrika,* **25,** 127–152.

Greenhouse, S. W., and S. Geisser (1959). On methods in the analysis of profile data. *Psychometrika*, **24**, 95–112.

Harter, H. L. (1957). Error rates and sample sizes for range tests in multiple comparisons. *Biometrics*, **13**, 511–536.

Harter, H. L. (1960). *Expected values of normal order statistics*. ARL tech. rep. 60–292, Wright-Patterson AFB, Ohio.

Harter, H. L., D. S. Clemm, and E. H. Guthrie (1959). *The probability integrals of the range and of the studentized range*. WADC tech. rep. 58-484, vol. 2. Wright Air Development Center, Ohio.

Hartley, H. O. (1940). Testing the homogeneity of a set of variances. *Biometrika*, **31**, 249–255.

Hartley, H. O. (1950). The maximum *F* ratio as a short-cut test for heterogeneity of variance. *Biometrika*, **37**, 308–312.

Hays, W. L. (1981). *Statistics*. New York: Holt, Rinehart, and Winston.

Hedges, L. V. (1981). Distribution theory of Glass's estimator of effect size and related estimators. *Journal of Educational Statistics*, **6**, 107–128.

Hedges, L. V., and I. Olkin (1985). *Statistical methods for meta-analysis*. Orlando: Academic Press.

Henderson, C. R. (1953). Estimation of variance and covariance components. *Biometrics*, **9**, 226–252.

Horst, P. (1963). *Matrix algebra for social scientists*. New York: Holt, Rinehart, Winston.

Hotelling, H. (1931). The generalization of Student's ratio. *Annals of Mathematical Statistics*, **2**.

Hughes, H. M., and M. B. Danford (1958). *Repeated measurement designs, assuming equal variances and covariances*. Rep. 59-40, Air University, School of Aviation Medicine, USAF, Randolph AFB, Texas.

Huynh, H. (1978). Some approximate tests for repeated measurement designs. *Psychometrika*, **43**, 161–175.

Huynh, H., and Feldt, L. S. (1970). Conditions under which mean square ratios in repeated measurements designs have exact *F* distributions. *Journal of the American Statistical Association*, **65**, pp. 1582–1589.

Huynh, H., and L. S. Feldt (1976). Estimation of the Box corrections for degrees of freedom from sample data in randomized block and split-plot designs. *Journal of Educational Statistics*, **1**, 69–82.

Huynh, H., and L. S. Feldt (1979). Estimation of the Box correction for degrees of freedom in randomized block and split-plot designs. *Journal of Educational Statistics*, **1**, 62–82.

Huynh, H., and G. K. Mandeville (1979). Validity conditions in repeated measures design. *Psychological Bulletin*, **86**, 964–973.

Imhof, J. P. (1962). Testing the hypothesis of no fixed main-effects in Scheffe's mixed model. *Annals of Mathematical Statistics*, **33**, 1085–1095.

Johnson, N. L., and Welch, B. L. (1940). Applications of the noncentral *t* distribution. *Biometrika*, **31**, 362–389.

Kempthorne, O. (1952). *The design and analysis of experiments*. New York: Wiley.

Keuls, M. (1952). The use of studentized range in connection with an analysis of variance. *Euphytica*, **1**, 112–122.

Kirk, R. E. (1982). *Experimental design*. 2nd ed. Monterey, CA: Brooks/Cole.

Koele, P. (1982). Calculating power in analysis of variance. *Psychological Bulletin*, **92**, 513–516.

Kraemer, H. C., and S. Thiemann (1987). *How many subjects: statistical power analysis in research*. Newbury Park, CA: Sage Publications.

Krantz, D. H., and A. Tversky (1971). A conjoint-measurement analysis of composition rules in psychology. *Psychological Review*, **78**, 151–169.

Levison, B., and H. P. Zeigler (1959). The effects of neonatal X irradiation upon learning in the rat. *Journal of Comparative and Physiological Psychology*, **52**, 53–55.

Lewis, D. J., and J. W. Cotton (1958). Partial reinforcement and nonresponse acquisition. *Journal of Comparative and Physiological Psychology*, **51**, pp. 251–257.

Lindquist, E. F. (1953). *Design and analysis of experiments in psychology and education*. Boston: Houghton-Mifflin.

Lord, F. M. (1969). Statistical adjustments when comparing pre-existing groups. *Psychological Bulletin*, **72**, 336–337.

Luce, R. D., R. R. Bush, and E. Galanter (1963). *Handbook of mathematical psychology*. New York: Wiley.

Lunneborg, C. E., and R. D. Abbott (1983). *Elementary multivariate analysis for the behavioral sciences: applications of basic structure*. Amsterdam: Elsevier.

Lunney, G. H. (1970). Using analysis of variance with a dichotomous dependent variable: an empirical study. *Journal of Educational Measurement*, **7**, 263–269.

Marascuilo, L. A., and J. R. Levin (1970). Appropriate post hoc comparisons for interactions and nested hypotheses in analysis of variance designs: the elimination of type IV errors. *American Educational Research Journal*, **7**, 397–421.

Mauchley, J. W. (1940). Significance test for sphericity of a normal n-variate distribution. *Annals of Mathematical Statistics*, **11**, 204–209.

Maxwell, S. E., and H. D. Delaney (1990). *Designing experiments and analyzing data: a model comparisons approach*. Belmont, CA: Wadsworth.

Maxwell, S. E., H. D. Delaney, and J. M. Manheimer (1985). Analysis of residuals and ANOVA: correcting an illusion by using model comparisons and graphs. *Journal of Educational Statistics*, 10, **3**, 197–209.

Meyer, D. R., and Noble, M. E. (1958). Summation of manifest anxiety and muscular tension. *Journal of Experimental Psychology*, **55**, 599–602.

Mielke, P. W., Jr., and R. B. McHugh (1965). Non-orthogonality in the two-way classification for the mixed effects finite population model. *Biometrics*, **21**, 308–323.

Mitchell, J. (1986). Measurement scales and statistics: a clash of paradigms. *Psychological Bulletin*, **100**, 398–407.

Morrison, D. F. (1967). *Multivariate statistical methods*. New York: McGraw-Hill.

Nagarsenker, B. N., and K. C. S. Pillai (1973). The distribution of the sphericity test criterion. *Journal of Multivariate Analysis*, **3**, 226–235.

Newman, D. (1939). The distribution of the range in samples from a normal population, expressed in terms of an independent estimate of standard deviation. *Biometrika*, **31**, 20–30.

Odeh, R. E. and E. G. Olds (1959). *Notes on the analysis of variance of logarithms of variances*. WADC Tech. Note 59-82, Wright–Patterson AFB, Ohio.

Olds, E. G., T. B. Mattson, and R. E. Odeh (1956). *Notes on the use of transformations in the analysis of variance*. WADC Tech. Rep. 56-308, Wright Air Development Center, Ohio.

Overall, J. E., and D. K. Spiegel (1969). Concerning least-squares analysis of experimental data. *Psychological Bulletin*, **72**, 311–322.

Owen, D. B. (1965). The power of Student's t test. *Journal of the American Statistical Association*, **60**, 320–333.

Patnaik, P. B. (1949). The noncentral χ^2 and F-distributions and their approximations. *Biometrika*, **36**, 202–232.

Pearson, E. S., and H. O. Hartley (1958). F distribution, *Biometrika Tables for Statisticians*, **1**. 2nd ed. New York: Cambridge.

Rao, C. R. (1952). *Advanced statistical methods in biometric research*. New York: Wiley.

Rao, C. R. (1958). Some statistical methods for the comparison of growth curves. *Biometrics*, **14**, 1–17.

Rao, C. R. (1965). *Linear statistical inference and its applications*. New York: Wiley.

Rider, P. R., H. L. Harter, and M. D. Lum (1956). *An elementary approach to the analysis of variance*. WADC Tech. Rep. 56-20, Wright Air Development Center, Ohio.

Robson, D. S. (1959). A simple method for construction of orthogonal polynomials when the independent variable is unequally spaced. *Biometrics*, **15**, 187–191.

Rosenthal, R., and D. B. Rubin (1982). A simple, general purpose display of magnitude of experimental effect. *Journal of Educational Psychology*, **74**, 166–169.

Satterthwaite, F. E. (1946). An approximate distribution of estimates of variance components. *Biometrics Bulletin,* **2,** 110–114.

Scheffé, H. A. (1953). A method for judging all possible contrasts in the analysis of variance. *Biometrika,* **40,** 87–104.

Scheffé, H. A. (1959). *The analysis of variance.* New York: Wiley.

Seal, K. C. (1951). On errors of estimates in double sampling procedure. *Sankhya,* **11,** pt. 2, 125–144.

Searle, S. R. (1966). Matrix algebra for the biological sciences. New York: Wiley.

Searle, S. R. (1968). Another look at Henderson's methods of estimating variance components. *Biometrics,* **24,** 749–788.

Šidák, Z. (1967). Rectangular confidence regions for the means of multivariate normal distributions. *Journal of the American Statistical Association,* **62,** 626–633.

Siegel, S. (1956). *Nonparametric statistics.* New York: McGraw-Hill.

Smith, H. F. (1957). Interpretation of adjusted treatment means and regressions in analysis of cavariance. *Biometrics,* **13,** 3, 282–297.

Smith, R. A. (1968). An empirical analysis of the effect of unequal sample size on the Tukey studentized range technique. Unpublished doctoral dissertation. University of Colorado, Boulder.

Snedecor, G. W. (1934). *Analysis of variance and covariance.* Ames, Iowa: Iowa State University Press.

Spjøtvoll, E., and M. R. Stoline (1973). An extension of the T method of multiple comparisons to include the cases with unequal sample sizes. *Journal of the American Statistical Association,* **68,** 975–978.

Steel, R. G. D. (1959). A multiple comparison rank sum test: treatments versus control. *Biometrics,* **15,** 560–572.

Stevens, S. S. (1946). On the theory of scales of measurement. *Science,* **103,** pp. 667–680.

Stevens, S. S. (1951). Mathematics, measurement and psychophysics. *Handbook of Experimental Psychology,* S. S. Stevens, ed., 1–49. New York: Wiley.

Stevens, S. S. (1959). Measurement, psychophysics and utility. *Measurement: Definitions and Theories,* Churchman, C. W. and Ratbosh, P., ed., 18–63. New York: Wiley.

Stoline, M. R. (1978). Tables of the studentized augmented range and applications to problems of multiple comparisons. *Journal of the American Statistical Association,* **73,** 656–660.

Student (1927). Errors of routine analysis. *Biometrika,* **19,** 151–164.

Suppes, P. (1951). A set of independent axioms for extensive quantities. *Portugaliae Mathematica,* **10,** 163–172.

Suppes, P., and J. L. Zinnes (1963). Basic measurement theory. *Handbook of Mathematical Psychology,* vol. 1, 3–76, Luce, R. D., R. R. Bush, and E. Galanter, ed. New York: Wiley.

Sutcliffe, J. P. (1957). A general method of analysis of frequency data for multiple classification designs. *Psychological Bulletin,* **54,** 134–137.

Tiku, M. L. (1967). Tables of the power of the F test. *Journal of the American Statistical Association,* **62,** 525–539.

Timm, N. H. (1975). *Multivariate analysis with applications in education and psychology.* Monterey, CA: Brooks/Cole.

Tong, X. L. (1980). *Probability of inequalities in multivariate distributions.* New York: Academic Press.

Townsend, J. T. and F. G. Ashby (1984). Measurement scales and statistics: the misconception misconceived. *Psychological Bulletin,* **96,** 394–401.

Tukey, J. W. (1949). One degree of freedom for nonadditivity. *Biometrics,* **5,** 232–242.

Tukey, J. W. (1953). The problem of multiple comparisons. Ditto, Princeton University.

Tukey, J. W. (1955). Answer to query. *Biometrics,* **11,** 111–113.

Tukey, J. W. (1956). Variance of variance components; I. balanced designs. *The Annals of Mathematical Statistics,* **27,** 722–736.

Tukey, J. W. (1957). The comparative anatomy of transformations. *The Annals of Mathematical Statistics,* **28,** 602–632.

Tukey, J. W. (1962). The future of data analysis. *The Annals of Mathematical Statistics,* **33,** 1–67.

Vaughn, G. M., and M. C. Corballis (1969). Beyond tests of significance: estimating strength of effects in selected ANOVA designs. *Psychological Bulletin,* 72, **3,** 204–213.

Vonesh, E. F., and M. A. Schork (1986). Sample sizes in the multivariate analysis of repeated measurements. *Biometrics,* **42,** 601–610.

Walker, H., and J. Lev (1953). *Statistical inference.* New York: Holt.

Wallace, D. L. (1959). Simplified beta approximations to the Kruskal–Wallis *H* test. *Journal of the American Statistical Association,* **54,** 225–230.

Wallenstein, S., and J. L. Fleiss (1979). Repeated measurements analysis of variance when the correlations have a certain pattern. *Psychometrika,* **44,** 229–233.

Welch, B. L. (1947). The generalization of Student's problem when several different population variances are involved. *Biometrika,* **34,** 28–35.

Wherry, R. J. (1931). A new formula for predicting the shrinkage of the coefficient of multiple correlation. *Annals of Mathematical Statistics,* **2,** 440–457.

Wilcox, R. R. (1987). New designs in analysis of variance. *Annual Review of Psychology,* Rosenzweig, M. R. and Porter, L. W., ed., pp. 29–60. Palo Alto, CA: Annual Reviews, Inc.

Wilk, M. B., and O. Kempthorne (1955). Fixed, mixed, and random models. *Journal of the American Statistical Association,* **50,** 1144–1167.

Wilk, M. B., and O. Kempthorne (1957). Nonadditivities in a Latin square design. *Journal of the American Statistical Association,* **52,** 218–236.

AUTHOR INDEX

SUBJECT INDEX